Brink's Modern Internal Auditing

Eighth Edition

The Wiley Corporate F&A series provides information, tools, and insights to corporate professionals responsible for issues affecting the profitability of their company, from accounting and finance to internal controls and performance management.

Founded in 1807, John Wiley & Sons is the oldest independent publishing company in the United States. With offices in North America, Europe, Asia, and Australia, Wiley is globally committed to developing and marketing print and electronic products and services for our customers' professional and personal knowledge and understanding.

Brink's Modern Internal Auditing

Eighth Edition

A Common Body of Knowledge

ROBERT R. MOELLER

WILEY

Cover design: Wiley

Published by John Wiley & Sons, Inc., Hoboken, New Jersey.

The Seventh Edition was published by Wiley in 2009.

Published simultaneously in Canada.

For general information on our other products and services or for technical support, please contact our Customer Care Department within the United States at (800) 762-2974, outside the United States at (317) 572-3993 or fax (317) 572-4002.

Wiley publishes in a variety of print and electronic formats and by print-on-demand. Some material included with standard print versions of this book may not be included in e-books or in print-on-demand. If this book refers to media such as a CD or DVD that is not included in the version you purchased, you may download this material at http://booksupport.wiley.com. For more information about Wiley products, visit www.wiley.com.

Library of Congress Cataloging-in-Publication Data:

Moeller, Robert R.
Brink's modern internal auditing : a common body of knowledge / Robert R. Moeller. — Eighth edition.
pages cm. — (Wiley corporate F&A)
Revised edition of the author's Brink's modern internal auditing, 2009.
Includes index.
ISBN 978-1-119-01698-4 (hardback) — ISBN 978-1-119-18000-5 (ePDF) — ISBN 978-1-119-17999-3 (ePub) — ISBN 978-1-119-18001-2 (oBook) 1. Auditing, Internal. I. Title.
HF5668.25.M64 2015
657'.458—dc23

2015023640

10 9 8 7 6 5 4 3 2 1

Dedicated to my best friend and wife, Lois Moeller.
Lois has been my companion and partner for over 45 years,
whether we are somewhere in the world visiting an interesting historical location,
attending one of Chicago's many music and theater events,
gardening vegetables in the backyard,
or finding the right wine and cooking the produce.

Contents

Preface

THIS BOOK IS A COMPLETE guide and a definition of a common body of knowledge (CBOK) for the processes and profession of internal auditing—what professionals need to know to successfully perform individual internal audits and what an enterprise needs to know to launch an effective internal audit function. With a heritage that goes back to the first days of internal auditing after World War II when Victor Brink produced the first edition, the chapters following outline a professional CBOK and describe internal auditing today. Although it is often misused, the word *modern* beginning with the title of the first edition says a lot about this book's heritage and the contemporary practice of internal auditing. In the first edition it described a new and evolving profession. The early internal auditors were often little more than accounting clerks or clerical support staff for their external auditors. Brink envisioned them as professionals performing much broader services to management.

Due to the pervasiveness of information technology processes and the Internet in all areas of commerce, the rules for a consistent definition of internal controls, and our evolution to a truly global economy, internal auditors today must operate in an ever-changing environment. Internal auditors need increasing levels of knowledge and understanding in many areas, but sorting through what is important and what is just nice to know represents challenges for internal auditors at all levels. This newly revised eighth edition discusses modern internal auditing in terms of areas where there is a strong knowledge requirement as well as other areas where only a general level of knowledge is needed. This edition updates our three common CBOKs for the profession of internal auditing.

The practice of internal auditing is important to enterprises today worldwide, and senior management members, government regulators, and other professionals need to have a general understanding and set of expectations of the roles and capabilities of internal auditors. That is, just as internal auditors need a CBOK to better define their profession, the outside world needs to better understand internal auditors and how they can serve management at all levels.

The following chapters describe this CBOK for internal auditors—knowledge areas that should be important to all internal auditors, no matter their level of experience, their business area, or where they are working in the world. The CBOK topics presented here are not based on surveys of what other internal auditors are doing today; they are based on this author's long-term, 40-plus years of experience in internal auditing as well as his extensive professional activities and research.

The following are some of the CBOK elements found in each chapter:

Part One: Foundations of Modern Internal Auditing. These two introductory chapters highlight the importance of internal auditing today in all aspects of business, government, and other activities, as well as why a CBOK is important.

1. **Significance of Internal Auditing in Enterprises Today.** This introductory chapter talks about the origins of internal auditing. It does not contain key CBOK information, but provides important background knowledge and history for today's internal auditor and explains what led Victor Brink to write the first edition.
2. **An Internal Audit Common Body of Knowledge.** In this chapter, we explain and expand the concept of an internal auditing CBOK and why it is important to the profession.

Part Two: Importance of Internal Controls. The review and assessment of internal controls are key internal audit activities. The five chapters in this part describe internal control reviews in terms of the newly revised COSO internal control framework, the Sarbanes-Oxley Act (SOx) requirements, and several internal control frameworks including COBIT.

3. **The COSO Internal Control Framework.** This recently revised internal control framework has become the worldwide standard for assessing internal controls; every internal auditor needs to understand the Committee of Sponsoring Organizations (COSO) internal control framework and how to use it in internal audit assessments of internal controls.
4. **The 17 COSO Internal Control Principles.** These principles were introduced as part of the newly revised framework and provide guidance to better help internal auditors to plan and perform their reviews of internal controls.
5. **Sarbanes-Oxley Act (SOx) and Beyond.** SOx became law in the United States in 2002 and has massively changed how we assess and measure internal accounting controls almost worldwide. The chapter discusses the current status of SOx including its AS5 auditing standards and other elements of this extensive set of legislation that are particularly important to internal auditors.
6. **COBIT and Other ISACA Guidance.** In our very IT-dependent world, internal auditors need a more IT-oriented framework to help them measure and assess internal controls as part of their review efforts. The Control Objectives for Information and related Technology (COBIT) tool is important here, and all internal auditors should have a least a general understanding of this worldwide-recognized internal control framework.
7. **Enterprise Risk Management: COSO ERM.** Risk management is an important internal audit knowledge area, and internal auditors need to understand and make use of COSO Enterprise Risk Management (COSO ERM) as part of their internal audit planning and assessment activities. The chapter describes this risk assessment framework and why it is important for internal auditors.

Part Three: Planning and Performing Internal Audits. The six chapters in this part discuss some important general concepts and elements of the practice of modern internal auditing, ranging from professional governing standards to assessing those areas in the enterprise that should be candidates for internal audits.

8. **Performing Effective Internal Audits.** This chapter contains an introduction on the overall practice of planning, performing, and completing an effective internal audit. These are the steps of what it takes to perform an internal audit.
9. **Standards for the Professional Practice of Internal Auditing.** All internal auditors need to have a strong knowledge and understanding of these Institute of Internal Auditors (IIA)–issued standards. The chapter provides an overview of the more important elements of the standards and where to search for more information.
10. **Testing, Assessing, and Evaluating Audit Evidence.** A major activity in internal auditing is to examine a record or artifact of audit evidence and then to decide if it meets audit review criteria. This is a basic internal audit knowledge area that must follow internal auditing best practices.
11. **Continuous Auditing and Computer-Assisted Audit Techniques.** The ongoing growth of 24/7 systems and processes is changing the way that internal auditors should assess and evaluate internal controls. This chapter introduces online continuous monitoring tools that internal auditors should consider a key CBOK knowledge area.
12. **Control Self-Assessments and Internal Audit Benchmarking.** The IIA has developed some extensive criteria for internal auditors at any level to look at what they are doing at a point in time and then to make an assessment of that work. The chapter describes these processes as well as guidance for improving and reviewing the quality of internal audit work.
13. **Areas to Audit: Establishing an Audit Universe and Audit Programs.** There are a wide variety of areas in any enterprise that are potential candidates for review, but internal auditors should tailor that list down to what is generally known as an audit universe. The chapter provides some guidance on how to build and assess potential review areas necessary to plan and perform internal audits.

Part Four: Organizing and Managing Internal Audit Activities. The five chapters in this part discuss the process of launching, performing, and completing internal audits.

14. **Charters and Building the Internal Audit Function.** Best practices here cover the building and managing of an effective internal audit function. The chapter's theme is on how a new enterprise would launch and build its own internal audit function, including an audit committee–approved audit charter.
15. **Managing the Internal Audit Universe and Key Competencies.** Beyond the knowledge and technical skills involved in understanding the COSO internal control framework and IT general controls, internal auditors must possess some core key

competencies, such as interviewing and writing skills. These apply to all levels of an internal audit function, ranging from audit management to audit staff members. The chapter will focus on some necessary CBOK skills for all levels of internal auditors.

16. **Planning Audits and Understanding Project Management.** Whether building an audit schedule for an upcoming fiscal period or planning a specific audit engagement, internal auditors at all levels need to have an understanding of good project management techniques. This chapter discusses project management for internal auditors.
17. **Documenting Audit Results through Process Modeling and Workpapers.** As another specialized internal audit skill, internal auditors need efficient and cost-effective procedures to review and document overall business processes of all types. While many alternatives are available, this chapter will introduce some good internal audit–based approaches to understand various processes and then to document that work through audit workpapers.
18. **Reporting Internal Audit Results.** Reporting the results of audit work as well as developing recommendations for corrective actions is a major task. Whether reports are developed in hard- or soft-copy formats, this chapter will suggest approaches and guidelines for producing them effectively.

Part Five: Impact of Information Systems on Internal Auditing. Internal auditors must know how to evaluate IT controls as well as how to use IT in performing their internal audits. The six chapters in this part outline some important internal audit IT–related CBOK areas.

19. **ITIL® Best Practices, the IT Infrastructure, and General Controls.** The chapter will explain processes for reviewing IT general controls, the overall controls that cover the IT infrastructure and all aspects of IT operations. In addition, the chapter will introduce the Information Technology Infrastructure Library (ITIL®), an internationally recognized set of best practices that promote a partnership between business operations and IT functions, and explain why knowledge of ITIL® is important for internal auditors.
20. **BYOD Practices and Social Media Internal Audit Issues.** The growth of the Internet, the Internet-based nature of many systems today, and our increasing personal use of smartphones and tablet devices have introduced many changes in the manner that IT systems are managed and controlled. This chapter discusses some of the issues from an internal audit perspective and areas where internal auditors should develop a good CBOK understanding.
21. **Big Data and Enterprise Content Management.** The growth of massive IT systems coupled with legal and government requirements to capture and return this system data has led to the environment known as big data. This chapter discusses some internal control concerns in this environment as well as some internal audit knowledge needs.
22. **Reviewing Application and Software Management Controls.** In addition to the general controls covering IT operations, internal auditors need to understand how to review internal controls covering specific applications ranging from

local-office handheld and desktop procedures to larger enterprise-wide applications. This chapter will introduce some internal audit knowledge areas and some IT audit best practices.

23. **Cybersecurity, Hacking Risks, and Privacy Controls.** IT security and privacy issues are major knowledge areas that often require specialized technical skills beyond those of many internal auditors. However, this chapter will introduce some fundamental security and privacy control concepts as well as some basic internal auditor knowledge requirements in this area.
24. **Business Continuity and Disaster Recovery Planning.** Concepts such as backing up major computer files have a long internal audit–related history, with the objective of allowing the restoration of operations in the event of a calamitous interruption in IT services. This chapter will look at an expanded view of continuity planning with an emphasis on tools and procedures to get the business back in operation.

Part Six: Internal Audit and Enterprise Governance. The four chapters in this part go beyond just internal audits and discuss the relationship of an internal audit function with its board audit committee as well as the importance of such areas as governance, risk, and compliance (GRC) issues, ethics and whistleblower procedures, and fraud investigations.

25. **Board Audit Committee Communications.** Internal audit functions report to their board of directors' audit committees, per SOx rules. While this is very much an audit management responsibility, all internal auditors need to have a better understanding of their roles and responsibilities with regard to the audit committee.
26. **Ethics and Whistleblower Programs.** SOx requirements and other good enterprise governance practices call for these types of programs. There are many areas described here where internal audit can help make strong improvements to operations.
27. **Fraud Detection and Prevention.** Understanding how to recognize and detect fraud is an important internal audit skill. This chapter will discuss some basic fraud understanding techniques for internal auditors.
28. **Internal Audit GRC Approaches and Other Compliance Requirements.** There are numerous compliance rules impacting today's enterprises, but the overall concept of strong and effective GRC principles is particularly important. This chapter will provide internal auditors with some of the more important of these concepts for enterprise governance purposes.

Part Seven: The Professional Internal Auditor. The two chapters in this part focus on professional certifications for internal auditors—important career objectives—as well as internal audit's role as an internal consultant to its enterprise organization.

29. **Professional Certifications: CIA, CISA, and More.** Certifications such as the IIA's Certified Internal Auditor (CIA) are important for building professional credentials. This chapter will look at some of the more important certifications of interest to internal auditors, along with their requirements.

30. **The Modern Internal Auditor as an Enterprise Consultant.** Until very recent times, IIA standards prohibited internal auditors from acting as consultants in the same areas where they were performing internal audits. Revised IIA standards now allow an internal auditor to act as a consultant to his or her enterprise, and this chapter will discuss this internal audit role and responsibility.

Part Eight: The Other Sides of Auditing: Professional Convergence. The final part will conclude with four chapters on the importance of quality assurance auditing and the impact of International Organization for Standardization (ISO) standards on internal auditors. In addition, we will conclude by summarizing our internal audit CBOK.

31. **Quality Assurance Auditing and ASQ Standards.** The more production- and process-oriented American Society for Quality (ASQ) has its own internal audit section with audit procedures that are close to but not the same as IIA internal audit standards. We expect more professional convergence here going forward, and the chapter will discuss ASQ internal auditing procedures and their similarity to IIA materials.
32. **Six Sigma and Lean Techniques for Internal Audit.** Enterprises worldwide have adopted techniques, such as Six Sigma, to create all levels of operational efficiencies. The chapter will look at several that should be important knowledge areas for internal auditors and will consider how some of these programs can be used to enrich and expand internal audit activities.
33. **ISO and Worldwide Internal Audit Standards.** ISO quality systems standards are becoming increasingly important to most enterprises as they operate on a worldwide basis. This chapter will discuss the ISO process and will review some of the more important of these to internal auditors, no matter where they are working. The chapter will look at some important differences in internal auditing and other related global standards and will discuss the impact of internal accounting standards on all internal auditors. Although the IIA got its start as primarily a U.S.-based organization, it has now expanded to become truly global.
34. **A CBOK for the Modern Internal Auditor.** This final chapter will summarize the various topics from other chapters that highlight areas where internal auditors should have a strong knowledge, as well as others calling for a good general but less specific understanding. The result is our proposed internal audit CBOK.

While some topics and issues may change over time, with this eighth edition we are taking a stronger and more focused view on the knowledge areas that are essential to being a successful and outstanding internal auditor today.

PART ONE

Foundations of Modern Internal Auditing

CHAPTER ONE

Significance of Internal Auditing in Enterprises Today: An Update

THE PROFESSION OF AUDITING HAS been with us for a long time. Mesopotamian scribes in around 3000 BC utilized elaborate systems of internal controls using stone documents that contained ticks, dots, and checkmarks. Auditing has evolved over the millennia, and today we generally think of two basic types of business enterprise auditors: external and internal. An external auditor is chartered by a regulatory authority, with authority to visit an enterprise or entity to independently review and report on the results of that review. Those reviews generally cover financial statements but may involve other compliance areas. In the United States, financial external auditors are Certified Public Accountants (CPAs), who are state-licensed and follow the standards of the American Institute of Certified Public Accountants (AICPA; www.aicpa.org). However, there are many other types of external auditors in fields such as medical equipment devices, television viewer ratings, and multiple governmental areas.

Internal auditing, as discussed throughout this book, is a broader and often more interesting field. As an employee or member of an enterprise, an internal auditor independently reviews and assesses operations in a wide variety of areas, such as accounting office procedures, information technology systems controls, or manufacturing quality processes. Most internal auditors follow high-level standards established by their prime professional enterprise, the Institute of Internal Auditors (IIA; www.theiia.org), but there are many different practices and approaches to internal auditing today due to its worldwide nature and wide range of auditing activities.

The primary objective of this book is to define and describe internal auditing as it is or should be performed today—modern internal auditing—as well as to describe a *common body of knowledge (CBOK)* for internal auditing. Because of modern internal auditing's many variations and nuances, the chapters following describe and discuss it in terms of this CBOK, the key tools and knowledge areas that all internal auditors should generally use in their internal audit activities or at least know, as well as some other knowledge areas where internal auditors should have at least a good general understanding. These are the common practices that are essential to the profession of modern internal auditing.

An effective way to begin to understand internal auditing and its key CBOK areas is to refer to the internationally recognized internal audit professional organization, the IIA, and its published professional standards that define the practice:

> Internal auditing is an independent appraisal function established within an organization to examine and evaluate its activities as a service to the organization.

This statement becomes more meaningful when one focuses on its key terms. *Auditing* suggests a variety of ideas. It can be viewed very narrowly, such as the checking of arithmetical accuracy or physical existence of accounting records, or more broadly as a thoughtful review and appraisal at the highest organizational level. Throughout this book, the term *auditing* will be used to include this total range of levels of service, from detailed checking to higher-level appraisals. The term *internal* defines work carried on within an enterprise, by its own employees, in contrast to external auditors, outside public accountants, or other parties such as government regulators who are not directly a part of the particular enterprise.

The remainder of the IIA's definition of internal auditing covers a number of important terms that apply to the profession:

- *Independent* is used for auditing that is free of restrictions that could significantly limit the scope and effectiveness of any internal auditor review or the later reporting of resultant findings and conclusions.
- *Appraisal* confirms the need for an evaluation that is the thrust of internal auditors as they develop their conclusions.
- *Established* confirms that internal audit is a formal, definitive function in the modern enterprise.
- *Examine and evaluate* describe the active roles of internal auditors, first for fact-finding inquiries and then for judgmental evaluations.
- *Its activities* confirm the broad jurisdictional scope of internal audit work that applies to all of the processes and activities of the modern enterprise.
- *Service* reveals that the help and assistance to the audit committee, management, and other members of the enterprise are the end products of all internal auditing work.
- *To the organization* confirms that internal audit's total service scope pertains to the entire enterprise, including all personnel, the board of directors, and their audit committee, stockholders, and other stakeholders.

As a small terminology point, the chapters following will generally use the term *enterprise* to refer to the whole company or business, and the term *organization* or *function* to reference an individual department or unit within an enterprise. In the chapters to come, we describe a variety of other terminology and usage conventions as we discuss a CBOK for internal auditing and internal audit professionals.

Internal auditing should also be recognized as an organizational control within an enterprise that functions by measuring and evaluating the effectiveness of other controls. When an enterprise establishes its planning and then proceeds to implement its plans in terms of operations, it must do something to monitor the operations to assure the achievement of its established objectives. These further efforts can be thought of as *controls.* While the internal audit function is itself one of the types of controls used, there is a wide range of other organization- or function-level controls. The special role of internal audit is to help measure and evaluate those other controls. Thus internal auditors must understand both their own role as control function and the nature and scope of other types of controls in the overall enterprise.

Internal auditors who do their job effectively become experts in what makes for the best possible design and implementation of all types of controls and preferred practices. This expertise includes understanding the interrelationships of various controls and their best possible integration in the total system of internal control. It is thus through the internal control door that internal auditors come to examine and evaluate all organization activities and to provide maximum service to the overall enterprise. Internal auditors cannot be expected to equal, let alone exceed, the technical and operational expertise pertaining to the many various activities of an enterprise. However, they can help the responsible individuals achieve more effective results by appraising existing controls and providing a basis for helping to improve them. In addition, because internal auditors often have a good knowledge and understanding of many organizational units or special activities within a total enterprise, their levels of understanding often exceed those of other people.

1.1 INTERNAL AUDITING HISTORY AND BACKGROUND

The need for effective control processes created the concept of internal auditing. Despite its ancient roots, however, internal auditing was not recognized as an important process by many enterprises and their external auditors until the 1930s. This recognition was primarily due to the establishment of the U.S. Securities and Exchange Commission (SEC) in 1934 and changing external audit objectives and techniques at that time. The United States as well as the rest of the world had just gone through a major economic depression. As a legislative corrective action, the SEC required that all enterprises registered with it must provide financial statements certified by independent auditors. This requirement also prompted corporations to establish internal auditing departments, but with the objective primarily to assist their independent auditors. At that time, external financial auditors were focused on expressing an opinion on the fairness of an enterprise's financial statements rather than on detecting internal control weaknesses or even clerical errors. The SEC rules precipitated auditing based on a limited sample of transactions, along with greater reliance on internal control procedures.

At that time, internal auditors were primarily concerned with checking accounting records and detecting financial errors and irregularities and often were little more than shadows or assistants to their independent external auditors. Walter B. Meigs, writing about the status of internal auditors during the 1930s, observed that "internal auditors were either clerks assigned to the routine task of a perpetual search for clerical errors in accounting documents, or they were traveling representatives of corporations having branches in widely scattered locations."[1] Those early internal auditors were often little more than clerical helpers who carried out routine accounting reconciliations or served as clerical support personnel. Vestiges of this old definition of internal auditing continued in some places even into the early 1970s. For example, in many retail organizations in the 1970s, the "auditors" were the people who balanced cash registers (remember those?) at the close of the business day.

Although other voices said something should be done to improve and better utilize the potential of internal auditors, things really got started after Victor Z. Brink completed his college thesis on internal auditing just before going off to serve in World War II. After the war ended, Brink returned to organize and head internal auditing for Ford Motor, and his college thesis was published as the now long-out-of-print first edition of *Modern Internal Auditing.*

About that same time, in 1942, the IIA was launched. Its first chapter was started in New York City, with Chicago soon to follow. The IIA was formed by people who had been given the title of internal auditor by their enterprises and wanted to both share their experiences and gain knowledge with others in this new professional field. A profession was born that has undergone many changes over the years and has resulted in the multifaceted profession of the modern internal auditor discussed in this book.

The typical business enterprise of the 1940s, when modern internal auditing was just getting started, required a very different skill set than today. For example, aside from some electromechanical devices and activities in research laboratories, digital computer systems did not exist. Enterprises had no need for computer programmers until these machines started to become useful for record-keeping and other computational and accounting functions. Similarly, enterprises had very rudimentary telephone connections where switchboard operators routed all incoming calls to a limited number of desktop telephones. Today, we are all connected through a vast, automated worldwide web of often wireless telecommunications and the Internet. The increasing complexity of modern business and other enterprises has created the need for internal auditors to become ever-greater specialists in various business controls. We can also better understand the nature of internal auditing today if we know something about the changing conditions in the past and the different needs those changes created. What is the simplest or most primitive form of internal auditing and how did it come into existence? How has internal auditing responded to changing needs?

At its most primitive level, a self-assessment or internal auditing function can exist when any single person sits back and surveys something that he or she has done. At that point, the individual asks himself or herself how well a particular task has been accomplished, and perhaps how it might be done better. If a second person is involved in this activity, the assessment function would be expanded to include an evaluation of that second person's participation in the endeavor. In a small business, the owner or manager will be doing this review to some extent for all enterprise employees. In all of these situations, the assessment or internal audit function is being carried out directly as a part of a basic management role. However, as the operations of an enterprise become more voluminous and complex, it is no longer practicable for the owner or top manager to have enough contact with all operations to satisfactorily review the effectiveness of enterprise performance. These responsibilities need to be delegated.

Although this hypothetical senior manager could build a supervisory system to try to provide a personal overview of operations, he or she will find it increasingly difficult to know whether the interests of the enterprise are being properly served as the enterprise grows larger and more complex. Are established procedures being complied with? Are assets being properly safeguarded? Are the various employees functioning efficiently? Are the current approaches still effective in the light of changing conditions?

The ultimate response to these questions is that the manager must obtain further help by assigning one or more individuals to be directly responsible for reviewing activities and reporting on the previously mentioned types of questions. It is here that the internal auditing activity comes into being in a formal and explicit sense. The first internal auditing assignments usually originated to satisfy very basic and sharply defined operational needs. The earliest special concern of management was whether the assets of the enterprise were being properly protected, whether company procedures and policies were being complied with, and whether financial records were being accurately maintained. There was also considerable emphasis on maintenance of the status quo. To a great extent, this internal auditing effort can be viewed as a closely related extension of the work of external auditors.

The result of all of these factors was that the early internal auditors were viewed as playing a narrow role in their enterprises, with relatively limited responsibility in the total managerial spectrum. Their body of knowledge needs were increasing. An early internal auditor was viewed as a financially oriented checker of records and more of a police officer than a coworker. In some enterprises, internal auditors once had major responsibilities for reconciling canceled payroll checks with bank statements or checking the mathematics in regular business documents. As mentioned, internal auditors in smaller retail enterprises are often still responsible for reconciling daily cash sales to recorded sales receipts.

Understanding the *history of internal auditing* is important because this old image of internal auditors still exists to some extent in various places in the world. This is so even though the character of the internal auditing function is now very different. Over time, the operations of various enterprises increased in volume and complexity, creating managerial problems and new pressures on senior management. In response to these pressures, many senior managers recognized the possibilities for better utilization of their internal auditors. Here were individuals already set up in an enterprise internal audit function, and there seemed to be every good reason for getting greater value from them with relatively little increase in cost.

Internal auditors perceived these opportunities and initiated new types of services themselves. Thus they gradually took on broader and more management-oriented responsibilities in their work efforts. Because internal auditing was initially largely accounting-oriented, this upward trend was felt first in the accounting and financial-control areas. Rather than just report the same accounting-related exceptions, such as some item of documentation lacking a supervisor's initial, internal auditors now usually questioned the overall control processes they were reviewing. Subsequently, internal audit valuation work began to be extended to include many nonfinancial areas in the enterprise.

New business initiatives, such as the COSO (Committee of Sponsoring Organizations) internal control framework discussed in Chapters 3 and 4 or the Sarbanes-Oxley Act (SOx) requirements, highlighted in Chapter 5, have caused a continuing increase in the need for the services of internal auditors. In addition, internal auditors today should be very much interested in governance, risk, and compliance (GRC) issues that are emphasized in our chapters on COSO internal controls and discussed in other chapters.

Internal auditors in past years often felt that fraud detection and prevention were not their responsibility but were an issue for legal authorities. Similarly, risk management in the past was often viewed as a concern only for the insurance department and not internal audit. But the profession has changed, and an understanding of both of these issues should be part of an internal auditors' common body of knowledge; risk management is discussed in Chapter 7, and fraud detection and prevention in Chapter 27.

Ethics and social responsibility issues are another concern for the modern internal auditor and are discussed in Chapter 26. As a result of these new pressures, the skills and services of internal auditors have become more important to all interested parties. There are now more and better-qualified internal auditing personnel and a higher level of enterprise status and importance attached to the position. The IIA has grown from its first New York City, 25-member charter chapter in 1942 to an international association with about 150,000 members and hundreds of local chapters worldwide. At the same time, the importance of internal audit has been recognized by external auditors through their auditing standards, as discussed in Chapter 9. The internal audit profession has reached a major level of maturity and is well positioned for continuing dynamic growth.

Internal auditing today involves a broad spectrum of types of operational activity and levels of coverage. Today, internal audit's role is constantly being redefined. Internal auditing has moved beyond being a staff activity often roughly tied to the controller's department, to a function reporting to the audit committee of the board, and SOx, discussed in Chapter 5, has been a major driver of change for internal auditors in the United States and worldwide. While they once had a nominal reporting relationship to the audit committee of the board, SOx has strengthened and formalized that reporting relationship. However, in some other enterprises, internal audit continues to function at just a routine compliance level. In other situations, it still suffers from being integrated too closely with regular accounting activities and limits virtually all of its audit work to strictly financial areas. These are all exceptions that do not reflect the potential capabilities of modern internal auditors. They may also reflect a lack of progressive attitudes in the overall enterprise.

Today, internal audit has expanded its activities to all operational areas of the modern enterprise and has established itself as a valued and respected part of the senior management resources. The modern internal auditor is formally and actively serving the board of directors' audit committee, and the person responsible for an internal audit function, the chief audit executive, today has direct and active communication with the audit committee. This situation reflects major progress in the scope of internal audit's coverage and level of service to all areas of the enterprise. The internal auditing profession itself, through its own self-development and dedication, has contributed to this progress and has set the stage for a continuing upward trend.

1.2 MISSION OF INTERNAL AUDITING

Management authors over the years have talked about the need for and importance of enterprises and organizations at all levels to establish formal *mission statements* to help management and all members of the enterprise team set consistent goals in their activities. Formal mission statements are an important and now well-recognized concept. This author in past editions of this book has talked about the importance of mission statements and how internal auditors should look for them when reviewing enterprise operations.

However, many internal audit professionals and certainly this author did not give sufficient attention to the fact that internal auditors lacked their own mission statement. Perhaps the definition of internal auditing and internal auditors' long history of reviewing internal controls and assisting management with its recommendations caused internal auditors themselves to assume that their mission is understood by all.

The internal auditors' professional organization, the IIA, has now decided that all internal auditors need to have a mission statement that supports the profession. The IIA ties internal audit standards and other important internal auditing attributes into what is called the *International Professional Practices Framework (IPPF)*, an effort to bring standards and other internal audit attributes together. The mission of internal auditing is:

> To enhance and protect organizational value by providing stakeholders with risk-based objective and reliable assurance, advice and insight.

These are valuable concepts to help understand the role and importance of internal auditing that we will reference in the chapters going forward. The purpose of this internal auditing mission statement is to provide internal auditors with a clear understanding of what they should aspire to achieve in their enterprises. Along with the definition of internal auditing introduced in this chapter, internal audit standards from Chapter 9, and other materials in the following chapters, this mission statement should help them better understand their roles. An understating of this internal audit mission statement is a strong internal audit CBOK requirement.

1.3 ORGANIZATION OF THIS BOOK

The object of this book is to define the practice of modern internal auditing as it exists today and to describe a common body of knowledge (CBOK) for the profession. While we generally think of an internal auditor as a professional affiliated with the IIA and its standards, he or she is really a larger, broader person today. Many enterprises have a parallel—almost a shadow—group of quality auditors who primarily follow the internal audit standards of the American Society for Quality (ASQ; www.asq.org). These are internal auditors with different backgrounds but similar approaches to IIA-background internal auditors; we should hopefully see greater convergence of these two in the years ahead.

This book's 34 chapters endeavor to define the practice of modern internal auditing today and to describe an internal audit CBOK. Relying on the internal auditing insights and a heritage, going back to *Victor Brink*'s earliest editions, but with a focus on new and evolving trends and technologies, the chapters are organized into eight parts or sections as discussed in Chapter 2.

The chapters following define a professional CBOK for internal auditors, the areas that all internal auditors should know and understand. When Victor Brink developed this first edition many years ago, he was defining a modern internal auditor as a new and important professional who was more than just an external auditor's helper. How the profession has grown and changed! Our modern internal auditing CBOK emphasizes the roles and responsibilities of today's modern internal auditor. It is our objective that the materials in the following chapters will help all internal auditors to gain knowledge and expertise in this profession and for management and others to better understand the practice of modern internal auditing.

NOTE

1. Walter B. Meigs, *Accounting Review* 35, no. 2 (April 1960): 377.

CHAPTER TWO

An Internal Audit Common Body of Knowledge

INTERNAL AUDIT PROFESSIONALS CONSTANTLY ENCOUNTER areas where they are expected to gain personal and professional knowledge to assist them in performing internal audits. These knowledge areas come from industry developments, standards changes introduced by the Institute of Internal Auditors (IIA) or others, technology changes such as use of new Internet Web services, or just good ideas developed from other internal auditors through the IIA's "Progress through Sharing" motto. Some of this knowledge comes from learning more about industry-specific regulatory requirements; other ideas are just good ways to make internal audits more effective and efficient. The bottom line, though, is that internal auditors at all levels are expected to have knowledge in a wide variety of areas, some unique to an individual enterprise or product area and others covering the general practice of internal auditing. There are a lot of knowledge area needs, and a new internal auditor might ask, "What do I need to know to become an experienced, qualified, and well-recognized internal auditor?"

Over time experienced internal auditors have given differing answers to this question. Victor Brink in the first edition of this book introduced a variety of internal audit knowledge areas, but that was before the days of information technology (IT) systems and processes, the Internet, and the massive changes in world businesses over the last 60-plus years. Other authors have tried to define internal auditor knowledge requirements, and this author certainly tried to explain many internal audit knowledge areas in the previous editions of this book. However, until our seventh edition, there was no recognized minimal set of *internal audit knowledge requirements*. That is, there had been no published *common body of knowledge (CBOK)* for the professional of internal auditing.

This lack of a CBOK for the professional practice of internal auditing was recognized by William G. Bishop III, CIA (Certified Internal Auditor), who served as president of the IIA from 1992 until his untimely death in 2004. Subsequent to Bishop's death, the IIA recognized this need for a CBOK for the profession and contracted with a team of researchers to survey the practices that might define such a CBOK for internal auditing. The results of their efforts to date will be discussed later in this chapter.

Given this book's historical background and ongoing attempts to describe all aspects of the profession of internal auditing, "A Common Body of Knowledge" was the subtitle and a major theme for the prior, seventh edition, and even more so for this one. The following chapters describe the major common knowledge requirements for today's modern internal auditor—some of these are areas where an internal auditor *must* have a strong knowledge and understanding. Others are areas where an internal auditor *should* develop a good general awareness. An example of the former is Chapter 9 on internal audit professional standards. That is an essential internal must-have knowledge area. Other topics, such as Chapter 32 on Six Sigma and what are called lean techniques, cover areas where an internal auditor should have a good general awareness. Taken together, however, the following chapters define an internal auditing common body of knowledge.

2.1 WHAT IS A CBOK? EXPERIENCES FROM OTHER PROFESSIONS

Business and professional terms and acronyms are often used and reused so often that we sometimes miss their true meanings. The phrase *common body of knowledge* falls in that category. A CBOK for any profession defines the minimum level of proficiency needed for effective performance within that profession. Rather than embodying all the knowledge domains that a practitioner, such as an internal auditor, might need in order to be viewed as an expert in that profession, a CBOK focuses on the minimal knowledge needed by any professional in that discipline to perform effectively.

A Web search for "CBOK" on Google or other search engines gives references to multiple professional organizations that have developed or attempted to develop their own CBOKs. For example, the Association of Business Process Management Professionals International (ABPMP; www.abpmp.org), a relatively small professional organization with roots in the European Union, has released its own CBOK and published several guidance books describing its approach.

The Bank Administration Institute (BAI; www.bai.org) also has released a CBOK for banking industry risk professionals. With risk management an important knowledge area of banking, BAI felt that a CBOK was necessary to define knowledge needs and expectations for banking professionals specializing in that area. Knowledge and an understanding of the areas described in this CBOK have enhanced the professional credibility of some professionals. Sometimes, however, the development of a CBOK started as a good idea that fizzled out for lack of funding or interest. The once-prominent Institute for the Certification of Computer Professionals (ICCP)[1] had attempted to develop its own IT-oriented CBOK, but IT processes and knowledge areas move faster than any group has been able to document and describe. Never really fully launched, the ICCP CBOK is little more than a historical footnote on the Web today.

Other professional organizations have dubiosly added the "BOK" suffix onto a set of practices common to their profession. For example, the Project Management

Institute (PMI) has published a set of knowledge requirements for project managers, its Project Management Body of Knowledge (PMBOK).[2] Many specialized professional organizations have tried to capture all of the terms or concepts that a professional operating in that field should know. Even the U.S. Department of Homeland Security has developed an IT-based cybersecurity standard that they call the Essential Body of Knowledge (EBK).[3]

The formats and contents of these various published BOK documents vary. Some are little more than fairly general outlines, while others are very detailed descriptions of specific knowledge areas where a professional will be expected to have some skills or to operate. The PMI's PMBOK is a good example of what a professional should expect in a body of knowledge compendium. The guide breaks down all elements of the project management process, describing inputs, tools, and techniques, and then outputs for each element. The elements are then linked to other activities in the project management process. Knowledge or understanding is an important internal audit skill, whether it is planning a comprehensive plan of internal audits over the year or outlining the requirements and tasks for a specific audit. Chapter 16 on understanding project management references this PMI PMBOK as part of an internal audit CBOK requirement area.

No type of published CBOK can simply stand by itself, no matter how detailed its descriptions. For internal auditors, a CBOK will cover a wide variety of internal audit–specific practice areas, an understanding of general management practices, and some general application knowledge areas. These requirements must be considered or linked, as shown in Exhibit 2.1. This concept should be considered for all published bodies of knowledge.

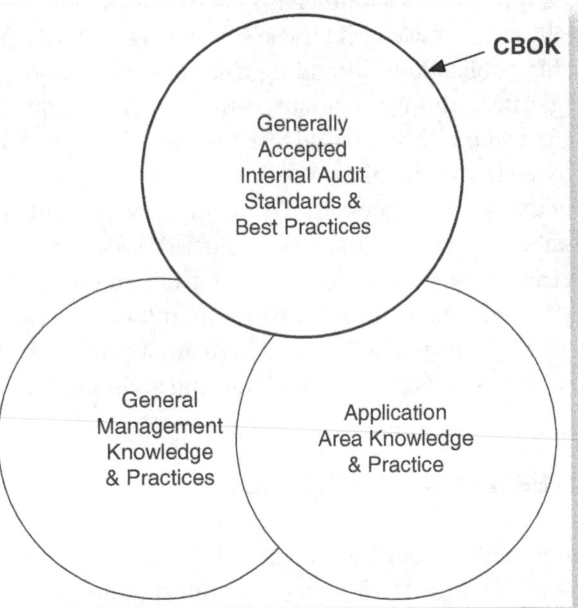

EXHIBIT 2.1 Relationship of a CBOK to Other Knowledge Areas

2.2 WHAT DOES AN INTERNAL AUDITOR NEED TO KNOW?

Victor Brink's first edition of this book, way back in the 1940s, greatly expanded the profession of internal auditing and outlined many areas where this then-new, developing profession can be a help to enterprises and to society. As business practices and technologies have changed over the years, Brink, in his first several early editions, and certainly this current author in subsequent editions, tried to introduce these newer, evolving areas that are important to today's internal auditors.

The chapters following have combined these into areas that an internal auditor should know and others where there at least should be a good general understanding as an internal audit CBOK. We highlighted these topic areas in the preface to this book and will describe them in greater detail in the chapters to come. Does every internal auditor need to have a detailed understanding of all of the topics summarized in the preface? We would argue an answer of no, but we feel an internal auditor should develop a general understanding of essentially all the issues and topics we discuss. Some of these may be specialized, but an internal auditor must have at least an awareness of them. All internal auditors, and especially the new internal auditor, should be familiar with materials such as the Committee of Sponsoring Organizations (COSO) internal control framework, discussed in Chapter 3, as well as Chapter 8's discussion on planning and performing internal audits and Chapter 9 on the IIA internal audit standards. Other chapters may only point to areas where an internal auditor can gain some support information. However, internal auditors can use this material to gain a better understanding of the depth and breadth of modern internal auditing.

The more experienced internal auditor will specialize in some areas as well as gain more industry-specific knowledge. Whether the enterprise manufactures heavy industrial equipment or provides financial services, an experienced internal auditor should develop skills and knowledge of those specific areas. This can come from reading industry-specific publications, attending trade shows, or just listening, listening, and more listening. After gaining that industry-specific knowledge, an internal auditor should be able to use some of this knowledge to merge with internal audit principles, as appropriate, discussed in the chapters to come.

It is an objective of this book that internal auditors at all levels gain an understanding—albeit sometimes just a very general understanding—of some of the many topic areas that impact the profession of internal auditing. When encountering a topic such as ITIL® internal control concerns, an internal auditor should be able to turn to the index of this book and find some general information on ITIL®, as discussed in Chapter 19, as well as some ITIL®-related internal audit issues.

2.3 AN INTERNAL AUDITING CBOK

The field of internal auditing is very broad, and this book covers what are the most important knowledge areas for today's modern internal auditor. These include both topics where it is essential that today's modern internal auditor have a strong understanding and knowledge to use and apply in internal audit activities and other areas where an internal auditor should have a general knowledge. These CBOK areas come from industry developments, standards changes introduced by the Institute of Internal Auditors (IIA) or others, technology developments such as audit issues surrounding the use of wireless and cloud computing, and other well-recognized practices developed from internal auditors worldwide through the IIA's "Progress through Sharing" motto. Some of this internal audit knowledge comes from an understanding of industry-specific regulatory requirements as well as just good ideas to make internal audits more effective and efficient. The bottom line, though, is that internal auditors at all levels should have knowledge in a wide variety of areas, some unique to an individual enterprise or product area, and others covering the general practice of internal auditing. There are a lot of knowledge area needs, and a new internal auditor might ask, "What do I need to know to become an experienced, qualified, and well-recognized internal auditor?"

This author first was exposed to this profession by enrolling in a 1975 evening hours college course on internal auditing in Minneapolis taught by Leon Radde, while working as an IT systems analyst for the computer manufacturer Sperry UNIVAC. Radde, who went on to become the IIA's chairman of the board, used Larry Sawyer's book[4] to introduce him to the topic, and this author used that internal audit knowledge to join a team that launched a worldwide IT audit practice first for Sperry. As the author's biography shows, he went on to accept internal audit positions of increasing responsibility, became an author on his own, and then met with Victor Brink to write an earlier edition of this book. He has also been an active member of the IIA over the years, serving in IIA chapter leadership positions and speaking at conferences.

With a broad and continuing experience in many aspects of internal auditing, this edition and the seventh edition have assembled a wide range of internal auditing guidance and information to develop this internal audit CBOK.

CBOK Requirements: Importance of Internal Controls

The four chapters in Part Two of this book introduce some common practices that are essential knowledge requirements for every internal auditor. Chapter 3 discusses how enterprises and their internal auditors went for many years without a clear and consistent understanding of the meaning and concept of internal controls. These definitions were resolved and clarified, however, through the Committee of Sponsoring Organizations (COSO) internal control framework, a three-dimensional description or model of how an enterprise should organize and think of its internal controls. Originally launched as sort of best practices description of good internal controls, the COSO internal control framework has become first the U.S. and now a worldwide standard for defining and establishing good internal controls. Whether operating in an industry environment, as an IT specialist internal auditor, or in not-for-profit or governmental sectors, every internal auditor should possess a CBOK understanding of the COSO internal control framework.

The COSO internal control framework was revised and updated in 2014, with the need for a greater emphasis on fraud management and understanding risks as well as evolving worldwide enterprise organizational structures. COSO is now supported by a set of 17 internal control principles, a key internal audit knowledge requirement. The revised COSO framework and its supporting principles are introduced in Chapters 3 and 4.

In the early part of this century, a series of major accounting frauds and business failures in the United States and elsewhere became a clarion call for external auditing and corporate governance reforms. The result was the Sarbanes-Oxley Act (SOx) in the United States, discussed in Chapter 5. SOx defines mandatory rules and reporting standards for many enterprises, large and small, in the United States and worldwide. Although the SOx legislation is very broad and has regulations and rules in some areas that may be of little interest to most internal auditors, a knowledge and understanding of the SOx internal control review procedures should be a CBOK requirement for all internal auditors working at least with public corporations. In addition, all internal auditors should have general CBOK understanding of the SOx internal control and its corporate governance rules.

Chapter 6 introduces another very important internal control framework, the control objectives for IT, or COBIT. An internal control framework with origins tied to IT audit specialists, COBIT is important for all internal auditors because IT systems and processes are pervasive in all aspects of virtually every enterprise today. Whether operational, financial, or IT specialists, all internal auditors should have at least a high-level CBOK understanding of the COBIT framework and how it might apply to their internal audit activities.

Part Two ends with a description of the COSO Enterprise Risk Management (COSO ERM) framework, a model to help understand and describe enterprise risk management. A basic understanding of the concepts and principles of risk management is important to internal auditors today, as support to assess various areas to review and make other internal audit decisions. Every internal auditor should have a high-level CBOK understanding of COSO ERM as discussed in Chapter 7.

CBOK Requirements: Planning and Performing Internal Audits

Having a good knowledge and understanding of COSO internal controls helps an internal auditor to understand important basic principles, but an internal auditor needs the knowledge of how to plan and perform internal audits. The six chapters in Part Three include some of this CBOK background information, starting with Chapter 8 on performing effective internal audits. The ability to plan and perform an individual internal audit is a key CBOK requirement.

A very strong understanding of the IIA's *International Standards for the Professional Practice of Internal Auditing* is a very key internal audit CBOK requirement. These are the rules, summarized in Chapter 9, that outline how an internal auditor should launch, conduct, and manage any review, whether in an audit attest engagement or while serving as an internal consultant. These are internal audit's marching orders, and a good knowledge and understanding of them is an essential CBOK requirement.

While its technical details can be a challenge for some internal auditors, all should have a CBOK high-level of understanding of internal audit testing and evaluation procedures, including statistical and nonstatistical audit sampling, as discussed in Chapter 10. Internal auditors should know how to appropriately look at a body of audit evidence, pull and review an appropriate sample from that evidence, and then make an audit decision and recommendations from that sample.

The modern internal auditor today should not always perform reviews as a one-time scheduled visit, but should take advantage of the automated processes that are installed in many enterprises and build continuous auditing processes where appropriate, a CBOK knowledge and awareness need discussed in Chapter 11. Internal auditors should perform their reviews using what are called audit programs, documented steps covering the audit procedures to follow. Internal auditors at all levels should understand how to construct and use audit programs, to serve as a guide for constructing consistent internal audit reviews.

Chapter 12 covers another important area where internal auditors should perform self-audits and to assess how peer groups are performing similar internal audit functions. Called control self-assessments and benchmarking, these are CBOK knowledge areas, and internal auditors should have a good CBOK understanding of them.

CBOK Requirements: Organizing and Managing Internal Audit Activities

Part Four covers important CBOK areas on managing and performing individual audits as well as other individual internal audit skills. For example, Chapter 14 discusses audit charters, the official enterprise audit committee authorizations of an internal audit function. Chapter 15 discusses some key internal audit effectiveness competencies. Both of these are CBOK areas essential for effective internal auditing.

Project management is presented and discussed in Chapter 16. Every internal audit project should be planned and organized in a well-structured, consistent manner, and the chapter provides an overview of understanding project management—a CBOK general knowledge requirement.

Chapter 17 covers an essential internal auditor CBOK area, documenting audit results through workpapers. Although detailed processes and techniques may vary from one internal audit function to another, all internal auditors should have the knowledge and understanding of how to develop effective workpapers to describe individual audit activities.

Although formats can vary from one internal audit function to another, the ability to report internal audit results effectively is a key CBOK requirement. Although much of the effort in developing and delivering formal internal audit reports is often delegated to more senior members in the internal audit team, all internal auditors should have a strong CBOK understanding of the purposes and roles of their enterprise's internal audit reports, as discussed in Chapter 18.

CBOK Requirements: Impact of Information Technology on Internal Auditing

Because IT processes are so critical to all areas of business operations today, the six chapters of Part Five describe some very important CBOK areas. Chapter 19 discusses performing IT general-controls reviews as well the Information Technology Infrastructure Library (ITIL®) best practices for understanding and installing IT infrastructure control procedures. These are CBOK areas in which every internal auditor should have a good general understanding.

Technology changes and handheld and wireless devices are common today both for enterprise applications and as internal auditor tools. Chapter 20 introduces internal control issues in this internal audit environment. Chapter 21 introduces two other newer, important and evolving internal control issues—what we call big data and enterprise content management. For years, internal auditors have recommended that IT applications have appropriate backups. Because systems and applications generate so much data today, internal auditors need to understand the management of these processes in a well-controlled manner.

While the general controls that cover the overall IT function are important, internal controls covering specific IT applications are at least as crucial. For virtually all internal auditors, a CBOK understanding of these IT control concepts is particularly vital, as many IT applications and their internal control responsibilities have moved from traditional centralized IT functions to individual user-managed controls. Internal auditors should have a good CBOK understanding of IT application controls as discussed in Chapter 22.

With our heavy reliance on IT applications and processes as well as the use of the Internet, networked applications, and IT resources, these same applications face a multitude of security and privacy threats. Chapter 23 discusses cybersecurity and IT privacy controls. While IT security issues are often a very special and complex area, internal auditors should try to gain an overall high-level CBOK understanding of cybersecurity internal control issues.

The last chapter in Part Five, Chapter 24, discusses business continuity planning and disaster recovery, areas where technology has made it much easier than in past years for an enterprise to save its IT-stored data to recover operations after some unexpected event. Though this area was once very much the realm of IT specialist auditors, every internal auditor today should have a CBOK general understanding of continuity planning and recovery operations.

CBOK Requirements: Internal Audit and Enterprise Governance

Events such as the enactment of SOx, a growing recognition of the importance of enterprise-level fraud, and other new laws have made many aspects of the business world increasingly complex and have added to an internal auditor's CBOK needs. The four chapters in Part Six look at several areas where internal auditors should develop a CBOK understanding. Chapter 25 reviews internal audit communications and relationships with the board of directors' audit committee. While this is a critical requirement, particularly for the CAE, all members of an internal audit function should have a general CBOK understanding of the role of the audit committee in internal audit operations, and especially that role in their own specific enterprise. In a similar sense, Chapter 26 discusses ethics and whistleblower programs, important initiatives in many enterprises. Again, these are areas where internal auditors need to develop a good CBOK understanding of effective programs and why they are important to internal audit.

Understanding basic fraud detection and prevention controls, as introduced in Chapter 27, should be a basic CBOK requirement for all internal auditors. This is an area where in past years internal auditors were not been expected to have the skills to look for fraud. While the typical internal auditor today may not be a Sherlock Holmes–level fraud investigator, all internal auditors should gain a good CBOK level of understanding of both the red flags that indicate a possibility of fraud and general internal audit fraud investigation review procedures.

Chapter 28 covers the importance of overall governance, reporting, and compliance (GRC) issues in today's internal audit and internal controls environments. The chapter reviews the importance of GRC issues in general for the modern internal auditor, and looks at several U.S. laws—HIPAA and the Gramm-Leach-Bliley Act—that have some strong enterprise-level compliance requirements. While U.S.-based internal auditors should gain a CBOK general understanding of these and related compliance regulations, internal auditors worldwide should always develop similar CBOK understandings of the rules that govern compliance in their own countries and locations.

CBOK Requirements: Internal Auditor Professional Certifications

While it is certainly not an internal auditor CBOK requirement, all internal auditors should be aware of the more important and well-recognized internal audit professional certifications. Chapter 29 reviews the requirements for several of these—the CIA and CISA certifications—and discusses some other related certifications as well.

Chapter 30 discusses the role of the internal auditor as an internal enterprise business consultant. A practice that was banned by internal audit standards until recent years, serving as an internal consultant can be an important role for internal audit and its enterprise organization in many situations. Internal auditors should have a good general CBOK understanding of the internal audit standards for serving as an enterprise consultant.

CBOK Requirements: Internal Auditing Professional Convergence

The last part of our CBOK requirements discussion introduces the need for internal auditors to have a greater understanding of some internal audit issues that go beyond just IIA-related internal auditing and its standards. For example, Chapter 31 introduces the area of quality internal auditing. These are internal audit procedures that are defined and described in the United States by the American Society for Quality (ASQ). All internal auditors should develop at least a CBOK understanding of the ASQ quality internal audit standards and procedures.

Related to ASQ quality audit procedures, Chapter 32 discusses two quality efficiency process methodologies: lean techniques and Six Sigma. Both are valuable internal control process improvement approaches that an internal auditor will most frequently encounter on the shop or production floor. However, an internal auditor working in a process or manufacturing systems environment should have a general CBOK awareness or understanding of these important methodologies.

Chapter 33 introduces International Organization for Standardization (ISO) international standards, with an emphasis on quality and IT management standards. These standards and the compliance efforts to meet them have been in place worldwide for some years. They are increasingly appearing in U.S. environments, and internal auditors who have worked in an IIA standards environment over the years should gain a greater CBOK understanding of these ISO standards and their supporting concepts.

Chapter 33 also very briefly introduces some worldwide accounting and auditing standards. In particular, what are called international accounting standards have been preferred almost everywhere in the world, with the exception of the United States, where what have been called generally accepted accounting principles (GAAP) are used. Although it is not yet official, the United States is now slowly moving from GAAP to the international standards. While this does not have a major impact on internal audit procedures, all internal auditors should gain a CBOK understanding of the implications of this change.

2.4 ANOTHER ATTEMPT: THE IIA RESEARCH FOUNDATION'S CBOK

Chapter 1 highlighted the origins of internal auditing and discussed how the profession has evolved from one of primarily accounting support and mathematical-accuracy checking to today's internal control evaluation specialists. The profession has come a long way. Following the IIA's *International Standards for the Professional Practice of Internal Auditing,* described in Chapter 9, internal auditors today work in corporate, not-for-profit, and governmental agencies worldwide. They work in all sizes of enterprises, in all industry areas, and under many different conditions.

Going beyond the IIA standards and some legal requirements for internal audit reviews, there had not been many defined rules of right and wrong guidance for internal audit practices. However, over the years, internal audit professionals have expressed a need to better formalize things and develop an internal audit CBOK. Although there had been several limited attempts to develop such a body of knowledge, the *IIA Research Foundation (IIARF)* contracted with a consulting group in 2007 to develop such a CBOK for the internal audit profession. This occurred at about the same time we were developing our CBOK for the prior, seventh edition of this book. The original 2007 IIARF CBOK was based on e-mail surveys and was called *A Global Summary of the Common Body of Knowledge.*[5]

The stated objective of this IIA consultant–led survey was to capture and describe the state of the internal auditing professional practices throughout the world, including:

- The knowledge and skills that internal auditors possess
- The skill and organizational levels used for the practice of internal auditing work
- The actual duties performed by internal auditors
- The structure of internal audit organizations
- The types of industries that practice internal audit
- The regulatory environment of various countries

The IIARF CBOK had the stated objective of documenting the unique value-added role of internal auditing in enterprises throughout the world. It sought to better define the profession of internal auditing and ensure that it remains a "vibrant and relevant contribution to enterprises." The IIA has stated that it plans to use the results of its not very well defined CBOK study to improve standards, procedures, and other offerings in future years in areas including revised internal audit certifications and examinations, revised standards, and other internal audit publications. However, at the time of this 2015 publication, the organization has done essentially nothing to keep this concept alive.

The IIARF's CBOK 2007 objective, however, was not a set of high-level standards for performing internal audits, such as the approach used in the PMI's PMBOK, discussed further in Chapter 16, or the Information Technology Infrastructure Library (ITIL®) best practices that can be found in Chapter 19. It did not cover areas where internal auditors should have a good knowledge as well as others where they should have awareness, as will be presented in these chapters. Rather, the IIARF sought to gain a better knowledge of the current duties and activities of internal auditors in various IIA chapter units worldwide and of individuals operating as heads of internal audit functions, including chief audit executives, audit managers, internal audit seniors/supervisors, staff members, and others affiliated with internal audit.

Although it was called a CBOK, the IIARF's approach did not define or recommend internal audit common knowledge best practices but was based instead on internal auditors' responses to a questionnaire. Contractors developed a detailed survey form that was sent to some 9,000 individual internal audit functions around the world. The summarized results provided a view of what internal audit departments—what the IIARF CBOK document calls Internal Auditing Activities (IAAs)—were doing as part of their work. Significantly, there was no split between IIARF CBOK's defined IAAs in larger countries, such as the United States and the United Kingdom, and those in smaller-country internal audit functions.

The 2007 IIARF CBOK surveys were assembled similar to a consumer-type survey where participants were asked to respond to questions based on a score ranging from 1 to 5 for each question. That is, a response of 5 meant the respondent strongly agreed to a survey question, 4 meant they somewhat agreed, and a 1 indicated that they strongly disagreed. The results were published as a single mean value of the various 1-to-5 responses but with no standard deviation values to show the variances or ranges of those responses. For example, the IIRF CBOK study asked for responses to the statement "Your internal audit activity brings a systematic approach to evaluate the effectiveness of internal controls." A reported 2,374 CAEs responded to this question, with a mean value of 4.35. Does this mean that some internal audit functions *do not* follow a systematic approach in their reviews of internal controls, and does such a response mean this is by design or default? If true, these would have been disturbing results.

A problem with these reported results is that we do not have any further information to support the types of responses or the variances in the reported scores. While the CAE for an effective internal audit function would be expected to respond to such a question with a score of 5, the published CBOK begs the question of why a certain portion of CAEs report that their internal audit function did not have a "strongly agree" score of 5 in place in response to the question about evaluating internal controls. Is it because a certain portion of internal audit functions are not very effective, or is it because of a natural tendency—this author is one of them—not to rate such a survey score on the total high or low end of the range? From our perspective, this is a problem with many of the now obsolete IIARF CBOK's reported responses. From CAEs to audit staff members, almost everything is reported with scores somewhat greater than 4.0 but less than 5.0. Three IIARF CBOK evaluation statements were ranked under 4.0 but above 3.5:

1. Your internal audit activity brings a systematic approach to evaluate the effectiveness of governance processes.
2. The way your internal audit activity adds value to the governance process is through direct access to the audit committee.
3. Compliance with the IIA's *International Standards for the Professional Practice of Internal Auditing* is a key factor for your internal audit activity to add value to governance processes.

With all levels of respondents reporting relatively low scores for these three questions, there would appear to be some internal audit management concerns here. Of course, decoding responses to these types of statements is always problematic. To the second statement in the list, does this say that a large number of the CBOK respondents do not feel their internal audit activities add value to their enterprise's governance activities, that they do not have sufficient access to their audit committees, or both? One almost has the feeling that no one at the IIARF read their CBOK consultants' study and asked some hard questions before its publication. There was much here contrary to the IIA CBOK guidance discussed in the following chapters.

The IIARF CBOK study was filled with some interesting survey results that showed what internal audit functions were doing across the world. If nothing else, this type of information will allow a CAE to assess whether his or her internal audit function is performing activities in line with other internal audit functions worldwide. We have extracted the results from two of CBOK's published table results, but the interested reader should contact the IIARF to receive a copy of these IIRF CBOK results.

As an example of the IIARF's CBOK reported materials, Exhibit 2.2 shows the relative internal audit usage, ranked both overall and by level of internal auditor, for a series of common internal audit tools and techniques. CBOK selected 15 internal audit tools and techniques and ranked them by their utilization. These important tools and techniques are also the basis for many of our chapters going forward. Not unexpectedly, the Internet and related e-mail processes were then found to be the most important internal auditing tools and techniques. The IIA has very much emphasized quality management processes over recent years and built them into their standards, and Chapter 31 discusses the importance of quality assurance internal auditing procedures.

As another example of the old IIARF CBOK materials, Exhibit 2.3 contains a series of survey statements that were directed to CAEs and to internal audit managers asking if the statement currently applied to their internal audit function, would they likely install the practice in the future, or if it was not applicable or not planned. While certain of these survey questions surely would not apply to some not-for-profit and other internal audit groups, many of the results here are surprising. For example, to the statement "The organization has implemented an internal control framework," only about 70% of internal audit mangers responded that they had such

EXHIBIT 2.2 Internal Audit Tools and Techniques Ranked by Overall Usage

Tools & Techniques	Overall	CAE	Audit Manager	Senior/ Supervisor	Audit Staff	Others
Internet & E-mail	1	1	1	1	1	1
Risk-Based Audit Planning	2	2	2	2	2	2
Analytical Reviews	3	3	4	3/4	4	3
Electronic Workpapers	4	4	3	3/4	3	4
Statistical Audit Sampling	5	5	6	5	5	5
Computer-Assisted Audit Techniques	6	6	5	6	6	6
Flowchart Software	7	7/8	7	7	8/9	7/8
Benchmarking	8	7/8	8	9/10	11	7/8
Process Mapping Applications	9	9	9	8	8/9	7/8
Control Self-Assessments	10	1	10	9/10	10	9
Data Mining	11	10	11	12	12	12
Continuous/Real-Time Auditing	12	12	13	11	7	11
IIA Quality Assessment Review Tools	13	13	12	14	14	14
Balanced Scorecard	14	14	14	13	15	15
Total Quality Management Techniques	15	15	15	15	13	16

Source: Based on results of IIARF's 2007 CBOK survey.

an internal control evaluation process currently in place, with the bulk of the others planning to do something within the next three years. With IIA standards calling for such activities to be in place as part of an effective and compliant internal audit function, it appears that much more work is needed. Chapters 3 through 6 discuss the importance of internal controls and a framework for establishing and measuring them. Beyond the tables extracted here, the 2007 IIARF CBOK was filled with other perhaps disturbing observations. At the time of this publication, the IIARF has deleted all references to its 2007 CBOK, acting as if it never happened. Perhaps, this is good for the profession. The interested reader should review the planned IIARF CBOK new study (not yet released at the time of this publication).

Although not directly summarized in these tables, some of the IIARF CBOK responses are professionally disturbing on several levels. For example, only some 82% of all IIARF CBOK respondents state that they use IIA standards in whole or in part. These are the ground rules for internal auditing, and one really wonders about the nearly 20% who say they do not use these standards, even in part. The importance of IIA standards will be discussed in Chapter 9, where we argue that knowledge of them is essential to drive and develop internal audits.

EXHIBIT 2.3 Internal Audit Management Responses to IIARF Survey Questions

Statement	Number of Respondents	Currently Applied	Likely to Apply Within the Next 3 Years	Will Not Apply in the Foreseeable Future	Not Applicable
Internal audit is required by law or regulation where the enterprise is based.	3,464	61.2	43.1	12.9	12.8
Internal auditors have an advisory role in enterprise strategy development.	3,445	28.9	32.7	30.3	8.0
Internal audit complies with a corporate governance code.	3,447	67.7	22.7	4.3	5.3
Internal audit has implemented an internal control framework.	3,443	70.5	24.3	3.5	1.7
Internal audit has implemented a knowledge management system.	3,423	25.6	43.9	20.6	9.9
The internal audit function has provided training to audit committee members.	3,424	34.0	32.3	18.5	15.1
Internal audit assumes an important role in the integrity of financial reporting.	3,437	55.7	25.6	13.7	4.9
Internal audit educates enterprise personnel regarding internal controls, corporate governance, and compliance issues.	3,437	64.3	25.3	7.3	3.1
Internal audit places more emphasis on assurance activities rather than on consulting services.	3,448	71.5	15.2	844.0	4.9

Source: Based on results of IIARF's 1997 CBOK survey.

Note: These findings were extracted from Table 2-14 from the IIARF's 2006 CBOK study.

The IIA had stated that it planned to update its IIARF CBOK study every three years and also expressed plans to release other products and offerings to enhance and build IIARF CBOK. However, nothing much happened following those plans, the IIA contracted for a new CBOK survey study in 2014, and questionnaires were sent to IIA members asking them for their CBOK practice opinions. At the time of this publication, the new IIARF has not yet been released and, as mentioned earlier, the IIARF has purged its 2007 study from its library of publications, as if it had never existed.

The 2007 IIARF CBOK survey was never a common body of knowledge study in the way other professional organizations define the concept or the way we define it in this book. The IIARF's CBOK was not a guide to internal auditor best practices. Rather, it described a wide range of internal audit activities and how they were then practiced. For the CAE as well as the audit committee and management responsible for internal audit within an enterprise, this original 2007 IIARF CBOK should be viewed as perhaps something of a wake-up call regarding how individual internal audit groups are performing in relationship to survey results and to IIA standards. In general, the IIARF CBOK points out many areas where an internal audit function should improve.

2.5 ESSENTIAL INTERNAL AUDIT KNOWLEDGE AREAS

Does every internal auditor need to have a detailed understanding of all of the topics summarized in the preface to this book? We would argue an answer of no, but we feel that any internal auditor should develop of general understanding of essentially all of the issues and topics discussed in this book. Some of these may be specialized, but an internal auditor must have at least awareness. For all internal auditors, and especially the new internal auditor, materials such as the Committee of Sponsoring Organization (COSO) internal control framework, discussed in Chapter 3, are essential, as well as Chapter 7's discussion on planning and performing internal audits and Chapter 9 on the IIA internal audit standards. Other chapter topics may only point to areas where an internal auditor can gain some support information. However, that same newer internal auditor can use this material to gain a better understanding of the depth and breadth of modern internal auditing.

The field and profession of internal auditing is broad, and this book only tries to cover what we feel are perhaps some of the most important knowledge areas for today's modern internal auditor. The chapters going forward define a CBOK for today's modern internal auditor.

NOTES

1. The organization, at www.iccp.org, was one of the early proponents of testing and certifying IT professionals through its Certificate in Data Processing (CDP) program from the 1970s. It attempted to develop a CBOK for computer professionals, but the project evidently ran out of steam in the late 1990s.

2. *A Guide to the Project Management Body of Knowledge* (*PMBOK Guide*), 5th ed. (Newtown Square, PA: Project Management Institute, 2013).
3. Information Technology (IT) Security Essential Body of Knowledge (EBK), U.S. Department of Homeland Security, October 2007.
4. Lawrence B. Sawyer, *Sawyer's Internal Auditing: The Practice of Modern Internal Auditing* (Altamonte Springs, FL: Institute of Internal Auditors, 1973). This author accessed the first edition of this book. It is still published by the IIA, but later editions are very much changed.
5. *A Global Summary of the Common Body of Knowledge* (Altamonte Springs, FL: Institute of Internal Auditors Research Foundation, 2007).

PART TWO

Importance of Internal Controls

CHAPTER THREE

The COSO Internal Control Framework

BUSINESS EXECUTIVES AND SOME internal auditors may ask, "Who or what is *COSO*"? It's not a standard or a detailed requirement but only a framework. In our business world of multiple rules and regulations that have requirements from multiple governmental and other regulatory agencies often using hard-to-remember acronyms, it is easy to roll our eyes or shrug our shoulders at yet another acronym and set of requirements. COSO *internal controls* is a framework outlining professional practices for establishing preferred business systems and processes that promote efficient and effective internal controls. The sponsoring organizations that issue and publish this material are neither governmental nor some other type of regulatory agencies. Nevertheless, the *COSO internal control framework* is an important set or model of guidance materials that enterprises should follow when developing their business processes, systems, and procedures as well as in establishing *Sarbanes-Oxley Act (SOx)* compliance. An understanding of the COSO internal control framework is an internal audit CBOK *must* requirement.

The COSO internal control framework was originally launched in the United States in 1992, now a long time ago. This was a period of some significant fraudulent business practices in the United States and elsewhere that revealed a well-recognized need for improved internal control processes and procedures guidance. This 1992 COSO internal control framework soon became a fundamental element of the American Institute of Certified Public Accountants (AICPA) auditing standards in the United States and eventually became the standard for enterprise external auditors in their reviews certifying that *enterprise internal controls* were adequate following the SOx rules discussed in Chapter 5. Because of its general nature describing good internal control practices, the COSO framework had never been revised until 2014.

Since the release of that original COSO framework, there have been many changes in business organizations and particularly in enterprise structures and IT processes. For example, mainframe computer systems with lots of batch processing procedures were common then but have all but gone away today, to be replaced by client-server and wireless systems. Also, the World Wide Web was barely getting started then and not nearly as prevalent as it is today. Because of the Internet, enterprise organizational structures have become much more fluid, flexible, and international. In addition, things like social network computing, powerful handheld devices, and cloud computing did not exist back then.

Although some might wonder why it took so long, COSO announced in 2011 that they were revising their internal control framework, and the final, revised COSO internal control framework description was finally released in mid-May 2014, with a full compliance requirement by the beginning of 2015. This chapter will first discuss the importance of internal control concepts and then will describe the newly revised COSO internal control framework and how internal auditors can use it to improve their internal control reviews.

3.1 UNDERSTANDING INTERNAL CONTROLS

In years past, business executives as well as internal and external auditors all viewed internal controls as one of those concepts that everyone agreed was important in business, but few could define consistently. Part of the problem was that many persons looked at internal controls in the manner of a classic organization chart, with its levels of senior and middle management in its multiple operating units or within different activities. At each level, people looked at internal controls within their own lines of authority. However, control procedures are often somewhat different at each of these organization levels and components. For example, one unit may operate in a regulated business environment where its control processes are very structured, while another divisional unit of the same core enterprise may be an entrepreneurial start-up operation with a less formal structure. Different levels of management in these enterprises will have different control concern perspectives. The question "How do you describe your system of internal controls?" could receive different answers from persons in various levels or components in each of these enterprise organizational units.

This whole internal control definition issue was resolved in the early 1990s when a consortium of professional accounting and auditing organizations—the AICPA, the Institute of Internal Auditors (IIA), and others—got together to develop a common definition of what was meant by good internal controls. These professional organizations became the Committee of Sponsoring Organizations (COSO) and were given authority by governmental organizations and others to develop a common definition of what is meant by good or adequate internal controls. COSO hired PricewaterhouseCoopers, did an extensive user organization survey, and began its work to develop a common internal control definition.

The original COSO internal control framework, released in 1992, provided an excellent description of this multidimensional concept, defining internal control as follows:

> Internal control is a *process*, effected by an entity's board of directors, management, and other personnel, designed to provide reasonable assurance regarding the achievement of objectives in the following categories:

- Effectiveness and efficiency of operations
- Reliability of *financial reporting*
- Compliance with applicable laws and regulations

This is the COSO definition of internal controls, and it has really not changed since its release. COSO originally used a three-dimensional model to describe an internal control system in an enterprise. Exhibit 3.1 illustrates the original COSO model of internal control as a pyramid with five layers or interconnected components comprising the overall internal control system. These are shown with a component called the *control environment* serving as the foundation for the entire structure. Four of these internal components are described as horizontal layers, with another component of internal control, called communication and information, acting as an interface channel for the other four layers.

The COSO model was quickly adopted by the auditing and accounting profession, first in the United States and then worldwide. It became particularly significant after the Sarbanes-Oxley Act (SOx) became law. SOx requires that public reporting organizations must attest to the adequacy of their internal controls, using the COSO framework as a measure.

While the basic concepts of internal controls have not much changed since that COSO framework was first released many years ago, the overall environment where business operates and internal auditors perform their reviews has changed a lot, including some of the following:

- **The rise of using contracted services, new organizational structures, and increased international connections.** While the single monolithic corporation, such as Ford Motor of some 100 years ago, is largely a thing of the past, organizational relationships today are often increasingly complex, with the use of contracted services, joint ventures, and different international business arrangements.

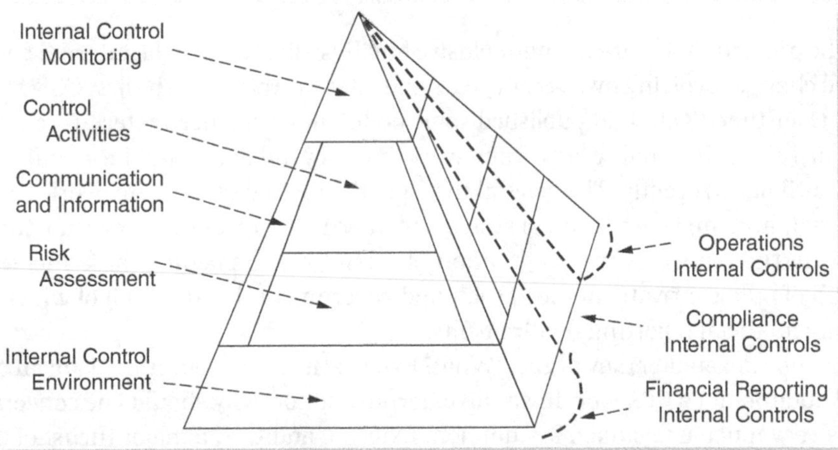

EXHIBIT 3.1 COSO Internal Controls Pyramid View

- **Increased compliance and regulatory requirements beyond just annual financial reporting.** Enterprises today are faced with multiple requirements to build and manage systems that are in compliance with a vast range of standards and legal and regulatory requirements, both in their own country and internationally.
- **Recognition that fraud prevention and detection is necessary for effective internal controls.** In years past, *fraud detection* and prevention measures were not considered to be accounting and auditing concerns but legal and enterprise security issues. These matters were still not part of the original COSO framework, but our attitudes have totally changed in recent years and internal auditors now have major responsibilities for fraud-related issues.
- **Increased needs for understanding and assessing risk as part of internal control operations on all levels.** Understanding and managing risk has become an increased requirement for internal auditors since the original COSO framework. While that original framework highlighted understanding risks as an internal control component, our understanding and concerns here have grown dramatically.
- **The constant changes in IT technologies and the way we use IT to build and manage processes.** If there is any area that has changed the most since the original COSO framework, it is the growth and prevalence of IT-related processes and technologies.
- **Ever-increasing security concerns, particularly IT security in today's big data era.** At the time of the original COSO framework, enterprise security concerns in general were far less of an issue and IT security often represented little more than a secure lock on the mainframe computer center door. How things have changed! A mixture of various Internet-based threats and general terrorism concerns worldwide have expanded internal control concerns.
- **Internal control implications associated with social media and wireless systems.** This is a totally new and evolving area since the original COSO framework was released. Social media systems such as Facebook now allow enterprise associates and others to get around enterprise rules and also to communicate with handheld wireless devices.

The previous items are not all-inclusive but illustrate some of the internal control–related changes evolving over recent years and after the release of the first COSO framework. Over time COSO had published some additional guidance materials to support and clarify their internal control framework, but they did not revise the overall framework until more recently. The general thrust of the revised COSO framework has been the design and implementation of systems of internal controls over external financial reporting that supports the preparation of financial statements. These include the breadth of public, private, not-for-profit, and governmental entities, all of which have external financial reporting requirements.

An internal auditor may argue, "What? External financial reporting? I am an operational auditor, not a CPA working as an external auditor; why should I be concerned?" This is very much a mistaken assumption. External auditors, a major thrust of COSO, review and assess the internal financial controls that have been installed in enterprise systems, but internal audit and enterprise management are responsible for monitoring as well as designing and installing these internal control processes. The COSO internal control framework is very relevant here, and business executives as well as their internal auditors, IT specialists, the finance and accounting staffs, and others should also be aware of and understand the COSO internal control framework. All should focus on the five basic principles that support enterprise COSO internal controls:

1. An organization should demonstrate a commitment to integrity and ethical values.
2. The board of directors should demonstrate independence from management and exercise oversight of the development and performance of internal controls.
3. Management should establish, with board oversight, structures, reporting lines, and appropriate authorities and responsibilities in the pursuit of objectives.
4. The organization should demonstrate a commitment to attract, develop, and retain competent individuals in alignment with objectives.
5. An organization should hold individuals accountable for their internal control responsibilities in the pursuit of objectives.

Each of these principles was part of the original framework and has continued with the new, revised framework described in greater detail in the following sections. As a CBOK must, internal auditors should always remember the three major components of internal controls—effectiveness and efficiency of operations, reliability of financial reporting, and compliance with applicable laws and regulations—to give three dimensions to this model. Just as the pyramid structure showed the internal control structure as the environment for all internal control processes, this view adds equal weight to each of these three components. The revised COSO internal control model and its components for the separate entities and activities in an enterprise will be discussed in more detail in the sections and other chapters following.

3.2 REVISED COSO FRAMEWORK BUSINESS AND OPERATING ENVIRONMENT CHANGES

It is important to remember who or what COSO is and the authority of its published guidance materials. As discussed previously, COSO, or the Committee of Sponsoring Organizations of the *Treadway Commission*, is a joint initiative of five private-sector professional accounting, auditing, and finance organizations. COSO is dedicated to providing thought leadership through the development of frameworks and guidance on enterprise risk management, internal control, and fraud deterrence. An important point here is that COSO does not have the authority to issue standards such as are found in government rules or professional organization guidance. Rather, this guidance, including the COSO internal control framework, outlines only an approach or recommended best practices that others should generally follow.

These COSO framework concepts have become the basis for standards-setting entities in other areas or requirements. Importantly, the Sarbanes-Oxley Act (SOx), discussed in Chapter 5, requires enterprises to have effective internal control systems in place that are consistent with the COSO internal control framework. Until recently, when an enterprise attested that its internal controls are in compliance with COSO, they were attesting to the original, 1992 COSO framework. As a result, both enterprise management and their external auditors seeking to establish SOx legal compliance have relied on the original COSO framework to assert their legal compliance. Enterprises at all levels, and certainly internal auditors, have kept this concept in mind when building, implementing, and monitoring their internal control systems and processes. Internal auditors should be aware that all of their existing audit programs and processes now should reflect the revised COSO framework. The new COSO internal control framework and its supporting guidance materials contain changes in the following areas:

- **Expanded expectations for governance oversight.** Increasing regulatory requirements and stakeholder expectations require boards of directors to increase their emphasis on the adequacy of internal financial controls in their enterprises.
- **Increased globalization of markets and operations.** Enterprises today increasingly expand beyond their traditional domestic markets in pursuit of value, often entering into international markets and engaging in cross-border mergers and acquisitions.
- **Changes and greater complexities in enterprise business operations.** Enterprises change their business models and enter into complex transactions in the pursuit of growth, greater quality, or productivity, as well as in response to changes in markets or regulatory environments. These changes may involve entering into joint ventures, strategic alliances, or other complex arrangements with external parties, implementing shared services, and engaging with outsourced service providers.
- **Increased demands and complexities in laws, rules, regulations, and standards.** Governmental authorities are increasingly releasing complex rules and legislation where compliance is often difficult to achieve and where these rules do not directly follow classic internal control approaches.
- **Ever-increasing use of and reliance on evolving technologies.** As we have highlighted in our introduction to this chapter, the growth of IT systems and related technologies has very much changed our approaches to implementing and managing internal control processes. Today's IT systems are increasingly based on automated internal controls and processes to build, install, and monitor these automated controls.
- **Increased need to prevent and detect corruption.** The U.S. Foreign Corrupt Practices Act, introduced many years ago and discussed in Chapter 2, was an earlier example of legislation to increase internal control and other legal requirements. Today, there is a wide range of anticorruption and antifraud rules and legislation in place, including international as well as often differing rules in many U.S. states.

Each of these COSO changes requires an enterprise to evaluate these implications on its systems of internal control with an emphasis on its external financial reporting, and to design and implement appropriate responses so that systems of internal control adapt and remain effective over time.

Internal auditors have a key role here in their understandings and evaluations of their organization's systems of internal controls. Such a system of internal control does not refer to a self-contained set of procedures, such as might be found in a smartphone application, but the overall processes and procedures necessary to perform some regular ongoing business function. An example might be the processes necessary to evaluate, acquire, and purchase production goods. Many people and functions may be involved in this purchasing process, but it should be done with consistent and adequate internal controls. Those internal controls should have been evaluated and assessed as part of the COSO internal control framework following the original 1992 version.

For any existing, ongoing enterprise, internal auditors should have been evaluating and assessing these internal controls in designated significant areas. Now with the current revised COSO internal control framework, internal auditors should evaluate what they have done in the past and make any necessary changes to comply with the COSO framework. The sections following describe the revised COSO internal control framework. Knowledge and understanding here is an essential CBOK requirement.

3.3 THE REVISED COSO INTERNAL CONTROL FRAMEWORK

In addition to the three internal control objective categories of operations, reporting, and compliance just described, the COSO framework defines internal controls from two other dimensions or perspectives: separate components of internal control and organization factors. Looking similar to but slightly different from the original COSO internal control framework that was introduced in 1992, Exhibit 3.2 shows the revised three-dimensional COSO internal control framework.

We will be using this internal control cube relationship here and in other chapters going forward. The three categories of *internal control objectives*—operations, reporting, and compliance—are represented by the columns defined at the top in this diagram. The front-facing side of this COSO cube diagram defines five key components or levels of internal control:

1. Control environment
2. Risk assessment
3. Internal control activities
4. Information and communication
5. Monitoring activities

This is the area where there have been the most changes in the new, revised COSO internal control framework. Each of these internal control activity levels or key components will be introduced and discussed in the chapters to come.

Shown on the right-facing side of the model, an enterprise's organizational structure is the third important dimension of internal control. It represents the internal control–related components of the overall organization structure: the enterprise entity itself, its divisions, subsidiaries, operating units, or functions, including business processes such as sales, purchasing, production, and marketing. As a key point here, we should keep in mind the components of overall organization entity starting with the overall or total enterprise in total and then breaking down to all business units and

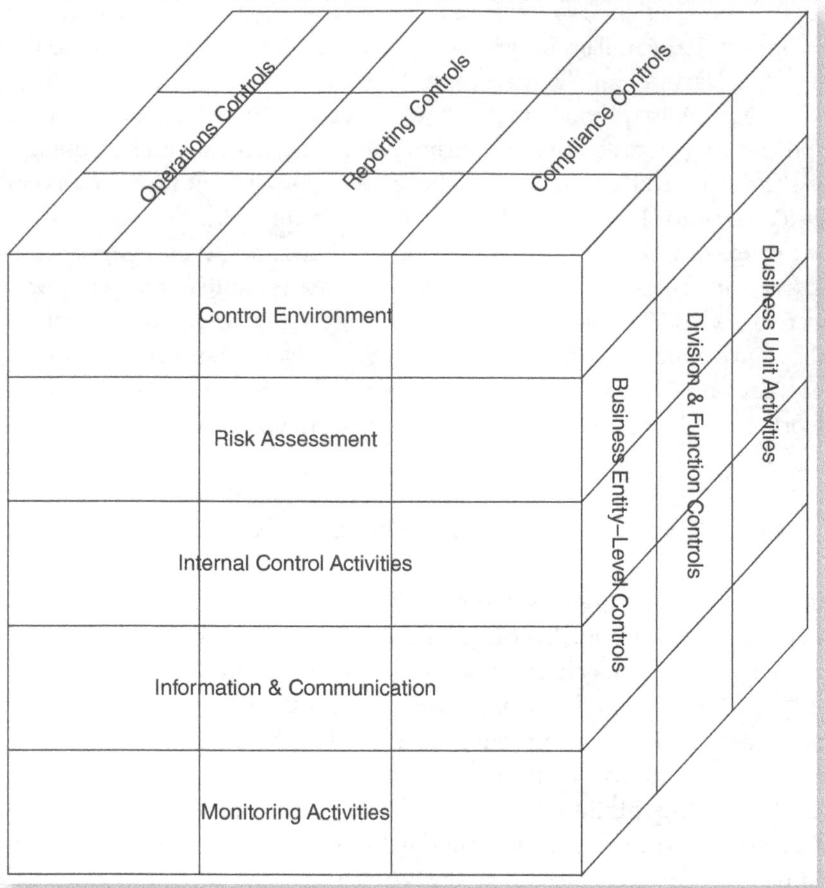

EXHIBIT 3.2 COSO Internal Controls

individual components as well. Some individual control activities may differ from one another in some operating details, but they all should fit into the control environment for the total entity.

As an example, assume that a European Union–based enterprise has launched a new business product sales venture in Myanmar (Burma), a country that had been closed to the outside world until recently. With limited IT resources and telecommunication connections, we can expect some different control processes in the Myanmar facility than would be found in the entity's headquarters operations. However, additional processes—such as the use of supporting manual control procedures—should be established to achieve internal controls at the overall entity level. These manual processes may have been all but abandoned.

The whole idea behind this model is that internal control for today's enterprise is not a single control objective but a multilevel, multifaceted concept with each unit in the COSO model having a relationship to other components in all three dimensions. Enterprise management should be clear about its internal control objectives, such as specifying suitable external reporting objectives relating to the preparation of financial statements. Some of these objectives can be very specific based on some enterprise planned business activity. Others should define well-understood or assumed objectives. For example, management may set an entity-level external financial reporting objective as follows: "Our Company prepares reliable financial statements reflecting activities in accordance with generally accepted accounting principles." This may have been assumed by members of the management team, but there is a value in clearly defining such matters. Management should also specify suitable sub-objectives for enterprise divisions, subsidiaries, operating units, and functions with sufficient clarity to support entity-level objectives. Internal auditors should understand this new, revised framework and use it as a basis for their internal control reviews.

3.4 COSO INTERNAL CONTROL PRINCIPLES

In addition to its three-dimensional elements, the revised COSO framework now codifies a set of principles that support the five components of internal control. While the 1992 version implicitly reflected some of these core internal control principles, the revised version explicitly defines 17 internal control principles representing fundamental concepts associated with the 5 components of internal control. COSO makes these principles explicit to increase management's understanding as to what constitutes effective internal control. These principles are outlined and discussed from an internal auditor's perspective in Chapter 4. They are broad concepts intended to apply to a wide range of enterprises, including for-profit and not-for-profit, publicly traded and private, both government bodies and other organizations.

Supporting each COSO principle are points of focus, representing important characteristics associated with each. These points of focus are intended to provide helpful guidance to assist management in designing, implementing, and conducting their internal control processes and in assessing whether relevant principles are present and functioning. However, the revised COSO framework does not require separate evaluations of whether they are in place. Management has the latitude to exercise judgment in determining the suitability or relevancy of these points of focus provided in the revised COSO framework and may identify and consider other important characteristics germane to a particular principle based on the enterprise's specific circumstances.

Taken together, these COSO internal control components and the COSO principles constitute the criteria and the points of focus to provide guidance that will assist management as well as internal auditors in assessing whether these components of internal control are present, functioning, and operating together within an enterprise. Each of the points of focus is mapped directly over the 17 principles, and each is also mapped directly to one of the five internal control components. These concepts should become much clearer as we discuss the COSO framework in more detail in the sections following and in Chapter 4.

The key for internal auditors to understanding when using the COSO framework is to keep in mind the three-dimensional nature of the framework where every internal control element, up and down and across the other sides of the COSO cube, should be considered in terms of its relationships with other components—easy to say but often hard to visualize when performing and developing internal audit reviews. In the following sections, we will look at the five COSO elements on the front-facing side of the COSO cube. We will then conclude by flipping this three-dimensional COSO cube around to look at internal audit issues from the perspective of its other dimensions.

3.5 COSO INTERNAL CONTROL COMPONENTS: THE CONTROL ENVIRONMENT

The front-facing side of the COSO internal control framework model shows five levels of internal control categories. The top-level category is called the control environment—the set of standards, processes, and structures that provide a basis or structure for carrying out effective internal control activities across an enterprise. The control environment includes the actions of the board of directors and senior management who take responsibility for overall internal controls and expected standards of conduct. The control environment comprises the integrity and ethical values of the enterprise; the parameters enabling the board of directors to carry out its oversight responsibilities; the organizational structure and assignment of authority and responsibility; the processes for attracting, developing, and retaining competent individuals; and the rigor around performance measures, incentives, and rewards to drive accountability for performance. The resulting control environment has a pervasive impact on the overall system of internal control.

The COSO control environment component is influenced by a variety of internal and external factors, including the entity's history, values, market, and the competitive and regulatory landscape. It is defined by the standards, processes, and structures that guide people at various levels in carrying out their responsibilities for internal control and making decisions in pursuit of the entity's objectives. An effective control environment creates the discipline that supports the assessment of risks necessary for the achievement of the entity's objectives, performance of control activities, use of information and communication systems, and conduct of monitoring activities. The COSO control framework introduces four internal control environment principles as described next and discussed further in Chapter 4:

1. An enterprise should specify objectives with sufficient clarity to enable the identification and assessment of risks relating to objectives.
2. The enterprise should identify risks to the achievement of its objectives across the entity and analyze risks as a basis for determining how they should be managed.
3. The organization should consider the potential for fraud in assessing risks to the achievement of objectives.
4. The organization should identify and assess changes that could significantly impact the system of internal control.

An enterprise that establishes and maintains a strong control environment positions itself to be more resilient in the ever-changing face of internal and external pressures. It does this by demonstrating behaviors of integrity and ethical values, adequate oversight processes and structures, and organizational design that enables the achievement of the entity's objectives with an appropriate assignment of authority and responsibility, a high degree of competence, and a strong sense of accountability for the achievement of objectives. In both the short and long term, effective control environment processes should position an enterprise and its key elements to be more resilient in the face of external pressures.

An enterprise's control environment is also synonymous with its internal control culture. Elements of a strong culture, such as integrity and ethical values, oversight, accountability, and performance evaluations, make the control environment strong as well. Culture is part of an enterprise's control environment, but also encompasses elements of other components of internal control, such as establishing effective policies and procedures, ease of security controls or access to information, and responsiveness to the results of monitoring activities. These issues will be discussed further in our review of other elements of the COSO internal control framework. Internal auditors should recognize that their organization's culture is influenced by the control environment that has been installed and established as well as other components of internal control.

This important internal control objective emphasizes that senior management, the board of directors, or an equivalent oversight body should lead by example in developing values, an enterprise philosophy, and an operating style in the pursuit of the enterprise's objectives. What senior management does and says really sends a message to everyone associated with the enterprise.

Some internal auditors as well as business managers today often do not consider these control environment factors when assessing internal control systems, but they should, as this is an important first step. If management is setting the right example and employees know that management values ethics and integrity, that attitude will be passed down to the employees and the business will have a strong foundation.

The strength of any system is based on its underlying foundations. No matter how complex the structure, if it doesn't have a solid foundation, its integrity will be unreliable. The foundation of a control system is the philosophy of the business and the people controlling it. Before designing the controls, one must consider the foundation—its environment. The COSO control environment framework asks enterprise management to consider the following questions:

- Does management take undue business risks to achieve objectives? Does it encourage risk taking or an "achieve at all costs" attitude?
- Does management attempt to manipulate performance measures so they appear more favorable? Does it bend the truth?
- Does management pressure employees to achieve results regardless of the methods or with little concern for those methods? Do they believe that the financial ends justify the means?
- Is management open and honest with employees about performance and results?

Enterprises are led from the top by senior management and the board of directors, and their business ethics and philosophies will be passed down to all levels of employees and stakeholders. The more ethical and responsible the management style, the more likely that employees will respond to that style and behave in an ethical and responsible manner. Alternately, if management shows little concern for honest and ethical behavior, the employees will follow that lead.

The COSO framework control environment and its supporting principles is a key and very important element for establishing effective internal controls in an enterprise. COSO describes the importance of setting the tone of an enterprise and influencing the control consciousness of its people. An effective control environment supports and strengthens the other control elements, whereas a weak control environment undermines these elements, rendering them useless. In an effective control environment, personnel and all stakeholders know that doing the right thing is expected and will be supported by upper-level management, even if it hurts the bottom line. In a weak environment, control procedures can be frequently overridden or ignored, providing an opportunity for fraud.

This control environment is perhaps the most important component in the COSO internal control framework. Its emphasis on the *tone at the top* provides guidance on how enterprise management should incorporate risk awareness and control activities into their daily work routines in their areas of responsibility. By maintaining a positive attitude toward internal controls and compliance with established enterprise policies as well as various legal requirements, management sets the tone for the entire area. The control environment also encompasses the culture, ethical values, teamwork, morale, and development of administrative employees.

A totally weak or deficient enterprise control environment can present some significant challenges for internal auditors. Many of their findings and assessments, as will be discussed in the other chapters going forward, are based on assessments of control environment strengths. Internal auditors should regularly highlight these issues in their audit report findings and recommendations. In the case of total, ongoing deficiencies, an enterprise's head of internal audit, the chief audit executive, should report these concerns to the audit committee of the board.

3.6 COSO INTERNAL CONTROL COMPONENTS: RISK ASSESSMENT

Risk assessment is a key element in the COSO internal control framework, located as a component of the three-dimensional COSO cube. Risks are defined here as the possibility that an event may occur that will adversely affect the achievement of enterprise objectives. The management of internal control risks affects an enterprise's ability to succeed, compete within its industry, maintain its financial strength and positive reputation, and maintain the overall quality of its products, services, and people. There are always some risks in any business activity and there is no practical way to reduce all of them. Management, however, must determine how much risk is to be prudently accepted and strive to maintain risk within these limits, understanding how much tolerance it has for exceeding its target risk levels.

COSO's internal control risk assessment component is the process for determining how all levels of risks will be managed, and a precondition to risk assessment is the establishment of risk-related objectives, linked at different levels of enterprise operations. Because of the types and nature of the risks an enterprise will encounter, management should identify and specify their risk objectives within operations, reporting, and compliance categories with sufficient clarity to be able to identify and analyze the risks to those objectives. Management also should consider the suitability of the objectives for the entity. Risk assessment also requires management to consider the impact of possible changes in the external environment and within its own business model that may render its internal controls ineffective.

While COSO internal control risk assessment defines important points for general management to consider, internal auditors should keep these risk management issues in mind in all of their ongoing internal control review activities. Chapter 15 on internal audit key competencies discusses these internal audit risk management issues for performing internal audits. The COSO internal guidance materials outline a series of risk assessment principles discussed in Chapter 5 with the following four key concepts:

1. The enterprise should specify objectives with sufficient clarity to enable the identification and assessment of risks relating to those objectives.
2. The enterprise should identify risks to the achievement of its objectives across the entity and should analyze risks as a basis for determining how those risks should be managed.
3. The enterprise should consider the potential for fraud in assessing risks to the achievement of objectives.
4. The enterprise should identify and assess changes that could significantly impact its system of internal controls.

The first of these and a key internal control principle calls for an enterprise to specify its risk objectives with sufficient clarity to enable the identification and assessment of risks relating to those objectives. This point is important for internal auditors both in their internal audit reviews as well as in their understanding of their own internal audit activities.

An internal auditor can recognize that this sounds good but may wonder what COSO means by a *risk objective*. We can think of a risk objective as the commitment of managerial resources, using both human capital and other expenditures, to achieve some uncertain or risk-based goal. A clear set of risk objectives should provide a targeted focus on where an enterprise should commit the often substantial resources needed to achieve desired performance goals. This is often an area where things can break down. It is easy for any senior manager, from the CEO on down, to state that they want to accomplish some warm-and-fuzzy-sounding risk-based goal in some future period, but such goals are of little value unless they are backed up by some substantial plans and activities.

Risk Identification and Analysis

Enterprise management at all levels should endeavor to identify all possible risks that may impact the success of the enterprise, ranging from the larger or more significant risks to the overall business down to the less major risks associated with individual projects or smaller business units. This requires a studied, deliberate approach to looking at potential risks in each area of operations and then identifying the more significant risk areas that may impact each operation in a reasonable time period. The idea is not to just list *every possible risk* but to identify those that might impact operations, with some level of probability, within a reasonable time period. This can be a difficult exercise because we often do not know the probability of the risk occurring or the nature of the consequences if the enterprise has to face the risk.

The risk identification process should occur at multiple levels in an enterprise. A risk that impacts an individual business unit or project may not have that great of an impact on the entire enterprise, but a major risk that impacts the entire economy will flow down to the individual enterprise and the separate business units. Some major risks are so infrequent but can still be so cataclysmic that it is difficult to identify them as a possible future event. Internal auditors should consider risk-related issues as part of their ongoing review activities.

Identifying and analyzing risks should be an ongoing iterative process conducted to enhance an enterprise's ability to achieve its objectives. Internal audit can often play a powerful role here as it builds and establishes what is often called an audit universe, as discussed in Chapter 13. Although an enterprise may not explicitly state all of its risk-related objectives, this does not mean that an implied objective is without either internal or external risk, and the enterprise should consider all risks that may occur.

To be effective, an enterprise risk identification process should be supported by a variety of activities, techniques, and mechanisms, each relevant to the overall risk assessment. Management should consider these risks at all levels and take necessary steps to manage them. The risk assessment should consider factors that influence the severity, velocity, and persistence of the risk, the likelihood of the loss of assets, and the related impact on operations, reporting, and compliance activities. In addition, the enterprise needs to understand its tolerance for accepting risks and its ability to operate within those risk levels. While certainly not all-inclusive, Exhibit 3.3 lists some major risk areas that may impact the enterprise, including strategic, operations, and finance risks. This is the type of high-level list that a chief executive officer might jot down and use to respond to a stockholder annual meeting question, such as "What worries you at the end of the day?" Certainly not listing all risks facing the enterprise, this is the type of first-pass list that an enterprise can use to get started on a detailed identification of risks. The people responsible for risk management in the enterprise—often an enterprise risk management team—can meet with senior management and ask some of these "What worries you . . ." types of questions to identify such high-level risks.

Once the enterprise has performed this preliminary risk identification, it should consider all significant risk-related interactions—including goods, services, and information—internal to the enterprise and between it and relevant external parties. Those external parties can include potential and existing suppliers, investors, creditors, shareholders, and other stakeholders as well as customers, intermediaries, and competitors. In addition, the enterprise should consider such external issues as new laws and regulations, environmental issues, and potential natural events, among many others.

EXHIBIT 3.3 Types of Enterprise Business Risks

Strategic Risks		
External Factors Risks	**Internal Factors Risks**	
■ Industry Risk ■ Economy Risk ■ Competitor Risk ■ Legal and Regulatory Change Risk ■ Customer Needs and Wants Risk	■ Reputation Risk ■ Strategic Focus Risk ■ Parent Company Support Risk ■ Patent/Trademark Protection Risk	
Operations Risks		
Process Risks	**Compliance Risks**	**People Risks**
■ Supply Chain Risk ■ Customer Satisfaction Risk ■ Cycle Time Risk ■ Process Execution Risk	■ Environmental Risk ■ Regulatory Risk ■ Policy and Procedures Risk ■ Litigation Risk	■ Human Resources Risk ■ Employee Turnover Risk ■ Performance Incentive Risk ■ Training Risk
Finance Risks		
Treasury Risks	**Credit Risks**	**Trading Risks**
■ Interest Rate Risk ■ Foreign Exchange Risk ■ Capital Availability Risk	■ Capacity Risk ■ Collateral Risk ■ Concentration Risk ■ Default Risk ■ Settlement Risk	■ Commodity Price Risk ■ Duration Risk ■ Measurement Risk
Information Risks		
Financial Risks	**Operational Risks**	**Technology Risks**
■ Accounting Standards Risk ■ Budgeting Risk ■ Financial Reporting Risk ■ Taxation Risk ■ Regulatory Reporting Risk	■ Pricing Risk ■ Performance Measurement Risk ■ Employee Safety Risk	■ Information Access Risk ■ Business Continuity Risk ■ Availability Risk ■ Infrastructure Risk

The risk identification process should attempt to consider all risks within an enterprise, including its subunits and operational functions, such as finance, human resources, marketing, production, purchasing, and IT management. In addition, this process should consider risks originating from outsourced service providers, key suppliers, and channel partners that directly or indirectly impact an enterprise's achievement of objectives. COSO suggests that management should consider risks in relation to internal and external factors.

Risk Response Strategies

As part of establishing effective COSO internal controls, enterprises also should develop risk management strategies to address how they intend to assess, respond, and monitor risk. This often involves judgments based on assumptions about the risk and a reasonable analysis of the costs associated with reducing the levels of risk. COSO internal control guidance materials identify four basic risk response strategies approaches:

1. **Avoidance.** This is a strategy of walking away from the risk—such as selling a business unit that gives rise to the risk, exiting from a geographical area of concern, or dropping a product line. The difficulty here is that enterprises often do not drop a product line or walk away until after the risk event has occurred with its associated costs. Unless an enterprise has a very low appetite for risk, it is difficult to walk away from a business area or product line just on the basis of a potential future risk if all is going well at the present in other respects. Avoidance can be a potentially costly strategy if investments were made to get into an area with a subsequent pullout to avoid the risk.
2. **Reduction.** A wide range of business decisions may be able to reduce certain risks. Product line diversification may reduce the risk of too strong a reliance on one key product line. Splitting an IT operations center into two geographically separate locations may reduce the risk of some catastrophic failure. There are a wide range of often effective strategies to reduce risks at all levels that go down to the mundane but operationally important step of cross-training employees.
3. **Sharing.** Virtually all enterprises as well as individuals regularly hedge or share some of their risks by purchasing insurance. Many other techniques are available here as well. For financial transactions, an enterprise can engage in hedging operations to protect from possible price fluctuations. The idea is to arrange to have another party accept some of a potential risk, with the recognition that there will be costs associated with that activity.
4. **Acceptance.** This is the strategy of no action. An enterprise can "self-insure" itself rather than purchase an insurance policy. Essentially, an enterprise should look at a risk's likelihood and impact in light of its established risk tolerance and then decide whether or not to accept that risk. For the many and varied risks that approach an enterprise, acceptance is often the appropriate strategy for some risks.

These four general strategies are key concepts in understanding risk management, and internal auditors should develop a general response strategy for each of the risks using an approach built around one of these. In doing so, the costs versus the benefits of potential risk responses should be considered to best align them with the enterprise's overall risk appetite or willingness to accept that risk. For example, an enterprise's recognition that the impact of a given risk is relatively low would be balanced against a low risk tolerance that suggests that insurance should be purchased to provide a potential risk response. For many risks, appropriate responses are obvious and almost universally understood. An IT operation, for example, spends the time and resources to back up its key data files and implement a business continuity plan. There should be no question regarding this basic approach, but various levels of management may question the frequency of backup processes or how often the continuity plan needs to be tested.

The basic message here is that an enterprise and of course internal audit need an overall risk response plan in order to be compliant with the COSO internal control framework. Risk management is a very important part of the COSO internal control framework, and an understanding of risk management concepts and concerns should be part of every internal auditor's CBOK. Risk management issues will be discussed in other chapters, and particularly in Chapter 7 on COSO ERM, the enterprise risk management framework.

As we have stated in our introductory comments, the basic concepts in the risk assessment component of the COSO internal control framework have not changed much since the original framework, but the internal control guidance very much has. Management should build and tailor their risk management processes following the four principles listed at the beginning of this section and discussed in more detail in Chapter 4.

3.7 COSO INTERNAL CONTROL COMPONENTS: INTERNAL CONTROL ACTIVITIES

Perhaps the core element in the overall COSO internal control framework, control activities are the actions—established through enterprise policies and procedures—that help ensure that management's directives to mitigate risks to the achievement of objectives are carried out. Control activities are performed at all levels of an enterprise, at various stages within business units and processes, and over the technology environment. These control activities may be preventive or detective in nature and may encompass a range of manual and automated activities such as authorizations and approvals, verifications, reconciliations, and business performance reviews. A basic or fundamental internal control, segregation of duties is typically built into the selection and development of COSO control activities. Where segregation of duties internal controls are not effective or even practical, management must select and develop alternative control activities.

Control activities are an area where, on one hand, basic internal control activity concepts have not changed all that much from the original COSO internal control framework. For example, segregation of duties is a basic internal control concept that still remains as an important internal control in many areas. That is, the person or automated function that initiates a financial transaction should not be the same person or process that approves it. On the other hand, there have been massive changes in control activities guidance since the original COSO framework. The guidance behind that original framework goes back to the long-gone days of mainframe computer systems with lots of batch processing procedures.

Control activities support all of COSO's internal control components in the COSO cube, but the revised COSO internal control framework guidance particularly aligns control activities more with the risk assessment element. Along with assessing risks, management should identify and put into effect actions that are needed when an enterprise chooses to either accept or avoid a specific risk, and chooses to develop control activities to avoid that risk. This action to reduce or share some risk serves as a focal point for developing and selecting control activities for that risk element. The nature and extent of the risk response and associated control activities will depend, at least in part, on the desired level of risk mitigation acceptable to enterprise management. By *mitigation*, we mean some management action that either reduces exposure to the identified risk or the likelihood of its occurrence.

Control activities include actions that ensure that responses to assessed risks, as well as other management directives, are carried out properly and in a timely manner. For example, a member of senior management may set an operations objective to "meet or exceed operating unit sales targets for the ensuring reporting period," but senior staff management may subsequently identify a risk that their key personnel have insufficient knowledge about current and potential customer needs to easily meet this objective. Management responses to identify this recognized risk may include reviews of sales histories from existing customers and developing market research initiatives to better attract potential customers. Control activities here might include tracking the progress of customer buying histories against established timetables as well as taking steps to improve the quality of the reported marketing data.

When determining recommended actions to take to mitigate risk, internal auditors should consider all aspects of the enterprise's system of internal control as well as its relevant business processes, IT systems, and locations where control activities are needed. This may include considering control activities outside the operating unit, including shared service, data centers, or processes performed by outsourced service providers. For example, an enterprise may need to establish control activities to address the integrity of information sent to and received from an outsourced service provider.

Business Process Control Activities

Important areas for internal audit understandings, business processes are established across an enterprise to enable them to achieve their objectives. These processes may be common to all business activities—such as purchasing, payables, or sales—or may be unique to a particular industry. Each of these processes transforms inputs into output through a series of related transactions or activities. Control activities that directly support actions to mitigate transaction processing risks in an enterprise are usually called *application controls* or *transaction controls*.

Transaction controls are often the most fundamental control activities in an enterprise since they directly address the risk responses to business processes in place to meet management's objectives. Transaction controls should be selected and developed wherever the business process may reside, ranging from centralized enterprise financial consolidation processes to customer support processes at local operating units.

A typical business process will cover many objectives and sub-objectives, each with its own set of risks and risk responses. A common way to consolidate these business process risks into a manageable form is to group them according to the business process objectives of completeness, accuracy, and availability. If the objectives are achieved for each of the transactions within a particular business process, then the business process sub-objectives will likely be achieved.

The control activities element of the COSO internal control framework uses the following information-processing objectives:

- **Completeness.** Transactions that occur should be recorded. For example, an enterprise can mitigate the risk of not processing all transactions with vendors by selecting actions and transaction controls that support the processing of all invoice transactions within appropriate business procedures.
- **Accuracy.** Transactions should be recorded in a correct amount in the right account and on a timely basis. For example, transaction controls over key system elements, such as an item price or vendor master database, can address the accuracy of processing a purchasing transaction. Accuracy in the context of an operational process can be defined to cover the broader concepts of quality, including the accuracy and precision of the recorded part.
- **Validity.** Recorded transactions represent an economic event that actually occurred and then was executed according to prescribed procedures. Validity is generally achieved through control activities that include the authorization of transactions as specified by enterprise policies and procedures.

These concepts are particularly important for internal auditors. Internal auditors should keep these in mind when reviewing and assessing the transaction-supporting control processes and applications.

Risk of untimely transaction processing may be considered a separate risk or be included as part of the completeness or accuracy of overall information processing objectives. Restricted access may also be considered an IT processing objective, because without appropriately restricting access over transactions in a business process, the control activities in that business process can be overridden and segregation of duties controls may not be achieved.

While IT objectives are most often associated with financial processes and transactions, the concept can be applied to any enterprise activity. For example, IT processing objectives and related control activities apply to management's decision-making processes over critical judgments and estimates. In this environment, management should consider the completeness of the identification of significant factors affecting estimates for which it must develop and support these assumptions. Similarly, management should consider the validity and reasonableness of those assumptions and the accuracy of its estimation models.

This does not mean that if management considers and pays close attention to these established objectives, the enterprise will never make a faulty judgment or estimate, since these are all subject to human error. However, when appropriate control activities are in place and when management uses good and well-thought-out judgments, the likelihood of better decision making is improved.

Types of Transaction Control Activities

Sometimes basic internal control concepts that have been with us many years are almost forgotten or dropped from our everyday dialogue regarding the designing and building of effective internal controls. The revised COSO internal control guidance material does a good job of outlining basic internal control activities that will be discussed further in the chapters to come. For example, the COSO internal control framework guidance material highlights the following types of transaction control activities:

- **Verifications.** This is a transaction type of control that compares two or more items with each other or compares an item with policy rules, and performs a follow-up action when the items compared do not match or are considered inconsistent with policy. Examples here include IT applications with programs, including matching or programmed reasonableness tests. Verifications generally address the completeness, accuracy, or validity of processing transactions.
- **Reconciliations.** This transaction process compares two or more data elements, and if differences are identified, actions are taken to bring the data into agreement. Reconciliations generally address the completeness and/or accuracy of processing transactions.
- **Authorizations and approvals.** An authorization process affirms that a transaction is valid, particularly one representing an actual economic event. An authorization typically takes the form of an approval by a higher level of management or of a system-generated verification and determination that a transaction is valid.
- **Physical controls.** Equipment inventories, securities, cash, and other assets are typically secured physically in locked or guarded storage areas. The physical control transactions here should be periodically counted and compared with supporting control records.
- **Controls over standing data.** *Standing data*—a term first introduced some years ago by one of the major public accounting firms—is the data elements developed from outside the enterprise (often from a standards organization) that support the processing of transactions within that enterprise. Control activities over the processes to populate, update, and maintain the accuracy, completeness, and validity of this standing data should be established by the enterprise.
- **Supervisory controls.** These transaction control processes assess whether other transaction control activities, such as verifications, approvals, controls over standing data, and physical control activities are being performed completely, accurately, and according to enterprise policy and procedures. Management normally should judgmentally select and develop supervisory controls over higher-risk transactions, including high-level reviews, to see if any reconciling items have been either followed up on or corrected, or to determine whether an appropriate explanation was provided.

These comments about control activity transactions say much about the supporting guidance provided as part of the revised COSO internal control framework. Many of the words about common transaction types make sense to experienced internal auditors, but the new COSO guidance emphasizes that they are all necessary for effective internal controls. Internal auditors are often very involved with reviewing and assessing enterprise control activities, and there will be many references to them in other chapters going forward.

3.8 COSO INTERNAL CONTROL COMPONENTS: INFORMATION AND COMMUNICATION

As another COSO element, information is necessary for an enterprise to carry out its internal control responsibilities to support the achievement of its objectives. Management obtains or generates and then uses relevant and quality information from both internal and external sources to support the functioning of other components of internal control, and internal auditors review and assess that same management information. Communication, the other component of this COSO element, is defined here as the continual, iterative process of providing, sharing, and obtaining necessary information. Internal communication is the means by which information is disseminated throughout an enterprise, flowing up, down, and across the entity. It enables personnel to receive clear messages from senior management that control responsibilities must be taken seriously. External communication also enables inbound communications of relevant external information and provides information to external parties in response to requirements and expectations.

Although its principles have not changed very much since the original COSO internal control framework, the revised COSO information and communication element is structured and looks a bit different in this revised COSO internal control framework. In addition, information and communication concepts have changed in today's world of using such practices as outsourced service providers in our Internet-driven global economy. The COSO's information and communication element is a key component for developing and implementing effective internal control processes.

The overall concept supporting COSO information and communication is that an enterprise needs to develop and deliver many forms and types of competent information, from and to management. This concept is more than the information flow described on a classic IT flowchart and calls for the delivery of effective messages, understood by all parties and with effective internal controls. That is, processes should be in place to identify, capture, and distribute the key elements of all types of information and then communicate relevant elements of this information to appropriate parties.

This COSO component describes the importance of the information stored by an enterprise and how it should be communicated to various parties. The information system portion of this element records, processes, stores, and reports data. The communication system dictates how information is reported, who gets it, and how it is used in fraud control. This information and communication process should:

- Record transactions as they occur, breaking them into their component parts (dates, amounts, names, accounts, authorizations, etc.).
- Process, summarize, and report that information for management purposes and pure accounting purposes.
- Store captured and processed data in formats that can be summarized, audited, reviewed, and reported quickly and easily.
- Report that information in a format that can be used for management analysis and internal control purposes.

The information and communication component of the COSO framework primarily supports the functioning of other internal control components, including objectives relevant to internal and external reporting. Internal auditors reviewing internal controls associated with the COSO internal control framework should differentiate their reporting objectives from the somewhat separate information and communication components of this internal control element in assessing systems of internal control.

Terminology changes over time, and today we too often think of the term *information* as just an IT issue. However, the COSO internal control framework defines it in a broader sense, stating that information encompasses *all* of the data that is combined and summarized based on their relevance to enterprise information requirements. These information requirements are determined by the ongoing functioning of other internal control components, taking into consideration the expectations of all users, both internal and external. Information systems, as defined by COSO, support decision making by supporting the processing of relevant, timely, and quality information from internal and external sources.

The COSO communication element component calls for an enterprise to share relevant and quality information internally and externally. Management communicates information internally to enable its personnel to better understand the enterprise's objectives and the importance of their control responsibilities. Internal communication facilitates the functioning of other components of internal control by sharing information up, down, and across the enterprise. External communications enable management to obtain and share information between the enterprise and external parties about risk, regulatory matters, and changes in circumstances, customer satisfaction, and other information relevant to the functioning of other internal control components.

Importance of Using Relevant Information

With the mass of information, including an enterprise's formal published systems and procedures, memos, multiple e-mail communications, external vendor news postings, and communications from social media sources, internal auditors are often bombarded with information when beginning to review and assess internal controls in some area. An internal auditor should obtain or generate and use relevant, quality information to support the functioning of components of internal control under review. Information is necessary for an enterprise to carry out their internal control responsibilities in support of the achievement of objectives. Information about an enterprise's higher-level objectives should be gathered from the board of directors and senior management activities and summarized in a way that line management and others can understand these objectives and their role in their achievements. For example, in a not uncommon situation, senior managers may find that their line managers do not have a solid understanding of an enterprise's key objectives. Supporting business plans here are sometimes far too broad and vague or may have been too detailed or difficult to concisely communicate. The internal auditors performing high-level reviews should summarize these key objectives into a clear narrative document that strongly outlines and emphasizes review objectives.

Communication problems, as defined in the COSO internal control framework, are often a "Management 101" type of basic issue, where internal audit should always remember that this relevant information is a key component of effective internal controls. However, internal audit, working together as a team with senior management, should be able to survey past operational and financial management results as well as inputs to identify and define better relevant information requirements.

Obtaining relevant information, as defined in the COSO internal control framework, requires management to identify and define information requirements at a strong level of detail and specificity. Identifying information requirements is an iterative and ongoing process that occurs throughout the performance of an effective internal control system. Exhibit 3.4 shows examples of various types of external and external relevant information in support of the COSO internal control components.

Information requirements are established through activities performed in support of the other internal control components. These requirements facilitate and direct management and other personnel to identify relevant and reliable sources of information and underlying data. The amount of information and underlying data available to management may often be more than is needed because of increased sources of information and advances in data collection, processing, and storage. In other cases, data may be difficult

EXHIBIT 3.4 Relevant Source of Information Examples

Info. Source	Example of Relevant Information	Data Example
Internal	E-mail communications	Organization changes
Internal	Inspection reports from production floor	Online and quality production informaton
Internal	Minutes of notes from operations committee meeting	Actions in response to reported metrics
Internal	Personnel time reporting system	Hours incurred on time-based projects
Internal	Reports from manufacturing systems	Production results: number of units shipped
Internal	Responses to customer surveys	Factors impacting customer repeat purchases
Internal	Whistleblower hotline	Complaints on management behaviors
External	Data from outsourced service provider	Products shipped from contract manufacturer
External	Industry research reports	Competitor product information
External	Peer company earning releases	Market and industry metrics
External	Regulatory bodies	New or expanded requirements
External	Social media, blog, or other posts	Opinions about the enterprise
External	Trade shows	Evolving customer interests and preferences
External	Whistleblower hotline	Claims of fraud, bribery, etc.

to obtain at the relevant or level or requisite specificity. Therefore, a clear understanding of the COSO-defined information requirements directs management and other personnel to identify relevant and reliable sources of information and data.

This COSO internal control concept of relevant data is important for internal auditors. We will discuss this further in the chapters going forward, but all too often internal auditors have requested documentation to support some area or controls being reviewed. Whether it is old-fashioned paper documentation or today's Internet-based documents, internal auditors have requested documentation covering some area and management cleans out their files, giving them way too much, some of it extraneous and much more than an internal auditor has the time and resources to review. An internal auditor may think, "Omigosh, I'll never have time to review all of this stuff." But the auditor may add a workpaper note to say that documentation has been supplied and go forward. A better approach is to take a quick look at all of the stuff that has been supplied and ask some hard questions about whether all of this is relevant and supports the internal audit review.

Importance of Internal Communications

COSO suggests that an enterprise should internally communicate its objectives and the responsibilities of good internal controls. This information-related communication should be initiated and endorsed by senior management and conveyed to all elements across an enterprise organization, including:

- The importance, relevance, and benefits of effective internal controls
- The roles and responsibilities of management and other personnel in performing those internal control processes
- The expectations of the enterprise to communicate up, down, and across any matters of significance relating to internal control, including instances of weakness, deterioration, or nonadherence

An enterprise should establish and implement policies and procedures that facilitate effective internal communication. This includes specific and directed communications that address individual authorities, responsibilities, and standards of conduct across the enterprise. Senior management should communicate the enterprise's objectives clearly throughout so that other management and personnel, including such nonemployees as contractors, understand their individual roles in the organization. Such communication occurs regardless of where personnel are located, their level of authority, or their functional responsibility.

Internal communication begins with the communication of objectives. As management cascades communication of enterprise-specific objectives throughout the organization, it is important that related sub-objectives or specific requirements are communicated to personnel in a manner that allows them to understand how their roles and responsibilities impact the achievement of an enterprise's objectives. Internal auditors should keep these needs in mind as they are performing internal audit control reviews.

All personnel should also receive a clear message from senior management that their individual or operating unit internal control responsibilities must be taken seriously. Through the communication of objectives and sub-objectives, personnel should understand how their roles, responsibilities, and actions relate to the work of others in the enterprise, their responsibilities for internal control, and what is deemed as acceptable and unacceptable behavior. However, communication about internal control responsibilities may not on its own be sufficient to ensure that management and other personnel embrace their accountability responsibilities and respond as intended. Often, management must take timely action that is consistent with such communication to enforce the messages conveyed.

In addition, information that is shared through internal communications helps management and other personnel to recognize any problems or potential problems, to determine their cause, and to take corrective actions. For example, assume that an internal audit department conducts an audit over commissions paid to distributors in one international location. The audit, in this example, may reveal instances of the fraudulent reporting of sales through certain distributors. Further investigation exposes payments by the distributor to the sales representative responsible for the related distributors. This information would be published by the internal audit in an audit report addressed to the board and senior management. Once these internal audit findings have been confirmed, the control weakness should be shared with sales management in other locations, enabling them to analyze information more critically to determine if the issue is more pervasive and to take any necessary actions.

Communications between management and the board of directors provides the board with information needed to exercise its oversight responsibility for internal control. Information relating to internal control that is communicated to the board generally should include significant matters about adherence to, changes in, or issues arising from the system of internal control. The frequency and level of detail of the communication to management and the board of directors must be sufficient to enable these parties to understand the results of management's separate and ongoing assessments and the impact of those results on the achievement of objectives. Additionally, the frequency and level of detail must be sufficient to enable the board of directors to respond to indications of ineffective internal control on a timely basis.

COSO internal control guidance encourages direct communication between board members and other personnel. Members of the board of directors should have direct access to employees without reference to management. This is the type of guidance that sounds good in theory but is often not very effective in practice. With the exception of open forum sessions at annual meetings, most employees and other stakeholders of all but the very smallest of corporations do not have much opportunity to directly interact with their board members. Management-led open forum sessions may change this relationship, but communication barriers will continue to exist despite COSO's good intentions.

3.9 COSO INTERNAL CONTROL COMPONENTS: MONITORING ACTIVITIES

Monitoring activities assess whether each of the other five objectives or components of COSO internal control, including the control environment, risk assessment, and others, are present and functioning. An enterprise and its internal auditors should use ongoing and separate evaluation processes to ascertain whether established internal control principles, both across the enterprise and its subunits, are in effect, present, and functioning. Monitoring here is a key input into the organization's assessment of the effectiveness of internal control. The revised COSO internal control framework identifies two principles, discussed in Chapter 4, for the monitoring activities' internal control component:

1. The organization selects, develops, and performs ongoing and/or separate evaluations to ascertain whether the components of internal control are present and functioning.
2. The organization evaluates and communicates internal control deficiencies in a timely manner to those parties responsible for taking corrective action, including senior management and the board of directors, as appropriate.

An enterprise's system of internal control will often change, and the entity's objectives and its components of internal control may change over time as well. Also, procedures may become less effective or obsolete, may no longer be in place and functioning, or may be deemed insufficient to support the achievement of new or updated internal control objectives. Monitoring activities should be selected, developed, and performed to ascertain whether each control component or principle from the five internal control components is present and functioning, and that some forms of internal control deficiencies exist. Management also needs to determine whether the system of internal control continues to be relevant and able to address new risks.

Where appropriate, monitoring activities identify and examine expectation gaps relating to internal control anomalies and abnormalities, which may indicate that one or more components of internal control, including controls to affect principles across the enterprise and its subunits, are not present and functioning. Monitoring activities will generally identify root causes of such breakdowns and may operate within various business processes across the enterprise and its subunits. These words are adapted from the supporting COSO internal control guidance materials. They mean that appropriate monitoring processes help to dig out and identify potential problems that have been all but ignored, and scheduled internal audits frequently point to this role.

Enterprises need to consider underlying details in determining whether an activity is a control activity, as was discussed previously, versus a monitoring activity, and especially where the activity involves some level of supervisory review. Review activities are not automatically classified as monitoring activities. For example, the intent of a monthly completeness control activity would be to detect and correct errors, where a corresponding monitoring activity would only be to ask why there were errors in the first place, and then to task management with fixing the process to prevent future errors. In simple terms, a control activity responds to a specific risk, whereas a monitoring activity assesses whether controls within each of the five components of internal control are operating as intended, among other things. As always, when we consider any aspect of COSO internal controls, we should always take into account the three-dimensional nature of the COSO framework and control relationships up, down, and across.

The COSO revised framework monitoring activities guidance materials emphasize that an enterprise should conduct ongoing evaluations to support its monitoring activities and that an enterprise should identify and communicate any known internal control deficiencies as part of its monitoring activities. Installation of appropriate monitoring activities brings to completion a full circle of internal control processes, as illustrated in Exhibit 3.5. The idea behind this exhibit is that when an enterprise develops and implements enterprise objectives, that action should go through each of the COSO control components. In a circular fashion, moving from establishing or building an appropriate control environment, this cycle moves to monitoring activities, and those monitoring activities act as a review factor over all other internal control components.

An enterprise should select, develop, and perform ongoing and/or separate evaluations to monitor or ascertain whether their internal control components of are present and functioning. Monitoring can be done through separate management-initiated evaluations or through an effective internal audit process. Internal audit reviews over some area of operations or internal controls is an example of a separate monitoring activity and a reason why the internal audit process is so important for establishing effective internal controls under the COSO framework. As discussed in Chapter 8 on performing effective internal audits, internal control reviews should be initially planned and scheduled based on internal audit's risk assessment processes, but internal auditors then may return to review that same area again, based on any internal control

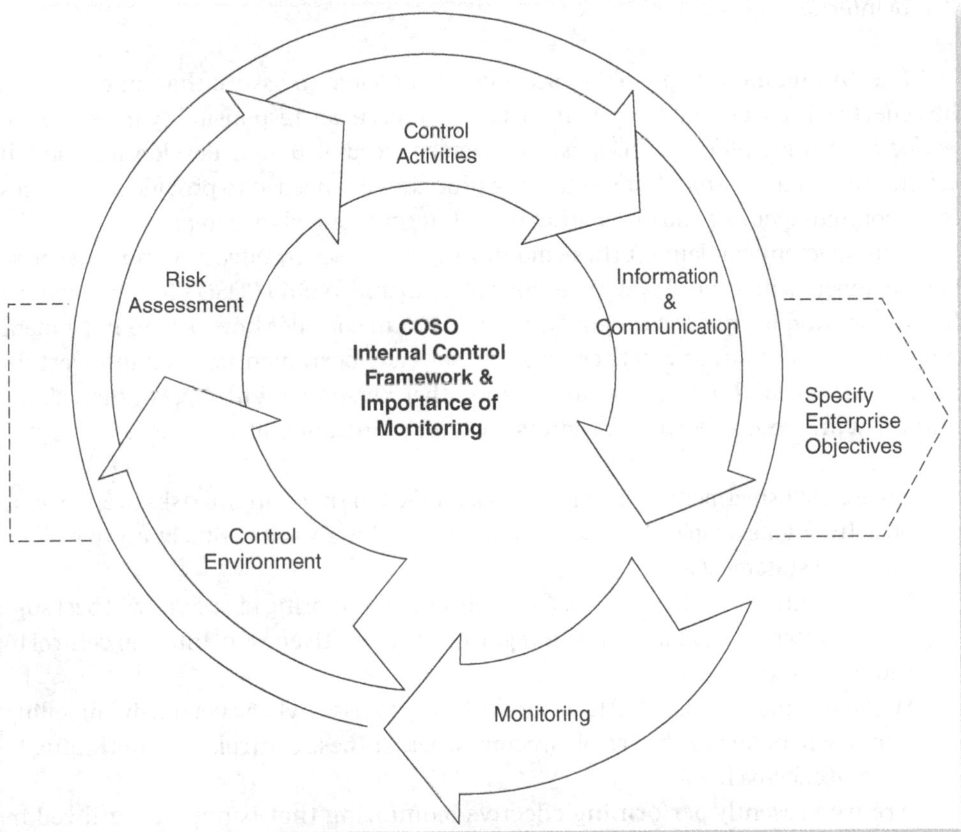

EXHIBIT 3.5 COSO Monitoring Activities

deficiencies found in the first review. In addition, separate monitoring evaluations may be conducted periodically by management, internal audit, or external parties, among others, with scope and frequency a matter of management judgment.

Continuous COSO monitoring processes are similar to the continuous internal audit processes discussed in Chapter 11. They also are like an oil pressure light in an automobile that only flashes a warning if the pressure is out of bounds. Ongoing evaluations are generally defined, routine operations built into business processes and performed on a real-time basis, reacting to changed conditions. Where ongoing evaluations are built into business processes, their internal control components are usually structured to monitor themselves on an ongoing basis.

Unmonitored controls tend to deteriorate over time. The COSO framework defines monitoring as processes to help ensure that internal control continues to operate effectively. When monitoring is designed and implemented appropriately, an enterprise should benefit because it is more likely to:

- Identify and correct internal control problems on a timely basis
- Produce more accurate and reliable information for use in decision making
- Prepare accurate and timely financial statements
- Be in a position to provide periodic certifications or assertions on the effectiveness of internal control

Effective monitoring processes are a key component to assure that an enterprise has effective internal controls and internal audit has a key responsibility in helping to perform many monitoring processes. Management needs to design, develop, and launch effective internal controls, but monitoring processes are needed to provide assurances to senior management and others that those internal controls are in place.

Management can launch these monitoring processes by encouraging enterprise staff members with control system responsibility to understand COSO's internal control framework and its monitoring guidance and then to consider how best to implement monitoring processes or whether they have already been incorporated into certain areas. Further, both internal auditors and other personnel with appropriate skills, authority, and resources should address these four fundamental questions:

1. Have established monitoring processes identified the meaningful risks to enterprise objectives, for example, the risks related to producing accurate, timely, and complete financial statements?
2. Which controls are "key controls" that effective monitoring processes will best support an internal audit assessment regarding the effectiveness of internal control in those risk areas?
3. What information collected from monitoring processes will be persuasive in telling management and the board of directors whether these controls are continuing to operate effectively?
4. Are we presently performing effective monitoring that is not well-utilized in the evaluation of internal control, resulting in unnecessary and costly further testing?

Management and the board of directors should understand these concepts of effective monitoring and how they can serve their respective enterprise interests. Internal audit review activities should provide senior management with assurances that their internal control systems are working and that installed monitoring processes are providing that guidance.

COSO's internal control monitoring objective should help enterprises answer these and other questions within the context of their own unique circumstances—circumstances that will change over time. As they progress in achieving effectiveness in monitoring, enterprises likely will have the opportunity to further improve the process through the use of such tools as continuous monitoring or auditing tools and exception reports tailored to their processes. Over time, effective COSO monitoring processes should lead to organizational efficiencies and reduced costs associated with public reporting on internal control because internal control problems can be identified and addressed in a proactive rather than reactive manner.

3.10 THE COSO FRAMEWORK'S OTHER DIMENSIONS

The prior sections have described the more important components of the COSO internal control framework, from the control environment to monitoring. Each of these describes important components or elements of internal control that must be individually effective and must work with the other related internal control elements. For example, COSO risk assessment elements should drive and help manage control activities. However, the major feature of the COSO framework that is sometimes all but ignored is its three-dimensional nature.

Exhibit 3.6 has flipped the COSO internal control framework and shows operations, reporting, and compliance controls from a front-facing perspective. There is no change here in the concept of effective COSO internal controls, but the exhibit provides a different way of looking at them. That is, an internal auditor reviewing and assessing the effectiveness of an organization's business reporting controls, such as may be found in a manufacturing resource control system, should think about the effectiveness of those controls with regard to internal control elements ranging from the overall control environment to monitoring activities.

In a similar manner, each of these internal controls should be considered with respect to the organization-size side of the COSO cube. That is, an internal control should be effective in an individual business unit or department, at a larger business or functional level, and for an entire business entity. As we will find as we explore internal audit processes and internal control procedures in the chapters following, these concepts are sometimes difficult to apply consistently across the overall enterprise. While there can be some minor and even justifiable variations, management should try to apply these COSO internal controls consistently across an overall business entity.

As we have stated previously, a strong knowledge and understanding of the COSO internal control framework should be an internal auditor CBOK requirement. COSO does not contain rules, as found surrounding Chapter 5's description of SOx, or recommended

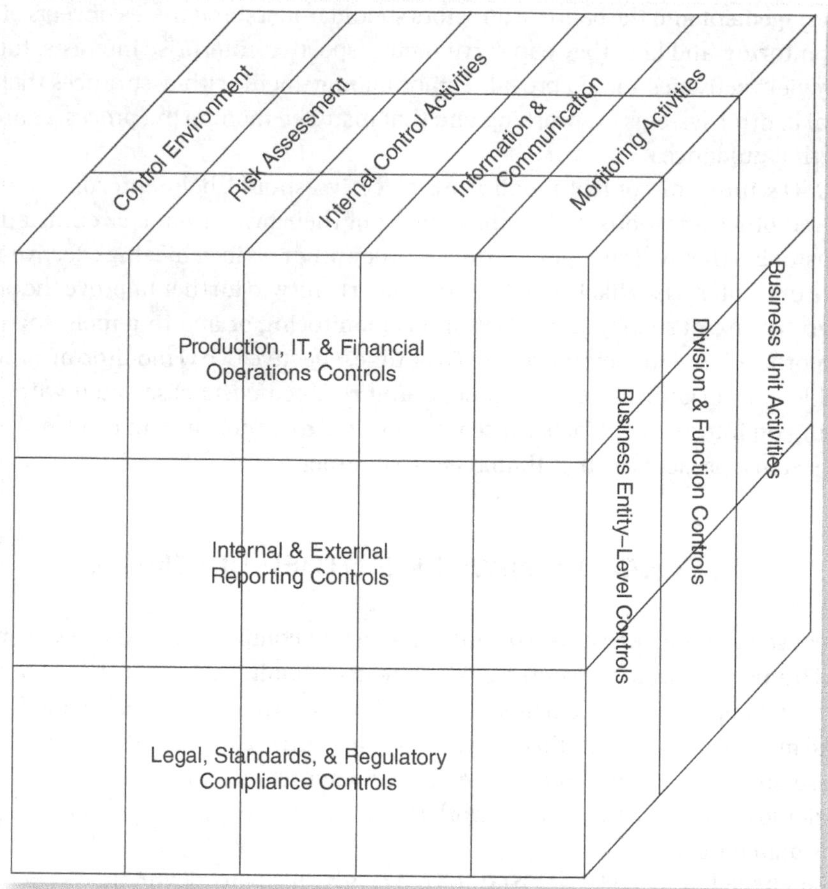

EXHIBIT 3.6 COSO Internal Controls—Reporting Perspective

best practices, as will be discussed in Chapter 19 on ITIL®, but the COSO internal control framework contains some strong guidance for building and assessing all levels of enterprise internal controls, ranging from those in a smaller business unit IT application system to overall corporate-level processes.

CHAPTER FOUR

The 17 COSO Internal Control Principles

CHAPTER 3 DESCRIBED THE REVISED COSO internal control framework. A key component of that framework is COSO's 17 internal control principles, guidance to help managers and internal auditors better understand and utilize COSO internal controls. These principles are a new concept that was not included in the original COSO framework, and they are helpful for internal auditors in their reviews and understandings of COSO internal controls. This chapter will introduce these COSO internal control principles and why they are important for management and internal auditors in building effective internal controls.

Rather different from COSO, the Institute of Internal Auditors (IIA) has established a set of 12 core principles that describe internal audit effectiveness to support the principles in their standards and *code of ethics*, both discussed in Chapter 9. They are a key component in their International Professional Practices Framework (IPPF). These principles, both for COSO internal controls and for the IIA's IPPF, represent key goals or talking points that internal auditors should use in planning, performing, and evaluating their internal control reviews.

4.1 COSO INTERNAL CONTROL FRAMEWORK PRINCIPLES

The COSO internal control framework, introduced in Chapter 3, is supported by 17 principles. For some managers who have looked at the COSO three-dimensional framework and walked away confused, these principles supply more guidance and understanding of internal control concepts, though they do not exactly track to the elements of the framework. These elements are listed in Exhibit 4.1 and will be described in greater detail further on.

EXHIBIT 4.1 COSO Internal Control Principles

Element	Principle
Control environment	1. Demonstrate commitment to integrity and ethical values 2. Ensure that board exercises oversight responsibility 3. Establish structures, reporting lines, authorities, and responsibilities 4. Demonstrate commitment to a competent workforce 5. Hold people accountable
Risk assessment	6. Specify appropriate objectives 7. Identify and analyze risks 8. Evaluate fraud risks 9. Identify and analyze changes that could significantly affect internal controls
Control activities	10. Select and develop control activities that mitigate risks 11. Select and develop technology controls 12. Deploy control activities through policies and procedures
Information and communication	13. Use relevant, quality information to support the internal control function 14. Communicate internal control information internally 15. Communicate internal control information externally
Monitoring	16. Perform ongoing or periodic evaluations of internal controls (or a combination of the two) 17. Communicate internal control deficiencies

Internal auditors should develop an understanding of these principles as a CBOK *must*. These concepts should assist internal auditors to better develop and perform their internal control reviews.

4.2 CONTROL ENVIRONMENT PRINCIPLE 1: INTEGRITY AND ETHICAL VALUES

The first principle of the COSO control environment calls for an enterprise to demonstrate a commitment to *integrity and ethical values*. Enterprise history and culture often play a major role in forming this internal *control environment*. When an enterprise historically has had a strong management emphasis on producing error-free products, when senior management continues to emphasize the importance of high-quality products, and when this message is communicated to all levels, this becomes a major enterprise control environment factor. The messages from the CEO or other very senior managers are known as the *tone at the top*—management's messages to all stakeholders. The message from the top should be more than just "we will comply with the law" types of statements. The messages should be far broader and emphasize that an enterprise is committed to the highest ethical standards in every aspect of its business, including not just compliance but in its business, sales, legal counseling, and human resources practices as well as its treatment of employees and customers.

These are the messages and repeated commitments from senior leadership throughout the enterprise to emphasize the importance of compliance and ethical conduct that should be embraced and integrated into every level of business operations. However, if senior management gains a reputation for looking the other way at policy violations and makes dubious-sounding statements, this negative message will be communicated to other levels of the enterprise. A positive tone at the top calls for senior management to lead by example on matters of integrity and ethics; positive actions here are a foundation stone establishing a strong control environment for the enterprise.

While the tone at the top is very important, an effective enterprise-wide code of ethics—once typically called a code of conduct because of the emphasis on rules—is equally or even more important in establishing an effective internal control environment. Codes of ethics have been with business organizations for many years, but have traditionally been more focused on lower-level staff members than on senior management. They should be an important component of an effective system of internal controls for all members of an enterprise, from senior management to the operations staff and other stakeholders.

The effective enterprise today should develop and enforce a code of that covers applicable ethical, business, and legal rules for all enterprise stakeholders, whether they be the officers, all other employees, or a larger group of stakeholders including vendors and consultants. A code of ethics should be a clear, unambiguous set of rules or guidance that outlines what is expected of all enterprise stakeholders. The code should be based on the values and legal issues surrounding an enterprise. That is, while all enterprises can expect to have a code of prohibitions against sexual and racial discrimination, a defense contractor with many contract-related rules issues might have a somewhat different code of ethics than a fast-food store operation. However, the code should apply to all members of the enterprise from the most senior level to a part-time clerical employee. For example, a code of conduct rule prohibiting erroneous financial reporting should be the same whether directed at the CFO for deliberately incorrect quarterly financial reporting or the part-timer for an incorrect or fraudulent weekly time card. Punishments and remedial measures should be applied to both. Exhibit 4.2 contains some of the topics that are typically included in an enterprise code of ethics.

Affirming Adherence to the Code of Ethics

An enterprise's code of ethics must be a *living document*. It has little value if it has been developed, delivered to all stakeholders with much hullabaloo, and then essentially filed away and forgotten after that initial launch. If there is a new code of ethics or even a major revision of the existing code, the enterprise should undertake a major effort to deliver a copy of that code to all employees and stakeholders. An important step would be to formally present the new code of ethics to the enterprise's top managers, and particularly the financial officers. Codes of ethics in the past sometimes received only token acceptance from the senior officer group, with a feeling that they were really for the staff and not for them.

Enterprise senior management should be required to formally acknowledge that it has read, understands, and will abide by the enterprise's code of ethics. With the

EXHIBIT 4.2 Example Code of Ethics Topics

The following are topic areas found in a typical enterprise code of ethics. The actual code should have specific rules in each of these areas.

I. INTRODUCTION
   A. Purpose of This Code of Ethics: A general statement about the background of the code of ethics, emphasizing enterprise traditions.
   B. The Enterprise's Commitment to Strong Ethical Standards: A restatement of the mission statement and a supporting message from the CEO.
   C. Where to Seek Guidance: A description of the ethics hotline process.
   D. Reporting Noncompliance: Guidance for whistleblowers–how to report.
   E. Your Responsibility to Acknowledge the Code: A description of the code acknowledgement process for all stakeholders.

II. FAIR DEALING STANDARDS
   A. Enterprise Selling Practices: Guidance for dealing with customers.
   B. Enterprise Buying Practices: Guidance and policies for dealing with vendors.

III. CONDUCT IN THE WORKPLACE
   A. Equal Employment Opportunity Standards: A strong commitment statement.
   B. Workplace and Sexual Harassment Policies: An equally strong commitment statement.
   C. Alcohol and Substance Abuse: A policy statement in this area.

IV. CONFLICTS OF INTEREST
   A. Outside Employment: Limitations on accepting employment from competitors.
   B. Personal Investments: Rules regarding using enterprise data to make personal investment decisions.
   C. Gifts and Other Benefits: Rules regarding receiving bribes and improper gifts.
   D. Former Employees: Rules prohibiting giving favors to ex-employees in business.
   E. Family Members: Rules about giving business to family members, creating potential conflicts of interest, and family-member employee relationships.

V. ENTERPRISE PROPERTY AND RECORDS
   A. Enterprise Assets: A strong statement on the employees' responsibility to protect assets.
   B. Computer Systems Resources: An expansion of the enterprise assets statement to reflect all aspects of computer systems resources.
   C. Use of the Enterprise's Name: A rule that the enterprise name should only be used for normal business dealings.
   D. Enterprise Records: A rule regarding employee responsibility for records integrity.
   E. Confidential Information: Rules on the importance of keeping all enterprise information confidential and not disclosing it to outsiders.
   F. Employee Privacy: A strong statement on the importance of keeping employee's personal information confidential from outsiders and even other employees.
   G. Enterprise Benefits: Employees must not take enterprise benefits where they are not entitled.

VI. COMPLYING WITH THE LAW
   A. Inside Information and Insider Trading: A strong rule prohibiting insider trading or otherwise benefiting from inside information.
   B. Political Contributions and Activities: A strong statement on political activity rules.
   C. Bribery and Kickbacks: A firm rule on using bribes or accepting kickbacks.
   D. Foreign Business Dealings: Rules regarding dealing with foreign agents in line with the Foreign Corrupt Practices Act.
   E. Workplace Safety: A statement on the enterprise's policy to comply with OSHA rules.
   F. Product Safety: A statement on the enterprise's commitment to product safety.
   G. Environmental Protection: A rule regarding the enterprise's commitment to comply with applicable environmental laws.

management team standing behind it, the enterprise should next roll out the code of ethics to all enterprise stakeholders. This can be done in multiple phases, with delivery to local or more major facilities first, followed by smaller units, foreign locations, and other stakeholders. Rather than just including a copy of the code with payroll documents, an enterprise should make a formal effort to present it in a manner that will gain attention.

A new code of ethics can be communicated through a video by the CEO, by webcasts, training sessions, or other means to emphasize its importance and meaning. Special communication methods might be used for other groups such as vendors or contractors, but an enterprise objective should be to get all stakeholders to formally acknowledge that they will abide by the enterprise's code of ethics. This can be accomplished by an Internet or telephone response type of system where every enterprise stakeholder is asked to respond to these three questions:

1. Have you received and read a copy of the code of ethics? Answer yes or no.
2. Do you understand the contents of this code of ethics? Answer yes if you understand this code of ethics or no if you have questions.
3. Do you agree to abide by the policies and guidelines in this code of ethics? Answer yes if you agree to abide by the code and no if you do not.

Every employee and stakeholder should be required to acknowledge acceptance of their enterprise's code of ethics, with responses recorded on a database listing the employee name and the date of their review and acceptance or nonacceptance. The idea is to have everyone—all of the stakeholders—buy into the code and agree to its terms. If someone refuses to accept the code because of questions, supervisors or others should discuss the matter with that person to gain eventual resolution. The final issue here is that the enterprise should expect all employees to agree to accept and abide by the enterprise's code of ethics. Following that code should be just another enterprise work rule, and consistent failure to abide by the rules should be grounds for termination.

The purpose of this code acknowledgment requirement is to avoid any "I didn't know that was the rule" excuses in the future when code violations are encountered. It is a good idea to go through a code acceptance process on an annual basis, or at least after any revision to the code document. The files documenting these code acknowledgments should be retained in a secure manner.

Code Violations and Corrective Actions

An enterprise-wide code of ethics lays out a set of expected behaviors. In addition to publishing a code of ethics and obtaining stakeholder acceptance, there also needs to be a mechanism for reporting code violations and for investigating and handling those violations. The objective here is that if the enterprise issues a strong code along with a message from the CEO about the importance of good ethical practices, all stakeholders are expected to follow those rules. However, we all know that people are people and there will always be some who violate the rules or run on the edge. An enterprise needs to establish a mechanism to allow employees or even outsiders to report potential violations of the code in a secure and confidential manner. Much of that reporting mechanism can be handled through a whistleblower facility, as discussed in Chapter 26.

A code of ethics describes a series of rules for expected actions in the enterprise. When violations are found, the matter should be investigated and actions taken on a consistent basis, no matter the rank of the stakeholders. If the code of ethics prohibits making copies of corporate software—and it should—the penalties for a staff analyst in a remote sales office or a senior manager in corporate headquarters should be the same. Assuming they both read the prohibition in the code and acknowledged acceptance, penalties for violations should be consistent. Otherwise, there can be an atmosphere in which the rules appear to apply only to some. This supports COSO's integrity and ethical values principle.

4.3 CONTROL ENVIRONMENT PRINCIPLE 2: ROLE OF THE BOARD OF DIRECTORS

The control environment is very much influenced by the actions of an enterprise's *board of directors* and its audit committee, with the principle "Ensure that the board exercises oversight responsibility."

In the years prior to the Sarbanes-Oxley Act (SOx), boards and their audit committees often were dominated by senior management inside directors, often with limited representation from outside, minority board members. This created situations where the boards were not totally independent of management. Enterprise officers sat on the board and were in effect managing themselves, often with less concern for the outside investors. SOx changed this and requires that audit committees be truly independent. An active and independent board is an essential component of the COSO control environment. By setting high-level policies and by reviewing overall enterprise conduct, the board and its audit committee have the ultimate responsibility for setting the tone at the top.

An independent board must have a close relationship with senior management to ensure effective and successful enterprise operations and a strong internal control environment. The board of directors and its audit committee should identify and understand the expectations of stakeholders, including customers, employees, investors, and the general public, as well as enterprise legal and regulatory requirements. These expectations should help shape the objectives of the enterprise and the oversight responsibilities of the board. The following board of directors' activities may assist management in determining whether this COSO control environment principle is present and functioning.

- **Establish oversight responsibilities.** The board of directors should identify and accept its oversight responsibilities in relation to established legal requirements and stakeholder, investor, and public expectations.
- **Apply relevant expertise.** The board of directors should define, maintain, and periodically evaluate the skills and expertise needed among its members to enable them to ask probing questions of senior management and take commensurate actions.

- **Operate independently.** The board of directors should have sufficient members who are independent from management and are objective in their evaluations and decision making.
- **Provide oversight for the system of internal controls.** The board of directors should retain oversight responsibility for management's development and performance of internal controls.

The board of directors should review and approve policies and practices that support the performance of internal controls across the enterprise in regular meetings between management and the board. The processes and structures particularly relevant to the audit committee of the board are those that provide an oversight for the system of internal controls, and the joint efforts of the board and senior management can demonstrate that this internal control environment principle is present and functioning.

4.4 CONTROL ENVIRONMENT PRINCIPLE 3: AUTHORITY AND RESPONSIBILITY NEEDS

Management should establish, with appropriate board oversight, structures, reporting lines, and appropriate authorities and responsibilities in the pursuit of its internal control objectives. There should be an organizational structure in place to plan, execute, control, and periodically assess the activities of the overall enterprise. This control environment goal is to provide for clear accountability and information flows within and across the overall enterprise and all of its subunits.

In order to determine that this enterprise internal control principle is functioning, management and the board of directors should consider the multiple operating units, legal entities, geographical locations, and outsourced service providers in the enterprise to support the achievement of these internal control objectives. With today's complex international enterprises, with multiple agreements between operating units and outside providers, this can be a complex mix, but management should then design and evaluate lines of reporting for each entity structure to enable execution of authorities and responsibilities and flow of information to manage the activities of the entity.

Many enterprises of all types and sizes today have streamlined their operations and pushed their decision-making authority downward and closer to the frontline personnel. A strong control environment says that frontline employees should have the knowledge and power to make appropriate decisions in their own area of operations rather than be required to pass the request for a decision up through more senior enterprise channels. The critical challenge that goes with this delegation or empowerment is that although they can delegate some authority in order to achieve objectives, senior management is ultimately responsible for the decisions made by those subordinates. An enterprise can place itself at risk if too many decisions involving higher-level objectives are assigned at inappropriately lower levels without adequate management review. In addition, each person in the enterprise must have a good understanding of the enterprise's overall objectives as well as how individual actions interrelate to achieve those objectives. Enterprise management should recognize that this control environment component of the COSO framework is greatly influenced by the extent to which individuals recognize that they will be held accountable. This holds true for all members of the enterprise, from staff members all the way up to the chief executive, who has ultimate responsibility for all activities within an entity, including the internal control system.

4.5 CONTROL ENVIRONMENT PRINCIPLE 4: COMMITMENT TO A COMPETENT WORKFORCE

The enterprise should demonstrate a commitment to attract, develop, and retain competent individuals in alignment with its objectives. This COSO control environment principle calls for policies and measures that qualify stakeholders to carry out their assigned responsibilities, and it requires relevant skills and expertise, which are gained largely from professional experience, training, and certifications. A commitment to competence is expressed in individual attitudes and behaviors in carrying out one's responsibilities. A human resources function can often help define competence and staffing levels by job role, facilitating training and maintaining completion records as well as evaluating the relevance and adequacy of individual professional development in relation to the enterprise's needs. This COSO principle goes a bit stronger on individual competence issues than does the typical enterprise human resources function today, which is often more wrapped up in such matters as diversity issues than in concerns with employee skills. This control environment principle calls for enterprises to define their competence requirements as needed to support the achievement of their internal control objectives, with consideration given to:

- Knowledge, skills, and experience needs
- The nature and degree of judgment and limitations of authority to be applied to specific positions
- Cost-benefit analyses of different levels of skills and experience
- Trade-offs between the extent of supervision and the requisite competence levels of individual employees

The listed topics raise some hard issues that are often not truly considered by management when evaluating their employees. The control environment is enhanced when we have only the right people in the right jobs.

This principle goes on to say that the board of directors should evaluate the competence of the CEO, and in turn, management should evaluate competencies across the enterprise and outsourced service providers in relation to established *policies and procedures* as well as acting as necessary to address any shortcomings or excesses. The supporting COSO guidance uses the example that a changing risk portfolio may cause an enterprise to shift resources toward areas of the business that require greater attention. Here, as an enterprise brings a new product to market, it may elect to increase staffing in its sales and marketing teams, or as a new applicable regulation is issued, it may focus on those individuals responsible for its implementation. Shortcomings may arise relating to staffing levels, skills, expertise, or a combination of such factors. Management is responsible for acting on such shortcomings in a timely manner.

A key word in this principle and others is *demonstrate*. In all cases, management must take steps to implement the control principle. This is important for internal auditors, who as part of their reviews should be looking for what an enterprise unit has done to implement some internal control principle.

4.6 CONTROL ENVIRONMENT PRINCIPLE 5: HOLDING PEOPLE ACCOUNTABLE

Management and the board of directors should establish the mechanisms to communicate and hold individuals accountable for the performance of internal control responsibilities across the organization and implement corrective action as necessary. As part of this they should establish performance measures, incentives, and other rewards appropriate for responsibilities at all levels of the entity, reflecting appropriate dimensions of performance and expected standards of conduct and performance.

In particular, the board of directors ultimately holds the CEO accountable for internal control in the enterprise's achievement of objectives, and the CEO and other senior management in turn are responsible for designing, implementing, conducting, and periodically evaluating whether the defined structures, authorities, and responsibilities establish accountability for internal control at all levels of the enterprise. Accountability here refers to the level of ownership for and the commitment to the performance of internal control in the pursuit of objectives. Management and the board should establish the mechanism to communicate and hold personnel accountable for their performance of internal control responsibilities across the enterprise and should take appropriate corrective actions as necessary.

Accountability for internal control is interconnected with leadership, and tone-at-the-top leadership messages as well as related management messages throughout the enterprise should be strong where internal control responsibilities are understood, carried out, and reinforced. However, as this COSO principle suggests, people should be held accountable for their actions. All too often today, we face situations where no one is designated to be in charge. Senior managers may look at an internal control problem, and if it is relatively minor in its impact, they will roll their eyes and say that it is an inexperienced staff problem and do nothing about it. Similarly, staff-level personnel may blame the same problem on their management but take no steps to point out their concerns to management or petition for revision or change.

This COSO internal control principle emphasizes that management and all levels of the enterprise should hold people responsible for internal control management as well as all related strengths and weaknesses. This is an important concept that we ignore too often, and an important internal control principle.

4.7 RISK ASSESSMENT PRINCIPLE 6: SPECIFYING APPROPRIATE OBJECTIVES

Risk assessment, a key element in the COSO internal control framework, is defined here as the possibility that an event may occur that will adversely affect the achievement of some enterprise objective. The management of internal control risks affects an enterprise's ability to succeed, compete effectively in its industry, maintain its financial strength and positive reputation, and maintain the overall quality of its products, services, and people. There are always some risks in any business activity and there is no practical way to reduce all of them. Management, however, must determine how much risk is to be prudently accepted and strive to maintain risk within these limits, understanding how much tolerance it has for exceeding its target risk levels.

We all face a variety of risks, some regularly probable and others preposterous. The latter refer to once-in-a-thousand-years events such as major floods or earthquakes. Yes, they may happen at some time in the future, but establishing objectives and potential remedial practices is often of little value. Rather, management as well as internal audit should ask themselves what potential situations worry them in the relatively near term. This can form the basis for establishing a set of risk objectives.

For example, a manufacturer of a technical product may have an objective to launch a new product, using an evolving technology that may face some strong competitors in a very price-competitive market, and with some uncertainties about whether the market will accept the product as much as hoped. This type of scenario can introduce a large number of potential risks and should be identified and documented.

4.8 RISK ASSESSMENT PRINCIPLE 7: IDENTIFYING AND ANALYZING RISKS

Enterprise management with the support of internal audit should endeavor to identify all possible internal control risks that may impact an enterprise, ranging from the larger or more significant risks down to the less major risks associated with individual projects or smaller business units. The risk identification process requires a studied, deliberate approach to looking at potential risks in each area of operations and then identifying the more significant risk areas that may impact each operation in a reasonable time period. The idea is not to just list every possible risk but to identify those that might impact operations, with some level of probability, within a reasonable time period. This can be a difficult exercise because we often do not know the probability of the risk occurring or the nature of the consequences if the enterprise has to face the risk.

While COSO's focus is on external financial reporting, the risk identification process should occur at multiple levels in an enterprise. A risk that impacts an individual business unit or project may not have that great of an impact on the entire enterprise or beyond. Conversely, a major risk that impacts the entire economy will flow down to the individual enterprise and the separate business units.

While identifying and analyzing risks should be an ongoing iterative process conducted to enhance an enterprise's ability to achieve its objectives, it is an important area that should be considered as part of internal audit planning, as discussed in Chapter 8. Although an enterprise may not explicitly state all of its risk-related objectives, this does not mean that an implied objective is without either internal or external risk, and the enterprise should consider all risks that may occur.

To be effective, an enterprise risk identification process should be supported by a variety of activities, techniques, and mechanisms, each relevant to the overall risk assessment. Management should consider these risks at all levels and take necessary steps to manage them. The risk assessment should consider factors that influence the severity, velocity, and persistence of the risk, its likelihood of the loss of assets, and the related impact on operations, reporting, and compliance activities. In addition, both internal audit and the overall enterprise need to understand the enterprise's tolerance for accepting risks and its ability to operate within those risk levels.

COSO's *risk identification and analysis* principle call for the consideration of all risks within an enterprise, including its subunits and operational functions, such as finance, human resources, marketing, production, purchasing, and IT management. In addition, this process should consider internal and external risks originating from outsourced service providers, key suppliers, and channel partners that directly or indirectly impact an enterprise's achievement of objectives. In conducting these risk assessments, management should consider the rate of change in determining the frequency of the risk assessment process. While risk assessment is a dynamic process, enterprises should use a combination of ongoing and periodic risk assessments. Internal audit can play an important role here in both their risk-based internal audit planning and "boots on the ground" identification of potential risk areas as part of internal audits at field locations.

4.9 RISK ASSESSMENT PRINCIPLE 8: EVALUATING FRAUD RISKS

As we discussed in Chapter 3, internal auditors in the past had minimal involvement with fraud-related issues, but this has very much changed. Internal auditors are often in a very good position to evaluate *fraud risk* due to their ongoing review activities throughout an enterprise. Fraud detection and prevention processes will be discussed more thoroughly in Chapter 27, and they are an important COSO internal control principle.

A fraud risk assessment is a process that an enterprise should utilize to determine its exposure to internal and external fraud. The assessment should review operations and controls, including policies and procedures, to determine where gaps exist that could allow a person or group of persons to carry out a fraud against the enterprise. A fraud risk assessment should then look at key areas of the enterprise to determine if actions have been taken that would alert management to a fraud or to effectively deter the execution of a fraud. Each enterprise has different levels of risk and mitigation techniques depending on their industry. A manufacturing firm with high unit value inventory has different risks than a software technology company with valuable intellectual property. A retail establishment with stores has a different set of

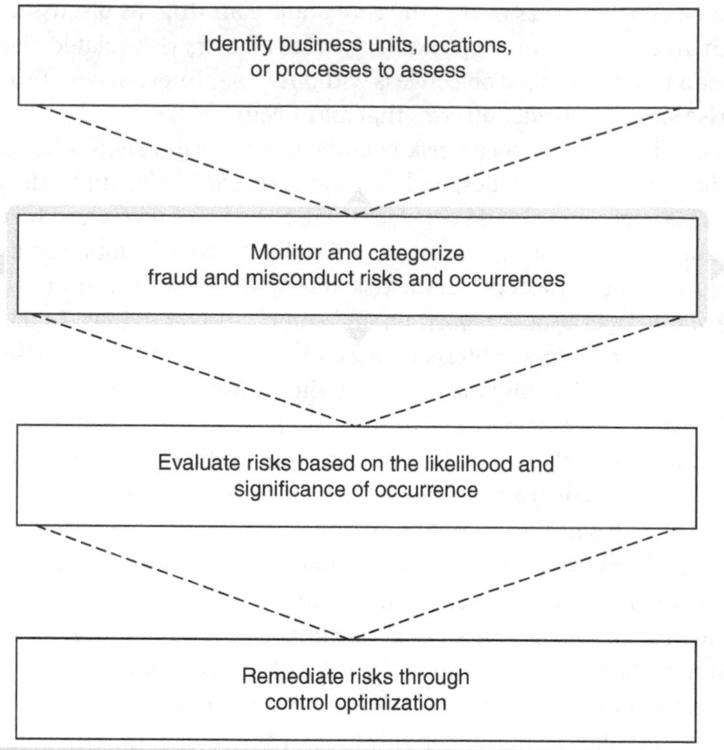

EXHIBIT 4.3 Fraud Risk Assessment

risks than a professional services firm. Each risk assessment needs to be tailored to the organization and the specific risks it faces. Exhibit 4.3 shows this general fraud risk assessment process.

Internal auditors run into many such awareness concerns and potential fraud issues in the ongoing course of their scheduled reviews. They also typically get involved in much more detailed, transaction-level reviews than their external audit counterparts and see questionable documents or transactions more frequently. If management feels there may be a potential fraud in the enterprise, the first step is almost always to contact internal audit, which also will have some connection and communication with the corporate legal department. They can discuss any potential concerns there and get a quick opinion on whether some concern requires more attention. If there are strong signs of an active fraud, corporate legal will almost always be ready to jump into the matter and help.

The IIA standards emphasize that internal audit has a role to play regarding fraud detection and prevention, but the primary responsibility falls on management. Although this sounds simple in theory, the problem lies in communicating that message to management. The evaluation of fraud risks is an important internal control principle.

4.10 RISK ASSESSMENT PRINCIPLE 9: IDENTIFYING CHANGES AFFECTING INTERNAL CONTROLS

Risk assessment principles are of little value if an enterprise goes through an extensive analysis to identify risks but then does essentially nothing to take action to mitigate the identified risks. This really calls for a risk response plan with the final principle for COSO internal controls risk assessment:

> Identify and analyze changes that could significantly affect internal controls.

Enterprises should develop risk management strategies as part of their risk management processes. Risk management strategies address how an enterprise intends to assess identified risks, plan responses, and monitor those risks—making explicit and transparent the risk perceptions that an enterprise routinely uses in making both investment and operational decisions. Risk identification and analysis strategies are a key part of enterprise risk management.

Response strategies are a key component of COSO internal controls. Once the potential significance of risks has been assessed, management should consider how those risks should be managed. This often involves judgments based on assumptions about the risk and a reasonable analysis of the costs associated with reducing the levels of risk. Management should consider acting on each of the four basic *risk response strategies* discussed in Chapter 3: avoidance, reduction, sharing, and risk acceptance.

Management should develop a general risk response strategy for each of its risks using an approach built around one of these four general strategies. In doing so, it should consider the costs versus benefits of each potential risk responses to best align them with the enterprise's overall risk appetite. For example, an enterprise's recognition that the impact of a given risk is relatively low would be balanced against a low risk tolerance that suggests that insurance should be purchased to provide a potential risk response. For many risks, appropriate responses are obvious and almost universally understood. An IT operation, for example, spends the time and resources to back up its key data files and implement a business continuity plan. There should be no question regarding this basic approach, but various levels of management may question the frequency of backup processes or how often the continuity plan needs to be tested.

An enterprise at this point should go back to the several risk objectives that have been established as well as the tolerance ranges for those objectives. Then it should readdress both the likelihoods and the impacts associated with each of the identified risks within those risk objectives to develop an assessment of both of those risk categories as well as an overall assessment of the planned risk responses and how those risks will align with overall enterprise risk tolerances. The basic message here is that an enterprise needs an overall risk response plan in order to be complaint with its COSO internal control framework.

4.11 CONTROL ACTIVITIES PRINCIPLE 10: SELECTING CONTROL ACTIVITIES THAT MITIGATE RISKS

This important COSO control activity principle states that, as part of its overall internal controls environment, an enterprise should select and develop *control activities* that contribute to the mitigation of internal control risks to the achievement of their objectives to acceptable levels. Control activities include actions that ensure that responses to assessed risks, as well as other management directives—such as establishing an enterprise code of ethics—are carried out properly and in a timely manner.

Because every enterprise has its own set of objectives and implementation approaches, there will always be differences in their objectives, risks, responses, and related control activities. Every enterprise is managed by different people with different skills who use their individual techniques in effecting internal controls. In addition, controls reflect the environment and industry in which the enterprise operates as well as the complexity of its organization, its history, culture, and scope of operations.

Enterprise-specific factors can impact the control activities needed to support their systems of internal control:

- The enterprise's environment and complexity as well as the nature and scope of its operations, both physically and logically, can all affect enterprise control activities.
- Highly regulated enterprises generally have more complex risk responses and control activities than less regulated entities.
- The scope and nature of risk responses and control activities for multinational enterprises with diverse operations generally address a more complex internal control structure than those of a domestic enterprise with less varied activities.
- An enterprise with a fairly sophisticated enterprise resource planning system, as discussed further in the sections following, will have different control activities than one using less sophisticated IT systems.
- An enterprise with decentralized operations and an emphasis on local autonomy and innovation presents a different control environment than another whose operations are constant and highly centralized.

The previous points highlight an obvious issue regarding the COSO internal control framework. When establishing internal control processes, an enterprise always needs to think of the relative size and complexity of the enterprise. One size does not fit all, and management must consider the relative size of the enterprise and should make internal control accommodations based on relative size and other operating environment considerations.

The selection and development of strong enterprise control activities that mitigate overall risk is an important COSO internal control principle. For internal auditors, this will lead to developing and performing effective internal audits, as are discussed in Chapter 8, as well as other internal audit activities found in other chapters.

4.12 CONTROL ACTIVITIES PRINCIPLE 11: SELECTING AND DEVELOPING TECHNOLOGY CONTROLS

COSO uses the term *technology* in this principle, and it could include such areas as manufacturing robotics, pharmaceutical testing instruments, and the development of consumer-oriented electronic video products. All of these technology products and more go beyond what we normally call IT systems, and many of their internal control concerns and issues are really outside of the range of many internal auditors. Given space limitations here, when COSO referenced *technology controls*, we will be referencing IT systems applications and general controls. Both of these IT control areas cover a wide range of topics and are discussed in Part Five of this book, Chapters 19 through 24.

There are many different types of technical-, management-, and governance-related IT controls covering everything from high-level management IT policies to control processes for specific applications and even running on handheld devices. Exhibit 4.4 describes this overall IT control hierarchy, much of which will be discussed in other chapters going forward. Our point here is that there is one COSO internal control principle talking about the importance of IT controls, but an enterprise has a challenge to select and develop appropriate IT controls.

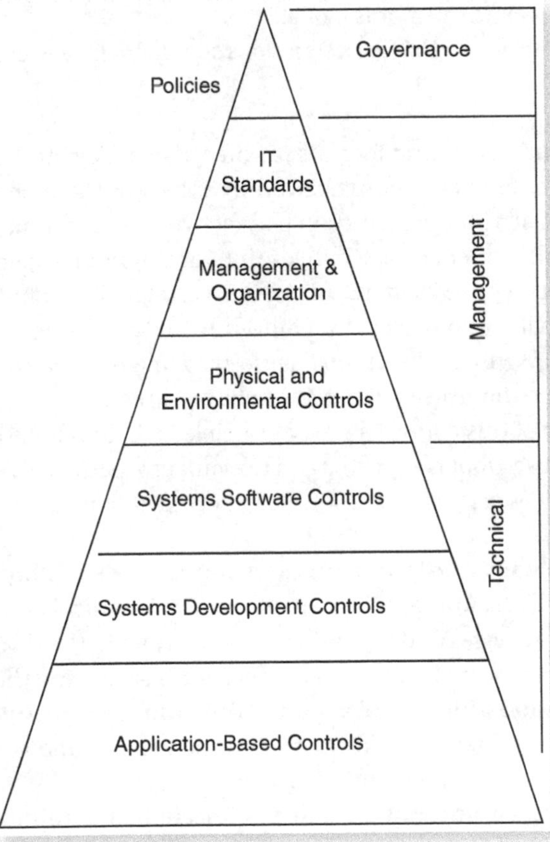

EXHIBIT 4.4 IT Control Hierarchy

4.13 CONTROL ACTIVITIES PRINCIPLE 12: POLICIES AND PROCEDURES

The third of the COSO control activities principles calls for an enterprise to deploy its control activities through policies and procedures. Control activity policies specify and establish what is expected, and procedures put those policies into action. While an enterprise will normally have many policies and procedures in place to achieve its objectives, control activities should be initiated that specifically relate to those policies and procedures and contribute to the mitigation of risks for the achievement of objectives at acceptable levels.

A policy should be more than just the CEO saying he or she generally wants to do something or take some action without any more specific details. In going through a formal review and approval process, an enterprise should publish statements outlining management's intention to implement some policy or take some action. Often published on a customer service database, enterprise-published policies should have the following elements:

- **Policy purpose.** There should be a high-level statement outlining the intent or high-level objectives of the policy.
- **Location and applicability.** There should be a definition of whether the policy applies only to some units or is global.
- **Roles and responsibilities.** Descriptions should include everyone involved in the policy.

There are many styles and formats of enterprise policy statements, and in some cases policies can even be communicated orally as long as the supporting messages are well understood. Unwritten policies can be effective where communications channels involve limited management layers and close interactions with supervision of personnel. But whether or not they are written, policies must establish clear individual responsibility and accountability and be deployed diligently and consistently by competent personnel. A procedure will not be useful if performed in a rote manner, without a sharp, continuing focus on the risks to which the policy is directed.

A key element of this control activity principle is that an enterprise should deploy policies that establish what is expected and relevant procedures to reflect these policies. This control activities principle calls for the following action steps:

- **Establish policies and procedures to support the deployment of management's directives.** Management should establish control activities that are built into business processes and employees' day-to-day activities through policies establishing what is expected and relevant procedures specifying those actions.
- **Establish responsibility and accountability for executing policies and procedures.** Management should establish responsibility and accountability for all relevant control activities of the enterprise.
- **Perform using competent personnel.** Selection and training processes should be in place such that competent personnel are assigned to perform control activities with diligence and focus.

- **Perform in a timely manner.** Responsible personnel should perform control activities in a timely manner as defined by enterprise policies and procedures.
- **Take corrective actions when appropriate.** Responsible personnel should investigate and act on matters identified as a result of executing control activities.
- **Reassess policies and procedures.** Management should periodically review control activities to determine their continued relevance and should refresh them when necessary.

4.14 INFORMATION AND COMMUNICATION PRINCIPLE 13: USING RELEVANT, QUALITY INFORMATION

An enterprise should obtain and use relevant, quality information to support the functioning of its internal control components. Information is necessary for an enterprise to carry out its internal control responsibilities in support of the achievement of objectives. Information about an enterprise's objectives should be gathered from the board of directors and senior management activities and summarized in a way that line management and others can understand these objectives and their role in their achievements. This communication problem is often a "Management 101" type of basic issue, where we should always remember that relevant information is a key component of effective internal controls. Senior management, IT specialists, internal auditors, and others, working as a team, should survey past operational and financial management information input and output resources to identify and better define relevant information requirements.

Obtaining relevant information, as defined in the COSO guidance materials, requires management to identify and define information requirements at a strong level of detail and specificity. Identifying information requirements is an iterative and ongoing process that occurs throughout the performance of an effective internal control system.

Information requirements are established through activities performed in support of the other internal control elements or components. These requirements facilitate and direct management and other personnel to identify relevant and reliable sources of information and underlying data. The amount of information and underlying data available to management may often be more than is needed because of increased sources of information and advances in data collection, processing, and storage. In other cases, data may be difficult to obtain at the relevant level or requisite specificity. Therefore, a clear understanding of the COSO-defined information requirements directs management and other personnel to identify relevant and reliable sources of information and data.

Information from Relevant Sources

With our growing use of video, voice, and communications over the Internet and wireless sources, in addition to more traditional printed reports, internal and external information is received from a variety of sources and in a variety of forms and formats. Exhibit 4.5 shows some examples of types of information that enterprise management encounters on a regular basis.

EXHIBIT 4.5 Information from Relevant Sources Example

Info. Source	Example of Relevant Information	Data Example
Internal	Senior or supervisory management communications	Organization changes
Internal	Inspection reports from production floor.	Online and quality production informaton
Internal	Internal audit report finding and recommendations	Planned corrective actions based on audit findings
Internal	Personnel time reporting system	Hours incurred on time-based projects
Internal	Reports from manufacturing systems	Production results: number of units shipped
Internal	Responses to customer surveys	Factors impacting customer repeat purchases
Internal	Whistleblower hotline reported concerns and issues	Complaints on management behaviors
External	Data from outsourced service provider	Products shipped from contract manufacturer
External	Industry research reports	Competitor product information
External	Peer company earning releases	Market and industry metrics
External	Governmental or trade association rules and new standards	New or expanded requirements
External	Social media, blog, or other posts	Opinions about the enterprise
External	Trade show surveys and attendee recorded comments	Evolving customer interests and preferences
External	Whistleblower hotline	Claims of fraud, bribery, etc.

In managing their information from external sources, management should consider them in terms of a comprehensive scope of potential events, activities, and data sources available internally and from reliable sources, and select those that are most relevant and useful to the current organizational structure, business model, or objectives. As changes to an enterprise occur, their information requirements also change. For example, an enterprise operating in a highly dynamic business or economic environment may experience continual changes, often caused by the activities of highly innovative and quick-moving competitors who shift customer expectations. In addition, this type of enterprise may face evolving regulatory issues, globalization issues, and challenges from technology innovations. Thus management must regularly reevaluate its information requirements and adjust to the nature, extent, and sources of information and underlying data to meet its ongoing needs.

Processing Data through Information Systems

COSO uses the phrase *information system* in a rather broad sense, meaning both information technology (IT) systems and other overall related processes—both manual and IT-based—for capturing, analyzing, storing, and distributing all types of business information. Enterprises develop information systems to source, capture, and process large volumes of data from internal and external sources into meaningful, actionable information to meet defined information requirements. Information systems encompass a combination of people, processes, and technology that support a business's basic or fundamental processes managed internally as well as those supported through relationships with outsourced service providers and other external parties.

Information can be obtained through a variety of forms, including manual input or compilation, or through the use of IT processes such as application programming interfaces automated links. Conversations with customers, suppliers, regulators, and employees are also sources of critical data and information needed to identify and assess both risks and opportunities. In some instances, information and underlying data captured requires specificity. In other cases, information may be obtained directly from an internal or external source.

The volume of information accessible to an enterprise presents both opportunities and risks. Greater access to information will generally enhance internal controls. The increased volume of information and underlying data, however, may create additional risks such as operational risks caused by inefficiency due to data overloads, or compliance risks associated with the laws and regulations around data protection, retention, privacy, and security issues arising from the nature of data stored by or on behalf of the enterprise.

The nature and extent of information requirements, the complexity and volume of this information, and the dependence on external parties impacts the range of sophistication of information systems, including the extent of technology deployed. Regardless of the level of sophistication adopted, all types of information systems support the end-to-end processing of transactions and data that enable the enterprise to collect, store, and summarize quality and consistent information across relevant processes, whether manual, automated, or a combination of both.

Information systems developed with integrated, technology-enabled processes provide opportunities for an enterprise to enhance the efficiency, speed, and accessibility of information to users. Additionally, such information systems may enhance internal controls over security and privacy risks associated with the information obtained and generated by the enterprise. Information systems should be designed and implemented to restrict the access to information only to those who need it and to reduce the number of access points to enhance the effectiveness of migrating risks associated with the security and privacy of information.

Achieving the right balance between the benefits and the costs to obtain and manage information and supporting systems is a key consideration in establishing an information system that meets an enterprise's needs. This COSO internal control principle elevates the importance of all enterprise information systems—both IT and other processes—in establishing effective internal controls. Enterprise management should think about the importance of the information systems not just in terms of processes, often primarily just managed by an IT function or department, but in terms of overall enterprise information flows as a vehicle for improving enterprise internal controls.

4.15 INFORMATION AND COMMUNICATION PRINCIPLE 14: INTERNAL COMMUNICATIONS

An enterprise should internally communicate internal control information, including its objectives and responsibilities, to support the functioning of other components of internal control. Endorsed by senior management, this communication of information should be conveyed to all elements across an enterprise and include:

- The importance, relevance, and benefits of effective internal controls
- The roles and responsibilities of management and other personnel in performing those internal control processes
- The expectations of the enterprise to communicate up, down, and across any matters of significance relating to internal control, including instances of weakness, deterioration, or nonadherence

An enterprise should establish and implement policies and procedures that facilitate effective *internal communication*. This includes specific and directed communication that addresses individual authorities, responsibilities, and standards of conduct across the enterprise. Senior management should communicate the enterprise's objectives clearly throughout so that other management and personnel, including such nonemployees as contractors, understand their individual roles in the organization. Such communication occurs regardless of where personnel are located, their level of authority, or their functional responsibility.

Internal Control Communication

Internal control communication begins with the delivery and communication of objectives. As management cascades communication of enterprise-specific objectives throughout the organization, it is important that related sub-objectives or specific requirements are communicated to personnel in a manner that allows them to understand how their roles and responsibilities impact the achievement of an enterprise's high-level objectives.

All personnel should also receive a clear message from senior management that their internal control responsibilities must be taken seriously. Through the communication of objectives and sub-objectives, personnel should understand how their roles, responsibilities, and actions relate to the work of others in the enterprise, their responsibilities for internal control, and what is deemed as acceptable and nonacceptable behavior. By establishing appropriate control structures, authorities, and responsibilities, communication to personnel on their expectations for practicing and implementing effective internal controls is affected. However, communication about internal control responsibilities may not on its own be sufficient to ensure that management and other personnel embrace their accountability responsibilities and respond as intended. Often management must take timely action that is consistent with such communication to enforce the messages conveyed.

In addition, information that is shared through internal communications helps management and other personnel to recognize any problems or potential problems, determine their cause, and take corrective action. For example, an internal audit department conducts an audit over the commissions paid to distributors in one international location. If this audit reveals instances of the fraudulent reporting of sales through certain distributors and a further investigation exposes payments by the distributor to the sales representative responsible for the related distributors, this information would be published by the internal audit department in a report addressed to the board and senior management. Once the internal audit findings have been confirmed, the control weakness should be shared with sales management in other locations, enabling them to analyze information more critically to determine whether the issue is more pervasive and to take any necessary actions.

Communications between management and the board of directors provide the board with the information it needs to exercise its oversight responsibility for internal control. Information relating to internal control that is communicated to the board generally should include significant matters about adherence to, changes in, or issues arising from the system of internal controls. The frequency and level of detail of the communication to management and the board of directors must be sufficient to enable the board members to understand the results of management's separate and ongoing assessments and the impact of those results on the achievement of objectives. Additionally, the frequency and level of detail must be sufficient to enable the board of directors to respond to indications of ineffective internal control on a timely basis.

Internal Communication beyond Normal Channels

For information to flow up, down, and across the enterprise, there must be open channels of communication and a clear-cut willingness to report and listen. Management and other personnel must believe that their supervisors truly want to know about internal control–related problems and that they will deal with them as necessary. In most cases, normal established reporting lines, such as a traditional organization chart in an enterprise, are the appropriate channels of communication. However, personnel are usually quick to pick up signals if management does not have the time or interest to deal with problems they have uncovered. Compounding this problem, an unreceptive manager may be the last to know that the normal communication channel is inoperative or ineffective.

In some circumstances, separate lines of communication are needed to establish a fail-safe mechanism for anonymous or confidential communications when normal channels are inoperative or ineffective. Some smaller enterprises have provided and made employees aware of a channel for such communication to be received by a member of the board, or a member of the audit committee. Many larger enterprises have established an ethics function and some type of a hotline function where personnel at all levels can call in their concerns on a 24/7 basis, and report them, ask questions, or even act as whistleblowers to report on some issue. This author played a major role in launching an ethics function and establishing an ethics hotline for a major U.S. corporation some years ago, and a number of these concepts are described in his book on SOx internal controls.[1]

Enterprise stakeholders should fully understand how these communication channels operate and how they will be confidentially protected for their use. Policies and procedures should be in place requiring that all communication through these channels be assessed, prioritized, and investigated. Escalation procedures should be in place to ensure that necessary communications will be made to a designated board member, the head of internal audit, or the chief ethics officer, if such a function exists, who would be responsible for ensuring that timely and proper assessments, investigations, and appropriate actions are performed. These separate mechanisms encourage employees and affiliated stakeholders to report suspected violations of an enterprise's code of conduct without fear of reprisal, and send a clear message that senior management is committed to open communication channels and will act based on the information that is reported to it.

Methods of Communication

Both clarity and effectiveness of any information communicated is important to ensuring that these messages are received as intended. Active forms of communication such as face-to-face meetings are often more effective than passive forms such as broadcast e-mails or Web postings. Periodic evaluation of the effectiveness of enterprise communication practices helps to ensure that these methods are working. This can be done through a variety of existing processes, such as employee performance evaluations, annual management reviews, and feedback programs.

Management should select appropriate methods of communication, taking into account the audience, nature of the communication, timeliness, cost, and security and privacy requirements as well as any legal or regulatory requirements. Exhibit 4.6 shows an example of various internal control–related communication formats. Not one of these is necessarily better than another as long as the method selected appropriately communicates desired messages to intended recipients.

When choosing a method or format for communication, management should consider the environment where the messages are transmitted. For example, cultural, ethnic, and generational differences can affect how messages are received, and the method of communication should be adjusted based on those factors. Regardless of the method of communication used, management should consider their requirements to deliver

EXHIBIT 4.6 Methods of Internal Communication Examples

Communication Type	Typical Purpose
Private Network Pages	Policies and Procedures
E-mail Messages	Presentations
Live or Online Training	Web Site Postings
Twitter or Facebook	Social Media Postings
Memoranda	Text Messages
One-on-One Discussions	Webcasts and Video
Performance Evaluations	Secure Employee Database

communications to both internal parties particularly those external parties where the messages relate to compliance with laws and regulations. Given the potential volume and ability to store and retrieve such information, these communication requirements may be challenging when management relies on the masses of e-mails associated with real-time technology-enabled communications. Control activity principles over the retention of internal control information should consider the challenges of advances in technology, including communication and collaboration technologies used to support internal control.

Communication of information related to internal control responsibilities alone may not be sufficient to ensure that management and other personnel receive and respond as intended. Consistent and timely actions taken by management regarding such communications reinforces the messages conveyed. With ever-changing technologies, management today has many options in their choice of delivering effective messages to all involved personnel regarding internal control matters. However, management should consider the environment and the intended recipients of these messages, and use what they consider to be the more effective methods given the planned recipients.

4.16 INFORMATION AND COMMUNICATION PRINCIPLE 15: EXTERNAL COMMUNICATIONS

An important COSO principle an enterprise should establish and implement are policies and procedures that facilitate effective *external communication*. This includes mechanisms to obtain or receive information from external parties and to share that information internally, allowing management and other personnel to identify trends, events, or circumstances that may impact their achievement of internal control objectives.

Communication with external parties allows others to readily understand events, activities, and other circumstances that may affect how they should interact with an enterprise. Management's communication to external parties should send a message about the importance of internal controls in the enterprise by demonstrating open lines of communication. Communication to external suppliers and customers is critical for establishing an appropriate control environment and to help these external parties understand an enterprise's values and culture. They should be informed of such things as an organization's code of conduct and recognize their responsibilities in helping to ensure compliance with this and other values. For example, management may distribute their policies and practices for business dealings with vendors upon approval of a new vendor and may require the vendor to acknowledge its adherence prior to the approval of an initial purchase order with the vendor.

Communication complexity issues may arise between an enterprise and external parties through service providers and other outsourcing arrangements, joint ventures and alliances, and other transactions that create mutual dependencies between these parties. Such complexities may create concerns over how business is being conducted between the parties. In this case, an enterprise should consider making separate communication channels available to external service providers to allow them to communicate directly with management and other personnel. For example, a customer of products developed through a joint venture may learn that one of the joint venture partners sold products in a country that was not agreed to under the joint venture arrangements. Such a breach may affect the customer's ability to use or resell the products, impacting that customer's business. The enterprise should facilitate channels in which it can communicate concerns to others in the enterprise without disrupting ongoing operations.

Similar to internal communications, the means by which management should communicate externally impacts its ability to obtain information needed as well as to ensure that key messages about the enterprise are received and understood. Management should consider the many forms and methods of communications used, taking into account the audience, the nature of the communication, its timeliness, and any legal or regulatory requirements. The communication of internal control information and data to external parties is an important but often ignored principle.

4.17 MONITORING PRINCIPLE 16: INTERNAL CONTROL EVALUATIONS

Monitoring activities assess whether COSO's internal control objectives are present and functioning. An enterprise should use ongoing and separate evaluation processes to ascertain whether established internal control principles, both across the enterprise and its subunits, are in effect, present, and functioning. Monitoring is a key factor in an assessment of the effectiveness of internal controls. An enterprise, often with the support of internal audit, should conduct ongoing control monitoring activities and identify and communicate any known internal control deficiencies in a full circle of internal control processes. The idea here is that an enterprise should go through each of the COSO control components, and as this cycle moves to monitoring activities, they act as a review factor over all other internal control components.

As a key control principle, an enterprise should select, develop, and perform ongoing and/or separate evaluations to monitor or ascertain whether its internal control components are present and functioning. Monitoring can be done through some combination of separate evaluations or continuous monitoring processes. An independent, one-time internal audit over some area of operations or internal controls is an example of a separate monitoring activity. Internal audit may schedule a single review of an area, based on their risk assessment, and then may return to review that same area again, based on any internal control deficiencies found in the first review. Separate evaluations should be conducted periodically by management, internal audit, or external parties, among others.

Continuous monitoring processes are similar to the continuous internal audit processes discussed in Chapter 11. They are like warning lights in a production measurement device that only flash if some measurement is out of bounds. Ongoing evaluations are generally defined, routine operations built into business processes and performed on a real-time basis, reacting to changed conditions. Where ongoing evaluations are built into business processes, their internal control components are usually structured to monitor themselves on an ongoing basis.

Unmonitored controls tend to deteriorate over time, and an enterprise should implement monitoring processes to help ensure that internal control continues to operate effectively. When monitoring is designed and implemented appropriately, an enterprise should benefit because it is more likely to:

- Identify and correct internal control problems on a timely basis
- Produce more accurate and reliable information for use in decision making
- Prepare accurate and timely financial statements
- Be in a position to provide periodic certifications or assertions on the effectiveness of internal control

Over time, effective monitoring can lead to organizational efficiencies and reduced costs associated with public reporting on internal control, because monitoring-related problems are identified and addressed in a proactive rather than reactive manner.

4.18 MONITORING PRINCIPLE 17: COMMUNICATING INTERNAL CONTROL DEFICIENCIES

An enterprise should communicate its internal control deficiencies in a timely manner to all parties responsible for taking corrective actions, including senior management and the board of directors. The enterprise should identify monitoring-related matters worthy of attention that represent both potential or real shortcomings in some aspect of the enterprise's system of internal controls and that have the potential to adversely affect the ability of the enterprise to achieve its objectives. In addition, an enterprise should strive to identify opportunities to improve the efficiency of its internal controls.

The results of ongoing and separate monitoring evaluations should be assessed against management's criteria to determine to whom to report and what is to be discussed, and all identified internal control deficiencies should be communicated to those members of the enterprise management in positions to take timely corrective actions. After any identified deficiencies are evaluated, management should determine that remediation efforts are conducted on a timely basis.

Internal control deficiencies, such as those identified by internal audit, should be reported both to responsible parties for taking corrective actions and to at least one level of upper management. These actions are discussed in Chapter 18 on reporting internal audit results. Where findings cut across organizational boundaries, the deficiencies should be reported to all relevant parties and to a sufficiently high level to drive appropriate action. That is, deficiencies relating to the board of directors where the board is not independent to the extent required or where the board did not provide sufficient oversight should be reported as prescribed by established reporting protocols to the full board, the chair of the board, and appropriate board reporting committees.

Processes to report internal control deficiencies are a key component to assure that an enterprise has effective internal controls. Management needs to design, develop, and launch effective internal control processes, but there needs to be some forms of monitoring process in place to provide assurances that those internal controls are in place.

The 17 COSO internal control principles were not included in the original framework but now are an important guide to help management and internal audit to focus on the internal control guidance contained in the three-dimensional COSO framework. We will be concentrating on these principles in various chapters going forward, and a general knowledge of these 17 COSO internal control principles should be part of every internal auditor's CBOK operating activities.

NOTE

1. Robert R. Moeller, *Sarbanes-Oxley Internal Controls, Effective Auditing with AS5, COBIT and ITIL®* (Hoboken, NJ: John Wiley & Sons, 2008).

CHAPTER FIVE

Sarbanes-Oxley (SOx) and Beyond

THE *SARBANES-OXLEY ACT (SOX)* IS a U.S. law enacted in 2002 to improve financial reporting audit processes and to correct a series of board of director, public accounting, and other practices. It has had a major impact on businesses first in the United States and now worldwide. While many of SOx's new auditing and internal control rules directly changed many financial reporting and external auditor practices, SOx also had a major impact on internal auditors. A general understanding of SOx, with an emphasis on its *Section 404 internal accounting control rules*, is a key CBOK requirement for all internal auditors.

SOx became law in the United States as a response to a series of accounting misdeeds and financial failures at some once-major corporations such as Enron and WorldCom. A major component of SOx is the *Public Company Accounting Oversight Board (PCAOB)*, an independent entity that sets U.S. external auditing standards and regulates the public accounting industry. Those auditing standards are set at very high levels. For example, the sections following will introduce the PCAOB's Auditing Standard No. 5, or *AS5*. SOx introduced major changes that have impacted corporate governance, accounting, and financial reporting audit processes. SOx is a wide-ranging set of requirements that has redefined both how we govern public enterprises and how we attest that their reported financial results are fairly stated.

Most of the business and auditor attention to SOx requirements has focused on its Section 404 internal control attestation rules. Internal auditors should be aware of these requirements for SOx Section 404 reviews as well as what are called the *Section 302* rules, making management responsible for its reported financial statements. Both of these rules have caused a lot of effort and concern as corporations began to establish compliance with SOx. Other portions of the legislation have not received much attention or caused major compliance concerns. An example is a SOx requirement that audit committees establish what are called whistleblower programs, discussed in Chapter 26, to report fraudulent accounting anonymously.

This chapter will provide an overview of SOx today, with an emphasis on Section 404 and other areas that are most important to internal auditors and corporations. With an emphasis on internal auditor CBOK needs, this chapter will focus on three aspects of SOx:

1. **Key SOx elements: overview of the legislation.** We will summarize SOx rules in such areas as audit committee procedures and new external auditor rules. These should help internal auditors to better understand these SOx rules.
2. **Section 404 internal accounting control reviews.** The SOx requirements for reviews of internal accounting controls have caused much toil and turmoil in corporations since the law became active. We will describe this process and why it is important for internal auditors.
3. **SOx's AS5 risk-based approaches.** The previously referenced set of PCAOB auditing standards called AS5 has suggested more risk-based auditing approaches. More important here, AS5 emphasizes the importance of internal audit's work in performing financial reporting internal control reviews.

Much of the impact of SOx depends on detailed rules released by the PCAOB to interpret the legislation. SOx legislation was drafted in a one-size-fits-all manner, suggesting that SOx and SEC rules applied to any entity, despite its size or home country, that has a security registered with the SEC. Those practices are changing, and we will also look at how SOx is evolving into a worldwide global standard. A general knowledge of SOx should be part of every internal auditor's CBOK.

5.1 KEY SARBANES-OXLEY ACT (SOx) ELEMENTS

The official name for this U.S. federal law is the Public Accounting Reform and Investor Protection Act. It became law in August 2002, with most of the final detailed rules and regulations released by the end of the following year. Its title being a bit l ong, business professionals refer to it as the Sarbanes-Oxley Act, from the names of its principal congressional sponsors. As this is still too long of a name, most generally refer to it as SOx, SOX, or even Sarbox, among many other variations.

SOx introduced a series of totally changed processes for external auditing and gave new governance responsibilities to senior executives and board members. It also established the PCAOB, as rule-setting authority under the SEC that issues financial auditing standards and monitors external auditor governance. As happens with all comprehensive federal laws, an extensive set of specific regulations and administrative rules has been developed by the Securities and Exchange Commission (SEC) based on the SOx legislation.

U.S. federal laws are organized and issued as separate sections of legislation called titles, with numbered sections and subsections under each. Much of the SOx legislation contains rules that are not very significant for most internal auditors and business professionals. For example, Section 602 (d) of Title I states that the SEC "shall establish" minimum professional conduct standards or rules for SEC practicing attorneys. While this is perhaps good to know, it does not have any internal audit impact. Exhibit 5.1 summarizes the major sections of SOx, and a discussion of key SOx titles follows. Our intent is not to reproduce the full text of this legislation—it can be found on the Web[1]—but to highlight portions of the law that are significant to internal audit and business professionals. Of interest, even though internal control processes very much rely on both external and internal auditors, the original SOx legislation makes almost no direct reference to the important roles and responsibilities of internal auditors. The importance of internal audit in SOx internal control reviews was subsequently highlighted in the AS5 rules, released in mid-2007 and discussed later. The emphasis throughout this chapter will be on the role of internal audit in today's SOx environment.

EXHIBIT 5.1 Sarbanes-Oxley Act Key Provisions Summary

Section	Subject	Rule or Requirement
101	Establishment of PCAOB	Overall rules for the establishment of the PCAOB, including its membership requirements.
104	Accounting Firm Inspections	Schedule for PCAOB inspections of registered public accounting firms.
108	Auditing Standards	The PCAOB will accept current but will issue its own new auditing standards.
201	Out of Scope Practices	Outlines prohibited accounting firm practices such as internal audit outsourcing, bookkeeping, and financial systems design.
203	Audit Partner Rotations	The audit partner and the reviewing partner must rotate off an assignment every five years.
301	Audit Committee Independence	All audit committee members must be independent directors.
302	Corp. Responsibility for Financial Reports	The CEO and CFO must personally certify their periodic financial reports.
305	Officer and Director Bars	If compensation is received as part of fraudulent/ illegal accounting, the benefiting officers or director is required to personally reimburse funds received.
404	Internal Control Reports	Management is responsible for an annual assessment of internal controls.
407	Financial Expert	One audit committee director must be a designated financial expert.
408	Enhanced Review of Financial Disclosures	The SEC may schedule extended reviews of reported information based on certain specified factors.
409	Real-Time Disclosure	Financial reports must be distributed in a rapid and current manner.
1105	Officer or Director Prohibitions	The SEC may prohibit an officer or director from serving in another public company if found guilty of a violation.

Title I: Public Company Accounting Oversight Board

The SOx legislation contained new rules for external auditors. Prior to SOx, the American Institute of Certified Public Accountants (AICPA) had guidance-setting responsibility for all external auditors and their public accounting firms through its administration of the Certified Public Accountant (CPA) test and its restriction of AICPA membership to CPAs. While state boards of accountancy actually licensed CPAs, the AICPA had overall responsibility for the profession. External audit standards were then set by the AICPA's Auditing Standards Board (ASB). Although basic standards—called generally accepted auditing standards (GAAS)—have been in place over the years, newer standards were later released by the AICPA and called Statements on Auditing Standards (SAS). While much of GAAS was just good auditing practices, such as that accounting transactions must be backed by appropriate documentation, the SAS covered specific areas requiring better definition. SAS No. 79, for example, defined early internal control standards, and SAS No. 99 covered the consideration of fraud in a financial statement audit. The AICPA's code of professional conduct required CPAs to follow and comply with all applicable auditing standards.

The AICPA's GAAS and its numbered SAS standards had been accepted by the SEC, and they define audit reviews and tests necessary for a certified audited financial statement. However, the accounting scandals that led to the passage of SOx signaled that the process of establishing auditing standards was broken, and SOx took this audit standards-setting process away from the AICPA, which was dominated by the major public accounting firms, and created the PCAOB, a nonfederal, nonprofit corporation with the responsibility to oversee all audits of corporations subject to the SEC.

The PCAOB does not replace the AICPA but assumes responsibility for the external auditing practices that were formerly managed by AICPA members. The AICPA continues to administer the CPA examination, with its certificates awarded on a state-by-state basis, and sets auditing standards for U.S. private, non-SEC organizations. While SOx Title I defines PCAOB auditing practices for external auditors, other audit process and corporate governance rules have changed how internal auditors coordinate their work with external auditors. The PCAOB releases rules to support SOx legislation, and as this book goes to press, there have been five new standards up through the very important AS5 discussed later in this chapter (see www.pcaobus.org).

The following paragraphs provide some background on SOx Title I external audit process rules and the origins of SOx. An understanding of these SOx rules will help internal auditors in their ongoing dealings with their external auditors and business management.

PCAOB Administration and Public Accounting Firm Registration

The PCAOB is administered through a board of five members appointed by the SEC, with three members *required* to be public, non-CPA members. SOx requires that the PCAOB not be dominated by CPA and public accounting firm interests, and its chairperson must not have been a practicing CPA for at least the past five years. The PCAOB is responsible for overseeing and regulating all public accounting firms that practice before the SEC, including:

- **Registering the public accounting firms that perform audits of corporations.** Much more detailed than just filling out an application form and beginning audits, a registering external audit firm must disclose the audit fees collected, describe its audit and quality standards, provide detailed information on its CPAs performing audits, and disclose any pending criminal, civil, or administrative actions. A firm can be denied the right to register due to any PCAOB questions regarding its background.
- **Establishing auditing standards.** These standards include auditing, quality control, ethics, independence, and other key audit areas. Although many continue to follow earlier AICPA standards, new PCAOB standards are gradually being released. Perhaps the most significant to date has been the Auditing Standard No. 5 (AS5) introduced later in this chapter. As there are frequent calls for more continuous auditing and health and safety sustainability reporting audits, we can probably expect a whole different dimension of these standards in the future.
- **Conducting inspections of registered public accounting firms.** The AICPA had a peer review process in the past, but the public accounting firms often found little to say in criticism of their peers. The PCAOB now performs the quality-related reviews of registered firms.
- **Conducting investigations and disciplinary procedures.** Individual auditors' or an entire registered firm's wrongdoing discovered in formal investigations can result in sanctions that would prohibit a firm or an individual auditor from performing audits under the PCAOB.
- **Performing other standards and quality functions as the board determines.** The PCAOB has indicated that it may get into other areas to protect investors and the public interest. There has been little activity here, but as the need for auditing services evolves, these standards will certainly change and evolve.
- **Enforcing SOx compliance.** The PCAOB is responsible for enforcing compliance to SEC auditing rules beyond the SOx overall legislation. This results in a variety of administrative law actions or other procedures as appropriate.

Information and results on this public accounting firm registration process can be found at www.pcaob.gov. This published registration data may be of particular value for an enterprise that is not using one of the major public accounting firms. There are many highly credible medium-sized and smaller public accounting firms that can provide an enterprise with excellent, high-quality service, but it is always prudent to check the PCAOB registration records.

Auditing, Quality Control, and Independence Standards

Title I, Section 103 gives the PCAOB authority to establish auditing and related attestation standards, quality control standards, and ethics standards for registered public accounting firms. SOx recognizes the previously issued AICPA auditing standards and states that new auditing standards may be based on "proposals from one or more professional groups of accountants or advisory groups." As we move to a greater global economy and as SOx becomes more of a worldwide standard, we can expect to see international auditing standards, as discussed in Chapter 33, have an increasing influence.

The Institute of Internal Auditors' (IIA) *International Standards for the Professional Practice of Internal Auditing*, discussed in Chapter 9, falls into the PCAOB's "standards by other professional groups" category as well. IIA standards are designed to support all internal auditor review work but are not for an external auditor's audit and attest work. When an internal auditor had been working in support of external audit counterparts on some audit task, this work should follow PCAOB audit guidelines. While the frequency of issuance has been somewhat limited to date, PCAOB standards cover some of the following areas:

- **Audit workpapers retention.** The PCAOB standard AS3, *Audit Documentation*, mandates that audit workpapers and other supporting materials should be maintained for a period of not less than seven years. This requirement is certainly in response to an infamous event just prior to the fall of what was once a large and prominent corporation, Enron, and the subsequent end of its auditor, Arthur Andersen. After spectacular growth and almost too good to be true financial results, Enron was under some financial pressure in 2001 when the SEC announced that it was going to conduct an on-site investigation. Enron's then external auditor, Arthur Andersen, used an internal firm policy to justify the destruction of all but the most current of its Enron audit documentation. This was a motivating factor that led to the SOx rule.
- **Concurring partner approval.** While external audit standards had required a concurring or second-party approval for each audit report issued, these were often done more for an after-the-fact quality control review. Under SOx rules, a second external audit partner is required to personally and professionally commit to the findings and conclusions in any audit. This concurring opinion here refers to the external auditor's formal opinion, in the conclusion of an audit, that the client's financial reports are "fairly stated" in accordance with what have been known as generally accepted accounting principles (GAAP).
- **Scope of internal control testing.** PCAOB rules require external auditors to describe the scope of both their testing processes and test findings. Prior to SOx, external auditors had sometimes used internal firm policies to justify the most minimal of test sizes and they frequently tested only a very small number of items despite being faced with very large test populations. If no problems were found, they expressed an opinion for the entire population based on the results of a very limited sample. They now must pay greater attention to the scope and reasonableness of their testing procedures, and the supporting documentation must clearly describe the scope and extent of testing activities.
- **Evaluation of internal control structure and procedures.** Although there were other standards in the first years of SOx, the PCAOB today requires use of AS5, discussed later, for the review and evaluation of financial systems internal controls. SOx rules further specify that an external auditor's evaluation must contain a description of material weaknesses as well as any material noncompliance matters found. External auditors are required to update the effectiveness of internal controls, and an absence of this documentation should be considered a weakness of internal controls.

- **Audit quality control standards.** The PCAOB has only issued audit quality standards called interim,[2] not yet issued its own specific quality standards. SOx requires that every registered public accounting firm have quality standards related to:
  - Monitoring of professional ethics and independence
  - Procedures for resolving accounting and auditing issues within the firm
  - Supervision of audit work
  - Hiring, professional development, and advancement of personnel
  - Acceptance and continuation of engagements
  - Internal quality inspections
  - Other quality standards to be prescribed by the PCAOB

These are general quality standards, and the PCAOB may release a specific set of quality standards that apply to all registered public accounting firms. In a similar sense, we also can expect the IIA to establish quality standards applicable to all internal auditors. Quality standards based on the internationally recognized ISO 9000 are introduced in Chapter 33.

Some internal auditors might question the applicability of these PCAOB standards. Internal auditors have their IIA *International Standards for the Professional Practice of Internal Auditing* and may feel there is little need to become concerned here. However, PCAOB auditing standards impact business professionals and internal as well as external auditors. With external auditors working under SOx rules, the audit committee will expect its external and internal auditors to operate in a consistent manner. Whether it is quality standards, effective internal controls testing, or concurrent approvals, an internal audit department should modify its procedures to comply with the PCAOB standards.

Inspections, Investigations, and Disciplinary Procedures

The PCAOB conducts accounting firm inspections to assess compliance with SOx rules and professional standards; these occur annually at larger public accounting firms and once every three years if a registered firm conducts less than 100 financial statement audits. The reviews evaluate the quality control system of the firm as well as its documentation and communication standards. The inspections are documented in formal reports to the SEC and state boards of accountancy. When appropriate, the PCAOB may initiate public accounting firm investigations and disciplinary procedures and can compel testimony, require the production of audit work, and conduct disciplinary proceedings. The latter may range from temporary suspension of an individual or firm to substantial fines, or even to being barred from the profession.

Title I, Section 106 consists of one brief paragraph on foreign public accounting firms that has resulted in much controversy. It says that if any foreign public accounting firm prepares an audit report for an SEC-registered corporation, that foreign public accounting firm is subject to the rules of SOx, the PCAOB, and related SEC rules, including a requirement of those foreign firms to register under SOx rules. Our multinational world is filled with many non-U.S. public accounting firms, some governed by their own national public accounting standards but most by the International Accounting Standards discussed in Chapter 33. We are seeing convergence in these standards, and the rules are changing.

Accounting Standards

Title I concludes by affirming that the SEC has authority over the PCAOB, including final approval of rules, the ability to modify PCAOB actions, and the removal of board members. While the PCAOB is an independent entity responsible for regulating the public accounting industry, the SEC is really the final authority. SOx recognizes the U.S. accounting standards-setting body, the Financial Accounting Standards Board (FASB), by saying that the SEC may recognize "generally accepted" accounting standards set by "a private entity" that meets certain criteria. The act then goes on to outline the general criteria that the FASB has used for setting accounting standards.

There is and always has been a major difference between accounting and auditing standards. The former define some very precise accounting rules, such as saying a certain type of asset can be written off or depreciated over no more than *X* years. These are the principles called generally accepted accounting principles (GAAP) and are today being replaced by international accounting standards. Auditing standards are much more conceptual, highlighting areas that an auditor *should consider* when evaluating controls in some area. These standards became increasingly loosely interpreted as we went into the 1990s, when management was frequently under pressure to continually report short-term earnings growth, and the external auditors often refused to say no. The result was the financial scandals of Enron and others as well as Andersen's audit document destruction when it received news that the SEC was coming. SOx and the PCAOB now oversee public accounting companies.

Title II: Auditor Independence

Internal and external auditors are separate and independent resources, with external auditors responsible for assessing the fairness of an enterprise's published financial reports, while internal auditors serve management in a wide variety of other areas. In the early 1990s, this separation began to change, with external audit firms taking responsibility for some internal audit functions as well. This started when larger enterprises began to outsource some of their noncore functions such as an employee cafeteria or plant janitorial function. The thinking was that employees working in these specialized areas were not really part of core enterprise operations, and all should benefit if people responsible for noncore functions were outsourced to another company that specialized in their special areas, such as for janitorial services. The previous in-house janitors would be transferred to the janitorial services company, and in theory, everyone would benefit. The enterprise that initiated the outsourcing would experience lower costs by giving a noncore function, janitorial services, to someone who better understood it. The outsourced janitor, in this example, also might have both better career possibilities and better supervision.

Internal auditor outsourcing started in the late 1980s following this same line of reasoning. External audit firms began offering to outsource or take over a client's existing internal audit functions. The idea made sense to senior management and their audit committees because they often did not really understand the distinctions between the two audit functions and were sometimes more comfortable with their external auditors. In addition, senior management and their audit committees were often enticed by the promised lower costs of internal audit outsourcing. Although the IIA initially fought against the concept, internal audit outsourcing continued to grow through the 1990s. Although a few independent firms made efforts as well, internal auditor outsourcing continued to be the realm of the major public accounting firms.

Internal audit outsourcing became an issue during investigations after the Enron failure. Their internal auditor function had been almost totally outsourced to its once well-respected external audit firm, Arthur Andersen, and the two audit groups worked side by side in Enron's offices. After Enron's fall, after-the-fact questions were raised about how that outsourced internal audit department could have been independent of Andersen. Enron investigators felt it would have been very difficult in that environment for internal audit to raise any concerns to the audit committee about their external auditors. This potential conflict became a reform issue for SOx.

Limitations on External Auditor Services

SOx Section 201, covering services outside the scope of past traditional external auditor activities, forbids a registered public accounting firms from contemporaneously performing both audit and nonaudit services at a client. The prohibition includes internal auditing, many areas of consulting, and senior officer financial planning. For the internal audit professional, it is now illegal for a registered public accounting firm to provide internal audit services if it is also doing the audit work. This means that the major public accounting firms are out of the internal audit outsourcing business for their audit clients. Other firms, including independent spin-offs from public accounting firms, can still provide internal audit outsourcing, but the era when an internal auditor became an employee of his or her public accounting firm is over.

In addition to the ban on providing outsourced internal audit services, SOx prohibits public accounting firms from providing other services, including:

- **Financial information systems design and implementations.** Public accounting firms previously installed IT financial systems, often of their own design, at their clients' offices. They then returned to review the internal controls of the systems they had just installed—a significant conflict of interest. This is no longer allowed.
- **Bookkeeping and financial statement services.** Public accounting firms previously offered accounting services to their clients in addition to doing the audits. Even for major corporations, it was not unusual for the team responsible for the overall financial statement audit to also do much of the work necessary to build those same consolidated financial statements. Again, this is a potential conflict of interest that is no longer allowed.
- **Management and human resources functions.** Prior to SOx, external audit firms often helped their own professionals to move to client management positions. As a result, accounting managers in some enterprises often were alumni of their external auditors. This was sometimes frustrating for internal auditors or others who were not from that same public accounting firm, and avenues of promotion seemed limited because of "old-boy" network connections with the external audit firm.

- **Other prohibited services.** Although this does not have much impact on internal audit, SOx also specifically prohibits external audit firms from offering actuarial services, investment advisor, and audit-related legal services.

Under SOx, external auditors audit the financial statements of their client enterprises, and that is about all. Beyond the prohibited activities, external auditors can engage in other nonaudit services only if those services are approved in advance by the audit committee, which may be wary of approving anything that appears to be at all out of the ordinary.

SOx external audit service prohibitions have also had a major impact on internal audit professionals. Because external audit firms can only be *just the auditors,* internal audit professionals are finding increased levels of respect and responsibility for their role in assessing internal controls and promoting good corporate governance practices. Internal audit's relationship with audit committees also has been strengthened, as they will seek increasing help for services that were sometimes assumed by their external audit firms.

Audit Committee Preapproval of Services

Section 202 of SOx's Title II specifies that the audit committee must approve all external audit and nonaudit services *in advance.* While most audit committees had been doing this all along, this SOx approval requirement was often little more than a formality. Audit committees in the old days often received little more than a brief report from their external auditors and then approved it in a perfunctory manner similar to how a volunteer business organization's meeting minutes are often approved. SOx changed this, and audit committee members can now expose themselves to criminal liabilities or stockholder litigation for allowing a prohibited action to take place. Of course, there are many minor external auditor activities that do not have to go through these formal audit committee approvals in advance. SOx sets *de minimus*[3] exception rules for audit committee permission requirements, stating that they are not required for nonauditing services if:

- The aggregate dollar value of the service does not exceed 5% of the total external audit fees paid by the enterprise during the fiscal year.
- The services were not recognized as nonaudit services by the enterprise at the time the overall audit engagement was initiated.
- The services are brought to the attention of the audit committee and approved by them prior to the completion of the audit.

These exceptions give an audit committee some flexibility, but the nature and accumulated dollar value of additional nonaudit services must be carefully monitored throughout the course of a fiscal year to maintain a level of compliance. Internal audit can help their audit committee in this process to help ascertain that all services continue in compliance with the SOx rules.

External Audit Partner Rotation

Title II makes it unlawful for a public accounting lead partner to head an engagement for over five years. The major public accounting firms had corrected this well before

SOx, and while lead partner rotation had been common, SOx makes the failure of a firm to rotate a criminal act. Audit partner rotation has sometimes brought challenges to internal auditors who may have been working comfortably with a designated audit partner over extended periods and will need to become accustomed to working with a new external audit team lead from time to time.

External Auditor Reports to Audit Committees

While external auditors have always communicated with their audit committees in the course of the audit engagement, this communication was sometimes very limited. Management might negotiate a "pass" from their external auditors on some accounting change, but the matter would only be reported to the audit committee in the most general of terms if at all. External auditors are now required to report on a timely basis all accounting policies and practices used, alternative treatments of financial information discussed with management, the possible alternative treatments, and the approach preferred by the external auditor. If there are disputed accounting treatments, the audit committee should be made well aware of the actions taken.

Conflicts of Interest and Mandatory Rotations of External Audit Firms

SOx Title II, Section 206 prohibits external auditors from providing any audit services to a firm where the CEO, CFO, or chief accounting officer participated as a member of that external audit firm on the same audit within the past year. This really says that an audit partner cannot leave an audit engagement to begin working as a senior executive of the same firm that was just audited. There were some outrageous examples of this role switching back at the time of the Enron scandal. The prohibition is now limited to public accounting partners, but staff members and managers can still move to positions in the auditee enterprise. It still continues to be valuable for persons beginning their careers in public accounting and then moving to such enterprise positions as members of internal audit.

Title III: Corporate Responsibility

While SOx Title II set up new rules for external auditor independence, Title III describes major new regulatory changes for audit committees. This is an area where internal auditors should have a greater level of interest and role. Although audit committees were generally composed of independent directors, there were many exceptions. SOx introduced a wide range of governance rules covering corporate boards and their audit committees.

Audit Committee Governance Rules

All registered enterprises must have an audit committee composed of only independent directors. The external audit firm reports directly to that audit committee, which is responsible for their compensation, oversight of the audit work, and the resolution of any audit disagreements. While major corporations in the United States have had audit committees in the past, SOx tightened these rules. In addition, while internal audit often had only a nominal reporting relationship to their audit committee, SOx requires a strong, direct-line internal audit reporting relationship to the audit committee. Audit committee communications will be discussed in Chapter 25.

SOx calls for audit committees to establish procedures to receive, retain, and treat complaints and to handle whistleblower information regarding questionable accounting and auditing matters. During the Enron debacle that precipitated SOx, an employee tried to get the attention of the external auditors or an Enron financial officer to disclose some improper accounting transactions. The employee's concerns were rebuffed. An audit committee–led ethics whistleblower or hotline function could be a resource to respond to these types of issues, and internal audit can act as a conduit for SOx accounting and auditing whistleblower reports. Ethics and whistleblower programs, from an internal audit perspective, are discussed in Chapter 26.

Section 302: Corporate Responsibility for Financial Reports

Prior to SOx, enterprises filed their financial statements with the SEC and investors, but the responsible corporate officers who "signed" those reports could argue that they were not really personally responsible for them in the event of any errors. They could claim that any errors or problems were the responsibility of their subordinates. SOx has raised this bar. The CEO, CFO, or other persons performing similar functions now must personally certify each annual and quarterly report filed. The signing officer must certify that:

- The signing officer has reviewed the report.
- Based on that signing officer's knowledge, the financial statements do not contain any materially untrue or misleading information.
- Again based on the signing officer's knowledge, the financial statements fairly represent the financial conditions and results of operations of the enterprise.
- The signing officer is responsible for:
  1. Establishing and maintaining internal controls.
  2. Having designed these internal controls to ensure that material information about the enterprise and its subsidiaries was made known to the signing officer during the period when the reports are prepared.
  3. Evaluating the enterprise's internal controls within 90 days prior to the release of the report.
  4. Presenting in these financial reports the signing officer's evaluation of the effectiveness of these internal controls as of that report date.
- The signing officer has disclosed to the auditors, audit committee, and other directors:
  1. All significant deficiencies in the design and operation of internal controls that could affect the reliability of the reported financial data, and further, have disclosed these material control weaknesses to the enterprise's auditors.
  2. Any fraud, material or not material, that involves management or other employees who have a significant role in the enterprise's internal controls.
- The signing officer has indicated in the report whether there were internal controls or other changes that could significantly impact those controls, including corrective actions, subsequent to the date of the internal control evaluation.

Given that SOx imposes potential criminal penalties of fines or jail time on individual violators of the act, the report signer requirement places a heavy burden on responsible corporate officers who must take all reasonable steps to make certain that they are in compliance.

This personal sign-off requirement has been a major concern for CEOs and CFOs, and an enterprise needs to set up detailed paper-trail procedures such that the signing officers are comfortable that effective processes have been used and the calculations to build the reports are all well documented. An enterprise may want to consider using an extended sign-off process where staff members submitting the financial reports sign off on what they are submitting. Internal audit should be able to act here as an internal consultant and help senior officers establish effective processes. The audit workpaper model, with extensive cross-references, might be a good approach. Exhibit 5.2 provides an example of an officer disclosure sign-off type of statement for senior officers. This exhibit is not an official PCAOB form, but shows the type of letter an officer might be asked to certify. It also references a sample organization name, Global Computer Products, which we will use in other examples throughout this book. Under SOx, the CEO or CFO is asked to personally assert to these types of representations and could be held criminally liable if incorrect. While the officer is at risk, the support staff—including internal audit—should take every step possible to make certain the package presented to the senior officer is correct.

Internal auditors should take particular care, given SOx rules, on the nature and description of any findings encountered during the course of audits, on follow-up reporting regarding the status of corrective actions taken, and on the distributions of these audit reports. Many internal audits may identify significant weaknesses in areas of the enterprise that are not material to overall operations. A breakdown in the invoicing process at one regional sales office may be significant to the performance of that sales region for the corporation, but will not be a materially significant internal control weakness if the problem is local and does not reflect a wider, more pervasive problem, and if the problem was corrected after being discovered by internal audit. The chief audit executive should establish good communications links with the audit committee and key financial officers such that they are aware of audits performed, the key findings, and corrective actions taken. Internal audit should also provide some guidance as to whether reported audit findings are material to the enterprise's overall system of internal control.

Improper Influence over the Conduct of Audits

SOx makes it unlawful for any officer, director, or related subordinate person to take any action, in contravention of an SEC rule, to "fraudulently influence, coerce, manipulate, or mislead" any external CPA auditor engaged in the audit for the purpose of rendering the financial statements materially misleading. These are strong words in an environment where there often was a high level of discussion and compromise between the auditors and senior management when a significant problem was found during the course of an audit.

Prior to SOx, there were many "friendly" discussions between management and external auditors regarding a financial interpretation dispute or proposed adjustment. The result was often some level of compromise. This is not unlike an internal audit team in the field that circulates a draft audit report with local management before departing.

EXHIBIT 5.2 Sarbanes-Oxley Section 302 Officer Certification

Sarbanes-Oxley Section 302
Officer Certification

I, (*Name of Officer*), certify that:

1. I have reviewed this quarterly report on Form 10-K of Global Computer Products;
2. Based on my knowledge, this quarterly report does not contain any untrue statement of a material fact or omit to state a material fact necessary to make the statements made, in light of the circumstances under which such statements were made, not misleading with respect to the period covered by this quarterly report;
3. Based on my knowledge, the financial statements, and other financial information included in this quarterly report, fairly present in all material respects the financial condition, results of operations, and the cash flows of, and for, the periods presented in this quarterly report;
4. The Global Computer Products' other certifying officers and I are responsible for establishing and maintaining disclosure controls and procedures (as defined in Exchange Act Rules 13a-14 and 15d-14) for the corporation and we have:
   a. designed such disclosure controls and procedures to ensure that material information relating to Global Computer Products, including its consolidated subsidiaries, is made known to us by others within those entities, particularly during the period in which this quarterly report is being prepared;
   b. evaluated the effectiveness of Global Computer Products, disclosure controls and procedures as of a date within 90 days prior to the filing date of this quarterly report (the "Evaluation Date"); and
   c. presented in this quarterly report our conclusions about the effectiveness of the disclosure controls and procedures based on our evaluation as of the Evaluation Date;
5. The Global Computer Products' other certifying officers and I have disclosed, based on our most recent evaluation, to Global Computer Products and the audit committee of our board of directors (or persons performing the equivalent function):
   a. all significant deficiencies in the design or operation of internal controls that could adversely affect Global Computer Products, ability to record, process, summarize, and report financial data and have identified for Global Computer Products' auditors any material weaknesses in internal controls; and
   b. any fraud, whether or not material, that involves management or other employees who have a significant role in Global Computer Products' internal controls; and
6. Global Computer Products' other certifying officers and I have indicated in this quarterly report whether or not there were significant changes in internal controls or in other factors that could significantly affect internal controls subsequent to the date of our most recent evaluation, including any corrective actions with regard to significant deficiencies and material weaknesses.

After much discussion and sometimes other follow-up work, that draft internal audit report might have been changed before its final issue. The same things often happened in external auditor draft reports covering quarterly or annual preliminary results. SOx rules now prohibit such practices for external auditors. These rules evolved during the congressional hearings leading up to the passage of SOx, where testimony included tales of strong CEOs essentially demanding that external auditors accept certain questionable accounting entries or lose the audit business. There can still be friendly disputes and debates, but if an SEC ruling is explicit in some area and if the external auditors propose a financial statement adjustment because of that SEC rule, management *must* accept it without an additional fight.

There can be a fine line between management disagreeing with external auditors over some estimate or interpretation and management trying to improperly influence its auditors. External audit may have done some limited internal control testing in an area and then proposed an adjustment based on the results of that test. This type of scenario could result in management disagreeing with that adjustment and claiming the results of the test were "not representative." While the external auditors under SOx have the last word in such a dispute, internal audit can sometimes play a facilitating role here as well. Internal audit resources, for example, can be used to expand the population of an audit sampling test, perform other extended observations, or perform other testing regarding the disputed area. When this is done, internal audit is not helping to improperly influence the conduct of an audit but helping to resolve the matter. AS5 encourages these practices.

Forfeitures, Bars, and Penalties

Title III concludes with a series of detailed rules and penalties covering corporate governance. Their purpose is to tighten existing rules that were in place before SOx or to add new rules for what often seemed to be some outrageous or at least very improper business practices prior to SOx. These rules, outlined next, do not impact the audit committee or internal or external auditors directly, as they are directed at other areas of what was believed to be corporate governance excess.

- **Forfeiture of improper bonuses.** Section 304 requires that if an enterprise is required to restate its earnings due to some material violation of securities laws, the CEO and CFO *must reimburse* the company for any bonuses or incentives received on the basis of any original, incorrect statements issued during the past 12 months. The same applies for any profits received from the sale of enterprise securities during that same period. During the SOx hearings, multiple instances were cited where a company had issued an aggressive but unsupportable earnings statement, its key officers had benefited from bonuses or the sale of stock from that reported good news, and then the company soon had to restate its earnings due to some material noncompliance matter. There would not have been those CEO and CFO bonuses under the revised, correct interpretations. SOx places a personal penalty on senior corporate officers who benefit from materially noncompliant financial statements.
- **Bars to officer or director service.** Section 305 is another example of how SOx tightened up the rules. Prior to SOx, federal courts were empowered to bar any person from serving as a corporate officer or director if that person's conduct demonstrates "substantial unfitness to serve as an officer or director." SOx changed the standard here by eliminating the word *substantial,* saying that the courts can bar someone from serving as a director or officer for *any* conduct violation.
- **Pension fund blackout periods.** A standard rule for 401(k) and similar retirement plans has been that a fund administrator can establish a blackout period over a time period that prohibits plan participants from making investment adjustments

to their plans. A participant with a substantial amount of his or her retirement funds in company stock could, because of bad company news, transfer funds from that stock to a cash-based money market fund or some other investment option. These blackout periods are usually instituted for purely legitimate reasons, such as a change in plan administrators. A complaint during the SOx hearings, based on the Enron failure, was that there was a blackout in place during the final weeks before Enron's bankruptcy, preventing employees from making changes to their plans. However, those same blackout rules did not apply to the corporate officers, who had their own plans and who in some cases got out of Enron stock before things totally collapsed. SOx rules now state that the same blackout periods must apply to everyone in the company, from staff to corporate officer.

- **Attorney professional responsibility.** Section 307 covers revised rules for attorney professional conduct and was initially very controversial. An attorney is required to report evidence of a material violation of securities law or a similar company violation to the chief legal counsel or the CEO. If those parties do not respond, the attorney is required to report the evidence up the ladder to the *board audit committee*. SOx's initial rules also allowed that if an attorney discovered such a securities law violation, the attorney should withdraw from the engagement while reporting the violation particulars, what is called a "noisy withdrawal."

  The controversy here was that SOx effectively required an attorney to violate the rules of attorney-client privilege. Under traditional rules, if a subsidiary executive met with an attorney to discuss some matter that constituted a potential violation of SOx, the attorney and the subsidiary manager client would work out the issues. The initial concern was that an attorney was supposed to blow the whistle on such a discussion and bring the matter potentially all the way to the audit committee. The final rules, however, softened things to narrow the scope of attorneys and otherwise limit the rules impact.
- **Fair funds for investors.** The final section of Title III states that if an individual or group is fined for a violation through administrative or legal action, the funds collected will go to a "disgorgement" fund for distribution to investors who suffered because of the fraud or improper accounting actions. The same rule applies to funds collected through a settlement in advance of court proceedings. Properties and other assets seized will be sold and also go into that disgorgement fund. The whole idea here is that investors who lost because of individual corporate wrongdoing may be subject to some financial settlement from such a fund.

Title IV: Enhanced Financial Disclosures

Title IV of SOx is designed to correct some financial reporting disclosure problems, to tighten up conflict-of-interest rules for corporate officers and directors, to mandate a management assessment of internal controls, to require senior officer codes of conduct, and other matters. There is a lot of material here. Many unexpected bankruptcies and sudden earnings failures around the time of the Enron failure were attributed to extremely aggressive, if not questionable, financial reporting. With the approval of their external auditors, many companies pushed to the limits and used such tactics as issuing questionable pro forma earnings to report their results or moving their corporate headquarters offshore to minimize taxes. While these tactics had been in accordance with GAAP, SOx tightened up many rules and made these financial disclosure tactics difficult or illegal.

So-called pro forma financial reports were frequently used to present an as-if picture of a firm's financial status by leaving out nonrecurring earnings expenses such as restructuring charges or merger-related costs. However, because there was no standard definition or consistent format for reporting pro forma earnings, depending on the assumptions used, it was possible for an operating loss to become a profit under pro forma earnings reporting. For example, under older, pre-SOx accepted practices in 2001, Cisco Systems, Inc., the San Jose, California–based maker of computer networking systems, reported net income of $3.09 billion on a pro forma basis but simultaneously reported a net loss of $1.01 billion on a GAAP basis. Cisco's pro forma profit specifically excluded acquisition charges, payroll tax on the exercise of stock options, restructuring costs and other special charges, an excess inventory charge, and net gains on minority investments. Cisco certainly was not alone here, as many companies had reported pro forma earnings showing ever-increasing growth while their true, GAAP results were not so favorable. The problem with these two sets of numbers is that investors and the press frequently ignored the GAAP numbers, focusing on the more favorable pro forma results. SOx requires that pro forma, published financial statements must not contain any material untrue statements or omit any fact that makes the reports misleading. Further, the pro forma results also must reconcile to the financial conditions and results of operations under GAAP. A common reporting technique prior to SOx, they are not at all common today.

Perhaps the major issue that brought Enron down was a large number of off-balance-sheet transactions that, if consolidated with regular financial reports, would have shown major financial problems. Once they were identified and included with Enron's other financial results, the disclosure pushed Enron toward bankruptcy. SOx requires that quarterly and annual financial reports must disclose all such off-balance-sheet transactions that may have a material effect on the current or future financial reports. These transactions may include contingent obligations, financial relationships with unconsolidated entities, or other items that could have material effects on operations. While many of the SOx financial disclosure rules are really the responsibility of external auditors, this is an area where internal auditors might be of help. It is often the internal auditor, on a visit to a distant unit of the company, who encounters these types of off-balance-sheet arrangements in discussions with field personnel. If they find something significant, internal audit should communicate the appropriate details to the audit committee. The final rules here after passage of SOx require an enterprise to provide an explanation of its off-balance-sheet arrangements in a separately captioned subsection of the "Management's Discussion and Analysis" (MD&A) section of its annual Form 10-K.

Expanded Conflict-of-Interest Provisions and Disclosures

The SOx legislative hearings often pictured corporate officers and directors as a rather greedy lot. In arrangements that frequently appeared to be conflicts of interest, large relocation allowances or corporate executive personal loans were granted and then subsequently forgiven by corporate boards. A CEO, for example, who requests the board to grant his CFO a large personal loan with vague repayment terms and the right to either demand payment or forgive certainly creates a conflict of interest. Although exceptions are allowed, SOx makes it unlawful for any corporation to directly or indirectly extend credit, in the form of a personal loan, to any officer or director.

Another section of Title IV requires that all disclosures under SOx, as discussed previously, must be filed electronically and posted "near real time" on the SEC's web site. This makes the filing of such information much more current. Internal audit should potentially consider evaluating the control systems in place to handle such SEC online reporting. This is an area where reporting was often hard-copy-based in the past, and there could be a risk of improper transmission or security leaks without proper internal control procedures.

Section 404: Management's Assessment of Internal Controls

SOx requires that all annual 10-K reports must contain an internal control report stating management's responsibility for establishing and maintaining an adequate system of internal controls as well as management's assessment, as of the fiscal year ending date, on the effectiveness of those installed internal control procedures. This is what has popularly been known as the Section 404 rules. Internal audit, outside consultants, or even the management team—but not the external auditors—have the responsibility to review and assess the effectiveness of their internal controls, and external auditors are then to attest to the sufficiency of these internal control reviews built and controlled by management. From an internal audit perspective, Section 404 is perhaps the most important element of SOx, and a general understanding of its requirements should be part of every internal auditor's CBOK.

Section 404 internal control reviews are described in more detail and are supported by AS5 standards discussed later in this chapter. These AS5 rules are particularly important to internal auditors because the standards specify that external auditors may elect to use the work of internal auditors in their internal control reviews. As the following sections explain, internal auditors may act as consultants to their enterprises in helping to build these internal accounting controls, or they can support their external auditors by auditing the internal accounting controls.

Financial Officer Codes of Ethics

SOx requires that enterprises adopt a *code of ethics* for their CEO, CFO, and other senior officers that discloses their compliance with this code as part of their annual financial reporting. While SOx has made this a requirement for senior officers, employee codes of ethics or conduct have been in place in some enterprises for many years but were often established for employees and supervisors rather than corporate officers. These codes defined rules or policies that were designed to apply to all employees, and they covered such matters as policies on the protection of company records or on gifts and other benefit issues. Codes of conduct will be discussed in Chapter 26 on ethics and whistleblower programs.

With growing public concern about the need for strong ethical practices, many enterprises have appointed an ethics officer to launch such an initiative along with a code of conduct as a first step. However, those codes of conduct were often directed at the overall population of employees, not the senior officers. SOx has brought enterprise codes of conduct to new levels. SOx does not specify the content of enterprise-wide codes of ethics and focuses on the need for standards to apply for senior officers. SOx requires that an enterprise's senior officer code of ethics or conduct must reasonably promote:

- Honest and ethical conduct, including the handling of actual or apparent conflicts of interest between personal and professional relationships
- Full, fair, accurate, timely, and understandable disclosure in the enterprise financial reports
- Compliance with applicable governmental rules and regulations

Many larger enterprises today have established ethics-type functions, but if such an ethics function is not in place, internal audit can play an important role in helping its enterprise achieve compliance with SOx ethical rules.

If an enterprise has a code of conduct, management should assure that it applies to all members of the enterprise, is consistent with SOx, and that these ethical rules are communicated to all members of the enterprise, including senior managers. An enterprise should make sure that its existing code of conduct covers the SOx rules just discussed, that it has been communicated to senior management, and that these officers have agreed to comply with it. While SOx compliance rules were established only for senior officers, this is the ideal time to launch an ethics function throughout the enterprise that applies to senior management and to all employees as well. A strong ethics function should be promoted throughout the enterprise and not just as a SOx legal requirement.

Other Title IV Required Disclosures

All SEC registered entities are required to file annual Form 10-Ks as well as other SEC financial reports. While the issuing enterprises filing those reports would anticipate an SEC review in some detail, the hearings leading to SOx revealed that these SEC reviews were not always very timely or comprehensive. Section 408 mandates the SEC to perform "enhanced reviews" of the disclosures included in *all* company filings on a regular and systematic basis and no less often than once every three years. The SEC can decide to either perform an enhanced review of disclosures as soon as possible or to wait to schedule the review through the three-year window. This enhanced review could be triggered by *any one* of the following situations:

- If the corporation has issued a material restatement of its financial results
- If there has been significant volatility in its stock prices compared to others'
- If the corporation has a large market capitalization
- If this is an emerging company with significant disparities in its stock price-to-earnings ratio

- If the corporation's operations significantly affect material sectors of the national economy
- Any other factors the SEC may consider relevant

The SEC has the authority to schedule such an extended disclosure review for large Fortune 500–size companies, leaders in some sectors of the economy, or where stock prices are out of average ranges. Of course, with the "other factors" consideration, virtually any corporation could potentially move to the head of the list for such an extended review.

In general these rules say that enterprises should be prepared for their public filings to be reviewed by the SEC more thoroughly and frequently than in the past. These financial statement disclosures are included in the MD&A section of an enterprise's 10-K report. This reporting covers a wide range of issues, including transactions with unaffiliated subsidiaries or derivative trading activities.

The last Title IV section, 409, mandates that enterprises must disclose "on a rapid and current basis" any additional information containing material financial statement issues. An enterprise can include trend and quantitative reporting approaches as well as graphics for those disclosures. This is a change from traditional SEC report formats, which allowed only text, with the exception of corporate logos. The concept is to get key data to investors as soon as possible, not through slow, paper-based reports. Section 409 points to the concept of a real-time financial close that has become a reality for many enterprises.

Title V: Analyst Conflicts of Interest

This SOx title and other subsequent sections do not directly cover financial reporting, corporate governance, audit committees, or external and internal audit issues, but were drafted to correct other perceived abuses encountered during the SOx congressional hearings. Title V is designed to rectify some securities analyst abuses. Investors have relied on the recommendations of securities analysts for years, but these analysts were often tied to large brokerage houses and investment banks, and were analyzing and recommending securities both to investors and their financial institution employers. When they looked at securities where their employer had an interest, there were supposed to be strong separations of responsibility between the people recommending a stock for investment and those selling it to investors. In the frenzy of the late-1990s dot-com bubble, these traditional analyst controls and ethical practices broke down. In the aftermath of the market downturns, analysts sometimes recommended stocks seemingly only because their investment bank employer was managing the initial public offering. Also, investigators found analysts publicly recommending a stock to investors as a "great growth opportunity" while simultaneously telling their investment banking peers that the stock was a very poor investment or worse.

Abuses of this manner existed in many circumstances. While investment analysts once relied on their own self-governing professional standards, the SOx hearings revealed that many of these standards were ignored by strong and prominent securities analysts. Title V attempts to correct these securities analyst abuses. Rules of conduct have been established with legal punishments for violations. SOx has reformed and regulated the practices of securities analysts. The result should be better-informed investors.

Titles VI through X: Fraud Accountability and White-Collar Crime

These SOx titles cover a series of issues ranging from the funding of SEC appropriations to plans for future studies, and they include new rules to tighten up what in the past had been viewed as regulatory loopholes. Among these, the SEC can now ban persons from promoting or trading penny stocks because of past SEC misconduct or can bar someone from practicing before the SEC because of improper professional conduct. The latter rule gives the SEC the authority to effectively ban a public accounting firm from acting as an external auditor for corporations.

This SEC professional misconduct ban would be a major penalty to any public accounting firm or individual CPA who was found to have violated professional or ethical public accounting standards. Although SOx outlines a process of hearings before any action is taken, individual CPAs or entire firms can be banned temporarily or permanently. This takes this monitoring and policing process away from the AICPA's peer review processes of the past and gives the regulatory authority to the SEC. While an individual negligent CPA can still work in non-SEC practice areas such as small business accounting or, for that matter, internal audit, even a temporary ban can be a death knell for a practicing CPA or public accounting firm. All concerned must be aware of and follow SEC rules and procedures, particularly this new set authorized by SOx.

SOx Titles VIII and IX seem to be very much a reaction to the failure of Enron and the subsequent demise of Arthur Andersen. We have discussed some of the events surrounding the failure of Enron, including the conviction of Arthur Andersen for its destruction of Enron's accounting records. At that time, even though Andersen seemed very culpable to outside observers for its massive efforts to shred company accounting records, the courts eventually found Andersen innocent of criminal conspiracy, but the firm ultimately ceased operating anyway. Now Title VIII of SOx has established specific rules and penalties for the destruction of corporate audit records.

The words in the statute are much broader than just the problematic activities related to Andersen and apply to all auditors and accountants, including internal auditors. SOx is particularly strong regarding the destruction, alteration, or falsification of records involved in federal investigations or bankruptcies: "Whoever knowingly alters, destroys, mutilates, conceals, covers up, falsifies or makes false entry in any record, document, or tangible object with the intent to impede, obstruct, or influence the investigation . . . shall be fined . . . [or] imprisoned not more than 20 years, or both." Strong words taken directly from the statute! This says that any enterprise should have a strong records retention policy. While records can be destroyed in the course of normal business cycles, any hint of a coming federal investigation or the filing of bankruptcy papers for some affiliated unit should trigger activation of that records retention policy.

In a separate section, SOx establishes rules for corporate audit records. Although we tend to think of SOx primarily in terms of rules for external auditors, it very much applies to internal auditors as well. Workpapers and supporting review papers must be maintained for a period of five years from the end of the fiscal year of the audit. SOx clearly states that these rules apply to "any accountant who conducts an audit" of an SEC-registered corporation. While internal auditors have sometimes argued in the past that they only do operational audits that do not apply to the formal financial audit process, the prudent internal audit group should closely align their workpaper record retention rules to comply with this SOx five-year mandate.

Several of the sections of the legislation are designed to tighten up things and to correct what were viewed by others as excesses. One such excess was corporate officers getting large loans from their board of directors based on stock manipulation and performance that was later found to be improper. In the past, boards of directors regularly forgave those loans after some period, but now SOx mandates that debts incurred are in violation of securities fraud laws and cannot be forgiven or discharged. The executive—now probably ex-executive—who received the forgiven loan is now obligated to repay the corporation. Another section here extends the statute of limitations for securities law violations. Now legal action may be brought no later than two years after discovery or five years after the actual violation. Since securities fraud can take some time to discover, this change gives prosecutors a bit more time.

The Organizational Sentencing Guidelines is a published list of corporate penalties for violations of certain federal laws. If an enterprise is found to be guilty, the punishment or sentencing could be shortened if there had been an ethics program in place that should normally reduce the possibility of such a violation. While the basic concepts of the sentencing guidelines are still in place, SOx modifies them to include the destruction or alteration of documents as offenses.

Section 806 adds whistleblower protection for employees of publicly traded enterprises who observe and detect some fraudulent action and then independently report it to the SEC or some other outside party. By employee, we mean officers, contractors, or agents as well. Any person who observes an illegal act can blow the whistle and report the action with legal protection from retaliation. The SOx whistleblower rules cover securities law violations and do not include the provisions in other federal contract whistleblower rules where the person reporting something may be rewarded with some percentage of the reported recovery.

Title VIII's Section 807 defines criminal penalties for shareholders of publicly traded companies, stating that whoever executes or attempts to execute a scheme to defraud any persons in connection with a corporation's securities or fraudulently receives money or property from that sale shall be fined or imprisoned not more than 25 years, or both. This is a strong potential penalty for securities fraud. The regulations, rules, and penalties outlined in SOx have made following the rule extremely important. Title IX then goes through existing white-collar criminal law penalties and raises maximum punishments. For example, the maximum imprisonment for mail fraud has now grown from 5 years to 20, and the maximum fines for various violations have increased as well. These increased penalties coupled with the provisions of the Organizational Sentencing Guidelines create an environment where an increasing number of persons found guilty of white-collar crimes may have to spend time in prison.

Finally, Section 906 of SOx Title IX contains a requirement that CEOs and CFOs must sign a supplemental statement with their annual financial report that certifies that the information contained in the report "fairly represents, in all material respects, the financial condition and results of operations." These effectively personal certifications are coupled with penalties of fines up to $5 million and 10 years for anyone who certifies such statements while knowing they are false. Since these are personal penalties, the prudent CEO and CFO must take *extreme care* to make certain that all issues are resolved and that the annual financial statements are correct and fully representative of operations. Title X then is a "sense of the Senate" comment that corporate income tax returns should be signed by the CEO. Again, responsibility is placed on the individual officer, not the anonymous corporate entity.

Title XI: Corporate Fraud Accountability

While prior sections of SOx focused on the individual responsibilities of the CEO, CFO, and others, the last SOx title covers corporate responsibilities for fraudulent financial reporting. Here the SEC is given authority to impose a temporary freeze on the transfer of corporate funds to officers and others in a corporation that is subject to an SEC investigation. This was done to correct some reported abuses where some corporations were being investigated for financial fraud while they simultaneously dispensed huge cash payments to individuals. A corporation in trouble should retain some funds until the matter is resolved.

Section 1105 also gives the SEC the authority to prohibit persons who have violated certain SOx rules from serving as corporate officers and directors. While it is not an automatic ban, the SEC has the authority to impose this when it feels appropriate. The idea is to punish the corporate wrongdoer who has been found culpable of securities law violations at one corporation, only to leave that troubled corporation to serve at another.

5.2 PERFORMING SECTION 404 REVIEWS UNDER AS5

The prior section summarized significant contents and requirements in the SOx legislation. It is an important law, and every internal auditor should have a general CBOK understanding of its content. Going beyond just this general understanding, SOx's Section 404 on reviews of internal accounting controls should receive the most internal audit attention and understanding. Section 404 mandates that an enterprise is responsible for reviewing, documenting, and testing its own internal accounting controls, with the results then being passed on to the enterprise's external auditors, who are charged with reviewing and attesting to that work as part of their review of the reported financial statements. When SOx first became the law, Section 404 reviews were a major pain point for many enterprises because external auditors were following a very detailed set of financial accounting audit procedures under SOx, called Auditing Standard No. 2 (AS2). These auditing standards required very detailed reviews that left no room for small errors or omissions.

In 2007, these Section 404 auditing rules changed with the release of AS5, a more risk-based audit approach that also allows external auditors to better use the work of internal auditors in their assessments. This section will provide a summary of Section

404 rules today and will discuss approaches for performing such reviews using AS5's more risk-based approach. In addition, we will look at approaches to keep supporting SOx Section 404 documentation up to date. SOx rules require that internal controls documentation should be updated on an ongoing basis, but this important requirement too often slips between the cracks. Business professionals and internal auditors need to understand the Section 404 rules and to take appropriate steps to keep their enterprises in compliance. These rules impact enterprises that have achieved SOx compliance in a previous period as well as those that are now coming under registration requirements.

Section 404 Internal Control Assessments Today

Management has had an ongoing responsibility for designing and implementing internal controls over its enterprise's operations. Although the standards for what constituted good internal controls were not always very well defined in the past, they have remained a fundamental management concept. SOx Section 404 requires the preparation of an annual internal control report as part of an enterprise's SEC-mandated 10-K annual report. In addition to the financial statements and other 10-K disclosures, Section 404 requirements call for two information elements in each of these 10-Ks:

1. A formal management statement acknowledging their responsibility for establishing and maintaining an adequate internal control structure and procedures for financial reporting
2. An assessment, as of the end of the most recent fiscal year, of the effectiveness of the enterprise's internal control structure and procedures for financial reporting

In addition, the external audit firm that issued the supporting audit report is required to review and report on management's assessment of its internal financial controls. Simply put, management is required to report on the quality of their internal controls, and their public accounting firm must audit or attest to that management-developed internal control report in addition to their normal financial statement audit. Management has always been responsible for preparing their periodic financial reports, and the external auditors then audited those financial numbers and certified that they were fairly stated. With SOx Section 404, management is now responsible for documenting and testing its internal financial controls as well as reporting on their effectiveness. External auditors then review the supporting materials leading up to that internal financial control report to assert that the report is an accurate description of the internal control environment.

To the nonauditor, this might appear to be an obscure or almost trivial requirement. Even some internal auditors who primarily perform operational audits may wonder about the nuances in this process. However, audit reports on the status of internal controls have been an ongoing and simmering issue between the public accounting community, the SEC, and other interested parties going back to at least 1974. Much of the problem then was that there was no recognized definition for what is meant by internal controls. The release of the new COSO internal control framework, released in 2014 and discussed in Chapter 3, establishes an accepted standard for understanding internal controls. Under SOx Section 404, management is required to report on the adequacy of their internal controls with their external auditors attesting to the management-developed internal controls reports.

This process follows a basic internal control on the importance of maintaining a separation of duties where the person who develops transactions should not be the person who approves them. Under Section 404 procedures, the enterprise builds and documents its own internal control processes, then an independent party such as internal audit reviews and tests those internal controls, and finally the external auditors review and attest to the adequacy of this overall process. Their financial audit procedures will be based on these internal controls. This Section 404 process improves things from pre-SOx days when external auditors frequently built, documented, and then audited their own internal controls—a separation-of-duties shortcoming.

Launching the Section 404 Compliance Review: Identifying Key Processes

Every enterprise uses a series of processes to conduct its normal business activities. Some may be represented by automated systems, others are primarily manual procedures performed on a regular basis, while still others are a combination of automated and manual. These processes are normally considered in terms of basic accounting cycles and include the:

- **Revenue cycle.** Processes dealing with sales or other revenue to the enterprise.
- **Direct expenditures cycle.** Covers expenditures of material or direct production costs.
- **Indirect expenditures cycle.** Operating costs that cannot be directly tied to production activities but are necessary for overall business operations.
- **Payroll cycle.** Covers all personnel compensation.
- **Inventory cycle.** Although inventory will eventually be applied to production as direct expenditures, special processes are needed due to the time-based holding nature of inventory until it is applied to production.
- **Fixed assets cycle.** Property and equipment require separate accounting processes, such as periodic depreciation accounting over time.
- **General IT cycle.** This set of processes covers information technology (IT) controls that are general or applicable to all IT operations.

We will be discussing these processes in Chapter 8 in the discussion of planning and performing effective internal audits. The identification of these key processes is an initial Section 404 compliance step. While they will differ depending upon the nature of an enterprise, Exhibit 5.3 describes a set of key processes for a distribution company. A term that is frequently used by many professional without too much thought of its meaning, a *process* is a particular course of action intended to achieve a result, such as the process of obtaining a driver's license. It is a series of actions that have clearly defined starting points, consistent operational steps, and defined output points. We call the series a process because they are set of defined steps that can be repeated and followed consistently. A first compliance step here is to document, understand, and then test key processes, whether in a distribution company, a manufacturer, a research laboratory, a minerals extraction enterprise, or something else. The idea is to identify only the key processes. During SOx's first years, many enterprises—often with the encouragement of their external auditors—attempted to define *every* process. They did not have guidelines for eliminating the less risky ones and often went through to a high level of minutiae. AS5 now has established a level of reasonableness here.

Internal audit often can be a major help here. For many enterprises, internal audit may have already defined key processes through its annual audit planning, reviews of specific areas, and overall audit documentation efforts. After discussions with management as well as with internal auditors who understand enterprise internal control systems, such a process list should be developed to become a basis for launching a stream of internal control reviews for the enterprise.

Launching the SOx Section 404 Compliance Review: Internal Audit's Role

With the exception of SOx's prohibition of external audit firms from performing internal audit services for their audit clients, there are few specific references to internal audit in the text of the SOx legislation. Even though SOx does not give any specific

EXHIBIT 5.3 Sample Key Processes for a Distribution Company

1. **Purchase order management**. Processes must be in place to purchase or acquire the goods to be distributed.
2. **Inventory management**. Once goods have been purchased, there is a need for processes to manage them in inventory before distribution to customers.
3. **Warehouse management**. Processes must be in place to store product inventory in secure and well-organized facilities, with subprocesses for the inspection and placement of goods.
4. **Demand planning**. An enterprise needs to know how customers will demand existing and new products. This may include marketing-based processes including customer surveys.
5. **Order processing**. Whether paper-based or not paper-based, processes should be in place to receive new orders, approve customer credit histories, and pick and pack the received orders.
6. **Shipping and receiving**. Processes should be in place to ship goods to customers as well as to inspect and receive incoming ordered goods.
7. **Logistics management**. A distribution company is typically faced with requirements for special shipping arrangements, movement of goods between warehouse facilities, and other arrangements where logistics processes are needed.
8. **Billing and invoicing**. After orders are received and shipped, processes are needed to bill customers for payment and then to manage those accounts.
9. **Accounting systems**. Beyond accounts receivable, an enterprise needs accounting and financial processes for all of its accounting functions.
10. **Information systems**. Processes are needed for all aspects of IT operations, including IT service design, service operations, delivery of all aspects of IT services, and processes for continual IT improvements.
11. **Human resources**. Processes are needed to manage all people associated with the distribution enterprise, including compensation, benefits, related taxes, and all human resources-based legal requirements.
12. **Internal audit**. The enterprise needs an effective internal audit function to review and assess controls governing these processes.

responsibility to internal audit, they have become an important resource in many enterprises for the completion of their Section 404 internal control assessments. Under SOx, a separate and independent function within the enterprise—often internal audit—reviews and documents the internal controls covering key processes, identifies key control points, and then tests those identified controls. External audit would then review that work and attest to its adequacy. For many enterprises, internal audit has been a key resource for performing these internal control reviews. Internal audit functions originally distanced themselves from Section 404 reviews because of potential internal auditor independence standards, but the current IIA standards, as discussed in Chapter 9, now allow them to act as consultants to help document and establish effective internal control processes. Internal audit's role in Section 404 reviews can take three different forms, as follows:

1. Internal auditors can act as internal consultants for their enterprise by identifying key processes, documenting their internal controls, and performing appropriate tests of those controls. This review work would be subject to management approval for subsequent attestation by external audit.
2. Internal auditors can review and test internal control processes similar to their normal internal audit reviews but acting as an assistant or contractor for their external auditors. Another in-house or outside consulting resource could be designated by the enterprise to perform the Section 404 reviews, and internal audit would act as a resource to support their external auditors in reviewing the Section 404 work results. This approach is now allowed under the newer AS5 rules that allow external auditors to rely on internal audit materials.
3. Internal audit can work with and help other corporate resources—either internal or external—that are performing the Section 404 reviews but not get directly involved with those reviews, either as independent internal auditors or as agents for their external audit firm. This approach allows internal audit to devote more time and resources to other internal audit projects. This may also be the only alternative for a very small internal audit function.

The CAE, financial management, and the audit committee should work with the enterprise's external auditors to define responsibilities for these Section 404 internal control reviews. In some cases, the decision will be that it is most efficient for resources other than internal audit to take the second approach described earlier. External audit might make arrangements with internal audit to review and assess the adequacy of those internal controls. In this situation, internal audit would be working for external audit in reviewing and attesting to the results of internal control reviews but would not be performing the actual reviews. As mentioned, this type of arrangement will give internal audit an important role in helping external audit achieve their Section 404 review objectives. The negative side of this arrangement is that the consultants assigned may not have the time, resources, or process knowledge to perform these internal control assessments. This often works best when an enterprise has another internal audit–like function such as a strong quality assurance or risk assessment function that can review, document, and test internal control processes.

As an alternative to the first item just listed, internal audit performs the review work for enterprise financial management for a subsequent but separate and independent assessment by the external auditors. The positive side of this arrangement is that internal audit is often the best and most qualified enterprise resource to perform these reviews. They understand internal controls as well as good documentation techniques. Although this arrangement will involve more external audit resources, this may be an effective way to complete this Section 404 review requirement, but all parties must realize their roles and responsibilities.

Section 404 reviews are an annual process, and internal audit should update and change their review strategy over the years. Documentation prepared and tested in the first year should be updated and retested in future periods as required. While there is no reason the strategy selected may be the same every year going forward, changes always introduce increased costs and added time spent relearning approaches. All parties should develop a cost-effective approach to achieve these SOx requirements. While we are now taking a more risk-based approach under AS5, the basic SOx Section 404 requirements have not changed.

Launching the Section 404 Compliance Review: Organizing the Project

Establishing Section 404 compliance places a major challenge on SOx-registered enterprises. Even though an enterprise has evaluated their internal controls using the COSO internal control framework and its 17 principles, discussed in Chapters 3 and 4, they may still face some challenging tasks ahead in documenting their internal control environment for SOx Section 404 compliance. On a positive side, however, this was a *very* challenging task in the first days of SOx, and with the more risk-based AS5 approach to SOx today, the approach is now more constrained.

Internal audit can play a major role in helping senior management to get ready for Section 404 compliance, both in reviewing existing or new documented processes. Based on the internal audit standards discussed in Chapter 9, internal audit should recommend internal control improvements as the new processes are being developed, or they can separately act as consultants for installing those new internal control processes.

Whether performed by internal audit or independent parties, Section 404 *compliance reviews* should develop a formal project following the project management approach discussed in Chapter 16. While larger SOx-registered public enterprises have already gone through multiple rounds of their SOx compliance work today, there are always newer entities that have not. The amount of effort required for new registrants would be based on the strength and sophistication of an enterprise's internal control processes, but should follow the steps.

Step 1: Organize the Section 404 Compliance Project. Assign a project team to lead the effort. A senior executive such as the CFO should act as the project sponsor, with a team of both internal and external resources to participate in the effort. Roles, responsibilities, and resource requirements should be estimated as well. Internal audit can often assume major responsibilities in helping here.

Step 2: Develop the Section 404 Compliance Project Plan. The internal control compliance project should be well in process prior to the financial year end. While an existing plan can be updated in subsequent years, there will be a major challenge and time crunch during earlier years. The plan should focus on significant areas of enterprise operations with coverage over all significant business units. Although there can be many plan variations here, Exhibit 5.4 outlines planning considerations for a Section 404 compliance review. Although work steps described here are at a high level, the team should develop a detailed plan document to begin the SOx Section 404 internal financial controls review.

Step 3: Select Key Processes for Review. Every enterprise depends on a wide range of financial and operational processes in order to execute and manage its essential operations. The overall nature of business objectives says a lot about an organization's key

EXHIBIT 5.4 Planning Considerations for a Section 404 Internal Control Review

1. Determine status of review. Is this the first round of Section 404 review for this entity or a subsequent year follow-up?
2. If a new review, follow the work steps to understand, document, and test key processes. Otherwise, plan for a review in a subsequent period.
3. Review and update existing documentation covering prior 404 reviews, including process flow charts and internal control gaps identified and remediated.
4. If any key process documentation is missing or inadequate, initiate steps to redocument these processes
5. Meet with the external audit firm responsible for the current Section 404 attestations and determine if there are any changes in their key process documentation and testing philosophy, with an emphasis on AS5 rules.
6. Consider any organization changes since the past review, including acquisitions or major reorganizations, and modify review coverage, if necessary.
7. Through meetings with senior and IT management, identify if significant new systems or processes have been installed over the past period and if those new changes have been reflected in updated documentation.
8. Review any internal control weaknesses identified in the past review and assess whether internal control corrections reported as installed appear to be working.
9. Develop preliminary testing strategies for key processes, and discuss these plans with both the external auditors and appropriate enterprise management to affirm the appropriateness of the testing approaches,
10. Assuming the prior Section 404 review was done by internal audit; determine that appropriate, knowledgeable trained resources are available to perform the upcoming review.
11. Interview all parties involved in the prior Section 404 review exercise to assess any lessons learned and develop plans for corrective actions in the upcoming review.
12. Based on discussions with external auditors and senior management, determine scope materiality parameters for the upcoming review.
13. Determine that the software, if any, used to document prior review is still current, and make any changes necessary to have adequate tools in place to perform the upcoming review.
14. Prepare a detailed project plan for the upcoming Section 404 review, with considerations given to coordination of review activities at business entity units and external auditors.

processes, but some possess greater risks than others. For a distribution company, for example, inventory processes would be a critical key to its operations.

For many enterprises, the payroll system process is a key set of automated and manual routines that take time and attendance data and produce payroll checks or transfers to employees' checking accounts. The total payroll process is much larger and includes steps necessary to add employees, to process a pay increase, and to communicate with accounting and benefits systems. There can be numerous transaction flows in this overall process. However, with every employee regularly checking his or her own personal compensation, most payrolls are highly controlled. This is very different from some complex automated processes where many staff members may not have a good understanding of a complex automated system.

Internal audit, as part of a Section 404 compliance team, should review all enterprise processes, focus on the more significant, and select the ones that are higher-risk or financially important. The selection should focus on processes where there is a risk that a failure could cause a major financial or operational risk to the enterprise. These processes should then be ranked by the size of assets controlled and other measures, with an overall consideration given to their risk of failure. For example, in raising the question of whether the application software was purchased or built in-house, the enterprise might—and probably should—decide that purchased software often has a lower risk. Internal audit can assist in developing documented procedure to justify why one process was more worthy or significant for detailed review than another. However, the enterprise should develop some risk-based criteria for why they have or have not selected some process for review. The approach should then be applied consistently.

Step 4: Document Selected Process Transaction Flows. A next and very important Section 404 step is to prepare transaction flow documentation for the key processes selected. If documentation had been previously prepared as part of a COSO internal control review, it should also be reviewed to determine if it is still accurate. Documentation is much more of a challenge for an entity if this is the first SOx 404 review, and if the enterprise has never documented its processes. There are a variety of accepted documentation protocols, and a goal should be to select some notation or automated support system that is simple to prepare and update and easily understood by all interested parties. The documentation should show important transaction flows and control points. A key need for any documentation is a supporting process to keep it updated. Three-ring notebooks full of process documentation that were often used in the old days are of little value for future use, as these books are almost never updated, despite the best intentions of internal audit or whoever prepared the documentation materials.

An enterprise should have a good understanding of why it decided to document some processes and not others. It is best to concentrate on documenting processes where certain controls are not easily and quickly understood due to their complexity or automated methods. Exhibit 5.5 lists some typical application control process areas for establishing Section 404 compliance. This exhibit highlights areas such as cloud computing and wireless applications that should be considered in any risk assessment in today's environments and are covered in other chapters going forward.

EXHIBIT 5.5 Application Control Process Areas for Establishing Section 404 Compliance

1. **Automated process controls.** Many complex applications, such as ERP systems, contain multiple detailed decision steps often embedded in the application software that become candidates' compliance reviews.
2. **Manual processes needing automation.** Controls here are often loose, at times almost manual-link interfaces between automated systems, or they operate outside of usual automated processes.
3. **Interface/integration controls.** Risks exist where applications are loosely integrated and depend upon data transmitted across nonsecure facilities or where reconciliation processes are weak.
4. **Internal and external reporting controls.** Automated applications frequently generate reports to internal business, regulatory, and governmental agencies that contain risks ranging from legal to reputational issues if controls are weak or reported results incorrect.
5. **Application security separation of duties controls.** In today's IT applications, a wide range of stakeholders, including vendors and other parties, may have been given access to certain critical applications. These parties may be allowed systems accesses with proper separation of duties controls. Strong application process controls are often needed here.
6. **Application and processes based on cloud technology.** Still a newer, evolving set of technologies, processes using cloud technologies may be greater candidates for Section 404 compliance reviews.
7. **Highly distributed wireless application processes.** The growth of wireless applications, using smartphones, tablet computers, and RFID devices, introduces new internal control risks as possible candidates for specialized internal control reviews.
8. **General IT control processes.** Pervasive IT processes such as IT configuration management, security administration including password management, new systems project management, and others could all be candidates for separate process reviews.

Enterprises should establish procedures to ensure that all changes to previously documented systems are updated when required. The groups or functions that initially documented these SOx processes should be given the responsibility to maintain this documentation. Documentation can be done as verbal descriptions, but it is usually best to use some type of flowcharting technique. The idea is to show the inputs, outputs, process steps, and key decision points for any process. There are many different approaches that can be used here, and Chapter 17 on internal auditor process modeling techniques contains some examples. The documentation should be prepared in a manner that can easily be understood by all interested parties and, more important, can be easily updated for process changes.

Step 5: Assess Selected Process Risks. Once key processes have been defined and documented, the next step is to assess risks through a detailed "What could go wrong?" type of analysis. The idea is to ask questions about the potential risks surrounding each reviewed process. For example, in an accounts payable process, could someone gain access to the system and then arrange to cut an unauthorized check? Could system controls be sufficiently weak that multiple payments might be generated to the same authorized vendor? There could be numerous risks of this sort. The SOx review team should go through each of the selected processes and highlight potential risks in such an open-ended set of questions and then focus on the expected supporting controls. Based on their backgrounds, internal audit can play a very valuable role in this type of analysis.

Step 6: Assess Control Effectiveness through Appropriate Test Procedures. System controls are of little value if they are not working effectively. Interviews and the preparation of process documentation can sometimes determine if appropriate controls do not appear to be in place or are ineffective. In that case, the conclusions from the assessment should be documented and discussed with the process owners, and an action plan developed to take corrective actions to improve the controls.

In most instances, the documented controls should be tested to determine that they are operating effectively. This is called audit testing, and it has been a common process over the years for both internal and external auditor reviews of controls. At one time these audit tests were extremely extensive and expensive, with large sample transaction sizes. Evaluation of the results of these samples allowed internal or external auditors to draw conclusions regarding whether financial results were fairly stated or internal controls appeared to be working. Statistically based audit sampling is less common today due to audit efficiency pressures.

Whether a statistically based sample is used or not, the SOx process reviewer should use one or more sample transactions to test whether the controls are in place and working on a consistent basis. Exhibit 5.6 contains suggested sample sizes, based on the frequency of the control performance. The idea here is that if a control covers many repetitive items, the sample size to determine that it is operating effectively should be larger. The size of the sample can present a challenge for some processes, but if it is a largely paper-based process with many people-based approval steps, the SOx reviewer might borrow from other classic internal audit techniques and try a "walk-through" type of test. The idea here is to take a single transaction—such as a vendor invoice requiring approval—and individually walk that transaction through each of the processing steps prior to cutting the accounts payable check. Again, this is a test to assess internal controls over a process. If the results of the test are positive, the process reviewer could determine whether the process appears to be working with adequate internal controls. This exercise is discussed in greater detail in Chapter 10 on assessing audit evidence and should be part of an internal auditor's CBOK.

EXHIBIT 5.6 Recommended Sample Sizes by Control Frequency

Frequency the Control Operates	Recommended Minimum Sample Size
▪ Multiple times per day	At least 30 items
▪ Daily	At least 25 items
▪ Weekly	At least 10 items
▪ Monthly	At least 5 items
▪ Quarterly	At least 2 items

Step 7: Review Compliance Results with Key Stakeholders. Senior management is ultimately responsible for an enterprise's final Section 404 report. The project team should review their progress with senior management, highlighting their review approaches and short-term corrective actions initiated. Similarly, since they must formally attest to the results of this internal control review, the external auditors should be kept informed of progress and any outstanding issues in process of resolution.

Coordination with key stakeholders is important here. All too often, assessments have identified some potential internal control weakness at a local facility, documented it on site with little follow-up, and then raised it as a potentially significant weakness back at headquarters. In many cases, the potential weakness had minimal impact to the overall enterprise and could have been resolved and corrected at the local level. Stakeholder communication at all levels is important here.

Step 8: Complete Report on the Effectiveness of the Internal Control Structure. This is the final step in a Section 404 compliance review. This is the report, along with the external auditor's attest work, that will be filed with the SEC as part of the enterprise's 10-K annual report. Since these internal control reviews are not a onetime exercise, all work should be documented similar to internal audit workpapers documenting audit evidence, discussed in Chapter 10.

A first-time SOx Section 404 compliance project can be a major undertaking, and for most enterprises today certainly requires considerably more time and effort than is expressed in the short set of work steps described here. However, AS5 rules have made this review process a bit easier. It is now not necessary to go back to almost square one in each review-cycle year but to rely on the work from prior periods. The old-timer, now experienced with multiple years of these reviews, might look at AS5 and say something along the lines of "You should see how bad it was in the old days!" AS5 has simplified and more rationalized the internal control review process, but we still must keep these basic entity-level internal control review processes in place.

As has been discussed, this is also really a key area where internal audit can play a very significant but advisory role. The effort required will depend on the level of internal control work that has previously been performed in the enterprise. Many, except for new entities, have already gone through multiple cycles of their Section 404 reviews and are today in maintenance mode. Often through the leadership of internal audit, these enterprises have reviewed, tested, and documented their internal controls following the COSO framework standard, and have the ongoing task today of achieving Section 404 compliance.

Also, if an automated system control was found to be effective in the first year and if there were no known changes to this process, it is no longer necessary to go back and redocument and retest in subsequent review periods. This is an example of exercising more of a risk-based approach. As another major change, management now has the flexibility to exercise judgment to tailor review approaches to enterprise facts and circumstances. Section 404 reviews continue to be important, and AS5 rules offer more flexibility and should be used to establish a more risk-based reasoned approach to these assessments.

5.3 AS5 RULES AND INTERNAL AUDIT

Shortly after SOx became the law in the United States, the PCAOB released Auditing Standard No. 2 (AS2), new guidance that called for external auditors to take conservative and detailed approaches on their audits of financial statements. AS2 mandated a look-at-everything audit approach, and enterprise external audit bills became much more expensive. While many larger enterprises gritted their teeth and lived with the new rules, industry leaders, academics, and others loudly proclaimed that AS2 needed some revisions. The SEC and the PCAOB agreed to revise AS2, with an objective of making the auditing standard more scalable for the 6,000 or more so-called nonaccelerated filers that had yet to comply with SOx as of 2007. Those publicly traded enterprises with a public float of $75 million or less were required to have their Section 404 auditor attestation reports completed in upcoming fiscal years, and many felt they needed some relief from AS2 audit rules. As a result, Auditing Standard No. 5 (AS5) was issued in late May 2007.

While AS5 is really a set of standards for the external auditors who review and certify published financial statements, these new rules are important for internal auditors and financial managers as well. AS5 introduces risk-based rules with an emphasis on the effectiveness of enterprise-level controls that are more oriented to enterprise facts and circumstances. In addition, the new auditing standard calls for external auditors to consider including reviews of appropriate internal audit reports in their financial statement audit reviews. AS5 allows external auditors to place more emphasis on management's ability to establish and document key internal controls, and both financial management and internal auditors need to understand these risk-based rules for the financial audits of their enterprises.

It is not our objective in this book to provide an overview of the AS5 rules; our previously published book on Sarbanes-Oxley internal controls has a chapter describing AS5 in some detail,[4] and these rules are particularly important for internal auditors because they stress that external auditors can rely on the work of internal auditors in their Section 404 assessments. AS5 has four broad objectives:

1. **Focus internal control audits on the most important matters.** AS5 calls on external auditors to focus their reviews on areas that present the greatest risk that an internal control will fail to prevent or detect a material misstatement in the financial statements. This approach calls for external auditors to focus on identifying material weaknesses in internal control in their audits, before they result in material misstatements of financial statements. AS5 also emphasizes the importance of auditing higher-risk areas, such as the financial statement period-end close process and controls designed to prevent fraud by management. At the same time, the new standard provides external auditors a range of alternatives for addressing lower-risk areas, such as by more clearly demonstrating how to calibrate the nature, timing, and extent of testing based on risk, as well as how to incorporate knowledge accumulated in previous years' audits into the auditors' assessment of risk. Also and very important to our internal auditor CBOK, AS5 also allows external auditors to use the work performed by an enterprise's internal auditors or financial staff when appropriate.

2. **Eliminate audit procedures that are unnecessary to achieve their intended benefits.** AS5 does not include the previous AS2 standard's detailed requirements to evaluate management's own evaluation process and clarifies that an internal control audit does not require an opinion on the adequacy of management's process. For example, AS5 focuses on the multilocation dimensions of risk in an enterprise and reduces requirements that external auditors should test a "large portion" of an enterprise's operations or financial positions. This should allow a reduction in financial audit work.
3. **Make the audit clearly scalable to fit the size and the complexity of any enterprise.** In order to provide guidance for audits of smaller, less complex companies, AS5 calls for tailoring internal control audits to fit the size and complexity of the enterprise being audited. The standard has guidance on how to apply AS5's principles to smaller, less complex enterprises as well as the less complex units of larger enterprises.
4. **Simplify the text of the standard.** AS5 is shorter and easier to read than its AS2 predecessor. This is in part because the standard has been streamlined and reorganized to begin with the audit itself; definitions and other background information are included only as appendices. For example, AS5 eliminates the previous standard's discussion of materiality, clarifying that the auditor's evaluation of materiality is based on the same long-standing principles applicable to financial statement audits.

With AS5, external auditors may consider using the work of others to help perform their enterprise SOx financial statement internal control audits. This practice was not as well defined under previous SOx rules, but AS5 explicitly allows it. AS5 states that an external auditor may use the work performed by, or receive direct assistance from, internal auditors, other company personnel, or third parties working under the direction of management or the audit committee to provide evidence about the effectiveness of financial reporting internal controls. This is a major change for internal auditors.

Of course, the external auditors are signing off on or attesting to the audit results, and they must assess the competence and objectivity of the persons whose work they plan to use. The higher the degree of competence and objectivity of others, the greater use an auditor may make of their work. In particular, AS5 calls for an assessment of the competence and objectivity of internal auditors. *Competence* means the attainment and maintenance of a level of understanding and knowledge that enables persons to perform the tasks assigned to them, and *objectivity* means the ability to perform those tasks impartially and with intellectual honesty. To assess competence, an external auditor should evaluate the qualifications and ability of their internal auditors or others to perform the work the external auditor plans to use. To assess objectivity, AS5 calls for an external auditor evaluation of whether factors are present that either inhibit or promote a person's ability to perform with the necessary degree of objectivity the work the auditor plans to use.

AS5 also states that external auditors should not use the work of persons who have "a low degree of objectivity, regardless of their level of competence," and also should not use the work of persons who have a low level of competence regardless of their degree of objectivity. Personnel whose core function is to serve as a testing or compliance authority at the company, such as internal auditors, normally are expected to have greater competence and objectivity in performing the type of work that will be useful to the external auditor. This may be an area where the CAE, as well as the audit committee and senior management, may want to challenge their external auditors if they see no role for internal audit in the financial statement audit planning process.

Although AS5 talks about internal auditors in an almost generic fashion, the role of the professional IIA-member internal auditor is important here. Based on the *International Standards for the Professional Practice of Internal Auditing*, as summarized in Chapter 9, an IIA internal auditor can be expected to have the competence and objectivity necessary for help in supporting an external auditor's review of Section 404 internal controls. While other persons, such as outside consultants, can be used to assist external auditors in their financial statement internal control reviews, internal auditors should have a major role here in assisting with Section 404 and AS5 audit compliance.

Internal audit's ongoing role here should be viewed with a level of caution. We have discussed how internal auditors can often be excellent resources to identify, document, and test key Section 404 processes. They could do this in a support role for the external auditor's attestation reviews. However, pure separation-of-duties independence rules say that they cannot perform these reviews within the enterprise and then act as third-party helpmates for the external auditors to help attest to that same work. This conflict of duties should be clearly understood by all parties, and care should be exercised by internal auditors and management to prevent it.

5.4 IMPACT OF THE SARBANES-OXLEY ACT

The previous sections have provided a general overview of the Sarbanes-Oxley Act. While this discussion did not cover all sections or details of SOx, our intent is to give internal auditors an overall understanding of key sections that will have an impact on the annual audit of an enterprise and its audit committee. Whether a large, Fortune 500–sized U.S.-based corporation, a smaller company not even traded on NASDAQ, or a private company with a bond issue registered through the SEC, all come under SOx rules.

SOx is an important law, and every internal auditor should have a general understanding of its content as CBOK requirement. Going beyond just this general understanding, SOx's Section 404 on reviews of internal accounting controls should receive the most internal audit attention and understanding. In Section 404, an enterprise is made responsible for reviewing, documenting, and testing its own internal accounting controls, with those review results then being passed on to the enterprise's external auditors, who are charged with reviewing and attesting to that work as part of their review of the reported financial statements. When SOx first became law, Section 404 reviews were a major difficulty for many enterprises because external auditors were required to follow the very detailed AS2 set of financial accounting audit procedures. These auditing standards left little room for small errors or omissions.

SOx has caused multiple changes to enterprises, particularly in the United States, and also worldwide. The roles and responsibilities of both external and internal auditors have changed, and enterprises certainly look at internal controls and business ethics from a much different perspective. A general knowledge of SOx and its procedures for performing Section 404 internal control reviews should be every internal auditor's CBOK repository.

NOTES

1. The text of the law can be found in many locations online. One source is http://fl1.findlaw.com/news.findlaw.com/hdocs/docs/gwbush/sarbanesoxley072302.pdf.
2. The PCAOB Quality Standards were described as interim when issued in 2003 and remained interim at the time of this book's publication in 2015.
3. A principle of law: Even if a technical violation of a law appears to exist according to the letter of the law, if the effect is too small to be of consequence, the violation of the law will not be considered as a sufficient cause of action, whether in civil or criminal proceedings.
4. Robert Moeller, *Sarbanes-Oxley Internal Controls: Effective Auditing with AS5, CobiT, and ITIL®* (Hoboken, NJ: John Wiley & Sons, 2008).

CHAPTER SIX

COBIT and Other ISACA Guidance

THE COMMITTEE OF SPONSORING ORGANIZATIONS' (COSO) internal control framework, as introduced and discussed in Chapter 3, has become the standard mechanism for measuring and evaluating internal accounting controls under the Sarbanes-Oxley Act (SOx), as was introduced in Chapter 5. However, SOx does not *mandate* the strict use of the COSO internal control framework but only calls for its utilization for understanding and evaluating internal controls. Prior to the release of the recently revised COSO framework, some professionals had expressed concerns about the original COSO internal control framework, and had criticized it because it did not give enough emphasis to information technology (IT) tools and processes.

As an alternative, another more IT-oriented internal control framework is called Control Objectives for Information and related Technology (COBIT). This framework has been in place since well before SOx, and many enterprises began to use COBIT when SOx became the law as a preferred tool for complying with its Section 404 internal control procedures. The COBIT internal control framework provides guidance on evaluating and understanding internal controls, with an emphasis on enterprise IT resources and governance issues. COBIT is not a replacement for the COSO internal control framework but is a different way to look at COSO-mandated internal controls in today's IT-centric world.

Although originally launched as a tool to help what were once called "computer auditors"—specialist internal and external auditors who long ago reviewed IT-related internal controls—COBIT today is a very helpful tool for evaluating all internal controls as well as IT governance processes across an enterprise. It provides emphasis and guidance on the linkage of IT with other business resources to deliver overall value to an enterprise today. This chapter will provide an overview of the current version, 5, of the COBIT framework and its key components. More important, this chapter will describe the relationship between COBIT objectives and the COSO internal control framework for use in internal audit reviews. Even if an internal auditor does not use the COBIT framework in reviews of internal controls, all internal auditors should have a high-level common body of knowledge (CBOK) of the basic COBIT framework. Knowledge of COBIT, in addition to the COSO internal control framework, will help internal auditors to better understand the role of IT controls and risks in many enterprise environments.

6.1 INTRODUCTION TO COBIT

COBIT (originally written as CobiT) is an acronym that is becoming increasingly recognized by many internal and external auditors and IT professionals. COBIT is an important internal control framework that can stand by itself, but it is also an important support tool for documenting and understanding both COSO and SOx internal controls. Although COBIT's original emphasis was IT-oriented, the framework has been broadened, and internal auditors in many enterprises today should at least have an understanding of the COBIT framework and its use as a tool for documenting, reviewing, and understanding SOx internal controls. A general knowledge of COBIT should be an internal auditor CBOK requirement.

The COBIT standards and framework are issued and regularly updated by the *IT Governance Institute* (*ITGI;* www.itgi.org) and the closely affiliated professional organization *Information Systems Audit and Control Association (ISACA)*. ISACA is more focused on IT auditing, while ITGI's emphasis is on research and governance processes. ISACA also directs the Certified Information Systems Auditor examination and professional designation as well as its newer Certified Information Security Manager certification and examination. These audit-related professional certifications are discussed in Chapter 29. ISACA was originally known as the Electronic Data Processing Auditors Association (EDPAA), a professional group that was started in 1967 by internal auditors who felt their professional organization, the Institute of Internal Auditors (IIA), was not giving sufficient attention to the importance of IT systems and technology controls as part of internal audit activities. EDP once stood for electronic data processing, today an almost archaic term for IT. Over time, this professional enterprise broadened its focus and became ISACA, while the IIA has also long since embraced strong technology issues.

The EDPAA, originally an upstart IT audit professional organization, began to develop IT audit professional guidance materials shortly after its formation. Just as the EDPAA evolved into ISACA and now the ITGI, its original IT audit standards became a very excellent set of internal control objectives that evolved into COBIT, now in its 2012 version 5 edition.[1] With virtually all enterprise processes today tied to IT-related matters, an understanding of the overall area of IT governance is critical. The COBIT framework principles are often described as a pentagon covering five broad and interconnected areas of internal controls, as illustrated in Exhibit 6.1. These show COBIT's five major areas of emphasis arranged around the important core concept of IT governance:

1. **Strategic alignment.** Efforts should be in place to align IT operations and activities with all other enterprise operations. These include establishing linkages between

enterprise business operations and IT plans as well as processes for defining, maintaining, and validating quality and value relationships.

2. **Value delivery.** Processes should be in place to ensure that IT and other operating units deliver promised benefits throughout a delivery cycle and with a strategy that optimizes costs while emphasizing the intrinsic values of IT and related activities.
3. **Risk management.** Management at all levels should have a clear understanding of an enterprise's appetite for risk, compliance requirements, and the impact of significant risks. Both IT and other operations have their own and joint risk management responsibilities that may individually or in combination impact the entire enterprise.
4. **Resource management.** With an emphasis on IT, there should be an optimal investment in, and the proper management of, critical IT resources, applications, information, infrastructure, and people. Effective IT governance depends on the optimization of knowledge and infrastructure.
5. **Performance measurement.** Processes should be in place to track and monitor strategy implementation, project completions, resource usage, process performance, and service delivery. IT governance mechanisms should translate implementation strategies into actions and measurements to achieve these goals.

These five COBIT internal control concerns or areas of emphasis are the framework's elements and define IT governance. The COBIT framework is an effective tool for documenting IT and all other internal controls, and this chapter looks at the framework

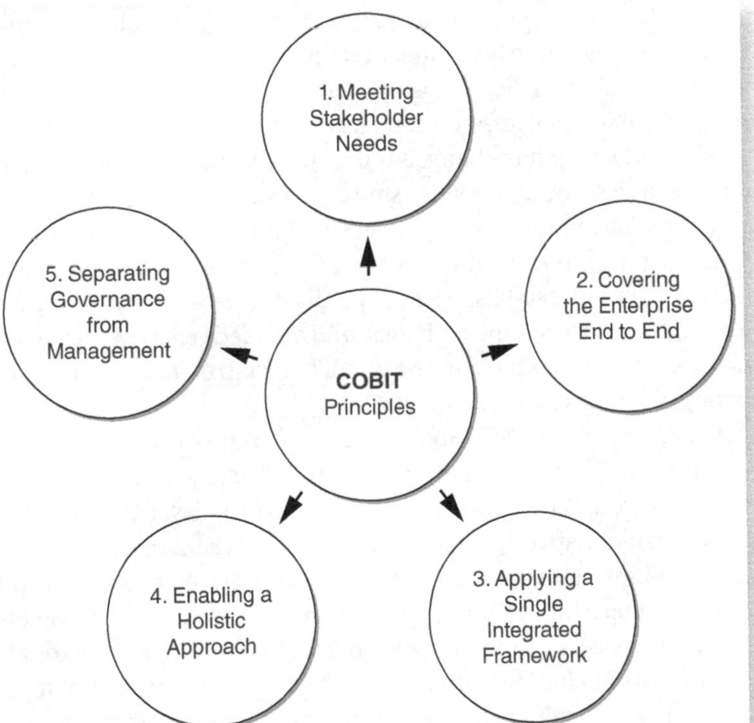

EXHIBIT 6.1 Five Principles of Internal Controls

in the broader perspective of using COBIT to assist in the IT governance processes of management, enterprise, and internal auditing.

The following sections provide an overall description of the COBIT framework and its elements to link business with IT goals through key controls and effective measurement metrics. In addition, this chapter will describe mapping COBIT standards with the COSO internal control framework, discussed in Chapter 3; the Information Technology Infrastructure Library (ITIL®) service management best practices introduced in Chapter 19; and for overall IT and corporate governance. Elements and key components of IT governance will be discussed as well. The COBIT framework is an effective mechanism for documenting and understanding internal controls at all levels. Although COBIT first started primarily as a set of "IT audit" guidance materials, it is a much more powerful tool today.

6.2 COBIT FRAMEWORK

IT processes and their supporting software applications and hardware devices are key components in any enterprise today. Whether a small retail business with a need to keep track of its inventory and pay employees, or a Fortune 500 corporation, all need a wide set of interconnected and often complex IT processes that are closely tied to their business operations. That is, business processes and their supporting IT resources work in a close information-sharing relationship. IT cannot and certainly should not tell business operations what types of IT processes and systems they should consider implementing, but IT provides information to help influence business decisions. In the very early days of computer systems, IT managers sometimes felt they had lots of answers and promoted systems solutions to their businesses, sometimes with very counterproductive results. However, this relationship has changed today and IT and business operations generally should have a close mutual relationship of shared requirements and information. Internal auditors must understand the needs and information-sharing requirements on both sides. IT has responsibilities over a series of other related process areas that are audited by or through established audit guidelines, are measured by a series of performance indicator measures and activities, and are made effective through a series of activity goals. All of these become part of COBIT, a control framework including both IT and business processes.

Chapter 3 described the COSO internal control framework and its importance in defining SOx internal controls. An internal auditor might ask, "I understand and use COSO internal controls. Why another framework?" The answer to this question is that COBIT provides an alternative approach to define and describe internal controls that has more of an IT emphasis than even the newly revised COSO internal control framework. Information and supporting IT processes often are the most valuable assets of virtually all enterprises today, and management has a major responsibility to safeguard its supporting IT assets, including automated systems. A combination of management, users of IT, and internal auditors all need to understand these information-related processes and the controls that support them. This combination is concerned about the effectiveness and efficiency of their IT resources, its IT processes, and overall business requirements, as shown in Exhibit 6.1 describing COBIT's five basic principles, with business requirements driving the demand for IT resources and those resources initiating IT processes and enterprise information in a continuous circular manner. These principles are discussed in more detail in the sections following. Management should be interested in the quality, cost, and appropriate delivery of its IT-related resources whose control components are the same as the COSO internal control elements discussed in Chapter 3. Internal controls over IT resources are very much based on the effectiveness and efficiency interdependencies of these IT components.

As a point of clarification, all of our references to COBIT in this chapter cover the current version, 5. Earlier editions of this book referenced previous version of COBIT, which contained some difficult-to-understand concepts. Prior versions of COBIT had much more of an IT orientation, making it difficult to grasp for many non-IT professionals. COBIT has been streamlined over the years, and version 5 is an important and useful tool for evaluating and understanding internal controls.

The following sections will discuss each of COBIT's five principles, ranging from principle 1 of meeting stakeholder needs, to principle 5 on separating governance from management. IT governance is now a key COBIT concept that was not strongly emphasized as an important internal control element in either the original COSO framework or in SOx. An important internal control concept today, COBIT defines IT governance as a series of key areas ranging from keeping focus on strategic alignments to the importance of both risk and performance measurement when managing IT resources.

While COBIT has an objective of covering all enterprise operation internal controls, it primarily provides a comprehensive framework designed to assist enterprises in achieving their objectives for the governance and management of enterprise IT. Simply stated, it helps enterprises create optimal value from IT by maintaining a balance between realizing benefits and optimizing risk levels and resource use. COBIT has an objective of enabling IT to be governed and managed in a holistic manner for the entire enterprise, taking in the full end-to-end business and IT functional areas of responsibility, considering the IT-related interests of internal and external stakeholders. COBIT is generic and useful for enterprises of all sizes, whether commercial, not-for-profit, or in the public sector.

COBIT approaches internal controls and enterprise governance from a different perspective than we have introduced through COSO in previous chapters. In addition, although it purports to cover all *enterprise internal controls* and governance issues, it is heavily IT-oriented. COBIT is an important and useful tool and reference source for internal auditors.

The following five sections will introduce and discuss COSO's five key principles. These principles have been extracted and summarized from ISACA published documentation.[2] An understanding of each is important for using COBIT in evaluating and understanding enterprise internal controls. Internal auditors should consider using COBIT and version 5 when reviewing and assessing internal controls in any heavily IT-oriented environment. Perhaps a major concern with using COBIT and its current version, however, is that many of its diagram descriptions have changed significantly. In contrast, the COSO internal control framework has continued to look about the same from its original 1992 introduction until today. This is not at all true with ongoing versions of COBIT over the years. Nevertheless, it is a valuable tool for reviewing and assessing internal controls in heavily IT-oriented environments.

6.3 PRINCIPLE 1: MEETING STAKEHOLDER NEEDS

COBIT's first principle is almost obvious, stating that an enterprise and its key management should recognize that their enterprise exists to create value for their stakeholders, whether they are investors, customers, employees, users, or others. Consequently, any enterprise, commercial or not, should have this concept of value creation as a major management and governance objective. This is an obvious-sounding statement that unfortunately is not always true. Too often, enterprise leaders at all levels keep their personal and organization priorities ahead of those that meet the greater good of the overall enterprise.

Value creation, as defined in COBIT, means realizing a wide range of benefits at optimal resource costs, risks, and resource utilization. These benefits can take many forms, including financial for commercial enterprises or public service for governmental entities. COBIT calls for stakeholder needs to be transformed into an actionable strategy that translates stakeholder needs into specific and customized enterprise- and IT-related goals, what COBIT calls *enabler* goals. This calls for setting specific goals at every level and in every area of the enterprise in support of the overall goals and stakeholder requirements, and thus effectively supports alignment between enterprise needs and IT solutions and services. COBIT defines this as a process of identifying IT and management needs and then building goals from those needs.

When initiating a review following *COBIT principles*, the internal auditor should step back and develop an understanding of the financial, customer, internal, and enterprise needs of the enterprise. COBIT's concept of identifying "needs" as opposed to the need to establish goals is, in the opinion this author, a rather fuzzy concept. Asking IT managers, "What are your needs for improving your organization's internal controls?" will surely prompt them to answer in terms of their goals, thinking most are about the same. Nevertheless, Exhibit 6.2 outlines some potential stakeholder needs questions extracted from COBIT reference materials that an internal auditor might identify through IT and other management reviews. The whole idea is to use these or related questions to develop identified needs into a series of enterprise goals that can be used to support COBIT's assessment on internal controls.

COBIT next suggests that these identified IT and management needs should be formalized and converted into more established goals. This can often be effectively accomplished using a balanced scorecard approach, as introduced in Chapter 17. A balanced scorecard is an important tool that should be part of an internal auditor's CBOK. COBIT suggests that first a set of enterprise goals should be established, followed by a similar exercise of establishing IT goals. This goal-setting process reflects COBIT's heavy IT orientation despite its protestations of being an overall management internal control evaluation tool.

Exhibit 6.3 shows a list of 17 generic financial, customer, internal, and learning enterprise goals as defined by COBIT. Each of these goals is contrasted against COBIT's

EXHIBIT 6.2 Questions for Developing Enterprise IT Governance and Management

1. How does the enterprise get value from its use of IT? Are end users satisfied with the quality of IT service?
2. How does the enterprise manage the performance of IT?
3. What processes are in place to best exploit new technology for new strategic opportunities?
4. What goals should be employed to best build and structure the IT department?
5. How well are IT outsourcing agreements managed and what processes are in place to obtain assurance over external providers?
6. Have control requirements been established for IT information and related IT risks?
7. Have processes been established to control IT costs and use IT resources in an effective and efficient manner?
8. Are IT human resources practices in place to develop and maintain resources as well as to manage performance?
9. Are processes in place to assure IT systems processes?
10. How does the enterprise improve its business agility through using a more flexible IT environment?
11. Does the lack of strong business strategies cause IT projects to fail?
12. How critical is IT to sustaining the enterprise and what processes are used if IT resources are not available?
13. Have requirements been defined for primary business processes dependent on IT?
14. How often and how much do IT projects go over budget and what is the average overrun of these IT operational budgets?
15. How much of the IT effort goes to fighting fires rather than to enabling more major business improvements?
16. Are sufficient IT resources available to meet required enterprise strategic objectives?
17. How long does it take senior and IT management to make major IT decisions?
18. Does IT support the enterprise in complying with regulations and service level requirements?

governance objectives of benefits realization and both risk and resource optimization. A letter P on the exhibit indicates that the goal is of primary importance to objective, while an S indicates that it is of secondary or of lesser importance.

As a last step in implementing this first principle, COBIT calls for the team implementing this process to cascade these established goals into COBIT's enabler goals. This COBIT goals cascade is important for allowing the definition of priorities for implementation, improvement, and assurance of enterprise IT governance based on strategic enterprise objectives of the related risks. In practice, this goals cascade should help an enterprise to define its relevant and tangible goals and objectives at various levels of responsibility.

6.4 PRINCIPLE 2: COVERING THE ENTERPRISE END TO END

COBIT states that it addresses the governance and management of information and related technology from an enterprise-wide end-to-end perspective—not a very common expression for most internal auditors. This means that COBIT calls for the integration of enterprise IT governance, and that the governance system for enterprise IT proposed by COBIT

EXHIBIT 6.3 COBIT Generic Enterprise Goals

Goal Dimensions	Generic Enterprise Goals	Relation to Governace Objectives		
		Benefits Realization	Risk Optimization	Resource Optimization
Financial	1. Stakeholder value of business objectives	P		S
	2. Portfolio of competitive products and services	P	P	S
	3. Managed business risk (safeguarding of assets)		P	S
	4. Compliance with external laws and regulations		P	
	5. Financial transparency	P	S	S
Customer	6. Customer-oriented service culture	P		S
	7. Business service continuity and availability		P	
	8. Agile responses to a changing business environment	P		S
	9. Information-based strategic decision making	P	P	P
	10. Optimization of service delivery costs	P		P
Internal	11. Optimization of business process functionality	P		P
	12. Optimization of business process costs	P		P
	13. Managed business change programs	P	P	S
	14. Operational and staff productivity	P		P
	15. Complinace with internal policies		P	
Learning and Growth	16. Skilled and motivated people	S	P	P
	17. Product and buisiness culture	P		

should integrate seamlessly in any governance system. COBIT aligns with views on IT governance covering all functions and processes required to govern and manage enterprise information and related technologies wherever that information may be processed. Given this extended enterprise scope, COBIT also addresses all the relevant internal and external IT services, as well as internal and external business processes.

COBIT provides a holistic and systemic view on governance and management of enterprise IT based on a number of enablers. We have taken the term *holistic* from COBIT. It is one of those terms often used by academics but not by internal auditors as they discuss the progress of their reviews, nor by many enterprise managers. It refers to taking an all-encompassing view of things based on the nature, functions, and properties of the components and their interactions. In other words, we should take a big-picture look at things.

The whole idea here is that COBIT's value creation objectives of benefits realizations, risk, and resource optimization should drive some governance enablers. These enablers should be enterprise-wide and end to end. That is, they should be inclusive of everything and everyone, internal and external, that is relevant to governance and management of enterprise information and related IT, including the activities and responsibilities of both the IT functions and non-IT business functions.

Information is one of the COBIT enabler categories, the model by which COBIT 5 defines enablers and allows every stakeholder to define extensive and complete requirements for information and the information-processing life cycle, thus connecting the business and its need for adequate information and the IT function, and supporting the business and context focus.

Governance enablers are the organizational resources for governance, such as frameworks, principles, structures, processes, and practices, through or toward which action is directed and objectives can be attained. Enablers also include the enterprise's resources—for example, service capabilities (IT infrastructure, applications, and so on), people, and information. A lack of resources or enablers may affect the ability of the enterprise to create value.

6.5 PRINCIPLE 3: A SINGLE INTEGRATED FRAMEWORK

COBIT is a single and integrated framework as it aligns with other current relevant standards and frameworks, such as ITIL®, discussed in Chapter 19, and allows the enterprise to use COBIT as an overarching governance and management framework integrator. It is complete in enterprise coverage, providing a basis to integrate effectively other frameworks, standards, and practices. A single overarching framework serves as a consistent and integrated source of guidance in a nontechnical, technology-agnostic common language.

COBIT provides a simple *architecture* for structuring guidance materials and producing a consistent product set. It has an objective of integrating knowledge previously dispersed over different frameworks such as COSO. There is no mention in the COBIT documentation of its relationship with the IIA's *International Standards for the Professional Practice of Internal Auditing*, as discussed in Chapter 9. However, COBIT is an alternative tool that an internal auditor should consider as an alternative internal control review framework, particularly given COBIT's emphasis on IT systems and processes. The COBIT framework delivers guidance on governance and the management of enterprise IT by aligning to other relevant standards and frameworks, such as ITIL® and ISO standards. Exhibit 6.4 describes the overall COBIT goals and metrics flow.

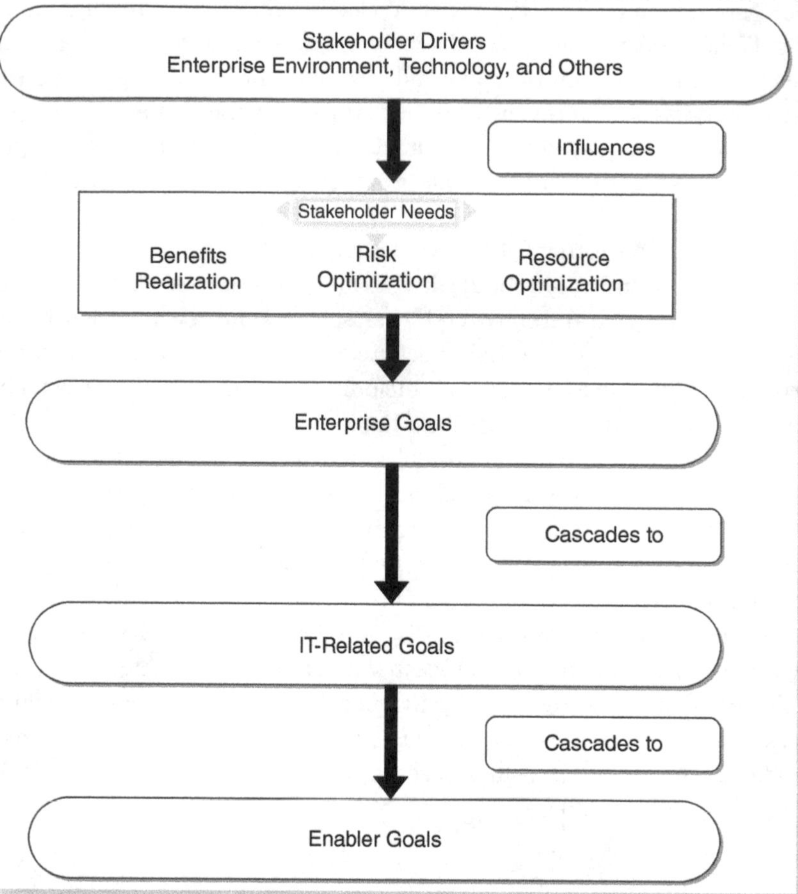

EXHIBIT 6.4 COBIT Goals and Metrics

6.6 PRINCIPLE 4: ENABLING A HOLISTIC APPROACH

Enablers are factors that, individually and collectively, influence whether something will work—in this case, the governance and management over enterprise IT. Enablers are driven by the goals that cascade from principle 3, where higher-level IT-related goals define what the different enablers should achieve. Exhibit 6.5 describes these classes or types of enablers:

- **Principles, policies, and frameworks** are enabler vehicles to translate the desired behavior into practical guidance for day-to-day management.
- **Organizational structure** enablers are the key decision-making entities in an enterprise.
- **Culture, ethics, and behavior** of individuals and of the enterprise are enablers often underestimated as a success factor in governance and management activities.

- **Information** enablers are pervasive throughout any organization and include all information produced and used by the enterprise. Information is required for keeping the organization running and well governed, but at the operational level, information is very often the key product of the enterprise itself.
- **Service, infrastructure, and application** enablers include the infrastructure, technology, and applications that provide the enterprise with information technology processing and services.
- **Personal professional skills and competencies** are required for successful completion of all activities and for making correct decisions and taking corrective actions.

What COBIT is really saying is that information, which needs to be managed as a resource, and other information, such as management reports and business intelligence information, are important enablers for the governance and management of the enterprise. This also includes service, infrastructure, and applications as well as people and their skills and competencies.

There are four common dimensions to enablers: (1) the internal stakeholders, (2) external stakeholder goals, (3) the stakeholder enabler life cycle, and (4) just

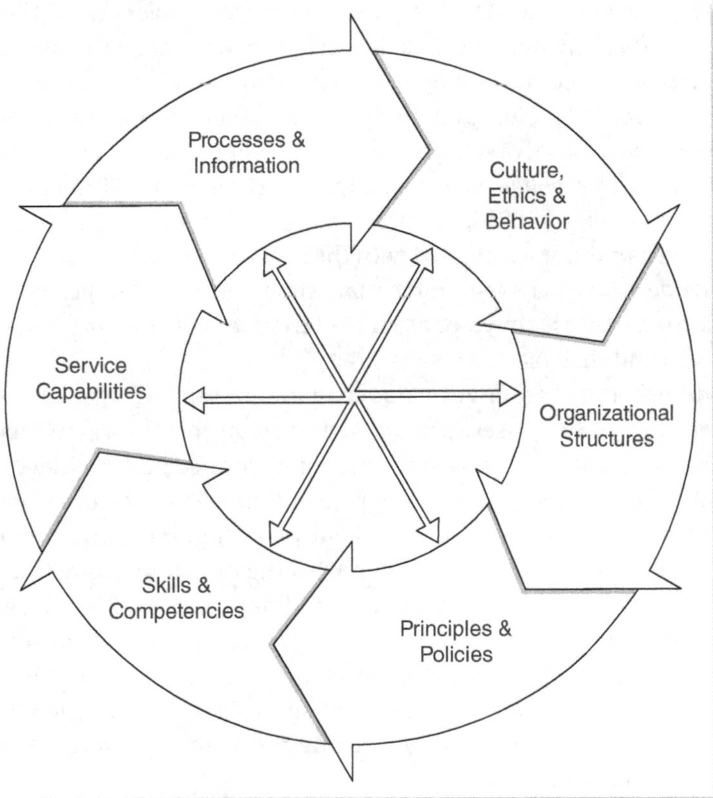

EXHIBIT 6.5 COBIT Enabler Types

good practices. That is, each enabler has stakeholders who play an active role and/or have an interest. For example, processes have different parties who execute process activities and/or who have an interest in the process outcomes; organizational structures have stakeholders, each with his or her own roles and interests that are part of the structures. Stakeholders can be internal or external to the enterprise, all having their own, sometimes conflicting interests and needs. Stakeholders' needs translate to enterprise goals, which in turn translate to IT-related goals for the enterprise.

6.7 PRINCIPLE 5: SEPARATING GOVERNANCE FROM MANAGEMENT

COBIT's remaining and fifth principle focuses on the importance of separate but related concepts of management and governance in an IT-oriented enterprise. The COBIT framework makes a clear distinction between governance and management. These two disciplines include different types of activities, require different organizational structures, and serve different purposes. This distinction is a key to COBIT's view of governance and management.

We often forget that *governance*, a popular term in business today, is derived from the Greek verb meaning "to steer." A governance system refers to all the means and mechanisms that enable multiple stakeholders in an enterprise to have an organized say in evaluating conditions and options; setting direction; and monitoring compliance, performance, and progress against plans, to satisfy specific enterprise objectives. This all refers to a major set of steering activities. Means and mechanisms here include frameworks, principles, policies, sponsorship, structures, and decision mechanisms, as well as roles and responsibilities, processes, and practices to set direction and monitor compliance and performance aligned with the overall objectives. This is a rather large and extensive definition of IT governance, but we should always remember that in most enterprises, governance is the responsibility of the board of directors under the leadership of the CEO and chairman.

Often differentiated from governance, management entails the judicious use of resources, people, processes, practices, and so on to achieve an identified end. It is the means or instrument by which the governance body achieves a result or objective. Management is responsible for execution within the direction set by the guiding body or unit. Management is about planning, building, organizing, and controlling operational activities to align with the direction set by the governance body. From the definitions of governance and management, it is clear that they comprise different types of activities, with different responsibilities; however, given the role of governance—to evaluate, direct, and monitor—a set of interactions is required between governance and management to result in an efficient and effective governance system. These interactions, using the enabler structure, are shown at a high level in Exhibit 6.6.

COBIT emphasizes that governance and management are different types of activities, with different responsibilities. However, given the role of governance—to

EXHIBIT 6.6 COBIT Governance and Management Interactions

Enabler	Governance and Management Interactions
Processes	COBIT makes a distinction between governance and management processes, including specific sets of practices and activities for each. This process model also includes RACI charts describing the responsibilities of different orgaizational structures within the enterprise.
Information	The process model describes inputs to and outputs from different process practices to other processes, including information exchanged between governance and management processes. Information used for evaluating, directing, and monitoring enterprise IT is exchanged between governance and management as described in the process model inputs and outputs.
Organizational structures	The number of organizational structures are defined in each enterprise; structures can sit in the governance space or the management space, depending on their composition and scope of decisions. Because governance is about setting the direction, interaction takes place between the decisions taken by the governance structures–e.g., deciding about the investment portfolio and setting risk appetite–and the decisions and operations implementing the former.
Principles, policies, and frameworks	Principles, policies, and frameworks are the vehicles by which governance decisions are institutionalized within the enterprise, and for that reason are an interaction between governance decisions and management.
Culture, ethics, and behavior	Behavior is also a key enabler of good governance and management of the enterprise. It is set on top–leading by example–and is therefore an important interaction between governance and management.
People, skills, and competencies	Governance and management activities require different skill sets, but an essential skill for both governance body members and management is to understand both tasks and how they are different.
Services, infrastructure, and applications	Services are required, supported by applications, and infrastructure to provide the governance body with adequate information and to support the governance activities of evaluating, setting, and monitoring.

evaluate, direct, and monitor—a set of interactions is required between governance and management to result in an efficient and effective governance system. These interactions, using the enabler structure, are then tied to specific internal control review processes, the real strength of the COBIT framework.

6.8 USING COBIT TO ASSESS INTERNAL CONTROLS

While *COSO internal controls* are built around only a single framework model and some general guidance for evaluating and assessing these internal controls, there is an extensive and detailed set of published materials supporting COBIT internal control assessments. In this section, we provide a limited summary of some of the COBIT guidance materials to give an internal auditor a flavor of COBIT, but interested professionals may want to consult the ISACA web site for more information and to request full copies of supporting materials. Downloadable versions are free to ISACA members or can be purchased at a nominal cost.

COBIT divides the steps necessary to evaluate IT controls and processes into what COBIT calls five domain areas:

1. Evaluate, Direct, and Monitor (EDM)
2. Align, Plan, and Organize (APO)
3. Build, Acquire, and Implement (BAI)
4. Deliver, Service, and Support (DSS)
5. Monitor, Evaluate, and Assess (MEA)

These five domain areas' identifying initials, such as MEA for the fifth domain, will be used as part of our description of COBIT elements during our brief introduction to COBIT in the next section in this chapter. These domain areas are further summarized into an overall process map for the management of enterprise IT, and we emphasize here that COBIT is a tool for controlling and evaluating all enterprise internal controls, even though its focus is primarily IT-oriented.

For each of these process domain areas, COBIT defines what it calls specific key management practices. For example, the Deliver, Service, and Support (DSS) domain area, shown on the lower line of items in Exhibit 6.7, shows six process areas for that domain, from DSS 01, Manage Operations, through DSS 06, Manage Process Controls. The COBIT documentation then drills down with detailed Enabling Process descriptions for each. For example, the COBIT calls Enabling Process DSS 04 Manage Continuity, then drills down to DSS 04.01, Define the Business Continuity Policy.

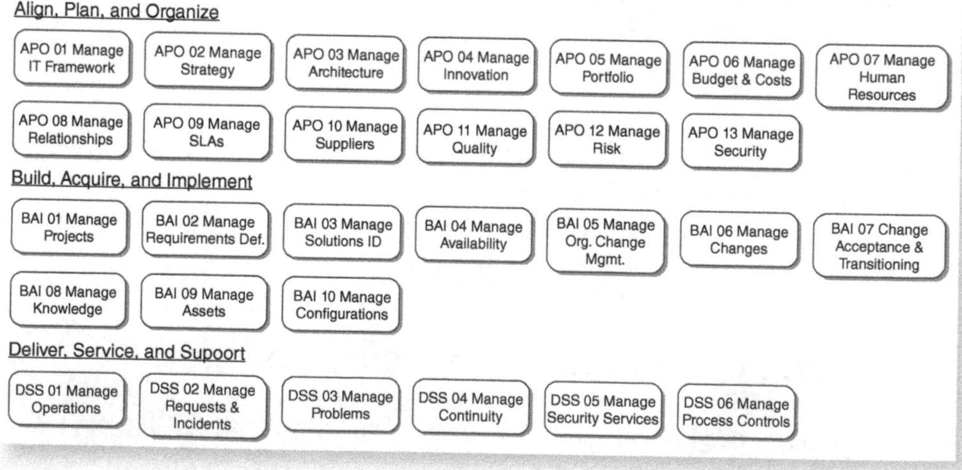

EXHIBIT 6.7 Process Reference Model

Exhibit 6.7 is just a brief example of the extensive materials that are part of COBIT guidance materials. COBIT provides enterprise-level and IT goals throughout as well as an extensive set of inputs and outputs for virtually every management practice. The published COBIT material may appear almost overwhelming for some business professionals, but it works excellently in helping to better define IT-related controls.

Similar sets of control objective process categories have been defined for each of COBIT's process categories. The purpose of the detailed but fairly specific control processes is to help make a business case for the implementation and improvement of the governance and management of IT. Their objective is to recognize both their typical pain points and trigger events, with an overall objective of creating the right environment for IT operations and implementations.

COBIT defines a set of 17 IT-related goals that can be mapped to each of these processes, with the goals divided into categories labeled Corporate, Customer, Internal, and one called Learning and Growth. These COBIT IT-related goals are then mapped to the factors for two COBIT processes, EDM (Evaluate, Direct, and Monitor) and DSS (Deliver, Service, and Support). A mapping on how each IT-related goal is supported by a COBIT-related process is illustrated in Exhibit 6.7 and expressed using a scale where:

- *P* stands for a primary connection between the IT-related goal and the connected COBIT-related process, when there is an important relationship where the designated COBIT process is a primary support for the achievement of an IT-related goal.
- *S* stands for secondary, when there is a less important relationship and the COBIT process is a secondary support for the IT-related goal.
- A blank space on the exhibit says there is no strong relationship here.

For example, the DSS 07 COBIT process to Manage Security has a strong or primary relationship with the IT-related goal designated as compliance and support for business-related laws and regulations. That same DSS 07 process also has secondary relationships with several other IT goals, such as number 7, the delivery of IT services in line with business requirements (Exhibit 6.8).

The COBIT framework may seem almost too detailed for an internal auditor and often appears to be far too complex with its multiple objectives and goals. Optimal value can only be realized from leveraging COBIT if it is effectively adopted and adapted to suit each enterprise's unique environment. Each implementation approach will also need to address specific challenges, including managing changes to culture and behavior.

The COBIT guidance emphasizes that governance and management are different types of activities, each with different responsibilities. However, given governance's steering role—to evaluate, direct, and monitor—a set of interactions is required between governance and management to create an efficient and effective governance system. These interactions, using the enabler structure, are then tied to specific internal control review processes, the real strength of the COBIT framework.

		COBIT Processes	IT-Related Goals																
			Alignment of IT & business strategy	IT compliance & support for business compliance with laws & regulations	Commitment of executive management for making IT-related decisions	Managed IT-related business risks	Realized benefits from IT-related investments & services portfolio	Transparency of IT costs, benefits & tasks	Delivery of IT services in line with business requirements	Adequate use of applications, information & technology solutions	IT agility	Security of information, IT processing infrastructure & applications	Optimization of IT assets, resources & capabilities	Enablement & support of integrating applications & technology into business processes	Optimization of IT resources & capabilities	Availability of reliable & useful information	IT compliance with internal policies	Competent & motivated IT personnel	Knowledge, expertise & initiatives for business innovation
			1	2	3	4	5	6	7	8	9	10	11	12	13	14	15	16	17
			Corporate						Customer		Internal							Learning & Growth	
Evaluate, Direct & Monitor	EDM 01	Set and Maintain the Governance Framework	P	S	P	S	S	S	P		S	S	S	S	S	S	S	S	S
	EDM 02	Ensure Value Optimization	P		S		P	P	P	S			S	S	S	S		S	P
	EDM 03	Ensure Risk Optimization	S	S	S	P		P	S	S		P			S	S	P	S	S
	EDM 04	Ensure Resource Optimization	S		S		S	S	S	S	P		P		S			P	S
	EDM 05	Ensure Stakeholder Transparency	S	S	P			P	P						S	S	S		S
Deliver, Service & Support	DSS 01	Manage Operations		S		P	S		S	S	S	S	P			S	S		
	DSS 02	Manage Processes		S		P	S		S	S	P			S	S		S	S	
	DSS 03	Manage Configuration		S		S				S	S	S	S			S			
	DSS 04	Manage Service Requests & Incidents				P			S	S		S						S	
	DSS 05	Manage Problems		S		P	S		S	S	S		P	P	P	P	S		S
	DSS 06	Manage Continuity	S	S		P	S		P	S	S	S	S			P	S	S	S
	DSS 07	Manage Security	S	P		P			S	S		P			S	S			
	DSS 08	Manage Business Process Controls		S		P			P	S		S		S		S	S	S	S

EXHIBIT 6.8 COBIT Goal and IT Objective Mapping Example

6.9 MAPPING COBIT TO COSO INTERNAL CONTROLS

The COSO internal control framework states that internal control is a process—established by an entity's board of directors, senior management, and other personnel—designed to provide reasonable assurance regarding the achievement of stated objectives. While having similar objectives, COBIT approaches IT controls by looking at information—not just COSO's financial information—that is needed to support business requirements and the associated IT resources and processes.

COSO control objectives cover effectiveness, efficiency of operations, reliable financial reporting, and compliance with laws and regulations. Its primary role is for fiduciary and financial internal controls. On the other hand, while both ISACA and ITGI acknowledge and make explicit reference to COSO's financial internal controls role, they extend COBIT's role to cover quality and security requirements in the overlapping categories of effectiveness, efficiency, confidentiality, integrity, availability, compliance, and reliability of information. These categories form the foundation of COBIT's control objectives within its five domain areas.

COSO and COBIT cater to different audiences. While COSO's target audience is general and directed to senior management, COBIT is more intended for IT management, IT users, and IT internal and external auditors. Both COSO and COBIT view internal control as an entity-wide process, but COBIT specifically focuses on IT controls. This distinction in effect defines and determines to a large extent the scope of each control framework.

Because of these differences, senior management should not necessarily expect a direct one-to-one relationship among the 5 COSO control components, the 17 COSO principles, and the 5 COBIT objective domains. Although the use of COBIT is often concentrated in the IT function at many enterprises and COSO internal controls are more of a senior management concern, both enterprise functions should realize and recognize the importance of each framework for assessing and implementing effective internal controls.

NOTES

1. *COBIT: Governance, Control and Audit for Information and Related Technology*, 4th ed. (Rolling Meadows, IL: IT Governance Institute, 2000).
2. *COBIT* 5 (Rolling Meadows, IL: IT Governance Institute, 2014).

CHAPTER SEVEN

Enterprise Risk Management: COSO ERM

ENTERPRISES NEED TO IDENTIFY ALL the business risks they face—financial and operational as well as social, ethical, and environmental—and to manage them at an acceptable level. Understanding risks is a major component of achieving Sarbanes-Oxley (SOx) and *internal controls* compliance, through the *COSO* internal control framework and *AS5* auditing standards; internal audit, in both its assurance and its consulting roles, can play a significant role in contributing to this management of risk. A frequently used term in internal control standards and procedures, *risk* has too often been one of those terms where many internal auditors have said, "Yes, we must consider risks!" even though their understandings and assessments of risk have not been consistently well understood or defined. One professional's concept and understanding of risk may be very different from someone else's, even though they are both working for the same enterprise and in similar areas. This has been particularly true for managers and internal auditors working to improve both COSO internal controls and SOx-related compliance; there has not been a consistent understanding of what is meant by this concept of risk.

Particularly to support an understanding of both COSO and SOx internal controls, internal auditors need to have a good understanding of risk management on an enterprise level and how it impacts their skills for building and developing effective internal control processes. The revised COSO internal control framework introduced in Chapter 3 and the material in Chapter 5 on SOx describe how the AS5 external auditing standard has introduced risk-based considerations to the process. As discussed in those chapters, external auditors are required to assess relative risks when selecting the internal accounting control areas to review and consider when performing their reviews.

A major consideration here is that management and external auditors should consider relative risks when implementing and assessing internal controls to achieve compliance with the *SOx Section 404* internal control rules. In order to use these new AS5 auditing standards effectively, all parties should understand the risks surrounding their enterprise and should be able to document and attest to when they did or did not raise an internal controls exception issue, based on relative risks. However, an ongoing problem in our use and understanding of this concept of risk has been the lack of a consistent definition of what is really meant by *risk*. While the word has origins in the insurance industry, its concept goes beyond insurance issues and is important for internal auditors and other business professionals. Many have talked about how they had "considered risk" when implementing an internal control or process, but they often had no consistent definitions here. The question of what steps were followed in such a risk consideration might produce a wide range of answers.

This all changed when COSO released their *Enterprise Risk Management* Integrated Framework (COSO ERM).[1] This is an approach to allow an enterprise and internal audit to consider and assess its risks at all levels, whether it be in an individual area such as an information technology (IT) development project, or global risks regarding an international expansion. While released by the same COSO guidance-setting function that has developed and maintains the COSO internal controls framework, COSO ERM sometimes looks like its internal controls brother, but it has a much different feel and approach.

This chapter will introduce the COSO ERM framework and its elements, but the emphasis will be on why COSO ERM can be an important internal audit tool to better understand and evaluate the risks surrounding internal controls at all levels. The chapter also will describe major elements of the COSO ERM framework and look at how internal auditors can better build COSO ERM into their audit processes as well as steps for auditing the effectiveness of an enterprise's risk management processes. Although the basic framework models look similar, COSO ERM is different from the COSO internal control framework discussed in Chapter 3.

An understanding of risk assessment approaches and overall risk management, with an emphasis on COSO ERM, should be important elements in every internal auditor's CBOK. This chapter will discuss risk management fundamentals, introduce COSO ERM, and present internal audit techniques for understanding and assessing risks in many areas, ranging from selecting areas to review to evaluating risks as part of internal audit reviews. While this chapter emphasizes risks on a total enterprise level, Chapters 3 and 4 discuss risk issues from the perspective of the COSO internal control framework, and Chapter 16 will use some of these same risk management techniques to discuss risk-based audit planning within an individual internal audit group.

7.1 RISK MANAGEMENT FUNDAMENTALS

Every enterprise exists to provide value for its stakeholders, but that value can be eroded through unexpected events at all levels of the enterprise and in all activities, ranging from day-to-day operations to setting strategy for some future but uncertain endeavor. All of these activities are subject to uncertainties or risks, whether it is the challenge caused by a new and aggressive competitor or the damage and even loss of life caused by a major weather disturbance. Risk management is an insurance-related concept where an individual or enterprise typically uses insurance mechanisms to provide a shield or protection from those risks. We make these insurance-related decisions based on assessments of the relative risks and the costs to cover them through the purchase insurance. Risks and insurance costs also change over time. Fire insurance to cover an individual's home is an example of this. Back in the days of oil lanterns and straw stored in a nearby stable, there was always a high risk of fires. We only need to think of the Great Chicago Fire of 1871 in which, as legend has it, a cow kicked over a lantern and caused a fire that devastated the city. The risk of fire is not as great today, and fire insurance is not very expensive, in a relative sense. However, there is always the possibility of a lightning strike or electrical malfunction to cause a fire in a structure, and mortgage finance companies require fire insurance coverage. Even if there is no mortgage, all prudent persons today will purchase such fire insurance although it is not required. A destructive fire to one's home presents a low-level but consistent risk. While the cost of homeowners' fire insurance is relatively low, an individual homeowner might assess other potential risks, such as for earthquakes, and often not purchase insurance for that risk. In a given geographical area, the possibility of an earthquake appears so low that an owner would not even consider purchasing insurance despite the low cost of such a policy. In another situation, an individual may live by a body of water where there are damaging floods every several years. Even if one can purchase flood insurance—and most insurance companies will not even offer it—the insurance coverage will be very expensive. Some may decide to accept the risk of a flood in future years and will go without insurance coverage. In all of these cases, the insurance purchaser makes a risk management decision.

Risk management as it is practiced today is essentially a post-1960s phenomenon. Moving beyond concerns about weather-related events, risk management began to emphasize protecting enterprises against a major catastrophe, such as a major computer system failure back in the mainframe days when most information systems assets were stored in one centralized system. The concern about managing risks surrounding that computer system moved to a general concern about managing a wide range of other business risks.

Enterprises today face a wide variety of risks and need some help and tools to sort through all of them in order to make rational cost- and risk-related decisions. This is the process of risk management. While some in business today typically just assess an area as high-, medium-, or low-risk and then make quick insurance or risk protection decisions based on those options, others use more sophisticated qualitative or quantitative tools to help them understand and evaluate their risks. The following sections will briefly survey some fundamental modern risk management approaches with an objective of helping to establish more effective enterprise risk management procedures.

An effective risk management process requires four steps: (1) risk identification, (2) quantitative or qualitative assessment of the documented risks, (3) risk prioritization and *response planning*, and (4) risk monitoring. There is always a need to identify and understand the various risks facing an enterprise, to assess those risks in terms of their cost or impact and *probability*, to develop responses in the event of a risk occurrence, and to develop documentation procedures to describe what happened as well as corrective actions going forward. The same is true for enterprise-wide risk management decisions or the decisions of an internal auditor in the course of a single review engagement. This section will focus on the management of risks across an enterprise.

This four-step risk management process should be implemented at all levels of the enterprise and with the participation of many different people. Whether in a small enterprise operating over a limited geographical area or a large worldwide enterprise, these risk management approaches should be developed for the total entity. This is particularly important for worldwide enterprises with multiple operating units engaged in different business operations and with facilities in different countries. Some risks in one unit may directly impact or be related to risks in another, but other risk considerations may be effectively independent from the whole. These common risks can occur because of a wide variety of circumstances ranging from poor financial decisions to changes in consumer tastes to new government regulations.

Risk Identification

Management should endeavor to identify all possible risks that may impact the success of the enterprise, ranging from the larger or more significant risks to the overall business down to the less major risks associated with individual projects or smaller business units. The risk identification process requires a studied, deliberate approach to looking at potential risks in each area of operations and then identifying the more significant risk areas that may impact each operation in a reasonable time period. The idea here is not to just list every possible risk but to identify those that might have more major impact on operations, within a reasonable time period. This can be a difficult exercise because we can only estimate the probability of the risk occurring or the nature of the consequences if the enterprise has to face the risk. This risk identification process should occur at multiple levels with an understanding that a risk that impacts an individual business unit or project may not have a great impact on the entire enterprise or beyond. Conversely, a major risk that impacts the entire economy will flow down to the individual enterprise and its separate business units. Some major risks are so infrequent but still can be so cataclysmic that it is difficult to identify them as a possible future event.

A good way to start the risk identification process is to begin with a high-level enterprise chart that lists corporate-level as well as operating units. Each of those units may have facilities in multiple global locations and also may consist of multiple and different types of operations. Each separate facility will then have its own departments or functions. Some of these facilities may be closely connected to one another, while others represent little more than corporate investments. A difficult and sometimes complicated task, an enterprise-wide initiative should be launched to identify all risks in various individual areas. This type of exercise can yield interesting and/or troubling results. For example, a corporate-level senior manager may be aware of some product liability risks, but a frontline supervisor in an operating unit may look at the same risks from an entirely different perspective.

Different members of the enterprise at different levels will look at some of the same risks from different viewpoints. A marketing manager may be concerned about competitor pricing strategies or the risk of pricing activities that would put the enterprise in violation of restraint-of-trade laws. An IT manager may be concerned about the risk of a computer virus attack on a key systems server but will have little knowledge of those pricing-issue risks. More senior management typically will be aware of a different level and set of risks than would be on the minds of the operations-oriented staff. Still, all of these risks should at least be identified and considered on a unit-by-unit basis and over the entire enterprise.

To be effective, this risk identification process requires much more than just sending out an e-mail to all operating units with a request for the recipients to list their key risks. Such a request will typically result in a wide range of inconsistent answers with no common strategy. A better approach is to identify people at all levels of the enterprise who would be asked to serve as risk assessors. Within each significant operating unit, key people should be identified from operations, finance/accounting, IT, and unit management. Their goal would be to identify and then help assess risks in their units built around a risk identification model framework. This is the type of initiative that can be led by the CEO and an enterprise risk management group, if one exists, or a function such as internal audit.

The idea here is to outline some high-level risks that may impact various operating units. Knowledgeable people can then look at these lists and expand or modify them as appropriate. Exhibit 7.1 shows some types of major risks that may impact an enterprise, including various strategic, operations, and finance risks. This is the type of high-level list that a CEO might jot down in response to the shareholder question "What worries you at the end of the day?" While certainly not listing all of the risks facing the enterprise, this is the type of first-pass list that an enterprise can use to get started on a detailed identification of risks. The people responsible in the enterprise—often the CEO and supporting staff—can meet with senior management and ask some of these "What worries you?" type of questions to identify such high-level risks.

This very general, high-level risk model can serve as a basis to better define the specific risks facing various units of an enterprise, such as the entry here of business continuity risk under technological risks. An IT manager should be able to expand this to a long list of detailed technology-related risks associated with business continuity. An operations manager who is the user of IT resources might look at business continuity risks from a different perspective and may introduce other new risks associated with what happens if IT services are not available. In order to have a better understanding of the risks facing an enterprise, it is often best to expand these lists to establish a more complete set.

An enterprise management team should then take this more complete list of potential enterprise risks and ask themselves questions along the lines of:

- Is the risk common across the overall enterprise or unique to one business group?
- Will the enterprise face this risk because of internal or external events?
- Are the risks related, such that one risk may cause another to occur?

The idea is to gain a strong understanding of the nature of enterprise-level risks and then to highlight major risks, including the risk of a significant fall in customer satisfaction ratings, the risk of a new and very large competitor entering the market,

EXHIBIT 7.1 Types of Enterprise Risks

Enterprise-Wide Strategic Risks		
External Factors Risks	**Internal Factors Risks**	
■ Industry Risk ■ Economy Risk ■ Competitor Risk ■ Legal and Regulatory Change Risk ■ Customer Needs and Wants Risk	■ Reputation Risk ■ Strategic Focus Risk ■ Parent Company Support Risk ■ Patent/Trademark Protection Risk	
Operations Risks		
Process Risks	**Compliance Risks**	**People Risks**
■ Supply Chain Risk ■ Customer Satisfaction Risk ■ Cycle Time Risk ■ Process Execution Risk	■ Environmental Risk ■ Regulatory Risk ■ Policy and Procedures Risk ■ Litigation Risk	■ Human Resources Risk ■ Employee Fraud or Malfeasance Risks ■ Employee Turnover Risk ■ Performance Incentive Risk ■ Training Risk
Finance Risks		
Treasury Risks	**Credit Risks**	**Trading Risks**
■ Interest Rate Risk ■ Foreign Exchange Risk ■ Capital Availability Risk	■ Capacity Risk ■ Collateral Risk ■ Concentration Risk ■ Default Risk ■ Settlement Risk	■ Commodity Price Risk ■ Duration Risk ■ Measurement Risk
Information Risks		
Financial Risks	**Operational Risks**	**Technological Risks**
■ Accounting Standards Risk ■ Budgeting Risk ■ Financial Reporting Risk ■ Taxation Risk ■ Regulatory Reporting Risk	■ Pricing Risk ■ Performance Measurement Risk ■ Employee Safety Risk	■ Information Access Risk ■ Business Continuity Risk ■ Availability Risk ■ IT Systems Obsolescence Risks ■ Infrastructure Risk

or the risk of an identified significant control weakness as part of the financial statement close. Any of these major risks could present significant challenges to the enterprise.

Enterprise management should review these identified risks and highlight those that appear to be most critical to the enterprise to prepare a final set of identified organization risks by the overall enterprise and its significant operating units. Because viewpoints and perspectives will vary across the enterprise, these identified risks should be shared with responsible operating and financial management, giving them opportunities to provide feedback. The idea here is to identify the population of risks that are threatening an enterprise, both at an individual unit level and on a total high-level corporate basis. These will not necessarily become the core risks but often are a starting point for enterprise risk assessments.

Key Risk Assessments

Having identified the significant enterprise risks, a next step should be to assess their likelihood and relative significance. A variety of approaches can be used here, ranging from best-guess qualitative approaches to some detailed, very mathematical quantitative analyses. The idea is to help decide which of a series of potentially risky events should give management the most to worry about.

A simple but often effective approach here is to take the list of identified risks discussed previously and circulate them to key managers with a questionnaire asking for each risk:

- What is the likelihood of this risk occurring over the next one-year period? Using a scoring range of 1 to 9, assign a best-guess score as follows:
  - Score 1 if you see *almost no chance* of that risk happening during the period.
  - Score 9 if you feel the event will *almost certainly happen* during the period.
  - Score 2 through 8 depending on where you feel the likelihood falls in this range.
- What is the significance of the risk in terms of cost to the enterprise? Again using a 1-to-9 scale, scoring should depend on the financial significance of the risk. A risk whose costs could lower earnings per share by perhaps 1 cent might qualify for the maximum score of 9.

Questionnaires here should be independently circulated to knowledgeable people to score each of the identified risks per these two measures. As an example, assume that an enterprise has identified six risks, R-1 through R-6, and four managers are asked to separately evaluate each risk in terms of likelihood and significance. These scores can then be averaged by both factors and plotted on a risk assessment analysis chart, as shown in Exhibit 7.2. In this hypothetical model, R-1 had an average likelihood score of about 3.75 and a significance score of 7.00, and this score is plotted in quadrant I of the example risk assessment analysis chart. This example shows R-1 as relatively significant but not very likely to occur. With all identified risks plotted in this manner, the high-likelihood and more significant risks in quadrant II should receive immediate management attention. This type of risk assessment analysis chart provides a good qualitative measure to understand significant risks surrounding an enterprise.

This high-risk assessment process works quite well when an enterprise has identified a relatively small number of risks. It is fairly easy to look at the risk assessment analysis chart and to focus on remediation planning for the high-likelihood and significant risks in the upper right-hand quadrant. Often, however, an enterprise may have identified a much larger set of risks, and ranges of only 1 to 9, as well as plots on the example chart, will not provide sufficient detail. A better approach is to express these significance and impact estimates in terms of a percentage estimate (e.g., 72%) of

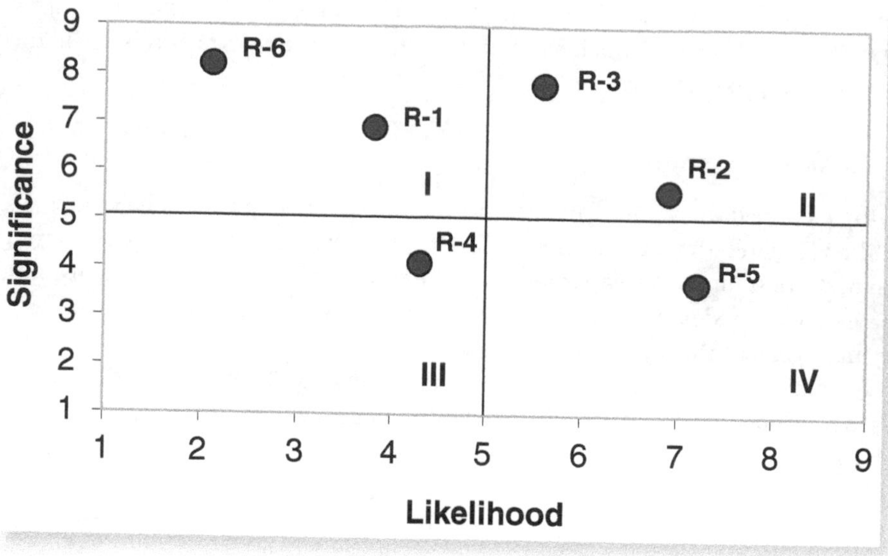

EXHIBIT 7.2 Risk Assessment Analysis Chart

achieving some risk or as a probability (e.g., 0.72). However, just increasing the number of digits, from a 7 to a full 72%, does not increase the accuracy of the assessment. More attention should be given to better understand the relationship between probabilities covering independent and related risk events.

Probability and Uncertainty

When a large number of risks have been identified, management should think of the individual estimated risk likelihoods and occurrences in terms of two-digit probabilities ranging from 0.01 to 0.99. We have used this range because risks never have a 0% chance or 100% chance of occurring—otherwise they would not be risks. A basic rule of probability is that we cannot add up independent probability estimates to yield a joint estimate. If the probability of risk A occurring is 60% and the probability of a separate but related risk B is also 60%, we *cannot* accurately say that the probability of both occurring is 0.60 + 0.60 = 1.20. This 120% does not make sense. Rather, the joint probability of two independent events is the product of the two separate probabilities using the formula:

$$\text{Pr(Event 1)} \times \text{Pr(Event 2)} = \text{Pr(Both Events)}$$

That is, if Event 1 is 0.60 and Event 2 also 0.60, the combined probability of both events occurring is (0.60) × (0.60) = 0.36. In terms of the assessments, if a risk has a 60% significance estimate or that we are 60% certain that the risk will occur and if the impact has been rated at 60%, there is a 36% probability that we will achieve both of those risks. We can also call this the risk score for the individual risk.

An accurate risk assessment process, however, requires more than just top-of-the-head estimates, whether stated in a single 1-to-9 range or as a full two-digit percentage. Enterprise management should take a hard look at their identified risks and should gather more information, if required. For example, during the risk identification process, one manager may have identified the consequences of a new tariff law as a serious risk. However, responsible managers may want to better understand its actual consequences. It may be something that is not at all applicable to the unit in question or that does not go into effect until some years into the future. The point here is that all identified risks may need some additional information before they can be accurately assessed.

Risk Interdependencies

We have discussed risks at an individual organizational unit level, but risk independencies must always be considered. Risk independencies must be considered and evaluated throughout the organizational structure. Any entity should be concerned about risks at all levels of the organization but only really has control over the risks within its own sphere. The 2002 fall of the accounting firm Arthur Andersen in the wake of the Enron collapse is an example. Each city-by-city and country-by-country unit of that once-esteemed public accounting firm had its own risk assessment procedures, following firm-wide standards. However, a risk event at one operating office, Houston, caused the firm to collapse worldwide. An operating office in another area, such as Toronto, might not even have fully anticipated such risks in faraway Houston. The point here is that risks are often very interdependent within an enterprise. Each operating unit is responsible for managing its own risks but may be subject to the consequences of risk events on units above or below in the organization structure.

Risk Ranking

While the examples used in this chapter show a short list of identified risks, a typical enterprise will end up with a very long list. A next step is to take the established significance and likelihood estimate, calculate risk rankings, and identify the most significant risks across the entity reviewed. Exhibit 7.3 is an example of this type of analysis. Using the likelihood and significance scores from Exhibit 7.2, the product of these two gives relative risk rankings. This hypothetical analysis shows that risks C and G have the highest risk rank scores and can be plotted in the upper right-hand quadrant as the most significant risks in this example. The risk significance and probabilities of occurrence are often called the *risk drivers* or the *primary risks* for a set of identified risks. An enterprise should then focus its attention going forward on these primary risks. These types of risk-ranked schedules can be organized on a unit-by-unit basis and adjusted to accommodate all related risks in parallel with as well as above or below the entity being ranked or evaluated.

Management must identify these unit-by-unit assessed risks to make certain that risk likelihood and significance estimates are appropriate throughout. All too often, risk events that occur far away from corporate headquarters can cause major problems. An example from over 30 years ago can be drawn from a risk event at the U.S. corporation Union Carbide. On the night of December 2, 1984, over 40 tons of poisonous gases leaked from a pesticide factory owned by *Union Carbide in Bhopal, India*, killing

EXHIBIT 7.3 Risk Scoring Schedule

Identified Risk	Significance Probability	Likelihood Probability	Risk Score (P x I)	Rank
A	0.55	0.30	0.17	8
B	0.88	0.24	0.21	7
C	0.79	0.66	0.52	1
D	0.77	0.45	0.35	4
E	0.35	0.88	0.31	5
F	0.54	0.49	0.26	6
G	0.62	0.72	0.45	2
H	0.66	0.20	0.13	9
I	0.90	0.45	0.41	3
J	0.12	0.88	0.11	10

Note: The actual identified risks shown here are only used as an example to illustrate that probabilities should be identified for each risk to establish a risk score ranking.

more than 20,000 residents.[2] After much legal wrangling, Union Carbide, which had built that plant in 1969, settled a civil suit brought by the Indian government in 1989 by agreeing to pay $470 million for damages suffered by the half million people who were exposed to the gas. The company maintained that this payment was made out of a sense of "moral" rather than any "legal" responsibility since the plant was operated by a separate Indian subsidiary, Union Carbide India Limited (UCIL), but court proceedings revealed that management's cost-cutting measures had effectively disabled safety procedures essential to preventing or alerting employees of such disasters. Dow Chemical has since taken over Union Carbide and denies responsibility for the disaster. However, because of the tremendous loss of life there and because Dow Chemical was much larger than what was Union Carbide and its UCIL subsidiary, ongoing litigation still continues to haunt Dow.

The Bhopal gas leak is an example of how a risk event at a distant and relatively small unit can have disastrous consequences for a major corporation. While the risk identification and assessment rules outlined in this chapter would not have accounted for this magnitude of a catastrophe, each unit in an enterprise needs to recognize the likelihoods and consequences of risks at individual unit levels. A risk event at a small foreign subsidiary can bring down the entire enterprise. While risk management at all levels should now recognize that catastrophes can happen, we can never predict risks of this major consequence; an enterprise should always be aware that the worst disaster can happen.

Quantitative Risk Analysis: Expected Values and Response Planning

There is little value in identifying significant risks unless an enterprise has at least some preliminary plans for the action steps necessary if they incur one of them. The idea is to estimate the cost impact of incurring some identified risk and then to apply that cost to a risk factor probability to derive an expected value of the risk. This is often an exercise that does not require detailed cost studies with lots of supporting historical trends and estimates. Rather, expected cost estimates should be performed by frontline people at various levels of the enterprise who would have a good level of knowledge of the area or risk implications.

The idea is to go through each of the identified risks—or if time is limited, only the key risks—and estimate the costs of incurring the risk. Because the kinds of risks discussed involve such matters as the failure of a hardware component, the drop in a market share, or the impact of a new government regulation, these are typically not the types of costs that one can just look up in a current vendor catalog. Some hypothetical risks, labeled A, B, and C, illustrate this type of thinking:

- **Risk A:** Loss of up to *X*% market share due to changing consumer tastes.
  - Estimate the reduction in sales and loss of profits due to the *X*% drop.
  - Estimate how much it will cost to begin to restore the lost market position.
- **Risk B:** Temporary loss of major manufacturing facility for *X* days due to hurricane.
  - Estimate the best- and worst-case costs to get the plant temporarily repaired and back in operation within *X* days.
  - Estimate the extra labor and production costs incurred during the interim.
- **Risk C:** Loss of information systems for *X* days due to a pernicious computer virus.
  - Estimate the business and profitability loss during the down period.
  - Estimate the cost to transfer operations to the business continuity site.

These factors illustrate the type of thinking needed to estimate the costs of recovering from some risk event. It is often difficult to determine what it would cost to recover from risks. While there is no need to perform detailed, time-consuming analyses here, knowledgeable people who understand the risk area often can provide good estimates on the basis of:

1. What is the best-case cost estimate if it is necessary to incur the risk? This is an assumption that there will be only limited impact if the risk occurs.
2. What would a sample of knowledgeable people estimate for the cost? For Risk A, as outlined, the director of marketing might be asked to supply an estimate.
3. What is the expected value or cost of incurring the risk? This is the type of risk that might include some base costs as well as such other factors as additional labor requirements.
4. What is the worst-case cost of incurring the risk? This is a what-if-everything-goes-wrong type of estimate.

We have suggested using four estimates as an idea of the ranges of costs in various people's thinking. However, one best-guess estimate should be selected from the four estimates—usually something between estimates 2 and 3 just listed. These estimates and supporting work should be documented, with the selected cost estimate entered as the cost impact on the Exhibit 7.4 risk response planning schedule. These are the same risks that were identified in the Exhibit 7.3 schedules, but are here ordered by risk rank. This reordering is important when an enterprise has a long list of identified risks.

EXHIBIT 7.4 Risk Ranking Expected Cost Example

Identified Risk	Significance Probability	Likelihood Probability	Risk Score (P × I)	Rankings	Cost Impact	Expect Cost (Cost × Score)
C	0.79	0.66	0.52	1	$120,600	$62,881
G	0.62	0.72	0.45	2	$785,000	$350,424
I	0.90	0.45	0.41	3	$15,000	$6,075
D	0.77	0.45	0.35	4	$27,250	$9,442
E	0.35	0.88	0.31	5	$52,350	$16,124
F	0.54	0.49	0.26	6	$1,200	$318
B	0.88	0.24	0.21	7	$12,650	$2,672
A	0.55	0.30	0.17	8	$98,660	$16,279
H	0.66	0.20	0.13	9	$1,200,980	$158,529
J	0.12	0.88	0.11	10	$88,600	$9,356

The expected cost in this exhibit is just the product of the cost impact and the risk score. This is an estimate of what it will cost an enterprise to incur some risk. Although the numbers selected for these samples are arbitrary, they show how a risk management specialist should interpret or act on this type of analysis. Risk C, for example, has a high likelihood and significance as well as a fairly high expected cost to correct. This is the type of risk that management should identify as a candidate for corrective action. However, the next risk on the schedule, Risk G, also belongs in the upper right quadrant but with a relatively low-cost impact and a high expected cost. This may be the type of risk where management decides to accept the risk or to develop some other form of remediation plan. Risk H is another with a high cost to implement, with fairly high significance and a low likelihood of occurrence. These are the kinds of numbers where management will frequently decide to hope for the best and live with the risk. It will be expensive if management incurs this risk but also expensive to install corrective action facilities.

Internal auditors should always be wary when dealing with such risk estimates, both in their work on audit engagements and in their own internal audit planning. It is often easy to be given wildly estimated risk probability estimates with no real support. Although we are sometimes forced to make some type of best-guess estimate, an estimate given with little support can sometimes become almost frozen over time.

Quantitative Risk Analysis: Risk Monitoring

The identification of key risks should never be a single, onetime process. The environments surrounding identified risks will soon change as surrounding conditions change. For some, conditions may change such that the risk becomes an even greater threat. For example, management may have identified potential political risks in some less developed country, but events can often happen quickly and political changes in that same country can make those concerns even riskier. An enterprise needs a mechanism to monitor these identified risks.

Risk identification processes are not continuous exercises. Just as an enterprise will prepare an annual budget with revisions perhaps once per quarter, a risk identification process should often be an annual or quarterly process. Once these risks have been identified, the enterprise needs to monitor them and make ongoing adjustments as needed. This risk monitoring can be performed by the process owner or by an independent reviewer. Internal audit is often a very credible and good source to monitor the current status of identified risks. It may gather this information through surveys or face-to-face reviews. Internal audit always has a level of extra credibility and authority. When the auditors ask about the status of some identified risk area, the people responsible for the area will quite probably provide accurate information. If internal audit is unable to easily receive good information regarding the status of some identified risk, it can always schedule a visit to better understand the nature of the risk area. Of course, internal auditors have their own audit project scheduling and risk assessment issues, and they typically cannot just schedule a review in a short time frame to understand the current status of some identified risk. However, if people in the enterprise know that internal auditors may sometimes pay a visit to better understand the status or some risk, there will be a strong tendency to provide some accurate status answers.

Accurate monitoring processes are an essential component of risk management. An enterprise may have gone through an elaborate process to identify its more significant risks. However, the current status of those risks needs to be monitored on a regular basis with changes made to the identified risks as necessary.

7.2 COSO ERM: ENTERPRISE RISK MANAGEMENT

COSO Enterprise Risk Management is a framework to help enterprises have a consistent definition of their risks. It also is an important tool for understanding and improving SOx internal controls. COSO ERM was launched in a manner similar to the development of the original COSO internal control framework, as discussed in Chapter 3. Similar to the need for a consistent definition of *internal controls*, there was also no consistent enterprise-level definition of *risk*. This concern was emphasized by the comments of John Flaherty, the first chairman of COSO: "Although a lot of people are talking about risk, there is no commonly accepted definition of *risk management* and no comprehensive framework outlining how the process should work, making risk communication among board members and management difficult and frustrating." [3] COSO contracted with PricewaterhouseCoopers to develop this risk framework, and the COSO ERM framework was published after the initial SOx rules in September 2004. Even though the COSO internal control framework was revised in 2014, there have been no changes or announced planned changes to COSO ERM. The remainder of this chapter summarizes COSO ERM in some detail.

Just as the original and now the current revised COSO internal control framework has an objective of proposing a consistent definition of its subject, the COSO ERM framework starts by defining enterprise risk management as follows:

> Enterprise risk management is a process, effected by an entity's board of directors, management and other personnel, applied in a strategy setting and across

the enterprise, designed to identify potential events that may affect the entity, and manage risk to be within its *risk appetite*, to provide reasonable assurance regarding the achievement of entity objectives.

Professionals should consider these key points and concepts supporting the COSO ERM framework definition, including:

- **ERM is a process.** The dictionary defines a *process*—an often misused word—as a set of actions designed to achieve a result. However, this definition does not provide much help for many professionals. The idea here is that a process is not a static procedure such as the use of an employee badge designed and built to allow only certain authorized persons to enter a locked facility. Such a badge procedure—like a key to a lock—only allows or does not allow someone entry to the facility. A process tends to be a more flexible arrangement. In a credit approval process, for example, acceptance rules are established with options to alter them given other considerations. An enterprise might bend the credit rules for an otherwise good credit customer who is experiencing a short-term problem. ERM is that type of process. An enterprise often cannot define its risk management rules through a small, tightly organized rule book. Rather there should be a series of documented steps to review and evaluate potential risks and to take action based on a wide range of factors across the entire enterprise.
- **The ERM process is implemented by people in the enterprise.** An ERM process will not be effective if it is only implemented through a set of rules sent in to an operating unit from a distant corporate headquarters, where the corporate people who drafted the rules may have little understanding of the various decision factors surrounding them. The risk management process must be managed by people who are close enough to the risk situation to understand the various factors surrounding that risk, including its implications.
- **ERM is applied through the setting of strategies across the overall enterprise.** Every enterprise is constantly faced with alternative strategies regarding a vast range of potential future actions. Should the entity acquire another complementary business or just build internally? Should they adopt a new technology in their manufacturing processes or stick with the tried and true? An effective ERM set of processes should play a major role in helping to establish those alternative strategies. Since many enterprises are large, with varied operating units, ERM should be applied across the entire enterprise using a portfolio type of approach that blends a mix of high- and low-risk activities.
- **An enterprise's risk appetite must be considered.** A relatively new concept or term for many, *risk appetite* is the amount of risk, on a broad level, that an enterprise and its individual managers are willing to accept in their pursuit of value. Risk appetite can be measured in a qualitative sense by looking at risks in such categories as high, medium, or low; alternatively, it can be defined in a qualitative manner. An understanding of an enterprise's risk appetite covers a wide variety of issues that will be discussed further in this chapter as part of implementing COSO ERM to strengthen an enterprise's SOx internal control environment. The basic idea is

that every manager and, collectively, every enterprise have some level or appetite for risk. Some will accept risky ventures that promise high returns, while others prefer a more guaranteed-return low-risk venture. One can think of this appetite for risk concept in terms of two investors. One may prefer very low-risk but typically low-return money market or index funds, while another may invest in low-cap start-up technology stocks. That latter investor can be described as having a high appetite for risk. As another example, at a pedestrian street intersection with a "Walk"/"Don't Walk" crossing light, the person who begins crossing the intersection when the light starts to flash "Walk," meaning it will soon change to "Don't Walk," has a higher appetite for risk.

- **ERM provides only reasonable, not positive, assurance on objective achievements.** The idea here is that an ERM, no matter how well thought out or implemented, cannot provide management or others with any assured guarantee of outcomes. A well-controlled enterprise, with people at all levels consistently working toward understood and achievable goals, may achieve those objectives period after period, even over multiple years. However, an unintentional human error, an unexpected action by another, or even a natural disaster can occur. Despite an effective ERM process, an enterprise can experience a major and totally unexpected catastrophic event. Reasonable assurance does not provide absolute assurance.
- **An ERM is designed to help attain the achievement of objectives.** An enterprise, through its management, should work to establish high-level common objectives that can be shared by all stakeholders. Examples here, as cited in COSO ERM's documentation, include such matters as achieving and maintaining a positive reputation within an enterprise's business and consumer communities, providing reliable financial reporting to all stakeholders, and operating in compliance with laws and regulations. The overall ERM program for an enterprise should help it to achieve those objectives.

ERM-related goals and objectives are of little value unless they can be organized and modeled together in a manner such that management can look at the various aspects of the task and understand, at least sort of, how they interact and relate in a multidimensional manner. This is a real strength of the COSO internal control framework model. It describes, for example, how an enterprise's compliance with laws and regulations impacts all levels of internal controls, from monitoring processes to the control environment, and how that compliance is important for all entities or units of the enterprise. The COSO ERM framework provides some common definitions of risk management and can help to achieve SOx internal control objectives as well as better risk management processes throughout the enterprise.

7.3 COSO ERM KEY ELEMENTS

The COSO ERM framework, as shown in Exhibit 7.5, has become a worldwide model for describing and defining internal controls, and has been the basis for establishing SOx Section 404 compliance. Perhaps because some of the same team members were initially involved with the COSO internal control framework and ERM, the COSO ERM framework, at first observation, looks very similar to the COSO internal control framework. This COSO ERM framework is shown in Exhibit 7.5 as a cube with the components of:

- Four columns representing the strategic objectives of enterprise risk;
- Eight horizontal rows or risk components; and
- Multiple levels to describe any enterprise, from a headquarters entity level to individual subsidiaries. Depending on organization size, there can be many slices of the model here.

This section will describe the horizontal components of COSO ERM, while later sections will discuss its other two dimensions and how they all relate to one another. The concept behind the ERM framework is to provide a model for enterprises to consider and understand their risk-related activities at all levels as well as how these risk components impact one another. An objective of this chapter is to help internal auditors at all levels, from the chief audit executive to staff auditors, to better understand COSO ERM and learn how it can help manage a wide range of internal audit risks facing enterprises.

Although the COSO ERM framework diagram looks very similar to the COSO internal control framework that has become familiar to many internal auditors over the years, it has been almost ignored by some, and others have incorrectly viewed COSO

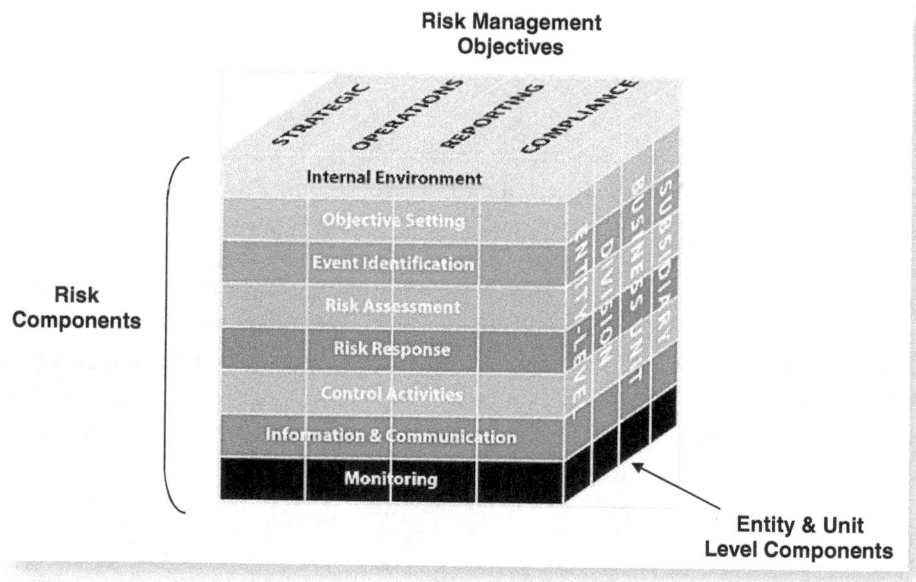

EXHIBIT 7.5 COSO ERM Framework

Source: COSO Enterprise Risk Management: Understanding the New Integrated ERM Framework, Robert R. Moeller. Copyright © 2007 John Wiley & Sons. Reprinted with the permission of John Wiley & Sons.

ERM as just an update or supplement to the more familiar COSO internal control framework. However, COSO ERM has different objectives and uses. *COSO ERM should not be considered just a new and improved or revised version of the COSO internal control framework.* It is much more. The following sections will outline this framework from a risk components perspective.

COSO ERM: The Internal Environment Component

Looking at the front or face of the COSO ERM cube, there are eight levels or factors, with the internal environment located at the top. This is similar to the revised COSO internal control framework. The internal environment should be thought of as the capstone to COSO ERM. Going back to when bridges were constructed of bricks, the capstone held the brick arches rising from each side of a span, keeping the overall bridge together. This capstone component is also similar to the box at the top of an organization chart that lists the chief executive officer as the designated head of a function. This level defines the basis for all other components in an enterprise's ERM model, influencing how strategies and objectives should be established, how risk-related business activities are structured, and how risks are identified and acted upon. The COSO ERM internal environment component consists of the following elements:

- **Risk management philosophy.** These are the shared attitudes and beliefs that characterize how the enterprise considers risk in everything it does. More than a message in a code of conduct, a risk management philosophy is the attitude that should allow stakeholders at all levels to respond to high-risk proposals with an answer along the lines of "No, that's not the kind of venture our company will be interested in." Of course, an enterprise with a different philosophy might respond to this same proposal with an answer along the lines of "Sounds interesting—what's the expected rate of return?" Neither response is really wrong, but an enterprise should try to develop a consistent philosophy and attitude to how it accepts risky ventures. This risk philosophy is important when internal auditors evaluate SOx internal controls.
- **Risk appetite.** As discussed previously, appetite is the amount of risk an enterprise is willing to accept in the pursuit of its objectives. An appetite for risk can be measured in either quantitative or qualitative terms, but all levels of management should have a general understanding of their enterprise's overall risk appetite. The term *appetite* was not often used by internal auditors and other managers prior to COSO ERM, but it is a useful expression that describes an overall risk philosophy.
- **Board of directors' attitudes.** The board and its committees have a very important role in overseeing and guiding an enterprise's risk environment. The independent, outside directors in particular should closely review management actions, ask appropriate questions, and serve as a check and balance control for the enterprise. When a senior enterprise officer has an "it can't happen here" attitude regarding possible risks at various levels, members of the board should ask the hard questions about how the enterprise would react if one of those events actually does happen.
- **Integrity and ethical values.** This important ERM internal environment element requires more than just a published code of conduct; it includes a

well-thought-out mission statement and integrity standards. These materials help to build a strong corporate culture to guide the enterprise at all levels in making risk-based decisions. A strong corporate culture, as well as a written code of conduct, is an important element of an enterprise's integrity and ethical values. Stronger ethical values might have helped enterprises such as the failed Enron and WorldCom, discussed previously, to better avoid the accounting scandals that led to the enactment of SOx. This area should be an essential component in every ERM framework today.

- **Commitment to competence.** *Competence* refers to the knowledge and skills necessary to perform assigned tasks. Management decides how these critical tasks will be accomplished through developing strategies and assigning the proper people to perform them. We have all seen enterprises that do not have this type of commitment. Senior management sometimes makes grand and loud plans to accomplish some goal but then does little to achieve it. The stock market frequently punishes failures in such activities. With a strong commitment to competence, managers at all levels should take steps to achieve their promised goals.
- **Organizational structure.** An enterprise should develop an organizational structure with clear lines of authority, responsibility, and appropriate reporting. Every professional has seen situations where the organization does not allow for appropriate lines of communication. For example, prior to SOx, many internal audit functions had published organizational charts showing them reporting to their board audit committees, but this relationship often was only on paper with limited communications beyond periodic but very brief audit committee meetings. While SOx has changed this, there remain environments where the audit committee still has only very limited interaction with its internal audit function, representing a failure in organizational structure.
- **Assignments of authority and responsibility.** This ERM component refers to the extent or degree to which authority and responsibility are assigned or delegated. The trend in many enterprises today is to push approval authority responsibilities down the organization chart, giving lower-level and even first-line employees greater authorization and approval authority. A related trend has been to flatten organizations by eliminating middle management levels. These structures usually encourage employee creativity, faster response times, and greater customer satisfaction. However, this type of customer-facing organization requires strong procedures and rules for the staff as well as ongoing management so that lower-level staff decisions can be overruled if necessary. All individuals should know how their actions interrelate and contribute to the overall objectives of the enterprise. A strong enterprise code of conduct is a critical element here.
- **Human resources standards.** Practices regarding employee hiring, training, compensation, promotion, disciplining, and all other actions send messages regarding what is favored, tolerated, or forbidden. When management winks at or ignores some gray-area activities rather than taking a strong stand, that message is informally and quickly communicated to others. Strong standards are needed to ensure that human resources rules are communicated to all stakeholders and are enforced.

Two internal environment components of COSO ERM, the enterprise's risk management philosophy and its relative appetite for risk, feed other elements of the COSO ERM framework. While a risk management philosophy can be considered in terms of board of directors' attitudes and human resources policies, among others, risk appetite is often a softer measure where an enterprise has determined that it will accept some risks but reject others in terms of their likelihood and impact. Exhibit 7.6 shows a risk appetite map illustrating where an enterprise should recognize the range in which it is willing to accept risks in terms of their likelihood and impact. This diagram says an enterprise may be willing to get involved in a high-negative-impact project if there is a low likelihood of an occurrence. There is a third dimension to this chart as well. An enterprise will sometimes have a greater appetite for a more risky endeavor if there is a higher potential return.

COSO ERM Objective Setting

Ranked right below the internal environment in the COSO ERM framework, *objective setting* outlines important conditions to help management create an effective ERM process. This ERM element says that in addition to an effective internal environment, an enterprise must establish a series of strategic objectives, aligned with its mission and covering operations, reporting, and compliance activities. COSO ERM emphasizes that a mission statement is a crucial element for setting objectives; it is a general, formalized statement of purpose and a building block for the development of specific functional strategies. Often just a simple, straightforward statement, a mission statement should summarize

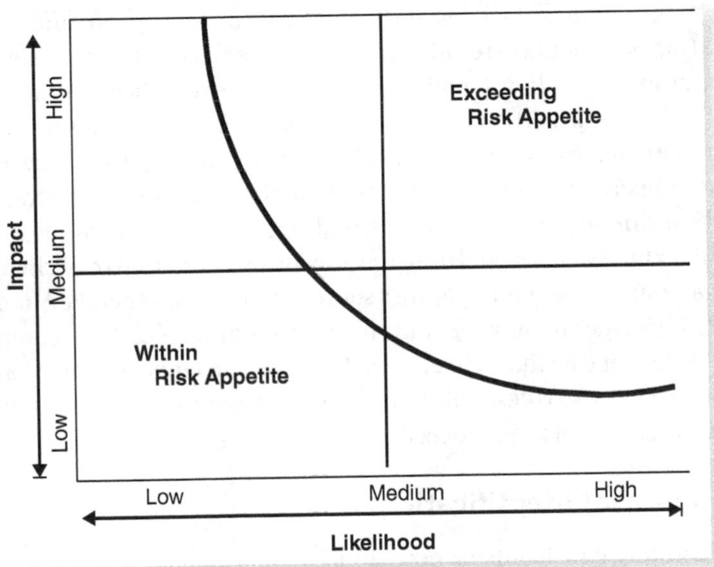

EXHIBIT 7.6 Risk Appetite Map

Source: COSO Enterprise Risk Management: Understanding the New Integrated ERM Framework, Robert R. Moeller. Copyright © 2007 John Wiley & Sons. Reprinted with the permission of John Wiley & Sons.

an enterprise's objectives and its overall attitude toward risks. Properly done and delivered, a mission statement should encourage an enterprise to develop high-level strategic objectives and then to help select and implement operations, reporting, and compliance objectives. While operations objectives pertain to the effectiveness and efficiency of the enterprise in achieving profitability and performance, reporting and compliance goals cover the reporting of performance and compliance with laws and regulations. COSO ERM calls for an enterprise to formally define its goals with a direct linkage to its mission statement, along with measurement criteria to assess if it is achieving these risk management objectives.

The ERM internal environment component of understanding the enterprise's risk management philosophy and its risk appetite calls for the objective-setting component to formally define that risk appetite in terms of a tolerance for risk. Tolerances are guidelines that an enterprise should use, at all levels, to assess whether or not it will accept risks. Establishing and enforcing risk tolerances can be very difficult, with potential problems if these rules are not clearly defined, well understood, and strictly enforced. An enterprise should establish tolerable ranges of acceptable risks in many areas. For example, products coming off production lines might have acceptable preestablished error rates of less than some value, such as an error rate no greater than 0.005%. That is an acceptably low error rate in many areas, and production management here would accept the risk of any product warranty claims or damage to their reputation if there were errors within that relatively narrow limit. Of course, today's quality assurance emphasis on Six Sigma programs brings those tolerance limits much tighter.[4]

The point here is that an enterprise should define its risk-related strategies and objectives. Within those guidelines, it should decide on its appetite and tolerances for these risks. That is, it should determine the level of risks it is willing to accept, and given those risk tolerance rules, how far it is willing to deviate from these preestablished measures. Exhibit 7.7 outlines the elements relationship of COSO ERM's objective-setting component. Starting with an overall mission, the approach is to (1) develop strategic objectives to support accomplishment of that mission, (2) establish a strategy to meet objectives, (3) define any related objectives, and (4) define risk appetites to complete that strategy. This exhibit was adapted from the previously referenced published COSO ERM guidance materials. These materials are a source to gain a more detailed understanding of COSO ERM. In order to manage and control risks at all levels, an enterprise needs to set its objectives and define its tolerances for having to engage in risky practices and for its adherence to these rules. Things will not work if the enterprise establishes some risk-related objectives but then proceeds to ignore them.

COSO ERM Event Identification

Events are enterprise incidents or occurrences, internal or external, that affect the implementation of an ERM strategy and the achievement of its objectives. While an internal auditor's tendency is to think of events in a negative sense—determining what went wrong—they can be positive as well. Many enterprises today have strong performance-monitoring tools in place, with the monitoring process of costs, budgets, quality

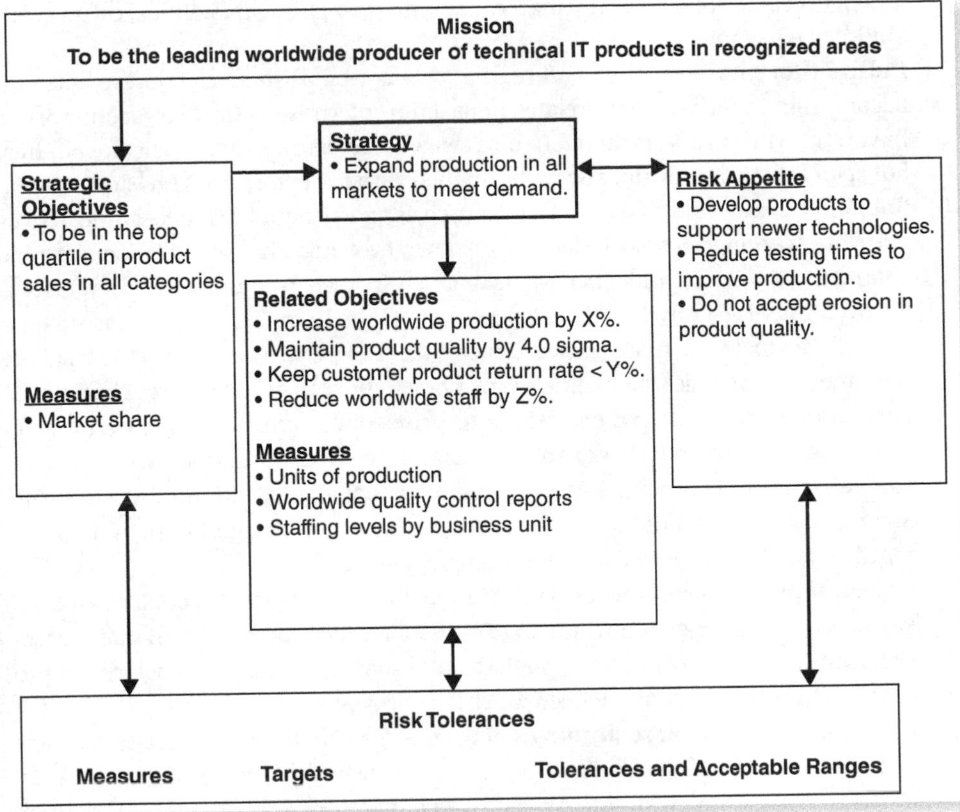

EXHIBIT 7.7 COSO ERM Risk Objective-Setting Component

Source: COSO Enterprise Risk Management: Understanding the New Integrated ERM Framework, Robert R. Moeller. Copyright © 2007 John Wiley & Sons. Reprinted with the permission of John Wiley & Sons.

assurance, compliance, and the like. However, going beyond a meter on a production assembly line, monitoring processes should include:

- **External economic events.** A wide range of external events need to be monitored to help achieve an enterprise's ERM objectives. Both short- and long-term events can impact an enterprise's strategic objectives. As an example, in December 2001, after some currency market turmoil, Argentina declared a major default of its public debt. This external event had a major impact on international credit markets, suppliers of agricultural commodities, and other business dealings in South America. External economic *event identification* here requires an enterprise to go beyond reported news headlines and raise the flag to suggest that yes, such a currency default may highlight an enterprise risk-related event.
- **Natural environmental events.** Whether fire, flood, or earthquakes, numerous events can become incidents in ERM risk identification. Impacts here may include

loss of access to some key raw material, damage to physical facilities, or unavailability of personnel.

- **Political events.** New laws and regulations as well as some election results can become significant risk event–related impacts on enterprises. Many larger enterprises have a government affairs function that reviews developments and lobbies for change, but such functions may not always be aligned with the enterprise's ERM objectives.
- **Social factors.** While an external event such as an earthquake is sudden and arrives with little warning, most social factors are slowly evolving. These include demographic changes, social mores, and other events that may impact an enterprise and its customers over time. The growth of the Hispanic population in the United States is such an example. As more and more Hispanic people move to a city, for example, the teaching requirements in public schools and the mix of selections in grocery stores changes.
- **Internal infrastructure events.** Enterprises often make changes that trigger other risk-related events. For example, a change in customer service arrangements can cause major complaints and a drop in customer satisfaction in a retail unit. Strong customer demand for a new product may cause changes in plant capacity requirements and the need for additional personnel.
- **Internal process–related events.** Similar to infrastructure events, changes in key processes can trigger a wide range of risk identification events. In many cases, risk identification may not be immediate, and some time may pass before the process-related events signal the need for risk identification.
- **External and internal technological events.** Every enterprise faces a wide assortment of technological events that may trigger the need for formal risk identification. Some may be gradual, while others, such as the shift to a Web environment, are more sudden. In other cases, a company may suddenly release a new improvement that causes competitors everywhere to jump into action. Although the idea seems commonplace today, when Merrill Lynch launched its Cash Management Account (CMA) concept in the mid-1980s, it caused a major stir in the financial services industries. CMA was a service that combined customer stock brokerage, bank checking accounts, and other financial services all under one roof. We forget today that in the past all such accounts required separate providers with essentially no linkages between them.

An enterprise needs to clearly define its significant risk events and then have processes in place to monitor them in order to take any necessary appropriate actions. This is a forward-thinking type of process that is often difficult to recognize in many enterprises, but looking at these internal and external potential risk events and deciding which require further attention can be a difficult process. Some are immediate needs, others future-directed. COSO ERM supporting materials suggest that an enterprise should establish processes to review potentially significant risks and then consider some of the following approaches:

- **Event inventories.** Management should develop risk-related listings of events common to the enterprise's specific industry and functional area and attempt to establish some type of "lessons learned" archive source. This is the type of data that can be supplied by longer tenure members of an enterprise who can offer "We tried this several years ago, but . . ." types of comments.

- **Facilitated workshops.** An enterprise can establish cross-functional workshops to discuss potential risk factors that may evolve from various internal or external events. This can result in action plans to correct the potential risks. While the approach sounds good, it is often a challenge to allocate sufficient time to meet in cross-functional groups to talk about such risks.
- **Interviews, questionnaires, and surveys.** Information regarding potential risk events can come from a wide variety of sources, such as customer satisfaction letters or employee exit interviews. This information should be captured and classified to identify anything that might point to a risk event.
- **Leading events and escalation triggers.** The idea here is to establish a series of business unit measurements to monitor risk tolerance objectives and promote remedial action. For example, an enterprise's IT group may establish an objective to maintain strong security controls over the risk of a system intrusion. With a measure of the number of identified intrusion attempts during a period, a trigger of perhaps three intrusions incidents in a given month might trigger further action. Dashboard-type software tools can often be used here. These increasingly common software tools are similar to the dashboard of an automobile, where indicators will flash signals for such conditions as low oil pressure or overheating. Risk status is reported through some simple, easy-to-comprehend graphics monitors, such as red, yellow, and green warning lights.
- **Loss event data tracking.** While the dashboard approach monitors risk events as they happen, it is often valuable to put things in more perspective after the passage of some time. Loss event tracking refers to using both internal and public database sources to track activity in areas of interest. These sources can also cover a wide variety of areas ranging from leading economic indicators to internal equipment failure rates. Again here, an enterprise should install effective risk identification processes to track both internal and external risk-related events.

The risk identification tools and approaches just discussed can yield some very valuable and useful information to an enterprise that identifies risks and opportunities. These require good analyses of the data as well as initiating plans for action, whether to shield from the risk or to take advantage of potential opportunities.

COSO ERM Risk Assessment

While the internal environment component is COSO ERM's cornerstone and a later section will discuss monitoring as its foundation, the risk assessment component is the ERM framework's core. Risk assessment allows an enterprise to consider the impact that potential risk-related events may have overall on an enterprise's achievement of its objectives. These risks should be assessed from two perspectives: the likelihood of the risk occurring, and its potential impact. A key part of this risk assessment process, however, is the need to consider the very important concepts of inherent and *residual risks* as well as:

- **Inherent risk.** As defined by the U.S. government's Office of Management and Budget, inherent risk is the "potential for waste, loss, unauthorized use, or misappropriation due to the nature of an activity itself." Major factors that affect enterprise-inherent risk are the size of its budget, the strength and sophistication of management, and simply the very nature of its activities. Inherent risk is outside the control of management and usually stems from external factors. For example, the major retailer Walmart is so large and dominant in its markets that it faces various inherent risks due to just its sheer size.

- **Residual risk.** This is the risk that remains after other management responses to risk threats and countermeasures have been applied. There will virtually always be some level of residual risk.

An enterprise will always face some mixture of inherent and residual risks. After management has addressed the risks that came out of the risk identification process, they will still have some residual risks to remedy. In addition, there always are some inherent risks where they can do little. Walmart, for example, can take some steps to reduce its market-dominance-related inherent risks, but can do essentially nothing regarding the inherent risk of a major natural disaster such as an earthquake covering an important area of its operations.

Risk likelihood and impact are two other key components necessary for performing risk assessments. *Likelihood* is the probability or possibility that the risk will occur. In many instances, this can be a key management assessment stated in the terms of high, medium, or low likelihood of the risk occurring. There are also some good quantitative tools to develop likelihood estimates, but it does little good to estimate the likelihood of a risk occurring unless there are strong supporting data.

Estimating the *impact* of a risk event occurrence is a bit easier. Some risk events may cause minor but not irrecoverable impacts on an enterprise. Others can be all but disastrous. The failure of a significant IT server and a related database can have a significant impact if not supported by appropriate backup and recovery processes. As part of an impact estimate, an enterprise can develop some relatively accurate estimates such as the cost of replacing facilities and equipment, the cost of restoring systems, and the cost of lost business due to the failure. However, the concept behind ERM is not to develop precise, actuarial-level calculations regarding these risks but to provide for an effective risk management framework. Detailed calculations can be delegated to insurance estimators and others.

An analysis of risk likelihoods and potential impacts can be developed through a series of quantitative and qualitative measures. The basic idea is to assess all of the identified risks and rank them in terms of likelihood and impact in a consistent manner. Without going through a detailed quantitative analysis, each identified risk can then be ranked on an overall relative scale of 1 to 10, with consideration given to the impact and likelihood of each. This can be achieved through a focused management group decision process where each of the identified risks is reviewed and ranked with respect to this scale. Exhibit 7.8 shows a series of risks for a sample company rated on high, medium, or low relative values. For a larger enterprise, the risks could be scaled 1 to 10 to allow greater granularity. The idea is to identify risks and assign some relative rankings and to identify the risks that should receive the most thorough management attention.

Overall approaches to reviewing these various likelihood and impact risks need to be considered. Risk assessment is a key component of the COSO ERM framework. This is where an enterprise evaluates all of the risks that might impact its various

EXHIBIT 7.8 Risk Likelihood and Impact Mapping Example

Risk Definition	Impact	Likelihood	Risk Ranking
Failure to record sales activity accurately and timely may misstate financial reports.	**High**: Accounting errors may have a material impact on financial and operational information.	**Medium:** Despite strong procedures, newer personnel in various location may make errors.	8
Failure to understand current and changing laws and regulations may result in inability to comply with laws in multiple operations jurisdictions.	**Medium:** Even small, technical violations of most regulations should not have a material effect on operations.	**High**: With worldwide operations in multiple jurisdictions, violations –if only technical–can occur.	7
Inadequately controlled segregation of duties may allow employees to process unauthorized, fraudulent transactions.	**High**: Fraudulent operations could have significant impacts on company operations.	**Low**: Ongoing internal audits and stronger management control practices should prevent such control breakdown events.	5

objectives, considers the potential likelihood and impact of each of these risks, considers their interrelationship on a unit-by-unit or total enterprise basis, and then develops strategies for appropriate responses. In some respects, this COSO ERM risk assessment process is not too different from the classic risk assessment techniques that have been used by internal auditors over the years. What is unique here is that COSO ERM suggests that an enterprise should take a total approach, across all units and all major strategic concerns, to identify its risks in a consistent and thorough manner.

COSO ERM Risk Response Elements

Having assessed and identified its more significant risks, the COSO ERM's *risk response process* calls for a careful review of estimated risk likelihoods and potential impacts, with consideration given to their associated costs and benefits, to develop appropriate risk response strategies, following any of four basic risk strategies:

1. **Avoidance.** This is a strategy of walking away from a risk—such as selling a business unit that gives rise to a risk, exiting from a risky geographical area, or dropping a product line. The difficulty is that enterprises often do not drop a product line or walk away until after the risk event has occurred with its associated costs. Unless an enterprise has a very low appetite for risk, it is difficult to walk away from an otherwise successful business area or product line just on the basis of a potential future risk. Avoidance can be a potentially costly strategy if investments were made to get into an area, followed by a subsequent pullout to avoid the risk.

A collective lessons-learned understanding of past activities can often help with this strategy. If the enterprise had been involved in some area in the past with unfavorable consequences, this may be a good way to avoid the risk once again. With the tendency of constant changes and short employment tenures, this collective history is too often lost and forgotten. An enterprise's well-understood and well-communicated appetite for risk is perhaps the most important consideration when deciding if a risk-avoidance strategy is appropriate.

2. **Reduction.** A wide range of business decisions may be able to reduce certain risks. For example, product diversification may reduce the risk of too strong of a reliance on one key product line, or splitting IT operations into two geographically separate locations will reduce the risk of some catastrophic failure. There are a wide range of often effective strategies to reduce risks at all levels that go down to the obvious and mundane, such as cross-training employees to reduce the risk of loss of productivity if someone departs unexpectedly.
3. **Sharing.** Virtually all enterprises regularly share some of their risks through the purchase of insurance, but other risk-sharing techniques are available as well. For financial transactions, an enterprise can engage in hedging operations to protect from possible price fluctuations, or an enterprise can share potential business risks and rewards through corporate joint venture agreements or other structural arrangements. The idea is to have another party accept some of a potential risk as well as share in any resultant rewards.
4. **Acceptance.** This is the strategy of no action, such as when an enterprise self-insures by taking no action to reduce a potential risk. Essentially, an enterprise should look at a risk's likelihood and impact in light of its established risk tolerance and then decide whether or not to accept that risk. For the many and varied risks that approach an enterprise, acceptance is often an appropriate strategy.

Management must develop a general response strategy for each of its risks using an approach built around one or a mixture of the just described risk-avoidance strategies. In doing so, it should consider the costs versus benefits of each potential risk response as well as strategies that best align with the enterprise's overall risk appetite. For example, an enterprise's recognition that the impact of a given risk is relatively low would be balanced against a low risk tolerance that suggests that insurance should be purchased to provide a potential risk response. For many risks, appropriate responses are obvious and almost universally understood. An IT operation, for example, spends the time and resources to back up its key data files and implements a business continuity plan. There are typically no questions regarding the need for these basic approaches, but management may question the frequency of backup processes or how often the continuity plan needs to be tested. That is, they may question the extent and cost of planned risk prevention measures.

An enterprise should go back to its established risk objectives as well as the tolerance ranges for those objectives, readdressing both the likelihoods and impacts associated with each to develop an overall set of the planned risk responses. This is perhaps the most difficult step in building an effective COSO ERM program. It is comparatively easy to identify a 5% likelihood risk that there may be a fire in the scrap materials bin and then to establish a risk response remedy to install a nearby fire extinguisher. However, responses to most risks are complex and require fairly detailed planning and analysis. If there is a risk that an enterprise could lose an entire manufacturing operation due to a key but old equipment plant production failure, potential risk responses might include:

- Acquire backup production equipment to serve as spare parts for cannibalization.
- Shut down the manufacturing production line with plans to move it elsewhere.
- Arrange for a specialized shop to rebuild/reconstruct the old equipment.
- Reengineer the manufactured product and plan for new product introduction.

Developing risk responses requires a significant amount of planning and strategic thinking. The several risk response alternatives may involve costs, time, and detailed project planning. For example, one of the older equipment response strategies outlined here is to acquire a set of backup equipment. If that is to be the approved strategy, action must be taken to acquire the old backup equipment before this activity can even be identified as an actual risk response strategy. The idea is that all risks listed on such an analysis should be measured against the same impact factors, based on an accept, avoid, share, or reduce risk strategy.

COSO ERM calls for risks to be considered and evaluated on an entity- or portfolio-wide basis. This can sometimes be a difficult process in a large, multiunit, multiproduct enterprise, but it provides a starting point in getting these various risks organized for identification of the more significant risk that may impact the enterprise. The idea is to look at these various potential risks, their probability of occurrence, and the impacts of each. A good analysis here should highlight areas for more detailed attention.

COSO ERM Control Activities

ERM's *control activities* are the policies and procedures necessary to ensure action on identified risk responses. Although some of these activities may only relate to an identified and approved risk response in an area of the enterprise, they often overlap across multiple functions and units. The control activities component of COSO ERM should be tightly linked with the risk response strategies and actions previously discussed.

Having selected appropriate risk responses, an enterprise should select control activities necessary to ensure that they are executed in a timely and efficient manner. The process of determining if control activities are performing properly is very similar to completing SOx Section 404 internal control assessments as discussed in Chapter 5. COSO ERM calls for approaches of identifying, documenting, testing, and then validating these risk protection controls. Having gone through the COSO ERM risk event identification, assessment, and response processes, risk monitoring requires the following steps:

1. Develop a strong understanding of the significant risks and establish control procedures to monitor or correct for them.
2. Create fire drill–type testing procedures to determine if those risk-related control procedures are working effectively.

3. Perform tests of risk-monitoring processes to determine if they are working effectively and as expected.
4. Make adjustments or improvements as necessary to improve risk-monitoring processes.

This four-element process includes steps to review, test, and then assert that internal control processes are working adequately. A major difference, of course, is that under SOx an enterprise *is legally required* to assert the adequacy of their internal controls. There are no such legal requirements with COSO ERM, but an enterprise should install risk-monitoring control activities to monitor the various risks it has identified. Because of the critical nature of many risks to an enterprise, risk monitoring can be very critical to an enterprise's overall health. Many control activities under COSO internal controls are fairly easy to identify and test due to the accounting nature of many internal controls and generally include the following areas:

- **Separation of duties.** Essentially, the person who initiates a transaction should not be the same person who authorizes that transaction.
- **Audit trails.** Processes should be organized such that final results can be easily traced back to the transactions that created those results.
- **Security and integrity.** Control processes should have appropriate control procedures such that only authorized persons can review or modify them.
- **Documentation.** Processes should be appropriately documented.

These control procedures and others are fairly well recognized and applicable to all internal control processes in an enterprise and also somewhat applicable to many risk-related events. Many professionals, whether or not they have a financial or internal auditing background, can often define some of the key controls that are necessary in most business processes. For example, if asked to identify the types of internal controls that should be built into an accounts payable system, many professionals would say that checks issued from the system must be authorized by independent persons, that accounting records must be in place to keep track of the checks issued, and that the check-issuing process should be such that only authorized persons can initiate such a financial transaction. These are generally well- and widely understood control procedures. An enterprise often faces a more difficult task in identifying control activities to support its ERM framework. Although there is no accepted or standard set of ERM control activities at this time, the COSO ERM documentation suggests several areas:

- **Top-level reviews.** Senior management should be very aware of the identified risk events within organizational units and perform regular top-level reviews on the status of identified risks.
- **Direct functional or activity management.** In addition to top-level reviews, functional and direct unit managers should have a key role in risk control activity monitoring. This is particularly important where control activities take place within separate operating units, with the need for communications and risk resolution across enterprise channels.

- **Information processing.** Whether it is IT systems–based processes or softer forms such a paper or messages, information processing represents a key component in an enterprise's risk-related control activities. Appropriate control procedures should be established with an emphasis on enterprise IT processes and risks.
- **Physical controls.** Many risk-related concerns involve physical assets such as equipment, inventories, security, and physical plants. Whether physical inventories, inspections, or plant security procedures, an enterprise should install appropriate risk-based physical control activity procedures.
- **Performance indicators.** The typical enterprise today employs a wide range of financial and operational reporting tools that also can support risk event–related performance reporting. Where necessary, performance tools should be modified to support this important ERM control activity component.
- **Segregation of duties.** A classic control activity; the person who initiates certain actions should not be the same person who approves them.

These control activities can be expanded to cover other key areas. Some will be specific to individual units within the enterprise, but each of them, singly and collectively, should be important components of supporting the enterprise's ERM framework.

COSO ERM Information and Communication

This COSO ERM component is a separate set of risk-related processes linking other COSO ERM components, as described in Exhibit 7.9 showing the information flows across the COSO ERM components. For example, the risk response component receives residual and inherent risk inputs from risk assessment as well as risk tolerance support from the objective-setting component. ERM risk response then provides risk response and risk portfolio data to control activities as well as feedback to risk assessment. Standing alone, the monitoring component does not have any direct information connections but has overall responsibility for reviewing all of these functions.

While it is relatively easy to describe how information should be communicated from one COSO ERM component to another in a simple flow diagram, this is a far more complex process in practice. Many enterprises have a complex web of often not very well linked operational and financial information systems for their basic processes. These linkages become even more complex for many ERM processes given that many basic enterprise applications do not directly lend themselves to risk identification, assessment, and risk response–type processes. Going beyond a comprehensive ERM information application for an enterprise, there is a need to develop risk monitoring and communication systems that link with customers, suppliers, and other stakeholders.

While the information half of the ERM information and communication component is normally thought of in terms of IT strategic and operational information systems, ERM communication is the second aspect of this component. It talks about communication beyond just IT applications, such as the need for mechanisms to assure that all stakeholders receive messages regarding the enterprise's interest in managing its risks. A major component of these communication messages should be the use of a common risk language throughout the enterprise regarding the roles and responsibilities of all

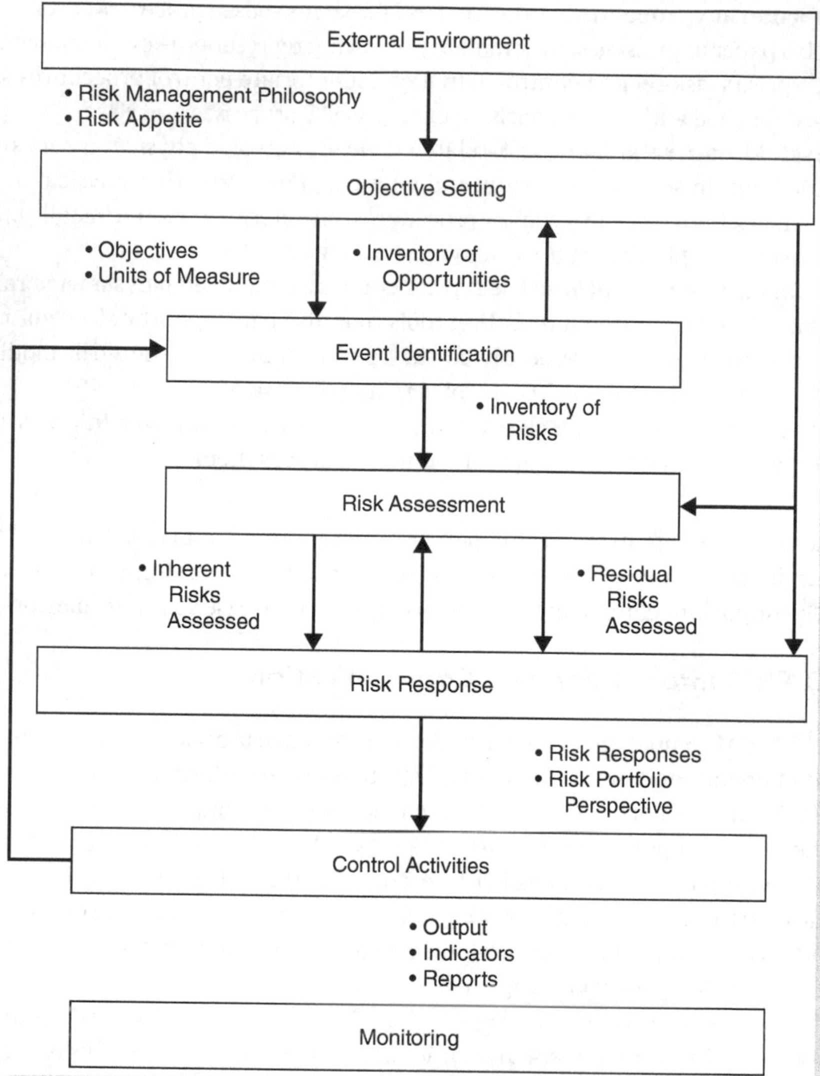

EXHIBIT 7.9 Information and Communication Flows in ERM Components

Source: COSO Enterprise Risk Management: Understanding the New Integrated ERM Framework, Robert R. Moeller. Copyright © 2007 John Wiley & Sons. Reprinted with the permission of John Wiley & Sons.

stakeholders regarding their risk management–related roles. COSO ERM will be of little value to an enterprise unless the overall message of its importance is communicated to all stakeholders in a common and consistent manner.

COSO ERM Monitoring

Placed at the base of the stack of ERM framework components, ERM monitoring is necessary to determine that all installed ERM components work effectively. People in an enterprise change, as do supporting processes and both internal and external conditions, but the monitoring component helps assure that ERM is working effectively on a continuous basis. These include processes to flag exceptions or violations in other components of the overall ERM process. For example, an accounts receivable billing function should identify the overall financial and operational risks if customer bills are not paid on a timely basis. An ongoing—almost real-time—credit collections monitoring tool could provide senior management with day-to-day and trending data on the status of collections. Dashboard monitoring tools, discussed in Chapter 11 on *continuous auditing*, are types of ERM monitors that can also work here.

Going beyond dashboard monitoring tools, enterprise management should take an overall responsibility for ERM monitoring. In order to establish an effective ERM framework, monitoring should include ongoing reviews of the overall ERM process ranging from identified objectives to the progress of ongoing ERM control activities, including the following types of activities:

- Implementation of ongoing management reporting mechanisms such as for cash positions, unit sales, and key financial data. An enterprise should not have to wait until fiscal month end for these types of status reports, and quick-response "flash reports" should be initiated.
- Periodic risk-related alert reporting processes that monitor key aspects of established risk criteria, including acceptable error rates or items held in suspense. Such reporting should emphasize statistical trends and comparisons both with prior periods and other industry sectors.
- Current and periodic status reporting of risk-related findings and recommendations from internal and external audit reports, including the status of ERM-related SOx-identified gaps and prior internal audit report recommendations.
- Updated risk-related information from sources such as government-revised rules, industry trends, and general economic news. Again, this type of economic and operational reporting should be available for managers at all levels.

Separate or individual evaluation monitoring refers to detailed reviews of individual risk processes by a qualified reviewer such as internal audit. Here the review can be limited to specific areas or cover the entire ERM process for an enterprise unit, and internal audit is often the best internal source to perform such specific ERM reviews. The role of internal audit in the ERM process and with monitoring in particular is discussed in the following sections.

7.4 OTHER DIMENSIONS OF COSO ERM: ENTERPRISE RISK OBJECTIVES

Although many look at COSO ERM from the perspective of the front-facing side of its three-dimensional framework, the two other dimensions—the operational and organizational levels—should always be considered. Each component of COSO ERM operates in this three-dimensional space where each must be considered in terms of the other related categories. The top-facing components of strategic, operations, reporting, and compliance risk objectives are important for understanding and implementing COSO ERM. In addition, while Exhibit 7.5 shows each of these top-facing risk objectives as having the same relative size or width, the category of operations-level risk objectives is often viewed as a much broader and higher-exposure risk category than the others.

Operations Risk Management Objectives

There are many types of operations risks that can impact an enterprise. Following the three-dimensioned ERM framework, the operations-level risk objective calls for the identification of risks for each enterprise unit or component. This identification of operations-level risk objectives often requires detailed information gathering and analysis, particularly for a larger enterprise covering multiple geographic areas, product lines, or business processes. Direct managers of individual units usually have the best understanding of their operational risks, and that information can become lost when consolidated for higher-level reporting. In order to gather more detailed background information on potential operations risks, information can often be gathered through internal audit reviews or surveys of persons directly impacted by these risks. A survey of direct on-the-floor members of the enterprise, along with follow-up questions, will allow the development of a consistent set of cataloged operations risks across all levels of the enterprise. The questions asked here would be similar to the types of detailed questions often used in internal audit internal control assessments, and the results of any available data here could become a basis for developing a better understanding.

Circulated through all levels of an enterprise, with a message encouraging stakeholders to respond in a candid manner, these types of surveys can often gather important information regarding potential risks at detailed operational levels. A manager of a remote operating plant may not have adequately communicated concerns about some plant-level operational risk. A broadly based and confidential survey often will better allow people to communicate those often local-level operations risks up through the enterprise.

With ERM's portfolio view of risks, an enterprise should avoid rolling things up to too much of a summary level, missing or rounding off important lower-level risks. Whatever the level in an organizational hierarchy or the geographic location, managers at all levels should be aware that they are responsible for accepting and managing the risks within their own operational units. Too often, unit managers may gain an impression that risk management is only some senior-level, headquarters type of concern. The importance of COSO ERM and operations risk management should be communicated to all levels of an enterprise. Internal auditors should act as eyes and ears here and report all observed operations risks.

Reporting Risk Management Objectives

This ERM objective covers the reliability of an enterprise's reporting, including the internal and external reporting of financial and nonfinancial data. Accurate reporting is critical to an enterprise's success in many dimensions. While we frequently see news reports regarding the discovery of inaccurate corporate financial reporting and the resultant stock market repercussions for the offending entity, that same inaccurate reporting can cause problems in many areas.

No matter what industry, an enterprise faces major risks from inaccurate reporting at any unit or area. Operating units must make certain that reported results are correct before they are passed up to the next level in the organization, and consolidated numbers must be accurate, whether financial reports, tax returns, or any of a myriad of other areas. While good internal controls are necessary to ensure accurate reporting, ERM is concerned about the risk of authorizing and releasing inaccurate reports. Strong internal controls should minimize the risk of errors, and an enterprise should always consider the risks associated with inaccurate reporting. Small errors and discrepancies can be ignored over time until there is a major error that needs to be disclosed. The risk of such inaccurate reporting should be a concern at all levels of the enterprise.

Legal and Regulatory Compliance Risk Objectives

Enterprises of any nature must comply with a wide range of laws and government-imposed or industry regulations. While compliance risks can be monitored and recognized, legal risks are sometimes totally unanticipated. In the United States, for example, an aggressive plaintiff legal system can pose a major risk to otherwise well-intentioned enterprises. Asbestos litigation during the 1990s and beyond is an example. A fibrous mineral, asbestos was a natural insulation material, once used extensively and considered totally benign. But too much direct contact with asbestos fibers over time was subsequently found to cause severe lung problems and even death. Miners engaged in the extraction of asbestos have met that fate. In the past, asbestos was used in many products, such as wrappers to insulate heating pipes or as fire protection barriers. While the risks to persons working or living in a structure with these asbestos-sealed pipes are fairly minimal, aggressive litigators have brought actions against corporations, claiming that anyone who could have had any contact, no matter how minimal, with a product that used asbestos could be at risk sometime in the future. The result was litigation directed against companies who had manufactured products containing even small amounts of asbestos, calling for damages based on potential human risks in future years. Because of huge damage awards, virtually all the major corporations that once used asbestos have gone bankrupt, out of business, or have had to pay huge court-imposed damage losses. This is a type of legal risk that is very difficult to anticipate but that can be disastrous to an enterprise.

COSO ERM recommends that compliance-related risks be considered for each of the risk framework components, whether in the context of the internal environment, objective setting, or risk monitoring, as well as across the enterprise. These are important elements of the risk management framework that need to be communicated and understood.

All enterprises face a wide range of legal and *regulatory compliance* requirements, with some impacting virtually all enterprises and others related to only single business units in a specialized industry sector. The nature of those compliance risks needs to be communicated and understood through all levels of an enterprise. This is an area where an enterprise may accept a certain level of risk in terms of its concerns regarding legal compliance.

While an enterprise should not deliberately ignore a major law because of a feeling that it will never be caught, it should always take a reasoned approach to risks in conjunction with its overall philosophy and risk appetites. For example, many regulatory rules specify that all expenditures must be supported by a receipt. While there usually are no reasonableness guidelines, one enterprise could decide that "all expenditures" goes down to an employee's travel expenses of less than $1, while another will require receipts for anything above $25. The latter enterprise has made a decision that the costs of documenting these small expenditures is greater than any fine it might receive if caught in a regulatory compliance issue. This type of risk-related decision is similar to the AS5 financial internal controls rules for SOx discussed in Chapter 5. In order to manage and establish legal and regulatory risk objectives, the board of directors, the CEO and members of management need to have an understanding of the nature and extent of all of the regulatory risks the enterprise faces. The legal department, key managers, internal audit, and others can help in assembling this information. There are many regulatory enterprise-level risks ranging from major to minor, but regulatory risks are never "minor" when an enterprise is found to be in violation of one or another of them.

7.5 ENTITY-LEVEL RISKS

The third dimension of the COSO ERM framework calls risks to be considered on an organization or entity level. The Exhibit 7.2 COSO ERM framework shows four divisions or slices in this framework dimension: entity-level, division, business unit, and subsidiary risks. This is not a prescribed company-type division, and ERM suggests that risks should closely follow the given enterprise's official organization chart. COSO ERM risks should be identified and managed within each significant organizational unit, including risks on an entity-wide basis through individual business units.

An enterprise with four major operating divisions and with multiple business units or subsidiary units under each would have an ERM framework that reflected all of these units. While these risks are important on an overall organizational level, there should be a level of consideration on a unit-by-unit basis to as low a level as necessary to allow the enterprise to understand and manage its risks. COSO ERM does not specify how thinly these unit-level risks should be sliced, and the criticality and materiality of individual business units should be given consideration. For a major fast-food restaurant chain with thousands of units, it almost certainly would not be reasonable to include each individual unit as a separate component in the risk model. Rather, management should define its organizational-level risks at a level of detail that will cover all significant, manageable risks.

Risks Encompassing the Entire Organization

Multiple risks at the business unit level should roll up to *entity-level risks*. While it is easy for an enterprise to consider some unit-level risks "not material"—using pre-SOx public accounting—consider a relatively small subsidiary in a third-world country that is manufacturing casual clothing. Often, such a unit would be so small in terms of corporate revenue contributions or its relative size that it can slip under the radar screen on a senior corporate level. However, if there were child labor issues at the host country, the enterprise may soon find itself at the center of attention regarding this small subsidiary operation. In such a situation, journalists may ask the CEO to publicly comment on policies and procedures at that subsidiary operation, even though the CEO may only vaguely know of its existence.

Our point here is that both major and seemingly small risks can impact an entire enterprise. The delivery of tainted food produced at one small unit of a large fast-food chain can impact the prospects and reputation of the total enterprise. While it is relatively easy to identify high-level entity-wide risks such as compliance with SOx Section 404, and to identify and monitor these as part of the COSO ERM process, care must be taken that smaller potential risks do not slip between the cracks. As risks are identified through organization-wide objective setting, they should be considered on an entity-wide basis as well as by individual operating units. Those individual unit risks should be first reviewed and consolidated to identify any key risks that may impact the overall organization. In addition, any organization-wide risks should be identified.

Business Unit–Level Risks

Risks occur at all levels of an enterprise, whether a major production division with multiple plants and thousands of employees or a minority ownership position in a foreign-country sales company. Risks must be considered in each significant organizational unit. The risks identified in the minority ownership position in a foreign-country sales company, for example, may be risks unique to that unit, but they should be rolled up to the overall entity. We have cited the example of entity-level risks that might result from failures in manufacturing or human rights standards at a small subsidiary in a third-world country. Risk events here can cause an embarrassment to the overall enterprise, but they should have been controlled all the way down to that small company unit. The previously discussed Bhopal, India, plant explosion disaster brought down the major parent corporation, Union Carbide, as mentioned.

Depending on the complexity and number of operating units, risk responsibility can often best start as a push-down process where corporate-level management will formally outline its major risk-related concerns and ask responsible management at each of the major divisions to survey risk objectives through the operating units within that division. In this manner, significant risks can be identified at all levels and then managed at levels where they can receive the most direct, local support.

A major concept surrounding COSO ERM is that an enterprise faces a wide range of significant risks at all levels. Some may be significant, while others may be just troubling annoyances and viewed as minor. The COSO ERM framework provides a mechanism to consider these risks; it is an important tool to help assure SOx compliance.

7.6 PUTTING IT ALL TOGETHER: AUDITING RISK AND COSO ERM PROCESSES

Easily confused with COSO internal controls, the COSO ERM framework outlines a risk management approach applicable to all industries and encompassing all types of risk. With its focus on recognizing an enterprise's appetite for risk, the need to look at an enterprise's overall portfolio of risks, and the need to apply risk management within the context of overall strategy setting, COSO ERM provides an excellent platform for considering an enterprise's overall risk environment. While COSO ERM is often ignored when looking at other internal control matters, internal auditors should have a CBOK general understanding of this important framework.

Internal auditors encounter risk and risk management issues in many audit review and analysis areas, and the effective internal auditor should understand risk management processes. All too often, an internal auditor will be performing an internal control review in some area and will be told that the area was or was not selected because of "risk considerations"—an easy set of words to use. The internal auditor should have a CBOK level of understanding of basic risk management processes to be able to ask the right questions and to review the adequacy of those risk management processes.

With a focus on the COSO ERM framework as well as general good risk management practices, internal audit can provide a service to their enterprise by planning and performing reviews of enterprise-level risk management processes. Whether acting as internal audit reviewers of controls or consultants to management, internal auditors should gain a good understanding of the COSO ERM framework. In addition, any internal audit review of enterprise ERM processes should be planned through risk-based internal audit project planning approaches as discussed in Chapter 16, using some of the following tools:

- **Process flowcharting.** As part of any identified ERM process, process flow charts can be useful in describing how risk management operates in an enterprise. This requires looking at documentation prepared for risk-related processes, determining if they are correct given current conditions, and describing the overall adequacy of all levels of enterprise risk processes. Internal audit process modeling and process flowcharts are discussed in Chapter 17.
- **Reviews of risk and control materials.** An ERM process often results in a large volume of guidance materials, documented procedures, report formats, and the like. There may often be value to an internal audit to review the risk and control materials from an effectiveness perspective.
- **Benchmarking.** Although an often misused term, *benchmarking* here is the process of looking at functions in another environment to assess their operations and to develop improved approaches based on the best practices of others. While gathering comparative information is often a difficult task due to the reluctance of competing enterprises to share it, adherence to the IIA's "Progress through Sharing" motto and traditions should promote this practice.
- **Questionnaires.** A good method for gathering information on ERM effectiveness from a wide range of people, questionnaires can be sent out to designated stakeholders with requests for specific information. This is often a valuable internal audit technique.

Internal audit should consider launching a high-level review of the effectiveness of its enterprise's COSO ERM processes, gather detailed implementation data, and then assess the effectiveness of overall COSO ERM in the enterprise and as a tool to support and enhance SOx and COSO internal control compliance. Exhibit 7.10 provides guidance for auditing and assessing the status of COSO ERM processes. Any areas where processes here appear weak should become a warning signal to senior management.

EXHIBIT 7.10 Auditing COSO ERM Procedures

Step	Internal Audit Procedure
1	Meet with appropriate managers to gain an understanding of the enterprise's ERM implementation strategy, its planned scope, project plans, and current implementation status.
2	Develop a strategy for reviewing ERM processes, perhaps with a focus emphasizing all internal environment processes on an entity level as well as the status of all components for a selected subsidiary or business unit.
3	Develop detailed internal audit plans for the components selected for reviews and publish engagement letters announcing the planned audits.
4	Review enterprise-wide ERM guidance materials in place to assess whether ERM objectives are being adequately communicated and assess areas where communication may be lacking.
5	Assessing ERM philosophy and appetite
5.1	Meet with appropriate senior members of management to assess whether a risk management philosophy has been defined and communicated.
5.2	Through surveys or interviews completed by selected members of the enterprise to determine if the risk appetite has been communicated.
6	Risk management integrity and ethical values
6.1	Review published codes of conduct and other materials to determine if risk-related ethical values are being communicated.
6.2	Review a sample of enterprise communications and assess whether attention is given to ERM philosophies.
7	Risk management organization structure
7.1	Meet with human resources management to assess whether processes are in place to communicate ERM philosophy to enterprise.
7.2	Review code of conduct records to determine that the code has been periodically updated, that all stakeholders have acknowledged it, and that code compliance records are in place.
7.3	Based on a review of organization charts and other documentation, assess whether ERM philosophy appears to be in place throughout selected units in the enterprise.
8	Select one subsidiary or enterprise unit to determine if enterprise-wide ERM objectives and risk components are in place for the selected unit.
8.1	Assess compliance with ERM internal objectives for the selected business unit.
8.2	Assess compliance with ERM objectives setting processes for the selected business unit.
8.3	Assess compliance with ERM event notification processes for the selected business unit.
8.4	Assess compliance with ERM risk assessment for the selected business unit.
8.5	Assess compliance with ERM risk response processes for the selected business unit.
8.6	Assess compliance with ERM control activity processes for the selected business unit.
8.7	Assess compliance with ERM information and communication processes for the selected business unit.
8.8	Assess compliance with ERM risk monitoring processes for the selected business unit.

Because the two framework models look quite similar on first observation, it is very easy to miss thinking about the unique characteristics of COSO ERM. Risk management, and COSO ERM in particular, are standards that should be part of every internal auditor's CBOK. Internal auditors should use risk management principles when deciding which areas to select for their reviews, as discussed in Chapter 16 on risk-based audit planning, and then to use risk principles when assessing audit evidence, as discussed in Chapter 10. Perhaps even more important, COSO ERM will grow in importance and recognition as more enterprises understand and adopt the ERM framework. Internal auditors should understand COSO ERM both in order to audit compliance with these processes and to consult with management to ensure more effective implementations.

NOTES

1. Robert Moeller, *COSO Enterprise Risk Management: Establishing Effective Governance, Risk, and Compliance (GRC) Processes*, 2nd ed. (Hoboken, NJ: Wiley, 2011).
2. Paul Vickers, "Bhopal 'Faces Risk of Poisoning,'" BBC News, November 14, 2004, http://news.bbc.co.uk/2/hi/south_asia/4010511.stm. This is one of many Web references on this issue. A search for "Bhopal, India," and "Dow Chemical" will yield a large amount of information on the subject.
3. Melissa Klein Aguilar, "COSO Releases a New Risk Management Framework," *Accounting Today*, October 25, 2004.
4. Six Sigma is a disciplined methodology for eliminating defects (driving toward six standard deviations between the mean and the nearest specification limit) in any process, from manufacturing to transactional and from product to service.

PART THREE

Planning and Performing Internal Audits

CHAPTER EIGHT

Performing Effective Internal Audits

THE MANY CHAPTERS OF THIS book outline our internal audit common body of knowledge (CBOK) and cover all aspects of modern internal auditing, including basic internal control standards, communicating with the board of directors' audit committee, and performing specialized *internal audits* in such areas as IT cybersecurity controls. This chapter goes through the basic steps and processes necessary to plan, perform, and complete individual internal audits. While internal audit organization matters are covered in other chapters, we will start this chapter with the assumption that an enterprise has an effective internal audit function, supported by an approved audit charter authorizing the function, as well as audit committee approval for an annual plan of internal audit activities as discussed in Chapter 14. This chapter will go through the internal audit steps necessary to perform an internal control review. Virtually all internal audits start with a reaffirmation of initial audit objectives, the development of a detailed individual audit plan, and then the actual internal audit, including the initial assessment review and the documentation of internal controls, tests to determine that key controls and other facilities are working as expected, and subsequent reports on the results of the audit. While other chapters discuss many different internal audit activities, this chapter describes one of internal audit's core CBOK requirements.

An effective internal auditor serves as a frontline set of eyes and ears for the audit committee and senior management, and must do more than just review the enterprise's compliance with published documented procedures. Internal auditors visit organization facilities where the actual work is performed and records are maintained, observing operations and providing management-level reports. Internal auditors can then develop an understanding of the processes in place and design and perform appropriate tests to evaluate supporting internal controls. This chapter introduces procedures to organize, plan, and perform internal audits, starting with an internal audit charter, and then includes surveys, the documentation of internal controls, workpaper documentation, and administrative controls for managing internal audits. These procedures are appropriate for virtually all operations, whether an audit of a remote operational area covering manufacturing resource planning or a corporate headquarters financial area such as an accounts payable function. These same procedures are also appropriate for specialized audits, such as reviews of telecommunications or information technology (IT) controls. The basic steps to perform internal audits discussed in this chapter—such as the *preliminary survey* to evaluate *audit evidence*, documentation, and controls testing techniques—are useful for performing most internal audits.

Our example audit will be based on a review of a hypothetical sample company, Global Computer Products, a manufacturer and distributor of IT security hardware and software with operations in the United States, India, and the Netherlands. There are references to Global Computer Products in other chapters throughout this book.

8.1 INITIATING AND LAUNCHING AN INTERNAL AUDIT

An internal charter, as discussed in Chapter 14, is the overall authorizing authority for an internal audit function, and provides a justification for launching and performing an internal audit in some area of enterprise operations. A credible internal audit function, based, for example, in a cold northern area, cannot just say, "Hey, it's springtime—let's go to our Florida operations and perform an internal audit." Rather, internal audits should be launched for any of a variety of reasons as outlined in the following list in descending order. That is, an occurrence's location at the top of this list means that an internal audit function should drop almost everything else and get to helping with the problem.

The justifications for initiating and launching an internal audit are:

1. **Corporate reorganizations, including legal or physical threat events.** The acquisition of a new business or the sale of a current operating unit often creates an immediate need for internal audit work. Despite prior approved plans, internal audit is often needed at once in these situations. Also, when an enterprise is suddenly faced with a major legal allegation or some such matter, it is time for internal audit to drop all regular activities and support the overall enterprise objectives. Many years ago, this author was the internal audit director for a large retail enterprise that was caught by state regulators in a major case of bad business practices. Faced with the threat of the shutdown of enterprise operations in several key states, this author dropped his regular internal audit activities to review and recommend solutions to fix the problem, despite the published audit plan and schedule.
2. **Audit committee formal requests.** As discussed in Chapter 25, the board audit committee is responsible for the internal audit function and approves an annual internal plan. That plan should be the main driver of internal audit activities.
3. **A request to schedule an audit by senior management or the external auditors.** Despite an audit committee–approved plan, a member of the board, senior management, or the external audit firm may request an internal audit covering

some activity. In such a case, internal audit may adjust its approved plan to allow for the requested review.

4. **Need for a follow-up audit based on the results of a prior audit.** Sometimes when a scheduled audit has been completed, there will be a need to dig deeper and explore *findings* in greater detail. Special audits should be scheduled to cover these areas in greater detail as internal audit's schedules and resources allow.
5. **A special audit performed at the request of local or unit management.** An internal audit team, working at various locations, often receives requests for additional or more detailed audits in some area. The CAE should vet these requests and plan such audits as they might fit into the current internal audit schedule or become candidates for the following year's internal audit plan.
6. **Other auditable areas identified in the audit universe as described in Chapter 15 but not in the regular, approved annual internal audit plan.** An audit universe schedule describes all of the potential auditable entities in an enterprise. If an internal audit function has some slack time—and that should typically never occur—such lower-priority internal audits can be scheduled.

Once internal audit has identified and selected an area for an internal audit review, the next steps are to allocate internal audit resources, gather additional supporting information as needed, and start the processes of announcing and launching the internal audit. Our point of emphasis with the six audit selection criteria above is that enterprises will encounter many differing needs to launch an internal audit review, and the CAE must work closely with the audit committee to ensure that all parties understand internal audit's mission and role in launching and performing an internal audit.

The following sections discuss the overall process of organizing and performing an individual internal audit. As a word of caution here, however, we are primarily discussing roles where internal audit acts in an attest function, where it reviews an area, performs tests to determine if the processes reviewed are in compliance with expectations, and then makes recommendations for corrective actions. In those situations where internal audit will be operating in a consultative role, a rather different approach is discussed in Chapter 30. However, whether internal audit is acting in a normal attest role or as an internal consultant, many of the planning and organization processes discussed in this section are similar.

8.2 ORGANIZING AND PLANNING INTERNAL AUDITS

The steps and processes for organizing and planning internal audits require a general understanding of the IIA's *International Standards for the Professional Practice of Internal Auditing*, discussed in Chapter 9, as well as knowledge of supporting internal audit guidance tools described in Chapters 10, 11, and 12. For example, this chapter walks us through the steps necessary to conduct an internal audit, but an auditor needs some support on preparing workpapers and communicating results through *audit reports*, as discussed in Chapter 17. Internal auditing requires a wide range of interrelated skill and knowledge areas that cannot simply be described as one sequential set of action steps but rather include many interrelated activities.

While this chapter will outline general steps for performing an internal audit, we will focus on an internal controls review of the purchasing and accounts payable processes at our example company, Global Computer Products. Our hypothetical company must purchase parts to add to its production cycle and pay for those goods through supporting accounting processes.

However, before an internal audit function can launch any planned audits, it needs to have some building blocks in place to establish an effective internal audit resource or function. Outlined in other chapters, these internal audit foundation building blocks include:

- **An effective plan or organization and a charter for launching internal audit activities.** Chapter 14 suggests procedures for building an effective internal audit function, and Chapter 25 on communications with the board of directors' audit committee describes securing planning approval for an internal audit function.
- **A long-range annual audit plan.** An individual internal audit should be based on an overall plan of activities for the internal audit group. Chapter 15 discusses risk-based audit planning, and of course, that long-range audit plan would have been approved by the audit committee. This chapter starts with the selection of long-range audit plans to begin the actual internal audit activities.
- **Standard and effective approaches for performing all internal audits.** Chapter 9 discusses the IIA's *International Standards for the Professional Practice of Internal Auditing*, fundamental requirements for all internal audits, and Chapter 15 outlines a series of key competencies necessary to perform internal audits.

Of course, the previous points are not the only key CBOK tools necessary to perform effective internal audits. Among other matters, internal auditors need to develop good approaches for evaluating audit evidence (see Chapter 10), effective audit results reporting (see Chapter 18), a strong understanding of the COSO internal control framework (see Chapter 3), and a consistent framework for evaluating those controls (see Chapter 5).

Starting with steps for planning an internal audit and then continuing through a variety of audit processes, this section will outline the steps necessary for an internal controls review of the production parts purchasing cycle at a unit of our sample company, a representative internal audit. Our objective here and in other supporting chapters is to suggest a series of internal audit procedures for performing reviews. Whether as an individual professional or as the enterprise's internal audit department or function, internal audit will be more effective if all members of the audit staff follow consistent, professional procedures in performing their reviews. They will become a strong enterprise resource in the eyes of management, who should expect consistent, quality approaches from the ongoing performance of their internal audit resources.

8.3 INTERNAL AUDIT PREPARATORY ACTIVITIES

Each internal audit project or assignment should be carefully planned prior to its start. Audits should be initiated as a scheduled element in internal audit's annual planning and risk assessment process through a management or audit committee special request or in response to unplanned events, such as the discovery of a fraud, new regulations, or unexpected economic events. Some internal audits will be updates or repeats of reviews performed in prior periods, such as an update of some internal controls and testing as part of a review of a SOx Section 404 key process, but internal audit has a need to regularly launch new internal audit reviews. Whether the new audit is a scheduled but first-time review or an audit requirement that was identified because of some unexpected event, internal audit needs to develop a plan for it.

Chapter 16 discusses project management and the importance of developing plans for individual internal audits as well as periodic plans for the overall audit function. Exhibit 8.1 is a sample authorizing charter for our Global Computer Products example enterprise. As discussed in Chapter 16, internal audit would use this charter authorization to build an annual internal audit plan to outline its activities over a future period. The plan would be approved by the audit committee and would be periodically updated as internal audit reports its progress to the audit committee. Later in this book, Exhibit 25.4 shows an example of a one-year summarized plan for upcoming internal audits. In this chapter, we will outline the steps necessary for a new internal audit plan covering purchasing and accounts payable internal controls at our Global Computer Products example enterprise. The audit was initially scheduled with some high-level stated objectives and hours estimates. This chapter brings us from the high-level annual internal audit plan to steps for getting ready to perform the actual audit.

After internal audit has developed an annual plan for the upcoming year, planning and scheduling individual internal audits can often be a challenge. Despite well-thought-out plans, unscheduled events, requests from management, or situations such as unfavorable results from other audits may cause changes in an internal audit's long-range plan. While there often are pressures to begin such special audits immediately, a properly planned audit will almost always produce better audit results. In addition, internal audit can obtain significant savings in time and effort with adequate advance planning and preparatory work.

Although a small element of the preparatory activities described in this chapter can be performed concurrent with the audit itself, most of these internal audit activities should take place in advance of visiting the audit site or beginning the internal audit. These important preparatory activities include defining the objectives, scope, and procedures or audit program to be used in an individual audit. This is particularly important in larger enterprises that are performing multiple concurrent audits with different mixes of audit personnel assigned to each. The following sections discuss steps required to plan and perform a typical internal audit. Based on Exhibit 8.2's example audit plan, assume that internal audit can begin work on a planned accounts payable systems review at Global Computer Products' Minneapolis production facilities. Also assume that this is a new audit that was scheduled in the prior year as part internal audit's risk assessment–based planning processes.

While no single internal audit is really typical, the planning outlined here should normally be done well in advance for most internal audits. Relative project management risks, as discussed in Chapter 16, should have been considered as part of the long-range audit plan leading up to each individual internal audit. Once the need for the new audit

EXHIBIT 8.1 Sample Internal Audit Charter

Internal Audit Department
Authorizing Charter

Internal Audit's Mission

The mission of Global Computer Products Internal Audit is to ensure that company operations follow high standards both by providing an independent, objective assurance function and by advising on best practices. By using a systematic and disciplined approach, Internal Audit helps Global Computer Products accomplish its objectives by evaluating and improving the effectiveness of risk management, internal control, and governance processes.

Independence and Objectivity

To ensure independence, Internal Audit reports directly to the Board of Directors Audit Committee, and to maintain objectivity, Internal Audit is not involved in day-to-day company operations or internal control procedures.

Scope and Responsibilities

The scope of Internal Audit's work includes the review of risk management procedures, internal control, information systems and governance processes. This work also involves periodic testing of transactions, best practice reviews, special investigations, appraisals of legal and regulatory requirements, and measures to help prevent and detect fraud.

To fulfill its responsibilities, Internal Audit shall:

— Identify and assess potential risks for all areas of enterprise operations.

— Review the adequacy of controls established to ensure compliance with policies, plans, procedures, and business objectives.

— Assess the reliability and security of financial and management information and supporting systems and operations that produce this information.

— Assess the means of safeguarding assets.

— Review established processes and propose improvements.

— Appraise the use of resources with regard to economy, efficiency, and effectiveness.

— Follow up recommendations to make sure that effective remedial action is taken.

— Carry out ad hoc appraisals, investigations, or reviews requested by the Audit Committee and Management.

Internal Audit's Authority

In order to promote effective controls at reasonable cost, Internal Audit is authorized, in the course of its activities, to:

— Enter all areas of Global Computer Products operations and have access to any documents and records considered necessary for the performance of its functions.

— Require all members of staff and Management to supply requested information and explanations within a reasonable period of time.

Accountability

Internal Audit shall prepare, in liaison with Management and the Audit Committee, an annual audit plan that is based on business risks, the results of other internal audits, and input from Management. The plan shall be presented to Senior Management, including the General Counsel, for approval by the Audit Committee. Any needed adjustments to the plan should be communicated to and approved by the Audit Committee.

Internal Audit is responsible for planning, conducting, reporting, and following up on audit projects included in the audit plan, and deciding on the scope and timing of these audits. The results of each internal audit will be reported through a detailed audit report that summarizes the objectives and scope of the audit as well as observations and recommendations. In all cases, follow-up work will be undertaken to ensure adequate response to Internal Audit's recommendations. Internal Audit also will submit an annual report to Senior Management and to the Audit Committee on the results of the audit work, including significant risk exposures and control issues.

Standards

Internal Audit adheres to the standards and professional practices published by both the Institute of Internal Auditors as well as the Information Technology Governance Institute.

has been identified, the next steps should be to define or reaffirm the specific audit objectives, work out logistics arrangements for the review, and then develop a detailed individual audit plan for that review. The following sections discuss the major components for performing such an internal audit.

Determine the Audit Objectives

Internal audit should generally establish plans for internal audit activities that typically cover a fiscal-year period. These long-range plans are based on management and audit committee requests, audit staff capabilities, the nature of prior audit work, available resources, and general risks facing the enterprise. This long-range, risk-based internal

EXHIBIT 8.2 Generic Individual Audit Plan

REF	Audit Activity	Week 1	Week 2	Week 3	Week 4	Week 5
1	Review past activity and assess risks	X				
2	Develop audit approach and preliminary plan	X				
3	Contact site to schedule audit	X				
4	Travel to location	X				
5	Review and document processes		X			
6	Perform walk-through to verify		X	X		
7	Develop and perform tests of internal controls			X	X	
8	Perform other audit procedures as planned				X	
9	Summarize and confirm audit results			X	X	
10	Complete audit workpapers				X	
11	Schedule audit closing meeting				X	
12	Prepare draft audit report with recommendations					X

audit planning process, discussed in Chapter 16, paints a sort of big-picture activity list for internal audit. However, changes in business operations and the general economy, problems identified through other internal audits, new laws and regulations, audit staff changes, or any of a variety of other issues may somewhat alter that long-range audit plan. These overall audit plans should include high-level objectives for each planned audit as well as an understanding of the surrounding risk environments.

A high-level objective statement should be established for each individual planned audit. These do not have to be detailed lists of requirements but should have sufficient information to tell the auditee, management, and others what internal audit is trying to accomplish when launching an internal audit in some area. Here are some examples of internal audit objective statements:

- To assess the adequacy of purchasing system internal accounting controls at the Global Computer Products Minneapolis facility as well as the purchasing processes at multiple branch facilities, interfaces to the accounts payable system at corporate headquarters, and automated systems to support these processes.
- To update documented processes and test internal controls, as necessary, for fixed asset management processes to satisfy their SOx Section 404 requirements.
- To review the internal controls in place over maintenance for the IT configuration management database and supporting procedures.

Each of these fairly brief example objective statements describes what internal audit is planning to accomplish in an upcoming review. While the project can be expanded as the reviews get started, these objective statements get an internal audit launched.

Closely tied to the objective statement, a scope statement is sometimes valuable to add as well. For example, an objective statement can identify a planned review of quality management production processes in international operations; a scope statement might limit the review to only Australia/New Zealand operations. The scope statement better defines what the new audit is trying to accomplish.

These internal audit preliminary objective and scope statements should be reviewed with management or others requesting the audit. An effective way to describe these internal audit plans is through an audit planning memo. While not a document presented directly to the auditee, this communication describes what internal audit is planning to accomplish, who will be doing the review, and its approximate timing. Such a memo is an essential starting document for the workpapers, as described in Chapter 17, documenting that internal audit. Exhibit 8.3 shows a sample audit planning memo where an internal audit supervisor outlines the objectives of a planned internal audit, who will be assigned to do the work, and its estimated timing. Of course, even though our exhibit shows this as a memo from the old hard-copy paper days, the planning memo today would almost certainly be an electronic document.

Audit Schedule and Time Estimates

The approved annual internal audit plan, discussed in Chapter 16, outlines which internal audits are to be performed in any given period. Key internal audit staff members and

EXHIBIT 8.3 Audit Planning Memo Sample

February 2, 20xx

To: Workpaper Files

From: L. C. Tuttle, Audit Supervisor

Subject: Accounts Payable Systems Audit Planning Memo

This memo is to document the planned review of key purchasing and accounts payable processes at Global Computer Products manufacturing facility in Minneapolis, MN. The review will be performed by two members of our internal audit staff with L. C. Tuttle as project leader and Herman Hollerith providing support for our review of network and IT systems controls.

The objective of this review will be to assess the adequacy of purchasing system internal accounting controls at the Global Computer Products Minneapolis facility as well as the purchasing processes at multiple branch facilities, interfaces to the accounts payable system at corporate headquarters, and automated systems to support these processes.

The audit is scheduled to begin on about March 15, 20xx, and has been budgeted for a total of XX hours of time from the on-site audit team. A detailed plan, including expected hours for each auditor, will be prepared prior to the start of this review.

The review will emphasize controls over linkages from the purchasing system to other enterprise manufacturing database systems. In addition, the review will update documentation and perform tests, as necessary, to support SOx Section 404 requirements covering this process. All recommendations and audit findings will be reported in a normal internal audit department report.

L. C. Tuttle, Audit Supervisor

W. J. Rawdon, Audit Manager

managers should have participated in this planning process and be aware of ongoing needs for any subsequent plan adjustments. Preliminary time estimates are established and time frames set for performing each audit. However, changes are often made to this annual plan during the course of the year due to the increased resource requirements of other audits in progress, revised audit scopes, personnel changes, and other management priorities.

In addition to the annual plan and any necessary revisions, individual audit schedules should be prepared based on this plan. Depending on the nature of the audits performed and audit staff size, these individual schedules may cover a month, a quarter, or a longer period. For a larger internal audit group, detailed audit schedules should be prepared for the entire audit department as well as individual auditors and reviewed at least monthly to reflect changes or adjustments. For example, an internal audit specialist in a key area may be unavailable for several weeks or months. This might require an overall shift in audit department plans.

Exhibit 8.4 shows a sample detailed schedule of audit activity for an entire department over a three-month period. The same type of plan can be reorganized to show

EXHIBIT 8.4 Audit Plan Project Schedule Example

Global Computer Products Internal Audit Department February, March, and April Audit Project Schedule Hours						
Project #	**Audit**	**Auditor**	**Activity**	**Feb (hrs.)**	**Mar (hrs.)**	**Apr (hrs.)**
A23-06	A/P—Purchasing Minneapolis Review	Hollerith	Test IT Controls	20	80	45
A23-06	A/P—Purchasing Minneapolis Review	Spatz	Document Processes	110	24	12
A23-06	A/P—Purchasing Minneapolis Review	Prusch	Tests of Transactions	36	80	12
A23-06	A/P—Purchasing Minneapolis Review	Tuttle	Manage Audit	12	18	20
A28-78	Branch Sales Offices	Bushman	US West Results	120	145	30
A28-78	Branch Sales Offices	Lester	US West Results	0	68	160
A31-01	Job Control Review	Doe	Document Processes	0	64	80
A31-01	Job Control Review	Hollerith	Test IT Controls	0	40	40
A31-01	Job Control Review	Tuttle	Manage Audit	8	12	12

project assignments for each auditor over a similar multimonth period and can also be used to show scheduled vacations, supervisory administrative time, and formal training. As a control device, a detailed audit plan can serve as a tool for the reconciliation of available auditor days with scheduled audit requirements.

The number and level of staff required for various audits depends on an evaluation of the nature and complexity of the audit projects as well as internal auditor abilities and time constraints. Audit projects should be broken down into individual tasks for making these audit project hour estimates. Overall estimates are then more reliable and can serve as a benchmark for comparing actual with budgeted audit performance. Of course, the plans developed at an early stage of the audit are often preliminary and must be adjusted once more information is obtained.

Auditor skills and developmental needs should be considered in selecting personnel for any audit project assignment. After deciding on the individual audit segments, the talents needed to perform the audit tasks must be determined. For example, one segment of a planned audit may require an information systems audit specialist to evaluate certain IT controls, while another segment may require audit sampling skills to construct and evaluate a statistical test.

Internal Audit Preliminary Surveys

The annual risk-based long-range audit plans discussed in Chapter 16 should of course be made with knowledge of the expected areas to be audited. For example, based on past experience, audit management would realize that a branch office review should take about X hours to complete; however, risk analysis for annual audit planning is often performed at a high or overview level. There is often a need to go beyond those annual plan-hours estimates before starting the actual audit. If plans are for a repetitive review of an area previously reviewed, a good first step should be a preliminary survey that gathers background materials regarding the entity to be audited. This survey is often the responsibility of audit management or the designated in-charge auditor. The following are items that should be reviewed, if available, during an internal audit preliminary survey:

- **Review of prior workpapers.** The prior audit objectives and scope, *audit workpapers*, and audit programs should be reviewed to gain familiarity with approaches used and the results of those audits. Internal audit critiques, prepared at the end of each review and discussed in Chapter 18, help to better understand the prior review approaches used and the alternatives available. Special attention should be given to any problems encountered in the prior audit and the suggested methods of solving them. The organization of internal audit workpapers is discussed in Chapter 17.
- **Knowing the amount of time from the prior audit.** Any internal problems encountered can help determine the planned resources needed. The results of prior tests performed should be reviewed, deciding whether any should be reduced, eliminated, expanded, or performed on a rotating basis in future audits. Prior workpapers may indicate that a large sample of test-count items was included as part of an inventory review, but due to generally good internal control procedures, few problems were encountered. Planning for the upcoming audit should focus on whether those same control procedures, still in place, can allow sample sizes to be reduced.
- **Review of prior audit reports.** Past audit findings and their significance should always be considered, including the extent of management commitments to take corrective actions. To obtain leads to other sensitive areas, the auditor should also study reports on similar entities or functions in the organization. For example, if a branch-level audit is planned in a multibranch unit, recent audit reports covering other branches may point to potential problem areas in the branch planned for review. Related findings in other areas may also be useful.
- **Significant recommended corrective actions.** Particular attention should be given if substantial corrective actions were required in that past audit, and the upcoming planned audit should include an examination of those areas as well. Attention should also be directed to any disputed items from a prior report. Although internal audit management should have an objective of clearing up all disputed items in an audit report, there may be situations where the auditor and auditee agree to disagree. These matters are discussed in Chapter 18 on reporting audit results. The auditor should note any such areas as a suggestion for a planned audit in an upcoming period.
- **Organization of the entity.** An internal auditor should obtain an organization chart of the planned audit entity to understand its structure and responsibilities.

Particular attention should be given to areas where there may be a potential separation-of-duties problem. In addition, the number of employees and the names of key employee contacts by major departments or sections should be obtained. This should include, if possible, the name of a key liaison person for contact during the planned audit. If applicable, the entity's mission statement or similar functional descriptions should be obtained to better understand its purpose. Budgets and financial performance data also should be reviewed as background material. The internal audit manager may want to gain this information through a telephone request or e-mail note and should advise the auditee that the requested information is to help in the planning of the potential audit. The areas reviewed when gaining an understanding of the organization of the entity will vary somewhat depending on the type of audit planned. In an operational audit of a manufacturing area, an internal auditor might want to gain an overall understanding of the manufacturing process. Similarly, a planned IT operations general-controls review would require the internal auditor to gain some background information about the operations environment, the telecommunications network, and the applications processed.

- **Other related audit materials.** Supporting data from related audits completed, planned, or in process should also be studied. This may include problems identified by external auditors in a prior-period SOx Section 404 review or any reviews by governmental regulatory auditors. The results of internal reviews by departmental or other organization officials, press releases, and other related reports provide additional useful background material. Any indication of known problem areas from these reviews should be noted. In some instances, it is beneficial to review articles in the professional literature—such as the Institute of Internal Auditors' publications—to discuss successful approaches used by other internal auditors.

8.4 STARTING THE INTERNAL AUDIT

As discussed in the prior sections, we have planned our internal audit at our Global Computer Products example company and defined its objectives. Now the first step in actually starting most internal audits is to inform the group or organization to be audited—the auditee—that an internal audit has been scheduled. Although internal audit would have prepared a planning memo, as shown in Exhibit 8.3, as documentation for the internal audit files, the group or function to be audited must be informed of this planned internal audit. The only exception to this rule would be a fraud-related investigation, where internal audit generally would appear at the auditee site unannounced. A different situation from internal audit, fraud detection reviews are discussed in Chapter 27. Otherwise, internal audit should inform appropriate persons at the facility or unit to be reviewed through an informal note followed up by a more formal notice.

This notice of a planned upcoming internal audit is called an engagement letter. It is an internal planning document that informs the auditee of when the internal audit is scheduled, who will be performing the review, and why the audit has been planned (regularly scheduled audit, management or auditor committee request, etc.). This who, what, and why approach should be used for all *engagement letters*. A sample engagement letter is shown in Exhibit 8.5. This letter should notify auditee management of the following:

1. **Addressee.** The communication should be addressed to the manager directly responsible for the unit being audited.
2. **Objectives and scope of the planned audit.** The auditee should be clearly advised of the purpose of the planned internal audit and the areas it will cover. For example, the letter might advise that internal audit plans to review internal controls over the shop floor labor collection system, including main-plant shop floor operations.
3. **Expected start date and planned duration of the audit.** As much as possible, the engagement letter should give the auditee some understanding of the timing of the audit.
4. **Persons responsible for performing the review.** At a minimum, the in-charge auditor should be identified for this planned audit. This will help auditee management to identify this key person if a team of auditors arrives on site.
5. **Advance preparation needs.** Any requirements needed in advance of the field visit or at the audit site should be outlined. This might include copies of certain reports in advance of the visit. This is also an appropriate place to request internal audit temporary office space, computer systems network access, and access to key IT systems or databases.
6. **Engagement letter copies.** Although the term *carbon copy* or *CC* is outdated today, copies of the engagement letter should be directed to appropriate persons in the enterprise with a need to know.

Based on the overall audit objectives, financial, statistical, and other reports relating to the entity being audited should also be requested in advance as part of the engagement memo. Reports of this nature can help identify trends or allow comparisons between entities to determine any significant variances. Appropriate levels of management should also be copied on this engagement memo. Although it is usually appropriate to inform auditee management that an internal audit has been scheduled, there may be circumstances where no formal engagement letter is released. For example, if the audit is fraud-related, the review might be performed on a surprise basis and only scheduled through appropriate levels of senior management. Small retail locations are also good candidates for surprise audits even though there is no suspicion of fraud. In most instances, however, auditee management should be informed of the planned audit visit and made aware of internal audit's planned objectives.

Some internal audit professionals have taken different stands on whether audits should be announced in advance. They argue that a surprise audit allows a review to see actual conditions without giving the auditee the benefit of cleaning up records, documentation, and other matters. However, the arrival of an audit team for an unannounced audit can cause serious disruptions to the auditee organization, with the possibility that the prime auditee may be on vacation or away at a seminar. Unless there is a suspected fraud or a need for a surprise cash count, unannounced audits should generally be avoided. There may even be reasons to postpone or reschedule the review as announced in the

EXHIBIT 8.5 Internal Audit Engagement Letter Example

February 2, 20xx

To: Red Buttons, Dept. 7702

From: L. C. Tuttle, Audit Supervisor

Subject: Accounts Payable Systems Audit

The internal audit department has scheduled a review of your purchasing systems and accounts payable processes. Our review will include internal controls over the key purchasing and accounts payable processes at the Global Computer Products manufacturing facility in Minneapolis, MN. The review has been scheduled as part of our annual internal audit planning process, approved by the Board of Directors Audit Committee.

The objective of our review will be to assess the adequacy of purchasing system internal accounting controls at this Global Computer Products Minneapolis facility as well as the purchasing processes at multiple branch facilities, interfaces to the accounts payable system at corporate headquarters, and automated systems to support these processes.

Our audit is scheduled to begin on about March 15, 20xx, with myself as the in-charge auditor, two other members of the internal audit staff, Judy Spatz and Marcie Prusch, as well as Herman Hollerith, who will lead a review of supporting network and IT systems controls. We plan to conclude our work in June, including the issuance of an internal audit report.

We will need access to your regular purchasing and accounts payable system records and files. In addition, please inform the vendors providing you with purchasing systems support that we may need to access some of their supporting systems as part of our internal audit testing.

Please arrange for systems access and temporary systems passwords for myself as well as our internal audit team of Spatz, Prusch, and Hollerith. We will also require some working space in your office area. Please contact me at lc.tuttle@globalcomputerprod.com or at ext. 9999 if you have any questions.

L. C. Tuttle, Audit Supervisor

W. J. Rawdon, Audit Manager

engagement letter. For example, a key manager or technical support authority may have a prescheduled vacation during the period of the planned audit. If that person is a key source of information and if there are no special reasons for the audit's planned time schedule, audit management should reschedule it to accommodate local management. In many situations, however, unit management may inform internal audit that "this is a bad time," with no strong reasons for postponing the audit. Because internal audit has a comprehensive schedule of planned audits and its own scheduling problems, it is appropriate to refuse such requests for postponement and insist on initiating the audit as planned.

Once the audit has been scheduled and auditee management informed, the assigned audit team should be ready to begin work at the auditee site. This phase of the audit is called *fieldwork*, an old term dating back to the early days of internal auditing. Even though the audit may not take place at a remote site and possibly will start just down the hall from internal audit or will mainly consist of reviews through Web screens, we still call this phase fieldwork. The term dates from earlier days when internal auditors traveled to remote locations—the field— to perform their internal audit reviews. At this point, the internal audit team has gathered such background information as relevant policies and procedures. Internal audit would next perform a *field survey* to improve the assigned audit team's understanding of the areas to be reviewed as well as to establish preliminary audit documentation of those procedures. We are describing this internal audit field survey as a first-time audit event. However, in many cases, internal audit will be returning to perform a repeat review after a lapse of time. In that case, workpaper documentation should be retrieved and updated for the newly scheduled internal audit.

Internal Audit Field Surveys

A preliminary survey is often critically important in determining the direction, detailed scope, and extent of the audit effort; it is the first step taken at the audit site. The auditor cannot just rush in with no clear purpose or objectives and begin examining documents and observing operations. A field survey allows auditors to (1) familiarize themselves with the major local processes in place, and (2) evaluate the control structure and level of control risk in the various processes and systems included within the audit. If members of the audit team are unfamiliar with the audit location and its management, this is the point to make introductions and clarify any questions that may have been raised through the engagement letter. It is also the appropriate time for the in-charge auditor to outline planned interview requirements and to establish a preliminary schedule. The following information elements should be assembled by the in-charge auditor and other members of the team during a typical field survey:

- **Organization.** During the field survey, the auditors should confirm that organization charts, whether online or on paper, are correct and include the names of key personnel. The auditor should become familiar with functional responsibilities and key people involved in the operations. Often a title on an organization chart does not reflect the true responsibilities of that position. Formal position descriptions should be requested whenever they may be appropriate. If the function does not have prepared charts available at the time of the preliminary survey, the auditor should draft a rough organization chart and review these assumptions with auditee management.
- **Manuals and directives.** Copies of applicable policy and procedure manuals, extracting data of interest for the audit workpapers, may be available through an online system, and appropriate access should be obtained. Applicable federal and state laws and regulations should be studied, as well as management directives to comply with them. Depending on the overall objectives of the audit, correspondence files should also be screened for applicable materials.
- **Reports.** Relevant management reports and minutes of meetings covering areas appropriate to the audit—budgeting, operations, cost studies, and personnel matters, and the results of any external inspections or management reviews as well

as actions taken—should be analyzed. Examples might include manufacturing cost performance reports or a fire inspector's review of computer server centers' physical security. Such reports may provide leads for the audit, as well as a summary of problems faced, recommendations made, and progress achieved in their implementation.

- **Personal observations.** A tour or walk-through of the activity familiarizes internal auditors with the entity, its basic operations, personnel, and space utilization. It also provides the audit team an opportunity to ask questions and observe operations. Auditors are sometimes guilty of visiting an operation, spending much of their time in an accounting or administrative office, and completing the audit without a clear understanding of the actual activity audited. This can result in serious omissions in the final audit work. The impressions gained from this tour should be documented in the audit workpapers as a narrative. Compliance with company procedures should also be observed and documented.
- **Discussions with key personnel.** Discussions with key personnel in the area being audited help to determine known problems, the current results of the unit's operations, and any planned changes or reorganizations. Questions should be raised based on preliminary data reviewed or tour observations.

The field survey should be the initial review contact point with the auditee; here, local management can meet the audit team and the assigned auditors have their first exposure to the entity to be reviewed. Problems or misunderstandings can potentially arise at this point. Although these matters should have been resolved at the time of the engagement letter release, unit management may not always understand what the internal auditors want, or internal audit may not have a correct understanding of the entity, despite their preliminary planning. The result may point to a need to somewhat adjust the scope of the planned review, the planned audit procedures, or even the overall audit. Small changes are appropriate, but this is not the time to revise internal audit plans. If changes are requested, the assigned in-charge auditor should contact internal audit management for guidance.

This section has referred to both "the internal auditor" and "the in-charge auditor." Depending on the size of the overall internal audit staff and the audit engagement, the review may be performed by one or several internal auditors. One assigned auditor should always be designated the in-charge auditor, with responsibility for making most on-site audit decisions. In-charge responsibilities are usually assigned to more senior members of the audit staff, but the responsibility should be rotated throughout the staff to give less experienced auditors some management experience. Internal audit staffing roles and responsibilities are discussed in Chapter 15.

Documenting the Internal Audit Field Survey

Normally, the field survey will occupy the first day or two at the audit site. For large reviews, the survey can be performed during a separate visit in advance of the auditor's detailed testing and analysis work. In either case, the work performed and summaries of data gathered through the field survey should be documented in audit workpapers. Copies of key reports and published procedures should be obtained, summary notes and observations recorded from all interviews and tours, and flowcharts prepared for all systems or processes. These materials should be part of the auditor's workpapers, as discussed in Chapter 17.

An internal auditor's field survey also can identify new or revised audit techniques in the light of changed auditee procedures or operating conditions. For example, a function that was once a traditional IT application processes may now be Web-based or use cloud technologies. Software to draft flowcharts should be prepared describing major processes including changes from any prior audits. Through their graphic summary of the flow of operations and data, flowcharts are often a key tool to illustrate complexities and control points in a system or process. The old adage that "a picture is worth a thousand words" very much applies here.

The concept of developing flowcharts for all major transaction processes is important for documenting many audit processes and is necessary for the SOx Section 404 documentation discussed in Chapter 5. There are many variations and approaches to developing flowcharts, but they are a good tool to show the relationships between different operational elements and where control points exist in a process. Once completed, these flowcharts become part of the auditor's permanent workpaper file for that entity. They also support requirements that organizations maintain documentation covering their internal controls. The ability to use software tools to construct a process flowchart should be part of every internal auditor's CBOK.

Field Survey Auditor Conclusions

The purpose of an internal audit field survey is to confirm the assumptions gained from the preliminary audit planning and to develop an understanding of key systems and processes. Because the information that supports the preliminary audit planning is often imperfect, this is an important point where the assigned audit team can make adjustments to the planned audit scope and objectives. For larger audits, it is often a good idea for internal audit management to visit the team performing the field survey and review its results. This way, any necessary management-approved scope changes can be made. This on-site presence can clear up any potential questions that could be raised later.

An internal auditor may encounter instances where the information gathered from a field survey may cause the audit team either to adjust the planned audit scope substantially or even to cancel the detailed audit work. Sometimes the audit team involved in the preliminary planning may call the auditee at a remote location and be advised that there are "no changes" in the area of the auditor's interest. When the audit team arrives, the field survey could point out significant changes, such as the introduction of a new information system, which changes the overall control environment and may require the internal audit team to add another specialist to the project, causing both staffing and audit test strategy adjustments. In other cases, the audit team may find that changes are so substantial that the planned audit should be canceled or postponed. In most instances, however, the field survey provides the audit team with additional data to help it adjust its planned procedures.

The materials gathered in an internal audit field survey should be used either to document or to update a workpaper permanent file. If a member of audit management is not on site, the results of the survey should be summarized in written form, communicated

EXHIBIT 8.6 Field Survey Conclusions Audit Report Example

April 1, 20XX

To: Sandra Smyth, Audit Manager

From: L. C. Tuttle, Audit Supervisor

Subject: Purchasing & Accounts Payable Minneapolis Field Survey

We have concluded our field survey at the Minneapolis site that included a review of active supporting processes as well as an observation of operations. While most of our preliminary internal audit plans to review internal controls are correct and will support our upcoming planned internal audit here, we identified several areas where our planned audit scope and planned procedures should be modified:

1. *Cash Discount System.* We were advised that with the low interest rates we have been experiencing in recent years, the unit has found little advantage in taking cash discounts from prompt payments. As a result, we were advised that these processes are not normally used today. We should modify our planned audit procedures in this area from the planned 20 hours to just a very limited 4-hour-internal audit documentation update.
2. *Prevalence of Web-Based Processes.* Local purchasing systems have moved from the more paper-forms based processes of just five years ago to a totally Web-oriented environment. Our planned hours should be expanded to document these new processes and to develop new testing procedures as appropriate. Herman Hollerith was budgeted for 145 hours over three months to review and test the old system. We should expand his planned 145 hours to 200 hours, and increase his planned 20 hours in the first month to 40 hours. That time would be spent on understanding, documenting, and developing testing procedures for the Web application.

Please advise if these proposed changes to our audit plan are acceptable.

____
L. C. Tuttle, Audit Supervisor

____
W. J. Rawdon, Audit Manager

through e-mail, and reviewed with internal audit management before proceeding with the audit. Exhibit 8.6 is an example of an internal audit report on field survey conclusions. This document is particularly important if the in-charge auditor feels there is a need to change audit scope or planned procedures.

8.5 DEVELOPING AND PREPARING AUDIT PROGRAMS

Internal audits should be organized and performed in a consistent manner with an objective of minimizing arbitrary or unnecessary auditor procedures. To help achieve this goal of audit consistency, internal auditors should use what are called *audit programs* to perform audit procedures in a consistent and effective manner for similar types of audits. The term *program* refers to a set of auditor procedures similar to the steps in a computer program, instructions that go through the same program instructions every time the process is run. For example, a computer program to calculate pay will include instructions to read the time card file of hours worked, look up the employee's rate where it is stored in another file, and then calculate the gross pay. The same steps apply for every employee unless there are exceptions such as overtime rates coded into the payroll program. Similarly, an audit program is a set of preestablished steps an internal auditor performs. An audit program is a tool for planning, directing, and controlling audit work and a blueprint for action, specifying the steps to be performed to meet audit objectives. It represents the auditor's selection of the best methods of getting the job done and serves as a basis for recording the work steps performed.

An effective internal audit department should have a series of generalized audit programs prepared for most of its recurring audit activities. Many of these programs, such as one covering an observation of the taking of physical inventories, are often used from year to year and enterprise entity to entity with little change. In other situations, the internal auditor may only have to modify a standard program to the unique aspects of a particular audit. In some situations, a standard audit program will not be applicable. For example, the internal auditor may want to review controls in a new business entity with some unique control characteristics, or audit management may want to take a different approach because of problems encountered with similar previous reviews. Based on planned audit objectives and data gathered in the preliminary and field surveys, the in-charge auditor may want to prepare a customized audit program for guiding the review. This may be little more than a standardized program with minimal local changes, or it may be a unique set of audit procedures based on the preliminary planning and the results from the field survey. In order to prepare this program, the internal auditor first should have an understanding of the characteristics of what constitutes an adequate audit program.

Audit Program Formats and Their Preparation

An audit program is a procedure describing the steps and tests to be performed by the auditor when actually doing fieldwork. The program should be finalized after the completion of the preliminary and field surveys and before starting the actual audit. It should be constructed with several criteria in mind, the most important of which is that the program should identify the aspects of the area to be further examined and the sensitive areas that require audit emphasis.

A second important purpose of an audit program is that it should guide both junior and more experienced internal auditors. For example, management may request that internal audit observe the taking of an annual physical inventory. This type of review consists of fairly standard procedures to assure, among other matters, that goods shipping and receiving cutoff procedures are proper. A less experienced internal auditor may not be aware of these procedure steps, and even experienced internal auditors may forget one or another. An audit program outlines the required audit steps. An established internal audit department will probably have built a library of programs, established over time, for tasks such as a physical inventory observation or a review of fixed assets. When planning a review where such established programs exist, audit management needs only to use these established programs with consideration given to any changed conditions that have been discovered through the preliminary or field surveys. The audit program is revised as necessary, with the changes approved by audit management prior to the start of the review.

For many internal audit departments, appropriate established audit programs may not be available for many areas. This is because internal auditors are typically faced with a wide and diverse set of areas for review, but they will not have the time or resources to review every area on a frequent basis. Established programs prepared for prior audits often become out of date due to new systems or changed processes. The auditor responsible for the field survey or another member of audit management should update any existing audit program or prepare a revised set of audit program steps for the planned review. Depending on the type of planned audit, programs usually follow one of three general formats: (1) a set of general audit procedures, (2) audit procedures with detailed instructions for the auditor, or (3) a checklist for compliance reviews.

The following examples illustrate these audit program types. Exhibit 8.7 is a general audit program for a review of the direct expenditure cycle, the product-related purchase process in an enterprise. The program outlines the high-level or general audit steps that internal auditors will need to follow when performing internal audits in that area. With a library of such high-level audit programs covering reviews of each major business cycle, such as direct expenditures, fixed assets, and others, internal audit needs to tailor these general audit programs to the specific unit or facility that it is reviewing. Often internal audit will take its general audit programs and tailor them to more specific areas or business units.

EXHIBIT 8.7 General Audit Program Instructions for Direct Expenditures

Step	Internal Audit Procedure	W/P Ref.
1	Determine that valid/authorized purchase orders exist for each purchasing transaction.	
2	Duplicate purchase orders should not exist and should not be processed.	
3	Open/outstanding purchase orders should be investigated and resolved.	
4	Receipts of goods should be processed and recorded once.	
5	Receipts of goods should be processed and recorded only if a valid purchase order exists.	
6	Vendor invoices are processed and recorded only for goods order and received.	
7	Vendor invoices should be processed and received once.	
8	Debit memos are generated only for real/authorized transactions.	
9	All receiving transactions are processed and recorded in the proper period.	
10	Purchase orders contain accurate price, units of measure, and other relevant data.	

Signature ____________ Date ____________

Exhibit 8.8 is an example of a more detailed audit program, this one covering audit steps for a review of petty cash controls at a branch unit. It consists of general audit procedures to review cash at any unit of a multifacility organization. Petty cash controls are one of the smaller, less critical internal control concerns for many enterprises, but internal auditors will often regularly perform this type of review. Internal audit will sometimes make these types of detailed audit programs even more specific or detailed. The program shows the steps that should be included in any such audit and illustrates an example audit program.

Exhibit 8.8 represents a typical internal audit program format where audit tasks are broken into numbered steps with space allowed for the internal auditor completing the audit step to initial and date it. Also included is a column for a reference to the workpaper that describes the audit step. For example, for the step 1 start of this process, the internal auditor performing the procedure would document cashier responsibilities. Typically, an established internal audit function would have developed these types of audit programs for many of its regular or periodic audits. The audit team visiting an organizational unit could then use standard programs to review internal controls in a consistent manner from one unit to the next. This is particularly important in a multiunit organization where audit management wants to have assurance that controls over the area were reviewed and evaluated in a consistent manner, no matter who the assigned auditor or the location. This sample audit program is shown as a printed document that could be developed and controlled by internal audit. In some instances, the in-charge auditor might prepare a custom program to evaluate certain special procedures encountered during the field survey.

The checklist format audit program was once internal audit's most common format. Often a more junior internal auditor would be given an audit program composed of a long list of questions requiring "yes," "no," or "not applicable" responses and would complete these program steps either through examinations of documents or through interviews. Exhibit 8.9 is an example of a checklist format audit program for reviewing ethics and business compliance policies. "Yes" and "no" responses, when asked in an information-gathering context, are often appropriate. A checklist format audit program has two weaknesses, however. First, while a series of yes-or-no type interview responses can cause an experienced auditor to look at problem areas or to ask other questions, a less experienced auditor may not go beyond the yeses and nos and dig a bit deeper into where they might lead. A procedures-oriented audit program better encourages follow-up inquiries in other areas where the information gathered may raise questions.

The questionnaire format audit program also tends to cause the auditor to miss examining necessary evidential matter when asking the questions. An inexperienced internal auditor can too easily check "yes" on the questionnaire without determining, for example, whether that response is properly supported by audit evidence. An example would be a question regarding whether some critical document is regularly approved. It is easy to ask the question, receive an answer of "yes," and never follow up to see if those documents were actually approved. Each of these audit program formats will work for different types of reviews, provided the internal auditor gives some thought to the program questions. The key concern is that all audits should be supported by an audit program that documents the review steps performed. This approach allows audit

EXHIBIT 8.8 Audit Program Standard Format: Review of Petty Cash

Audit: ________ **Location:** ________ **Date:** ________

#	Audit Step	Initial & Date	W/P Ref.
1.	Prior to review, determine who is the cashier responsible for the petty cash fund balances, receipt requirements, replenishment procedures, and guidelines for authorized disbursements.		
2.	Perform this petty cash review on a "surprise" basis. Identify yourself to cashier, request that the cashier function be closed but observe audit during your initial review, and make a detailed count of cash in the account as well as any included personal checks.		
3.	Having performed the count in the presence of cashier, ask the cashier to acknowledge the results of the auditor's cash count.		
4.	If any personal checks found in the cash count were over one day old, ask why they were not deposited or if they are being held as collateral for an employee short-term loan fund. If for such a fund, assess the propriety of this practice.		
5.	Reconcile the audited cash count with the fund's disbursement register, noting any differences.		
6.	Determine that all cash disbursements recorded have been made to valid employees for authorized purposed.		
7.	Observe office security procedures covering the fund and determine that funds are locked or otherwise secured.		
8.	Review procedures for fund replenishments. Select a prior period, review its supporting documentation, and reconcile activity to purchase journal.		
9.	Assess the overall control procedures, propriety, and efficiency of this petty cash process. Comment as appropriate.		
10.	Determine that the petty cash function is used only for authorized small cash disbursements rather than as a general change or short-term loan fund.		
11.	Document the results of the review and take steps to initiate immediate corrective actions if any problems were encountered during this review.		

________ Signature ________ Date

EXHIBIT 8.9 Checklist Format Audit Program: Review of Business Ethics

#	Internal Control Concern	Yes	No	N/a
1	Does the enterprise have a written code of business ethics/business conduct?			
2	Is the code distributed to all stakeholders?			
3	Are new stakeholders/employees provided an orientation for the code?			
4	Does the code assign responsibilities to operating personnel and others regarding compliance with it?			
5	Are all stakeholders required to acknowledge that they have read, understand, and agree to abide to the code?			
6	Are training program delivered to all stakeholders regarding compliance with the code?			
7	Does the code address standards that govern personnel conduct in their dealings with suppliers and customers?			
8	Is there an effective mechanism in place to allow employees and other stakeholders to confidentially report suspected violations of the code?			
9	Are there appropriate mechanisms in place to follow up on reports of suspected violations of the code?			
10	Is there an appropriate mechanism to allow employees and other stakeholders to find out the results of their reported code-related concerns?			
11	Is compliance with the code's provisions a standard used for measuring personnel performance at all levels?			
12	Is the code consistent with the requirements of the Sarbanes-Oxley Act?			
13	Are there procedures in place to update the code on a regular and periodic basis?			

____________ ____________

Signature Date

management to recognize what procedures the auditors did or did not perform in a given review. Strong and consistent audit programs are an important step in improving the overall quality of the internal audits performed.

Exhibit 8.9 is a checklist-format program for a review of enterprise business ethics. In this type of audit, the reviewer will be asking questions about whether the entity is or is not doing something. Yes-or-no responses are appropriate for this type of audit program, since there is not a very strong need to investigate corroborative evidence here.

The reliability of the planned materials and processes to be reviewed and internal audit's other understandings about an operation should also be considered when developing audit program for a specific facility or resource. There is little value in developing an audit program at a facility that calls for a review of systems and procedures when internal audit realizes that they are no longer in use. In developing an audit program, an internal auditor should try to select audit steps that are meaningful and that will produce reliable forms of audit evidence. For example, the audit program often needs to call for detailed tests in a given critical, high-risk area rather than suggesting that the information can be gathered through interviews.

Advanced audit techniques should also be incorporated into audit programs wherever practicable. Members of the audit staff who have IT audit or other technical skills should be consulted when preparing these audit program steps. There is no single best or set format for an audit program; however, the program should be a document that auditors can use to guide their efforts as well as to record activities. That audit program will then be included in the workpapers to serve as almost a table of contents of the audit activities described in those workpapers.

Types of Audit Evidence

As discussed in Chapter 9, the IIA professional standards state that an internal auditor should examine and evaluate information on all matters related to the planned audit objective. This information, called audit evidence, covers everything an internal auditor reviews or observes. The internal auditor should gather audit evidence in support of the auditor's evaluation—what internal audit standards call sufficient, competent, relevant, and useful audit evidence. A properly constructed audit program should guide an internal auditor in this evidence-gathering process. However, there multiple types of evidence that can be useful in developing audit conclusions. If an auditor actually observes an action or obtains an independent confirmation, this is one of the strongest forms of evidence. However, a casual response to an auditor's question covering that same area will be weaker. It is not that an auditor thinks the auditee is not telling the truth, but that actually observing some event is far superior to just hearing about it. Internal auditors will encounter different levels of audit evidence and should attempt to design their audit procedures to look for and rely on the best available audit evidence. Exhibit 8.10 provides some ranges of best evidence for different classifications of materials. The idea that a written, signed document is better evidence than a casual response should be no surprise to an internal auditor, but it is always good to keep these concepts in mind.

The field survey and the subsequent development of an audit program are preliminary activities to performing the actual internal audit. It is often more efficient to have supervisory

EXHIBIT 8.10 Internal Audit "Best Evidence" Classifications

Evidence Classification	Strongest	Weakest
Audit Procedures/ Technique	Observation/Confirmation	Casual Inquiry
Origin of the Evidence	Corroborative Materials	Underlying Statistics
Relationship of the Auditee	External Document	Auditee Internal Document
Form of Audit Evidence	Written with Signatures	Oral Comments
Sophistication of Evidence	Formal Documentation	Informal (i.e., Notes)
Location of Evidence	Connected to Area Reviewed	Derived/Supporting Materials
Source of Audit Evidence	Product of Internal Audit Work	Other Supporting Materials

personnel complete these preliminary steps before assigning staff auditors for the actual review. Supervisory internal auditors, whether audit management or experienced in-charge auditors, usually have the expertise to make quick assessments of field situations and to fine-tune the overall audit approach. However, once the survey and the completed audit programs have been reviewed and approved by internal audit management, the next challenge is performing the actual audit to meet its desired audit objectives. The preparatory work from the survey will play an important role in assuring the audit's success; however, the internal auditor will now be faced with the day-to-day problems of performing the actual audit.

The actual audit steps performed will depend on the characteristics of the entity audited. A financially oriented audit of a credit and collection department will be quite different from an operational review of a design engineering function. The audit might include independent confirmations of account balances, while the operational audit typically includes extensive interviews with management and supporting documentation to assess key internal controls. Despite these differences, all internal audits should be performed and supervised following a general set of principles or standards. This will assure that internal audits are properly directed and controlled.

8.6 PERFORMING THE INTERNAL AUDIT

This section discusses general steps necessary to perform any internal audit, and should be used in conjunction with other specific audit procedures discussed throughout this book. Understanding how to perform an internal audit is really *the key* CBOK internal audit requirement. While the previously discussed preliminary survey is an important planning step, an engagement letter, shown in Exhibit 8.5, is the important first step in announcing a planned audit, defining its objectives and scope, the assigned audit team, and the approximate time periods. A single engagement letter is usually sufficient; however, in some audit situations there may be a considerable time interval between an initial field survey and the actual audit. A second engagement letter would then be useful.

An engagement letter outlines the arrangements for the planned internal audit. As discussed previously, unannounced audits may be justified in cases where there is a suspicion of fraud or when a unit is very small, with records that can be easily altered. In most instances, however, audit management should start the review with this formal engagement letter that alerts local and line management of the planned review, allowing them to adjust their schedules as appropriate. In some instances, auditee management may request a postponement due to any number of reasons. With the exception of a potential fraud situation, internal audit management should always try to be flexible here.

The assigned internal auditors also have some advance work prior to actual fieldwork. If there was a separate field survey, those results should be reviewed, as should any audit permanent file workpapers. For larger audits with multiple auditors, audit program assignments should be made in advance. For out-of-town engagements, travel and lodging arrangements should be made in accordance with enterprise policies. Travel costs can be a major expense for an internal audit department, particularly if there are numerous, scattered audit locations, domestic and worldwide. Significant travel savings can often be realized by taking advantage of discount airfares and making other cost-effective travel arrangements. Internal audit management must recognize, however, that travel will always be a major budget expense and should not avoid trips to higher audit-risk locations just because of the cost. Internal audit has a responsibility to their audit committee and senior management to report on the status of the enterprise's internal control structure. Field visits should not be postponed or eliminated because of the cost of travel to remote locations.

Internal Audit Fieldwork Initial Procedures

An internal audit can cause interruptions and problems in the day-to-day operations of the auditee organization. The in-charge auditor and members of the audit team should begin by meeting with appropriate members of auditee management to outline preliminary plans for the audit, including areas to be tested, special reports or documentation needed, and personnel to be interviewed. This also is an appropriate time for the internal audit team to tour the unit and to meet other unit personnel. The auditors should request that management contact all affected members of the auditee organization to provide them with an auditor-prepared tentative schedule of the planned audit work. This will eliminate potential problems in securing the cooperation of auditee personnel.

Despite the best of plans, problems can still occur while conducting the audit. For example, a key auditee organization supervisor may claim to be too busy to talk to internal audit and will not supply necessary information. Similarly, a cycle from a key IT system file that was to have been saved for audit tests may have been deleted. These types of problems can either slow progress or require a revised testing and analysis strategy. Any problems should be detected early in the assignment and solved as soon as possible. Difficulties in obtaining cooperation of one department's personnel, for example, may slow work in that area and delay the completion of the entire audit.

When these types of potential problems occur, the in-charge auditor should meet with auditee management to discuss any problems and to find solutions. If local management appears to be uncooperative, the in-charge auditor may have to contact internal audit management to resolve the problem at a different level. If a key component of the planned audit is missing, such as a missing data file, audit management should develop a revised strategy to get around the problem. This might include:

- **Revising audit procedures to perform additional tests in other areas.** This type of change, however, should only be performed with care. If there was a strong reason for selecting the now missing file—such as the need to tie it to some other data—it may be necessary to reconstruct the missing balances.
- **Completing the audit without the missing data file.** The workpapers and the final report would indicate internal audit's inability to perform the planned tests. The in-charge auditor should always gain approval from internal audit management for this approach.
- **Completing other portions of the audit and rescheduling a later visit to perform tests.** (This is only an option if the missing data file cannot be reconstructed or if a different cycle of data would be sufficient.) Management should be informed, of course, of audit budget overruns because of this problem.

These or similar types of problems can be encountered in this manner for many field audits. It is important that such problems be detected and resolved as early in the audit as possible. If the internal audit team faces a total lack of cooperation, management should be informed at appropriate levels to resolve the matter. Both the internal auditors and auditees should always remember that both are members of the same overall enterprise with common general interests and goals.

The actual audit fieldwork should follow the established audit program. As each step is completed, the responsible auditor should initial and date the audit program. Documentation gathered from each audit step, as well as any audit analyses, should be organized and forwarded to the in-charge auditor, who performs a preliminary review of the audit work. The in-charge auditor monitors the performance of the audit work in progress and reviews workpapers as they are completed for each step. Exhibit 8.11 shows a field audit point sheet where the in-charge auditor has signed off on key audit program steps and suggested areas for additional work. The comments from this sheet go back to the audit program for a review of petty cash. Of course, petty cash is usually a relatively small, low-risk area, but this type of point sheet document is useful for larger audits.

Point sheets should always be supported by and cross-referenced to the specific audit workpapers, and the status of the points raised should be documented to show their eventual disposition. If developed into a finding, the point sheet can also be cross-referenced to that audit report finding. If the point sheet potential finding is dropped during the fieldwork or later, the reasons should be documented. The results of many audit steps will not yield specific audit findings but may raise questions for further investigation. The conditions in many areas reviewed can be subject to explanations or interpretations by local management. Rather than just writing them up, the field audit team should generally discuss their preliminary audit observations with the persons responsible for the area. The auditor can sometimes misinterpret something that is easily resolved. If questions still remain, the matter may become a preliminary audit finding, as discussed in the following section.

EXHIBIT 8.11 Preliminary Audit Findings: Minneapolis Facility Purchasing and Accounts Payable Audit

April 15, 20xx

To: Workpaper Files

From: L. C. Tuttle, Audit Supervisor

Subject: Purchasing & Accounts Payable Systems Audit Preliminary Findings

This memo is to document our preliminary observation from our recent review of key purchasing and accounts payable processes at Global Computer Products manufacturing facility in Minneapolis, MN. The objective of this review will be to assess the adequacy of purchasing system internal accounting controls at the Global Computer Products Minneapolis facility as well as the purchasing processes at multiple branch facilities, interfaces to the accounts payable system at corporate headquarters, and automated systems to support these processes.

Our preliminary findings and observations from this review are listed below. The observations may be subject to revision based on management comments or clarification regarding our observations. In addition, these observation will be supported by a full internal audit report to be issued on or about May 5, 20XX.

While we found internal controls and procedures to be generally adequate, we observed the following areas requiring corrective actions:

1. Valid purchase orders were missing for some equipment in the new products engineering laboratory.
2. Existing policies for investigating open purchase orders are not being followed and we observed a growing number of these documents.
3. Purchase orders issued for materials in the Speedo division were frequently missing part units of measure, creating an environment for potential errors.
4. The new Web-based purchasing system is lacking daily input balancing controls, creating an environment where duplicate purchase orders could be issued.
5. Purchasing and accounts payable records and systems are not regularly included in the new corporation business continuity plan.

L. C. Tuttle, Audit Supervisor

W. J. Rawdon, Audit Manager

Audit Fieldwork Technical Assistance

The field survey or the audit program development process may have identified any need for specialized technical help to perform an internal audit; however, other complex problems requiring technical support may arise in the course of the audit fieldwork. For example, the assigned auditor may question the accounting treatment of a certain set of transactions and want to get better information about normal practices for them. Similarly, the auditors may encounter a specialized IT application, with unique control considerations, that was not sufficiently identified or described in the survey.

If a technical issue is not familiar to the audit team, the in-charge auditor should seek assistance as soon as possible. An internal audit supervisor or specialist may have to research the audit or technical issue in order to provide the answer. In other instances, it may be necessary to bring an internal audit expert in the area in question to the field site to resolve the concern or problem. However, a typical internal audit department does not have resident experts ready to travel out to the field site to resolve a problem, and issues can normally be resolved through telephone calls, e-mails, or exchanges of documentation.

The important message that audit management should communicate to staff is that all technical audit problems should be brought to the attention of the in-charge auditor for resolution as soon as possible. Any cost and extra time requirements caused by these technical problems should be documented. If the technical problem cannot be promptly resolved, it may be necessary to reschedule the audit or to revise the strategy, as described earlier.

Audit Management Fieldwork Monitoring

If the internal audit covers an extended period of time or level of required resources, internal audit management should review the audit's progress and provide technical direction through visits and communications. These reviews supplement the ongoing work of the in-charge auditor, who is part of the field staff. The frequency and extent of these visits will depend on the criticality of the review, the experience of the assigned staff, and the size of the review. A medium-size review headed by an experienced in-charge auditor and covering familiar areas may not require a management review if communication lines are good. However, if the audit covers a critical area, if a new program or new techniques are used, or if the assigned in-charge auditor has limited experience in the area reviewed, an experienced member of audit management should visit the fieldwork project periodically.

The purpose of these visits should be to review the work in progress and to help resolve problems encountered. While audit management may feel that this is also an appropriate time to take the assigned field staff out to lunch or dinner to thank them for their efforts, all should realize this is not the purpose of audit field visits. Audit management should take this opportunity to understand any evolving issues in the audit and to suggest changes as appropriate. This is also a good time for management to start the review of completed audit workpapers, as discussed in Chapter 17.

Internal audit workpapers report on the work performed and provide a link between the procedures documented in the audit program and the results of audit tests. Because they will become the basis for findings and recommendations in final audit reports, the workpapers should appropriately document all audit work. While the in-charge auditor should have been reviewing and commenting on workpapers for larger audits through audit point sheets as illustrated in Exhibit 8.11, smaller reviews without a separate auditor will not have this type of feedback. Point sheets are an internal audit quality assurance tool and should be resolved by the auditors in the field as soon as there is an indication that a potentially substantive audit issue exists. This facilitates bringing these issues to the attention of both internal audit and auditee management at an early point in the review. It also serves as a control to assure that all leads are followed. In addition, the various auditor point sheets, developed by individual staff members, may bring out a number of minor issues that fall into a pattern, indicating a more serious overall condition.

The member of audit management visiting the field site should spend some time reviewing and approving the workpapers and preliminary finding sheets then prepared. These workpaper-review comments should be documented, cover such areas as additional work or explanations required, and suggest adjustments to the audit program if appropriate. The management review should typically not result in major changes to the audit approach. However, internal audit management can often bring some additional guidance or understanding to the audit in process.

The review comments should be documented in a manner that references pages or items in the workpapers where the management reviewer has questions or identifies missing items of audit documentation. Based on these review comments, the staff auditors should then perform the additional audit work required and make necessary changes to the workpapers, indicating the action taken on the review sheet. After completion of internal audit's comments, the additional work done, or corrections, the supervisor indicates on the review comment sheets his or her clearance of all items as well as any further actions to be taken.

Potential Audit Findings

Whenever an internal auditor discovers a potential audit deficiency, a brief summary of the conditions found and potential findings and recommendations should be prepared. This summary sometimes appears in what is called an audit preliminary findings sheet. Based on the Exhibit 8.5 engagement letter and partially on the general audit program steps outlined in Exhibit 8.7, Exhibit 8.11 is an audit preliminary findings sheet for our sample audit of accounts payable processes for Global Computer Products' operations in its Minneapolis facility. Whether or not the conditions described in such a preliminary document result in the final audit report findings depends on the results of additional review and analysis. These preliminary findings describe deficiencies or opportunities for improvement that were identified during the audit. These preliminary findings may have been developed through the auditor point sheets, described earlier, or through other internal audit-documented findings and observations. These items start the preliminary report writing process early in the audit, and help to assure that the essential facts for developing an audit report finding have been obtained. Although the contents of a preliminary audit finding can vary depending on the needs of the particular internal audit, preliminary audit findings typically have the following elements:

- **Identification of the findings.** This is just an identification number for the audit and a description of the potential findings.
- **The conditions of the completed audit.** The description is generally brief but sufficient to give local management an understanding of the conditions found.
- **References to the documented audit work.** The audit point sheet should contain cross-references to the step in the audit program that initiated the comment, as well as where it is documented in the audit workpapers.

- **Auditor's preliminary recommendations.** Audit report space should be used to document the nature of the potential audit finding and what was wrong. This might become the basis for a potential future audit report finding. Some notes on potential auditor-recommended corrective actions might be included here.
- **Results of discussing the findings with management.** The in-charge auditor should discuss all potential findings on an informal basis with the manager directly responsible for the matter. The results of this conversation should be documented here.
- **Recommended disposition of the matter.** On the basis of the conversation with management, the in-charge auditor should include comments on the recommended disposition of the findings. It might be recommended for inclusion in the audit report, dropped for a variety of reasons, or deferred until more information can be gathered.

Audit Program and Schedule Modifications

The audit program is the overall guide for conducting an internal audit. Developed from preliminary survey data and from any past internal audits on file, it may be subject to adjustment during the course of the review. Auditors must be responsive to new evidence, changes in supporting systems, and other changes in conditions. In the early stages of an audit, it may be necessary to redirect some of the planned staff assignments as well as to modify some audit program steps. Of course, the in-charge auditor in the field should always obtain approval from audit management before making any such changes.

The need for audit program modifications is most frequent when internal audit has developed a common audit program for use in reviews of similar but not identical units. For example, an audit program may have been developed to cover controls over the purchasing function for an organization with multiple independent manufacturing units, each with separate purchasing functions. Those purchasing function audit programs should reflect both organization policy and general internal control principles. Due to local differences, however, this audit program may contain steps that are not applicable to one or another specific purchasing area under audit. Any such steps that are bypassed on the individual audit program should be approved and documented as to the reasons.

Changes are often required in the audit schedule and plan as work progresses. Some flexibility should be factored into plans to meet unforeseen requirements. During the field audit assignment, situations may be encountered that affect the progress of its audit, such as an unexpected problem or event, the need to modify or drop an audit program segment, the discovery of a new area for review, or changes in audit personnel. In other instances, there may be slippage in the plan due to additional time requirements to finish an audit program step. In these circumstances, revised budgets are needed. Proper approvals for these changes should always be obtained from internal audit management.

Reporting Preliminary Audit Findings to Management

A major area of emphasis in any internal audit is the identification of areas where the unit reviewed is not in compliance with good internal control procedures and where improvements are needed. These areas would have been documented during the course of the audit through the use of a point or findings sheets and preliminary findings types of documents. Although these potential audit items should have been discussed with the unit supervisors directly responsible, the audit team should also review them with unit management before leaving the field audit assignment.

Potential audit findings should be reviewed with unit management during the audit to determine if they are factual and appear to be significant. Depending on the scope and size of the audit, these potential findings should be analyzed at several points during the course of the review. If an audit is scheduled over multiple weeks, the in-charge auditor might schedule a meeting with unit management at least at the end of each week to discuss all findings that developed over the course of that week. If the findings are of a minor, procedural nature, management can take necessary corrective actions at once. They can then be deemphasized or deleted in any final audit report. For other findings, the in-charge auditor should review proposed findings to ascertain that cost savings are indicated and properly reported and that findings are related to operational effectiveness.

Even though the audit's duration may be too short to have weekly status meetings, the field audit team should almost always review all potential findings with management before leaving the location. This will allow internal audit to present its preliminary findings and recommendations to local management to obtain their reactions and comments. It also gives both parties an opportunity to correct any errors in the preliminary audit report findings before internal audit leaves the location.

8.7 WRAPPING UP THE FIELD ENGAGEMENT INTERNAL AUDIT

Internal audits should be managed in the same manner as any large project requiring personnel time and other resources and resulting in a defined deliverable. Both personnel resources and other costs should be planned and budgeted on a detailed level, and Chapter 16 talks about project management for internal auditors. The audit's actual performance should be recorded and measured against established time- and cost-based budgets to analyze and correct for any significant variances. Significant project milestones, such as the completion of fieldwork or of the draft audit report, should also be tracked against plans. Of course, the most important internal audit work product is the formal audit report, with its findings and recommendations, which is delivered to the auditee after completion of the review as well as to the audit committee. Internal audit reporting processes, as well as some sample audit reports, are discussed in Chapter 18.

Chapter 15 discusses risk-based audit planning and the development of the annual audit plan, while this chapter considers the need for detailed plans for individual audit projects. Individual internal audits should be budgeted with time and other costs measured against those plans. No matter how large or small an enterprise's internal audit function, an audit project performance reporting system should be established. For audits greater than about two weeks' duration or those performed in multiple locations at the same time, progress reports should be required on a weekly or biweekly basis. These reports should be based on the time summaries from the assigned audit staff as well as commentaries from the in-charge auditor at the location. They can include such information as budgeted and actual time to date, estimated time to complete, and a summarized description of progress against the audit program. This data can be gathered by the supervising auditors at field sites and transmitted to the central internal audit department. The in-charge auditor should take responsibility for explaining any significant variances in audit actual versus budget performance. Such a report would be based on an overall internal audit time-reporting system that measures expended staff internal audit hours against established internal audit budgets.

The time expended on individual audit projects should be further summarized by internal audit management to provide an overview of all audits planned or in process. A three-month window is often a good time period for planned future activities, given the various senior management requests and other factors that can impact an internal audit plan. This type of report is used to provide control over audits scheduled or in process while a separate, more detailed report can be completed for each individual audit to assure that they are started and completed on a timely basis. The rolling three-month report can be a useful tool for communicating with the audit committee.

Any increases in audit time budgets should be carefully monitored, and reasons for the variance as well as any corrective action plans should be identified. Audit project monitoring indicates any audits not started on time or that are outside of budget parameters. In some cases, the problem may be inaccurate budgets; in others, the problem may lie in auditor performance. Close control of the audit will prevent slippage caused by inadequacies in staff, delays in solving problems, insufficient supervision, and excessive attention to detail.

As discussed in Chapter 16 on project management for internal auditors, automated techniques and tools should be developed and maintained for such an internal audit reporting and control system. Spreadsheet or database packages can provide a powerful structure for building such systems. Many paper-based reports can be eliminated, and the field auditors can transmit their time summaries and status report information to a central internal audit project reporting system.

8.8 PERFORMING AN INDIVIDUAL INTERNAL AUDIT

As discussed throughout this book, internal auditing is a large and complex process with many activities, and the concept behind our CBOK theme is to highlight the knowledge areas that are important to any internal auditor. While internal audit reports, discussed in Chapter 18, are internal audit's most important work product, the ability to plan and perform an individual internal audit is a key knowledge requirement. Whether a member of the internal audit staff, a more senior designated in-charge auditor, or any member of the internal audit management team, the professional should have a sufficient understanding to assess risks and plan the internal audit, to visit the audit site and start the engagement, to prepare workpapers documenting those audit activities, and to summarize results in preparation for the concluding internal audit report.

Because so many different types of internal audits are performed, we have not tried to outline the steps necessary to perform one generic internal audit. However, an internal auditor should have a good understanding of the *International Standards for the Professional Practice of Internal Auditing*, as summarized in Chapter 9, as well as many of the internal audit planning and performance tools summarized in other chapters. The standards are a key, however. They outline the steps of the procedure that an internal auditor must follow.

The most important values that the internal audit process provides to the audit committee and management are the reported results of the detailed audits performed in the field or as part of overall operations. Gathering initial evidence, performing the audit, and reporting initial findings to management are all part of this internal audit process. Exhibit 8.12 summarizes these steps for performing internal audits up through the completion of the fieldwork. Once the fieldwork has been completed, the next step will be the preparation of the actual audit report, as discussed in Chapter 18.

EXHIBIT 8.12 The Internal Audit Process: Summarized Steps

1. As part of audit planning, perform risk analysis to identify potential control risks.
2. Based on results of the risk analysis and other constraints, develop audit plan.
3. Preliminarily schedule internal audit and allocate resources.
4. Review any past audit reports and workpapers covering audit area.
5. Visit site and perform field survey covering area of planned audit.
6. Based on established workpapers and field survey, prepare audit programs.
7. Prepare and deliver engagement letter for audit, and plan to start internal audit.
8. Begin internal audit fieldwork and planned internal audit.
9. Document processes and perform planned audit procedures.
10. Develop audit point sheets covering preliminary internal audit findings.
11. Complete audit documentation and summarize potential audit findings.
12. Complete internal audit fieldwork and review proposed findings with auditee.

CHAPTER NINE

Standards for the Professional Practice of Internal Auditing

EVERY PROFESSION REQUIRES A SET of standards to provide rules and guidelines to govern their practices, general procedures, and ethics. These standards help the specialists performing similar work to call themselves professionals because they are following a recognized and consistent set of best practices standards. The key standards for internal auditors are found in the Institute of Internal Auditors' (IIA's) *International Standards for the Professional Practice of Internal Auditing* (IIA standards), a set of guidance materials that has been important to internal auditors for many years going back to the pre-Web paper-document days when the IIA standards where known as the *Red Book* by many internal auditors. The internal auditor's *code of ethics* is bundled with these practice standards. The IIA standards have gone through multiple revisions over the years. In 2015, the basic IIA standards, code of ethics, and other guidance materials were bundled into what is known as the *International Professional Practices Framework (IPPF)*.

This chapter will summarize the current required and recommended IIA standards as well as a description of the overall IPPF, including internal audit's core principles and its *mission statement*. It is important to note that IIA standards are just advisory. Although the organization can pull someone's CIA certificate, it does not have the power to prohibit someone from practicing internal auditing in the manner that the American Insitute of CPAs (AICPA) can prevent someone from practicing public accounting. However, some of these IIA standards are clearly marked as "Required," while others are just "Recommended." An internal auditor's work should be performed in compliance with all of these standards. A strong understanding of the IIA's *International Standards for the Professional Practice of Internal Auditing* and an overall knowledge of the IPPF is an absolute internal auditor common body of knowledge (CBOK) *must* requirement for all internal auditors. The IPPF and these standards provide support for many if not all internal audit professional activities.

The IIA code of ethics for internal auditors is an important supporting foundation for internal auditors in today's world of frequent open questions regarding professional ethics. This chapter will also consider the code of ethics of the Information Systems Audit and Control Association (ISACA) professional organization. ISACA members are often IIA or CPA members as well, and many are IT audit specialists, but their code of ethics places a special emphasis on their IT-related activities. Although ISACA does not have the same level of standards as IIA, their COBIT internal control framework and information regarding their related professional group, the IT Governance Institute, are discussed in Chapter 6. Chapter 31 also will introduce another very important set of *internal audit standards*, the quality audit guidance standards from the American Society for Quality (ASQ). ASQ's internal audit standards and its quality auditors represent a different dimension and discipline from the IIA's approaches and standards. It also represents an area that should be better understood in the overall world of internal auditing.

The IIA's *International Standards for the Professional Practice of Internal Auditing* and its IPPF represent a must-know set of requirements for internal auditors today, and this chapter will summarize these IIA standards, including a discussion of the most current, just-released changes to them. While the standards are an evolving set of rules that may not exactly reflect all industry practices at a point in time, they recognize a set of guidelines for internal auditors worldwide to follow in their service to management. The current IIA standards are available from the IIA.[1] They represent important guidance for today's internal auditor and must be in every internal auditor's professional library.

9.1 WHAT IS THE IPPF?

Over the years, the IIA has released many guidance materials that have gone beyond the long-standing practice standards, definitions, and ethics codes. In 2015 they brought all of these together into what is now the IPPF. Although the IPPF does not have the authority of all of the IIA's published documents, Exhibit 9.1 shows its key components, bundled together into either *required* or *recommended* elements:

- **An internal audit mission statement.** In prior editions of this book and others, we have talked about the importance of enterprise senior management's establishing mission statements to provide guidance for the overall enterprise. Perhaps this author and others never considered that internal auditors needed a formal mission statement to cover their work, too. However, it is a good summary statement to describe what an internal auditor actually does. The new IPPF mission is introduced in Chapter 1 on the significance of internal auditing.
- **Internal audit core principles.** These again are concepts understood by many internal auditors, which the IPPF has sought to more formally define. The IPPF internal audit core principles are introduced in this chapter.
- **Definition of internal auditing.** This important statement is found in Chapter 1.
- ***International Standards for the Professional Practice of Internal Auditing.*** First published by the IIA years ago as its *Red Book*, these standards are summarized later in this chapter.
- **Implementation and supplemental guidance.** These are concepts that have been described but were not released as part of the 2015 IPPF.

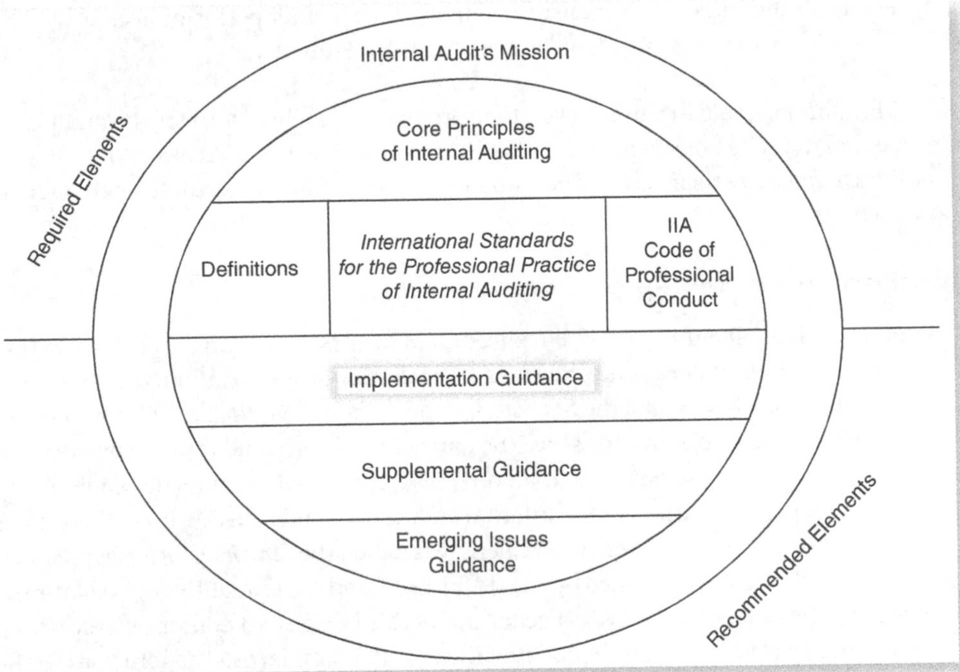

EXHIBIT 9.1 IPPF Extract

- **Emerging issues guidance.** While internal auditors have always been confronted with new and evolving technical, business, and legal issues, they have had to adapt to them as best as possible. Although the guidance has not yet been released, the IIA is proposing it here as part of the IPPF.

9.2 THE INTERNAL AUDITING PROFESSIONAL PRACTICE STANDARDS: A KEY IPPF COMPONENT

Internal auditors work in a large variety of enterprises and are asked to perform internal audit reviews in a diverse number of operational, IT, and financial areas. Despite this diversity, an enterprise audit committee and senior management expect their internal auditors to perform reviews in a competent and consistent manner. Internal audits should be performed using a set of recognized standards as a key approach to meet those management expectations. As the premier and leading worldwide internal audit professional organization, the IIA, through its IPPF, has developed and issued standards that define the basic practice of internal auditing. The *International Standards for the Professional Practice of Internal Auditing* are designed to:

- Delineate basic principles for the practice of internal auditing.
- Provide a framework for performing and promoting a broad range of value-added internal audit activities.

- Establish the basis for the measurement of internal audit performance.
- Foster improved organizational processes and operations.

The standards aid in this process; they provide a guideline both for the audit committee and management to measure their internal auditors as well as one for internal auditors to measure themselves. The standards also set some constraints upon internal audit activity.

Background of the IIA Standards

Chapter 1 talked about the early background of internal auditing, a profession that developed its own standards and processes. Its professional organization, the Institute of Internal Auditors, first issued the *Standards for the Professional Practice of Internal Auditing* in 1978 with an objective to "serve the entire profession in all types of business, in various levels of government, and in all other enterprises where internal auditors are found . . . to represent the practice of internal auditing as it must be." Prior to these 1978 standards, the most authoritative document was called the *Statement of Responsibilities of Internal Audit*, originally issued by the IIA in 1947 and subsequently revised over the years until the current standards. The author of this book's first edition, Victor Brink, played a major role in the development of the first IIA standards. The foreword to the 1978 IIA standards describes them as "the criteria by which the operations of an internal auditing department are evaluated and measured." It goes on to state, "Compliance with the concepts enunciated by the Standards is essential before the responsibilities of the internal auditor can be met."

The standards were developed by the IIA's Professional Standards Committee based on its own professional expertise as well as comments received from IIA members and other interested parties. Because of the diverse group of participants who developed the earlier standards, the final language often had some overlap, compromise, and incompleteness. As a result, some individual standards and guidelines still may be subject to varying interpretations.

All internal auditors today are expected to follow these standards. It would be a rare internal audit function that did not have an internal audit charter, as was discussed in Chapter 8, and those charters should strongly affirm adherence to the IIA's standards. While some internal auditors may have also come from some other professional area, such as banking or from an external audit firm, with their own disciplines and professional standards, those audit activities generally will not be in conflict with the IIA standards. They may use slightly different terminology, as will be discussed with the ISACA code of ethics, introduced later in this chapter, but must follow audit practices that generally fit under the IIA standards. As a matter of practice, however, the IIA's standards govern the work of internal audit and knowledge of them is an important CBOK requirement. When there appears to be a conflict and when the individual questioning that conflict is working as an internal auditor, the IIA's standards take precedence over any conflicting professional standards.

The IIA has historically published these standards, with the above title, in the previously mentioned small publication known as the *Red Book*. With a changing world and impressions of the role of internal auditors, the standards have changed over the years. There was a major update to them in 2001, a revised set was issued in 2004, and they were further updated in 2012 and have been included in today's IPPF.

9.3 CONTENT OF THE IIA STANDARDS

The following discussion is a summary and overview of the IIA standards. It is designed to help internal audit professionals better understand and use these standards in their internal audit work, but should not be considered an authoritative reference. Internal auditors should purchase a copy of the IIA's *Red Book* standards for their own guidance.

The standards consist of what are called *attribute standards, performance standards,* and *implementation standards*. The attribute standards address the characteristics of enterprises and parties performing internal audit activities. The performance standards describe the nature of internal audit activities and provide quality criteria against which the performance of these services can be evaluated. While the attribute and performance standards apply to all internal audit services, the implementation standards also apply to specific types of engagements and are further divided between standards for assurance and standards for consulting activities. This split reflects that internal auditors sometimes do strictly audit assurance–type projects, such as reviewing internal control effectiveness in some area, and sometimes do internal audit consulting–related work.

Many of the other chapters in this book cover internal audit assurance or attest activities, while Chapter 30 has a focus on internal auditors as enterprise consultants.

The attribute standards are numbered in sections as part of the 1000 series of standards, while performance standards are classified in the 2000 series. Implementation standards, further designated as (A) for assurance or (C) for consulting, are organized under each of these attribute and performance standards. The sections following describe the attribute and performance standards in some detail as well as some of the descriptive implementation standards. Recognizing that internal auditors may be asked just to review internal controls or to act more as internal consultants, there may be multiple sets of implementation standards: a set for each of the major types of internal audit activity. Implementation standards established for internal audit assurance activities are coded with an "A" following the standard number (e.g., 1130.A1), and those covering internal audit consulting activities are noted by a "C" following the standard number (e.g., nnnn.C1).

Our objective here is not, however, to just reproduce all of these IIA standards but to describe their content and how they have changed or are evolving over recent years. If not already in possession of them, all internal auditors should obtain a copy from the IIA or at least gain access to the standards and develop a good understanding of their contents. Knowledge of the standards is a CBOK requirement for all internal auditors. The IIA web site, www.theiia.org, is an official source for these IIA internal audit standards, and the reader is advised to consult it.

Internal Audit Attribute Standards

Attribute standards address the characteristics of enterprises and individuals performing internal audit activities. Numbered from paragraph 1000 to 13000, they cover broad areas that define the attributes of today's modern internal auditor. Here, along with the performance standards, we have listed and described these attribute standards (organized by their standards paragraph numbers):

1000—Purpose, Authority, and Responsibility. The purpose, authority, and responsibility of the internal audit activity should be formally defined in an internal audit charter, consistent with the standards, and approved by the board of directors. Separate implementation standards here state that internal auditing assurance and consulting services must be defined in the internal audit charter.

1100—Independence and Objectivity. The internal audit activity must be independent, and internal auditors must be objective in performing their work. Subsections under this discuss the importance of both individual and organizational objectivity as well as the need to disclose any impairment to internal audit independence or objectivity.

1110—Organizational Independence. While the IIA standards do not specify that internal audit should report to the audit committee, that reporting relationship must be free from any interference in determining the scope of internal auditing, performing work, and communicating results. While we often think of internal audit as a key component in today's Sarbanes and Oxley (SOx)–defined corporate world with board audit committees, internal audit can operate in many different international locations or for many different types of enterprises. Whether serving a not-for-profit organization in the United States or a governmental agency in a developing country, internal audit always must exhibit organizational independence.

1120—Individual Objectivity. This really repeats a basic principle of internal auditing: Internal auditors must have an impartial, unbiased attitude and avoid conflicts of interest.

1130—Impairments to Independence or Objectivity. If internal audit's independence or objectivity is impaired in fact or appearance, the details of the impairment must be disclosed as part of the audit work. This could be a management-imposed impairment or one due to the background or other circumstances surrounding an individual internal auditor.

There are several assurance and consulting attribute standards here, but one summarizes this standard:

1130.A1—Internal auditors should refrain from assessing specific operations for which they were previously responsible. Objectivity is presumed to be impaired if an internal auditor provides services (this is an assurance standard here, but consulting standards have a similar paragraph) for an activity for which the internal auditor had responsibility within the previous year.

This is an important standard. Because of their specialized knowledge, internal auditors are sometimes asked to go back to audit the group where they once worked. In such a case, no matter how hard they may try to act to the contrary, they will not be viewed as objective.

> **1200—Proficiency and Due Professional Care.** Engagements must be performed with proficiency and due professional care. There is an important proposed new implementation standard here:
>
> **1210.A1**—The CAE should obtain competent advice and assistance if the internal audit staff lacks the knowledge, skills, or other competencies needed to perform all or part of the engagement.
>
> **1210.A2**—An internal auditor must have sufficient knowledge to identify the indicators of fraud and the manner in which it is managed by the organization, but are not expected to have the expertise of a person whose primary responsibility is detecting and investigating fraud.

As discussed in Chapter 27, this internal auditor fraud audit guidance is somewhat weak. The AICPA under SAS No. 99 requires external auditors to aggressively think about red flags, indicators that might include the possibility of fraud, as well as to look for potential fraud in the course of their audits. Although this requirement is certainly an IIA professional standards decision, we feel that internal auditors should maintain a greater awareness about the possibility of fraud in the course of their internal audits. Internal auditors are often the best investigators to find these circumstances. For example, an external auditor may have little contact with a remote sales office, but internal audit may visit that same office as part of a regularly scheduled internal audit.

> **1210.A3**—Internal auditors must have general knowledge of key information technology risks and controls available to support technology-based audit techniques. However, not all internal auditors are expected to have the expertise of some specialized IT auditors whose primary responsibility is information technology.

Recognizing that there is a need for IT audit specialists, this standard states that *all* internal auditors *must* have a good general understanding of IT risks and controls. In addition, 1210.A2 substandard on due professional care specifies that internal auditors must consider the use of "technology-based audit" tools and techniques. Computer-assisted audit techniques have been part of the toolkits of many internal auditors.[2] While a good idea for all of these years, they now have risen to the level of internal audit standard.

> **1220—Due Professional Care.** Internal auditors must apply the care and skill expected of a reasonably prudent and competent internal auditor. Due professional care does not imply infallibility. Another section of the standards goes on to state that in exercising due professional care, an internal audit must consider:
>
> - Extent of work needed to achieve the engagement's objectives;
> - Relative complexity, materiality, or significance of matters to which assurance procedures are applied;
> - Adequacy and effectiveness of risk management, control, and governance processes;

- Probability of significant errors, irregularities, or noncompliance; and
- Cost of assurance in relation to potential benefits.

This internal audit standard really says that an internal auditor must be cautious in beginning and performing an internal audit. The first of these bullet points, the extent of work, says that an internal auditor, for example, must perform an adequate level of investigation and testing before coming to a final audit recommendation. As one of the new standards released in 2004, computer-assisted audit techniques appear once again:

1220.A2—In exercising due professional care, the internal auditor must consider the use of technology-based audit tools and other data analysis techniques.

1220.A3—The internal auditor must be alert to the significant risks that might affect objectives, operations, or resources. However, assurance procedures alone, even when performed with due professional care, do not guarantee that all significant risks will be identified. As discussed in Chapter 6, an understanding of risk assessment techniques is an increasingly import CBOK area for internal auditors. This guidance has been part of the IIA standards going back to its early versions and must be part of an internal auditor's procedures.

The standards continue in this section with 1230—Continuing Professional Development, a standard on the requirement for continuing professional education and development.

1300—Quality Assurance and Improvement Program. The CAE must develop and maintain a quality assurance and improvement program that covers all aspects of internal audit activity and continuously monitors its effectiveness. The quality assurance and improvement program must be designed to enable an evaluation of the internal audit activity's conformance with internal auditing standards as well as an evaluation of whether internal auditors apply the Code of Ethics. The program also assesses the efficiency and effectiveness of the internal audit activity and identifies opportunities for improvement.

The standards here call for both internal and external quality reviews and emphasize the importance of good quality assurance processes within internal audit. Quality assurances as well as quality audits are discussed in Chapter 31, and two important standards here are:

1311—Internal Assessments. Internal audit management must have an internal assessment process in place that includes both the ongoing monitoring of the performance of the internal audit activity and periodic reviews performed through self-assessment or by other persons within the enterprise with sufficient knowledge of internal audit practices.

1312—External Assessments. As discussed previously, external assessments must be conducted at least once every five years by a qualified, independent reviewer or review team from outside the organization. The CAE must discuss this need for more frequent external assessments with the board audit committee and the qualifications and independence of the external reviewer or review team, including any potential conflicts of interest.

This section of the standards has a requirement that the CAE may state that the internal audit activity conforms with the IIA internal auditing standards only if the results of the most recent quality assurance and improvement program support this statement.

Internal Audit Performance Standards

Performance standards describe the nature of internal audit activities and provide quality criteria against which these services can be measured. There are six performance standards, outlined next, along with substandards and implementation standards that apply to compliance audits, fraud investigations, or control self-assessment projects. While we are summarizing the standard here for the purpose of describing internal audit processes, the interested professional must contact the IIA to obtain the standards in either downloaded or printed format.

> **2000—Managing the Internal Audit Activity**. The CAE must effectively manage the internal audit activity to ensure it adds value to the enterprise.

This standard covers six substandards: Planning, Communication and Approval, Resource Management, Policies and Procedures, Coordination, and Reporting to the Board and Senior Management. These substandards generally describe such good internal audit management practices as 2040 on Policies and Procedures, stating that the CAE must establish such guides.

The substandard 2060 on Reporting to the Board and Senior Management contains guidance applicable to today's SOx rules: "The chief audit executive should report periodically to the board and senior management on the internal audit activity's purpose, authority, responsibility, and performance relative to its plan. Reporting must also include significant risk exposures and control issues, corporate governance issues, and other matters needed or requested by the board and senior management. Reporting must also include significant risk exposure and control issues, including fraud risks, governance issues, and other matters needed or requested by senior management and the board."

> **2100—Nature of Work.** Internal audit activity includes evaluations and contributions to the improvement of risk management, control, and governance systems using "a systematic and disciplined approach."

Earlier IIA standards did not really address the important area of risk management. Risk management is discussed in Chapter 7 and is outlined in the IIA standards as follows:

> **2110—Risk Management.** Internal audit must assist the enterprise by identifying and evaluating significant exposures to risk and contributing to the improvement of risk management and control systems. Determining whether risk management processes are effective is a judgment resulting from an internal auditor's assessment that:

- Organizational objectives support and align with an enterprise's mission;
- Significant risks are identified and assessed;
- Appropriate risk responses are selected that align risks with the enterprise's risk appetite; and
- Relevant risk information, enabling staff, management, and the board to carry out their responsibilities, is captured and communicated in a timely manner across the enterprise.

Risk management processes should be monitored through ongoing management activities, separate evaluations, or both.

2110.A1—Internal audit activity must monitor and evaluate the effectiveness of the enterprise's risk management system.

2110.A2—The internal audit activity must evaluate risk exposures relating to the enterprise's governance, operations, and IT regarding the COSO standards of internal control.

2110.C1—During consulting engagements, internal auditors must address risk consistent with the engagement's objectives and must be alert to the existence of other significant risks.

2110.C2—Internal auditors must incorporate knowledge of risks gained from consulting engagements into the process of identifying and evaluating significant risk exposures of the enterprise.

2110.C3—When assisting management in establishing or improving risk management processes, internal auditors must refrain from assuming any management responsibility by actually managing risks.

2130—Governance. Internal audit must assess and make appropriate recommendations for improving the governance process in its accomplishment of the following objectives:

- Promoting appropriate ethics and values within the enterprise;
- Ensuring effective organizational performance management and accountability;
- Communicating risk and control information to appropriate areas of the enterprise; and
- Coordinating the activities of and communicating information among the board, external and internal auditors, and management.

This IIA governance standard is very consistent with SOx requirements. These standards support our Chapter 26 discussion on ethics and whistleblower programs.

2200—Engagement Planning. Internal auditors must develop and record a plan for each engagement, including the scope, objectives, timing, and resource allocations.

An important aspect of all internal audits, planning is discussed in Chapter 8 on performing effective internal audits.

2201—Planning Considerations. In planning an audit engagement, internal auditors should consider:

- The objectives of the activity being reviewed and the means by which the activity controls its performance.
- The significant risks to the activity, its objectives, resources, and operations, and the means by which the potential impact of risk is kept to an acceptable level.
- The adequacy and effectiveness of the activity's risk management and internal control processes compared to a relevant control framework or model.
- The opportunities for making significant improvements to the activity's risk management and control processes.

2201.A1—When planning an engagement for parties outside the enterprise, internal auditors must establish a written understanding with them about objectives, scope, respective responsibilities, and other expectations, including restrictions on distribution of the results of the engagement and access to engagement records.

2201.C1—Internal auditors must establish, and generally document, an understanding with consulting engagement clients about objectives, scope, respective responsibilities, and other client expectations. For significant engagements, this understanding must be documented.

2210—Objectives Must Be Established for Each Engagement.

2210.A1—Internal auditors must conduct a preliminary assessment of the risks relevant to the activity under review, and engagement objectives must reflect the results of this assessment.

2210.A2—The internal auditor must consider the probability of significant errors, irregularities, noncompliance, and other exposures when developing the engagement objectives. This relates to the risk assessment considerations discussed previously.

2210.A3—Adequate criteria are needed to evaluate controls. Internal auditors must ascertain the extent to which management has established adequate criteria to determine whether objectives and goals have been accomplished. If adequate, internal auditors must use such criteria in their evaluation. If inadequate, internal auditors must work with management to develop appropriate evaluation criteria.

2210.C1—Consulting engagement objectives must address risks, controls, and governance processes to the extent agreed on with the client.

2220—Engagement Scope. The established scope must be sufficient to satisfy the objectives of the engagement.

2220.A1—The scope of the engagement must include consideration of relevant systems, records, personnel, and physical properties, including those under the control of third parties.

2220.A2—If significant consulting opportunities arise during an assurance engagement, a specific written understanding as to the objectives, scope, respective responsibilities, and other expectations must be reached and the results of the consulting engagement communicated in accordance with these consulting standards. This says that an internal auditor can begin an audit as a strictly assurance level of review but may expand it to a consulting-level audit if there is a need or management request.

2220.C1—In performing consulting engagements, internal auditors must ensure that the scope of the engagement is sufficient to address the agreed-upon objectives. If internal auditors develop reservations about the scope during the engagement, these reservations must be discussed with the auditee to determine whether to continue with the engagement.

2230—Engagement Resource Allocation. Internal auditors must determine the appropriate resources necessary to achieve the audit engagement objectives. Staffing must be based on an evaluation of the nature and complexity of each engagement, time constraints, and available resources.

2240—Engagement Work Program. Internal auditors must develop and document work programs that achieve the engagement objectives. These work programs must establish procedures for identifying, analyzing, evaluating, and recording information during the engagement. They must be approved prior to their implementation, and any adjustments approved promptly. Work programs for consulting engagements may vary in form and content depending upon the nature of the engagement.

2300—Performing the Engagement. Internal auditors must identify, analyze, evaluate, and record sufficient information to achieve an audit engagement's objectives and must base conclusions and engagement results on appropriate analyses and evaluations.

2310—Identifying Information. Internal auditors must identify sufficient, reliable, relevant, and useful information to achieve the engagement's objectives. Sufficient information is factual, adequate, and convincing so that a prudent, informed person would reach the same conclusions as the auditor. Reliable information is the best attainable information through the use of appropriate engagement techniques. Relevant information supports engagement observations and recommendations and is consistent with the objectives for the engagement. Useful information helps an enterprise meet its goals.

2320—Analysis and Evaluation. Internal auditors must base conclusions and engagement results on appropriate analyses and evaluations.

2330—Recording Information. Internal auditors must record relevant information to support the conclusions and engagement results.

2330.A1—The CAE must control access to engagement records, and must obtain the approval of senior management and/or legal counsel prior to releasing such records to external parties, as appropriate.

2330.A2—The CAE must develop retention requirements for engagement records, regardless of the medium in which each record is stored, that are consistent with the enterprise's guidelines and any pertinent regulatory or other requirements.

2330.C1—The CAE must develop policies governing the custody and retention of engagement records, as well as their release to internal and external parties. These policies must be consistent with the enterprise's guidelines and any pertinent regulatory or other requirements.

2340—Engagement Supervision. Engagements must be properly supervised to ensure that objectives are achieved, quality is assured, and staff is developed. The extent of supervision required will depend on the proficiency and experience of internal auditors and the complexity of the engagement. The CAE has overall responsibility for supervising the engagement, whether performed by or for the internal audit function, but may designate appropriately experienced members of the internal audit function to perform the review. Appropriate evidence of this supervision is documented and retained.

2400 and 2410—Communicating Results. Internal auditors must communicate their engagement results, including the audit's objectives and scope as well as applicable conclusions, recommendations, action plans, and the internal auditor's overall opinion and/or conclusions.

2410.A1—Final communication of engagement results must, where appropriate, contain the internal auditor's overall opinion and/or conclusions.

2410.A2—Internal auditors are encouraged to acknowledge satisfactory performance in engagement communications.

2410.A3—When releasing engagement results to parties outside the enterprise, the communication must include limitations on distribution and use of the results.

2410.C1—Communication of the progress and results of consulting engagements will vary in form and content depending upon the nature of the engagement and the needs of the client.

2420—Quality of Communications. Communications must be accurate, objective, clear, concise, constructive, complete, and timely.

2421—Errors and Omissions. If a final communication contains a significant error or omission, the CAE must communicate corrected information to all *parties* who received the original communication.

2430—Use of "Conducted in conformance with the *International Standards for the Professional Practice of Internal Auditing.*" Internal auditors are encouraged to report that their engagements are "conducted in conformance with the *International Standards for the Professional Practice of Internal Auditing.*" However, internal auditors may use the statement only if the results of the quality assurance and improvement program demonstrate that the internal audit activity conforms to the *Standards*.

2431—Engagement Disclosure of Noncompliance with IIA Standards. When noncompliance with the *Standards* impacts a specific engagement, communication of the results must disclose the:

- Principle or rule of conduct of the Code of Ethics or *Standard(s)* with which full conformance was not made;
- Reason(s) for noncompliance; and
- Impact of noncompliance on the engagement.

2440—Disseminating Results. The CAE is responsible for communicating the final results of audit work to appropriate parties who can ensure that the results are given due consideration.

2440.A1—The CAE is responsible for communicating the final results to parties who can ensure that the results are given due consideration.

2440.A2—If not otherwise mandated by legal, statutory, or regulatory requirements, prior to releasing results to parties outside the enterprise, the CAE must:

- Assess the potential risk to the enterprise;
- Consult with senior management and/or legal counsel as appropriate; and
- Control dissemination by restricting the use of the results.

2440.C1 and C2—The CAE is responsible for communicating the final results of consulting engagements to clients. During consulting engagements, risk management, control, and governance issues may be identified. Whenever these issues are significant to the enterprise, they must be communicated to senior management and the board.

2500—Monitoring Progress. The CAE must establish and maintain a system to monitor the disposition of results communicated to management as well as a follow-up process to monitor and ensure that management actions have been effectively implemented or that senior management has accepted the risk of not taking action.

2600—Resolution of Management's Acceptance of Risks. When the CAE believes that senior management has accepted a level of residual risk that *may be* unacceptable to the enterprise, the CAE must discuss the matter with senior management. If the decision regarding residual risk is not resolved, the CAE and senior management must report the matter to the board for resolution.

The current IIA standards represent a significant improvement over the older and very lengthy standards that were in place through the 1990s. The standards conclude with a glossary of terms to better define the roles and responsibilities of internal auditors. Various glossary terms are introduced in other subsequent chapters, but one that is important for internal auditors is the definition of *independence*. The word frequently appears in internal auditing literature, but the official definition of *internal auditor independence* is:

> Independence is the freedom from significant conflicts of interest that threaten objectivity. Such threats to objectivity must be managed at the individual auditor level, the engagement level, and the organizational level.

This is an important concept today. We again emphasize that these paragraphs are *not the verbatim IIA standards* but an edited and annotated version. Some of the more minor standards statements have not been included in this chapter, a few words in some cases have been changed, and descriptive comments have been added. As previously stated, internal auditors are advised to obtain the official version of these standards through the Institute of Internal Auditors at www.theiia.org.

9.4 CODES OF ETHICS: THE IIA AND ISACA

The IIA's code of ethics is displayed in Exhibit 9.2, with a purpose to promote an ethical culture in the profession of internal auditing. This code of ethics is divided into high-level

EXHIBIT 9.2 Internal Auditor Code of Ethics

PRINCIPLES Internal auditors are expected to apply and uphold the following principles:

- **Integrity**. The integrity of internal auditors establishes trust and thus provides the basis for reliance on their judgment.
- **Objectivity**. Internal auditors exhibit the highest level of professional objectivity in gathering, evaluating, and communicating information about the activity or process being examined. Internal auditors make a balanced assessment of all the relevant circumstances and are not unduly influenced by their own interests or by others in forming judgments.
- **Confidentiality.** Internal auditors respect the value and ownership of information they receive and do not disclose information without appropriate authority unless there is a legal or professional obligation to do so.
- **Competency.** Internal auditors apply the knowledge, skills, and experience needed in the performance of internal audit services.

RULES OF CONDUCT

1. **Integrity.** Internal Auditors:
   1.1. Shall perform their work with honesty, diligence, and responsibility.
   1.2. Shall observe the law and make disclosures expected by the law and the profession.
   1.3. Shall not knowingly be a party to any illegal activity, or engage in acts that are discreditable to the profession of internal auditing or to the organization.
   1.4. Shall respect and contribute to the legitimate and ethical objectives of the organization.
2. **Objectivity.** Internal Auditors:
   2.1. Shall not participate in any activity or relationship that may impair or be presumed to impair their unbiased assessment. This participation includes those activities or relationships that may be in conflict with the interests of the organization.
   2.2. Shall not accept anything that may impair or be presumed to impair their professional judgment.
   2.3. Shall disclose all material facts known to them that, if not disclosed, may distort the reporting of activities under review.
3. **Confidentiality.** Internal Auditors:
   3.1. Shall be prudent in the use and protection of information acquired in the course of their duties.
   3.2. Shall not use information for any personal gain or in any manner that would be contrary to the law or detrimental to the legitimate and ethical objectives of the organization.
4. **Competency.** Internal Auditors:
   4.1. Shall engage only in those services for which they have the necessary knowledge, skills, and experience.
   4.2. Shall perform internal audit services in accordance with the *International Standards for the Professional Practice of Internal Auditing*.
   4.3. Shall continually improve their proficiency and the effectiveness and quality of their services.

principles covering internal audit integrity, objectivity, confidentiality, and competency as well as rules of conduct covering these same areas. It is necessary and appropriate for a profession that depends on the trust placed on users of internal audit services to provide objective assurances about risk management, control, and governance. The IIA's current code of ethics was first released in 2000 and continues to be an important internal audit standard and a key element of the IPPF. Any person performing internal audit services, whether or not a member of the IIA, should follow this code of ethics. Professional certificates, including the Certified Internal Auditor (CIA) designation, will be discussed in Chapter 29.

The IIA code of ethics applies both to individuals and to entities that provide internal auditing services. For IIA members and recipients of or candidates for IIA professional certifications, breaches of the code of ethics will be evaluated and administered according to IIA Bylaws and Administrative Guidelines. The IIA goes on to state that even if a particular conduct is not mentioned in the code, this does not prevent the conduct or practice from being unacceptable or discreditable. Violators of the code, whether an IIA member, certification holder, or candidate, can be held liable for disciplinary action.

ISACA, as well as its affiliated research arm, the IT Governance Institute, is the professional audit enterprise that represents or speaks primarily for IT auditors. ISACA was originally known as the Electronic Data Processing Auditors Association (EDPAA), a professional group that was founded in 1969 by a group of internal auditors who felt the IIA was not giving sufficient attention to the importance of IT systems and their related technology-related internal controls. It still leads the IIA on technology-related issues. ISACA is also the professional enterprise that administers the CISA (Certified Information Systems Auditor) examination and program and is responsible for the COBIT internal control framework discussed in Chapter 6.

With its IT audit and IT governance orientation, ISACA represents a somewhat different group of auditors. Historically, ISACA drew a large number of members from IT audit specialists and public accounting external audit firms, and it also has had a very strong international membership in some areas of the world. Many IIA members are also ISACA members, and while the two groups do not have many joint meetings or other endeavors, each represents an important segment of the audit community.

While ISACA—fortuitously—does not have its own set of professional standards, it does have a code of ethics as shown in Exhibit 9.3. Because of its IT heritage, the ISACA code is more oriented to technology-related issues. It is a set of professional standards that applies to and should be of particular value to IT audit professionals. Although the wording is different, there is nothing in the ISACA code that is really contrary to the IIA code. Internal auditors, whether working primarily in IT areas or with a more general internal controls orientation, should exercise strong ethical practice in their work.

9.5 INTERNAL AUDIT PRINCIPLES

Neither COSO nor the IIA had used the concept of or term *principles* in the past, but these useful high-level objective statements are helpful in ongoing internal control and audit review activities. A *principle* is a high-level statement that will allow others to assess whether their activities in a given area are accomplishing overall objectives, and internal auditors should use them as kind of a one-line measure to assess activities in some area.

EXHIBIT 9.3 ISACA Code of Professional Ethics

The Information Systems Audit and Control Association, Inc. (ISACA) sets forth this Code of Professional Ethics to guide the professional and personal conduct of members of the association and/or its certification holders.

Members and ISACA certification holders shall:

1. Support the implementation of, and encourage compliance with, appropriate standards, procedures, and controls for information systems.
2. Perform their duties with objectivity, due diligence, and professional care, in accordance with professional standards and best practices.
3. Serve in the interest of stakeholders in a lawful and honest manner, while maintaining high standards of conduct and character, and not engage in acts discreditable to the profession.
4. Maintain the privacy and confidentiality of information obtained in the course of their duties unless disclosure is required by legal authority. Such information shall not be used for personal benefit or released to inappropriate parties.
5. Maintain competency in their respective fields and agree to undertake only those activities that they can reasonably expect to complete with professional competence.
6. Inform appropriate parties of the results of work performed, revealing all significant facts known to them.
7. Support the professional education of stakeholders in enhancing their understanding of information systems security and control.

Failure to comply with this Code of Professional Ethics can result in an investigation into a member's, and/or certification holder's, conduct and, ultimately, in disciplinary measures.

Exhibit 9.4 displays the IPPF's internal audit principles. They are organized with principles 1 to 3 describing areas for internal auditor input, principles 4 through 9 describing internal audit activity and processes, and principles 10 to 12 relating to the outcomes or results of internal audit activity. As shown in the exhibit, key words for each principle are set in bold type to indicate major points. For example, principle 2 emphasizes the importance of internal audit objectivity, a key internal auditor attribute.

The IIA's goal for these principles is to make it easier for internal audit professionals to understand and focus on the things that are most important. These principles should facilitate more effective communications with key stakeholders, including regulators, regarding the priorities that define internal audit effectiveness. This really says that when an internal auditor is reviewing or recommending a control activity in some area under review, the auditor should always keep these general, high-level principles in mind. For example, one of the IPPF principles on individual internal auditor activities says that an internal auditor should display "objectivity in mindset and approach." This is not really different from recognized internal audit standards, but, stated as a principle, it gives an internal auditor the opportunity to ask the question of whether an audit is really objective when recommending some approach. The answer should be a given, but the principle gives an internal auditor and the internal audit management team an opportunity to ask a follow-up hard, introspective question.

EXHIBIT 9.4 Internal Audit IPPF Principles

Internal auditor individual activity **inputs**

1. Demonstrate uncompromised **integrity**
2. Display **objectivity** in mindset and approach
3. Demonstrate commitment to **competence**

Internal audit **process** activities

4. Are **appropriately positioned** within the organization **with sufficient authority**
5. **Align strategically** with enterprise aims and goals
6. Have adequate **resources** to effectively address significant risks
7. Demonstrate quality and continuous improvement
8. Achieve **efficiency and effectiveness** in delivery
9. **Communicate effectively**

Internal auditor individual activity **outputs**

10. **Provide reliable assurance** to those charged with governance
11. **Are insightful, proactive, and future-focused**
12. **Promote positive change**

9.6 IPPF FUTURE DIRECTIONS

The IPPF is new and is an attempt to better tie the wide range of evolving issues and new internal control guidance needs impacting internal auditors today. The IIA has separately published often excellent supplemental guidance on various issues, as referenced where appropriate in other chapters. We must remember, though, that the IIA is largely a volunteer organization with no central research and administrative services. When it publishes guidance on new and evolving issues, it typically hires a contractor, but not necessarily a recognized internal auditor to do the work, often with little general membership feedback before publication. For example, around 2008 the IIA hired some researchers to develop their own CBOK. The work was done through a survey, but with little member follow-up and some questionable results.

A perhaps almost troubling element of the IPPF is that the IIA has seemingly unrealistic plans to more actively address emerging internal audit business and technical issues in an almost real-time manner. The IPPF documents state that when faced with new, developing, or emerging internal audit issues, the IIA plans to issue guidance "within a matter of weeks" to address such new internal audit issues or potential solutions. Understanding internal auditing issues associated with something like "bring your own device" internal controls, new internal issues discussed in Chapter 20, or internal controls over big data, an evolving controls issue discussed in Chapter 21, creates a challenge for an international organization such as the IIA to review internal control issues and get out timely guidance to its members. Although the IIA was slow in the past in getting information on new technologies and issues to its members on a prompt basis, the draft documents supporting the new IPPF claim it has changed its ways. We hope so.

Beyond our comments on the IIA's evolving issues aspirations, the overall IPPF seems to be a very good concept for internal auditors, improving internal definitions and emphasizing key principles along with an emphasis on the IIA's code of ethics and the *International Standards for the Professional Practice of Internal Auditing.* An overall understanding of all components of the IPPF should be a strong CBOK requirement.

NOTES

1. *International Standards for the Professional Practice of Internal Auditing* (Altamonte Springs, FL: Institute of Internal Auditors, 2004).
2. See Robert R. Moeller, *IT Audit, Control, and Security* (Hoboken, NJ: John Wiley & Sons, 2010).

CHAPTER TEN

Testing, Assessing, and Evaluating Audit Evidence

THE INTERNAL AUDIT PROCESS BEGINS with first establishing audit objectives, then planning and preparing the internal audit, performing planned audit procedures including gathering and examining audit evidence, and finally assessing the audited results to determine if the audit objectives have been satisfied, if supporting internal controls are adequate, if the materials reviewed are sufficient to develop an audit conclusion, and if there is a need for corrective action–based internal audit recommendations. This process of testing, assessing, and then evaluating audit evidence is often a challenge and a source of concerns for many internal auditors. For example, an internal auditor may review a sample of 100 items and find one error/exception but no problems with 99 of them. Should that one remaining internal control problem item cause an internal auditor to highlight matters as an internal control problem or should the internal auditor give that single exception a pass and go forward? There often are no easy answers, but a knowledgeable internal auditor should be able to evaluate this audit evidence and make the appropriate decision.

While Chapter 8 outlined the steps for performing an internal audit and Chapter 9 described the IIA international professional standards necessary for performing internal audits, this chapter reviews processes to test, assess, and evaluate audit evidence. These are key common body of knowledge (CBOK) steps necessary to look at audit evidence and then to develop appropriate audit conclusions based on that evidence. This stage is really a key step in the overall internal audit process.

In addition to the necessary skills to evaluate audit evidence, an internal auditor needs to understand some of the basics of *audit sampling*. Many internal auditors, however, back away from or try to ignore audit sampling because it is "too mathematical" and perhaps because they do not like the supporting statistics calculations, perhaps dating back to poor impressions of statistics in their college days. This chapter also will introduce some of the simple calculations and procedures necessary to perform audit sampling, a basic CBOK requirement.

10.1 GATHERING APPROPRIATE AUDIT EVIDENCE

Internal auditors make assessments about audit issues or satisfy their audit objectives through detailed reviews of what is called *audit evidence*. That is, an internal auditor usually is not able to look at every item in an area of audit concern to develop evidence to support an audit. This approach is much more difficult when internal audit is faced with a large population of items to examine—hundreds, thousands, or even more. Rather, the auditor must examine a limited set of sample files or reports to develop audit conclusions over the entire set or population of data.

In the early days of internal auditing, 100% examinations of transactions or documents were common to assess control procedures compliance. As enterprises grew larger and more complex, this 100% examination approach was often not feasible, so internal auditors would typically select a sample to develop an audit conclusion. In particular, given today's IT systems, internal auditors needed some way to review these large masses of computerized data. There is a major internal audit challenge here. An internal auditor needs a consistent approach to sample a portion of items from a large population of data and then to draw audit conclusions based on that limited sample.

The internal audit sampling challenge here is to extract a sample of items that will be representative of the entire population. If there are 100,000 transactions and if an internal auditor only looks at 50 of them, finding 10 exceptions (20% of the sample), can the auditor conclude that 20% of the entire population of transactions, or 20,000, are exceptions? This audit conclusion can only be considered true if the sample of 50 drawn is representative of the entire population. Audit sampling techniques can help an internal auditor determine an appropriate sample size and develop an opinion for this type of audit task.

Audit sampling has two major branches: statistical and nonstatistical. *Statistical sampling* is a mathematical-based method of selecting representative items that reflect the characteristics of the entire population. Using the results of audit tests on the statistically sampled items, an internal auditor can then express an opinion on the entire group. For example, an auditor could develop a statistical sample of items in an inventory, test those items in that sample for their physical quantity or value, and then express an opinion on the value or accuracy of the entire inventory. *Nonstatistical sampling*, also called *judgmental sampling*, is not supported by mathematical theory and does not allow an internal auditor to express *statistically precise* opinions on the entire population. Nevertheless, nonstatistical or judgmental sampling is often a useful audit tool.

10.2 AUDIT ASSESSMENT AND EVALUATION TECHNIQUES

When planning an audit that includes the examination of a large number of transactions or other evidence, an internal auditor should always ask the question "Should I use audit sampling?" The correct answer here is often not just a simple yes or no but may be complicated by such factors as the number or nature of items to be sampled, a lack of technical expertise or IT software availability to do the sampling, a fear of the mathematical focus of sampling, or the potential nonacceptance of the sampling results by management. "Sampling" also is an expression that is frequently misused by internal auditors. All too often, an internal auditor will be faced with a file cabinet filled with hundreds of documents to review, and the auditor will pull out one or two items from the front and perform audit procedures based on this limited selection. While this examination of two items may be appropriate for an audit observation, an internal auditor often *should not* try to draw conclusions for the entire population or contents of the file cabinet drawer based on that limited sample. To effectively develop this type of conclusion, internal auditors need a process where they should:

- Understand the total population of items of concern and develop a formal sampling plan regarding the population of items;
- Draw a sample from the population based on that sample selection plan;
- Evaluate the sampled items against audit objectives; and
- Develop conclusions for the entire population based on audit sample results.

These steps represent the process of audit sampling. Audit sampling is the process of examining less than 100% of the items within an account balance or class of transactions for the purpose of drawing some form of conclusion for the entire population based on the sample audit results. Audit sampling can often be a very attractive and effective option for internal auditors and should be a CBOK requirement.

Why use audit sampling? We often hear reports on the results of statistical sampling techniques in consumer research, government studies, or in the quality-control testing on a production assembly line, and audit sampling can be a very effective tool for internal auditors as well. While 100% examinations work for limited amounts of audit evidence, internal audit almost always finds itself looking at a sample—either very large or small—of the audit evidence. The internal auditor would then draw an audit conclusion based on the results of that sample. With formal audit sampling, internal audit can draw a conclusion along the lines of "Based on the results of our audit sample, we are 98% certain the true inventory balance is between *X* and *Y*." This type of statement and process will be discussed in greater detail in the paragraphs following.

Formal audit sampling is a powerful tool, and with some study and practice, internal auditors can easily and effectively begin to use audit sampling. Whenever an internal auditor needs to draw conclusions based on a population of multiple items but does not want to examine the entire population, audit sampling can introduce better and more efficient audits. The following reasons encourage the use of audit sampling and statistical sampling:

- **Conclusions may be drawn regarding an entire population of data.** If a statistical sampling method is used, information can be accurately projected over the entire population without performing a 100% check on the population, no matter how large. For example, an internal auditor may be interested in the occurrence of some error condition in a large volume of incoming product freight bills. The auditor could select a statistical sample of these freight bill documents, test the sample for the error condition, and then be able to make a 98% certain type of estimate about the occurrence of that error condition in the entire population of freight bills.

This technique typically will result in a strong audit position and significant audit savings.

- **Sample results are objective and defensible.** Internal control errors often occur on a random basis over the total items subject to error, and each error condition should have an equal opportunity of selection in an audit sample. An audit test based on random selection is objective and even defensible in a court of law. Conversely, a sample based on auditor judgment could be distorted due to intentional or unintentional bias in the selection process. An auditor looking for potential problems might examine only the larger or sensitive items, ignoring others.
- **Less sampling may be required through the use of audit sampling.** Using mathematics-based statistics, internal auditors need not increase the size of a sample directly in proportion to increases in the size of the population to be sampled. Even though a sample of 60 items may be needed to express an audit opinion over a population of 500 items, that same sample of 60 may still be sufficient for a population of 5,000. An internal auditor who does not use statistical approaches often will oversample large populations because of the incorrect belief that larger populations require proportionately larger samples. By using statistics-based sampling procedures, less testing may be required.
- **Statistical sampling may even provide for greater accuracy than a 100% test.** When voluminous amounts of data items are counted in their entirety, the risk of significant clerical or audit errors increases. However, a small, well-controlled sample will typically receive very close scrutiny and analysis. The more limited sample would be primarily subject only to sampling errors resulting from the statistical projection.
- **Audit coverage of multiple locations is often more convenient.** Audits can be performed at multiple locations with small samples taken at individual sites to complete an overall sampling plan. In addition, an audit using comprehensive statistical sampling may be started by one auditor and subsequently continued by another. Each of their sample results can be combined to yield one set of audit results.
- **Sampling procedures can be simple to apply.** In years past, internal auditors often were required to use either tables published in sampling manuals or complex computer systems to develop a sampling plan and sample selection. With the availability of laptop computer–based software packages, audit sampling has been simplified. The sampling tools and techniques discussed in this chapter should help to explain the process for internal auditors.

Despite the advantages of audit sampling, an internal auditor must keep in mind that *exact information* cannot be obtained about a population of items based on just a sample, whether it be judgmental or statistical. It is only through making a 100% test and following good audit procedures that an internal auditor can obtain exact information. With nonstatistical, judgmental sampling, information is only obtained about those items examined. With statistical sampling, regardless of the number of items examined, positive information can be obtained about all of the items in the population within a level of statistical confidence. The sections following will discuss judgmental and statistical audit sampling—both important internal audit tools. In addition, the discussion on statistical sampling provides guidance on attributes, monetary unit, and *variables sampling* techniques as well as other techniques for internal auditor use.

10.3 INTERNAL AUDIT JUDGMENTAL SAMPLING

Although we usually support a more statistical audit sampling approach for many internal audits, nonstatistical judgmental sampling can often also be a very appropriate internal audit procedure in many situations. As its name implies, this approach requires an internal auditor to use his or her best judgment to design and select a sample. No statistical decision rules are used and the auditor only selects a sampling plan approach that will provide a large enough sample to test the audit objectives, such as whether the internal controls reviewed are operating properly or if the procedures examined are being followed. Judgmental sampling requires an internal auditor to select a representative sample of items in a population of data or transactions for audit review. The sample will be less than 100% of the entire population of items included in the review but should be sufficient for internal audit to develop overall audit conclusions based on those sample results. For internal auditors, the methods for a judgmental sample selection may take many forms, including:

- **Fixed percentage selection.** An examination of a fixed percentage—such as 10%—of the items or dollars in an audit population. These sample items are then often selected haphazardly, with the auditor opening a file drawer, for example, and selecting every one or two items or files until the desired sample size is met.
- **Designated attribute selection.** A selection of all or part of the items active during a time period, such as one month in an audit covering a year's transactions. Alternatively, an auditor could select all items having a common characteristic, such as all accounts ending in a particular letter of the alphabet, as part of a review of vendor invoices.
- **Large value selection.** A selection for audit review of just those items with large monetary or other significant balances.
- **Designated area selection.** An examination of only items readily available, such as those stored in a particular file drawer. Such sample items may be selected because they looked "interesting."
- **Other selected attribute selection.** A review of only sensitive items or items with some other attribute of audit concern. In a review for inactive or obsolete inventory items, an auditor might select for review only those items that appear to be dusty or located in out-of-the-way locations in the inventory stores area.

Although useful data may be obtained from judgmental samples, the results can be misleading or inaccurate regarding overall conclusions about the whole population or account. An internal auditor may look at the accuracy of finance charges for the largest 10% of some account under the assumption that these are the most significant. Even though no significant problems were found for the 10% sampled, the auditor will not know of any significant control problems over the remaining accounts representing the other 90%. Similarly, an internal auditor can select a dusty corner of a storage space in a search for obsolete inventory. The items found in that area are probably candidates to scrap and be put in an internal audit report comment, but they cannot be assumed to represent the level of obsolescence throughout the facility.

When planning a review based on judgmental samples, an internal auditor should make three judgmental sampling decisions. First, the internal auditor must develop a method of selection, and decide what types of items to examine. Internal auditors can be subject to criticism if problems are encountered later that were not included in the sample selection. An examination of all account names starting with the arbitrary first letters *A* and *M* will not reveal a problem for an account with an account name starting with *S*.

The size of the sample is the second audit judgment decision. Auditors sometimes incorrectly select only two or three items located off the top of the deck, review them, and state that audit results are based on this very limited and nonrepresentative audit sample. This can be misleading, and managers who receive internal audit report findings often assume that a far larger sample was reviewed. The sample size should be reasonable compared to the entire population. Too small of a sample will not represent the overall population, while a too large sample may be extra time-consuming or otherwise expensive to evaluate.

The third decision is how to interpret and report the audit results from the limited judgmental sample. An internal audit review of excess and obsolete inventory that selects 20 dusty and dirty items from the stores area and finds that 10 are obsolete should not then conclude that 50% of the entire inventory is obsolete based on that sample. The bulk of the store's inventory may be active and appear to be clean. If those active items were not considered in the selection, conclusions from the judgmental sample may be inaccurate. Even though 50% of the dusty and dirty items examined may be obsolete, this does not mean that *the entire* inventory is obsolete. The results from a judgmental sample must be stated very carefully. Exhibit 10.1 provides examples of some problems with incorrectly reporting judgmental sampling results and the ambiguous audit report conclusions based on incomplete judgmental samples. All of these examples point out that the findings were based on some level of judgmental sample. The problem here is that internal auditors frequently refer to their audit sample and draw conclusions from the results even though there has been little statistical support for those sample conclusions. We are showing these

EXHIBIT 10.1 Problems with Judgmental Sampling Audit Findings

Example Audit Problem Finding 1: Based on our sample of inventory items, we found three items that were incorrectly labeled. Controls need to be improved to . . .

What Is Wrong Here: There is no reference to the number of items in the inventory, the size of the sample, or the implications of the sample results.

Example Audit Problem Finding 2: Based on our statistical sample of accounts receivable records, we found . . .

What Is Wrong Here: This is a judgmental sample finding with no reference to what is meant by a "statistical sample" and how the internal audit conclusion was developed.

Example Audit Problem Finding 3: We found seven incorrectly valued items in our sample of fixed asset items; based on the results of this sample, we recommend . . .

What Is Wrong Here: There is no explanation of what is meant by the "items in our sample." Reported audit findings should give some details on the size of the population and number of items sampled for the audit.

as examples of problems in reporting sampling results, but Chapter 18 contains a more extensive discussion of reporting internal audit results.

The whole concept behind internal audit judgmental sampling is that item selection is simply based on the internal auditor's judgment. An internal auditor can select as many or as few sample items that appear appropriate in the internal auditor's professional judgment. Often, a good internal auditor can "smell" a potential problem by looking at an area and selecting a series of items that represent potential problems. However, even though some internal auditors may be right on target when pulling their often arbitrary-size samples, many others may miss significant items or may focus on a few bad apples that do not represent an entire population of otherwise good items. Although there are multiple options on an approach here, the successful internal auditor is often better off using some form of statistical sampling for audit item selection, as discussed in the section following.

10.4 STATISTICAL AUDIT SAMPLING: AN INTRODUCTION

Statistical audit sampling is a powerful tool that allows an internal auditor to project the results of a statistically correct audit sample over the entire population with a strong degree of accuracy and confidence. Based on the rules of probability, statistical sampling requires the use of established mathematical selection techniques with results that can be projected over the entire population in a manner that will be accepted by the courts, government regulators, and others. Statistical sampling is also one of those often challenging topics that many internal auditors first encountered in an undergraduate college course; they finished the class and hoped never to encounter that subject again!

Statistical sampling was once a complex internal audit process requiring a high degree of mathematical and computational skills. Revised and accepted sampling approaches as well as software tools available today eliminate much of these past computational difficulties. As an important internal audit CBOK skill, we will discuss some of the statistical concepts supporting statistical sampling as well as more common approaches to internal audit statistical sampling. Examples are presented to help an internal auditor more effectively use statistical sampling.

A general understanding of probability and statistical concepts is an important first step for using statistical sampling. While this chapter does not attempt to be a statistics textbook, some basic statistical concepts and terminology are important. While we can draw a statistical sample without the need for an in-depth understanding, interested internal auditors should consult a book on statistical auditing[1] for more information. While some of these concepts are fairly easy, a general understanding is important.

We start with some of the important statistical sampling terms. First, the expression *population* refers to the total number of items that are subject to an audit, and a *random sample* is the process of selecting a sample where each unit in that population has an equal probability of selection. That random sample then represents the characteristics of the entire population. However, the characteristics of one random sample drawn by an internal auditor may be different from a sample from the same population drawn by another. To determine how far a sample result differs from that of a 100% test, an internal auditor should have an understanding of the behavior of all possible samples that might be drawn from a population.

Because multiple samples may bring different results, it is important to understand the statistical sampling terms for measures of central tendency. In audit sampling, the term *average value* is used to describe or measure sampled data, in terms of both their example and the mathematical descriptions. While internal auditors often work with much larger populations, consider a hypothetical population of 25 accounts receivable balances with a total value of $86,345.24, as shown in Exhibit 10.2.

Six different measures are commonly used by statisticians to look at the central tendencies of this data or the degree that the various values are dispersed around a central average. The most common statistical measures for looking at data are the called the

EXHIBIT 10.2 Sample Population of Accounts Receivable Balances

Item #	Accounts Receivable Balance	Rank
1	$275.00	3
2	$1,059.25	8
3	$2,564.78	15
4	$9,032.00	22
5	$1,750.00	12
6	$17,110.40	25
7	$1,713.99	11
8	$6,245.32	20
9	$534.89	5
10	$534.89	6
11	$2,564.78	16
12	$1,122.05	9
13	$3,025.88	17
14	$514.99	4
15	$10,554.58	24
16	$1,988.63	13
17	$7,026.50	23
18	$978.00	7
19	$1,654.54	10
20	$3,066.00	18
21	$35.87	1
22	$78.99	2
23	$2,003.00	14
24	$6,995.41	21
25	$3,915.50	12
Total	$86,345.24	

mean, median, mode, range of data values, variance, the *standard deviation,* and the *skewness of the data.* Although the calculation of these central-tendency measures can be performed today by pressing a function key on an auditor's business financial calculator, an internal auditor should understand their meaning and use, and how they are calculated. We will explain these values using the Exhibit 10.2 sample data.

1. The *mean* is the simple average of the values of items in a population. It is calculated by adding up the total amount in the population of interest—in this Exhibit 10.2 example, 25 individual balances for \$86,345.24—and then dividing this total by the number of observed items in the population. Although an internal auditor certainly does not need to worry about what the Greek symbol means, μ is often used to report the mean. In this example, the mean or μ is 86,345.24/25 = \$3,453.81
2. The *median* is the middle amount value when all of the items in the population are ranked by value, either smallest to largest or vice versa. Exhibit 10.2 contains a column on the right side, which shows the ranking of each item by its value or size. Item 21 has been ranked as number 1 because it is the smallest value in the population at \$35.87. Item 22 is ranked as number 2 because it is the next smallest. The median is calculated by counting the number of individual items in the population and selecting the one where 50% are larger and the other 50% are smaller. In this example, item 16 has been ranked as number 13, meaning twelve items are smaller and twelve are larger, and so item 16's corresponding value, \$1,988.63, is the median for this population. The median is rarely the same value as the mean. Here, the median value is smaller than the mean because there are more items of smaller value in the population.
3. The *mode* is the amount or value that occurs most frequently in a population. In this example, two items—numbers 9 and 10—each have a value of \$534.89. The mode is generally not a very meaningful measure in statistics. While sometimes useful in a larger population with many items bunched around the same general values, a mode is more useful when the data is summarized into a histogram. The histogram for this sample, in Exhibit 10.1, shows that the most common value for the sample data is less than \$500.
4. The *range* is the difference between the largest and the smallest values in a population. In this example, the range is the difference between item 6 (\$17,110.40) and item 21 (\$35.87), or \$17,074.53. This measure is primarily useful as an indicator of the breadth of the population data. The range will also be discussed as part of measuring dispersion through what is called the standard deviation.
5. The *variance* is a measure of the spread of a distribution, and it is computed as the average squared deviation of each number from its mean. The symbol σ^2, or sigma squared, is a measure of the variance or what is called the standard deviation. For example, for a population consisting of the numbers 1, 2, and 3, the mean is 2 and the variance is the square root of this standard deviation calculation:

$$\sigma^2 = \frac{(1-2)^2 + (2-2)^2 + (3-2)^2}{3} = .667$$

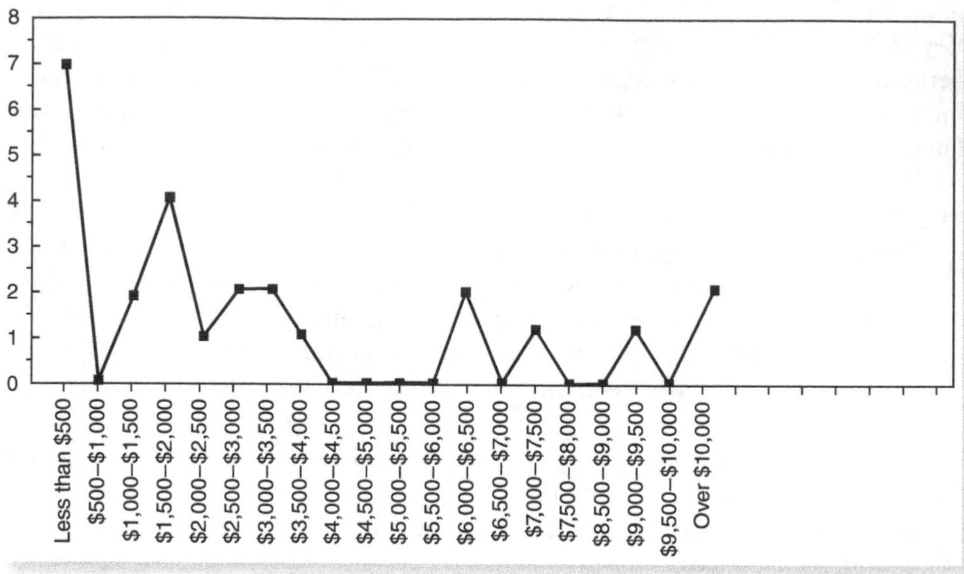

EXHIBIT 10.3 Accounts Receivable Balances Histogram

6. *Standard deviation.* Each of the measures discussed until now—such as mean and median—should be fairly easy to understand for most professionals, even those who have not had much background in statistics. In contrast, many find the concept of standard deviation more difficult. Standard deviation is an important measure of the dispersion or distribution of data around a central mean.

The standard deviation is a measure of the *variability* of values for individual items in a population. The symbol σ, or sigma, is often used for the standard deviation where:

$$\text{standard deviation} = \sqrt{\frac{\sum_{I=L}^{n}(X_i - \bar{X})^2}{n}}$$

Standard deviation tells the auditor how much variation of values exists around the mean or central point. Exhibit 10.4 shows a standard deviation calculation for our same 25-item accounts receivable balances example. One column in this exhibit shows the $x_i - X$ differences, and the next column in this exhibit shows differences as squared values of those differences. Following the formula, dividing the sum of these squared differences by the population size minus 1 (a correction because this is a sample) will compute the standard deviation here of $4,045.78

The properly skeptical internal auditor may ask, "What is all of this good for?" Standard deviation is a measure of the central tendency of a normally distributed population of data, and it shows how far the items in a population are from the mean or central point. A population of 50 items all with values of about $1,000 each as well as a population of another 50 with average values of less than $1 would have about the same mean value as a different population of 100, with 50 around $450 and the other 50 of around

EXHIBIT 10.4 Standard Deviation Sample Calculation

N	X_i	$x_i - \overline{X}$	$(x_i - \overline{x})^2$
1	275.00	(3,178.81)	10,104,833.02
2	1,059.25	(2,394.56)	5,733,917.59
3	2,564.78	(889.03)	790,374.34
4	9,032.00	5,578.19	31,116,203.68
5	1,750.00	(1,703.81)	2,902,968.52
6	17,110.40	13,656.59	186,502,450.43
7	1,713.99	(1,739.82)	3,026,973.63
8	6,245.32	2,791.51	7,792,528.08
9	534.89	(2,918.92)	8,520,093.97
10	534.89	(2,918.92)	8,520,093.97
11	2,564.78	(889.03)	790,374.34
12	1,122.05	(2,331.76)	5,437,104.70
13	3,025.88	(427.93)	183,124.08
14	514.99	(2,938.82)	8,636,662.99
15	10,554.58	7,100.77	50,420,934.59
16	1,988.63	(1,465.18)	2,146,752.43
17	7,026.50	3,572.69	12,764,113.84
18	978.00	(2,475.81)	6,129,635.16
19	1,654.54	(1,799.27)	3,237,372.53
20	3,066.00	(387.81)	150,396.60
21	35.87	(3,417.94)	11,682,313.84
22	78.99	(3,374.82)	11,389,410.03
23	2,003.00	(1,450.81)	2,104,849.66
24	6,995.41	3,541.60	12,542,930.56
25	3,915.50	461.69	213,157.66
Sum	86,345.24		392,839,570.23
Average,	3,453.81		16,368,315.43
X&c.ovline;		Std. Dev.	4045.78

$550. Although the mean for each would be around $500, they would be very different populations of data, and the standard deviation would help to explain those differences.

A *normal distribution* is the bell-shaped diagram used to show data; often it is organized with a few values very high, a few very low, and most in the middle. If a large supply of small pebbles were to be dropped, one by one, onto a flat surface, the pebbles would form in a mound the shape of a bell curve. Much of the data internal auditors deal with also follows this bell-curve shape. If we look at the population of an average large city and plot the number of people by age, a few will be either very old or newborn at any point in time—with perhaps an equal number less than five years and greater than

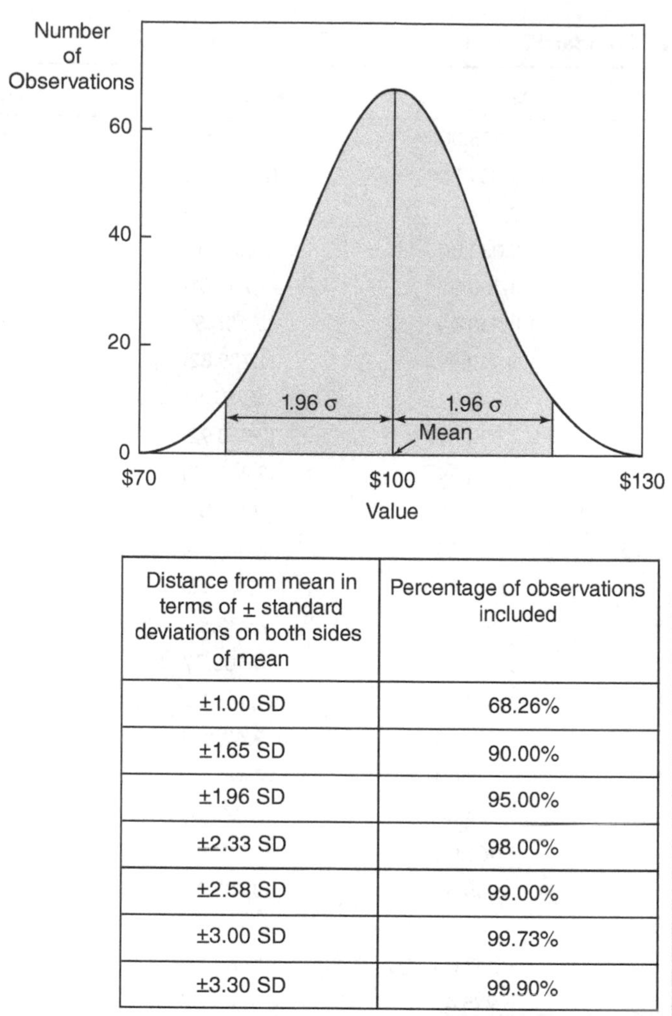

Distance from mean in terms of ± standard deviations on both sides of mean	Percentage of observations included
±1.00 SD	68.26%
±1.65 SD	90.00%
±1.96 SD	95.00%
±2.33 SD	98.00%
±2.58 SD	99.00%
±3.00 SD	99.73%
±3.30 SD	99.90%

EXHIBIT 10.5 Standard Deviation Sample Calculation

90 years—but the average or mean age may be about 45. These ages will be distributed into a bell-curve shape in what is called a normal distribution. The assumption that most populations follow a normal distribution is important for internal auditors involved in sampling. Exhibit 10.5 shows a normal distribution where the mean, median, and mode are all the same.

Standard deviation is a measure of how many items in a population will be disbursed around the central or mean point in a standard distribution. Statistical theory says that 68.2% of a normally distributed population will reside plus or minus one standard deviation around the mean; 95.4% will be within two standard deviations. How the items in the population are distributed around those central measures of mean and standard deviation is often of interest to the internal auditor. Is there an equal distribution of large and small values around the central measures? At times, a population will *not* follow this normal or symmetrical shape. If plotted by age, the population of a retirement community would be heavily weighted to older persons. We would say that this distribution by age is *skewed.* Many other business-related populations follow a skewed distribution, with a few items with very large values. It is important for internal auditors to understand if a population of data is skewed to either the right or left. Audit testing and evaluation procedures are often modified by this distribution of skewed data.

Because of its rather complex-looking formula, the importance of standard deviations does not seem very apparent, and the calculation of standard deviations may seem rather difficult or at least tedious. Various tools are available to perform these calculations, ranging from spreadsheet software to handheld calculators. An internal auditor who needs a better understanding of standard deviation concepts should dig into one of those old college textbooks that many of us have stored, or reference a good current statistical textbook. Exhibit 10.5 shows the concept of standard deviations around a mean value and the included percentages.

10.5 DEVELOPING A STATISTICAL SAMPLING PLAN

As a first step for audit sampling, an internal auditor should develop a sampling plan that will allow each item in a population to have an equal probability of selection. This involves a much more precise approach than that used in the judgmental sampling approaches discussed previously. The plan should attempt to remove any bias in the selection of items to assure that they are representative of the total population. An internal auditor is often faced with a challenge here in understanding any large amount of data, whether inventory records, accounts receivable payment histories, actual physical locations of assets, or other types of audit evidence. Statistical sampling allows an internal auditor to pull a representative sample of this data that will allow for an audit conclusion over the entire population of data. However, an internal auditor must understand the nature of the data to be reviewed when developing this sample selection strategy or audit plan, including:

- **The population (or universe or field) to be sampled must be clearly defined.** The *population* is the total number of units from which a sample can be drawn, including the scope or nature of items to be reviewed, such as all accounts payable vouchers for a year and the specific characteristics of audit interest. An example would be a large number of accounts payable vouchers where internal audit is only interested in materials purchases. Payables covering other areas—such as travel reimbursements or telecommunications charges—would not be included in this example audit population.
- **The population should be divided or stratified into groups if major variations exist between population items.** A population such as a materials inventory often includes only a few items of very high value and many of smaller values. Such a population would be skewed and not follow a normal distribution. When a population covers a few very large or significant items and many others with very small amounts, statistical conclusions based on the entire population will often not be valuable. Internal audit should perhaps consider stratifying the sample by

placing the smaller set of high-value items in one population and the balance in a separate population. Separate samples could be drawn from each.

- **Every item in a population must have an equal chance of being selected in the sample.** Every attempt should be made to eliminate bias in a sample selection when there is a lack of availability of particular items of interest. Auditors are sometimes guilty of bias when deciding to restrict some items from the sample selection even though the audit's conclusions are expressed in terms of the total population. They may decide arbitrarily to ignore some items in a population because of lack of easy access. For example, it is easy to ignore top-shelf, hard to reach items in an inventory audit. Auditors will pull the sample from readily available items and then state their audit conclusions as if they had looked at the entire population. If certain items must be ignored for logistical or other valid reasons, internal audit should always reveal that fact when reporting results.
- **There should be no bias in making the sample selection from the population.** Similar to the previous situation, an auditor may be faced with a population of items stored at both local and remote facilities but only looks at ones in the local facility. The auditor can then draw an audit conclusion based only on the items stored locally. Those items stored in remote warehouses that have been ignored may have different attributes than the central warehouse items. Sample result conclusions from the local items reviewed may not represent the remote warehouses.

The sampling plan used should be clearly documented and discussed with management, who with their knowledge of the items to be reviewed may suggest adjustments to the sampling plan. The development of a sampling plan is an important step for any audit sample.

There are four common methods for selecting an audit sample: *random number, interval, stratified,* and *cluster selection.* The latter two are also often referred to as types of sampling, but they are more properly identified as optional selection techniques. The following sections discuss very briefly each of these techniques. The modern internal auditor should have a general understanding of the most appropriate technique for a given audit situation.

Random Number Audit Sample Selection

Items here should be selected *at random,* with each in the population having an equal chance to be selected as a part of the sample. In theory, an internal auditor would place all the items from a population in a container (or numbers to identify them), mix them thoroughly, and independently draw the individual items for the sample from the container. Since this is generally not feasible, the auditor must find other means to draw the random sample. In the past, auditors often used time-consuming and somewhat complex processes. Today, however, an internal auditor can use any of a large number of computer tools to a select random number sample. An Internet search for "sampling random numbers" will reveal a wide variety of quite adequate software tools, some free and others selling for a small amount. The idea is to have a starting and ending number for all items in the population, determine the sample size, and then select random numbers based on that sample size. This process is easy with, for example, a population of 1,000 invoices where it is easy to identify each by number.

With larger or more complex populations, each item in the population to be sampled should be assigned a unique identifying tracking number, such as the voucher number on a paper document, part numbers for an inventory, or some sequential number. For example, if the population is described on a multiple-page IT-generated file report, items can be identified on the basis of the system's page number and line number per page. An inventory of 1,625 items could be displayed in a 30-page report with about 55 lines per page. Since the individual inventory items in such a report may not be numbered, they can be identified by their placement on this report. The items on page 1 would range from page 1, line 1 (or 0101 to 0155), followed by 0201 to 0255 for the entries on page 2. This scheme was easier in the old days of ponderous printed reports, but a review of system output files will define the items in the population subject to selection. The file used for the selections should be saved in a safe location to avoid inadvertent deletions or manipulations.

The sample size for such a selection should be large enough to recognize that some items cannot be selected and must be replaced. In our example of a population based on output report page and line numbers, where the highest number in a series would be 0155, the random number of 0199 might be drawn. Since that item does not exist based on the scheme used, the item number should be rejected and another random number drawn.

Although the major public accounting firms have developed a theoretical minimum sample size for their tests (often 60 or even 30), internal auditors generally should use *no minimum sample size* in an audit. An internal auditor may conservatively select a very large sample on the basis of seeking better results, with management more apt to accept the results of a large sample. Alternatively, a small sample size may be sufficient to arrive at adequate conclusions based on a limited amount of work. These internal audit sample-size decisions are made strictly on the basis of audit judgment and the objectives of the audit without regard to formal statistical sampling rules. Since they are formal and often very mathematical, sampling theory rules are beyond the scope of this book and can be found in an audit sampling text.

A random number–based population selection assumes that most populations follow a standard bell-curve distribution. Many actual populations do not follow such a normal distribution, raising the question of the feasibility of using audit sampling. Often a population may contain a small but significant group of very large items with the remainder having small balances distributed over a wide range. In other cases, most items, whether as errors or not, may be all nearly equal with respect to the audit attribute to be examined. They do not follow a standard distribution even though the basis of many of the statistical sampling methods discussed assumes that the distribution is in the form of a normal distribution. While there are mathematical techniques to get around non-normal distribution and to still take a valid sample, they are mathematically complex and not necessary for the typical internal auditor. However, a good method of assuring more accurate results when a sample is drawn from a badly skewed population is to increase the sample size. Mathematical theory says that as the sample size gets larger, the shape of the sampling distribution becomes closer to a normal distribution.

Interval Selection Audit Sample Selection

Another statistically sound technique for selecting sample items uses what is called *interval selection* or *systematic sampling*. This requires the selection of individual items based on uniform intervals from the items in the total population. This technique is especially useful for *monetary unit sampling*, discussed later in this chapter, where an internal auditor would develop a sample by selecting every *n*th item in the population, such as from an inventory listing. It is necessary that there be a reasonably homogeneous population, in terms of type of item, and no bias in the arrangement of the population that would result in a sample that is not statistically representative.

Interval selection should be related to the size of the sample and the total population. The planned sample size divided into the population size then establishes the interval. Thus a population of 5,000 and a needed sample of 200 would yield an interval requirement of 5,000/200 or every 25th item. An internal auditor would then examine every 25th item in the population series with the starting point in the first interval group established on a random number basis. In the event the actual population turns out to be larger than was estimated, a practical solution is to increase the sample by extending the interval selection on the same basis. If the actual population is less than estimated, it will be necessary to complete the sample through a new interval selection based on the number of items short in relation to the total population size. This problem can be avoided by always having a safety margin through a larger-than-needed sample estimate.

An interval selection where every *n*th item is selected is perhaps the easiest way to draw a sample from a population; however, the very nature of the method introduces the possibility of bias in the sample selection. For example, in a sample of daily transactions with an interval selection of every 30 days, if the starting random number pointed to the beginning of the month, a compliance error that normally took place later in the month might not be detected. The internal auditor could select day 5 of month 1, then move forward on the interval of 30 to perhaps day 6 of month 2 and so on. Based on this start, items from day 15 to about 30 will never be selected. Because of this bias, internal auditors should exercise caution before using this technique.

Stratified Selection Audit Sample Selection

With this selection approach a population is divided into two or more subgroups or strata, with each subgroup handled independently as a separate population. Stratified selection is an extension of random or interval selection techniques, because either can be applied to the smaller strata of the population. In some cases, one of the strata may be examined 100% while the others would be subject to random selection. The justification for stratification may be that one stratum has significantly different characteristics, and internal audit may wish to evaluate that subgroup on a more individual and precise basis. Through reducing variability, stratification can decrease the standard deviation and help to reduce sample sizes.

The data presented in the Exhibit 10.3 histogram shows where stratification might be useful. Internal audit might decide that all items in the population with balances greater than $10,000 should be examined 100%. In a purely random selection, using a random number table and a sample size of five, none of the three large items might be selected. Using stratification, internal audit could divide this population into two strata:

items over $10,000 and items under. The strata less than $10,000 would be subject to random selection, while the strata greater than $10,000 would receive 100% selection.

The most common populations requiring stratification are those that have a few items of very high value, such as inventories, accounts receivable, or invoices. Since these high-value items have much greater significance, internal audit may wish to subject them to higher standards of scrutiny. In other cases there may be a need for stratification since individual subgroups are processed in different ways, or by different groups, and the nature of the items may call for different standards of audit scrutiny, such as certain inventory subject to theft. Under these conditions, the larger variability in the total population makes a single type of testing and evaluation inapplicable.

Stratified sampling principles have long been well recognized, and audit sampling stratification provides more meaningful statistical measures together with the possibility of smaller sample sizes. Once the stratification selection technique has been adopted and the subgroups subjected to different standards of audit scrutiny, the results of each evaluation can be used independently, based on the sampling of the separate populations, or can be brought together to support a consolidated conclusion relative to the total population.

Cluster Selection Audit Sample Selection

Using a sampling approach called *cluster selection*, samples are made by systematically selecting subgroups or clusters from the total population. Cluster selection is useful when items are filed in shelves or in drawers, and it is physically more convenient to select subgroups based on the physical shelf area or individual file drawers. The rationale is that the items on particular portions of the shelf areas or in designated drawers are substantially similar in their nature and that a sample thus selected will be representative. However, the variability *within* the individual samples is frequently less than the variability *among* the samples. Hence, to offset this lesser variability, it is customary to use a larger sample when applying the cluster selection approach. A variation of the cluster selection approach, called *multistage sampling*, involves sampling the individual clusters instead of examining the sample as a whole.

Assume a population of 60,000 warehouse items located on 2,000 feet of shelves. If internal audit decides to review a sample of 600, the plan might be to divide the population into 20 clusters where each cluster would have 30 items. Since the average number of items on the shelves may be 30 per linear foot (60,000/2,000), each cluster would cover an area of one foot (30/30). These individual clusters would then be selected at intervals of 100 feet (2,000/20) and with a random start. Of course, the validity for this type of sample selection is dependent on the consistency of the population. That is, random number selection or regular interval selection would presumably assure a better representative sample. While sometimes useful, cluster sampling generally must be used with care.

10.6 AUDIT SAMPLING APPROACHES

An internal auditor can take several audit sampling approaches depending on the audit's objectives, whether it will be based on tests of compliance, financial statement controls, or on any special conditions. The three most common approaches here are *attributes sampling*, *variables sampling* (including monetary unit sampling), and *discovery sampling. Attributes sampling* is used to measure the extent or level of occurrence of various conditions or attributes—in other words, to assess internal controls. For example, an internal auditor might want to test for the attribute of whether invoice documents have received proper approval signatures. An invoice will either be correctly approved or not—a yes-or-no qualitative condition. Normally, the attribute measured here is the frequency of an error or other type of deficiency. The extent of the existence of the particular deficiency, such as improperly approved documents, determines the seriousness of the situation and how internal audit will report its findings and recommendations. Attributes or characteristics can be applied to any physical item, financial record, internal procedure, or operational activity. Attributes sampling often measures compliance with a designated policy, procedure, or established standard, and can be a strong test for internal controls. A control is either determined to be working or not working. "Sort of working" is not an appropriate conclusion. An internal auditor tests conditions in the selected items and then assesses whether the overall population is in compliance with the control attribute.

Variables sampling deals with the size of a specified population, such as account balances or tests in individual sample items. Here the auditor's focus is on "how much" as opposed to the yes-or-no focus of attributes sampling. The objective of variables sampling is to project total estimated quantities for some account or adjustments to the account on the basis of the auditor's statistical sample. Illustrative would be a sample to estimate the total value of an inventory based on sample results. Variables sampling is concerned with absolute amounts as opposed to the number or extent of a particular type of error.

Two important variables sampling approaches are *stratified sampling* and the now very common *monetary unit sampling*. Variables sampling procedures are closely related to attributes sampling, but include additional concepts and calculations. Because of the more complicated nature of variables sampling, a step-by-step analysis is given next for single-stage variables sampling. This example is based on a simplified manual estimate of the standard deviation when computer support tools or other information on the standard deviation are not available.

A third type of statistical sampling, *discovery sampling*, is similar to the nonstatistical judgmental sampling discussed earlier. Discovery sampling is used when an internal auditor wants to pull a sample from a large volume of data without the statistical processes associated with variables and attribute sampling. While the following sections discuss these sampling methods in some detail, our presentation here does not equip an internal auditor with enough information to become an expert in *statistical sampling concepts*. Appropriate additional training, experience, and specialized books and computer software tools are necessary. From a CBOK perspective, an internal auditor should have a general understanding of these sampling approaches and which are appropriate. More skilled help may be needed to perform statistical sampling–based internal audits.

Attributes Sampling Procedures

Attributes sampling is the process of pulling a sample to estimate the *proportion* of some characteristic or an attribute of interest in a population. For example, an internal auditor may be interested in the rate of occurrence of some monetary error or compliance exception that might exist in a population of accounts payable disbursement vouchers. The auditor here would be testing for the number of items that have some type of significant error, not the total monetary value of all of the errors. This type of test is very appropriate for assessing the level of internal control in some specific account, and can be a very important approach for Sarbanes-Oxley Act (SOx) Section 404 internal control tests. The starting point in attributes sampling is to estimate an expected rate of errors—that is, how many errors can internal audit and management tolerate? Depending on the items sampled and the culture of the enterprise, this expected error rate may be as little as 0.01% or as large as 5% or even more. Even if senior management states that no errors will be allowed in some highly critical operation, all parties often recognize that there always may be a small or very small possibility of an error, and depending on the criticality of the operation, such a very small error rate will be accepted. An expected error rate is the recognition that certain types of operations contain errors no matter how good the other controls and procedures are. If internal audit were to perform a 100% examination of an account but only find a small number of errors—say, 0.5%—it might be difficult to convince management that its controls are weak. Management might expect and tolerate a 1% error rate here and not express much concern at internal audit's findings. In an attribute-sampling test, internal audit must estimate the expected rate of errors in the population sampled, based on management's stated expectations, other audit tests, or just internal audit assumptions.

Along with estimating the expected error rate, internal audit should decide on the acceptable precision limits and the degree of wanted confidence for the sample. In other words, an internal auditor would like to be able to say, "I am 99% confident that the error rate of this account is less than 1%." These estimates will allow an internal auditor to determine the size of a sample that will provide a reliable conclusion regarding the condition tested. This determination is made through statistical methods and can be obtained from various statistical software packages or even by calculating using manual tables found in old statistical sampling books. These factors provide an initial basis for the size of the sample to be reviewed. The internal auditor now selects this sample and examines the items sampled to determine the number of errors that exist in the sample.

As can be expected, the error rate in a sample is normally higher or lower than the previously estimated acceptable error rate. If lower, the internal auditor has established that the condition tested is safely within the limits selected. If the sample shows a higher error rate, the auditor must determine whether the results are satisfactory and what further action, if any, is needed. Conceivably, the sample can be expanded, but internal audit will often feel there is an adequate basis for arriving at a conclusion. The key to meaningful attribute sampling is to take an appropriate sample and properly develop an audit conclusion based on the sample results.

Attributes sampling, once commonly used by both internal and external auditors, is now used less frequently because of the often difficult computational requirements and statistical knowledge required. However, it remains an effective tool to employ to report to management on the status of some control procedure. The internal auditor who wishes to obtain a greater understanding is encouraged to seek out Google references or a detailed book on the subject.

Attributes sampling is frequently used by governmental regulatory agencies, and its results are acceptable in a court of law. Although the process takes more work than the nonstatistical procedures discussed previously, when properly performed, attributes sampling will allow the auditor to express an opinion over the presence of some condition with a high degree of statistical authority.

Performing an Attributes Sampling Test

Attributes sampling is useful when an internal auditor is faced with a rather large number of items to be examined and wants to test whether certain controls are working or not working. The auditor must first define what is to be evaluated or the specific nature of the compliance tests to be performed, the nature of the sampling units, and the population characteristics. Attributes sampling is a yes-no type of audit test where the item or attribute sampled must either be correct or incorrect; there can be no measure of "almost correct" or "close enough." In a test of the completeness of travel report approvals, for example, enterprise procedures may state that the responsible manager must approve all travel reports greater than $100. Thus any voucher not approved by the responsible manager would be considered a compliance error. Internal audit should carefully define the types of tests to be performed as well as the acceptance and rejection rules. While it is possible to separately sample for two or more different attributes, each statistical test should concentrate on compliance with one such test criteria. If multiple ones are used in a single test, the failure of any one would mean that the entire item sampled is out of compliance.

The size of the population as well as the auditor's tolerance for errors will impact the number of items to be sampled. If an internal auditor is testing for travel policy compliance and if there is a requirement for manager approval for vouchers over a $25.00 limit, should internal audit treat a nonapproved $25.01 item as an error or should it allow for a perhaps 5% or 10% exception rate? As much as possible, these items should be defined in advance.

In addition, internal audit should have a clear understanding of the number and location of the items to be sampled. If initial plans are to sample *all* travel accounting reports, those reports must be available or readily accessible. If some items are filed at a remote, international location, internal audit may not be able to sample *all* such reports unless it gains access to the remote, international location reports as well as the national items filed centrally. Otherwise, internal audit should reduce the scope of the population sampled and look at only domestic travel accounting reports.

The auditor must first make some preliminary estimates, based on observations and other audits, of what is expected from the sample results and then pull an actual audit sample based on those expectations. For example, if a fairly high level of errors in the population is expected, the auditor's sample should be sufficient to confirm or refute those initial expectations. Internal auditors need to estimate the maximum tolerable error rate, the desired *confidence level* of the sample, the estimated population error rate, and then the initial sample size. These key attribute sampling parameters are:

- **Maximum tolerable error rate.** Statisticians also call this estimate the *desired upper precision limit*. This is the error rate an internal auditor will allow while still accepting the overall internal controls. The idea is that a typical population may have some errors. In the previously discussed audits of travel expense reports, which were reviewed for departmental management approvals, a realistic internal auditor recognizes that there may be *some* errors, such as the $25.01 vouchers that are above the $25.00 requirement. This is an error an internal auditor might accept but still feel that internal controls are generally adequate.

The maximum tolerable error rate is normally expressed as a percentage that can vary based on the nature of the items reviewed. In the previous example, an auditor might accept a 5% tolerable error rate or upper precision limit. In other instances, a smaller or larger estimate can be used, but this estimate should never be more than 10%. Such an estimate indicates major internal control problems, and the resultant attribute sample may provide little further information. If an internal auditor knows that internal controls are very bad, it is of little value to take an attribute sample to verify what the internal auditor has already determined through other audit procedures. Similarly, an internal auditor should normally expect some errors and establish a reasonable value for this rate, perhaps 1% or 2%.

- **Desired confidence level.** This is a measure of the auditor's confidence on the results of a sample. That is, internal auditors generally would like 95% or 98% certainty that the results of the sample are representative of the actual population. An internal auditor will never be 100% certain that a sample condition exists unless the auditor reviews essentially 100% of the items in the population. If a population of 100 items contains one error, an auditor might look at a sample of 10 items and find no errors. He or she may look at 20, 30, 50, or even 90 items and still not find more than that initial one error. The only way to be 100% certain that the population contains a 1% error rate is to look at 100% of the items. However, an internal auditor should typically look at a much smaller sample and still be able to state that he or she is 95% or 98% certain that the error rate is no more than 1%.

  The assumed confidence level value, usually 95% or 98%, along with the estimated population size, will determine the size of the sample needed to test the estimated population. Too large of a confidence level may require too large of a sample. Too low of a confidence level may reduce the size of the sample, but the results may be questionable. Management typically would not accept an internal audit finding that states they are "75% confident" that some condition is true.

- **Estimated population error rate.** In attributes sampling, an internal auditor estimates the level of errors in population and then takes a statistical sample to confirm or refute those assumptions. In order to calculate the sample size, the internal auditor also needs to estimate the expected rate of occurrence of errors in the population. This estimate, together with the confidence level and the maximum tolerable error rate, determines the size of the sample. For example, if the confidence level is 95% and the maximum tolerable error rate is 5%, the auditor should look at a sample of 1,000 items in a very large population if the estimated population error rate is 4%. A smaller estimated population error rate will reduce the sample size. Given the same parameters, an estimated population error rate of 1% will drive the sample size down from 1,000 to 100 items. If the expected population error rate is very large—greater than 50%—the required sample size will become very large.

Generally, the larger the difference between the maximum tolerable error rate and the estimated population error rate, the smaller the necessary sample size.

- **Initial sample size.** The preceding three factors, along with some statistical correction factors, determine the necessary sample size. While calculation formulas can be found in a statistical textbook, internal auditors normally use audit software to develop attribute sampling plans. A Web search for "attribute sampling software" will provide a wide range of options. Accessing such a statistical sample software package, an internal auditor only needs to provide the (1) maximum tolerable error rate, the (2) confidence level, the (3) estimated population error rate, and the (4) approximate sample size. The software will then provide the required sample size for the attributes test. Exhibit 10.6 contains some attributes sample sizes estimated using these values. The exhibit illustrates that if the confidence level is 99%, the maximum tolerable error rate is not over 5%, and the estimated error rate is 4%, an internal auditor should examine 142 items for an attributes test over a population of about 500 items.

This is a very brief introduction to the process of selecting a sample size when performing an attributes test. The real difficulty for internal auditors here is that sample sizes tend to be large. Because judgmental tests often sample perhaps only 50 items, it may be difficult to justify the larger sample sizes needed to perform a statistically correct attributes test. While in some instances an internal auditor can adjust the sample size by modifying sampling assumptions, this becomes part of the overall audit conclusions. In Exhibit 10.6, with a 1,000-item population and a desired reliability of 3%, an internal auditor will have to pull a sample of 260 items in order to express a 99% sample results opinion with an expected error rate not over 5%. This sample size will become much smaller if the confidence level is lowered from 99% to 95%. In such cases, there is the possibility that management may question audit findings with a 95% certainty, particularly when the auditee disagrees with the findings and is looking for a way to refute the sampling results.

Selecting the Sample to Perform Audit Procedures

Having made some audit sample assumptions and determined the sample size, the next step is for an internal auditor to pull the actual items for review. The random sampling procedures described previously can be used to select items to review. Multiple attributes also can be tested using the same set of sample items. The concept to remember is that the internal auditor will be performing a separate yes-or-no type of test for each of the individual attributes on each of the items in the sample.

Workpaper documentation should describe all items selected as part of the attributes test. Spreadsheet software is useful here for recording the results of the audit tests, but the internal audit procedures should be performed with great care. If an audit fails to recognize an error condition in the selected sample items, that fact will throw off the conclusions reached as part of the overall sample. With a large population, each sample item may speak for hundreds or even thousands of actual items. Each sample item should be evaluated carefully and consistently against the established attributes. An assessment of "close enough" should not be used. If some attribute measurement is too stringent for certain items, internal audit should consider reevaluating the entire

EXHIBIT 10.6 Attributes Sampling Size Examples

Sample Size Reliability of:						
Population Size	+/– 1%	+/– 1.5%	+/– 2%	+/– 2.5%	+/– 3%	+/– 4%
200						99
250						110
300						119
350					175	126
400					187	132
450					197	137
500					206	142
550				263	214	145
600				274	221	148
650				284	228	151
700				293	234	154
750				302	239	156
800			397	310	244	158
850			409	318	248	160
900			420	324	252	162
950			431	330	256	163
1,000			441	336	260	165
1,050		419	450	341	263	166
1,100		422	459	346	266	197

Confidence Level: 99%

Expected error rate not over 5%

sample set. An internal auditor may be looking for several error conditions but then find another error not included in the original test design. If significant, internal audit may want to redefine the overall attributes test.

Evaluating the Results of the Attributes Sampling Test

As discussed, prior to actually selecting and evaluating the sample items, an internal auditor will have made initial assumptions regarding the maximum tolerable error rate, the reliability, and the level of confidence, as well as about how many compliance errors would be tolerated to assess whether the controls are adequate. The next key step is to evaluate the sample results against those assumptions to determine if an internal control problem exists. Recall that an upper precision limit or maximum tolerable error rate and a confidence level formed the standards used to determine the sample size and perform the sampling test. An internal auditor should now assess the actual error rate of the sampled items and calculate an upper precision limit based on those sample errors. That precision limit, computed on the basis of the actual sample, should be less than or equal to the desired precision limits established at the beginning of the sample exercise in order for the auditor to report favorable results from the sample.

Normally, if the results of the sample do not meet the preliminary criteria, this condition points to a major audit finding. While these audit criteria should have been well thought out and approved before beginning the test, sometimes internal audit or management may decide that the original assumptions were too conservative. A new upper precision limit or confidence level could be used and the sample results measured against it. This approach should only be used with the greatest caution. In effect, the auditor here is attempting to explain some bad results. Were the matter ever to reach a court of law, internal audit would have a tough time justifying why it had altered its assumptions to make the sample results look good. A better approach when the results are unfavorable is to expand the sample size.

When attributes sampling results turn out unfavorably, management sometimes may claim that internal audit only looked at some very unusual items and that the remainder of the population is not that bad. An increase in the sample size will have the effect of decreasing the computed upper precision limit, assuming that the auditor does not find a substantial number of additional errors. However, internal audit should weigh the relative costs and benefits of this approach. A better approach is to report the internal control problem based on the current results and to expand the sample size in a subsequent audit review. It is hoped that management would take steps during the interim to improve internal controls in the area of interest.

Attributes sampling is a very useful technique for assessing one or several internal controls in an area of audit interest. Because estimates of such things as the maximum tolerable error rate are made in advance, it is difficult to dispute the audit test assumptions when compared to sample results. Similarly, because random number or similar techniques are typically used to select the sample items, it would be difficult to claim auditor bias in the selections. To better explain the attributes sampling process, an example follows.

10.7 ATTRIBUTES SAMPLING AUDIT EXAMPLE

This section discusses an example of attributes sampling at what we have called Gnossis, Inc., a large research and development sample enterprise. We assume in this hypothetical example that management has asked internal audit to assess whether the controls over its human resources records are correct. Certain employees have complained that they did not receive their scheduled increases on a timely basis, and Gnossis was recently fined in a court action when human resources records deficiencies were found during a legal discovery action. Senior management has asked internal audit to review payroll department internal controls.

Gnossis has about 4,000 employees, and internal audit has decided to perform an attributes test to assess the internal controls covering human resources records. The Gnossis human resources function uses two IT systems for employee records—one for pay calculations and one for benefits—and maintains a desktop spreadsheet-based system for such matters as employee health insurance declarations. Through a review of the human resources record-keeping process, internal audit found some 30 different record-keeping control issues, ranging from such major matters as whether pay is properly withheld for tax purposes to more minor items such as whether monthly deductions to pay for an employee credit union contribution are correct. Internal audit has combined all of these 30 record-keeping issues as a single attribute, as a single yes-or-no test. The problem here is that a few minor problems would force internal audit to conclude that internal controls are not working even though no problems were found over the major issues. This will often be difficult to communicate to management.

An audit strategy is to test the Gnossis human resources records for separate attributes. Although internal audit could have tested separately for all 30 attributes, a better approach is to decide which are the most significant and to test only for those separate attributes. Assume that internal audit has decided to test human resources records for the following five attributes:

1. Pay grade and status on the automated system should be the same as in manual files.
2. Authorizations for withholdings should be signed and dated by employees.
3. Preemployment background checks should have been completed.
4. If there were no life insurance deductions, employee-signed waivers should be recorded.
5. Pay increases are according to guidelines and are properly authorized.

While these are certainly not all of the areas where audit can test to determine if controls are adequate, in this example, internal audit has determined that it will statistically test employee records internal controls based on these five attributes. Internal audit would first discuss this approach with Gnossis management to obtain their consent. The next step is to establish sampling parameters and develop a sample plan. Based on the prior year's experiences and staff projections for the coming year, it was estimated that there would be approximately 4,000 employees in Gnossis payroll records. Using statistical sampling software, internal audit assumed an expected error rate of 2%, a desired precision of 1.25%, and a 90% confidence level to select a sample size of 339 items. The item of interest here would be an employee payroll file, and internal audit would separately review employee files for each of these five attributes.

Internal audit's next challenge is to select the 339 plus perhaps 40 extra payroll files for audit inspection. The physical records are stored alphabetically in the human resources department with eight-character employee numbers that are not sequential but assigned when an employee joins the enterprise. Because of turnover over the years, internal audit was not able to directly select the sample by matching selections from a random number table to a list of employees in sequence by their employee number. Rather, the sample employees were selected from a printed list of employees, a report 75 pages long and with about 55 items per page, using four-character random numbers 0101 through 0155 by page to 7555.

The sample items selected were listed on spreadsheets, as shown in the Exhibit 10.7 example, with space to list the results of each attributes test. Although largely manual procedures were used here to select the sample, internal audit could have made this selection using automated procedures as follows:

EXHIBIT 10.7 Attributes Test Worksheet for a Human Resources Test of Records

Random Number Selected	Matching Employee #	Employee Name	Audit Attributes Test Result # 1	# 2	# 3	# 4	# 5	Auditor Initials	Date Reviewed
0137	0266812	Archer, James Q.							
0402	0342201	Aston, Robert							
0988	0466587	Djuruick, Mary Jo							
1003	0502298	Eggbert, Katheran P.							
1256	0629870	Fitzgerald, Edward K.							
1298	030029	Gaddi, Emron							
1489	0687702	Horen, Rupert D.							
1788	1038321	Issac, Stanley L.							
1902	1189654	Jackson-Smith, Susan							
2263	1250982	Jerico, John							

1. Use a random number program to generate 379 numbers for the 339-count desired sample size, along with 40 extras. The range of the random numbers should be between 1 and 4,000.
2. Output the selected random numbers to a file and sort them in ascending order.
3. Using desktop software, match the sequential random numbers with the record counts on the employee master file. Thus if the first random number is 0137, the program would select the 137th record on the employee master file.
4. Output the selected record data to a spreadsheet file similar to the data shown in Exhibit 10.8.

This automated approach to attributes sample selection will take some initial effort and is best if internal audit also contemplates additional audit sampling procedures against the employee records files. Once the statistical sample is selected, these attributes are tested by pulling the designated employee personnel file. The procedures here are essentially the same as for any audit. The internal auditor checks each employee record selected against each attribute and then indicates on the worksheet whether the attribute is in compliance.

EXHIBIT 10.8 Attributes Sampling Size Examples

Random Number Selected	Matching Employee #	Employee Name	Audit Attributes Test Results # 1	# 2	# 3	# 4	# 5	Auditor Initials	Date Reviewed
0137	0266812	Archer, James Q.	*OK*	*OK*	*OK*	*OK*	*OK*	*RJK*	*11/16*
0402	0342201	Aston, Robert	*NO - 12.3*	*OK*	*NO - 14.02*	*OK*	*OK*	*RJK*	*11/17*
0988	0466587	Djuruick, Mary Jo	*OK*	*OK*	*NO - 14.12*	*OK*	*OK*	*RJK*	*11/16*
1003	0502298	Eggbert, Katheran P.	*OK*	*OK*	*OK*	*OK*	*OK*	*RJK*	*11/16*
1256	0629870	Fitzgerald, Edward K.	*OK*	*OK*	*OK*	*OK*	*OK*	*RJK*	*11/16*
1298	030029	Gaddi, Emron	*OK*	*NO - 13.2*	*NO - 14.32*	*OK*	*OK*	*RJK*	*11/16*
1489	0687702	Horen, Rupert D.	*OK*	*OK*	*OK*	*OK*	*OK*	*RJK*	*11/16*
1788	1038321	Issac, Stanley L.	*OK*	*OK*	*OK*	*OK*	*OK*	*RJK*	*11/16*
1902	1189654	Jackson-Smith, Susan	*OK*	*OK*	*OK*	*OK*	*OK*	*RJK*	*11/16*
2263	1250982	Jerico, John	*NO - 12.5*	*OK*	*OK*	*NO - 25.23*	*OK*	*RJK*	*11/16*

After reviewing these attributes for the 339 sample items, the final step is just to tabulate the exceptions or error rates. For Attribute 1 as described previously, internal audit finds that 10% of the employees in the sample had data errors between their manual payroll files and automated payroll records. At the 90% confidence level, this represents 7.3% to 13.3% of the total number of employees at Gnossis. Because sample results show an extensive error rate for this one important attribute, the results should be immediately disclosed to management without the need for further sampling.

Summary information on the results of these five attributes tests would be provided to management in a formal audit report, as discussed in Chapter 18. Only minor or insignificant problems appeared for three of the five attributes tested, while for the other two, Attributes 1 and 3, significant internal control problems were found. In internal audit's opinion, the internal control breakdown over these two attributes is sufficient to suggest major problems within the human resources record-keeping process. Based on these internal audit recommendations, management has the responsibility to analyze the entire file to determine the extent and frequency of these and other attribute errors throughout the system.

10.8 ATTRIBUTES SAMPLING ADVANTAGES AND LIMITATIONS

When there is a need to review a large number of items, attributes sampling procedures can provide a statistically accurate assessment of a control feature or attribute. Although statistical theory requires a relatively large sample size, internal audit can review some control or condition within a sample of that data and then can state that it is confident, within a preestablished confidence value or percentage, that the number of errors in a total population will not exceed a designated value or that the control is working. Attributes sampling is not useful for determining the estimated correct value on an account such as an inventory book value, but is an extremely useful tool for reviewing control procedures in a variety of operational areas. Some internal auditors feel the technique has some impediments to its use, including:

- **Attributes sampling computations are complex.** This chapter has only introduced some very basic attributes sampling concepts. The actual review and analysis of sample results can be very complex and may require the use of complex sampling software. An internal auditor needs to have a good understanding of the process or could be in danger of interpreting results incorrectly.
- **Appropriate definitions of attributes may be difficult.** In the previous human resources records example, internal audit sampled and evaluated controls on five attributes selected from a set of 30 actual attributes. The selection of attributes to be tested was based on either auditor judgment or management requests. However, an auditor may have missed one or another important attribute when analyzing the data.
- **Attributes sample results may be subject to misinterpretation.** Properly presented, the results of an attributes sample are stated very precisely, such as, "We are 95% confident that the percentage of error items in the account is between 2 and 7.3%." Despite this precision, people may hear these results and interpret them incorrectly, such as, "There is over a 7% error rate in the account." That is not what was communicated, but many listeners prefer easier answers.
- **Imperfect data requires corrections.** The basic theory surrounding an attributes sample assumes that the population of data follows a normal distribution, with no other unusual complications. While nonstandard data distributions can be corrected through adjustments in the sample size selection and evaluations, non-normal distributions complicate the process.

Despite these problems, attributes sampling equips internal audit with a very powerful tool to assess internal controls in a large population of data through the evaluation of a limited sample. While the technique often is too time-consuming or complex for many internal audit sampling approaches, an internal auditor should have at least a basic CBOK understanding of attributes sampling and make use of it when appropriate. The technique is particularly appropriate when the initial, judgmental results of an internal control review indicate problems in an area and when management disputes the preliminary results from audit's limited, judgmental sample as being "unrepresentative." A follow-up attributes sample will allow internal audit to take another look at the data and come back making a stronger statement about the status of internal controls surrounding the area in dispute.

10.9 MONETARY UNIT SAMPLING

Attributes sampling measures the extent of some condition, and variables sampling estimates the value of an account. Variables sampling can be further divided between the more traditional stratified sampling methods, discussed briefly in this chapter, and what is frequently called *monetary unit sampling*. Monetary unit sampling is a technique to determine if a financial account is fairly stated, and it is a good method for estimating the amount of any account overstatements. This technique is alternatively called dollar unit sampling or probabilities proportional to size (PPS) sampling. The concept is that every dollar or unit of currency in an account is treated as a member of the population and each has a chance of selection. A $1,000 voucher for an account will have 1,000 units of population, while a $100 voucher for the same account will have 100. Thus a $1,000 item in a population has 1,000 times greater chance of sample selection than a $1 item. This is a very popular form of sampling for public accounting firms, and although various texts and sources use different names, we will here call this approach monetary unit sampling.

As stated, the sampling unit is *each currency unit* rather than physical units, such as an invoice or payroll check. For example, if purchases are being tested for a year, the monetary unit sampling population will consist of the total dollar value of purchases made, and the sampling unit will be each dollar of purchases. If errors are found in the invoices, they are related to individual dollars in these invoices using various evaluation methods. A Google search will find multiple references on monetary unit sampling. Another good reference is the AICPA Audit Guide *Audit Sampling.*[2]

Selecting the Monetary Unit Sample: An Example

Assume that internal audit wants to review a series of accounts receivable balances to determine if they are fairly stated or recorded. Also assume there are 1,364 items or customer balances in this example account, with a total recorded balance of $54,902.25. The balances range from some large to others very small, with the first 30 of them listed in Exhibit 10.9. Assume that internal audit has initially either decided on a sample size of 60 or to look at only 60 individual dollars and the items these dollars represent. With this sample, the internal auditor can look at $54.902.25/60 = $915.034 or every 915th dollar in the account balance. Each time the items included in one of those dollars are selected, the auditor will examine that entire item.

Exhibit 10.9 has columns for the account numbers (here numbered from 1 to 30), the balance for each of these accounts, and the cumulative total. The additional columns in this exhibit show the process of making a monetary unit selection, as follows:

1. Although the auditor will select every 915th dollar, a starting point is needed somewhere between $1 and $915. To select this, a starting random number between 1 and 915 was selected; in this case, the number was 37.
2. The starting random number, 37, is then added to the first invoice of $123.58, rounded to 124 to yield 161. All values have been rounded to avoid pennies. Since 161 is less than 915, the next item, 754, is added to the accumulated value to yield 1039. Here, the auditor will encounter the 915th dollar, and this item will be selected for review.

3. A new starting number is now needed, and 915 is subtracted from 1039 to compute a starting number for the next item, 124. This is added to the third item, 589, to yield 713, not enough for selection.
4. The fourth item in this sample is large, 2056. The interval of 915 appears twice in this stream of dollars (915 × 2 = 1830) and the item is selection for two of the sample items.
5. The sample selection procedures are shown in Exhibit 10.9. The auditor can walk through these calculations using a pocket calculator.

The selection of items for a monetary unit sample is generally just as easy as that shown in Exhibit 10.9. An internal auditor can select a sample using a spreadsheet software package or even through a manual calculation using a calculator. The purpose is simply to determine the monetary interval based on the calculated sample size. Two key points and limitations of monetary unit sampling should be mentioned here. First, monetary unit sampling is only useful for testing for the presence of *overstatement*. In the extreme, monetary unit sampling will never select an account that has been incorrectly recorded at a zero value. If the auditor has selected dollars in a population that is

EXHIBIT 10.9 Monetary Unit Sampling Example

Acct. No.	Balance	Cum. Total	Start	Int. Tot.	-I-Mus SELECTs			-II-
1	$123.58	$123.58	37 +	124 =	161			
2	$754.22	$877.80	161 +	878 =	1039 SELECT	1039–	915 =	124
3	$588.85	$1,466.65	124 +	589 =	713			
4	$2,055.95	$3,522.60	713 +	2056 =	2769 SELECT(2)	2769–	1830 =	939
5	$341.00	$3,863.60	939 +	341 =	1280 SELECT	1280–	915 =	365
6	$855.20	$4,718.80	360 +	855 =	1215 SELECT	1215–	915 =	300
7	$12.55	$4,731.35	300 +	13 =	313			
8	$89.00	$4,820.35	313 +	89 =	402			
9	$250.00	$5,070.35	402 +	250 =	652			
10	$1,099.30	$6,169.65	652 +	1099 =	1751 SELECT	1751–	915 =	836
11	$87.33	$6,256.98	836 +	87 =	923 SELECT	923–	915 =	8
12	$788.99	$7,045.97	8 +	789 =	797			
13	$5,892.10	$12,938.07	797 +	5892 =	6689 SELECT(7)	6689–	6405 =	284
14	$669.90	$13,607.97	284 +	670 =	954 SELECT	954–	915 =	39
15	$24.89	$13,632.86	39 +	25 =	64			
16	$123.00	$13,755.86	64 +	123 =	187			
17	$123.00	$13,878.86	187 +	123 =	310			
18	$6.00	$13,884.86	310 +	6 =	316			
19	$540.90	$14,425.76	316 +	541 =	857			
20	$100.50	$14,526.26	857 +	101 =	958 SELECT	958–	915 =	43
21	$66.89	$14,593.15	43 +	67 =	110			

Acct. No.	Balance	Cum. Total	Start	Int. Tot.	-I-Mus SELECTs			-II-
22	$39.00	$14,632.15	110 +	39 =	149			
23	$35.00	$14,667.15	149 +	35 =	184			
24	$89.00	$14,756.15	184 +	89 =	273			
25	$100.00	$14,856.15	273 +	100 =	373			
26	$53.90	$14,910.05	373 +	54 =	427			
27	$436.09	$15,346.14	427 +	436 =	863			
28	$237.76	$15,583.90	863 +	238 =	1101 SELECT	1101–	915 =	186
29	$209.91	$15,793.81	186 +	210 =	396			
30	$28.89	$15,822.70	396 +	29 =	425			

Starting Random Seed = 37
Interval Selection = 915
Total Sample Items Selected = 10

understated, the selection method may never find those dollars. Second, the selection method described does not handle credit amounts correctly, so the sample selection procedure itself would not work correctly if the account included a large number of credit items. The best solution here is to pull out all recorded credit balances and treat them as a separate population to be evaluated. If there are only a small number, they might be ignored. Despite these limitations, monetary unit sampling is an effective way to evaluate the recorded balance in a large monetary account.

Performing the Monetary Unit Sampling Test

The number of dollars to be examined in a population determines the auditor's sample size. Similar to attributes sampling, a monetary unit sampling test requires that four things be known regarding the account to be sampled:

1. The maximum percentage of the recorded population value that the auditor will tolerate for errors. This is the same upper precision limit discussed previously for attributes sampling.
2. The expected confidence level.
3. An expected error rate for sampling errors.
4. The total recorded value of the account to be evaluated.

The first item in the list is the dollar value of the populations that may contain allowable errors divided by the recorded book value of the population. This is the same estimate discussed previously for attributes sampling, an error rate that an internal auditor could tolerate and still accept the overall controls in the system. Using public accounting terminology, an internal auditor should first think of the total amount of *material errors* that would be accepted. Although this number can be calculated, generally a small percentage rate of perhaps 2% is used.

The estimated confidence level follows the same general rule for attributes. An internal auditor cannot really say that he or she is *100% confident* unless the sample size is 100%. Too low of a confidence level, such as 80%, will cause management concern. Often 98% or 95% are good assumptions. These factors provide data to determine the recommended sample size, which again can be obtained from a table or from statistical sampling software. The values in Exhibit 10.6, based on a 95% confidence level, can be used here. As discussed previously, this is also an area where some public accounting firms have used a fixed sample size of 60 or sometimes 30, arguing that the mathematics does not require larger sample sizes.

The monetary unit sample size is then used to calculate the monetary interval by dividing the recorded book value of the account by the sample size to determine the every *n*th dollar interval. This interval sets a selection limit for larger items and all items greater than or equal to this interval will be selected. Each item represented by a selected dollar is then evaluated by the auditor to determine if it is correctly stated. The auditor calculates the correct amount for each selected account and records both that amount and the correct audited amount. This will point out how much each account is overstated.

Evaluating Monetary Unit Sample Results

Monetary unit sampling is an effective approach for evaluating account balances to determine if they have been overstated. Since every dollar in every item in an account will be subject to sample selection, overstated items may be discovered during the sampling process. The evaluation of the monetary unit sampling results to estimate the total error in the account is a more complex process. The basic idea is to document the recorded amounts and the audited amounts for each item selected and then to calculate the error percentage for each. Upper precision limits are calculated for each error item to determine the suggested amount of any audit adjustment.

The computations for a formal monetary unit sample evaluation have a series of statistical or theoretical options that go beyond the scope of this chapter. The process is often of more interest to external auditors, who can use this to propose a formal adjustment to a client's audited financial statements. For internal auditors, it is often sufficient to use the results of items selected through monetary unit sampling to gain an overall assessment as to whether an account is correctly stated. Books such as the AICPA Audit Guide, referenced previously, can walk the interested internal auditor through this formal sample evaluation process.

Monetary Unit Sampling Advantages and Limitations

The most important advantage of monetary unit sampling is that it focuses on the larger-value unit items in a population. A purely random sample could bypass large-dollar-value items based on a random selection. Because monetary unit sampling selects sample items proportional to their dollar values, there is less risk of failing to detect a material error since all the large dollar units are subject to selection based on the size of each. Any item in a population that is larger than the monetary interval will *always be selected.* Even though management will expect internal audit to take unbiased, random samples, it might express concern if an audit bypassed certain large-value items using other sample selection techniques. Monetary unit sampling assures that there will be a greater coverage of the larger-value items in a population. Another advantage is that if no errors are found in an initial sample and a very low expected error rate is established, relatively small sample sizes may be used. An internal auditor can readily determine the maximum possible overstatements and restrict the sample sizes in these circumstances. As discussed, public accounting firms often limit their monetary unit sample sizes to either 60 or 30 items. In addition, an internal auditor obtains the benefits of unlimited stratification by use of a monetary sampling unit.

Monetary unit sampling is also attractive because the item selection is computationally easy. As illustrated in the previous example, internal audit can effectively select a sample from a relatively large population using a spreadsheet program or even a pocket calculator, a good choice when at a field location and lacking computer-assisted audit tools. The main disadvantage of monetary unit sampling is that the procedure does not adequately test for financial statement understatements. Missing documents or transactions are a common problem in poorly controlled systems, and if items are missing from a population, dollar unit sampling procedures will not detect the missing items. They cannot be sampled. Accordingly, an internal auditor cannot project a value of the population using monetary unit sampling. A drawback to this method is that zero or negative values cause problems because there is no chance such items will be sampled. Another problem is that a total book value must be known in order to make interval calculations. The method cannot provide estimates of unknown population values. Finally, because monetary unit sampling is a relatively new concept for internal auditors, there are fewer training programs available compared to traditional methods such as attributes sampling.

Despite these concerns and limitations, monetary unit sampling is often the best method for auditing errors in some recorded book value. It can also be useful as a selection method for an internal control attributes test when all items in the population have some recorded monetary value. The approach is often superior to the random number selection previously discussed and will result in a very appropriate selection.

10.10 OTHER AUDIT SAMPLING TECHNIQUES

A fair amount of study, training, or experience is necessary to gain more than a minimum level of proficiency in any of these audit sampling methods. Attributes, monetary unit, and variables sampling—probably in that order—are the more important tools for internal auditors to understand and use. An internal auditor should have a high-level CBOK understanding of these techniques, but establishing expertise takes some additional work. Sampling, however, is a broad area with other less complex methods that can be used under certain circumstances. The following sections briefly describe some of these other internal audit sampling methods.

Multistage Sampling

This technique involves sampling at several levels. A random sample is first selected for some group of units and then another random sample is pulled from within the population of the units first selected. For example, assume each of 200 retail stores maintains its own inventory records, sending only summarized results to a headquarters office. Internal audit, interested in the age or condition of the inventory, might first select a sample of the stores and then at each store select a random sample of their inventory items. When all locations are examined with a sample selected at each location, the result can be treated as a variables or attributes sample.

Multistage sampling assumes that each primary sampling unit is homogeneous, but such assumptions can sometimes cause problems. If an internal auditor assumes that all of the example retail unit stores are essentially the same but subsequently finds that one or two of the units are very different from the others, such a failure to consider those unusual stores in the overall audit test can bias any overall sample projection. While this technique can be useful for a retail chain store environment, the formal mathematics for calculating sample sizes, reliability, and in particular for estimating the sampling error is complex. While practical for the chain store situation, the method can break down if the internal auditor wants to project the results of the sample test statistically.

Replicated Sampling

This is a variation of multistage sampling that requires the drawing of one overall random sample of size *X*, composed of *Y* separate random subsamples of size *X*/*Y*. If a sample of 150 items is to be taken from a very large population, rather than drawing a single sample, an internal auditor would select 15 samples of 10 items each. These primary samples from the overall population would be pulled from a series of random numbers. Then the same random numbers used to select each of the primary items would be used to select subsamples for items within those groups. The first random number would be assigned to subsample 1, the second to subsample 2, and so forth until a sufficient number had been apportioned.

Why would an internal auditor want to use replicated sampling rather than the multistage sampling previously described? The main reason is that the mathematics is easier. Again, this chapter will not devote space to a detailed discussion of this sampling procedure, but the technique may be useful to internal auditors in some situations.

Bayesian Sampling

A technique that is rarely used or seldom mentioned in audit sampling literature but that has great potential promise is *Bayesian sampling*. The procedure is named after the English mathematician Thomas Bayes, and is based on revised probabilities of sample sizes and the like, based on what are called *subjective probabilities* acquired from the results of prior tests. Very simply put, Bayesian sampling allows an auditor to adjust sample assumptions and probability factors based on the results of a prior audit. In other words, even though the size of the population is the same and the auditor's risks are unchanged, the sample can be modified based on the results of past audit work. While auditors tend to do this as a matter of course, Bayesian sampling allows an auditor to *formally* modify the sampling plan based on the results gathered in past audit tests.

An internal auditor will probably not encounter Bayesian sampling today either in internal audit publications or by contact with external auditors. However, detailed reviews of COSO internal controls, as described in Chapter 3, could make a Bayesian sampling approach potentially attractive. Internal auditors may encounter Bayesian sampling in the future.

10.11 MAKING EFFICIENT AND EFFECTIVE USE OF AUDIT SAMPLING

Audit sampling is a key, important part of the internal auditor's CBOK, but is not always an essential requirement to be included in all audits. An internal auditor may or may not decide to test transactions when performing an audit. The internal auditor decides, on the basis of overall comparisons and other auditing procedures, that a test of transactions is unnecessary or that the amounts involved are not sufficiently material to warrant testing. However, an internal auditor is often faced with situations that will require sampling of transactions. The best of control systems cannot eliminate errors resulting from system breakdowns, and overall reviews or tests of a few transactions may not be sufficient to disclose whether internal controls are operating effectively.

While procedures may appear to be adequate, an internal auditor generally must test actual transactions to determine whether those procedures have been followed in practice. If tests are made, audit sampling should be considered as a basis for arriving at more valid conclusions. If the test of transactions generated through the audit sample indicates that operations are acceptable, no further work may be required. Where errors are found, an internal auditor is generally faced with the following decisions in order to arrive at an audit conclusion:

- **Isolating errors.** Through a review of the types of errors and their causes, an internal auditor may be able to isolate the total amount of errors. For example, one vendor may be submitting erroneous invoices, and a review of all of the vendor's invoices may pinpoint all the errors. As another example, a particular automated system may appear to be causing the errors, and a special review of that system may be required. Either type of analysis can determine the amount of deficiency as well as the basic cause.
- **Reporting only on items examined.** When an internal auditor encounters significant errors, it may only be necessary to report the results of the tests to operating personnel. The nature of the errors may be such that it is the responsibility of operational managers to strengthen procedures and determine the magnitude of errors. As part of this review, an internal auditor should attempt to determine the causes for the condition and make specific recommendations for corrective action. Unless an internal auditor projects the results of a statistical sample, management is provided only with errors or amounts pertaining to the items examined.
- **Performing 100% audits.** Although an internal auditor typically will not perform a detailed examination of all transactions, there sometimes may be a need for an extended examination when significant errors are found. An example is where certain recoveries are due from vendors but where specific vendors and amounts have to be identified in order to file the claims. If not a 100% examination, the auditor's sampling plan would have to be based on a very high confidence level, perhaps greater than 99%, and a low risk of perhaps 1%. The result will be a very

large sample but with a very high acceptability of sample results. This large sample size or 100% examination may not be justified in terms of the costs involved, and a more conventional statistical sampling plan may suffice.

- **Projecting results of sample.** If the selection of items for the test is made on a random basis, the results can be evaluated using statistical tables. The number and dollar amount of errors can be projected to determine the range of errors in the entire field at a given confidence level. The projection can be used to make an adjustment, or as a basis for decisions of the kind described in the preceding paragraphs.

Audit sampling is a powerful internal audit tool, to support audit procedures such as inquiry, observation, vouching, confirmation, computation, and analysis. As a basis for extending its use of audit sampling, internal audit should review areas in which testing was performed in prior reviews along with an analysis of the objective of those tests, the period covered, the effective use of judgmental or audit sampling, the number of items in both the field and the sample, results of these tests, and the feasibility of using these audit sampling procedures in subsequent audits.

In past years, audit sampling was a difficult process both to understand and to use. Internal auditors needed to refer to published handbooks filled with extensive tables and then to use this tabled data to perform fairly detailed sample selection and test results calculations. The process was comparatively difficult and certainly was not understood by many auditors. Computerized sampling software has changed all of that. It simplifies the necessary calculations, eliminating the need for reference to formulas or tables. In addition, it facilitates the use of sophisticated techniques, thus enabling an internal auditor to obtain more precise and unbiased results. While an internal auditor can of course use the time-consuming manual calculation procedures to determine the sample size and to evaluate results in the rare situation when a computer is not available, today's laptop computers contain the tools to make this sampling process much easier. The following techniques also will facilitate the use of audit sampling for many audit procedures:

- **Combine audit steps.** Audit time savings can be achieved if various audit steps are performed as part of the same statistical sample. This can be done by testing for as many attributes or characteristics as possible in the sample. For instance, in a review of purchases, the primary audit objective may be to determine whether there is adequate documentary support. In addition, an internal auditor may decide to include statistical sampling tests to determine whether excess materials are being acquired.
- **Use a preliminary sample.** Auditors can devote considerable effort to developing a sampling plan based on an estimated confidence level, precision, and expected error rate or standard deviation; however, in many cases there is insufficient information in a first audit to develop the sampling plan. By taking a preliminary sample of 50 to 100 items, an internal auditor is in a better position to make decisions on the extent of sampling required. The preliminary sample can then be included as part of the final sample, and the results of the preliminary sample may lead an internal auditor to conclude that no further testing is required.

- **Perform interim audits.** When a sampling plan is prepared in advance—such as for the year of interest—the items to be tested can be examined on a monthly or other interim basis without waiting until the end of the year. Thus staff auditors can be utilized when available to perform the audit sampling on an interim basis. For example, if the sample plan calls for examination of every hundredth voucher, these can be selected for examination as the transactions are processed.
- **Enlarge the field size.** A basic consideration in audit sampling is that the sample size should not vary to a great extent with an increase in field size. Thus savings can be obtained by sampling for longer periods of time, or from a field composed of more than one department or division. In some cases an internal auditor may decide to test a particular account for a two-year period, with selection of items during the first year on an interim basis as part of that two-year test.
- **Apply simple audit sampling methods.** In most instances, a simple estimation sample will provide adequate results, without the need for techniques that are difficult to understand, apply, and explain. An internal auditor should not overlook judgmental sampling in the audit tests, and sensitive items should be examined in addition to a random selection of items. These can be examined on a 100% basis or sampled as part of a separate stratum.
- **Achieve an effective balance of audit costs and benefits.** An internal auditor should consider the costs of examining each sampling unit when considering extending a sample, with consideration given to the costs of additional work compared with benefits from obtaining increased confidence or precision in the final results. When an internal auditor first tries and then effectively uses some of the audit sampling techniques discussed in this chapter, the auditor will subsequently find other useful areas to use sampling in the course of operational audit, including production activity improvements, improved inventory management, or even records and document management.

Audit sampling is a powerful tool that is too often ignored by many internal auditors. In the past, auditors have not used audit sampling because it was viewed as being too difficult or too theoretical. Auditors found it easier to say, "You have a problem here," rather than saying, "Based on our audit sample, we are 95% certain that we have identified a control problem." Findings based on appropriate audit samples allow internal auditors to express concerns or opinions on a more solid basis. IT tools now make statistical sampling a simpler task than in earlier days when auditors relied on extensive tables of values and difficult formulae. Today, the effective modern internal auditor should have a CBOK understanding of the basics of audit sampling and use them when appropriate.

NOTES

1. Dan M. Guy, D. R. Carmichael, and O. Ray Whittington, *Practitioner's Guide to Audit Sampling* (New York: John Wiley & Sons, 2001).
2. *Audit Sampling* (AICPA, 2014), www.aicpa.org.

CHAPTER ELEVEN

Continuous Auditing and Computer-Assisted Audit Techniques

CONTINUOUS ASSURANCE AUDITING (CAA) IS the process of installing control-related monitors in IT systems that will send audit-related signals or messages to auditors—usually internal auditors—if the IT system's processing signals a deviation with one or another audit limit or parameter. This concept has been around since the earlier days of IT auditing when pioneer internal audit specialists developed audit monitoring tools known as Integrated Test Facilities (ITFs) or System Continuous Audit Review File (SCARF) facilities.[1] These processes date back to the days of mainframe computers and the almost primitive technology of that earlier era. Although these real-time audit monitor concepts sounded very interesting, they were seldom if ever implemented in that earlier era of batch processing and magnetic tape storage applications.

The older concepts of ITFs and SCARFs have long since evolved into CAA monitoring techniques, and while these older CAA tools and techniques are still effective, today they represent relatively advanced IT and internal audit procedures. This chapter will discuss CAA as an improved alternative approach for reviewing today's automated systems as well as what is known as *continuous monitoring (CM)*, business-controlled procedures that can be subject to periodic internal audits. Technology makes *continuous auditing* approaches much easier to implement, and evolving requirements for almost real-time financial reporting make them very attractive. The concept leads to the installation of audit monitors and the ability to "close" an enterprise's financial reports on almost a real-time basis. CAA represents a dramatic change in the internal audit model and may transform both auditor practices and skill requirements as it becomes more widely accepted.

Enterprises today have multiple needs to retain all forms of operating and historical information, stored on information systems databases. When this stored data is organized on a series of large, complex, and interrelated databases, the concept has come to be known as a data warehouse. A data warehouse environment is an almost necessary component for implementing CAA, as are the tools of data mining and online analytical processing. This chapter will briefly discuss these concepts and their applicability to internal audit processes.

The chapter will also discuss the importance of building and using *computer-assisted auditing tools and techniques (CAATTs)*. Back in the days when large computer systems files were stored on multiple reels of magnetic tape or later on disk or drum drives, internal auditors had difficulties in accessing and assessing the data stored on those files beyond the often ponderous printed reports produced by IT systems groups. Early internal and external auditors back in the 1970s developed some simple but effective software tools to select and sample items from what were then considered massive system files. That work became the foundation for information systems or IT auditing, once called computer auditing, and spurred the formation of ISACA's predecessor organizations.

Much has changed and files stored on reels of magnetic tape have gone away; this chapter will discuss some current methods for developing and using CAATTs in today's IT environments. CAATTs are still an important internal auditor tool, and knowledge of them should be part of every internal auditor's common body of knowledge (CBOK).

Finally, this chapter will introduce *XBRL*, the AICPA-initiated extensible business reporting language. XBRL is a standards-based way to communicate business and financial information across multiple enterprises. For example, if enterprises code a standard value on their financial reports in XBRL, such as the total assets or accumulated depreciations, it is very easy to identify the value despite differing physical report formats. XBRL is becoming an increasingly important tool that internal auditors should understand and will almost certainly be using in future years.

While many chapters of this book have highlighted internal audit CBOK areas that we feel should be internal audit requirements, the CAA, CAATT, and XBRL concepts discussed in this chapter are areas where internal auditors need just a general understanding. It may not be necessary for an internal auditor to have the skills, for example, to implement CAA or even some CAATT processes. However, internal auditors should understand that these are tools and concepts that may be useful in various internal audit processes.

11.1 IMPLEMENTING CONTINUOUS ASSURANCE AUDITING

Auditing has gone through a series of conceptual changes over time. In its earliest days, it was primarily a process of vouching and testing, a concept that goes back to the dictionary definitions of these terms. To "vouch" means to attest, guarantee, or certify something as being true or reliable, and auditors performed tests to support that vouching process. This often detailed type of audit process has been used for years. However, as processes became more highly automated, auditors began to rely primarily on reviews of internal controls to support their audit conclusions rather than old-fashioned vouching. If internal controls were adequate and found through tests to be working, there was less need to perform the detailed transaction testing. In this subsequent phase of internal auditing and through the early 1990s auditors placed a major emphasis on reviews of internal controls as the major component of their attest work.

With too many IT applications and their diverse controls to consider, coupled with an ongoing emphasis on increased audit efficiency, auditors—particularly external auditors—began perform formal risk analyses over their control environments, with their audit emphasis placed only on higher-risk internal control areas. This audit risk analysis process was discussed in Chapter 7, and could be considered a third phase of auditing after the first, "vouch and test," and the second, internal control reviews. Analyses of what caused the financial failures in the early part of this century, involving such corporations from that era before the Sarbanes-Oxley Act (SOx) such as Enron, WorldCom, Tyco, HealthSouth, and a host of others. These all raised many questions about the audit procedures then used. How could all of these failures have happened? Why didn't the external auditors see these internal control weaknesses and other problems? Why did internal auditors seem to be too in bed with their external auditors rather than being independent reviewers? A major concern here was that financial reports were frequently unreliable. A second concern and criticism was that the supporting final audited reports were often delivered well after the official statement closing dates and contained many pro forma numbers, as they were called then. SOx now requires that financial reports be closed and issued on a much tighter schedule, closer to the enterprise's period ending dates. That requirement points to the need for continuous close audits and auditor assurances—what may become the next phase or generation of audit techniques.

What Is a Continuous Assurance Auditing and Monitoring System?

CAA is an internal audit process that produces audit results simultaneously with, or shortly after, the occurrence of actual events. Auditor-supervised controls, for example, are installed in a major, enterprise-wide resource application that includes alarm monitors and continuous analytical analysis routines to either attest results or highlight items for immediate audit analysis. A CAA is generally independent of the underlying business application and includes processes that test transactional data against defined control parameters or rules. CAA processes today run automatically on a daily or weekly basis and generate exception reports or alerts for internal auditor follow-up. Similar to the traditional audit process, a CAA is more detective than preventive.

Although the underlying concepts are very similar, we can sometimes confuse what is called continuous assurance auditing and continuous monitoring. Their basic characteristics are:

Continuous Assurance Auditing

- Repetitive software audit monitors are built into IT applications. For example, if internal audit is interested in financial transactions in a general ledger account above some specified limit, a software change can be installed to monitor any activity that meets the criteria.
- Rather than scheduling periodic internal audits to review an area, CAA records areas of potential interest for internal audit's attention. It is then internal audit's responsibility to follow up on these items.

- Internal audit is generally responsible for the CAA software, often installed independently and without the knowledge of some users, and may face problems if application users make certain IT changes.

Continuous Monitoring

- In many respects, continuous monitoring (CM) is very similar to CAA except that the IT users—often management—install CM in an application of interest.
- Rather than being intended to detect individual exception items or unusual transactions, CM is often installed in the form of dashboard screens—similar to a gas gauge in an automobile—to monitor ongoing status.
- Internal audit may review CM processes on a periodic basis, but often only to gain assurance that the overall process is working.

CM and CAA are similar but different in their concepts. In its most basic design, a CAA is an independent application that monitors another critical application. Exhibit 11.1 shows a CAA audit monitoring application for an automated payments system. This is a separate parallel set of software that monitors all payment activity through periodic reviews of activity through a payments transaction file. Activity summaries are reported through periodic reports, and any unusual items are highlighted in an exception report, probably through an e-mail notice. This type of system is very similar to the kinds of password security monitors that are in place in many enterprises. High-level transaction activity would be reported on a regular basis, and any significant red-flag violations would be highlighted for immediate attention.

CAA applications imply more than just monitors that run against application transaction files and highlight exceptions. For many enterprises, applications are much more complex. Enterprise resource planning (ERP) systems are an example. These are the all-inclusive application packages, by vendors such as SAP, PeopleSoft, or Oracle, that provide total systems solutions including accounting, the general ledger, human resources, and purchasing, covering virtually all application areas in the enterprise. These are complex IT applications in which an average ERP implementation

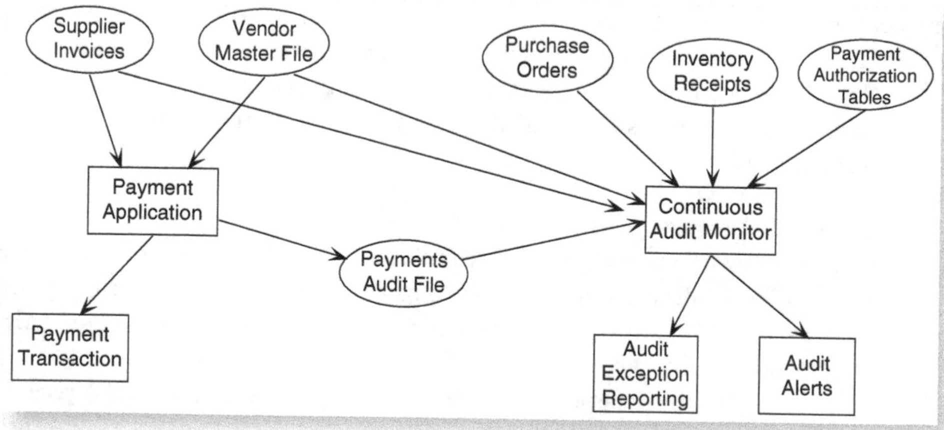

EXHIBIT 11.1 Payment System Continuous Audit Monitoring Application

often costs an enterprise more than $12 million and often takes almost two years to implement for a large enterprise. These implementations are built around a single or a closely federated set of databases. Any CAA set of monitors here must be much more complex, as multiple transactions may be updating or depending on multiple tables. The CAA process is very useful as it allows monitoring to be installed over a complex set of processes. This is also the ideal environment to install CAA, as the monitoring activity can be built around the common database structure of an ERP implementation.

Exhibit 11.2 provides a conceptual view of the multiple audit review processes that are elements of CAA. At the base of the exhibit is a stream of measurable IT application processes such as might occur in a complex ERP. The audit team would then establish some metrics it wishes to monitor as well as supporting standards for those metrics. As a simple example, internal audit might be interested in sales division office transactions over $10,000 because of a concern expressed by management of possible unapproved marketing activity. Metrics tools could be built into these processes to monitor all cash

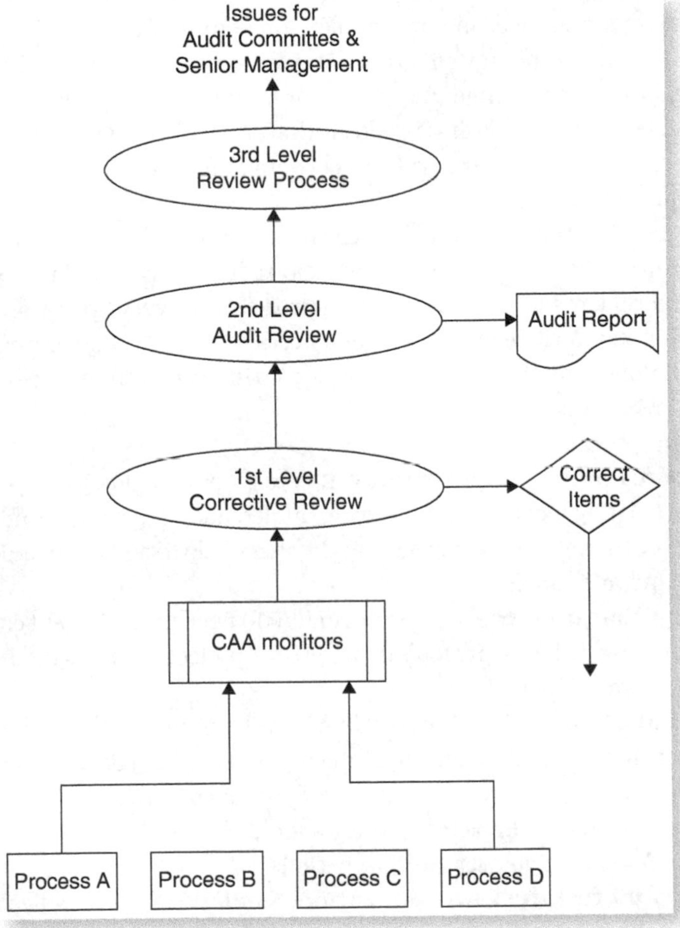

EXHIBIT 11.2 CAA Conceptual Model

transfer transactions with a standard that any amount over $10,000 should be flagged. The process could have multiple levels of metrics and standards, with exceptions fed up to a first-level assurance process that would monitor the difference and, in some instances, send back a correcting feedback transaction to the ongoing process. The first level of monitoring here might be similar to the warning notes that are sent to a corporate systems user when his or her e-mail account is over 90 percent full.

Other discrepancies would flow up to what Exhibit 11.2 shows as a second-level monitoring or auditing process. This level would produce the reports to management or emergency exception notices. Beyond reports, this level could produce more significant audit or assurance actions. In the e-mail account example, CAA would initiate a transaction to prevent further accesses to the offending user. There is also a third level to CAA to monitor the auditing process. Control procedures would additionally be built into the process to monitor ongoing CAA activity. This is the level that the enterprise could use to report CAA activities to external auditors.

The continuous audit monitoring processes just described can be performed on multiple levels. They are often initiated by key managers who are interested in the health and strong internal controls of their various automated systems. CAAs are typically implemented over major complex applications to support internal audit needs. A large, highly integrated purchasing system, an enterprise ERP application in a manufacturing environment, or a vendor management system are all examples where a CAA might be a good fit. The idea is that these are typically the types of applications where there may be large volumes of data and with many rules and decisions involved in processing steps.

However, an internal audit function cannot just build and implement a CAA application on its own. The successful implementation of an internal audit CAA requires the support of several key stakeholders in the enterprise. As a very first step, internal audit leadership should prioritize areas for audit coverage and select a continuous auditing approach. The following steps should be considered in the planning and implementation of internal CAA processes:

1. **Define CAA output requirements.** It is easy to read glowing reports about the power of CAA applications, but internal audit leadership should understand their potential needs and assess how they might better help to audit and understand some complex installed application.
2. **Select CAA analysis tools.** Internal audit will need to implement either in-house or vendor-provided software tools for their CAA project. Sections of this chapter will highlight some of them.
3. **Develop audit objectives for the CAA.** Similar to what other chapters have discussed for internal audit planning, internal audit should develop some high-level objectives for the planned CAA application. Because the CAA application will take time and resources to implement, there should be a continuing interest in the use of this CAA application over multiple periods.
4. **Prepare and test the CAA application.** Similar to the IT application software management systems discussed in Chapter 22, care should be given to plan, develop, and test the CAA prior to its implementation.

5. **Assess data integrity and prepare data.** The use of a CAA application is typically not a onetime audit exercise but something that will be used on a continuous basis. Internal audit should execute the CAA and initially follow up on any reported exception transactions to determine their validity.
6. **Review the results of the continuous monitoring approach with management.** Internal audit should first determine that its efforts to develop the CAA provided cost-effective results, and if it plans to use this approach further, it should explain and review this approach with both management and the audit committee.
7. **Develop continuous audit routines to assess controls and identify deficiencies.** The CAA should be rolled out, documented, and implemented as an internal audit tool for ongoing reviews of the application selected.

Exhibit 11.2 shows a CAA operating on multiple levels. The first CAA level might be to flag and extract all transactions that pass resources between the enterprise and some entity of interest, extracting all transactions that match auditor-defined criteria for further analysis, vouching, or reporting. An example might be installing monitors to screen for all financial transactions with some group of countries or companies of interest. A second level would be a bit more sophisticated and would include some limits or logical templates in the evaluation process, such as maximums and minimums in the monitors. On a third and more analytical level, the CAA could examine the formal rules relative to the process monitored. An example here might be the use of system generated values such as interest rates or asset returns and a comparison with internal auditor-initiated reasonableness tests of those assumptions compared with historical values.

At its most basic level, a CAA can introduce a heightened level of monitoring to application systems. Classic internal auditor points of control may even "disappear" into the processing system, changing recording and measurement tools. The cycle time for making audit-based decisions or actions will very much decrease as it is based on systems measures. A CAA can create an environment for 24/7 continuous auditing.

CAA processes have already been implemented at a variety of larger enterprises. AT&T, for example, was an early leader, and CAA has become quite common in the insurance, stock brokerage, and medical claims processing industries. Although neither enterprise management nor their internal auditors publically talk about the audit tools in use, we have seen references that such high-transaction retailers including Walmart, JC Penney, and Dollar General all have implemented CAA applications.[2] Built around an enterprise's ERP system, CAA is particularly useful for monitoring purchase and payment cycle applications with an emphasis on controls over potential vendor-related fraud. CAA is a valuable tool for any application area where cash is going out the door, including employee travel accounting, insurance claims, and money laundering controls.

Resources for Implementing a CAA

While the basic concept of implementing some form of audit monitor in an ERP or other business application seems relatively straightforward, the actual implementation of a CAA in an enterprise often presents challenges. In order to be independent of other IT applications, the CAA process must be installed with some level of independence from other persons and IT developers. That is, if a CAA has an objective to monitor all marketing expense transactions over *X* dollars and some certain other conditions, those marketing expense system monitoring controls must be installed independently such that they cannot be easily bypassed. However, installing a CAA process in an ERP or any other larger and complex applications requires some IT technical skills that may be beyond the technical capabilities of many internal auditors. Conversely, even if internal audit has the skills to install a CAA in an enterprise's applications, IT management will look at any such proposal with a high degree of skepticism. IT management will not trust its auditors to install their own CAA monitoring software in a production systems environment, but if IT agrees to take the CAA software module and test and modify it for production installation, the CAA's independence could potentially be compromised.

The market is always changing, but this section introduces several vendor- supplied software solutions for installing CAA. The products and approaches discussed are not the only solutions to installing CAA, but represent some good starting points for an enterprise that is considering the uses of CAA. Good sources for more information on CAA can be found in a Google search for information on continuous auditing. That will yield information from a variety of sources, particularly public accounting firms that are interested in promoting CAA approaches. Partially based on some past continuous auditing presentations, we have selected several CAA implementation examples.

11.2 ACL, NETSUITE, BUSINESSOBJECTS, AND OTHER CONTINUOUS ASSURANCE SYSTEMS

Many auditors over the years have used ACL,[3] a popular and effective software product for computer-assisted audit analysis and retrievals. ACL allows internal auditors to install and implement fully embedded and automated continuous auditing or monitoring applications. ACL's audit-related testing applications comprise a series of automated data analysis tests that are manually initiated and run on a regular basis. The ACL approach goes a step further such that the auditor does not need to formally start and run the monitoring program. ACL software is linked to enterprise files and applications so that it can run in the background. The software is useful for such areas as detecting unusual transaction indicators of fraud or identifying duplicate and other overpayments. While perhaps not truly continuous, ACL can be installed and run on completion of process steps and at periodic time intervals. It takes a slice of the data, capturing all transactions since the last test process. ACL continuous assurance software is used today by all the major public accounting firms in the United States. An organization today that is interested in implementing some beginning level of CAA might well consider starting with ACL's assurance product.

Complex information systems can be built with a wide variety of monitoring programs and displays to allow an operator to review performance and highlight any potential problems. This is similar to the driver of an automobile who faces a dashboard that monitors performance by showing speed, progress by miles traveled, status by fuel remaining, and problems by warnings for such items as low oil pressure. This dashboard approach allows the driver to monitor overall progress while the vehicle is in operation and to take action as required. That same dashboard approach can be used with business information systems.

The typical online application today has a continuous display for that application. In a sales order application, designated users can access the progress of sales recorded, perhaps by product line or region, through an online terminal. However, that monitoring typically just covers that one sales application, and another screen must be called up to review related activities handled by other applications, such as ongoing cash collections or returns. Today's IT applications provide a better environment for such cross-application monitoring, as all of the overall systems components, from receiving to general ledger processes, are under a common database structure. In addition, several good software products exist that allow an organization to install dashboard monitors to review overall progress of business transactions and other activities to facilitate prompt remedial action when necessary. Perhaps two of the better of these software tools today are BusinessObjects[4] and IBM's Cognos Business Intelligence and Financial products. They help an enterprise to tie a wide variety of diverse applications to a dashboard, allowing users to monitor overall activity.

The console monitors on the classic mainframe computers acted as dashboards and watched all system activity, with a constant stream of messages to the operator. The same concept can be applied to today's major, integrated applications. They allow an enterprise and internal audit to move from an environment of monitored controls to the real-time monitoring of systems operations with adjustments for continuous improvement.

11.3 BENEFITS OF CAA

CAA approaches allow internal audit to deal with IT-based issues on a real-time basis. Rather than waiting for an internal audit that is scheduled only once a year or later, a CAA process provides internal audit with an early warning for many areas of internal audit interest. CAA provides internal audit with a tool for proactive risk management. In addition, effective CAA processes allow internal auditors to develop a better understanding of their enterprise's business environment as well as to support compliance and drive business performance.

By changing traditional internal audit approaches and implementing CAA processes, internal auditors can develop a better understanding of their business environment and the risks to their enterprise to support compliance and drive improved performance. CAA processes can provide for the automation of testing through the verification of transaction integrity and validity and the generation of internal control alarms. CAA creates an environment of continuous testing where internal control failures can be detected and fixed immediately. Although there is some effort involved in implementing CAA, its approach of looking at full populations of data from areas of interest can very much increase the overall effectiveness of internal audit. Where once CAA processes were promoted by almost "voice in the wilderness" speakers at internal audit technical conferences, we are now seeing the internal audit functions of major enterprises adopt CAA approaches. CAA is a growing internal audit trend.

11.4 COMPUTER-ASSISTED AUDIT TOOLS AND TECHNIQUES

Historically, internal auditors gathered evidence from an enterprise's books and records to support their conclusions. Paper-based documents were used as audit evidence that showed supporting transactions were properly recorded in a timely manner and contained appropriate authorizing signatures or notations. Today, most documents are IT-based and paperless, and internal auditors have a challenge to review and understand these documents and procedures to support their audit conclusions. While internal auditors test and review the internal controls surrounding IT systems, they often need tools to better understand and evaluate the completeness and accuracy of the data stored in the IT applications' files and databases. While it is almost always more efficient to use IT techniques to examine all recorded items on the supporting computer files, internal auditors also can act with greater independence by developing their own specialized file retrievals. There are many approaches to retrieving data through the use of what are called computer-assisted audit tools and techniques (CAATTs), the independent auditor-controlled software to assist audit efforts.

A CAATT is a specialized computer program or process, controlled by internal audit, that is used to test or otherwise analyze data on computer files. Terminologies change over time, and an internal auditor will sometimes see the acronym CAAT or CAAP rather than CAATT, where the last letter in the first refers to just "technique," and in the second to "procedure." These acronyms can be used interchangeably. The AICPA uses CAATT, which is also our preferred term in this chapter.

As mentioned in the introduction to this chapter, in the early days of data processing systems, auditors typically just relied on the printed outputs from IT systems and used conventional audit procedures to read, test, and analyze these sometimes massive computer-generated reports. As IT systems became more pervasive with ever-larger data files, auditors needed better approaches to adequately evaluate the documentation and records stored in large IT systems.

The necessity for CAATT procedures first became evident with the now long-forgotten *Equity Funding fraud* in the early 1970s. Equity Funding Corporation, a California-based insurance company, was reporting very significant, almost unbelievable growth and earnings from the late 1960s up through the early 1970s. Their external auditors at that time relied on the printed report outputs generated by the company's computer systems rather than on the data recorded in computer files. Only after their external auditors looked at the contents of those computer files was a major fraud detected.

A member of Equity Funding's external audit team developed some independent software to read and analyze the firm's computer files and found that records had been manipulated to report incorrect financial results. Auditors were not able to easily access computer files at that time, and this examination of IT records with an auditor's own software was considered to be a very innovative approach. The Equity Funding fraud launched what was then called computer auditing—now IT auditing—and the use of CAATTs.

A CAATT is an auditor-controlled computer program that can be run against production IT files to analyze that data and perform audit tests. The Equity Funding analysis happened before today's powerful desktop software tools, and this CAATT application was considered to be an advanced audit technique. End users then typically relied on their data processing departments to write special retrieval programs to give them the various requested output reports. Both internal and external auditors later began to use what was called generalized audit software to develop their own programs independently for testing and analyzing data. This generalized software became the basis for CAATTs to define specialized IT systems and procedures to assist both internal and external auditors.

As an example of a typical CAATT, assume that internal audit is interested in testing the accuracy of the aging from an automated accounts receivable system, given that system data is only stored on IT files, with no significant paper reports describing those calculations. Internal audit may be concerned that the receivables, as reported on the aged trial balance report, may not be properly aged as to the number of days due. Thus the receivables account balances may be over- or understated. This is often a good area for the use of an internal audit–developed CAATT.

A CAATT application can be developed to recalculate independently all of the agings in the accounts receivable system, to verify accounts receivable balances and highlight any unusual exception items. Internal audit might perform this CAATT-oriented approach through the following steps:

1. **Determine CAATT objectives.** Internal audit should not just "use the computer" to test a system without a clear set of starting audit objectives for any CAATT. In this example, internal audit would have an objective of determining whether accounts receivable agings are correctly stated.
2. **Understand the supporting IT systems.** Internal audit should review IT systems documentation to determine how accounts receivable agings are calculated, where this data is stored in the system, and how items are described in system files.
3. **Develop CAATT programs.** Using a selected software retrieval package or IT language processor, internal audit would write their own programs to recalculate accounts receivable agings and to generate totals from accounts receivable files.
4. **Test and process the CAATT.** After testing the programs, the internal auditor would arrange to have the CAATTs processed against production accounts receivable files.
5. **Develop audit conclusions from CAATT results.** Similar to any audit test, audit conclusions would be drawn from the results of the CAATT processing, documented in the workpapers, and discussed in the audit report, as appropriate.

This is the general approach to developing and processing CAATTs. It follows the same steps internal audit would use for establishing audit objectives and performing appropriate tests for reviews on any system or process. As previously discussed, a CAATT is a specialized set of computer programs or procedures that are under the control of internal audit. The CAATT can be developed through generalized audit software programs run on the production computer system, specialized software run on the auditor's own laptop computer, or specialized auditor-use-only program code embedded in an otherwise normal production application. With our major reliance on IT processes in all areas of an enterprise today, CAATTs can enhance internal audit processes in some of the following areas:

- **Increase audit coverage.** CAATTs can allow an internal auditor to review and analyze such components as massive financial databases where internal auditors sometimes do not have easy access to online screen reports and where there are no paper reports.
- **Focus on risk areas.** Similar to the previous point and our example of testing accounts receivable agings, CAATTs often allow an internal auditor to review and investigate areas that have not received a high level of internal audit scrutiny.
- **Increase cost-effectiveness.** Although CAATTs may require some incremental time and cost to develop, they can be very effective for analyzing large volumes of IT-resident data over multiple periods.
- **Improve audit credibility.** CAATTs provide internal auditors with the ability to independently look at complex databases and provide detailed analyses and recommendations; that type of analysis can very much improve internal auditor credibility.
- **Improve integration of IT and financial and operational auditors.** CAATTs often are used to analyze financial and operational processes using IT processes. They will cause all interested parties to better talk and coordinate audit objectives and needs.
- **Encourage auditor independence from IT service support operations.** Internal auditors do not have to be heavily dependent on the IT systems and infrastructure to operate their CAATTs. Although strong coordination is essential, internal auditors can operate in a fairly independent manner.

Internal auditors should have a good understanding of when CAATTs should be used to enhance the audit process, the types of software tools available to an internal auditor, and how to use a CAATT in an audit. Although some CAATTs require an internal auditor to have specialized programming knowledge, most can be implemented by an auditor with only a general understanding of information systems.

11.5 DETERMINING THE NEED FOR CAATTs

CAATTs are powerful tools that can enhance both the audit process and internal auditor independence. However, these procedures can sometimes be time-consuming to develop and will not always be cost-effective unless properly planned and designed. This section discusses areas where CAATTs will enhance an audit and areas to consider when developing and implementing a CAATT.

Before developing a specific CAATT, an internal auditor should first determine if the planned approach is appropriate. All too often, a member of management may have concerns about audit efficiencies and then may ask the internal audit team to "do something" to improve audit efficiency by better using IT resources as part of internal audits. This type of improved audit efficiency directive often may result in disappointment for all parties. Similarly, a highly technical internal auditor may sometimes develop a "technically interesting" CAATT as part of an audit even though it really does not support or contribute to the overall effectiveness of the internal audit's objectives. The decision to develop and implement a CAATT in support of an internal audit will depend on the nature of the data and production programs being reviewed in the audit, the CAATT tools available to internal audit, and the objectives of the audit. Internal audit needs an overall understanding of CAATT procedures in order to make this decision, and should consider the following:

- **The nature or objectives of the audit.** Internal audit should initially evaluate the materials to be reviewed in a planned audit and consider the size and format of any IT-based data. Audits based on values or attributes of computerized data are typically good candidates for CAATTs. For example, the previously mentioned accounts receivable audit is a good CAATT candidate because there is generally a large volume of transactions but minimal paper records. Many of the operational and financial audit areas discussed throughout this book also are good candidates for CAATTs.
- **The nature of the data to be reviewed.** CAATTs are most effective when both data and decision-dependent information about that data are based on automated systems. For example, a manufacturing inventory system will have most of the descriptive information about its inventory on IT system files. Inventory-related data is input directly, and inventory status information is based on system reports on output screens. There are often only limited paper-based original records. Internal audit procedures for inventory here might include an analysis of manufacturing costs, and inventory system attributes can be summarized and analyzed through a CAATT. Only audits over areas where there is heavy dependence on IT files and data are good potential candidates for a CAATT.
- **The available CAATT tools and audit skills.** Internal audit should strive to develop its CAATTs using existing automation tools available within the audit department or the enterprise IT function. Internal audit should consider the types of software tools available for CAATT development before contacting outside vendors. That availability may be based on both audit budget constraints and product limitations.

Auditor skills should also be considered, and the internal audit function must assess whether technical audit specialists are needed and available for planned CAATT development projects. The three considerations listed here are stated in very general terms but are areas to be considered when planning the overall strategy for using CAATTs. Internal audit should recognize that a CAATT may be difficult to implement and is sometimes not very cost-effective. The challenge for internal audit is to identify appropriate areas for CAATTs.

Some years ago, there were special software products available to assist auditors in building and developing CAATTs. IT technology has changed extensively since those products were released, and those special computer audit software products have been replaced by report generators and other tools that are available with many standard software tools. An internal audit group often does not need to try to acquire a specialized audit software product today, but there are many excellent retrieval tools available to help an internal auditor to develop CAATTs. For example, the ACL software product discussed previously in this chapter for continuous auditing also has many capabilities as a CAATT tool. Internal audit–developed CAATTs can be effective in some of the areas discussed later.

- **Examining Records Based on Criteria Specified by Internal Audit.** Because records in a manual system are visible, internal audit can scan for inconsistencies or inaccuracies without difficulty. For records on computer data files, internal audit can specify audit software instructions to scan and print records that are exceptions to the criteria, so that follow-up actions can be taken. Examples of those specified areas are:
  - Accounts receivable balances for amounts over the credit limit
  - Inventory quantities for negative and unreasonably large balances
  - Payroll files for terminated employees
  - Bank demand deposit files for unusually large deposits or withdrawals
- **Testing calculations and making computations.** Internal audit can use software to perform quantitative analyses to evaluate the reasonableness of auditee representations. Such analyses might be for:
  - The extensions of inventory items
  - Recalculation of depreciation amounts
  - The accuracy of sales discounts
  - Interest calculations
  - Employees' net pay computations
- **Comparing data on separate files.** When records on separate files should contain compatible information, software can determine if the information agrees. Comparisons could be:
  - Changes in accounts receivable balances between two dates, comparing the details of sales and cash receipts on transaction files
  - Payroll details with personnel files
  - Current and prior period inventory files to assist in reviewing for obsolete or slow-moving items
- **Selecting and printing audit samples.** Multiple criteria may be used for selection, such as a judgmental sample of high-dollar and old items and a random sample of all other items, which can be printed in the auditor's workpaper format or on special confirmation forms. Examples are:
  - Accounts receivables balances for confirmations
  - Inventory items for observations
  - Fixed-asset additions for vouching
  - Paid voucher records for a review of expenses
  - Vendor records for accounts payable confirmations
- **Summarizing and resequencing data and performing analyses.** Audit software and reformat and aggregate data in a variety of ways to simulate processing or to determine the reasonableness of output results. Examples are:
  - Totaling transactions on an account file
  - Testing accounts receivables aging
  - Preparing general ledger trial balances

  - Summarizing inventory turnover statistics for excess or obsolescence analysis
  - Resequencing inventory items by location to facilitate physical observations
- **Comparing data obtained through other audit procedures with IT system data files.** Audit evidence gathered manually can be converted to a machine-readable form and compared to other data files. Examples are:
  - Inventory test counts with perpetual records
  - Creditor statements with accounts payable files

Although many of these were originally developed for external auditors and date from before the days of integrated database files, these techniques are generally still applicable for internal auditors. The number and sophistication of these CAATTs increases as the individual internal auditor becomes more experienced in their use.

11.6 STEPS TO BUILDING EFFECTIVE CAATTs

Internal auditors should follow the same approach for developing CAATTs whether using a report generator retrieval language or downloaded data to an auditor's laptop computer. This approach is similar to the systems development methodology approach discussed in Chapter 22. The difference here is that an internal auditor may develop a CAATT for a onetime or limited-use effort rather than for an ongoing production application. Because internal audit often draws conclusions and makes rather significant recommendations based on the results of a CAATT, it is important to use good systems development practices to design and test CAATTs. The following is a four-step approach to develop a CAATT:

1. **Determine the objectives of the computer-assisted audit tool.** It is not sufficient for internal audit just to audit the automated accounting system. All too often an internal audit manager will just direct a staff auditor to write a CAATT for some audit without fully defining its objectives. The desired audit objectives should be clearly defined; this will make the subsequent identification of testing procedures a much easier task. Once internal audit has defined a CAATT's objectives, file layouts and systems flowcharts should be obtained to select the appropriate data sources for testing. Sometimes, an internal auditor at this point encounters technical problems that might impede further progress. A CAATT documentation file or workpaper should also be started along with this step.
2. **Design the computer-assisted application.** The CAATT software tool used must be well understood, including its features, the overall program logic, and reporting formats. Any special codes or other data characteristics must be discussed with persons responsible for the IT application. Consideration should also be given to how internal audit will prove the results of audit tests by, for example, balancing to production application control totals. These matters should be outlined in the documentation audit workpapers.
3. **Program or code and then test the application.** This task usually follows step 2 very closely. Programming is performed using the selected software tool. Once

the CAATT has been programmed, internal audit should arrange to test it on a limited population of data. The results must be verified for both correctness of program logic and the achievement of desired audit objectives. This activity should also be documented in the workpapers. Correctness of program logic means the CAATT must *work*. Sometimes an error in coding will cause the application to fail to process. The failure to achieve audit objectives is a different kind of problem. For example, in a CAATT to survey conditions in an inventory file, an auditor may make too broad of a selection, producing an output report of thousands of minor exceptions. Such CAATT logic should be revised to produce a more reasonablely sized selection.

4. **Process and complete the CAATT.** Making arrangements for processing the CAATT often requires coordination between internal audit and IT operations. Internal audit is often interested in a specific generation of a data file, and it is necessary to arrange access to it. During the actual processing, internal audit must take steps to assure that the files tested are the correct versions.

Depending on the nature of the CAATT, an internal auditor should prove the results and follow up on any exceptions as required. If there are problems with the CAATT logic, internal audit should make corrections as required and repeat the steps. The CAATT application workpapers should be completed at this point, including follow-up points for improving the CAATT for future periods.

CAATs are powerful tools that should be available for use by any internal auditor, and should not be solely the responsibility of an IT audit specialist. Just as end users make increasing use of retrieval tools for their own IT needs, all members of an audit department should gain an understanding of available audit tools to allow them to develop their own CAATTs.

Of course, as more and more automated processes become paperless, the auditor's need to build and use CAATTs will increase. That is, the traditional paper trails that auditors use to trace and validate transactions are reduced or even eliminated in today's modern automated system. Audit tools ranging from application report generator software to continuous audit monitors will increasingly become the only options available to test and gather evidence about these paperless systems. Many operational systems have some very strong paperless elements. An internal auditor must be creative when designing a CAATT to gather evidence regarding these paperless applications, and many of the techniques described in this chapter apply.

11.7 IMPORTANCE OF USING CAATTs FOR AUDIT EVIDENCE GATHERING

Internal auditors often do not give sufficient attention to the need to gather evidence when reviewing automated applications. It is too often an interesting and challenging audit task to gain an understanding of an IT application and to evaluate its internal controls, but the detailed confirmations of account balances or other types of evidence-gathering tests are sometimes viewed by internal auditors as not as interesting and too time-consuming. However, these evidence-gathering procedures often provide internal audit with opportunities to implement the most creative portion of the audit project. Assume, for example, that internal audit has performed a detailed internal controls–oriented review of a large fixed-asset capital budgeting application where transactions are initiated from a variety of subsidiary systems and where the application eventually provides general ledger financial statement balances. Internal audit has tested system-to-system internal controls and concludes that these internal controls are adequate; they have also manually recalculated the depreciation expenses for several selected transactions and found them to be correct.

Can an internal auditor conclude that the fixed assets and accumulated depreciation numbers produced by this sample system are accurate? In a large enterprise, where fixed assets may represent a substantial portion of the balance sheet, an internal auditor may decide that there is far too great of a risk in relying solely on just this internal controls review. The several transactions selected for a recalculation compliance test may not be representative of the entire population, and there may be an error in certain classes of these transactions. Although application-to-application controls may have appeared proper, some types of transactions may be assigned to incorrect account groups. Without detailed CAATT-based testing of this example fixed-assets system, it is possible that these errors could go undetected.

Internal auditors should have an understanding of when it is cost-effective and appropriate to develop CAATTs to perform detailed tests of IT applications in order to verify the correctness of transactions or account balances. Some of the circumstances when internal audit should perform this more detailed application evidence gathering and testing include:

- There is a perception that the risk of relying just on internal controls is too high.
- Although internal audit may have performed limited walk-through or compliance types of tests, the results of these tests may be somewhat inconclusive and will suggest a need for more detailed tests.
- In some instances, certain internal controls may be weak or difficult to identify, and internal auditors may want to develop CAATTs to perform detailed tests of the automated applications.
- Some complex or large automated applications are involved, such as the comprehensive ERP systems discussed in Chapter 22.

In many instances, the decision whether to rely on just internal accounting controls and limited compliance testing or to perform detailed tests of transactions will be a decision of audit management. However, the use of CAATTs should be a key internal audit tool to employ in many situations. The nature of the audit tests to be performed, the extent of data, the complexity of the application, and the tools and skills available to internal audit should all be factors in this decision. Internal audit should become familiar with the various software products and techniques available for analyzing and testing computer system files. The implementation and processing of CAATTs should be part of the skill set requirement for all internal auditors.

11.8 XBRL: THE INTERNET-BASED EXTENSIBLE MARKING LANGUAGE

Business today is very much based on Internet-supported applications. Paper-based reports and the batch systems that once supported them have largely disappeared. Virtually all enterprises today are operating in an environment of Internet-supported processes. While a very flexible approach, relying on the Internet can raise concerns about document integrity from management and internal auditors. When reports were being produced in the classic closed-shop data center of past years, whether on paper or through online systems, there usually were few questions about the integrity of the reported data, provided that the supporting internal controls were adequate. As long as there were appropriate general and application controls in place, internal auditors had few questions about general data integrity and only had to perform traditional audit tests to acquire a level of assurance regarding the data. However, the free and open nature of the Internet can raise doubts or questions about the integrity of transmitted data. The question here is, how does the user know that the file of data transmitted through the Web is actually what it is represented to be?

Coding or marking languages solve some of those concerns, and XBRL, an industry standard approach for the publishing, exchange, and analysis of financial and business reports and data, offers an excellent solution. XBRL (eXtensible Business Reporting Language) is an open-standard marking language developed by a consortium of over 200 companies and agencies, and strongly supported by AICPA in the United States. Delivering benefits to investors, accountants, regulators, executives, business and financial analysts, and information providers, XBRL provides a common format for critical business reporting processes, simplifying the flow of financial statements, performance reports, accounting records, and other financial information between software programs. XBRL defines a consistent format for identifying data and for business reporting to streamline the preparation and dissemination of financial data, and to allow analysts, regulators, and investors to review and interpret it. As a result, XBRL can save time and money when information consumers within and outside of a company analyze complex operations and financial data. In the post-Enron era of SOx, XBRL is an important tool for providing consistent business and financial reporting.

XBRL Defined

XBRL is an Internet standard similar to the use of HTML for Internet browsing, MP3 for digital music, or XML, the eXtensible Markup Language standard, for electronic commerce. XBRL uses standard Internet XML data tags to describe financial information for public and private companies and other enterprises. Its controlling group, XBRL International, is a professional affiliation of many hundreds of enterprises as well as governmental jurisdictions that collaboratively produce standard specifications and taxonomies that anyone can license royalty-free for use in their applications. Just as there are established formats for Internet e-mail addresses or Web links, XBRL provides both a standard description and classification system for the contents of accounting reports. Data can be taken from an accounting information system and XRBL coded to produce an electronic annual report including all financial statements, the auditors' report, and 10-K notes. The document can then be read directly by computer programs and end users or, more likely, be coupled with a style sheet to produce a printed annual report, user-friendly Web pages, or an Adobe Acrobat file. Similarly, internal business reports and regulatory filings can be output in a variety of forms.

The Web is filled with many positive comments about XBRL, but the comment "XBRL is . . . perhaps the most revolutionary change in financial reporting since the first general ledger"[5] says a lot. XBRL provides a method for enterprises to report their financial information in a format that can be easily read and understood by others. It allows for efficient data collection and publishing as well as serving as a tool for improved data validation and analysis. Exhibit 11.3 illustrates how XBRL can improve the transfer of data and information across systems and entities. As the exhibit shows, financial data from an enterprise's ERP, general ledger, and other financial systems can be all coded in XRBL. That coded information then can be used, either at the present time or in the future, for reports to banks, annual reports, Securities and Exchange Commission (SEC) *EDGAR*[6] filings, and others. XBRL is a consistent approach for reporting to investors, credit agencies, governmental units, and others.

Implementing XBRL

Though visionaries have praised the concept, and tools and standards have been established, XBRL is still an evolving standard. There have been some but not many early XBRL adopters to date. For example, Microsoft Corporation has been filing its SEC 10-K report in XBRL format since 2002, and General Electric is using it for internal company reporting. Governmental regulators have seen the value of financial reports issued in

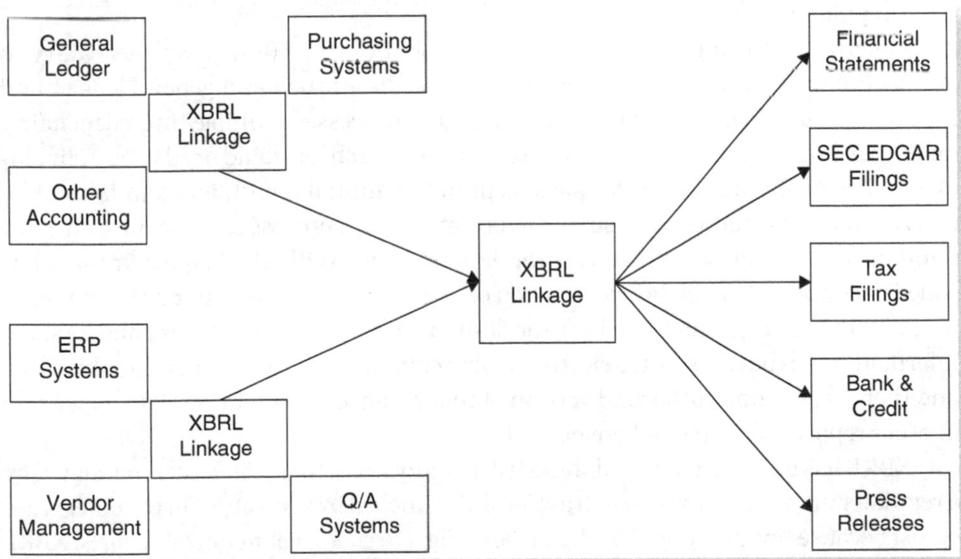

EXHIBIT 11.3 XBRL Interoperability Concepts

a consistent and traceable format, and the U.S. Federal Deposit Insurance Corporation now requires that federal bank status call reports be submitted in XBRL format. The standard can save on costs and provide reporting flexibility by eliminating proprietary accounting system dump formats and doing away with manual copy-and-paste consolidation and reporting. The SEC has converted its EDGAR financial information database to XBRL and requires all larger corporations to file their financial reports in XRBL, covering almost all reported issues and incidents today.

As an Internet markup language for financial data, XBRL is similar to HTML for browsers, where the Internet user clicks on some tagged reference to get pointed to another site. Under XBRL, Internet financial data is tagged in a manner to be recognized and properly interpreted by others using applications based on a standardized XBRL vocabulary of terms, called a taxonomy, to map results into agreed-on categories. An example of this XBRL taxonomy is the markup or coding for well-defined concepts within the current U.S. generally accepted accounting principles (GAAP), including "Accounts Receivable Trade" and "Allowance for Doubtful Accounts." No matter where it is located in the report format, a value can be recognized as the "Allowance for Doubtful Accounts," whether within an enterprise's reports or across multiple enterprises. However, GAAP may vary somewhat depending on whether the enterprise is a retailer, a minerals extraction mining company, or any of many other variations, and XBRL qualifiers set these categories. A major savings with XBRL is the reduction of the data manipulation required when the enterprise needs to reposition the output from their financial systems to meet the needs of diverse users. A quarterly IRS tax form is very different in format and content from the format in a quarterly SEC filing, although the information needed to file both documents typically comes from the same financial database. With XBRL, information will be entered once and the same information can be rendered as a printed financial statement, an HTML document for a web site, an EDGAR SEC file, a raw XML file, or a specialized reporting format such as periodic banking and other regulatory reports.

Paperless reporting is facilitated here as well. Prior to XBRL, it was necessary to extract financial information for reports from databases such as a general ledger, and that extracted information would then need to be processed multiple times depending on the needs of the user. For example, a typical balance sheet would need to be individually processed for SEC filings, for placement in the annual report, for examination by external auditors, and for analysis by management. Each process could require an extra handling of the information to create the desired report. With XBRL, the information is coded once and is then ready for extraction electronically into reports for all information users. With the proper tools in place, the desired output for all uses of the balance sheet information can be transmitted electronically, without the need for paper-based reports, and there is only one authorized version of that balance sheet with its data appearing in other reports or sources where needed.

XBRL has become a required standard in many areas today. Whether mandated by a regulatory reporting agency such as the SEC, launched by visionaries in the enterprise, or just because "everyone else" will soon be using it to code their financial reports, XBRL will soon be used by most enterprises as part of their financial reporting procedures. If there currently has been no action, an internal auditor should have conversations with appropriate persons in IT as well as financial management to determine enterprise plans for XBRL implementations. As a first step, however, the interested internal auditor should gain some knowledge about it. Since it is an XML-based, royalty-free, and open standard language, much information is available through the official web site (www.xbrl.org). That site will point interested persons to a wide variety of papers, presentation sets, and descriptions of XBRL's use.

Because XBRL is still an evolving language, there are some risks of error here. An enterprise needs to select an appropriate taxonomy and appropriately tag their data. Going back to our earlier example, there will be one taxonomy for a manufacturing and distribution enterprise and quite another for a petroleum refinery. While this would be a fairly broad error, starting with the wrong one will cause multiple control problems. Once an appropriate taxonomy is selected, procedures need to be in place to ensure that the tagging of data is complete and accurate. This the same type of control concern that Internet browser users occasionally encounter when one clicks on a link and gets pointed to the wrong or a nonexistent site. It is a frustrating occurrence when surfing through the Web, but a critical error when retrieving or reporting financial data. Internal audit should review procedures to ensure that controls are in place for that XBRL data tagging. Even though these kinds of endeavors often start as a pet project by some member of the IT group, that tagging should be documented in a controlled environment.

XBRL has become a new-rule standard for Web-based financial reporting and supporting systems in the United States, the European Union, and throughout the world. While it is not yet a CBOK requirement, internal auditors should have a familiarity with the technology and its uses. It may lead to many "Are you XBRL compliant?" questions in financial internal control reviews. XRBL is not only the future standard for the publishing, delivery, and use of financial information over the Web, but also a logical business choice.

NOTES

1. The first edition of Robert Moeller's *Computer Audit, Control, and Security* (New York: John Wiley & Sons, 1989) discussed how internal auditors can build ITF and SCARF facilities. This edition is now out of print.
2. Chun-Hsiu Yeh and Wei-Cheng Shen, *Using Continuous Auditing Life Cycle Management to Ensure Continuous Assurance* (Yuanlin, Taiwan: Chung Chou University of Technology, 2002).
3. ACL Services Ltd., 1550 Alberni Street, Vancouver, BC, V6G 1A5, Canada.
4. BusinessObjects Corporation, a division of SAP.
5. *Accounting Today*, September 2000.
6. A long acronym whose meaning does really not matter today, EDGAR is the SEC's forms and filing database; it can be found at www.sec.gov.edgar.

CHAPTER TWELVE

Control Self-Assessments and Internal Audit Benchmarking

MUCH OF THE INTERNAL AUDIT work described in this book discusses areas where an internal auditor will select some other area of operations and review the status of its internal controls. This chapter will look at two other aspects of internal audit reviews and internal control assessments: *control self-assessments (CSAs)* and internal audit benchmarking. These are each valuable and important common body of knowledge (CBOK) internal audit procedures.

CSAs are internal audit–led processes for ongoing internal controls improvements. Rather than internal auditors visiting an area of operations and performing a formal internal audit review, in a CSA an internal audit team works with some of its own internal audit team members in some area of operations and leads them in an effort to evaluate their current internal control procedures and then to use the results of the review to improve internal controls. To many, this is a process that is far less confrontational than a formal internal audit and also can be an effective way to improve and continue to improve internal controls in an enterprise.

In recent years, the Institute of Internal Auditors (IIA) has very much embraced the CSA concept and has even established formal certification examinations to recognize qualified internal auditors as leaders in this process. This chapter will review the internal audit CSA process and describe the use of this sometimes important evaluation tool for internal auditors. A good understanding of CSAs should be an internal auditor CBOK requirement.

Benchmarking is an internal audit technique that goes back to the IIA's "Progress through Sharing" original guidance. Back in the first days of internal auditing and when Victor Brink was launching the first edition of this book, internal auditors from different enterprises frequently met at IIA chapter meetings and elsewhere to share their approaches with peers in other businesses and to develop some internal audit best practices techniques. Benchmarking is a more formal internal audit practice of this same general nature. It is a process that allows internal auditors to compare how similar organizations are attempting to perform and execute similar practices. It can often be a useful internal audit tool, and an internal auditor should have a CBOK general level of knowledge on how to design and perform a successful benchmarking exercise.

12.1 IMPORTANCE OF CONTROL SELF-ASSESSMENTS

One of the Committee of Sponsoring Organizations (COSO) internal control framework's recommendations, mentioned briefly in Chapter 3, is that enterprises "should report on the effectiveness and efficiency of [their] system of internal control." That internal control reporting can either be at a total enterprise level or can be limited to individual enterprises departments or functions. Chapter 5 discussed internal accounting controls review from a Sarbanes-Oxley (SOx) perspective, and other chapters have covered various other aspects of internal controls reviews. Several years ago and even before SOx, the IIA introduced its CSA methodology, as a process for an internal audit function to look at its own controls or for helping others to review their internal controls. Based on the total quality management approaches of the early 1990s and highlighted in Chapter 31 as well as the COSO internal control framework discussed in Chapter 3, the CSA methodology has become a powerful tool for internal auditors and others to better understand an enterprise's internal control environment. The approach requires internal auditors to formally assemble a special team to assess those internal controls.

CSA was first developed by a team of internal auditors at Gulf Canada Resources Ltd. in 1987 as a tool to assess its internal control effectiveness as well as business processes. At that time, Gulf Canada was facing both a legal consent decree requiring the company to report on its internal controls as well as some difficulties resolving oil and gas measurement issues through traditional audit assessments. Gulf Canada's internal audit group launched a *facilitated meeting* self-assessment approach that involved gathering management and staff for interviews relating to and discussions of specific internal control issues or processes. The process became CSA, a mechanism to assess informal, or soft, controls as well as the more traditional hard controls such as accounting balances.

That CSA approach was published and has been adopted by a number of major corporations as well as becoming part of the IIA *International Standards for the Professional Practice of Internal Auditing* (see Chapter 9). This chapter describes the CSA process in more detail and discusses the potential value to an enterprise in using CSA, how internal audit can launch CSA, and how to evaluate the data and results from a CSA project. CSA can be an important and useful tool for many internal audit enterprises.

12.2 CSA MODEL

CSA is a process designed to help departments within an enterprise to assess and then evaluate their internal controls. In many respects, the CSA approach uses some of the same concepts found in the COSO internal control framework as discussed in Chapter 3. The CSA model says that an enterprise must implement strong control objectives and control activities in order to have an effective control environment. These two elements

EXHIBIT 12.1 The CSA Process

are surrounded by a good system of information and communication as well as processes for risk assessment and to monitor performance. This CSA model is shown in Exhibit 12.1.

CSA is a continuous improvement process similar to methods described and used by quality assurance, as discussed in Chapter 31. The concept calls for a team to establish and improve their control environment by establishing goals and objectives regarding those controls, then performing a risk assessment to better understand those designated control risks, to implement control activities to reduce identified risks, and then to monitor the performance of those improved controls. This is a continuous process where the CSA team can start in any quadrant of the Exhibit 12.1 CSA model and then move to the next phase in a clockwise manner.

The CSA is a control assessment process that for some has been viewed as more approachable than the COSO internal control framework or Chapter 6's COBIT model. While some business professionals, for example, look at a COSO internal control risk assessment process as too high-level and difficult to understand, CSA is an approach where individual departments in an enterprise can formally meet, in a facilitated group format, and assess the risks and internal controls within their individual departments or functions. Internal audit departments have used CSA as a method for internal auditors to better think about how to improve their internal controls.

12.3 LAUNCHING THE CSA PROCESS

The CSA process assesses and examines the effectiveness of internal control processes not by a team of outsiders such as consultants, or even internal auditors, but by people from within the function being assessed. Internal audit often takes a leadership role here. The CSA objective is to provide reasonable assurance that good internal control business objectives will be met. The CSA concept requires the gathering management and staff for interviews to assess their internal control environment—a control self-assessment. Because CSA requires all people in a function to participate in these sessions, from senior managers to staff, it often works best when someone outside of the department acts as a facilitator. While many people can take this CSA facilitator role, internal audit is often a key group, ideal for this role because of its internal control review background. A separate quality audit function, as discussed in Chapter 31, can often be a major help here as many of its approaches are similar to the CSA model approach.

The CSA process works particularly well when an enterprise has some business unit whose internal controls do not match exactly with the rest of operations. For example, assume that an enterprise manufactures some type of plant production equipment used by other manufacturing businesses. Also assume that there are good production and product internal controls for the main business, but because these are high-value components, customers may return these finished goods to a rework facility from time to time to upgrade them to a new version. The rework facility cleans up and upgrades the products for sale as used equipment to other markets. This type of rework facility would be an ideal candidate for a CSA review. It would probably have different but similar processes when compared to the prime manufacturing business. Because its work is specialized when compared to mainstream production business, the rework facility team members would understand both regular production and rework operations. We will reference this type of rework facility in our CSA descriptions here.

Regardless of who acts as a leader or facilitator, a CSA project should improve an enterprise's control environment by making involved stakeholders more aware of their specific departmental objectives and the role of internal controls in achieving goals and objectives. A basic concept behind the CSA process is to motivate members of an enterprise unit to design and implement their own internal control processes and then to continually improve them. Our example of a specialized rework facility would be a good fit for this type of CSA review process. A CSA review can be particularly effective, for example, when the internal control process reviewed is a large enterprise resource planning (ERP) system that covers all or most aspects of operations. Our example rework facility uses ERP IT components only partially. In an ERP, one basic automated system covers accounting, human resources, production, marketing, and more. The ERP covers many aspects across an enterprise, but the members of our example rework facility may not fully understand all of the internal control implications of such a large all-encompassing system and the results of their various individual actions.

As a good first step to launch CSA processes for an enterprise, the chief audit executive (CAE) or some other person leading the initiative will need to sell the CSA concept to senior management. In a smaller enterprise, the message may be that CSA should help the enterprise to improve internal control procedures and SOx Section 404 compliance while not embarking on a time-consuming, expensive exercise. Other potential benefits from such a CSA process are:

- Increasing the scope of internal control reporting during a given period
- Targeting internal control–related work by placing a greater focus on high-risk and unusual items discovered in the course of these CSA reviews

- Increasing the effectiveness of internal audit–recommended corrective actions by transferring internal control ownership and responsibility to operating employees

While published CSA results indicate that it is an effective technique for improving the internal control environment, perhaps the worst way for an enterprise to use CSA is for the internal audit management to attend an IIA-sponsored CSA seminar, to come back all enthused, and then to work with operations management to launch a big-picture, wide-ranging comprehensive CSA program in the enterprise without understanding the necessary detailed steps to make it successful. This is almost certainly a mistake. An enterprise should start small and initially designate some single business unit or entity where there is a general feeling that control improvements are needed. Internal audit should explain the process to management and obtain approvals to launch CSA, at least as a pilot program. Going beyond a traditional audit review, internal audit will normally run a CSA program with one person designated as the team lead.

The CSA team leader then needs to refine its review area even closer and decide what portion of the entity will use CSA, what functions or objectives to consider, and what level of stakeholders should be included in the assessments. The number and level of stakeholders will depend on the CSA approach selected. Three principal CSA approaches are *facilitated team meeting workshops, questionnaires,* and *management-produced analysis.* Internal audit–led CSA teams often combine a mixture of more than one approach to accommodate their self-assessments.

Facilitated team meetings gather internal control information from work teams that may represent multiple levels within an enterprise. A facilitator trained in internal control system design, often from internal audit, IT, or quality assurance, should lead these sessions. The questionnaire-based approach uses surveys that are usually based on simple yes/no or have/have not responses. Process owners use the survey results to assess their control structure. The third approach, a management-produced analysis, is really an internal audit type of analysis. Based on a management- or staff-produced study of the business process, a CSA specialist—probably an internal auditor—combines the results of the study with information gathered from sources such as interviews with other managers and key personnel. By synthesizing this material, the CSA specialist develops an analysis that process owners can use in better understanding and improving internal controls for the given process area.

The CSA approach and format used here will depend on the overall enterprise culture as well as senior management decisions. In the event a corporate culture does not support a participative CSA approach, questionnaire responses and internal control analysis can enhance the control environment. Ideally, the *facilitated session* works the best where all employees meet on a peer basis and discuss and evaluate their internal control issues and concerns in open facilitator-led discussions.

Just as there was some discussion (see Chapter 5) on the role of internal audit in SOx Section 404 reviews, the same issues may be raised for CSA processes. There must be a decision as to whether internal audit or operating management will drive the CSA process. Some CSA practitioners believe that internal audit, as the arm of senior management responsible for internal control oversight, may be the appropriate driver for CSA. The presence of internal auditors in CSA-facilitated meetings is in and of itself an oversight control. Others believe that a self-assessment can only be effectively performed by operating management and/or work units. The involvement of internal audit, in this view, means that management will be less accountable for internal controls. Internal auditors, in their roles as enterprise internal consultants, are very qualified to lead such efforts.

Performing the Facilitated CSA Review

The basic concept behind a CSA review of an internal control system or process is to organize a group of people, across multiple levels of the enterprise and from multiple units, and then to collectively gather extensive information about the internal controls for that selected system or process. The idea is to select a representative sample of stakeholders throughout the enterprise to meet and discuss the selected system's operations and controls. Our prior example of a rework facility in a manufacturing operation would be a good fit here. An internal auditor or some other communications specialist should then be designated to head these workshops, lead discussions, and help draw conclusions.

Facilitated team workshops gather information from work teams representing different levels in the business unit or function. The format of the workshop may be based on objectives, risks, controls, or processes. Each has distinct advantages depending on the internal control area reviewed. Assume as an example that an enterprise has installed a large, comprehensive ERP system that encompasses many major operational areas. Management has requested an internal control risk assessment of this major application. Because the ERP system covers many aspects of business operations, a decision is made to review systems controls through a series of focus-group users gathered to discuss and review systems operations. Planning steps for organizing these CSA reviews should be developed into a CSA enterprise plan. Based on the extensive set of CSA materials published by the IIA,[1] a facilitated CSA session can follow any of four meeting formats:

1. **Objective-based CSA-facilitated sessions.** These sessions focus on the best way to accomplish a business objective, such as accurate financial reporting. The workshop begins with the team identifying the controls presently in place to support the system objectives and then determining any residual risks remaining if controls are not working. The aim of this workshop format is to decide whether the control procedures are working effectively and that any remaining risks are within an acceptable level. This type of session could begin by the facilitator asking participants to identify their group's control environment, emphasizing such areas in the control environment as:
   a. The control consciousness of the enterprise
   b. The extent to which employees are committed to doing what is right or doing it the right way
   c. A wide variety of factors that encompass technical competence and ethical commitment
   d. Intangible factors that are often essential to effective internal control
2. **Risk-based CSA-facilitated sessions.** These sessions focus on the CSA teams listing risks to achieve internal control objectives. The workshop begins by listing

all possible barriers, obstacles, threats, and exposures that might prevent achieving an objective and then examining control procedures to determine if they are sufficient to manage any identified key risks. The aim of the workshop is to determine significant residual risks. This format takes the work team through the entire set of objectives, risks, and controls surrounding the entity reviewed. This would follow with risk-based discussions in which teams are asked to identify their risks through such questions as:

   a. What could go wrong?
   b. What assets do we need to protect?
   c. How could someone steal from us?
   d. What is our greatest legal exposure?

   Sessions would attempt to identify significant risks at department, activity, or process levels. For each identified risk, the groups should discuss the potential likelihood of occurrence and the potential impact. Those risks with a reasonable likelihood of occurrence and a large potential impact would be identified as significant.

3. **Control-based CSA-facilitated sessions.** These sessions focus on how well the controls in place are working. This format is different from the two sessions prior because the facilitator identifies the key risks and controls before the beginning of the workshop. During the CSA session, the work team assesses how well the controls mitigate risks and promote the achievement of objectives. The aim of the workshop is to produce an analysis of the gap between how controls are working and how well management expects those controls to work.
4. **Process-based CSA-facilitated sessions.** These sessions focus on selected activities that are elements of a chain of processes. Processes are a series of related activities that go from some beginning point to an end, such as the various steps in purchasing, product development, or revenue generation. This type of workshop usually covers the identification of the objectives of the whole process and the various intermediate steps. The aim of the workshop is to evaluate, update, validate, improve, and even streamline the whole process and its component activities. This session format may have a greater breadth of analysis than a control-based approach by covering multiple objectives within the process and by supporting concurrent management efforts, such as reengineering, quality improvement, and continuous improvement initiatives.

Each of these formats can be effective for developing and understanding both the hard and soft controls[2] in a function as well as the risks surrounding any significant internal control processes. The keys to success here are to have knowledgeable and well-prepared meeting facilitators ask appropriate questions and get all of the selected team members to participate. The other major key is to take detailed transcriptions of the meeting sessions. While not every word spoken has to be recorded, strong meeting highlights are needed. Recording major discussion points on a large pad in the front of the room often works well.

While the facilitator is a major driver here, CSA sessions can easily turn into disasters with the wrong mix of people. Lower-level stakeholders may feel reluctant to discuss control weaknesses if people who are more senior are in the session. Comments about risks or control weaknesses can get very personal if some of the team members have major responsibilities for the systems or process discussed. Despite all of this, the CSA process can be a very worthwhile, if expensive, tool to look at a comprehensive system or process from multiple perspectives and to understand any internal control weaknesses.

Performing the Questionnaire-Based CSA Review

A CSA-facilitated review can be difficult and time-consuming, no matter whether it is relative risk–, internal control–, or process-based. In many cases, a questionnaire format can be an effective way to gather internal controls information. A questionnaire is prepared covering the process or system of interest and then distributed to a selected group of stakeholders to gain an understanding of the risks and controls in the area of interest. Exhibit 12.2 is an example CSA questionnaire for planning and budgeting processes. It was developed from IIA materials. The IIA also has an extensive set of other sample CSA questionnaires on its web site: www.theiia.org.

EXHIBIT 12.2 CSA Specific Function Questionnaire: Planning and Budgeting

These questions can be used for a CSA review of planning and budgeting processes:

1. Do you ensure that completed budgets are consistent with the strategic plan of the company?
2. Are policies and procedures in place to avoid understatement of expenditures?
3. Do you investigate all variances between actual expenditures and budgeted amounts, and, for all variances, are explanations required?
4. Do you ensure that the finalized budget and all approved revisions are properly documented and approved?
5. Have you assigned a person to receive all information regarding changes to the company that may affect the budget?
6. Is the budget preparation procedure (including approval level requirements) fully documented, and is it distributed to all management involved in the budget process?
7. Are procedures in place to provide adequate information to departmental management for their use in developing a budget?
8. Do you monitor both short and longer term trends in expenses?
9. Are the calculation methods for expenses (including new categories) adequately explained?
10. Do you ensure that departments are given adequate time to complete and submit their budgets?
11. Have you identified one individual within each department that has the responsibility for completing the budget, and is assistance provided as needed?
12. Do you advise departments on what and how expenses are to be charged for acquisitions or disposed operations?
13. Are procedures in place to ensure that a limited number of authorized indiviuals have access to the budgets and that any additions, changes, and deletions are approved and traceable? If the budget is online, are all transactions identified by user ID, date, and transaction type?
14. Do you review the initial budgets and identify areas of possible cost reductions?
15. Are procedures in place to identify departments that consistently incur large expenditures at year end to bring actual costs up to budget?
16. Are procedures in place to handle cash forecasts?
17. Do you monitor and require approvals for all capital expenditures?
18. Have you identified all of the documentation required of departments when submitting numbers for budgets, return on investment calculations, etc.?
19. Do you monitor project breakdowns to ensure that large projects are not broken down into smaller projects to avoid approval requirements?

The CSA team would circulate these questionnaires, with the respondent's name attached, to a selected group of stakeholders, monitor results to assure that an appropriate number have been returned, and then compile the results. Questionnaires will not yield the discovery-type comments that would come out of focus groups, but will give an overall assessment of the soundness of processes and internal controls. This is an effective way to gather basic CSA background data.

Performing the Management-Produced Analysis CSA Review

As an alternative to a survey or a facilitated workshop, a management-produced analysis is very similar to the type of operational review that an internal auditor would perform. This is one of the three CSA analysis approaches suggested by the IIA, where management produces a staff study of the business process—almost a research study. The CSA specialist, who may be an internal auditor, combines the results of the study with information gathered from sources, such as other managers and key personnel. By synthesizing this material, the CSA specialist develops an analysis that process owners can use in their CSA efforts.

The management-produced analysis approach, although endorsed by the IIA as one of three suggested CSA approaches, is difficult to perform for the typical enterprise. It suggests an almost "academic" review by someone in the enterprise, followed by some comparative research for subsequent analysis. We generally do not suggest this IIA-endorsed alternative approach.

The IIA believes all the formats discussed here strengthen the entity's control structure. Each entity should perform an analysis of external opportunities or threats as well as internal strengths and weaknesses to determine which format is most appropriate in the enterprise. Many CSA users combine one or more formats within a given facilitated meeting to best meet their needs.

12.4 EVALUATING CSA RESULTS

A CSA analysis, particularly if it covers multiple processes or systems, will result in a large amount of data. Some may support existing process strengths, others will point to internal control weaknesses in need of correction, and still others may point to areas in need of further research. In many cases, the work will validate the integrity and controls of the systems and processes reviewed.

The results of a CSA review will be similar to a COSO review of internal accounting controls—a disciplined and thorough method to evaluate significant internal controls. This can also be a good first step to launch a SOx Section 404 analysis, as was described in Chapter 5. CSA provides a manner for reviewers to gain a better understanding of the many soft controls that surround many processes or systems. Published documentation or focused control review interviews may indicate that some controls exist. However, the back-and-forth from a facilitated session may reveal that "yes, there are control processes described in our systems documentation, but we always push the escape key to ignore the control warning messages." This can be an effective way to expose internal control vulnerabilities.

CSAs were introduced to the internal audit community in the late 1980s and subsequently were embraced by the IIA. Many private-sector enterprises worldwide have initiated successful CSA programs, and several state governments within the United States began requiring CSA-oriented internal control assessments. The auditing and accounting departments within those states complied with the regulations via questionnaires or management-produced analysis processes. The Federal Deposit Insurance Corporation and the Canadian Deposit Insurance Corporation, for example, now require financial institutions throughout the United States and Canada, respectively, to assess internal controls with specific CSA guidance compliance. Also, ISACA has launched a not dissimilar Risk and Control Self-Assessment that is similar to CSA and has been developed and supported by Stanford University.

To support the CSA process, the IIA has launched a specialty certification, the Certification in Control Self-Assessment (CCSA). This examination-based certificate is designed to enhance senior management's confidence of a reviewer's understanding, knowledge, and training in the CSA process. The CCSA certificate and its requirements, as well as other internal auditing professional certifications, are discussed in Chapter 29.

The IIA believes that CSA processes effectively augment the profession of internal auditing. One of the primary responsibilities of the board and officers of any enterprise is providing stakeholder assurance through oversight of the enterprise's activities. Internal auditing, by definition, assists members of the enterprise in the effective discharge of their responsibilities. Through CSA, internal auditing and operating staff can collaborate to produce an assessment of internal controls in an operation. This synergy helps internal auditing assist in management's oversight function by improving the quantity and quality of available information. The quantity is increased as internal auditing relies on operating employees to actively participate in CSA reviews, thus reducing time spent in information gathering and validation procedures performed during an internal audit. The quality is increased since participating employees have a more thorough understanding of the process than an auditor can develop over a relatively short period of time. As we discussed in our introduction to this chapter, a basic knowledge of how to organize and conduct a CSA process should be part of an internal auditor's CBOK.

12.5 BENCHMARKING AND INTERNAL AUDIT

Benchmarking is one of those professional concepts that is frequently misused. That is, it is often easy for a professional to say, "We benchmarked that process," when an internal auditor asks some process-related questions. However, if that same internal auditor asks to see the results of the benchmarking study, the response may become vague, and no formal documentation may be available to support the analysis.

Benchmarking is a "best practice where an enterprise evaluates various aspects of its own processes in relation to associated practices, usually within their other peer enterprises. After such an analysis and comparison, an enterprise can develop plans on how to adopt these other best practices, usually with the aim of increasing some aspect of performance. Benchmarking may sometimes be a one-time event, but it is often treated as a continuous process in which an enterprise continually seeks to challenge and improve its practices. In simplistic terms, it is a process where an organization compares its processes with other, hopefully better processes to try to improve process standards and to improve the overall quality of a system, product, or process.

Benchmarking can be a powerful management tool because it overcomes what some consultants call "paradigm blindness." This is the mode of thinking along the lines of "the way we do it is the best because this is the way we've always done it." Benchmarking can open an enterprise to new methods, ideas, and tools to improve its effectiveness. It helps crack through resistance to change by demonstrating other methods of solving problems than the one currently employed and demonstrating that they work, because they are being used by others.

Benchmarking approaches are important to internal auditors from two perspectives. First, the use of benchmarking can be a very powerful internal audit recommendation when reviewing operations in some area. An internal auditor often observes obvious internal control weaknesses in some area, but may not have the depth in an area to make comprehensive internal control improvement recommendations. A strong recommendation, however, would be for internal audit to recommend that some operating unit use benchmarking studies to achieve best practices in some area. We will discuss how to launch and implement benchmarking in the section following.

Internal auditors also need benchmarking to improve their own internal audit practices. The IIA has promoted the concept of "Progress through Sharing" to improve the practice of internal auditing since its founding in the late 1940s. Many ideas were then shared through both presentations and informal discussions at IIA chapter meetings, but the IIA is worldwide today, with many seeking this data and information to share, and Internet tools available to promote that sharing. The IIA has launched what it calls the *Global Audit Information Network (GAIN)*, a benchmarking tool to share best ideas and promote internal audit best practices. We will briefly review GAIN concepts and how it is designed to promote internal audit best practices.

Implementing Benchmarking to Improve Processes

There are no accepted standard professional procedures for launching an internal audit benchmarking process. Because of this, many variations exist of what professionals call benchmarking. With many loose definitions in place, we tend to forget that benchmarking is a process that allows an enterprise unit to compare how it is performing related to its peers in some area of operations. To better describe how benchmarking works, we will describe an effort that this author led for a large Chicago-area corporation in the mid-1990s.

For background, this author had a lead role in launching a business compliance and ethics function for this corporation. This was a new initiative for the corporation, and to his knowledge, at that time there were not many other major corporations that had similar compliance and ethics functions. This new process was essentially a service-type function with almost no fear of giving out trade secrets. An enterprise manufacturing a patented consumer shampoo product, for example, cannot try to visit a series of its competitors to see how they are manufacturing a similar product. There are too many confidentiality issues. However, many other enterprises are freely—and sometimes proudly—willing to share how well they are performing in some area. The steps following describe how this author launched a successful benchmarking study for a unit of his employer some years ago. We will describe the necessary steps to launch benchmarking from the perspective of this author's project. The author's actions are described using the word *we*, but these points should apply to all internal auditors acting as internal consultants and the team launching a benchmarking study.

1. **Define the objectives of the benchmarking study.** It sounds almost obvious, but the first step is to define what an internal auditor wants to learn from the benchmarking exercise. In this example, we wanted to launch an ethics function "help a service desk/hotline" function where employees could anonymously call in any observed code of conduct violations and also ask ethics and code of conduct questions. We were aware that some other corporations were doing this and wanted to develop an improved or best practices process.
2. **Establish a set of potential partners who may be willing to participate.** In this case, we were aware through professional meetings and publications of other companies that were doing something similar. This is an important benchmarking planning step. Too many partners can be difficult to manage, but too few may not give much representative information. Names and contacts can be gathered through professional meetings and conferences.
3. **Develop specific goals and objectives for the benchmark study—what do we want to learn?** This step defines what we want to learn from our study. Since time and logistics will typically prevent direct visits, much of our information will come from responses to questionnaires, with follow-ups by telephone later. Benchmarking surveys are usually designed to allow another enterprise to brag about some best practice; they are not exercises where outsiders typically talk about their problems or what didn't work.
4. **Clear up legal and confidentiality issues.** In a benchmarking study, we will be asking other enterprises to give us some potentially confidential company information, and by asking these questions we are admitting that we may have deficits in the area we are reviewing. The process should be reviewed with enterprise legal resources to avoid any pitfalls. This is an area where we will need to have some strong declarations out front. For example, we should strongly state that any data gathered will be kept strictly confidential.
5. **Contact potential benchmarking partners.** After all of the preliminary work, we should contact potential participants for the study. This often works best when professional personal contacts have been established. We should outline our proposed benchmarking project with the following objectives:
   a. The purpose of our benchmarking study—what are we trying to learn?
   b. Why have we selected this potential participant?
   c. What specific information are we seeking, how will we gather it (e.g., questionnaire), and how much time will it take?
   d. Strong statements on confidentiality—we will not reveal or compromise any company information.

e. An offer to give something as a result of participation. This is usually the promise to share the total results of the study with all participants.
f. A request for an acknowledgment that they will be willing to participate.

6. **Gather benchmarking information.** This is the step where we gather our benchmarking data from each participant. While it usually requires sending out fairly detailed interview questionnaires, telephone calls or even site visits are possibilities. The idea is to find out as much as we can about what our participants are doing in our area of interest.
7. **Gather and scrub results.** After we have completed our benchmarking surveys—care should be taken to not drag things out over too long a period—the survey information should be assembled and reviewed to answer our questions. Any potentially confidential information regarding other company names and identities should be scrubbed or removed.
8. **Publish benchmarking results and make changes, as appropriate**. The whole purpose of any benchmarking study is to see what others are doing as best practices in an area of interest. In the author's study cited from several years ago, we found we were doing a superior job in the area of interest, but there were still only a few enhancing recommendations from the study.

We have described a benchmarking study in very general terms. Benchmarking is often a very good way to gather best practices information from other enterprises. Professionals from other enterprises are often very willing to brag about how well they are doing some business practice.

Internal auditors can often launch benchmarking studies as a way to see how other internal audit functions are handling some practice or approach. Benchmarking here is a little beyond casual conversations about internal audit practices with other internal audit peers as part of an IIA chapter meeting. Here, an internal audit function may elect to launch a benchmarking study about some best practice with other internal audit chapters, even on a worldwide basis. Internal audit's sharing processes will encourage this and a formal benchmarking study will add some support to the results of any such study.

An internal auditor acting as an enterprise consultant, as discussed in Chapter 30, is an excellent vehicle for internal audit to help in implementing benchmarking. Internal auditors often make recommendations that some business unit improve its processes through benchmarking. As discussed, benchmarking is all too often a term that is used in business almost flippantly. Internal auditors with an understanding of the benchmarking process can engage in a separate internal consulting project to help their auditees establish effective benchmarking procedures.

Benchmarking and the IIA's GAIN Initiative

As discussed, the IIA was an early proponent of benchmarking approaches through its "Progress through Sharing" motto. While that was an appropriate approach, the IIA decided to better formalize things through its previously referenced GAIN benchmarking forum. First established by the IIA in 1992, GAIN did not receive a large amount of attention and has been better formalized in recent years. The IIA's GAIN is a knowledge exchange forum to:

- Share, compare, and validate internal audit practices
- Network with other internal audit functions
- Learn from the challenges and solutions of internal audit peers
- Gain leading internal audit practices from top organizations
- Enhance internal audit operational effectiveness and efficiency

As a separate IIA initiative, the GAIN conference publishes extensive and comprehensive benchmarking studies regarding internal audit activities on a global scale. The IIA GAIN initiative asks its member internal audit functions to register and to complete a fairly detailed questionnaire about their internal audit function. Exhibit 12.3 is an extract from this GAIN questionnaire. The IIA's GAIN function attempts to gather some fairly extensive information about each cooperating internal audit function.

EXHIBIT 12.3 IIA GAIN Annual Benchmarking Questionnaire Example

The following list the types of information that the IIA is requesting its GAIN participants to submit about their internal audit function. This information is then shared with other submissions to form annual internal audit benchmarking studies. The following topics may not be fully complete but have been pulled from the IIA's GAIN web site to show the types of benchmarking information that the IIA is attempting to collect.

Section A: Enterprise Information

- Revenues, assets, and expenses as of and for the most recent fiscal year end from the enterprise's financial statements.
- Total full-time personnel equivalents for the enterprise.

Section B: Internal Audit Resources

- Total costs of internal audit activities categorized as follows:
  - Salary (gross pay and bonuses)
  - Employee Benefits (if not tracked separately, averages 30% of salaries)
  - Travel and Training
  - Costs of sourced services (e.g., consultants, cosource providers, etc.)
- Total internal audit staff differentiating between in-house staff versus sourced staff using the following categories:
  - Chief Audit Executive
  - Directors and Managers
  - Seniors and Supervisors
  - Staff
  - Secretarial and Clerical

For each staff level outlined above (excluding clerical), provide information regarding the levels of education sought, average years in internal audit profession, average years in enterprise's primary industry, and the number of staff at each level with one or more professional designations (certifications).

. . .

Section D: Risk Assessment and Audit Planning

- Number of auditable activities or units in audit universe (all possible audits planned and actual audits for year).
- Components of audit plan categorized by assurance engagements, consulting engagements, management requests, fraud investigations, and follow-up audits.
- Percentage of management requests that were actually accomplished.
- Information on type and creation of audit plans.
- Information on type and creation of enterprise/internal audit risk assessments.
- Number of risk categories used and percentage coverage of those categories by the audit plan, if applicable.
- Information on type and creation of engagement-level audit plans.

Section E: Audit Implementation/Life Cycles/Reporting

- Total audit staff time categorized as follows:
  - Assurance engagements
  - Consulting engagements
  - Fraud investigations
  - Management requests
  - Follow-up audits
  - External audit assistance
  - Nonchargeable time—training and other
  - Absences
- Percentage of audit time spent on planning, fieldwork, and reporting.
- Calendar days (business days) to complete: planning, fieldwork, reporting, and follow-up.
- Calendar days that lapse between the end of fieldwork and the issuance of draft reports and the end of fieldwork and the issuance of final reports.
- Number of audit recommendations, major audit findings, and repeat findings identified during the year.
- Percentage of recommendations actually implemented.

Upon completion of an internal audit function's questionnaire, this response data is validated and added to the GAIN Annual Benchmarking Study database. From an internal function's answers and those of other similar internal audit groups, a variety of unique internal audit benchmarking reports are available through GAIN that reflect internal audit activities in contrast with its peers. While a wide variety of customized reports are available specific to industry groupings and other attributes, GAIN publishes an annual internal audit benchmarking report that really gives an internal audit function an understanding of how they are doing in contrast to their peer internal functions. These annual reports are available for purchase through the IIA. Exhibit 12.4 is a sample GAIN annual benchmarking survey table of contents. There is lots of good valuable internal audit benchmarking data here, and a CAE should use this data to better understand how his or her internal audit function is doing in contrast to others. One area that is rather surprising, however, is the lack of benchmarking data being gathered surrounding IT audit issues and practices. GAIN does not appear to be giving enough benchmarking attention to that very important area.

The IIA's GAIN function also does a wide variety of what the IIA calls Flash Surveys. For example, they will poll participating internal audit groups and ask, for

EXHIBIT 12.4 GAIN Annual Benchmarking Survey Table of Contents

The following table of contents lists the types of benchmarking data that can be included in an IIA GAIN benchmarking survey. GAIN gathers this type of contributed data from a range of worldwide internal audit functions.

Section 1: Demographic Information

- Demographic Information: Financial
- Respondents by Expense Class
- Demographic Information: Employees
- Respondents by Industry
- Organizational Demographics
- Sarbanes-Oxley Status

Section 2: Summary Information

- Revenues and Assets per Auditor
- Expenses and Employees per Auditor

Section 3: Internal Audit Costs

- Summary of Audit Costs
- Salary and Benefits as a Percentage of Total Audit Costs
- Travel and Training as a Percentage of Total Audit Costs
- Total Costs per Auditor (with and without Travel)
- Travel and Training Costs per Auditor

Section 4: Internal Audit Staffing

- Internal Audit Staff Profile
- Change in Internal Audit Staff Size
- Summary of Professional Audit Staff by Function
- General and IT Auditors as a Percentage of Total Auditors
- Fraud and ESH Auditors as a Percentage of Total Auditors
- Level of Education Sought for Auditors
- Internal Audit Experience of Auditors
- Industry Experience of Auditors
- Number of Staff with Professional Designations
- Percentage Staff with Professional Designations
- Professional Designation Mix
- Level of CIA Designation Required
- Internal Audit Hiring Practices
- Staff Turnover

Section 5: Sourcing

- Sourced Staff Profile
- Costs of Purchased Services
- Level of Sourcing
- Audit Activities Sourced
- Sourced Hours and Fees
- Fees for Purchased Services
- Future Reliance on Sourcing

Section 6: External Audit

- External Audit
- Internal Audit Assistance on External Audit
- External Audit Fees as Percentage of Total Revenues, Assets, and Expenses

Section 7: Internal Audit Oversight

IA Oversight and Areas of Focus

Section 7.1: Internal Audit Oversight—Chief Audit Executive

CAE Reporting Line
Title of Chief Audit Executive
Responsibilities of Chief Audit Executive

Section 7.2: Internal Audit Oversight—Audit Committee

Audit Committee
Audit Committee Chair
Audit Committee Meetings
Presence of Audit Committee Charter
Responsibilities of Audit Committee
Information Shared with Audit Committee
Professional Development of Audit Committee Provided by Internal Audit
Evaluations of Audit Committee and Charter

Section 8: Risk Assessment and Audit Planning

Section 8.1: Audit Universe

Audit Universe
Audit Performance
Percent of Audits Planned Actually Performed
Percent of Audit Universe Audited
Audits per Auditor
How Audit Universe Is Determined

Section 8.2: Audit Plan

Allocation of Audit Plan
Percent of Management Requests Completed
Type of Audit Plan
Years Covered by Audit Plan
How Audit Plan Is Created

Section 8.3: Risk Assessments

Presence of Formal Risk Assessment Process for Internal Audit
Frequency of Internal Audit Risk Assessment
Factors Influencing Risk Assessment
Risk Assessment Rating Criteria
Risk Categories
Percentage of Risk Categories Covered by Audit Plan
Presence of Engagement Level Risk Assessments
Engagement Level Risk Assessments—Information Gathering

Section 9: Audit Implementation/Life Cycles/Reporting

Allocation of Audit Staff Time
Audit Life Cycle
Audit Life Cycle—Reporting
Tools and Techniques Utilized on Audits.
Audit Engagement Reporting

Section 9.1: Observations and Follow-Up Audits

Expressing an Opinion on Internal Control
Audit Follow-Up Activities
Presence of Audit Recommendations
Audit Recommendations

(continued)

EXHIBIT 12.4 *(continued)*

Major Audit Findings Identified
Major Audit Findings—Metrics
Repeat Findings
Percent of Recommendations Actually Implemented

Section 9.2: Continuous Auditing

Continuous Auditing
Responsibility of Continuous Auditing
Continuous Auditing Operations
Benefits and Obstacles of Continuous Auditing

Section 10: IT Auditing

IT Audit Group
Integration of IT and General Audits

example, if they use automated or manual tools to develop and produce their internal audit reports. These surveys are generally limited to some 300 to 400 responses and provide some basic yes-or-no responses to the questions. While one can argue about the depth and auditor understanding of some of these responses, this is often good background information to allow a CAE to assess what other internal audit functions are doing.

The IIA GAIN function has come a long way in allowing internal auditors to better understand what their peers are doing as part of their internal audit practices. The responses to the GAIN questionnaires are only as good or accurate as the internal audit function by function data entered. However, this GAIN data provides an overview of many of the practices that are important to all internal auditors. A CAE should strongly consider enrolling in the GAIN benchmarking surveys and studies. This is an excellent way for internal functions as well as the overall internal audit staff to understand areas that other internal auditors are emphasizing. It really improves the sharing of information among internal auditors.

12.6 BETTER UNDERSTANDING INTERNAL AUDIT ACTIVITIES

This chapter has introduced two important internal auditor tools: control self-assessments and benchmarking. CSAs say that rather than internal auditors performing formal reviews in some areas, internal audit can often provide overall value to all parties by promoting this concept of a control self-assessment. While not appropriate in some areas, this approach encourages internal auditors to act as internal consultants and to lead efforts within their own enterprise to encourage teams of frontline people to look at their own internal controls and to implement improvements. This can be a very effective tool on many levels, and internal auditors should have a CBOK understating of how to launch controls assessment processes.

An understanding of both the CSA process and internal auditor benchmarking are important internal auditor CBOK requirements. As discussed, benchmarking is one of those terms that is used too often without a complete understanding of the process.

Internal auditors should have a basic CBOK understanding of both the CSA and benchmarking processes, whether using them to gain best practice information from other internal audit functions or to serve as an enterprise consultant to help enterprise personnel launch their own benchmarking studies.

NOTES

1. *Control Self-Assessment: Experience, Current Thinking, and Best Practices* (Altamonte Springs, FL: Institute of Internal Auditors, 1996).
2. *Hard controls* refer to controls built into IT or other formal systems, while *soft controls* are based on either published procedures or stakeholder recognition that they are the rules.

CHAPTER THIRTEEN

Areas to Audit: Establishing an Audit Universe and Audit Programs

WITH OVERALL OBJECTIVES TO REVIEW and improve internal controls as well as to promote the effectiveness and efficiency of operations, an internal audit function is presented with a wide variety of areas and activities to include in its internal audit reviews. It can concentrate on reviews of financial process internal controls, all worldwide operational areas in the enterprise, safety and security issues, information technology (IT) systems–related controls, or any of a series of other areas. Given the broad scope of enterprise operations, management, and audit committees demand for internal audit attest services, most internal audit functions find that there are just too many areas to include within internal audit's planning and performance scope given staff skill, budget, and timing constraints. Internal audit functions need to establish their own basis point or foundation to define the areas within their scope that they may consider for internal audits. This list of potential areas to audit is often called the *audit universe*.

Although the term *universe* sounds a little space age, the term and concept have been used by internal auditors for some time. With reviews and approvals by the audit committee and senior management, the audit universe is the established population of auditable entities for any internal audit function. Such an audit universe may not cover every unit in the enterprise, as some are just too small, low-risk, or technically complex to be considered for internal audit reviews. However, once an internal audit function has established its scope of potential areas to review, the chief audit executive (CAE) and other members of the audit team can subject these potential audit areas to risk analysis and otherwise develop overall internal audit activity plans.

This chapter looks at the concept of establishing and maintaining an audit universe for an enterprise's internal audit function as well as using that universe as a basis for outlining high-level internal audit procedures, performing risk assessments, and establishing an overall, effective internal *audit program*. Our common body of knowledge (CBOK) concept here is that internal auditors at all levels should understand this concept of having an enterprise-specific internal audit universe as a basis to guide their internal audit activities. That audit universe will help internal audit to better present planned activities to the audit committee, as discussed in Chapter 25, and to more effectively plan risk-based internal audits, as discussed in Chapter 8.

In addition, all members of an internal audit function should perform their internal audit procedures in a consistent and orderly manner. They will accomplish these audit procedures through documents called audit programs. While audit programs may follow different formats from one enterprise to another as well as for different specialized internal audit types, they should follow a consistent format within an internal audit function. All internal auditors should have a strong CBOK understanding of how to use and construct internal audit programs.

13.1 DEFINING THE SCOPE AND OBJECTIVES OF THE INTERNAL AUDIT UNIVERSE

An audit universe is the aggregate of all areas that are available to be audited within an enterprise. To define its audit universe, internal audit should review or understand the number of potential auditable entities in terms of both the business units or areas of operations within the enterprise and the number of auditable units or activities within and across those business units. These auditable entities can be defined in a number of ways, such as by function or activity, by organizational unit or division, or perhaps by project or program. Some examples of *auditable activities* include:

- Policies, procedures, and practices both on an enterprise level and specific to locations, such as at international units
- Manufacturing, distribution, or supply chain units
- Information systems on infrastructure and specific application levels
- Major contracts or product lines
- Social media activities, such as the use of Facebook or Twitter and others, that are common to enterprise personnel
- Functions such as purchasing, accounting, finance, marketing, and others

This list highlights some of the major processes that help drive the enterprise. Some may be centrally directed, while others are unique to a specific auditable entity. The idea is to define these in a manner such that specific internal audits can be planned and executed.

The second way of looking at these entities is by business units. In today's environment, an enterprise may have multiple lines of business with operations across the globe, and may exhibit a myriad of authority/responsibility and reporting structures. In order for an internal auditor not to get lost in the complexity of corporate structures, an organized inventory of all significant auditable units should be compiled. The definition of auditable entities units must depend on specific organizational characteristics and whether the enterprise is functionally organized or product-centered. The idea is not to get too big or—an even greater problem—too small in these definitions. We should define auditable entities in a manner where individual internal audits will be cost-effective. Some examples include:

- Consider a multiplant manufacturing facility with many small production units. It might make sense to define all manufacturing processes at each of these smaller production units as potential auditable units. These production plant audits would include all manufacturing activities at each, such as purchasing, receiving, factory floor routing, quality assurance, shipping, and the like. It would almost never make sense to send an audit team to review a single process, such as the receiving process, at just one production plant.
- For a multirestaurant chain with many small units, it might be best to define each individual restaurant as an auditable unit, with no plans to schedule specific processes at each restaurant as a separate audit. An internal audit team might review all operations at a particular restaurant, rather than a common process, such as cash control procedures, for an individual restaurant unit.
- In many instances, it is often most efficient to designate a common process covering all units as an overall auditable entity, particularly if common policies and procedures cover all individual units.

In building their audit universe description, the CAE and a supporting internal audit team might start with a fairly detailed organizational chart to describe the auditable entity units. This can sometimes be a complex process if the enterprise has many subsidiaries, international-based units, joint ventures, and the like as well as a complex audit department structure. However, the emphasis should be placed on units where the enterprise CAE has prime internal audit responsibility.

Although there are many different organization structures, Exhibit 13.1 shows how auditable entities might be identified in a sample enterprise organization. The idea is that internal audits may be planned and executed in an up-and-down sense in the organization chart. That is, potential audits can cover all operations in an operating division, a subsidiary unit, a plant facility, or major units under a plant. On a cross-dimension, internal audits could be scheduled across such an organizational chart, covering all functional operations—such as IT security management—for each unit that may have similar but common functions.

The internal audit team should also define several audit focal points to ensure consistency in the execution of all potential internal audits. These focal points, which serve as a general outline for audit planning documents and audit work programs, help produce trending reports regarding the status of controls in the enterprise's control environment.

For example, the four audit focal points for an information security universe, shown in Exhibit 13.1, are:

1. IT access controls
2. System security configuration
3. Monitoring and incident response
4. Security management and administration

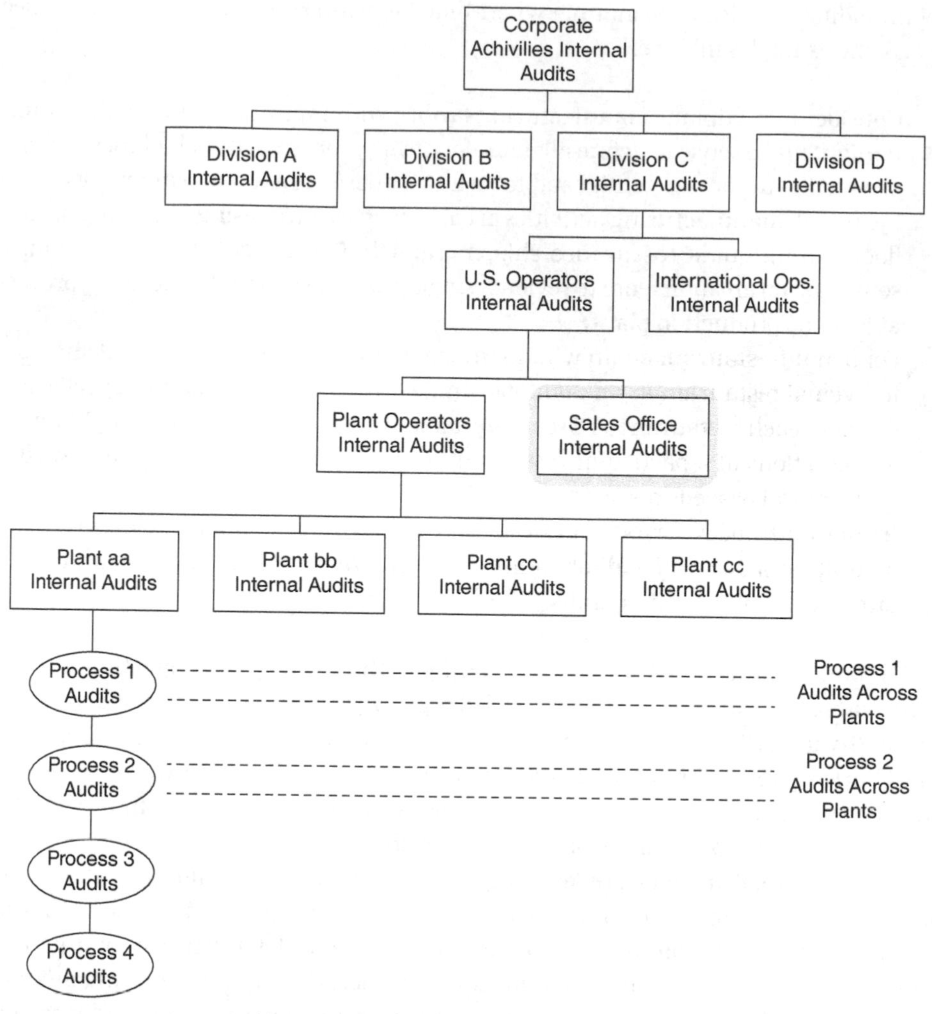

EXHIBIT 13.1 Audit Universe Organization Example

The four audit focal points for an IT infrastructure universe element might be:

1. Structure and strategy
2. Methodologies and procedures
3. Measurement and reporting
4. Tools and technology

Internal audit can use this list of potential auditable entities to share with members of management for their observations or corrections. The message along with this tentative audit universe compilation is that this list represents organizational units or activities in the enterprise where internal audit has prime internal audit responsibility. These are not necessarily current areas where internal audit might schedule a review, a potential picture of enterprise auditable units from an internal audit perspective.

This type of audit universe picture of enterprise auditable units should not be a onetime exercise, but continually maintained and updated as part of annual *internal audit planning* processes.

An Audit Universe Example: Global Computer Products

Various chapters throughout this book have referenced our example company, Global Computer Products. We will use it again in this chapter in our discussion on how to develop an internal audit universe.

Our example company is a hypothetical manufacturer and distributor of hardware- and software-based computer security products, with $2.4 billion in annual sales. It is a medium-sized high-technology manufacturing enterprise that operates internationally. Some key characteristics of Global Computer Products include:

- **Locations and operations.** The company has a headquarters office in the Chicago area in the United States with a computer security development facility in San Jose, California, and four product distribution centers in smaller U.S. cities as well as a distribution office in Belgium. In addition, the company has two hardware manufacturing facilities in China and a software production and distribution facility in India. All facilities are leased or licensed, and customer service functions have been outsourced.
- **Management team.** The company's chief executive officer was originally the founder of the company. He and three senior engineers are the only employees left over from the early days and the company's initial public stock offering. Due to turnover often typical in the industry, most employees have fairly short tenures. The chief financial officer is quite new, as the prior officer was asked to resign because of a Sarbanes-Oxley (SOx)–related dispute with the audit committee. The company makes extensive use of nonemployee contractors. Reporting to the CAE, Global has a relatively small internal audit department as well as a single general counsel.
- **Product description.** Global had developed a computer security product that consists of a hardware device plugged into a user's computer USB slot along with software drivers. The hardware device consists of a plug-in card based primarily on standard hardware chips along with some embedded programming. The software is based on proprietary algorithms. Elements of the product design are protected by patents, although these rights have been challenged in courts and also somewhat copied by some competitors.
- **Marketing.** Global's product is marketed by advertisements in professional publications as well as through a team of sales representatives. On a worldwide basis, 80% of sales are to individuals, with the balance to smaller businesses. The United States accounts for about 75% of product sales, with the balance from Europe. There is also a small but growing segment of sales from Brazil, where an independent agent is distributing the product. By agreement, Global has the right to audit these operations, but has never scheduled any work there. Global ships products from its distribution centers direct to computer equipment retailers as well as to individual customers, based on Internet, mail, or telephone orders.

- **Sales and finances.** Global's $2.4 billion in sales is split in the following categories:

Consumer cash sales through credit card purchases	41.0%	Export sales to agents	12.7%
Sales to wholesale distributors	23.4%	Licensing fees and royalties	4.9 %

As Global Computer Products is a relatively young enterprise, its internal audit function does not have a long history of continual audits through the enterprise. Rather, internal audit was launched when Global was formed, and most of its initial audit activity has been devoted to accounting and internal control processes at its Chicago headquarters, some operational process audits at its San Jose office, and reviews of general and application controls by an IT audit specialist at essentially just the U.S. locations. Exhibit 13.2 is an organization chart for the Global Computer Products sample enterprise.

Global Computer Products had never established a formal audit universe statement and had been planning and scheduling its reviews based on an informal audit planning process with management and audit committee requests to perform internal audits in one or another area. A member of the audit committee, in particular, has been questioning the CAE about the lack of internal audit coverage in several areas, particularly in international operations. As a result, the Global CAE has made plans to expand internal audit's staff size and coverage.

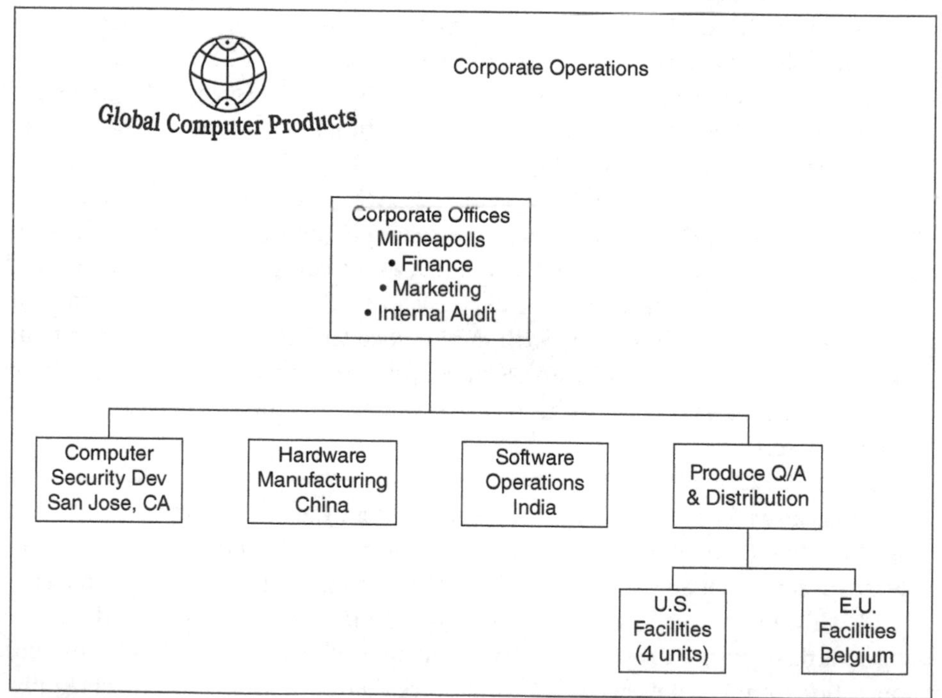

EXHIBIT 13.2 Global Computer Products Organization Example

13.2 ASSESSING INTERNAL AUDIT CAPABILITIES AND OBJECTIVES

A detailed list of enterprise units showing all of the areas that internal audit *could* review is of little value unless internal audit has the skills and resources to launch audits in those areas. In his earlier internal audit days, this author once was hired as the unit audit director of a large enterprise replacing an existing internal audit group that had spent too much time as part of an annual internal audit planning exercise preparing audit universe lists of all of the entities and units at this then very large enterprise. The result from his internal audit predecessors was extensive and impressive-looking lists of auditable entities, but the internal audit function had neither the capability nor even actual objectives to really perform audits at some of these auditable units.

To expand this example, the enterprise had a large group of remote distribution units as well businesses run by independent franchisees and contractors. An audit universe document had been prepared by the existing audit team that this author inherited that included all of these franchisee businesses as auditable units even though most had never been visited by corporate internal audit. An example of these was a small group of home improvement units whose whole function was to perform home pest removal services. On a contract basis, this franchisee unit would visit a home and remove rats, mice, or bats residing in attics.

This was a relatively small chain of operations that had little impact on or risk to overall parent enterprise operations. Aside from signing proper contracts and paying commissions to the parent, these franchisees had little connection with the parent corporation's operations. Did internal audit know anything about this type of business? Aside from commission transactions, was there any financial impact? The answer to this series of related questions should have been no. Units like this should never be included on internal audit universe lists.

The idea here is that internal audit should be realistic in developing its audit universe lists. It should develop high understanding of the business of control risks for each of the candidates on its universe list and assess whether there are internal audit risks and/or opportunities for each. Our Global Computer Products enterprise, described in Exhibit 13.2 shows a series of European sales and distribution functions. For example, assume there is a small sales office in Kiev in Ukraine. Since internal audit will almost certainly never visit that unit or have any direct contacts with it, these Kiev operations do not belong in the audit universe list. There should only be a reference that these units were not included as potential internal audit candidates and the reasons for that decision.

Based on the preliminary list of auditable units and candidates, internal audit should next go a step further to develop and enhance its audit resource lists. Although there still may be some uncertainly of the nature of some of these business units and their internal control issues, internal audit should analyze each of these potential internal audit candidates as follows:

- **Establish high-level control objectives for each of the audit universe candidates.** The idea is to determine why a unit is on such a list as well as internal audit's potential *control objectives* for such units. Our previous example of a franchisee household pest control service would probably be eliminated in such an exercise.

- **Assess high-level risks for audit universe candidates.** Following the COSO Enterprise Risk Management approach discussed in Chapter 7, internal audit should review each of these audit universe candidates and estimate the high-level risks to the enterprise if there was a major internal control failure associated with the audit universe candidate.
- **Coordinate the internal audit activity with other audit and governance interests.** While internal audit is or should be the prime reviewer of enterprise internal controls, any planned audit work should be coordinated with other interested parties. For example, external auditors may request a more complete SOx Section 404 internal controls review, as discussed in Chapter 5. The audit universe and internal audit planned activities should be coordinated with such external audit requests. Similarly, internal audit projects should be coordinated with planned work by any independent quality audit function, as discussed in Chapter 31. It is easy to say that internal audit should have a lead role here, but these planned audit efforts should be coordinated.
- **Develop high-level control objectives for audits designated by the audit universe.** While this will become more important in an annual planning process, as was discussed in Chapter 8, a high-level audit objective should be identified for each item included in the audit universe. This should be a simple statement of planned audit objectives for each item in the audit universe to help ensure that the strategy, objectives, and scope for each audit include relevant control objectives (i.e., a completeness check to identify gaps).
- **Develop a preliminary control assessment questionnaire for each audit.** In many cases, audits listed on the audit universe are repeats of internal audits from prior periods. In many situations, this audit guidance should be updated as processes change and reevaluated for future audits in each area. In other cases, internal audit should develop some high-level questionnaire steps to get them started in these potential audit universe reviews.

As a result of this review and analysis work, internal audit should develop a preliminary audit universe schedule that will show the areas for potential review. Such a list would include areas where there is a recurring internal audit interest, where there may be a higher internal control failure risk, and other high-level review objectives. This type of approach will give internal audit a beginning step to initiate its regular internal audit planning activities. Of course, a smaller internal audit group can face a daunting task when building an effective audit universe for a large-scale enterprise. Internal audit may not have the time or resources to perform reviews of items included in the audit universe without some other adjustments.

13.3 AUDIT UNIVERSE TIME AND RESOURCE LIMITATIONS

It is sometimes easy to build an audit universe document that includes many—often too many—potential internal audits that will never be executed. Our Global Computer Products example illustrates this problem. Global currently has a headquarters location–based internal audit group that does not have any regular international presence. Based on the size of the internal audit function, the audit committee should recognize that some of the auditable entities on its universe list can be essentially never reviewed, given internal audit's size and budget. The idea is to demonstrate potential review activities over upcoming periods and what can realistically be included in internal audit's scope of planned activities.

A next step should be to look at the preliminary audit universe list and determine those audits that are required on an annual or even a semiannual basis. These are audits, such as SOx Section 404 internal control reviews, that must be completed during a current period. There are other regular internal audits that are not mandated but are expected by senior management and the audit committee. For example, management may expect internal audit to maintain some presence in observing the taking of physical inventories in a manufacturing environment. As part of their audit universe and enterprise planning, internal audit should assume that they will need to schedule these reviews on a regular and periodic basis.

Although we are still dealing at a very high level here, a next step is to look at the remaining items in the preliminary audit universe and determine if time and resources are available for reviews of these remaining items. In some situations, this list of potential auditable entities will demonstrate that there are just too many audit entity items left in the audit universe to complete reviews over a reasonable period of time. Because of the ongoing enterprise and market changes that we all experience, a time span here should not be more than five years; three years is preferable. In addition, these internal audits set for scheduling in the current period or in a three- to five-year cycle may require specialized internal audit skills. There may need to have more internal audit resources on board for such areas as IT network security or continuity planning and testing. Where additional internal audit skills or additional resources will be needed, they should be documented and scheduled.

All of these gathered data and planning assumptions will help internal audit to build and publish a preliminary audit universe for the enterprise. This document shows the areas where internal audit plans on performing audits over upcoming periods, the high-level objectives of those audits, and their relative risks. The schedule should also document assumptions, such as audits that will be performed by quality assurance, or other reviews that have not been considered because they are low risk, they have been eliminated because of logistical difficulties, or they will be performed by other bodies. Regarding logistical difficulties, we are often referring to entities in some fairly distant or difficult-to-schedule location. Our creation of a sales office in Kiev, Ukraine, for Global Computer Products is an example. While Kiev is a European capital city and certainly not remote, such as the nation of Tonga in the South Pacific, and is easily accessed via regular airlines, such a location might present a logistical difficulty to our small sample company.

Internal audit should prepare an audit universe document for the current period. This should be reviewed with members of senior management and then presented to the audit committee for approval. Exhibit 13.3 is a portion of what would be a much larger audit universe schedule for our Global Computer Products example enterprise. Similar to an annual budget schedule or a capital funding request, this might normally be a much larger, more extensive type of analysis document. This exhibit is to provide an example of what such an internal audit universe schedule might look like.

EXHIBIT 13.3 Global Computer Products Sample Audit Universe Schedule

Business Unit	Location	Audit Area	Audit	Audit Risk	Prev. Audit	Scheduled
Headquarters	Minneapolis	Financial	Accounts Payable	Low		
Headquarters	Minneapolis	Financial	Banking Operations	Medium		
Headquarters	Minneapolis	Financial	Budgeting	Low		
Headquarters	Minneapolis	Financial	SOx 404 Internal Controls	High		
Headquarters	Minneapolis	Operations	Corporate Marketing	Medium		
Headquarters	Minneapolis	Operations	Advertising	Low		
Product Distribution	Fargo, ND	IT Infrastructure	Inventory System	Medium		
Product Distribution	Meriilville, IL	IT Infrastructure	Inventory System	Medium		
Product Distribution	Los Cruces, NM	IT Infrastructure	Inventory System	Medium		
Product Distribution	Midville, OH	IT Infrastructure	Inventory System	Medium		

13.4 "SELLING" AN AUDIT UNIVERSE CONCEPT TO THE AUDIT COMMITTEE AND MANAGEMENT

The CAE and a key internal audit team may go through massive efforts to initially build and maintain their internal audit universe and may have solicited the help and advice from senior management in the contents and assumptions of this audit universe, but the audit committee is the entity responsible for reviewing and approving such a document. In the end, the audit committee is responsible if there are any questions regarding why internal audit neither did nor did not look at some area, and the CAE should carefully brief the audit committee members and explain key assumptions.

The audit universe schedule should be prepared and updated on an annual basis for audit committee review and approval. Where the audit committee suggests different areas of emphasis or involvement, the CAE should initiate these internal audit planned changes and make appropriate adjustments to the internal audit annual plan and schedule. In addition, this is often the time for internal audit to seek authorization for changes to internal audit's budget, manpower, or other function changes. Internal audit would be operating under an annual enterprise budget, but it is the audit committee that can make a midstream change—for example, to add a new IT audit staff specialist to the internal audit group.

We have titled this section as the "selling" of the audit universe plan to the audit committee. Perhaps this is an inappropriate term. The audit committee is responsible for all internal audit activities and should rely on the CAE and other members of internal audit to perform all of these scheduled audits and to report results back to the audit committee. However, because the typical audit committee does not meet very often and may not be very close to many changes and new events, the CAE is the individual closest to the audit universe and other changes. The CAE is often the person who communicates changes in internal audit's schedule or changes in its emphasis. The CAE must keep the audit universe and the supporting annual plan in front of the audit committee and also convince or "sell" approval request concepts to the audit committee for their ongoing approval.

The audit universe is the basis for the annual audit plan, as described in Chapter 8, and will help to guide internal audit's ongoing activities and performance. Chapter 25 describes audit committee communications and contains some examples of internal audit progress communication with the audit committee. These are all based on the very important audit universe schedule, a key document that describes internal audit's planned and potential activities over an extended period.

13.5 ASSEMBLING AUDIT PROGRAMS: AUDIT UNIVERSE KEY COMPONENTS

An audit universe and its supporting information describe internal audit's high-level review objectives in an area. We have also discussed how internal audit should define and document some high-level objectives for each planned review, but it will not be enough to assign the work to a staff-level auditor; they will need some step-by-step guidance to perform internal audits in a consistent manner. Internal audits should be organized and performed with an objective of minimizing arbitrary or unnecessary procedures. Of course, an internal auditor will not recognize those arbitrary or unnecessary procedures until an auditor has gained some experience in performing reviews. To provide help and guidance, internal auditors use what are called *audit programs* to perform their internal audit procedures in a consistent and effective manner for similar types of audits. The term *program* refers to a set of auditor procedures similar to the steps in a computer program, instructions that go through the same program actions every time the process is run. For example, a computer program to calculate pay will include instructions to read the time card file of hours worked, look up the employee's rate stored in another file, and then calculate the gross pay. The same steps apply for every employee unless there are exceptions such as overtime rates coded into the payroll program. Similarly, an audit program is a set of preestablished steps an internal auditor performs. An audit program is a tool for planning, directing, and controlling audit work and a blueprint for action, specifying the steps to be performed to meet audit objectives. It represents the auditor's selection of the best methods for getting the job done and serves as a basis for recording the work steps performed.

An effective internal audit department should have a series of generalized audit programs prepared for recurring audit activities. Many of these programs, such as one covering an observation of the taking of physical inventories, are often used from year to year and entity to entity with little change. In other situations, the internal auditor may only have to modify a standard program to the unique aspects of a particular audit. In some situations, a standard audit program will not be applicable. For example, the internal auditor may want to review controls in a new business entity with some unique control characteristics, or audit management may want to take a different approach because of problems encountered with similar previous reviews. Based on planned audit objectives and data gathered in the preliminary and field surveys, the in-charge auditor may want to prepare a customized audit program for guiding the review. This may be little more than a standardized program with minimal local changes, or it may be a unique set of audit procedures based on the preliminary planning and the results from a field survey, as discussed in Chapter 8. In order to prepare this program, the internal auditor first should have an understanding of the characteristics of what constitutes an adequate audit program.

Audit Program Formats and Their Preparation

An audit program is a procedure describing the steps and tests to be performed by the internal auditor when actually doing fieldwork. The program should be finalized after the completion of the preliminary and field surveys and before starting the actual audit fieldwork. It should be constructed with several criteria in mind, the most important of which is that the program should identify the aspects of the area to be further examined and the sensitive areas that require audit emphasis.

A second important purpose of an audit program is that it should provide guidance to both less and more experienced internal auditors. For example, management may request that an internal audit department observe the taking of the annual physical inventory. This type of review consists of fairly standard procedures to assure, among other matters, that shipping and receiving cutoff procedures are proper. A less experienced internal auditor may not be aware of these procedure steps, and even experienced internal auditors may forget one or another. An audit program outlines the required audit steps. An established internal audit department will probably have built a library of programs, established over time, for tasks such as a physical inventory observation or a review of fixed assets. When planning a review where such established programs exist, audit management needs only to use this established program with consideration given to any changed conditions that have been discovered through the preliminary or field surveys. The audit program is revised as necessary, with the changes approved by audit management prior to the start of the review.

For many internal audit departments, appropriate established audit programs may not be available for many areas. This is because internal auditors are typically faced with a wide and diverse set of areas for review, but they will not have the time or resources to review every area on a frequent basis. Established programs prepared for prior audits often become out of date due to new systems or changed processes. The auditor responsible for the field survey or another member of audit management should update any existing audit program or prepare a revised set of audit program steps for a current newly planned review. Depending on the type of audit, programs usually follow one of three general formats: a set of general audit procedures, audit procedures with detailed instructions for the auditor, and a checklist for compliance reviews.

Some examples may better illustrate these audit program types. Exhibit 13.4 is an audit program for a review of petty cash controls at a small branch unit. It consists of general audit procedures to review cash at any unit of a multifacility organization.

EXHIBIT 13.4 Audit Program for a Review of Petty Cash

Audit: ______ **Location:** ______ **Date:** ______

AUDIT STEP	Initials & Date	W/P Reference
1. Prior to review, determine who is the cashier responsible for the petty cash fund, the authorized fund balances, receipt requirements, replenishment procedures, and guidelines for authorized disbursements.	______	
2. Perform the petty cash review on a "surprise" basis. Identify yourself to the cashier, ask that the cashier function be closed during your initial review, and make a detailed count of the cash in the account as well as any personal checks included. Perform this count in the presence of the cashier and ask the cashier to acknowledge your results.	______	
3. If personal checks were included that are over one day old, inquire why they were not deposited on a prompt basis. If the fund is being used as an employee short-term loan fund, with checks held as collateral, assess the propriety of this practice.	______	
4. Reconcile the cash count with the fund's disbursement register, noting any differences.	______	
5. Determine that all disbursements recorded have been made to valid employees for authorized purposes.	______	
6. Observe office security procedures covering the fund. Determine that the funds are locked or otherwise secured.	______	
7. Review procedures for fund replenishments. Select a prior period, review supporting documentation, and reconcile to purchases journal.	______	
8. Assess the overall control procedures, propriety, and efficiency of the petty cash process.	______	
9. Determine that the function is used only for authorized small cash disbursements rather than as an employee change or short-term loan fund.	______	
10. Document the results of the review and initiate corrective actions if any problems were encountered during the review.	______	

Petty cash controls are one of the smaller, less critical internal control concerns in many organizations. However, this is a step that an internal auditor will regularly perform in many cases. The program shows the rather simple steps that should be included in any such audit and illustrates an example audit program.

This audit program is shown as a traditional paper document. However, with today's world of auditor computer systems, this and essentially all such programs would be a library resource on the internal auditor's laptop computer. The basic program will be constructed as secure form, such that an internal auditor can use these steps to perform a review but does not have the authority to make changes to the documented procedures. The Exhibit 13.4 checklist audit program was once internal audit's most common format. The auditor would be given an audit program composed of a long list of questions requiring "yes," "no," or "not applicable" responses and would complete these program steps either through examinations of documents or through interviews.

This checklist-format audit program has two weaknesses, however. First, while a series of auditee yes-or-no–type interview responses can lead an experienced auditor to look at problem areas or to ask other questions, these same points may be missed when a less experienced internal auditor is just completing the questionnaire and not going beyond the yeses and nos and digging a bit deeper as to where they might lead. A procedures-oriented audit program better encourages follow-up inquiries in other areas where information gathered may raise questions.

This questionnaire format audit program also tends to cause the auditor to miss examining necessary evidential matter. The more inexperienced auditor can too easily check "yes" on the questionnaire without determining, for example, whether that response is properly supported by *audit evidence*. An example would be a question regarding whether some critical document is regularly approved. It is easy to ask the question, receive an answer of "yes," and never follow up to see if those documents were actually approved. Each of these audit program formats will work for different types of reviews provided the internal auditor gives some thought to the program questions. The key concern is that all audits should be supported by some type of audit program that documents the review steps performed. This approach allows audit management to recognize what procedures the auditors did or did not perform in a given review. Strong and consistent audit programs are an important step to improving the overall quality of the internal audits performed.

Exhibit 8.9 represents a typical, more general internal audit program format. This program describes steps in a review of business ethics processes. For each internal audit, the tasks are broken into numbered steps with space allowed for the internal auditor completing the audit step to initial and date it, as well as a column for a reference to the workpaper that describes the audit step. The audit team visiting an enterprise unit could then use these standard programs to review internal controls in a consistent manner from one unit to the next. This is particularly important in a multiunit organization where audit management wants to have assurance that controls over the area were reviewed and evaluated in a consistent manner, no matter who the assigned auditor or the location. This sample audit program is shown as a printed document that would typically be developed and controlled by internal audit. In other instances, the in-charge auditor might prepare a custom program to evaluate certain special procedures encountered during the field survey.

An audit program with detailed instructions or procedures assumes that the auditor using it lacks some of the technical knowledge necessary to perform the review. Such audit programs are often developed for onetime reviews of fairly specialized areas and prepared by audit management or a knowledgeable audit specialist with adequate knowledge to plan all of the required audit procedures. This step-by-step audit program format is useful when a centralized audit management group with remote auditors in the field wishes to have all of those field auditors perform the same audit procedures.

There is no best or set format for an audit program; however, the program should be a document that auditors can use to guide their efforts as well as to record activities. The results of the audit program, shown in Exhibit 8.9, would then be included in the workpapers to serve as almost a table of contents of the audit activities described in those workpapers. Word processing packages and other related software can be used to prepare audit programs.

Types of Programs Obtaining Audit Evidence

As discussed in Chapter 9, IIA standards state that an internal auditor should examine and evaluate information on all matters related to the planned audit objective. The internal auditor should gather audit evidence in support of the evaluation, what internal audit standards call *sufficient, competent, relevant,* and *useful.* An audit program, properly constructed, should guide the auditor in this evidence-gathering process. An internal auditor will encounter multiple types of evidence that can be useful in developing audit conclusions. Actually observing an action or obtaining an independent confirmation is one of the strongest forms of evidence. However, an auditee's often casual response to an auditor's question covering the same area will be the weakest. It is not that an auditor thinks the auditee is not telling the truth, but actually observing some event is far superior to just hearing about it. Internal auditors will encounter different levels of audit evidence and should attempt to design their audit procedures to look for and rely on the best available audit evidence.

The field survey and the subsequent development of an audit program are preliminary activities to performing the actual audit. It is often more efficient to have supervisory personnel complete these preliminary steps before assigning staff auditors for the actual review. These supervisory auditors, either audit management or experienced in-charge auditors, usually have the experience to make quick assessments of field situations and to fine-tune the overall audit approach. However, once the survey and final audit program are complete and have been reviewed and approved by internal audit management, internal audit is faced with the challenge of performing the actual audit to meet the desired audit objectives. The preparatory work from the survey will play an important role in assuring the audit's success; however, the internal auditor will now be faced with the day-to-day problems of performing the actual audit.

The actual audit steps performed will depend on the characteristics of the entity audited. A financially oriented audit of a credit and collection function will be quite different from an operational review of a design engineering department. The financial audit might include independent confirmations of account balances, while the operational audit might include extensive interviews with management and supporting documentation to assess key internal controls. Despite these differences, all internal audits should be performed and supervised following a general set of principles or standards. This will assure that internal audits are properly directed and controlled (see Exhibit 13.5).

EXHIBIT 13.5 Internal Audit "Best Evidence" Classifications

Evidence Classification	Strongest	Weakest
Audit Technique	Observations/Confirmation	Inquiry
Origin of Evidence	Corroborative	Underlying Statistics
Relationship to Auditee	External Department	Internal Group
Form of Evidence	Written/Secure System	Oral
Sophistication of Evidence	Formal/Documented	Informal
Location of Evidence	Created in Actual System	Derived or from Support System
Source of Audit Evidence	Personal Audit Work	Supplied "Second-Hand"

13.6 AUDIT UNIVERSE AND PROGRAM MAINTENANCE

The audit universe document is a general description of all of the audit units that an enterprise internal audit function may review or perform. It is a plan that defines the breadth and scope of an internal audit function's activities. To some extent, if questioned after the fact why an internal audit group has never scheduled a review in some area, they can point out that the area was not included in annual internal audit plans but, more important, was never defined as part of their internal audit universe description. The universe is the big-picture map covering internal audit's territories and boundaries. It should be used as a basis for communication with the audit committee and for planning ongoing internal audit activities.

The audit universe document is not something that should be changed on a constant and regular basis whenever there is some small enterprise change. However, internal audit should have processes in place to keep its audit universe current and updated with perhaps regular quarterly or annual update reviews. This is often a good time for the CAE to explain to the audit committee any changes in internal audit's scope and operations. An effective audit universe defines internal audit annual planning and becomes a vehicle to describe an internal audit function's activities.

This chapter has also discussed the importance of establishing an audit universe along with introducing some formats of effective audit programs. An effective internal audit function needs to establish a series of standard audit programs covering all of their regular audit activities. While some internal audits are done on a specialized, almost onetime basis, many others cover regular internal audit activities that may be repeated annually or even quarterly. Internal audit needs to develop a standard audit program format for all reviews as well as standard procedures for some regular, repetitive internal audits. Audit programs were once paper documents that were sometimes lost or improperly modified. Today, however, they can be electronic documents that are centrally controlled and located on auditor laptops. They can be a learning tool for incoming internal auditors and a tool to prepare consistent and more effective internal audits.

An understanding of how to build and use both an audit universe for an internal audit function as well as supporting audit programs are key internal audit CBOK requirements. Senior members of the internal audit team should have an overall understanding of how to build and use these tools. Internal audit staff members should understand their use and how they fit in overall internal audit processes. Perhaps even more important, internal auditors at all levels should have a strong CBOK understanding of building and using audit programs that are consistent with their audit department's established standards.

IV

PART FOUR

Organizing and Managing Internal Audit Activities

CHAPTER FOURTEEN

Charters and Building the Internal Audit Function

THIS CHAPTER AND THE OTHER chapters in Part Four that follow it cover the essential activities of an internal audit department, through launching an internal audit department, as described in this chapter, to reporting internal audit results through effective audit reports in Chapter 18. This chapter introduces some key practices necessary to build an effective internal audit function, starting with an authorizing charter as well as the basic processes of building, staffing, and managing an effective internal audit department. We start by describing the need to establish a formal internal audit charter, a basic authorizing document that has some common elements no matter whether internal audit is serving a large corporate structure or a smaller not-for-profit entity. This is the *audit committee* approved document that outlines internal audit's authority and responsibility to operate within an enterprise.

The chapter discusses other important steps to building an effective internal audit function, including typical internal audit position descriptions and effective organizational structures. No matter the industry, geographic location, or size of the enterprise, all internal audit departments or functions need to follow some of these similar good practice procedures.

Most of this book's common body of knowledge (CBOK) theme covers technical internal audit areas such as information technology (IT) application control reviews or guidance for assessing the results of audit evidence. This chapter and the others in Part Four discuss steps for launching and managing the effective internal audit function or department. When Victor Brink launched the first edition of this book shortly after World War II, many enterprises had heard of the potential benefits of internal auditing and wanted to learn more about how to establish such a function. While that first edition of *Brink's Modern Internal Auditing* helped to launch the internal auditing profession, the world of professional internal auditing today is now widely recognized and much more complex. Today, virtually all medium and large public, private, governmental, and not-for-profit enterprises worldwide have established internal audit functions.

This chapter reviews the steps necessary to start an effective internal audit function, including the importance of establishing a formal audit committee–authorized charter and building an effective internal audit staff. The chapter will also review important internal audit policies and procedures as well as the first steps to review auditable entities within the enterprise. This material, as well as the content of the other chapters in Part Four, should help an enterprise launch an internal audit function that follows some recommended best practices.

14.1 ESTABLISHING AN INTERNAL AUDIT FUNCTION

There is no one optimal way to organize an internal audit function in an enterprise today. There can be many differences in type of business, geographic span, and organizational structure, with differing internal audit needs for each. Each enterprise, however, must follow the *International Standards for the Professional Practice of Internal Auditing* and should operate under the International Professional Practices Framework (IPPF), both discussed in Chapter 9, and must have the support and recognition of enterprise senior management. The need for an internal audit function comes from corporate requirements such as the Securities and Exchange Commission and the Sarbanes-Oxley (SOx) Act rules, or legal requirements from governmental agencies. If a newly launched entity does not have an internal audit function, senior management should take steps to initiate one.

A senior manager, designated the *chief audit executive (CAE)*, who has been challenged to establish a new internal audit function is faced with a variety of options, depending on the enterprise's overall business, its geographic and logistical structures, the various control risks it faces, and the overall enterprise culture. Whether a corporation structure with a requirement for an audit committee or some other type of enterprise, there is almost always a need and justification to establish an internal audit function. This section will discuss some of the elements required to build and manage an effective internal audit function.

A key requirement for any effective organization is a strong leader; for internal audit, that leader is a CAE who understands the needs of the overall organization and its potential control risks as well as the contributions that internal audit can make. This person must have the support of both the audit committee and senior management. Most large enterprises today have multiple units spread across the world. Even if geographically positioned in a single location, the larger enterprise will almost always have multiple specialty functions with control risks potentially requiring separate internal audit emphasis. The effective internal audit department must be organized in a manner that serves senior management and the audit committee by providing the best, most cost-effective audit services to the entire organization. We will consider the benefits and difficulties in having a centralized or a decentralized internal audit organization as well as some alternative internal audit organization structures.

This chapter will again reference our hypothetical example company, Global Computer Products. As also discussed in other chapters, we have defined this as a relatively small IT software and hardware manufacturer and distributor, headquartered in the United States but with some worldwide operations. We will assume here that the company was incorporated not too long ago, but because of its small size never had an effective internal audit function. An important first step is to have an approved internal audit charter—the formal marching orders authorizing internal audit for the enterprise.

14.2 AUDIT COMMITTEE AND MANAGEMENT AUTHORIZATION OF AN AUDIT CHARTER

An internal audit charter is a formal document, approved by the audit committee, to describe the mission, independence, objectivity, scope, responsibilities, authority, accountability, and standards of the internal audit function. Internal audit has free rein to look at a wide range of records and to ask questions at all levels. Internal auditors have a lot of responsibility in an enterprise, and some type of authorizing authority is needed. Because in a corporate structure the internal audit function reports to the audit committee of the board, that audit committee would normally authorize the rights and responsibilities of internal audit through a formal authorizing document or resolution—what is usually called an internal audit charter.

There are no fixed requirements for such an authorizing document, but an internal audit charter should affirm internal audit's:

- Independence and objectivity
- Scope of responsibility
- Authority and accountability

An internal audit charter, then, is the authorizing document for an enterprise internal audit function that can be used when a manager in a separate and sometimes remote organizational unit questions why an internal auditor is asking to see or review certain documents or to gain access to an enterprise facility. Such an internal audit charter would say that senior management—the board of directors' audit committee—has granted that internal auditor access to enterprise records. More important, the charter provides a high level of authorization for the enterprise's internal audit function.

There is no fixed format for the contents of a charter. The IIA's internal audit standards, as discussed in Chapter 9, reference the need for an internal audit charter, but the IIA's web site (www.theiia.org) does not provide any specific guidance as to its content or format. A general Web search for "internal audit charters" will provide a variety of examples, but most today are primarily from government and academic institutions. Exhibit 8.1 is an example of a typical internal audit charter from our Global Computer Products company. It clearly outlines internal audit's authority as well as such responsibilities as developing a risk-based audit plan and issuing timely audit reports. A knowledge and understanding of charters should be part of an internal audit CBOK.

An internal audit charter, as was described in Exhibit 8.1, should be much more than a nice-sounding document; it should outline a strong internal audit function to launch and perform key internal audit activities. These include understanding the areas in any enterprise that should be candidates for internal audit reviews, building an effective internal audit organization and team, and establishing supporting procedures to allow those internal audits. While an internal audit charter is an essential authorization to launch a new internal audit function, many if not most internal audit functions today have a charter that may have been developed and approved many years ago. If one is in place, it is often a good idea for the CAE to periodically review that existing charter and present it to the audit committee to reaffirm their understanding of the role and responsibilities of internal audit.

14.3 ESTABLISHING AN INTERNAL AUDIT FUNCTION

With exception of a very small single-person internal audit facility, every internal audit function needs to have someone to be in charge and responsible for internal audit—the CAE—as well as some supporting and administrative staff. While there can be many variations in position descriptions and titles, this section will provide some model internal auditor position descriptions for various levels and types of internal auditors in an enterprise. Those same position titles will map to the various internal audit organization structures discussed next. In addition, there are different CBOK requirements for each of these internal audit position descriptions.

Role of the CAE

Someone should be responsible for any internal audit function or group—this is usually the boss. Although the title internal audit director was more common in years past, IIA standards today support the title of chief audit executive, the most senior internal audit officer in the enterprise, with ultimate responsibility for the entire internal audit function.

No matter whether the CAE works at a Fortune 500 major corporation or a relatively small private or not-for-profit enterprise, he or she is the designated person to lead and direct the enterprise's internal audit function or department. While we are presenting an example CAE position description here, the following are important topics and responsibilities that should be part of any CAE's CBOK and also be reflected in the internal audit charter:

- **Enterprise operations and risk issues.** In addition to managing the internal audit function, the CAE should have knowledge regarding all aspects of the enterprise's operations, whether financial, operational, or market matters.
- **Human resources and internal audit administration.** The CAE is responsible for the internal audit staff and must build an effective organization and both recruit and lead an effective internal audit team.

- **Relationships with the audit committee and management.** The CAE is the internal audit spokesperson for the audit committee and all levels of enterprise management.
- **Corporate governance, accounting, compliance, and regulatory issues.** Whether dealing with SOx, accounting, finance issues, or other regulatory issues impacting the enterprise, the CAE should have at least a general understanding and knowledge.
- **Internal audit team building and administration.** No matter what size the team is, the CAE is responsible for building an effective internal audit function that receives admiration and respect from the recipients of internal audit services.
- **Technology.** The CAE should have a general understanding of how technology is used within the enterprise as well as how it can be applied to promote internal audit services.
- **Risk-based audit planning.** The CAE should understand risk assessment processes as they are applied to enterprise operations, and also should be able to think of operations in terms of these key processes.
- **Social media issues.** Through the use of products such as Facebook, Twitter, or others, social media tools and processes are introducing major changes in enterprises today; the CAE should understand these changes and how they impact an enterprise.
- **Negotiating skills and relationship management.** The CAE will often be drawn between issues raised by the internal audit team and a sometimes hostile management that may take exception to internal audit's findings and recommendations. The CAE is often called on to negotiate an appropriate resolution to these issues as part of building an effective internal audit team.
- **Internal audit's assurance and consulting roles.** Although these roles can sometimes become blurred, the CAE should always emphasize to both the internal audit team and management the separate roles of providing internal audit assurance services and providing consulting services, as discussed in Chapter 9.
- ***International Standards for the Professional Practice of Internal Auditing.*** The CAE should be an expert on these IIA standards, should understand IPPF concepts, and should help to apply them to all aspects of internal audit activities.

The CAE has an important job both in leading an effective internal audit department and in delivering internal audit services to the enterprise. Although many members of the internal audit team may have stronger or more specialized knowledge in some areas, the CAE is the key person who represents internal audit to the enterprise.

Internal Audit Management Responsibilities

Depending on the overall enterprise size, beyond the CAE, an internal audit function may have multiple levels of internal audit supervisors or managers to closely monitor and manage the internal audit function. These are the resources that create an effective internal audit function through close planning, monitoring, and supervising the

EXHIBIT 14.1 Internal Audit Manager Position Description

Job Responsibilities

The Manager of Internal Audit has responsibility for assisting the Chief Audit Executive (CAE) in providing guidance and supervision of the Internal Audit Department (the "Department"). Additionally, the Internal Audit Manager is responsible for: (1) executing the financial/operational audit portion of the Department's Annual Audit Plan; (2) assisting the CAE in preparing regular updates of internal audit activity to the Audit Committee; (3) providing advice and counsel on new systems, initiatives, and services under development from an internal control perspective; (4) assisting the CAE in the coordination of financial internal audit activities, including Sarbanes-Oxley Section 404 internal controls assessments, with the independent registered public accountants; (5) effectively and efficiently managing financial internal audit function resources; (6) hiring, training, and professionally developing the financial internal audit team; and (7) overseeing the quality of work performed by the financial internal audit team, ensuring compliance with applicable standards.

Internal Audit Key Competencies

- In-depth technical knowledge of internal audit practices and principles including IIA International Standards and their IPPF framework
- Strong knowledge of accounting principles and a thorough understanding of financial statements
- Solid knowledge and experience with regulatory rules and compliance requirements affecting the internal auditing and accounting professions (e.g., Sarbanes-Oxley Act)
- Good knowledge of all aspects of the IT systems and controls as used in the enterprise
- Detail oriented with strong analytical and problem-solving abilities
- Solid leadership, management, and administrative skills
- Broad-based business knowledge including financial/operational practices and procedures from a company operations perspective
- Strong interpersonal, communication, and presentation skills

Required Skills

A Bachelor of Science Degree in Business Administration with a major in Accounting or Finance; a minimum of seven years of progressive internal audit and/or public accounting experience; and a Certified Internal Auditor (CIA) certificate. A Certified Public Accounting (CPA) certificate is also highly recommended.

field audit staffs that are actually performing internal audits. While the CAE should normally be an internal audit generalist with a good knowledge of enterprise internal controls issues and internal audit practices, the *internal audit managers* and supervisors will generally be specialists in such areas as financial or IT internal audit issues. As an example, Exhibit 14.1 is a sample position description for an internal audit manager with both financial and operational audit skills. Such an internal audit manager often would be expected to be a Certified Public Accountant (CPA) in addition to a Certified Internal Auditor (CIA) to enable that manager to better communicate and understand finance and accounting issues with both enterprise management and the internal audit staff. The manager should also have good IT internal controls skills.

We perhaps too often insist that a certification such as a CPA, CIA, or CISA must be a *requirement* for certain types of internal audit positions. While they certainly are a measure of demonstrated skills, a CAE building an effective internal audit organization should always consider the skills and aptitudes of the candidates for any internal audit manager position rather than just the initials after their name on their business card. For example, an internal audit staff member may have joined an enterprise internal audit group with a strong BA in economics. If that same new professional joined the internal audit department, acquired a CIA, and performed well in accounting and financial internal control audits, the lack of a CPA should not necessarily prevent that person from being a candidate for an internal audit manager position performing financial reviews.

Enterprise human resources functions may impose requirements here, but the CAE should play a lead in insisting that there are appropriate position descriptions in place for all members of the internal audit management team. They should be structured in such a manner that all members of the internal audit staff can recognize the requirements to move from one level to the next. For example, an internal audit field supervisor should clearly understand the additional requirements to move up to an internal auditor manager level if such a position becomes available.

Internal Audit Staff Responsibilities

In many enterprises, internal audit is an excellent entry place for new, just-out-of-college, nonspecialist staff members. That is, an enterprise may have requirements for engineers and will want to hire new engineering degree graduates or may have needs for people in advertising and will want to add new candidates with appropriate advertising or communications skills, but entry-level staff internal audit candidates can come from a wide range of degree areas. However, while many general degree programs can provide excellent internal auditor candidates, an excellent source for internal audit candidates is colleges that offer specialized bachelor-level internal audit degree programs. While they are not very common today, the programs at Loyola University in Chicago[1] and at Louisiana State University[2] are excellent examples of well-regarded internal audit training programs. Students there can receive a bachelor's degree in internal auditing. However, because there are not many specific internal audit training programs, an enterprise should seek candidates with degrees in such area as finance, accounting, economics, or information systems.

What should be the requirements for an entry-level internal audit position? We would argue that candidates do not necessarily need to have an accounting degree, the historically typical entry point for many internal auditors, but should have a strong ability to understand systems and process flows coupled with superb speaking and writing skills. Even at a staff level, a beginning internal auditor should be someone who can quickly review often complex processes, assess potential weaknesses, and then communicate those concerns to internal audit management and overall enterprise management.

Exhibit 14.2 is a position description for an entry-level operational internal auditor. That is, this listing would identify the type of candidate who does not necessarily have strong CPA-like accounting and auditing skills, but rather can understand and analyze business processes, perform tests, develop descriptive documentation, and make appropriate recommendations. This staff-level operational audit position can be an entry-level slot into the internal audit function. Of course, if a new candidate has a degree in internal auditing, has passed at least portions of the CPA or CIA examinations, or did some internal audit in another enterprise, the candidate should be brought in on a more senior level.

EXHIBIT 14.2 Staff Internal Auditor Position Description

Responsibilities

As a member of the Internal Audit Department and under the direction of an assigned Internal Audit Manager, a Staff Internal Auditor is responsible for planning, developing, performing, reporting, and following up on specific internal audit assignments as directed. Staff Internal Auditor responsibilities must be carried out in accordance with Internal Audit Department procedures, following IIA *International Standards for the Professional Practice of Internal Auditing.*

Specific Duties and Responsibilities

- Prepare or revise audit programs to accomplish objectives, and perform internal audits in accordance with approved audit programs.
- Review and appraise the soundness of internal controls and determine the adequacy of these controls.
- Conduct periodic reviews and tests to ensure compliance with procedures and regulatory requirements, making recommendations for improving current and proposed procedures.
- Review and report on possible internal control weaknesses, violations of corporate business practices, policies, or procedures.
- Perform other job-related internal audit duties as assigned.
- Attend internal/external meetings to expand professional expertise and maintain professional contacts that support assigned functions.

Knowledge and Skills

- Education: B.S. degree or the equivalent of experience and education.
- Interpersonal Skills: A significant level of trust and diplomacy is required, in addition to normal courtesy and tact. Work involves extensive personal contact with others and/or is usually of a personal or sensitive nature. Work may involve motivating or influencing others. Outside contacts become important and fostering sound relationships with other entities (companies and/or individuals) becomes necessary.

Other Skills

- General knowledge of accounting and audit procedures and the ability to work independently
- Must have strong Internet skills, including the ability to search and perform analyses
- Must have a working knowledge of spreadsheets and word processing software; must be able to operate a laptop computer and general office equipment

Where does that entry-level hire go from here? This can often be a challenge, as internal auditors often must have specialized knowledge in accounting and finance or other specialized areas. Many of these knowledge areas can be gained through a strong program of training seminars or just on-the-job experience. As discussed later in this chapter, an internal audit function should implement a strong and ongoing training program for all members of the internal audit function.

Information Systems Audit Specialists

While we have suggested that many staff internal auditors can be successful in an enterprise with only a general knowledge and can learn much more through training, IT specialist internal auditors need extra training and skills. Most if not all internal audit functions need at least one specialist on the internal audit staff with strong IT-related internal control skills covering such areas as systems security, application internal controls, and computer systems operations management. This type of internal auditor skill requirement goes beyond entry-level positions where an entry-level auditor candidate has a bachelor's degree in computer science but little more than a basic understanding of spreadsheets.

The skill requirements for the information systems audit specialists in an internal audit group will very much depend on the technical maturity of the enterprise's IT functions. An enterprise that has its applications based on what is called an enterprise resource planning set of linked applications tied to complex databases will require a different set of information systems audit specialist skills than would an enterprise where most of its IT resources are based on Web-based applications. Due to the span and breadth of ever-changing IT technologies, information systems auditors are faced with a wide range of knowledge requirements. Exhibit 14.3 outlines the basic knowledge requirements that would be expected from an experienced or seasoned information systems audit specialist. These internal audit IT control knowledge requirements will be outlined in greater detailed in Part Five (Chapters 19 through 24).

EXHIBIT 14.3 IT Systems Auditor Basic Knowledge Requirements

An IT systems internal auditor specialist should be expected to have at least a high-level working knowledge of the following areas as demonstrated through past work experiences:

- Business application systems—whether for accounting, business, or other purposes—and the basic balancing and integrity controls surrounding all automated systems.
- Data management processes—whether a formal database or spreadsheet tabled data—and the importance of validating and maintaining that data.
- Computer and Internet security skills. While IT security can be a very complex and specialized skill area, an IT systems auditor should have a basic knowledge of the importance of backups, password controls, and other IT security procedures.
- Storage management and the importance of backup and recovery processes.
- Computer operating systems basic functions—whether on a laptop system or larger system—and the potential risks and vulnerabilities if such systems are not updated or maintained.
- Computer systems architectures, with an emphasis on use of the Web, Information Technology Infrastructure Library, client-server configurations, and telecommunications.
- IT service operations processes, with an emphasis on problem management, access controls, and general application management.
- IT service design processes, with an emphasis on continuity, capacity, and information security management processes.
- Governance and service strategy processes, including essential IT financial management processes.
- Programming or coding techniques sufficient to construct and implement computer-assisted audit procedures appropriate to the enterprise environment.
- Ongoing interest and curiosity to understand and explore newer and evolving technology concepts, such as storage management virtualization.

Finding and recruiting an internal auditor with information systems skills and knowledge can sometimes be a challenge. It is often difficult to find professionals with the appropriate technical skills and then to correctly screen and identify the better candidates. Internal audit hiring managers or CAEs who may have come from more of a CPA-oriented finance and accounting background sometimes have difficulty in identifying appropriate information systems audit specialist candidates. Of course, if the internal audit function has already established an information systems audit function, peer-level interviews for the recruitment process often will be of great help. An enterprise may seek candidates who have achieved Certified Information Systems Auditor (CISA) credentials. The CISA and other internal auditor professional credentials will be discussed in Chapter 29.

In addition to the IT information systems internal auditor controls requirements outlined in Exhibit 14.4, every member of an internal audit function—from the CAE to junior staff auditors—should have some minimal or CBOK level of knowledge covering IT control procedures. With our almost pervasive use of automated and Web tools today, this is fairly common, but there still are a few otherwise competent internal auditors who tend to avoid IT technical matters. In the concluding chapter of this book, Exhibit 34.1 outlines a set of CBOK information systems knowledge requirements for all internal auditors, with explanations of these areas covered in other chapters going forward.

Other Internal Auditor Specialists

Typical internal audit positions range from the CAE in charge of the function to supporting internal audit managers to the internal audit staff to information systems audit specialists. However, depending on the size of the enterprise and the overall nature of internal audit activities, there can be other specialty positions in internal auditor support roles. Much depends on how the responsibilities of internal audit have been defined through its charter. For example, IIA standards define the roles where internal auditors can act as an in-house consultant to their enterprises and when they can act as assurance-level internal auditors. Some enterprises may want to expand that role and establish a full in-house consulting function as part of internal audit. These roles are discussed in Chapter 30 on the role of an internal auditor as an enterprise consultant.

Similarly, there is a whole other branch of internal auditing called quality auditing. These are internal auditors who tend to be more production shop floor–oriented and follow a complementary set of standards from the American Society for Quality in the United States. Quality auditors traditionally have operated as a totally separate function from the IIA-oriented internal auditors who are the main topic of this book. However, we are beginning to see a greater integration between these two audit functions, with those auditors included as part of the normal internal function but serving as specialists. Quality assurance auditing is discussed in Chapter 31.

In addition to internal audit specialists, an enterprise may want to add other support personnel to the internal audit group for such tasks as monitoring and organizing internal control documentation or, for a larger internal audit group, to just support the laptop computers and other resources need by the overall internal audit group. These other professionals would be able to support internal audit's overall mission to review and help improve internal controls in the enterprise—the real purpose for an effective internal audit function in an enterprise.

NOTES

1. Quinlan School of Business, Loyola University Chicago, www.luc.edu/quinlan/undergraduate/majorsminors/accounting/.
2. Louisiana State University, E. J. Ourso, College of Business, Center for Internal Auditing, http://www.bus.lsu.edu/Internal-Audit/Pages/About.aspx.

CHAPTER FIFTEEN

Managing the Internal Audit Universe and Key Competencies

THE OVERALL EMPHASIS THROUGHOUT THIS book has been the common body of knowledge (CBOK) areas that internal auditors should know and understand. Most of these cover areas where internal auditors should gain a great knowledge and understanding, such as Chapter 9 on internal audit professional standards, Chapter 13 on defining an audit scope document or audit universe, Chapter 17 on documenting results through effective workpapers, or Chapter 23 on cybersecurity and privacy controls. Each of these chapters presents an overview of the subject area and points to concepts and issues where an internal auditor can gain a better understanding through additional study, experience, and internal audit activities. However, in addition to these important areas of internal audit understanding, there is a major internal auditor need. In all areas that may be potentially reviewed, internal audit management must have a high-level understanding of the potential auditable areas within the auditor's enterprise and areas of responsibility. This generally is called the audit universe, as was described in Chapter 13; it is a compendium of all areas and processes in an enterprise that may be subject to audit.

Using this audit universe concept can sometimes create problems if there is too much enterprise turmoil, such as frequent organization acquisitions or dispositions. Also, sometimes areas described in the universe are almost too far off the beaten track, and management at various levels sometimes strongly wishes that internal audit would all but stay away. This chapter describes this author's experiences some years ago and problems in trying to use an audit universe document for enterprises that were often in a state of turmoil. We are calling this situation auditing in the weeds, and while company names have been suppressed, these comments are based on this author's experiences of more than 40 years performing and directing internal audits.

To better understand the many specialized internal audit areas included in an audit universe, all internal auditors must establish some key professional competencies. This includes the ability to conduct an effective audit interview and to operate in a professional and credible manner when conducting internal audits. A discussion of these essential internal audit competencies is the second overall theme of this chapter.

Many of our key competency areas cover things that an internal auditor perhaps should have learned well before starting a career and even during the years of acquiring a basic education. This chapter cannot really explain how an internal auditor should conduct an auditee interview, for example, as any such interview depends on the individual internal auditor and the surrounding circumstances. However, a goal of this chapter is to remind internal auditors of subjects and areas that are important to the practice of modern internal auditing. Building an internal audit CBOK has been our ongoing chapter-by-chapter topic, and the internal audit key competencies discussed in this chapter should be fundamental CBOK requirements for all internal auditors. Using the established audit universe and applying these key competencies, an internal auditor should be able to better plan and manage internal audits, as discussed in Chapter 16 on project management, internal audit planning, and other topics.

15.1 AUDITING IN THE WEEDS: PROBLEMS WITH REVIEWS OF NONMAINSTREAM AUDIT AREAS

Enterprises of all sizes and areas of operations grow by acquisition. This typically happens when a corporation wants the products, technology, or even key people that are affiliated with a competitor. Sometimes the smaller unit will be purchased using cash or stock. When the acquisition units are of similar size, the combination will be a merger with one or the other remaining in charge. In almost all cases, the merged unit does not disappear at once but typically becomes a division or some other component of the parent. From an audit universe perspective, such mergers almost always create new auditable entities for the central parent corporation.

These mergers create very different internal control environments, depending on central corporate cultures. Sometimes, the acquiring corporation will send out teams of its own resources to aid and smooth the merger. In other situations, the acquired units will remain almost totally independent with their own functions and operations such that the only evidence of the merger will be the top-level financial reporting arrangements. In his years of managing information technology (IT) internal audit functions and directing the overall internal audit process, this author worked in four different corporate environments, among others, where extensive audit universe lists were used or should have been used to plan and perform internal audits throughout an enterprise.

The paragraphs following describe four corporate environments where this author either directed the overall internal audit function, launched and established an IT audit function, or worked as an IT internal auditor. In the interest of confidentiality, we have not disclosed actual corporate names, but one of this author's example enterprises was eventually acquired by an even larger entity, two went bankrupt and have disappeared, and the fourth is sort of still in operation. Our internal audit experiences with two of these were before the Sarbanes-Oxley Act, but they all point to areas where internal audit functions and processes can always be improved. The following list describes these four corporate entities in general, and the paragraphs that follow describe some of the problems encountered with each when using a sometimes not well-defined audit universe list to drive audit planning activities.

- **Corporation 1, a large international industrial manufacturer later acquired by an even a larger entity.** Years ago, this author was a senior IT internal auditor working at a corporate level. Each of this corporation's major division operating units had its own internal audit functions, with only limited coordination between them and corporate internal audit. Internal audit planning then was before the days of publishing an audit universe when this internal auditor developed his own audit plan and, for example, told his manager, "Hey, I'm finishing that IT controls review in Milan—how about if I review the facility at the Naples plant before flying home?" After a quick telephone call, the Naples audit was launched without too much advance planning.
- **Corporation 2, a now-bankrupt, fairly large, old-line U.S. manufacturing company that had some old-technology dying product lines and products with some international operations. With cash remaining from some declining but still viable products and older good times, the corporation had embarked on a spree of technology-related acquisitions.** This author was in charge of a small IT audit function and reported to a chief audit executive (CAE) who tended to change plans and ground rules on an arbitrary, nonstop basis. Most of the newly acquired entities had weak controls with seemingly little central corporate direction.
- **Corporation 3, another now-bankrupt Midwestern U.S. manufacturing corporation that had old-line roots but more recently had embarked on a wide range of retail, manufacturing, agriculture, and distribution acquisitions.** This author launched their corporation's IT audit function and was responsible for an operational audit team. Although there was an audit universe document that had been developed in earlier, quieter times, corporate acquisitions and dispositions were so frequent that the audit scope was constantly changing.
- **Corporation 4, a once major U.S. corporation with operations in retail, finance, real estate, and insurance.** The author launched the corporate-level IT and finally assumed audit director responsibility for the entire internal audit function. The corporation was very large and had developed and regularly updated an extensive audit universe document that covered many company-owned and company-controlled operations.

We are using these example corporations to discuss some things that can go wrong with the use of just an established audit universe as an aid for effective audit planning. Much more is needed than a list of auditable entities that never can realistically be reviewed. In addition, there is need for strong central management direction to establish an effective internal auditor function for a larger corporation. We have titled this section "Auditing in the Weeds" because a poorly designed or even lack of an overall audit scope can lead an internal audit function off into inappropriate areas—often the weeds in a large corporate enterprise.

The need for some understandings on internal audit review requirements at example corporation 1. As an IT analyst many years ago, this author first became involved with internal audit after being asked to join a newly formed corporate level IT audit function at what we are calling corporation 1. This was years ago and the concept of an audit universe never entered the vernacular. The corporation had separate internal audit functions and staffs at each of its major divisions, but there was no coordination between them at the staff level except for friendly words at a few joint social gatherings. The different audit functions performed similar reviews at various operating units with no attempt to review overall enterprise internal control strengths and weaknesses. Although this took place years ago when this author was not in an internal audit decision-making position, his recollection points out the need for an overall understanding of common internal audit review candidates across an enterprise, even though there may have been common internal control concerns across different operating units within the overall enterprise. We didn't talk about the concept of establishing an audit universe then but it sure would have helped.

No clear understanding of internal audit's scope and responsibilities at example corporation 2. Leaving the large but uncoordinated internal audit function after 10 years with example corporation 1, this author was next asked to form an IT internal audit function for an old technology corporation that was trying to bootstrap itself into the modern world through numerous new technology acquisitions. New IT audit resources were hired and attempts were made to launch effective internal control audit processes. However, the corporation was a mix of the older businesses that were tied to archaic and failing technologies and the recently acquired new businesses that had no connection to the core corporation and looked at headquarters only as a source of funds. The author reported to a CAE who ran things in a cycling crisis mode. There were attempts to institute some good internal audit procedures, but too much time was spent trying to put out multiple raging fires. This author and the IT audit staff he hired soon left for other opportunities, and the corporation was declared bankrupt in the following year or two.

Multiple newer acquisitions lacking corporate guidance and IT support at example corporation 3. This author spent three years with what we are calling example corporation 3 during the era of go-go creative financing in which this enterprise acquired a large array of smaller independent companies ranging from regional retail chains to farm-building manufacturing to machine tools to lumber and agricultural products and more. Corporation 3 easily got the financing to buy these businesses, and the original owners probably did well, but there was little follow-up from corporation 3 except for monthly financial reporting rules and a copy of the corporate human resources manual. For example, there was essentially no corporate IT support.

Although there was never a formal audit universe document, internal audit was expected to visit and survey these new units. Even though Institute of Internal Auditors standards at that time prohibited internal auditors from acting as consultants, the internal auditors visiting these newly acquired units were encouraged by senior management to act like consultants and discuss their thoughts and observations.

Corporation 3 was growing rapidly by acquisition, and internal audit support was fairly haphazard across these business units. Internal audit plans were assembled but were usually not met due to rapid enterprise changes. Shortly after this author left the company, corporation 3 attempted to acquire an even bigger target, got in over its head perhaps, and was eventually forced into bankruptcy. The internal audit department was dissolved except for the CAE, who was given a "turn out the lights" type of job to help to wind things down.

The problems with too large an audit universe at example corporation 4. After the continual crises at our example corporation 3, we spent the next eight years at a major public accounting firm taking roles as a national director of IT audit and managing a consulting practice. We were then invited to launch a corporate-level IT audit function at a very large major company that had been in business for many years. Although internal audit operated independently at the major divisions, there had been no central, corporate-level IT audit function even though the company's IT resources were centralized. There was an established and annually updated audit universe schedule for this example corporation #4 that was very large, consisting of a number of retail and distribution units, business processing centers, and customer service centers, as well as a plethora of others where the corporation had effective financial interests. There also was a sizable internal audit staff but poor risk-based planning processes in place. Some units received frequent internal audits, perhaps because they were close to the homes of nearby field auditors, while others never hit the audit candidate radar scope.

When this author took responsibility for this immense audit universe, a plan was developed to divide the universe into certain high-risk and must-perform internal audit candidates and the rest. Most of those other units had been on the audit universe list for years but were never considered as internal audit candidates. This author wanted to establish some internal audit coverage over these smaller units. A plan was developed to use statistical sampling, following the same techniques described in Chapter 10, to select remaining audit candidates from the large and diverse audit universe list.

The sample selection plan and approach were sold to and accepted by senior management and external audit. Our first implementation, however, resulted in several problems. Although audit sampling theory says that every item in the population should have an equal probability of selection, the first attempt to use this plan resulted in some really strange audit candidates. For example, the audit selection identified an operational facility audit at a very small company-owned termite eradication service in rural West Texas.

From a cost and risk perspective, it was very hard to justify an internal audit at such a facility. The recommendation here was to suggest organizing this termite eradication facility with other small freestanding units into some business group. Also, the audit universe selection process was modified so that such very small, low-risk potential operational audits would have some, but a very minimal, chance of audit selection. They could still remain on the audit universe list with a minimal chance of audit selection.

15.2 IMPORTANCE OF AN AUDIT UNIVERSE SCHEDULE: WHAT IS RIGHT OR WRONG

Based on our work and internal audit experiences over the years, the previous paragraphs describe how an enterprise internal audit function can have problems if it does not have adequate planning procedures supported by an audit universe schedule. Problems also occur if such an audit universe schedule is too detailed, listing areas that will never or should never be subject to an internal audit review. Of course, the audit universe schedule should list the entities that internal audit should include in its plans and reviews. If the enterprise is so flexible that everything is constantly changing, there may be some need to rethink overall internal audit strategy.

An enterprise internal audit function, led by its CAE, should develop an audit universe schedule subject to reviews and approvals by the audit committee and senior management. Such an audit universe may not cover every unit in the enterprise, as some are just too small, low-risk, or too technically complex to be considered for regular internal audit reviews. However, once an internal audit function has established its scope of potential areas to review, the CAE and other members of the audit team can subject these potential audit areas to risk analysis and otherwise develop overall internal audit activity plans.

Chapter 13 contains some descriptions and examples of developing and applying an audit universe schedule. The audit universe is a scope description of internal audit's auditable entities for an enterprise—not what is necessarily included in the current annual audit plan but what internal audit management considers being within their scope. In some respects, it can be considered a defense mechanism for when management or a member of the audit committee asks why internal audit did not review some area after some sort of crisis. However, the current audit universe should not be used as a crutch. The audit universe defines overall internal audit scope in a big picture manner.

There is no formal publication requirement, format, or approval process for an internal audit universe schedule. Internal audit should assess the current universe when reviewing annual audit plans with the audit committee. The CAE and other members of the internal audit management team should be responsible for changes to this schedule, and any updates should be given to the audit committee.

15.3 IMPORTANCE OF INTERNAL AUDIT KEY COMPETENCIES

What skills are essential to be a successful internal auditor? There are many, and they usually include having attained at least a four-year college degree in an area that will give the new auditor an understanding of the importance of business operations as well as the ability to be able to easily observe areas of operations and to describe them through written and verbal methods. More importantly and even more fundamentally, an internal auditor must have strong personal ethics and a work-related commitment. That is, when an internal auditor is sent to some auditee site or location to perform a review, the internal auditor must maintain a professional demeanor and conduct his or her work in an honest and ethical manner. These things are fundamental and necessary to build a set of internal auditor key competencies.

We have defined internal audit key competencies as some of the skills necessary to conduct effective internal audits. While some internal audit professionals may look at these selections differently, adding or deleting some, our recommendation for internal audit key competencies include:

- **Interview skills.** Whether interviewing a unit manager or staff members on a production floor, an internal auditor should be able to easily meet with these people, ask appropriate questions, and then gain the desired information.
- **Analytical skills.** The internal auditor should have the ability to look at a series of sometimes disconnected events and data and to draw some preliminary conclusions from that material.
- **Testing and analysis skills.** Related to analytical skills, being able to review a series of events or populations of data to perform tests that will determine if audit objectives are effective is another tool an internal auditor should have.

- **Documentation skills.** An internal auditor should be able to take the results of audit observations as well as any tests and to document those results, both verbally and graphically, to describe the environment that was observed.
- **Recommending results and corrective actions.** Based on documented testing and analysis results, an internal auditor should be able to develop effective recommendations for corrective actions.
- **Communication skills.** Whether to the staff that was subject to the audit or to senior management, an internal auditor should be able to communicate the results of the audit work along with recommendations for corrective actions.
- **Negotiating skills.** Since there can always be differences of opinion on internal audit findings and recommendations, an internal auditor should have the ability to negotiate successful final results.
- **Commitments to learning.** Internal auditors are always experiencing new changes and materials in their enterprise operations and the profession; they must have a passion for learning and continuing their education.

These listed points represent some really key competencies and skills that are necessary to perform effective internal audits, no matter what industry, geographic area, or type of internal audit. The sections following discuss some of these key competencies in greater detail.

15.4 IMPORTANCE OF INTERNAL AUDIT RISK MANAGEMENT

Risk management was not a commonly recognized internal audit skill in its earlier days. In the 1982, fourth edition of this book, and before this author became a participant, it was not even mentioned. However, today risk management should be viewed as an important internal auditor CBOK competency requirement. Risk management is discussed in Chapter 7 on COSO ERM and should be considered as a four-step process: (1) risk identification, (2) quantitative or qualitative assessments of the documented risks, (3) risk prioritization and response planning, and (4) risk monitoring. This process should be implemented at all levels of the enterprise and as part of virtually all internal audit reviews. These common risks can occur because of a wide variety of circumstances ranging from poor financial decisions to changes in consumer tastes to new government regulations.

Whether an enterprise is small, with few facilities in a limited geographic area, or is a large, global enterprise, it should develop internal risk management approaches. This is particularly important for the worldwide enterprises so common today. They may have multiple units engaged in different business operations and facilities in different countries. Some risks in one unit may directly impact or be related to risks in another, but other risk considerations may be effectively independent from the whole. Internal auditors should strive to identify and understand the various risks facing an enterprise in the course of their internal audit work, to assess those risks in terms of their cost or impact and probability, to develop responses in the event of a risk occurrence, and to develop documentation procedures to describe what happened as well as appropriate corrective actions going forward.

15.5 INTERNAL AUDITOR INTERVIEW SKILLS

Internal auditor interviews with members of auditee management are an important first step in the internal audit process. Based on the established audit universe, as discussed previously, internal audit functions will plan to perform a review of some area, whether an assessment of internal controls, a review of operational controls, or any of many other types of audit assessments. The internal audit function will structure some preliminary plans for those planned reviews, including identifying the audit objectives, timing, and internal audit resources to be assigned. These planning steps are discussed in Chapter 16. The next step in this process is for the assigned in-charge internal auditor to meet with designated members of the auditee organization for an initial internal audit interview.

That initial interview and all others that follow are keys in the internal audit process. They are valuable first steps to launch an internal audit and to gather information, but a poorly prepared or organized auditee interview can throw the internal audit so far off course that it may be difficult to complete things as planned or contemplated. All internal audit interview meetings, whether with auditee management and team associates, should receive some internal audit preparation before launching the meeting.

Once an internal auditor has scheduled an auditee interview, the auditor should begin to focus on interview preparation. An internal auditor should never be fooled into thinking that he or she can simply walk into an auditee interview and just inform them of the planned audit. The auditee manager may have comments that "the timing is bad," the audit objectives seem misstated, or "all of that was covered" in some past period review. An internal auditor's goal must be to demonstrate the objectives of the planned review, as well as the auditor's knowledge and qualifications for the planned internal audit. Adequate preparation is key!

Internal auditors will be involved with auditee and other management group meetings or interviews on a regular, ongoing basis. These meetings are the contact points to launch new internal audits as well as to review the status and continuing progress of internal audits. Such meetings are generally not formal and often involve an internal auditor just meeting a manager at a nearby office desk or in a canteen over coffee. The real skill and competency need here is that an internal auditor should carefully plan objectives and even expected outcomes from such sessions, and then should conduct them in a planned, orderly manner. The last thing a professional internal auditor should do is to burst in on an auditee manager with no warning and then just blurt out some internal auditor concerns. The internal auditor's objectives will not be met in that situation, and internal audit will lose credibility in the eyes of enterprise management.

15.6 INTERNAL AUDIT ANALYTICAL AND TESTING SKILLS COMPETENCIES

According to a definition from the Web source Wikipedia, *analytical skills* refers to the ability to visualize, articulate, and solve complex problems and concepts, and come to decisions that make sense based on available information. Such skills include demonstration of the ability to apply logical thinking to gathering and analyzing information, designing and testing solutions to problems, and formulating plans. To test for analytical skills, an internal auditor might be asked to look for inconsistencies in some production report, to put a series of events in their proper order, or to critically read a project status report and identify potential errors. An analytical review usually requires an internal auditor to review some audit evidence materials and then to use logic to pick apart a problem and come up with a solution.

Internal auditors are expected to use analytical processes on a regular basis. The idea is not to jump into an audit with an already assumed conclusion, but to break down the elements of whatever data or series of events is being analyzed in order to reach a conclusion, and this may very well not always be the conclusion the auditor expected to reach. To be truly analytical, an internal auditor needs to think about all of the factors involved in a situation and then evaluate the pluses and minuses in order to develop a recommended solution.

There are a large number of analytical tools, some simple and others very complex, that an internal auditor can use to support internal control reviews. At a very basic level, an internal auditor can check whether some account either is or is not approved or an account either does or does not balance. The auditor's analytical skill comes from accumulating these results and reporting them in terms of statistical measures. In other cases, an ever-greater number of decision criteria are not that clear-cut, and an auditor might have the task of reviewing whether the separate documentation packages for a large set of product descriptions was adequate. While some packages may be missing, causing a failed audit test for that condition, many other documentation packages may be only sort of in place.

Internal auditor analytical skills are a key CBOK competency that can aid internal audit decisions to be developed in a consistent, organized manner. Too often, some professionals think of the terms *analytics* and *analytical analysis* as being related to a detailed, mathematically oriented process. Internal auditors should use analysis to describe their use of a well-documented, well-reasoned decision approach in their internal audit activities.

While internal auditors should use an analytical approach to develop their initial decision strategies, their next challenge and required key competency is to develop tests to review and assess the materials. Chapter 10 discusses audit sampling, with an emphasis on statistical and judgmental sampling. As a key internal audit competency, testing or sampling can be viewed in a broader perspective as a key CBOK competency, and Exhibit 15.1 describes some alternative audit testing approaches. The first of these, observation, is often not thought of in terms of the concept of testing. While an analytical approach, with established review and acceptance criteria, is often used to organize an observation-based testing process, other valid testing approaches can be used as well.

No matter what method is selected, internal auditors should always take appropriate steps to make certain that the samples they are testing are representative of the overall population analyzed. In the past, internal auditors sometimes just selected a couple of items of audit evidence from the top or head of a group of items and then made their audit recommendations based on this "sample" even though it may not have been

EXHIBIT 15.1 Selected Audit Alternative Testing Approaches

Physical Observation

A testing approach is used for processes that are difficult to formally document or control, for example, IT service desk problem analysis, stockroom cleanliness, or customer service practices that are important to the enterprise's image, but usually are not formally controlled. These factors can be especially important to organizational success when considered in broader contexts, such as assessments of employee morale or the professional tone of an office. Because these areas are somewhat subjective, developing internal audit recommendations can be difficult.

Independent Evaluations

An audit confirmation is an example of an independent confirmation. While this technique is more common with external auditors, internal auditors can sometimes find it useful as well. For example, confirmation letters can be sent to enterprise vendors to verify their compliance with some matter.

Compliance Tests

Compliance testing helps determine whether controls are functioning as intended. When conducting compliance tests, internal auditors often use one broad sample to test several items concurrently. However, multiple samples are sometimes very effective. As an example, for disbursement testing, an auditor can use one sample to test documentation and approval of disbursements, another to assess contract approvals and agreement to payments, and a third to test personal reimbursements. Such targeted tests can yield much clearer results than using one sample to test all three items.

Exception or Deficiency Testing

If a reporting system shows deficient performance, exceptions can be reviewed in detail to understand root causes and determine possible resolutions. Many process improvements require coordination with other departments or persons involved in the process; internal audit involvement in deficiency resolution frequently facilitates such coordination.

Accuracy Testing

Tests for accuracy help determine whether reviewed processes are measuring or assessing the right things and calculating results correctly. Much of today's reporting contains significant "black box" elements, where the underlying calculations are embedded in computer programs and intermediate files. By using CAATT procedures and gaining an understanding of the reporting objectives, internal auditors can effectively verify systems reporting accuracy.

particularly representative of the entire population. An understanding of the sampling and testing process should be a key internal audit competency.

The other requirement for this internal audit competency is the appropriate analysis of the test results. Once an internal auditor has selected a sample and performed an internal audit test, the results should be analyzed. Having taken or pulled such a sample according to the established audit objectives, an internal auditor should then review sample results for any possible errors to determine whether they are actually errors and, if appropriate, the nature and cause of the errors. For those that are assessed as errors, the errors found should be projected, as appropriate, to the item population, if a statistically based sampling method is used. Any possible errors detected in the sample should be reviewed to determine whether they are actually errors. Internal auditors should consider the qualitative aspects of the errors, including the nature and cause of the errors and the possible effect of the errors on the other phases of the audit. Internal auditors should also realize that errors that are the result of the breakdown of an IT process ordinarily have wider implications for error rates than do human errors.

Internal auditors should always take care to analyze and document their test sample results. Every effort should be devoted to making sure that the test results are representative of the overall population of items reviewed. When the audit results, as sometimes occurs, just do not "smell" right, an internal auditor should conduct any follow-up procedures that are necessary. However, the process of establishing audit objectives, pulling a sample of items of interest to ascertain if audit objectives are being met, and then reporting these results is a key internal audit internal audit competency.

15.7 INTERNAL AUDITOR DOCUMENTATION SKILLS

Internal auditors have a major challenge to prepare meaningful and helpful documentation covering all of their work, whether informal notes from a meeting to audit workpapers or the final issued audit report. Internal auditors have an ongoing need to develop strong audit work documentation skills. However, in our electronic world of powerful word processing, wireless, and social media communications, that documentation can sometimes get out of hand. Developing effective workpapers and internal audit reports is discussed in Chapters 17 and 18, respectively, and the section following in this chapter discusses documenting results in workpapers.

Perhaps every internal auditor has received a documentation-oriented word processing message describing an area of audit interest with some sort of supporting message attached. Documentation becomes a challenge when the first supporting attachment has its own attachment, several of which have more attachments, and on and on. Perhaps this type of a stream of attached documents provides the necessary and supporting information, but all too often such trails of attachments lead to ambiguities and problems. An internal audit function should establish some best practice standards for its internal electronic documentation. In some cases, the major automation software tools—such as Microsoft Office—will make this easy, but in other situations, there is a need to work around the vendor-supplied software. For example, Microsoft's Excel spreadsheet package does not have a strong revision control facility, and internal auditors will often need to establish their own revision control processes.

Exhibit 15.2 describes some internal audit e-office documentation best practices. We are using the term *e-office* to refer to the many word processing, spreadsheet, e-mail, and other forms of electronic documentation that an internal audit function will need to support the internal audit work beyond formal workpaper binders and issued audit reports both within the audit office and for auditor laptop systems. Whenever possible, these standards should be consistent with IT department standards, but the objective should always be to support the overall internal audit effort. If all members of the internal audit team use standard practices, such as Microsoft Word document revision

EXHIBIT 15.2 Internal Audit E-office Documentation Best Practices

A substantial amount of internal audit supporting documentation and other activities takes place on computer systems, whether auditor laptops, desktop machines tied to an audit office wireless network, or even on terminals connected to a central server processor. All of these comprise the e-office—the use of e-mail, word-processing, spreadsheets, databases, graphics, and other tools. The following are some best practices that internal audit should consider when implementing an effective internal audit e-office:

1. **Establish hardware and software standards.** Whether they are at an internal audit office in a remote, developing region or at corporate headquarters, all members of internal audit should use the same general hardware and software product suite.
2. **Use password-based security rules with regular updates.** Because of the sensitive information that internal audit encounters, password controls, with requirements for frequent changes, should be implemented on all systems—even auditor's personal laptops.
3. **Build security awareness.** All members of the audit team should be instructed in the sensitive nature of audit documents. For example, when documents are printed on a remote office printer, establish rules that the initiator must be present during the printing process. Even better, avoid printing internal audit documents at a remote location.
4. **Backup, backup, and backup.** Strong procedures should be established for at least 100% daily backups of internal audit file folders. A rotating stream of several cycles of backups should be established.
5. **Establish file revision control procedures.** Through the use of file naming conventions or software system controls, conventions should be established to identify all documents with the date created and a revision number.
6. **Build templates and establish style protocols.** All memos, audit programs, audit plans, and other key internal audit documents should be required to use the same common formats.
7. **Establish e-mail style rules.** While there are many needs and requirements for e-mail messages, some general style rules should be established. In addition, define and recognize areas that should be released as a controlled document rather that an e-mail message subject to forwarding.
8. **Establish e-mail attachment rules.** While attaching documents is an easy way to convey information, it can get out of hand with attachments attached to attachments, and so on. Guidance rules should be established here.
9. **Actively implement and monitor antivirus and firewall tools.** Effective software should be installed, regularly updated, and violations monitored, as appropriate.
10. **Limit personal use.** Whether a laptop brought to the auditor's home, downloaded music files, or a night-school paper typed in the office, personal use of e-office resources should be limited, if not prohibited.
11. **Establish locks and security rules for portable machines.** All auditor laptop machines should be configured with locking devices and guidance in their use should be provided. In addition, security audit guidance should be established for all portable machines.
12. **Monitor compliance.** A member of the internal audit team should periodically review and monitor compliance with auditor e-office procedures. Process and performance improvements should be installed as appropriate.

controls, internal audit will have greater success in controlling its own automation processes. As we have stressed several times in other chapters, internal audit standards in such areas as office documentation should try to be at least as good as if not better than the enterprise's overall standards.

Going beyond our comments about effective internal audit e-documentation, all internal auditors should develop strong skills and competencies in documenting every aspect of their work. Internal auditors should always keep in mind that their documentation, at all levels, may be subject to other reviews or disclosures. Whether it is a request from an audit committee member, an external audit, a court order, or even a government action, poorly prepared or inaccurate documentation could embarrass or even endanger the enterprise and damage both the internal audit function and the internal auditor (see Exhibit 15.3).

EXHIBIT 15.3 Internal Audit Documentation Best Practices

Best practices for increasing the quality of internal audit documentation include:

1. **Writing Narratives and Descriptions**
   - Describe all work in a narrative fashion such that an outsider can review some materials in place and understand the activities or processes.
   - Document the audit concepts observed or performed, but do not describe assumptions of speculative ideas.
   - Generate systems-related documentation with use of hyperlinks where appropriate.
2. **Simplification**
   - Keep documentation just simple enough, but not too simple—this is often an internal audit challenge.
   - Write the fewest documents with the least overlap.
   - Put information in the most appropriate places—that is, allow the reader to quickly grasp the main elements of a documentation package without having to go through multiple addendums.
   - Display key information publicly by including summaries and brief descriptions where appropriate.
   - Use a whiteboard, corkboard, or an internal web site—whatever is necessary to promote the transfer of information and thus communication.
3. **Determining What to Document**
   - Document with a purpose. For example, documentation describing test results should have a whole different focus and content than material designed for the audit staff.
   - Focus on the needs of the actual intended users(s) of the documentation, who would determine its sufficiency.
4. **Determining When to Document**
   - Iterate, iterate, iterate. Take evolutionary (iterative and incremental) approaches to gain feedback for materials under scrutiny.
   - Find better ways to communicate, recognizing that documentation supports knowledge transfer, but it is only one of several options available.
   - Keep documentation current. Materials that aren't kept up to date are of little value to most users.
   - Update documentation regularly, but internal audit should not devote too much time and resources to almost trivial issues. That is, documentation preparation resources must be balanced with other key internal audit activities.
5. **General**
   - Always recognize documentation as a requirement. It should not be postponed as a "when time is available" activity.
   - Require users to justify documentation requests. Check-out and back-in processes should be established.
   - Build a recognition throughout internal audit of the need for strong supporting documentation.
   - Provide documentation preparation training to all members of the internal audit team.

15.8 RECOMMENDING RESULTS AND CORRECTIVE ACTIONS

A very strong role—perhaps the most important—of an internal auditor is reporting the results of the internal audit work and developing strong recommendations for corrective actions, as appropriate. Internal auditors go through this exercise when creating their audit reports, as discussed in Chapter 18, or when serving as an enterprise internal consultant, discussed in Chapter 30. In all cases, an internal auditor needs to have the key skills to summarize the results of some audit work, to discuss what was wrong, and to develop some recommendations for effective corrective action.

While developing audit reports and their recommendations is often the responsibility of only senior, in-charge internal auditors or even the CAE, all members of the audit team should establish a competency to describe an audit finding and to make a recommendation for improvement. In some cases, a staff auditor will only go through this exercise as part of a workpaper note, but all internal auditors should think of much of their audit work in terms of:

- What were the objectives of this audit or exercise?
- What was found?
- Why were those audit findings incorrect or not in compliance?
- What can be done to correct this error or control breakdown?
- What are internal audit's recommendations for corrective action?

This is a review that is very much part of the overall internal audit process. Internal auditors at all levels should develop competencies to think of much of their work along those lines. Of course, it is always important that an internal auditor can think of or answer these questions in clear and simple enough terms that recipients can understand the issue and the nature of the suggested corrective action. This concept can become particularly difficult if the audit finding covers a complex or potentially obscure area. For example, an audit finding that covers an internal control weakness caused by an incorrect setting in an IT operating system production library will be difficult for many to comprehend. However, using analogies or other mechanisms, internal auditors should strive to prepare findings and recommendations in a way that is easily understood.

The preparation of effective internal audit reports, with meaningful findings and recommendations, is a very import competency area for all internal auditors. However, internal auditors at all levels should develop the skills to discuss and present audit findings and the related internal audit recommendations. This communication can take place in the workplace at all levels.

Internal auditors typically receive, review, and have access to a large amount of potentially confidential information. For that reason, it is very important that strong security controls be placed over all internal audit files and retained data. However, internal auditors at all levels should develop the skills and demeanor to interact with others in the enterprise to communicate about their work as appropriate and to help allow others in the enterprise to understand the value of internal auditing to an enterprise.

These comments were somewhat due to this author's experience where he encountered, as part of his enterprise consulting work, some totally noncommunicative internal audit functions. Involved in several recent IT consulting assignments, we encountered internal audit functions that were quite properly located in secure facilities but where audit staff members had essentially no contact with other enterprise members. The internal auditors, in both cases, checked into the office, went to their internal audit office area, closed doors, and were not seen until the end of the work day. Perhaps working on other critical projects, other members of those enterprises were not at all impressed with this total lack of communication. Whether presenting the results of an internal audit to local management or dealing with others on a day-to-day basis, all internal auditors should develop some strong communication skills. This is another internal audit key competency.

15.9 INTERNAL AUDITOR NEGOTIATION SKILLS

Whether it is the recommendations developed in an audit report or those developed in the process of reviewing audit evidence on the shop floor, internal auditors will encounter many areas where management and others will disagree with the auditor's assumptions or potential audit findings. There is seldom a need for an "I'm right because I'm the auditor" type of attitude. There can be many areas where an internal auditor will encounter a difference of opinion during a review or even where the internal auditor is just wrong.

Negotiation is something that we do all the time and is not used only for business or internal audit purposes. For example, we use it in our social lives perhaps for deciding a time to meet, or where to go on a rainy day. Negotiation is usually considered as a compromise to settle an argument or issue to benefit the internal auditor and others as much as possible.

Communication is always the link that internal auditors should use to negotiate issues or arguments, whether it is done face-to-face, on the telephone, or in writing. However, internal auditors as all levels should recognize the negotiation is not always between two people; it can involve an internal auditor with multiple members of an auditee group.

Internal auditors at all levels should learn negotiation skills as they complete their audit reports and prepare recommendations. There are always issues here, but internal auditors should recognize that any type of audit finding, no matter how seemingly inconsequential, will be viewed as a criticism by auditee management. Sometimes an internal auditor will encounter a situation where auditee management wants to fight internal audit on every point, no matter how trivial or how solid the audit finding. Internal auditors should develop skills to negotiate and compromise on some items or areas, but should always reserve the right to say that something is wrong and it needs to be reported; any disagreement from the auditee can be covered in the responses to the audit report and interactions with the audit committee, if necessary.

Exhibit 15.4 outlines some elements of the negotiating process. Although prepared to describe the overall negotiation process in a very general manner, internal auditors should keep these processes in mind when discussing any disputed audit findings and recommendations. Many of the points in this exhibit describe the kinds of issues that internal auditors should have in mind when presenting a draft audit report and wrapping things up. That is, even though internal auditors will expect agreement with recommendations, they should go into a closing meeting fully understanding possible objections and why internal audit is making the recommendation. As a cautionary note here, when an internal auditor agrees to modify a suggested recommendation or even drop an audit finding, the matter should always be documented in as much detail as possible and with an emphasis on why the internal audit or decided to change some matter.

EXHIBIT 15.4 Key Elements of the Negotiating Process

This schedule describes the negotiation process in a very general manner. Internal auditors should consider this approach in such areas as discussed disputed audit evidence and making disputed audit report recommendations.

Phase I: Beginning the Negotiation—Prebargaining

1. **Information**: Learn as much as you can about the audit issue or problem to be discussed. What information do you need from the other side?
2. **Leverage evaluation**: Evaluate your leverage or relative negotiating power and the other party's leverage at the outset. This is important because there may be a number of things you can do to improve your leverage or diminish the leverage of the other side. What will you do to enhance your leverage?
3. **Analysis**: What are the issues? This is particularly important when beginning a review of what might be a contentious audit report.
4. **Rapport**: Establish rapport with the auditee and your opponent(s). Internal audit needs to determine early on if your opponents are going to be cooperative; if not, consider employing a senior member of management as a possible mediator as soon as practical.
5. **Goals and expectations**: Goals are one thing; expectations are something else. What does internal audit expect to get out of the session?
6. **Type of negotiation**: What type of negotiation do you expect? Will this be highly competitive, cooperative, or something unusual? Will you be negotiating face to face, by fax, through a mediator, or in some other manner?
7. **Budget**: Every negotiation has its costs. Internal audit may have to divert staff and management time that it could be spending on other audit efforts to meet and negotiate. Unless you are willing to allocate unlimited time and resources, you will have to make some hard choices, which should be designed to give you the "most bang for your buck."
8. **Plan**: Develop a tentative negotiation plan.

Phase II: Bargaining Phase

1. **Logistics**: When, where, and how will you negotiate? This can be especially important when multiple units or locations are involved in the process.
2. **Opening offers**: What is the best offer you can justify? For example, should you modify or throw out one of several disputed audit recommendations? Should you make an offer, or wait to let another party go first?
3. **Subsequent offers**: How should you adjust your negotiating plan when responding to unanticipated moves by your opponent?
4. **Tactics**: What sort of tactics will you employ? What sort of tactics is your opponent using on you?
5. **Concessions**: What concessions will you make? How will you make them?
6. **Resolution**: What is the best way to resolve the problem? Is there an elegant solution? Be on constant lookout for compromise and creative solutions.

Phase III: Closure Phase

1. **Logistics**: How and when will you close the negotiation meeting? At this meeting or later on when internal audit presents a revised draft document?
2. **Documentation**: Prepare detailed documentation describing the session, with an emphasis on planned changes and agreements by both parties.
3. **Emotional closure**: In wrapping up a meeting, it is important to address the underlying interests and needs of the parties. If you neglect the latter, the agreement will probably not sustain.
4. **Implementation**: Whether internal audit agrees to make some changes in a draft audit report and the auditee agrees to change some disputed practice, the negotiated agreement is of little value unless matters are implemented promptly.

15.10 AN INTERNAL AUDITOR COMMITMENT TO LEARNING

A very significant internal auditor key competency is that all internal auditors should develop a strong commitment to learning. This really should go beyond the 40 hours of continuing education requirement for Certified Internal Auditors as outlined in Chapter 29. Business and technology are always changing, as are the political and regulatory climates in which enterprises operate. All internal auditors should embrace this commitment to constant and ongoing learning as a very key competency.

In many respects, the topics in many of the chapters of this book should help expand an internal auditor's commitment to learning. Two examples of this type of learning need can be found in Chapter 19 on IT general controls and ITIL (formerly Information Technology Infrastructure Library) best practices. While many internal auditors understand the importance of IT general controls, the ITIL best practices have not been a common area of interest among internal auditors, let alone IT functions in the United States. That chapter describes ITIL on a high level and why it is important from an IT internal control perspective. Similarly, Chapter 34 introduces International Accounting Standards and Internal Audit Worldwide. International accounting standards, as a substitute for the U.S.-based generally accepted accounting principles (GAAP), have been growing in acceptance in the world, country by country and region by region, with the United States as the only major holdout. In 2008, the Securities and Exchange Commission in the United States set some tentative rules for a conversion from GAAP to these international standards, but they were followed by many objections. As of this publication date, the United States still has not converted to the international standards. Chapter 34 gives a very high-level overview of these international standards, and although many internal auditors will not be involved in these accounting standard rules at all, they impact the reporting of financial results; and in making a commitment to learning, internal auditors should at least learn a little more about the international standards and how they will impact processes in the United States. This is an example of an issue where an internal auditor should be aware and have some general knowledge of the issues.

15.11 IMPORTANCE OF INTERNAL AUDITOR CORE COMPETENCIES

In this chapter we have tried to emphasize both the concept of an audit universe and some key internal auditor competencies that go beyond such areas as internal audit standards or planning and performing effective internal audits. While some may want to place more emphasis or less on certain competency areas, these are generally areas in which all internal auditors will need to operate successfully.

Following our overall chapter-by-chapter internal auditor CBOK theme, these competencies are essential to all internal auditors. While topics such as good communication skills or a commitment to learning are less knowledge areas than good practices, a strong familiarity and use of the key internal audit competencies discussed in this chapter should be required elements in every internal auditor's CBOK.

CHAPTER SIXTEEN

Planning Audits and Understanding Project Management

INTERNAL AUDITORS ARE FACED WITH their own and management demands to plan and complete their internal audits in a timely fashion, making efficient use of available audit resources, and to complete internal audit reviews of the overall array of internal audit candidates in their audit universe. Even though the audit committee, senior enterprise management, or even internal audit management may request that some area or function should be audited, internal audit needs a plan to perform such individual reviews. Internal auditors should think of performing an individual internal audit as a project, a special effort that requires planning, budgeting, and the allocation of resources. Each audit is a one-time effort that requires planning, execution, and a formal audit report. This chapter first discusses the overall process of project planning and then expands those general project planning techniques to planning for individual internal audits.

Internal auditors will need to assess the effectiveness of project management internal controls in many of their operational reviews, as well as use good project management techniques in many of their internal audit activities. Effective project planning techniques are important in many areas of enterprise activity, whether it be moving office facilities, launching a new marketing effort, or implementing a new IT system, and internal auditors should have a common body of knowledge (CBOK) understanding of project management best practices. These are important when planning and executing an individual internal audit and also when reviewing project planning activities in many operational areas in an enterprise.

While this and many other chapters describe a body of knowledge for internal auditors—our often referenced CBOK—this chapter will first introduce the Project Management Institute's Project Management Body of Knowledge (PMBOK) standards and discuss why these concepts are also important for internal auditors. Project management best practices should be an important tool for planning and performing all levels of internal audits. A project-based internal audit approach should generally improve internal audit's management and performance processes.

The project management concepts described in this chapter should help to plan and perform individual internal audits, as discussed in Chapter 15. Whether working at a staff planning individual internal audits or planning for more major audit activities, the use of good project management techniques should improve the internal audit function. These skills should be part of every internal auditor's CBOK, and the chapter will conclude with a discussion of the importance of planning and organizing individual internal audit efforts as projects.

16.1 THE PROJECT MANAGEMENT PROCESS

In past years, the term *project* was often used rather loosely and did not mean much to many internal auditors. While they talked about their reviews as "audits" and did not think of them as projects, people in other areas of the enterprise would be asked to organize a "project" to implement some special effort, and the organization and planning efforts for such a venture meant different things to different people. Those efforts often involved a designated lead person calling the project group together and doing little more than organizing the effort along the lines of "I want you, you, and you" to perform various project tasks, with little thought given to project enterprise and planning. These informal efforts often failed because the project team did not understand their individual as well as overall objectives, and neither time requirements nor the project scope were defined. In many instances, there were project time and budget overruns or the project failed for other reasons. Often that failure was due to the lack of a consistent, structured project management approach.

Several other project-related definitions are important here. Project managers often use the term *program* when discussing multiple projects. A program usually refers to a senior-level project used to manage or control a series of related or connected projects. For example, an enterprise may want to implement some fairly large initiative that is divided into a series of separate projects. Each of these projects can operate independently, but a program structure will manage all of them together. This chapter will generally refer to a project both as one single effort and as a program of multiple projects. An annual internal audit plan, consisting of multiple planned internal audits, can be called the annual program of planned audits for a period.

Historically, project management had been a poorly defined concept. Except for some U.S. government–led approaches, there was no consistent approach to project management. Matters changed in the mid-1990s when the *Project Management Institute (PMI)* (www.pmi.org), a project management professional organization, was launched. Started by a small group of U.S. professionals looking for a more consistent definition of their work, PMI today is an international professional organization of over 2.9 million members in virtually every country worldwide. PMI has researched, developed, and published a wide range of project management guidance materials. Its most significant document is a standards-like document called *A Guide to the Project*

Management Body of Knowledge (PMBOK), a comprehensive guide to all aspects of the project management process. Although not published as a government rules–type document, PMBOK has become the worldwide professional standard for project management practices. Exhibit 16.1 contains elements of the PMI's definition of a project. It is a fairly extensive description covering many activities, but an internal auditor should think of this definition in terms of how an individual internal audit is organized and managed. We will be discussing more of this project management process in the sections to follow.

In addition to the PMBOK guidance covering individual projects, additional PMI materials include guidance for program and *portfolio management* as well as a standard for organizational project management, OPM3. *Program management* generally refers to a series of related projects, while portfolio management covers standards for a suite of projects and programs within an enterprise. The concepts of OPM3 can be useful for organizing and managing an internal audit function and will be discussed in a later section.

PMI also has a certification program in which a PMI member who completes a professional examination and satisfies experience requirements can be certified as a PMP, or Project Management Professional.

EXHIBIT 16.1 PMI Definition of a Project

A project is a temporary endeavor undertaken to create a unique product, service, or result. The temporary nature of projects indicates that a project has a definite beginning and end. The end is reached when the project's objectives have been achieved or when the project is terminated because its objectives will not or cannot be met, or when the need for the project no longer exists. A project may also be terminated if the client (customer, sponsor, or champion) wishes to terminate it. *Temporary* does not necessarily mean the duration of the project is short. It refers to the project's engagement and its longevity. This term does not typically apply to the product, service, or result created by the project; most projects are undertaken to create a lasting outcome. For example, a project to build a national monument will create a result expected to last for centuries. Projects can also have social, economic, and environmental impacts that far outlive the projects themselves.

Every project creates a unique product, service, or result. The outcome of the project may be tangible or intangible. Although repetitive elements may be present in some project deliverable and activities, this repetition does not change the fundamental, unique characteristics of the project work. For example, office buildings can be constructed with the same or similar materials and by the same or different teams. However, each building project remains unique with a different location, different design, different circumstances and situations, different stakeholders, and so on.

An ongoing work effort is generally a repetitive process that follows an organization's existing procedures. In contrast, because of the unique nature of projects, there may be uncertainties or differences in the products, services, or results that the project creates. Project activities can be new to members of a project team, which may necessitate more dedicated planning than other routine work. In addition, projects are undertaken at all organizational levels. A project can involve a single individual or multiple individuals, a single or multiple organizational units.

16.2 PMBOK: THE PROJECT MANAGEMENT BOOK OF KNOWLEDGE

A search for books on project management at a supplier such as Amazon will yield thousands of titles, covering all aspects and variations of project management. The better ones, however, are based on the previously referenced *Project Management Body of Knowledge* (PMBOK). PMBOK has also become a standard under the American National Standards Institute (ANSI).[1] Chapter 33 provides some background on ANSI standards, and PMBOK describes all aspects of project management. The following sections provide an overview of the PMBOK project management process and the description of project management along with an emphasis on how it can be useful for managing internal audit functions. Exhibit 16.1 provides an overview of PMBOK. Overall, internal audit competencies should be improved by following these principles of good project management.

PMBOK defines the project management as a set of five basic process groups and nine knowledge areas that are the elements of almost all projects. Concepts applicable to projects, programs, portfolios, and operations, they have become a framework for effectively launching and executing projects. These five basic project management process groups are:

1. **Initiating.** There should be formal processes in place to launch any project effort, including a description of the project's objectives, estimated budgeting, and appropriate approvals. From an internal audit perspective, these initiating processes are discussed in Chapter 8 on launching effective internal audits.
2. **Planning.** Every project requires planning in terms of its time and resource estimates as well as for the linkages between components and other projects that require coordination. Chapter 15 on risk-based *audit planning* will provide insights here.
3. **Executing.** These are the actual project activities—what needs to be done to accomplish project goals. From an internal audit perspective, these activities may range from individual reviews to executing an ongoing program of internal audit activities.
4. **Controlling.** An ongoing set of processes should be in place to monitor the appropriate completion of project elements, determining that budgets and objectives are being met. This is an important component in overall internal audit management.
5. **Closing.** The final process requires wrapping up the project effort and both delivering the project components as well as summarizing and reporting the project results. For many internal audit activities, this is the production of internal audit reports, discussed in Chapter 18.

PMBOK matches each of these five project management processes with nine project management knowledge areas in terms of their inputs, outputs, and tools and techniques. Project inputs include the documents, plans, and necessary resources to do the project, and the outputs are the completed project materials. To go from the project inputs to the completed end product, a wide range of tools and mechanisms are necessary. A project to build a house, for example, would need lumber, a plan, and supplies such as nails and roofing as the inputs. A hammer and a saw as well as knowledge of carpentry are tools necessary to get started on the construction. The output is the completed house.

Although much more complex than just lumber, a hammer, and nails, the launching of an internal audit project also includes a set of key components, including a plan to conduct the audit, access to documentation and other materials to gain an understanding of the areas of concern, tools such as IT systems to perform the audit, and knowledgeable internal auditors to perform the review. In many respects, the construction of a frame house is a relatively small and simple project compared to many internal audit efforts. Most enterprise projects of any type are complex, and this complexity is what has led to the PMI and its PMBOK standards. Enterprises had too often launched major project efforts that were developed as if they were little more than this example of lumber, nails, a few tools, and hopefully a plan as the project components to build a house. The results were often massive cost and time overruns as well as failures to even complete the project. IT systems implementation projects of the past, as discussed in Chapter 19, were once examples of poor project management techniques. Massive amounts of resources were expended, and the final project results were often late and over budget, and missed original objectives. Many other non-IT projects had the same enterprise problems. All lacked consistent and thorough project management approaches.

PMBOK has defined the project management process in a consistent and well-controlled manner. In addition to the five basic project management process groups, as discussed, the PMBOK guidance material defines nine of what are called project management knowledge areas:

1. Project integration management
2. Project scope management
3. Project time management
4. Project cost management
5. Project quality management
6. Project human resources management
7. Project communications management
8. Project risk management
9. Project procurement management

PMBOK guidance describes each of these knowledge areas, in terms of their inputs, tools, and outputs, with a considerable level of detail. For example, Exhibit 16.2 shows the summarized inputs, tools, and techniques and the outputs for PMBOK's project risk management, and Exhibit 16.3 shows the data flow for PMI's risk management components. PMBOK provides very detailed guidance for each of these project management components, and an internal auditor seeking to learn

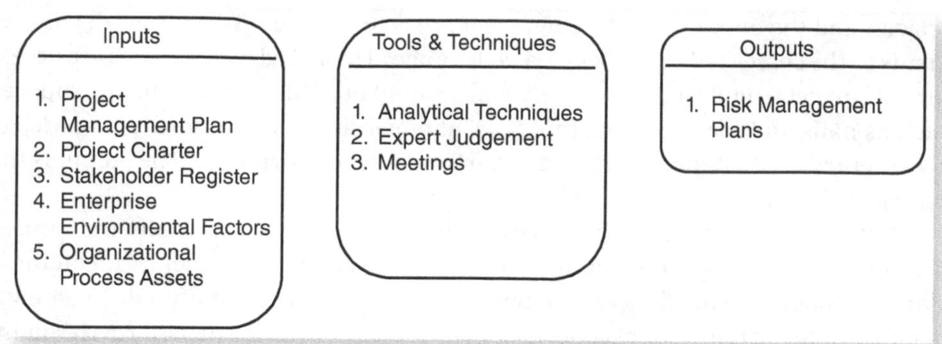

EXHIBIT 16.2 PMI Risk Management Components

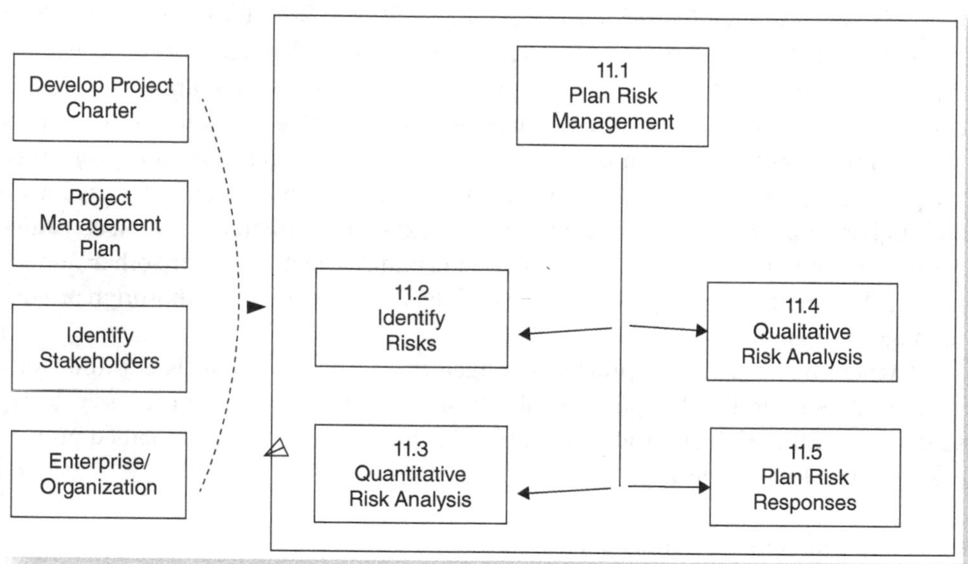

EXHIBIT 16.3 PMI Risk Management Data Flow

more about effective project management techniques is encouraged to secure a copy of the current edition of the PMBOK guide. It contains basic guidance steps to manage and organize virtually any project, and these are certainly the steps an internal auditor should consider when planning the time and resource requirements for any internal audit.

In addition to guidance on general management, the PMBOK contains a fair degree of detail on the project management tools and processes needed in each of these knowledge areas. Exhibit 16.4 summarizes these PMBOK processes and knowledge areas. The purpose of this chapter is not to provide a detailed overview of all of PMBOK's process and knowledge areas but to emphasize the role of this tool for planning and implementing effective project management processes for internal auditors. PMBOK is widely recognized today as the standard for managing a project.

EXHIBIT 16.4 PMBOK Process Groups and Knowledge Areas Summary

	Project Management Process Groups				
Knowledge Area	**Initiating Process Group**	**Planning Process Group**	**Executing Process Group**	**Monitoring and Controlling Process Group**	**Closing Process Group**
4	Project Integration Management	4.1 Develop Project Charter	4.2 Develop Project Management Plan	4.3 Direct and Manage Project Execution	4.4 Monitor and Control Project. Work 4.5 Perform Integrated Change Control 4.6 Close Project or Phase
5	Project Scope Management		5.1 Collect Requirements 5.2 Define Scope 5.3 Create Work Breakdown Struct.		5.4 Verify Scope 5.5 Control Scope
6	Project Time Management		6.1 Define Activities 6.2 Estimate Resources 6.3 Estimate Activity Resources 6.4 Estimate Durations 6.5 Develop Schedule		6.6 Control Schedule
7	Project Cost Management		7.1 Estimate Costs 7.2 Determine Budget		7.3 Control Costs

(continued)

EXHIBIT 16.4 *(continued)*

Knowledge Area	Initiating Process Group	Planning Process Group	Executing Process Group	Monitoring and Controlling Process Group	Closing Process Group
8	Project Quality Management		8.1 Plan Quality	8.2 Perform Quality Assurance	8.3 Perform Quality Control
9	Project Human Resources Management		9.1 Develop Human Resources Plan	9.2 Acquire Project Team 9.3 Develop Project Team 9.4 Manage Project Team	
10	Project Communications Management		10.2 Plan Communications	10.3 Distribute Information 10.4 Manage Stakeholder Expectations	10.5 Report Performance
11	Project Risk Management		11.1 Plan Risk Management 11.2 Identify Risks 11.3 Perform Quantitative Risk Analysis 11.4 Qualitative Risk Analysis		11.6 Monitor and Control Risks
12	Project Procurement Management		12.1 Plan Procurements	12.2 Conduct Requirements	12.3 Administer Procurements 12.4 Close Procurements

In addition to being an internal audit tool, knowledge of PMBOK will allow an internal auditor reviewing a project-related area in business operations to ask some questions about how an enterprise area has used PMBOK principles in a review of any project-related area.

To provide a better explanation of how PMBOK is organized and how it can become a tool to help internal auditors, we have selected a portion of PMBOK element 4.2, as an example on developing a project plan. While the PMBOK guidance is more oriented to the IT developer or manufacturing product developer, these concepts apply to an internal auditor as well. PMBOK describes this area as "the process of documenting the actions necessary to define, prepare, integrate, and coordinate all subsidiary plans." While the guidance here covers multiple plan areas or objectives, an internal auditor should think of this as preliminary guidance for building an internal audit plan. For example, assume that enterprise management has just purchased or acquired a company that will be folded into main operations. That purchase would only have taken place after there had been some due diligence work to gain a high-level understanding of the proposed acquisition, but this example assumes a situation where senior management requests that internal audit perform a detailed internal controls review of their new subsidiary acquisition.

As illustrated in Exhibit 16.4, every element of PMBOK is described in terms of the inputs, outputs, and tool and techniques to that process area. Develop Project Management Plan is numbered 4.2 and is at the intersection of the Project Integration Management knowledge area and the Executing Process Group, as shown in Exhibit 16.4. Again thinking of this detailed internal control review of the new subsidiary acquisition example, the required inputs for this process, following PMBOK guidance materials' numbering, are:

- **4.2.1 Project Charter.** PMBOK emphasizes the importance of a project charter similar to internal audit charters discussed in Chapter 14.
- **4.2.2 Project Scope Statement.** This is a key document in the audit planning process, as discussed in Chapter 15. The internal audit team launching any review needs to have a strong understanding of their audit scope.
- **4.2.3 Outputs from Planning Process.** This step is less of an issue for internal audits because internal audit will go into any audit engagement with plans to document processes reviewed as well as to deliver an appropriate audit report. This also is an example where PMBOK guidance does not entirely match internal audit procedures.
- **4.2.4 Enterprise Environment Factors.** These are PMBOK terms but include such areas as supporting information systems, any facilities issues, or any applicable governmental standards. Internal audit should gain knowledge of these input factors and should incorporate them into the internal audit planning as applicable. They include any other factors that can influence this audit plan. In this example, internal audit would use the results of the prior due diligence review as well as any internal audit work that may have been performed as part of preacquisition due diligence.

The project management plan here is the single output from this process work step. In our internal audit context, this would be an approved plan to initiate the internal audit. PMBOK's tools and techniques section here only calls for the need for "expert judgment." In our context, these would be the internal audit management skills to tailor processes to meet the audit's needs, to allocate necessary resources and skill levels, and to manage the audit's change management and configuration requirements.

PMBOK's Develop Project Management Plan process, as with all such elements, is not a single, freestanding process but is linked to other key PMBOK components. Exhibit 16.5 is a data flow diagram, adapted from the PMBOK guidance materials, that supports this key process and shows related linkages. Although at first perhaps appearing as a fairly complex diagram to the internal auditor lacking a more extensive understanding of PMBOK, this

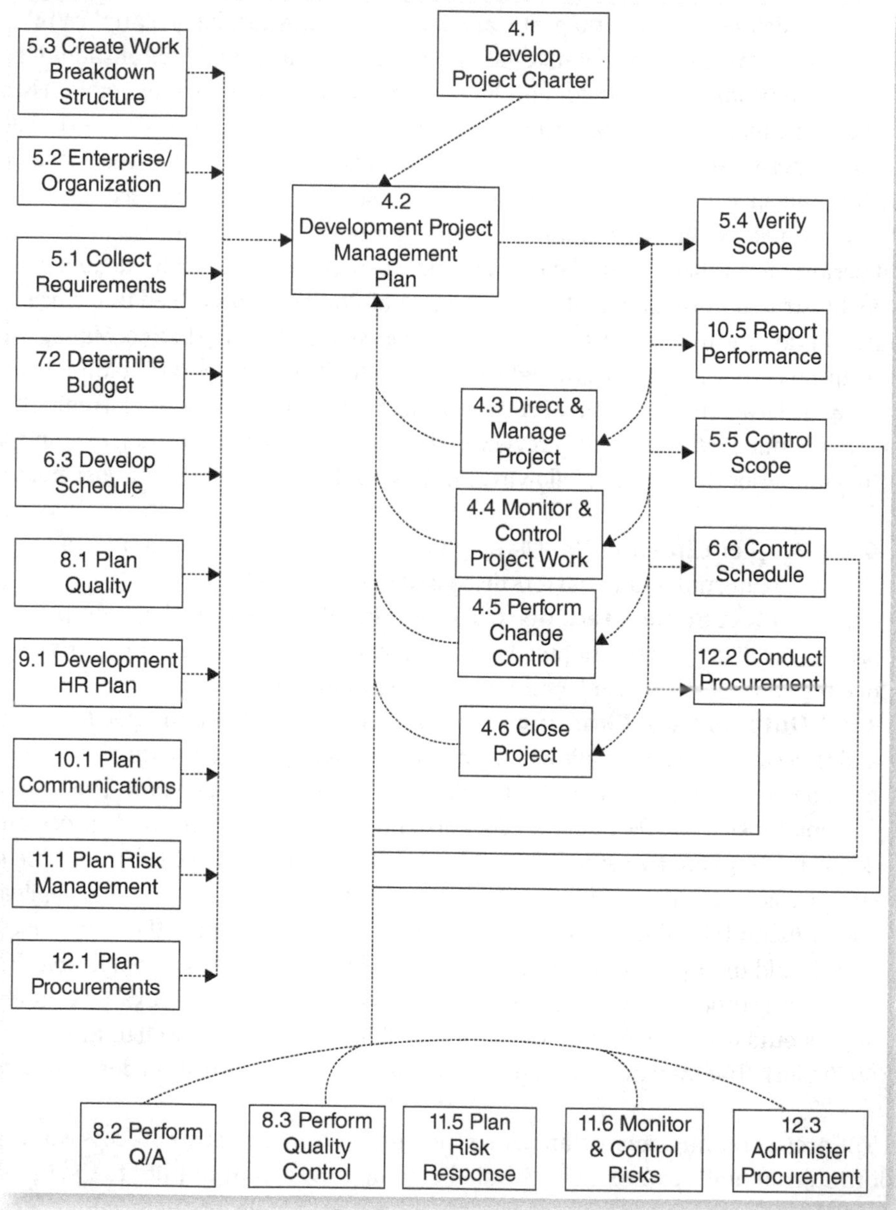

EXHIBIT 16.5 PMBOK Project Management Plan

exhibit shows how various PMBOK processes interact to develop a project management plan. For example, number 4.1, Develop Project Charter component, is the major input to this 4.2 process, with steps 4.3 through 4.6 describing the processes to manage, monitor, and close out the project. Just as Exhibit 16.5 shows a data flow diagram for the PMBOK 4.2 component, there are similar data flows for 4.1 as well as 4.3 to 4.6. Again, this process guidance also should be considered in the steps necessary to manage, perform, and complete an internal audit. The activities to the right and at the bottom of the exhibit show the procedures that feed this project integration management process to develop the project management plan. For example, there is a left-hand process on 16.5 labeled 8.1, Plan Quality. The related processes noted here are a Quality Management Plan and a Process Improvement Plan. These are the types of internal audit quality processes that are discussed in Chapter 12. The reader who may have found the three-dimensional COSO internal control framework, discussed in Chapter 3, to initially appear complex will find that PMBOK at first seems even more complex. The idea, however, is that are many interconnected elements necessary to build and maintain effective project management processes.

The PMBOK guidance materials discuss the inputs, outputs, and supporting tools for each of the numbered components, and they are all interrelated. These are standards necessary to effectively manage any project, and internal auditors should think of their more major audit activities in terms of formal PMBOK-type projects. While this guidance material sometimes may be too broad for some smaller audits, it will serve as an excellent guide for managing most larger and complex internal audits. PMBOK provides almost a checklist covering important and essential steps for planning and performing successful individual internal audits.

16.3 PMBOK PROGRAM AND PORTFOLIO MANAGEMENT

The PMBOK guidance focuses on individual projects and is useful for performing single internal audits. However, just as an internal audit function or department will be responsible for a series of internal audits over a period of time, any function managing a series of projects needs to think of them as a series of program projects as well as their relationships with other similar or related projects. Multiple and related projects are usually grouped together into what are called programs and project portfolios. A project management program consists of a series of related projects managed in a coordinated way to obtain benefits and controls that would not be available from managing them separately and individually. Programs generally consist of related work that may be outside the scope of the individual projects.

The need for program management generally occurs when an enterprise has some single objective that can only be achieved through a series of separate projects. For example, a plan to move a manufacturing facility to a new location would require a series of separate projects that all require coordination. One project here might require moving and setting up production equipment, another would move necessary raw materials, with still another doing IT systems conversions. Although someone should be in charge of coordinating all of these efforts, each project will have separate needs and requirements. They would be managed separately but grouped together as a program.

Internal auditors should think of requirements for a series of related internal audit projects as a program. For example, the enterprise may be asked to review Sarbanes-Oxley Act (SOx) Section 404 internal controls at a series of facilities within the enterprise. Even though each of these audits would take place at different types of facilities with different geographic locations and responsible internal audit teams, they each have similar high-level objectives and a senior manager might be responsible for the overall completion of each. These groupings of projects might be organized and managed as a program, with the individual internal audit project managers all reporting to a program manager for this overall compliance effort.

Moving up to a higher level, portfolio management refers to collections of projects, programs, and other work that are grouped together to facilitate their effective management. If internal audit groups existed for two units of a corporation, perhaps one covering internal audits in European Union countries and the other for the United States, the internal audit activities for each could be considered an internal audit portfolio with both of these classified under a higher-level portfolio at the corporate headquarters. This portfolio and program approach to project management is described in Exhibit 16.6. The idea is that reporting relationships should be established when necessary to promote efficiency and achieve overall objectives.

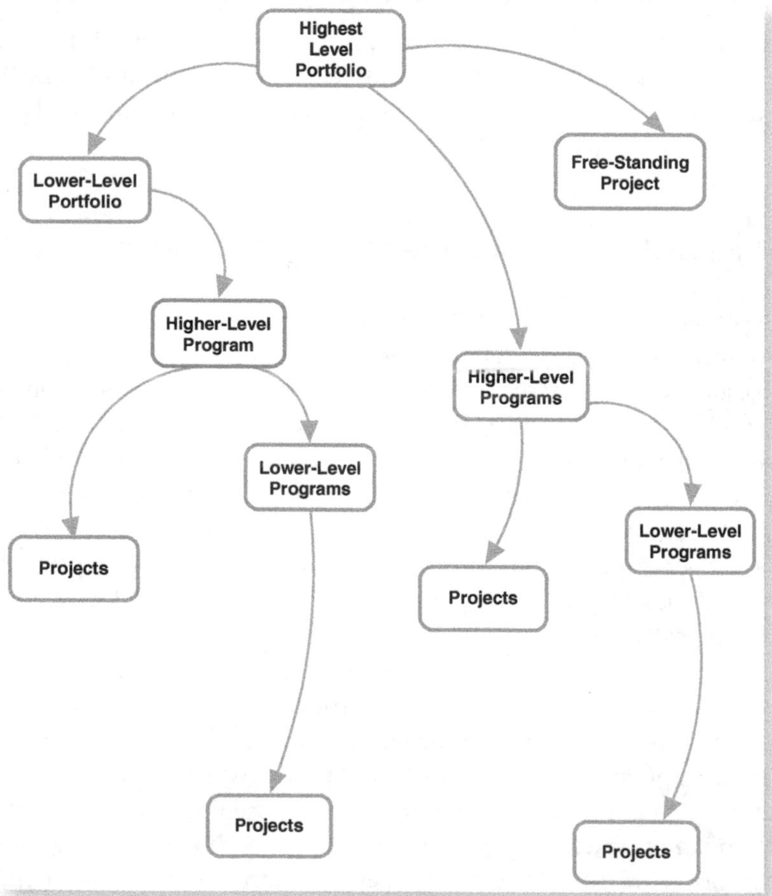

EXHIBIT 16.6 Project, Program, and Portfolio Management Interactions

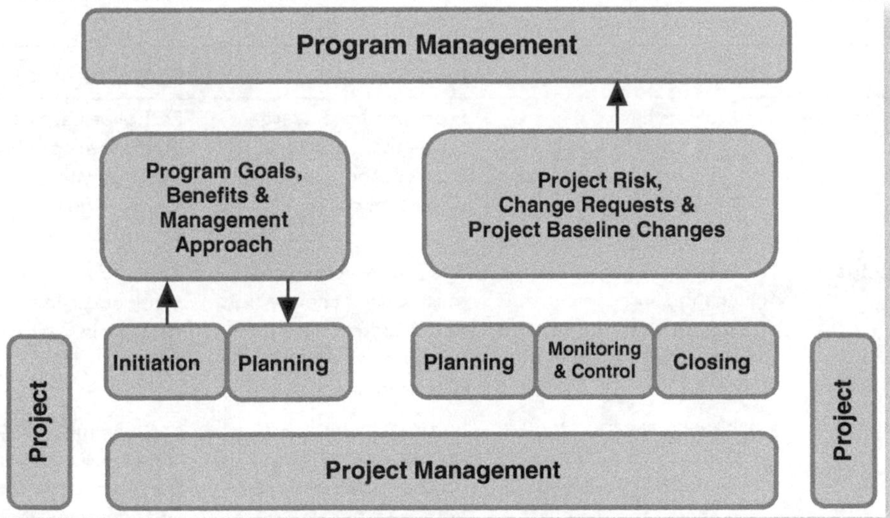

EXHIBIT 16.7 Interaction between Program Management and Project Management

Just as the PMI-issued PMBOK has become the standard for project management, the organization has subsequently released standards for program and portfolio management. The PMI *Standard for Program Management* is a set of best practices for the management of multiple, related projects that are measured and evaluated as a program. PMI has a similar standard for portfolio management. This guidance is also useful to internal audit where multiple but similar internal audit projects can be managed as a program or considered as a portfolio. Exhibit 16.7 shows this interaction between projects and program. The idea is that there should be a tight interaction between the two. Program management does not totally drive or dictate individual project activity, and the separate projects will help to define the overall structure of the supporting programs. The analogy between a series of individual internal audits and the overall audit function is very strong.

PMI program and portfolio management standards are important elements of the PMBOK project management guidance. Somewhat related to our Chapter 13 discussions on the importance of an audit universe is PMI's portfolio management set of best practices that takes both the project and program materials and defines them for high-level program management best practices. There are numerous relationships between these three, and although the PMI best practices have been tailored to a pure project management environment, internal auditors should consider PMI's best practices as a guide to managing both typical projects and internal audits.

Exhibit 16.8 shows the relationship between project, program, and portfolio management practices in terms of such factors as their scope, change management considerations, planning, success factors, management, and monitoring. This table, as well as many of the other exhibits in this chapter, has been extracted or modified from the PMI best practices materials for project, program, and portfolios. Although PMI uses terms such as *project manager*, much of its guidance material is very applicable to managing separate as well as either programs or portfolios of internal audits. Internal

EXHIBIT 16.8 Project, Program, and Portfolio Management Overview

	Projects	Programs	Portfolios
Scope	Projects have defined objectives. Scope is progressively elaborated throughout the project life cycle.	Programs have a larger scope than individual projects and provide more significant benefits.	Portfolios have a business scope that changes with the strategic goals of the enterprise.
Change	Project managers expect change and implement processes to keep change managed and controlled.	The program manager must expect change from both inside and outside the program and be prepared to manage it.	Portfolio managers continuously monitor changes in the broad environment.
Planning	Project managers require planning to evolve from high level to detailed planning throughout the project life cycle.	Program managers develop the overall program plan and create high-level plans to guide detailed planning at the component level.	Portfolio managers create and maintain necessary processes and communication relative to the aggregate portfolio.
Management	Project managers manage project teams to meet the project objectives.	Program managers manage the program staff and the project managers; they provide vision and overall ownership.	Portfolio managers may manage or coordinate portfolio management staff.
Success	Success is measured by product and project quality, timeliness, budget compliance, and degree of customer satisfaction.	Success is measured by the degree to which the program satisfies the needs and benefits for which it was undertaken.	Success is measured in terms of aggregate performance of portfolio components.
Monitoring	Project managers monitor and control the work of producing the products, services, or results that the project was undertaken to produce.	Program managers monitor the progress of program components to ensure that overall goals, schedules, budget, and benefits of the program will be met.	Portfolio managers monitor aggregate performance and value indicators.

auditors should develop a greater understanding of project management concepts, with an emphasis on the PMI PMBOK. This has become the worldwide standard for managing and understanding the project management process and is also becoming a strong tool for managing internal audits.

16.4 PLANNING AN INTERNAL AUDIT

The overall PMBOK guidance is important for internal auditors in the understanding and use of good project management practices. Its concepts are particularly useful when internal audit is reviewing virtually any enterprise project-related activity, whether it be an IT systems development effort, the move to a new office complex, the introduction of a new product offering, or many others. The internal auditor involved in reviewing any such area should ask if the project is following PMBOK standards and should ask to see evidence of the project's adherence to PMBOK, an effective project plan, and time and expense records. If such compliance records are not in place, there may be a solid internal finding here.

Past chapters have focused on components to build an effective internal audit function in an enterprise, internal audit practice standards, and other factors for assessing an array of potential internal audit candidates in an enterprise and selecting appropriate candidates for an internal audit. This section will focus on the steps necessary to plan and perform an individual internal audit beyond the broad PMBOK standards. While of course nothing is ever fully typical in the vast and varied world of internal auditing, this chapter here will use the same example company that has been cited in other chapters, Global Computer Products, to describe some of the processes necessary for planning and launching an internal audit.

The next section will focus on the necessary planning steps for a financial/operational internal audit review of the material receiving and accounts payables functions at a Global Computer Products manufacturing plant. While the chapter certainly cannot cover all of the many control risks and other aspects of such a theoretical plant operation, this section will attempt to walk through some of the important characteristics of such an internal audit. Our assumption here is that our example internal audit team focuses primarily on operational internal controls with some emphasis on financial issues and its supporting IT systems.

Although our discussion of PMBOK standards paints an environment that may not be typical for many internal auditors, these concepts provide excellent guidance for managing individual internal audits. All internal auditors must have a strong CBOK understanding if not hands-on experience in this process of planning and performing an individual internal audit.

16.5 UNDERSTANDING THE ENVIRONMENT: PLANNING AND LAUNCHING AN INTERNAL AUDIT

Chapter 13 talked about the importance of building an audit universe, an approved and documented description of all of the potential candidates for internal audits within an enterprise. The idea of such an audit universe document is not to describe everything where internal audit might launch an internal audit during a current period but to describe the scope of internal audit's planned activities. For example, assume our Global Computer Products example company has a small advanced product manufacturing plant in the city of Muddville, but assume that the company has a small advanced products research facility at that same location. When assembling its audit universe description, internal audit management may have decided that the Muddville advanced products facility was too small, too specialized, or otherwise out of the scope for internal audit. However, in our example, assume that internal audit has decided to focus on a review of the manufacturing plant operations. In this example, however, they are planning a review of the Muddville plant manufacturing direct materials cycle, the internal controls covering their purchasing, receiving, accounts payable, and overall accounting cycle operations. In addition, because the accounting cycle will be covered as part of SOx review procedures and the external audit later at year end, our example here has decided to focus on purchasing and receiving processes.

Although these processes are highlighted on the audit universe list, further assume that internal audit has never performed a purchasing and receiving processes review at this company facility, but has decided that its relative growth has pointed to a need for some internal audit work there. This example is not unusual for many internal audit functions. A large number of potentially auditable resources should be listed on the audit universe documentation, but because of the lack of time, resources, and other matters, some of these potential auditable entities never come up as candidates for planned internal audit reviews. They may remain on the back burner until their growth or other issues attract management attention or until a member of senior management or the audit committee asks if internal audit has ever done any work at that facility.

In this example, assume that internal audit has decided to launch a review of the Muddville facility operations, as part of their annual internal audit planning process. We will assume that internal audit has established audit programs for reviews of these areas, as discussed in Chapter 15, and has enough general knowledge about their operations to get started in launching the internal audit.

An important first step in any internal audit is to look at other internal audits either in process or short-term planned, to consider the availability of internal audit resources, and then to prepare a preliminary internal audit plan. Let us assume that the Muddville facility is out of town but will not require any long-distance travel to visit the location. We will also assume that the chief audit executive's (CAE's) and other internal audit team members' knowledge of plan operations there is sufficient that a preliminary visit is not necessary. However, based on what information is available, internal audit would prepare a preliminary plan for the upcoming Muddville audit.

Exhibit 16.9 is an example of the type of preliminary plan that might be developed for such a review of these Muddville purchasing and receiving operations. Because the information here is only very preliminary, the plan does not use specific dates but assumes that two internal audit staff members will be assigned to do the work. The preliminary plan shown only uses approximate estimated hours at this time, but care should always be given to not seal such preliminary plans "in cement," as more information may force all planned estimates up or down.

Having developed preliminary plans for this audit, a next step is to inform the responsible management at that facility through an internal audit engagement letter, as was discussed in Chapter 8. Usually launched along with some high-level preliminary discussions, the engagement letter announces the planned audit along with its objectives, its approximate dates, and the assigned internal auditors. While local management will often claim that the audit's timing is bad or other problems exist, the final audit plan may have to be adjusted, but then the audit can begin.

EXHIBIT 16.9 Muddville Purchasing and Receiving Preliminary Internal Audit Plan

Location: Muddville Plant Facility

Assigned Audit Team:

Ref No.	Audit Activity	Week 1	Week 2	Week 3	Week 4	Week 5
1	Review past activity and assess risks	X				
2	Develop audit approach and plan	X				
3	Contact site to schedule audit	X				
4	Travel	X			X	
5	Review and document processes		X			
6	Perform walk-throughs to confirm understandings		X	X		
7	Perform tests of internal controls		X	X		
8	Perform other audit procedures per audit plan			X	X	
9	Summarize and confirm audit results				X	
10	Complete audit workpapers				X	
11	Schedule audit closing meeting				X	
12	Prepare draft audit report for corrective action					X

16.6 AUDIT PLANNING: DOCUMENTING AND UNDERSTANDING THE INTERNAL CONTROL ENVIRONMENT

We have stated that our example internal audit function has never performed a review of purchasing and receiving operations at its Muddville facility but that it has audit programs and experience in performing similar reviews at other Global Computer Products facilities. However, because local processes and even supporting systems may differ from one plant to another, internal audit will need to gather more data and information about operations at Muddville. In an ideal world, internal audit can simply contact the local facility to be audited, ask them to send copies of flowcharts and other documentation, and then go from there to begin their preliminary internal audit work.

We are characterizing an ideal world, however, as such documentation may be sparse, out of date, or nonexistent. Internal audit may want to ask some questions to gather more information about these processes. Exhibit 16.10 is an example

EXHIBIT 16.10 Muddville Purchasing and Receiving Internal Audit Information Questionnaire

1. Are all material purchases authorized through formal, approved purchase orders?
2. Is purchasing based on a set of authorized, approved vendors?
3. Are approved vendors screened periodically for performance factors, such as on time delivery, compliance to specifications, etc.?
4. Are there any monetary or quantity limits on purchase orders that require additional approvals?
5. Do all purchase orders comply with authorized payment and delivery expectation standard terms?
6. Is the approved corporate purchasing system used for all material purchases?
7. Do all material receipts go through regular receiving operations?
8. Are there limits over the times when receipts are accepted?
9. Are approved corporate receiving systems used for the receiving process?
10. If incoming materials do not match to a purchase order in terms of purchase order documentation, quantity, approved deliver dates, or other factors, are processes are in place to resolve these issues?
11. Are all critical materials subject to inspection?
12. Are there standard documented processes in place for materials that do not match inspection criteria?

And other detailed questions to allow internal audit to gain an understanding of these processes.

questionnaire that internal audit could circulate to gain great information about an organizational unit and its environment where they plan to perform an internal audit. The results of that questionnaire should help internal audit to plan its review, including such things as the size and types of items to sample as well as the need for any IT application control reviews as discussed in Chapter 22.

Effective internal audits cannot generally be performed by internal audit working just in the corporate office and gathering audit evidence through e-mail messages and file queries. In almost all cases, internal auditors need to have their feet on the ground and spend some time visiting the auditee site and observing operations. Although it is sometimes only the result of general impressions, an internal auditor can typically learn a lot by spending time at an auditee site. Whether it's noticing a manager who always arrives very late, an analyst who does not appear to be following good IT security procedures, or any of many other internal auditor observations, an on-site internal auditor should observe these activities and actions while performing audit fieldwork. Many of these observations may not result in formal internal audit recommendations, but they will help an internal auditor to gain an overall sense of the unit being audited. Some of these matters can be formally documented in internal audit workpapers, while others are just impressions that an internal auditor can use to support the overall audit conclusions.

A far more important task that auditors have than making observations is to develop a good understanding of the materials they are reviewing, prepare documentation to support or update any existing materials, and then use that material to identify any internal control vulnerabilities or to help in internal audit's understanding of the processes being reviewed. Chapter 17 discusses documenting results through process modeling and stresses the importance of preparing preliminary process documentation, whether through high-level flowcharts or descriptions of the operations slated to receive detailed reviews and testing. The idea is to show decision points in the process that are often areas for audit tests.

Our point here is not to describe a hypothetical process in any detail, but to show how appropriate internal audit process documentation can define key decision points. In this example, if local management was concerned that bad, defective material was improperly entering into the production process, the internal auditor could use such a process flow to identify a point where, if materials were not given proper inspections, bad materials could enter into the production process. Simple flowchart diagrams describe an internal auditor's understanding of processes at the facility being audited. The internal auditor needs to confirm that such a documented description is correct. However, many processes and their supporting flowcharts are so complex that an internal auditor cannot just expect to show the flowchart to a manager at the site to ask for a yes or no response if everything on the flowchart is okay. More supporting information is often needed.

A walk-through exercise is often an effective way to verify that the process documentation is correct. This type of exercise is often most effective in very complex processes with many twists and turns and multiple decision points as well as multiple people-dependent decision points along the way. The idea is that an auditor would take a document, such as a material receiving report, and manually walk it through each of the steps being reviewed to determine that the personnel at each step in such a decision chain actually perform the process as described. Results here can sometimes be interesting. The internal auditor may present the document being analyzed to floor personnel to ask how they would process it. Sometimes the internal auditor will find that the process is not always quite working as had been documented.

If an internal auditor finds that a documented process is not accurate, in most cases the prepared documentation needs to be revised. However, in some situations, interviews during a walk-through may identify potential internal control weaknesses. These are situations where unit management appears to think how a process should be working but an internal auditor, through interviews with people actually performing procedures, may find that the reality is quite different. Situations like this may require some rethinking or revisiting.

16.7 PERFORMING APPROPRIATE INTERNAL AUDIT PROCEDURES AND WRAPPING UP THE AUDIT

Assuming that the documented processes are correct and complete, internal audit needs to identify key internal control areas here and then to develop audit tests to verify that those controls are working. The size and type of these tests depends very much on the nature and criticality of the processes reviewed. However, it is usually not sufficient to select one item to walk through the process, and then to say that everything is okay as long as those items met this audit test.

Chapter 10 discusses audit sampling, including using statistical and nonstatistical procedures to sample and evaluate audit evidence. Although some aspects of statistical sampling are complex and can lead an internal auditor into trouble, Chapter 10 suggests and we affirm again here that all internal auditors should have a least a CBOK general understanding of statistical audit sampling processes. These will allow an internal auditor to state with some confidence whether an internal controls appear to be working or whether an account balance is correct.

In our example audit here, the internal audit team would have arrived at the Muddville plant audit site, confirmed the process documentation that they prepared prior to their arrival at the audit field site, or created documentation during their first audit steps. Next, after reaffirming that documentation through walk-throughs, internal audit needs to refine their own internal audit procedures and then perform the audit tests.

We have described an environment where the internal audit function may have arrived at the audit site with some established audit programs, as were introduced in Chapter 15, for the areas that they will be testing and evaluating. However, in just as many cases, the internal audit team on site may find the need to make some small adjustments to their audit programs that had been prepared by internal audit management. In all such circumstances, the internal audit team should obtain approval for any audit program or procedure changes from internal audit management, and then go on to perform the actual audit steps as documented.

In our example internal audit, we are describing a relatively small set of procedures that would be performed with a small internal audit team—here two internal auditors—and over a fairly short time span. There are many other internal audit situations, however, where an internal audit will be much larger in terms of the areas reviewed, the size of the audit team, the time duration, and many other factors. Strong project management tools are essential for such an extended review. No matter what size, the internal audit team needs to develop effective internal audit workpapers, whether in traditional hard-copy files or auditor laptop computer–based soft-copy workpapers. Workpaper formats as well as other formats to control and better manage internal audit are discussed in Chapter 17.

After the on-site internal audit team has completed its audit tests and performed other internal audit procedures, there is a need to wrap up the audit fieldwork before departing from the audit site. Although the final audit report and even a final draft report may not be complete prior to internal audit's completion of their fieldwork, it is almost essential that the on-site internal auditors provide local management with at least a summary of their audit observations and potential finding and recommendations as discussed in Chapter 18 on the importance of internal audit reports.

Even though it may take some additional effort and audit resources to prepare even a draft audit report prior to the end of the audit fieldwork, internal audit should at least issue a potential audit findings point sheet that outlines the internal audit's observations and potential recommendations. We have cautioned against the field auditors even trying to prepare a draft audit report before a more detailed review and approval by audit management. Although internal audit reports have always been important, SOx requirements have made them even more critical because the audit committee now has full access to all internal audit reports. In our era of e-mail attachments, it is quite easy for a report—even labeled "draft"—to be somewhat circulated and misinterpreted. A draft report that contains some incorrect or even embarrassing conclusions should be tightly controlled and monitored.

There are some situations, of course, where an internal audit team can leave an audit engagement with a strong draft or almost final audit report. For example, when an enterprise has a large number of small retail or restaurant locations, the internal auditors performing the review will often be doing an almost checklist-compliance type of review, looking for such matters as whether required daily documents have been properly kept up to date. A full, final audit report makes sense in such situations.

For larger, perhaps more comprehensive internal audits, such as our Global Computer Products review of the Muddville plant facility, it is often a better idea to allow internal audit management to review and approve even the draft report. However, an internal audit point sheet is sometimes very effective. This is a document that does not at all look like an audit report but one that summarizes internal audit preliminary findings along with their potential recommendations. Exhibit 16.11 is an example of such a point sheet. This would essentially be a discussion-level document. If management has some significant areas of dispute, internal audit can document and agree to re-review draft findings or to make potential changes to clear up any management areas of concern.

EXHIBIT 16.11 Audit Fieldwork Preliminary Findings Point Sheet

Internal Audit Point Sheet

Audit: Muddville Plant Purchasing and Receiving Operations

Date: February 2, 20xx

Internal Audit Team Lead:

Note: These comments are preliminary internal audit findings and potential recommendations as a result of the recent internal audit review. The final results will be published in a soon to be issued internal audit report. While the final findings and recommendations may be somewhat subject to change, internal audit recommends that operations management begin corrective action steps in advance of their formal internal audit report.

Audit Finding #1: Incoming materials are not receiving required quality inspections, per established procedures. Although procedures require detailed inspections for finished electronic subassemblies, we found that some goods are being moved directly to production operations. In a sample of 15 incoming finished subassemblies, we found that receipt packages for 33% had been moved directly to the production area, bypassing quality inspections.

Recommendation: ________________

Audit Finding #2: ________________

Internal audit's objectives here are not to come home with a dazzling audit report filled with findings and recommendations but to review an area and to make recommendations to improve the overall internal control environment there. These objectives can be missed as internal auditors too often get involved with "gotcha" kinds of audit findings. As we have discussed throughout these chapters, internal auditors should try to provide overall service to management.

From a very high-level perspective, this section has tried to revisit some of the considerations that are necessary to plan individual internal audits. There are many different audit approaches to consider, and internal auditors should use any of the procedures discussed in here and in other chapters. No matter what best practices have been or will be discussed in other chapters, internal audits are only effective when an internal audit team establishes audit objectives, visits the area to be audited and gathers information to document and describe internal controls, tests those controls to determine whether they are effective, and then wraps up the audit by making recommendations for controls improvements, as appropriate.

Although some members of internal audit management get involved in desk-related jobs away from field activities and do not directly perform internal audits, every member of an internal audit function should have a strong CBOK level of knowledge of what it takes to plan and perform effective internal audits. That is perhaps the fundamental skill in the internal audit process, and every internal auditor from the CAE to audit staff members should be familiar and comfortable with the basic internal audit process.

16.8 PROJECT MANAGEMENT BEST PRACTICES AND INTERNAL AUDIT

Internal auditors should think of virtually every internal audit they plan and perform as a project similar to the best management practices that we have described on a high level here and that can be found in the PMBOK standard. The analogies between good internal audit practices and project management are strong. Exhibit 16.1 outlined the PMBOK-defined project management knowledge areas. These translate to the process of planning and performing an internal audit, using PMBOK terminology but from an internal audit perspective, as follows:

- **Project integration management.** Detailed plans need to be prepared for every internal audit, including processes to implement changes and alter that audit plan in light of new findings or other developments during the course of the audit.
- **Internal audit project scope management.** Every internal audit needs to establish and document a clear statement of the audit's scope at the beginning of the review. This scope will become a baseline for measuring internal audit progress, accomplishment of the scope's objectives, and any necessary change control.
- **Internal audit project time management.** The time and activities of all internal auditors involved in a review need to be budgeted, recorded, monitored, and assessed.

- **Internal audit project cost management.** Internal audit costs need to be budgeted, collected, and controlled.
- **Internal audit project quality management.** Every internal audit project needs to include appropriate quality planning, assurance, and control processes. These measures assess a particular audit as well as the overall internal audit function.
- **Internal audit project human resources management.** Proper attention must be given to all members of the team performing the internal audit, including audit team organization planning and all levels of staff development and training.
- **Internal audit project communications management.** Communications factors are important elements in any internal audit, whether in documenting results in workpapers, reporting status and results to both enterprise and audit management, and development of the final audit report.
- **Internal audit project risk management.** Every internal audit faces a variety of risks, and the internal audit team needs to have processes in place to formally identify and quantify those risks as well as to have procedures in place to respond to and control any risks associated with an internal audit.
- **Internal audit project procurement management.** Although they are perhaps the least significant of the PMBOK knowledge areas when compared to other aspects of an internal audit, processes should be in place during any audit contract for any outside services and goods as necessary.

Effective project management best practices, as defined in PMBOK, are an important CBOK skill requirement for all internal auditors, both in developing internal audit projects and in assessing the maturity of project management practices in the course of their reviews. This chapter has provided a high-level overview of the PMBOK and project management, but an internal auditor should take steps to increase skills and knowledge in this very important discipline. Internal auditors should use project management tools and methods as an aid for more efficient and effective internal audits.

NOTE

1. *A Guide to the Project Management Body of Knowledge* (*PMBOK Guide*), 5th ed. (Newtown Square, PA: Project Management Institute, 2013).

CHAPTER SEVENTEEN

Documenting Audit Results through Process Modeling and Workpapers

INTERNAL AUDITORS OBSERVE AND IDENTIFY many process-related problems, internal control weaknesses, or errors in data and operations as part of their internal audit reviews. However, those concerns and findings will not be fully recognized by enterprise management unless they are supported by strong supporting documentation to describe an internal auditor's findings or assertions. An internal auditor can describe a high-level internal control concern in a summary of audit results, but if managers responsible for the area audited only question the internal auditor's finding, they will respond to the internal auditor with a "show me" type of request. Internal audits need strong documentation to support their audit findings and observations. In addition to effective internal audit reports, as discussed in Chapter 18, good documentation must support the internal audit work.

The ability to effectively document audit evidence is a very important internal audit skill. There are two dimensions here. First, an internal auditor is often exposed to a wide range of information on the business and its operations at some site. In order to better understand control strengths and weaknesses, an internal auditor needs to think of these activities in terms of their often not-well-documented supporting processes. This chapter will review procedures for describing and documenting these activities through what is called process modeling. Auditor workpapers describe the activities. Other IT professionals use process modeling techniques with special diagrams and flowcharts that are complex and sometimes look not unlike ancient Egyptian hieroglyphics, but this chapter will explore simplified, effective process modeling techniques for internal auditors—an important CBOK skill.

The chapter also outlines techniques for documenting internal audit work in what are traditionally called audit workpapers. Called audit evidence, these are the materials that are assembled to describe the results of an internal audit. Audit workpapers are very important for individual internal audits as well as for the total enterprise.

In some situations, they can even become a source of evidence in a litigation matter. Once organized in voluminous paper-based files, audit workpapers now are often best organized in a digital format and assembled on laptop computers. This chapter will discuss some best practices for organizing internal audit workpapers today.

Internal audit has a Sarbanes-Oxley Act (SOx)–mandated legal requirement to retain its audit workpaper documentation for seven or more years. This can be a challenge when technology changes, sometimes make accessing these old records difficult, and physical space limitations present a challenge to keeping track of old internal audit activity records. The chapter will conclude with a discussion of internal audit record management and records retention best practices. Describing, documenting, and maintaining records of internal audit activities are all internal audit CBOK requirements.

17.1 INTERNAL AUDIT DOCUMENTATION REQUIREMENTS

Internal auditors spend most of their time reviewing records, performing analyses based on those records, and interviewing people at all levels in the enterprise to gain information. Auditors use all of this information to develop audit conclusions and to make appropriate recommendations. However, this effort is of little value unless the audit work is documented in an orderly manner to both support the current audit effort and provide a historical record. If internal auditors did not cover all of the details at the conclusion of a current review, they can always rely on personal memory to fill in some missing detail or observation when wrapping up and concluding an audit. However, those undocumented observations are of little value if the audit work is called into question—sometimes even for legal proceedings—months or even up to years into the future. The internal auditor who originally did the work may have moved on, and the internal audit work cannot be corroborated without supporting evidence. Strong, ongoing internal audit documentation is essential.

Internal audit documentation refers to published audit reports, action plans, and other materials supporting the reports, audit workpapers, key meeting minutes, special IT extract files, or reports. Of course, internal audit documentation cannot be retained in perpetuity, and an internal audit function should establish and follow some minimum documentation retention standards. While different countries and governmental units may have different rules, a good rule of thumb for internal audit document retention is the U.S. Securities and Exchange Commission (SEC) rules for external audit financial records.

The SEC requires that "records be retained for seven years after the auditor concludes the audit or review of the financial statements." For an internal audit, the records retention period would also be a minimum of seven years after the audit report is released. While public accounting firms are subject to Public Company Accounting Oversight Board rules as well as potential shareholder legal action, internal audit is not quite under the same spotlight. Nevertheless, an internal audit function should make arrangements to keep all significant records for this retention period.

The sections following discuss three important aspects of internal audit documentation: process modeling, audit workpapers, and document retention. In the first of these, an internal auditor will often begin a review in a new process area where there may have been no previous audits and even limited enterprise documentation. The internal auditor needs to observe operations, review reports and procedures, and ask questions to develop an understanding of that new process. This documentation is important for understanding the internal control environment and for making consulting-related recommendations when appropriate.

Workpapers are the second major topic of this chapter. These are the documents that describe an internal auditor's work and provide the basis and understanding for the internal audit. This chapter will discuss approaches for developing effective internal audit workpapers and will conclude with a section discussing workpaper document retention. We have moved from the printed and handwritten paper documents of the past to an era where audit work is assembled on laptop computers but where good documentation security and retention procedures are critical. A basic understanding of all three of these areas should be basic internal auditor CBOK requirements.

17.2 PROCESS MODELING FOR INTERNAL AUDITORS

Business process models or descriptions are maps that help an internal auditor to navigate through business activities:

- Where we are right now
- Where we need to go
- Where we came from
- How we got to where we are

Process models are really a sort of map or flowchart to help an internal auditor navigate through a series of observed activities. However, good process modeling is more than just a simple road map showing how to get from one point to another. Such a map will not help if we make a wrong turn somewhere along the way, and we need a more detailed road map to get back to the initial intended course. Exhibit 17.1 shows a very simple process model for a custom products manufacturing process that an internal auditor has been asked to review. Here, the design operations group receives inputs or orders from its customers and delivers the completed products to them. However, in order to produce the output, it must coordinate with suppliers, and there must be a measurement system feedback loop to promote product improvements.

This is the type of simplified chart that an internal auditor might draft on a first visit to a facility when asking questions about the unit's activities. Using this, an internal auditor can gather more information such as detailed input and output requirements between the process owners, the activities that transform a supplier's input into an output that meets customer requirements, and the feedback and measurement systems that are necessary to make the process work. It is necessary to go a level or more beyond this simplified model. For example, the operations processes could be defined in terms of planning, engineering, procurement, order entry, accounts payable, and accounts receivable.

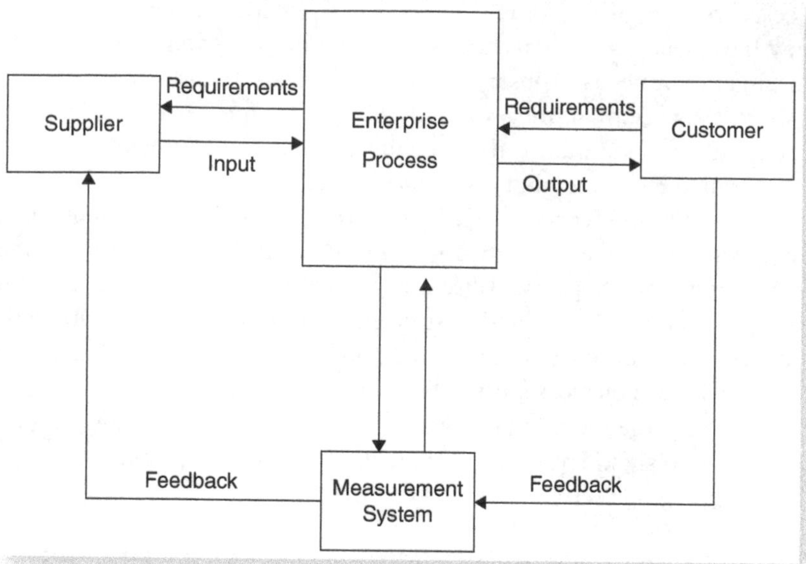

EXHIBIT 17.1 Process Model for Manufacturing Custom Products

Understanding the Process Modeling Hierarchy

While a business unit has sometimes developed its own process charts covering key activities, an internal auditor will frequently have to develop them as part of an initial visit to gain an understanding of operations. Some key process definitions will help the internal auditor to better communicate with others, particularly those who have been trained and understand process management concepts, such as:

- **Systems.** Related processes that may or may not be connected.
- **Processes.** Logically interconnected, related activities that take an input, add value to it, and produce an output to another internal process or output customer.
- **Activities.** Small parts of a process that are performed by a single department or an individual.
- **Tasks.** Steps that are required to perform specific activities.
- **External customers.** Entities outside of the process supplier's unit that receive a product, service, or information from the supplier.
- **Internal customers.** A person, department, or process within the enterprise that receives output from another process.

As part of understanding and describing processes, an internal auditor needs to understand how these process elements are related to one another. For example, Exhibit 17.2 shows a process hierarchy breakdown for what should be familiar for an internal auditor—the elements for performing an internal audit. While an actual process description would be much more detailed, this example shows that the process of evaluating internal controls points to a stream of subprocesses leading to the process activity of conducting audit tests.

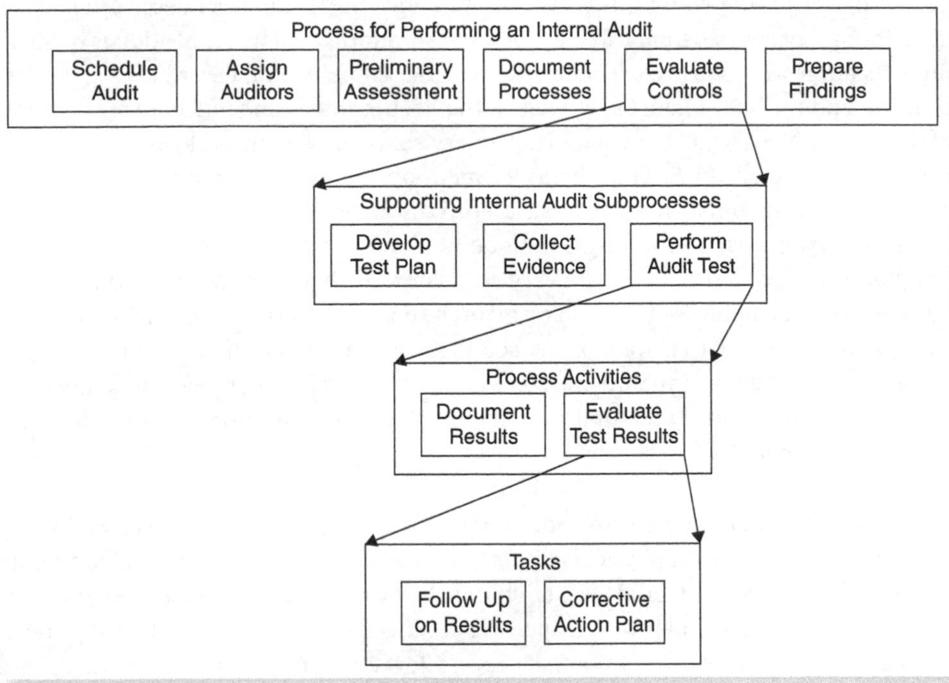

EXHIBIT 17.2 Workflow Process for an Internal Audit

Performing a process analysis and documenting key elements will require much more effort than the preliminary auditor walk-throughs described in Chapter 8 on performing effective internal audits. An internal auditor will need to assemble a team of personnel involved in the process area and go through a process area in some detail, defining such things as input and output criteria, potential errors associated with each link, and feedback processes to correct those errors. This can be a time-intensive process, but it should provide benefits to the current and future internal audits in the review area.

Describing and Documenting Key Processes

Process descriptions prepared by internal auditors should be part of the audit workpapers for any review, as discussed in the section following. Their purpose is to describe the flow of inputs and outputs between process activities, and they require strong descriptive material as well as flowchart diagrams. Although process descriptions were once prepared with pencil-and-paper methods that caused them to quickly get out of date, we now have powerful automated tools on laptop computers that will easily allow an auditor to develop process flowcharts. There are many strong products on the market, and while the objective of this book is not to endorse one product over another, we will say that SmartDraw and Visio are both excellent software products to consider. Before acquiring such graphics software, an internal auditor should meet with IT or quality assurance mangers to ascertain what software they are using.

Based on other modeling products in place, internal audit should develop diagramming standards to use in describing enterprise processes and their internal controls.

These diagramming standards will consist of flowcharts and brief descriptions. The descriptions, of course, should follow the same standards that internal audit is using in all of its audit workpaper descriptions, often bulleted notes that describe an interview that the auditor has conducted as well as the documented time and date of the interview. These notes should be reviewed for supervisor approval and protected from future unauthorized alterations. They are an element of the internal audit workpapers and require the same controls as discussed later in this chapter.

A survey of process modeling techniques will show numerous alternative diagramming approaches in use. Many are very complex and should be avoided, while others place too much emphasis on describing all of the detailed decision points in a process—similar to flowcharts that were once used to document a COBOL program.[1] Internal audit should develop a standard and consistent approach for its process modeling flowcharts. Two easy-to-use and -understand approaches are input/output flow diagrams and workflow charts.

1. **Input/output process flowcharts.** The flow description approach is best for processes that deal with physical objects. Its focus is on the passive participants that are being consumed, produced, or changed by the process activities. This type of a flowchart is a road map for transporting process steps from one activity to the next. Exhibit 17.3 shows an input/output process flow for manufacturing a wooden chair. Using an established blueprint, the various part inputs are transferred to an assembly process. Once completed, the chair moves to a painting process. This is a simple diagram, but it shows how process inputs and outputs move through an operation.
2. **Workflow description process flowcharts.** This type of diagram places its emphasis on the order of activities rather than what activity does the work. Exhibit 17.4 is an example of this type of flowchart showing a payment and shipping flow. Here, all activities must be done in a specified order, such as in the example

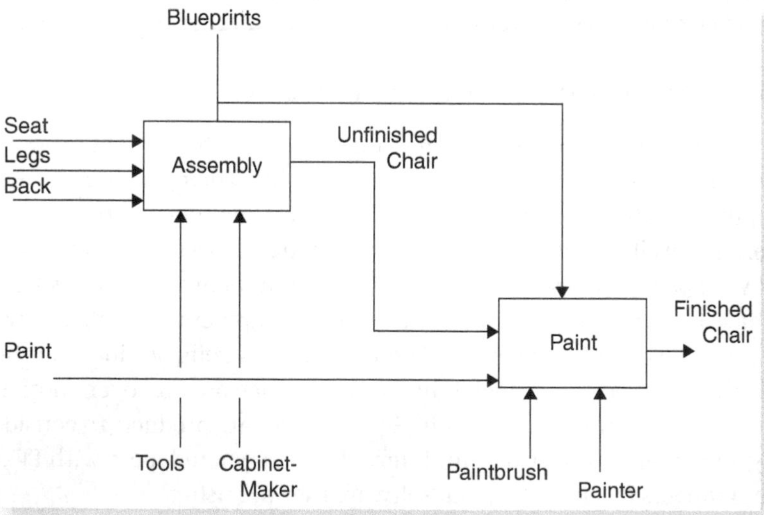

EXHIBIT 17.3 Input/Output Process Flowchart

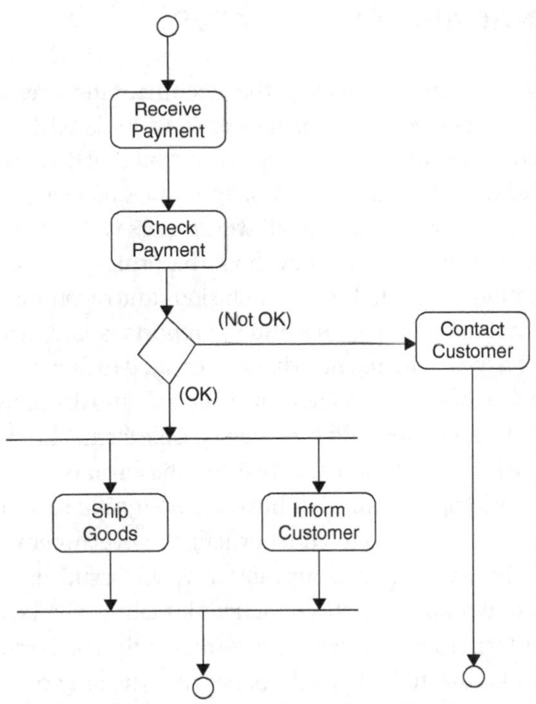

EXHIBIT 17.4 Workflow Description Process Flowchart

flowchart where it is essential to receive payment before shipping the goods. In this type of diagram, the emphasis is not on the participants but on the order that the process should flow. Because many internal audits involve office-type activities rather than manufacturing work steps, this form of process flowchart often best provides a road map of the types of activities that an internal auditor will encounter.

Process Modeling and the Internal Auditor

Process modeling in an important internal auditor tool both for reviews of existing enterprise processes and to suggest areas for improvement. Chapter 30 discusses the role of an internal auditor as an enterprise consultant; an understanding of process modeling tools and techniques is essential there. An internal auditor can meet with enterprise teams and identify areas for improvement.

We have provided a very high-level description of process modeling here. While the workflow type of flowchart described is not very complex, an internal auditor may want to gather more information to increase process modeling skills. While Institute of Internal Auditors (IIA)–heritage internal auditors may not be experienced in process modeling techniques, any member of the enterprise involved with quality assurance processes should be familiar with the techniques here. Chapter 31 discusses quality assurance auditing and approaches, and every internal auditor should have at least a minimum level of process modeling and flowcharting knowledge.

17.3 INTERNAL AUDIT WORKPAPERS

Workpapers are the written records kept to gather documentation, reports, correspondence, and other sample materials—the evidential matter—accumulated during an internal audit. The term *workpaper* is a rather archaic auditing expression that describes a physical or computer file that includes the schedules, analyses, and copies of documents prepared as part of an audit. The common characteristic of all workpapers is that they are the evidence to describe the results of the internal audit. They should be formally retained for subsequent reference and substantiation of reported audit conclusions and recommendations. As a bridge between actual internal audit procedures and the reports issued, workpapers are not an end in themselves but a means to an end. They are created to fit particular audit tasks and are subject to a great deal of flexibility. They must support and document the purposes and activities of an internal auditor, regardless of their specific form. Thus workpaper principles and concepts are more important than just their specific formats.

Internal audit workpapers can also have legal significance. In some situations, they have been handed over, through court orders, to government, legal, or regulatory authorities as supporting evidence in some matter. When scrutinized by outsiders in this context, inappropriate workpaper notes or schedules can easily be taken in the wrong context. Workpapers form the documented record of both who performed the audit and who reviewed the work. Internal audit workpapers are the only record of the audit work performed, and they may provide future evidence of what did or did not happen in an audit.

This section provides general guidance for preparing, organizing, reviewing, and retaining internal audit workpapers. Once organized in bulky legal-size paper folders, audit workpapers today are usually stored as computer-based folders or in a combination of paper and computer documents. The preparation of workpapers is a basic internal auditor CBOK requirement. As a side note, this chapter as well as other chapters use the term *workpaper*. Others in the field have used *working paper* or *work paper*. All mean the same thing.

As discussed in previous chapters, internal auditing is an objective-directed process of reviewing selected business documentation as well as interviewing members of the enterprise to gather information about an activity to support the audit objective. The internal auditor then evaluates these materials and information gathered from interviews to determine if the objectives of the audit are being met and whether appropriate standards and procedures are being properly followed. Based on this examination, the auditor forms an audit conclusion and opinion that is reported to management, usually in the form of audit findings and recommendations published in an internal audit report, as discussed in Chapter 18. An internal auditor, however, should not just casually flip through some reports or observe operations to give management impressions of what was found. The audit evidence, documented in the internal auditor's workpapers, must be sufficient to support the auditor's assertions and conclusions.

The overall objective of workpapers is to document that an adequate audit was conducted following IIA-defined professional standards. The major functions of auditor workpapers include:

- **Basis for planning an audit.** Workpapers from a prior audit provide an auditor with background information for conducting a current review in the same overall area. They may contain descriptions of the entity, evaluations of internal controls, time budgets, audit programs used, and other results of past audit work.

- **Record of audit work performed.** Workpapers describe the current audit work performed and reference it to an established audit program (see Chapter 15 on preparing audit programs). Even if the audit is of a special nature, such as a fraud investigation where there may not be a formal audit program, a record should be established of the auditing work actually carried out. This workpaper record should include a description of activities reviewed, copies of representative documents, the extent of the audit coverage, and the results obtained.
- **Use during the audit.** In many instances, the workpapers prepared play a direct role in carrying out the specific audit effort. For example, the workpapers can contain various control logs used by members of the audit team for such areas as the controls over responses received as part of an accounts receivable customer balance independent confirmation audit. Similarly, a flowchart might be prepared and then used to provide guidance for a further review of the actual activities in some process. Each of these would have been included in the workpapers in a previous audit step.
- **Description of situations of special interest.** As the audit work is carried out, situations may occur that have special significance in such areas as compliance with established policies and procedures, accuracy, efficiency, personnel performance, or potential cost savings.
- **Support for specific audit conclusions.** The final product of most internal audits is a formal audit report, as discussed in Chapter 18, containing audit findings and recommendations. The documentation supporting the findings may be actual evidence, such as a copy of a purchase order lacking a required signature, or derived evidence, such as the output report from a computer-assisted procedure against a data file or notes from an interview. The workpapers should provide sufficient evidential matter to support the specific audit findings that would be included in an audit report.
- **Reference source.** Workpapers can answer additional questions raised by management or by external auditors. Such questions may be in connection with a particular audit report finding or its recommendation, or they may relate to other inquiries. For example, management may ask internal audit if a reported problem also exists at another location that is not part of the current audit. The workpapers from that review may provide the answer. Workpapers also provide basic background materials that may be applicable to future audits of the particular entity or activity.
- **Staff appraisal.** The performance of a staff member during an audit—including the auditor's ability to gather and organize data, evaluate it, and arrive at conclusions—is directly reflected in or demonstrated by the workpapers.
- **Audit coordination.** An internal auditor may exchange workpapers with their external auditors, each relying on the other's work. In addition, government auditors, in their regulatory reviews of internal controls, may request to examine the internal auditor's workpapers.

In some respects, audit workpapers are no different from the formal files of correspondence, e-mails, and notes that are part of any well-managed enterprise. A manager would keep files of incoming and outgoing correspondence, notes based on telephone conversations, and the like. However, these files are based on good practices and may vary from one manager to another in an enterprise. The manager may never be called on to retrieve these personal files to support some enterprise decision or other action.

Internal audit workpapers are different in that they may also be used to support or defend the conclusions reached from the audit. They may be reviewed by others for various reasons. Members of an internal audit enterprise may work on common projects and need to share workpapers to support their individual components of a larger audit project or to take over an audit performed previously by another member of the audit staff. It is essential that an internal audit department have a set of standards to assure consistent workpaper preparation.

Workpaper Standards

There is no specific form or format for internal audit workpapers. The Institute of Internal Auditors international professional standards, outlined in Chapter 9, contain only high-level guidance for audit workpapers through their 2330 standard:[2]

> Internal auditors should record relevant information to support the conclusions and engagement results.

This very broad standard is supported by a series of what the IIA calls Practice Advisories that provide additional supporting information on internal audit workpaper issues including their preparation, control of the documentation, and retention requirements. The actual style and format of workpapers, however, will vary from one internal audit department to another and, to a lesser extent, sometimes even from one audit to another. An internal audit department will often establish workpaper standards that are consistent with their external auditors. However, internal audit should always recognize the differences between the financial statement attestation work of external auditors and the operational aspects of internal auditing. While there is no requirement to adopt external audit workpaper standards, many internal audit functions find it convenient to follow the general format of their external auditor's workpaper approaches.

Workpapers are not designed for general reading or as non–internal audit management reports. They are primarily designed to support individual internal audits but sometimes may be used by other members of the internal audit function, including management and quality assurance, as well as external auditors and corporate legal functions. The workpapers should follow a consistent set of standards and be able to stand alone so that an authorized outside party, such as an external auditor, can read through them and understand the objectives of the internal audit, the work performed, and any outstanding issues or findings. Internal audit workpaper standards should cover the following areas:

- **Relevance to audit objectives.** The content of the workpaper must be relevant to both the total audit assignment and any specific objectives of the particular portion of the review. There is no need for materials that do not contribute to the objectives of the specific audit performed.

- **Condensation of detail.** An internal auditor typically gathers a considerable amount of detailed data and information on any review, but that material should be carefully summarized in the audit workpapers to reduce their bulk to better describe the audit. For example, an audit may use IT retrieval tools to confirm balances on a data file, but it is often not necessary to include the entire retrieval report–produced output in the workpapers. A totals summary with test results, some sample details, and a copy of the computer program used may be sufficient.
- **Clarity of presentation.** To present clear and understandable material, internal auditors and their supervisors should review workpaper presentations on an ongoing basis and make recommendations for improvements.
- **Workpaper accuracy.** Workpaper accuracy is essential for all audit schedules and other quantitative data. Workpapers may be used at any time in the future to answer questions and to substantiate later internal audit representations.
- **Action on open items.** Questions are frequently raised during an audit, as part of the internal auditor's workpaper notes, or information is disclosed that requires follow-up. There should be no open items documented workpapers on completion of the audit. All workpaper items should either be cleared or formally documented for future audit actions.
- **Standards of form.** For workpapers to accurately describe the audit work performed, they must be prepared in a consistent format within any audit workpaper or from one to another within the internal audit department. An internal audit manager should, for example, know where to find an auditor hours schedule for any workpaper reviewed. The standards of form should include:
    - **Preparation of headings.** Individual workpaper pages or formats should have a heading with the title of the total audit, the particular component of that total audit assignment contained in a given workpaper sheet, and the date. A smaller heading on one side should indicate the name or initials of the person who prepared the workpaper and the date of preparation.
    - **Enterprise.** The use of appropriate headings, spacing, and adequacy of margins facilitates reading and understanding. The auditor might think of this enterprise along the lines of the manner in which a textbook is organized.
    - **Neatness and legibility.** These qualities not only make the workpapers more useful to all readers, but also confirm the care that went into their preparation.
    - **Cross-indexing.** All workpapers should be indexed and cross-indexed when feasible. Cross-indexing provides a trail for the auditor and assures the accuracy of information in the workpapers, as well as in the subsequent audit report.

Workpaper Formats

As mentioned, workpapers were once lengthy manual documents, handwritten by auditors with samples of any reports and other exhibits included in the package. With the now pervasive use of auditor laptop computers to develop and document internal audit work, those older manual workpapers are far less common today. Exhibit 17.5 shows a manually prepared workpaper page from an operational audit of a physical inventory observation. The important point here is this is a brief description of an internal auditor's observations. This form can stand on its own. The workpaper reader can determine the entity it covers, who did the work and when, and how this workpaper sheet relates to others in the audit. This basic format will be used in other figures in this chapter and in examples throughout the book. The internal auditor must be particularly careful to document all work steps and all audit decisions. For example, if an audit program had a work step that the in-charge auditor determined was not appropriate for a given review, the auditor should explain why that step was deleted rather than just marking it "N/A." In some situations, the initial of the audit supervisor who approved the change should also be included. Similarly, if the auditor was following up on a matter from a prior audit, the workpapers should document the manner in which the problem was corrected or else who advised the auditor that it had been fixed. It is not sufficient just to mark it "corrected" with no further references.

An internal auditor should always remember that situations may change and workpapers may be called into question many years after they have been prepared. It is possible for a regulatory agency, such as the SEC, to obtain as part of an investigation the rights to see a set of workpapers prepared years earlier. They might ask further questions or take other steps based on the audit work and observations recorded in those quite old workpapers. Memories often fade, and in this type of situation the audit workpapers may be the only credible record.

As discussed, internal audit workpaper formats will generally be based on word processing–based files and folders or may be organized as 8½-by-11-inch sheets secured in three-ring binders. Some may even use the much older format of folders prepared on legal-size sheets bound at the top. Today, most internal auditors prepare their workpapers

EXHIBIT 17.5 Manually Prepared Workpaper Sheet Example

	Global Computer Products Internal Audit	
AR-2.5.1	*Audit: MAXXAM Plant Inventory Observation*	*RRM*
	Location: South Bluff—March 4, 20xx	*3/4/xx*

Internal audit observed the taking of a finished goods physical inventory at the MAXXAM div. plant in South Bluff, OH. We reviewed the physical inventory instructions issued by the plant controller's office (see X-Ref-01) and found them complete and satisfactory. Plant personnel started the inventory at 8:00 AM on March 3. Internal Audit observed that all other plant activities were shut down during the inventory taking and that counting proceeded in an orderly manner.

Worksheets for recording the counts were prepared Global Computer's inventory system—they listed the parts assigned to designated storeroom locations but with no actual quantities (see X-Ref-02). A representative from the controller's office—Lester Tuttle—headed the control desk, issued count sheets, and logged them upon receipt.

As part of the inventory observation, Internal Audit selected a series of random stock keeping numbers and independently took test counts. We compared these counts to the counts recorded by the inventory team. Test counts and results were summarized (see X-Ref-03).

As a result of this physical inventory observation, internal audit found ________________

on their laptop computers where many of the auditor commentaries and schedules are maintained in secure files and folders. Regardless of page size or media, the purpose of a workpaper sheet is to provide a standard framework for documenting internal audit activities. As discussed previously, workpaper pages should be titled, dated, initialed by the preparer, and prepared in a neat and orderly manner. The next sections expand on this basic workpaper format.

17.4 WORKPAPER DOCUMENT ORGANIZATION

A typical internal audit includes the gathering of a large amount of materials to document some internal control process or the results of audit testing. With the wide range of activities reviewed and the equally wide range of audit procedures, the form and content of those individual workpapers may vary greatly. The major categories depend on the nature of the audit materials and the work performed, and the workpaper standards should be built around some specialized types of files. This chapter refers to these as *files*, while the term *folders* also is common today. Some internal audit departments still use the older term *binders* to refer to different workpaper groupings. Just as in any manual filing system, workpaper materials are classified by their basic type and grouped together in a file or bound together in a binder in a manner that aids their retrieval. For most internal audits, the workpapers can be separated into the following broad audit areas:

1. **Permanent files.** Many audits are performed on a periodic basis and follow repetitive procedures. Rather than capture all of the data necessary every time a periodic audit is performed, certain data can be gathered into what is called a permanent workpaper file, which contains data of a *historical or continuing nature* pertinent to current audits. Some of this data may include:
   - Overall enterprise charts of the audit unit
   - Charts of accounts (if a financial audit) and copies of major policies and procedures
   - Copies of the last audit report, the audit program used, and any follow-up comments
   - Financial statements about the entity as well as other potentially useful analytical data
   - Information about the audit unit (descriptions of major products, production processes, and other newsworthy matters)
   - Logistical information to help the next auditors, including notes regarding logistics and travel arrangements

   A permanent file is not meant to be *permanent* in the sense that that there will never be changes; rather, it provides an internal auditor starting a new assignment a source of background material to help plan a new audit. The permanent file is a source of continuity to tie audits together over time, but auditors are sometimes guilty of loading up these audit files with materials that do not deserve permanent status—for example, copies of various procedures that will have changed by the time of the next audit. Materials readily available at the time of the next audit need not be retained in permanent files unless certain ongoing procedures were based on those earlier materials. Similarly, internal auditors sometimes fill up paper-based permanent files for out-of-town locations with maps and menus of local restaurants. These units will change, as will both individual auditor preferences and department policies. This administrative planning material should be kept to a minimum.

2. **Administrative files.** Although a separate workpaper administrative file may not be necessary for a smaller audit, the same general administrative workpaper materials should be incorporated somewhere in all audit workpaper sets. If there is only a single auditor or limited review, this material may be incorporated into the single workpaper.
3. **Audit procedures files.** Records should be maintained of the actual audit work performed, depending on the type and nature of the audit assignment. For example, a financial audit may contain detailed spreadsheet schedules with auditor commentary on tests performed. An operational audit may contain interview notes and commentary on auditor observations. This file is generally the largest for any audit and often contains the following elements:
   - **Listings of completed audit procedures.** Workpapers are a central repository documenting the audit procedures, and include copies of the audit programs along with the initials of the auditors and the dates of the audit steps (see Exhibit 17.6). Commentary notes may be on the programs or attached as cross-referenced supplementary notes.
   - **Completed questionnaires.** Some internal audit functions use standard questionnaires covering particular types of internal control procedures. These questionnaires normally provide for yes and no answers and appropriate supplementary comments.
   - **Descriptions of operational procedures.** Workpapers should briefly describe the nature and scope of a specific type of operational activity. This description can be a process flowchart, as discussed earlier in this chapter, or a verbal narrative. An internal auditor should always note on the workpaper the source of the information used to develop this description. A member of auditee management may have described the process, or the auditor may have gathered this information through observation.
   - **Review activities.** Many internal audit workpapers cover specific investigations that appraise selected activities. These can include testing of data, observations of performance, inquiries to designated individuals, and the like. This is perhaps the most common type of workpaper prepared by the internal auditor. It follows no one form but only serves to describe the audit activities performed and the results. Exhibit 17.7 shows a workpaper covering tests of an audit of travel and entertainment expenses. As shown here, an internal auditor would provide some details of the audit work even though the final audit report will only summarize these findings.
   - **Analyses and schedules pertaining to financial statements.** In a financially oriented audit, a special variety of workpapers relates to attesting to the accuracy of financial statement or account balances. This type of workpaper schedule is an appropriate documentation for the SOx Section 404 reviews discussed in Chapter 5.

- **Enterprise documents.** There are often basic enterprise documents such as enterprise charts, minutes of meetings, particular policy statements or procedures, contracts, and the like. While some of these might be more appropriate for the permanent file, others are unique to a particular audit. However, the auditor should not include all material in the workpapers. For example, it may be sufficient to include a table of contents and have relevant extracts rather than incorporating an entire procedures manual in the workpapers. The purpose of these documents is to help future auditors in their decisions or processes.
- **Findings point sheets, supervisor notes, or drafts of reports.** Point sheets describing the nature of the audit finding as well as reference to the detailed audit work should be included in audit procedures files even though a copy has been forwarded to the administrative file. During an audit, the in-charge auditor or audit supervisor prepares review comments that may require explanation by the auditor. In some cases, further audit work is needed. A workpaper point sheet is shown in Exhibit 17.8. For smaller audits that do not have an administrative file, draft versions of the written report should be included here. These drafts can be annotated to show major changes, the persons responsible for authorizing those changes, and in some cases the reasons for the changes.
- **Audit bulk files.** Internal audits often produce large amounts of evidential materials that should be retained but are not included in the primary workpapers. For example, internal audit may perform a survey that results in a large number of returned questionnaires. These materials should be classified as workpapers but should be retrieved from the bulk file as necessary.

EXHIBIT 17.6 Workpaper Audit Program Example

	Global Computer Products Internal Audit **Audit: Headquarters Direct Sales** **AUDIT PROGRAM–CASH**	**LCT** **10/31/xx**
B25		
Ref.	**Audit Procedure**	**Disposition**
1.a	Review sources of reducing difficult-to-control cash conditions.	W/P B.32 LCT 10/30/xx
1.b	Determine that physical safeguards exist and are adequate for any cash maintained in any areas of operations.	
1.c	Review procedures to keep cash on hand—in all forms and levels.	
2.a	Determine that petty cash and branch funds are utilized and operated on an impress basis.	
2.b	Assess adequacy of documentary support for petty and miscellaneous cash disbursements.	W/P B.37 LCT 10/29/xx
2.c	Review controls surrounding issuance and use of company credit cards.	
3.a	Determine all employees who handle or have direct access to cash are adequately bonded.	
4.a	Select one of the petty cash funds and independently observe a cash count, reconciling results to recorded records.	W/P B.26 LCT 11/05/xx

EXHIBIT 17.7 Travel Audit Workpaper Example

Global Computer Products Internal Audit
Audit: Headquarters Travel & Entertainment
Z12.4 AUDIT PROGRAM—CASH 10/31/xx

Internal Audit reviewed a sample of employee travel and entertainment reports filed electronically during the 3rd quarter, 20xx. During that period, 987 reports were filed. We selected a sample of 45 of these reports for our review based on these criteria:

- All reports for the 6 senior officers—16 reports reviewed.
- Reports involving international travel—2 reports reviewed.
- All other reports having total reported expenses > $5,000—7 reports reviewed.
- A sample of the remaining 987 reports filed—27 reports reviewed.

Our review was based on Global Computer Product's travel and entertainment procedures, dated 03/12/xx. Selected sample reports were reviewed for these criteria:

- Reported expenses with policy guidelines.
- Use of the company credit card where appropriate.
- Use of company designated air carriers and rental cars.
- Appropriate levels of management approvals.

The results of the review are summarized on ______

EXHIBIT 17.8 Workpaper Supervisor Point Sheet Example

A.4.2	***Global Computer Products Internal Audit*** ***Audit: Axylotl Plant Production Control*** ***Workpaper Review Notes***	***RRM*** ***11/08/xx***
W/P Ref.	***Supervisor Review Notes***	***Auditor Actions***
B-21 & C-21	*Missing W/P X-references.*	*Corrected*
B-16	*Schedule does not cross-foot to D-02 summary. Please revise and correct.*	*OK—See D.02.1*
D-20	*Does the ref. point to larger control problem?*	*OK—See D.02.1*
D-21	*W/P sheet not signed or corrected.*	*Corrected*
D-36	*Evidence does not support your recommendation—Clarify!*	
D-41 to 5	*Missing W/P X-references*	*Corrected*
—	*Where is the X-Cat software located?*	*See XCM folder*

Workpapers are the basis for communicating audit documentation from one audit or auditor to the next and are also a means of communication with the enterprise's external auditors. An internal audit department should establish some overall standards covering the style, format, and content of the workpapers used in various audits. Some specific details do not need to be frozen, given the various types of audits performed and evolving audit automation procedures, as discussed later. However, workpaper content should be prepared consistently for all audits. The audit procedures workpaper file, for example, should contain materials covering each of the just discussed areas.

17.5 WORKPAPER PREPARATION TECHNIQUES

Much of the process of preparing workpapers involves the drafting of audit comments and developing schedules to describe the audit work and support its conclusions. This is a detailed process that requires internal auditors to follow the overall audit department standards for the preparation of workpapers, and also to make the workpapers easy to follow and understand. An important aspect is to ensure that all members of the internal audit staff have an understanding of the purposes for and the criticality of their audit workpapers. These schedules will be reviewed by internal audit management and others, who may question the type and extent of the work performed based on whatever is documented in the workpapers. This section discusses some of the basic techniques needed for preparing adequate workpapers. These comments are largely based on today's more common laptop-prepared workpaper templates but also include more traditional, manually prepared workpapers. Whether prepared manually or using a computer-based system, audit workpapers should contain certain indexing and notation standards that will allow for easy review by other interested internal audit professionals.

- **Workpaper indexing and cross-referencing.** Similar to reference notations in textbooks, sufficient cross-references and notations should allow an auditor or reviewer to take a significant reference in a workpaper commentary and trace it back to its original citation or source. For example, a workpaper document describing a financial review of fixed assets might mention that the IT application that calculates depreciation has adequate controls. It is sufficient to provide a cross-reference so that the interested reader could easily find those depreciation computation control auditor review workpapers. Index numbers on workpapers are the same as volume and page numbers in a published book. Workpaper index numbers should tie into a table of contents, which usually appears on the first page of the workpaper folder or manual binder. The number identifies the specific page in the workpaper binder. References to this number elsewhere allow an auditor to immediately select the correct workpaper binder and page. The system used for index numbers in a set of workpapers can be as simple or as complex as desired. Many internal audit departments adopt the same general indexing system used by their external auditors so that all members of the audit staff can understand the correct reference to a volume in a given workpaper set. A method for indexing manually prepared internal audit workpapers might follow a set of three digits so that "AP-5-26" would mean the 26th page of the 5th step in a given set of audit procedures. If multiple pages were required for page 26, they would be expressed as AP-5-26.01, AP-5-26.02, and so forth. Any numbering system should be easy to use and adaptable to change. With laptop-based workpaper documents, Microsoft Word hyperlinks can be a useful tool.

  Cross-referencing refers to placing other reference workpaper index numbers within a given workpaper schedule. For example, a workpaper schedule may discuss controls over fixed-asset additions and state that all additions above some specified limit receive proper approval by management. That workpaper statement would parenthetically reference another workpaper index number denoting fixed-asset tests and indicating evidence of management approvals. Cross-reference numbers are particularly important in financial audits where all numbers on various schedules should be tied together to assure consistency.

- **Tick marks.** Back in the early days of manually prepared audit workpapers, auditors often prepared a financial or statistical schedule and then selected various numbers from that schedule on which to perform one or more additional tests. For example, an auditor may review a sample of purchase orders to determine if they (1) represent vendors on the approved list, (2) are subject to competitive bids, (3) are computed correctly, and so forth. Rather than list this sample of purchase orders on multiple workpaper sheets for each of the tests, auditors normally used one schedule, employing what are called *tick marks* to footnote various tests performed.

  Tick marks are a form of auditor manual or pencil shorthand notation that have evolved over the years, particularly for financial audits. An auditor can develop a particular check mark to indicate that a given value on the financial schedule cross-foots to other related values, and another tick mark to indicate that it ties to the trial balance. The auditor need only note somewhere in the workpapers the tick mark used for each. Rather than asking the auditor to develop a legend, many internal audit departments have used a standard set of tick mark symbols in all workpapers. For example, a check mark with a line through it may mean that the workpaper item was traced to a supporting schedule and the numbers tied. These standard tick marks should be used by all members of the audit staff for all audits.

  Standard manually prepared tick marks improve communication, as audit management can easily review and understand workpapers. Exhibit 17.9 illustrates a set of traditional tick marks that were first used in the pencil-and-paper days. Although these same symbols may not be available through Microsoft Word, similar special characters can be designated for the same purpose. In developing these tick marks, the internal audit department might want to adopt the notation used by its external auditors. Of course, the auditor might develop another mark to indicate some other type of cross-check performed in the course of an individual audit, which would then be clearly explained.

✓̶	Agreed to mm/dd/yy workpapers
≈	Confirmed with maker of transaction—no exceptions
✓	Examined during audit procedures
ƒ	Footed
ƒƒ	Footed and cross-footed
^	Traced to ledger balance
CR	Traced to cash receipts deposit slips
ℊ	Verified computation

EXHIBIT 17.9 Workpaper Auditor Tick Marks Examples

- **References to external audit sources.** Internal auditors often record information taken from outside sources. For example, an internal auditor may gather an understanding of an operational area through an interview with management. The auditor would record that interview through workpaper notes and rely on that information as the basis of further audit tests or conclusions. It is always important to record the source of such commentary directly in the workpapers. For example, a workpaper exhibit could show how the auditor gained an understanding of a sample system, and the source that provided that information should be documented.

  Auditors may need to reference laws or regulations to support their audit work. Similarly, they may perform a vendor-related review and access a Web search to verify vendor existence. It is usually not necessary to include in the workpapers a copy of what may be a voluminous regulation, nor a copy of a page from the search. However, workpapers should clearly indicate the title and source of all external references, including the Internet address if appropriate. Extract page copies can be included to make a specific point when necessary, but a reference notation is normally sufficient.

- **Workpaper rough notes.** When conducting interviews, internal auditors often make their own very rough notes, often written in a personal form of shorthand easily readable only by the author. Auditors subsequently should rewrite or reenter these rough notes into workpaper commentary understandable by others. Because there may be a reason to review them again, these original note sheets should also be included in the workpapers, placed in the back of the workpaper manual binder or even in a separate file.

  Historically, most workpapers were prepared using pencil and paper. Schedules were recorded on accounting spreadsheet forms, commentaries were written in longhand, and any exhibits were attached. Most internal audit departments have now automated their workpapers through the use of spreadsheet and word processing software. This automation does not change the workpaper standards, but it usually makes the workpapers easier to read and to access. The typical workpaper today may use a mix of manual and automated schedules and audit commentaries. However, today's workpaper is usually a computer systems folder with perhaps some references to paper documents.

  Technology is always changing, and we may be seeing different formats of audit evidence in future years. Digital image scanners are very common today. They can be passed over a paper document, creating a digital image of that document for later retrieval. Similarly, some computers are now equipped with a pen stylus for the user to "write" directly on the computer screen. The data is captured in computer files. These and other evolving technologies offer opportunities for audit workpaper automation.

Workpaper Review Processes

All workpapers should go through an independent internal audit review process to assure that necessary work has been performed, that it is properly described, and that audit findings are adequately supported. The chief audit executive, reporting to the audit committee, has the overall responsibility for this review but usually delegates that work to supervisory members of the internal audit department. Depending on the size of the audit staff and the relative importance of a given audit, there may be multiple reviews of a set of workpapers, one by the in-charge auditor and another by a more senior member of internal audit management.

Evidence of this supervisory review should consist of the reviewer's initials and dates on each workpaper sheet reviewed. Some internal audit functions prepare a memorandum or workpaper review checklist to document the nature and extent of their reviews. In any case, there should be documented evidence that all workpapers have received a proper level of supervisory review. In addition to initialing completed workpapers, the supervisory reviewer should prepare a set of review notes with any questions raised during the review process to give to the responsible auditor for resolution. Some of these review points or questions may simply highlight clerical errors such as missing cross-references. Others may be of a more significant nature and may require the auditor to do some additional follow-up work. Review questions should be cleared promptly, and the reviewer should take the responsibility to assure that any open questions are resolved. This workpaper review process should *always* take place prior to the issuance of the final audit report. This will ensure that all report findings have been properly supported by audit evidence as documented in the workpapers.

17.6 INTERNAL AUDIT DOCUMENT RECORDS MANAGEMENT

Efforts to document processes or to describe an internal audit through effective workpapers are of little value unless an internal audit function has strong document retention controls covering all of its work products, including auditor notes, copies of meeting minutes, IT files, and many others. As we move to largely paperless business and internal audit environments, this document retention need has become much more of a challenge than the old days of paper-and-pencil records. In those old days, documents were often retained in formal filing cabinets requiring access to a key from an office administrator, supervisor reviews were evidenced by a familiar initial on the form, and attempts to make unauthorized changes required smudged erasures. The ease and flexibility of things today raises document risks such as the loss of audit workpapers due to a stolen auditor laptop or process errors in an IT analysis process developed by internal audit.

In the first section of this chapter, we discussed internal audit documentation requirements and outlined the need to keep all relevant internal audit documentation for a period of seven years after the completion of an internal audit. Again, this can sometimes cause a challenge in today's paperless auditing environment. Operating systems or file formats may change, and we may suddenly not be able to access or read a document. Documents can disappear due to someone mistakenly hitting the delete key, or documents can disappear because of a failure to download an auditor's laptop system to a central server system. An internal audit function needs strong and consistent document management policies with assigned administrative responsibilities for these tasks.

Chapter 19 discusses IT general controls and ITIL® best practices. Many of the latter ITIL® best practices cover such areas establishing configuration management controls over IT resources and IT change management processes. While ITIL® is focused on the

IT infrastructure, many best practice concepts apply to internal audit document management. The following sections discuss some important or even essential document management practices for an internal audit function in today's environment of auditor laptops and wireless networks:

- **Document standards and review processes.** Internal audit needs to establish standards for the software used, laptop computer configurations, and general document and template standards. The goal should be that every member of the internal audit team is using the same equipment and—with the exception of some specialized IT tools—everyone is following the same formats and standards. An objective of an internal auditor's documentation processes should be to eliminate all separate paper documents, and when an internal auditor needs to use paper forms or other evidential matters, digital scanning tools should be used to capture the material.

  Formal and secure processes should be set for each scheduled audit. An internal auditor at a field location may be assigned a laptop with a preliminary audit program as well as workpapers from a prior review all secured and loaded. The lead auditor certainly may encounter situations where an established audit program needs to be modified, but these proposed changes can be passed through a secure virtual private network for review and approval by audit management. That audit work, loaded on the lead auditor's laptop and shared with others on the audit team, should be the prime records repository for a given internal audit. At the conclusion of the audit, the workpaper materials—including the audit report—should be downloaded to the audit department's central server system.

- **Backup, security, and continuity.** This is perhaps the most critical and high-risk area for laptop-based internal audit systems. Many of the cybersecurity and privacy controls discussed in Chapter 23 are highly appropriate for automated internal audit work as well. A good starting idea here is to configure and assign auditor laptop systems as strictly internal audit tools only. There should be no outside links to the Internet or permitted downloads to USB devices. For personal e-mails back home and the like, an internal auditor can use one of the many small portable devices available.

  While we cannot chain an audit laptop or tablet system to the internal auditor's body, measures should be applied to keep the system secure, and in the event of a theft, strong security and password controls should be installed such that if a system is stolen, its contents cannot be easily accessed. (We use the word *easily* because computer forensics experts can access almost anything.) Procedures should also be established for internal audit files to be backed up and downloaded to the internal audit server system on a regular basis.

- **Hardware and software resource management.** There once was a day when some internal audit functions used central IT records for their automated workpapers. Today, with relatively efficient and lower-cost resources available, there is really no reason an internal audit function should not have a server system dedicated to just internal audit purposes. A secure system should be installed as a repository for all internal audit activities. The system's key file folders should be folded in with the IT function's continuity planning processes, as discussed in Chapter 24.

- **Audit reports, risk management, and internal audit administration.** Internal audit has a need to prepare and distribute a large body of materials, including audit reports, risk management analyses, budgets, and communications with the audit committee. The same seven-year document retention rule should apply to these internal audit administrative records, and they should be placed in secure folders on the audit department server system.

While we have discussed processes for retaining ongoing internal audit documentation, the seven-year retention rule can place demands on storage facilities, even despite the ever-lower costs of storage facilities. Many enterprises have used secure storage facilities for off-site storage of their older paper documents that have retention requirements. Vendors will pick up an enterprise's critical documents, catalog them by some broad retrieval categories, and then store them in secure, fire-protected facilities. These vendors provide insurance-company protection of stored documents and will deliver any document requested in a relatively short time frame. Although originally oriented to paper documents, similar vendors provide retention facilities for electronic documents. Internal audit should make arrangements for some type of secure off-site storage for key internal audit digital and paper documents.

17.7 IMPORTANCE OF INTERNAL AUDIT DOCUMENTATION

Virtually all of the internal audit processes in other chapters of this book must be supported by adequate documentation. This chapter has tried to emphasize the importance of audit workpapers to document internal audit activities as well as process modeling to describe enterprise activities. The ability to prepare descriptive and effective workpapers is a key internal CBOK requirement. In addition, all internal auditors from the chief audit executive to audit staff should be comfortable and familiar with the many IT tools available to describe and document internal audit processes.

NOTES

1. We are describing a detailed flowchart approach here that is seldom used today but was common in the earlier days of computer programming.
2. IIA standards are summarized in Chapter 9, and complete information regarding them can be obtained at www.theiia.org.

CHAPTER EIGHTEEN

Reporting Internal Audit Results

AN INTERNAL AUDIT REPORT IS a formal document where an internal audit function summarizes its work on an audit project by reporting its observations and *recommendations* based on that audit. *Audit reports* are the most important end product of the internal auditing process and are a major vehicle to describe internal audit's activities for people both inside and outside of the enterprise. Audit reports provide evidence about the professional character of internal audit activities and allow others to evaluate this contribution. Effective audit reports, of course, must be supported by high-quality audit fieldwork and evidence evaluation, as discussed in Chapter 10, but that same audit fieldwork can be nullified by poorly written or prepared reports. The preparation of clear and effective reports should be a major concern for internal auditors at all levels, from the chief audit executive (CAE) to audit team staff members. The understanding of how to construct and draft an effective internal audit report is a basic common body of knowledge (CBOK) requirement.

Good internal audit reporting is more than just report preparation and appearance. Audit reports should reflect the basic philosophy of an enterprise's total internal audit approach, including its underlying review objectives, supporting strategies and major policies, procedures covering the audit work, and the professional performance of the audit staff. While the audit report is the major means of communication, internal auditors will be less effective if their communications with the rest of the enterprise are limited only to published reports. Communication also must be effected through interviews during the course of fieldwork, closing meetings when *audit findings* are first presented, meetings with senior management and the audit committee to apprise them of the results of audits, and through many other contacts throughout the enterprise. All members of an internal audit organization must be effective communicators in both their written and spoken words. This chapter will discuss the purpose and presentation styles of internal audit reports, including various formats and methods of presenting the results of audit work to management and others in the enterprise. Audit reports are a major component of internal audit communication.

18.1 THE AUDIT REPORT FRAMEWORK

An effective audit report should engage its audience—ranging from members of the board audit committee to involved management—by discussing the risks and issues that were part of the report's themes and then developing a call for action based on the report's recommendations. While the next sections will discuss audit reports in more detail, Exhibit 18.1 outlines a general audit report framework.

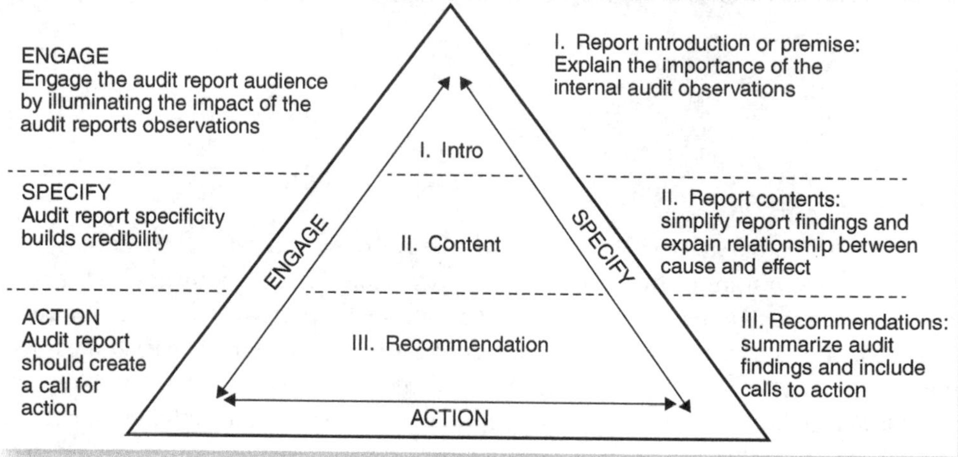

EXHIBIT 18.1 Audit Report Framework

The core of this diagram shows the three major elements of any internal audit report:

1. A report introduction to explain the reasons for initiating the audit and the importance of the report's observations.
2. The report's content or body that explains the audit work performed and discusses any related cause-and-effect matters.
3. Report recommendations. This review section summarizes internal audit's premises and includes calls for action.

The framework also is surrounded by three important objectives. First, any audit report must engage its readers and the overall interested audience by illuminating the impact of internal audit's observations. Second, an audit report must include a high level of specificity in order to support its findings and recommendations. Finally, any audit report must contain a call for action where audit report recommendations are summarized in greater detail. The next sections will discuss audit report elements and objectives in greater detail based on this overall internal audit report framework.

18.2 PURPOSES AND TYPES OF INTERNAL AUDIT REPORTS

Internal audit reports have a basic purpose to describe a planned audit's objectives and to communicate the results and recommendations from that audit. By their nature, internal audit reports are generally critical in their content and tend to emphasize such matters as internal control weaknesses. While it is perfectly proper to report that internal audit reviewed some area and found no problems, if the audit department or some individual consistently found no problems in most of the scheduled audits, there may be a need to review internal audit's risk assessment approach and their reviews following internal audit standards. Whether a formal written document circulated to senior and board level management or an informal or even verbal presentation at the end of the audit fieldwork, internal audit reports should always have four basic components:

1. **Audit objectives, timing, and scope of the review.** The audit report should summarize the high-level objectives of the review, where and when the review took place, and the high-level scope of the internal audit. A scope statement, for example, might disclose that the audit was performed at the request of the audit committee or was initiated as the result of a discovered fraud.
2. **Description of audit report findings.** Based on the conditions observed and found during the review, the audit report should engage its reader by describing the results of the internal audit. This is often where the report describes what, if anything, is wrong with the conditions found, as well as why it is wrong. The term *wrong* here includes internal control weaknesses, violations of company procedures, or any of a wide variety of other internal audit concerns.
3. **Suggestions for corrective actions.** Audit reports should include recommendations, based on the audit findings, for correcting the conditions observed and their causes. The objectives of these report suggestions include statements about fixing an observed condition as well as recommendations to improve operations.
4. **Documentation of plans and a clarification of views of the auditee.** The auditee, or function that has been audited, may wish to state mitigating circumstances or provide a clarification of issues for any reported matters in disagreement. Depending on the report format, this is often a place where the auditee can formally file a response to the internal audit findings and state plans for corrective actions in response to those audit findings and recommendations.

This four-step process—(1) why internal audit launched the review, (2) what internal audit found to be wrong and why it is wrong, (3) what should be done to correct matters, and (4) what will be done by the auditee based on internal *audit recommendations*—forms the basis of virtually all internal audit reports. Internal auditors should always keep these four steps in mind when drafting audit reports and the separate audit findings that provide the basis for them.

While internal audit functions often spend considerable time in preparing their audit reports, they sometimes lose sight of who is the report reader. An internal audit report should be prepared for the audit committee and senior management. While audit committees are much more visible and prominent today, due to Sarbanes-Oxley

Act (SOx) requirements, the audit report management readership exists at all levels, including the direct management of the component reviewed and more senior levels of management up to the audit committee at the highest level. Each management group has special needs and interests, and the question becomes one of which needs best serve overall organization interests. In more specific terms, the question comes down to what internal audit's respective responsibilities are to the direct auditee, or the management group with overall or higher-level responsibility for the area being audited.

The auditee—that is, the staff and management group that was audited—will be motivated by a combination of organization and local-entity interests. Direct auditee management knows that its ultimate welfare is closely related to total enterprise success but also knows that these rewards are largely determined by its own performance. This perception of performance is a combination of the operational results achieved and how more-senior management thinks the directly responsible managers are actually contributing. In everyday parlance, local or unit management strives to look good to upper-level management. What this all means in terms of internal audit is that the local managers often want help, but want it on a basis that does not discredit them with more senior levels of management. Ideally, they might like to have internal audit work with them on a private consultantcy basis but not report finding any dirty linen to senior management. While the internal audit professional standards discussed in Chapters 9 and 30 recognize that internal auditors may sometimes act as internal consultants, that is not internal audit's prime role.

Internal audit should try to help local management do a more effective job, knowing that in order to identify internal control problems and recommend potential solutions, internal audit must have the full cooperation and a near-partnership relationship with local management. However, this cooperative attitude can place pressure on internal audit if it is asked to pull its punches in audit reports with copies to senior management. Internal audit may feel that its reported concerns will be implemented sooner if it does not criticize local management too harshly in its published audit reports. However, internal audit has a major responsibility to report the audit's objectives on the conditions found or observed. While providing service to local management, internal audit's obligations reach all the way up to the audit committee of the board.

As a starting point for resolving these potentially conflicting demands, all management levels must be provided with a comprehensive understanding of each other's needs and internal audit's responsibility to serve them. There is often a need to increase the level of tolerance and flexibility by raising the level of findings and issues considered sufficiently significant to warrant inclusion in an audit report. This way, internal audit can eliminate many of the more minor matters that should be, and can be, finalized at the local level without involving higher-level managers. A determined joint effort is needed between the local managers and internal audit to work out needed follow-up actions during the course of an internal audit.

The general effect of these actions is to push internal audit more toward being seen as a service to local management in its work and away from being viewed as just a headquarters spy. This approach must continue to recognize that internal audit always has its important reporting responsibility to senior management and the audit committee.

18.3 PUBLISHED AUDIT REPORTS

Although audit reports have been discussed as almost a single concept, they can take a variety of different formats and styles, ranging from Web-based documents to hard-copy paper reports. In any format, an audit report is a formal report document outlining internal audit's concerns and recommendations following the four objectives previously discussed. In past years, management in the days before SOx sometimes placed restrictions or constraints on internal audit that limited it from preparing effective audit reports. For example, some senior managers in the past, and going back to the days of paper documents, may have declared that all audit reports must be one page or less in size. This type of request sometimes took place because internal audit functions had gotten too carried away with writing up pages and pages of audit report findings that may have seemed significant to the internal auditor but not to senior management.

Audit reporting attitudes also have changed after SOx. In the congressional hearings leading to the act, there was criticism directed at audit committees for sometimes receiving only summarized reports, at best, and not any level of detail regarding audit findings, whether from internal or external auditors. With SOx, audit committee members, and of course senior management, are to receive or have access to full copies of all audit reports. While it is their right to request summarized reports as well, they are still responsible for receiving and understanding all reported audit findings. Internal control findings must be clearly described in an internal audit report. This section will discuss formal published audit reports as well as alternative mechanisms for internal audit reporting.

Published Audit Report Formats

The form and content of internal audit reports can vary widely. An audit report covering a review of internal controls may appear different than a report on business continuity controls or one on fraud investigation procedures. However, no matter the subject of the internal audit, formal audit reports should always cover a similar general format, starting with a cover page, a description of the work performed, and then the internal audit findings and recommendations. We are describing an audit report here in the sense of an older, multipage type of paper document. Today, a report would typically be a Web-based document that may never even be formally printed. However, just as the words in a printed book cannot be changed once printed, software-copy versions of audit reports should be protected in such a manner that no one but the author—internal audit—can change them after release or publication.

Just as a traditional book will begin with a cover page and preface, an audit report should begin with an introductory page. Exhibit 18.2 is an example of an introductory page for a formal audit report covering a review of the purchasing function in our Global Computer Products sample enterprise. This report's introductory page or pages should have the following elements:

- **Report addressees and carbonees.** An audit report should always be addressed to one person responsible for drafting report responses, often someone usually at least one organizational level above the auditee. There should also be a selected list of carbonees, as determined by internal audit. The latter will include the auditee's manager, members of senior management, and other interested persons such as the partner in charge of the external audit team. (As an aside, *carbonees* refers to the old days when carbon paper was used to make copies. Carbon paper has all but vanished, but we still use the term.)

- **Title of report and objectives of review.** A brief, definitive title tells the reader what is contained in the audit report and also will be useful for various summary reports. Similarly, an audit report should have a brief but clear statement of the objectives of the review.
- **Audit scope and date of the fieldwork.** Usually included with the statement of audit objectives is some abbreviated information on the general scope of the audit and the approximate date of the audit fieldwork. A statement that a given report covers a review of the "purchasing function for electronic components at the XYZ division" will lead the reader to expect a different report than a statement that the audit covered just the "purchasing function."
- **Locations visited and timing of audit.** Because of potential delays in wrapping up audit reports due, time may pass between the conducting of the fieldwork and the publishing of the final audit report. The report cover page should clearly state when the audit fieldwork was performed and also mention the locations visited.
- **Audit procedures performed.** A brief paragraph describing the audit procedures performed is often very helpful to the report reader. This information is particularly useful if internal audit has performed some special testing procedures in order to arrive at its opinion.
- **Auditor's opinion based on the results of the review.** An internal audit report should *always* have some fairly general assessment of the overall adequacy of the controls or other concerns in the area reviewed. For example, the opinion statement might be worded using one of the following examples:
  - "We found the controls in the area reviewed to be adequate except for . . ."
  - "We found that most controls were good and were operating as installed . . ."
  - "We identified significant control problems in the areas reviewed. Our findings . . ."

Internal audit reports often follow one of several common approaches. Depending on the type of enterprise, its overall management style, the skills of the internal audit staff, and many other factors, each of the audit report formats described has its own merits as well as disadvantages. Internal audit wants to communicate what it did, what it found, and what needs to be corrected in a manner that will gain the attention of key managers in the enterprise. All professionals are faced with a barrage of paper documents as well as electronic communications, which they are asked to read, understand, and act on. Internal audit wants to provide the readers of its reports with enough information to explain the issues but not so much that members of management will place the report on an office credenza or e-mail inbox with little more than good intentions of reading it later. Without enough information, the reader may not know if a serious problem or other issues requiring action exist given the summarized report format. In an overly detailed report, the reader may miss significant points given the large volume of the

EXHIBIT 18.2 Formal Audit Report Introductory Page

Internal Audit Department Audit Report
Peerless Division Purchasing Function

To: Malcolm Muddle, Director of Operations

CC: Amos Arrons, Peerless Division Finance
Cecelia Clark, Peerless Vendor Management
Sam Sneed, Debits & Credits, CPAs

The Global Computer Products Internal Audit Department has performed an internal control review of the Peerless Division purchasing function. The objective of our review was to assess the quality of the internal control environment and the control procedures operating over the Peerless headquarters facility at Burning Stump, NE. Our work was restricted to operations at the Burning Stump facility and did not include purchasing activities at the facility in Malaysia. We completed the fieldwork for this audit on XX, 20xx.

Our review included an assessment of the adequacy of Peerless Division purchasing processes in place and their compliance with overall Global Computer Products procedures. We performed detailed tests of procedures, as we felt appropriate, and also reviewed controls over key Peerless Division IT systems. In addition, we performed a detailed confirmation and quality assurance assessment of a sample of Peerless vendors.

We generally found the internal controls over the Peerless purchasing function to be adequate. We did find some areas where we recommend that corrective actions are necessary to improve the internal control structures. Our internal audit findings and recommendations and Management's planned corrective actions are included in this report.

Samantha Smith
Internal Audit, Nov 7, 20xx

materials presented. Effective internal audit reports, however, should always include the following key elements:

- **A brief summary of the overall audit report.** The report should start with the main elements of the audit performed, discuss the critical issues, and then summarize the details. This will capture the attention of management readers before it is necessary to get into the report's details.
- **The central message of the report.** The report should discuss the results of the audit work, the related risks, and management concerns to consider. It should highlight why the reader should be concerned about the internal auditor's recommendations as well as the risks of not following those recommendations.
- **Elements of the audit findings.** Depending upon the audit's scope and nature, its findings can cover many details. However, the effective audit report should summarize its findings using such techniques as graphics and illustrative charts to help deliver messages.
- **Short, simple sentences and words the audience understands.** Internal audits covering an area such as IT operating systems security can get involved in some very technical areas. However, the report should attempt to use words and phrases that most readers can understand.

The approaches to developing and issuing internal audit reports depend very much on the nature and scope of the audit and present the internal audit department, the audit committee, and management with a variety of alternatives. For example, some internal audit reports strive to present a great deal of information about the activity area reviewed. Their objective is to provide an in-depth reference source to the report user. The information can be of a historical nature or pertain to the current situation. It may cover operational practices and results or may deal with financial information. An example here might be a review of a complex finance-oriented automated system or a description of a complex manufacturing process.

In other instances, audit reports sometimes provide a great deal—sometimes too much—of information about the audit procedures performed. Audit steps should be described in limited detail, such as the scope of actual verifications and testing. Sometimes this audit report coverage almost repeats the materials contained in audit standards and procedural manuals, as discussed in Chapters 8 and 9. With this type of audit report, there may be a question as to how interested the reader of the report will be in these procedural details and what purpose they really serve. Most users of audit reports should be willing to rely on the competence of internal audit for those technical dimensions. Detailed descriptions are only of value when internal audit needs to describe a complex area such as the decision logic of an opinion based on audit statistical sampling parameters. On balance, such detailed accounts of technical procedures should be excluded, or at least minimized.

Internal audit reports sometimes go into fairly voluminous detail about the results of the various audit efforts. Although the coverage here may look impressive, it is doubtful whether an extensive amount of detail describing the audit findings serves a useful purpose. With a very large audit report "book," the reader may be turned off and thus miss the important materials. Web-based audit reports with lots of hyperlinks allow this, and a report should not bury the reader with more information than most need. Audit reports should give only a necessary and sufficient amount of information about audit findings and allow the reader to understand the detailed issues involved.

In the other extreme, some internal audit departments have released only highly summarized reports that provide information that internal audit has reviewed some topic area and usually found no control exceptions of significance. This same style of report often mentions that control exceptions were found and they were corrected, with no details. These reports often do little more than state that internal audit has reviewed an area and found some "minor items," which were not included in the report even though they might be interesting to a reader. Unless these summarized reports reference longer, more detailed explanatory materials, they are not effective for most internal audit reporting needs. In addition, the summarized report may put the audit committee reader at risk by glossing over potentially significant internal control weaknesses, and by not providing the details required under today's SOx rules.

The more common report format—often the best—is one that focuses only on significant issues that have potentially important bearings on internal control weaknesses, policies, operational approaches, the utilization of resources, employee performance, and the results achieved or achievable. More senior enterprise managers are interested primarily in problems that are of such a nature and scope, and they typically wish to be informed and given the opportunity to contribute to solutions. If these significant issues relate to completed actions, the issues would have to be still more significant to merit the reporting. The advantage of this focus on significant issues is that senior managers can get the information they need without wading through excessive detail.

The actual audit report format and method of presentation will vary from one enterprise to another. Exhibit 18.2 shows an example of a brief but positive-sounding audit report. Although this is a memo format report and only one page in length for the purposes of this book, multiple-page reports should follow the same general style. While audit reports were once hard-copy typed documents (remember typewriters?), desktop- or laptop-based word processing software has changed the style and format of audit reports today. They can now be issued with interesting typeface fonts, with supporting graphics, or in a totally electronic format over a proprietary intranet. However, no matter the basic format, an audit report should always contain the elements of (1) what internal audit did, (2) when it did the work, and (3) what it found. A very key portion of an internal audit report should be the auditor's findings and recommendations.

Elements of an Audit Report Finding

During a review, the internal auditors assigned to the project may encounter exceptions or internal control weaknesses in some of the areas reviewed, as outlined in the established audit program. Those audit programs should have helped to identify exceptions as well as other internal audit observations that are the subject of the audit report's findings. For example, the audit program may direct the auditor to review a sample of travel expense vouchers to check that they are properly approved and to verify that the reported expenses are consistent with published travel policies. If internal audit finds that some of the sample selected is not properly approved or not in compliance with travel policy, internal audit will have one or more potential findings to report.

Auditors typically will encounter a large number and variety of exceptions in the course of almost any review. Some of these may be relatively important—such as the discovery of significant numbers of vouchers submitted for payment but lacking proper approval signatures. Others may be relatively minor—such as the discovery of an employee who reported \$25.50 for meal expenses when policy requires that such expenses must be less than \$25.00. While the latter is a violation of policy, senior management may not be much interested in an audit report that is filled with these relatively minor infractions. This is not to say that an internal auditor should look the other way at such minor internal control items. Such smaller internal control exceptions should be documented and discussed with management at the conclusion of fieldwork, but they may not necessarily be the types of issues to report to the audit committee and senior management through a formal audit report unless a series of them represent a trend. In such a case, internal audit might consider reporting them through a summarized finding covering the overall condition.

An internal auditor must analyze the bits and pieces of information gathered during a review to select findings and recommendations for inclusion in the final report. At the conclusion of the audit fieldwork, internal audit should always ask itself whether there is sufficient information to develop an audit finding, and if so, how these matters of concern should be presented. Options for the latter range from informal discussions with local management to a formal presentation in the audit report.

Audit report findings presented in a common format allow the report reader to understand the issues easily. No matter what the nature of the audit work or the finding, readers should be able to scan an audit finding and quickly decide what is wrong and what needs to be corrected. While important to both the internal auditors who drafted a finding and to report readers, audit report findings are sometimes not well constructed. Poorly drafted audit findings often make the report reader question what the problem is and why they should be concerned. Good audit report findings should contain the following:

- **Statement of condition.** The first sentence in a report finding should usually summarize the results of internal audit's review of the area of concern. It can give a comparison of "what is" with "what should be." The what-is sentence summarizes the condition or appraisal made by internal audit based on the facts disclosed in the review. The purpose is to capture the report reader's attention. Examples of audit report finding statements of condition include:
  - "Obsolete production equipment is being sold at bargain rates and in a manner that does not follow fixed-asset disposition policies."
  - "The backup and continuity plan for the new customer billing system has not been tested and does not follow enterprise security standards."
  - "The ABC division work-in-process inventory is not correctly valued according to generally accepted accounting principles."
- **What was found?** The finding should discuss both the procedures and the results of those procedures. Depending on its complexity, the finding may be summarized in little more than one sentence, or it may require an extensive discussion describing the audit procedures. This what-was-found statement can be as simple as, "Based on a sample of employee expense reports filed for fourth quarter 20XX, the enterprise's preferred rental car agency was not used in over 65% of the expense reports reviewed." Often this portion of the finding will be much more extensive, as internal audit describes the procedures performed and what was found. Examples can be found in the Exhibit 18.3 audit report findings.
- **Internal audit's criteria for presenting the finding.** Audit findings should always have a criterion, or a statement of what should be used in judging the statement of condition. Without strong criteria there cannot be an audit finding. Criteria vary according to the area audited and the audit objectives. The criteria may be the policies, procedures, and standards of an enterprise. In some instances, internal audit must develop the criteria. In an audit of the effectiveness of some procedure, there may not be preestablished targets or measurements that can be used as indicators, and standards may be couched in general or vague terms. Internal audit should consider the following:
  - **Criteria of extremes.** Clearly inadequate or outstanding performance is relatively easy to appraise. However, when performance moves closer to the average, it becomes more difficult to judge. Internal audit can sometimes use extreme cases of inadequate performance as criteria for the report finding. Although usually too extreme or incendiary, this might cause internal audit to state that some observed condition was "almost as bad as . . . [an extreme case]."

EXHIBIT 18.3 Audit Report Findings Examples

The following represent some typical findings that might be published in enterprise internal audit reports. While there can be multiple types and formats of internal audits, these represent the styles and topics that may be published in some representative internal audit reports.

I. ***Blanket Purchase Orders***. Blanket purchase orders should allow the enterprise to receive supplies of frequently used common parts without the need to issue separate purchase orders for commodity replenishments. Company purchase order policies allow and even encourage the use of these blanket orders at the buyer's discretion. However, we found that several buyers have never used this blanket purchase order concept. They generally advised internal audit that they thought they could get better prices by negotiating each purchase separately.

We reviewed the pattern of purchase orders for several frequently used commodities and found significant opportunities for potential savings. For example, we reviewed separate purchase order arrangements with different vendors made for certain electronic switch units at the Turbo Division. We found that vendor prices varied up or down by about 5% over the nine months reviewed. A blanket purchase order might have provided a guaranteed price, based on total aggregate quantities purchased.

Recommendation. Existing blanket purchase order policies should be strengthened and a program of blanket purchase orders should be initiated for frequently used commodity-type parts. The purchasing department should monitor the cost savings and other benefits from this program.

II. ***Professional Employee Travel Expenses***. Company travel policy specifies that all employees should work with the company travel agent to find the lowest airfares for business travel. In addition, policy specifies that travelling employees should always attempt to be at their business destination by noon on the first business day for domestic travel. We found that this travel policy is largely ignored by employees in several headquarters departments. We found several employees who did not arrive at their destination sites until late that day even though alternative flights were readily available. In addition, we found that a significant number of department 22-88 employees have made their travel arrangements as individuals, ignoring the travel agent policy requirements. In addition, these expenses were charged to individual charge cards with no evidence of efforts to seek minimal air travel costs. Similarly, in our review of travel records over the past six months, we found that over 5% of employees ignored the travel agent's lowest-cost recommendations and often selected higher-cost air tickets.

Recommendation. Policies should be strengthened to encourage least-cost air travel. A revised policy statement should be developed and issued to all travel employees emphasizing the need for lowest-cost travel. When employees do not accept the travel agent's recommendations, that act should be printed on the employee's air ticket itinerary and included with employee expense reports. Departmental managers should be assigned the first-tier responsibility to reduce their employees' air travel expenses.

III. ***After-Hours Office Security***. Company policy specifies that all employees should clear their desks of all reports, memos, and other business papers at the end of the business day and also sign off from desktop computers and terminals. In our review of office areas in three successive evenings at the Purchasing Department, we found numerous desks covered with materials and numerous computer systems still running. These practices compromise company security due to the possibility of an unauthorized person viewing and accessing materials left in office areas.

Recommendation. All employees should be reminded of these after-hours desktop policies. The Security Department should visit office areas from time to time in the evening. Persons not in compliance with the after-hours policy should be initially reminded with a desktop Security Department note, and supervisors will be informed of any repeat offenders.

  - **Criteria of comparables.** Comparisons can be made between similar operations or activities, determining their success or lack of success and causes for the differences. While it is never good to state specifically that Department A is X% worse than Department B, the report might compare the conditions found to average or typical conditions throughout the enterprise.
  - **Criteria of the elements.** In some cases, internal auditors incorrectly state their performance criteria in such broad terms that it is impossible to evaluate the reported condition. This type of vague criterion states that "all managers should make good decisions." While that would be ideal, we all know exceptions exist regularly. The reported measure should be broken down on a functional, organizational basis, or by elements of cost related to specific activities.
  - **Criteria of expertise.** In some cases, internal audit may find it useful to rely on other experts to evaluate an activity. These experts may be outside the enterprise or may be part of the audited enterprise's staff. This type of supporting reference often strengthens the overall audit finding.
- **Effect of the reported finding.** Internal audit should always consider the question "How important?" when deciding whether to include an item in the audit report. Internal audit must weigh materiality—if the finding is of no significance, it may not be a finding at all. Once a decision has been made to include it as a finding in the audit report, the effect of the reported condition should be communicated. Findings that will result in monetary savings or that affect enterprise operations and achievement of goals are always of special interest to management.
- **Cause or reason for the audit deviation.** The answer to the question "Why?" is especially important to management when reading an audit report. The reasons for a deviation from requirements, standards, or policy should be explained briefly but as well as possible. Identifying a cause for the condition gives a basis for taking needed management action.
- **Internal audit's recommendation.** Audit report findings should conclude by recommending appropriate corrective actions. This is the audit finding's conclusion of "What should be done?" A recommendation can be a simple admonition to fix something or can be a fairly detailed set of suggested corrective actions.

Although internal audit's description of objectives, audit procedures performed, and opinion of the controls as a result of the review are all important elements in an internal audit report, members of management will evaluate the quality of the report on the basis of the reported findings and recommendations. If any facts reported in an audit finding are incorrect, no matter how close to the real truth, an auditee may often challenge the credibility of the overall audit report. Any misstatement can place the entire audit report into question. Internal audit should take extreme care to report its audit findings factually and accurately. Otherwise, a significant amount of good internal audit work can be ignored. Care should also be taken in developing strong, meaningful, and realistic recommendations. The recommendations should generally give some consideration to the costs and benefits of various alternative recommended actions. Of course, if the audit finding is highlighting a potential violation of the law, the recommendation should always be to take prompt and complete corrective action.

If an internal audit's objective was to evaluate the efficiency, economy, and effectiveness by which management has accomplished its objectives, then internal audit has a responsibility to disclose both the satisfactory and unsatisfactory conditions found during an audit. While conditions needing improvement should always be described, communications here should avoid describing audit findings in totally negative terms. Rather, internal audit should strive to encourage management to take needed corrective action and to produce results. An internal audit report cannot be fully successful if the auditee is not receptive to the results of the audit, but a report with findings that just talks about what was right also provides little help to management. Consequently, internal audit should adopt a positive reporting style that is balanced with a mixture of favorable as well as appropriate unfavorable comments, that always presents matters in perspective, and that emphasizes constructive rather than just negative comments.

To provide a level of balance, internal audit must sort through the various positive and negative data gathered during the course of a review and ask itself the question "What should be the type and extent of favorable comments to be reported as a result of this audit?" The answer cannot be laid down in precise terms. The same criteria used in identifying significant findings can be used to report items considered significant based on standards of performance. For example, assume that an audit objective was to evaluate the timeliness of completing purchase requisitions. Comments in a report finding should relate to the enterprise's ability or inability to complete these purchase requisitions in a timely manner and ignore other unrelated issues. Some techniques to provide better audit report balance are:

- **Provide audit reports with perspective.** Internal audit should avoid the temptation to cite only those factors that support its conclusions and to ignore those that distract from it. Perspective is always added when listing the monetary effect of a finding as well as the value of the entire account under review. A $1,000 error sounds much more severe when it is part of a $100,000 account than it does for a $10 million account. The report finding should disclose, as appropriate, the total monetary amount audited or recorded in relationship to the total value of errors encountered. The significance of the finding is made evident by this procedure. Also, when deficiencies are disclosed in only part of the area examined, balance will be added to the report by identifying those areas examined that did not contain deficiencies. This practice should be in accordance with an internal audit policy of disclosing accomplishments as well as deficiencies.
- **Report auditee accomplishments.** Since the evaluation process involves weighing both satisfactory and unsatisfactory aspects of auditee operations in light of the audit objectives, mentioning auditee accomplishments in improving controls or correcting errors together with the noted deficiencies or aspects in need of improvement can add much to the usefulness of the audit report as a management tool. Auditee accomplishments should be disclosed in the summary of the report when the conclusions of the audit may be affected by their significance and in the findings when a detailed disclosure of the accomplishments is desired or necessary.

- **Show planned actions.** In situations where the auditee has taken, or has made plans to take, corrective action prior to the completion of the audit, the audit report should disclose this fact. In addition, other steps taken by the auditee in an attempt to correct a reported deficiency may not be so obvious but nevertheless should be considered as a positive reportable action. For example, the auditee may have contracted with an outside consultant to help implement the internal controls needed in an IT application covered in an audit report. Such arrangements should be included in the report along with those control weaknesses.
- **Report mitigating circumstances.** Mitigating circumstances generally consist of factors relating to the problems or conditions discussed in the audit report over which management has little or no control. Since these factors lessen management responsibility for the condition, they should be reported as part of the cause. Mitigating circumstances, for example, may include the very short time frame in which a program was required to be implemented, business conditions requiring immediate changes, or a lack of adequate budget funds for adding personnel or other resources to accomplish objectives.
- **Include the audit responses as part of the audit report**. Auditee responses to a finding may contain information that provides additional balance to an audit report. In addition to planned corrective action, the auditee may indicate other related accomplishments or cite additional facts and other circumstances. In instances where agreement has not been reached on the finding or recommendation, the auditee should be given the opportunity to explain the basis for nonoccurrence.
- **Improve audit report tonal quality.** The use of positive and constructive words and ideas rather than negative and condemning language will give a positive tone to the report. Unless deserved, audit reports should avoid phrases indicating that the auditee "failed to accomplish," "did not perform," or "was not adequate," and should state audit report ideas in a positive and constructive manner. Audit reports with negative titles and captions should be avoided since they do not add to the finding and may even misrepresent the actual situation. Thus a negative-sounding title for a finding such as "Inadequate Controls over Company Cash Controls" might be replaced by "Cash Controls Need Improvements" or just "Cash Collection Procedures" followed by a discussion of the internal audit concern.

These comments are not meant to suggest that all audit reports should be sugarcoated and that internal audit should never make strong critical statements about auditees. An internal audit and its subsequent audit report can often be a very critical process where internal audit investigates an area that perhaps has not received much management attention. If internal audit finds serious problems in the area reviewed, it should clearly identify problems that might be significant unless prompt corrective actions are taken. When possible, however, internal audit should give credit where due and discuss either positive or mitigating circumstances as would be appropriate. Exhibit 18.4 contains some examples of (n) negative- and (p) positive-toned audit report findings. The idea is neither to sugarcoat an audit finding nor to all but call the auditee guilty of a particular misstep.

EXHIBIT 18.4 Audit Report Negative and Positive Statement Examples

Negative Audit Findings Examples	Positive Audit Findings Examples
n.1 We found that controls in the area were generally poor.	p.1 We identified areas where controls need improvement.
n.2 Little management attention has been given to keeping documentation current.	p.2 The documentation was not current and other priorities have prevented it from being updated.
n.3 The failure to reconcile these accounts was caused by a lack of management attention.	p.3 We observed that these accounts had not been reconciled for several past periods.
n.4 Documentation was either out of date or nonexistent.	p.4 We found only minimal current documentation in the area.
n.5 The new inventory system is poorly designed.	p.5 The inventory system has some major control weaknesses in its design.
n.6 This failure to protect passwords could result in a management fraud.	p.6 Poor password controls represent weak internal controls.
n.7 No attention has been given to protecting stockroom inventories.	p.7 Better controls should be established over stockroom inventories.
n.8 The responsible manager did not seem to understand company procedures in this area.	p.8 Training in the use of these procedures needs to be strengthened.
n.9 The department failed in several of its training program operations.	n.9 Several opportunities exist for strengthening controls in training program operations.
n.10 The budgetary system was not adequate to assist management in the control of project funds.	n.10 The establishment of a proper budgetary system would assist management in the control of project funds.

18.4 ALTERNATIVE AUDIT REPORT FORMATS

With today's technology, audit results can be reported in a wide spectrum of formats. While the standard text-based audit report format described here is certainly the most familiar and often the best way to describe audit work, internal audit can use other approaches to describe the results of its audit findings and recommendations. That standard report becomes a record of corporate governance activity, allowing an enterprise to certify what internal audit did, what it found, and what was recommended. In our litigation-prone society, it is essential that an enterprise and its audit committee have formal, secure records of its internal audit activities. However, internal audit may elect to consider some alternative approaches, particularly for interim audit results reporting. Some of the less formal and more abbreviated alternative means by which internal audit can report the results of its work include:

- **Oral reports.** In a few situations, internal audit may want to report the interim (but not the final) results of its work and any recommendations orally. This reporting mode should always occur when an on-site audit team reports the results of its work at an end of audit fieldwork closing conference. In other cases, an oral report may be the result of emergency action needs, and an oral presentation may also be a prelude to a more formal written report. To some extent there may always be oral reporting as a means of supplementing or explaining written reports, especially when individuals being served have special needs. Oral reporting is often useful but should only be a supplementary form of audit reporting.

An oral report should not be a substitute for the formal written report, as there generally is no permanent record beyond any meeting notes. The auditor may think that local management agrees to correct some problem, but management may not really say that. As a result, there are more likely to be later misunderstandings unless detailed, contemporaneous notes are taken for workpaper documentation or if the meeting is recorded. However, the appearance of a video recording unit sometimes causes distrust. Oral audit reports should be used carefully and not in lieu of later written reports.

- **Interim or informal memo reports.** In situations where it is deemed advisable to inform management of significant developments during the course of the audit, or at least preceding the release of the regular report, internal audit may want to prepare some form of interim written report. These reports may only pertain to especially significant problems where there is a need for prompt corrective action, or they may be a type of progress report. A memo report should be used, at a minimum, to describe the results of an oral presentation, as discussed previously. An interim or memo report is often released to record the results of an oral presentation and to call local management's attention to a potential audit finding. The material discussed in this example report will eventually be included in a more formal audit report discussing the total results of an internal audit.
- **Questionnaire-type audit reports.** Not a common report format, a questionnaire type of report can be a useful interim summary to the formal audit report or serve as an appendix to the formal report document. This format works best where the scope of the audit review deals with fairly specific procedural matters, and usually at a fairly low operational level. However, this type of report usually has a fairly limited range of overall usefulness. Exhibit 18.5 is an example of a questionnaire audit report. It is often best used as an educational tool to inform management of internal audit's concerns.
- **Regular descriptive audit reports.** In most audit assignments, the work should be concluded with the preparation of a formal descriptive audit report. The exact form and certainly the content of such written reports will vary widely, both as between individual audit assignments and individual internal audit departments. They may be short or long and presented in many different formats, including differing approaches for quantitative or financial data presentations. The whole idea is that they represent a documented record of internal audit's work on an assignment.
- **Summary audit reports.** Internal audit functions frequently issue an annual or a more periodic report summarizing the various individual reports issued and describing the range of their content. These summary reports are often primarily prepared for the audit committees or other members of senior management. Summary reports are especially useful to top-level managers, but they must be

EXHIBIT 18.5 Questionnaire-Format Audit Report Example

ExampleCo Heavy Iron Division

Purchasing Department Internal Control Strengths and Weaknesses

Audit Controls Review	**Result**
1. Are departmental operating procedures current and adequate?	Yes
2. Are purchasing requirements properly specified by requesting departments?	Yes
3. Are multiple bids sought for all regular, noncustom purchases?	No
Multiple bid procedures are regularly ignored.	
4. Do requesting groups regularly send specifications with purchase requests?	Yes
5. Are blanket purchase orders used for volume-use parts?	No
Although procedures exist, blanket purchase order procedures are often ignored.	
6. Have dollar-based authorization limits been set for all P/Os and are they followed?	Yes

Note: This type of report will have a series of internal control strength and weakness questions along with yes-and-no responses based on the audit findings. A yes response indicates internal controls were found to be adequate for the area reviewed. The no responses indicate an internal control weakness and in general should have some collaborating explanations. These questions are from a Purchasing Department strengths and weaknesses audit review.

only cover pages for the senior managers and board members who have a SOx responsibility to have access to the full reports. In a larger internal audit enterprise, summary reports also allow the CAE to see the total reporting effort with more perspective, and on an integrated basis.

18.5 INTERNAL AUDIT REPORTING CYCLE

Starting in the early stages of an internal audit, it is often desirable to develop a framework for the final report, filling in as much of it as possible as the audit moves along. Information and statistics on the area to be audited can be gathered during the survey stage and included in the workpapers, as discussed in Chapter 17. This will assure that needed information is obtained early in the audit, and it will prevent delays in the final report-writing process. In addition, the objectives and scope of the review, defined at the start of the audit, should be fine-tuned as the audit moves along.

As audit findings are developed and completed, they can be inserted in the proper sections of the report, together with any comments by the auditee. The completed audit report is then just one step—although a very important one—in internal audit's overall process of evaluating and commenting on the adequacy of internal controls in order to serve management needs. The audit report process starts with the identification of findings, the preparation of a draft report to discuss those findings and their related recommendations, a discussion of the audit issues identified with management along with the presentation of the draft report, the completion of management responses to audit report findings, and the publication of the formal audit report covering the area under review. Exhibit 18.6 outlines suggested critical phases and action steps for the preparation of an audit report. Although a given internal audit department may alter some of these steps slightly to modify the report for its own needs, this generally is the process necessary to issue an appropriate internal audit report.

As findings are developed, internal auditors responsible for a review should analyze them with members of auditee management, soliciting their perspectives on the evolving audit findings. Possible causes for audit findings should also be discussed and additional information gathered to prove or disprove the potential audit report condition. In some instances, enterprise personnel will assist in obtaining information to develop the findings. They will often provide useful feedback as to whether internal audit's facts are correct or whether they are on the right track. Areas of disagreement can be pinpointed and resolved. Discussing findings with enterprise personnel at a staff level helps to get agreement and encourages implementing actions. When an agreement is reached, internal audit may be able to limit the amount of detail included in the audit report finding, thus shortening the audit report.

Preparing and Delivering Audit Reports

Once the audit fieldwork has been completed and internal audit has discussed its proposed audit findings with the auditee, a draft audit report should generally be prepared. We have used the word *generally* since sometimes a draft report will not be necessary if a special, investigative report is to be made for presentation to management. For example, internal audit would typically not prepare a fraud investigation draft report to review with persons involved in the potential fraud. In most other cases, internal audit should prepare a report draft with its proposed findings and recommendations along with a space for preliminary management responses. The draft is then sent to the manager directly responsible for the area that was audited. This is the party who responds and outlines the corrective actions to be taken. Internal audit will then combine these auditee responses with the original report header pages and the draft findings and recommendations to produce the final audit report. This final draft report is typically presented as a last opportunity for the auditee to read and understand the tone and contents of the audit report to be issued.

Closing meetings and a draft report are important steps to validate the adequacy and accuracy of the reported internal audit findings and the soundness of the related recommendations prior to the release of the final audit report. While the major foundation for this validation is the audit work performed by internal audit, work needs to be supplemented by the review and confirmation of the auditee personnel. The benefits of this supplementary validation are twofold. First, it provides a cross-check on the accuracy, completeness, and quality of the audit work. Important facts may have been overlooked or erroneously interpreted. There may also be other factors affecting some particular matter that are known only to certain people. The exposure to the auditee thus provides an important check on whether the findings and recommendations will stand up under later scrutiny. The second benefit is to help promote a partnership relationship with local management that will create both a cooperative spirit and a commitment to working out adequate solutions.

EXHIBIT 18.6 Audit Report Preparation Steps

The following are guidelines for summarizing internal audit fieldwork and preparing effective internal audit reports that summarize audit findings and make effective internal audit recommendations.

A. Outline Audit Findings
   a. Determine if there is sufficient support to warrant the audit findings.
   b. Review the findings to determine where additional evidence may be needed.
   c. Ascertain that the causes and effects of findings have been considered.
   d. Determine whether there is a pattern of deficiencies requiring procedural changes or whether the findings represent isolated cases.

B. Preparation of Audit Report First Draft
   a. Review findings drafts for adequate development.
   b. Ascertain whether the findings are stated in specific rather than in general terms.
   c. Ensure that figures and other facts have been checked and cross-referenced in the workpapers.
   d. Review workpapers supporting all findings for adequacy of support and disclosure of items of significance.
   e. Check for adequacy of tone, punctuation, and spelling (Note: Do not rely just on Microsoft Word spell-checks!).
   f. Ascertain whether there is sufficient support for the expression of the auditor's opinion or if a qualification is needed.
   g. Determine whether the cause, effect, and recommendations are adequately developed.
   h. Discuss methods of improving content and writing style with internal audit team.

C. Discussion with Management
   a. Determine whether management was aware of the problem and already was taking corrective action.
   b. Find out management's reasons for the conditions.
   c. Ascertain whether there are facts or mitigating circumstances of which the auditor was unaware.
   d. Determine management's ideas on how to correct the conditions.
   e. Ensure that management is aware of all significant items that will be present in the report.
   f. Ensure that efforts are made to obtain management's agreement on the facts and conditions.

D. Preparation of Audit Report Final Draft
   a. Ascertain that all prior recommendations for changes in the report have been made.
   b. Ensure that management's viewpoints have been adequately considered.
   c. Determine that the report is well written and easily understood.
   d. Ascertain that summaries are consistent with the body of the report.
   e. Ensure that recommendations are based on conditions and causes stated in the findings.
   f. See that management's viewpoints are fairly stated and adequately rebutted, if necessary.
   g. Review the report for use of graphics, tables, and schedules to clarify conditions represented.
   h. Ensure that auditors who wrote the findings agree with any changes made.

E. Audit Report Closing Conference
   a. Ensure that management has had an opportunity to study the final report.
   b. Attempt to obtain agreement on any points of difference.
   c. Consider any suggestions for changing content of report, as well as specific wording.
   d. Obtain current plans for follow-up action from management.

F. Issuance of Final Report
   a. Ensure that final changes are made in accordance with the closing conference.
   b. Check the report once again for typographical errors.
   c. Review the report for a balanced presentation, with positive comments included on results of the audit when applicable.
   d. Make a final reading of the report for content, clarity, consistency, and compliance with the Institute of Internal Auditors professional standards.

While this type of validation should go on during all stages of a review, one of the most important ways it is effected is through the presentation of a draft report to auditee management. Depending on the nature of the audit objectives and the complexity of the audit findings, such a draft report can be presented at either the closing conference at the end of the fieldwork, or just before the departure of the field audit personnel, or delivered to the auditee after the completion of the fieldwork.

At such an internal audit exit meeting, internal audit may generally find it difficult to deliver a full draft audit report at the end of fieldwork exit conference. Many audits are just too complex, there may be too many final questions, clarifications, or needed editorial skills to allow draft audit reports to be delivered at the time of the exit conference. This draft report exit conference strategy typically only works for compliance-type audits of smaller field or branch locations where recommendations are to correct a less significant problem, such as incorrectly priced goods at a local retail branch.

Before departure of the field audit team, internal audit may have discussed its concerns with local management in a formal exit conference and then prepared the draft report, including any additional comments or clarifications that may result from that conference. In most situations, this approach is more realistic than presenting the draft report at the time of the exit conference. However, the pressure to wrap up the audit work and for an out of town audit team to get home may cause them to take shortcuts in its desire to complete the field engagement.

With this strategy, the audit team has its exit conference but returns to the home office to draft the audit report over the next few days or even weeks. Many internal audit enterprises find that this approach works best. Audit management has an opportunity to review the field team's work and to make adjustments, as appropriate, to the draft audit report. The risk here is that the internal audit team responsible for the review will be pulled in other directions and will not complete the draft audit report in a timely fashion.

Audit exit or closing conferences should include members of the audit team and the local management responsible for the area reviewed. At the conference, major findings and proposed recommendations are reviewed and, to the extent that an agreement has already been reached between audit and local enterprise on particular matters, an opportunity is provided to inform responsible management in the area reviewed and to secure further agreement on audit findings and recommendations. The closing conference provides internal audit with a major opportunity to confirm the soundness of the audit results and to make any necessary modifications to the audit report draft as justified. This is also a major opportunity to demonstrate the constructive and professional services internal audit can provide. These meetings, although sometimes contentious, can be a major means for building sound partnership relations with the auditee. The objective should be to get as much agreement as possible so that the audit report can indicate the completed actions.

In many situations, the draft report should be forwarded to the local management for its review and any corrective action comments prior to the finalization of the formal or final report. Local management and the actual auditees will typically be given a limited amount of time to review this draft report, to suggest changes to its overall tone or to specific findings, and to prepare their audit responses. While internal audit should encourage auditee management to request changes to the draft report, the emphasis should be on the substantive issues in the draft report rather than on its wording.

Internal audit should request formal responses within perhaps 14 days after the receipt of the draft report. Although this is a relatively short time, given the time that the audit team often has spent on its fieldwork and draft report preparation, auditee management should be in a position to develop a rather rapid response since it is aware of the findings and suggested recommendations from the exit conference. However, both internal audit and auditee management should try to operate in the same general time frame. That is, if internal audit spends an inordinate amount of time preparing its draft report, it should give auditee management an even greater amount of time to prepare its audit report responses.

The submission of draft reports to auditee management at a later stage has merit through the demonstration of genuine consideration for the auditee. However, internal audit should work with auditee management to avoid excessive delay in finalizing the report. A major part of the effectiveness of the report is the extent to which it is issued promptly.

Audit Report Follow-Up and Summarization

Once management has submitted its audit report responses, internal audit should combine these responses with its draft findings and recommendations to release a final audit report addressed to management at least one level above auditee management, with copies to the board audit committee and other appropriate officers of the enterprise. Once the final audit report has been issued, internal audit should subsequently schedule a follow-up review to ensure that needed actions based on the audit were actually taken. In some cases, management may request this procedure. While the desirability of follow-up action in itself is very clear, questions can be raised about whether this is the proper responsibility of internal audit, and whether such action by internal audit will undermine the basic responsibilities of the managers in charge of the particular activities. Although internal audit standards, as discussed in Chapter 9, call for follow-up reviews, they can put internal audit in the role of a police officer and could conflict with its ongoing partnership relationship with the auditee.

Internal audit should play only a limited specific role after the audit report has been released, such as making itself available to respond to questions, and to review again the situation at the time of the next scheduled audit in the area. Many enterprises have adopted an intermediate type of approach where the coordination for audit report recommendation follow-up is placed in the hands of another office—usually within the controller's function or some more neutral administrative services group. The corrective actions are then initiated by the responsible line or staff manager, but responses are made to the coordinating group. If there are undue delays in dealing with the recommendation, the coordinating office can issue a follow-up status report. Under this approach, copies of these responses can also be supplied to internal audit for information, or internal audit can maintain a liaison with the coordinating group. There is no single best answer as to how this follow-up effort should be handled, but on balance it seems best to subordinate internal audit's formal role in it. Internal audit's help can always be requested on a special basis, either by the coordinating office or by individual managers. In addition, any lack of action can be highlighted at the time of the next scheduled internal audit review.

Internal audit has a responsibility to produce audit reports that are readable, understandable, and persuasive. The objective is to issue reports that will command the attention of the managers who have the responsibilities for the various operational activities, and to induce them to take appropriate corrective action. A secondary objective is for audit reports that will build respect for the internal auditing effort.

Internal audit receives a final payoff in its knowledge of the actions taken by auditees based on the internal audit report recommendations. Good audit reporting combines internal audit technical skills and the ability to communicate results to people in a way that will best assure their acceptance and active support. The importance of this part of internal audit's work underlines the need to give audit reports careful attention. It means that the CAE should be actively involved in the audit report process, and all levels of the internal audit staff should think in terms of ultimate report needs. In this connection, the problems of report development should also be given proper attention in internal audit training programs. The reports become a statement of internal audit's credentials when reports are subsequently circulated, referred to, and implemented. Audit reports are usually the major factor by which the reputation of an internal audit department is established.

Audit Report and Workpaper Retention

Formal internal audit reports and their workpapers are important documents supporting internal audit's activities. Procedures should be implemented to retain the records for each audit performed as part of regular enterprise-wide records storage procedures. All paper-based audit reports and supporting workpapers should be deposited in a secure corporate records storage facility. While some enterprises have their own procedures for this storage, many others use outside providers who place these documents in secure areas for later retrieval as required. While these external sources provide references to aid any later retrieval, internal audit should establish its own internal procedures to cross-reference their audit work with the storage titles of the stored items.

While we often think of stored internal audit records as tangible binders of workpaper files, much internal audit work today is developed on computer-based digital records, ranging from auditor notes entered on a laptop to digital photos of factory conditions captured on a cell phone camera. This material should be saved and then downloaded to a secure storage media. Material on audit laptop computers should be burned onto disks or other more permanent storage devices. For internal audit materials located on corporate servers or legacy systems, internal audit should make arrangements with the information systems enterprise to download and store internal audit records following the same procedures used for other centralized systems.

The issue here is that internal audit reports and supporting workpapers can become supporting materials in future litigation or even government legal actions. An enterprise may be required to produce records of its internal audit work to prove, in a court of law, what they did or did not do in some area. Also, a court order may require that the enterprise disclose records supporting some matter. The SOx seven-year records retention rule says that an enterprise must take care to preserve and organize all supporting records covering many areas. Internal audit reports and supporting workpapers are important enterprise records that are subject to those same record retention rules.

18.6 INTERNAL AUDIT COMMUNICATIONS PROBLEMS AND OPPORTUNITIES

Communications are an important element of every phase of internal audit activities. Internal auditors communicate with others through formal audit reports, through face-to-face encounters in audit fieldwork or meetings, and through a wide range of other formal and informal communications. When there is a misunderstanding or conflict on an audit assignment or when the auditor's recommendations are not correctly understood, an analysis of the difficulty usually points to some type of communication problem. Internal auditors should always keep in mind that communications are a basic ingredient of almost every type of audit activity, and they should work to improve these communications and reduce organization-level conflicts.

Effective communication both on a person-to-person basis and with larger groups is a key component to internal audit success. An internal auditor should have a good understanding of the problems associated with effective communications and how to cope with them. Situations continuously arise in an internal audit function when individuals need to communicate with one another. These include giving an oral instruction to a staff auditor, discussing an operational problem during an audit exit meeting, counseling a subordinate, interviewing a prospective employee, or conducting a staff performance review. All of these situations involve differing personal relationships, but consist of a continuing two-way flow of messages. An internal auditor should understand this process in order to identify the kinds of problems that can distort or prevent effective communication. These problems affect all steps in the communication process and include:

- **Not giving proper consideration to the power relationships of message senders and receivers.** Communication with a line supervisor will often be different than that with a senior manager.
- **Ignoring temporary emotional stress by either the sender or receiver.** An audit exit meeting can often turn into a situation filled with conflict and stress unless the internal audit communicator takes care to consider these potential emotional issues.
- **Failure to properly evaluate the capacity of the recipient to receive and understand the message.** If internal audit encounters a severe control problem in a technical area in the course of its work, those issues must be communicated properly.
- **Use of words that can have multiple meanings or can convey unintended meanings.** We have discussed this concern when preparing audit reports, but this is all the more critical in verbal communications.
- **Undue haste in the transmission of messages that undermine clarity and/or credibility.** Messages often need to be communicated slowly so that all parties will understand.
- **Perception that the sender wishes to satisfy personal needs, thus inducing emotional resistance and blocks.** Often an internal auditor will be viewed by others as having a personal agenda. Others quickly recognize this and communication may become blocked.

- **Failure to build needed foundations for the core message, and related bad timing.** Internal audit concerns are not effectively communicated when they are just thrown in the lap of the auditee.
- **Lack of clarity or conviction because of a reluctance to cause the receiver dissatisfaction.** While an internal auditor must build a case to describe a concern convincingly, the auditor should never mince words to avoid describing a problem situation but should always clearly communicate a control concern.
- **Impact of nonverbal actions such as tone of voice, facial expressions, and manner of communication.** In some parts of the world, a crossed leg with the sole of the foot pointing to the listener can be viewed as an extreme insult.
- **Not giving consideration to the perceptions and related feelings of the recipient.** Auditors should try to understand how messages will be received and decoded by their receivers.

All of these problems are part of the larger need for internal auditors to put themselves in the receiver's perspective and to consider how a message will be received. When it is done with some empathy, the result should be effective two-way conversation. The communicator must do everything practicable to understand how the receiver thinks and feels and then to communicate in a manner that gives all possible consideration to that knowledge. While the communicator often has conflicting higher-priority needs that prevent fully satisfying the receiver, it is still important to have a good understanding of the total communication process in order to make choices that are most consistent with the enterprise's overall welfare.

Both parties in communications—especially the main activator—learn from the questions and comments made by the receiver in response to a series of messages. This is called feedback. Part of effective two-way communication is to induce feedback so that an internal auditor has the best possible basis for determining whether managerial objectives are achieved. Different approaches may be necessary to induce and utilize good feedback. A related component—listening—is important in order to utilize any feedback better and to demonstrate interest in the other person's views. Otherwise, the result can be to create an emotional response that significantly blocks the receiver's acceptance and understanding of the sender's intended message.

People's varying needs relate alternatively to competition, conflict, and cooperation. Traditionally, conflict has been viewed as destructive and undesirable. However, when properly administered, conflict can be useful in achieving organizational welfare. Internal auditors need to learn to utilize conflict to the point where it is constructive but to control it when it threatens to get out of hand. Internal audit's responsibilities unavoidably generate situations that create competition and potential conflict. Both enterprise units and individuals continuously compete in terms of job performance, recognition, management support, and other needs. That competition should induce imaginative, sound thinking and high-level work performance. At the same time, the forces generated can be so intense that the competitors seek any means to win, irrespective of the questionable propriety and legitimacy of those means. At that point, competition ceases to benefit the enterprise and appropriate corrective actions are needed. Management then has a challenge to exploit the benefits of competition and healthy conflict in a legitimate professional sense but to control the process to avoid excesses. Internal audit becomes very much part of this set of competition and conflict concerns. In the course of their reviews, auditors often find themselves in conflict with various elements of an enterprise. Auditors can cause auditees to lose a level of competitive standing within their enterprises, and auditees may disagree with internal audit on just that basis. In the course of a review, conflict often occurs, and the effective auditor should use this conflict to communicate with management and convince it to take appropriate actions. However, the effective internal auditor needs to understand how to control that conflict.

Although the goal to win is an important and desirable motivation, it is the responsibility of every internal audit manager to make subordinates understand that there are sometimes other things more important than that particular victory. Put in other terms, people need to understand that how one wins is more important than the fact of winning. These principles also need to be reinforced often by the rejection of approaches that are not in the common interest. This means that internal audit must both be continuously alert and watch for red flags that indicate potential problems. When problem situations are observed, decisive actions may be necessary. Rules may be amended, particular individuals disciplined, personnel assignments readjusted. Ideally, conflict should not be allowed to develop to the point where these more dramatic direct actions are necessary. There is a challenge to utilize this conflict but not to let it get out of control to such an extent that it is counterproductive.

In the typical enterprise, there is a continuing need for properly balancing stabilization and change. Management seeks stabilization through the development policies and procedures whereby operations are standardized to improve internal controls and to assure the best handling of recurring similar types of events. However, changing conditions call for amended policies and procedures. The problem is to find a balance between stabilization and needed change. This is complicated because the perception and resolution of changes are often very difficult and controversial—that is, the factors involved are usually hard to analyze and measure. One obstacle to change is that enterprises often become used to the existing policies and procedures and tend to become biased in their favor, thus making them unaware of and unresponsive to the need for change. Internal audit often encounters this when it recommends policy or procedural changes through its audit reports. Additionally, people typically do not like to accept change even when the need for it is reasonably clear. Somehow, convenience tends to triumph over objectivity. This means that internal auditors often face a great deal of resistance when suggesting changes, irrespective of their real merits.

At the highest level, the need for change may involve new strategies, new business ventures, changes in products, or new supporting policies. Related changes may involve new organizational structures, relocation of plants, new production processes, or changes in people, but internal auditors often do not make recommendations for change at that level. In some cases, these changes involve only established habits or convenience, while others require more substantial adjustments. There is often some built-in resistance to change, ranging from minor attitudes to deliberate defensive action—including, in its most extreme form, sabotage. The managerial challenge is that when a decision involving change has been properly made, any resistance, whatever it may be, should be minimized, eliminated, or at least reasonably controlled.

When making their recommendations, internal auditors should understand how the enterprise will deal with that recommended change. How can internal audit achieve needed changes in a manner that will best serve the higher-level enterprise welfare? In all cases, the nature and scope of the necessary actions depend on the significance of the particular recommended change. Because individuals place a high priority on their freedom of action, the design and implementation of these controls is an area where human considerations are especially important. Since all managers are responsible for internal controls and at the same time are subject to them, the impact of recommended control improvements on people should be carefully considered. Perhaps in no phase of the management process is an understanding and consideration of people so critical.

18.7 AUDIT REPORTS AND UNDERSTANDING PEOPLE IN INTERNAL AUDITING

This discussion on creating effective internal audit reports has focused on the interests of all internal auditors in connection with their relations with management and with each other. While all of this is of interest to internal auditors as a part of their review and analysis of internal controls, it should also be of interest to the CAE and the audit committee. Some unique and specific problems confront internal auditors in their activities, including an image problem because an internal auditor is often thought of as focusing excessively on detailed compliance or control issues and is viewed as threatening. As has been discussed in earlier chapters, this image may have been earned in the past because of the manner in which internal auditors were once used in enterprises. To some extent, the image has also resulted because some internal auditors today do not do enough through their audit work and mode of personal relations to build a better one.

The modern internal auditor faces some serious problems in changing this image. Internal audit is charged with protective responsibilities that tend to make others in the enterprise see them as an antagonist or police officer. But internal audit's total role goes far beyond the narrow role of providing protective services. The modern internal auditor today is no longer the police officer or the person with the green eyeshade who is buried in what are sometimes viewed by others as trivial details. Instead, the modern internal auditor should be concerned with total enterprise welfare at all levels and in relation to all activities. In all aspects, communications and relations with people are continuing challenges that involve a target for internal audit that is always moving forward. Internal audit's success in meeting that challenge provides one of the greatest available opportunities to serve the enterprise and to achieve its maximum welfare.

We have stressed the internal auditor CBOK theme throughout the chapters of this book. The ability to describe internal audit work and to make effective audit report recommendations is a key internal audit CBOK requirement. However, going beyond the task of preparing and delivering effective internal audit reports, all internal auditors should strive to be excellent communicators to and with the fellow internal audit teams and all members of their overall enterprise.

PART FIVE

Impact of Information Systems on Internal Auditing

CHAPTER NINETEEN

ITIL® Best Practices, the IT Infrastructure, and General Controls

TODAY'S INTERNAL AUDITORS MUST HAVE a strong understanding of IT internal control techniques supporting enterprise IT processes and systems, ranging from financial applications to control an accounting general ledger to social media processes and the all-pervasive Internet. Although the lines of separation are sometimes difficult, we can generally think of IT controls on two broad levels: application controls that cover a specific process, such as an accounts payable application to pay invoices from purchases, and what are called general IT controls. This latter category covers internal controls that do not relate only to specific IT applications but are important for all aspects of an enterprise's IT operations infrastructure.

The concept of IT *general controls* goes back to the early days of centralized mainframe computers when internal auditors looked for such things as a lock on a computer center door as a general control that prevented unauthorized access to the hardware and the supporting tape and punch-card files. Today, we often think of the many and varied processes that cover all IT operations for an enterprise as the *IT infrastructure*. Because of the many possible variations in techniques employed, there is really no one set or rights and wrongs here, and an enterprise should establish and implement a set of best practices that will serve as guidance for establishing IT general controls.

This chapter will look at IT general or infrastructure controls from an internal audit perspective with an emphasis on the worldwide recognized set of best practices called the *Information Technology Infrastructure Library (ITIL®)*. These outline the type of framework an internal audit should consider when reviewing IT internal control risks and recommending effective IT general control improvements.

A knowledge of IT general or infrastructure controls is an essential CBOK requirement for all internal auditors. Many years ago, some internal auditors argued, "I'm a financial or operational internal auditor and don't review IT stuff—the IT audit techs should review those general control issues." With our use of IT and the Internet for all aspects of enterprise operations, all internal auditors should have a CBOK level of understanding of IT general or infrastrucuture controls as well as the other IT issues discussed in the other Part Five chapters following.

19.1 IMPORTANCE OF IT GENERAL CONTROLS

Internal auditors became involved with early IT procedures—then called data-processing controls—when accounting applications were first installed on early punch-card computer systems. Those early systems were often installed in glass-walled rooms within corporate lobbies to impress visitors with the enterprise's sophistication. However, those early systems were not particularly sophisticated by today's standards, and internal auditors, who were often unfamiliar with data-processing technology, would "audit around the computer." That is, an internal auditor might look at input control procedures and the application's outputs to check whether the inputs balanced to the output reports. In this era there was little question about accuracy and controls of reports produced by IT systems. The internal auditor would just go around the actual computer program processing procedures.

As we discussed in Chapter 11, things changed in the early 1970s with the Equity Funding fraud. External auditors ran their own audit software programs against Equity Funding's files to discover a massive fraud with invalid data recorded on system files. In the aftermath of the Equity Funding affair, organizations such as the American Institute of Certified Public Accountants (AICPA) and the Institute of Internal Auditors (IIA) began to emphasize the importance of reviewing what were then called data-processing operations and application controls. A new professional specialty, called *computer auditing*, was launched.

In those early days of business data processing, most computer systems were considered to be "large," and standard sets of auditor control objectives and procedures were developed for reviewing controls. While many are still applicable today, internal auditors must look at these IT control objectives from a somewhat different perspective when reviewing controls in a modern IT environment. The profession began to think of IT controls in terms of the controls within a specific application and what are called general or infrastructure controls, the pervasive controls surrounding all information systems operations. IT general or infrastructure controls cover all IT operations and include:

- **Reliability of information systems processing.** Good controls need to be in place over all IT systems operations. Discussed throughout this chapter, these controls often depend on the nature and management of the specific size and type of systems used.
- **Integrity of data.** Processes should be in place to ensure a level of integrity over all data used in various application programs. This is a combination of the general operations controls in this chapter as well as specific application controls discussed in Chapter 22.
- **Integrity of programs.** New or revised programs should be developed and managed in a well-controlled manner to provide accurate processing results. These

control issues include the overall process of application program development and are part of our discussion of ITIL® best practices.

- **Controls of the proper development and implementation of systems.** Controls should be in place to ensure the orderly development of new and revised information systems. These control issues also are discussed in Chapter 22.
- **Continuity of processing.** Controls should be in place to back up key systems and to recover operations in the event of an unexpected outage—what was called disaster recovery planning and is often known today as business continuity planning. These control issues are discussed in Chapter 24.

This chapter discusses general controls over in-house information systems operations ranging from client-server systems to desktop operations as well as older, larger mainframe computer systems operations that still exist in some environments. While there are differences between the sizes and management of these different systems, all should be subject to the same general control needs. In addition to discussing general control procedures, this chapter also discusses some related computer hardware types and characteristics. This discussion will hopefully encourage an internal auditor to ask or look for the correct information in an information systems environment.

19.2 CLIENT-SERVER AND SMALL SYSTEMS GENERAL IT CONTROLS

Internal auditors traditionally have had problems evaluating general controls in a small IT operation, ranging from *client-server systems* to enterprise desktop systems and smartphone-based wireless applications. These general controls awareness problems arise because small systems are often installed with limited staffs in a more user-friendly type of environment. Internal auditors, however, sometimes still look for general IT controls in terms of the more traditional, large mainframe IT environment discussed in the sections following. That is, internal auditors are looking for the strong physical security, good revision, and proper separation-of-duties controls that often do not exist or are only partially implemented in the typical small systems environment. This less formal approach was perhaps adequate when these small business or desktop systems were used primarily for single office accounting or similar low-audit-risk applications. The large capacity and capability of small systems today, the growth of the Internet, and the transition to client-server computing has made these small systems important parts of the IT control framework. When faced with evaluating controls in these small computer systems settings, internal auditors have sometimes reverted to the traditional, almost cookbook types of controls recommendations. That is, they have recommended that desktop systems be placed in locked rooms or that a small, two-person IT development staff be expanded to four in order to ensure proper separation of duties. While there may be situations where such controls are appropriate, often they are not applicable in a small business setting. Internal audit can easily lose credibility if their control recommendations are not appropriate to the risks found in the small computer systems setting.

Internal controls over the smallest of these IT systems, such as smartphone- and tablet-based applications, are discussed in Chapter 20 on wireless computing internal controls.

This chapter began with a discussion of differences between general, interdependent controls and application controls in large systems. These differences are equally applicable for small, Internet-based systems and client-server configurations. Internal auditors should understand the general controls surrounding a small computer system. Adequate general controls are necessary in order to place reliance on specific application controls. Enterprises are implementing increasing numbers, networks, and systems to support small business units, specific departmental computing, or provide IT for the entire enterprise. Despite their small size, these systems can often represent significant general control concerns.

General Controls for Small Business Systems

Although some internal auditors once thought of small business computers and client-server systems as one generic IT system class (as opposed to larger, mainframe computers), technological changes have introduced significant differences in control procedures and in related internal audit concerns. Small systems can be implemented in a variety of ways, depending on the system configuration and the size of the enterprise. Internal auditors should be able to recognize these differences and develop appropriate general internal control procedures to review their general controls. This chapter will discuss these general controls in terms of small business IT systems, Internet and networked systems, and client-server systems, as well as the classic large systems.

Internal auditors may encounter a wide range of small-scale as well as large IT systems in a typical modern enterprise. Small business computer systems provide total IT support for a small business function or unit; these systems may also support unit or departmental computing functions in a larger enterprise in support of central computer systems resources.

Client-server systems, defined in greater detail in a later section, are often a combination of various types and sizes of interconnected IT systems and may be found in all types and sizes of enterprises. Process or nonbusiness systems include the numerous types of small computers used increasingly for manufacturing, distribution, and other various operational control applications. Internal audit will frequently find these specialized control machines in many areas of an enterprise's operations.

If an IT system is located in a secure facility, has a multitask operating system, or has a relative large application support staff, internal audit should probably consider it to be a "large" computer system for purposes of audit planning and should review for appropriate large system general control procedures as discussed in Chapter 21. While not particularly precise, this definition covers the typical major IT system. This same type of attribute-based description can be more difficult in the small system environment. A strict computer hardware architecture definition often does not help internal audit to decide when to apply smaller system internal control review procedures. For example, small desktop computers can be coupled together with attached peripheral devices to provide more computer power than many traditional mainframe machines. When reviewing controls in such an environment, internal audit should consider these linked computers to be the same as the legacy *mainframe systems* discussed later in this chapter. Another problem in identifying small computers is that they often look like a large processor. For example, IBM's Power System line of computers was first implemented in 1988 as a small business computer called the AS/400 and then renamed System i. This product line and the individual machine capacities have been expanded many times to make many of these systems effectively operate as classic mainframe systems.

Small systems, which were once known as minicomputers, have been used for business applications since about the late 1960s. They are a product of the increased miniaturization of electronic components as well as of different approaches used by computer engineers. Because they were relatively inexpensive, easy to use, and did not require elaborate power or air-conditioning support, minicomputers were once used by many small business enterprises as well as for specialized IT applications. Long before the introduction of today's desktop systems, they brought IT capabilities to enterprises that could not afford the large investments required by classic mainframe systems.

Today's desktop, laptop, or tablet systems have had a rapid growth curve. Starting with hobbyists building their own microcomputers using newly available integrated circuit chips in the mid-1970s, things really got started in the late 1970s when Apple Computer Corporation was formed and produced the Apple II microcomputer. Although the machine was initially viewed as a curious toy, a spreadsheet software package, VISICALC, introduced about a year later, made the Apple II a serious tool for business decision making. Several years later, in the early 1980s, IBM introduced its personal computer and legitimized the microcomputer as a serious business-processing tool. Today, many machines are still said to be "IBM compatible" even though IBM neither has its name on these products nor even manufactures them.

Today, personal computers, often connected to wireless networks, are used for many business IT applications. They are often the only computer system resource for a small enterprise, and have replaced small "mainframe" systems. They may also be used for specialized departmental computing even though there may also be a larger, mainframe computer capability. In particular, these specialized computers are used for such applications as research laboratory or manufacturing process control rather than for pure business IT. These same machines may also be used for some business-processing applications in addition to their intended specialized purposes.

Ever-increasing speed and capacity have done much to promote the use of these server systems. When the first Apple II was released, it had an internal memory of 48 KB (kilobytes) of random access memory (RAM). By the mid-1990s, in contrast, off-the-shelf machines typically came with RAM capacities of 32 million megabytes or 32 MB. Today, memory sizes and capabilities are considerably larger by virtually every measure, whether it be processing speed, capability of running multiple tasks, or memory capacity.

These small business unit systems can cause difficulties for some internal auditors who have stated in their plans to the audit committee that they plan to review the general controls surrounding "all" IT systems in the enterprise. Clearly, this type of objective was once thought to cover just the mainframe computers and freestanding divisional minicomputer systems. The directive may also cover the enterprise's departmental desktop computers, sometimes freestanding but more often connected to the

Internet. However, internal audit may wonder if such an objective really covers the specialized IT workstations in the engineering laboratory used for recording test results or systems at the end of the distribution line that weighs the package and routes it to the correct shipping dock. These definition problems only get worse as embedded systems today take a greater role in controlling business processes. Embedded systems are the computers that reside behind such things as the dashboard of a car or on the control panel of a video recorder or even in the kitchen microwave. As consumers, we press these flat-panel screens and generally do not think we are submitting computer system commands. However, embedded systems will take greater roles in business processes as their capacities and applications increase.

While all of the above IT systems should be part of a general internal audit IT objective to review internal controls in all IT systems, internal audit's reviews should emphasize the systems used for *business IT* purposes. To follow an example just mentioned, the processor at the end of the distribution line probably uses a standard set of embedded software that cannot be modified by the local staff. It was very possibly purchased from an outside systems vendor, and after initial installation and testing, it simply works, with no programmer interaction. Such a machine generally has limited business or control risk implications.

Internal audit will often work in an environment where only small business systems are used, particularly when the enterprise is relatively small. An example would be a not-for-profit enterprise whose only systems needs are a server and desktop systems to support direct mailing and limited accounting-related applications. Internal audit should review general controls over such a server configuration as if it were a classic, large enterprise system. That is, there is still a need for systems security, integrity, and backup procedures. These types of small business systems will generally have the following common characteristics:

- **Limited IT staff.** The small business computer system, whether a single desktop system or a series of wireless units connected to a local or cloud-based server, will have a very limited dedicated IT staff, if any. A desktop system to provide accounting reports for a small company may be maintained by a single person. A small business or server system may have a manager/administrator and perhaps one or two systems administrators as its total IT department. Such a small IT operation creates a control risk because it is dependent on some separate small consulting firm for much of its IT support, and requirements such as backing up critical files may be ignored. However, a small staff size will not in itself create internal control concerns. Internal audit should be able to look for compensating controls just as it does when reviewing a small accounting department where a classic separation of duties is lacking.
- **Limited programming capability.** The typical small business computer system makes extensive use of purchased software packages. The enterprise's only "programming" responsibilities may be for loading update programs for the purchased software packages, maintaining systems parameter tables, and writing simple retrieval programs. If internal audit finds a large programming staff or extensive in-house development activity, some of the control procedures discussed in later sections for large systems development functions should be considered.

- **Limited environmental controls.** Small business systems can generally be plugged into normal power systems and operate within a fairly wide range of temperatures. Because of these limited requirements, they are sometimes installed without important, easy-to-install environmental controls such as backup drives, uninterruptable battery-based power supply systems, or electrical power surge protectors. While some small business computer installations or file servers may be housed in formal, environmentally controlled computer rooms, this is not a necessary attribute of these systems.
- **Limited physical security controls.** Because of less need for environmental controls, these systems are often installed directly in office areas. The level of auditor concern regarding physical security controls depends on the type of equipment and the applications processed. Internal audit may sometimes recommend that physical security be improved, particularly where critical applications are being processed. In many other instances, however, this lack of physical security controls should not present a significant internal control problem.
- **Extensive telecommunications network.** Virtually all desktop systems today have wireless connections to the Internet. Data and applications can be easily uploaded or downloaded. In addition, materials can be easily downloaded through common, easy-to-use USB devices. A combination of controls and policies should be established to protect the enterprise.

These characteristics certainly do not *define* a small business computer system, but only explain some of its common attributes. However, they should help internal audit to better decide on the control procedures to be used. As noted, when in doubt, internal audit should consider the system to be a large, more complex one.

19.3 CLIENT-SERVER COMPUTER SYSTEMS

The term *client-server* first appeared in IT literature in the late 1980s. To non-IT specialists, including many internal auditors, it is one of those specialized IT terms that is often difficult to understand, let alone describe. However, client-server architecture has become a very popular IT configuration in all sizes of enterprises and systems. In a local network environment, for example, each of the workstations is a *client*, and a centralized processor, which contains common shared files and other resources, is called the *server*. There also may be specialized servers for such tasks as storage management or printing. Workstation users submit requests from client machines to a server, which then serves that client by doing the necessary processing.

This client-server architecture, however, goes beyond just a workstation and a server. An application that queries a centralized database can be considered the client, while the database that develops the view of the database is the server to all workstations requesting database service. Similarly, an application program can request services from an operating system communications server. Exhibit 19.1 shows a client-server system sample configuration where a single server handles requests from multiple clients across a network. This client-server configuration, though very general, represents the typical IT system of today.

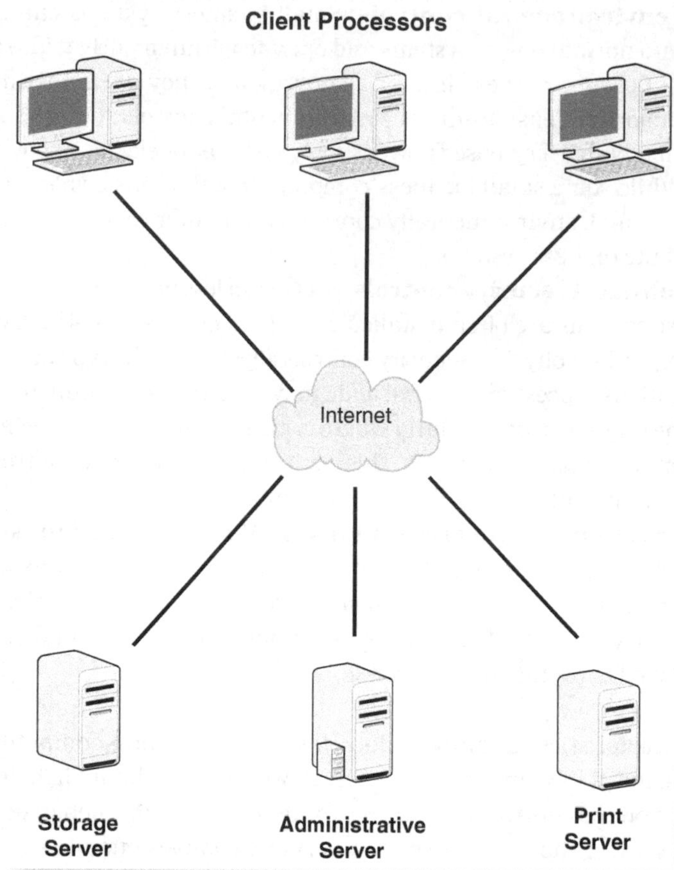

EXHIBIT 19.1 Client-Server System Configuration

In many enterprises today, other, often client-server-configured systems can be found in areas beyond IT operations and may be located in engineering laboratories, manufacturing control operations, marketing departments, and elsewhere. These systems may be used for process control, automated design work, statistical analysis processing, or many other applications. Some are totally dedicated to specific applications, while others may be used for a variety of tasks within their assigned functions. This multitude of IT machines has come about in many enterprises because of the relatively low cost of such machines, the familiarity of many professionals with IT techniques today, and the inability of traditional IT departments to support specialized IT needs.

Although these systems are not used for traditional business information needs, such as maintaining accounts receivable records, they often support critical applications for the enterprise. These systems are often found in the quality assurance environments discussed in Chapter 31. For example, an engineering computer may support computer-aided design work. Systems backup and integrity concerns in this environment may be as great as in the typical business IT center. Internal audit's role in regard to specialized IT operations will vary with both management's direction and internal audit's review objectives. While some audit enterprises will have little involvement with reviews over specialized computer systems, IT controls reviewed here can often play an important role in support of internal audit's understanding of control procedures and in other operational audit activities.

Before attempting any review of such a specialized computer system, internal audit should obtain a rough familiarity with the functions of that operation. For example, an internal auditor who plans to review a dedicated computer-aided design and manufacturing computer operation needs a general understanding of the terminology, general workings, and objectives of these systems. Reviews of specialized IT systems are not recommended for the less experienced internal auditor. In order to find control analogies from normal business IT situations and translate them to specialized control environments, an auditor must be fairly experienced in reviewing business IT computer centers, whether they are large or small operations. Over time, internal audit will encounter more of these specialized computer operations. The creative internal auditor can make increasing contributions to management by performing operational reviews over these computer centers on a periodic basis.

19.4 SMALL SYSTEMS OPERATIONS INTERNAL CONTROLS

As discussed, internal auditors have traditionally looked for a proper separation of duties as a first procedure for evaluating internal controls and IT general controls. This control, however, is also often lacking in a small business IT function. While good IT control objectives call for a proper separation of responsibilities between users and operators, these controls are often difficult to establish in a small department. When internal auditors first began to review general controls in small IT departments and tried to apply traditional large-system control remedies, those earlier recommendations were hard to sell to a cost-conscious management and would be treated with derision today.

The responsible manager for a small client-server system today may also be the principal technical specialist and operate the equipment for such tasks as backup processing. Separation-of-duties controls found in a large shop do not exist in this small environment, but there should be compensating controls, including:

- **Purchased software.** Nearly all small computer systems today operate with purchased software packages where "programmers" do not have access or have very limited access to source code. A major task may be to just install vendor software upgrades on the local system.
- **Increased management attention to system reports and consultant activities.** Although small business enterprise management may have very little knowledge of IT techniques, they often should give considerable attention to the key computer-generated reports. In a small company, it is not unusual for top management to review, for example, an accounts receivable aged trial balance in detail and on a regular basis. In this environment, many small businesses are very dependent on consulting management help from equally very small consulting firms. Care should be given to monitoring such consulting activities in terms of time spent, access to other enterprise records, and other matters.

- **Separation of input and processing duties.** In virtually all modern small business IT systems, users submit data inputs through their individual workstations and receive outputs on their terminals or remote printers. Internal auditors should look for some level of compensating controls if possible, including wireless firewalls to prevent access to other nearby unauthorized systems.

Even with these compensating controls in the modern small business IT system, internal audit should also be aware of potential control risks and weaknesses. There still exist IT departments in which the responsible manager implements many of the applications, has responsibility for the network management, controls all passwords, and appears to be the only person in the enterprise who understands the IT applications. While a limited staff may be acceptable in some circumstances, the enterprise faces a control risk if all IT knowledge is vested in only one person. Other control weakness symptoms in a small IT enterprise that do not typically exist in a large department include:

- "Loyal" employees who do not take their personal time off
- The use of special, undocumented programs known only to the IT manager
- Direct IT department participation in system input transactions, such as adjustments to the inventory system

Control risk may be a major consideration when audit procedures have identified significant control weaknesses in small business systems. In large enterprises, internal auditors often look for documented position descriptions in their internal controls reviews as evidence of good management controls over the IT function. Many small enterprises often do not have such descriptions for *any employee*. An internal auditor will not be effective in suggesting that such position descriptions be drafted just for the IT function while ignoring the rest of the enterprise when overall control risk is minimal because of the small size of the enterprise.

As discussed, planned organization and related management practices are often among the strongest control procedures in a large IT enterprise. In the small enterprise, the size and informality typically associated with such a group will tend to weaken controls. Senior management should have a good understanding of the IT function, its plans, and its objectives. A very important general control for the small IT enterprise is adequate documentation over its systems and procedures. There have been instances where both members of a two-person IT organization suddenly resigned due to a disagreement or better employment offer. Without adequate documentation, it is very difficult for someone else suddenly to take over. This is true even if the enterprise primarily runs packaged software, since there may be many special procedures associated with those packages. The risk is equally high if the enterprise uses desktop or tablet systems where users do much of their own work. The network administrator who configures the system and backs up files has a key control responsibility.

Sometimes a small IT system operation is an operating unit of a large enterprise with centralized IT facilities. Even though the small IT enterprise may be entirely freestanding, it may receive central direction as to appropriate standards and procedures. In order to ensure compliance with these standards, internal audit should have a general understanding of them and the level at which they are expected to be followed. Sometimes a large enterprise will issue mandatory standards applicable to all of its operating units, no matter their size, even though the standards may not be practicable for small units. While central management may look the other way regarding local compliance with these standards, internal audit often feels compelled to bring up violations found at a smaller unit. If such problems exist, internal audit should discuss these concerns with the central IT management group responsible for the standards. Very little is accomplished if an internal auditor brings up a violation of a corporate standard found at a remote unit when central management does not expect full compliance. This may be more of a topic for a centralized review of standards.

19.5 AUDITING IT GENERAL CONTROLS FOR SMALL IT SYSTEMS

Some small IT systems may be separate operating units of a large enterprise and provide support for the total enterprise. Such systems may have many of the attributes of a larger, mainframe computer system, including a limited but formal IT enterprise, production schedules, and a responsibility for implementing new applications. However, the small IT system enterprise often has no other specialized functions. Internal audit will encounter a variety of computer hardware brands or product names in a small systems environment, but most will be open systems with a common operating system that can operate no matter what brand of hardware is used. This is different from classic mainframe computers, where the manufacturer generally built the computer hardware as well as an operating system. Numerous vendors supply such small computer systems with both improved functionality and price performance, and internal auditors will be more effective in reviewing small business computer system controls if they have an overall knowledge of some of their capabilities.

Despite the small and informal nature of a typical small business computer system, internal audit should still expect to have general control objectives with the following internal control concerns:

Weak system controls over access to data and programs. When unauthorized persons are allowed to access and modify computer files, general controls are very much weakened, and internal audit should consider access to data and programs to be *the major general controls objective* when reviewing the small IT enterprise. This is true whether the IT department uses packaged software products or spreadsheets or databases developed in-house.

Controls over access to data can be considered in terms of both specific applications and general controls. However, in small IT systems, general controls often have a greater importance than specific application data access controls because applications operating on a single small business computer system will typically all operate under the same set of data-access controls. In a small system, data can be improperly accessed and modified through improper data-access attempts by way of user terminals, unauthorized use of specialized utility programs, or invalid IT requests.

Improper data access through user workstations. Small systems, whether a series of laptops connected through a wireless system or a powerful server system, often do not have the sophisticated security controls found on large mainframe-type systems. Rather, small systems have a user log-on/password identification coupled with menu-based information security. A systems user typically enters the assigned log-on or user ID identification code onto the terminal and receives a menu screen with the applications available to that code. The user can only then access the applications assigned to that menu.

These menu-based security systems, historically found in systems such as a version or model of an older IBM AS/400, can provide a fairly effective control against improper access attempts. However, they can break down due to the informality and lack of formal rules and procedures in many small enterprises. Log-on codes are often not changed on a regular basis, one general menu is given to virtually all employees, or terminals with more privileged IDs are left on for virtually all to use. Because users are often not aware of potential data vulnerabilities, management may give only minimal attention to such security issues. In order to review controls in this area, internal audit should first gain a general understanding of the data security system installed, which may range from a good password-based system to a highly structured set of procedures. The next step is to understand how that security system has been implemented and is being used. The latter step implies that the internal auditor should spend some time reviewing the use of the application controls in user areas.

A small business computer system may not have the logging mechanisms to monitor invalid access attempts. Instead, internal audit should review the overall administration procedures covering the security system. These can include reviewing how often log-ons are changed, who has access to the system administrator's menu, and local management's general appreciation of IT access controls.

Unauthorized use of utility programs. Modern small systems are often equipped with powerful utility programs that can easily change any application data file. These programs are designed to be used for special problem-solving situations, and often produce only a limited audit trail report. All too often, these utilities serve as substitutes for normal production update programs or are used by an IT manager for these special updates, and sometimes are even given to users. For example, an enterprise may have installed an inventory status system. While the system normally provides proper stock-keeping records, the inventory status may become misstated from time to time due to a variety of reasons. In order to help users correct these inventory status record-keeping problems, the IT administrator may have developed the practice of correcting inventory balances through the use of a utility program. While the IT manager may be following proper management direction in the normal use of such a program, there may be no audit trails over its use.

These utility programs go by a variety of names depending on the type of computer operating system. For example, in a Unix operating system environment, the *su* (super-user) command has some powerful attributes that should be protected. Internal audit should understand the types of standard utility programs available for the system under review. The usage of the particular program can best be determined through inquiry and observation.

Improper IT data and program access requests. The informality of small enterprises often allows data to be accessed improperly through normal IT operations procedures. For example, someone known to the IT function may initiate a special computer run, which results in improper access to confidential data. In larger, more formal enterprises, such a request would often require some type of special management permission, but small, informal enterprises often waive such requirements. This type of access may be a greater control risk than access through use of improper programs.

Internal audit should look for controls to prevent such casual IT requests. The best control could be a formal "request for data services" type of form, approved by management. In addition, logs should be maintained listing all production IT activities as well as the name of the requester and the report recipient. Many of the control concerns over improper access to data also apply to small-system program libraries. Small business systems typically do not have the sophisticated software control tools over program libraries found in large systems, but they generally do have menu-based systems that offer some security types of controls. Without such a proper menu type of security system to limit improper access, it can often be relatively easy for someone with a little knowledge to locate and potentially modify program library files.

Internal audit may also find weak controls over program library updates. The one or two personnel in a small IT department who act as network administrators typically can update program libraries with little concern for documenting those changes or obtaining any type of upper management authorization. While some of these changes may be justified in order to respond to user emergency requests, others may not be properly authorized. It is difficult, if not impossible, to install separation-of-duties enterprise controls over small business system program libraries. In addition, it probably will not work for internal audit to suggest that management formally review and approve all program library updates—they will neither be interested nor have the technical skills to perform such reviews. The best control method here might be to install procedures that require the logging of all changes or software package updates to the production program library, with such logs subject to periodic internal auditor reviews.

This type of control takes advantage of the fact that many small business IT systems maintain a hash[1] total count of the program sizes in bytes and also have the ability to retain some form of date or version number within the program name. Internal audit might then suggest a small business computer system program library control as follows:

- Establish program naming conventions that include the date or version number included with the program name. When not available in commercially purchased software, a separate control file with this data can be established. This feature is becoming increasingly common; for example, it can be implemented within the Windows operating systems.

- Have the persons authorized to make program table or parameter changes log in the version number, date, program size, and reason for the change in a manual listing subject to periodic management. If the application was developed in-house, the source code should contain comments explaining the change.
- Maintain at least one backup copy of the program library and rotate a copy of the program library file to secure portable disk drive in an off-site location at least once per week.
- Strengthen access controls such that nonauthorized personnel cannot easily access program library files.
- Perform an internal audit review of the library change log on a periodic basis. That review should match logged program versions, dates, and sizes with data reported on the program library file.

These steps will not provide complete assurance that all program changes have been authorized; however, if internal audit periodically reviews logged changes and questions any discrepancies, enterprise systems personnel will probably take care to better and consistently document and log any production program changes.

Our message throughout this section is that there are or should be some general IT internal control concerns for all small IT systems, whether a network of laptops coupled to a server over wireless links or even a freestanding office desktop system. There are many variations in the types of small-system IT configurations, but internal auditors should use some general internal control objectives to review general controls in these IT environments. Exhibit 19.2 contains general control objectives for reviews of small business IT systems.

19.6 MAINFRAME LEGACY SYSTEM COMPONENTS AND CONTROLS

As discussed in the introduction to this chapter, the UNIVAC II, one of the first successful business IT computers, was introduced in 1951 and helped predict the results of the 1952 U.S. presidential election. It required a huge amount of physical space, weighed 15 tons, and cost $1.3 million (in 1950 dollars). Its central processing unit was housed in a cabinet with doors on both ends so a technician could walk through it to make any required repairs but it had less memory capabilities than today's smartphones. Was the UNIVAC II a "large" computer system? In today's terms, although it was physically large, based on its cost and the floor space it occupied, with respect to its memory, speed, and functional capabilities, the answer is no. The term *large* as it applies to computer systems becomes even more difficult today. Once described by their manufacturers as "minicomputers," small systems may appear to be "large computers" to an auditor because they operate as servers to support a large variety of IT equipment such as multiple workstations, disk and storage devices, and the many other devices attached to the system. The large-system computer hardware may also be supported by a big operations staff and will handle many varied processing tasks. Different professionals each have their own definitions of what a large computer system is. The technical programmer

EXHIBIT 19.2 General Control Objectives for Small Business IT Systems

1. Determine if there is a complete and current inventory of systems hardware, including servers, printers, and network controllers as well as a complete inventory of application and systems software.
2. If employees and other stakeholders have been authorized to use personal smartphones and tablets for systems processes, review controls over who has been issued this equipment and assess adequacy of management and use of these facilities.
3. The network hardware inventory report should contain model and identification numbers. Review a limited sample of these items to determine the equipment is installed as described.
4. Trace a sample of the listed application and systems software to determine that current versions are installed, that appropriate documentation is in place, and that vendor licenses are current.
5. Review file and data backup procedures and determine that these resources are regularly backed up to secure locations.
6. Observe computer server facilities and verify the equipment is located in limited access secure facilities with adequate power and environmental controls.
7. Observe storage processes for backups of key files to determine that media are regularly backed up to secure off-site locations.
8. Assess the adequacy of access control security procedures to determine that key systems and files are adequately protected by passwords that are regularly changed and difficult to easily detect.
9. Review procedures in place for restricting, identifying, and reporting on unauthorized users of the network environment and assess the adequacy of processes to investigate and correct security violations.
10. Assess the adequacy of systems security monitoring processes as well as new employee training practices in place to emphasize application security.
11. Review the adequacy of procedures for installing new software in the systems environment and assess that controls are in place to prevent the introduction of unauthorized software products.
12. Review a sample of key applications and verify they are supported by adequate continuity plans for disaster recovery purposes. Also, determine that continuity plans are tested periodically.
13. Interview persons responsible for network security administration to determine that adequate firewall tools have been installed.
14. Review records of systems downtime over a recent period and determine that adequate short and long range measures are in place to continual improvements.
15. If available, obtain application operating schedules covering key financial and operational applications and determine that adequate attention is given to application internal controls.
16. Interview systems manger/administrator to assess whether this person is knowledgeable and properly trained. Also, if system is managed by outside consultants, review the adequacy of systems support efforts.
17. Interview a sample of systems users and determine if they are satisfied with systems performance, including response times and availability.

may define a large computer system in terms of the central processor's internal design or architecture. Management may define the same computer system's size in terms of what the equipment configuration and the size of the IT staff necessary to support it. Some auditors not familiar with IT systems may observe an older, or what is now called a legacy, system located inside a secure facility with a raised floor, and on that basis will conclude that it must be large. This is particularly true if the auditor's experience is limited to small laptops, desktop and server devices, or cloud computing connections.

Internal auditors were once more interested in the size of the computer system to be reviewed than they are now because of its impact on internal audit's approach and the audit control procedures. This has changed with the forward rush of technology developments, and there is no longer a direct relationship between machine size and audit complexity. Nevertheless, some of the controls that internal audit would expect to find in a very large computer center operation would not necessarily apply to the small business computer system discussed in previous sections. For example, a technical or systems programming staff, responsible for monitoring performance and maintaining a large computer's operating systems, is often not necessary for a small, modern computer system.

Characteristics of Large IT Systems

Large systems usually have some common characteristics, whether a classic IBM mainframe requiring chilled-water cooling or several interconnected Unix file server processors. While not all IT internal control characteristics may apply to every large computer system, the following should help an internal auditor understand the characteristics of the large business IT system:

- **Physical security controls.** A large computer center with multiple servers and significant data files is usually located in a room with locked access controls and no windows to the outside. This security helps to protect the equipment as well as the programs and data. Locked doors to the computer room prevent unauthorized persons, both employees and outsiders, from entering the area to ask distracting questions of the operators or to cause malicious damage.

  In former days, large-scale computer systems first required extensive magnetic tape drive arrays, then magnetic storage cartridges, and extensive numbers of rotating-head disk drive storage units. Today, with the massive capabilities of cheap and miniaturized storage devices, there are typically minimal needs for operations personnel to mount, load, or remove to a storage media library these older devices.

  While all business operations are subject to terrorism, fires, or floods, a large system computer center has a particular vulnerability because the equipment cannot easily handle these stresses. Because of the type and extent of data processed in the modern large-scale computer system, systems operations should be located in unobtrusive locations and built to minimize exposure to fires, floods, or other acts of God.
- **Environmental control requirements.** Specialized electrical power systems as well as dedicated air-conditioning or water-cooling chiller systems are often necessary because miniature electrical components operating at full power generate a considerable amount of heat. Because of these special needs and because IT systems consist of multiple pieces of equipment connected by communications cables, the system hardware is often located in specialized rooms with dedicated environment monitoring controls and false floors that provide space for power cables and ventilation. Large systems, vulnerable to electrical power outages or fluctuations, are almost always equipped

with emergency power supplies that can smooth out power fluctuations or provide a source of emergency power to allow the computer system an orderly shutdown.

Some systems may be supported by independent generators to provide power over an extended period in the event of an outage. Weaknesses in environmental controls can potentially result in failures in the operation of key IT applications. Internal audit should always be aware of control procedures in this area and make recommendations where appropriate.

- **Multitask operating systems.** Virtually all computers use some type of master operating system to control the various programs run by the computer and other tasks such as reading various files and other folders or supplying report data or print server facilities. Typically these operating systems can run many programs in parallel as well as other tasks such as printing. A multitask operating system on a large computer must be managed and usually requires specialized personnel, called systems programmers.
- **In-house programming capabilities.** While small staff enterprises purchase the majority of their applications from software vendors or have their systems supplied by an enterprise headquarters staff, enterprises with large computer systems are often supported by an in-house systems and programming department ranging in size from a group of perhaps several hundred employees or more to others with limited in-house programming capabilities. Programmers are different as well. Until the early 1990s, many used the COBOL language, but programmers today may only develop parameters for specialized purchased software packages or may do some custom work in languages such as C++ or Visual BASIC. In-house programmers almost never write custom inventory control or payroll applications. A large enterprise with its own programming and systems analysis staff should have a fairly formal systems development methodology or systems development life cycle (SDLC) procedure to develop and implement new applications. SDLCs are discussed in Chapter 22. There should be specialized library files to control computer programs as well as technical documentation covering the programmers' work.
- **Extensive telecommunications networks.** Virtually all modern systems have an extensive telecommunications network, both wireless and cable-connected, to support multiple online terminals located throughout the enterprise and connected either directly to the central computer system or to the Internet. The network may also require specialized technical personnel within the IT enterprise to manage telecommunications.
- **Very large or critical files.** Although an IT system may be rather small in many respects, it may have one or more applications that maintain critical data on very large databases. While these critical files once consisted of many reels of magnetic tape, disk-oriented database management systems or hard storage drives are used today. Because of the criticality of such large databases, the IT system—whatever its actual hardware configuration—takes on characteristics of a large system. The need for backup copies and the integrity of critical files is crucial to the IT function. The enterprise should require strong file backup procedures and database administrators to help ensure the accuracy, integrity, and completeness of the database.

- **Input-output control sections.** Although they are not at all common today, some systems once had input-output control functions to receive any batch input data (such as tapes mailed from remote sources), to distribute any inputs, and to schedule and set up production jobs. In the earlier days of IT, when most production jobs were run in a batch mode, such control functions often balanced input batches to system outputs and resolved many problems. Today, users generally take responsibility for their own data, submitted through terminals in user areas with outputs transmitted back to them, and the controls should be built into the systems receiving or transmitting this data.

These characteristics, although not specific only to large *legacy systems*, provide some guidance to help determine whether an internal auditor is working with a large IT systems environment. There are many variations in what can be defined as either a large or small computer system. While internal audit's control objectives will remain essentially the same for both, control procedures will differ. Techniques for auditing small systems were discussed previously in section 19.2. If an internal auditor has doubts about whether an IT review should be tailored to a large or small system, the safest approach is to consider the system to be reviewed as a large, complex one.

19.7 INTERNAL CONTROL REVIEWS OF CLASSIC MAINFRAME OR LEGACY IT SYSTEMS

Large IT systems typically have their own unique control characteristics. Although much has been published about today's client-server and desktop systems, significant changes have also taken place over the years for large mainframe computer operations. For internal auditors, internal control issues that were once frequent audit concerns are now an almost accepted part of today's large systems operating procedures. Other, newer control issues have now become part of internal audit's review process. In the early days of older, classic mainframe systems, a common internal audit concern was that computer operators should neither have access to computer operating programs nor the knowledge to change them. The reasoning was that if programmers could operate the equipment, they could improperly modify or run unauthorized programs. Checklists and audit programs were published—including in earlier editions of this book—that directed internal auditors to attest that, among other matters, computer operators did not execute programs and programmers did not operate the equipment. Although the system configurations and organization procedures may be very diverse today because of the different types and ages of hardware and software in a modern large systems operations area, Exhibit 19.3 discusses some of the areas an internal auditor should consider in order to gather some base information regarding the operations and control procedures in a large data center operation.

There is no typical hardware configuration for the modern, large IT enterprise. Often the inexperienced internal auditor will be given a tour through a room filled with central processors, servers, storage devices, and other equipment and may complete the tour with little understanding of what was seen. Because of the miniaturization of

EXHIBIT 19.3 Information Systems Large IT General Controls Preliminary Survey

1. Obtain basic information about the environment through initial exploratory discussions with information systems (IS) management.
2. Review published organizational charts to determine that appropriate separation of functions exists between operations, systems, and database management. Discuss any potential conflicts with IS management.
3. Obtain job descriptions of key IS personnel and review this personnel documentation for adequate and appropriate qualifications, task definitions, and responsibilities. Ensure that security and control accountability are appropriately assigned to key personnel.
4. Based on discussions within management both inside and outside the IS organization, assess whether the organizational structure is aligned with business strategies to ensure expected IS service delivery.
5. Review IS policies and selected procedures for completeness and relevance with specific emphasis on security, business continuity planning, operations, and new systems development.
6. Inquire whether responsibilities have been assigned to keep the policies and procedures current, to educate/communicate them to staff members, and to monitor compliance with them.
7. Based on discussions with senior IS management, assess whether strategic, operational, and tactical IS plans are in place to ensure alignment with the organization's overall business plans.
8. Determine the existence of a new applications and hardware IS steering committee and gauge this committee's functions through a limited review of steering committee meeting minutes.
9. Ensure that a formal methodology is used in the development of new systems developments, major equipment installations, or major enhancements to systems in production. The methodology should include formal steps for definition, feasibility assessment, design, construction, testing, and implementation as well as formal approvals at every stage.
10. Determine that processes are in place for making changes to application programs in production, including testing and documentation sign-off, and formal approvals to implement the change into production.
11. Ensure that responsibility for physical and logical security has been appropriately apportioned and that appropriate documented procedures exist.
12. Review procedures in place for operating and maintaining the network along with attached routers, in terms of device configuration and software parameter changes, and ensure that procedures for allocating and maintaining the network configuration are performed on a scheduled basis and under proper change management.
13. Review the disaster-recovery/continuity plan to ensure that detailed plans for recovery of operations have been prepared, that the plans are documented, communicated to the appropriate personnel, and properly tested on a periodic basis.
14. Review both IS budget and actual costs as well as performance against those measured to assess financial performance. Discuss reasons for any variances.

electronic components, the modern computer center takes up much less space than was previously required. For example, the large IBM legacy mainframe system up until the mid-1990s often required water-cooling systems that called for extensive plumbing. Advances in technology have eliminated the need for many of these elaborate, large, and expensive systems.

In addition, there have been significant changes in the design of many IT peripheral components. The once common magnetic tape drives, for example, have now all but gone away, and even the cartridges that later became more common are now often configured as small solid-state drives. Disk drives are still in use but are often configured as arrays of small disks with considerably greater data storage capacity. Output printing is still done on remote high-speed laser printers, but enterprises increasingly strive to go paperless and communicate reports as digital files. An internal auditor should gain an understanding of the types of IT equipment used by requesting a hardware configuration chart from operations management. While internal audit will typically not be in a position to determine, for example, the correct models of disk drives, such a chart will indicate that management has done some planning in their computer hardware configuration. These charts are often filled with model numbers rather than explanations of the equipment. The internal auditor should always ask questions about the nature of this equipment.

While the number and type of storage devices and other equipment will vary, an internal auditor can expect to find similar characteristics in all operating facilities. They should help internal audit to develop procedures to test the appropriate controls. When auditors first started to review IT general controls, they often looked for such things as locked computer room doors, fire extinguishers, and proper batch controls. Such controls are now in place as a matter of course in large computer centers. While internal audit should always keep these controls in mind, other general control objectives and procedures must also be considered.

Operating System Software

Early business computer systems had little more than a single basic master program—what came to be called an operating system—to load and schedule application programs, with those application programs taking care of their own utility functions, such as tape file label checking or sorting data. The IBM 1401 computer of the mid-1960s had only 8 KB (8,000 bytes) of memory to contain its operating system. The basic 1401 operating system did little more than load programs and communicate with input and output devices. Modern operating system software is much more complex than older systems and capable of handling many users and systems functions. The typical user with a laptop system today can be overwhelmed the complexity of that computer's operating system, whether it is Microsoft Windows or Apple's Mac OS.

IT operating systems are the basic software tools that provide interfaces between systems users, application programs, and other IT hardware. In addition to the basic operating system, an internal auditor will encounter various monitors and controllers, including specialized software to schedule jobs or handle logical security. Operating systems software includes the central operating system, control programs, various programming aids, and application-related support software.

An internal auditor should develop a general understanding of the various types of installed operating system software that may be on a given system as well as the high-level control risks, including:

- **Central operating systems.** The operating system supervises the processing of all systems resources and programs. IBM's older large MVS operating system is an example. Because these operating systems were often so closely tied to the hardware they control, operating systems traditionally have been unique to the computer vendor's equipment. Today the trend is toward common or open operating systems. The Unix operating system, for example, has been implemented on virtually all sizes and models of computer systems. Although less common on large mainframes, Unix is found on many small to midsize computers and is a major controller for Internet systems. Unix provides common user interface functions with the hardware where it is installed. There are other versions of Unix that differ slightly. In addition, the open source operating system Linux is becoming increasingly common today.

- **System monitors.** A variety of basic operating system support software products help schedule jobs, monitor systems activities, and help solve operator problems or system errors. These products are very closely tied to the basic operating system but are usually sold and installed separately. Monitors provide internal signals to other operating system functions—that is, they are similar to a semaphore signal once found on a railroad track. Once a train enters a stretch of track, a control monitor detects the train and raises various semaphores to signal other trains that one is already on the track. Some monitors just log operating system activity for historical purposes. An example is IBM's system management facility (SMF) utility on what is now known as IBM's System z. The SMF software facility monitors virtually all systems activities, including which programs are processed and the various disk files used. Operating system memory dumps are another example of a monitor. Here, the contents of the affected system memory are reported when a program goes into an error status.
- **Network controllers and teleprocessing monitors.** These are specialized operating system programs that supervise and control transmissions between the host computer system and peripheral devices. These devices allow the applications processing on a host computer system to communicate with multiple network connections. Software programs that support the interaction between online terminals and the host computer also fall into this class of operating software. IBM's online monitor, the CICS (Customer Information Control System)—often called "kicks"—allows user terminals to access and process online programs. An internal auditor may find the name CICS somewhat curious, as it is generally used for much more than customer information applications. CICS was originally developed by IBM in the early days of its old 360 series computers for a specific customer who needed a method to access programs in an online manner. IBM did not have such an online software product at the time, although its mainframe computer system competition did. So it created CICS as a special product that has since become its basic online processing control product; many have forgotten what the acronym CICS really means.

All of these special names or acronyms can cause an auditor some communication problems. Computer systems users may know what the product does but may forget what the acronym really represents. As long as the systems specialist and the auditor understand the functions of a software product, there is little need to worry about the specific meaning of the acronym. Internal auditors should not become discouraged by this foreign language of specialized computer software terms and names. When IT technical personnel speak in their own techno-jargon, an internal auditor should always ask for clarifications when uncertain.

19.8 LEGACY OF LARGE SYSTEM GENERAL CONTROL REVIEWS

In an older, traditional IT environment, the computer operations area was often internal audit's prime area of internal control concern. In those days, computer operators had considerable power to make changes or to bypass systems controls such as overriding data file label controls, making changes to program processing sequences, or inserting unauthorized program instructions into production applications. While these are still possible today, both the complexity of large computer operating systems and the sheer volume of work passing through the modern IT operations center makes such unauthorized actions difficult. Internal audit has greater risks to consider.

Many once common internal audit IT operations control improvement recommendations are no longer feasible today. For example, older business data center legacy computers had a console printer attached to record operator commands, and internal auditors traditionally recommended that these console logs be reviewed on a regular basis. The logs were often ignored but were useful for tracing inappropriate operator activities. Today this console activity is recorded onto log files, but the sheer volume of that data makes a periodic human review of console log reports all but totally unrealistic; other tools and controls are available to help internal auditors understand operations controls. Internal audit should initially gain an understanding of the information system enterprise, its established control procedures, and specialized duties and responsibilities.

An important first step in an internal audit review of IT operations large system general controls is to clearly define that review's objectives. All too often, a member of the audit committee or senior management may ask internal audit to "review the computer system controls" in some enterprise data center. That request may be based on IT controls as they once existed in older systems. An internal auditor should consider the following questions when planning such a data center review:

- What is the purpose of the information system operations review?
- Which specific controls and procedures are expected to be in place?
- How can evidence be gathered to determine if controls work?

Based on the results of this exercise, internal audit should develop a set of control objectives specifically tailored for the planned review rather than just use a standard set of internal control questions. Whether an IT or any other review, the internal audit objectives identified depend on the purpose of the review.

If management has requested a review of the costs and efficiency of data center operations, for example, internal audit procedures might include such areas as the chargeback and the job-scheduling systems. Although a large system IT general controls review can have a variety of purposes, it will often fit into one of the following four review types.

1. Preliminary reviews of IT general controls. This is the type of review that outside auditors sometimes call a *preliminary survey* or an *assessment of control risk*. Its purpose is to gain a general understanding or overview of the IT controls environment.

Internal audit asks questions, observes operations, and reviews documentation, but there is typically only very limited testing, if any. For example, internal audit might inquire about the procedures for updating production program libraries and might review the forms used for the approval process. However, the auditor would probably not select a sample of the programs in the production library to determine if they had followed proper library update procedures.

A preliminary review can help determine the need for a more detailed general controls review or extended control risk assessment at a later date, or can gather preliminary controls information for a specific applications review. This type of review is limited in scope and may not cover all aspects of the IT enterprise. Some areas where a preliminary review would be appropriate might include a preliminary controls review of IT operations at a new acquisition or a follow-up review after a very detailed general controls review from an earlier period; the review here would emphasize changes in control procedures as well as actions taken on prior audit recommendations.

Although there can be many changes based on the review's specific purpose, Exhibit 19.4 outlines steps for a preliminary survey of IT general controls. These steps should guide an internal auditor to gain information about the general structure of IT operations, how it plans and organizes resources, its management reporting tools, and procedures for security and contingency planning. These audit steps will not help in understanding the types of applications in place, but will assess how that IT function is organized and managed.

2. Detailed general controls reviews of IT operations. A comprehensive, detailed review of IT large systems general controls should cover all aspects of IT operations, including systems programming, routers and telecommunications controls, firewall devices, and storage administration. A detailed general controls review, including tests of controls, often requires internal audit to spend considerable fieldwork time in both the IT operations and systems development functions. While the preliminary review can sometimes be performed by a less experienced auditor who is developing IT audit skills, a detailed general controls review is best performed by more senior audit staff members with good understandings of IT controls and procedures.

Based on a preliminary IT operations walk-through review, internal audit should develop a general understanding of the IT control procedures in place. Questions internal audit might pose could include:

- **How is work scheduled?** Some large system computer operators do little more than initiate jobs from a production job queue file, while others have considerable authority in deciding which jobs to run. In the latter situation, internal audit might want to spend time reviewing control log reports and operator instructions. If these procedures have been automated, internal audit may want to consider a specialized review of the production control software area.
- **How is storage media managed?** Automated tools are often used here. In addition, some operations have a separate library facility where production media cartridges are mounted. Even when software has been installed, computer operators often can bypass label controls and introduce incorrect files into a production environment.

- **What types of operator procedures or instructions are used?** Large systems operations documentation can take a variety of formats; internal audit should have a general understanding of this documentation format and content to help in the design of specific audit tests.
- **How is work initiated and how does it flow through operations?** In many large IT systems operations, production is initiated through remote job entry user terminals. In others, the production-control function funnels all necessary input data to machine operations. Some functions rely on users to initiate most inputs through their online terminals. The type and nature of internal audit's tests will depend on the customary procedures.

The basic idea is for internal audit to understand how IT operations function in the data center reviewed. The effective internal auditor should go through a set of these types of questions prior to each review. A large systems operations function may install new procedures from time to time, changing or adding complexities to the control structure. The audit procedures to be performed in a detailed review of general controls for a legacy computer system can be extensive, depending on the size and scope of the audit. Exhibit 19.4 contains a limited set of control objectives for this type of large systems review.

EXHIBIT 19.4 Large IT Systems General Controls Review Objectives

1. Determine that the IT equipment is located in a secure, environmentally controlled facility.
2. Discuss physical and environmental control procedures with information systems management to determine current policies, major changes, and other future plans.
3. Tour computer room server facilities and observe physical security strengths and weaknesses, including:
   a. The existence of locking mechanisms to limit computer room access only to authorized individuals
   b. The placement of computer room perimeter walls and windows to limit access
   c. The location of power transformers, water chiller units if appropriate, and air-conditioning units to provide proper protection
   d. The general location of the computer room facilities within the overall building to minimize traffic
   e. The existence of fire detection equipment, including zone-controlled heat and smoke detectors and local extinguishers
4. Review computer room temperature, humidity, and other environmental controls and assess their adequacy.
5. Briefly review maintenance records to ascertain that physical and environmental controls are regularly inspected and maintained.
6. Production processing should be scheduled to promote efficient use of computer equipment consistent with the requirements of systems users. Through interviews with operations management, develop an overall understanding of computer processing demands, including online and other production work as well as any end-user social computing.
7. Also through interviews, describe the telecommunications network surrounding the computer system, including routers, connections to workstations, computer centers, and the outside.
8. Review procedures for scheduling regular production jobs including the use of automated job scheduling tools.

9. Match a limited number of scheduled production jobs against actual completion times to determine whether actual schedules are followed.
10. Determine that operating system job classes or priority codes are used to give proper priority to critical production jobs, and evaluate procedures for rush or rerun jobs.
11. Review documentation standards for production applications to determine that they provide operators with information regarding:
    a. Normal operations, including instructions for special forms, tape files, and report disposition
    b. Application restart and recovery procedures.
12. Review procedures, automated or manual, for turning new applications or revisions over to production to determine there is a review by operations following standards.
13. Determine that policies prohibit computer operations personnel from performing programming tasks or running unauthorized jobs.
14. Determine that production source libraries and table files cannot be accessed by operations personnel.
15. Assess information systems procedures for periodically reviewing the contents of log files or otherwise monitoring improper operator use of computer equipment.
16. Review and document procedures for changing production programs or procedure libraries when emergency situations require special handling.
17. Determine that all emergency processing activities are properly documented and are subject to subsequent management review.
18. Select several documented emergency program fixes and determine that the necessary changes were added to production processing libraries and were documented.
19. Determine that an automated system is in place to log all computer systems activity, including all jobs and programs run, any reruns, abnormal terminations, or operator commands and data entered through system consoles.
20. Determine that computer activity logs are at least high-level reviewed periodically, that exception situations are investigated, and that the results of investigations are documented.
21. Determine that files produced from the computer operating system's log monitor are retained long enough to allow investigation of unusual activities.
22. Review procedures for logging problems to determine that all abnormal software and hardware operating conditions are documented.
23. Determine that schedules exist for the submission of critical input batch files and that procedures exist to follow up on missing data.
24. Review procedures to prohibit unauthorized input or access to production files and programs.
25. Review a limited sample of production batch applications to determine that appropriate systems control techniques are used.
26. Determine whether users or information systems personnel are responsible for reviewing output controls and assess whether those control reviews are being performed.
27. Assess procedures for reviewing distributed output reports to determine whether they are complete.

3. Specialized or limited-scope-oriented reviews. Because of management requests and perceived risks, auditors often perform limited reviews over specialized areas within an overall IT function. These specialized reviews can be limited to one function, such as database administration, or a specialty area, such as output report distribution. Often, management will request that internal audit perform this type of review due to some identified problem, such as a well-publicized security violation.

An audit of a highly specialized or technical area of IT operations often takes considerable auditor creativity in planning the work. Management may be concerned about the equity of the computer chargeback system and may ask internal audit to look at it. There will be a need to gain a general understanding of the systems used, spend time planning the additional procedures and tests to be performed, and then return to the actual testing.

As IT has grown in complexity and importance to the enterprise, internal auditors can expect to perform more of these specialized, limited reviews. With the IT function as a major resource in many enterprises, it may be inappropriate to attempt to review *all* IT general controls in *all* operational areas as one single detailed review. This would be the same as if internal audit attempted to perform a review of "manufacturing" in a major plant environment. Rather than cover all manufacturing functions, internal audit might review production control one year and receiving and inspection the next, and eventually cover most significant functions. For a specialized review of a specific IT control area, such as memory media library management, internal audit should expand on the procedures developed for a general controls review in that area and add additional audit tests as necessary.

4. Reviews to assess compliance with laws or regulations. One of the major objectives of internal control, as discussed in Chapter 3 on COSO internal control fundamentals, is compliance with laws and regulations. Internal auditors should always be aware of objectives in this area and include appropriate tests in their reviews. Auditors working with governmental agencies or in enterprises that do extensive governmental contracting may often be required to perform IT-related compliance audits to determine if appropriate laws and regulations are being followed. These will differ very much from agency to agency and from one political division to another.

A compliance-related IT review can often be combined with a preliminary or detailed general controls review, but internal auditors must be aware of the relevant procedures and regulations, such as those published by the governmental agency requiring the audit. Most bank-examination agencies, for example, have published IT controls guidelines. When operating in this type of environment, internal auditors must become aware of the regulatory environment as well as any published procedures.

19.9 ITIL® SERVICE SUPPORT AND DELIVERY IT INFRASTRUCTURE BEST PRACTICES

As defined previously, ITIL® is the acronym for the Information Technology Infrastructure Library, a set of best practices first developed in the 1980s by the British government's Office of Government Commerce (OGC)—formerly called the Central Computer and Telecommunications Agency. It is a vendor/supplier independent collection of best practices that has become widely recognized in IT operations, first in the United Kingdom, followed by the European Union, then in Canada and Australia, and now increasingly in the United States. ITIL® is a detailed framework of significant IT best practices, with comprehensive checklists, tasks, procedures, and responsibilities designed to be tailored to any IT organization. Dividing key processes between those covering IT service delivery and those for service support, ITIL® has become the de facto standard for describing many fundamental processes in IT service management, such as configuration or *change management*.

ITIL® is a formal "library" of technical publications published by the British OGC.[2] The publications and their contents are tightly controlled, similar to the International Organization for Standardization (ISO) international standards publications discussed in Chapter 33. Internal auditors should be aware of the existence of ITIL® and should ask their IT functions how much they have embraced or adopted ITIL® best practices. Our intent here is not to provide a detailed description of the components of ITIL® but to give internal auditors a high-level understanding of some of its elements. A general knowledge of ITIL® will allow internal auditors to better understand some key IT processes and to make more effective recommendations when they review IT general controls.

ITIL® processes cover what we frequently call the IT infrastructure—the supporting processes that allow IT applications to function and deliver their results to systems users. All too often, internal auditors have focused their attention on the application development side of IT and ignored important supporting service delivery and support IT processes. An enterprise can put massive effort, for example, into building and implementing a new budget forecasting system, but that application will be of little value unless there are good processes in place, such as problem and *incident management*, to allow the users of the system to report systems difficulties. Also needed are good capacity and availability processes to allow the new application to run as expected. These ITIL® processes are all part of what is called the *IT infrastructure*, and a well-designed and well-controlled application is of little value to its users without strong service support and delivery processes in place. Internal auditors should have a good understanding of these enterprise processes and then develop an appropriate test of controls. These may have been covered in an IT general controls review, and ITIL® provides a good general best practices model to follow.

While they have become fairly common elsewhere in the world, ITIL® processes are now widely recognized in the United States and have not yet been adequately recognized by internal auditors. The following sections will provide an overview of some ITIL® processes important for an internal auditor, including such areas as capacity or service level management. This should give an internal auditor some guidance on how IT functions, such as a help desk, should provide areas for internal controls improvements in this very important IT process area.

ITIL® processes have traditionally been split between those covering what ITIL® defines as service support and those for service delivery. Service support processes help make IT applications operate in an efficient and customer-satisfying manner, while service delivery processes improve the efficiency and performance of IT infrastructure elements. There are five ITIL® service support best practice processes, ranging from release management, for placing a process into production, to incident management, for the orderly reporting of IT problems or events. ITIL service support processes cover good practices for any IT enterprise, whether it is a centralized operation using primarily classic legacy mainframe systems as its IT central control point, to highly distributed client-server operations. Because of the many variations possible in an IT operations function, ITIL® does not prescribe the details of "how" to implement service support processes such as configuration or change management. Rather, it suggests good practices and ways to manage inputs and relationships between these processes. There is no order or precedence among each. They can be considered and managed separately, but all of them are somewhat linked to one another. Exhibit 19.5 shows a high-level view of

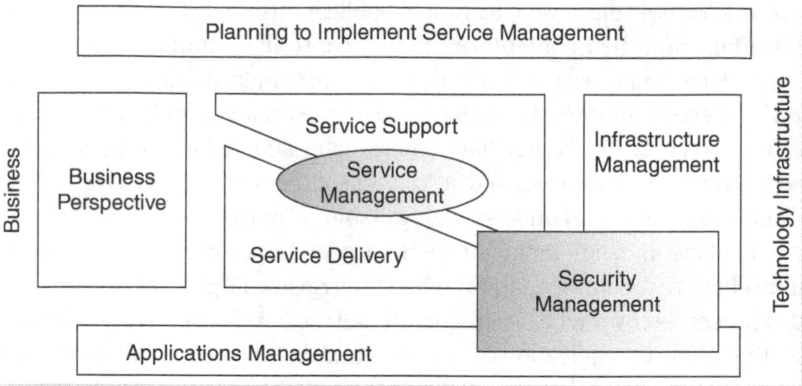

EXHIBIT 19.5 The ITIL® Framework

Source: Sarbanes-Oxley Internal Controls: Effective Auditing with AS5, COBIT, and ITIL, Robert R. Moeller. Copyright © 2008 John Wiley & Sons. Reprinted with permission of John Wiley & Sons, Inc.

the ITIL® framework. It shows that the service management areas of service delivery and support, along with security management, provide a linkage between the business operations and IT technology and infrastructure management.

Although there are many components and elements to ITIL®, this section will only discuss its five defined service support processes, areas that are important for an internal auditor performing an IT general controls review. They suggest preferred approaches for an IT operations function to organize and operate its productions systems in a manner that will promote efficient operation and will deliver quality services to the ultimate user or customer of those services. These are particularly useful for an internal auditor performing a review and making recommendations in an IT operations area.

When an internal auditor is observing and reviewing IT operations internal controls, a useful approach is to think of things in terms of these separate ITIL® processes. For example, the ITIL® process called incident management, or what has traditionally been called the help desk, is a facility where systems users or customers can call in with a question or problem. While a help desk function can be very useful, it is often a source of grousing when, for example, a similar problem is called in repeatedly with no evident efforts to analyze things and initiate a solution. Going beyond just a casual help desk and thinking of this as an overall process where matters are reported to other supporting processes will improve performance and the overall quality of IT operations.

ITIL Service Support Incident Management

Incident management processes cover the activities necessary for restoring an IT service following a disruption. ITIL® defines a disruption as any type of problem that prevents an IT user from receiving adequate services, whether it is an overall system failure, the user's inability to access the application for any of a wide variety of reasons, a password failure due to a "fat fingers" typing error, or any other problem. The reported problem is called an *incident*, some type of deviation from standard operations. We will use this terminology and refer to incidents throughout our discussion of ITIL®. Although many IT functions have a function called a help desk or a customer support group, we refer to this general function here as the *service desk.* The service desk is usually the owner for the incident management process, although all service support groups across IT may have a role.

The objective of effective incident management processes is to restore normal operations as quickly as possible in a cost-effective manner with minimal impact on either the overall business or the user. How quickly is "quickly" should not be subject to interpretation, and ITIL® calls for restoration time-frame standards to be defined in what are called *service level agreements (SLAs)* between IT and the customer or user. Effective SLAs are an important component of the IT infrastructure and are discussed later as one of the ITIL® service delivery processes; their existence should be on an internal auditor's radar screen. The first component of the ITIL® incident management process is the detection and documentation of the incident by the service desk, as a single point of contact. These incidents can include such matters as a user calling in some specific application problem to IT operations informing the service desk of an application processing problem.

Once the service desk receives a reported incident, it should classify it in terms of its priority, impact, and urgency. The definition of a reported incident's priority is one of the most important aspects of managing IT incidents. Every person who calls in an incident thinks that his or hers is the most important, and the incident management function has the difficult task of defining the relative priority of the reported incident, its importance, and its impact on the business. Exhibit 19.6 shows the life cycle of an incident from the initial call through resolution and closure. Our point here is to help internal audit understand not how to manage a service desk process but rather its recommended best practices. An understanding of ITIL® best practices allows an internal auditor to ask some probing questions when reviewing IT general controls. For example, internal auditors should look for formal SLAs, as part of the service level management process, to define the priority with which incidents need to be resolved and the effort put into the resolution of and recovery from incidents. These SLAs should depend upon:

- **The *impact or criticality* of the incident on the reporting entity or overall enterprise.** Incident management should assess, for example, how many users will suffer as a result of a reported technical failure of a hardware component. Similarly, a call regarding a problem with the month-end close process should be assigned a higher level of criticality than a problem with the system that generates purchase orders.
- **The *urgency* of the reported incident.** *Urgency* refers to the speed necessary to solve an incident of a certain impact. A high-impact incident does not, by default, always have to be solved immediately. An incident call reporting that some user group can't work at all because of a service outage is often of greater urgency than a senior manager calling to request a functionality change.
- **The *size, scope,* and *complexity* of the incident.** The incident management team should investigate the reported incident as soon as possible to determine its extent. A reported failure of some component may just mean that a device is out of service or that a server is down. Those types of incidents often are not very complex and can be repaired relatively easily. A telecommunications failure that might impact multiple international units and thus might delay the monthly financial close can be much larger in size and scope.

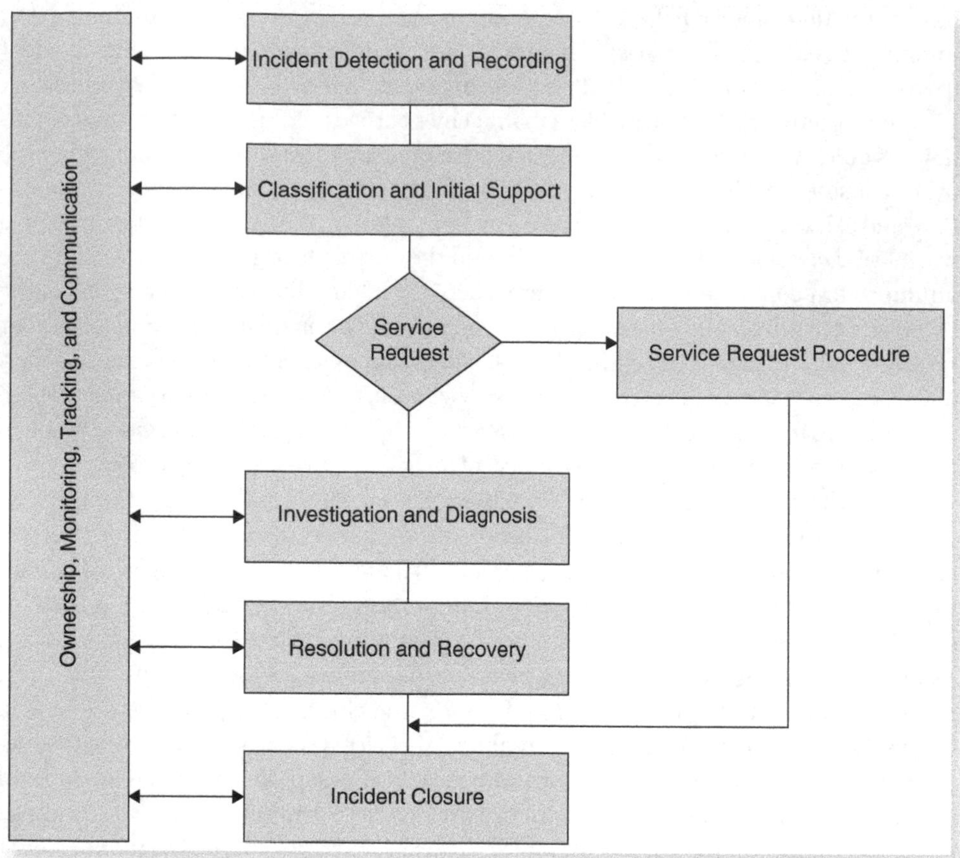

EXHIBIT 19.6 ITIL® Incident Management Life Cycle

Once an incident has been logged in, the process of investigation and diagnosis should begin. If the service desk cannot resolve the incident, it should be assigned to other IT support levels for resolution. However, all parties that work on the incident should keep records of their actions by updating a common incident log file.

Some incidents can be resolved through a "quick fix" by the service desk, others by a more formal problem solution, or in the case of more significant problems, by a work-around to get things back in partial operation coupled with a formal request for change (RFC) to systems, to a vendor, or whatever parties are need to correct such a significant problem. In any event, efforts should be marshaled to correct the problem with the incident management function retaining ownership of the matter until resolution. Solid documentation should be maintained to track the incident until its resolution. The incident can be formally closed once matters have been fixed, or if not easily solved, it should be passed to the *problem management* process function as discussed later.

All ITIL® processes are somewhat related to one another, and we have selected incident management as one to discuss. In many instances, incident management represents the first line between users of IT services and IT itself. Properly organized, incident management should be much more than the help desks of an earlier time when users called in with problems but did not get much help beyond perhaps password resets. Incident management is a first point of contact between the customers—users—and the overall IT function. Incidents, the result of failures or errors within the IT infrastructure, result in actual or potential variations from the planned operation of services. Sometimes the cause of these incidents may be apparent and can be addressed or fixed without the need for further investigation. In other situations there may be a need for a hardware or software repair, a matter that often takes some time to implement. Short-run solutions may be a work-around, a quick fix to get back in operation, or a formal RFC to the change management process to remove the error. Examples of short-term work-arounds might be just instructing a customer to reboot a personal computer or reset a communications line, without directly addressing the underlying cause of the incident.

Where the underlying cause of the incident is not identifiable, it is often appropriate to raise a problem record for the unknown error within the infrastructure. Normally a problem record is raised only if investigation is warranted, and its actual and potential impact should be assessed. Successful processing of a problem record will result in the identification of the underlying error, and the record can then be converted into a known error once a work-around has been developed and/or an RFC submitted.

Service Support Problem Management

When the incident management process encounters a deviation with an unknown cause or reason, that incident should be passed on to the problem management process for resolution. The objective here is to minimize the total impact of problems through a formal process of detection and repair as well as taking actions to prevent any reoccurrence. The problem management process is the next step in the criticality of some reported incident and should be considered in terms of three subprocesses: problem control, error control, and proactive problem management. ITIL® defines a "problem" as an unknown underlying cause resulting from one or more incidents, and a "known error" is a problem that has been successfully diagnosed and for which a work-around has been identified. The idea is not to necessarily create a second administrative function in an IT enterprise to take reported help desk incidents, but to identify when and how some reported help desk incidents should be passed to another person or authority to better diagnose the reported matter and treat it as a problem. An effective problem management process can do much to improve overall IT customer service.

In addition to resolving any single incident that was bumped up to the problem management process, IT should try to establish processes for better problem and error control, including maintaining data to help identify trends and suggesting improved procedures for the proactive prevention of problems. Data should be maintained on solutions and/or any available workarounds for a resolved problem and closed problem records. In many instances, problem management may encounter a situation where it is necessary to go a step further and file a formal request for change either through IT development function or through a hardware or software vendor.

The problem management process focuses on finding patterns between incidents, problems, and known errors. A detailed review of these patterns allows an analyst to solve the problem by considering the many possibilities and narrowing things down to a solution, what is called root cause analysis. There are many good techniques for resolving and correcting problems, often caused by a combination of technical and nontechnical factors. An internal auditor reviewing problem management processes should look for documented formal procedures to support problem analysis and resolution. Problem management is a good area for internal audit to diagnose IT service delivery processes in order to better understand the overall health of IT operations. Areas where internal audit may ask some questions here include:

1. The number of RFCs raised and the impact of those RFCs on the availability and reliability of the overall IT services covered.
2. The amount of time worked on investigations and diagnoses for various types of problems by organization unit or vendor.
3. The number and impact of incidents occurring before a root problem is solved or a known error is confirmed.
4. The plans for resolution of open problems with regard to people and other resource requirements as well as related costs and budgeted amounts.

The ITIL® service support problem management process is an important area for internal auditors to consider and understand when assessing the overall health of IT infrastructure operations. An efficient incident management process is necessary to receive customer calls and take immediate corrective actions, but an effective problem management process will go a step further to analyze and solve the problem, initiating RFCs where necessary and otherwise improving IT customer satisfaction.

Service Support Configuration Management

Whatever their relative size, IT operations functions are complex, with multiple types and versions of systems components that must work together in an orderly, well-managed manner. This is certainly true for both small IT systems operations and for major corporations with classic mainframe systems, "farms" of servers, and a multitude of storage devices and communications gear. A formal *configuration management* function is an important service delivery process that supports the identification, recording, and reporting of IT components and their versions, constituent components, and relationships. Items that should be under the control of configuration management include hardware, software, and associated documentation. Configuration management is not the same concept as the depreciation accounting process for asset management, although the two are related. Asset management systems maintain details on IT gear above a certain value, their business unit, and their location. Configuration management also maintains relationships between assets, which asset management usually does not. Some enterprises start with asset management and then move on to configuration management.

The basic activity of the configuration management process is to identify the various individual components in IT operations, called configuration items (CIs), and then to identify key supporting data for these CIs, including their owners, identifying data, and version numbers, as well as systems interrelationships. This data should be captured, organized, and recorded in what is often known as a configuration management database (CMDB). The team responsible for configuration management should select and identify these configuration structures for the entire infrastructure's CIs, including establishing relationships between each CI and connected components in the overall IT infrastructure configuration. Going beyond just entry in the CMDB, the process should ensure that only authorized CIs have been accepted and that no CI is added, modified, replaced, or removed without an appropriate change request and an updated specification.

An internal auditor can think of the importance of the configuration management process in terms of desktop applications in the audit department. Every internal auditor today probably has a laptop computer, but unless each has consistent versions of software, there may be difficulties in systems communicating with one another. This is where configuration management is important. It is even more important when attempting to understand the various versions or even types of software and equipment in a large IT operation.

The configuration management process also includes some control elements. A series of reviews and audits should be implemented to verify the physical existence of CIs and check that they are correctly recorded in the configuration management system. Although we have used the word *audit* here, this is not an internal audit process but the ITIL®-defined term for the IT team responsible for the configuration management process. Configuration management should also maintain records for CI status accounting to track the status of a CI as it changes from one state to another, for instance from under development, to being tested, to going live, and then to being withdrawn.

A CMDB does not have to be a complex, specialized application. An enterprise can establish a very basic level of CMDB just by using spreadsheets, local databases, or even paper-based systems. In today's large and complex IT infrastructures, however, configuration management requires the use of physical and electronic libraries along with the CMDB to hold definitive copies of software and documentation. The CMDB should be based upon database technology that provides flexible and powerful interrogation facilities. It should contain details about the relationships between all system components, including incidents, problems, known errors, changes, and releases.

The existence and controls supporting a CMDB can be a good point for internal audit to understand an enterprise's IT configuration management process and its supporting controls. If the enterprise IT function does not have a good CMDB, internal audit can anticipate seeing strong internal control problems throughout the IT infrastructure. Exhibit 19.7 outlines audit procedures for reviewing an enterprise's configuration management process.

The configuration management process interfaces directly with systems development, testing, change management, and release management to incorporate new and updated product deliverables. Control should be passed from the project or supplier to the service provider at the scheduled time with accurate configuration records. In addition, the CMDB can be used by the service level management process to hold details of services and relate them to the underlying IT components. The CMDB can also be used to store inventory details of CIs, such as supplier, cost, purchase date, and renewal date for a license. An additional bonus is the use of the CMDB to cover the legal aspects associated with the maintenance of licenses and contracts.

EXHIBIT 19.7 ITIL® Configuration Management Internal Audit Steps

1. Review and understand existing enterprise configuration management practices as well as their interfaces to the service management processes, procurement, and development.
2. Assess the knowledge and capability of existing IT functions and its staff in terms of controls and processes for configuration, change, and release management processes.
3. Review extent and complexity of existing configuration software and systems support data, whether held in hard-copy form, in local spreadsheets, or in configuration management databases (CMDB), and develop an understanding of that database and its retrieval tools.
4. Select a production application and understand its definition on the CMDB in detail, including interfaces to change management, release management, other service management processes, procurement, and development.
5. Using the installed CMDB reporting tool, define the inventory of configuration items (CIs) for one selected system and physically trace a sample of reported CIs to actual configuration components.
6. Determine processes are in place to link configuration management business processes and procedures with the CMDB tools.
7. Test the CMDB and other support tool(s) to determine key components, software, and documentation have been implemented and controlled on the CMDB.
8. Review adequacy of facilities to provide secure storage areas to manage CIs (e.g., cabinets, controlled libraries, and directories).
9. Assess adequacy of processes to communicate and train staff in the importance and use of configuration management.
10. Review problem management processes to determine the extent and appropriateness of their use of the CMDB for resolving problems.
11. Determine that appropriate access and update controls are in place to prevent unauthorized or inappropriate use of the CMDB.
12. Determine that the CMDB receives adequate backups and that it is part of the continuity plan key resources backup and recovery procedures.

Service Support Change Management

The problem management process, discussed earlier, often results in the need for IT changes, ranging from program changes to process revisions that improve service or reduce costs. The goal of ITIL® change management is to utilize standardized methods and procedures for the efficient and prompt handling of all changes, in order to minimize their impact on service quality and the day-to-day operations. ITIL® change management processes include:

- IT hardware and system software
- Communications equipment and software
- All applications software
- All documentation and procedures associated with the running, support, and maintenance of live systems

The last point here is of particular concern to internal auditors. All too often, IT hardware and software is changed with little concern given to also changing the supporting documentation. Changes to any IT components—for example, applications software, documentation, or procedures—should be subject to a formal change management process.

Internal auditors often encounter IT functions where the change management process is haphazard at best. Examples here are changes to applications without thinking through their implications on the overall IT infrastructure, incident management fixes that create other changes, or senior management requests for changes to solve short-term or immediate problems. A formal change management process that reviews and approves any proposed changes will almost always improve IT and enterprise internal control processes. The ITIL® change management process should be tightly linked to configuration management, discussed previously, to ensure that information regarding the possible implications of a proposed change is made available, and any possible impacts are detected and presented appropriately.

Change management processes should have high visibility and open channels of communication in order to promote smooth transitions when changes take place. To improve this process, many IT functions have instituted a formal change advisory board (CAB), made up of people from both IT and other functions within the enterprise, to review and approve changes. A CAB also assists in the assessment and prioritization of changes. It should be given the responsibility of ensuring that all changes are adequately assessed from both a business and a technical perspective. To achieve this mix, the CAB should consist of a team with a clear understanding of the customer's business needs as well as the technical development and support functions. Chaired by a responsible change manager, a CAB should comprise IT customers, applications developers, various experts/technical consultants as appropriate, and any contractor or third parties' representatives if in an outsourcing situation. Although a CAB should meet regularly to review and schedule proposed changes, it should not act as an impediment to IT operations. It should exist to provide orderly scheduling and introduction of all types of IT infrastructure changes.

Efficient overall service management processes require a capability to change things in an orderly way, without making errors and wrong decisions. An effective change management process is indispensable for an effective IT infrastructure. When reviewing IT internal controls, internal auditors should look for an effective change management process that provides:

- Better alignment of IT services to business requirements
- Increased visibility and communication of changes to both business and service support staff
- Improved risk assessments
- A reduced adverse impact of changes on the quality of services
- Better assessments of the cost of proposed changes before they are incurred
- Fewer changes that have to be backed out, along with an increased ability to do this more easily when necessary
- Increased productivity of IT customers, through less disruption and higher-quality services
- A greater ability of IT to absorb a large volume of changes

An effective change management process is an important component of IT infrastructure controls. The process must align tightly with other key processes in the IT infrastructure: change, configuration, capacity, and release management.

Service Support Release Management

IT functions need effective processes to ensure that changes are introduced to all impacted parties in an orderly and well-controlled manner. Release management covers the introduction of authorized changes to an IT service. A release will typically consist of a number of problem fixes and enhancements to the service, including new or changed software and hardware needed to implement the required approved changes.

Releases will normally be implemented as a full release, where all of the components being changed are built, tested, distributed, and implemented together. This eliminates the danger that obsolete versions of CIs (discussed in configuration management earlier in this chapter) will be incorrectly assumed to be unchanged and used within the release. With a full release, all components supporting some application area or system are released as a single component. With all new and existing components bundled together, any problems are more likely to be detected and rectified before entry into the live environment. The disadvantage is that the time, effort, and computing resources needed to build, test, distribute, and implement the full release will increase.

An alternative approach to release management is a delta or partial release, which includes only those CIs that changed since the last full or delta release. A delta release may be more appropriate when a full release cannot be justified due to such factors as the urgency for needed facilities or the size and related resource requirements of a delta release in comparison with a full release. There is no single correct choice, and a decision to do a delta release should be taken on a case-by-case basis, with the CAB making the recommendation. Internal auditors should understand the importance of well-ordered release processes and should look for well-ordered and established processes as they perform IT general controls reviews.

These sections in this part of the chapter have outlined ITIL® service support processes at a very high level. When reviewing IT general controls, an internal auditor should think of the importance of processes such as configuration management. An internal auditor does not need to be an expert in these ITIL® service support areas, but should keep them in mind when reviewing IT general controls. An internal auditor should become sufficiently familiar with these processes to better understand controls and procedures supporting IT service support.

19.10 SERVICE DELIVERY BEST PRACTICES

The preceding paragraphs have outlined the five ITIL® service support processes. In addition, there are five ITIL® service delivery processes. Service support covered the accurate processing of IT applications and components ranging from receiving a reported incident to defining the problem to introducing the change and then releasing it into production. The equally important ITIL® service delivery processes cover areas more closely aligned with the smooth and efficient operation of the overall IT infrastructure. Some of these, such as the continuity management process, have traditionally been near and dear to the hearts of many internal auditors. Others, such as service level agreements that define performance and expectations between IT and its customers, should be familiar to internal auditors who encounter similar arrangements in other areas.

Service Delivery Service Level Management

Service level management is the name given to the ITIL® processes of planning, coordinating, drafting, agreeing, monitoring, and reporting on formal agreements between IT and both the providers and recipients of IT services. As explained previously, these agreements are called service level agreements (SLAs), and they represent a formal agreement between IT and both providers of services to IT as well as IT end-user customers. When the first ITIL® service level best practices materials were published in 1989, an SLA was an interesting but not very common concept. Today many enterprises have introduced them—although with varying degrees of success—and internal auditors should be familiar with and understand the importance of SLAs when reviewing internal IT infrastructure controls.

In an example of an SLA, IT contracts with an outside provider, such as for disaster recovery backups. The arrangement will be covered by a formal contract where the disaster recovery provider agrees to provide certain levels of service, following some time-response-based schedule. The governing contract here is an SLA between IT and the provider of continuity services. SLAs between IT and their customers are even more important here, from an internal control perspective. We have used the term *customer* to represent the historical and still common term *IT users*. There are many groups in an enterprise that use IT's services, and as customers, they have expectations of certain levels of service and responsiveness. These arrangements are defined through an SLA, a written agreement between an IT and its customers defining the key service targets and responsibilities of both parties. The emphasis should be on an agreement, and SLAs should not be used as a way of holding one side or the other to ransom. A true partnership should be developed between the IT provider and the customer for a mutually beneficial agreement; otherwise the SLA could quickly fall into disrepute and a culture of blame may prevent any true service quality improvements from taking place.

In an SLA, IT promises to deliver services per an agreed-upon set of schedules and understands that there will be penalties if these service standards are not met. The goal is to maintain and improve service quality through a constant cycle of agreeing, monitoring, reporting, and improving the current levels of IT service. SLAs should be strategically focused on the business and maintaining the alignment between the business and IT.

While there is no format requirement for a SLA, Exhibit 19.8 outlines the contents of a typical SLA. This should not be the type of exhaustive document that an internal auditor might find as part of a personal mortgage house closing. Rather, the IT customers will negotiate the IT service requirements that they are seeking, such as "average response times no more than . . ." or "financial systems close processing completed by . . ." or other factors. To temper expectations and show what could be available, an IT function usually provides a service offerings catalog. Customer IT services requirements should be negotiated and formal SLAs established. Performance against these SLAs should be monitored on an ongoing basis with performance reported regularly. Failure to meet these SLA standards could result in additional negotiations and SLA adjustments. This SLA process provides benefits for the business and IT, including:

- Because IT should be working to meet negotiated standards, IT services will tend to be of a higher quality, causing fewer interruptions. The productivity of the IT customers should improve as well.
- IT staff resources will tend to be used more efficiently when IT provides services that better meet the expectations of its customers.
- By using SLAs, IT and its customers can measure the services provided and the perception of IT operations will generally improve.
- Services provided by the third parties are more manageable with the underpinning contracts in place and any possibility of negative influence on the IT service provided is reduced.
- Monitoring overall IT services under SLAs makes it possible to identify weak spots that can be improved.

EXHIBIT 19.8 Sample IT Service Level Agreement Contents

While there is not one commonly accepted form or format for an SLA document, the following set of contents should be considered as key elements for most SLAs:

Agreement Introduction Pages

- Parties to this agreement
- Title and brief description of the agreement
- Signatories
- Dates: start, end, review
- Scope of the agreement: what is covered and what is excluded
- Responsibilities of both the service provider and the customer
- Description of the services covered.

Service Hours

- Hours that each service is normally required (e.g. 24 × 7, Monday to Friday 8 am to 6 pm)
- Arrangements for requesting service extensions, including required notice periods (e.g., request must be made to the service desk by noon for an evening extension, by noon on Thursday for a weekend extension)
- Special hours allowances (e.g., public holidays)
- Service calendar

Availability

- Availability targets within agreed hours, normally expressed as percentages. The measurement period and method should be stipulated and may be expressed for the overall service, underpinning services, and critical components, or all three. Since it is difficult to relate to a simplistic percentage, availability can be measured in terms of the customer's inability to carry out its business activities.

Reliability

- Usually expressed as the number of service breaks, or the mean time between failures (MTBF) or mean time between system incidents (MTBSI).

Support

- Support hours (where these are not the same as service hours), including arrangements for requesting support extensions
- Required notice periods (e.g., request must be made to the service desk by noon for an evening extension, by noon on Thursday for a weekend extension)
- Special hours allowances (e.g., public holidays)

- Target time to respond to incidents, either physically or by other method (e.g., telephone contact, e-mail)
- Target time to resolve incidents, within each incident priority (targets varies depending upon incident priorities)

Throughput

- Indication of likely traffic volumes and throughput activity (e.g., the number of transactions to be processed, number of concurrent users, amount of data to be transmitted over the network)

Transaction Response Times

- Target times for average, or maximum workstation response times (sometimes expressed as a percentile (e.g., 95% within two seconds).

Batch Turnaround Times

- Times for delivery of input and the time and place for delivery of output

Changes

- Targets for approving, handling, and implementing RFCs, usually based upon the category or urgency/priority of the change.

IT Service Continuity and Security

- Brief mention of IT service continuity plans and how to invoke them, and coverage of any security issues, particularly any responsibilities of the customer (e.g., backup of freestanding PCs, password changes)
- Details of any diminished or amended service targets should a disaster situation occur (if no separate SLA exists for such a situation).

Charging

- Details of the charging formula and periods (if charges are being made). If the SLA covers an outsourcing relationship, charges should be detailed in an annex that may not be publicly available due to potential confidence provisions.

Service Reporting and Reviewing

- The content, frequency, and distribution of service reports, and the frequency of service review meetings.

Performance Incentives/Penalties

- Details of any agreement regarding financial incentives or penalties based upon performance against service levels. These are more likely to be included if the services are being provided by a third-party organization. It should be noted that penalty clauses can create their own difficulties.

The SLA process should be an important component of IT operations. If an enterprise does not use formal SLAs, internal auditors reviewing IT operations general controls should consider recommending that the enterprise IT function initiate formal SLA processes. SLAs can create a totally new environment within IT, where all parties will better understand their responsibilities and service obligations, with the SLA as a basis for resolving many issues. Internal audit can use them as a basis for assessing internal controls in a variety of areas and for making strong controls improvement recommendations.

Service Delivery Financial Management for IT Services

In its earlier days, the IT function in most enterprises was operated as a "free" support service. Its expenses were handled through central management with its cost allocated to benefiting users. There was little attention given to costs in those early days. If a department wanted some new application, it would pressure management to purchase the package and add any additional necessary people to manage it. Over time, IT enterprises began to establish chargeback processes, but these were too often viewed as a series of "funny money" transactions where no one paid too much attention to the actual costs and pricing of IT services.

Today, the costs and pricing of IT services are or should be a much more important consideration. The well-managed IT function should operate as a business, and financial management is a key ITIL® process to help manage the financial controls for that business. The objective of the service delivery financial management process is to suggest guidance for the cost-effective stewardship of the assets and resources used in providing IT services. IT should be able to account fully for its spending on IT services and to attribute these costs of services delivered to the enterprise's customers. There are three separate subprocesses associated with ITIL® financial management:

1. **IT budgeting** is the process of predicting and controlling the spending of money for IT resources. Budgeting consists of a periodic, usually annual, negotiation cycle to set budgets along with the ongoing day-to-day monitoring of current budgets. Budgeting ensures that there has been planning and funding for appropriate IT services and that IT operates within this budget during the period. Other business functions will have periodic negotiations with IT to establish expenditure plans and agreed investment programs; these ultimately set the budgets for IT.
2. **IT accounting** is the set of processes that enable IT to account fully for the way its money is spent by customers, services, and activities. IT functions often do not always do a good job in this area. They have a wide variety of external costs, including software, equipment lease agreements, telecommunications costs, and others, but these costs are often not well managed or reported. They have enough data to pay the bills and evaluate some specific area costs, but IT functions often lack the level of detailed accounting that can be found in a large manufacturing enterprise, for example. The manufacturing cost accounting or activity-based accounting model has applicability there.
3. **Charging** is the set of pricing and billing processes to charge customers for the services supplied. This requires sound IT accounting and needs to be done in a simple, fair, and well-controlled manner. The IT charging process sometimes breaks down in an IT function because billing reports of IT services are too complex or technical for many customers to understand. IT needs to produce clear, understandable reports of the IT services used such that customers can verify details, understand enough to ask questions regarding service, and negotiate adjustments if necessary.

Financial management for IT services provides important information to the service level management process, discussed previously, about the IT costing, pricing, and charging strategies. While generally not operated as a profit center, the financial management process allows both IT and its customers to think of IT service operations in business terms. The financial management process may allow IT and overall management to make decisions about what, if any, functions should be retained in-house or outsourced to an external provider.

EXHIBIT 19.9 Costs and Pricing Internal Audit Review Steps

1. Develop and document a general understanding of the cost structure for IT operations, including costs of equipment leases, vendor leases, IT supplies, and personnel costs.
2. Review and understand enterprise costing philosophy for IT operations–is it an overhead function, cost recovery, or revenue generating?
3. Review processes for costing and pricing IT services:
   a. Are all IT costs covered?
   b. Based on interviews with IT users, does the costing and pricing system appear to be understandable?
   c. Is there a process in place to administer the costing process and to make adjustments if necessary?
4. Review the negotiation process with IT users to understand pricing process–are expected costs included in SLAs?
5. Select pricing reports during a period for several processes and check to determine the prices are included in SLAs.
6. Review appropriateness of adjustment process of over a period to determine the corrections are investigated and applied when appropriate.
7. Review data processing services billed for one accounting period and determine whether they cover all actual IT costs. Investigate and report on any differences.
8. For a selected accounting period, trace IT pricing charges to appropriate accounting system entries.

The ITIL® financial management process allows accurate cost-benefit analyses of the IT services provided and allows the IT enterprise to set and meet financial targets. It also provides timely reporting to the service level management process, such that customers can understand the charging and pricing methods used. Of all of the ITIL® service support and delivery processes, financial management is one that frequently gets short shrift. IT people have a technical orientation and tend to think of financial management as an *accounting issue*, almost beneath them. On the other side of the coin, finance and accounting professionals tend to look at these issues as being too technical and beyond such transactions as equipment lease accounting or facility space charges. Internal auditors should use their financial skills as well as IT knowledge to review and assess financial management process internal controls. Exhibit 19.9 provides procedures for an internal audit review of the costs and pricing of IT processes. This is not a common review area for internal audit, but given the large costs distributed to customers as well as the importance of an enterprise's IT resources, it can be an important internal audit area.

Service Delivery Capacity Management

ITIL® capacity management ensures that the capacity of the IT infrastructure is aligned to business needs to maintain the required level of service delivery at an acceptable cost through appropriate levels of capacity. Through the gathering of business and technical capacity data, this process should result in a capacity plan to deliver cost justified capacity requirements for the enterprise. In addition to being a prime objective for understanding an enterprise's IT capacity requirements and to deliver against them, capacity management is responsible for assessing the potential advantages new technologies could have for the enterprise.

The capacity management process is generally considered in terms of three subprocesses covering business, service, and resource capacity management. Business capacity management is a long-term process to ensure that the future business requirements are taken into consideration and then planned and implemented as necessary. Service delivery capacity management is responsible for ensuring that the performance of all current IT services falls within the parameters defined in existing SLAs. Finally, resource capacity management has a more technical focus and is responsible for the management of the individual components within the IT infrastructure. The multiple inputs to these three capacity management subprocesses include:

- SLAs and SLA breaches
- Business plans and strategies
- Operational schedules and schedule changes
- Application development issues
- Technology constraints and acquisitions
- Incidents and problems
- Budgets and financial plans

As a result of these multiple inputs, the capacity management process—often under a single designated capacity manager—will manage IT processes, develop and maintain a formal capacity plan, and make certain that capacity records are up to date. In addition, the capacity manager must be involved in evaluating all changes to establish the effect on capacity and performance. This capacity evaluation should happen both when changes are proposed and after they are implemented. Capacity management must pay particular attention to the cumulative effect of changes over a period of time that may cause degraded response times, file storage problems, and excess demand for processing capacity. Other capacity management process responsibilities include some duties of the network, application, and system managers. They are responsible for translating the business requirements into the required capacity to be able to meet these requirements and to optimize IT performance.

The implementation of an effective capacity management process offers IT the benefits of an actual overview of the current capacity in place and the ability to plan capacity in advance. Effective capacity management should be able to estimate the impact of new applications or modifications as well as provide cost savings that are in tune with the requirements of the business. Proper capacity planning can significantly reduce the overall cost of ownership of an IT system. Although formal capacity planning takes time, internal and external staff resources, and software and hardware tools, the potential losses incurred without capacity planning can be significant. Lost productivity of end users in critical business functions, overpaying for network equipment or services, and the costs of upgrading systems already in production can more than justify the cost of capacity planning. This is an important ITIL® process, and internal auditors should consider the capacity management processes in place when reviewing IT infrastructure controls and processes.

Service Delivery Availability Management

Enterprises are increasingly dependent on IT services on a 24/7 availability. When IT services are unavailable, in many cases the business stops as well. It is therefore vital that an IT function manage and control the availability of its services. This can be accomplished by defining the requirements from the business regarding the availability of the IT services and then matching them with the possibilities of the IT enterprise.

Availability management depends on multiple inputs: requirements regarding the availability of the business; information on reliability, maintainability, recoverability, and serviceability of the CIs; and information from the other processes, incidents, problems, and achieved service levels. The outputs of the availability management process are:

- Recommendations regarding the IT infrastructure to ensure its resilience
- Reports about the availability of IT services
- Procedures to ensure that availability and recovery are dealt with for every new or improved IT service
- Plans to improve the availability of the IT services

Availability management activities can be described as planning, improving, and measuring actions. Planning involves determining the availability requirements to find out if and how IT can meet them. The service level management process, discussed previously, maintains contact with the business and will be able to provide the availability expectations to availability management. The business may have unrealistic expectations with respect to availability without understanding what this means in real terms. For example, they may want 99.9% availability yet not realize that this will cost five times more than providing 98% availability. It is the responsibility of service level management and the availability management process to manage such expectations.

An IT function can either design for availability or recovery. When the business cannot afford a particular service downtime for any length of time, IT will need to build resilience into the infrastructure and ensure that preventive maintenance can be performed to keep services in operation. In many cases building extra availability into the infrastructure is an expensive task that can be justified by business needs. Designing for availability is a proactive approach to avoiding downtime in IT services.

When the business can tolerate some downtime of services or a cost justification cannot be made for building additional resilience into the infrastructure, designing for recovery is the appropriate approach. Here, the infrastructure will be designed such that in the event of a service failure, recovery will be "as fast as possible." Designing for recovery is a reactive management approach for availability. In any event, processes such as incident management need to be in place to recover as soon as possible in case of a service interruption.

The main benefit of availability management is a structured process to deliver IT services according to the agreed requirements of the customers. This should result in a higher availability of the IT services and increased customer satisfaction. This covers an area where internal auditors can often ask some hard questions as part of their IT general controls reviews.

Service Delivery Continuity Management

As businesses are becoming ever more dependent on IT, the impact of any unavailability of IT services has drastically increased. Every time the availability or performance of a service is reduced, IT customers cannot continue with their normal work. This trend toward a high dependency on IT support and services will continue and will increasingly influence direct customers, managers, and decision makers. ITIL® continuity management emphasizes that the impact of a total or even partial loss of IT services should be estimated and continuity plans established to ensure that the business, and its supporting IT infrastructure, will always be able to continue.

ITIL® calls for an appropriate strategy to be developed that contains an optimal balance of risk reduction and recovery options. It calls for some of the same business continuity and disaster recovery strategies as are discussed in Chapter 24 of this book. Using the approaches outlined there, an IT enterprise can implement an effective set of service continuity processes, and internal auditors should refer to that chapter to better understand and evaluate continuity and disaster recovery planning processes.

19.11 AUDITING IT INFRASTRUCTURE MANAGEMENT

The ITIL® service support and service delivery processes introduce an expanded and improved approach for looking at all aspects of the IT infrastructure. These processes are not independent and freestanding. While each process can somewhat operate by itself, they all depend upon the input and support from other related processes. We have tried to show these interdependencies in several of the process descriptions, and an internal auditor reviewing controls over any of the ITIL® processes must think of these controls in relation to other connected processes.

ITIL® service delivery and service support are two interrelated and side-by-side elements. They support the management of the IT infrastructure and management of the enterprises. IT applications are in the center of this puzzle and a key area of internal controls concern.

Our previous discussions of problem management, incident management, and change management ITIL® processes, among others, tend to call for a very large IT function with multiple levels of staff and management resources. An internal auditor might ask how these ITIL® standards apply to an enterprise that is much smaller. Our answer here is very much that *yes*, ITIL® applies to all sizes of IT functions. In order to be ITIL®-compliant an enterprise does not need multiple levels of support staff. Rather, it needs to think of the various service support and service delivery processes from an ITIL® best practices perspective. A small IT function may not need to establish separate incident management and problem management functions, but must think of each as a separate process with unique controls procedures. Even in a very small IT function, each ITIL® process area should be treated as a separate area for process improvement.

Internal auditors should give this area particular care when making recommendations. The size and scope of the area being audited and the scope of operations should always be considered. This author thinks of the early days of IT controls, back when many applications were developed in-house for production applications. To promote adequate separation of duties, many audit guidance materials have recommended that there be a separation of duties between people who operated the computer and those who programmed it. Otherwise, in the days of far simpler systems, there was a risk that an individual of fraudulent intent might change an application program—to write himself an unauthorized check, for example—and then produce this personal check when operating the system. This was good control in the early days of IT, but it is not as relevant today. Today, internal auditors should think about the adequacy and appropriateness of IT controls in terms of the controls built into individual applications as well as the infrastructure process controls discussed in this chapter.

The IT infrastructure area is an important area for internal audit reviews. All too often internal auditors have concentrated their attention on the applications controls and IT general controls of the past. In today's world of complex processes supporting the IT infrastructure, the ITIL® processes outlined in this chapter offer some excellent areas for internal audit attention. When reviewing internal controls for any IT enterprise, whether a major corporate-level IT operation or the smaller function found in many of today's enterprises, the effective internal auditor should concentrate on reviewing controls over key infrastructure processes.

19.12 INTERNAL AUDITOR CBOK NEEDS FOR IT GENERAL CONTROLS

The need for an internal auditor common body of knowledge (CBOK) is an ongoing theme throughout these chapters. In some instances, such as understanding the *International Standards for the Professional Practice of Internal Auditing*, as discussed in Chapter 9, this knowledge should be an essential internal auditor CBOK requirement. Other topic areas, such as our Chapter 33 discussion of ISO 9000 and other quality system standards, internal auditors should have a CBOK basic understanding of the area but do not necessarily need a detailed level of knowledge. This chapter has discussed internal audit reviews of IT general controls and the IT infrastructure. These areas represent a strong CBOK requirement for all internal auditors.

As we have discussed, the world of IT general controls is seemingly constantly changing and evolving as we have moved from the classic mainframe computers of an earlier era to today's multiple server devices connected through wireless networks and the Internet. There can be a lot of technical issues here that may be best reserved for IT audit specialists, but all internal auditors today should have a strong CBOK level of knowledge of IT general controls and the supporting infrastructures that allow those general controls to operate and function.

The next chapters will discuss other IT-related issues that are also important to internal auditors, such as cybersecurity and continuity planning, but an internal audit understanding of IT general controls is essential. No matter the size or scope of IT operations, certain controls procedures—such as program revision controls—are general and apply to all operations. In addition, an overall understanding of ITIL® best practices should allow internal auditors to comprehend and evaluate IT general controls in many environments.

NOTES

1. A hash total is a summation of the numeric and alphabetic values for some computer value. It is used as a control total.
2. ITIL® publications are available from the UK agency called the Stationery Office and can be found through www.tsoshop.co.uk.

CHAPTER TWENTY

BYOD Practices and Social Media Internal Audit Issues

IN OUR EVER-CHANGING WORLD OF new business technologies and the way we adopt and use them, internal auditors face ongoing challenges in understanding these new approaches, developing internal procedures to review and assess them, and adopting practices to accept and work with the manner in which these new changes are installed. At any point in time there are always a wide range of new technology issues, some of which cause all of us to rethink our internal audit approaches, while others just go away either because the new technology does not cause much of an internal control impact or because the new approach ends up having a very short life span. Other new technology approaches stay with us, grow, and effectively establish their own internal control practices.

This chapter discusses two broad technology issues that are becoming increasingly important and changing the ways that internal auditors should understand, review, and assess them. The first is what has been called BYOD (bring your own device) practices, or what we generically refer to as business operations where stakeholders are allowed or encouraged to bring their own personal tablet computers, smartphones, laptops, or other personal systems when attending meetings to access and communicate with corporate systems or other client systems. These handheld devices were once quite expensive for individuals to own and their issuance and use was often controlled by central IT departments. Today there are handheld computing device options that are cheap and very powerful. Enterprises have to recognize and should openly permit, restrict, tolerate, or promote the use of these personal devices in the workplace. This chapter discusses some internal control and internal audit issues surrounding the BYOD phenomenon.

Our second chapter topic on social media audit issues is related to BYOD matters and is perhaps larger and more significant than the BYOD phenomenon in the workplace. This is the concept of social computing with software tools such as Facebook, Twitter, and others both for personal and workplace use. While generally not used for enterprise systems, these software products can have internal control implications for an enterprise. The chapter discusses the use and misuse of social media tools in the enterprise as well as recommended internal audit control procedures.

20.1 THE GROWTH AND IMPACT OF BYOD

The business use of personal devices, such as tablet computers, BlackBerrys, iPhones, and other smartphones, has continued to surge dramatically. Just focusing on one device, the number of smartphones in use across the globe reached over two billion by mid-2015, according to many estimates. While many of these are only for personal use, other employee-owned devices allow access, at the very least, to corporate e-mail, calendars, and many contact systems. We refer to these handheld devices today as BYODs. Enterprises once issued laptop computers to their employees to allow them to access systems on corporate networks. Today these systems are linked to the Internet and can be accessed through a wide variety of Web-enabled handheld devices. Since one does not need a special or enterprise IT–approved system to access the Web, enterprises began to realize that it was okay for staff to bring their own devices to meetings as long as they were using them for access to Web-enabled systems. Whether a company meeting, professional event, or other activity, management or event sponsors began to allow participants to bring their own laptops, tablets, smartphones, or other computing devices. "BYOD" became a familiar invitation to many meetings, similar to the way college-age people see the designation "BYOB" on party invitations. Today, BYOD or BYODs is a generic term for all of these handheld computing devices.

Whether used as a personal system or for workplace tasks, BYOD systems are common today. While BYODs can raise concerns about security or about managing the vast amounts of data these devices generate, they also raise internal control issues beyond IT security to encompass a wide range of endpoint management issues. The issue reaches beyond data loads to encompass a broader impact the devices have on IT infrastructure and operations. The heavy use of BYODs in an enterprise can raise some key issues that enterprise IT management and internal audit should be ready to address.

From an organizational perspective, the rapid adoption of smartphones and tablets is eroding cultures in many enterprises where IT functions once managed IT technology and controlled access to resources by selecting, purchasing, deploying, and supporting employees' mobile devices. In many enterprises today, BYOD scenarios and the robust, application-based focus of smartphones and tablets are taking over. This change points to more complex heterogeneous environments for IT and more productive functionality opportunities for business users than in the past.

Whether used for collecting global positioning data, supporting business transactions, or interfacing with the network to ensure optimal performance for enterprise technology functions, BYOD activities are at the heart of many of today's IT services and operations. The power, freedom, and popularity of these devices can create some internal control concerns for general and IT management as well as highlight some review area concerns for internal audit.

The explosion in the number and types of BYODs, as a result, spawns questions that enterprises must address if they are to gain the most benefits possible from employees, their devices, and the business network. It is true that an increase in the number of devices does not increase the amount of data employees can handle by the same rate. After all, each employee uses only one device at a time. But more devices means more opportunities for gathering data and more opportunities for connecting with the network. The network, as a result, has to grow and evolve to meet those increased demands.

In a BYOD scenario, an enterprise can achieve cost savings when it is not purchasing company-owned devices but rather expecting employees to bring in their own units. But without strong enterprise BYOD policies, as discussed in the next section, the employee use of multiple BYOD operating systems and hardware platforms can cause increased expenses—and significant IT headaches. For while applications on smartphones and tablets move mobile business connectivity beyond voice mail and e-mail, they also increase the need for more bandwidth and larger infrastructures.

Beyond the BYODs in place for their own internal audit departmental use, internal auditors will encounter them in various levels of use in virtually every enterprise or operating department that internal audit will review. Internal audit should always look for appropriate enterprise policies covering BYOD use and should look for an enterprise's level of BYOD risk tolerance.

20.2 UNDERSTANDING THE ENTERPRISE BYOD ENVIRONMENT

For virtually every review of enterprise operations or review conducted in a specific business unit or department, internal audit should gain a general understanding of the unit's BYOD risk tolerances and overall policies in place covering these activities. Understanding an enterprise's tolerance for risk, as discussed in Chapter 7, is the first step to understanding how BYOD works in an enterprise. A company's industry may be a primary indicator for this risk tolerance. For instance, organizations in health care, financial services, government, or security services will likely adopt a more defensive position toward BYOD than Internet-based tech companies. Exhibit 20.1 shows the levels of risk for several different categories. For example, an enterprise may have a very tight BYOD policy that only allows a certain model of device in the workplace. For others, the policy may be a little less restrictive, going all the way to being wide open.

Once upon a time, corporate-owned desktops were among the few employee devices enterprises needed to manage. Today, the average employee uses several devices for work, including desktop computers, laptops, tablets, and smartphones. Managing the sheer number and range of these devices—whether owned by the employee or company—has introduced extremely dynamic and complex security issues. Therefore, it is absolutely essential that internal auditors in their reviews of BYOD activities look for policies leading to a trust model that identifies how and when a device falls out of compliance, steps for remediation, and the extent to which these actions are acceptable to users. A trust model should:

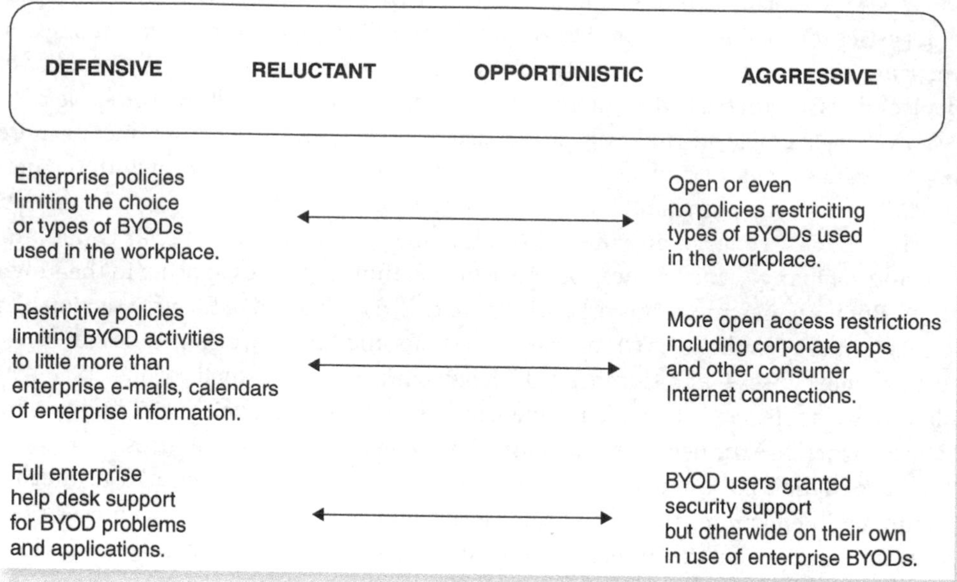

EXHIBIT 20.1 BYOD Risk Tolerances

- Assess the risks for common security issues on personal devices.
- Outline remediation options—such as notification, access control, quarantine, or selective wipe—that will be issued depending on security concerns and whether the device is owned by the company or employee.
- Set tiered policies for security, privacy, and application distribution based on device ownership.
- Clearly establish the identity of the user and device through certificates or other means.
- Ensure that security policies are sustainable and flexible enough to support a positive user experience without compromising data security.

This trust model should translate into strong enterprise BYOD security policies. While the BYOD field is still new and evolving with no really commonly recognized best practices, internal auditors should look for an effective enterprise-wide BYOD policy that has been approved and is understood by key players, including general management, IT, BYOD users, and internal audit.

20.3 BYOD SECURITY POLICY ELEMENTS

BYOD is a relatively new trend that is still used for establishing IT best practices. As a result, many enterprises are still rushing to create policies and processes that are simply unsustainable over the long term. Understandably, enterprises are mainly concerned about implementation costs and security, and tend to focus on those issues in the beginning. But without respect for the user experience, an enterprise BYOD program may never even get off the ground. If BYOD policies are overly restrictive, lack adequate support for employees' preferred devices, or are simply too complex and confusing, employees will find a way to either circumvent the policies or end their participation altogether. This is not unlike when enterprise stakeholders were given access to the Internet in the workplace but were told to not use it except for enterprise business. These rules were regularly violated. In these instances, the needs of the company are not met—either security is compromised or business value was lost. So while cost and security concerns are important issues to manage, BYOD program sustainability depends completely on delivering a consistently positive user experience over the long haul. In their reviews of IT activities, internal auditors should look for the following elements in an enterprise BYOD policy.

Mitigate Enterprise BYOD Security Risks

Today, the average employee uses several devices for work, including desktop computers, laptops, tablets, and smartphones. Managing the sheer number and range of these devices—whether owned by the employee or company—has introduced extremely dynamic and complex security issues. Therefore, it is absolutely essential that any BYOD security policy attempt to build a trust model that identifies if, how, and when a device falls out of compliance, steps for remediation, and the extent to which these actions are acceptable to users. A BYOD trust model should:

- Assess the risk for common security issues on personal devices.
- Outline remediation options—such as notification, access control, quarantine, or selective wipe—that will be issued depending on security concerns and whether the device is owned by the company or employee.
- Set tiered policies for security, privacy, and app distribution based on device ownership.
- Clearly establish the identity of the user and device through certificates or other means.
- Ensure that security policies are sustainable and flexible enough to support a positive user experience without compromising data security.

Enforce Enterprise BYOD Security

In a BYOD environment, the enterprise applications used may involve sensitive enterprise data, which can easily be compromised if the device is lost or infected with malware. An enterprise will need some level of control to prevent data from falling into the wrong hands. And yet employees don't want to feel that the company is tracking their every move, post, and tweet, especially on their own devices. To gain employee trust and protect critical data, an enterprise BYOD program must implement application design and governance procedures that:

- Modify application availability based on security requirements.
- Communicate and justify to all stakeholders the extent to which IT supports or restricts personal applications.

- Define application availability based on device ownership, because certain internal applications may not be appropriate on personal devices for security reasons.
- Define enforcement or remediation levels for application usage violations, such as user notifications, improper access control violation, or centralized IT system quarantines.

BYOD security should be tied to overall enterprise IT security policies and practices. Whether concerning a personal device or an enterprise IT system, good security processes should apply to both, with a somewhat heavier emphasis on the BYODs in the enterprise IT environment.

Emphasize Stakeholder Experience and Privacy

Optimizing the user experience should be a top priority for an enterprise BYOD program. Policies should include clear communication over sensitive topics such as BYOD system privacy that will be critical for establishing employee trust. A BYOD policy should aim for a social contract that clearly defines the BYOD relationship between the enterprise and its employees or stakeholders. Internal audit should look for such a contract in any review of BYOD policies that includes well-defined agreements that help to:

- Identify the activities and data that enterprise IT will monitor on a stakeholder BYOD, such as an applications inventory, and tools to protect against rogue applications that could compromise enterprise data.
- Clarify which security actions IT will take in response to certain circumstances.
- Define granular controls over any enterprise BYOD policy, such as activity monitoring, location tracking, and application visibility.
- Critically assess all IT security policies and restrictions to ensure that they are not overly restrictive.
- Identify core services, such as e-mail and mission-critical applications, that the enterprise can deploy to the employee's device.
- Communicate when employee devices are out of compliance, the possible consequences, and proactive notifications to help users remediate issues quickly.

Protect the Enterprise from BYOD Legal Actions

Introducing a BYOD program may also introduce new liability concerns to an enterprise. As part of any BYOD program, an enterprise needs clear policies and procedures to protect from threats ranging from the loss of intellectual property and confidential customer data to legal action, fines, and reputation damage resulting from data leaks. While every business needs to seek specific legal counsel on their BYOD liability issues, an enterprise mobile device policy or end-user agreement should include, at minimum:

- Security policies for enterprise data on differing personal devices. For example, differing levels of protection against overprivileged consumer applications might be required on Android versus iOS smartphone operating systems.

- Policies for personal Web and application usage during and after business hours, on- and off-site.
- Clear limitations for company liability due to the device owner's personal data loss.
- Definition and understanding of how BYOD reimbursement partial stipend versus full payment of service costs affects enterprise liability.
- Extent of the enterprise's liability for personal data loss (for example, if IT accidentally administers a full wipe of data on someone's personal device).

As part of any overall internal controls or a specific IT review, internal audit should assess whether there are effective BYOD policies in place.

BYOD is still rapidly evolving in enterprises today. In a BYOD program, the old-school model of help desk calls and tickets, as discussed in Chapter 19, introduces a new era of user-based IT self-service. Although the need for an IT help desk will never go away, a core component of BYOD is a comprehensive support service that allows users to resolve the majority of incidents without help desk intervention. The BYOD-based self-service model should allow users to:

- Self-register new devices, monitor and manage current devices, and wipe or retire devices as needed. That is, an employee must register any BYOD to gain access to corporate IT resources.
- Implement policies to self-remediate hardware, software, application, and compliance issues through clear notifications and resolution instructions.
- Keep the enterprise BYOD program productive and efficient while maintaining security and compliance controls. The same general policies that an enterprise has established for overall Sarbanes-Oxley Act internal control compliance should apply to the installed BYODs as well.

Allowing the use of BYODs in an enterprise means more than just saying yes to employee preferences to use whatever new device appears in the marketplace. It means putting into place policies that govern how these devices will be used and managed. Many of these policies regulate issues that are unique to portable devices—from which telecommunications carrier to use, to who pays for the service, to how data will be removed from the device if it is lost or stolen.

Internal auditors should recognize the importance of effective BYOD policies as part of their internal controls reviews. Compliance and policy settings, along with policy enforcement, are the control features most frequently cited as important. But as important as policies are, enterprises should have written policies and procedures that directly address the issues surrounding the use of mobile devices and all BYODs.

Procedures for managing these devices are similarly important, ranking nearly as high as policies among organizational priorities. In a heterogeneous BYOD environment, the selection of management tools can be critical. Large numbers of differing proposed solutions can create management chaos. An enterprise should reduce complexity, with mobile device management solutions that integrate with its existing management infrastructure—just as BYOD smartphones and tablet computers integrate into regular business processes.

Many internal auditors currently have their own personal BYOD systems, whether a smartphone, tablet device, or something else. They should understand some of the internal control issues surrounding BYODs and should incorporate that knowledge into their internal control reviews. Internal auditors should have a knowledge-level understanding of BYOD issues.

20.4 SOCIAL MEDIA COMPUTING

One use of BYOD handheld devices and their supporting applications is part of what is called social media computing. Whether accessed on a personal handheld device or another type of terminal, these applications or online service systems focus on building what we today call networks or relations among groups of people or users who share common interests and/or activities. Not too many years ago this was an unknown or undefined IT concept. Earlier social media systems had many more features and sometimes risks than the traditional e-mail system where each user on a network is identified by little more than an e-mail address with no further information. Today, people with common interests or connections can log on to such a social media system by establishing their own automated calling card or a brief biographical type of profile. Members of a network may post their photographs, biographical information, and descriptions of their activities, family, sometimes political opinions, or other attributes or materials. Virtually all social media services today are Web-based and allow users to interact over the Internet, through e-mail, or instant text messaging facilities. Social media sites allow users to share ideas, activities, events, and interests within their individual networks.

Social media IT applications got their start well before today's era of the all-pervasive Internet and even before today's laptop personal computers, BlackBerrys, or iPhones. The following are some of the major trends in the development of social media computing from the beginning to the present:

- **1978 to 1989—the era of one-to-few applications.** In the very early days of personal computers (e.g., the Apple II or IBM PC or earlier models), the first recognized social media application was called the Computerized Bulletin Board System, created in February 1978 by Ward Christianson of IBM. It was used by an IBM software development group to post messages about meeting times and locations, saving the time that had been spent in telephone calls. This was perhaps the first example in which posted messages moved beyond a one-to-one to a one-to-few type of interactive application. This was the era before the Internet was popularized, and thousands of bulletin board systems, with names such as FidoNet, soon sprang up across North America and elsewhere, becoming useful and increasingly popular tools for communication between the geographically dispersed users who accessed these systems over telephone-line modems.
- **1990 to 1994—the growth of the Internet.** In the early 1990s, Internet use was primarily available only to government, military, and academic organizations. This author, who was writing his first IT audit book at that time, had to find an acquaintance at a local university to give him *written permission to establish an*

Internet account in order to access some IT audit–related documents. However, several consumer-based Internet applications soon appeared, with names like Prodigy and CompuServe. These services, found in most major U.S. cities, became what were called Internet service providers. Internet consumer acceptance soon received a major thrust from America Online (AOL), a company that aggressively marketed the Internet by sending out millions of AOL signup disks that allowed participants to hook up to their telephone lines to access the Internet and send e-mail messages, shop for goods, and participate in the new concept of online discussion forums. With the interactive opportunity to join online forums and broadcast e-mails, these applications were the first scalable social media applications.

- **1995 to 1999—the dot-com bubble.** This era saw a major boom in Web technologies and Internet tools. Although most of the early applications were based on new consumer products and merchandising, there was not much growth here in social media applications beyond the existing bulletin board sites. An exception from this era is SixDegrees.com, an early social network service web site that lasted from 1997 to 2001 and is now all but forgotten. It was named after the six degrees of separation concept that allowed users to list their friends, family members, and acquaintances on the site, and allowed external contacts to join members' circles as well. Users could send messages and post bulletin board items to people in their first, second, and third degrees, and see their connection to any other user on the site. It was one of the first manifestations of social networking web sites in the format now seen today.
- **2000 to 2004—the growth of social media.** After none of the concerns about an IT calamity at the beginning of the year 2000 (Y2K) materialized and the dot-com bubble began to recede, a series of new social media applications were launched during this period, with names such as MySpace, Facebook, Friendster, LinkedIn, and many others. We will be discussing some of these applications in greater detail in the following sections. Many of these new applications were widely used by people inside enterprise organizations and outside of the enterprise-controlled applications. Although there always had been some low-level chatter within enterprise systems, social media applications allowed people to create content and participate in discussions without organization participation—an almost subversive trend! Another Internet platform application launched around the turn of this century, WordPress, allowed individuals with no programming knowledge to build and launch blogs, web sites, personal diaries, or content sites. Using such a tool, a person could host a blog on their own domain site and have essentially full control over its design and contents. This was a major move toward personal journalism.
- **2005 to 2009—the growth of social networking applications.** Social media applications continued to grow and evolve, including applications such as YouTube, a video-sharing web site where anyone can become a publisher of video content. The BYODs we call smartphones became very popular. With them, a user could download a wide variety of applications. Perhaps the most significant new social media application during this era was the launch of Twitter, a microblogging application in which a user can publish short content-based messages and follow others through their own short bursts of information. We will introduce Twitter further in a later section.

- **2010 and beyond.** Our use of social media applications continues to grow, causing many IT governance issues and concerns in today's enterprises. For example, in the events during the first months of 2011 that are popularly known as the Arab Spring, autocratic political leaders in Tunisia, Egypt, and Libya were brought down. In each of these cases, the antigovernment protests were initiated after massive social media chatter over Facebook and other such vehicles. People saw events that enraged them and posted their comments and photos to others, who passed them on to still others. The results were surges of popular protest that soon toppled these governments. Also, the Middle Eastern Islamic terrorist group ISIS has captured large portions of Syria and Iraq and took hostages—often Western journalists—whom they beheaded if they did not collect the ransoms they demanded. The beheadings were broadcast online worldwide using social media tools.

While people using the likes of Facebook to help topple an autocratic government is a strong example of the power of social media, these tools continue to present IT governance and internal control challenges to business enterprises today. For many today, these systems are almost too new, and enterprises with traditionally controlled IT systems and applications are often not in a position to easily adapt to the open, flexible nature usually associated with social media systems. Also, individual members of an enterprise will often be individual users of their own social media computing application. This can present IT governance problems if an enterprise has not established appropriate rules and procedures covering their social media operations.

The following sections discuss three very popular but quite different social media applications—Facebook, LinkedIn, and Twitter—as well as some of the unique governance issues surrounding each of these applications. Each of these started as personal applications, but people have moved them into the workplace through their workplace communications on individual laptop systems or smartphones.

Social Media Example: Facebook

Facebook is a social media service and web site that was launched in February 2004 by Mark Zuckerberg along with several of his Harvard University dormitory roommates as a means to better communicate and share information among fellow students. Originally limited to just Harvard, Facebook was quickly expanded to other colleges in the Boston area, the Ivy League, and then Stanford University. Growing by word of mouth, it gradually added support for students at other universities before opening to high school students and others. Today, Facebook has become a very popular system used by many people worldwide. In addition, for many it has somewhat replaced e-mail as a means of communication among individuals. From its limited college dormitory start in 2004, Facebook had more than 1.4 billion active users as of January 2015, with that number continually growing. Starting as a private company, Facebook has long since become an actively traded public company.

Individual users of Facebook often first get started by someone, usually a friend, sending them an e-mail message and asking them to become their Facebook "friend."

The new user will then be asked to create a personal profile, add other users as friends, and exchange messages, including automatic notifications when they update their profile. Additionally, users may join common-interest user groups, organized by workplace, school or college, or other characteristics.

Steps to Joining Facebook

For many senior-level business professionals, Facebook is more than just an IT application. It is a concept that a senior business professional may have read about, even though that same senior executive often has no understanding of the system beyond the comments and Facebook activities of their usually IT-savvy children. This is particularly true if one has no college-age or high school–age children who understand and use Facebook. Of its more than a billion users, some 60% are under the age of 35.

Business professionals often become involved with Facebook through receiving an e-mail from a business associate, friend, or relative asking the recipient to become a "friend" of that person on Facebook. The idea is that one logs on based on the initial invitation and can then connect with other Facebook users in a cascading manner such that friends of friends can be connected to create an expanding network. Exhibit 20.2 outlines the steps to joining Facebook.

Using Facebook

Much more than just an alternative to e-mail, Facebook is a system to build up a profile about oneself, to post status updates to everyone on your friends list, to send personal messages to other individuals who are your Facebook friends, and much more. These status updates and private messages, whether text or images, can be posted to Facebook from a smartphone. Of course, in its college dormitory original environment, the posted messages were often descriptions and pictures from a recent party or some other event. They typically are just a note and do not require or solicit a response. A Facebook user can send private messages to his or her friends, which can be forwarded to others. Posting

EXHIBIT 20.2 Steps to Joining Facebook

Step 1. Visit Facebook's website at www.facebook.com.

Step 2. Fill in your full name, a valid email address or mobile number, password (at least six characters), birthday, and click whether male or female. Then click the green "Sign Up" button. When you click "Sign Up," you're agreeing to Facebook's Statement of Rights and Responsibilities and Privacy Policy.

Step 3. You will receive an email from Facebook. Open it and click "Confirm Your Account."

Step 4. You will be taken back to Facebook where you now can find people you know already on Facebook by searching your email account(s), add a profile picture, take the privacy tour, and complete your profile by adding your company name and location, the city and state you reside in, your education background, personal interests, and other personal information. You can add as little or as much information about yourself as you'd like.

to friends' walls depends on that particular friend's privacy settings. Those postings can be seen by others.

Facebook postings can give a detailed depiction of one's personal life and activities, depending upon the level of privacy selected. For example, after logging on to Facebook, one can enter the name of an acquaintance who is registered in Facebook—or anyone for that matter—and look at that person's posted profile and recent Facebook postings from others. One can gain access to that person's Facebook friends, even looking at their postings as well. We will talk more about business privacy concerns in a following section, but if a Facebook user has not designated his or her activity as private, one can sometimes find out more about a person than that person would want. For example, one can see "Thank you for inviting me to . . ." types of posts that have been made to a person's wall, sometimes with a photo, and one can go to that sender's Facebook page, again depending on the privacy settings. These posts remain on a person's Facebook wall forever, unless deliberate steps are taken to delete records. While this is all great for college student life, postings and the recordings of activities could cause privacy and even security concerns in a business environment.

The Facebook concept can be useful in a business environment as means to build and manage workforce teams. For example, for a large systems implementation project—along the lines of an effort described in Chapter 16 on project and program management—the project administrator can ask all project team members to create or update their Facebook profiles and establish them as members of the project team. Project events can easily be scheduled and communicated and the manager interested in the backgrounds of team members can access their profiles in a friendlier manner than allowed by the typical human resources records.

Our description here only highlights only a few of the ever-expanding Facebook features. One can subscribe to download postings from selected web sites, post status updates, send private messages, and upload photos and videos. You can even talk to someone on Facebook using your smartphone. For a business enterprise, Facebook can present some internal control risks. For example, an employee can complain in a Facebook post about the quality of some enterprise product or even the competence of a manager. What was intended as a personal message to a Facebook friend can be picked up by that friend and then sent to other friends of friends to establish widespread, and sometimes damaging, nets of communications about the enterprise product or specific issues. As will be discussed in the section following on social media legal issues, there are multiple IT governance issues here.

Although Facebook has a component for building enterprise business pages, which is a powerful tool for marketing all aspects of an enterprise's business operations, and despite a current surge in the use Facebook as a business communications tool, its typical use today is not for business but for personal communications. However, creating a Facebook business page is a good method of promotion, because Facebook business pages are viewable by millions of users. These pages are an effective advertising platform offering innovative methods of Web marketing, allowing for interaction among business owners and customers. They go beyond the IT governance issues theme of this chapter, as they represent a strong and powerful enterprise application.

Social Media Example: LinkedIn

This very popular social media application is based around business-related social or professional networking concepts that are similar to networking-type communications among multiple professional groups, such as members of an Institute of Internal Auditors local chapter or college alumni groups. LinkedIn is also a popular communications platform for many professionals such as project managers, civil engineers, geologists, auditors, and others. It operates worldwide and in multiple languages. At the time of our publication, there were over 350 million registered LinkedIn users.

Most professionals first encounter LinkedIn through an e-mail note from a professional associate with an invitation to join some LinkedIn group or establish a LinkedIn connection of common professional interest. If new to LinkedIn, that invitee is asked to register by posting some personal information and often a professional résumé. This is a bit more formal than Facebook, where one is simply asked to become someone's Facebook "friend."

When registering in LinkedIn as part of a professional group, the user is asked to provide professional résumé-type information, such as current and past employers as well the dates of those jobs, and other personal professional information. There is also space to post a full résumé, advertisements, and other materials. The system also has a process where the new registrant can request past employers and professional contacts to provide personal references.

LinkedIn allows registered users to maintain a list of contact details of people with whom they have some level of relationship, called connections. Users can invite anyone (whether a site user or not) to become a connection, but the recipient of an invitation can select "I don't know" to reject or count against the person's invitation. LinkedIn connections can be used in some of the following ways:

- A contact network can be built up consisting of someone's direct connections, the connections termed second-degree connections, and also the connections of second-degree connections termed third-degree connections. This can be used to gain an introduction to someone a person wishes to know through a mutual contact.
- LinkedIn can then be used to find jobs, people, and business opportunities recommended by someone in one's contact network.
- Employers can list jobs and search for potential candidates.
- Job seekers can review the profile of hiring managers and discover which of their existing contacts can introduce them.
- Users can post their own photos and view photos of others to aid in identification.

LinkedIn's "gated access approach" allows contacts with professionals requiring either a preexisting relationship or the intervention of a contact of theirs. The system is intended to build trust among the service's users.

Within its various specialized topic areas, LinkedIn sites can become active discussion forums covering LinkedIn specialty areas. For example, a LinkedIn site for the National Association of Corporate Controllers has a series of active discussions. A LinkedIn member of that group may pose question, such as "How should my board better manage its internal auditors?" Others then may enter a response, and the result may be a hot back-and-forth discussion.

Perhaps more important than its professional contacts features, LinkedIn includes a series of specialized applications with objectives to get leads, analyze traffic, promote product sales, promote brand awareness, handle ticket sales, communicate with investors, and more. The LinkedIn Polls application is a good example. It allows users to easily find answers to business and market-research questions. It allows an enterprise to ask some question and LinkedIn will distribute it to your connections and millions of other professionals on LinkedIn. The poll results can be shared with Facebook or Twitter integrations, or embedded in an enterprise's web site. It operates just like any other polling service: LinkedIn users can ask a question, add up to five potential responses, and choose how long it will run. Once responses have been received within the specified time period, LinkedIn shares them with established social networks or enterprise web sites. Because of this link, poll responses can be broken down by age, gender, or seniority, allowing management to analyze such questions as "Do 25-year-olds answer differently from 45-year-olds?" or "Do men and women answer differently?"

LinkedIn is more of a business-related application and does not have the same almost open-environment exposure risks that can be found in Facebook, where posts can be seen by friends, friends of friends, and even strangers, depending on privacy settings. However, because it is a professional communication and discussion vehicle among various professional specialized groups, enterprise confidential data can easily slip through LinkedIn discussion sites. A product development engineer, for example, may have subscribed to a LinkedIn site for enterprise product development engineers. As part of LinkedIn's ongoing online discussions, that development engineer might inappropriately respond to an online discussion by giving some enterprise confidential information to make a technical point, not realizing the nature of the data released. In addition, that engineer's résumé may be open to outside recruiters, a potential drain on company resources.

Social Media Example: Twitter

Many in the United States first heard about Twitter in 2011 when a then U.S. congressman, Anthony Weiner, claims his account was hacked and the public became aware of his exchanging lewd photos of himself on Twitter with women. Weiner was forced to resign, and his shenanigans certainly caused many to hear about the potential power of Twitter.

Twitter is a free service that allows anyone to say almost anything to anybody in 140 characters or less—it is a "what are you doing right now" system that permeates online social communication. Twitter enables its users to send and read these short text-based posts, informally known as "tweets" because of the bluebird logo, often via mobile phone using the Twitter app released for certain smartphones. With all of this message traffic, Twitter is one of the ten most visited web sites worldwide. A February 2009 survey by Compete.com referenced Twitter as the third most used social network based on their count of 6 million unique monthly visitors and 55 million monthly visits. To help explain Twitter's terminology and concepts, Exhibit 20.3 lists a few Twitter terms and concepts. A more senior manager may find their staff members using these terms as they tweet messages to others.

EXHIBIT 20.3 Twitter Terms and Concepts

- **Tweet**—When you post or write your 140 characters on Twitter and hit send it's called a tweet or tweeting.
- **Handle**—The term used for a user's Twitter name in the format @ducttape, a short personal name.
- **Follow**—This is the act of adding someone to your list of the people you are following, making their tweets show up on your homepage.
- **Replies**—This is what it is called when someone writes a tweet directly at a user's handle—@ducttape cool post today blah blah—and this also is often an invite to engage with another follower.
- **Retweet**—This is a tactic of republishing someone else's tweet—the original tweet along with the author's handle stays intact, but you are basically showing someone's tweet to your followers. Many use this to add content and acknowledge material from the people they follow.
- **DM**—This is the term for a message that is sent directly to another user. They must be following you for you to DM them, but this is a very useful tool for private messages and generally a good choice when a Twitter user starts going back and forth with someone on something your entire base of followers might not find interesting.
- **Hashtag**—This is a way people categorize tweets so to effectively create a way for people to view related tweets under the same tag.

With Twitter's ability to track and carry a range of messages about a wide variety of people and subjects, a user and sometimes an employee often may be spending too much time reading and sending tweets. For example a San Antonio–based market research firm, Pear Analytics, analyzed 2,000 tweets (originating from the United States and in English) over a two-week period in August 2009 and separated the messages into six categories:

- Pointless babble—40%
- Conversational—38%
- Pass-along value—9%
- Self-promotion—6%
- Spam—4%
- News—4%

These results indicate that Twitter often contains too much "pointless babble," the first item on the list. Perhaps the advantage here is that these messages allow Twitter correspondents to know what the people around them are thinking and doing and feeling. However, a lot of this activity is similar to company staff talk sessions around the watercooler from a past era. The astute manager back then frowned on or limited such watercooler chat. Attempts should be made to treat staff social media workday usage in the same manner.

Twitter is a powerful tool that can present risks to an enterprise if used inappropriately whether as in the case of ex-congressman Weiner, discussed previously, or any number of other current examples. We discuss the importance of enterprise codes of conduct in Chapter 26 and the need to determine that all impacted stakeholders have read, understand, and agree to comply with that code of conduct, and it's clear that an enterprise should launch a similar policy for social media applications such as Twitter.

Exhibit 20.4 is an example enterprise policy for employee use of Twitter, Facebook, and other social media products. Similar policies could be implemented for other social media software, and the policy could be structured in a manner that includes all enterprise social media applications. The key here is that any such policy must be launched in a manner such that all employees and other stakeholders understand its purposes and the potential risks of any such social media applications.

EXHIBIT 20.4 Enterprise Social Media Policy

This policy applies to all social media tools, used both on and off the job for enterprise business operations. Beyond the more specific guidance discussed here, anyone using social media tools on either personal or enterprise devices should:

- Treat others as you would like to be treated.
- Add value to your consumers, your industry, and your business.
- Be respectful, professional, and courteous.
- Provide insight, expertise, and relevant conversation.
- Communicate ethically and morally in support of your professional goals.

In addition, all enterprise stakeholders should keep the following principles in mind:

Think before You Post

Keep in mind that most online social computing platforms are like public marketplaces—what's out there is available for all to see. On social platforms, the boundaries of professional and personal information are not always very clear. In these days of shifting privacy policies and powerful search engine indexing, you can't always be sure what is being shared, viewed, or archived. Note that what you publish online will be public for a very long time. What you post will reflect on you, so be consistent with the way you would wish to portray yourself to the company, friends, family, colleagues, and clients.

If you are unsure whether certain content is appropriate to share online, then don't post it. It's better to be safe than sorry.

Responsibility

You are personally responsible for your words and actions, no matter where you are, even in the online world. Please remember that when you participate in social media, you are speaking as an individual and not on behalf of the company. Always identify yourself using the first person singular.

When you discuss company-related information online, be transparent by giving your name and role and mentioning that you work for the company. If you have an individual site that refers to or has an impact on the company, use a disclaimer such as "The views expressed on this site are my own and not those of [*company name*]."

Where applicable law permits, know that the company reserves the right to monitor use of social platforms and take appropriate action to protect against misuse that may be harmful to the company's reputation.

Establishing a company account or becoming an official representative that shares information about the company and the areas we work in requires approval from appropriate levels of management. Only these accounts may display the company logo.

Conduct

Your behavior online should be consistent with Our Code of Business Ethics.

You have the opportunity to help shape the company's reputation online. Use your expert knowledge to enrich discussions, help solve problems, share the excitement of our work environment, and promote learning and idea-sharing.

Always remember that the tone you use online can be interpreted in different ways by your readers, due to nonverbal communication or cultural differences. Some participants may not be familiar with abbreviations, emoticons, and other common codes used in online communication. Remember also that comments are often taken out of context, so stick to the facts.

Trust is the key element in building relationships online. Build trust by keeping a respectful tone, even when disagreeing with others, and by responding to comments in a timely manner. If you realize that you've make a mistake, try to correct it promptly.

Do not engage in any conduct online that would not be acceptable in your workplace or that is unlawful. For example, do not make derogatory remarks, bully, intimidate, harass other users, use insults, or post content that is hateful, slanderous, threatening, discriminating, or pornographic.

Confidentiality

Always protect our companies', clients', and suppliers' confidential and other proprietary information. Don't put anything online you wouldn't share with a journalist, client, analyst, or competitor.

Make sure any reference to business information, customers, and suppliers does not violate any nondisclosure obligations. Please also remember your confidentiality obligations under your employment agreement.

Don't disclose information about colleagues or other persons, misuse their personal data, or publish their photos without their permission.

Always use good judgment regarding information that could be of a sensitive nature. Don't use social computing platforms to exchange information that is company, customer, or supplier confidential, unless access has been cleared for receipt of such information, and the platform has been cleared for appropriate security levels. Public sites are not appropriate sites for internal communication with other company employees.

Copyrights

Comply with laws and regulations and more particularly with laws governing intellectual property rights, including copyrights and trademarks.

You must not post content or take any action that violates the law or infringes company or any third party's intellectual property rights.

Final Thoughts

Use of social computing platforms in accordance with this policy can be a very effective and powerful communication tool. Be proud of what you do and enjoy a sense of accomplishment in the search for better quality and greater efficiency. Above all, please use good judgment, be attentive to others, and take the trouble to listen and be understood.

20.5 ENTERPRISE SOCIAL MEDIA COMPUTING RISKS AND VULNERABILITIES

A very valid senior executive question might be "I am an enterprise senior manager. Why should I be concerned about our employees and other stakeholders using Facebook, Twitter, and other social media tools in our business work environment?" That is the type of question that many senior managers may ask when they do not really understand these ostensibly friendly applications.

Social media sites often seem friendly and exist outside of the radar screen of many business systems, processes, and concerns. They are too often viewed as an employee diversion, like the joint efforts of a planning committee for the annual holiday party. However, social media issues can get out of control as other people can see the message traffic and initiate actions based on the communications.

A *Chicago Tribune* article highlighted how employee Facebook chatter can cause trouble to an enterprise. The staff members at an auto dealer talked flippantly among themselves through Facebook about how their employer was "probably ignoring U.S. labor laws." Their supposedly private messages were eventually passed on to U.S. labor law authorities, through someone copying someone, who then used the message to copy someone else, and so on. This eventually resulted in legal actions against the employer. Messages sent through social media systems present some risks.

Sometimes social media systems are viewed as almost a human resources–related resource, such as an almost unofficial company newsletter. However, an enterprise faces many risks in social media systems, including loss of reputation and possible liability suits when employees blab or post photos and videos about what they shouldn't. There are also the computer security risks of malware, identity theft, phishing, and the privacy breach of sensitive data that will be introduced in Chapter 23.

The risks associated with employee use of Facebook, Twitter, and other social media should be considered primarily the responsibility of enterprise management, and beyond that the IT security department. These applications are generally operated over the Internet and outside enterprise-controlled systems.

Many of social media's risks and management concerns are tied to the individual behavior that takes place outside the infrastructure boundaries of the enterprise and its IT systems. However, social media systems carry with them issues related to content and freedom of speech. These social media practices tie very much to the issues in Chapter 26's discussion on the need for an ethical workplace culture. That chapter discusses the importance of strong management messages and policies such as codes of conduct and mission statements to help get an enterprise and its stakeholders thinking in a correct and positive manner. However, an enterprise should be aware of some of the following social media risks and concerns:

- **Employee productivity issues.** This is perhaps more of a management issue in terms of setting employee goals and responsibilities, but employees at all levels can sometimes spend excessive amounts of time sending notes and pictures to friends, both inside and outside of the enterprise, whether over Twitter, Facebook, or some other social media application. In some respects this is not too different from people spending excessive amounts of time on personal telephone calls, but this social media activity is sometimes hard to detect and monitor.
- **Lack of control over corporate content.** Employees and other stakeholders may innocently or deliberately post wrong or improper information on social media sites. This type of information can be passed on to many others through the cascading

nature of many social media tools. Once the false information has started to spread, it is difficult to stop it.

- **Noncompliance with record management regulations.** Despite copyright and data protection rules, it is often very easy for stakeholders to copy and communicate protected documents over social media systems. An enterprise faces risks if such records are improperly or illegally communicated.
- **Viruses and spyware.** There have been reported incidents where social media or related networking sites have been used to spread malware such as viruses, and social media systems are certainly not unique here. Realistically, however, social networking sites probably pose no more of a threat than any other type of web site.
- **Bandwidth problems.** This was much more of an issue in the earlier days of Internet using voice-level telecommunications. *Bandwidth* refers to the "size of the pipe" or the amount of data transmitted over communications lines. People sending large volumes of digital photographs or other high-volume material can choke a system. While this is not so great of an issue over the Internet as a whole, high-volume materials can all but clog communication lines for a smaller enterprise.
- **Enterprise security issues.** There is much vulnerability here. A perpetrator, for example, can use a cell phone to take a picture of a confidential document, product, or facility and then easily transmit that material to one or many over a tool such as Facebook with just a few quick keystrokes. Physical controls, well-communicated policy statements, and a strong enterprise ethical environment are needed here.
- **Liability issues.** An enterprise could be held liable for postings by an employee made on company time through enterprise IT resources. While the law really isn't clear at this point in time, individuals have been found liable for incautious postings to social networking sites, and it's possible that businesses could too. It's a risk to certainly consider.

As our use of social media tools grows, we can only expect this trend to continue. Because most enterprise stakeholders have their own smartphone device as well as a home system with Internet connections, virtually all of them have access to social media sites. Some will make extensive use of these tools and the boundary between personal activities and office systems can quickly become fuzzy. An enterprise is looking through rose-colored glasses if it tries to implement only a workplace policy of no social media activities while on the job. We generally work not only at a facility on a nine-to-five basis, but in the home office or while traveling as well. We cannot draw lines here.

Social media tools are growing in the workplace. Our earlier discussion of LinkedIn mentioned its polling tool, which can be a common and frequently used social media application in the workplace. We will increasingly be seeing the lines become more closely linked between social media applications for primarily personal purposes and the use of these applications as business tools. The only way, we feel, to limit risks and to have a better IT governance understanding of the use of social medial tools in the workplace is to establish and effectively communicate some policies about the use of social media tools to all stakeholders in the enterprise workplace, as discussed next.

20.6 SOCIAL MEDIA POLICIES

Internal audit and enterprise management need to understand and establish, when appropriate, educational practices outlining the dos and don'ts for various social media systems as well as some very specific policies covering the stakeholder use of these tools. These social media policies should be almost a subset of corporate policies such as codes of conduct as well as IT security and privacy policies that are communicated to all employees and stakeholders. For example and discussed in greater detail in Chapter 26, an enterprise should develop an overall stakeholder code that outlines company policies in a very high-level but easy-to-understand manner. The code should be refreshed and updated regularly and all stakeholders should be asked to periodically affirm that they have read it, understand it, and agree to abide by it. Implementing such a code of conduct is important for strong and effective enterprise IT governance practices. Exhibit 20.4 provided an example of a general enterprise social media policy designed to apply to all stakeholders using enterprise social media applications, ranging from staff members to senior management, and applicable to all social media applications that have an impact on the enterprise, whether an enterprise-based initiative and an application based on the system at home or a personal device.

An enterprise should implement policies for social media as well as for specific applications. Because there are substantial differences between many of these applications, using Facebook and Twitter as examples, an enterprise should implement a general policy on the use of social media applications in the workplace as well as some rules for specific popular applications.

Depending on the level of use of Facebook or other social media applications in the enterprise, similar policies can be launched. The idea is to get the message to all stakeholders that their use of various social media applications in the workplace carries some risks as well as opportunities for the enterprise and their career paths.

Social media applications present some strong internal control and governance issues for today's enterprise. While the Facebook, Twitter, and LinkedIn applications that have been briefly introduced in this chapter are perhaps the most common today, this is no guarantee that they will be as prominent a few years hence. However, their concepts represent a sea change regarding the manner in which information is developed and processed that almost certainly will not change. Although many senior managers may look on most of these applications as tools for their teenage children and younger associates on staff, every senior manager and certainly every internal auditor should at least become hands-on familiar with and have a CBOK understanding of these tools in order to better understand them and communicate with others in the enterprise.

CHAPTER TWENTY-ONE

Big Data and Enterprise Content Management

WITH OUR INCREASING EMPHASIS ON all types of automated systems and the convenient tools available to save this data as well as the low cost of data storage, industries on all levels have come to the era of what we call *big data*, the massive amounts of information or even just pure data captured in all types of automated systems. Enterprises, customers, and certainly government regulators often seek access to all of the data covering transactions over time and then expect this data to be available for access and analysis over prior periods.

The ability to capture and store so much data has become easier over recent years because of the relatively low cost of data storage today. However, while the costs of data storage have gone down, the amounts or volumes of data to capture and store have increased massively. With an emphasis on internal auditor knowledge needs, this chapter provides an overview of big data concepts and a discussion of governance, *risk and compliance issues* regarding big data, related security information, and internal audit processes for internal control reviews in a big data environment.

In addition, this chapter also will introduce *enterprise content management (ECM)* issues. This is again a big data–related issue where enterprises should install appropriate transactional and business controls to effectively manage the data and information contained in their key systems. Internal auditors should have a general CBOK understanding of big data and ECM issues and internal controls as well as of how to perform effective internal audits in these environments.

21.1 BIG DATA OVERVIEW

Managing and controlling big data issues has become one of the most important new trends in information usage for both business and IT functions since our last edition of this book and over about the past 10 years. With the growth of automated systems and our ability to capture vast amounts of data, the effective use of this big data is changing the way an enterprise makes decisions, does business, and succeeds or fails. It is causing both management and its IT functions to look beyond traditional technologies and to establish new tools to process the increasingly larger data volumes in an efficient and well-controlled manner. Of course, big data issues are changing many internal audit processes as well.

Anyone involved with IT systems today as well as most consumers have been impacted by big data issues. There was once a time when IT resources placed limitations on how much data one could store (remember floppy disks?), but today very cheap tools are available to store massive amounts of data. Even our terminology has changed. We once talked about kilobytes, or 1,000 bytes of data, and soon thereafter megabytes, or 1 million bytes. Now we are using the term *petabytes*, or 10^{15} bytes of data, about half of all the information stored in U.S. research libraries.

When a large enterprise attempts to keep all data for its many sales transactions over multiple periods of time, it can quickly move into a big data environment. In past times, we kept this data on old IT tape files or even on printed paper. Because it was very difficult to retrieve this stored data, it was often eventually just discarded. Today, however, regulations and even customer demand have created a requirement that this stored data be available almost in perpetuity. Exhibit 21.1 describes this big data environment from a sales and marketing systems perspective. We will be discussing other big data concerns and issues in the sections going forward.

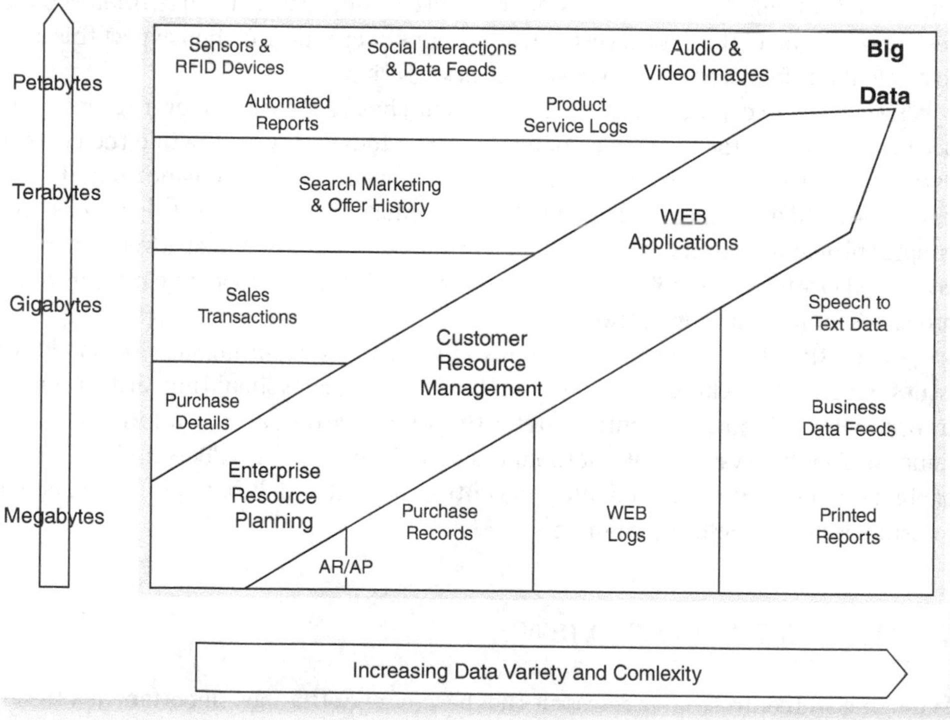

EXHIBIT 21.1 Big Data Spectrum

There are multiple earlier different definitions here, but the IT research firm, Gartner has the best or most recognized:[1]

> *"Big data" is high-volume, -velocity and -variety information assets that demand cost-effective, innovative forms of information processing for enhanced insight and decision making.*

These three V's of high *volume*, *velocity*, and *variety* have traditionally defined the common environment that had previously been used to define and describe big data issues. Many sources today, however, add a fourth V, *veracity*, as an additional important big data factor. Veracity refers to the accuracy and correctness of these masses of big data, and the concept is particularly important for internal auditors when considering big data from an audit and control perspective.

An internal auditor should remember that big data internal control covers much more than just large volumes of transactional data. It concerns such things as video messages, messages over smartphones using a software tool such as Twitter, and global positioning system coordinate transactions. By digging into this four-V definition a bit deeper, an internal auditor should develop a better understanding of the implications of each of these big data internal control concepts.

Volume

Volume refers to the sheer amount of common data for a given application or system and depends upon the relative size of the enterprise. In many cases, data of extreme volume has a common format and can be counted in traditional "rows" records, and/or in terms of the storage space required. An example of extremely voluminous data is the raw event logs for a high-volume server. Another might be the volume of holiday season sales transactions for a multiunit retailer.

Although what constitutes big data may vary by industry and business operations, an enterprise should have control procedures in place to manage situations when they encounter high volumes of data. These might include special monitoring processes for known high-volume periods, limiting the data collected to elements necessary to current or expected business processes, profiling data sources to identify and subsequently eliminate redundancies, or monitoring data usage to determine "cold spots" of unused data that can be eliminated or offloaded to a special storage resource.

Data and transaction volume issues are a very important defining element of big data. When encountering big data volumes when reviewing some IT application, an internal auditor might ask some questions about what both management and IT are doing to process any unexpected high volumes of data. There is no single correct answer here, but an internal auditor should look for analysis and good internal control procedures to manage both current and unexpected high volumes of data.

Velocity

Velocity refers to the speed at which the data is delivered and/or changes. The problem of velocity is one of capture and response. When a massive number of transactions or messages are rapidly coming into an enterprise's application or web site, that enterprise needs to capture and process this high velocity of data. This is not a content problem and is often not associated as big data volume and/or variety problems as well. A common example of high-velocity data is the so-called Twitter firehose—the continuous stream of all the tweets passed through the Twitter system. Some incident or a Twitter comment may cause massive numbers of response transactions. While Twitter's only requirement is to categorize and capture this mass of messages, too much velocity can cause system challenges.

The importance of data's velocity—the increasing rate at which data flows into an organization—often follows a similar pattern to that of volume. Specialized companies such as financial traders or even travel booking and reservation sites all must have systems that cope with fast-moving data to their advantage. Many Internet and mobile applications deliver and consume products and services that require rapid responses generating a data flow back to their providers. Online retailers, for example, should have facilities to compile large histories of customers' every click and interaction beyond just the final sales transactions and during busy periods. Enterprises that are able to quickly utilize that information, by recommending additional purchases, for instance, gain competitive advantage. The smartphone era has increased again the rate of data inflow, as consumers carry with them a streaming source of location imagery and audio data.

It's not just the velocity of the incoming data that's the issue: it's possible to stream fast-moving data into bulk storage for later batch processing, for example. The importance here often lies in the speed of the feedback loop, taking data from input through and back to a decision point. Industry terminology for such fast-moving, high-velocity data is often called *streaming data*, or *complex event processing*. This latter term was more established in product categories before streaming processing data gained more widespread relevance, and now seems likely to diminish in favor of streaming.

We can envision this whole process as a floodgate being opened and some system or process being subjected to a massive stream of incoming objects or materials. With big data, an enterprise application may be subjected to a massive amount of similar but differing transactions. It must be sufficiently agile to respond to all of these in a timely and correct manner. An IT application may have been tested to handle a wide variety of differing transaction types correctly. But when massive amounts of these transactions are input in about the same time frame, sometimes with interconnections with one another, there can be some severe and critical big data concerns.

Variety

Big data variety refers to the many sources and types of both structured and unstructured data from sources such as spreadsheets, databases, video links, graphics, monitoring devices, and more. Rarely does data present itself in a form perfectly ordered and ready for processing, and this variety of unstructured data can create problems for storage, processing, and analysis.

A common theme in big data systems is that the source data is diverse and doesn't fall into neat relational structures. It could be text from social networks, image data, or a raw feed directly from a sensor source. None of these things come ready for integration into an application.

Data variety is the challenge of having disparate data sets, from different sources in different formats, all in silos, thereby failing to gain from the benefits a unified view of data brings. A great example of this is marketing data: social media, sales, and advertising data all saved and kept separate. Facebook and Twitter data on their own can only tell you how well one part of your campaign did, but cannot give you an insightful and holistic picture of the whole campaign. To get to the bottom of how your different social media tactics have impacted your web site visits or how your media spend influences your online sales, you need to combine various data sets. No marketing campaign is single-channel anymore, so your data approach shouldn't be either.

Veracity

Veracity deals with concerns regarding uncertain or imprecise data as well as the biases, noise, and abnormality in data. IT, general management, and certainly internal audit when dealing with big data systems situations should ask whether the data that is being processed and stored is meaningful to the problem being analyzed. In traditional database systems and certainly in systems where internal audit has reviewed its internal controls and found them adequate, there has always been the assumption that the application's data is certain, clean, and precise.

Big data veracity refers to situations where data may be in doubt due to inconsistencies, ambiguities, incorrect approximations, or a variety of other issues. This is not a problem that is unique to big data applications. Data veracity problems in even some single small application can turn out to be a massive problem when one is faced with major big data applications. An enterprise IT team needs to develop a big data veracity strategy to help keep data clean and processes to keep "dirty data" from accumulating in systems.

All in all, as IT systems grow larger with increased data volumes and activities, enterprises at all levels face big data internal control issues. However, an order entry system that receives perhaps 100 automated product orders a day faces a much different challenge than if it were to begin to receive 100,000 orders during the same period. Certainly management should be making adjustments as business grows, but the growth of big data poses some challenges for management and internal auditors in meriting and effectively operating their big data applications. Exhibit 21.2 summarizes these major big data issues, and the sections following discuss some of the associated big data audit and internal control issues.

21.2 BIG DATA GOVERNANCE, RISK, AND COMPLIANCE ISSUES

Big data brings new challenges in the form of governance and security issues as well as increased regulations. While many IT governance, risk, and compliance issues remain unchanged no matter the size of systems or volumes of data employed, systems and enterprises operating in a big data environment provide some additional issues and

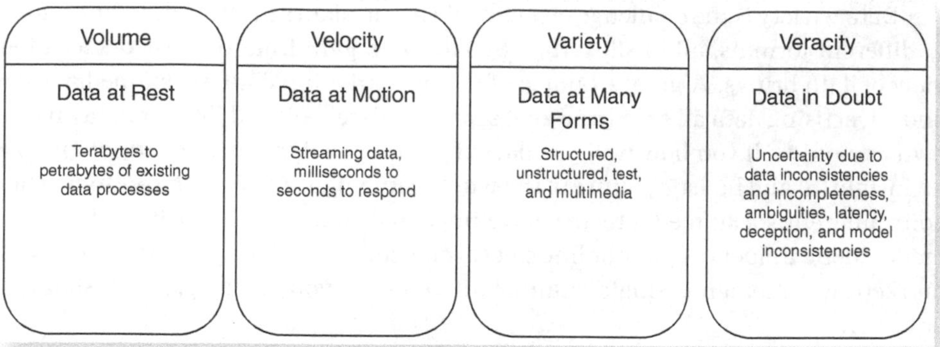

EXHIBIT 21.2 Big Data Internal Control Issues

challenges for internal auditors performing internal control reviews in such a big data environment. Our point here is that internal auditors should have a good CBOK understanding and level of knowledge of big data internal control issues. As businesses and systems grow, internal auditors will increasingly encounter big data systems and need to understand the appropriate internal control issues.

Big data's existing applications and the IT initiatives to build and operate in those environments offer significant opportunities for enterprises to develop a thorough and insightful understanding of their business, but also significant governance and internal control risks. As a preliminary review step, an internal auditor should understand the four big data facets or elements of volume, velocity, variety, and veracity, as discussed in prior sections, and how they apply to a given application as well as an IT data function under review. The level of activity in any or all of these areas can help internal auditors ascertain whether they are facing a big data situation.

Internal auditors should look for appropriate governance controls and well-architected data governance sets of processes when reviewing internal controls in a big data environment. These should often include:

- **A documented directory of all enterprise data assets.** An enterprise's IT function, directly responsible to the chief information officer (CIO), should be given responsibility for periodic inventories of all IT files, application programs, and other *data assets*.For example, Chapter 24 on continuity planning talks about the importance of having records of all key IT assets for business recovery purposes. This type of directory is even more important in an era of big data with large-volume files and often many transaction interconnections.
- **Identification of the owners of all data assets.** Similar to the need for directory records of data assets, the era of big data says that an IT function should have an understanding of the "owners" of all its data assets. That is, who has the rights to update and maintain various elements and to vouch for data asset integrity? This should also be a responsibility of the CIO's function. Data identification issues are particularly significant with big data veracity issues.
- **Responsibility assignments for ensuring the accuracy, accessibility, and other characteristics of data.** Big data resources should not present too great

of a data governance issue when the key files are part of a strong enterprise IT function with an active internal audit resources to assess and test internal controls. However, all too often multiple organization resources, sometimes based in multiple geographic areas, may have somewhat mixed involvement with accessing and updating various data elements of some big data resource. While internal audit can assess its internal controls on critical applications, internal audit functions typically do not have the resources to cover everything, and there should be assigned owners to assess the accuracy and quality of data on a regular ongoing basis. This can be accomplished by installing data access and input controls on the front end, by performing analytical reviews to assess overall characteristics, and by performing regular random samples of file data to test for accuracy and other expected characteristics. The owners of big data assets should assign certain persons to review big data resource quality and integrity. Any of the issues here come under the ITIL® best practices discussed in Chapter 19, with particular attention given to big data systems.

- **Processes for storing, archiving, and creating backup data.** Whether they are for an individual internal auditor's laptop system or large corporate system databases, backup processes both for IT and other business activities are essential good internal control requirements. However, big data systems and applications often introduce complexities into backup processes. With massive numbers of transactions streaming into the big data application, a duplicate clone system, as discussed in the section following on big data storage management, can be a solution, but this can present a logistical problem when dealing a really massive data source. There are multiple potential solutions here for big data backup processes, but some may not present full 100% assurance. Big data management processes should attempt to maximize their effectivity at reasonable costs.
- **Control mechanisms to prevent data leakages.** *Data leakage* is a concern in today's era of big data. Data leakage is the unauthorized transmission of data or information from within an organization to an external destination or recipient. Data leakage is defined as the accidental or intentional distribution of private or sensitive data to an unauthorized entity. With big data, an information security or other data leakage break can result in millions of records transferred to unauthorized parties.

  Sensitive data includes intellectual property, financial information, medical patient information, personal credit card data, and other information depending upon the business and the industry. Furthermore, in many cases, sensitive data may be shared among various stakeholders such as employees working from outside the organizational premises, business partners, and customers, increasing the risk of confidential information falling into unauthorized hands.

  Chapter 23 addresses IT and cybersecurity issues of concern for internal auditors. These issues are even more critical when dealing with a big data environment. We should think of big data as a huge reservoir of water contained by a dam. A controlled process, such as a power generator, may drain some of the contents of that dam in a controlled manner. However, the dam should protect that reservoir from an unauthorized leakage. Even a small leak in the dam could cause a torrent, a deluge of that previously protected water. This is what can happen with a big data leakage. The security and integrity of IT assets is even more critical in a big data environment.

- **Standards and procedures for handling of data by authorized personnel.** As every internal auditor knows, properly documented internal control standards and procedures are always important. In a big data environment, they are particularly important, along with the need for adequately trained personnel. This can cause a major challenge for an enterprise with systems operating in a big data environment. From the perspective of all four of the big data V's introduced here, personnel at all levels need to understand the big data systems they are working with. Too often it is easy for an enterprise's IT functions to develop what becomes a big data application without stress-testing that application in a big data environment. Strong personnel security procedures are very important here. This includes not only adequate job history, education, criminal, and security background checks, but also sufficient training and mentoring of the personnel accessing and updating big data applications.

21.3 BIG DATA MANAGEMENT, HADOOP, AND SECURITY ISSUES

Given the impact of big data's four V's tidal waves, enterprise CIOs need strong controls to manage big data resources, to establish appropriate internal controls, and to recognize and manage big data security issues. Massive security breaches are a regularly reported problem in which perpetrators gain access to major data facilities and steal massive amounts of personal and private data, such as credit card numbers, U.S. Social Security numbers, personal information, and much more.

Our era of big data has led to the growth of two major open source big data management software products, *Hadoop* and NoSQL. These are called open source software products because they were developed in a collaborative manner by interested computer scientists who develop, test, and make suggested improvements to a software tool available through the Internet. These tools evolved similar to the Linux database of some time ago. An internal auditor working with big data issues should at least be familiar with these terms and concepts.

Hadoop is a tool that allows enterprises to process and analyze large volumes of unstructured and semistructured data, heretofore inaccessible to them, in a cost- and time-effective manner. Because Hadoop can scale huge clusters of data, enterprises do not need to rely on just sample data sets but can process and analyze all relevant data. IT specialists can apply an iterative approach to data analysis, continually refining and testing queries to uncover previously unknown insights.

The downside to Hadoop and its myriad components is that they are immature and still developing, although there is a new generation of Hadoop developers and data scientists coming of age. Firms such as IBM and Microsoft are currently offering Hadoop tools and services to make deploying and managing the technology a practical reality for the traditional enterprise.

NoSQL is a new style of database (the acronym stands for not only SQL) that has emerged, like Hadoop, to process large volumes of multistructured data. However, whereas Hadoop is adept at supporting large-scale, batch-style historical analysis, NoSQL databases are aimed at serving up discrete data stored among large volumes of multistructured data to end-user and automated big data applications. This capability is lacking from current enterprise relational database technology, which simply can't maintain needed application performance levels at big data scale.

Most internal auditors will certainly not be experts, and perhaps do not need to know the technical aspects of the systems and security controls built into major big data systems such as Hadoop and NoSQL. When an internal auditor reviewing big data controls finds out that the enterprise is using Hadoop and NoSQL, the auditor should at least have a general familiarity with the tool and its purposes.

Moreover, despite major investments by many enterprises in IT security controls and information security, attackers appear to be getting the upper hand. There are a number of factors that explain this:

- Big data systems as well as all attackers are becoming more organized and better funded. But while attacks have become dynamic and exploit the weaknesses in user-centric, hyperconnected infrastructures, many enterprises' IT defenses have remained static.
- IT-enabled organizations continue to grow more complex and frequently demand much more open and agile systems, creating opportunities for collaboration, communication, and innovation. This also results in new vulnerabilities that cybercriminals, "hacktivist" groups, and nation-states have learned to exploit.
- Compliance is often far-reaching, with regulators and legislators who are getting more prescriptive. Enterprises, particularly those with multiple lines of business or international operations, have an increasingly hard time keeping track of current controls that are in place, those that are needed, and how to ensure that they are being managed properly.

Just as enterprises grow along with their IT systems and resources, and as we increasingly link with other big data resources, big data issues have become a concern for many enterprises. As part of audit planning, an internal auditor should assess an enterprise's current and planned big data file management and security concerns. Security organizations today need to take a big data approach, including understanding potential adversaries, determining what data they need to support decisions, and building and operationalizing a model to support these activities.

Through discussions with the enterprise CIO and the IT support team, internal audit should assess the planning and readiness for the big data era that, if not now, may soon impact many enterprises and their IT functions. Many of these points are controls issues that perhaps should have already been in place as part of normal IT operations; the big data era to come will emphasize them. The following are some issues that an enterprise internal auditor should consider in a review and assessment of big data and IT security and control risks.

Eliminate and Simplify Tedious Manual Data Entry Tasks

A typical enterprise has multiple applications that have been developed and implemented over time and that may require a fair amount of data input. To improve security controls, an enterprise should review existing applications and take steps to eliminate tedious manual tasks in routine response or assessment activities. Systems needs to reduce the number of manual, repetitive tasks associated with investigating an issue—like toggling between consoles and executing the same search in five different tools. While these tasks will not be eliminated overnight, the system should consistently reduce the number of steps per incident. These are all things that create problems that will be even more significant in a big data era.

Review and Identify Higher-Criticality Applications

Internal auditors and certainly business analysts should focus on their highest-impact issues with an objective of minimizing risks and improving internal controls. IT security teams should map the systems they monitor and manage back to the critical applications and business processes they support. Particularly important when there are links to other systems and people, an enterprise needs to understand the dependencies between these systems and third parties, like service providers, and understand the current state of their environment from a vulnerability and compliance standpoint. Internal audit should focus its review efforts on these higher-criticality applications, as are discussed in Chapter 8 on planning for effective internal audits, and perhaps more important, IT management should focus its IT security and control efforts on them as well.

Focus on the Most Relevant Application Data

Security professionals often refer to the importance of "reducing false positives"—that is, focusing on the potential red flags that may represent a security or data leakage violation before concentrating on the otherwise seemingly valid data. The analysis and review of application data should focus on eliminating noise, and provide pointers for analysts to home in on the most high-impact issues. Big data applications also need to provide supporting data in a way that highlights what are likely the biggest problems and why.

Augment Human Knowledge

A big data application should be designed to help both business analysts and internal auditors spend time analyzing the most critical items. This includes providing built-in techniques for identifying the most high-priority issues, as well as current threat intelligence that uses those techniques to identify the latest tools, techniques, and procedures in use by the attacker community. From a security perspective, this requires an enterprise IT security and internal audit to monitor current published security incidents and to make changes to existing applications as necessary. For example, in January 2014 up to 110 million customer accounts at Target stores were compromised through a data breach. Analysts published what went wrong and suggested corrective actions.[2] Both IT and internal audit should be aware of these issues and should use them as lessons for corrective actions.

Maintain an "Over the Horizon" Perspective to Big Data Security Issues

Any defense against modern big data security and data integrity threats is a race against time. Big data systems need to provide early warning—and eventually predictive models—marrying external threat intelligence with internal situational awareness to move the security team from passive defense to active defense and prevention. Internal auditors working with both management and IT security functions in reviewing big data application internal controls should take a big-picture view to solve problems and take corrective actions. We have used the description "over the horizon" here because both IT management and internal auditors need to take more of a big-picture look when assessing security issues in a big data environment.

Managing big data and navigating today's threat environment is challenging. The rapid consumerization of IT has escalated these challenges. The average end user accesses myriad web sites and employs a growing number of operating systems and applications daily utilizing a variety of mobile and desktop devices. This translates to an overwhelming and ever-increasing volume, velocity, and variety as well as veracity issues of data generated, shared, and propagated.

Successful protection relies on the right combination of methodologies, human insight, an expert understanding of the threat landscape, and the efficient processing of big data to create actionable intelligence. Chapter 23 discusses some important cybersecurity issues that should be part of an internal auditor's CBOK information requirements. A major problem here, however, is that enterprises too often have taken a piecemeal approach to security. They use antivirus software to weed out malware and firewalls to keep the bad guys out, but none of these systems communicate with each other in an intelligible way. When meaningful messages do emerge, it's often too late—trade secrets are long gone or customers' credit card data has already been compromised.

But going beyond IT security controls over individual applications and IT functions, big data issues call for a much broader view of risks and internal controls. Critical components of a big data environment are an understanding of how an enterprise's data is organized, an analysis of the often complex relationships using specialized search algorithms, and the employment of custom models.

21.4 COMPLIANCE MONITORING AND BIG DATA ANALYTICS

Internal auditors have long been familiar with audit sampling issues—that is, selecting a few representative items from a population of data, analyzing those selected items to find any possible internal control deviations, and then drawing an overall conclusion on internal controls in that overall population of data based on the results of the sample. These techniques are discussed in Chapter 10 on audit evaluation techniques and should be part of an internal auditor's CBOK. However, things become a bit more complex when dealing with a big data population of sometimes hundreds of millions of data items with many interconnections. Specialized monitoring and analysis tools are needed.

Coupled with the growth of big data, there are currently a growing number of big data monitoring and analytical tools offered by major vendors such as IBM and EMC as well as host of specialized consulting firms. Monitoring the performance of big data repositories is just as important as monitoring the performance of any other type of database. Applications that want to use the data stored in these repositories will submit queries in much the same way as traditional applications querying relational databases like Oracle, SQL Server, Sybase, DB2, and others. When reviewing internal controls in this area, an internal auditor should ask the IT function to explain what monitoring tools have been installed, what types of conditions are being monitored, and what actions are taken to correct and remediate monitored exceptions.

Exhibit 21.3 describes the types of *compliance monitoring* life cycle that an internal auditor should look for when operating in a big data environment. It is really a simple process, but an internal auditor should look for installed software to detect errors and unusual condition. There should be processes in place to investigate and then to remediate the reported conditions. The final and fourth step is to install processes to both correct the reported condition and prevent future occurrences.

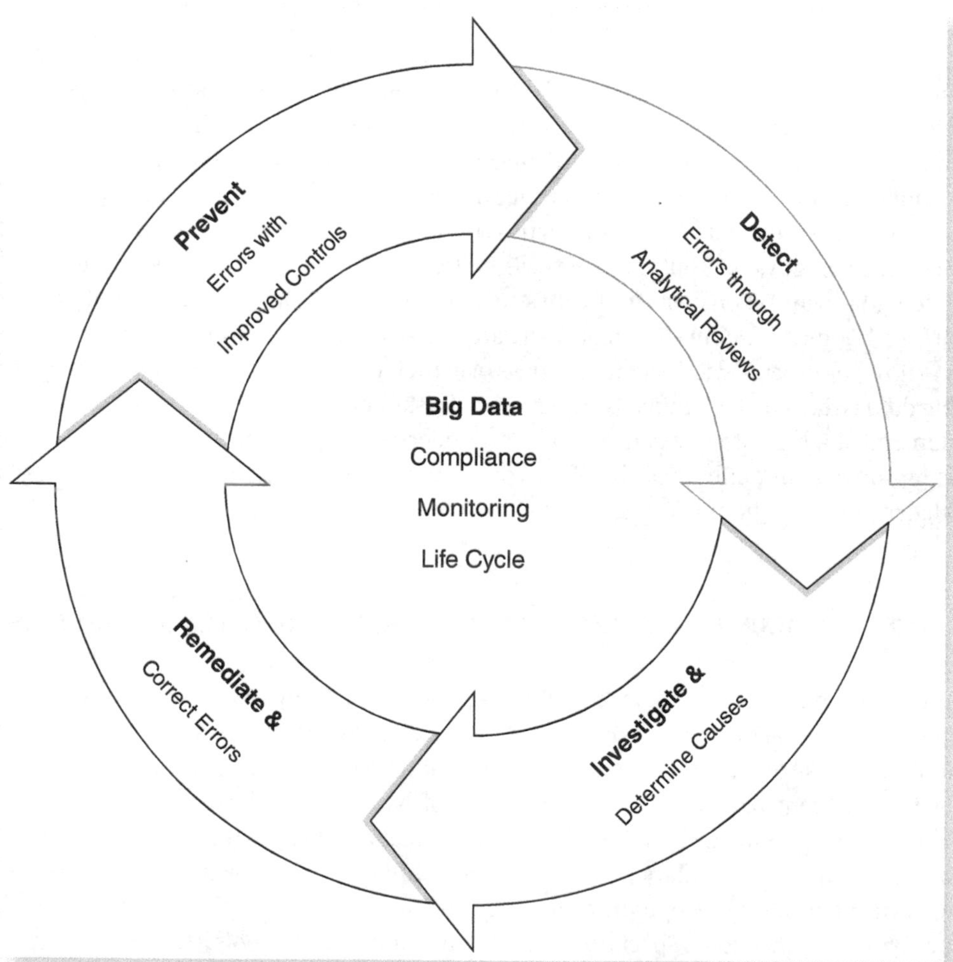

EXHIBIT 21.3 Compliance Monitoring Life Cycle

21.5 INTERNAL AUDITING IN A BIG DATA ENVIRONMENT

There are important risk and internal control issues in this new, evolving, and growing big data environment area. Many of the internal audit procedures discussed in other chapters are the same, whether dealing with more conventional IT applications and processes or big data environments. However, big data raises some additional audit and control concerns simply because of issues surrounding the four big data issues of velocity, volume, variety, and veracity as outlined previously in this chapter. Exhibit 21.4 lists some internal audit considerations that should be used when reviewing systems and controls in a big data environment.

With a good *big data governance* mechanism in place, enterprises can benefit from enhanced productivity, more efficient processes, a stronger competitive position, and greater innovation. Internal auditors should be aware of the multiple internal control issues they may face when reviewing systems and processes in a big data environment.

21.6 ENTERPRISE CONTENT MANAGEMENT INTERNAL CONTROLS

Just as big data has become an important and evolving concept for enterprise IT functions and their internal auditors, enterprise content management (ECM) also is a new and rapidly evolving concept that should become part of an internal auditor's CBOK area of understanding and familiarity. ECM describes the strategies, methods and tools used to capture, manage, store, preserve, and deliver content and documents related to enterprise processes. ECM covers processes to aid in the management of information within the entire scope of an enterprise, whether in the form of a paper document, an electronic file, a database print stream, bar code images, or even an e-mail.

ECM is an umbrella term covering document management, Web content management, search, collaboration, records management, digital asset and workflow management, documents capture and scanning processes, and much more. ECM is primarily aimed at managing the life cycle of information from initial publication or creation all the way through archival and eventually disposal. Well-managed and well-controlled ECM processes aim to make the management of enterprise information easier through simplifying storage, security, version control, process routing, and retention. The benefits to an organization include improved efficiency, better internal controls, and reduced costs. For example, many banks use ECM processes to store copies of customer-written checks as opposed to the older method of keeping physical checks in massive paper warehouses. Under the old system, a customer request for a copy of a check might take weeks, as the bank had to contact the warehouse to find where the right box, file, and check would need to be located. The check would then need to be pulled and a copy made and mailed to the bank, where it would finally be mailed to the customer. With an ECM system in place, a bank employee simply queries the system for the customer's account number and the number of the requested check. When the image of the check appears on a screen, the bank is able to mail or e-mail it immediately to the customer, usually while the customer is still on the phone.

EXHIBIT 21.4 Auditing Big Data Internal Controls

I. Big data application selection criteria.
   a. Review data volume, transaction activity statistics, and other factors to identify enterprise big data applications.
   b. Document scope of identified big data applications, including other system feeds and Internet connections.
   c. Use internal audit planning risk assessment tools to evaluate big data application risks and appropriateness for reviews.

II. Big data enterprise environment factors.
   a. Document special software used for big data applications and determine that versions are regularly updated.
   b. Determine that general IT controls from other reviews are in place and operative for identified big data applications.

III. Applicability and relevance of big data sources.
   a. Review and document the types and sources of processes that supply date to identified big data applications.
   b. Review controls in place to accept only data from relevant sources.
   c. Determine that data governance rules have been established and have been appropriately communicated to application users.

IV. Collect information from appropriate sources.
   a. Determine that security controls have been installed to only accept valid, authorized input transactions.
   b. Review procedures for authorizing and validating input transactions to determine that transactions appear to come from only valid sources.

V. Integration and verification of collected information.
   a. Review logging and cut-off procedures to determine that the timing of input transactions are tracked.
   b. Review error logging procedures for selected application and determine that appropriate accept/reject processes are in place.
   c. Review customer service processes to assess controls to adjust errors and correct system input problems.

VI. Information storage and retrieval processes.
   a. Determine that transaction and process activity is sufficiently retained and is consistent with enterprise continuity management controls.
   b. Assess whether clear audit trails are part of the selected big data application.

VII. Information classification and analysis.
   a. Assess and review analytical review processes in place.
   b. Determine that the big data system reviewed places input information into various and appropriate buckets.
   c. Determine that data quality rules have been implemented that appear appropriate for the application reviewed.
   d. Interview several big data application users to assess whether they have a good understanding of the supplication reviewed and its controls and error review techniques.

VIII. Identification of big data user controls.
   a. Review controls to allow various classifications of users to access the big data application reviewed.
   b. Select a sample of several recently recorded application transactions and determine that they were performed by authorized persons.

   c. Determine that input and application controls have been documented and communicated to the user community as appropriate.

IX. Linkages with other related applications.
   a. Through discussions with the IT database administration function and other users, identify other applications that interface with this big data application and assess whether linkages appear appropriate.
   b. Determine that adequate traffic reports are available to monitor activities with other applications.

X. Cut-off and balancing controls.
   a. Determine that automated balancing procedures are in place to determine that balancing controls are adequate.
   b. Assess the appropriateness and relevance of the big data application reviewed as an element of the enterprise's IT assets.

ECM operations cover many areas in the modern enterprise. Exhibit 21.5 shows an overview of key ECM processes. Any given enterprise may have installed some, if not all, of these processes to manage its enterprise systems information and data. A large number of vendors, such as EMC, IBM, Microsoft, and Oracle, are offering sites of ECM product solutions. An internal auditor should gather some information on the type and status of any ECM software installed as part of an IT general and infrastructure control review and gain some general knowledge about its features and capabilities. This whole ECM field is rapidly changing as new technologies evolve and as we move away from our historic dependence on primarily paper documents and toward digital image–based records.

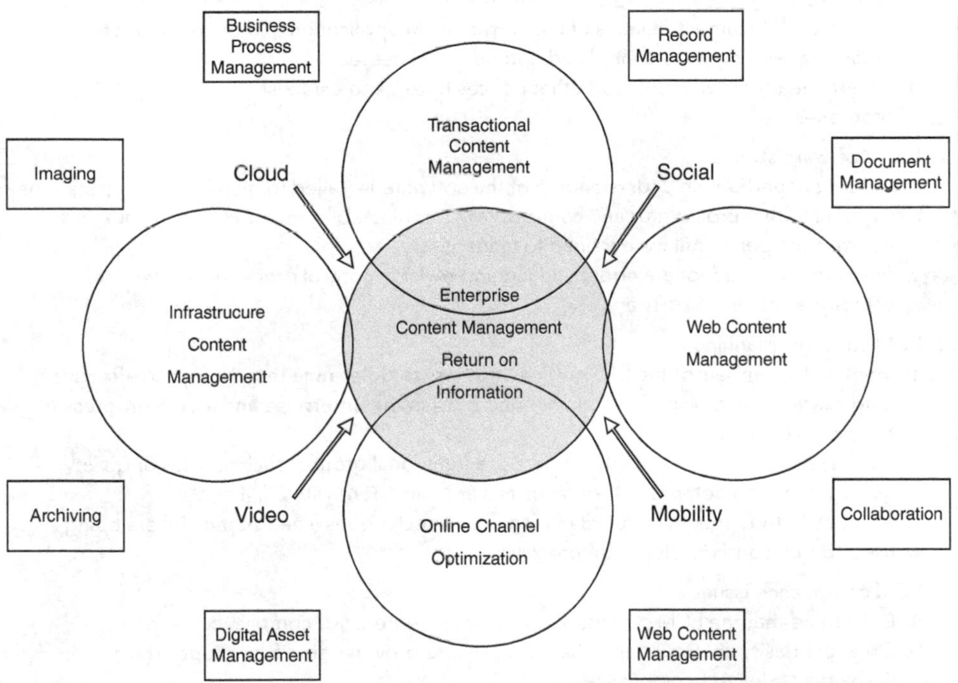

EXHIBIT 21.5 ECM Overview

21.7 AUDITING ENTERPRISE CONTENT MANAGEMENT PROCESSES

ECM requirements are driven by enterprise productivity goals as well as their compliance needs. Many enterprises today have installed some but not all of the ECM components described in Exhibit 21.5. Some of these, such as imaging components or collaboration processes, may not be needed for an enterprise at a current point in time. Others, such as business process management, are really key internal control elements, as described in Chapter 3 on the COSO internal control framework, but virtually all enterprises today need to have strong records and document management processes in place as well record archival processes. Exhibit 21.6 outlines some key ECM internal audit steps.

EXHIBIT 21.6 Enterprise Content Management Internal Audit Review Procedures

The following procedures outline steps for an internal audit review of enterprise content management (ECM) processes in an enterprise. These steps may vary depending the nature and business objectives of the enterprise as well its past and current document and enterprise content activities.

1. Organization ECM status.
   a. Meet with enterprise IT management to review the current software installed and the status of ECM current plans and activities.
   b. Review and assess the adequacy of current and long-range plans for enterprise ECM activities.
   c. Review and document features of the current ECM application and the number of personnel with rights to control and update its processes.
   d. Determine that procedures and other polices have been established to manage ECM processes.
2. ECM software stratus.
   a. Document and obtain understanding of the software installed to manage ECM operations.
   b. Determine that procedures and controls have been established for ECM software and appropriate personnel were trained to manage it.
   c. Assess whether adequate error handling and revision control procedures have been established for ECM software.
3. ECM strategic planning.
   a. Meet with members of the CIO's office or others to determine that there is an effective long-range plan in place for implementing ECM in the enterprise and assess progress toward any plan goals.
   b. Meet with key members of other enterprise functional groups, such as sales or quality management, to determine their activities are consistent with ECM goals.
   c. Assess whether effective project management techniques (see Chapter 16) are being used to build and develop ECM processes.
4. ECM compliance issues.
   a. Determine that the ECM process supports major enterprise compliance issues.
   b. On a test basis, determine that the ECM process provides significant support for Sarbanes-Oxley Act compliance issues.

5. ECM cost issues.
   a. Review enterprise processes to monitor the hourly human resources, and software and equipment costs of building and maintaining ECM facilities.
   b. Determine that return on investment or similar techniques are used to evaluate installed ECM components.
6. ECM collaboration.
   a. Assess whether the installed ECM allows collaboration across multiple technologies, such as instant messaging, whiteboards, social media, and others.
   b. Assess whether goals have been established implementing collaboration techniques, such as better records management, knowledge capture, and improved compliance.
7. ECM continuity issues.
   a. Determine that ECM processes have been closely integrated with enterprise continuity planning processes (see Chapter 24).
   b. Determine that ECM continuity processes are tested at least annually and that processes are updated to the plan with application changes.
8. ECM internal controls.
   a. Assess whether the ECM is consistent with the COSO internal control framework.
   b. Determine that all processes tied to the enterprise ECM process have been mapped, with an ongoing objective of streamlining them for minimum results.

ECM is a broad and wide-ranging topic, but internal auditors should be aware of the multiple information resources flowing into their organization and how they should be managed and controlled. Internal auditors should be aware that implementing an ECM can result in significant improvement to enterprise operations, including improved enterprise organizational readiness, the repurposing of valuable information assets, and both improved information interdependencies and automation technologies. For many enterprises today, ECM is still an almost blue sky goal for the future. Internal auditors should try to have a CBOK understanding of ECM concepts, and when implemented, know how it can improve overall enterprise internal controls.

NOTES

1. Svetlana Sicular, "Gartner's Big Data Definition Consists of Three Parts, Not to Be Confused with Three 'V's,'" *Forbes*, March 27, 2013, http://www.forbes.com/sites/gartnergroup/2013/03/27/gartners-big-data-definition-consists-of-three-parts-not-to-be-confused-with-three-vs.
2. Rick Robinson, "Three Lessons from the Target Hack of Encrypted PIN Data," *Security Intelligence*, January 9, 2014, http://securityintelligence.com/target-hack-encrypted-pin-data-three-lessons/#.VDBZX_nIYd0.

CHAPTER TWENTY-TWO

Reviewing Application and Software Management Controls

IT APPLICATIONS DRIVE MANY IF not most of today's enterprise processes. These applications range from the relatively simple, such as an accounts payable system to pay vendor invoices, to the highly complex, such as enterprise resource planning (ERP) database applications to control virtually all enterprise business processes. While these applications were once based primarily on enterprise central IT systems, today they may be based on client-server, tablet, and even linked smartphone systems. Many if not most IT applications today are based on software purchased from vendors, and an increasing number come from Web-based services. Some IT applications today are still developed by in-house teams, but many others may be based on spreadsheet or database desktop applications. While the IT general control procedures discussed in Chapter 19 cover best practices over all IT operations, specific control processes are also associated with each installed application. In order to perform internal control reviews in specific areas such as accounting, distribution, or engineering, internal auditors must have the skills to understand, evaluate, and test the controls over the supporting IT applications. Reviews of specific application controls can often be more critical to achieving overall audit objectives than reviews of general IT controls.

Even though an internal audit review may find good general IT systems controls, each specific application must itself have good application control procedures in place under the umbrella of the general controls. For example, even if there are inadequate general controls over key IT systems management processes, it will be very difficult for an internal auditor to rely on the controls built into a specific application. A weakness in a specific application control may be an indictment of all general controls, but the control weakness may be unique to that specific application.

A typical enterprise may have a large and diverse number of production IT applications that may support a wide variety of enterprise functions, starting with the financially significant but also including such areas as manufacturing, marketing, engineering, and others. These supporting application systems may be implemented using a variety of IT technologies, such as centralized systems with telecommunication networks, Internet-based network systems, client-server applications, and even older mainframe batch processing systems. Some of these applications may have been developed in-house, but increasingly large numbers of them are based on purchased software packages installed locally or accessed through Web-based service providers.

The concepts for building and installing IT applications have very much changed in recent years, particularly due to the growth of the Internet and integrated converged databases. While members of management may not have a good understanding of today's IT general controls issues, they are typically interested in internal audit findings covering specific application controls reviews and any identified weaknesses. For example, while an audit finding on general controls over computer operating systems program libraries may not generate management interest, a finding of an incorrect discount calculation based on a foreign currency conversion problem in an accounts payable application is sure to draw attention. However, because of the relative complexity of many IT applications and because their controls often reside both within the application and in supporting user areas, audits of many IT applications can often be a challenge to the modern internal auditor.

This chapter discusses how internal auditors should effectively review internal accounting controls in IT applications, including assessing the risks in selecting applications for review, developing an understanding of application controls as well as evaluating and testing those controls, and techniques for reviewing new applications. This chapter will focus on the internal control characteristics of different types of applications and then how to select appropriate applications in internal controls reviews. While there are many differences from one application to another, this chapter will focus on how an internal auditor should select higher-risk applications as candidates for internal audit reviews, the tools and skills needed to understand and document application internal controls, and finally, processes to test and evaluate those applications. Though this was once an area reserved for IT-specialist internal auditors, today all internal auditors should have the knowledge and skills to evaluate and assess IT application internal controls as part of their basic CBOK skills.

22.1 IT APPLICATION COMPONENTS

An internal auditor should understand the elements of a typical IT application. People not familiar with IT sometimes think of an application in terms of today's smartphone apps or just in terms of any system output reports or data displayed on terminal screens. However, every application, whether a Web-based service facility, an older mainframe system, a client-server application, or an office productivity package installed on a local desktop system, has three basic components: (1) the system inputs, (2) the programs used for processing the relevant data, and (3) the system outputs. Each of these has an important role in an application's internal control structure.

Early IT applications could easily be separated into these three components. The traditional computerized payroll system from long ago used time cards and a personnel paymaster file as its inputs and a set of programs to calculate pay and benefits as well as to update pay history records. The outputs from that old payroll system were the printed checks, payroll register reports, and updated paymaster files. Today that same payroll system might accept inputs from an automated plant badge reader that controls accesses and tracks attendance, a shop-floor production system that performs incentive pay calculations, various other online inputs, and a human resources database. A series of computer programs, some located at a Web-based service provider and others distributed to remote workstations, would do the processing. In many cases today, much of the payroll processing may be handled by an outside service function that does most of these activities. The modern payroll system's outputs will include transactions to transmit compensation to employee bank accounts, pay vouchers mailed to employees, input files to assorted tax and benefit sources, various display screens, and an updated human resources database.

While the input, output, and computer processing system components may not at first be all that clear to an internal auditor performing an initial review, the three elements exist in all applications, and no matter how complex the application may appear to be, an internal auditor should always develop an understanding of an application by breaking down its input, output, and processing components. The following sections briefly discuss some of the control aspects of these application components to give an overview of modern IT applications. All internal auditors should have, at the very least, a general understanding of IT applications and supporting processes—a basic CBOK requirement.

Application Input Components

Every IT application needs some form of input, whether data are manually input from transaction vouchers or supplied from some other automated system. Think of a common handheld calculator: the device will generate no results unless data of some sort is input through the key panel. Although the computer programs in an application process the data, determine the outputs, and have a major impact on controls, an internal auditor should always understand the nature and sources of the input components. In traditional batch-oriented systems, this was a fairly easy process as inputs often were sequential records on a magnetic tape file or even 80-column punch cards. Today, inputs are often generated from various automated sources, including wireless data collection devices and specialized bar code readers.

Data Collection and Other Input Devices

Almost forgotten now, the very early IT applications used punch cards as their input source. A single card carried 80 or 90 columns of alphanumeric encoded punched data, and users entered their transactions on data collection sheets for keypunching onto these card formats. The original data collection sheet was the first step in the input chain, and internal auditors were concerned that all transactions were keypunched correctly. These cards were then machine-sorted or otherwise manipulated prior to entry into a system, either read directly into a computer program or copied to magnetic tape for subsequent processing on a batch basis. That is, 500 lines of transactions may have been prepared on data collection sheets and processed as a batch. The need for all transactions to be correctly keypunched and subsequently read into the computer program made input transaction controls a key component of an application's overall internal controls.

Technological improvements have of course eliminated those punch cards and the keypunched input records. Batch-type transactions that must be entered into a computer application are no longer entered by a specialized keypunch or data-entry department. Rather, operational departments use online terminals to enter their transactions for collection and subsequent processing. Following a processing schedule, these transactions may be applied upon input or collected and updated later in a batch mode. The data-entry programs used to capture them often have some transaction-screening capabilities to eliminate any low-level errors common to earlier batch input systems. In many other situations, the entry of a transaction updates files in a real-time mode.

Transaction input data comes from many sources. A retail store captures sales inputs through a combination of sales entries entered on the point of sale (POS) terminal and product sales are entered through barcode readers. Similarly, data is captured on a manufacturing shop floor through various tickets and badges that are entered in readers by workers directly on the shop floor. A small RFID (radio frequency identification) chip embedded on the label of the component may provide inputs as to the product's identification and any subsequent movements. These are all input devices generating transactions for updating to some type of processing application. Input transactions are increasingly generated not from within the enterprise but from applications located in different physical locations and controlled by others. Enterprises today receive a wide variety of data transactions through the Internet, or electronic data interchange systems, or wireless systems. Here, another enterprise may submit purchase order transactions, accounts payable remittances, or other significant business transactions. Individuals initiate sales transactions, trade securities, and perform other business activities through their home computers via the Internet. All of these represent input transactions to various IT applications, and each has its own unique control considerations.

An internal auditor reviewing input controls over IT applications should always look for some of the same basic internal control elements found in all enterprise processes. For example, there should be some means of checking that only correct data are entered. An IT program that, through its supporting validation tables, can verify that a part or employee number is or is not valid, cannot easily verify that the current quantity should have been entered as 100 as opposed to 10. The older batch systems had hash total checks to help look for these possible errors. A hash total is a nonmonetary value such as the "sum" of all account numbers. Modern systems need reasonableness checks built into their data collection procedures, and the programs processing the transactions need controls to prevent errors or to provide warning signals.

Application Inputs from Other Automated Systems

Computer applications are often highly integrated, with one application unit generating an output file of data for processing by another. Transactions entered into one application may impact a variety of other interrelated applications. Thus an error or omission of an input at one point in a chain of applications may impact the processing of another connected application. In addition to understanding the sources of the transactions to an application, an internal auditor should understand the nature of other automated inputs to that same application. For example, a modern payroll system may receive inputs from a sales performance system to calculate commissions. The sales performance file that feeds the payroll system is another input. The controls there are based on the input, processing, and output controls of the sales performance system. If sales performance data represent a significant input to the payroll system, an internal auditor needs to be concerned about the controls over it, as well as over any other supporting applications.

A large network of interconnected applications can present a challenge to the auditor attempting to review the input controls for just one of these. An internal auditor may be interested in understanding application input controls for application X. However, files from applications A, B, and C may provide inputs to X, while D and E provide inputs to applications A and C, respectively. In order to review input controls, an internal auditor typically does not have the time or resources to review all of these processes and must decide on the most critical of them and assume the other less critical supporting applications are generating appropriate transactions.

Files and Databases

Although usually generated by some other supporting application or updated by the application under review itself, an application's files and databases represent important inputs. In some instances, these files represent tables of data used for the validation of program data. As part of gaining an understanding of an application, the internal auditor should understand the nature and content of all supporting application files. The software that controls these files generally has various record-counting and other logical controls to determine that all transactions are correctly written onto and can be retrieved from the supporting electronic media. Files also have their own date and label-checking controls to prevent them from being improperly input to a wrong processing cycle or an incorrect application. Once written as streams of sequential records on magnetic tape, today's files are input onto storage disks or USB higher-density thumb drives. An internal auditor needs a general understanding not only of the type and nature of inputs to a computer application but also of the source of the file data and any controls over it, as will be discussed in greater detail later in this chapter.

Databases can represent a particular challenge to an internal auditor. Although the term *database* is often misused to refer to almost any type of computer file, an IT database is a system for organizing data in a format such that all important data elements point or relate to each other. In years past, many mainframe computers used what were called *hierarchical databases,* where data was organized in a grandfather-father-son "family tree" type of structure. IBM's mainframe product of years ago, called IMS (Integrated Management System), was once a popular hierarchical database in the days of mainframe systems. When it was used in a manufacturing enterprise, for example, each product might be organized as a header record that would point to each of its parts. Those components in turn would each have a hierarchy of records comprising its individual parts. File integrity was very important here because a program error that breaks one of the connecting chains would make it difficult to retrieve the lost data.

Today what is called the relational database is the most common file structure and is found on all types and sizes of computers. A relational database is like a multidimensional Excel spreadsheet. That is, the user can retrieve data across various database rows, columns, and pages rather than having to go to the head of each tree and then search down through that tree to retrieve the desired data. In addition to being a very effective way to organize input data to application systems, these databases allow for easy retrieval of end user–oriented reports. Two common examples of this relational database model are Oracle Corporation's database products and IBM's DB2 database.

Application Programs

Applications are processed through a series of computer programs or sets of machine instructions. The traditional payroll system example mentioned earlier in this chapter would consist of a series of computer programs: one would read the employee's time card data, store the number of hours worked, and then use the employee number on that input time card to look up the employee's rate and scheduled deductions. Based on this match, the program looks up the employee's rate of pay and multiplies this by the number of hours worked to calculate the gross pay.

A computer program is a set of instructions covering every detail of a process. Writing a program is the process of writing detailed instructions and then following them to the letter. As an experiment to comprehend the details involved in writing a larger computer program, an internal auditor should try to write down each step to follow in the morning from the time the alarm goes off until his or her arrival at the office. Do this one day, documenting all normal actions as well as alternate decision paths, such as whether to dress normally for work or for "casual Friday." The following morning, use those same instructions *exactly* as they are written to get up, wash and dress, and then go off to work. Most will arrive at work missing an item of clothing or worse. This is the difficulty of writing detailed computer programs. It is usually not necessary for internal auditors to know how to write formal computer programs today beyond the simple audit-retrieval applications, but the effective internal auditor should understand how computer application programs are built and what their capabilities are, in order to define appropriate control procedures.

Traditional Mainframe and Client-Server Programs

Mainframes, or what we often call legacy computers today, had been used extensively for business applications since the early 1960s. Although these applications were first programmed in early computer languages based on what are now called first-generation actual machine languages using binary 1s and 0s, we quickly moved to second-generation symbolic languages that used codes to represent instructions such as to add or to store a value. Third-generation languages soon followed. They used actual English-like instruction statements such as "ADD A TO B" to describe the actions to be taken. Programs called *compilers* translated these instructions into machine language. Although a large variety of these third-generation or compiler languages were introduced in the

1960s, COBOL,[1] with its English-like instructions, was the almost standard language for business data processing well into the 1980s. It is still in limited use today for some business applications, but specialized database and report-generator languages as well as object-oriented languages are dominant today.

A wide range of computer languages are used today, such as Visual Basic and Java. In addition, many applications are developed through English language–like report-generator languages that reside on top of a supporting computer language. Apart from the skills to write an audit retrieval request, an internal auditor today does not need to have skills in programming languages.

Modern Computer Program Architectures

Although in the mainframe computer days of years past most business applications developed in-house would be written in COBOL, that has gone away. While most enterprises today generally purchase or lease their software packages or access them through a Web service provider, some IT functions still do develop their own applications in-house, using a wide variety of programming tools beyond the traditional COBOL, called object-oriented programming languages. In-house development normally occurs when an enterprise has business requirements for which no commercial software package seems correct, or, more significantly, when an enterprise has plans for some strategic software-based initiative. An internal auditor today, even with a fundamental knowledge of a language such as Visual Basic, COBOL, or C, may have some initial difficulties understanding how these object-oriented applications are programmed and constructed. Often they consist of many very small program code modules that pass data to one another, sometimes over remote telecommunication lines. Some high-level concepts of object-oriented programming, which are certainly not an internal audit CBOK need, are described in Exhibit 22.1. With names such as Java and C++, these are the programming languages of today's Web-based applications.[2]

An internal auditor reviewing application controls should ascertain the level of application development programming done within the IT organization and determine what languages and tools are used. The auditor should rely on the level of overall application program standards in place as well as on other programming development and maintenance controls, and rather than looking for these in each given application reviewed, should review the general systems development controls in the IT enterprise. These might be included in a general review of IT operations, as discussed in Chapter 19.

When an enterprise plans to build and launch a major new or revised in-house software application, internal audit should request the right to perform a preimplementation review of the new application development project. This is an environment where the internal auditor serves as an ongoing reviewer of the application development process, assessing the evolving internal controls environment and making consulting recommendations, as discussed in Chapter 30 on the internal auditor as an enterprise consultant.

Reviews of the application development process and preimplementation internal audit reviews are most effective for large development efforts that cover an extended

EXHIBIT 22.1 Object-Oriented Programming Language Concepts

Object-oriented programming (OOP) programming languages, such as JAVA or C++, are organized around *objects* of data rather than logic-based actions. Programs using languages such as COBOL were based on logical procedures that took input data, processed it, and produced output data. These older programming approaches described the processing logic but did not define the data. OOP focuses on the data objects we want to manipulate rather than the logic required to manipulate them. Examples of objects range from human beings (described by name, address, and so forth) to buildings and floors (whose properties can be described and managed) or the little individual parts in a manufactured produce.

The first step in OOP is to go through a data modeling exercise and identify all the objects you want to manipulate and how they relate to each other. Think of all of the furniture in the board of director's meeting room. There will be a major table for board meetings and side tables for the supporting staff. The chairs in that room will be *objects* with each director, around the table, having one *class* of chair, the support staff another class, and the CEO at the end of the table with still another. These objects are then generalized into *classes of objects*. OOP defines the logical sequences of these classes of objects. The director's chairs are arranged around the board conference table, the CEO at the end, and support staff off to the sides. OOP provides computer instructions, based on the relevant data in the class object characteristics, to allow the objects and their characteristics to communicate with each other in well-defined interfaces called *messages*. For example, the CEO's chair will be at the head or the table, and if the CEO is present, messages will be delivered to other board members.

The concepts and rules used in OOP provide these important benefits:

- The concept of a data class makes it possible to define subclasses of data objects that share or all of the main class characteristics. Called *inheritance*, this property of OOP forces a thorough data analysis, reduces development time, and ensures more accurate coding.
- Since a class defines only the data it needs to be concerned with, when an instance of that class (an object) is run, the OOP program will not be able to accidentally access other program data. This characteristic of *data hiding* provides greater system security and avoids unintended data corruption.
- The definition of a class is reusable both by the program for which it is initially created but also by other object-oriented programs (and, for this reason, can be more easily distributed for use in networks).
- The concept of data classes allows a programmer to create new *data types* not already defined in the language itself.

The OOP languages C++ and JAVA are the most popular object-oriented languages today, with JAVA designed especially for use in distributed applications on corporate networks and the Internet.

span of time and cover primarily components developed in-house. Exhibit 22.2 contains internal audit guidelines for a review of a new application systems development control. These control processes are closely linked to the IT general controls discussed in Chapter 19. Control processes should be put in place for the overall IT functions, and an internal auditor should look for them to exist in each application selected for review. Of course, today most new application development projects do not just consist of new programs developed in-house but rather the building of tables for use with purchased

EXHIBIT 22.2 Internal Audit IT Application Development Review Guidelines

These guidelines cover circumstances where an enterprise IT organization is in the process of developing an IT application requiring some in-house programming development and where internal audit performs internal control reviews of those efforts.

1. All requests for new or revised applications should follow IT standards and receive prior authorization.
2. The application development process should include sufficient requesting user interviews to develop a firm understanding of needs.
3. All new application projects should receive a detailed statement of requirements along with a formal cost-benefit analysis.
4. Project plans should be prepared for all IT department development work as well as for individual application development projects.
5. Care should be given to ensuring that application development projects meet the long-range objectives of the enterprise.
6. The responsibilities for application development work should be assigned with adequate time allowed to complete development assignments.
7. The application development process should include sufficient user interviews to obtain a full understanding of requirements.
8. Attention must be given to internal controls, audit trails, and continuity procedures.
9. Adequate resource and capacity planning should be in place to ensure that all hardware and software is sufficient when the application is place in production.
10. Sufficient attention must be paid to backup, storage, and continuity planning for the new application.
11. Adequate controls must be installed to provide strong assurances regarding the integrity of the data processes and outputs from the application.
12. The application should be built with adequate controls for the identification and correction or processing errors.
13. All application processing data and transactions should contain strong audit trails.
14. Adequate documentation should be prepared on a technical as well as an application user level.
15. Test data should be prepared following a predetermined test plan that outlines expected results and satisfies user expectations.
16. When data is converted from an existing application, strong control procedures should be established over the conversion process.
17. If the application is critical, internal audit should be given an opportunity to participate in a formal preimplementation audit.
18. There should be a formal sign-off and approval process as part of the completion of the application development process.

software applications as well as interfaces between some new purchased application and other existing components. Proper attention must be devoted to preserving internal controls and performing adequate testing in these situations, and the internal audit guidelines outlined here can provide service to the enterprise.

Vendor-Supplied Software

Most IT applications today are based on vendor-supplied software. An outside vendor will supply the basic, usually Web-based, system elements, and the enterprise's IT development function only has the responsibility of building custom tables, file interfaces, and output report formats around the purchased application. The actual program source code for the purchased software is often protected by the vendor to prevent improper access and changes. Both the internal auditor and IT management should be concerned that the software vendor has a reputation for quality, error-free software. Often small entrepreneurial software suppliers can provide some very cost-effective solutions, but there can be risks in using an undercapitalized software developer. If there is any doubt that the software vendor lacks stability, arrangements should be made at the time of the software purchase contract to place a version of the vendor's source code "in escrow" in the event of a vendor business failure. A bank or some other agency would hold a version of the protected source code for release to customers if the software vendor were to fail.

The decision to lease or purchase a software package is too often based on an IT manager meeting a software salesperson at a trade show or being mesmerized by the vendor's Web pages, establishing a need, and the purchase of the software package without a full analysis of the costs and benefits. While it is different than the traditional IT preimplementation review, internal auditors often can play a strong consulting-level role in the acquisition of a new software package. There are often many internal control issues beyond what is listed in sales brochures, and Exhibit 22.3 is a checklist that an

EXHIBIT 22.3 Purchased Software Internal Controls Audit Checklist

1. Determine the requirements and objective for the new application have been clearly approved and defined.
2. Assess whether application requirements have been clearly defined and whether they can be satisfied by modification of current application.
3. If requirements call for new application, determine whether an IT analysis has been performed to determine if it may be most cost-effective to develop in-house or to purchase.
4. If a search for a potential purchased application, determine that detailed requirements have been defined through a request for proposal (RFP) approach.
5. Determine if the RFP requirements clearly match the exiting enterprise IT environment.
6. A review procedure for distribution of RFP's to assure that its distribution covered all appropriate vendor candidates.
7. Assess whether documentation is in place to review all vendor proposals on a consistent basis.
8. For application software vendors that appear to meet preliminary requirements, determine that the software has been effectively demonstrated through testing.
9. Where multiple vendors are presenting competing software products, consistent evaluation procedures should be in place.
10. Enterprise financial and legal resources should be in place to participate in software selection.
11. The selected software product should have adequate documentation, "help" facilities, and a regular update program in place.
12. Determine that an implementation plan is in place to either convert data or an existing application to the new software application.
13. Where appropriate, develop preliminary plans for CAATT procedures covering new application.
14. Establish internal audit workpaper records for new purchased software application.

internal auditor can use both when providing consulting help and when reviewing the decision to purchase a major new software package. An internal auditor should have as good an understanding of the internal controls surrounding major purchased software applications as of any application developed in-house.

Large, integrated packages such as the ERP systems mentioned previously can have a major impact on all aspects of an enterprise. These database application packages may include production, purchasing, inventory, human resources, accounting, and all other business applications implemented as a linked series of databases. Data introduced to one application component, such as a revised standard cost for a manufactured part, will connect to other systems as necessary. For example, that revised standard cost will be reflected in inventory and financial systems, among others.

IT Application Output Components

In addition to our discussion of computer application inputs and the programs to process that input data, no discussion of an application system's key components would be complete without a description of its outputs. These usually consist of output screens or updated files as well as printed reports. This is an important area to survey in an application review, as in many instances the controls of internal audit concern in an application are contained on the output screens of control files. Older applications once produced large volumes of output reports indicating the results of their processing and any control or error problems. The sheer volume and frequency of those output reports often prevented users from giving adequate attention to many reported control problems, and internal auditors frequently identified control concerns that users could have identified by just reviewing their output reports.

Today's applications produce few if any paper-based output reports, with results reported on online data retrieval screens. In some cases, special online reports signal control problems and data errors, while in others the user is responsible for calling up the appropriate screen to review any problems. All too often this step may be ignored and processing errors can go undetected. Internal auditors should always review the scope of application output reports and their user dispositions. Reports or screens are not the only application outputs, as transactions or updated files are typically passed to a variety of other integrated applications. Just as a modern IT application may receive its inputs from a highly integrated set of input systems, it may be one more link in a chain to still others. Again and always, the internal auditor should develop a good understanding of the application reviewed as well as all of its inputs and outputs.

22.2 SELECTING APPLICATIONS FOR INTERNAL AUDIT REVIEWS

While all major IT operations and key applications should be subject to regular reviews, internal audit typically does not have the resources or time to regularly review the controls for all of its IT applications. In addition, many IT applications represent a minimal level of control risk. As part of a specific operational review or as part of a general IT controls review, internal audit should attempt to select only the more critical applications for review. The audit process for selecting these applications should focus on the selection of more enterprise critical applications as discussed in Chapter 15 on the audit candidate selection process. Because IT applications are so critical to enterprise operations, internal auditors often identify these as targets as part of their audit planning, or sometimes receive specific requests from the audit committee or senior management to review specific application controls.

Internal audit should typically be faced with requests for reviews of a large number of application candidates at any time, and care should be taken in documenting the reasons for selecting one application over another. This will help if internal audit is questioned subsequent to completing a series of reviews. Audits of the controls over representative IT applications are sometimes included as part of a general controls review of the IT function. Internal audit should develop a detailed understanding of the general controls surrounding IT operations as discussed in Chapter 19, and then review the controls surrounding one or more selected applications following the application selection processes discussed in Chapter 15.

Internal auditors often perform reviews of the specific applications that support an overall functional area. For example, internal audit may schedule a combined operational and financial review of the purchasing department. This may also be the appropriate time to review the application controls for the major automated purchasing systems supporting that department. In this integrated audit approach, internal auditors can concentrate on both the more technical issues surrounding the applications and on other supporting operational controls.

22.3 PRELIMINARY STEPS TO PERFORMING APPLICATION CONTROLS REVIEWS

Once an application has been selected for review, internal audit should gain an understanding of the purpose or objectives of that application, the technology approaches used, and the relationship of the application to other significant processes. It may be necessary for the internal auditor to do some background reading and study special technical aspects of that application. This auditor understanding can often be accomplished through reviews of any past audit workpapers, interviews with IT and user personnel, and reviews of application documentation. While prior audit workpapers can be very helpful and the interview process will allow an auditor to ask relevant controls-related questions, a review of applications documentation is often a useful first step in reviewing and evaluating the controls over an IT application. Chapter 17 discusses preparing and making effective of audit workpapers. As an early step in this review process, internal audit should perform a walk-through of the application to better understand how it works and how its controls function. These preliminary steps will allow an internal auditor to develop specific audit tests of the application's more significant controls.

In the early days of enterprise-developed IT applications, documentation often consisted of detailed system flowcharts with supporting record layouts and little else. This helped the programmer but was of little use to application users or internal auditors attempting to understand the application's controls. In addition, the early flowcharts were often hand-prepared and quickly became out of date. When a relatively small change was subsequently added to a complex system flowchart, designers were often reluctant to redraw their pencil-and-paper-based charts. Perhaps they remembered the changes, but other interested persons reviewing this documentation, such as internal auditors, would not be aware of them.

Over time, application documentation evolved into a more text- and functional chart–oriented format. Decision tables and logic charts described the functions of individual programs, while text described the overall system. Although this type of documentation was more functional and less technical, it too had a tendency to quickly become out of date. Programmers and system designers often would not take the time to incorporate later changes into this systems documentation. Today, powerful documentation tools such as flowchart generators are available. A real strength of these automated documentation tools is that detailed flowcharts can be combined into summarized versions with changes introduced on one chart updating all others.

Internal audit can expect to find various types and quantities of application documentation depending on the relative age and complexity of the application to be reviewed. Due to poor IT management procedures, complex in-house-developed applications sometimes have very limited documentation. The published documentation covering other vendor-supplied applications, however, will often cover many dozens of volumes of descriptive text. Users will treat such documentation as almost encyclopedic reference materials. A review of the published documentation should be a first step to gaining an audit understanding of an application. If aspects of the documentation are missing or out of date, the internal auditor will probably have a finding at the conclusion of the review. However, this lack of documentation should not necessarily prevent an internal auditor from performing an application review. When performing the review, internal audit should normally look for the following documentation elements:

- **Systems development methodology initiating documents.** These refer to initial project requests, any cost-benefit justifications, and the general systems design requirements. Although many initial assumptions may have changed during the systems design and implementation process, these documents often will help internal audit understand why the application was designed and controlled in the manner it is.
- **Functional design specifications.** This documentation should describe the application in some detail. Each of the program elements, database specifications, and systems controls should be described. If major changes have been made to the application since its original implementation, these changes should also be reflected in the design documentation. Their purpose is to allow an IT analyst to be able to make changes or respond to user questions regarding the application.
- **Program change histories.** There should be some type of log or documented record listing all program changes within an application. Some IT departments keep this with the application documentation, while others maintain it in a central file cross-referenced to the program source code. While this type of documentation is an essential element to control program changes, it will also provide internal

audit with some feeling for the application's relative stability. A large number of ongoing change requests for a given application may mean that the application system is not achieving user objectives. Revision service support controls should follow ITIL® best practices, as discussed in Chapter 19.

- **User documentation manuals.** Along with technical documentation, appropriate user documentation should be available for any application. In a modern, Web-based system, much of this user documentation may be in the form of "HELP" or "READ ME" types of online screens. However, this documentation should be sufficiently comprehensive to answer user questions. It should also be supported by evidence of a user training program, as appropriate.

Internal audit should review selected application documentation to gain an understanding of the controls to be reviewed, and may also want to use these materials to develop questions for later interviews. Copies of key or representative sections should also be taken for workpaper documentation. However, internal audit should not normally attempt to copy the entire documentation file for workpaper purposes. This was done all too often by internal auditors in the past, adding considerable bulk to workpaper files, but doing little to accomplish audit objectives.

Conducting an Application Walk-Through Review

Once internal audit has reviewed prior workpapers and the application documentation, and interviewed users and IT personnel to clarify any questions raised through the documentation review, a next step is to verify internal audit's understanding of the application by a *walk-through* review. An IT application walk-through review is the same type of internal audit process as an initial review of an operational facility, in which the auditor would tour a facility, such as a production floor. The purpose of the walk-through is to confirm internal audit's general understanding about how the IT application operates and to preliminarily test application controls through sample transactions.

As an example of an application walk-through process, assume that internal audit has been asked to review the controls over an older in-house-developed accounts payable application operating on an in-house server system. The enterprise is a manufacturing firm with other fairly sophisticated IT applications, and this accounts payable application was installed several years before and had never been reviewed when it was under development. Based upon a review of this example application documentation, internal audit should attempt to determine that the application receives inputs from the following sources:

- Purchase order commitments from the manufacturing material requirements planning purchasing system
- Notifications of goods received from the materials-receiving system
- Various online terminal payment transactions for indirect goods and services that are not recorded through the materials-receiving system
- Payment approval transactions entered through an input screen
- Miscellaneous payables journal transactions entered as batch data

Assume that application data is recorded on a relational database along with tables of values for validating purchase terms, including the calculation of any purchase discounts. Based on the review of documentation, application outputs include the accounts payable electronic fund transfer transactions as well as any paper checks, transactions to the general ledger, cost accounting application materials, and various control and accounting summary screens and reports.

The prime system users are personnel from the general accounting as well as the purchasing department, who set up automatic vendor payments under preagreed terms. The example application flowchart in Exhibit 22.4 describes internal auditor steps for an application walk-through. The steps to performing an application walk-through for the example accounts payable application are as follows:

1. **Briefly describe the application in the audit workpapers.** Based on internal audit's review of the application's documentation, a brief description of the application should be prepared for later inclusion in the audit workpapers. This workpaper documentation follows the general format of the walk-through description except there should be greater detail, identifying key subsystems, input screen formats, key data file names, and output report formats. (For a discussion of internal audit workpapers, see Chapter 17.)
2. **Develop a block diagram description of the application.** A block diagram is a very high-level, abbreviated auditor-level systems or functional-level flowchart for an application. It should reflect major concepts following the above-written description and also illustrate some application flow concepts. This often can be a hand-drawn document that will help increase auditor understanding of the application reviewed. Exhibit 22.5 is an example of such a system block diagram that

EXHIBIT 22.4 IT Applications Walk-Through Internal Auditor Steps

1. Develop a general understanding of the application, its inputs, outputs, and any procedures requiring manual or other system interactions.
2. For an application with a large number of steps requiring manual processing procedures, select a sample of key transaction types to be processed from a normal production cycle. For workpaper documentation purposes, document identifying control numbers or other characteristics to tract transaction through application processes.
3. Observe or use software tools to monitor the processing of each module or workstation step, noting situations where the walk-through transaction is:
   a. Inputs to another application or supporting process are passed on through the node processing module.
   b. Transactions are held for further cycles in process or rejected as errors during the specific processing module.
4. Follow selected transactions through each processing module step, documenting instances where the documented control procedures are not being followed or where the transaction causes application errors or manual operator difficulties.
5. At the end of the walk-through, discuss with appropriate IT or user administrators any unusual or unexpected problems and document internal control status.
6. For an automated application with essentially no paper trail, follow essentially the same procedures but making appropriate inquiries and using software query tools to determine the application is processing with appropriate controls and as expected.

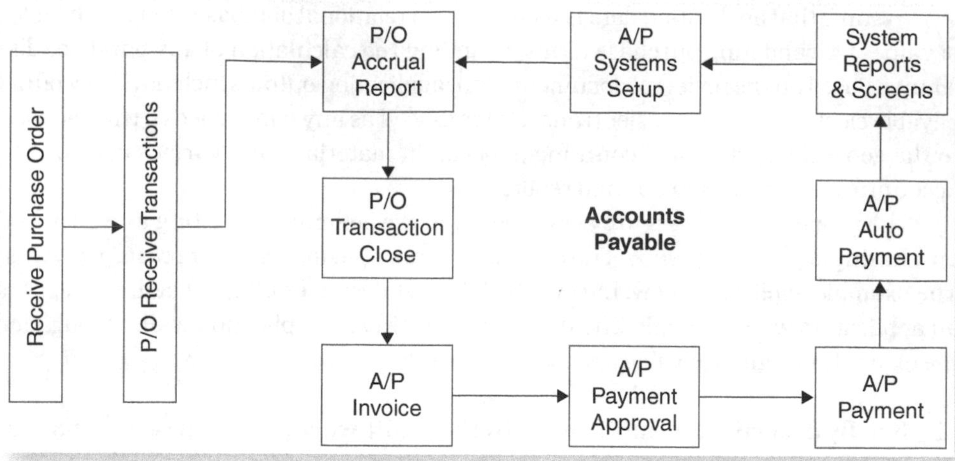

EXHIBIT 22.5 Accounts Payable Block Diagram

can be useful to confirm an understanding of the application with key IT and user personnel.

3. **Select key application transactions.** One or several representative transactions should be selected to walk or to trace through the application. This selection would be based on discussions with users and fellow members of the audit team. In this example of an accounts payable system walk-through review, the internal auditor may select automated transactions that the receiving system should match against the payables purchase order records to initiate payment.
4. **Walk a selected transaction through the system processes.** In the older days of manual or simpler IT applications, a walk-through amounted to just what the words say. That is, an auditor would take an input transaction form and walk it through each of the clerical desks or steps normally used to process the transaction to verify the processing procedures. In a modern application, this walk-through process typically requires recording screen shot prints of a transaction as it is entered into a terminal, and then following the transaction through its subsequent steps. In this accounts payable example, the walk-through transaction is a receiving report entry indicating that a valid open purchase commitment had been received. Internal audit would then review the open commitments module of the system to determine whether the transaction was recorded on a transaction report or screen. It should then be traced to a properly computed accounts payable check or to a funds-transfer transaction and then to general ledger system transactions for the correct amount.

This type of application testing is often called *compliance testing.* That is, internal audit is verifying that the application is operating in compliance with preestablished control procedures. If internal audit wished to verify that all accounts payable checks had been input to the general ledger through a comparison of account balances or other methods, this would be called *substantive testing,* or a test of financial statement balances. Tests in support of Sarbanes-Oxley Act Section 404 controls typically tie a single item test to financial statement general ledger accounts.

5. **Modify the system understanding as required.** Since the purpose of an application walk-through is to develop a basic understanding of its functions and controls, a walk-through review does not allow internal audit to determine whether *all* transactions are working as described. However, if internal audit discovers that the selected walk-through transactions are not working as assumed, the preliminary auditor-prepared application documentation may need to be revised. Once revised, internal audit may want to repeat the steps just explained to determine that internal audit has a proper understanding of system transaction flows.

   The walk-through allows internal audit to gain a preliminary understanding not only of the application and its controls, but also its relationship with other automated systems. Limited compliance testing allows the internal auditor to confirm that the application is operating as described. While this is not a substitute for detailed, substantive application testing, the walk-through allows an internal auditor to identify major control weaknesses as well as to gain a sufficient understanding of the application to define control objectives for subsequent, detailed audit testing and evaluation procedures.

Developing Application Control Objectives

After the review of documentation and walk-through compliance testing, an internal auditor should next develop detailed audit objectives and procedures for completing the application review. This depends upon the type of review planned, the characteristics of the application, and the results of the preliminary review steps. A given review might be concerned with the level of control risk and the ability of the application to support financial statements correctly. The procedures associated with these audit objectives would be tests of the financial statement balances built up from detailed application transactions.

An internal auditor also could have other objectives in reviewing an IT application. Management may have asked internal audit to perform a review to determine if user personnel have received sufficient training to operate it or to review another application to determine if related discount and interest calculations associated with accounts payable are correctly performed. The walk-through compliance testing may have identified significant problems, and the auditor may want to do little more than to confirm those preliminary but troubling observations. Before proceeding any further with the review, the internal auditor should now confirm or revise the specific review objectives.

Specific application review audit objectives should be clearly defined. The auditor responsible for the detailed review might wish to summarize these objectives for the review and approval by appropriate members of management. This may help prevent an internal auditor from devoting resources to testing an area not considered significant. In the accounts payable system discussed here, an internal auditor may have established several specific objectives for this review as follows:

- The accounts payable system should have adequate internal controls, such that all receipts recorded from the receiving system are correctly matched to vendor files before the preparation of disbursements.
- Vendor terms should be correctly computed with controls to eliminate potential duplicate payments.

- Controls should be in place to prevent or at least flag improper or unusual disbursements.
- All systems-generated disbursements should be recorded on general ledger files using correct account numbers and other descriptive codes.

Depending on management's direction, internal audit might develop other objectives for performing such a review. For example, the review could focus on database integrity or on control procedures over miscellaneous disbursements. Any review may have multiple objectives. For example, if management had asked internal audit to review the accounts payable system to assure that no illegal or improper payments have been made, internal audit would probably also want to add a general objective to assess control risk and to determine that the system of internal controls is adequate.

Before actually starting any detailed application review, internal audit should document the specific objectives of the review and discuss them with the management requesting the application review to determine if the planned review approach is on target and will satisfy the audit request. This same procedure should also take place even if the application review has been initiated by the audit department as part of a total review of an IT function. Exhibit 22.6 contains suggested control objectives for an IT application review.

EXHIBIT 22.6 Control Objectives for an IT Application Review

1. Develop a general understanding of the application to be reviewed: its principle business purposes, inputs, outputs, and the technology environment.
2. Based on the general understanding of the application, develop a general process flowchart that identifies key decision points: its inputs, outputs, and internal controls.
3. Develop an understanding of the general controls surrounding the application and its processing environment, with an emphasis on ITIL® Service Support and Service Delivery general controls (see Chapter 19).
4. Discuss the application and its performance with key system users and IT to understand any concerns or outstanding issues regarding the application.
5. Develop a testing plan for the application that emphasizes:
   a. Identification of significant transactions, accounting, and business-related controls within and surrounding the application's environment.
   b. Identify control objectives covering each of those significant controls as well as areas of concern that should satisfy the auditor that key controls are effective.
   c. Develop testing and sampling approaches for each of the key controls.
6. Gather evidence to perform tests of identified key controls, including:
   a. Copies of key files and extracts of transactions to reperform application functions.
   b. Special application transaction to test key or critical application controls.
   c. Audit software procedures or package software functions to review application transactions and special functions.
   d. Manual or paper-based documentation to support the application's controls testing.
7. Schedule and perform tests of key application controls using the test materials gathered.
8. Evaluate all test results in a pass/fail context and communicate testing results with key systems users and IT to verify and validate the testing approach and its results.
9. Maintain copies of all testing plans and evidence, documenting the results in internal audit workpapers.
10. Develop appropriate corrective action plan, where appropriate, to correct any problems encountered in the testing or application review.

22.4 COMPLETING THE IT APPLICATION CONTROLS AUDIT

Usually more difficult to define than an internal audit's general objectives, supporting detailed IT application audit procedures vary and depend on (1) whether the application primarily uses purchased or in-house-developed software components; (2) whether the application is integrated with others or is a separate process; (3) whether it uses Web-based service providers, client-server, or older, legacy computer system methods; and (4) whether its controls are largely automated or require extensive human intervention. The exact nature of an application can also vary considerably. Although the emphasis of internal audits was once primarily over controls in accounting-related applications, internal auditors today should also review applications over other areas as well, such as manufacturing resource planning or loan portfolio analysis. All of these areas require knowledge of the application's specific attributes as well as the supporting technologies. That is, an internal auditor should understand how the application works by first documenting the IT applications, then defining specific audit test objectives, and finally performing a series of audit tests to verify that the application controls are in place and working as expected.

Besides the review of documentation and the walk-through, discussions with key user personnel and responsible systems personnel can aid the auditor's understanding. The amount of effort spent here depends both on the type of application reviewed and the number of users who can be of help. For example, a capital budgeting decision support application will probably have a small group of key users who have a thorough understanding of its procedures. A logistical support system, such as factory floor data collection, may be used by a large group where it may be difficult to identify the key system users.

A next step is to complete the documentation of the application for audit purposes. Internal audit should have been making workpaper notes throughout. The documentation procedure here is largely one of summarization where workpapers describe the understanding gained and include notes for potential follow-up review work.

Clarifying and Testing Audit Control Objectives

The previous section discussed the importance of establishing test objectives as part of an application review—the types of controls an auditor would expect to be in place for an application. The next step of clarifying the objectives of the review is often a major area where internal audit has been known to fail. Management may expect internal audit to review accounting controls, but an internal audit review may have put too much emphasis on logical security controls, giving less attention to other established control objectives. This misunderstanding of audit objectives becomes especially critical when the review is not typically in the auditor's more common realm of accounting applications. For example, if management has asked internal audit to review a new manufacturing resource planning system, its objectives could include validating internal accounting controls, reviewing for materials parts flow efficiencies, checking for system compliance with applicable regulations, or a combination of these. These should be summarized into a brief statement and discussed with both audit management and application user management.

Although the need for a clear statement of review objectives may appear to be an obvious early step, auditors often omit it. Of course, the objectives of an application review may change if internal audit encounters evidence of other control problems during the course of a review that would suggest audit scope or procedure changes. In a manufacturing resource review, for example, the initial objective of affirming the adequacy of the application's internal controls might change to one of fraud detection if potentially invalid transactions were encountered.

Internal audit should next test the key control points within the application. With limited compliance testing having already been done as part of gaining an understanding and the walk-through, these test procedures can now be expanded to make a more definitive assessment of the application's controls. In older and simpler batch-oriented systems, this task was fairly easy. Internal audit looked for input data acceptance controls, for any computer-processing decision points, and for output data verification controls. Since there are only a few processes associated with such an older batch application, today this identification of test procedures could often be accomplished with minimal analysis. Modern applications today with online updating, close integration with other applications, and sophisticated programming techniques all combine to make identifying test procedures difficult. Other factors include:

- Inputs to the application may have been generated by external sources, such as Web linkages, or from other applications at partner enterprises.
- Controls once performed by data input personnel are now built into programs.
- Modern optical scanning input devices and output documents with multidimensional barcodes make visual inspection difficult.
- Database files may be shared with other applications, making it difficult to determine where a change or transaction originated.
- The application may make extensive use of Web interfaces and will appear to be paperless to internal audit.

There are numerous other reasons why an internal auditor may have difficulty initially identifying IT application audit test procedures, and the application's description, along with key user discussions, should help to identify some of these controls. As a rule of thumb, an internal auditor should look for points where system logic or control decisions are made within an application and then develop test procedures to verify that those decision points are correct. These points include the key controls within an application, such as checks on the completeness of transactions or the accuracy of calculations. Exhibit 22.7 lists some typical test procedures oriented to more modern client-server applications.

Tests of Application Inputs and Outputs

In the very early days of IT auditing, many audit-related tests were little more than checks to verify that all inputs to a program were correctly accounted for and that the correct number of output transactions was produced based upon these inputs. An auditor's review of an automated payroll system is an example here. The internal auditor would test to determine that all time cards input were either accepted or rejected and

EXHIBIT 22.7 Sample IT Application Audit Test Procedures

The following are test procedures that an internal auditor might use when assessing IT application internal controls. Based on the nature and objectives of the application, these may not apply to all applications, and the auditor needs to have a detailed understanding of the application and its key internal controls before developing a test plan.

- *Foot key files.* Using available purchased software tools or CAATTs, determine that key data file values, reported total foot to supporting totals, and appropriate totals and balances are correct.
- *Test key calculations.* Using sample transactions, determine that results and totals are correct as predicted.
- *Consider running special audit-only updates.* Prepare a set of transactions covering key aspects of the application and arrange for a special, internal audit–controlled update. Review the results of the special internal audit–only update for controls and processing accuracy, and take care to remove the special audit-updated transaction-processed results from the production cycle.
- *Perform transaction balancing.* Using the transaction totals from a production process, independently calculate and reconcile audit control totals to reported application totals from the same cycle.
- *Review application logical security.* Review application's embedded security levels to determine that all users are granted proper levels of read and write access.
- *Document internal controls.* Test for controls of key documents (ID #s, etc.) to determine that updates can be traced back to their point of origination.
- *Review for unauthorized changes.* Review program library update logs, determine that application program versions on production libraries are the same as those retained in documentation files.
- *Assess contingency planning provisions.* Depending on audit risk, review the continuity and contingency planning provisions and review the results of any appropriate testing processes.

that the number of output payroll checks produced could be reconciled to those system input time cards. This was a test of system inputs and outputs.

Although time cards have gone away, automated applications have become much more complex, and many audit test procedures today are little more than those same tests of inputs and outputs. An internal auditor should examine the outputs generated from an application, such as invoices produced by a billing system, to determine that the input data and automated computations are correct. This type of audit test is limited in nature and will not cover all transactions or functions within an application.

The purpose of a control risk assessment or compliance test is to determine if application controls appear to be working. If all transactions or all data are to be reviewed, substantive testing procedures or tests of financial statement balances, as discussed in Chapter 10, should be used. The extent of this testing depends upon the audit objectives. For example, an external auditor will tend to perform compliance tests over those aspects of an application that cover financial statement–related internal accounting controls. An internal auditor may also want to perform compliance tests over other areas, such as the efficiency of administrative controls.

For older applications, tests of inputs and outputs are often quite easy to perform. The auditor would select a sample of input transactions and then determine that the number of inputs was equal to the count of processed items plus any rejected or error

EXHIBIT 22.8 Automated Purchasing System Compliance Tests Example

1. Select a series of purchase orders generated by the application reviewed and trace them back to either the requirements generated by the manufacturing system or by authorized manual purchase inputs, determining that all new purchase orders have been properly authorized.
2. From the sample, trace the purchase orders selected back to established records for vendor terms and prices, resolving any differences.
3. Select and trace a cycle of automated purchase orders to Web control logs to determine that all documents were transmitted without error and on a timely basis.
4. Using a sample of purchase orders received from the Web log, determine that vendors are documented through current, signed purchase agreements.
5. Select a sample of receiving reports and determine that the application is working properly by matching receipts to open purchase orders and accounts payable records.
6. Select a sample of recent accounts payable vouchers and any actual checks generated for parts and materials, tracing the payments to valid receiving reports and purchase orders.
7. Using sample transactions that were either held upon receipt for noncompliance with terms or improper timing, verify that transactions are handled correctly and per established procedures.
8. Balance a full cycle of purchase transactions from the manufacturing system providing inputs to the control logs, Web logs, and printed purchase order documents.

items. This type of audit test is not nearly as easy for today's applications, where the auditor often will not encounter a one-to-one relationship between inputs and outputs. Test transaction approaches, discussed next, are often much easier to perform and even more meaningful. Nevertheless, tests of inputs and outputs are sometimes useful for reviews of applications. Audit procedures for an example automated purchasing application compliance tests is outlined in Exhibit 22.8.

Test Transaction Evaluation Approaches

An internal auditor may want to ascertain that transactions entered into a system are correctly processed. For example, when reviewing a plant floor manufacturing application, an internal auditor might record several shop materials transactions as they are entered on manufacturing floor terminals, and after an overnight processing cycle, the auditor can verify that those transactions have correctly made adjustments to inventory records and that work-in-process cost reports have also been properly updated. This verification can take place by reviewing special retrieval reports against data files. As part of the test transaction process, an auditor can also test whether error screening controls are operating as described. The emphasis here should be on the testing of the error-verification routines within the application. Internal audit can select transactions input to an application that appear to be invalid and then trace them through the application to determine that they have been properly reported on exception reports. Internal audit can also consider submitting test error transactions to a system to verify that they are being properly rejected by the application.

Other Application Review Techniques

The computer-assisted audit tools can be useful in reviewing application controls. All too often, internal auditors use these tools to test some accounting control, such as an accounts receivable billing calculation, but not to evaluate other application controls. Audit software can match files from different periods, identify unusual data items, perform footings and recalculations, and simulate selected functions of an application. Other useful techniques are:

- **Reperformance of application functions or calculations.** This type of test is applicable for both the automated and the manual aspects of application systems. For example, if a fixed-assets application performs automatic depreciation calculations, internal audit can use automated tools to recalculate depreciation values for selected transactions as a compliance test.
- **Reviews of program source code.** For applications developed in-house, internal audit can verify that a certain logic check is performed within a program by verifying the source code. However, this type of compliance test should be used with only the *greatest amount of caution.* Because of the potential complexity of trying to read and understand program source code, it is very easy to miss a program branch around the area being tested. There are specialized programs available to compare program source code with the compiled versions in production libraries.
- **Observation of procedures.** Observations may be useful when reviewing both automated applications and manual processes. For example, a remote workstation receiving downloaded data from a central system may require extensive manual procedures in order to make the proper download connection. Internal audit can observe this on a test basis to determine if these manual procedures are being correctly performed.

Completing the Application Controls Review

Although compliance tests are powerful methods to test application controls, internal audit should be aware that this level of assurance is not absolute. There is a risk that an internal auditor may test an application control and find it to be working when in fact it does not normally work as tested. Because of the risks associated with such compliance tests, therefore, internal audit should always be careful to condition its audit report to management with a comment about the risks of incorrect results due to limited audit tests. Sometimes the controls tested do not appear to be working correctly because internal audit does not understand some aspects of the application system. Internal audit may want to review the application description and identification of controls to verify that they are correct. It may be necessary to revise internal audit's understanding of application controls and then to reperform the audit risk assessment procedures.

If internal audit finds through compliance testing that the application controls are not working, it will probably be necessary to report these findings. The nature of this report very much depends on the severity of the control weaknesses and the nature of the review. For example, if the application is being reviewed at the request of the external auditors, the identified control weaknesses may prevent them from placing any level of reliance on the financial results produced by the application. If the control weaknesses are primarily efficiency-related or operational, internal audit may want to just report them to IT management for future corrective action.

Applications can be primarily financial or operational. They can be implemented using purchased software, be custom-developed applications located on in-house systems with extensive database and telecommunications facilities, operate in a client-server environment, or exist in numerous other variations. As noted, this diversity makes it difficult to provide just one set of audit procedures for all applications. While internal audit can develop a general approach to reviewing most data-processing applications, it is usually necessary to tailor that approach to the specific features of a given application. The following section describes how an internal auditor might perform a review of a capital budgeting application operating in a client-server environment with telecommunication links through a network to a larger server.

22.5 APPLICATION REVIEW EXAMPLE: CLIENT-SERVER BUDGETING SYSTEM

As an application review example, assume internal audit has been asked to review the controls over an in-house client-server architecture capital budgeting system. The financial planning department has developed the capital budgeting analysis portion of the application using a popular desktop spreadsheet software package. Although it is built around a purchased software spreadsheet package, the users have coded a series of macro instructions for running the programs. The workstation portion of the system communicates with a server file containing mainframe budgeting system data.

Internal audit has been asked by management to review general controls over both local networks and their client-server computer operations. Following the audit procedures in Chapter 19, internal audit found that general controls in these areas were adequate. That is, users documented their desktop applications; adequate backups of files and programs were performed on server files; password procedures limited access to only authorized personnel; and other good control procedures were followed. Among internal audit's recommendations was to place stronger controls over telecommunications access to the local network and to install virus-scanning procedures.

Sometime after that general controls review, this capital budgeting system was implemented on the administrative office network. Because this system provides direct input to the corporate budgeting system, management has asked internal audit to review its application controls. After discussing this review request with senior and IT management, internal audit developed the following review objectives:

- The spreadsheet capital budgeting system should have good internal accounting controls.
- The application should properly make capital budgeting decisions based upon both the parameters input to the system and programmed macro formulas.
- The system should provide accurate inputs to the central or corporate budgeting system through the local file server.
- The capital budgeting system should promote efficiency within the financial planning department.

These objectives represent the general format for developing objectives for this type of internal audit review application. Management will often not state its objectives in quite these words but may be looking for performance or features objectives. It is the responsibility of internal audit to listen to management's requests and to translate them to review objectives, as in the example we just explained.

Reviewing Capital Budgeting System Documentation

Internal audit's first step should be to review the documentation available for this example application. Since it is built around a commercial desktop software product, internal audit might expect to find or should ask for some of the following:

- Documentation for the capital budgeting software package, including spreadsheet macro procedures, and formulas.
- Procedures for uploading capital budget data to the central system budgeting application through network server files, as well as procedures for accepting the input data to the mainframe IT function.
- Procedures to ensure the integrity of the data resident on server files. Internal audit will probably not find documented procedures covering exactly all of the five elements. However, there should be documentation covering the software product used, the interfaces with other applications, and the necessary manual procedures.

These materials should be reviewed to determine that they are complete and that internal audit has gained a general understanding of the overall application. Then, after reviewing this documentation and discussing it with its financial planning users, internal audit should describe the allocation for audit workpaper documentation purposes. Since the application is built around a spreadsheet software product, this description primarily covers its manual interfaces. Control descriptions over file server applications and their network connections to client systems have been covered as part of the previously mentioned general controls review. Auditors often find it convenient to describe such an application in the form of a flowchart, although a written description may be just as adequate. The purpose of this type of description is to provide internal audit with workpaper documentation of the application and to provide a basis for the identification of significant control points.

Identifying Capital Budgeting Application Key Controls

Although a rather simple but compact application, this example capital budgeting application has some critical control points. For example, if the spreadsheet macro procedures are incorrectly calculating capital costs, present values, and such related factors, management may very well take incorrect actions regarding their investment decisions. If data is incorrectly transmitted to the mainframe budgeting system, financial statement records may be incorrect. If the application is not properly documented, a change of key users in the financial-planning department may make the system nearly inoperable.

Based on internal audit's understanding of this example system, key system controls are now defined and documented. Here, because internal audit has recently performed

EXHIBIT 22.9 Capital Budgeting Application Input and Output Audit Tests

1. Develop a detailed understanding of all significant application input transactions—their nature, timing, and source.
2. Develop a strong understanding of transaction error correction procedures, both the nature of the tables or rules used for verification as well in any built-in system logic; determine that formal turnaround procedures exist to control any initial error items.
3. Using documentation or database descriptions, trace all input to output data flows with the application showing how many input elements (e.g., orders from the inventory application.) will change or modify other system elements and document this understanding in workpapers through audit data process flow diagrams (see Chapter 17.).
4. Determine that controls exist for comparing the number of items input to those that have been either accepted or rejected; review error identification procedures to determine if users can easily understand the cause and nature of any errors.
5. Review procedures for the correction and resubmission of rejected items; determine if errors are held in suspense files for analysis and corrective actions.
6. Develop a detailed understanding of all significant system output control totals and review the nature of supporting controls for a selected single application update processing cycle and from cycle to cycle.
7. Select an input update cycle for review, and if the number of items input, less any rejected errors, ties to application output control totals.
8. For the test cycle selected for review, determine that all error items from the cycle have been corrected, resubmitted, or received proper disposition.
9. Review control totals in the subsequent processing cycle to determine if file totals have remained consistent from one cycle to the next, investigating any discrepancies.
10. Review existing error suspense files to ascertain that all error items have been investigated and corrected in a timely manner; investigate any items remaining in the error cycle to determine reasons for any delays.
11. Review any preliminary concerns or errors with IT and responsible management to make any necessary changes to audit test procedures.
12. Document all testing activity in workpapers.

a general controls review, it is not necessary to reconsider those general controls during the application review. The audit review procedures can now be developed similar to those shown in Exhibit 22.9.

Performing Application Tests of Compliance

For the final step in this application review, internal audit should perform tests of the established audit procedures. Depending on management's and internal audit's relative interest in the application, it may not be necessary to test all of the controls as listed. Many are related to one another. If no problems or weaknesses are identified in one control area, internal audit may decide to pass on the related control areas. Some of the tests of application controls might include:

- **Reperformance of computations.** Capital budgeting is based on some very specific computations, such as the estimation of the present value of future cash flows based on discount factors. Using another spreadsheet tool or even a desk calculator, internal audit could select one or several present value computations generated by the system and recalculate them to determine the reasonableness of system processes. Any major differences should be resolved.

- **Comparison of transactions.** Internal audit can select several sets of application budget schedules and trace them through the file server budget system to determine that they have been correctly transmitted.
- **Proper approval of transactions.** Before any system-generated budget schedule is transmitted to the central budget system, it should have had proper management approvals. Internal audit should select a sample of them for review.

There are numerous other similar compliance tests that can be performed for such an application. The imaginative internal auditor will be able to perform these depending upon the nature of the audit and the objectives of management. Control weaknesses should be reported to management for corrective action.

22.6 AUDITING APPLICATIONS UNDER DEVELOPMENT

Many internal auditors recognize that it is much more efficient to review an IT application for its internal controls while it is being developed and implemented than after it has been placed into production. The role of the internal auditor here is similar to that of a building inspector reviewing a new construction project: it would be difficult to make constructive recommendations regarding the completed building. Even if some problems were found, the inspector would be under considerable pressure not to identify problems that would require significant portions of the building to be torn down and rebuilt. Rather, the building inspector identifies problems during construction and suggests how they can be corrected before completion. Similar to that building inspector, the effective internal auditor should also suggest corrective actions to improve system controls along the way. It is easier to implement changes during an application implementation process than after it has been completed and the system placed into production.

To continue with the analogy, an internal auditor must be careful not to take responsibility for *designing* the new application's controls. The building inspector points out problems but certainly does not take responsibility for a building's construction. The discussion on the foundations of internal auditing, in Chapter 1, emphasize that it is internal audit's task to review and recommend but not to design or build the controls in any area reviewed. When reviewing new applications under development, an internal auditor should point out internal control weaknesses to the application developers but only recommend they implement those recommendations.

Application development groups, user management, and auditors all tend to agree that, in reviewing new IT applications under development, internal audit provides another set of eyes to look at the new and soon-to-be-implemented application. This section offers approaches to reviewing new applications under development as well as a discussion of some of the pitfalls internal audit may encounter when attempting to do so.

Objectives and Obstacles of Application Preimplementation Auditing

When the concept of preimplementation reviews was first proposed by the then new profession of EDP auditors in the early 1970s, many traditional internal auditors were opposed to the approach. Traditionalists argued that if an auditor reviewed an application in advance of its implementation, it would be difficult to come back later and review that same application after implementation. The argument was that if an internal auditor had "blessed" the internal controls of a system under development, how could that same auditor come back later and perform a critical review? Over the years, internal auditors have grown to accept preimplementation reviews, acting as auditors and not consultants. Internal auditors, however, face four major obstacles when reviewing new applications under development:

1. **Them versus-us-attitudes.** Although internal audit and general management may both accept the concept, IT management may often express a wariness or even resentment when internal audit announces its plan to review an application that is under development and still has many details yet to be worked out. The announcement "Hello, I'm from internal audit, and I am here to help you" may not be favorably received. Good preimplementation review procedures can establish respect for internal audit's role and add value in the development process. An internal auditor who spends many hours reviewing a complex new application with some potential control-related issues and who concludes only with a "Documentation needs to be improved" recommendation will not be seen as having added much value to the process.
2. **Internal auditor role problems.** The internal auditor's role must be clearly understood by all parties and might be defined as one of the following:
   - **An extra member of the implementation team.** The systems design team invites the auditor to various design review meetings. However, that internal auditor will be more of an observer than a normal member of the design team. The auditor's objective is to gather data regarding key controls and processing procedures for a subsequent audit report.
   - **A specialized consultant.** Sometimes an internal auditor can become so involved in the systems design and development process that he or she is viewed as just another design team consultant making recommendations during the course of the implementation process. Internal audit should take care to not be viewed in that light. Following the standards for an internal auditor as an enterprise consultant, as discussed in Chapter 30, an internal auditor should act primarily as an independent reviewer providing help to the team, not as a specialized consultant who is part of the design process.
   - **An internal controls expert.** In any review, internal audit should always make certain that a review of internal controls is included in the new project. However, the auditor should not be the primary designer of those controls. Otherwise, he or she may have problems reviewing the completed application and its controls at some later date.

- **An occupant of the extra chair.** Sometimes an internal auditor does not do a proper level of preparatory work as part of a preimplementation review. Systems management may request an auditor to review various materials and attend design review meetings. An internal auditor who does not prepare but simply attends these meetings provides no real contributions. Nevertheless, if problems occur in the future, management may say, "But internal audit was there!"
- **State-of-the-art awareness needs.** New systems applications often involve new technologies or business processes. A general understanding of new technologies may require additional auditor homework to read vendor manuals and other documentation.
- **Many and varied preimplementation candidates.** The typical large enterprise may have a significant number of new application projects that are potential candidates for preimplementation reviews. These projects will all have different start times, durations, and completion dates. An internal auditor needs to perform an ongoing risk assessment to select the most appropriate new review candidates.

Despite these potential obstacles, there are strong reasons for an internal audit function to become actively involved in preimplementation reviews of major or critical new applications before they are placed into production. This is particularly true in today's era of major enterprise-wide applications that require detailed planning and testing in all areas of the enterprise.

Preimplementation Review Objectives

A key important objective of application preimplementation auditing is to identify and recommend controls improvements such that they can be potentially installed during the application development process. However, rather than just assuming that a new IT project is a given and then reviewing its controls, internal audit should also have an objective of reviewing the justification and definition of the new development project. There should be a good project management system in place that properly plans development steps and measures actual progress against those planned steps. For more major projects, internal audit can evaluate the adequacy of project development controls used for the particular application. This preimplementation phase also is an excellent time for an internal auditor to gain an understanding of the new application sufficient to design future automated audit tests. Whether it is an in-house or cloud-developed application or the implementation of a vendor package, internal auditors reviewing new applications under development should gain an overall understanding of all aspects of that application project.

Some internal auditors are faced with a statutory requirement for reviewing new applications under development. Several U.S. states and other countries have legislation requiring that all new significant state agency applications be reviewed by their internal audit departments for controls prior to implementation. Auditors in state governments can expect such legislation to appear in their own states in the future.

Preimplementation Review Problems

Preimplementation reviews often present internal audit with some very serious implementation problems, including a frequent challenge of too many review candidates given limited internal audit resources. Internal auditors sometimes make the mistake of announcing their intention of reviewing *all* new applications and all major modifications prior to their implementation. In a large enterprise, there may be dozens or even hundreds of user requests for new or major revision applications projects initiated regularly. Internal audit will find no time for comprehensive preimplementation reviews and only time for little more than nominal rubber-stamp approval signatures. To overcome these difficulties, internal audit should consider the following:

- **Selecting the right applications to review.** Auditors are faced with the problem of selecting only those applications of audit significance. Rather than rely on a simple value judgment or an arbitrary process, internal auditors should follow a risk-based, structured selection method for identifying those applications to review, similar to what was discussed in Chapter 15. A development group, for example, maybe working on applications A, B, and C. Given the relative application risks as well as limited audit time and resources, internal audit may decide to perform preimplementation reviews only for application B. However, if significant postimplementation problems appear in C, management might later second-guess internal audit and ask why system C had not been selected for review. An internal auditor with a consistent selection approach will be able to justify the decision to review B rather than C.
- **Determining the proper auditor's role.** As discussed, when an application has been selected for preimplementation review, internal audit can all too often become overly involved in its systems-development and implementation processes. Particularly for applications based on vendor software or developed with rapid application development methods, new IT projects require extensive user and systems development team efforts, with numerous design review meetings. While internal audit will often be asked to participate in these design review meetings, they may cause an auditor role problem. Actively involved in the typical design review meetings where design compromises may be negotiated, internal audit may find it difficult to comment on these same decisions later as audit points. However, if internal audit is excluded from design meetings, it may have a hard time performing the review. To be effective in reviewing new applications under development, the internal auditor's role needs to be carefully defined.
- **Review objectives can be difficult to define.** When an auditor informs the IT department that a given application has been selected for preimplementation review and requests supporting documentation, he or she may receive hundreds of pages of requirements studies, general design review documentation, meeting minutes, and other materials. Internal audit may then be asked to review and comment on this mass of materials. An audit objectives and control procedures approach can help an auditor choose the relevant materials to review.

Multiple implementation projects and new technologies present some major challenges to internal audit to perform effective IT application preimplementation reviews. However, whether for new applications developed in-house or installed purchased software, internal audit preimplementation reviews will add value to the internal controls environment in the enterprise. In addition, auditors, who have been accused in an old joke of being the ones who "join the battlefield after the action is over to shoot the wounded," can now play a proactive role in the application development process through preimplementation reviews.

Preimplementation Review Procedures

Many of the same audit procedures used in other reviews should be followed for reviews of new applications under development. All too often, internal auditors argue that applications under development are somehow different. However, as fluid and subject to ongoing developmental change as applications under development are, many of the same control objectives and procedures discussed previously for IT applications are still quite appropriate for these reviews. Auditors should tailor their preimplementation reviews along the various phases of a new project's development, starting at initial project initiation, to requirements definition, to development and testing, and finally to implementation. These same basic steps apply whether to a major application developed in-house, a vendor software package, or a user-led set of desktop applications. There will only be a difference in emphasis depending upon the application development approach.

When internal audit has selected a given application for preimplementation review, an important first step is to review the overall planned audit program with IT management so that there is an understanding of what the internal auditor expects to find, as well as the review approach. Some procedures may be tailored to fit a given application, but the objectives discussed in the next subsections should apply for most preimplementation reviews.

Application Requirements Definition Objectives

When possible, internal audit should get involved in a preimplementation review early in the development phase. Here, internal audit should review the detailed requirements study to determine the overall control status of the new application. If internal audit can identify control concerns during this phase of application development, it will be relatively easy for system designers to address and correct them.

Exhibit 22.10 is a set of audit procedures for the requirements definition phase of any project. Internal audit should look for similar requirements no matter how the new application is developed. Some of these procedures, of course, may require modification if the application under review is composed of specialized technologies or will be a major modification to an existing system. However, internal audit should perform control procedures necessary to satisfy all of the control objectives listed here.

Internal audit may need to decide if any special skills are required to complete the review. If the application involves the use of new or unique systems technologies and specialized supporting software, internal audit may want to enroll in training on the software product to be used—such as through classes offered by the vendor to the development staff—or internal audit may bring in someone with specialized skills or training.

EXHIBIT 22.10 Preimplementation Review Requirements Definition Checklist

Audit Step	REFERENCE
1. Obtain a general understanding of the IT department's system development methodology standards for both developing new applications and installing purchased software to assure an appropriate requirements definition study.	______
2. Obtain user approved request documentation authorizing the detailed application development or purchase.	______
3. Review detailed project plan for new application and ascertain, through discussions with IT and requesting users, that estimates of time and resources seem reasonable and achievable.	______
4. Determine there was an appropriate analysis, including cost and timing considerations, to determine whether the application should be built in-house or purchased/leased.	______
5. Determine if any special skills are needed to review application internal controls, such as RFID wireless connections or an understanding of ERP databases. If appropriate, arrange for internal audit staff members to learn new skills through seminars, etc.	______
6. Identify and review significant internal controls surrounding the new application. Discuss controls with both key users and IT to develop testing procedures.	______
7. If significant portions of the application involve in-house developed modules, assess whether appropriate consideration is given to purchase software alternatives.	______
8. Assess whether the impact of manual aspects of the application have been given proper consideration as part of the requirements definition, such as training needs or process changes.	______
9. If the application appears to be a candidate for automated testing procedures, begin preliminary audit planning for installation.	______
10. Review the extent of user sign-offs on the requirements study; based on selected interviews, assess whether users understand the new application and its ramification.	______

For example, with some large projects that take years to develop and implement, it can be effective to add a specialist to the staff to cover just the review of such a large project. At the completion of this phase, internal audit might write an informal audit report outlining any preliminary observations and concerns. In addition, workpapers should be started to document the new application controls procedures.

Detailed Design and Program Development Objectives

This is typically the longest phase of a new application project, and internal audit may want to schedule several reviews during this phase. While each of the periodic reviews should probably focus on a specific area of the new application development project, the overall purpose should be to satisfy some of the following questions:

- Does the detailed design comply with the objectives of the general requirements definition?
- Do users understand the controls and objectives of the new application under development?
- Has proper consideration been given to application controls and security?
- Is the application being developed according to the IT department's own systems development standards?
- Is the application development process supported by a well-organized project plan, similar to internal audit planning discussed in Chapter 16?
- Have any earlier audit recommendations been incorporated into the detailed design?

During this phase, care should be taken not to become too buried in detail. Some IT enterprises may attempt to use internal audit as a quality assurance function for the project. However, overall audit effectiveness will be diminished if internal audit's time is spent reviewing such things as compliance with detailed programming standards.

Reviews of this nature should be limited to periodic testing. Any control-related concerns encountered should be brought to the attention of management so that corrective action can be taken in a timely manner. If the new application is purchased software, there will often be limited in-house design and programming requirements. However, the IT enterprise may have to build file conversion programs, or interfaces with existing systems, or table files, or report generator definitions. These can represent major efforts, and internal audit still should review controls over the purchased software before it is installed and implemented.

Application Testing and Implementation Objectives

This phase includes testing of the new application, completion of documentation, user training, and conversion of data files. Internal audit often will be able to see if system controls appear to be working as expected and will want to test any embedded audit modules incorporated into the application. Exhibit 22.11 is a preimplementation review application testing checklist for this phase to help internal audit recommend whether the new application is ready for final implementation. Significant system control problems, coupled with management pressures to implement the application as soon as possible, can make this phase difficult. IT often promises to correct control problems in the new application during what it calls a "phase two." Auditors often find that because of other priorities, this promised phase two never seems to occur. Internal audit should consider the severity of such control problems and either document them for follow-up review or inform management of the need for corrective action during the current implementation.

At the conclusion of the application testing and implementation phase, the responsible auditor should prepare a final report that documents significant control issues identified by internal audit and subsequently corrected by the IT development function. This report should also outline any outstanding control recommendations that have not been implemented. While reports up to this point have been informal, this final report should follow normal audit department reporting standards, as discussed in Chapter 18.

EXHIBIT 22.11 Preimplementation Review Application Testing Checklist

Audit Preimplementation Step	Auditor Init.
1. Determine if a formal test plan exists, including an outline by key application modules detailing expected data conditions, the business rules tested, the type of test, and the expected results for each module condition tested.	______
2. Review the results of several recent unit tests to determine if results have been mapped to the test plan, exceptions researched, and errors corrected as appropriate.	______
3. Determine is the application being tested satisfies original application design requirements; if exceptions exist, determine they are properly documented, reviewed, and approved by key users.	______
4. Interview representative key users to understand their participation in the testing process; where participation appears to be lacking, discuss and document the need for user participation to assure successful implementations.	______
5. Review the extent of overall systems testing, including key interfaces with other applications and outside service providers.	______
6. If any original requirements have not been achieved by the completed application, assess procedures in place to determine whether to add procedures later or to otherwise allow for discrepancies.	______
7. If appropriate, initiate a series of internal audit developed test transactions that emphasize key controls, defined in earlier review steps; review the test results and assess application performance.	______
8. Summarize the results of application testing activities and make an internal audit recommendation for the appropriateness of the application implementation.	______

Postimplementation Review Objectives and Reports

Although the new application is no longer in development, this phase of a postimplementation audit is still important. The postimplementation review should take place shortly after a new application has been implemented and has had time to settle down. In other words, internal audit should perform the review after the users have had an opportunity to understand the application and information systems have had time to resolve any final implementation difficulties. The postimplementation review here determines if application design objectives have been met and if established applications controls are working. It also should look at project controls to determine if the application was completed within budget. Ideally, this review should be performed by another member of the audit staff to provide an independent assessment of the new application.

Internal audit departments should have a fairly formal procedure for issuing audit reports. Draft reports are prepared, auditees prepare their responses after some discussion and negotiation on the draft, and a final audit report is issued, with copies distributed to various levels of management (see Chapter 18). This audit report format is sometimes inappropriate for reviews of new applications under development. An individual internal controls problem with a particular program or output report, which may be identified by an auditor when performing a preimplementation review, can be corrected by the applications developer almost at once. There is little need to discuss such a finding in the format of a formal audit report draft. The control concern should have been corrected long before the audit report was issued. Audit and general management, which might expect the more formal audit report with its findings and recommendations, should both understand the special report format used for preimplementation reviews.

Informal, memo-type reports should be issued after each phase of the preimplementation reviews to discuss the scope of review activities and document any audit concerns. If some of the prior concerns have been corrected, the actions taken and current status of the controls issue should be discussed. Of course, internal audit should also develop workpaper documentation covering these review activities, which will serve both to document preimplementation activities and to provide a basis for later application reviews.

At the conclusion of the preimplementation review, internal audit should issue a formal audit report following board audit and department standards following the report formats discussed in Chapter 18. Where appropriate, this report can discuss preimplementation audit findings and corrective actions taken. However, the main function of this final report is to highlight outstanding control issues that still need to be corrected within the new applications system.

22.7 IMPORTANCE OF REVIEWING IT APPLICATION CONTROLS

Internal auditors should place a major emphasis on reviewing their supporting IT applications when performing reviews in other areas of the enterprise. Even though good general or interdependent IT control procedures may often be in place, individual applications controls may not all be very strong. An enterprise's applications may have been developed through a series of compromises among users or without any level of proper quality assurance. To evaluate IT application controls properly, internal audit needs a good understanding of both IT procedures and the specific control and procedural characteristics of each application area.

The effective internal auditor should spend a substantial amount of audit effort reviewing and testing controls over specific IT applications as well as new applications in the development process. Such reviews will provide assurance to general management that applications are operating properly, and to IT management that their design and controls standards are being followed, allowing them to place greater reliance on the output results of such applications. An understanding of application control reviews should be a key component in the modern internal auditor's CBOK toolkit.

NOTES

1. Developed in the 1960s, the computer programming language COBOL stands for *COmmon Business Oriented Language*, and it is still used today as a key programming language for systems on many types and sizes of computers and applications.
2. There are numerous textbooks and references describing object-oriented programming. A search engine such as Google will provide many further references.

CHAPTER TWENTY-THREE

Cybersecurity, Hacking Risks, and Privacy Controls

IN TODAY'S WORLD OF WEB-DOMINATED IT systems as well as ever more complex networked and wireless communications, security and privacy controls over data and information are important for enterprises as well as individual systems users. Almost every day we hear about, or sometimes experience ourselves, situations where our key systems files and data have been improperly accessed or hacked, or vital personal files and records have been stolen, altered, or given to an unauthorized perpetrator. Some of these, what we call *cybersecurity* breaches, are often simply the result of poor internal controls, but others are the products of highly sophisticated data penetration schemes. While such complex cybersecurity breaches are beyond the technical skills of many to forestall, others can be prevented by strong IT cybersecurity controls, which make up a very important area of internal audit IT controls concerns.

This chapter describes some of the more significant cybersecurity issues and risks of today and discusses IT cybersecurity and privacy controls in two broad areas. First, we will focus on some of the many cybersecurity and privacy threats that internal auditors should consider in their reviews of IT-based systems and processes. We have limited our focus to only "some" of these process areas because the field of IT security controls is vast and sometimes raises highly technical issues beyond the skills of many internal auditors. Nevertheless, all internal auditors should have a general CBOK understanding of these risks and effective internal control procedures.

The chapter will discuss some effective cybersecurity control processes that internal auditors can review and recommend in their work. We also will introduce the NIST (National Institute of Standards and Technology) cybersecurity framework, an effective tool to help manage enterprise cybersecurity issues. Cybersecurity today goes beyond the traditional four walls around the IT operations center and includes such matters as effective vendor management where an outside contractor or other entity may be using enterprise IT resources and can pose an additional cybersecurity risk.

The chapter includes a summary of the *Payment Card Industry Data Security Standard (PCI DSS)*, a guideline that has been developed by major credit card companies such as Visa and American Express to help enterprises that process card payments prevent fraud and to provide some protection from various credit security vulnerabilities and threats. Because credit cards are so pervasive, an enterprise processing, storing, or transmitting payment card data must now be PCI DSS compliant or risk losing their ability to process credit card payments. Internal auditors should understand the high-level key elements of this standard and incorporate it in their reviews where appropriate.

The chapter will conclude with a discussion of cybersecurity and privacy controls that should be part of internal audit departmental and operating procedures. Following the old saying that "the shoemaker's children have no shoes," internal audit functions sometimes fail to implement appropriate security and privacy protection controls over their own internal audit processes. This includes adequate controls over audit evidence materials, internal audit workpapers, auditor laptop computer resources, and many others. While every audit department is different, this chapter will suggest best practices for an internal audit function.

Because there is a great level of complexity to IT cybersecurity practices, most internal auditors may not view themselves as technical experts in many of these areas. Many of these concerns, though, just require a good understanding of effective internal control processes as discussed throughout this book. All internal auditors should acquire a high-level common body of knowledge (CBOK) understanding of cybersecurity risks, related internal controls, and preventive mechanisms. Also, an internal auditor should understand when he or she needs to seek the help and advice of seasoned security experts when performing internal audits.

23.1 HACKING AND IT NETWORK SECURITY FUNDAMENTALS

We do not hear much about major bank robberies today. In past times, when bank vaults held large amounts of cash and were locked up at night but open and protected by guards during the day, it was not uncommon for gangsters to arrive at a bank, overpower staff and guards, and depart carrying bags of cash from the vault. Today the environment is very different. While a bank may control a huge amount of assets, they are only recorded on computer files so a potential thief cannot easily stage a holdup and run off with a bag full of cash. In addition, where the bank does have some cash potentially subject to theft, there are extremely strong controls in place, including surveillance cameras, the ability to trace currency serial numbers, and a wide variety of other controls.

Today most of those financial records and related assets are carried and stored as electronic records protected by password-based security systems, but they can be easily converted to cash if a perpetrator is able to penetrate the password controls and access these key electronic records. Perpetrators usually gain access to these electronic records through what is called *hacking*, a systems violation by someone who seeks and exploits weaknesses in a computer system or computer networks. The term goes back to the early days of small microcomputer systems and has had many subvariations. However, for an internal auditor and many enterprise managers, hacking means the improper access and theft of IT systems files and records.

Internal auditors should have an understanding that IT security procedures today are sometimes a little closer to those past days of bank robberies. It is sometimes easy for a perpetrator to gain electronic access to valuable data records without detection or at least any level of active surveillance. The thief can sometimes directly download this valuable data over the Internet or a wireless network without an immediate trace in order to use it for criminal purposes. The IT thief may also be taking assets more valuable than just cash, such as credit card authorization numbers that will allow massive purchases elsewhere, passwords to gain access to other even more valuable systems, or even the identities of people to then use for further fraudulent transactions.

Lacking proper internal control procedures, an enterprise's IT systems hardware, software, and data may face any or all four of the following basic classes of IT threats:

1. **Interruptions.** A system asset can become lost, unavailable, or unusable through the malicious destruction of a program, theft of a hardware component, or improper use of network resources.
2. **Interceptions.** An outside party, such a person, program, or renegade computer system, can gain access to an IT file or other assets. An example of this type of threat may be a rogue Internet program that gains access to key files and downloads their contents to another party. Interceptions can often take place with few traces and can in the short run be difficult to detect.
3. **Modification.** Here, an unauthorized intruder not only accesses but makes changes to data, programs, or even hardware components. While modifications can often be quickly detected, in some cases they can go on almost unnoticed.
4. **Fabrication.** This threat occurs when an unauthorized person introduces counterfeit objects into an IT environment. These might include spurious transactions to a new work communications system or inserting records in an established database.

These threats were serious in the earlier days of large legacy IT systems with batch transactions, major usage mass storage disk and tape drives, and limited fixed-line telecommunications connections. They have risen exponentially in our current environment of the Internet, wireless communications, enterprise resource planning (ERP) databases, and computing devices ranging from sophisticated server systems to small handheld devices. Internal auditors reviewing internal controls in these environments should be aware of these systems and processes.

Just as IT systems have become more sophisticated and better controlled, threats against them have also increased. On a regular basis, we see press accounts of some computer security breach and the theft or destruction of sensitive data. As a single example and certainly not a unique one, during the November and December 2013 holiday shopping season in the United States, the retailer *Target Corporation* discovered that perpetrators had hacked into its IT systems and stolen credit card information from 40 million customers, and taken other personal information from about 70 million customers as well. As this book went to press, Target had already incurred a $61 million loss in attempting to correct matters and was subject to 90 major lawsuits, with almost certainly more to come.

The Target breach was national in scope and happened in all of its stores, not just online, and involved tampering with the machines customers use to swipe their cards when making purchases. Although Target had its own security processes, it subcontracted some IT services to an outside vendor who was given access to Target's systems. A perpetrator breached that subcontractor's controls and gained access to Target's card scanning processes. The importance of establishing third-party vendor controls will be discussed below.

Just as bank robbers in the old days ran off with stolen cash, sometimes in small bills that were never to be recovered, the perpetrator who has thousands and thousands of credit card numbers and other personal information can use them in ways that are difficult to trace. The Target theft took place over the weeks before and after the holiday shopping season. The data was stolen through the daily transfers of sales data from many of the company's stores. Target might not have initially detected this breach because to it the daily sales transmittals from stores over a communications network seemed to show no problems. The perpetrators just made duplicate copies of the personal sales data for their own use.

This is just one example of the many computer security breaches that occur worldwide regularly. Many of these involve highly technical exploitations of what might appear to be good internal technical controls. Internal auditors may not have the technical skills to assess security risks in many of these IT environments and to make appropriate technical recommendations, but they should still have a basic CBOK understanding of computer security concepts for use in a wide range of internal audit reviews.

23.2 DATA SECURITY CONCEPTS

Enterprise data, whether it is customer account data located in a major data server center ERP system database or field data collected on a staff member's laptop, needs to be protected. Although there can be multiple variations and configurations, Exhibit 23.1 illustrates some basic data security concepts, showing four ways that IT data should be protected. Not all of these modes are necessary for all data, but internal auditors may find it useful to think of data security along these lines.

In some instances, data may require some basic confidentiality protections. As the exhibit illustrates, the control emphasis here is not on confidentiality and integrity threats through the outside protective walls; rather, availability controls are needed to protect programs and data. The extreme example of data confidentiality here is the building cornerstone where some key records are sealed in a foundation stone and never seen again while the building is standing. We no longer construct buildings with that level of permanence, and a foundation cornerstone generally does little good in most situations today. The data must be available in a protected, confidential manner. Although there always can be threats, the data should be protected from any unexpected spillage or seepage.

Data integrity is a great concern. For any data repository, there are always outsiders who try to breach the wall to gain access. In our Target example earlier, a perpetrator gained access to customer data and destroyed its integrity by making unauthorized

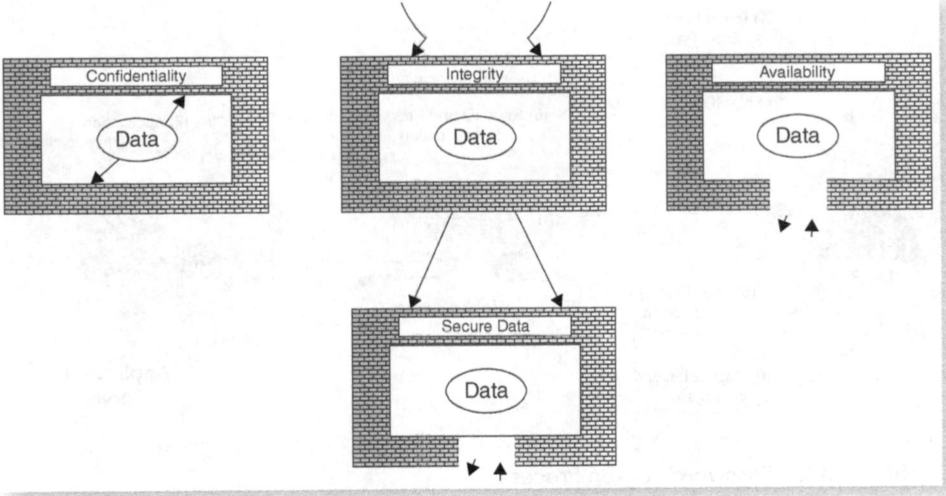

EXHIBIT 23.1 Data Security Concepts

copies. While the wall of confidentiality is important, the data generally must become available to others. This is a two-way portal, and the programs and processes controlling the data should make it available only to proper, authorized sources. Password-type controls are very important here and are discussed in the following sections.

The bottom case in Exhibit 23.1, secure data, combines the other three strategies into a secure data environment. Two other data security concepts are very important here, including what are known as firewalls and protections against *viruses*. Both of these are discussed further in later sections. Although this exhibit is quite conceptual, internal auditors should think about computer security in terms of the three concepts of confidentiality, availability, and integrity.

23.3 IMPORTANCE OF IT PASSWORDS

Passwords are a basic IT control in which a user of a system or data must enter some personal code or password known only to that user to gain access to the IT resource. There can be other, more complex configurations than the basic IT password log-on exchange shown in Exhibit 23.2; internal auditors should look for this type of process in their internal control reviews. A user enters a password to gain application acceptance, but if the password is incorrect, system access is denied.

When reviewing IT applications' internal controls, an internal auditor should always look for the effective use of passwords. The IT security literature is filled with guidance on the use of passwords, and some best practices in the use of IT passwords include:

- Passwords are a user's responsibility to create, but administrative rules should be established to make them hard for others to guess. For example, controls and

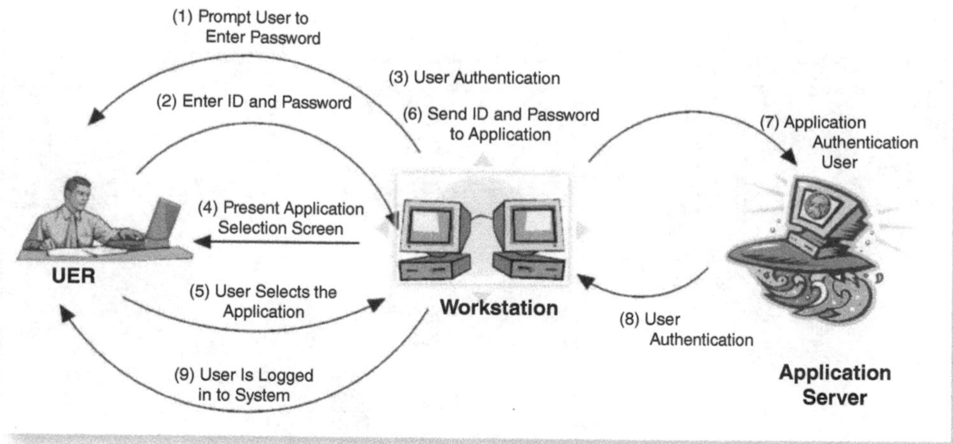

EXHIBIT 23.2 Password Log-on Process

guidance should be in place to prevent the use of employee birth dates or nicknames as passwords.

- Passwords should be structured such that they are difficult to easily guess. For example, IT security can set rules requiring a mix of upper- and lowercase letters and numerals in a password.
- Processes should be in place to require frequent password changes. Sometimes computer operating systems administer this control; if not, procedures should otherwise be in place requiring regular password changes.
- Processes should be in place to monitor passwords, deny access after perhaps two or three invalid password attempts, and allow passwords to be reset through an administrative procedure. These processes also should allow a user to receive a replacement if a password has been forgotten.
- Systems that generate or require extremely long or complex passwords should never be installed. If passwords are too complex and difficult to remember, users will write them down and post them as a reminder, and the purpose of a confidential password will be lost.
- Strong enterprise people-oriented procedures should be in place on the use of passwords. That is, guidance should prohibit the sharing of passwords or storing them in easy-to-see places.

The effective use of passwords is an important IT security authentication control. There are other authentication systems, such fingerprint or even iris scanners for some highly sensitive applications, but effective password systems are perhaps the best for regular business applications. Internal auditors should be aware of the requirements for good password controls and should look for effective password systems as part of their many reviews of IT application internal controls. Internal auditors should always keep in mind that passwords are a first line of defense for protecting an IT resource. They should be kept secure and private, changed frequently, and their usage and improper access attempts monitored.

23.4 VIRUSES AND MALICIOUS PROGRAM CODE

A computer virus is typically a very small computer program routine that can make multiple copies of itself and infect another computer without permission or knowledge of the user. The term *virus* is used because it is the kind of program that can attach itself to another system and then spread itself to others as they come in contact with that same set of virus code. A virus can only spread from one computer to another when the virus code is taken to some other uninfected computer, for instance, by a user sending it over a network or the Internet, or by carrying it on a removable medium such as a CD or a USB drive. Viruses can also spread to other computers by infecting files on a network file system that is accessed by another computer.

Computer viruses first came into the world in what was called the ARPANET, the early 1970s forerunner of the Internet. Someone—the identity of the author is subject to speculation—introduced a program on the network that displayed the message I'M THE CREEPER: CATCH ME IF YOU CAN, which began to appear on many ARPANET system programs.

In the early 1980s days of Apple II and IBM PC desktop computers, viruses reappeared on the floppy disks that were used to share programs and data from computer to computer. Although the Creeper messages were perhaps viewed as cute by some early users, virus programs soon began to become malicious. For example, some of the early viruses inhabited and took over the memory space of someone's computer, and then were ready to move to another if the infected user tried to solve the problem by sending a floppy disk to another system to seek help. We often forget that these were the days when a popular system such as the Apple II had only 32 KB of memory, and blocking that memory disabled the system.

As time passed, viruses became even more nasty and destructive, and the term *malware* was introduced as a name for bad or dangerous software. Some are Trojan horses, a type of malware named after Greek mythology, that attach to a computer and then sit silently until some date or event is met. Another example is called a logic bomb, an unknown program that only triggers when some other event occurs. As an example, a programmer worried about being fired could insert a logic bomb routine into the employer's payroll system to delete all systems files if that programmer's ID is ever deleted from payroll records.

Exhibit 23.3 lists some of the more common types of malicious code. There are many other examples of and stories about new types of malware, but the objective of this chapter is not to describe such incidents. An Internet search will provide an extensive list of other current malicious malware types. The software industry has responded to these malware threats with a variety of commercial products that constantly monitor for bad software and when it is encountered either block it or repair the bad program code. There are evidently many people around the world who are constantly trying to build more complex and difficult-to-detect malware routing, and the virus prevention software vendors are working just as fast to catch their code and prevent introductions.

Malware threats have evolved into a wide range of increasingly widespread and often quite sophisticated cybersecurity risks given our heavy dependence on and use of all types of IT systems. A significant threat has been the explosion of tactics designed

EXHIBIT 23.3 Types of Malicious Program Code

Code Type	Characteristics
Virus	Attaches itself to programs and propagates copies of itself to other programs.
Trojan Horse	Contains unexpected functionality that later performs a disguised function.
Logic Bomb	Program that only triggers when some other specified event occurs.
Time Bomb	Program that only triggers when some other specified time period is met.
Trapdoor	Undocumented software entry point that circumvents system protections.
Worm	Propagates copies of itself through a network.
Rabbit	Software code that replicates itself again and again without limit to exhaust the resource.
Scareware	Sometimes called ransomware, can lock up software and then demand a ransom.

to trick users into divulging their usernames, passwords, and other confidential information, which can then be used to commit crimes based on identity fraud. A goal of some of these malware threats has been to clean out the victim's bank account, and the information is also often used to help perpetrators commit further fraud and gain unauthorized access to networks.

Internal auditors should recognize that software viruses are a constant threat and look for the effective implementation of antivirus software for every computer system reviewed, whether it is a corporate-level central IT system or a business laptop. An internal auditor should determine that a current version of the software protection software is installed, that it is regularly updated, and that actions are taken when viruses are detected. Policies and software controls should be in place to restrict unauthorized software from being introduced into IT systems operations, whether in the form of attempts to download unauthorized programs from the Internet or flash drives and CDs that employees want to load on their home laptops.

23.5 SYSTEM FIREWALL CONTROLS

A common type of IT software security is called a systems firewall, a software process that filters traffic between protected "inside" and less protected or untrusted "outside" environments. It is a specialized type of software that either allows or prevents certain types of transactions. Exhibit 23.4 is an example of a very simple firewall configuration. An enterprise needs to install firewalls both between its systems network and the outside world through the Internet or other resources. Firewalls monitor traffic, route some to designated network locations, and block others.

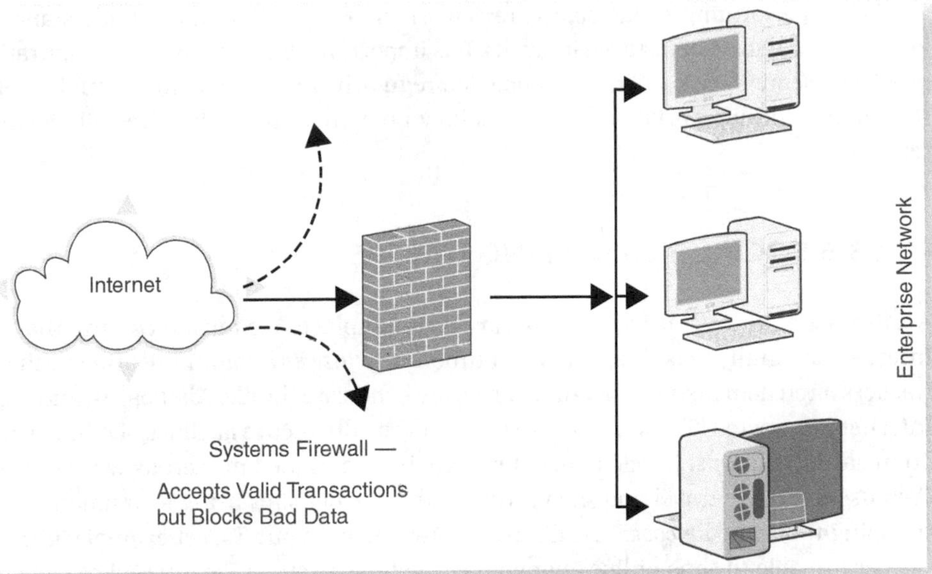

EXHIBIT 23.4 Firewall Diagram

Firewalls are often set up as what is called a screening router, a proxy gateway, or a guard. From an internal audit perspective, however, rather than understanding the technical details of the configurations, internal auditors should ask questions and determine how firewalls have been installed in the enterprise area reviewed. For example, screening router configuration firewalls can be used when an enterprise has, for example, three local area networks (LANs), one for its corporate offices, one for U.S. operations, and a third for European Union (EU) facilities. Corporate is allowed to send and receive messages to both facility LANs, but perhaps the United States and EU are only allowed to send certain specified things to corporate and are not allowed full access across the two facility LANs.

Similarly, a proxy gateway firewall is used when an enterprise wants to set up online price lists and product offerings for outsiders, but prevent those outsiders from modifying the price and product information or accessing supporting files connected with the product offerings. Another configuration, a guard firewall, is used when an enterprise allows its employees to access most areas of the Web, but prohibits access to such things as sports scores or online gambling sites.

In addition to screening or monitoring network addresses and Web addresses, firewalls can also monitor the specific content in a message or Web page. They can audit this activity and even report improper access attempts. Firewalls must be correctly configured, but the configuration must be regularly updated for the internal and external environments. Firewalls protect an environment only if they control all access to a network perimeter. For example, if a firewall was set up to control all access to a LAN but if one of the devices on that LAN had a dial-up modem connection, security could be breached. Firewalls are strong security controls, but are often the targets of penetrators.

When performing a data security review, an internal auditor should understand the location and nature of installed firewalls. It is important that the firewall configuration provides adequate protection and is updated regularly. In addition, an internal auditor should look for appropriate review and follow-up activity regarding firewall violation reports.

23.6 SOCIAL ENGINEERING IT RISKS

As discussed, Internet privacy threats are commonplace. We must recognize that the Internet originally was designed as an inherently *insecure* communications vehicle. Hackers often demonstrate that they can easily penetrate the files, databases, and other Internet-connected IT resources in the most physically secure facilities of military and financial institutions. In addition, enterprises have designed numerous ways to track Web users as they travel and shop throughout Internet sites using a common cyber-snooping tool called a *cookie*. As discussed previously in our Target example, identity thieves are able to shop online anonymously using the credit identities of others, and Web-based information brokers can sell sensitive personal data, including Social Security numbers, relatively cheaply.

Software products such as Facebook and Twitter started out as personal software tools but are now found in many enterprise workplaces. These as well as the growth of smartphones have changed the overall complexion of IT systems and have introduced a wide range of *social engineering* IT risks and concerns. Many of these involve a perpetrator gaining confidential information through some kind of a "friendly" but improper access attempt. New terminology appears regularly, but IT social engineering perpetrators often use one of the methods highlighted in Exhibit 23.5.

There has been extensive media coverage of these issues, with a growing public awareness of online privacy issues. Some form of U.S. Internet privacy law is expected to be passed in the coming years that will provide strong consumer protections in this area. Although our comments are speculative, such legislation could mandate that every commercial web site provide a privacy policy, clearly explain its data collection practices, and provide meaningful ways for visitors to prevent their personal data from being captured and sold to other enterprises.

Criminals frequently are looking for social engineering ways to dupe a user and steal that user's identity. Effective controls are not necessarily very complex. For example, users should beware of e-mail messages with a URL address in them asking the recipient to contact the sender via that Internet link. A very simple control is to always call the supposed sender, using a number from the phone book or online, to confirm they sent the message before responding via the Internet. Failing to respond in that manner lessens the chance of having one's identity and authentication information stolen or bank account rifled.

Internal auditors should be aware that these evolving IT social risks and issues are a growing concern. While it is an enterprise's responsibility to educate their user community and warn people to avoid such frauds, internal auditors should be aware of such schemes and look for appropriate warnings when asked. Many of these vulnerabilities can be triggered by an individual enterprise employee just trying to do the right thing

EXHIBIT 23.5 IT Social Engineering Security Risk Methods

Code Type	Characteristics
Baiting	Attacker leaves a malware-infected CD-ROM or USB flash drive in a location sure to be found (bathroom, elevator, sidewalk, parking lot, etc.), gives it a legitimate-looking and curiosity-piquing label, and simply waits for the victim to use the device.
Phishing	The attempt to acquire sensitive information such as usernames, passwords, and credit card details (and sometimes, indirectly, money) by masquerading as a trustworthy entity in an electronic communication.
Pretexting	The practice of deceiving individuals into surrendering personal information for fraudulent purposes.
Quid Pro Quo	An attacker calls random numbers at a company, claiming to be calling back from technical support. Eventually this person will hit someone with a legitimate problem, grateful that someone is calling back to help them. The attacker will "help" solve the problem and, in the process, have the user type commands that give the attacker access or launch malware.
Shoulder Surfing	Involves observing an employee's private information over his or her shoulder. This type of attack is common in public places such as airports, airplanes, or coffee shops.
Tailgating	An attacker, seeking entry to a restricted area secured by unattended, electronic access control (e.g., by RFID card), simply walks in behind a person who has legitimate access. Following common courtesy, the legitimate person will usually hold the door open for the attacker or the attackers themselves may ask the employee to hold it open for them. The legitimate person may fail to ask for identification for any of several reasons, or may accept an assertion that the attacker has forgotten or lost the appropriate identity token.

by responding, for example, to a legitimate-looking e-mail asking for help. There is a need for strong enterprise education programs that outline risks here and the steps to take to report suspicious activity.

Malicious code, passwords, and firewalls are only a few of the many security issues that IT systems and networks face today. Others include elaborate access controls, the need to use encryption when transmitting data, multilevel security in database administration, and many more. From an internal audit perspective, some of the most important computer security issues center on the need to establish strong management support for the IT security programs in place and on overall stakeholder education programs concerning IT network security threats and vulnerabilities.

Whether it is an active program to monitor for malware software, the placement of firewalls, or other issues, internal auditors should have a good CBOK general understanding of network and cybersecurity control procedures in their ongoing IT internal control reviews. In many respects, as these issues become more technically complex, the IT security risks increase. Internal auditors may not be strong IT security specialists, and they should always be able to request help from the enterprise IT organization's security specialists.

23.7 IT SYSTEMS PRIVACY CONCERNS

Privacy is the expectation that confidential personal information disclosed in a private place will not be disclosed to third parties, when that disclosure would cause either embarrassment or emotional distress to a person of reasonable sensitivities. *Information* should be interpreted broadly to include images (e.g., digital images, photographs) and text. It certainly covers all aspects of IT systems and networks.

In our complex world of IT networks, Internet-connected systems, and ever-advancing technologies, privacy issues on many levels are growing concerns. There are multiple issues here about how much personal data and information individuals should allow to be given to interested enterprises, government authorities, and even other individuals. Similarly, from a privacy and security perspective, an enterprise wants adequate levels of protection. Two U.S. laws, the Health Insurance Portability and Accountability Act (HIPAA) and the Gramm-Leach-Bliley Act, establish some privacy-based rules that internal auditors should be aware of, and there are other IT-related privacy issues that belong on an internal auditor's radar screen. In some instances, these are just evolving issues, but internal auditors should at least be aware of them as they perform internal control reviews, particularly in IT network–related areas. The following sections describe some evolving privacy issues in today's world of network cybersecurity concerns (though these issues are not always internal control audit ones).

Data Profiling Privacy Issues

As part of everyday life, data is collected from individuals and enterprises, frequently without their consent and often without their realization. For individuals, data is collected and stored in a computer system where:

- Bills paid with credit cards leave a data trail consisting of the purchase amount, type, date, and time.
- The use of supermarket discount cards creates a comprehensive database of all consumer purchases.
- Data is collected when a car equipped with a radio transponder from an electronic toll-collection system passes through an electronic tollbooth. The owner's account with the toll-collection company is debited and a record is created of the location, date, time, and account identification.
- We leave a significant data trail when we surf the Internet and visit web sites.
- Data also is collected when we subscribe to a magazine, sign up for a newsletter, join a professional association, fill out a warranty card, give money to charities, donate to a political candidate, tithe to a religious organization, invest in a mutual fund, make a telephone call, or interact with a government agency. With all of these transactions we leave a data trail that is stored in some computer file.

We are not yet to the point where the contents of all these many databases can be easily merged, but in the aftermath of the 9/11 terrorist attacks, U.S. government and law enforcement authorities proposed the development of an airline traveler screening program that would compile information from many consumer data files. That proposal was highly controversial and was not implemented, but a limited version could be developed in the future.

The legal protections for data privacy vary across the world. In the United States they are weak, and the unfettered collection of data from numerous sources, in an environment where there are few legal restrictions on how the data can be used and merged, can violate privacy and trample on civil liberties. There are few restrictions in the United States on how data can be collected and merged, although stronger laws exist in EU countries, Canada, New Zealand, and Australia. Internal auditors should have a general understanding of these issues.

Online Privacy and E-Commerce Issues

There has been extensive media coverage of online privacy issues. Starting with the Electronic Communications Privacy Act, passed in the United States in 1986, a variety of privacy laws have been enacted over the years, including the Cyber Intelligence Sharing and Protection Act and the Computer Fraud and Abuse Act. None of these laws has fully kept up with changing technology, and all suffer from financial freedom advocates' criticisms. Other U.S. Internet privacy laws may be passed in the coming years that will provide strong consumer protections in this area, and internal auditors should be aware of these changing rules. While our comments are speculative, such legislation could mandate that every commercial web site provide a privacy policy and require that commercial web sites clearly explain their data collection practices and provide meaningful methods for visitors to prevent their personal data from being captured and sold to other enterprises. Internal auditors should be aware of any evolving issues here. Knowledgeable individuals can take steps to prevent their Web-surfing practices from being captured by the web sites they visit. But, realistically, few people have the requisite knowledge or patience to take advantage of such privacy-enhancing strategies.

Radio Frequency Identification (RFID)

When consumers wave their keychain or an embedded credit card in front of the gasoline pump's meter to automatically pay for fuel, they are likely using radio frequency identification (RFID) technology. Attached to the keychain or card is a small data chip that contains a radio frequency ID sensor. RFID technology also is frequently used in building access cards (ID cards that enable individuals to gain entry to a building or to an office area within a building). Yet another application is the employee identification cards issued by many companies. These are often called contactless ID cards because the user need only wave the card within a few inches of the reader in order to gain entry to the building or office.

In the applications described here—paying for fuel and gaining entry into a secured building—the individual is well aware of each and every use in which the RFID tag is accessed. But RFID tags are tiny and can be embedded in items in ways that are virtually invisible. And reading devices can also be invisible. In the future, RFID readers could possibly be embedded in streetlight poles, and an RFID tag associated with an individual—perhaps embedded in one's driver's license—could record the transactions that person engages in throughout each day, such as buying a newspaper at the corner vending machine, purchasing groceries, using public transit, entering the workplace, and so on. If RFID tags were embedded in driver's licenses, which most people carry with them at all times, we could live in a society where location privacy and anonymity are a thing of the past.

Could such a scenario actually happen? Many people find it hard to imagine that we would allow such uses of RFID to actually occur. However, this is an example of the types of evolving concerns that internal auditors might confront. The challenge for many internal auditors performing reviews in these areas is that auditee management and their staffs may have different expectations. There should be a high level of concern about some of the privacy issues discussed throughout this chapter.

U.S. Federal Privacy Protection Laws

Citizens of most developed countries enjoy rights to privacy through laws that are called data protection acts. In most such nations, comprehensive, or omnibus, data protection laws govern how personal information can be used by government agencies as well as commercial-sector entities. The use of personal information is usually an opt-in or opt-out personal decision under most such laws. In other words, an individual's personal information cannot be used, say, for marketing unless that person gives affirmative consent.

The United States has no such law, but there are multiple laws covering specific industry sectors, such as the Telephone Consumer Protection Act (telemarketing), the Fair Credit Reporting Act (credit reports and employment background checks), the previously referenced HIPAA (medical records privacy), and other financial privacy rules. Gaps here leave many uses of personal information unprotected. For example, the junk mail one often receives when subscribing to magazines is not covered by a specific law.

The privacy approach taken in the United States is referred to as an opt-out right. For example, a consumer's personal information is used to send them unsolicited ads until and unless the consumer signs up to stop this through the direct marketing industry's Mail Preference Service (MPS). And even that does not guarantee that your mailbox will be junk free. The MPS is a voluntary standard. Although members of the Direct Marketing Association must subscribe to it as a condition of membership, not all companies that market to individuals are members. Most internal auditors need only to witness the spam in their e-mail inboxes to understand this point.

23.8 THE NIST CYBERSECURITY FRAMEWORK

The U.S. government's National Institute for Standards and Technology (NIST) has been responsible for developing standards and guidelines in many areas over the years and, more recently, some IT-related guidance material. In early 2014, NIST released its cybersecurity framework, a risk-based compilation of guidelines designed to help enterprises assess their current capabilities and to draft a prioritized road map toward improved cybersecurity practices. Similar to the COSO internal control framework introduced in Chapter 3, this NIST document is not a standard requirement but rather a set of recommended best practices to help enterprises better understand and internal auditors to review enterprise cybersecurity controls.

As an area where internal auditors can assist in their assessment activities, the NIST framework calls for IT and management to initially assess the quality of their cybersecurity practices. Once this assessment is completed, an enterprise can use NIST's criteria to improve its cybersecurity posture and develop an enterprise cybersecurity target profile. Each enterprise will have unique requirements based on its industry, customers, and business partners. The NIST target profile can identify gaps that should be closed to enhance cybersecurity practices and provide the basis for a prioritized road map to help achieve improvements. Exhibit 23.6 outlines NIST's recommended layers of cybersecurity maturity. The idea here is for an enterprise IT function to use these tiers to take a good hard look at where it stands on cybersecurity maturity and where the next need to go. Implementation tiers help create a context that enables organizations to understand how their current cybersecurity risk management capabilities stack up against the characteristics described by the framework. That is, if an internal audit review indicates that an enterprise is currently only at Tier 1, it is often most effective to take steps to move to Tier 2 rather than try to jump straight to Tier 4.

In reviewing where an enterprise's cybersecurity maturity and capabilities fit around these suggested tiers, the NIST framework adds functions:

1. **Policies.** Formal, up-to-date documented policies should exist that are readily available to employees. The policies should establish a continuing cycle of assessing risk and implementation and use monitoring for program effectiveness. These policies should be written to cover all major facilities and operations and should clearly assign IT security responsibilities, and lay the foundation necessary to reliably measure progress and compliance. In addition, policies should identify specific penalties and disciplinary actions if the policy is not followed.
2. **Procedures.** Formal, up-to-date, documented procedures should be in place to implement the security controls identified by the defined policies. These procedures

EXHIBIT 23.6 NIST Tiers of Cybersecurity Maturity

- Tier 1 Partial Risk: management is ad hoc, with limited enterprise awareness of risks and no collaboration with others.
- Tier 2 Risk Informed Risk: management processes and program are in place but are not integrated enterprise-wide; collaboration is understood but enterprise lacks formal capabilities.
- Tier 3 Repeatable Formal: policies for risk-management processes and programs are in place enterprise-wide, with partial external collaboration.
- Tier 4 Adaptive Risk: management processes and programs are based on lessons learned and embedded in culture, with proactive collaboration.

should outline what is to be performed, who is to perform the procedure, and on what the procedure is to be performed. Procedures clearly define IT security responsibilities and expected behaviors for IT asset owners and IT management and security administrators. The procedures should contain appropriate individuals to be contacted for further information, guidance, and compliance.

3. **Implementation.** Procedures are communicated to individuals who are required to follow them. IT security procedures and controls are implemented in a consistent manner everywhere that the procedure applies and are reinforced through training. Ad hoc approaches that tend to be applied on an individual or case-by-case basis are discouraged. Policies are approved by key affected parties. Initial testing is performed to ensure controls are operating as intended.
4. **Test.** Tests are routinely conducted to evaluate the adequacy and effectiveness of all implementations and to ensure that all policies, procedures, and controls are acting as intended and that they ensure the appropriate IT security level. Effective corrective actions should be taken to address identified weaknesses, including those identified as a result of potential or actual IT security incidents.

   The frequency and rigor with which individual controls are tested depend on the risks that will be posed if the controls are not operating effectively.
5. **Integration.** Policies, procedures, implementations, and tests should be continually reviewed with improvements made as required. Security vulnerabilities should be understood and managed. Threats should be continually reevaluated, and controls adapted to changing IT security environment. Additional or more cost-effective IT security alternatives are identified as the need arises. Costs and benefits of IT security are measured as precisely as practicable. Status metrics for the IT security program are established and met.

This NIST framework has created a common language to facilitate conversation about cybersecurity processes, policies, and technologies, both internally and with external entities such as third-party service providers and partners. NIST encourages organizations to share current intelligence on vulnerabilities, threat information, and response strategies.

Although it will require some initial education, the potential benefits of a common cybersecurity language and increased collaboration are strong for internal audit, IT, and operations management. The NIST framework casts its discussion of cybersecurity in the vocabulary of risk management. In that context, executive leaders and board members, who typically are better versed in risk management, should be able to more effectively articulate the importance and goals of cybersecurity. It can also help enterprises to better prioritize and validate investments based on risk management.

The *NIST cybersecurity framework* is a relatively new U.S. government set of cybersecurity guidance that balances IT security compliance with risk management standards. While the framework is voluntary, enterprises in many industries may gain significant benefits by adopting the guidelines at the highest possible risk tolerance level. Doing so should not only help improve cybersecurity programs, but also potentially advance regulatory and legal standing for the future. Exhibit 23.7 illustrates

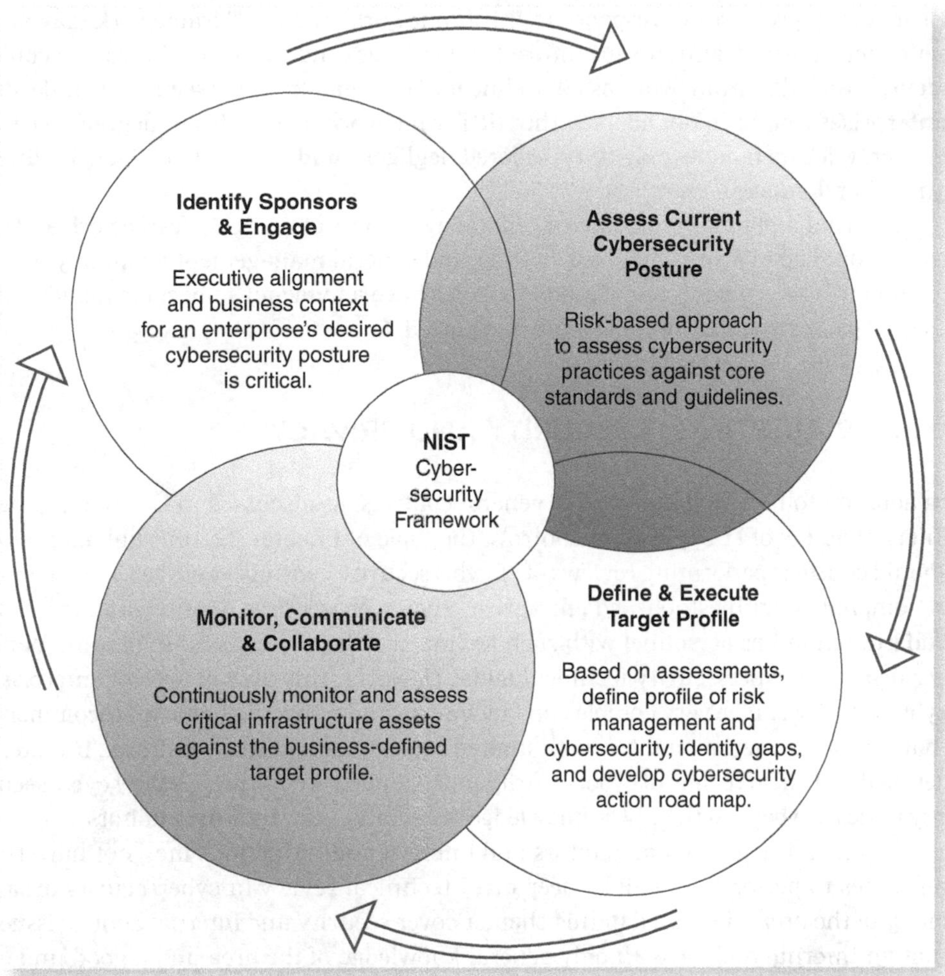

EXHIBIT 23.7 NIST Implementation Steps

this NIST framework implementation process. The reader can get more detailed information on this public resource as well as other valuable material available free from www.nist.gov.

The executive order that originally created the NIST framework stipulated that regulatory agencies will determine which aspects of the framework should be incorporated into existing regulatory mandates across industry sectors. In effect, the framework may become the de facto standard for cybersecurity and privacy regulation and may impact legal definitions and enforcement guidelines for cybersecurity moving forward. As a result, enterprises that adopt the framework at the highest possible risk tolerance level may be better positioned to comply with future cybersecurity and privacy regulations.

At a minimum, businesses that operate in regulated industries should begin monitoring how regulators, examiners, and other sector-specific entities are changing their review processes in response to this framework. The NIST framework may also set cybersecurity standards for future legal rulings, and in future the courts could identify the NIST framework as a baseline for "reasonable" cybersecurity standards. Enterprises that have not adopted the NIST framework to a sufficient degree—Tier 3 or Tier 4, for instance—may be considered negligent and may be held liable for fines and other damages.

Internal auditors should have a general awareness of the NIST framework and at least should be in a position to ask both IT and general management about any plans to adopt it. Government-issued guidance rules have a tendency to become mandatory as time passes and they become more recognized.

23.9 AUDITING IT SECURITY AND PRIVACY

In addition to handling audits of IT general controls, as discussed in Chapter 19, and internal audits of IT application controls, the topic of Chapter 22, internal audit also should consider performing reviews of IT cybersecurity controls as well as assessments of compliance with established enterprise privacy procedures. If an overall internal audit function has personnel with such technical skills, it can assist in planning and performing a cybersecurity technical audit. However, this overall area of enterprise cybersecurity can be very complex and technical, and we would not at all recommend that a typical internal auditor, with limited specialized technical training, initiate a detailed technical review of cybersecurity in the auditor's enterprise. Many cybersecurity issues are beyond the CBOK knowledge expectations for internal auditors.

While many individual auditors and internal audit functions may not have the resources to perform a credible "deep dive" technical review in cybersecurity areas, many of the areas discussed in this chapter cover security and internal control issues that an internal auditor with only general knowledge of the area and a good understanding of the associated IT risks can perform an effective cybersecurity audit that will protect an enterprise from many risks and exposures.

The use and implementation of IT firewalls, as previously discussed, is a good example of an effective internal audit review area. We have discussed, for example, the types or configurations of IT firewalls that can be implemented. In many instances, however, internal auditors do not need to know, for example, the technical attributes of a proxy firewall. Rather, effective internal auditors should ask some general but very control-specific questions that will enable them to obtain an understanding of cybersecurity internal controls in this area.

For example, let us assume that an internal auditor is reviewing cybersecurity controls covering a local wireless network system at a small enterprise operating division. The internal auditor might ask some questions along the lines of:

1. Can you give me a diagram of your IT systems configuration here showing all internal and external cable and wireless router connections within the network?
2. Have you installed firewalls throughout the network to protect all and various classes of access points?

3. Is there any way that devices on the network can communicate with other facilities, such as a dial-up line through a modem that can bypass the firewall barriers?
4. What types of actions or transactions does the firewall screen for?
5. Are firewall parameters regularly updated? When was the last time?
6. What types of improper access attempts are monitored through the various levels of firewalls?
7. What types of corrective action procedures are in place for attempted firewall violations?
8. Can I review some recent firewall violation documentation?

None of these questions really requires an internal auditor to have a super-strong level of technical knowledge. Rather, the internal auditor is recognizing here that firewalls are an effective security control and is asking, in a general manner, how they have been installed for the enterprise's wireless configuration. Of course, an internal auditor always faces the risk of receiving a techno-babble answer from an IT person who either really wants to impress the auditor or resents the internal audit process. In that case, the best solution is to write down the response and follow up later with some other enterprise technical resource personnel. However, the general responses to these questions might indicate some control strengths and weaknesses in the area reviewed.

A good internal audit first step in any cybersecurity review is to understand the IT network to be reviewed. Over time, IT networks grow, and even members of management can lose track of the many interconnections that can be attached to a network. There are a variety of commercial software and even freeware Internet tools available to look at an overall network and identify all of its devices and network connections. Internal audit should work with IT management to run such an analysis tool over their IT network and ask appropriate question to gain an understanding of this environment.

Many cybersecurity internal control issues are more related to good internal control issues rather than just heavy technical natters. The 2013 Target data breach, discussed earlier in this chapter, was primarily caused by poor management procedures covering third-party vendors who were allowed access but not adequately vetted or reviewed. Internal audit should plan and schedule reviews of their enterprise's cybersecurity procedures. If an internal audit function lacks necessary technical skills in a complex technical environment, consideration should be given to contracting with outside technical consulting help.

Exhibit 23.8 contains some cybersecurity internal control audit procedures, covering the areas discussed in this chapter. These procedures may not provide complete coverage of all of the cybersecurity issues facing an enterprise and do not cover some of the evolving privacy issues; as such, internal auditors should develop a high-level understanding of the risks and controls in this important area. As we more and more become a highly networked and interconnected world, enterprises need to build and establish strong and effective controls. An internal auditor may not be an all-knowing technical guru here, but an internal auditor's general understanding of risks and control issues in these areas will help make him or her a more effective aid to enterprise management.

EXHIBIT 23.8 Cybersecurity Internal Controls Audit Procedures

1. Document and understand the IT network.
   a. Use software tools available through IT departmental resources to document and describe the key enterprise network. If no such tools are in place, use one of the several freeware tools available.
   b. Through inquiry and discussion, determine that there are no other rogue networks, perhaps at a foreign facility but loosely connected to the main corporate network or through a telephone modem.
2. Network configuration security controls.
   a. Review network configuration diagrams to determine that connections to other networks and computer systems are minimized.
   b. Determine that connections to the Internet are limited and only used when necessary.
   c. Assess the extent of wireless networks and determine they are appropriately secured.
   d. Review the extent of dial-up connections in place and determine they are secured and their usage monitored.
3. Network system access controls.
   a. Assess the adequacy of physical security controls surrounding prime or main data centers.
   b. Review any remote facilities, such as research lab sites, and determine they are following approved central IT processes.
   c. Review configuration to determine that there are no unattended, unsecure workstations attached to the network.
   d. Assess whether suitable physical protections–including hardware, telecommunications equipment, cables, and wiring–are in place for all data centers.
   e. Review the adequacy of backup provisions for electrical power, communication, and storage.
4. Understand who has access to the network.
   a. Through a discussion with IT security administration, determine that adequate procedures are in place to limit network access to only authorized employees.
   b. Review any procedures in place to grant network access to outside third parties, such as vendors, and determine that appropriate vetting procedures are in place to determine that these outsiders have an adequate understanding of enterprise network security procedures.
   c. On a test basis, select a sample of direct employees and any outside parties granted access to the network to determine that they are still active participants and appear appropriate.
5. Review the extent and currency of written cyber-security procedures covering:
   a. Personnel screening for new hires;
   b. Information protection and key document controls;
   c. Password and system access procedures;
   d. Utilizations of facilities for business use and restrictions on personal use of system resources; and
   e. Disposal of sensitive information.
6. Security prevention countermeasure controls.
   a. Review overall password policies to determine that there are procedures in place to monitor password violations, to require regular password changes, and to monitor violations.
   b. Determine an effective password reset policy is in place where appropriate measures are taken to indentify the true owner before granting new passwords.
   c. Review the location and purpose of all installed firewalls and assess their appropriateness.
   d. Determine that firewall activity is audited and that corrective actions are taken when required.
   e. Review the adequacy of protection procedures in place to prevent sniffing and spoofing.
   f. Assess policies in place for using encryption and assess whether encryptions procedures are adequate.

7. Security incident monitoring and investigation techniques.
   a. Determine there are formal incident reporting and investigation procedures in place.
   b. Determine that appropriate investigation and action plans are implemented in the event of security breaches.
   c. On a test basis, review actions taken on any reported suspicious events to determine that applicable corrective actions were taken.
   d. Review the skills, training, and documented actions of the established incident response team to assess effectiveness.
   e. Determine there has been adequate coordination with law enforcement agencies to, at a minimum, support cyber-security issues.
8. Cyber-security training.
   a. Determine that all affected staff members are trained in cyber-security risks and issues, as appropriate.
   b. Look for a program of enterprise-wide security training to raise awareness and highlight potential risks.

23.10 PCI DSS FUNDAMENTALS

PCI DSS is a cybersecurity standard that was launched 2007 by the Payment Card Industry Security Standards Council, a worldwide industry group led by American Express, Discover, MasterCard, Visa, and others. The PCI DSS data security standard must be used by anyone wanting to accept credit cards as a form of payment. Such credit cards are so pervasive in enterprise commerce worldwide, and the failure to comply with the standard can result in a variety of fines and potentially the loss of the right of an enterprise to accept credit cards at all. This section provides an overview of this important cybersecurity standard.

PCI DSS has been established to comply with the massive number of local and national credit card payment rules and also to follow the guidelines of the major credit card companies. The standard contains configuration and audit guidelines, and these standards cover any IT device that accepts credit cards as payment. The phrase "any IT device" is quite broad, because beyond the more standard computer systems, it applies to the point of sale devices found in retail stores, any site accepting e-mail payments, residential parking meters, and a wide range of others.

Exhibit 23.9 shows the 12 basic requirements for a PCI DSS implementation. While very high level and oriented to the credit card industry, many of these apply to good general network security and include many of the areas discussed in this chapter, such as installing effective firewalls, the use of antivirus software, and the importance of security policies.

Effective use of these requirements means going a little further in understanding cybersecurity control needs. For example, Requirement 11 in Exhibit 23.9 is the need to regularly test security systems and processes. This might require an enterprise to:

- Test security controls annually
- Run internal and external data scans quarterly
- Perform annual penetration tests on systems and applications
- Use tools for network and host intrusion detection
- Implement file integrity monitoring procedures

EXHIBIT 23.9 PCI DSS Goals and Requirements

Goals	PCI DSS Requirements
Build and maintain a secure network	1. Install and maintain a firewall configuration to protect cardholder data
	2. Do not use vendor-supplied defaults for system passwords and other security parameters
Protect cardholder data	3. Protect stored data and do not store card and transaction data unnecessarily
	4. Encrypt transmission of cardholder data and sensitive information across public networks
Maintain a vulnerability management program	5. Use and regularly update antivirus software
	6. Develop and maintain secure systems and applications
Implement strong access control measures	7. Restrict access to data by business need-to-know
	8. Assign a unique ID to each person with computer access
Regularly monitor and test networks	9. Restrict physical access to cardholder data
	10. Track and monitor all access to network resources and cardholder data
	11. Regularly test security systems and processes
Maintain an information security policy	12. Establish and maintain high-level security principles and procedures

Many enterprises worldwide are involved with credit card transactions and working to achieve PCI DSS compliance. It is a hybrid mix of a standard, such as the Institute of Internal Auditors international standards discussed in Chapter 9, and a governmental regulation, where the rule of law requires compliance. It is also a good example of the growing importance of cybersecurity issues.

Internal auditors whose enterprises use credit card payment transactions may be involved with compliance efforts here, but if not, they should make appropriate communications within their organizations. Audit procedures should be adjusted to assure PCI DSS compliance.

23.11 SECURITY AND PRIVACY IN THE INTERNAL AUDIT DEPARTMENT

As we alluded to previously in our "the shoemaker's children have no shoes" saying, internal auditors as an operating function in the enterprise and as individual internal auditors need to establish their own security and privacy procedures and best practices. Internal auditors regularly visit a site and capture information and data, either in a hard- or soft-copy format, covering their review activities as well as supporting information from the site audited. Depending on the nature of a review, that captured audit evidence material must be maintained in a secure and confidential manner.

Most if not all internal audit functions today have moved from the old days of pencil-and-paper-based workpaper records and voluminous manual supporting records to today's world of laptop and tablet computers and the use of extensive automated processes. In those past years, internal auditors kept their work in thick workpaper binders, and after an individual audit was completed, the approved workpapers were filed in an often fairly secure audit department library. There was always a risk that a workpaper binder could become lost, but in today's era of electronic record-keeping on tablets and laptops, there may be greater internal audit privacy and security risks.

Internal auditors carry their laptop or tablet IT systems, work on them while on flights to audit assignments, and bring them to auditee locations. While an auditor's laptop system may carry critical files and information at any one time, the machine also has intrinsic value. Carried about through airport lounges or tossed into the backseat of rental cars, these machines are subject to loss or theft. While there is some cost associated with the laptop itself, the major cost of any system loss is the internal audit data contained in the system's files. Some important techniques for protecting auditor laptops include:

- **Establish personal responsibility for auditor laptops.** Through training, audit department standards, and just good guidance, all internal auditors who have been assigned a tablet or laptop system should be reminded that they have a strong responsibility for the security of their system. This can include such simple guidance as to keep it in the trunk of their automobile rather than the backseat, to not leave it sitting unattended, and to not allow family members to use it to prevent files being erased or corrupted.
- **Initiate periodic file backup procedures.** Whether using a backup site at the headquarters internal audit office or a special USB drive, auditor laptop computers should be regularly backed up. Storage devices have become very cheap and software tools for backups are readily available today. Procedures should be established for internal auditors to perform a 100% daily backup of their systems. There is no need to keep multiple versions, but the current backup copy can replace the current day's version.
- **Use physical locks and security mechanisms.** There are numerous small devices that are similar to a cable bicycle lock where the laptop can be connected to the desk or some other difficult-to-move object. As these are relatively inexpensive devices, an internal audit function should adopt them for internal auditor use. Tablet systems or smartphones used in audit work should always be secured as well.
- **Use antivirus systems and other tools.** This chapter earlier discussed computer malware and the need for antivirus protection. The same types of software tools should be installed in all internal auditor laptops as well.

An internal auditor's laptop computer is often a repository for auditor narratives, copies of documents, and other key items of audit evidence. Good security procedures should be established to protect these important internal audit resources. Even when an internal audit function does not use laptops and relies on desktop machines, similar security practices should be installed.

Workpaper Security

Workpapers are the key documents that carry evidence and the results of the internal audit assignment work. Chapter 17 talks about good workpaper documentation procedures, and audit department security over those workpapers is very important. Sarbanes-Oxley Act rules discussed in Chapter 5 require that, as audit evidence, workpaper files should be retained for a seven-year period. Also, in a litigation situation, internal audit workpapers can become legal evidence in civil or even criminal court proceedings.

In today's environment, workpaper internal audit documentation can be a combination of soft-copy automated files and hard-copy documents. Internal audit needs strong procedures to catalog, store, and secure its internal audit workpapers. Just as a catalog number identifies where a library book is stacked on the library's shelves for ease of retrieval, an internal audit function should develop some kind of numbering scheme for cataloging its workpapers. There is not one best approach here, but the chief audit executive in launching such a program should realize that seven years is a long time and there can be many changes in the enterprise and its operating units.

Audit workpapers should be organized in such a manner that a workpaper binder can be checked out for use. This use should be limited to other members of the internal audit staff as well as external auditors on request. Tracking records should be maintained to identify the location of any checked-out workpapers at any time.

Workpaper security is always a concern, and whether in hard- or soft-copy format, procedures should be installed to back up and protect workpaper files. For hard-copy documents, they should be kept in a secure, locked facility with access limited. Because seven years' accumulation can create quite a volume of materials, arrangements should be made to secure older workpapers with one of the secure document repository services that are common in today's business environments. Soft-copy workpaper materials should be backed up as well. There can be a particular concern here, however, as such things as file formats can change. As this book goes to press in 2015, consider the IT formats that were standard formats perhaps five years earlier. Those were days of floppy disk files and earlier versions of word-processing software, and a backup storage of those older devices would present problems today if needed. We cannot predict the future, but if technology changes appear to be making old soft-copy versions hard to use, arrangements should be made to convert them before it becomes too late.

Exhibit 23.10 contains some internal audit workpaper security best practices. As important documentation describing internal audit activities, their security is important. While it is always necessary to allow other members of the audit team to review old workpapers for following procedures and the like, extreme attention should be given to preventing any alteration of these workpapers once the audit assignment has been completed and the documentation approved. There is always the danger of a rogue member of the internal audit team making after-the-fact changes to the evidence gathered through audit workpapers, for any of several reasons, often those of self-protection. This can be prevented through read-only controls installed on soft-copy versions, but is difficult to control with hard-copy versions.

EXHIBIT 23.10 Internal Audit Workpaper Security Best Practices

- Establish general internal audit department workpaper standards defining best practices for such areas as capturing audit evidence, recording volume bulk evidence materials, and others.
- Develop general procedures for preparing workpapers in either hard-copy paper–based formats as well as office systems–based soft copies and establish guidelines for when either should be used.
- Establish a general indexing or numbering system for all workpapers that identifies the unit, type of audit, and year of audit as well as general workpaper cross-referencing guidance.
  - For tablet, laptop, or desktop computer based soft-copy workpapers:
    - Develop consistent file and file folder naming conventions that identify originators and dates of last changes.
    - Establish information access and data update security controls.
    - Back up files to a secure server or other facility at least daily.
    - Establish workpaper update procedures such that when a printed version of a workpaper is updated, the automated version is subsequently updated as well.
    - Copy workpapers of completed audits to a secure repository such that the data can be later accessed, given the seven-year minimum retention requirements.
  - For hard-copy, paper–based workpapers:
    - Establish consistent content naming conventions with descriptive names, dates, and auditor initials included on all workpaper sheets.
    - Establish security rules for paper-based workpapers during the audit process to prevent unauthorized persons from accessing workpaper files left on auditor desks, etc.
    - Develop consistent procedures for transporting and shipping workpaper files.
    - Because subsequent content alterations are sometimes difficult to trace, establish strong audit staff standards and guidelines on the improper alteration of workpapers.
    - Place all current workpapers in a secure facility with strong check-in and check-out rules.
    - Make arrangement for all older workpapers to be retained in a bulk storage repository.
- Build a comprehensive database to link all workpapers to the audit, completed report, and significant findings.
- Whether hard or soft copy, establish consistent workpaper review practices to identify the timing of supervisory reviews and nature of any changes.
- On a limited and test basis, perform quality reviews of older audit workpaper files to determine their ongoing accessibility.
- On a ten-year periodic basis, review a sample of old workpaper files to determine they are still compatible with the software versions used. If problems, take steps to revise and correct old versions.

Internal Audit Reports and Privacy

Internal audit reports, as described in Chapter 18, are documents that describe internal audit's activities for a planned audit project, the procedures performed, findings and recommendations, and auditee management's responses to those findings along with its recommendations for corrective action. By their nature, audit reports are not documents for mass distribution. They should only be shared with auditee management, enterprise senior management, external audit, and the audit committee. Disclaimers should be added to report documents stating that they are not to be copied or shared, and the chief audit executive (CAE) and members of the audit team should regularly emphasize the confidentiality needs for these documents.

Our comments here on workpapers have emphasized related security issues. Published audit reports raise a privacy issue as well. Comments in the findings section of an audit report can very much damage the professional credibility of portions of the enterprise and members of management. Care should be given to securing and protecting audit reports from access to unauthorized persons.

Our comments on internal audit security and privacy procedures represent some best practices that should be considered by internal audit functions, no matter their size, industry, or geographic location. However, while it is one matter for the CAE to agree and install such procedures, all members of internal audit should be aware of these practices on an ongoing basis.

Internal audit should establish departmental standards for workpaper security and privacy. Arrangements for a formal library repository should be established within the enterprise. This would typically be located near the CAE and enterprise headquarters; however, for a large, multiunit enterprise and large internal audit function, off-site or multiple workpaper library repositories could be established. The locations should be secure, with overall administrative control assigned to an administrative staff member. With ongoing seven-year retention requirements, the hard- and soft-copy workpaper repositories and libraries should be organized such that later retrieval will be comparatively easy.

Audit department security and privacy standards should be included in audit department standards and training. In particular, as discussed, every member of the internal audit team should be asked to recognize the privacy and protection needs of their assigned audit computers. Although internal auditors make security and privacy related recommendations in many audit areas, they also should always remember that these rules are extremely important for internal audit itself.

23.12 INTERNAL AUDIT'S PRIVACY AND CYBERSECURITY ROLES

Internal auditors should be aware of the growing and evolving cybersecurity and privacy issues both in their enterprises and worldwide. As discussed, many of the issues here can become quite technical, but all internal auditors should acquire at least a CBOK general understanding of many of the areas discussed in this chapter. For example, most if not all laptop computer users today are at least aware of the risks of computer viruses or other malware. An internal auditor should go a step further and understand the kinds of controls that can be applied to eliminate such risks and then take actions to prevent them.

The cybersecurity and privacy risks and issues discussed in this chapter are constantly changing and evolving. Software vendors, for example, will develop a new protection technique for some type of malware virus, only to have someone beat or get around the protection almost as soon as it is released. Most internal auditors will not become experts on many of these often highly technical issues, but all internal auditors should have a CBOK understanding of cybersecurity and related *IT privacy* risks.

CHAPTER TWENTY-FOUR

Business Continuity and Disaster Recovery Planning

VIRTUALLY NO ENTERPRISE TODAY WOULD be able to function without its IT systems, Internet connections, supporting communication networks, data repositories, and overall IT infrastructure. However, those same IT systems could be subject to any of a wide range of failures, and the enterprise needs the facilities and resources in place to recover and restore IT operations in a prompt and orderly manner. In the early days, the IT systems data protection process was called disaster recovery planning with an emphasis then on the recovery of mainframe IT systems, applications, and data files.

With a focus on IT files and programs, enterprises have regularly established what have been called disaster recovery procedures for keeping backup versions of older files in secure locations along with processes for restoring those backup data files if some sort of disaster limited access to current versions. While earlier backup processes were often based on fairly simple systems configurations, today's large-scale integrated and Internet-based systems have made backup and recovery much more complex. In the years up to the beginning of this century, internal audit often reviewed these procedures and found them to be weak. Processes for strong business continuity planning were often very limited and lacked adequate testing. However, despite frequent comments in many internal audit reports over the years, the issue often did not receive much high-level management and audit committee attention.

The terrorist attacks of September 11, 2001, changed everything. In addition to the massive loss of life and property, telephone lines were clogged, bridges and tunnels to get out of Manhattan were closed, and airlines across North America were shut down. The attacks of 9/11 triggered the activation of a series of enterprise *IT disaster recovery plans*. The World Trade Center was populated with a large number of IT systems–based financial institutions, most with what were thought to be adequate IT disaster recovery plans in place, but many of those plans were later found to be wanting.

This chapter introduces some best practices for effective IT business continuity and disaster recovery planning for internal auditors to use when reviewing internal controls in this enterprise-critical area. In past years, internal audit often was one of the few voices in an enterprise raising IT disaster recovery concerns, and this internal audit role continues to be an important internal control concern today. In addition, many U.S. federal regulations now contain requirements for effective IT business continuity programs, and management at all levels generally recognizes the need for effective IT continuity and recovery provisions. Along with other groups such as legal and IT security, internal auditors continue to have a key role in reviewing, testing, and evaluating their enterprise's business continuity planning processes.

This chapter briefly introduces some of today's technical tools that improve business continuity procedures. While not engaging in a deep technical discussion, we will review some tools in place today, areas where an internal auditor should at least have a good general understanding. For example, the chapter will introduce *data mirroring* techniques—a process where all duplicates of IT application transactions are simultaneously processed on the main system while also being routed to another backup site. Internal auditors often do not need to understand the technical configurations of such a process, but should have enough knowledge to ask some high-level questions about whether it has been considered. While all internal auditors should only have a general knowledge of IT continuity management standards, they should have the skills to assess and recommend effective general IT continuity procedures, an important internal audit CBOK knowledge requirement.

24.1 IT DISASTER AND BUSINESS CONTINUITY PLANNING TODAY

Internal audit reports over the years have discussed the risks of an enterprise losing a substantial element of its IT resources due to some disaster event. Many of these internal audit concerns go back to the early days when most IT resources were based in centralized data centers, but raising internal audit concerns then was often a hard sell. This author recalls leading an internal audit of disaster recovery planning a review for a then major U.S. corporation in the early 1990s. One of its major data centers was located close to a major high-traffic airport, with the potential risk of an airline accident incident nearby, and yet there was no effective recovery plan in place. When internal audit concerns about the lack of an effective IT recovery plan were first raised, the chief information officer shrugged it off, saying such a disaster could "never happen." In the end, this author as an internal audit director had to raise these concerns in a meeting with the audit committee to get the corporation to launch such a disaster planning effort.

Throughout the 1980s and early 1990s, a common IT disaster recovery solution was to make arrangements with a remote disaster recovery data processing facility to handle any emergency processing. Key backup files and programs were stored at off-site locations, with plans calling for the IT staff to shift to that alternate facility in the event of a disaster event. Professionals thought of IT disasters just in terms of fires, floods, or other bad weather situations. In those earlier, primarily mainframe systems days, enterprises sometimes even took what today sounds like rather bizarre actions for developing their IT disaster recovery plans. These included signing "reciprocal agreements" with nearby locations having similar IT resources so that each could move to the other location for processing in the event of an emergency at one. Reciprocal agreements between two CIOs then sounded good in theory, but they have never really worked beyond low-level, almost humanitarian help. That nearby reciprocal agreement site might be out of service for the same weather-related disaster, and probably would not be interested in someone else running their systems in off-shift periods. As a final impediment, corporate legal counsel would have a dozen reasons to say no to such a reciprocal agreement.

Others established raised-floor vacant space at one of their facilities and secured an agreement with their IT system hardware and network providers to quickly move in a replacement system in the event of an emergency. Computer hardware vendors will still agree to replace equipment in an emergency. In fact, this is easier today, as computer hardware is usually off-the-shelf rather than being mostly custom manufactured as was common in the past.

Those disaster recovery plans of the 1980s and early 1990s often were not sound, but a series of specialized disaster recovery vendors soon appeared with fully equipped computer systems sites operating at idle or what are called *hot* sites to serve as emergency backup facilities. In those days of centralized IT facilities, enterprises contracted to use those sites as their disaster recovery facility, ran periodic tests, and kept key backup files there. Even though technology changes have caused some challenges to these disaster recovery operations, these specialized hot site backup vendors still provide the primary IT backup solution for many enterprises in the twenty-first century.

With our era today of client-server and software as a service Web-based applications, an enterprise today faces a new set of risks around its IT assets. For most enterprises, there is no longer one or several major or central computer facilities for handling major IT applications but rather a wide range of desktop devices, servers, and other computer systems connected through often very complex communications and storage management networks, and linked to the Internet. Enterprises do not have all of their IT resources tied around one or several central data centers, and management is more interested in keeping its IT up and running than worrying about the risk of losing a central computer system's facility. The concept of IT disaster recovery planning, going back to the 1970s, was based on having processes in place to resume operations if some single disaster made the computer center inoperable. That is just not true today, but an enterprise needs to establish business continuity processes when faced with unexpected events.

The language and strategic approaches to IT business continuity and disaster recovery planning have changed today. While we certainly cannot deny that the events of 9/11 represented a major disaster, professionals today more typically think in terms of the importance of a business continuity plan, the procedures and processes necessary to restore overall business operations. The user of an online order processing system cares less about whether the server is operating than if a customer order, submitted through an Internet site, can be processed properly and efficiently. The application should be restored and operating as quickly and efficiently as possible, but the key objective is to support and restore the business processes.

In addition to concerns about restoring operations in the case of some disaster or business continuity event, enterprises today are typically more concerned about the continued availability of their IT resources, recognizing that any form of IT systems downtime can be very costly to an enterprise. The Web is filled with estimates of the business cost of IT downtime to an enterprise. For example, CA Technologies, in a study published by the *InformationWeek* newsletter in 2011,[1] surveyed some 200 companies across North America and Europe to calculate the losses incurred from an IT outage. What it found was more than $26.5 billion in revenue is lost each year from IT downtime, which translates to roughly $150,000 annually for each business.

The data from *InformationWeek* is just one recent estimate, and a Google search will yield many similar estimates. Improper or poorly planned *business continuity plans* can be very expensive for enterprises, and internal auditors should understand, review, and test these programs for compliance when performing specific application, general IT, or other internal control reviews. A systems failure will interrupt normal business processing, but a disaster that causes the loss of key records can be even more severe. The message here is that high systems availability and business continuity are very important to an enterprise, and internal auditors should have a CBOK understanding to continually look for areas where they can suggest business continuity planning and IT availability improvements. The following sections outline suggested internal audit activities and procedures in this very key area called business continuity planning (BCP), a more descriptive and important process than what was known as the older, more traditional concept of what we once called IT disaster recovery planning.

24.2 AUDITING BUSINESS CONTINUITY PLANNING PROCESSES

Internal auditors should always look for the existence of current and tested BCP, whether they are performing a review of general controls over an office server system, of a major IT operation, or of a desktop spreadsheet application used for office records. With the strong IT management awareness to have some levels of processes in place, internal auditors generally will not be breaking new ground when they look for the existence of BCP procedures. However, they may often find them out of date, not tested, or too often just ineffective.

The following sections describe procedures for internal audit BCP reviews from the perspectives of a centralized IT operation serving multiple units in an enterprise, a single but smaller server lever system serving a business unit, and BCP procedures for smaller, individual systems, such as a financial analysis system on a key manager's laptop system. The objective of each of these environments is to assure that business continuity processes are in place. Although there is room for that type of assistance, the internal auditor's role in each of these descriptions should be to assess the adequacy of BCP procedures and to make effective recommendations.

No matter the size of the IT environment and the business areas covered, an internal auditor should develop a good understanding of the relative risks associated with a loss or unexpected interruption in IT services, the technologies used and employed, and the technical and business nature of the environment. While there is really no one-size-fits-all here, an internal auditor needs to understand the BCP environment and the nature of ongoing testing and evaluations in order to make appropriate internal audit recommendations.

Internal Auditor Centralized Server Center BCP Reviews

A BCP is an outline of the steps necessary to help an enterprise recover from major service disruptions, whether from a fire or serious weather emergency, a computer equipment or network equipment failure, or any other form of major disruption. The goal of a BCP is to help an enterprise reduce the impact of a disaster outage or extended service interruption to an acceptable level and to bring business operations back online. As discussed, a BCP represents a change in emphasis from what IT professionals once called a disaster recovery plan. The prime emphasis of those older plans was to get IT systems and data processing operations working while the BCP emphasizes needs for continuous operation of the business unit.

As discussed, while many IT operations functions have had disaster recovery plans in place for some time, those approaches were often not very effective in actually getting key business processes operating again. Just as there are key separate steps necessary for planning and for conducting an internal audit, there are some key steps necessary for building an effective BCP. Several professional enterprises, such as the U.S.-based Disaster Recovery Institute and its London- based counterpart, have adopted a frequently published and well-recognized set of 10 BCP-recommended professional practices, as outlined in Exhibit 24.1. These have become the universally accepted standards in the industry for the key steps or components in a BCP, and the following sections discuss some of these steps in greater detail. An effective BCP is critical for an enterprise, and management is responsible for the survivability and sustainability of total operations to serve customers and service recipients. Many companies and most government enterprises are required by law to develop these business continuity plans. In other instances, legislation effectively requires a BCP. The Sarbanes-Oxley Act (SOx), for example, requires registered enterprises to be able to report their financial results in a timely manner. A systems failure is not an excuse, and an effective BCP will help to support the enterprise here.

BCP Audit Procedures, Project Management, Risk Analysis, and Impact Analysis

We have combined the first three elements of Exhibit 24.1 into one internal audit step. When reviewing the BCP in place for an IT unit, internal auditors will normally not be involved in the very important project management processes to build such a plan. Unless internal audit is involved in a BCP build preimplementation process, similar to the approaches used for auditing software management and application internal controls highlighted in Chapter 22, internal audit will generally not be involved in the project management processes for building the BCP materials but will only review the completed

EXHIBIT 24.1 Key Steps to Building a BCP

The following recommended professional practices or steps were initially developed by the Disaster Recovery Institute:

1. **Project Initiation and Management.** BCP processes should be managed through formal project management processes and within agreed time and budget limits.
2. **Risk Evaluation and Control.** A formal BCP risk evaluation process should be used to determine the events that can adversely affect the organization and its facilities with disruption as well as disaster, the damage such events can cause, and the controls needed to prevent or minimize the effects of potential loss. This should include a cost-benefit analysis to justify investments in controls to mitigate these risks.
3. **Business Impact Analysis.** Managers should understand the overall impacts resulting from disruptions and disaster events that can affect the organization as well as techniques that can be used to quantify and qualify them. This requires establishing critical functions, their recovery priorities, and interdependencies such that a recovery time objective can be set.
4. **Developing Business Continuity Strategies**. One single BCP is not applicable for all circumstances, and management should develop an appropriate strategy to determine and guide the selection of alternative business recovery operating strategies for the recovery of business and information resources within the recovery time objective, while maintaining the organization's critical functions.
5. **Emergency Response and Operations.** Emergency procedures should be in place to respond to and stabilize the situation following an incident or event, including establishing and managing an Emergency Operations Center to be used as a command center during the emergency.
6. **Developing and Implementing Business Continuity Plans**. The BCP should be developed, documented, and implemented using a formal, best practices–based process that provides recovery within established recovery time objectives.
7. **Awareness and Training Programs**. Processes should be implemented to train and educate all key members of the organization on the activation and use of appropriate BCP procedures.
8. **Maintaining and Exercising Business Continuity Plans.** The BCP and its key elements should be kept up to date with periodic testing of critical plan elements. Processes should be implemented to maintain and update the BCP in accordance with the organization's strategic direction.
9. **Public Relations and Crisis Coordination.** Processes should be in place to communicate all events surrounding a contingency event and to communicate with and, as appropriate, provide trauma counseling for employees and their families, key customers, critical suppliers, owners/stockholders, and corporate management during crisis. All stakeholders should be kept informed on an as-needed basis.
10. **Coordination with Public Authorities.** Processes should be in place for coordinating continuity and restoration activities with local authorities while ensuring compliance with applicable statutes or regulations.

BCP documentation. An enterprise IT function, often in cooperation with key application owners, will usually be involved with launching a project for developing a BCP.

When reviewing IT BCP internal controls, particularly a newly launched one, the internal auditor should ask to see the project plans that were created to build the multiple application BCPs covering major applications. More important, an internal auditor should look for evidence of a risk assessment to determine why certain applications require full recovery treatment in the BCP.

To clarify things, the entire configuration of hardware and software should be set up for full recovery in a BCP program. Once restored, all of the IT hardware and software should operate again. However, it may not be necessary to restore all application transactions or processes for some lower-risk applications. Business continuity procedures refer to procedures that capture any active transactions that were in process during a system outage. In an airline reservations system, for example, BCP procedures should be designed to capture all transactions in process throughout the processing cycle. Streaming technologies that allow this are discussed later in this chapter. However, other files and processes may be fairly static and may not require immediate BCP restoration. An account validation file that contains valid general ledger (G/L) codes would be an example here. Such account values are generally only updated periodically, and if a system failed at 3 a.m. on Tuesday, it would generally be sufficient to restore the G/L code file from a past update.

Exhibit 24.2 contains BCP internal audit procedures for an internal audit review of a major or centralized data center review. While there are few common hardware and software configurations today, an internal auditor should look for evidence that IT management has considered business continuity risks on an application-by-application basis for major applications and built a series of BCPs that cover those key applications. A major subset of a centralized facility is an *emergency response plan*. These are processes in a fire drill–like mode that allow the IT facility to react in the event of an unexpected emergency. Emergency response plans do not promote business continuity. They are last-ditch efforts to abandon ship in the event of an emergency. Backup files and other procedures should be in place, but an immediate priority should be to preserve the health and safety of the IT personnel located at the centralized IT facility.

Emergency Response Plan Operations

As part of any continuity planning review, internal auditors should attempt to gain assurance that appropriate emergency procedures are in place to respond to and stabilize the situation following an incident or event. In the older days of IT, disaster recovery plans were often published in thick books located on the desks of a few key enterprise managers. The idea was that in the event of some emergency, people would pull out their disaster recovery manuals to look up such data as the telephone number of the designated backup site to report the emergency or instructions for other emergency procedures. The material in these thick books might have worked in theory if the manuals were always kept up to date and the nature of the crisis event allowed time to review the manual first and then react. Many real-life events are much more crisis-oriented, with little time to dig out the disaster recovery manual and read its documented information. When the building is on fire, for example, human nature says that one should get out of the building as soon as possible, not spend time studying the published evacuation instructions. Enterprises need to think through these various possible situations in advance, and internal auditors should review existing published materials with some skepticism.

Enterprises should establish emergency response plans with an emphasis on two significant types of emergency incidents. The first is a fire-in-the-building type of emergency where the supporting emergency response plan would include posted fire exits

EXHIBIT 24.2 Centralized IT Facilities Internal Audit BCP Review Procedures

1 Understand BCP Objectives and Status

- Determine that IT and management understand the objectives of their BCP and expectations for recovery.
- Review procedures for assessing risks and estimating costs with alternative BCP actions.
- Understand the scope of the BCP, including equipment and processes covered and the scope of enterprise units.
- Identify the equipment, floor plan, procedures, and other items necessary for the recovery.

2 Continuity Planning

- Determine that the plan covers potential events including: weather, fire and flood, computer crime, and sabotage.
- Determine that decisions have been implemented and arrangements made for backup processing facilities—whether a hot site or other facility.
- Review risk assessments made, and their supporting analyses, to determine that the BCP coverage appears complete.
- Determine that service level agreements have been executed between applications users and key IT operations areas and that both understand their roles and responsibilities.
- On a test basis, determine that backup processes are installed and working per DRP specifications.

3 Review Emergency Procedures

- Review the emergency response plan and, on a test basis, assess whether stakeholders are aware of the plan.
- Review the results of the most recent two emergency response plan tests and determine if they met expectations and that corrective actions were installed if appropriate.
- Assess whether current and appropriate contracts have been executed with BCP service providers, such a hot site facilities.
- Assess whether communications have been established and action plans installed with outside providers, such as local fire and police facilities.
- Determine that disaster recovery teams have been assigned and are aware of their responsibilities.
- Determine that formal processes have been established for defining a disaster event and initiating the BCP.

4 Initiation of Recovery Procedures

- Select several critical applications, and on a test basis, determine that appropriate backups are being executed.
- For those same critical applications, meeting with key members of the business teams to determine they understand their responsibilities for operating in a BCP environment.
- Review the adequacy of processes for reviewing the BCP and keeping it current.
- Review the BCP critical application testing programs and assess adequacy.
- On a test basis, review the results of a critical process BCP test and determine that business operations have been adequately restored.

5 Maintaining the BCP

- Assess the adequacy of processes in place to keep BCP current given differing application and technology changes.
- Determine that procedures are in place to keep BCP documentation current, including communications with BCP providers.

and frequent fire drills. This type of emergency response plan should cover all enterprise operations, including IT resources, and should be regularly tested. A second level of emergency response plan should cover specific individual incidents that may or may not turn out to be significant, but must be corrected at once followed by an investigation and a plan of corrective action to prevent further incidents. These are called emergency *incidents,* and they often include such matters as security breaches or the theft of hardware or software. A good emergency incident response plan should be acted on quickly to minimize the effects of any further breaches. It should also be formulated to reduce any negative publicity and to focus attention on quick reaction time. The emergency incident response plan can be separated into four sections:

1. **Immediate response activities.** Whether an incident that occurs is a security breach, a theft of assets, or a physical intrusion, resources should be in place to investigate the matter and take immediate corrective action.
2. **Incident investigation.** All reported matters should be fully investigated to determine the situation that caused the emergency and possible future corrective actions going forward.
3. **Correction or restoration.** Resources should be available to correct or restore things as necessary. Since emergency incidents can cover a wide variety of areas, these resources may include information systems security specialists, building security managers, or others.
4. **Emergency incident reporting.** The entire emergency incident and the actions subsequently taken should be documented along with an analysis of lessons learned and any further plans for corrective actions.

Emergency incident responses must be decisive and executed quickly. Internal auditors should assess established plans, recognizing the need to first act quickly and then only later to build short-term strategies. Quick actions are needed, with little room for error. By staging fire drill–like practices and measuring response times, response time speed and accuracy can be improved. Reacting quickly may minimize the impact of resource unavailability and the potential damage caused by any future systems or facility compromises. An enterprise faces many potential emergency incidents or threats beyond a massive 9/11 type of emergency that causes the overall failure of IT resources. While the focus should always be on more major business continuity planning issues, an enterprise needs to have mechanisms in place to respond to every level of unexpected emergency event.

Internal auditors should look for appropriate emergency response plans as a component of many internal audit reviews. These plans will exist at a total facility level, such as a fire escape plan, or at an individual level, such as a plan to respond to a security breach. In many areas of the enterprise, auditors should ask if appropriate emergency response plans are in place, whether they are regularly updated and current, and whether have they been tested.

Client-Server Continuity Planning Internal Audit Procedures

A client-server IT environment may contain multiple server systems covering applications, databases, and Web operations. It is a characteristic of small enterprises where there is limited IT support for the enterprise but where IT systems are critical for ongoing business operations. These are the types of IT applications that support activities as distribution and billing for a small enterprise, or even a unit of a large enterprise with a limited in-house IT staff. These types of critical applications are often installed by an outside provider who gets the key applications with an admonition to establish a BCP. However, all too often, such BCP efforts are never launched or, if once published, they quickly become out of date and are ignored.

The small or medium-sized enterprise that does not have an effective BCP for its IT operations faces a substantial risk. The Web is filled with testimony that reveals that a major IT failure at a small enterprise that lacks an effective BCP can easily force the enterprise to fail. The internal audit resources in such an enterprise can often serve as major voices in alerting enterprise management to the risk of a key application failure and the need for effective BCP procedures.

The basic steps to build an effective BCP for a small or medium-sized enterprise are essentially the same as for building such a plan for a large enterprise. A key activity is to back up, back up, and continue to back up key files and applications, and internal audit can be a vital resource to review existing BCP processes and to make appropriate internal audit recommendations. The small to medium-sized enterprise often will not have arrangements for a formal hot site for its emergency backup processing, reasoning that the supporting hardware and software vendors can install replacement facilities in a short span of time. This process is relatively easy today with the many low-cost, high-capacity storage devices available.

There are often fewer internal audit resources in small-system client-server environments. However, as part of its general controls reviews of IT operations or reviews of internal controls surrounding other operations, internal audit should be sensitive to the need for an effective BCP. There are many variations here in terms of the size and business of the enterprise. Exhibit 24.3 is an internal audit readiness checklist for a client-server environment BCP. The idea here is that internal audit should survey and assess BCP readiness and make recommendations for improvements as appropriate.

Continuity Planning for Desktop, Laptop, and Handheld Device Applications

Technology is constantly increasing the power and capabilities of desktop, laptop, and even some handheld device applications and systems. USB devices about the size of pencil erasers can plug into a laptop computer to provide sometimes up to 64 gigabytes of memory or more. Although such devices are very cheap today, their size and capacity was almost unheard of not many years ago. Similarly, while desktop and laptop devices once had to be connected to larger systems through bulky cable arrangements, technologies today allow these devices to be connected wirelessly.

Because of this power and flexibility, key managers in many enterprises have built critical files and other information repositories on their personal laptop and desktop devices. Whiles these systems typically do not contain customer business transactions, they are often repositories for other key enterprise documents, such as capital budgeting

EXHIBIT 24.3 Internal Audit Steps for a BCP Client-Server Readiness Review

1. Has a BCP been developed, approved, and tested for central or headquarters IT facilities?
2. Develop and document an understanding, from an internal audit perspective, of the enterprise's IT environment, including the identification of application, Web, and database servers as well as networks and Internet connections.
3. Based on an internal audit review, does the existing central BCP cover all supporting server systems and networked facilities?
4. Is the environment multitiered with, for example, an application server linking to another nested operating environment? If so, determine that the existing BCP covers these extended resources.
5. Since a client-server environment will typically depend on networked connections provided by communications vendors, has the BCP allowed for the failure of any of those elements?
6. Does the client-server appropriately link with any older legacy applications and does the existing BCP cover that overall environment?
7. Where elements in the enterprise and the client-server environment are not included in the overall BCP, have provisions been made to include them?
8. Has a risk analysis been performed to identify the most critical applications, data repositories, and business functions?
9. Have interdependencies in the network been identified? For example, what would be the implications of the failure of a remote server in the operating environment?
10. Are backup processes in place for all key elements of the operating environment and have efforts been established to coordinate those backups?
11. Is there a comprehensive BCP testing program in place covering all critical elements of the systems environment?
12. Does the BCP contain provisions for the potential loss of system elements—such as key server systems—and the ongoing recovery of the IT environment?
13. Does the BCP testing cover business operations as well as IT resources, and has internal audit been involved with observing critical portions of that testing?
14. On a test basis, determine that emergency response plans are in place and have been tested for critical elements of the network.
15. Is there an ongoing, enterprise-wide training program in place to inform all enterprise stakeholders of their BCP risks and responsibilities?

analyses, new product plans, and key product engineering data. An effective BCP is just as important, if not more so, for these data files than for the supporting databases for business applications. These personal systems, particularly laptop and handheld devices that can easily slip into an airline bag, with control often limited to the owner of the system, can raise BCP concerns and certainly cause potential security risks.

Internal auditors should be aware of the BCP risks surrounding laptop devices in particular. Many internal auditors today are using laptop audit computers to record their results, store test data, and carry many other audit report–related data. While the internal audit department should have strong procedures regularly requiring internal auditors to back up their work to a centralized location, an incident such as a stolen or damaged audit computer—even with appropriate backup resources—can impact internal audit progress and even represent a security breach. Just as an internal audit function should have strong procedures for the backup and retention of work on single desktop and laptop devices, an enterprise should have some strong enterprise-wide backup and BCP procedures for all stakeholders using laptops and other portable

EXHIBIT 24.4 Desktop and Laptop Systems BCP Processes

1. Does the enterprise restrict business data and applications to company controlled devices?
2. Are inventory records maintained regarding the number of desktop and laptop systems in use, their owners, and the application activities?
3. Are enterprise policies in place restricting or limiting the use of desktop or laptop devices for sensitive data?
4. Has the enterprise-wide BCP considered organization IT risks and resources located on desktop or laptop devices?
5. Are there enterprise-wide procedures in place that require employees to download their key files and programs to remote storage devices?
6. Where such backup procedures are in place, are associates following these system download and backup rules? Asses this functionality by reviews of procedures on a test basis.
7. Are there active training programs in place to inform desktop and laptop system users of the risks of data loss?
8. On a test basis, determine whether the business operations from the backup storage files system can be restored to replacement systems for continued business operations.
9. Along with desktop and laptop system BCP processes, has proper attention been given to systems security and integrity concerns?
10. Are there processes in place to integrate and coordinate desktop and laptop processes with normal enterprise process resources?

devices. Exhibit 24.4 outlines some best practices for effective BCP processes and backup procedures for desktop and laptop personal computer systems.

24.3 BUILDING THE IT BUSINESS CONTINUITY PLAN

As mentioned in the first two sections of this chapter, what were once called disaster recovery plans were in the past published in thick notebooks that got out of date almost as soon as they were distributed. In addition, they focused primarily on recovering IT operations from a disaster event, not on recovering the business and its key operations. Many enterprises have established some form of disaster recovery plan for good business and internal control reasons, but enterprises that established disaster recovery plans following those old rules probably do not have an effective BCP in place today.

This section outlines steps to build an effective BCP for today's IT enterprise. Internal auditors can often play a key role in this process, with their knowledge of business systems and the internal control requirements of COSO or the COBIT frameworks, as outlined in Chapters 3 and 6. Although the words *disaster recovery* and *BCP* are not found specifically in the SOx legislation, the astute board audit committee or CFO should realize that an enterprise must have an effective BCP in place and working both in order to attest that internal controls are effective as required in SOx Section 404 and to release its financial results in a timely manner.

If an enterprise already has a BCP for part or all of its business activities, this BCP needs to be reviewed to determine whether it can effectively meet projected business continuity needs—and we have emphasized the business recovery aspect of the plan here. All too often, enterprises have simply taken their old-style disaster recovery plans and renamed them, giving minimal thought to business continuity requirements. That BCP should be current or have been regularly updated. It should have a detailed section on incident and risk assessment covering all key business activities, and should contain a strategy for recovery of all significant business processes, including applications, communications resources, and other IT assets. There should be assignments for disaster and business teams as discussed next. The BCP should contain detailed instructions for the business recovery process, including the overall project enterprise notification and reporting procedures. Once an existing BCP has been reviewed and an assessment made of its adequacy, it should be enhanced and updated as required.

If no BCP exists or the current version is very much in need of help, a project should be launched to create a new BCP with a designated project manager appointed to lead the effort. This individual should have good leadership qualities, an understanding of business processes, skills with IT security management, and strong project management capabilities. An ideal candidate might have Project Management Professional credentials.[2] In some enterprises, the information security officer may be an ideal candidate for this role. In other cases, internal auditors may be requested to act as consultants. The objectives and deliverables for such a BCP project need to be clearly defined to enable the assigned overall BCP project team to ensure that its work is consistent with original project expectations.

A BCP project's principal objective should be the development and testing of a well-structured and coherent plan that will enable the enterprise to recover normal business operations as quickly and effectively as possible from any unforeseen disaster or emergency that interrupts normal IT services. There also should be sub-objectives to ensure that all employees and other related stakeholders fully understand their duties in implementing the BCP, that information security policies are adhered to within all planned activities, and that the proposed business continuity arrangements are cost-effective. The BCP deliverables should consist of:

- Business risk and impact analysis
- Documented activities necessary to prepare the enterprise for various possible emergencies
- Detailed activities for dealing initially with a disaster event
- Procedures for managing the business recovery processes, including testing plans
- Plans for BCP training at multiple levels in the enterprise
- Procedures for keeping the BCP up to date

Each of these major BCP components is discussed in the following sections. A major objective here is to allow the enterprise to restore business operations as quickly and effectively as possible after a disaster event. This is an activity that requires active participation on many levels, and one where internal auditors should understand these processes and should make appropriate recommendations for improving the effectiveness of an enterprise's BCP.

Risks, Business Impact Analysis, and the Impact of Potential Emergencies

The identification and analysis of risks, as part of internal audit planning and discussed in Chapter 8, is an important BCP analysis tool. Risk or business impact analysis is a particularly important process for determining what applications and processes to include in the overall BCP. The thinking here is different from the past when recovery analysts and sometimes internal auditors focused too much on the subjective probabilities of some event occurring. That is, there were extensive discussions covering the potential probability of a tornado, an earthquake, or some other catastrophic event at a data center location. Those analyses focused on the loss of a centralized data center but not on the continuity and recovery of the business applications.

Today's BCP should include a descriptive list of the enterprise's key business areas, typically ranked in order of importance to the business, as well as a brief description of the business process and its main dependencies on systems, communications, personnel, and data. If the enterprise has already prepared an assessment of its key business processes, this can be an excellent time for the BCP team to update that documentation and to evaluate the relative importance of each. It should be emphasized that this is an inventory of *business processes*, not critical application systems. While the two are often one and the same, it is important that they be considered as the key processes necessary to keep the business operating.

A next step here is to look at those key business processes in terms of potential business outage failure impacts. Exhibit 24.5 outlines review procedures for this type of internal audit analysis. Each separate key business process should be considered, with attention given to such key business process factors as the impact on customer services, loss of customers, and the like. The results of such a review and analysis should help to outline the steps necessary to identify the components of what is usually called a business impact analysis (BIA). A newer term in the world of disaster recovery and business continuity planning, BIA is the process of defining the key business process risks that will impact business operations as a result of a loss of services. The concept behind this type of schedule is to look at all significant enterprise applications or processes and assess their time-based failure impacts.

Based on the outage risks, the BCP team should study and document its recovery requirements for its key business processes. This includes business process procedures, automated systems, and hardware plus software requirements. In addition, any existing backup and recovery procedures should be reevaluated. In larger enterprises, BCP-like arrangements are sometimes made by individual business units that may not be consistent with overall enterprise-wide BCP arrangements. Again, the emphasis should be on recovering business operations, not just on getting the automated systems reloaded and operating again.

Preparing for Possible Contingencies

Once the BCP project team has reviewed and completed its business processes, completed its initial processes, and assessed the business risks, the next steps should be to minimize the effects of potential emergencies. An objective here is to identify ways of preventing an emergency situation from turning into an even more severe disaster

EXHIBIT 24.5 Internal Audit Review Points for a BCP Audit

1. Plan and schedule the review following internal audit's planning risk assessment approaches.
   - Review the results of any past internal audit BCP reviews, noting audit findings and corrective action plans.
   - Determine the scope of the BCP review—specific business units or enterprise-wide.
   - Schedule staff to initiate the internal audit.
2. Review the existing BCP with the responsible manager.
   - Does the BCP appear to be current and up to date?
   - Does the BCP cover all areas of the enterprise, including business processes, or just primarily IT operations?
   - Are there open BCP issues to be resolved?
   - Has the BCP been reviewed with key members of management and do they appear to understand their responsibilities under the BCP?
   - Has internal audit's BCP review plan been reviewed with the audit committee?
3. Examine the contents and format of the BCP.
   - Based on internal audit's understanding of enterprise operations, does the BCP appear to cover key business processes and their supporting IT tools?
   - Are there adequate levels of business impact analysis and risk assessments as part of the BCP documentation?
   - Does the plan appear to cover appropriate procedures for backups—such as the use of mirroring—and off-site storage?
   - Does the BCP carry step-by-step outlined procedures for executing the BCP in the event of an emergency?
   - Are there call list chains included in the BCP?
   - Does the BCP include key vendor and emergency supply contacts?
   - Does the BCP document contacts for fire, police, and external media contacts?
   - Is there a process in place to provide for regular and automatic updates of the BCP?
4. Business and IT service level agreements (SLAs) covering BCP activities.
   - Determine that the enterprise has established appropriate SLAs covering the BCP.
   - Interview several interested parties to assess that they understand their BCP roles and responsibilities.
5. Overall training and understanding of the BCP.
   - Discuss the BCP with several members of the team designated to execute the plan to determine their understanding.
   - Do members in IT operations and systems appear to understand the roles and responsibilities?
   - Based on discussions with key persons in critical business process areas, does there appear to be a general understanding of their business recovery roles?
   - Based on an interview with the CFO, or designee, assess whether there is adequate understanding of the BCP and how it will operate.
   - Review BCP training records to determine if the training appears to be adequate, timely, and regularly scheduled.
6. Review the results of recent BCP tests.
   - Is there a formal program of testing critical BCP elements?
   - Are testing results documented in a lessons-learned format?
   - Does BCP testing cover both business recovery as well as IT functions?
7. Review of BCP backup procedures.
   - If a remote hot site vendor is used, review the contract and related documentation for currency.
   - Review the documented results of hot site tests.
   - Review the adequacy of other backup vendor or location procedures.
8. Prepare internal audit documentation assessing the overall adequacy of the enterprise's BCP.

for the enterprise due to lack of preparedness. The BCP project team should focus on activities that are essential to the continued viability of the business and should develop appropriate backup and recovery procedures for the identified critical applications. The complexity and related cost of these backup business continuity procedures will depend on the identified business process restoration needs as outlined in Exhibit 24.5.

Enterprises have a variety of options for establishing a backup strategy. Larger enterprises often have the resources to do much of this on their own, although many rely on outside vendors to provide backup processing services. An enterprise should consider implementing one of the following strategies:

- **Fully mirrored recovery operations.** This approach, discussed later in this chapter, requires building what is called a fully mirrored duplicate site with linkages between the live site and the backup, mirrored alternate facility. This requires specialized storage management hardware and software and is almost always the most expensive option. Fully mirrored strategies will provide the greatest level of recovery assurance.
- **Switchable hot site facility.** Here arrangements are made with a vendor who will guarantee to maintain an identical site with communications to enable the transfer of all data processing operations to this hot recovery site within an agreed time period, usually less than one or two hours. Because of the need to keep the equivalent of an exact duplicate site in waiting, the costs here can be almost as high as a fully mirrored arrangement.
- **Traditional hot site.** Here the enterprise will contract with a disaster recovery vendor with a compatible site to enable the switching of IT operations to that site within an agreed time period, usually less than eight hours after notification. This was a very common recovery approach back in the days of more traditional mainframes and server centers. While not a common strategy today, there still are a few vendors that can provide such a solution.
- **Cold site facility.** This was a more frequent approach in the classic mainframe days when disaster recovery sites were viewed as being very expensive and yet enterprise IT management wanted some possible solution. The strategy involves establishing emergency site space to allow the enterprise to begin processing as well as a standby arrangement with vendors to deliver minimum hardware configuration. This strategy also goes back to mainframe computers that required air-conditioning and water-cooling operations that were located under raised-floor computer room sites. In theory, those *cold sites* today could be operational within two to three days; today they represent little more than some space in the enterprise facility.
- **Relocate and restore.** This is the weakest level of backup strategy. It involves the identification of a suitable location, hardware and peripherals, and the reinstallation of systems and backed-up software and data *after* an emergency has occurred. Some managers were once guilty of advocating this approach. They backed up their software and data with no firm plans beyond just making arrangements if something happened. This strategy is inadequate for today's business processes.
- **No strategy**. This is almost unheard of today, yet there are still some enterprises that have no backup and recovery strategy for their IT operations. This is often

an "I'll get to building my BCP later, I'm too busy right now!" type of approach. This approach carries the highest risk of all, and in the event of a disaster it usually results in the enterprise going out of business. The internal auditor who encounters this situation should make it a strong business risk warning to the audit committee.

An enterprise BCP must contain appropriate strategy for the backup and recovery of an enterprise's IT and for business continuity. These BCP procedures, especially for key business processes, should be designed to get business operations back in operation per management requirements. While in some instances a decision to use a hot site strategy will be the major direction for almost all applications, some highly critical processes may require full mirroring capabilities. Such a mixed mode of backup strategies can be appropriate if the enterprise decides that full mirroring is only justified for that one highly critical process, while the others will rely on an adequate but appropriate hot site strategy.

An enterprise may have a mixed set of backup strategies, with some being stronger than others. However, all key processes in an enterprise should have some level of backup and restoration policy that allows the overall business to remain in operation. While not all processes may require full mirroring, for example, all should be part of a consistent, comprehensive approach that will allow the overall business to get back in operation in the event of a serious disruption. The cost of recovery can be a major factor here, and the BCP team should outline cost options and get the application owners to buy into an option through appropriate agreements. Internal audit, in its periodic reviews of BCP procedures throughout the enterprise, should highlight any discrepancies encountered here.

The BCP should have a high-priority objective to provide an adequate level of service to all customers throughout an emergency. Critical customer service activities should be included in the BCP, ordered in a priority sequence with restoration steps outlined in some level of detail. There are business managers who understand customer needs, but they may not necessarily be part of the recovery site BCP team, particularly if it would be operating at a remote hot site. Documentation describing key customers and customer service activities should be essential components of the BCP. The emphasis should be on getting the enterprise back in operation.

No matter what backup strategy is used, key files and documents should always be stored in secure off-site locations. Disaster recovery and business recovery teams should be designated and trained, with periodic tests to assure their ongoing familiarity with processes.

Disaster Recovery: Handling the Emergency

Building a BCP is a relatively easy process when the team sits in a closed room, brainstorms, talks through, and plots a business continuity recovery strategy. It suddenly becomes more difficult when alarm bells ring, signifying that an emergency event has occurred. One of the first tasks is to determine to what level the emergency situation requires activation of the full BCP and notification of the emergency response team. This notification should normally be communicated in a preagreed call list–driven format with members of the disaster recovery team instructed to assemble at a designated off-site location. In addition, management and key employees should be kept informed of developments affecting the BCP activation and its impact on their areas of responsibility. The BCP project team leader would be responsible for this notification activity.

The objective of this BCP phase is to get IT enterprise operations back in operation. This almost always involves contacting the designated alternate processing site, activating communications lines, making arrangements to get the team to that site, and otherwise taking steps to restore operations. Assuming the team is using a hot site vendor, the disaster recovery team should arrive at a backup site, get operating systems versions and key databases loaded, and begin production operations. These steps are often far easier said than done, and it is sometimes a challenge to get communications lines connected and up and running in the new environment. This is processing that must be handled in a tight time frame with the objective of having as many as possible critical business processes restored and operating quickly.

For the BCP and its resultant recovery to be effective, the recovery team must carefully consider and plan for the potentially complex series of activities needed to recover from a serious emergency. A planned approach is likely to result in a more coherent and structured recovery. It is likely that a serious disruptive event will produce unexpected results that may differ in some ways from the predicted outcomes contained within the plan. The recovery team should review any predefined procedures or strategies in the light of the actual situation arising following the emergency event and modify these procedures as appropriate.

Business Continuity Plan Enterprise Training

Extensive BCP processes and published documents are of little value unless the people responsible for executing those processes are regularly trained in their use. While many traditional disaster recovery plans were in the past published in thick books full of data, with the idea that team members would look up critical references, telephone numbers, and the like after a disaster event, this approach was not practical in a 9/11 type of disaster where the entire building suddenly collapsed into dust. Secure online plans will provide some help here, but what is needed is a BCP team familiar with the emergency response plans discussed earlier and trained in the general processes necessary in the event of an extreme emergency. Certain BCP team members must know enough about the plan so they will react almost instinctively in the event of a severe emergency situation.

In order to act without having to flip through a published plan to decide the next step, the BCP project team needs to launch a business continuity planning training program for members of the enterprise on many need-to-know levels, with four suggested levels of BCP training:

- **Level 1: General management overview.** Training here should be given to a wide range of people, starting with the audit committee, to outline the overall strategy for recovery in the event of an emergency event and to describe expectations of how the enterprise would operate in a business continuity environment.

- **Level 2: Key application systems users.** Training here should be focused on recovery procedures for critical applications. In many instances, critical applications should function in a business-as-usual sense except that processing will take place at the alternate hot site. However, some normal resources, such as user help desks, often will not work in the same manner. The training here should be oriented to designated critical applications and how they are planned to operate and should operate in a case analysis mode where users can review BCP processes for their applications and ask detailed questions or point out areas where corrective action may be needed.
- **Level 3: IT operations and systems staffs.** The IT staff, including operations, systems software, and IT security specialists, are the persons who usually will be most impacted by a business continuity that requires operations in a recovery mode. Training here should emphasize and reemphasize key elements of the BCP; it should take the format of regular and periodic fire drills. In some instances, this training can be based on actual BCP tests, while game-type simulations may be effective in others.
- **Level 4: BCP team members.** The team that built and launched the BCP should have the greatest familiarity with established BCP procedures. Nevertheless, their knowledge needs to be refreshed and updated on an ongoing basis.

An effective training program is a final step to building an effective BCP. While internal auditors, in their normal assurance level of activities, will typically not be leading an enterprise project to build and launch an enterprise BCP, they will often be very involved in its development and practices. In addition, they should include the status of continuity planning in the regular audits of both IT operations and other business areas.

24.4 BUSINESS CONTINUITY PLANNING AND SERVICE LEVEL AGREEMENTS

An enterprise and its IT function cannot just arbitrarily publish and release a BCP for its business process and application areas. There must be a strong buy-in from the users and application owners as well as their joint assurances of expectations and service delivery. If a senior executive in a specific user department feels that some of his or her business processes must *always* be operational with a full backup capability for significant transactions, that department should negotiate with IT to provide that level of business continuity service and also must recognize the necessary costs of additional hardware and software to provide that capability. In the past days of downloaded file copies periodically transmitted to a remote location, anything close to an immediate backup was only a theoretical concept. A transaction had to be written first in the main system and its database and then copied to a backup facility. There was always a delay, ranging from weekly or daily backup files to almost immediate real-time systems approaches. Newer mirroring storage management approaches can provide immediate backups. These techniques are described in the following sections. They are very effective but certainly more expensive.

In order to make a BCP work between IT and business units, they should consider jointly negotiating their recovery expectations through formal service level agreements (SLAs). An SLA is a contract between the business process owner and the provider of IT services for specified service objectives. SLAs are discussed as part of the ITIL® (Information Technology Infrastructure Library) service delivery best practices in Chapter 19 and can be fundamental to business continuity activities. Internal auditors should be aware of the importance of SLAs and should look for effective SLA implementations. An SLA is an agreement between IT and business operations to define minimum levels of expected computer systems backup and recovery. They are effectively a contract between IT and key user areas to support both normal day-to-day operations as well as the actions to be taken in the event of a serious service disruption. SLAs describe expected and promised levels of business continuity services and are basic building blocks for establishing effective business continuity plans.

While all IT organizations should establish internal SLAs, they are encountered most frequently in contracts for the services of outside IT providers. For example, an IT services vendor may agree to handle the processing of some application at a rate of *X* cents per transaction and may also agree to process those transactions within a specified turnaround time. The enterprise pays for these services based on the transaction rate and recognizes adjustments if expected turnaround time standards are missed. Similar SLA arrangements between users of services and information systems should be made within the enterprise, but the internal costs are normally based on internal budget amounts. For a BCP-related SLA, the benefiting user business function will specify its backup needs and will accept a periodic budget charge for those information systems and related services. If promised SLA targets are missed, a budget credit would be issued. Even though these SLA debit and credit amounts are often based on enterprise internal "funny money" transactions, they can become an important measure of management performance.

Business recovery SLAs are frequently structured to cover most if not all departments or functions in the enterprise. As part of these charges, they are also receiving an information systems function commitment or promise to provide an agreed-on level of business continuity services. When a business area has specific needs, special or unique SLAs should be created. Internal auditors should be aware of the importance of SLAs when reviewing business continuity planning and the enterprise's BCP. As mentioned, Chapter 19 has more information on building and launching SLAs. This is the type of contract that sets appropriate rules and expectations.

24.5 AUDITING BUSINESS CONTINUITY PLANS

Internal audit can and should play an important role in an enterprise's BCP development as well as its testing processes. Internal audit might offer its resources to observe and comment on the results of BCP tests, to suggest testing scenarios, or to offer consultative advice on the progress of the BCP development. While internal audit can be part of these BCP processes, they should periodically step back, assert their independence, and schedule periodic audits regarding the adequacy of BCP processes and business recovery procedures in general. Audits should be planned and scheduled as part of internal audit's regular risk assessment and audit planning process.

While internal audit may play the role of observers in the BCP testing process, formal internal audits should be scheduled to periodically assess all aspects of BCP readiness and the adequacy processes in place. Internal audit must be careful of the fine line between acting as an advisor to the BCP team and auditing their processes, where the audit committee may be the party interested in the overall adequacy of the BCP process for the continuance of the corporation. Internal audit's review of enterprise BCP processes should be based on such matters as the adequacy and currency of its BCP documentation, the results of scheduled tests, and a host of other issues. Exhibit 24.5 contains review points for an internal audit review of enterprise BCP processes. While every enterprise is different, the exhibit points out some general areas that should be considered in an internal audit review of enterprise BCP procedures. These focus on an audit of one self-contained set of resources and processes but can be expanded for a larger, multilocation enterprise.

The establishment of adequate business continuity processes is an important component of an enterprise's internal control structure, as discussed in Chapters 3 and 4 on COSO and SOx Section 404 internal controls. Internal audit should communicate the results of its reviews here with senior enterprise management as well as the audit committee. The results of the BCP audit should be included in the internal materials that would be part of the enterprise's Section 404 assessment of internal controls.

24.6 BUSINESS CONTINUITY PLANNING GOING FORWARD

As enterprises become ever more dependent on their IT automated business systems, procedures to keep those processes in operation in light of some emergency or other disaster have become increasingly important. The enterprise's staff can no longer get by claiming that everything is backed up with no real evidence of the effectiveness of these backups. Modern automated systems are tied to complex in-house and Internet-based databases where those old procedures are no longer applicable and effective BCPs are essential.

The old "disaster recovery" rules have long since changed as well. It is no longer sufficient for IT operations to move to a hot site backup location to begin processing and assume the enterprise will soon up and running. Processes must focus on restoring business operations in light of an extended interruption in IT services. Business requires the ability to get all of its processes back in operation with minimal delay. Internal auditors have an important role here in helping management to implement effective BCP processes and regularly assess their operations and controls. Although there can be many variations and approaches to an effective implementation, all internal auditors should have at least a general knowledge of BCP requirements and how to assess such a process. In today's highly automated world, an understanding of BCP requirements and best practices should be a requirement for an internal auditor's CBOK.

NOTES

1. Chandler Harris, "IT Downtime Costs $26.5 Billion in Lost Revenue," *InformationWeek*, May 24, 2011, http://www.informationweek.com/it-downtime-costs-$265-billion-in-lost-revenue/d/d-id/1097919?.
2. PMP is an examination- and experience-based qualification administered by the Project Management Institute (www.pmi.org).

VI

PART SIX

Internal Audit and Enterprise Governance

CHAPTER TWENTY-FIVE

Board Audit Committee Communications

OTHER CHAPTERS HAVE TALKED ABOUT how to execute and manage many internal audit processes and procedures as well as internal audit common body of knowledge (CBOK) information needs and knowledge areas. Internal audit's reporting relationship to the board of directors' *audit committee* presents a different challenge to all members of the internal audit team. Internal audit reports to the audit committee, which approves its overall planning activities and reviews the results of internal audits. However, the relationship here is often a bit different from a classic supervisor/subordinate type of relationship. Although they are much more active since the launch of the *Sarbanes-Oxley Act (SOx)*, members of an audit committee also have other board of directors responsibilities and usually will not be present in enterprise operations on a day-to-day basis. Internal audit's *chief audit executive (CAE)* is often the main contact with the audit committee and frequently must educate and advise the committee on internal auditing issues. Although it is an evolving issue, many audit committees understand the financial reporting issues associated with their external auditors but sometimes view internal audit as an almost unfamiliar resource.

This chapter will review the role of today's audit committee and its responsibilities for internal audit. We will discuss its roles in approving the audit charter, appointing the CAE, approving audit plans, and reviewing the results of internal audits. The chapter will also discuss the types of reporting that internal audit should be presenting to the audit committee to present the results of its work and to highlight issues that may require further action. SOx has also mandated other audit committee responsibilities, such as its role in managing a financial violation *whistleblower* program. While this role is discussed further in Chapter 26, this chapter will discuss how internal audit can aid the audit committee in such initiatives.

The audit committee has the responsibility to set the overall direction for internal audit. While members of internal audit often may not have much day-to-day contact with audit committee members, everyone there must realize that the audit committee is the final source to report matters of unusual concern and to seek resolutions. All internal auditors should have a CBOK high-level understanding of the role and responsibility of the audit committee in today's enterprise.

Many of our comments in this chapter refer to the failure of a major corporation, *Enron*, in the early years of this century, whose misdeeds led to the passage of SOx. Time passes quickly, and many ready readers have now all but forgotten the saga of this once high-flying corporation. An Internet search will provide much more information.

25.1 ROLE OF THE AUDIT COMMITTEE

A significant step in organizing an effective internal audit function is to obtain authorization and approval by the enterprise's audit committee of the *board of directors*. The audit committee provides this broad authorization for an internal audit function through the formal audit charter document that was discussed in Chapter 14. An enterprise corporate audit committee also approves internal audit's overall plans for continuing activities through the current period and beyond. As one of the several operating committees established by the board, the audit committee has a unique role compared to other board committees. It consists of only outside directors—giving it independence from management—and should be composed of specially qualified outside directors who understand, monitor, coordinate, and interpret the internal control and related financial activities for the entire board. As discussed in Chapter 5, one of those audit committee members must be designated as a financial expert per SOx rules. In order to fulfill its responsibilities to the overall board of directors, to the stockholders, and to the public, an audit committee needs to launch and manage an internal audit function that should become an independent set of eyes and ears inside the enterprise, providing assessments of internal controls and other matters.

The comments in this chapter are based on a corporate structure such as one with Securities and Exchange Commission (SEC)–registered stock. Nonpublic enterprises will benefit from this audit committee structure as well. For example, many not-for-profit or private enterprises are large enough to have a formal board of directors and an internal audit function. Although not mandated to do so by SOx and SEC rules, these types of organizations will benefit from a board audit committee of only independent directors. An internal auditor in that form of enterprise would benefit both the internal audit function and the overall enterprise management by suggesting this type of audit committee approach.

While external auditors have a prime responsibility to an enterprise's board of directors for attesting to the accuracy and fairness of financial statements, internal audit has an even larger role in assessing internal controls over the reliability of financial reporting, the effectiveness and efficiency of operations, and the enterprise's compliance with applicable laws and regulations. Corporate boards of directors have had formal audit committees for some time, and internal audit has always had a long-term reporting relationship to their board of directors' audit committee. However, much has changed since SOx in 2002. In past years, many audit committees met only quarterly for brief sessions in conjunction with regular board meetings; those meetings were often limited to little more than approving the external auditor's annual plan, their quarterly and year-end reports, and reviewing internal audit activities on what appeared to be little more than a perfunctory basis. While New York Stock Exchange (NYSE) rules, even prior to SOx, required that audit committees should consist of only outside directors, many audit committee directors were often buddies of the chief executive officer (CEO) with apparently little evidence of true independent actions. While internal audit's CAE has always had a direct reporting relationship to the audit committee, this often was little more than a theoretical relationship where the CAE had limited contact with the audit committee beyond scheduled board meetings. SOx rules have now changed much of that.

Although it is rapidly becoming history, a major issue that evolved from the collapse of Enron and the related financial scandals in the early years of this century was that boards and their audit committees were not exercising a sufficient level of independent corporate governance. The Enron audit committee was frequently highlighted as an example of what was wrong. It was reported to have met some 30 minutes per calendar quarter prior to the company's fall. Given the size of the corporation at that time and the many directions it was pursuing, the Enron audit committee's attention appeared to be limited at best.

Even before the fall of Enron, at around the turn of this century the SEC was becoming interested in seeing audit committees act as more independent, effective managers of a company's external and internal auditors. For example, what was called the Blue Ribbon Committee on Improving the Effectiveness of Corporate Audit Committees was formed in 1999 by the NYSE, the SEC, the American Institute of Certified Public Accountants (AICPA), and others. It issued a series of recommendations on improving the independence, operations, and effectiveness of audit committees. The major stock exchanges then adopted new independent director audit committee standards as listing requirements, and the then Auditing Standards Board of the AICPA raised standards for external auditors with respect to their audit committees. The subsequent financial failures of Enron and others showed that these earlier audit committee initiatives were not enough. The result was the legislative work that led to SOx.

Today, audit committees have greatly expanded responsibilities since the passage of SOx, and internal audit has a greater responsibility to best serve its audit committee. Although an audit committee will typically have regular contacts primarily with the CAE, all internal auditors should have an understanding of this very important relationship. We will discuss heightened audit committee responsibilities and how internal audit can better work with an audit committee under SOx rules.

25.2 AUDIT COMMITTEE ORGANIZATION AND CHARTERS

An audit committee is an operating component of the board of directors with responsibility for internal controls and financial reporting oversight. Because of this oversight responsibility, audit committee members must be independent directors with no connection to enterprise management. There are no size restrictions, but a full board with 12 to 16 members will often have a five- or six-member audit committee. An audit committee may invite members of management or others to attend its meetings and even to join in on the committee's deliberations. However, any such invited outside guests cannot be full voting members. An enterprise's board of directors is a formal entity given responsibility for the overall governance of that enterprise for its owner investors or lenders. All members of the board can be held legally liable through their actions on any issue, and a board and its committees enact most of its formal business through resolutions, which become matters of enterprise record. The enterprise of the board's various committees, including the audit committee, is established through such a resolution. Exhibit 25.1 is a sample board resolution to establish an audit committee.

EXHIBIT 25.1 Board Resolution Example: Authorizing the Audit Committee

ExampleCo Corp Board of Directors

Board Resolution No. XX, MM DD, 20YY

The Board of Directors authorizes an audit committee to consist of five directors who are not officers of ExampleCo. The Board will designate one member of the Audit Committee as a Financial Expert, per the requirements of the Sarbanes-Oxley Act, and elect one member to serve as its chair for a term of three years. The ExampleCo Chief Executive Officer may attend Audit Committee meetings as a nonvoting member at the invitation of the Audit Committee.

The ExampleCo Audit Committee is responsible for:

- Determining that ExampleCo internal controls are effective and formally reporting on the status of those controls on an annual basis with quarterly updates.
- Recommending an external auditor to be selected on an annual basis through a vote by the shareholders.
- Taking action, where appropriate, on significant control weaknesses reported by internal audit, the external auditors, and others.
- Approving an annual plan and budget submitted by the external auditor.
- Approving annual audit plans to be submitted by the outside auditor as well as by internal audit.
- Approving the appointment and ongoing service of Internal Audit's Chief Audit Executive.
- Approving the annual internal audit plan and recommending areas for additional internal audit work as appropriate.
- Reviewing and distributing the audited financial statements submitted by the outside auditor.
- Establishing an ExampleCo whistleblower program that allows officers, employees, and other stakeholders to report financial accounting errors or improper actions and to investigate and resolve those whistleblower calls without any retribution to the original whistleblower.
- Circulating a Code of Ethics to senior officers and obtaining their assent on a quarterly basis.
- Initiating appropriate actions based upon any recommendations by the outside auditor or the Director of Internal Audit.
- Maintaining records on other consulting activities as mandated by the Sarbanes-Oxley Act.

An Audit Committee meeting will be held at least concurrently with each scheduled Board meeting and at other times as required.

The Audit Committee will meet privately with the outside auditor or the Chief Audit Executive to assess the overall internal control environment and to evaluate the independence of the audit function.

Approved: Corporate Secretary

This type of resolution is documented in the records of the board and not revised unless some circumstances require a change.

Exhibit 25.1 is an example of the manner in which a board of directors sets rules for itself. Such resolutions are an example of corporate governance—setting the rules by which a corporation operates. Not published in annual reports and the like, appropriate board resolutions only become issues in matters of regulation and litigation when a board needs to rely on an authorizing resolution. After SOx first became U.S. law in 2002, many corporate board audit committee authorizing resolutions were updated to make them compliant. Otherwise, such resolutions are often onetime things.

While it is not a necessary requirement, corporate internal audit functions regularly operate through a formal internal audit charter, a document discussed in Chapter 14 that is approved by the audit committee to outline internal audit's role and responsibilities. The Institute of Internal Auditors (IIA) has provided some guidance for drafting an internal audit charter, but such charters do not follow any specific standards or format. However, they should formally state, among other matters, that internal audit has full access to all records and facilities within the enterprise. Internal audit charters cover the activities of the internal audit function but not the corporate board audit committee. The NYSE suggested proposed board *audit committee charters* in December 1999, but with no requirement that an audit committee should have such a charter. SOx, however, has now mandated that each board audit committee must develop its own formal audit charter to be published as part of the annual proxy statement.

The purpose of a board audit committee charter is to define the audit committee's responsibilities regarding:

- The identification, assessment, and management of financial risks and uncertainties
- The continuous improvement of financial systems
- The integrity of financial statements and financial disclosures
- Compliance with legal and regulatory requirements
- The qualifications, independence, and performance of independent outside auditors
- The capabilities, resources, and performance of the internal audit department
- The full and open communication with and among the independent accountants, management, internal auditors, counsel, employees, audit committee, and board

The audit committee is required to go before its overall board of directors and obtain authorization, through this charter document, for board audit committee activities just as the CAE, representing the enterprise's internal audit function, has regularly gone before the board audit committee. This audit committee charter is to be published annually as part of the enterprise's annual meeting proxy statement.

While some may look on this audit committee charter requirement as just some additional pages to add bulk to the already thick proxy statement, it is a formal commitment by the board audit committee to ensure the integrity of financial statements and to supervise the internal and external audit functions. There is no single required format for this charter document, but the NYSE has published a model charter that has been adopted by many public corporations today. While formats vary from one enterprise to another, audit committee charters generally include:

1. Purpose and power of audit committee
2. Audit committee composition
3. Meetings schedule
4. Audit committee procedures
5. Audit committee primary activities:
   a. Corporate governance
   b. Public reporting
   c. Independent accountants
   d. Audits and accounting
   e. Other activities
6. Discretionary activities:
   a. Independent accountants
   b. Internal audits
   c. Accounting
   d. Controls and systems
   e. Public reporting
   f. Compliance oversight responsibilities
   g. Risk assessments
   h. Financial oversight responsibilities
   i. Employee benefit plans investment fiduciary responsibilities
7. Audit committee limitations

Although audit committee charters vary, many contain activities and responsibilities as just described. Some appear to have been developed by corporate legal counsels with language to cover every possible contingency, while others are more clear and succinct. An excellent example of an easy-to-follow charter is Microsoft Corporation's 2014[1] audit committee charter, found on the company's web site, and shown in part in Exhibit 25.2. Although not included in our exhibit, the full text of that charter also outlines some 30 specific activities for the audit committee. For example, number 29 in that list states, "Meet with the General Auditor in executive sessions to discuss any matters that the Committee or the General Auditor believes should be discussed privately with the Audit Committee" and highlights that this activity will occur two times per year.

Few corporations are like Microsoft in terms of size and resources, but all corporations with SEC registration must conform to SOx rules. Smaller entities will not have the resources or need to release a Microsoft-like web-based audit committee charter. But a small corporation must still have an independent directors' audit committee, as mandated by SOx, as well as an audit committee charter. This is the type of board of directors' resolution document that would be part of corporate records.

Whether large or small, an enterprise needs to have effective internal controls as well as an internal audit function. This is especially important today, as a limited internal audit resource can no longer rely on its external auditors to perform required

EXHIBIT 25.2 Microsoft Corporation 2007 Audit Committee Charter

Role

The Audit Committee of the Board of Directors assists the Board of Directors in fulfilling its responsibility for oversight of the quality and integrity of the accounting, auditing, and reporting practices of the Company, and such other duties as directed by the Board. The Committee's purpose is to oversee the accounting and financial reporting processes of the Company, the audits of the Company's financial statements, the qualifications of the public accounting firm engaged as the Company's independent auditor to prepare or issue an audit report on the financial statements of the Company and internal control over financial reporting, and the performance of the Company's internal audit function and independent auditor. The Committee reviews and assesses the qualitative aspects of financial reporting to shareholders, the Company's processes to manage business and financial risk, and compliance with significant applicable legal, ethical, and regulatory requirements. The Committee is directly responsible for the appointment (subject to shareholder ratification), compensation, retention, and oversight of the independent auditor.

Membership

The membership of the Committee consists of at least three directors, all of whom shall meet the independence requirements established by the Board and applicable laws, regulations, and listing requirements. Each member shall in the judgment of the Board have the ability to read and understand fundamental financial statements and otherwise meet the financial sophistication standard established by the requirements of the NASDAQ Stock Market, LLC. At least one member of the Committee shall in the judgment of the Board be an "audit committee financial expert" as defined by the rules and regulations of the Securities and Exchange Commission. The Board appoints the members of the Committee and the chairperson. The Board may remove any member from the Committee at any time with or without cause.

Generally, no member of the Committee may serve on more than three audit committees of publicly traded companies (including the Audit Committee of the Company) at the same time. For this purpose, service on the audit committees of a parent and its substantially owned subsidiaries counts as service on a single audit committee.

Operations

The Committee meets at least six times a year. Additional meetings may occur as the Committee or its chair deems advisable. The Committee will cause to be kept adequate minutes of its proceedings, and will report on its actions and activities at the next quarterly meeting of the Board. Committee members will be furnished with copies of the minutes of each meeting and any action taken by unanimous consent. The Committee is governed by the same rules regarding meetings (including meetings by conference telephone or similar communications equipment), action without meetings, notice, waiver of notice, and quorum and voting requirements as are applicable to the Board. The Committee is authorized and empowered to adopt its own rules of procedure not inconsistent with (a) any provision of this Charter, (b) any provision of the Bylaws of the Company, or (c) the laws of the state of Washington.

Communications

The independent auditor reports directly to the Committee. The Committee is expected to maintain free and open communication with the independent auditor, the internal auditors, and management. This communication will include periodic private executive sessions with each of these parties.

(continued)

EXHIBIT 25.2 *(continued)*

Education

The Company is responsible for providing new members with appropriate orientation briefings and educational opportunities, and the full Committee with educational resources related to accounting principles and procedures, current accounting topics pertinent to the Company, and other matters as may be requested by the Committee. The Company will assist the Committee in maintaining appropriate financial literacy.

Authority

The Committee will have the resources and authority necessary to discharge its duties and responsibilities. The Committee has sole authority to retain and terminate outside counsel or other experts or consultants, as it deems appropriate, including sole authority to approve the firms' fees and other retention terms. The Company will provide the Committee with appropriate funding, as the Committee determines, for the payment of compensation to the Company's independent auditor, outside counsel, and other advisors as it deems appropriate, and administrative expenses of the Committee that are necessary or appropriate in carrying out its duties. In discharging its oversight role, the Committee is empowered to investigate any matter brought to its attention. The Committee will have access to the Company's books, records, facilities, and personnel. Any communications between the Committee and legal counsel in the course of obtaining legal advice will be considered privileged communications of the Company, and the Committee will take all necessary steps to preserve the privileged nature of those communications.

The Committee may form and delegate authority to subcommittees and may delegate authority to one or more designated members of the Committee.

Responsibilities

The Committee's specific responsibilities in carrying out its oversight role are delineated in the Audit Committee Responsibilities Calendar. The Responsibilities Calendar will be updated annually as necessary to reflect changes in regulatory requirements, authoritative guidance, and evolving oversight practices. The most recently updated Responsibilities Calendar will be considered to be an addendum to this Charter. The Committee relies on the expertise and knowledge of management, the internal auditors, and the independent auditor in carrying out its oversight responsibilities. Management of the Company is responsible for determining the Company's financial statements are complete, accurate, and in accordance with generally accepted accounting principles and establishing satisfactory internal control over financial reporting. The independent auditor is responsible for auditing the Company's financial statements and the effectiveness of the Company's internal control over financial reporting. It is not the duty of the Committee to plan or conduct audits, to determine that the financial statements are complete and accurate and in accordance with generally accepted accounting principles, to conduct investigations, or to assure compliance with laws and regulations or the Company's standards of business conduct, codes of ethics, internal policies, procedures, and controls.

tasks they may have performed in the past. The CAE for that smaller corporation should review materials published by the IIA, AICPA, or the Information Systems Audit and Control Association, and work with internal auditors from other smaller firms in the auditor's community to develop ideas and approaches. The local IIA chapter will typically have member CAEs from other nearby similar-sized companies who should be willing to share thoughts and ideas. The IIA's Global Audit Information Network program, discussed in Chapter 12, can be a source for reviewing other approaches for developing this material.

25.3 AUDIT COMMITTEE'S FINANCIAL EXPERT AND INTERNAL AUDIT

A major audit committee criticism in those pre-SOx days but after the fall of Enron was that many board members serving on audit committees had been elected because of their business or professional backgrounds, but they did not understand complex financial or internal control issues. SOx now requires that at least one of the audit committee independent directors must be what is called a financial expert with some fairly specific requirements for that role, as outlined in the Chapter 5 overview of SOx. This financial expert board member could very well be internal audit's best or closest audit committee ally and may be the starting point for the CAE to closely bind internal audit to the board's audit committee. The typical audit committee member today and certainly that financial expert are in a new and challenging position with legal mandates and lots of pressure.

SOx has caused many changes to corporate governance, the board of directors, and certainly the audit committee. In many situations, the CAE and internal audit may be a unique thread of corporate governance continuity, and internal audit can help the audit committee in this new era through a three-step approach:

1. Through a report and presentation, provide a detailed summary of current internal audit processes for risk assessments, planning and performing audits, and reporting results through audit reports.
2. Working with human resources and other resources, present plans to the audit committee to assist in launching the SOx required ethics and whistleblower program as discussed in Chapter 26.
3. Develop detailed plans for reviewing and assessing internal controls in the enterprise. This is a key component of SOx Section 404, internal control assessment requirements, as discussed in Chapter 5.

The first step here is that internal audit should make a concerted effort to explain its processes and procedures to the audit committee, the overall board, and to senior management with an emphasis on SOx's internal audit requirements. Once this board presentation is launched, it should become part of the annual internal audit planning process with ongoing changes reported. However, even before launching any such presentation, internal audit should go through its own processes and perform what might be called a health check to assess current internal audit practices. This might point to areas where there is room for internal audit improvement. Exhibit 25.3 shows an internal audit health check assessment survey that can be expanded or modified depending on current conditions. The idea here is that internal audit should go through a rapid self-assessment, asking itself how it is doing at present and what it should do to improve, and then making improvements as required. This is also along the lines of a control self-assessment, as discussed in Chapter 12.

EXHIBIT 25.3 Internal Audit Health Check Assessment

Internal Audit (IA) Processes	Yes/No
1. Does IA have a formal set of standards and are those standards consistent with IIA standards (as outlined in Chapter 8)?	
2. Are new IA members educated on the use of IA standards and is overall compliance to standards monitored regularly?	
3. Does IA prepare an annual audit plan and is performance against the plan regularly monitored by the audit committee?	
4. Are audit plans developed through a formal risk assessment process (see Chapter 7 on risk assessments)?	
5. Are individual audits planned and supervised with sufficient attention given to risks, adequate resources, and staffing (discussed in Chapter 16)?	
6. Is all IA work documented through a formal set of workpapers and are those workpapers reviewed by appropriate levels of management (workpaper procedures are discussed in Chapter 17)?	
7. Are audit findings reviewed, as appropriate, with management before release of final audit reports?	
8. Are recipients of audit reports required to respond to recommendations with plans for corrective action and are those responses monitored (see Chapter 18)?	
9. Are there special IA procedures in place in the event of fraud or suspected fraud encountered during reviews (fraud detection is discussed in Chapter 27)?	
10. Does IA report the results of its activities regularly to the audit committee?	
11. Are overall budgets developed for all IA work and is performance monitored against those budgets?	
12. Do all members of IA receive adequate training on accounting, internal controls, and technology issues?	

Once internal audit has gone through such a self-correction exercise, audit processes and ongoing activities should be presented to the audit committee as well as the overall board and management. The idea is to make certain that all parties are aware of internal audit's processes as well as ongoing issues. The session should be given to key members of management first, before the audit committee presentation, to ensure that internal audit's message is well understood and consistent with other management initiatives. Depending on the enterprise and its past history, internal audit may receive too little or even too much credit for its role in the corporate governance process.

25.4 AUDIT COMMITTEE RESPONSIBILITIES FOR INTERNAL AUDIT

The board of directors' audit committee has a primary responsibility for an enterprise's internal audit function. Prior to SOx, this had often been little more than a theoretical concept where internal audit reported to the audit committee "on paper" but effectively reported to the chief financial officer (CFO) or some other senior corporate officer. The modern internal audit function should have a charter-defined very active relationship with the enterprise's audit committee. These charters are often very specific regarding relationships with internal audit and typically require the audit committee to:

1. Review the resources, plans, activities, staffing, and organizational structure of internal audit. These areas are discussed in Chapters 14 and 15.
2. Review the appointment, performance, and replacement of the CAE.
3. Review all audits and reports prepared by internal audit together with management's response. Audit reports and communications are discussed in Chapter 18.
4. Review with management, the CAE, and the independent accountants the adequacy of financial reporting and internal control systems. The review should include the scope and results of the internal audit program and the cooperation afforded or limitations, if any, imposed by management on the conduct of the internal audit program.

These reviews have been part of the relationship between internal audit and its audit committee over time, but the audit committee charter published in the proxy formalizes this arrangement. The CAE should work closely with the audit committee to ensure that effective communication links are in place. The third point above on audit reports is an example. While some internal audit departments in the past supplied their audit committees with only summaries of internal audit report findings or just decided what they felt were significant audit report findings, SOx now mandates that internal audit should provide the audit committee with *all* audit reports and their supporting management responses. Even when internal audit generates a large number of audit reports, such as for a retail enterprise with audits of many smaller store units that often have few significant findings, the audit committee should receive detailed information on all audits performed. Even though summary reports are provided, complete reports for all audits should be provided as well.

Appointment of the Chief Audit Executive

While the CAE typically reports administratively to enterprise management, the audit committee is responsible for the hiring and dismissal of this internal audit executive. The board's compensation committee may also be involved when the CAE is designated as an officer of the enterprise. The objective here is not to deny enterprise management the right to name the person who will administer the internal audit department, which serves the combined needs of enterprise management and the audit committee. Rather, the significance of the audit committee's participation is to assure the independence of the internal audit function when there is a need to speak out regarding issues identified in the review and appraisal of internal controls and other enterprise activities.

The actual participation of the audit committee in the selection of the CAE can take a number of forms but typically involves a review of the proposed director's credentials followed by a formal interview. Enterprise management—often primarily the CFO—typically consults with the chair of the audit committee regarding potential CAE candidates, allowing the audit committee time to review and comment, and sometimes interview, before any change is actually made. In many instances, the enterprise will be faced with the need to name a new CAE because the existing person has resigned or has been promoted. Management may suggest the promotion of someone from within the enterprise or to recruit an outsider, but the audit committee will have the final decision. Agreement on the adequacy of the qualifications to serve the needs of both management and the board of directors is an essential condition of an ongoing effective relationship between senior management and the audit committee.

The audit committee is usually not involved in day-to-day administrative matters regarding the CAE and the entire internal audit function but must take care to ensure the ongoing quality of the internal audit function. For example, an incumbent CAE should continue to have opportunities for receiving a promotion or be given other responsibilities as a part of a management development program. In other instances, senior management may express strong feelings that the CAE should be transferred or terminated because of some strong management concern. In the latter situation, the audit committee should review the suggested personnel action and provide the affected CAE with a fair hearing on the issues involved. The audit committee may also feel that the CAE is not doing an adequate job in either complying with the audit committee's requests or in directing the internal audit function, or both. In such a case, the chair of the audit committee would typically express those concerns to enterprise management and start the process for a change in personnel. In an extreme case where there is disagreement regarding the CAE, the audit committee can always hire an outside consultant to perform the audit review work desired by the committee or can direct management, through board directives, to make a change.

The overall issue here is that the audit committee has the ability to hire or fire the CAE, but there must be an ongoing level of cooperation here. The audit committee is not on-site on a daily basis to provide detailed internal audit supervision and must rely on management for some detailed support. The CAE or any member of internal audit cannot just ignore an appropriate management request by claiming they only report the audit committee and are not responsible to enterprise line management. Similarly, enterprise management must make certain that internal audit is part of the enterprise and not some almost outsider because of the audit committee relationship.

Approval of Internal Audit Charter

As discussed in Chapter 14, an internal audit charter serves as a basis or authorization for every effective internal audit program. An adequate charter is particularly important to define the roles and responsibilities of internal audit and its responsibility to serve the audit committee properly. It is here that the mission of internal audit must clearly provide for service to the audit committee as well as to senior management. An internal audit charter is a broad but general document that defines the responsibilities of internal audit within the enterprise, describes the standards followed, and defines the relationship between the audit committee and internal audit. The latter point is particularly important as it sends a special message to senior management that the CAE can go to a higher authority—the audit committee—in the event of a significant controversy or internal control issue.

The audit committee is responsible for approving this internal audit charter, just as the full board is responsible for approving the audit committee's charter. We are discussing internal audit charters here because of this audit committee responsibility, but internal audit charters are discussed in greater detail in Chapter 14, in the section on charters and building an effective internal audit function. Who is responsible for drafting this internal audit charter? In theory, perhaps, the audit committee might draft this document as a board committee activity. In reality, the CAE will usually take the lead in drafting this charter and/or will suggest appropriate updates to an existing charter to the chair of the audit committee.

While the internal audit charter authorizes the work that should be performed, the audit committee members may not be in a position to draft detailed audit charter requirements. The CAE typically works closely with the chair of the audit committee to draft this document for audit committee and overall board approval. In addition to the charter, the specific nature and scope of internal audit's service responsibilities to the audit committee should be formalized and outlined. These could include periodic written audit status reports, regularly scheduled meetings with the audit committee, and both the right and obligation of internal audit's direct access to the audit committee. While this understanding typically does not require a formal audit committee resolution, both parties should have a clear understanding of the responsibilities of internal audit to present reports and to attend audit committee meetings. The acceptance of the internal audit charter and related provisions by all parties of interest means that internal audit is freed from barriers that might otherwise prevent it from making needed disclosures to the audit committee, even those of a very sensitive nature.

This charter statement of internal audit's relationship to the audit committee is especially important since internal audit also has a day-to-day working relationship with enterprise management. While the audit committee selects the CAE, other members of the audit team are hired and paid by the enterprise, not the independent audit committee. Senior management often may forget that internal audit also has this special reporting relationship within the enterprise. This need for an adequate internal audit charter is somctimes discounted by enterprise management on the grounds that there are *no restrictions* to internal audit's independence. Nevertheless, a strong internal audit charter, approved by the audit committee, is an important provision of corporate governance.

Approval of Internal Audit Plans and Budgets

The audit committee should ideally have developed an overall understanding of the total audit needs of the enterprise. This high-level appraisal covers various special control and financial reporting issues, allowing the audit committee to determine the portion of audit or risk assessment needs to be performed by either the internal or other providers. As part of this role, the audit committee is responsible for reviewing and approving all internal audit higher-level plans and budgets. This audit committee responsibility is consistent with its role as the ultimate coordinator of the total audit effort. While enterprise management may have its own ideas about the total audit effort and how it should be carried out, and while the CAE has views as to what needs to be done, this is an audit committee responsibility. It is essential that the varying views of the key parties be jointly considered and appropriately reconciled, but the audit committee will have the final word here.

The review of all internal audit plans by the committee is essential if the policies and plans for the future are to be determined most effectively. The introduction of new audit responsibilities since SOx has changed roles that had been in place for years, and all interested parties should understand the nature of the total audit plan. Enterprise management, internal auditors, and external audit alike then will know what to expect from the suppliers of audit services. The audit committee should assume a high-level coordination role. Although there are practical limitations as to how actively the audit committee can become involved in the detailed planning process, some involvement has a demonstrated high value. Typically, the chair of the audit committee is the most active person in this plan review, but even this person is subject to time limitations. Internal audit should prepare a comprehensive set of annual planning documents for the committee that give detailed plans for the upcoming year as well as longer-range plans for the future. Suggested formats for these plans are discussed in Chapter 8 on performing effective internal audits and in Chapter 15 on organizing internal audit activities. In addition, internal audit should prepare summarized reports of past audit activities and reassessments of its coverage to give the audit committee an understanding of significant areas covered in past reviews. Although internal audit should report its activities to the audit committee on a regular basis, this summary reporting of past activity gives an overview of past areas for audit emphasis as well as highlighting any potential gaps in audit coverage. Exhibit 25.4 is an example of a one-year audit plan for presentation to the audit committee of our example company, Global Computer Products. The CAE would present this type of report to the audit committee, listing particulars for each planned audit, with supporting details to answer questions and discuss supporting details. The summary report on past activities is particularly important in that it shows the areas that had been scheduled in the prior year's plan and the accomplishments against that plan.

In many enterprises, the annual audit plan is developed through both internal audit's risk analysis process and discussions with both senior management and the audit committee. Management and the committee may suggest areas for potential internal audit review, and internal audit should develop plans within the constraints of budget and resource limitations. If the audit committee has suggested a review of some specialized area but internal audit is unable to perform the planned audit due to some known constraints, the CAE should clearly communicate that deficiency to the audit committee.

25.5 AUDIT COMMITTEE REVIEW AND ACTION ON SIGNIFICANT AUDIT FINDINGS

An audit committee's most important responsibility is to review and take action on reported significant *audit findings* that are reported to them by internal and external auditors, management, and others. While the audit committee has responsibility for all of these areas, our focus here is on the importance of internal audit to report all significant findings to the audit committee on a regular and prompt basis. Part of this will occur through internal audit's distribution of all audit reports to the audit committee as part of the SOx requirements outlined in Chapter 5. While internal audit and others

EXHIBIT 25.4 One-Year Audit Plan Summary for Audit Committee Review

Global Computer Products 20xx Summarized Audit Plan

Division	Audit	Risk Rank	Est. Start	Planned Finish	Total Hours	Total Costs	Comments
Electro	Inv. Planning Controls	8.4					Carry-over—from 20xx
Electro	Phys. Inv. Observation	9.5					
Electro	B-Plant Security	7.4					
Electro	Materials Receiving	6.2					Physical & Logical Security
Electro	Procurement Controls	6.8					Operational Assessment
Electro	New Marketing System	7.8					
Distribution	XML Order Controls	9.1					First Audit of Process
Distribution	Whse. Physical Security	5.3					Financial Controls
Distribution	Factory Labor Reporting	7.2					Operational Controls
Distribution	Product Incentive System	8.6					Audit Committee Request
Distribution	Prod. Warranty Returns	8.8					Operational Controls
Distribution	Business Continuity Planning	9.1					
Distribution	A/R Control Proceed	7.5					
Asia Pacific	G/L System Integrity	8.6					First Review of Unit
Asia Pacific	Labor Relations Stds.	8.2					First Review of Unit
Asia Pacific	Mfg. Control System	9.2					First Review of Unit
Corporate	Government Relations Dept.	5.3					
Corporate	Construction Contracts	7.3					

(continued)

EXHIBIT 25.4 *(continued)*

Global Computer Products 20xx Summarized Audit Plan							
Division	**Audit**	**Risk Rank**	**Est. Start**	**Planned Finish**	**Total Hours**	**Total Costs**	**Comments**
Total Internal Audit Projects							
Nonaudit	Training						
Nonaudit	Audit Administration						
Total Internal Audit for 20xx							

should certainly not filter audit findings and only tell the audit committee what they feel is "significant," the interests and efficiencies of all will be better served by internal audit regularly reporting significant audit findings as well as the status and disposition of those findings. Exhibit 25.5 is an example of such a significant findings report from our Global Computer Products example company.

Reacting to significant audit findings requires a combination of understanding, competence, and cooperation by all of the major parties of interest—internal audit, management, external auditors, and the audit committee itself. Total enterprise welfare then becomes the standard by which to judge all internal audit services, as opposed to more provincial views that the interests of management and the audit committee may be to some extent conflicting. Within its own area of responsibility, internal audit should act aggressively in not just reporting the significant findings and stopping there but exercising ongoing monitoring actions to assess whether appropriate corrective actions are taken.

EXHIBIT 25.5 Internal Audit Significant Findings Audit Committee Report

Global Computer Products, Inc. Audit Committee of the Board of Directors Internal Audit Signficant Audit Findings—May 31, 20xx		
Status of Findings Reported in Prior Reports		*Current Status*
JAN XX	San Jose plant continuity plans have not been tested	Open
JUL XX	Physical security at ABC plant space	In Process
OCT XX	U.S Federal Form S-1 Incomplete	Corrected
NOV XX	Poor project planning at Maxx Division	In Process
DEC XX	Poor overall plant scrap accounting controls	Corrected
New Significant Audit Report Findings Added		
MAR XY	Poor controls over new WIP system	Open
APR XY	U.S. Federal EEOC reports not filed	Open

25.6 AUDIT COMMITTEE AND ITS EXTERNAL AUDITORS

The audit committee has a major responsibility for hiring the external audit firm, approving their proposed budget and audit plan, and releasing their audited financial statements. While many aspects of this arrangement have remained unchanged over time, SOx has caused some significant changes. As discussed in Chapter 5 on SOx Section 404 internal control assessments, the external auditors no longer can both perform and approve internal control assessments, nor are any consulting arms of the public accounting firms allowed to install financial applications that would be subject to external audit review. The major public accounting firms no longer have these consulting divisions, and, as discussed in several sections, public accounting firms are prohibited from outsourcing the internal audit services for the enterprises they audit. Audit committees need to be aware and sensitive to these changes.

SOx requires that the audit committee approve all external audit services, including comfort letters, as well as any nonaudit services provided by the external auditors. External auditors are still allowed to provide tax services as well as certain *de minimus* service exceptions, but they are prohibited from providing the following nonaudit services contemporaneously with their financial statement audits:

- Bookkeeping and other services related to the accounting records or financial statements of the audit client
- Financial IT design and implementation
- Appraisal or valuation services, fairness opinions, or contribution-in-kind reports
- Internal audit outsourcing services
- Management function or human resources support activities
- Broker or dealer, investment advisor, or investment banking services
- Legal services and other expert services unrelated to the audit
- Any other services that the Public Company Accounting Oversight Board determines to be not permitted

Even though their external auditors are prohibited from performing these activities, corporations will still need to contract for and acquire many of these types of services. These must be treated as special contracting arrangements, reported as part the annual financial reports. While it is in the best interest of the external audit firm to not get involved with such nonaudit services, internal audit should consider offering its services where appropriate and consistent with internal audit's charter.

25.7 WHISTLEBLOWER PROGRAMS AND CODES OF CONDUCT

As discussed in Chapter 5, SOx rules state that the audit committee must establish procedures for the receipt, retention, and treatment of complaints regarding accounting, internal accounting controls, or auditing matters, including procedures for the confidential, anonymous submission by employees of concerns regarding questionable accounting or auditing matters. This can be a documentation challenge since much of this material must be held in a secure, confidential manner. The CAE as well as enterprise legal counsel will often be the only non-CEO and CFO links between the audit committee and the corporation. Internal audit should offer its services to the audit committee—often to the designated financial expert—to establish documentation and communication procedures in the following areas:

- **Documentation logging whistleblower calls.** SOx mandates that the audit committee establish a formal whistleblower program where employees can raise their concerns regarding improper audit and controls matters with no fear of retribution. A large enterprise may already have an ethics function, as discussed in Chapter 26, where these matters can be handled in a secure manner. When a small enterprise does not have such a resource, internal audit should offer its facilities to log in such whistleblower communications, recording the date, time, and name of the caller for investigation and disposition. With a heritage of handling secure internal audit reports, internal audit is often the best resource in an enterprise to handle such matters. In all instances, SOx gives the audit committee the responsibility for launching and administering such a whistleblower program.
- **Disposition of whistleblower matters.** Even more important than logging in initial whistleblower calls, documentation must be maintained to record the nature of any follow-up investigations and related dispositions. Although the SOx-mandated whistleblower program does not have a cash reward program, complete documentation covering actions taken as well as any net savings should be maintained. Again, with its tradition of handling confidential matters, internal audit should offer to provide secure, confidential services here. This can be a very important activity, because if an employee calls in a whistleblower matter where it is later proven that this reported information got out and the whistleblower was subject to retaliation, the reporting employee can bring legal action against the corporation.
- **Codes of ethics.** SOx gives the audit committee the responsibility to implement a code of ethics for a corporation's senior officers such as the CEO and CFO. The concept is to outline a set of rules for proper conduct and to have these senior officers acknowledge that they have read, understand, and agree to abide by them. Chapter 26 discusses these ethics and whistleblower programs, and internal audit should play a leading role in helping the audit committee to implement such programs, not just for a limited set of senior officers but for the entire enterprise.

25.8 OTHER AUDIT COMMITTEE ROLES

The audit committee may frequently receive questions and queries regarding various accounting and auditing matters, and internal audit can offer to act as a secretary to the audit committee in documenting and handling these matters. Many of the points discussed in this chapter outline areas where internal audit can help the audit committee in handling some of its SOx-related administrative chores. Even for a very large corporation, the audit committee may consist of perhaps six persons, and the number will typically only be two in a smaller corporation. In addition, the typical independent director audit committee member is a busy person possibly serving on multiple boards and with little direct administrative support. While the CEO's or CFO's administrative support staff usually handles many administrative duties for board members, SOx rules require that the audit committee must act independently. Internal audit could be a natural resource to provide this help.

Under SOx, the audit committee takes on a new and important role, which internal audit is in perhaps one of the best positions to help facilitate. The CAE has an opportunity for open access to the audit committee through presentations at regular meetings and confidential one-on-one meetings. However, in the past, these meetings were often little more than formalities with limited true communications. As discussed throughout this book, SOx has changed these rules.

The audit committee and certainly its designated financial expert have been assigned a whole series of new responsibilities. Internal audit is an excellent source to help audit committee members to fulfill their SOx-related responsibilities through close communications as well as by offering to take on certain audit committee documentation tasks. The broad acceleration of social expectations, the resulting impact on the areas of enterprise responsibility, and the related growth of audit committees have generated new needs for the enterprise. As a result, there are new and expanding requirements for internal audit services that constitute both challenges and opportunities. SOx has changed much here, and the modern internal auditor should be aware of this expanded level of audit committee importance. Internal auditors should both understand these SOx-mandated service needs and actively serve and work with their audit committees as part of an overall objective to provide maximum service to the enterprise.

NOTE

1. Microsoft Corporation Audit Committee Charter and Responsibilities Calendar, July 1, 2014, http://www.microsoft.com/investor/corporategovernance/boardofdirectors/committees/audit.aspx.

CHAPTER TWENTY-SIX

Ethics and Whistleblower Programs

INTERNAL AUDITORS HAVE ALWAYS BEEN viewed as the ethical leaders in an enterprise. Whenever there have been questions of questionable dealings or fraud in operations, for example, the management response has almost always been to call on internal audit to investigate the matter. Because of their strong professional standards, supported by well-recognized professional codes of conduct, internal auditors are recognized and should be ethical leaders in the enterprise. They should be viewed as the enterprise's ethical leaders.

A knowledge and understanding of an internal auditor's professional code of ethics or conduct, as discussed in Chapter 9 along with both IIA and ISACA internal audit professional standards, are a key internal audit common body of knowledge (CBOK) requirement. Ethics and enterprise-wide codes of conduct have a much larger role in today's enterprise beyond just the internal audit function. In years past, many enterprises mouthed words about their commitment to ethics but often never went much further. However, since the launch of the revised Committee of Sponsoring Organizations internal control framework, discussed in Chapter 3, as well as today's Sarbanes-Oxley Act (SOx) rules, there has been an almost worldwide emphasis on the importance of establishing an ethical environment throughout the enterprise. While internal audit has had a continuing role here, many of these initiatives have been launched through enterprise human resources and corporate legal initiatives. Beyond just promoting an ethical environment for all enterprise stakeholders, these enterprise-wide initiatives have emphasized strong individual stakeholder codes of ethics or conduct, a recognition of enterprise core values, and what are frequently known as whistleblower programs. Employees and stakeholders at all levels are encouraged to think and act differently.

Moving beyond codes of ethics for individual professionals, whistleblower programs are an important facility for an overall enterprise. The concept behind them is that any employee or other stakeholder who has observed a work environment matter that appears to be significantly wrong should have the ability to report the matter to senior management without fear of recrimination. Whistleblower programs have been a standard in many U.S. legal rules and are an element of SOx, as discussed in Chapter 5. While internal auditors are not necessarily the designated recipients of whistleblower reports, they need to understand them and how they fit in the control environment of the enterprise.

This chapter discusses internal auditor ethics, compliance, and governance issues with an emphasis on the IIA and ISACA codes of conduct introduced in Chapter 9. Internal auditors need to understand these concepts and how they should be applied to their overall enterprise. In addition, in some smaller enterprises with more limited resources, internal audit may be called upon to launch and administer many, if not all, aspects of an enterprise's ethics and whistleblower programs. While knowledge of the IIA's code of conduct is a basic CBOK requirement, an overall understanding of whistleblower programs and enterprise ethics is important to the total enterprise and should be a key CBOK internal audit knowledge area as well.

This chapter also describes how to establish ethics and whistleblower functions that are consistent with SOx but also of value to all stakeholders in the enterprise: employees, officers, vendors, and contractors. Going beyond the SOx objectives to prevent fraudulent financial reporting, an effective ethics program is an important governance and compliance tool for the entire enterprise. Although they have been a component of U.S. defense contracting labor laws for years, SOx now mandates the establishment of whistleblower programs in all registered public corporations. We will look at the guidelines here and things internal audit can do to establish effective programs in the enterprise.

26.1 ENTERPRISE ETHICS, COMPLIANCE, AND GOVERNANCE

Many of the high-profile business failures over the years in the United States and elsewhere were characterized by investigators, regulators, and journalists to have occurred because of unethical behavior by business managers at all levels. Historically, such failures are nothing new. Ethical lapses have occurred since the early days of business and trade—at least over the past 1,000 years if not earlier. However, today's lapses often seem different, as our access to information widely publicizes them, and many more people may be hurt due to their stock market investments, retirement accounts, and other financial interests. While the so-called robber barons of the late nineteenth century had an attitude of "Let the public be damned!" in an era when there were few legal restrictions, this is not acceptable in today's society, with our need for compliance with a plethora of rules and regulations as well as an increased interest in business ethics, codes of conduct, and enterprise governance issues.

Internal auditors have been familiar with ethics programs and codes of conduct over the years. Internal audit's professional standards, as discussed in Chapter 9, make a code of conduct a prominent component, and many internal auditors have become involved with reviewing and helping to enhance their enterprise's ethics programs. This area became even more important when the SOx mandated signed ethics or code of conduct statements from senior officers and called for whistleblower programs directed by the audit committee.

As outlined in Chapter 5, SOx mandates that corporate audit committees must have their chief financial officer (CFO) sign an ethics statement. While this is no guarantee that the CFO will always follow ethical business practices, the threat of a major fine or even prison are strong compliance inducements. However, a strong set of personal values throughout the enterprise as well as an ongoing commitment to always do the right thing are often even more important. While SOx's requirements are limited to senior financial officers, an enterprise will generally find more value in launching and implementing such a program for the entire enterprise and its key stakeholders. While some ethics and code of conduct rules can be very specific to just the financial officers, enterprises will find greater value in having one set of rules apply to all, and internal audit may want to consider advising management to move in that direction.

Enterprises of all sizes and areas of business today should establish effective *ethics functions*, including a *mission statement* and a code of conduct. Although an ethics program is important today, an enterprise cannot claim to have implemented it just by publishing a code of business conduct and instructing all employees to read it. An effective ethics program requires a formal commitment between the enterprise and its employees and agents to do the right thing. Many enterprises today already have elements of an ethics program in place, while others assume they have good ethics practices because there have been no recent problems. All too often, those established "ethics programs" amount to little more than an employee code of conduct given to new hires on their first day on the job plus sometimes a few posters hung where employees can read them, or more typically Web postings on the enterprise's intranet system. A new employee is asked to read and sign the enterprise's code of conduct as part of completing such new-hire materials as tax withholding forms, medical plan selections, and other employee options. All too often this stakeholder signed code of conduct is simply filed away and forgotten by all involved parties. This does not constitute an effective ethics program for an enterprise.

The following sections outline some of the elements of an effective ethics program for an enterprise, starting with understanding the risk environment and moving to launching an effective enterprise code of conduct. An enterprise should consider launching an ethics program that applies to all stakeholders throughout its operations. While the emphasis may be a bit different at various levels, all should be aware of the enterprise's values and overall mission. As a natural party interested in good, ethical business practices, internal audit should be in a key position to help launch an enterprise-wide ethics function if one does not exist or to help to improve any current programs. Just as internal auditors should understand how to evaluate and recommend effective internal accounting controls, they should have a basic understanding of the elements of an effective organization ethics program.

As a clarification here, Chapter 9 introduced and discussed the importance of a code of ethics as part of an internal auditor's personal professional standards, including both the IIA and ISACA. This chapter discusses the importance of having an effective code and ethics program for an enterprise as a whole. While these enterprise-specific codes and standards should not be in conflict with an internal auditor's own professional standards, internal auditors should always determine, as part of internal control reviews, that effective enterprise-level codes exist.

26.2 ETHICS FIRST STEPS: DEVELOPING A MISSION STATEMENT

Every enterprise, no matter its size, should have a formal mission statement to describe its overall objectives and values. Properly developed, a mission statement should be a source of direction—a compass—to let employees, customers, stockholders, and other stakeholders know what the enterprise stands for and what it does not. Once little more than a nice-sounding slogan for many enterprises, effective mission statements are today important for promoting strong organizational ethics and good corporate governance. Effective mission statements can be a great asset to an enterprise, allowing it to better achieve organizational goals and purposes.

The Johnson & Johnson Tylenol crisis of the early 1980s provides a good example of the importance of a strong *corporate mission statement* as a compass to provide direction. Johnson & Johnson, a major medical products provider, manufactures a popular pain medication called Tylenol. At the time, such medications were sold in screw-top bottles with no tamper-proofing. Someone in the Chicago area opened a series of these Tylenol bottles, adulterated their contents with cyanide, and placed the bottles back on store shelves. Several people who purchased this tainted Tylenol subsequently died from cyanide poisoning. An investigation of the deaths quickly pointed to Johnson & Johnson and the poison-tainted Tylenol.

The matter put Johnson & Johnson under massive pressure. The corporation knew that it had extremely strong quality control processes in place that would prevent such poison contamination from occurring within its own manufacturing facilities. It also knew that the contaminated products had appeared only in the Chicago area, while Tylenol was found on store shelves worldwide. A worldwide product recall would be extremely expensive. However, rather than going through a long series of internal investigations, Johnson & Johnson quickly did the right thing. It recalled all Tylenol products from store shelves worldwide and subsequently released future products in a newly designed sealed package. When asked why it was able to make such a very expensive recall decision so quickly even though the company knew it was not at fault, Johnson & Johnson stated that there was no need for a delayed decision. The Johnson & Johnson credo, their mission statement, dictated that decision. That credo, found on the Johnson & Johnson web site,[1] states very strongly that the company's first responsibility is to supply high-quality products to its customers. At the time of the Tylenol crisis, everyone at Johnson & Johnson knew this. The credo had been posted widely in enterprise facilities, and there was no need for the enterprise to explore multiple potential alternatives before making a decision. The whole unfortunate matter highlighted the importance of a strong mission statement for an enterprise.

A strong corporate mission statement is an important element in any ethics and corporate governance initiative. Although most enterprises will not face a crisis on the level of Johnson & Johnson's tainted Tylenol in the 1980s, a stronger anchor of this sort might have helped some enterprises to better avoid the accounting scandals around the turn of this most recent century that led to the creation of SOx.

Working with an ethics officer function and senior management, internal audit can help to evaluate mission statements or rewrite and launch new ones. Stakeholder ethics surveys, discussed in the next section, will highlight potential problems in any existing mission statement. If employees or other stakeholders are not really aware of the corporate mission statement or if they view it as little more than a set of meaningless words, there is a need to revisit and revise that document. A poorly crafted mission statement can often do more harm than good, creating cynical and unhappy organization members who resist change. If the enterprise has no mission or values statement, there can be considerable value to assembling a team to develop a statement that reflects the enterprise's overall values and purposes. If an existing statement was met with cynicism during the ethics survey, it is time to rework and revise that statement. However, any revised statement should be carefully crafted and delivered. If just rolled out with no preparation, it may be viewed with even more cynicism. A good mission statement is also a good starting point for senior management tone-at-the-top messages in today's corporation.

A good mission statement should make a positive statement about an enterprise and hopefully inspire enterprise stakeholders to harness their energy, passion, and commitment to achieving goals and objectives. The idea is to create a sense of purpose and direction that will be shared throughout the enterprise. Perhaps one of the best examples of a mission statement was expressed by U.S. president John F. Kennedy in the early 1960s:

> This nation should dedicate itself to achieving the goal, before this decade is out, of landing a man on the moon and returning him safely to Earth.

Those simple words describe a mission and vision much better than an extensive document of many pages. Sometimes called values statements or credos, mission statements can be found in the annual reports of many enterprises. Some are lengthy, while others seem to be little more than fluff. The best are closer to the Johnson & Johnson credo explained earlier in this chapter or JFK's moon landing statement in their style.

Once an enterprise has developed a new mission statement or has revised an existing one, it should be rolled out to all enterprise members with a good level of publicity. Using a tone-at-the-top approach, senior managers should explain the reasons for the new mission statement and why it will be important for the enterprise. It should be posted on facility billboards, in the annual report, on the enterprise's homepage, and in other places to encourage all stakeholders to understand and accept it. The mission statement, however, should just not stand by itself; a series of other key steps are needed to build an effective ethics and compliance function.

Sometimes an internal auditor might argue, "I'm an internal auditor—I just review the internal controls that are in place. What do I have to do with launching an ethics function?" This is true, and internal audit should always be involved with reviewing and commenting on the controls that others have established. However, due to the unique nature of ethics and compliance programs and their relationship to the overall enterprise, internal audit can take an even more active role in helping to implement them.

26.3 UNDERSTANDING THE ETHICS RISK ENVIRONMENT

Virtually every enterprise faces a mix of risks that limit its business operations, growth, profitability, or other areas. When business or the economy is booming, there will always be downturns, but in order to keep showing ever-increasing growth when business is beginning to slow down, enterprises sometimes bend the rules with regard to their ethical and financial performance. This was the path of Enron, WorldCom, and other once prominent and now failed enterprises, and which led the U.S. Congress to pass SOx. Understanding an enterprise's risk environment should always be a first step to launching an effective ethics program.

While an effective ethics program cannot shield an enterprise from the risk of a major earthquake or some other cataclysmic event, it can help to protect it from a variety of other operational and business risks. Just as some accounting officers decided to bend the rules prior to SOx, these kinds of attitudes can present risks in many other areas. The office worker who copies company software or records for use on the home computer, the factory worker who skips product final inspection procedures to save time, or the vendor who ships fewer items than ordered because "they never check" shipping notices are all examples of bending the rules and increasing risks to the enterprise. These kinds of practices often develop because of perceived disparities between senior management and staff. The employee who regularly sees managers exceed expense account limits with no evident repercussions may soon try to bend the rules in other areas.

Internal audit can take a major lead here in surveying employee attitudes and practices. Ethics attitudes and risks can be assessed through either a targeted review of findings from past audits or through special reviews based on employee and stakeholder *ethics attitude surveys*. Internal audit can accomplish such an ethics survey through coordination with the enterprise's ethics function, if such a group exists. The nature of such an ethics function will be discussed in the following paragraphs, and if there is a formal ethics function, internal audit should review the results of any other ethics surveys that may have been performed there, making plans to revise or update as necessary. An ethics survey is a very good way to understand enterprise attitudes and is an aid to support corporate governance processes.

Ethics-Related Findings from Past Audits or Special Audits

If internal audit has completed a large number of compliance-related operational and financial audits over recent years, a reexamination of workpaper and audit report findings or even audit report responses may provide insights into overall enterprise ethical attitudes. Consistent workpaper findings covering "minor" infractions may point to overall trends in ethical attitudes. An example here would be an ongoing failure of employees to follow some relatively minor process or procedures such as securing a second approval signature on smaller-value transactions, despite a policy calling for this second signature, or the failure to document new IT applications, despite systems development documentation requirements. The responsible audit team may have decided the matter was "too minor" to include in summarized final audit reports, but such findings often point to potential ethical attitude problems. Even worse, sometimes these types of findings are reported in audit reports only to be brushed off in the report responses.

Some of the ongoing "minor" findings mentioned may not point to ongoing ethical violations but to areas where rules just need to be changed. Some enterprises, for example, may have travel expense rules calling for *every* travel expense to be reported by a receipt, even if this includes highway tollbooth fares of 50 cents each. The driver can get this postage-stamp-size toll receipt only by waiting in the cashier line rather than driving through a faster line that accepts coins without receipts. Because managers and others may feel that rules requiring such minimal-value receipts do not add value, expense reports lacking these receipts may be frequently submitted and approved without these receipts. Such a matter may be noted but not reported in audit reports. From an internal audit perspective, does this situation represent an ethical violation for the enterprise? On one level, the answer may be yes, because a rule is a rule. However, an internal auditor reviewing past audit reports and workpapers for ethical problems might best work with the appropriate unit in the enterprise to get such unreasonable rule procedures changed. Internal audit might also consider launching a special audit to assess such ethical attitudes. This would be a strong compliance review covering some key areas across the enterprise or a highly focused review in one department or group. This type of internal audit–initiated review will provide an overall assessment of ethical attitudes in the enterprise.

Employee and Stakeholder Ethics Attitude Surveys

Properly done, employee, officer, and stakeholder surveys can be an excellent way to assess enterprise ethical attitudes. The idea is to gather as much information as possible about ethical attitudes and practices from broad groups in the enterprise, such as factory workers (if appropriate), office staff, senior managers, vendors, and others. While the ethics attitude survey would include some common questions, each group would also receive specific questions directed to their responsibilities. The senior officer group, for example, would receive the same set of organizational attitude questions given to all, but also get specific SOx internal control–related questions.

Drafting a fact-gathering survey that receives a high response level is never easy, and the use specialized help should be considered. Rather than a series of questions requiring just yes-or-no responses, the survey should consist of many "Have you ever . . ." types of questions where persons completing the survey can provide as long or as short an answer as they wish. This open-ended response makes it more difficult to compile results, but interesting and valuable information may be retained. Exhibit 26.1 is an example of an ethics attitude survey that might be directed to supervisory, management, and other professional members of the enterprise.

A key requirement of this type of survey is that it must be as anonymous as possible. The surveys should be sent directly to employee homes along with a cover letter from the chief executive officer (CEO) explaining the objectives and purpose of the survey exercise. Return envelopes, prestamped, to a special post office box should be included. The survey document would be set with a primary objective to survey ethics attitudes; however, if the enterprise has already established a whistleblower hotline function, as discussed next, the survey could allow people to report such matters as well. Summarizing survey results can be a major challenge with this type of survey, particularly if respondents have provided free-form responses. Internal audit or the ethics officer would be responsible for preparing such a report, with the objective of reviewing the results with the audit committee and senior management. For confidentiality reasons, respondents would not receive this summary report; they should only receive a general thank-you letter.

EXHIBIT 26.1 Ethics Attitude Survey Questions

These questions might be used by an internal auditor in a survey of managers, supervisors, and other enterprise professionals in order to gain a better understanding their enterprise's ethics environment.

1. Do you have access to current enterprise policies and procedures?
2. If you have questions or need clarifications regarding these procedures, do you have a mechanism to ask questions or seek advice?
3. When an established procedure does not appear applicable, given current conditions, is there a process for submitting it for review?
4. Do you feel the rules and procedures apply just to other groups, such as regular employees if you are part-time or the headquarters operation if you are at a remote subsidiary?
5. Do you feel your senior managers follow the same types and levels of rules that you follow?
6. Has your supervisor ever told you to ignore some rule or procedure?
7. Do you feel some of the published rules and procedures are trivial or out of date?
8. Do you feel the CEO and other senior officers have delivered clear and strong messages on the importance of enterprise ethics?
9. Are you familiar with the enterprise's mission statement?
10. What does the mission statement mean to you?
11. Are you familiar with the code of business conduct?
12. Do you feel this code of conduct is regularly updated to reflect current business activities and issues?
13. Do you feel the code of conduct is applicable to all stakeholders, such as officers, contractors, or vendors?
14. Do you feel the rules are clear for violations of the code of conduct?
15. Have you ever reported an observed code of conduct violation? Were you satisfied with the results of that reporting?
16. Have you ever participated in any enterprise-sponsored ethics training?
17. Do you feel that training was relevant to your work environment as well as your duties and responsibilities?
18. Do you understand how to report accounting, internal control, or auditing concerns under the enterprise's whistleblower program?
19. Do you feel there is an effective mechanism in place to confidentially report violations of the code or other questionable acts?
20. Do you feel there are effective processes in place to investigate reported compliance violations and then to resolve them?
21. Have you observed any evidence that reported ethics compliance violations are subject to disciplinary actions?
22. Would you be reluctant to report a violation for fear of potential employer retaliatory actions?

Either of these approaches will allow internal audit, a designated ethics office team, or others to gain a general understanding of the ethics environment in the enterprise. This can be a first step to launching a formal ethics function or upgrading and enhancing an existing one. These surveys will provide general management some insights into the overall ethics atmosphere in their enterprise. While not required under SOx, this information will bolster corporate governance practices by highlighting areas where improvements are needed.

26.4 SUMMARIZING ETHICS SURVEY RESULTS: DO WE HAVE A PROBLEM?

The results of an ethics attitude survey or assessments from past internal audits may provide some assurances that things appear to be pretty good throughout the enterprise. More often, however, they can raise some troubling signs, ranging from small but ongoing compliance deviations, to surveyed vendors claiming heavy-handed negotiation tactics, to employees stating they have been asked to bend rules. The hard question with any such results is whether they represent troubling exceptions or the tip of a much larger ethics problem iceberg. At this point, internal audit and the enterprise's ethics officer should meet with senior management to develop some next steps.

Based on any potential disturbing red flags from the surveys, it may be best to expand the mail survey process. Also, concerns that came out of those initial surveys may point to a need to expand the assessments to such groups as customers, agents, or vendors. If the survey results ended with inconclusive or mixed messages, another appropriate step would be to set up a series of focus group sessions. Small groups of employees and stakeholders would be randomly selected and asked to meet in an off-site location to discuss their perceptions of enterprise ethical values. With a strong emphasis that any responses from such sessions are anonymous, a skilled facilitator could lead the selected group through a discussion. The resultant data may form the basis for launching an enterprise-wide ethics program or enhancing any existing programs. As discussed in the following sections, an ethics program effort requires a strong code of conduct as well as a whistleblower process to allow for reporting of ethics violations.

While SOx talks about these ethics and whistleblower issues only in terms of senior financial officers and potential financial fraud, a strong ethics program will benefit the entire enterprise in addition to providing SOx compliance. If an enterprise does not already have an ethics program, internal audit can be a natural party to helping establish one.

26.5 ENTERPRISE CODES OF CONDUCT

While a mission statement is a keystone to hold together the overall structure of corporate governance, an enterprise-wide code of conduct provides the supporting guidance for all related stakeholders. While SOx refers to this as a *code of ethics,* we are using the more traditional name *code of conduct.* Although such codes have been in place at major corporations for many years, SOx requires that registrants must develop them for their senior financial officers to promote the honest and ethical handling of any conflicts of interest and compliance with applicable governmental rules and regulations. Even if an enterprise does not come under SOx rules, there are many benefits to developing and issuing an appropriate code of conduct. The SOx code is mandated, but all enterprises can benefit from a code that covers all stakeholders.

The effective enterprise today should develop and enforce a code of conduct that covers applicable ethical, business, and legal rules for all enterprise stakeholders, whether the financial officers highlighted in SOx, all other salaried and hourly employees, or a larger group stakeholders. While internal audit is not typically the catalyst group to draft or launch such a code of conduct, internal audit can be a key participant in both helping to launch and then determining that the enterprise has an effective code of conduct that promotes ethical business practices.

Code of Conduct Contents: What Should Be the Code's Message?

A code of conduct should be a clear, unambiguous set of rules or guidance that outlines what is expected of all enterprise stakeholders, whether officers, employees, contractors, vendors, or others. The code should be based on both the values and legal issues surrounding an enterprise. That is, while all enterprises can expect to have code of conduct prohibitions against sexual and racial discrimination, a defense contractor with many contract-related rules issues might have a somewhat different code of conduct than a fast-food store operation. However, the code should apply to all members of the enterprise from the most senior level to a part-time clerical employee. For example, a code of conduct rule prohibiting erroneous financial reporting is the same whether directed at the CFO for incorrect quarterly financial reporting or the part-timer for an incorrect or fraudulent weekly time card.

If the enterprise already has a code of conduct, internal audit may want to schedule a review from time to time to revisit that code. All too often, older codes were originally drafted as rules for lower-level employees, with little attention given to the more senior members of the enterprise. SOx and its overall corporate governance guidance was meant for those senior officers but should be delivered in such a manner that it will apply to all enterprise stakeholders. Working with senior members of management and the audit committee, internal audit can examine any existing code of conduct to determine if those rules still fit the SOx era of today.

A joint team from a cross section of management, including legal and human resources, should be assembled to develop the code. The team should examine the business issues facing the enterprise and then draft a set of rules that are applicable to that enterprise. The code must be written in a clear manner such that the points can be easily understood by all. Exhibit 26.2 lists some example code of conduct topics. This list, although it does not apply to all enterprises, includes topics that are appropriate for many modern enterprises. The key is that messages delivered in the code must be clear and unambiguous.

Some years ago, this author led a project to develop and implement a code of conduct for a large U.S. corporation. An extract from the code's section covering company assets reads:

> We all have a responsibility to care for all of the company's assets including inventory, cash, supplies, facilities, and the services of other employees and computer systems resources. If you see or suspect that another employee is stealing, engaging in fraudulent activities, or otherwise not properly protecting company assets, you may report these activities to your manager or to the ethics office.

These words are an example of the tone and style of a good code of conduct. It places the responsibility on the recipient of the code, tries to explain the issues in an unambiguous manner, and suggests expected responses and actions.

EXHIBIT 26.2 Example Code of Conduct Topics

The following are topic areas found in a typical enterprise stakeholder code of conduct. The actual code should have specific rules in each of these areas.

1. Introduction
   a. Purpose of this Code of Conduct: A general statement about the background of the code of conduct, emphasizing enterprise traditions.
   b. The Enterprise's Commitment to Strong Ethical Standards: A restatement of the Mission Statement and a supporting message from the CEO.
   c. Where to Seek Guidance: A description of the ethics hot-line process.
   d. Reporting Noncompliance: Guidance for whistleblowers—How to report.
   e. Your Responsibility to Acknowledge the Code: A description of the code acknowledgement process for all stakeholders.
2. Fair Dealing Standards
   a. Enterprise Selling Practices: Guidance for dealing with customers.
   b. Enterprise Buying Practices: Guidance and policies for dealing with vendors.
3. Conduct in the Workplace
   a. Equal Employment Opportunity Standards: A strong commitment statement.
   b. Workplace and Sexual Harassment Policies: An equally strong commitment statement.
   c. Alcohol and Substance Abuse: A policy statement in this area.
4. Conflicts of Interest
   a. Outside Employment: Limitations on accepting employment from competitors.
   b. Personal Investments: Rules regarding using enterprise data to make personal investment decisions.
   c. Gifts and Other Benefits: Rules regarding receiving bribes and improper gifts.
   d. Former Employees: Rules prohibiting giving favors to ex-employees in business.
   e. Family Members: Rules about giving business to family members, creating potential conflicts of interest, and family member employee relating relationships.
5. Enterprise Property and Records
   a. Enterprise Assets: A strong statement on the employees' responsibility to protect assets.
   b. Computer Systems Resources: An expansion of the enterprise assets statement to reflect all aspects of computer systems resources.
   c. Use of the Enterprise's Name: A rule that the enterprise name should only be used for normal business dealings.
   d. Enterprise Records: A rule regarding employee responsibility for records integrity.
   e. Confidential Information: Rules on the importance of keeping all enterprise information confidential and not disclosing it to outsiders.
   f. Employee Privacy: A strong statement in the importance of keeping employee personal confidential to outsiders and even other employees.
   g. Enterprise Benefits: Employees must not take enterprise benefits where they are not entitled.
6. Complying with the Law
   a. Inside Information and Insider Trading: A strong rule prohibiting insider trading or otherwise benefiting from inside information.
   b. Political Contributions and Activities: A strong statement on political activity rules.
   c. Bribery and Kickbacks: A firm rule of using bribes or accepting kickbacks.
   d. Foreign Business Dealings: Rules regarding dealing with foreign agents in line with the Foreign Corrupt Practices Act.
   e. Workplace Safety: A statement on the enterprise policy to comply with OSHA rules.
   f. Product Safety: A statement on the enterprise commitment to product safety.
   g. Environmental Protection: A rule regarding the enterprise commitment to comply with applicable environmental laws.

Many enterprises have found value in adding a set of frequently asked questions to the code, along with suggested answers. These allow the code's readers to better understand the issues as well as the types of questions that a perhaps more unsophisticated employee might ask regarding a code rule. The key to a clear set of code of conduct rules is that they must be understood by all. This can be a real editing challenge.

Codes of conduct for different enterprises look different in style, format, and size. Some are elaborate, while others are bare-bones. *Enterprise codes of conduct*, by their nature, are certainly not company trade secrets, and corporate information or public relations offices will typically give out copies of their codes of conduct. Start with enterprises in your industry that you respect to see how they have built their code of conduct.

Global-scale enterprises have another issue when developing a code of conduct. Although a corporation may be headquartered in the United States, it may have significant operations worldwide in which key managers, employees, and other stakeholders do not use English as their primary language. Despite the added costs of translation, firms should consider producing a version of the code in at least the major languages used in corporate operations. If there are many locations and just small numbers of foreign-language stakeholders, a summary of the main code of conduct in each of the local languages might be appropriate. However, those summary versions should emphasize the same SOx financial fraud guidance contained in the primary code of conduct.

Communications to Stakeholders and Assuring Compliance

An enterprise's code of conduct must be a *living document*. It has little value if it had been developed, delivered to all stakeholders with much hullabaloo, and then filed and forgotten. If the document represents a new code of conduct or even a major revision, the enterprise should undertake a major effort to deliver a copy to all employees and stakeholders. Given the current SOx rules, a good first step would be to formally present the new code of conduct to the enterprise's top managers, and particularly the financial officers.

Codes of conduct in the past sometimes received only token acceptance from senior officers, who felt that they were really for the staff and not for them. The financial scandals that prompted SOx highlighted this discrepancy. Both Enron and WorldCom had adequate corporate codes of conduct, but their corporate officers evidently did not feel that these rules applied to them. A disturbing example of high-level corporate officer code of conduct avoidance can be found in the actions of former Enron CFO Andrew Fastow.[2] Because he knew that he would be violating the Enron corporate code of conduct with a series of fraudulent off-balance-sheet schemes, Fastow went to the Enron audit committee and asked them to formally vote him an exemption from their code of conduct rules. The audit committee granted this exemption.

The senior management group should formally acknowledge that they have read, understand, and will abide by the code of conduct. With the management team standing behind it, the enterprise should next roll out and then deliver the code of conduct to all enterprise stakeholders. This can be done in multiple phases, with delivery to local or more major facilities first, followed by smaller units, foreign locations, and other stakeholders. Rather than just including a copy of the code with payroll documents, an enterprise should make a formal effort to present it in a manner that will gain attention.

A new code of conduct can be communicated through a video by the CEO, webcasts, training sessions, or other means to communicate its importance and meaning. Special communication methods might be used for other groups such as vendors or contractors, but an enterprise objective should be to get all stakeholders to formally acknowledge that they will abide by the code of conduct. This can be accomplished by an Internet or telephone response type of system where every enterprise stakeholder is asked to respond to these three questions:

1. Have you received and read a copy of the code of conduct? Answer yes or no.
2. Do you understand the contents of the code of conduct? Answer yes if you understand this code of conduct or no if you have questions.
3. Do you agree to abide by the policies and guidelines in this code of conduct? Answer yes if you agree to abide by the code and no if you do not.

Responses should be recorded on a database listing the employee name and the date of their review and acceptance or nonacceptance. Any questions resulting from question number 2 can be handled through the whistleblower program described next. The idea is to have everyone—all of the stakeholders—buy into the code of conduct and agree to its terms. If someone refuses to accept the code because of questions, supervisors or others should discuss the matter with that person to gain eventual resolution. The enterprise should expect all employees to agree to accept and abide by its code of conduct. Following the code of conduct is just another work rule, and consistent failure to abide by its rules should be grounds for termination.

The point of this code acknowledgment requirement is to avoid any "I didn't know that was the rule" excuses when code violations are encountered. It is a good idea to go through a code acceptance process on an annual basis or at least after any revisions to the code document. The files documenting code acknowledgments should be retained in a secure manner.

Code Violations and Corrective Actions

An enterprise-wide code of conduct lays out a set of rules for expected behavior in the enterprise. SOx requires that financial officers must subscribe to a code containing rules prohibiting fraudulent financial reporting, but an enterprise should release one code of conduct with guidance for all stakeholders—the SOx impacted financial officers as well as all others, including employees at all levels, contractors, vendors, and others. In addition to publishing a code of conduct and obtaining stakeholder acceptance, there also is a need for a mechanism to report code violations and for investigating and handling those violations.

If the enterprise issues a strong code of conduct along with a message from the CEO about the importance of good ethical practices, all stakeholders are expected to follow those rules. However, we all know that people are people and there will always be some who violate the rules or run on the edge. An enterprise needs to establish a mechanism to allow employees or even outsiders to report potential violations of the code in a secure and confidential manner. Much of that reporting mechanism can be handled through the whistleblower facility, as discussed in this chapter. Other potential violations must be handled on a different level. Consider the female staff employee with a male supervisor who hints that sexual favors with him are a good way to advance in the enterprise. A code of conduct sexual harassment prohibition will not necessarily stop the supervisor, and the employee can often not easily report the situation to a manager one level above the supervisor. A process should be established for reporting all types of ethics violations.

In addition to the whistleblower facility, the enterprise should establish other mechanisms for reporting potential *code of conduct violations*. Since some people may not want to call an ethics hotline function, a well-publicized post office box address is sometimes very effective. Stakeholders could be encouraged to write to such an address, anonymously or not, to report ethics violations. Based on these responses, the ethics function, human resources, or some other appropriate function in the enterprise should investigate the matter and take action as necessary.

A code of conduct describes a series of rules for expected actions in the enterprise. When violations are found, the matter should be investigated and actions taken on a consistent basis, no matter the rank of the enterprise stakeholders. If the code of conduct prohibits making copies of corporate software—and it should—the penalties for a staff analyst in a remote sales office or a senior manager in corporate headquarters should be the same. Assuming they both read the prohibition in the code and acknowledged acceptance, penalties for violations should be consistent. Otherwise there can be an atmosphere in which the rules appear to apply only to some.

Most code of conduct violations can be handled through the enterprise's normal human resources procedures, which should have established processes where a first offense might result in verbal counseling or probation, with termination for repeat offenses. Some matters must be reported to outside authorities. A violation of SOx rules, such as an undocumented off-balance-sheet arrangement, would be reported to the Securities and Exchange Commission (SEC); the theft of goods from a warehouse would be reported to a county prosecutor. When these matters are discovered and reported to outside authorities, the matter moves outside of the enterprise's hands. The goal here is for the enterprise to have some process in place to encourage all stakeholders to follow good ethical practices, as defined in the code of conduct, and to provide a consistent mechanism for reporting violations and taking disciplinary action when necessary.

Keeping the Code of Conduct Current

Many of the basic rules of good ethical behavior as well as many enterprise-specific rules will not change from year to year. For example, the rule about protection of company assets, cited previously, stated that all stakeholders have a responsibility to care for their enterprise's assets, whether property, cash, IT resources, or others. That type of ethical rule will not change over time, but others may change due to business or other conditions. Enterprises should review their published codes of conduct on a periodic basis and at least once every two years to make certain the guidance is still applicable and current. This might include a code statement regarding the need for accurate and timely financial reporting at all levels or the enterprise's commitment to avoid any type of financial fraud. Changes to the code of conduct should not be treated lightly. Any revision should go through the same announcement and rollout process described previously for code introductions. The revised code should be issued to all stakeholders along with an explanation of the changes and a requirement to reacknowledge acceptance.

As new employees and other stakeholders join the enterprise, they should be given the existing code of conduct with the same requirement that they read and affirm the document. Consideration might be given to a webcast to explain and educate new employees regarding the code of conduct and the enterprise's commitment to it. Also, whether the code is revised or not, all stakeholders should be asked on a periodic basis to reaffirm that they have read and will continue to abide by the code.

A new code of conduct revision and request for stakeholder reaffirmation can be an expensive task requiring dedicated enterprise resources from the ethics function, human resources, internal audit, and others. Along with the mission statement, an enterprise should keep its code of conduct and supporting principles in front of all stakeholders at all times. This can be accomplished through constant references to the code of conduct, such as in bulletin board posters in all facilities, instructive questions and answers in publications, or as segments in employee training classes. Internal audit should play a key role in promoting the code and monitoring compliance through audit reviews and ongoing contacts through the enterprise. Internal auditors should be very aware of their enterprise's code of conduct and use it as a basis for reporting violations and making recommendations in the course of all other internal audits.

26.6 WHISTLEBLOWER AND HOTLINE FUNCTIONS

During the tumultuous period prior to the failures of Enron and WorldCom in the early years of this century, employees at those companies saw some of the severe accounting problems that eventually caused their companies' failures. Several employees did not feel they could communicate these concerns to their immediate supervisors and instead reported to senior management. Even though those reports were all but ignored, whistleblower protections have been part of many federal labor laws as a means to help regulators ferret out violations and wrongdoing. As outlined in Chapter 5, SOx mandates that enterprise audit committees establish procedures to "handle whistleblower information regarding questionable accounting or auditing matters." The whistleblower provisions of SOx are patterned after similar statutory schemes for protecting workers in the airline and nuclear power industries.

As outlined earlier in this chapter, a whistleblower function is a facility where an employee or any stakeholder who sees some form of wrongdoing can independently and anonymously report it to the enterprise or to regulatory authorities with no fear of retribution. While whistleblower programs have been around for some years to support U.S. federal contracting laws, health and safety regulations, and others, SOx moves these rules into the business offices of all U.S. publicly traded enterprises. While the audit committee is required to establish these whistleblower procedures, other functions, such as the ethics department, human resources, or internal audit, actually set them up.

Many enterprises that have established ethics functions also have hotline or similar ethics question telephone lines. These ethics hotlines can provide a starting point for the SOx whistleblower function, but they typically need adjustments or fine-tuning. Too often, reported incidents are not investigated in a proper manner or their confidentiality is not sufficiently strong. A slip-up here can cause major problems for an enterprise if the whistleblowing stakeholder feels that matters have not been resolved or individual confidentiality has been compromised. Internal audit often can be a major aid in this process through reviews of the existing process, recommending appropriate controls, and providing guidance to the audit committee.

Following the U.S. whistleblower rules for federal contracting and other federal regulations, any employee or stakeholder who observes some type of improper activity can blow the whistle and report the incident. The matter is then to be investigated and corrected if the allegations prove true, and the original whistleblower may receive a proportionate reward from the savings. An employee whistleblower, for example, who observes that a manufactured food ingredient appears to be lacking proper safety inspections can blow the whistle, informing his or her employer of this potential violation.

The SOx-mandated whistleblower program throws another new challenge to the responsible audit committee member. The typical board of directors audit committee member *may* be aware of such an enterprise function through past presentations, but almost certainly will not be aware of the necessary processes to establish an effective whistleblower program. Internal audit groups can often help the audit committee to establish an effective whistleblower program that will comply with SOx. This section discusses how to establish effective whistleblower programs and how internal audit can help to launch or refresh the function.

Federal Whistleblower Rules

The U.S. Department of Labor (DOL) administers and enforces more than 200 federal laws covering many workplace activities for about 10 million employers and 125 million workers. Most labor and public safety laws and many environmental laws mandate whistleblower protections for employees who complain about violations of the law by their employers. SOx has expanded this federal whistleblower protection. SOx Section 806 establishes whistleblower protection for stakeholders in publicly traded companies, allowing that no public company or any officer, employee, contractor, or agent of such company "may discharge, demote, suspend, threaten, harass, or in any other manner discriminate against an employee in the terms and conditions of employment because of any lawful act done by the employee." Those lawful acts are when the employee provides information or otherwise assists in an investigation conducted by a federal regulatory or law enforcement agency, Congress, or company personnel regarding any conduct that the employee "reasonably believes" constitutes a violation of SEC rules and regulations or fraud statutes, or files, testifies, participates in, or otherwise assists in a proceeding—pending or about to be filed—relating to an alleged violation. In other words, the employee or stakeholder who perceives some financial wrongdoing and then reports the matter is legally protected as part of the whistleblower investigation and resolution.

In many respects, whistleblower provisions are designed primarily to protect employees who think they have discovered some wrongdoing rather than to increase enterprise internal controls. Virtually any personnel action taken against a whistleblower employee, including a demotion or suspension, can potentially be subject to legal action under this provision. Although there have been limited whistleblower actions to date, it is still an open issue that should be on management's radar screen. An employee or stakeholder who registers a whistleblower complaint will be protected until the matter is resolved. SOx does seek to avoid frivolous complaints here by requiring that the whistleblower must have a "reasonable" belief that the practice reported constitutes a violation.

Under SOx rules, it is a crime for anyone "knowingly, with the intent to retaliate," to interfere with the employment or livelihood of any person—a whistleblower—who provides a law enforcement officer any truthful information relating to the possible commission of a SOx violation offense. Any whistleblower employee who then faces adverse employment action could potentially become a "protected informant" witness. Several legal sources have emphasized that this employee protection legislation is extraordinary and underscores the seriousness with which Congress views this subject.

SOx requires audit committees to establish a process for the receipt and treatment of complaints received regarding accounting, internal accounting controls, or auditing matters, and for "the confidential, anonymous submission by employees" regarding questionable accounting or auditing matters. Stakeholders who believe they have been unlawfully discharged or discriminated against due to their whistleblower action may seek relief by filing a complaint, within 90 days after the date of the violation, with the DOL or through initiating federal district court action. The aggrieved will typically need to secure legal help to seek relief. The process can be time-consuming and expensive for the accused corporation. The procedural rules here, including the burdens of proof for the employer and employee, will follow the Air 21 statute[3] for airline employees. For example, to prevail on a complaint before DOL, the employee must demonstrate that discriminatory reasons were a "contributing factor" in the unfavorable personnel action. Relief will be denied, however, if the employer demonstrates by "clear and convincing evidence" that it would have taken the same personnel action in the absence of protected activity.

An employee prevailing in such an action is entitled to full compensatory damages, including reinstatement, back pay with interest, and compensation for the litigation costs and attorney fees. However, if DOL does not issue a final decision within 180 days of the whistleblower's complaint filing, the matter may be moved to federal district court. Complicating matters further, the harmed whistleblower can take action on several fronts, seeking protection under federal and state laws as well as any collective bargaining agreement. Employers are exposed to potential "double jeopardy" for whistleblower actions, with liability under both SOx as well as state or federal laws on wrongful discharge and similar causes of action. In addition, the aggrieved whistleblower can seek punitive damages through separate court actions.

Based on administrative and judicial experiences in the nuclear energy and airlines industries, whistleblower protection laws can become a potential enterprise litigation minefield. If an employee raises any sort of accounting or auditing concern regarding an improper or illegal act, that whistleblower is totally protected until the matter is investigated and resolved. There are lots of trial lawyers in the wings eager to help the whistleblower and to file actions, particularly against major corporations with deep pockets. In addition, a substantial body of DOL and court precedent exists here to support regulatory sanctions and personal remedies.

Based on over 25 years of experience with whistleblower protection laws, this author believes that an impacted enterprise should attempt to strike a balance between the rights of employees to raise whistleblower concerns and the ability to manage the workforce. A positive work environment is needed in which employees feel free to raise concerns to management coupled with effective mechanisms to deal with any concerns raised. The strong ethics-related programs discussed earlier in this chapter, including mission statements and codes of conduct, will support this strategy.

SOx Whistleblower Rules and Internal Audit

Under SOx, any employee or stakeholder can become a whistleblower by reporting an illegal or improper accounting, internal control, and auditing activity. This should be an effective process when the potential whistleblower is a member of the corporate accounting staff who hears of plans for some fraudulent transactions or an employee at a remote unit that is not frequently visited by corporate staff, such as internal audit. Whistleblower rules are designed to encourage stakeholders to report these fraudulent or illegal acts and to very much protect the person who reported the matter. This raises a series of issues regarding internal auditors and their internal audit reviews.

An objective of internal auditing is to review and discover the types of accounting, internal control, and auditing issues specified in SOx. Internal audit findings are reviewed with management and presented in a formal audit report where management can outline their plans for corrective action. However, what if the internal audit team discovers an accounting, internal control, or auditing matter that is not formally reported to management in the audit report? Can one of the audit team members independently report the matter under SOx whistleblower procedures? Can an internal auditor who encounters a SOx accounting and internal control matter that is not part of a scheduled audit go through the whistleblower protection route to report the matter? What if the internal audit team member has not been performing well and fears termination? Can that poorly performing auditor dig up some potential findings, perhaps from past workpapers, and report them outside of the audit department to obtain whistleblower protection and job security until the matter is resolved?

The internal audit team is clearly part of management, and internal auditors have a first responsibility to report any improper or illegal matters encountered during an audit to internal audit management for disposition. Internal audit team members should not attempt to work as independent whistleblowers as part of their internal audit work.

Internal audit should develop a clear policy stating that any SOx accounting, internal control, or auditing matters encountered during the course of a scheduled audit review should be documented in the audit workpapers and communicated to internal audit management for resolution. Both the internal audit team and the management of the functions audited should understand that the purpose of internal audit is not to let loose a team of potential whistleblowers in a department's books and records. Any illegal or improper items should be investigated and reported through the normal internal audit process.

A situation could exist where an internal auditor does find some accounting or internal controls matter that somehow was dropped from the audit process, perhaps in a senior auditor's workpaper review. The internal auditor has a first responsibility to get resolution on the matter up through the chief audit executive or the audit committee. If the internal auditor documents and reports an issue, but internal audit management elects to drop or ignore the matter, the internal auditor certainly then has the right and responsibility to report it through, hopefully, the enterprise's audit committee or even SEC. Audit management and other processes should be in place to prevent such a frustrated internal auditor whistleblower situation.

Launching an Enterprise Help or Hotline Function

Many enterprises have help or *hotline functions*, administered through their ethics department, human resources, or an independent provider, that allow any employee or stakeholder to call anonymously and either ask a question, report a concern, or blow the whistle on some matter. The idea is to provide an independent facility where all stakeholders can ask questions or report possible wrongdoings at any level. These are not legally required functions, but allow employees or other stakeholders to ask questions, report possible wrongdoings, and even seek advice. The items reported may range from allegations of theft of company property, human resources complaints, or troubling questions. In most cases the telephone operator will take all of the necessary information, asking questions when needed, and then pass the reported incident to an appropriate authority for investigation and resolution. The hotline operator will typically assign the reported incident a case number so the caller can later check on resolution.

These employee hotlines got established in many larger enterprises a long time ago, beginning in the mid-1990s. Often staffed with knowledgeable human resources veterans who are particularly skilled at answering human resources–related issues, such as treatment in the workplace, these hotlines can be effective mechanisms to improve enterprise ethics and governance processes. Where hotline calls include allegations of wrongdoing, the recorded case should be shifted to others for investigation, such as to the legal department. In some instances these lines have turned into little more than corporate "snitch" lines where many minor gripes or infractions are reported; in general, however, hotlines have been very successful.

While many established ethics hotlines were set up to be "friendly" in answering employee questions and giving some advice in addition to investigating reported incidents, using this type of facility for the SOx whistleblower program places new controls and responsibilities on an enterprise. While the more friendly aspects of an ethics hotline can still apply, *federal whistleblower rules* require much more formalized processes, particularly in areas such as confidentiality, documentation requirements for all records, and efficient processing of any investigations. In addition, the employee calling in a SOx whistleblower allegation is legally protected from any future recrimination. In some respects, a legal bubble has to be encapsulated around the whistleblower employee such that there can be no actions of any sort directed at that whistleblower by the employer until the allegation is resolved. There have been situations, under other federal whistleblower laws, where an employee who called in an issue had her desk moved and successfully brought legal action for whistleblower discrimination. There is no reason to establish separate ethics help lines and SOx whistleblower lines. Callers would be confused about which to call in any event. However, with the SOx whistleblower requirement, control procedures need to be enhanced in any established ethics hotline facility. Exhibit 26.3 contains guidelines for setting up a SOx whistleblower call center.

An ethics hotline and whistleblower facility will be of little value unless it is communicated and sold to all members of the enterprise. A good way to initially launch these processes is through the employee code of conduct, discussed previously. Even if such a hotline has already been launched, the fact that the line can be used for any potential SOx whistleblowers needs to be communicated. The goal should be to investigate and promptly resolve all calls—and especially whistleblower calls—internally to avoid outside investigators and lawyers.

EXHIBIT 26.3 Guidelines for Setting Up a Whistleblower Call Center

- Establish independent—preferably toll-free—telephone line facility for the calls. The lines should not go through other enterprise "switchboards."
- Train all operators for the facility with the basic provisions of federal whistleblower rules. Also, establish scripts such that call operators can respond and ask the same general questions.
- Advertise and promote the facility throughout the enterprise with an emphasis that for all items reported, the caller will be eventually able to check status, all callers will be treated anonymously, and there will be no recrimination for caller actions.
- Implement a logging form to record all incoming calls. Maintain the date and time of the call, the caller's name or identification, and a summary of the details reported.
- Establish a routing and disposition process such as the status of who has the call information and the status of any investigation can be determined.
- Establish a secure database for all recorded whistleblower data with appropriate password protection.
- Working with the enterprise's human resources function, develop procedures to fully but anonymously protect all whistleblower reports from recrimination of any sort.
- Develop processes for closing out all whistleblower calls and documenting all actions, if any.

26.7 AUDITING THE ENTERPRISE'S ETHICS FUNCTIONS

The ethics and hotline function should not be exempted from the same types of operational or financial reviews that internal audit performs in all other segments of the enterprise. Different from asset management, marketing, or design engineering, which are periodically subject to operational or financial reviews based on potential audit risks, the ethics function should nevertheless be included in the same type of risk analysis model used by internal audit for audit planning and discussed in Chapter 15. Although the ethics code of conduct function may introduce minimal risks, the whistleblower function—particularly if administered internally—may present some major security and confidentiality risks. In addition, the CFO and other key officers are very much at risk if there are problems here.

The purpose of an internal audit review of the ethics and whistleblower function is to assess whether that ethics group is following good internal control procedures, making effective use of its resources, complying with good confidentiality procedures, and following its department charter authorizing the ethics function. While every ethics and whistleblower function may be a little different, internal audit should gain a detailed understanding of how the function operates and the procedures normally performed. As the enterprise's *ethics function,* internal audit should expect to find procedures at least as good as internal audit regarding compliance with such areas as document confidentiality and compliance with enterprise policies such as travel expenses. Other ethics functions responsibilities may point to areas where internal audit can suggest improvements. For example, the ethics department's code of conduct normally should have an acknowledgment form or process where employees indicate that they have read and understand the code. An ethics function may not have established appropriate procedures here to ensure that all newly hired employees go through this code acknowledgment process. Internal audit can assess this process and recommend improvements where appropriate.

Exhibit 26.4 describes internal audit procedures for a review of an enterprise's ethics and whistleblower functions. Because of the close, ongoing relationship that should exist between the ethics function and internal audit, if an operational review of ethics does come up as part of audit's risk analysis, the CAE should discuss the planned review with the ethics director in some detail to explain the reasons for and the objectives of the planned operational review. Privacy and confidentiality may become an issue in this type of review. A call to the hotline may have pointed to some form of potential employee malfeasance or a SOx whistleblower revelation, which the ethics function will want to keep highly confidential until the matter is resolved. Despite internal audit's ongoing exposure to other sensitive areas and issues in the enterprise, the director of the ethics function may be reluctant to have internal auditors review certain materials. The CAE should point out internal audit's ongoing exposure to other sensitive information and the requirements that it follow appropriate professional standards.

Assuming that these matters can be resolved appropriately, an operational review of an ethics function will give management additional assurances as to the integrity of controls in the ethics function, a component of operations where most managers have had little exposure or experience.

EXHIBIT 26.4 Audit Steps for a Review of Ethics and Whistleblower Functions

1. Enterprise Mission Statements
   - Review the enterprise's mission statement to assess whether it is actively communicated and emphasizes the importance of governance and business ethics practices.
   - If the mission statement appears to be lacking or in need of an update, discuss areas or plans for improvement with the audit committee.
   - Meet with appropriate members of management to assess ongoing programs to promote the mission statement throughout the enterprise.
2. Ethics Function Administration
   - Determine if the enterprise has established a formal ethics function, whether a separate unit, part of human resources, legal, or some other function, and develop an understanding of the function's leadership and responsibilities.
   - Determine who has responsibility for administering the overall ethics program in the enterprise and meet with that function to assess ongoing activities and programs.
   - Develop an understanding of and document the structure of the ethics function, including its structure and reporting relationships.
   - Review the ethics function's charter and other key process documentation and determine whether they are consistent with other enterprise initiatives.
   - Determine whether there is some form of hotline function in place and assess its span of activities.
   - Assess the ethics function's office security procedures for the adequacy of such matters as records, file, and workstation security.
   - If outside contractors are used to provide ethics or hotline services, review and document contractual arrangements.
3. Code of Conduct Processes.
   - Obtain a copy of current code of conduct.
     - Determine whether code is current and regularly updated.
     - Discuss the code with a sample of the enterprise staff to determine that they understand the code document.
     - Discuss the code with selected managers at all levels to determine if there are concerns about the code's issues or content.
   - Assess the adequacy of processes for obtaining code acknowledgments.
     - Select a sample of employees and determine that they acknowledged acceptance of the code.
     - Determine that all officers have accepted the code.
     - Assess adequacy of procedures for any employees who fail/refuse code acknowledgment.
     - Assess adequacy of code acknowledgment records.
   - Assess adequacy of processes for updating the code of conduct as required.
   - Assess processes in place to distribute code to all enterprise stakeholders, including remote locations, vendors, and others.
4. Hotline/Whistleblower Processes.
   - Develop a general understanding of whistleblower processes in place and determine whether they cover audit committee SOx requirements.
   - Assess the adequacy of procedures to communicate the whistleblower program to all stakeholders.
   - Assess adequacy of processes for logging whistleblower messages or calls received and documenting interactions.
   - Review process for disposition of calls and select of sample of recent calls to determine if processes appear adequate.

- Review overall security processes in place, including protection of key documents and individual whistleblower stakeholders.
- Meet with human resources to determine that adequate procedures are in place to protect/encapsulate any whistleblowers.

5. Audit committee responsibilities. Meet with audit committee representative to determine knowledge and understanding of the ethics and whistleblower programs in place.

26.8 IMPROVING CORPORATE GOVERNANCE PRACTICES

A strong ethics program, based on a meaningful mission statement and a code of conduct, are key elements for any overall program of enterprise corporate governance. The accounting scandals that led to SOx were in many respects scandals at the top levels of the enterprise, whether caused by a scheming financial officer, a greedy CEO, or a don't-ask-any-questions public accounting firm. The executive teams at the companies set their own rules, with little consideration given to the rest of the enterprise. The result has been Sox, which is highly focused on this same senior group. However, a strong overall ethics program will improve corporate governance practices for the entire enterprise, not just the people in the executive suite.

As part of their role as the ethics leaders in their enterprise, internal auditors should be very aware of the need for overall enterprise-wide corporate governance and ethics policies. Internal auditors should have strong ethics and compliance programs in place within their own internal audit group, and they should look for similar practices within the total enterprise. These include such things as enterprise senior management policy statements to emphasize that all stakeholders are encouraged, indeed have an obligation, to bring concerns about accounting and financial practices to the attention of management. Such policy statements should also stress that management will not tolerate retaliation against employees who raise concerns. The policy can help foster an open-door process for addressing issues, which after all is the most effective management approach.

Whether the enterprise is a large or a small one, the ethics and whistleblower processes discussed in this chapter are important both for SOx compliance and good corporate governance practices. Internal auditors should be aware of these ethics and whistleblower practices as part of their CBOK and should play a key role in helping to launch as well as review them.

NOTES

1. "Our Credo Values," Johnson & Johnson, http://www.jnj.com/about-jnj/jnj-credo.
2. Space here does not allow for a full account of the Enron saga. An online search will provide many references to the Enron failure.
3. The Wendell H. Ford Aviation Investment and Reform Act for the 21st Century (commonly known as Air 21) protects whistleblowers in the airline industry. A related act is the 1978 Energy Reorganization Act, which protects employees in the nuclear power industry from retaliation for their reporting of safety concerns.

27

CHAPTER TWENTY-SEVEN

Fraud Detection and Prevention

SEEMINGLY ALMOST LIKE CLOCKWORK, BUSINESSES in the United States and elsewhere regularly go through periods of business failures; often they are based on poor general economic conditions, but sometimes on questionable business activities or just fraud. The financial scandals at Enron and others that led to the enactment of the Sarbanes-Oxley Act (SOx) are examples of financial fraud by senior corporate officers. Fraudulent activity can occur at all levels of the enterprise, but in mid-2002, around the time of the enactment of SOx, corporate officers appeared to be real troublemakers in a slew of financial frauds. However, despite the publicity surrounding corrupt senior corporate officers, fraud can take place at all levels. Just as a chief executive officer (CEO), in cooperation with the chief financial officer (CFO), may fraudulently manipulate earnings to boost reported profits and their individual bonus compensation, a midlevel manager or even a staff-level employee may be tempted to initiate some fraudulent action for personal gain or just to get even with someone because of job frustration. Unfortunately, the publicity surrounding these incidents of fraud has since then created an almost everybody-does-it attitude. However, Ernst & Young in its annual Global Fraud Survey[1] reports that 85% of the worst frauds were caused by insiders on the payroll and over half of those frauds were initiated by members of management. Exhibit 27.1 summarizes some major enterprise fraud events, some before the market collapse that led to SOx and some after. Enterprise fraud is an issue that will always be with us, but internal auditors can help to prevent and detect fraud through effective internal control reviews.

EXHIBIT 27.1 Early Twenty-First-Century Business Fraud Examples

Company & Date	What Happened	How They Did It	How They Got Caught
Waste Management, 1998. A Houston-based publically traded waste management company.	Reported $1.7 billion in fake earnings.	Company falsely increased the asset property, plant, and equipment time lengths on their financial statements.	A new CEO and management team went through the books.
Enron Corporation, 2001. A Houston-based commodities, energy, and service company.	$74 billion in shareholder losses after discovery of frauds and bankruptcy.	Kept huge debts off the balance sheet.	Internal audit whistleblower and general investment community suspicions.
Worldcom Corporation, 2002. A telecommunications company.	$11 billion in shareholder losses after discovery of frauds and bankruptcy.	Fraudulent financial reporting through incorrect accounting entries, inflated revenues, and incorrect capitalizations.	Internal audit review discovered $1.8 billion of the fraud.
TYCO, 1982. New Jersey–based home security and home and industrial devices corporation.	CEO and CFO stole $150 million and inflated reported income by $500 million.	Money was siphoned through fraudulent stock sales as well as improper executive bonuses.	Investigation by the SEC and New York State Attorney General.
HealthSouth. 2003. Then the largest publicly traded healthcare company in the United States.	Earnings numbers were inflated by $1.4 billion to meet stockholder expectations.	CEO demanded that underlings make up transactions and reported earnings to boost overall profits.	Large CEO stock transactions led to SEC investigation.
Freddie Mac, 2003. U.S. government—backed mortgage financing resource.	$5 billion of earnings misstated.	Intentionally misstated and understated earnings.	SEC investigation.
Bernard Madoff Investment Securities, 2008. Small investment advisory firm.	Tricked investors out of $65 billion through a Ponzi investment scheme.	Gained investor trust and deliberately gave false investment information.	Principal player Madoff told his sons about scheme and he was arrested.
SAYTAM Consulting, 2009. An India-based IT consulting and systems services firm.	$1.5 billion in falsely reported revenues.	CEO falsified revenues, margins, and cash balances for company internal financial reporting.	CEO admitted the fraud in a letter to company board of directors.

An effective internal auditor needs to recognize potential fraudulent business practices as part of any audit and then should recommend controls and procedures to limit exposure to the fraudulent activity. This chapter outlines some of the *red flags*—common conditions that an internal audit might encounter when faced with a potential fraud and then discusses steps to identify, test, and properly process fraudulent activities. In addition, the chapter will introduce the standards and activities of the Association of Certified Fraud Examiners (ACFE) and their joint publication in conjunction with the AICPA and the IIA, *Managing the Business Risk of Fraud: A Practical Guide.*[2] Fraud investigation can be a very detailed and specialized activity, but all internal auditors should have a high-level common book of knowledge (CBOK) understanding of how to potentially sniff out circumstances, how to audit for potentially fraudulent activities, and processes for investigating and reporting fraud. Fraudulent activities represent a breakdown in a wide range of good practices and procedures, but internal auditors must recognize that fraudulent activities may always exist.

27.1 UNDERSTANDING AND RECOGNIZING FRAUD

Fraud is one of those terms that many people use even though they may not fully understand what they are talking about. An important internal auditor first step here should be to understand the dictionary or legal definition of what we call fraud. Its common-law definition is "the obtaining of money or property by means of false token, symbol, or device." In other words, someone improperly authorizes some document that causes a transfer of money. Fraud can be costly for any victim enterprise, and effective internal controls are an enterprise's first line of defense against fraud. A comprehensive, fully implemented, and regularly monitored system of internal controls is essential for the prevention and detection of losses that arise from fraud, and internal auditors often find themselves involved in fraud-related issues. When a fraud is discovered in the enterprise, internal audit is often almost the first resource called by management to conduct an investigation to determine the extent of the reported fraud. In other situations, internal auditors sometimes discover a fraud through the course of a scheduled audit and then investigate and report the matter to senior management, their corporate counsel, or other legal authorities. However, historically, neither internal nor external auditors have regularly looked for fraud as part of their scheduled audits. This is changing.

Auditors today, both internal and external, are taking on a more important role in the detection and prevention of fraud. This chapter discusses controls to prevent and detect fraud and introduces the AICPA auditing standard on fraud, AU-C, Section 240, titled *Consideration of Fraud in a Financial Statement Audit.* This guidance was part the AICPA's accounting standards and previously known as SAS No. 99.[3] We also discuss IIA initiatives to review for fraud in internal audits as well as procedures to detect and prevent fraud in IT systems. Fraud has been with us since time immemorial, but auditors in the past have claimed that detecting it was beyond their responsibilities. Today they are finding themselves with an increasing responsibility to detect fraud in the course of their review activities as well as to recommend appropriate controls to prevent future frauds. Joint guidance material on the impact of fraud in auditing also has been referenced by the previously mentioned AICPA, IIA, and ACFE guidance materials on the importance of fraud considerations for internal auditors and others.

27.2 RED FLAGS: FRAUD DETECTION SIGNS FOR INTERNAL AUDITORS

Many fraudulent activities are only easy to identify *after the fraud has been uncovered.* An employee of an enterprise who has been embezzling money over an extended period often will eventually be caught through some slip-up that reveals the fraud. After such a fraud is discovered, it is often easy to look at the situation and say such things as "But she was such a good employee—she hasn't missed a day of work for nearly two years! How could she have done this?" or "Now that I think about it, I wondered how he could afford all of those long weekend trips to expensive places!" It is easy to analyze the facts after a fraud has been discovered, but internal auditors and management should look for indicators of possible fraudulent activities in advance with a skeptical eye. They should look for what are called red flags.

For example, the first corporation (along with its CEO Richard M. Scrushy) to be indicted for accounting fraud under SOx was a health care provider called HealthSouth Corporation, an event briefly summarized in Exhibit 27.1. Then the largest U.S. provider of outpatient surgery, diagnostic, and rehabilitative services, HealthSouth operated in approximately 1,900 locations in all 50 states as well as in multiple international facilities. It reported in excess of $1.4 billion of fictitious earnings over a six-year period in order to meet investment analyst estimates and to keep its stock price high. Several of its financial and other officers pleaded guilty, claiming and testifying against the CEO and asserting that he demanded they report the fraudulent earnings. While this accounting fraud had been going on for at least 10 years at that time, there had been numerous signs of possible fraud that were seemingly ignored by the company's external auditors and others:

- HealthSouth's year 2000 pretax earnings more than doubled to $559 million, although its sales grew only 3%. Pretax earnings for 2001 were nearly twice 1999 levels, although sales rose just 8%. While there is nothing wrong with fantastic earnings growth, analysts and certainly auditors might have asked some hard questions.
- In late 2002, HealthSouth's internal auditors were denied access to key corporate financial records. Internal audit reported this to their outside auditors and to their audit committee; neither party took any action on these internal audit concerns.
- The CEO spent a considerable amount of time and attention on sports and popular music performers, flying his management staff off to events and bringing sports stars in to work with the company.

These examples are just a few of the activities that were occurring around the company, suggesting possible fraud. Fantastic reported earnings gains do not necessarily mean fraud, but can raise questions. Similarly, elaborate corporate-sponsored social events may only raise questions about how the enterprise is managing its resources rather than pointing to fraud. However, these kinds of activities can be suspicious. At HealthSouth, an ex-employee sent an e-mail to the external auditors suggesting they look at three specific accounts for fraudulent activity. This is more than a red flag; it is an attempt to blow the whistle. Based on this tip, a high-level investigation was launched by the external auditors, but again nothing was found. Many red flags were raised, but internal management pressure on a normally dominant CEO to back off from some fictitious financial reports eventually started a chain of events that soon exposed the fraud.

What we call a red flag here is a warning signal to the noninvolved observer that something does not look right. A huge increase in reported profits with not that much of an increase in unit sales may sound wonderful and be totally plausible. However, when faced with this type of data or red flag indicator, auditors or fraud examiners should ask the question "This seems unusual—how can it be so?"

Red flags are normally the first indications of a potential fraud. Someone sees something that does not look right and then often begins a low-level investigation. Internal auditors are often the first people to become involved. Exhibit 27.2 lists some typical red flags that potentially could point to possible financial fraud activities. None of these are absolute indicators of fraud, but internal auditors should always be skeptical in their reviews and be aware of such warning signals. When an internal auditor sees evidence of one or more of these or other red flags, it may be time to dig a little deeper. Unfortunately, internal auditors often fail to detect frauds for one of the following reasons:

- **There is an unwillingness to look for fraud.** Due to their training and past experience, internal auditors have historically not actively looked for fraud. They have often tended to view fraud investigation as a policing type of activity and not a prime internal audit responsibility.
- **Too much trust is placed in auditees.** Internal auditors, in particular, try to maintain a friendly, cordial attitude toward the auditees in their enterprise. Because they encounter these same people in the cafeteria or at an annual company picnic, there is usually a level of trust involved. Internal auditors quite correctly try to give their auditees the benefit of the doubt.
- **Not enough emphasis is placed on potential fraud issues in audit findings.** Internal audit findings often point to the same red flags as mentioned in Exhibit 27.2. They are included as audit report findings pointing out such matters as missing records or accounts that were not reconciled. However, internal auditors often fail to consider potential fraud in audit findings. Unless it is a glaringly large issue, they do not even think about fraud issues when developing audit report findings.
- **Fraud concerns often receive inadequate support from management.** The hint of possible fraud requires auditors to extend their procedures and dig a lot deeper. However, general and even audit management may be reluctant to give an individual auditor extra time to do so. Unless there are strong suspicions to the contrary, management will often want the audit team to move on and stop spending time in what they feel is an extremely low-risk area.

- **Auditors sometimes fail to focus on high-risk fraud areas.** Fraud can occur in many areas, ranging from employee travel expense reporting to treasury function relations with offshore banks. There can often be a much greater risk in the latter, while auditors often tend to focus on the former. While it may be comparatively easy to find problems in travel expenses, internal audits often do not include such high-risk areas as, for example, a review of treasury function relations with offshore banks, an often complex and difficult area to review.

Fraud is a word that can have many meanings, but we are referring to it in terms of a criminal act. There are over 300 references to fraud in federal criminal statutes, and the term appears throughout the SOx legislation. Most of those federal references are based on federal general fraud statute:[4]

EXHIBIT 27.2 Red Flags Indicating Potential Financial Fraud

The following list represent "red flags" that may be warning signals for evidence of financial fraud. These were adapted from the AICPA web site, www.aicpa.org.

- Lack of written corporate policies and standard operating procedures.
- Based on interviews at multiple levels, lack of compliance with organization's internal control policies.
- Weak internal control policies, especially in the division of duties.
- Disorganized operations in such areas as purchasing, receiving, warehousing, or regional offices.
- Unrecorded transactions or missing records.
- Counterfeit documents or evidence of alterations to documents.
- Photocopied or questionable handwriting on documents.
- Sales records with excessive voids or credits.
- Bank accounts not reconciled on a timely basis or stale items on bank reconciliations.
- Continuous out-of-balance conditions on subsidiary ledgers.
- Unusual financial statement relationships.
- Continuous unexplained differences between physical inventory counts and perpetual inventory records.
- Bank checks written to cash in large amounts.
- Handwritten checks in a computer environment
- Continuous or unusual fund transfers among company bank accounts.
- Fund transfers to offshore banks.
- Transactions not consistent with the entity's business.
- Poor screening procedures for new employees including no background or reference checks.
- Reluctance by management to report criminal wrongdoing.
- Unusual transfers of personal assets.
- Officers or employees with lifestyles apparently beyond their means.
- Unused vacation time.
- Frequent or unusual related-party transactions.
- Employees in close association with suppliers.
- Employees in close relationship with one another in areas where separation of duties could be circumvented.
- Expense-account abuse such as managers not following established rules.
- Business assets dissipating without explanation.

> Whoever, in any manner within the jurisdiction of any department or agency of the United States, knowingly and willfully falsifies, conceals, or covers up by any trick, scheme, or device a material fact, or makes any false, fictitious, or fraudulent writing or document knowingly the same to contain any false, fictitious, or fraudulent statement or entry, shall be fined not more than . . . or imprisoned not more than . . . or both.

Although this quoted text is stated in legalese, it is a strong message to management at all levels and their internal auditors. The auditor's word *material* is not emphasized here, and anything false, fictitious, or fraudulent could be considered a violation. There are multiple state statutes generally modeled after these federal rules, and an internal auditor should be aware of his or her state rules.

To help detect fraud, auditors need to have an understanding of why people commit fraud. An enterprise can display the red flags described in the previous section, but it will not necessarily be subject to fraudulent activities unless one or more employees decide to engage in fraud. Exhibit 27.3 lists some typical motivations, reasons, or excuses for committing a fraud. These are all reasons where strong internal controls are in place and the fraud is only committed by one person. *Fraud detection* is much harder when there is collusion between multiple persons. In the HealthSouth fraud described previously, a very aggressive CEO assembled a top management team he called "the company" to prepare the fraudulent financial reports. Members of "the company" at HealthSouth were highly compensated and received many incentives. The fraud did not become public until one member of "the company" began to have personal concerns about this growing accounting fraud. Whenever multiple people are involved in the same fraud, there is a possibility that someone will break ranks.

While major frauds involving senior management participation are difficult to sniff out, frauds that occur at lower levels in the enterprise are often easier to detect with a proper level of internal auditor investigation. For example, a payroll process can present a wide range of opportunities for fraud through the use of such mechanisms as inflating the actual hours worked for an employee, generating payment vouchers for fictitious or terminated employees, or issuing duplicate vouchers for an employee. These are the classic types of issues that are part of many internal audit procedures. However, rather than just as internal control violations, an internal auditor should think of these items in terms of potential areas for employee fraud. Auditors have performed these procedures for years but sometimes forget that there could be a fraud issue as well. In the HealthSouth fraud discussed here, it was later discovered that the external auditors did not even do a classic bank balance confirmation with HealthSouth's banks. This is a standard test in which the auditor asks the bank to independently confirm an enterprise's bank balance as of a certain date. In their promotion of audit efficiency over the years, auditors—particularly external auditors—have dropped many of these traditional procedures. It may be time to revisit some of them.

27.3 PUBLIC ACCOUNTING'S ROLE IN FRAUD DETECTION

The external auditor's responsibility for the detection of fraud in financial statements has been an ongoing but contentious issue over the years. The very first AICPA Statement on Auditing Standards (SAS No. 1) from many years ago stated, "The auditor

EXHIBIT 27.3 Motivations and Reasons for Committing Fraud

- **An employee has a desperate need for money.** This is probably the major motivator of fraud and the most difficult to detect. Whether because of a nasty divorce or a drug problem, the need for money can cause employees to resort to criminal actions.
- **Job frustrations.** Employees can become frustrated and feel their company "doesn't give a damn" about them and feel free to act inappropriately. Job layoffs or pay-grade freezes can foster such feelings.
- **"Everybody does it" attitudes.** This type of situation is often common in a smaller retail type environment where an employee thinks that everyone else is stealing as well. This attitude can also come up when senior managers seem to be living extravagantly at the same time the company is incurring losses.
- **Challenges to "beat the system."** This is a particular problem with would-be hackers in an automated systems environment. However, there can be many other cases where an employee, for example, tries to set up a fictitious account to see if he or she can bill the company and receive cash in return.
- **Lax internal controls making fraud easy.** This is a basic motivation that encourages many frauds. Poor internal controls often predict that the fraud will not be detected.
- **Low probability of detection.** Similar to the weak internal controls point, if an employee knows that chances of getting caught are nil, the temptation to commit fraud is greater.
- **Low probability of prosecution.** When a company seemingly never takes any action to bring criminal charges against someone, the word gets out, and people may view getting caught as an acceptable risk with little worry about prosecution.
- **Top management that does not seem to care.** Employees can often collectively determine when an employee seems to get away with breaking some rule or when otherwise very appropriate behavior is not rewarded.
- **Low organizational loyalty or feelings of ownership.** In today's complex world, we often have situations where the owners of some business operation are a continent and many organizational layers away. It is easy to have attitudes where no one really seems to care on a day-by-day basis.
- **Unreasonable budget expectations or other financial targets.** Organizations sometimes establish expectations that are all but impossible to meet. This can create an environment where people will bend the rules to meet those targets.
- **Less-than-competitive compensation and poor promotion opportunities.** If they cannot receive what they feel are appropriate rewards through normal compensation, people may bend rules to benefit themselves.

has no responsibility to plan and perform the audit to obtain reasonable assurance that misstatements, whether caused by errors or fraud, that are not material to the financial statements are detected." In other words, external auditors then were only responsible to determine if the financial statements were fairly stated; they had *no responsibility* to detect errors or fraudulent activity. The public accounting profession stood by this increasingly untenable position for many years. Even during the period of numerous financial frauds that led to the 1987 Treadway Commission Report on Fraudulent Financial Reporting (see Chapter 3), AICPA audit standards still did not require external audit include to assume any responsibility for the detection of fraud.

Despite continuing pressure for change over the years, AICPA audit standards regarding the external auditor's responsibility for fraud did not change until 1997 when this responsibility for fraud was restated in SAS No. 82: "The auditor has a responsibility to plan and perform the audit to obtain reasonable assurance about whether the financial statements are free of material misstatement, whether caused by error or fraud." This revised but tighter standard was released, after much professional discussion, at the peak of the turn-of-the-century dot-com bubble, when the investing public was concerned primarily about their investments surging forward and not as much with fraud.

Early in the twenty-first century with the failures of Enron, WorldCom, and a host of others, concerns about fraudulent financial reporting changed. Given SOx along with the PCAOB, it was perhaps now too late, and the AICPA released SAS No. 99 in December 2002 on the auditor's responsibility for detecting fraudulent financial reporting. Reworked today as accounting standard AU-C Section 240, it states that an external auditor is now responsible for providing reasonable assurance that audited financial statements are free of material misstatement, *whether caused by error or fraud.* We have used italics here because this was a major change in external auditor responsibilities.

The AU-C public accounting standard calls on external financial statement auditors to take on an attitude of professional skepticism regarding possible fraud. Putting aside any prior beliefs about management's honesty, the standard calls for the external audit team to exchange ideas or brainstorm on how frauds could occur in the enterprise they are about to audit. These discussions should identify fraud risks and should always keep in mind the characteristics that are present when frauds occur: incentives, opportunities, and ability to rationalize. Throughout the audit, the engagement team should think about and explore the question "If someone wanted to perpetrate a fraud here, how would it be done?" From these discussions, the external audit team should be in a better position to design audit tests that are responsive to the risks of fraud. The guidance here is that the external audit team should *always* go in to an audit engagement anticipating that there may be some level of fraudulent activity. This is in direct contrast with internal audit activities where members of internal audit and their auditees are part of the same enterprise and there should not be a suspicion of fraud unless it is found during a review or because of allegations reported by some level of enterprise management.

An external auditor engagement team now is expected to inquire of management and others in the enterprise as to their perceptions of the risk of fraud and whether they are aware of any ongoing fraud *investigations* or open issues. External auditors should make a point of talking to all levels of employees, both managers and others, giving them an opportunity to blow the whistle and encouraging someone to step forward. It might also help deter others from committing fraud if they are concerned that a coworker may turn them in during a subsequent audit. During a financial statement external audit, the audit engagement team should test areas, locations, and accounts that otherwise might not be tested. The team should design tests that would be unpredictable and unexpected by the client. This represented a major change in external auditing standards.

External accounting standards now recognize that management is often in a position to override controls in order to commit financial-statement fraud. Their auditing standard calls for procedures to test for management override of controls on every audit. It calls for a major external audit emphasis in detecting fraud, including procedures that external auditors are expected to perform in every audit engagement. This can be a major change from the "let's take the afternoon off and talk about things over a game of golf" approach that was common in years past on many external audit engagements.

In addition to imposing a very tough fraud detection auditing standard on its members, the AICPA has taken strong steps to bring external auditors up to speed regarding situations that encourage fraud as well as providing both educational materials and case studies. Its Web pages are filled with case studies, publications, continuing professional education courses, and other references on management fraud issues. You do not have to be an AICPA member to access the site, and there are member and nonmember prices for purchasing reference materials. As an example of the AICPA fraud-related materials, Exhibit 27.4 shows a checklist for auditors on misappropriation of assets. From an auditing and accounting professional organization that avoided getting involved in fraud prevention and detection work for many years, AICPA's fraud-related accounting standards as well as its published antifraud guidance materials very much raises the bar for all certified public accountants (CPAs). Given SOx and other recent events, it is unfortunate that the release of these audit standards did not happen sooner. Internal auditors will be seeing more fraud-related audit guidance going forward.

27.4 IIA STANDARDS FOR DETECTING AND INVESTIGATING FRAUD

Internal auditors are often in a better position to detect fraud in enterprise operations than are external auditors. While external auditors typically limit most of their client visits to around the quarterly and annual financial statement dates, internal auditors are just that—internal to the enterprise and often at enterprise sites on a daily basis. Just through their own observation, internal auditors may be in a much better position to see a red flag that could easily be missed by external auditors, despite the AICPA fraud standards. The shipping supervisor who shows up at the annual holiday party wearing an expensive Italian suit and sporting a brand-name gold wristwatch might raise a blip on the radar screen of another party participant, an internal auditor. There are many very valid reasons to justify expensive clothes, but such a show of wealth could be something for an internal auditor to remember when going forward with an internal controls review scheduled in that area.

Internal auditors run into many such awareness concerns and potential fraud issues in the course of their scheduled reviews. They also typically get involved in much more detailed, transaction-level reviews than their external audit counterparts and see questionable documents or transactions more frequently. If management feels there may be a potential fraud in some unit of the enterprise, the first step is almost always to contact internal audit, which will also have some connection and communication with their corporate legal department. They can discuss any potential concerns there and get a quick opinion on whether some concern requires more attention. If there are strong signs of an active fraud, corporate legal will almost always be ready to jump into the matter and help.

The IIA international standards emphasize that although internal audit has a role to play regarding fraud detection and prevention, the primary responsibility falls on management. Although this sounds simple in theory, the problem lies in communicating

EXHIBIT 27.4 Fraud Risk Factors Relating to Misappropriation of Assets

Risk factors that relate to misstatements arising from misappropriation of assets are classified according to the three conditions generally present when fraud exists: (1) incentives/pressures, (2) opportunities, and (3) attitudes/rationalizations. Some of the risk factors related to misstatements arising from fraudulent financial reporting also may be present when misstatements arising from misappropriation of assets occur. For example, ineffective monitoring of management and weaknesses in internal control may be present when misstatements due to either fraudulent financial reporting or misappropriation of assets exist. The following are examples of risk factors related to misstatements arising from misappropriation of assets.

Incentives/Pressures

A. Personal financial obligations may create pressure on management or employees with access to cash or other assets susceptible to theft to misappropriate those assets.
B. Adverse relationships between the entity and employees with access to cash or other assets susceptible to theft may motivate those employees to misappropriate those assets. For example, adverse relationships may be created by the following:
   - Known or anticipated future employee layoffs
   - Recent or anticipated changes to employee compensation or benefit plans
   - Promotions, compensation, or other rewards inconsistent with expectations

Opportunities

A. Certain characteristics or circumstances may increase the susceptibility of assets to misappropriation. For example, opportunities to misappropriate assets increase when there are the following:
   - Large amounts of cash on hand or processed
   - Inventory items that are small in size, of high value, or in high demand
   - Easily convertible assets, such as bearer bonds, diamonds, or computer chips
   - Fixed assets that are small in size, marketable, or lacking observable identification of ownership
B. Inadequate internal control over assets may increase the susceptibility of misappropriation of those assets. For example, misappropriation of assets may occur because there is the following:
   - Inadequate segregation of duties or independent checks
   - Inadequate management oversight of employees responsible for assets, for example, inadequate supervision or monitoring of remote locations
   - Inadequate job applicant screening of employees with access to assets
   - Inadequate recordkeeping with respect to assets
   - Inadequate system of authorization and approval of transactions (for example, in purchasing)
   - Inadequate physical safeguards over cash, investments, inventory, or fixed assets
   - Lack of complete and timely reconciliations of assets
   - Lack of timely and appropriate documentation of transactions, for example, credits for merchandise returns
   - Lack of mandatory vacations for employees performing key control functions
   - Inadequate management understanding of information technology, which enables information technology employees to perpetrate a misappropriation
   - Inadequate access controls over automated records, including controls over and review of computer systems event logs

Source: Printed with permission of the American Institute of Certified Public Accountants.

that message to management. IIA professional standards covering due professional care and scope of work cover fraud in a very general sense, as discussed in Chapter 9 on IIA professional standards. An internal auditor will be concerned about such matters as the possibility of wrongdoing and should consider evidence of any improper or illegal activities in an audit. However, the IIA standards that provide specific guidance on fraud seem to follow the older external audit standards just discussed. Recognizing that it may be difficult to detect fraud, the IIA standard 1210.A2 provides the guidance (our italics): "The internal auditor should have sufficient knowledge to identify the indicators of fraud *but is not expected to have the expertise of a person whose primary responsibility is detecting and investigating fraud.*" This is recognition that internal auditors may not have sufficient expertise for some fraud issues.

This same fraud standard is supported by IIA Practice Advisories 1210.A2-1 and 1210.A2-2, on the identification and investigation of fraud. Despite the words from the standard that internal auditors are *not expected to have the expertise,* the supporting Practice Advisory provides an internal auditor with some guidance on detecting and investigating fraud. We have included an edited portion of this Practice Advisory:

> Deterrence of fraud consists of those actions taken to discourage the perpetration of fraud and limit the exposure if fraud does occur. The principal mechanism for deterring fraud is control. Primary responsibility for establishing and maintaining control rests with management.

Internal auditors are responsible for assisting in the deterrence of fraud by examining and evaluating the adequacy and the effectiveness of the system of internal control, commensurate with the extent of the potential exposure/risk in the various segments of the enterprise's operations. In carrying out this responsibility, internal auditors should, for example, determine whether:

- The organization's environment fosters control consciousness, and realistic enterprise goals and objectives are set.
- Written policies, such as codes of conduct, exist that describe prohibited activities and the action required whenever violations are discovered.
- Appropriate authorization policies for transactions are established and maintained.
- Policies, practices, procedures, reports, and other mechanisms are developed to monitor activities and safeguard assets, particularly in high-risk areas.
- Communication channels provide management with adequate and reliable information.
- Recommendations need to be made for the establishment or enhancement of cost-effective controls to help deter fraud.

If an internal auditor suspects a potential fraudulent activity, appropriate enterprise authorities, usually the enterprise general counsel, should be informed. An internal auditor should only recommend whatever investigation appears necessary in the circumstances, but should rely on the recommendations of the general counsel. Thereafter, the auditor should follow up to see that the internal auditing activity's responsibilities have been met.

The previously referenced IIA Practice Advisories do not really educate an internal auditor on red-flag types of conditions that might suggest potential fraudulent activity. Rather, they suggest that if an enterprise does not have good policies and procedures or lacks a code of conduct, this could indicate an environment that encourages fraud. This is often true. But the lack of a current code of conduct or poorly drafted policy statements should not be the major reason for an internal auditor to go on a hunt for potential fraudulent activities. The red flags described in Exhibit 27.2 are better indicators.

The IIA has not taken the strong position on detecting fraud that the AICPA has. A 2015 search of the IIA web site using the key word *fraud* does not give an internal auditor the wealth of material that is now found on the AICPA site or can be found in the referenced IIA, AICPA, and ACFE guidance advisory. There are references to articles on fraud in older issues of the IIA publication *The Internal Auditor,* but not much more. Other fraud-related articles are listed but only available to IIA members. The previously referenced Practice Advisory is an example. The IIA also has special conferences on the topic, but the AICPA is taking a stronger professional lead here in providing guidance to auditors.

The IIA along with the AICPA, the Information Systems Audit and Control Association, the ACFE, Financial Executives International, the Institute of Management Accountants, and the Society for Human Resource Management have collaborated on and published a variety of fraud-related guidance materials. Other professional enterprises also have participated in reviewing and developing fraud guidance, including the American Accounting Association, the Defense Industry Initiative, and the National Association of Corporate Directors. However, the AICPA is clearly taking a lead role here, and good guidance materials are now categorized under their forensic and valuation services (FVS) offerings. Interested professionals should visit the FVS section on the AICPA web site,[5] where they can find a wide range of *auditing for fraud* guidance materials.

27.5 FRAUD INVESTIGATIONS FOR INTERNAL AUDITORS

In addition to helping to build and review controls to prevent and detect fraud, internal auditors sometimes become very involved in fraud investigations. While appropriate legal authorities should be used here for many fraud investigations, internal audit is often the first party asked to play a key role in other, less major matters. Internal auditors need not take the role of a Sherlock Holmes, but can help to gather information for smaller discoveries or provide supporting materials for larger matters. Internal audit often gets involved in potential fraud-related matters because of some troubling information encountered during an audit or an anonymous tip through a call or e-mail message.

When faced with potential fraud information, internal audit's first step should always be to consult with the enterprise's corporate counsel. Because of the nature of the allegation as well as the extent of initial information, the matter may also be turned over to legal authorities, such as the federal district attorney's office or state prosecutors. In some cases, legal advice will suggest that other authorities get involved in the matter at once. In smaller, seemingly less major matters, internal audit will sometimes be asked to take responsibility for the investigation. In many instances, these types of investigations just involve a detailed review of documents. The evidence gathered from that document review will become the basis for any further action.

Fraud-related investigations require an internal auditor to operate rather differently than during normal financial or operational internal audits. In any fraud-related review, an internal auditor should have three major objectives:

1. **Prove the loss.** Fraud-related reviews usually start out with the finding that someone stole something or did something in violation of established rules. The internal audit–led investigative review should assemble as much relevant material as necessary to determine the overall size and scope of the loss.
2. **Establish responsibility and intent.** This is a "Who did it?" step. As much as possible, the audit team should attempt to identify everyone who was responsible for the matter and if there was any special or different intent associated with the fraud action.
3. **Prove the audit investigative methods used.** The investigative team needs to be able to prove that their fraud-related conclusions were based on a detailed, step-by-step investigative process, not just an uncoordinated witch hunt. The review should be documented using the best internal audit review processes. Of particular importance here is that all documents to be used be secured.

There are many other procedures associated with a fraud-related examination. The objective of this chapter is not to describe the overall process of fraud examinations but to discuss the increased emphasis on fraud detection and prevention as outlined by newer standards, particularly the AICPA guidance as well as the previously referenced IIA fraud management publications. Internal auditors interested in learning more about fraud investigations should explore the activities and publications of the Association of Certified Fraud Examiners (www.cfenet.com). In addition to the previously referenced AICPA materials, this professional enterprise, as well as maintaining a formalized fraud investigation certification examination, has a variety of educational and guidance materials.

27.6 INFORMATION TECHNOLOGY FRAUD PREVENTION PROCESSES

Information technology or technology-related fraud covers a wide range of issues and concerns. In today's business environment, IT systems are virtually always a key component of modern financial or accounting-related fraud. Because IT systems and processes support so many areas and cross so many lines in the enterprise, we can think of IT-related fraud in multiple dimensions ranging from the minor to significant fraudulent activities:

- **Internet access issues.** Enterprises often establish both guidelines and sometimes controls to restrict Internet use, but the Web is so pervasive that it is difficult to separate personal from business use. Again, such rules are frequently ignored by employees and sometimes bypassed by software that will allow them to get around firewall barriers in systems. There can be a much greater possibility of abuse here, but the enterprise can potentially monitor employee Internet usage through software monitoring tools. Perhaps many will wink at such matters, but an enterprise associate should not be spending substantial amounts of workday time browsing the Internet or completing home shopping transactions.

- **Improper personal use of IT resources.** An enterprise should establish rules stating that there should be no personal files or programs on their work-supplied systems. Such rules are frequently ignored by employees, who may use word-processing or spreadsheet resources to perform some personal work as part of the business-related work that they may take home in the evenings. An enterprise should emphasize to employees that they should not be doing personal business while at the workplace. Perhaps even greater than the risk of fraud here is the possibility of introducing viruses or other harmful software to enterprise systems.
- **Illegal use of software.** Employees will sometimes attempt to steal or download copies of company software or will install their own software on enterprise computer resources. In doing so they are violating enterprise rules and often putting their employers in violation of software licensing agreements. In addition, they may be introducing viruses into enterprise systems. While an enterprise should have systems firewalls installed to protect from such improper software, there is always a risk of such malignant software slipping through.
- **Computer security and confidentiality fraud matters.** Employees can violate password protections and gain improper access to IT systems and files. Even if they are only trying to "see if it works," they are performing a fraudulent act by violating computer security rules.
- **Information theft through USB devices.** Today, storage devices about the size of a car ignition key can be plugged into a computer system and used to download multiple gigabytes[6] of recorded information. An enterprise can face a significant risk of the theft or loss of such data as customer records through these simple storage devices.
- **Information theft or other data abuse computer fraud.** It is one thing to improperly access a computer system by violating password controls, and another to improperly view, modify, or copy data or files. This can be a significant cause of computer crime.
- **Embezzlement or unauthorized electronic fund transfers.** Stealing money or other resources through improper or unauthorized transactions is perhaps the most significant cause of IT systems and network fraud issues. Whether initiating a transaction to send an accounts payable check to the home address or facilitating a major bank transfer, this can be a major area for computer fraud or crime.

These examples run the gamut from what might be considered fairly minor to significant IT abuses. We mention the more minor items to point out the range of items that can be considered IT-related fraud. If an employee is given a laptop computer for work and told it is only for business use, yet the employee uses that same laptop to write a book report as part of her child's homework, does this represents computer crime or fraud? The answer here is really yes, per the established rules. If the enterprise had set up rules, they were done for good reason, and employees should not violate them. However, should internal audit launch a review to discover violations in this area? Probably not; there are more important high-risk areas on which to spend limited time and resources. A strong code of conduct and ethics program, as discussed in Chapter 26, should be the predominant control procedure here.

We have used the book report example from the previous page to illustrate that there are many possibilities for computer fraud and abuse. It is often a very complex area where strong technical skills are needed to understand tools and methods. This is an area where the rules are continually changing. Individuals with a fraudulent intent are finding new ways to violate established automated controls, and skilled professionals are finding ways to detect and protect this fraudulent activity. Chapter 23 discusses IT security and privacy controls in a networked environment.

A related IT systems fraud detection area is computer forensics, the detailed examination of computers and their peripheral devices using computer investigation and analysis techniques for finding or determining potential legal evidence in a fraud situation. The idea here is that essentially anything written on a computer file can be recovered, even if it has been erased through an operating system command. The evidence required to be found covers a wide range of subjects such as theft of trade secrets, theft or destruction of intellectual property, fraud, and other civil cases involving wrongful dismissals, breaches of contracts, and discrimination issues. The previously referenced AICPA FVS web site is a source of considerable guidance materials on forensics auditing.

Recovered IT systems data can often be a gold mine in a fraud investigation. Perpetrators may feel that they have covered their tracks by deleting files, but computer forensics tools often allow full recovery. Forensic examinations involve the examination of computer media, such as CD-ROMs, hard disk drives, backup files, and other media used to store data. The forensic specialist uses specialized software to discover data that reside in a computer system, or can recover deleted/erased, encrypted, or damaged file information and passwords, so that documents can be read.

We have used this example of computer forensics as one approach to aid computer fraud investigations. This is an area that requires specialized tools and training, but internal auditors will probably not have the skills to perform such an analysis without necessary help. As an indicator of interest in this area, the AICPA has established a credential, Certified in Financial Forensics, that combines specialized forensic accounting expertise with the core knowledge and skills that make CPAs trusted business advisors in this area.

Other than direct testimony by an eyewitness, documentary evidence is usually the most compelling form of evidence, and paper trails have traditionally been rewarding for IT fraud investigators. In past years, documentary evidence was limited to paper. Where the best-evidence rule applied, the original document was produced. However, documents are rarely typed using typewriters or even printed today and are usually produced on personal computer word processors. Some of these documents are no longer printed and are e-mailed or faxed to the recipient directly from the computer. Because of the change in the way information is distributed and the way people communicate, copies of computer files are now as good as the original electronic document.

We have used computer forensics here as an example of new technology-based technique for fraud detection. Firewall software to protect a system or user from entering transactions or accessing systems beyond a fixed region is another example. Virus protection software is a third. A full discussion of the computer fraud aspects of these and other areas is beyond the scope of this book. The internal auditor must realize that computer fraud is a large and complex area.

27.7 FRAUD DETECTION AND THE INTERNAL AUDITOR

Fraud has always been with us, no matter how well we build strong standards for honesty, through codes of conduct and the like, as well as build ever stronger controls to prevent fraud. Badly burned by the accounting scandals that led to SOx, the AICPA and external auditors have taken on a major task to better detect fraudulent activities in their financial statement audits. Time will tell how effective are the new standards and guidance materials, but they call for a new dimension of thinking when planning and conducting financial statement as well as all levels of audits.

Internal auditors need to give greater consideration to fraud in their audit work. They have always been involved in some level of fraud investigation when called on by management, but fraud detection and prevention considerations need to become a more significant component of every internal audit. Internal auditors perhaps need to enter a new internal audit engagement by asking themselves some questions about where a new auditee might commit a fraudulent act. Internal auditors should retain a level of skepticism about the potential for fraud in their ongoing work assignments.

Internal auditors should have a general CBOK level of understanding of both the red flags that indicate the possibility of fraud as well general internal audit review procedures that include an investigation for fraud in the course of all internal audits. Internal auditors, however, should not begin a typical new internal audit with the expectation that the auditee is somehow fraudulent or dishonest. Rather, they should understand that fraud can exist at many levels, and where there is a suspicion in the course of a review, they should have the knowledge to report the matter to proper authorities and to assist in any fraud investigation as requested.

NOTES

1. Ernst & Young 12th Global Fraud Survey, New York, 2014.
2. IIA, AICPA, and ACFE, *Managing the Business Risk of Fraud: A Practical Guide,* 2010. It is available at each of their web sites, such as http://www.acfe.com/uploadedfiles/acfe_website/content/documents/managing-business-risk.pdf.
3. We use the word *was* because the PCAOB took over responsibility for issuing external auditing standards shortly after the release of SAS 99.
4. The federal fraud statute is referenced in a series of rules such as 18 U.S.C. 1341 on mail fraud and 18 U.S.C. 1344 on bank fraud.
5. There is a wide range of fraud materials at http://www.aicpa.org/InterestAreas/ForensicAndValuation/Resources/FraudPreventionDetectionResponse/Pages/FraudPreventionDetectionandResponse.aspx.
6. A gigabyte is a unit of information or computer storage meaning either exactly 1 billion bytes (1000^3, or 10^9) or approximately 1.07 billion bytes (1024^3, or 2^{30}). An internal auditor should think of a byte as a single character.

CHAPTER TWENTY-EIGHT

28

Internal Audit GRC Approaches and Other Compliance Requirements

ALL BUSINESSES, AND PUBLICLY TRADED corporations in particular, have faced governance needs and requirements issues going back to their earliest days. For many enterprises, senior management often initially took the lead in setting business and compliance rules and policies for their employees and others to follow. Internal auditors, of course, have made recommendations to improve *enterprise governance* through their reviews of internal controls. But while internal audit reviews and even management attention often focus on single operating units or corporate office issues, many of today's larger, multiunit enterprises need improved broad-based facilities for setting rules and procedures—they need efficient and effective governance processes.

Life would be easier for those same enterprises if they just had to rely on strong central leadership, such as a dominant CEO, to authorize and direct implementation of any required governance rules. However, enterprises today at any location or size are faced with ever increasing sets of rules and procedures ranging from local police and public safety ordinances to state, national and sometimes international government-issued rules and laws as well as some broad professional rules. An enterprise must comply with these laws and regulations on a whole series of levels, and compliance failures can potentially result in a variety of penalties. Internal audit can often raise issues here as part of specific reviews, but every enterprise needs processes to ensure that it is operating in compliance with the appropriate laws and regulations.

An enterprise always faces risks that it will misinterpret rules or be found in violation of one or another of these multiple laws and regulations. There are also risks that an enterprise's own established governance rules will not achieve their desired results or that it may face an event beyond its control, such as a significant economic downturn, a terrorist attack, an act of war, or a fire in a major facility, that impacts its sphere of operations. There is a need to understand and manage all of these risks at an overall enterprise level.

While enterprises in total and internal auditors in particular have always been concerned with various governance, risk, and *compliance issues*, enterprise management and internal auditors should bring all three of these concerns together into what have been called GRC principles. While other chapters throughout this book discuss such issues as the importance of enterprise governance practices, *risk management* fundamentals, and corporate governance practices, this chapter looks at the importance of establishing a strong set of enterprise governance, risk, and compliance—or GRC—principles, an important element of enterprise governance.

28.1 THE ROAD TO EFFECTIVE GRC PRINCIPLES

Internal auditors had not even heard about or used this now increasingly familiar GRC acronym until early in this century. The letter *G* stands for *governance*, concerns that cover the entire enterprise. In short, governance means taking care of business, making sure things are done according to an enterprise's standards, regulations, and board of directors' decisions, as well as governmental laws and rules. It also means setting forth clearly the stakeholder expectations of what should be done so that all stakeholders are on the same page with regard to how the enterprise is run. The *R* is *risk*. As discussed in Chapter 7 on COSO ERM, everything we do and all aspects of business operations involve some element of risk. When it comes to an individual running across a freeway or a child playing with matches, it's pretty clear that certain risks should just not be taken. When it comes to business, however, risk factors become a way to help both protect existing asset value and create value by strategically expanding an enterprise or adding new products and services.

Finally, the *C* is *compliance*, with the many laws and directives affecting businesses and internal auditors today. Sometimes internal auditors can also extend that letter to include *controls*, meaning that it is important to put certain controls in place to ensure that compliance is happening. For example, this might mean establishing good internal accounting controls, and effectively implementing legislative requirements such as the Sarbanes-Oxley Act (SOx) rules briefly discussed in Chapter 5. Or it might just mean monitoring a factory's air quality emissions or ensuring that its import and export papers are in order. Putting it all together, GRC is more than just a series of separate internal audit issues, but a paradigm to help grow the enterprise in the best possible way.

Enterprises and their internal auditors have historically not thought of or used the acronym GRC as a combined set of principles. As much as an enterprise managed or cared about any of these three combined GRC areas, they were often managed as separate areas concerns. Risk management is a classic case here. Enterprises years ago thought of risk management in terms of insurance coverage and managed their risks through an insurance department that often had little to do with other enterprise operations. Similarly, we always had a need to comply with all levels of established rules, including those to help govern the enterprise, but we have not historically combined them to form GRC concepts. Governance, risk, and compliance is an increasingly recognized concept that reflects a new way in which today's enterprises and internal audit are adopting an integrated approach to these aspects of their businesses, and also is a key component of effective internal control processes.

It is important to remember the core disciplines of governance, risk management, and compliance. Each consists of the four basic GRC components: strategy, processes, technology, and people. Exhibit 28.1 illustrates this GRC concept. Governance, risk management, and compliance principles are shown as being tightly bound to tie these principles together. The diagram shows that internal policies are just below governance in the top center of the diagram and are the key factors supporting governance, that external regulations drive compliance principles, and what we call an enterprise's risk appetite is a key element of risk management.

The lower left component of the GRC triangle is risk management, and this element should be closely tied to risk appetite, a relatively new term for many business and internal audit professionals in recent years. Discussed in Chapter 7, it refers to the amount and type of risk that an organization is prepared to pursue, retain, or take. The lower right component is compliance, an issue that is very close to many internal auditor review activities. However, while internal auditors are frequently involved with reviews of compliance with enterprise established procedures, external regulations are shown as being closely related to general compliance concerns.

The triangle in Exhibit 28.1 also highlights the components of an effective GRC strategy, including effective processes, technologies, including IT, and the people in the enterprise to make all of this work. Off to the left side, the exhibit says that an enterprise requires management attention and support, and that correct ethical behavior, organizational efficiency, and improved effectiveness are keys. The sections following discuss each of these GRC components further, and many of these basic components also are discussed in other chapters. These GRC concepts are all part of an internal auditor's CBOK, but it is important to think of all of them as part of this GRC triangle.

The three GRC principles or elements should be thought of in terms of one continuous and interconnecting flow of concepts, with neither the G, R, nor C elements any more important than the others. We started our discussion here with the governance aspect of GRC. Corporate or enterprise governance is a term that refers broadly to the

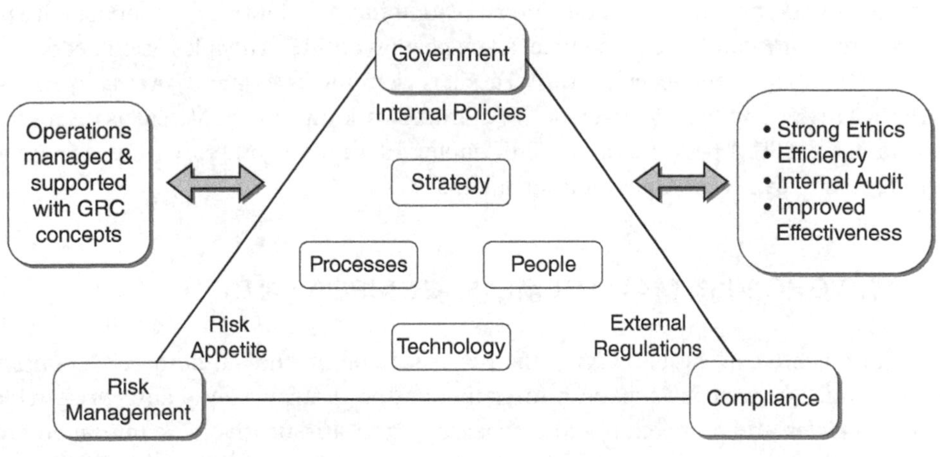

EXHIBIT 28.1 GRC Concepts

rules, processes, or laws by which businesses are operated, regulated, and controlled. The term can refer to internal factors defined by the officers, stockholders, or constitution of a corporation, as well as to external forces such as consumer groups, clients, and government regulations.

Moving on from senior corporate levels and into many areas of enterprise operations, enterprise governance is the responsibilities and practices exercised by the board, senior executive management, and all levels of functional management in many areas with the goals of providing strategic direction, ensuring that objectives are achieved, ascertaining that risks are managed appropriately, and verifying that the enterprise's resources are used responsibly. Governance really refers to the process of establishing rules and procedures within all levels of an enterprise, communicating those rules to appropriate levels of stakeholders, monitoring performance against the rules, and administering rewards and punishments based on the relative performance or compliance with the rules.

A well-defined and well-enforced set of corporate or enterprise governance principles provides a structure that, at least in theory, works for the benefit of everyone concerned by ensuring that the enterprise adheres to accepted ethical standards and best practices as well as to appropriate formal laws, rules, and standards. In recent years, corporate governance has received increased attention because of high-profile scandals involving abuse of corporate power and in some cases alleged criminal activity by corporate officers. An integral part of an effective corporate governance regime includes provisions for civil or criminal prosecution of individuals who conduct unethical or illegal acts in the name of the enterprise.

Although it is difficult to describe all of the concepts of corporate or enterprise governance in a few short paragraphs or a single picture, Exhibit 28.2 shows GRC enterprise governance concepts with an executive group in the center and their interlocking and related responsibilities for establishing controls, a strategic framework, performance, and accountability. The exhibit shows some of the key concepts within each of these responsibility areas. For example, for the strategic framework, there are the elements of planning corporate and business activities, risk management, business continuity, IT and network, and internal audit. Internal audit has a major role or responsibility in this strategic framework. Governance, a key portion of GRC principles, is embedded in many of the chapters on specific internal audit review and assessment *governance issues*. Whether reviewing the adequacy of COSO framework internal controls, as discussed in Chapter 4, ITIL® best practices from Chapter 19, or many others, GRC governance activities are key review areas for internal auditors.

28.2 GRC RISK MANAGEMENT COMPONENTS

A major objective of this book is to offer discussion of internal audit internal control review concepts to today's modern internal auditor. A strong set of enterprise-wide *GRC principles* and components are necessary and an effective risk management program is a key component of enterprise GRC principles and internal audit review processes. Chapter 7 discusses risk management and IT governance fundamentals in

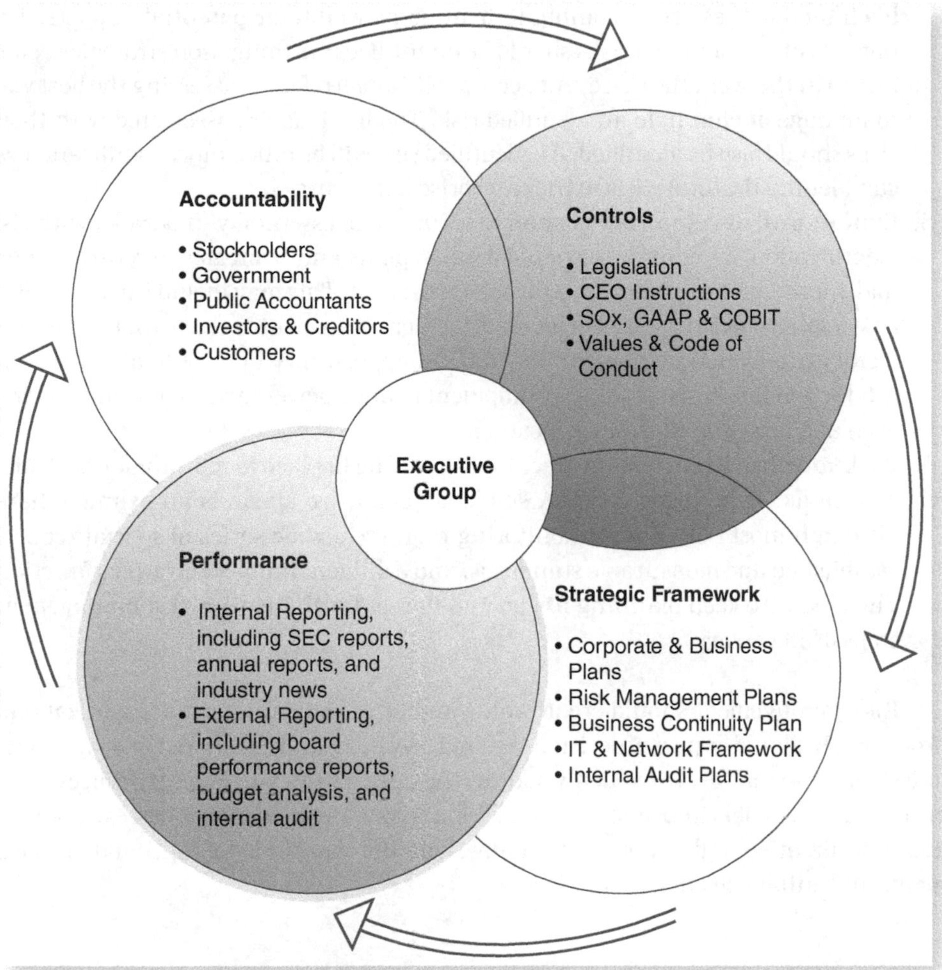

EXHIBIT 28.2 Elements of GRC Governance

greater detail, with an emphasis on COSO ERM, and risk management concepts and controls should be part of the overall enterprise culture from the board of directors and very senior officers down through the ranks. There are four interconnected steps in effective enterprise risk management GRC processes are shown in Exhibit 28.3 and as follows:

1. **Risk assessment planning.** An enterprise faces all levels of risks, whether global issues ranging from national economic or currency crises to product market competition factors and on to weather-related disruption at local operations. We cannot plan or identify every type of risk that might impact an enterprise, but there should be an ongoing analysis of these various potential risks.
2. **Risk identification and analysis.** Rather than just planning for the possibility of some risk event occurring, a more detailed analysis should be made on the

likelihood of these risks coming to fruition as well their potential impacts. The impacts of the identified risks should be quantified and mitigation strategies determined in the event the risk event occurs. *Mitigation* refers to assessing the best way to manage or eliminate an identified risk. The final factors associated with these risks should also be identified. An identified risk will be much more significant if we can identify the total costs to the enterprise if it occurs.

3. **Exploit and develop risk response strategies.** Essentially in parallel with risk identification, an enterprise should develop plans and strategies to return to normal operations and then recover from a risk event. This may include an analysis of risk-related opportunities. For example, if there is an identified risk that some older factory production equipment may fail, an opportunity may be to abandon that production line and install new equipment using a newer technology and possibly even at a newer or alternative location.
4. **Risk monitoring.** Tools and facilities should be in place to monitor for identified as well as other newer risks. A smoke detector fire alarm is an example here, although most risk-related monitoring requires a wide series of special reports, established and measurable standards, and a diligent human resources function. The idea is to keep planning ahead and to reenter these prior risk management steps as necessary.

Risk management should create value and be an integral part of organizational processes. It should be part of decision-making processes and be tailored in a systematic and structured manner to explicitly address the uncertainties an enterprise faces based on the best available information. In addition, risk management processes should be dynamic, iterative, and responsive to change with the capabilities of continual improvements and enhancements.

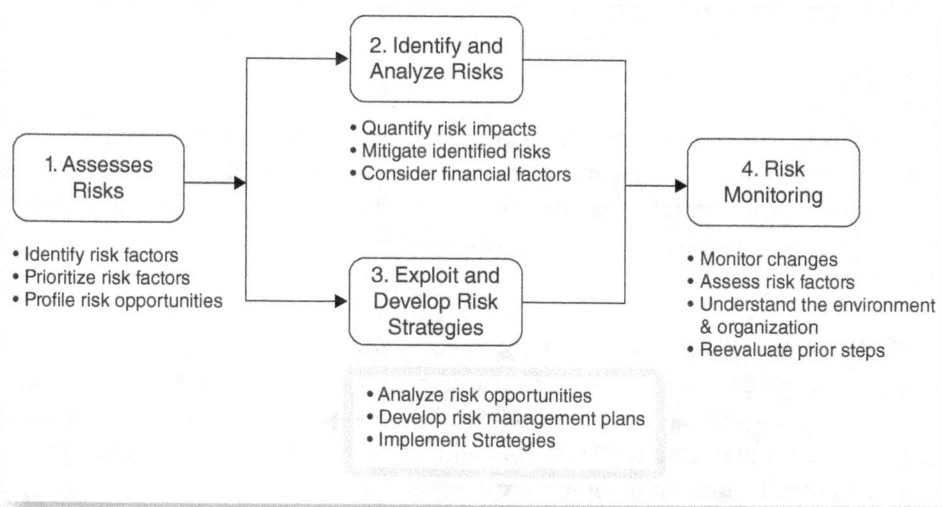

EXHIBIT 28.3 GRC Risk Management Strategies

28.3 GRC AND INTERNAL AUDIT ENTERPRISE COMPLIANCE ISSUES

Compliance is the process of adhering to the guidelines or rules established by either government agencies, standards, groups, or internal corporate policies. Adhering to these compliance-related requirements is a challenge for an enterprise, its related stakeholders, and internal auditors reviewing these processes because of:

- **The frequent introduction of new laws and regulations.** Using the United States as an example, a wide swath of agencies, such as the Environmental Protection Agency, regularly issue new rules that may have wide impacts on many enterprises, despite their prime business purposes. Companies have a challenge to monitor these rules and determine which ones appear to apply to them.
- **Vaguely written regulations that require interpretation.** Again using the United States as an example, in 2010 Congress passed a massive health care bill, the Affordable Care Act often called Obamacare. The legislation was printed on many thousands of pages covering issues and rules that the legislators who passed the bill never even read, let alone understood. Even today and several years later, we are still looking at these rules and interpreting what they were supposed to mean. The 2011 Dodd-Frank financial reform bill is a similar example. It is a very complex bill with many specific rules yet to be published as this book goes to press in 2015. Enterprise compliance with those types of rules can be very difficult, and when internal auditors have questions, they may need to consult with their legal department.
- **No consensus on best practice rules used for compliance.** Legislative rules are often filled with regulations stating such things as, "All transactions must be supported by a receipt." Does such a rule require receipts for transactions less than $1, less than $25, or some other value? There often are often no guidelines here and everyone seems to have their own interpretations.
- **Multiple overlapping compliance regulations.** U.S. states and local governmental units from different areas frequently issue rules that cover similar areas but have different requirements. These differences are typically eventually resolved in the courts, but compliance until matters are resolved can be a challenge.
- **Constantly changing regulations.** Regulatory agencies in particular are often constantly changing or reinterpreting their own rules, making strict compliance a challenge. Enterprise compliance must be viewed as a continuous process, not a onetime internal audit review project. However, compliance requirements continue to drive business agendas as enterprises are being held accountable for meeting the myriad mandates specific to their particular markets or areas of operations.

In addition, enterprises might also be required to address cross-industry legislation, such as the PCI DSS and other similar rules discussed in Chapter 23. Simply stated, the breadth and complexity of these compliance-related laws and regulations has caused challenges for many enterprises and internal auditors over the years.

Enterprises need to approach their GRC compliance principles from a strategic perspective that could help them move beyond simply meeting individual compliance mandates to realizing tangible business benefits from their infrastructure investments as a whole.

The scope of compliance permeates many aspects of enterprise activities and operations. Exhibit 28.4 illustrates some issues internal audit should consider as it attempts to establish its scope and approach to GRC compliance. An enterprise should not ignore some rules; it should always be aware that they exist. Nevertheless, a consistent approach on the use of compliance-driven capabilities and supporting technologies across an enterprise can provide an enterprise with potential benefits:

- **Flexibility.** One of the difficulties that internal auditors frequently encounter when reviewing compliance issues is that new regulations are introduced by authorizing authorities and existing regulations are changed on a frequent basis. By centrally managing compliance initiatives via organization-wide compliance architecture, an enterprise can more quickly adapt to these changes.
- **Reduced total cost of compliance ownership.** Investments can be leveraged across multiple regulations. For example, many regulations specify document retention requirements, which can be met by a single investment in a content database facility and records management system. This presents a requirement for internal auditors to make consistent recommendations.

EXHIBIT 28.4 Enterprise Internal Audit Review Considerations for Reviews of Compliance Activities

Scope of Compliance Area	Area for Considerations
Strategy	■ As an enterprise develops its compliance strategies, it must determine which regulations are the most relevant. ■ Compliance sustainability needs to be an integral part of any compliance strategy.
Organization	■ The organizational structure must be established to meet the specific requirements (or intent) of each regulation (e.g., the Sarbanes-Oxley Act recommends the chief executive officer and president be two different people).
Processes	■ Key processes must be documented and practiced. ■ Audits or reviews must take place to ensure documented processes are effectively being used to address compliance/regulation requirements.
Applications and Data	■ Applications must be designed, implemented, and continuously tested to support the requirements of each regulation. ■ Data must be properly protected and handled according to each regulation.
Facilities	■ Facilities must be designed and available to meet the needs of each regulation (i.e., some regulations may require records to be readily available at an off-site location).

- **Competitive advantage.** A broad and consistent enterprise compliance architecture allows internal auditors to better understand and control the business processes in the enterprises reviewed, allowing them to respond more quickly and accurately to external or internal compliance pressures. Furthermore, certain regulations may contain tangible business benefits through reduced minimum capital requirements, which could be enabled through an enterprise-wide compliance architecture.

Effective GRC compliance processes help internal audit to transform their business operations and gain deeper insight and predictability from their business information as they address regulatory-driven requirements. Key business drivers may include the ability to better manage information assets, demonstrate compliance with regulatory and legal obligations, reduce the risk of litigation, reduce the cost of storage and discovery, and demonstrate corporate accountability.

28.4 IMPORTANCE OF EFFECTIVE GRC PRACTICES AND PRINCIPLES

An enterprise needs to adopt strong governance, risk, and compliance processes, with the objective of establishing an effective GRC program. While many of the previous chapters of this book have focused more on IT governance processes, we should not forget the overall importance of combined strong governance, risk, and compliance processes that support all areas of enterprise operations.

Both as elements of the entities where internal audit performs its reviews as well as an internal auditor's own personal and professional standards, GRC principles and processes should be emphasized. All internal auditors should have a strong CBOK knowledge and understanding of GRC practices and principles. They should be fundamental foundation components and are important components of effective IT governance processes.

PART SEVEN

The Professional Internal Auditor

CHAPTER TWENTY-NINE

29

Professional Certifications: CIA, CISA, and More

WE LIVE IN A WORLD today increasingly filled with multiple and sometimes too many professional certification designations. Many are valuable and important, while others are perhaps only of value to their promoters. As an example of these contrasts and variations, a civil engineer designing highway bridges will seek a very important and well-recognized Professional Engineer (PE) certification, while a home interior designer may take a far less well-recognized examination to become a Certified Kitchen Designer (CKD). These certifications may be viewed positively by an employer or customer looking for a candidate to fill a position requiring appropriate job skills.

A PE certification is awarded only after the candidate has some solid job experience and has passed a difficult test. It is an important and well-recognized certification and is often a requirement in contract specifications. A CKD certification may give a candidate working for a local contracting firm some additional points to sell a remodeling job, but the designation is not very well recognized.

While many professional certifications are viewed as worthwhile, others do not appear to be very valuable. For example, and not to pick on an industry, but the insurance industry is filled with many types and levels of certifications. A potential purchaser of life insurance, for example, may encounter sales representatives with a stream of certification initials after their name on the business card, such as a Certified Life Underwriter (CLU). Will a consumer be more likely to buy life insurance from a CLU-designated salesperson over another salesperson? For many, the answer is probably no. The initials may help tell the consumer that the life insurance salesperson is experienced, but the sales pitch and price will often be the deciding factors on the purchase. Of course, a consumer will expect a greater knowledge of insurance processes from the salesperson with the CLU.

Internal auditors also have a need for strong and well-recognized professional certifications. Many have joined the profession with no specific certification requirements beyond their undergraduate college degrees. Others attained accounting degrees and prepared for the Certified Public Accountant (CPA) examination. Many hiring managers once assumed that potential internal auditor candidates must have a CPA to become qualified as internal auditors, but over time many realized the internal audit profession required people with more qualifications than just a CPA. Things changed at the urging of Institute of Internal Auditors (IIA) professionals, and the result was the Certified Internal Auditor (CIA) certification. Today, beyond or separate from the CIA, an internal auditor can become a Certified Information Systems Auditor (CISA), a Certified Fraud Examiner (CFE), or any of a number of other certifications. Some of these may be very valuable for a typical internal auditor, while others may receive little more than a ho-hum from management and peer professionals. This chapter will discuss some of the professional designations that are most important to the modern internal auditor. In particular, it will look at the CIA and CISA certifications, including their qualification and examination requirements. In addition, the chapter will consider some of the other certification options available to internal auditors.

This chapter will not discuss the CPA examination. While certainly more oriented to external auditors, the CPA exam is still the best and most recognized accounting, auditing, and internal control examination for all financial professionals, including internal auditors. It should be an objective for any internal auditor with a financial background. The other *professional examinations* discussed in this chapter, such as the CIA, also should be considered strong objectives for many modern internal auditors.

29.1 CERTIFIED INTERNAL AUDITOR RESPONSIBILITIES AND REQUIREMENTS

Sponsored by the IIA, the CIA designation is the only globally accepted certification for internal auditors and is the major standard by which individuals can demonstrate their competency and professionalism in internal auditing. The CIA examination was first offered in August 1974 to 654 candidates, and today there are about 100,000 CIAs worldwide. Administered by the IIA Board of Regents, the CIA is a three-part, eight-and-a-half-hour examination that is offered worldwide through computer-based testing services and consists of the following sections, as outlined in Exhibit 29.1:

Part I: Internal Audit Basics
Part II: Internal Audit Practices
Part III: Internal Audit Knowledge Elements

By applying to become a CIA candidate, an individual agrees to accept the conditions of the program including eligibility requirements, exam confidentiality, acceptance of the CIA's code of ethics, continuing professional education (CPE), and any other conditions enacted by the Board of Regents or its Certification Department.

To apply to take the CIA examination, candidates must hold a bachelor's degree or its equivalent, such as a Chartered Accountant, from an accredited college-level institution; a copy of the candidate's diploma, transcripts, or other written proof of completion

EXHIBIT 29.1 Current CIA Examination Summary

The Certified Internal Auditor (CIA) examination tests a candidate's knowledge of internal auditing practices and understandings, including internal audit issues, risks, and remedies. The CIA examination is nondisclosed, meaning that current exam questions and answers will not be published or divulged. The CIA examination now consists of three parts:

Certified Internal Auditor Examination Requirements

Part 1: Internal Audit Basics

Duration: 2.5 hours

Question Count: 125

Typical Part 1 focus areas:

- IIA Mandatory Guidance
- Internal Controls and Risks
- Tools and Techniques for Conducting Audit Engagements

Part 2: Internal Audit Practices

Duration: 2.0 hours

Question Count: 100

Typical Part 2 focus areas:

- Managing the Internal Audit Function
- Managing Individual Internal Audit Engagements
- Fraud Risks and Controls

Part 3: Internal Audit Knowledge Elements

Duration: 2.0 hours

Question Count: 100

Typical Part 3 focus areas:

- Governance
- Risk Management
- Organization Structure and Business Processes
- Communication
- Leadership
- IT and Business Continuity
- Financial Management
- Global Business Environments

of a degree program must accompany the candidate's application. With the exception of full-time undergraduate degree students in their senior year, candidates will not be allowed to sit for the exam until the educational requirement is met.

Applicants who do not possess a bachelor's degree and who are unsure whether their educational achievements or professional designations qualify as equivalents can apply for a waiver from these educational requirements through a formal request to the Board of Regents, the final judge of the acceptability of professional or educational attainment offered in lieu of a bachelor's degree and of equivalents. Extensive work experience can help a nondegreed internal auditor obtain permission to take the CIA examination. Information submitted should be sufficiently detailed to enable the Board of Regents to determine equivalency.

CIA candidates should exhibit high moral and professional standards and must submit in their certification application a character reference completed by another CIA, the candidate's supervisor or manager, or an appropriate educator. In addition, in order to receive their certificates, CIA candidates are required to have completed 24 months of internal auditing or equivalent experience in audit/assessment disciplines, external auditing, quality assurance, compliance, or internal control–related work. Either a master's degree or work experience in related business professions (such as accounting, law, or finance) can be substituted for one year of experience. Work experience must be verified by a CIA or the candidate's supervisor. Candidates may sit for the CIA exam prior to satisfying their experience requirement, but they will not be certified until the experience requirement has been met.

The CIA exam is nondisclosed and candidates must agree to keep the exam contents confidential. They should not discuss the specific exam content with anyone except the IIA's Certification Department. Unauthorized disclosure of exam material will be considered a breach of the code of ethics and could result in disqualification of the candidate or other appropriate censure.

The CIA examination covers a wide range of current topics that are significant to the modern internal auditor. Each of its three sections has multiple-choice questions that may or may not be covered in any particular examination offering. The examination is periodically updated and reflects current topics of interest to internal auditors. The internal auditor CBOK requirements outlined throughout this book are very close to Exhibit 29.1's internal auditor requirements. Virtually all of the CIA requirement topics outlined here are discussed in one of these chapters. As has been discussed in Chapter 6, an understanding of the COBIT framework should be a CBOK requirement for many if not all internal auditors.

While professionals can quibble about the extent of proficiency or awareness knowledge required for an internal auditor to become a CIA, the topics outlined in Exhibit 29.1 represent a comprehensive CBOK requirement for all internal auditors. These same subject areas are generally covered in the chapters throughout this book, and internal auditors should consider preparing for and taking the CIA examination to demonstrate their knowledge and understanding.

To give the reader a better understanding of the challenges found in the CIA examination, Exhibit 29.2 includes some IIA-published CIA sample examination questions. These questions were published in 2014 and certainly will not be replicated in the actual CIA test, but they give a flavor of the types of questions in the examination. Although not directly posted, information and solutions regarding each of these questions can be found in other chapters.

An internal auditor does not have to be a member of the IIA to take the CIA examination, although the IIA strongly encourages membership. All CIAs, IIA members and nonmembers, must be familiar with and agree to abide by the IIA's *International Standards for the Professional Practice of Internal Auditing* as well as the IIA's code of ethics. These two, outlined in Chapter 9, set the standards of practice and conduct for all internal auditors. These IIA standards are particularly important as they have recently been revised in 2014 from internal auditor best practices where the guidance said that an internal auditor "should" to a new internal audit standards requirement that an

EXHIBIT 29.2 Certified Internal Auditor (CIA) Sample Exam Questions

The following sample questions were published late 2014 on the IIA's web site (www.theiia.org) and represent the types of questions found in the CIA examination. Although questions from previous tests are posted, there several Web references such as this to help prepare for the examination.

Part 1: Sample Exam Questions

According to IIA guidance, independence of the internal audit activity is achieved through which of the following?

A. Staffing and supervision.
B. Continuing professional development and due professional care.
C. Human relations and communications.
D. Organizational status and objectivity.

Considering the differences between statistical and judgmental sampling, which of the following statements about statistical sampling is true?

A. No judgment is required, because everything is computed according to a formula.
B. A smaller sample can be used.
C. More accurate results are obtained.
D. Population estimates can be made with measurable reliability.

Part 2: Sample Exam Questions

Two internal auditors left the organization and cannot be replaced due to budget constraints. Which of the following is the least desirable option for completing future audit engagements?

A. Use self-assessment questionnaires to address audit objectives.
B. Employ IT solutions for audit planning, sampling, and documentation.
C. Eliminate consulting engagements from the audit plan.
D. Fill vacancies with personnel from operating departments that are not being audited.

Which of the following fraudulent entries is most likely to be made to conceal the theft of an asset?

A. Debit expenses, and credit the asset.
B. Debit the asset, and credit another asset account.
C. Debit revenue, and credit the asset.
D. Debit another asset account, and credit the asset

Part 3: Sample Exam Questions

Which of the following is the best strategy for limiting production delays caused by equipment breakdown and repair?

A. Schedule production based on capacity planning.
B. Plan maintenance activity based on an analysis of equipment repair work orders.
C. Preauthorize equipment maintenance and overtime pay.
D. Establish a preventive maintenance program for all production equipment.

Franchising and horizontal mergers are commonly used strategies in which of the following industry environments?

A. Emerging industries.
B. Declining industries.
C. Fragmented industries.
D. Mature industries.

Which of the following costs does management need to consider when introducing a new product or substituting a new product for an existing one?

1. Costs of retraining employees.
2. Costs of acquiring new ancillary equipment.

(continued)

EXHIBIT 29.2 *(continued)*

3. Write-offs due to undepreciated investment in old technology.
4. Capital requirements for changeover.

A. 1 and 3 only.
B. 1, 2, and 4 only.
C. 2, 3, and 4 only.
D. 1, 2, 3, and 4.

internal auditor "must." As another 2014 tool, the IIA has recently launched its Certification Candidate Management System (CCMS), a tool to keep track of a candidate's progress on various certification tests, as well as continuing education progress toward those certifications, that is related to the Qualification for Internal Audit Leadership certification discussed in a later section.

After certification, CIAs are required to maintain their knowledge and skills and to stay abreast of improvements and current developments in internal auditing standards, procedures, and techniques. Practicing CIAs must complete and report 80 hours of CPE credits every two years. They must report their CPE activities to the IIA per published deadlines, and any who fail to meet these requirements will be placed in inactive status and may not use their designation.

The CIA is a worldwide certification in contrast to the CPA, a U.S.-only certification, or various national versions of Chartered Accountant certifications. The CIA is the only internationally recognized designation for internal auditors. The CIA examination is offered in English, French, Spanish, Mandarin Chinese, Czech, German, Hebrew, Italian, Japanese, and Portuguese as well as an ever-growing set of other languages. While the examination once presented a challenge for many because candidates had to present themselves at testing sites for proctored sit-down examinations, today the CIA examination is offered through a worldwide chain of computer-based testing sites. A candidate must meet registration requirements, receive a testing site "ticket," and then arrange to visit an authorized testing site. (More information on the CIA process can be found in the IIA web site, www.theiia.org.)

29.2 BEYOND THE CIA: OTHER IIA CERTIFICATIONS

In addition to the CIA, the IIA's Board of Regents offers several other professional certification examinations and certificates: the Certification in Control Self-Assessment (CCSA), the Certified Government Auditing Professional (CGAP), and the Certified Financial Services Auditor (CFSA), and the Certification in Risk Management Assurance (CRMA). In addition, the IIA offers a Qualification for Internal Audit Leadership (QIAL) designation.

Each of these require separate examinations that are offered to candidates who have passed Part I of the CIA exam and have work experience appropriate to the specialty certification. For example, to earn the CRMA designation, the candidate must not just pass the special test but also gain work experience in that area. All are offered through the same computer-based training testing facilities as the CIA examination.

CCSA Requirements

Chapter 12 describes the IIA's control self-assessment (CSA) process. The CCSA exam tests a candidate's understanding of important CSA fundamentals, processes, and related topics such as risk, controls, and business objectives. As a means to promote and encourage CSA-related activities, the IIA has established this CCSA professional certification. In contrast to the experience requirements and overall rigor of the CIA examination, the CCSA is a single, two-hour-and-45-minute, 115-question examination that tests candidates on their knowledge of CSA processes in six broad domain areas:

Domain 1: CSA Fundamentals (5–10%)
Domain 2: CSA Program Integration (15–25%)
Domain 3: Elements of the CSA Process (15–25%)
Domain 4: Business Objectives/Organizational Performance (10–15%)
Domain 5: Risk Identification and Assessment (15–20%)
Domain 6: Control Theory and Application (20–25%)

Each of these domain testing areas requires the CCSA candidate to demonstrate CSA process knowledge in much more detail than is presented in Chapter 12 on control self-assessments. The topics tested on the CCSA exam are framed in the context of a variety of industry situations. Candidates are not expected to be familiar with industry-specific internal controls, but should be able to relate to risks and controls that generally apply to business processes in various industries. The IIA web site contains some sample CCSA examination questions. After completion of the CCSA examination, the successful candidate should be able to serve as an experienced CSA session facilitator, as was discussed in Chapter 12.

Candidates for the CCSA are not required to have CIA credentials, be members of the IIA, or even be internal auditors. The experience requirements for the CCSA are that a candidate must have had a strong level of experience in the control self-assessment field. Other requirements, however, such as accepting the IIA's code of ethics and continuing education are similar to the CIA. The CCSA alone will give a practitioner a level of expertise in this area, but it almost always needs to be combined with another certification such as the CIA. The CCSA is offered in the same array of testing sites as the CIA, but not in all of the same languages.

CGAP Requirements

There are numerous references throughout this book to government auditors, but with no explanation of their tasks and skills. Whether working for one of the many branches of the U.S. government or at a state or local level, an internal auditor working in a government environment is faced with a different set of knowledge and skill requirements than the typical internal auditor working in the private sector. Attainment of the CGAP allows a candidate to demonstrate these governmental auditing skills.

CGAP is a specialty certification designed specifically for and by government auditing practitioners working in the public sector at all levels—U.S. federal/national, state/provincial, local, quasi-governmental, or crown authority—and is a professional credential that prepares a candidate for the many challenges in this unique and demanding environment. This computer-based examination is currently available in English as well as Chinese (unsimplified), Polish, Spanish, and Turkish. It tests a candidate's comprehension of government auditing practices, methodologies, and environment, as well as related standards and control/risk models.

The requirements for the CGAP are similar to the CIA and CCSA just described. Here, candidates who register through CCMS for this two-hour-and-55-minute, 115-question examination must have had two years of auditing experience in a government environment (federal, state/provincial, local, quasi-governmental areas, authority/crown corporation). Candidates who register to take the exam in the United States will receive a local version with questions on U.S. Generally Accepted Government Auditing Standards (GAGAS/Yellow Book). Work experience must be verified by a CGAP, a CIA, a CCSA, a CFSA, or the candidate's supervisor. The CGAP examination and approximate concentration of questions covers the following areas or domains:

Domain 1: Standards and Control/Risk Models (5–10%)
Domain 2: Government Auditing Practice (35–45%)
Domain 3: Government Auditing Methodologies and Skills (20–25%)
Domain 4: Government Auditing Environment (25–35%)

Although this book does not cover the often very specialized field of governmental internal auditing, Exhibit 29.3 shows five sample CGAP questions, taken from the IIA

EXHIBIT 29.3 Certified Government Auditing Professional (CGAP) Sample Questions

The following sample questions were published late 2014 in the IIA's web site (www.theiia.org) and represent the types of questions found in the CGAP examination.

It is important that an internal audit department's statement of purpose, authority, and responsibility detail:
A. The delineation of responsibilities between the internal and external auditors.
B. The organizational status of the internal audit function.
C. Whether the agency head will present audit findings to the oversight committee.
D. Under what circumstances the internal audit director may have confidential access to the oversight committee.

An internal auditor plans an audit of a city's highway maintenance. The audit objective is to determine if fixed assets employed are properly reflected in the accounting records. Which of the following approaches is most effective?
A. Inspecting fixed assets used in the road maintenance process and tracing to the asset subsidiary ledger.
B. Scanning the asset subsidiary ledger for credit entries.
C. Selecting items from the asset subsidiary ledger and recalculating depreciation.
D. Examining documentation concerning the cost of fixed assets used in the road maintenance process.

An internal control that may be useful in the detection of integrity violations is:
A. Segregation of incompatible duties.
B. Periodic surprise cash counts.
C. Regularly scheduled site visits.
D. Properly designed forms.

web site, for this examination. These questions certainly are on topics that have not been discussed in this book, and they illustrate the specialized knowledge requirements of government auditors. The IIA lists a series of reference sources to help a candidate prepare for the CGAP examination.

CFSA Requirements

The Certified Financial Services Auditor (CFSA) is another of the IIA's specialty certifications and is tailored to demonstrate an individual internal auditor's competence and professionalism in banking institutions, thrift/savings and loan organizations, credit unions, insurance companies, security and commodity services, holding and investment companies, credit agencies, financial services regulatory agencies, and other financial services organizations.

The CFSA exam consists of 115 multiple-choice questions to be completed over a period of two hours and 55 minutes. It is offered through computer-based testing in Chinese, English, Italian, Portuguese (banking discipline only), and Spanish.

The exam questions for the CFSA are all multiple-choice, with 80% of the exam covering three disciplines—banking, insurance, and securities. The remaining 20% relate to the candidates' chosen discipline and will be at the proficiency level. CFSA candidates may choose any one of the three disciplines as part of their CFSA exam test, but may not choose to be tested on more than one discipline. The CFSA designation does not distinguish one chosen discipline from another. The examination covers the following domain areas:

Domain 1: Financial Services Auditing
Domain 2: Banking
Domain 3: Insurance
Domain 4: Securities

These financial domains can be very different, as the specialized knowledge requirements for banking often vary from the field of insurance. Exhibit 29.4 shows the topics syllabus for the CFSA's Domain 1, financial services auditing—a broad range of topics. Many of the topics cover areas where the candidate is expected to have a "proficiency" in the area. Other areas in the test are fields where the candidate should only be expected to just have an "awareness." This split between proficiency and awareness knowledge areas is similar to our CBOK guidelines throughout this book, where we point out that some areas are an internal auditor CBOK requirement while others are areas where an internal auditor should only have a CBOK general level of knowledge.

CRMA Requirements

The CRMA certification is designed for internal auditors and risk management professionals with responsibility for and experience in providing risk assurance, governance processes, quality assurance, or CSA. It demonstrates an individual's ability to evaluate the dynamic components that comprise an organization's governance and enterprise risk management program and provide advice and assurance around these issues. The

EXHIBIT 29.4 Certified Financial Services Auditor (CFSA) Domain 1 Exam Syllabus

Domain 1 of the CFSA examination covers financial services auditing topics that represent about 25 to 35% of the overall examination. The topics in this domain are areas where candidates must exhibit proficiency (P) thorough an understanding and ability to apply concepts in these topic areas. Other domains in the CFSA are areas where candidates only must exhibit an awareness (A) and knowledge of terminology and fundamentals) in the topic areas.

CFSA Domain 1 Topic Areas

A. IIA International Professional Practices Framework (P)
B. Internal Control/Risk Management/Governance (P)
  1. Internal Control Frameworks
  2. Risk Management Frameworks
  3. Governance Models
C. Audit Process (P)
  1. Audit Planning
  2. Audit Fieldwork
    a. Risk Assessment
    b. Analytical Review
    c. Data Gathering and Evaluation
    d. Testing
    e. Tools and Techniques
  3. Audit Communications
  4. Monitoring Outcomes
D. Implications of Information Technology (P)
E. Auditing Financial Statement Elements (P)
  1. Balance Sheet
  2. Statement of Cash Flows
  3. Income/Expense Statement
  4. Off Balance-Sheet Items

CRMA exam requires the candidate to complete Part I of the CIA examination as well as a separate CRMA exam, which consists of 100 multiple-choice questions covering four domains. The CRMA exam requires a completion time of two hours. Eligibility and experience requirements here are similar to the CIA, as discussed previously.

The CRMA exam core content covers four domains:

Domain 1: Organizational Governance Related to Risk Management (25–30%)
Domain 2: Principles of Risk Management Processes (25–30%)
Domain 3: Assurance Role of the Internal Auditor (20–25%)
Domain 4: Consulting Role of the Internal Auditor (20–25%)

The standards tested on the CRMA exam include CIA exam Part I topics, aspects of the IIA's international standards, discussed in Chapter 9, with an emphasis on internal audit independence and objectivity, governance concepts, risk identification and management, management controls, and audit planning. The CRMA exam topics also include governance aspects and principles of risk management assurance in addition to appropriate assurance and consulting roles for internal audit professionals.

QIAL Requirements

Not another certification, the QIAL designation is a new IIA-released path to promote professional growth and recognition. The IIA's idea here is that the growth and change in the internal auditing field is demanding a new type of leader—one who drives a high-performing audit team while delivering value by consistently addressing stakeholder needs, top-down risks, and expectations of an evolving marketplace. The QIAL has an objective to support internal audit professionals to rise to better-recognized positions to become what the IIA calls "the next generation of visionaries for the profession." The idea is that no matter whether an internal auditor is an aspiring leader or an audit executive, the IIA feels that the QIAL is the right qualification for the next stage in an internal audit professional's career progression.

As we have discussed in other chapters outlining internal auditor CBOK areas, the environment in which internal auditing operates is fast-moving, constantly changing, and hugely challenging. With ever-rising expectations and increased value attached to the role that internal auditing plays, much is required of those in leadership positions. Those who rely on the assurance and other services that internal auditing delivers should expect the activity to be led by individuals with a keen understanding of its role and nature alongside proven leadership capabilities.

The IIA introduced the QIAL member designation in 2014 as a qualification program that addresses the specific requirements for internal auditing leadership roles. This is a totally new program and approach. There is no formal examination to qualify, nor even a requirement to be a CIA. The QIAL has qualification classification categories of five years of internal audit experience as what is called an aspiring leader, 10 years to become a new leader, and 15 to become classified as an experienced leader. For each of these, candidates must complete three designated online case studies, make a presentation to a review panel, and participate in a panel interview.

At the time of this publication, the IIA's QIAL program is so new that we have little to report beyond its introductory documents. It appears to be a good approach for recognizing seasoned internal audit managers who may or may not have taken the CIA exam many years ago but have strong experience in internal audit leadership. The hard question here is whether that experienced internal auditor, often perhaps a chief audit executive, really personally needs that QIAL. This program, now in its very early days, looks very admirable, but time will tell about its future impact and importance.

29.3 IMPORTANCE OF THE CIA SPECIALTY CERTIFICATION EXAMINATIONS

This chapter began with some rather cynical comments about the plethora of professional certifications, using the Certified Kitchen Designer as perhaps an extreme example. While the CIA examination and its professional designation are important for internal auditors as professionals and for managers reviewing internal auditors' professsional credentials, we would somewhat question the value of, need for, or importance of these multiple IIA additional professional certifications as special, separate designations. For example, we highlighted the wide range of certifications in insurance industry professional designations. An internal auditor claiming he or she is also a CFSA beyond being a recognized CIA may not impress too many people at this time, because it is new and does not have a wide sphere of recognition.

The IIA currently has four professional certifications in addition to the new QIAL just discussed. Up until recent years, a candidate achieved these additional certifications by completing them through what was Part III of the CIA exam. As discussed in previous section, the CIA exam now has only three sections, and a candidate may achieve an additional IIA certification in some cases by completing Part I of the CIA as well as taking a specialized test for that internal audit specialty, or in other cases just taking the internal audit specialty certification exam.

Some of these specialty certifications, such as the CGAP, can be very important for an internal auditor working in a government environment at any level, while others such as the CCSA may be of less long-term value. Before embarking on one of these specialty certifications, an internal auditor might do an Internet search and local area search to check on the job market demands for persons with that specialty certification and then also question why an internal auditor wants to specialize in that niche. As an example, in December 2014 we did an Internet search for job postings for potential candidates with CFSA qualifications. With the exception of one in Australia and one in Canada, we found little. Things change, but an internal auditor should be cautious about the value here for future employment growth.

The overall or prime CIA examination should be an important test and measurement for all internal auditors. While this book has an objective of defining a CBOK for internal auditors, a knowledge of the CIA topic areas, as summarized in Exhibit 29.1 examination topic summary, contains an excellent set of CBOK requirements for internal auditors. All internal auditors should consider achieving the CIA as a prime professional objective. The other CIA related designations may be of lesser value.

29.4 CERTIFIED INFORMATION SYSTEMS AUDITOR

Previous chapters have mentioned the hopefully friendly rivalry between the IIA and what was once known as the EDP Auditors Association (now the Information Systems Audit and Control Association [ISACA]). As mentioned, what is now ISACA was founded by internal auditors who felt that the IIA was not giving enough attention to technology and information systems or IT issues. Over the years, these two professional groups have been operating in a somewhat parallel manner, and the ISACA has a certification examination that is similar but much more IT-focused than the IIA's CIA. The ISACA-led Certified Information Systems Auditor (CISA) examination and professional designation is open to all individuals who have interest and skills in information systems audit, control, and security. The examination is four hours in duration and consists of 200 multiple-choice questions. The test is offered each year in June and December at many worldwide locations and in a wide range of languages.

In addition to successfully passing the CISA examination, a candidate must have a minimum of five years of professional information systems auditing, control, or security-related work experience. A maximum of one year of information systems experience or one year of financial or operational auditing experience can be substituted for one of those five years of information systems auditing, control, or security experience. In addition, 60 to 120 completed college semester credit hours (the equivalent of an associate or bachelor's degree) can be substituted for one or two years, respectively, of information systems auditing, control, or security experience. Also, two years as a full-time university instructor in a related field (e.g., computer science, accounting, or information systems auditing) can be substituted for one year of information systems auditing, control, or security experience.

This experience must have been gained within the 10-year period preceding the application date for certification or within five years from the date of initially passing the examination. Retaking and passing the examination will be required if the application for certification is not submitted within five years from the passing date of the examination. All experience is verified independently with employers.

Per ISACA guidelines, the tasks and knowledge required of today's and tomorrow's information systems audit professional serve as the blueprint for the CISA examination. Exhibit 29.5 shows the five broad domain areas included in the CISA examination. More information about the requirements in each of these knowledge areas can be found on the ISACA web site (www.isaca.org) or in a variety of reference materials listed there as well. That same web site contains a set of sample questions.

The CISA examination has similar education, experience, and continuing education requirements as are found with the CIA examination discussed previously. This is a fairly technical level of examination; even though a candidate may have achieved CIA certifications, the CISA requires knowledge in an extensive set of areas. The CISA designation has been a globally accepted standard of achievement in the information systems (IS) audit, control, and security field since 1978, and has been recognized by many governments and major business groups around the world. At the time of this publication, more than 106,000 people have attained the CISA certification since its inception.

EXHIBIT 29.5 CISA Examination Domain Areas

1. **The IS Audit Process (14%)** Provide IS audit services in accordance with IS audit standards, guidelines, and best practices to assist the enterprise in ensuring that its information technology and business systems are protected and controlled.
2. **IT Governance and Managemenmt (14%)** Provide assurance that the organization has the structure, policies, accountability, mechanisms, and monitoring practices in place to achieve the requirements of corporate governance of IT.
3. **Information Systems Acquisition, Development, and Implementation (19%)** Provide assurance that the IT service management practices for the development/acquisition, testing, implementation, maintenance, and disposal of systems and infrastructure will meet the enterprise's objectives.
4. **Information Systems Operations, Maintenance, and Support (23%)** Provide assurance that the IT service management practices will ensure delivery of the level of services required to meet the enterprise's objectives.
5. **Protection of Information Assets (30%)** Provide assurance that the security architecture (policies, standards, procedures, and controls) ensures the confidentially, integrity, and availability of information assets.

Similar to the IIA with its CIA-related other certifications, ISACA also offers separate examination certificates for a Certified Information Security Manager (CISM), Certified in the Governance of Enterprise IT (CGEIT), and Certified in Risk and Information Systems Control (CRISC). Each of these are separate examinations requiring several levels of experience in the particular practice field but offered today in a more limited set of languages.

29.5 CERTIFIED INFORMATION SECURITY MANAGER

The Certified Information Security Manager (CISM) program and examination promotes international security practices and recognizes individuals who manage, design, oversee, and assess an enterprise's information security.

The CISM is a 200-question, four-hour examination that is offered in five different languages two times per year and covers five information security management areas. This is an examination covering the work performed by information security managers, as validated by prominent industry leaders, subject matter experts, and industry practitioners. The following is a description of these areas and the approximate percentage of test questions allocated to each area:

Domain 1: Information Security Governance (24%)
Domain 2: Information Risk Management and Compliance (33%)
Domain 3: Information Security Program Development and Management (25%)
Domain 4: Information Security Incident Management (18%)

Each of these content areas is discussed on the ISACA web site, with a fairly detailed outline of areas that a CISM manager would be expected to perform and know. The requirements for taking this worldwide certification examination are similar to the CISA, although it is not offered at present in very many languages.

The CISM is supported by the very strong and credible ISACA organization, and it has grown in terms of status and recognition. However, these examinations and certifications often take time to become highly recognized among managers and professionals. While preparing and sitting for any professional examination is an excellent learning exercise for any professional, an internal auditor may want to review the number of Internet job openings for candidates with a CISM. At the time of this publication, there are quite a few openings looking for a CISA with a CISM as well.

29.6 CERTIFIED IN THE GOVERNANCE OF ENTERPRISE IT

Certified in the Governance of Enterprise IT (CGEIT) recognizes a wide range of professionals for their knowledge and application of enterprise IT governance principles and practices. It requires five or more years of experience managing, serving in an advisory or oversight role, and/or otherwise supporting the governance of the IT-related contribution to an enterprise, including a minimum of one year of experience relating to the definition, establishment, and management of a framework for the governance of IT. While waivers are available for other certification, there are no substitutions for these CGEIT experience requirements. Certification here is based on successful completion of a 150-question, four-hour examination, available only in English, covering the following domain areas:

Domain 1: Framework for the Governance of Enterprise IT (25%)
Domain 2: Strategic Management (20%)
Domain 3: Benefits Realization (16%)
Domain 4: Risk Optimization (24%)
Domain 5: Resource Optimization (15%)

29.7 CERTIFIED IN RISK AND INFORMATION SYSTEMS CONTROL

The Certified in Risk and Information Systems Control (CRISC) certification is designed for those experienced in business and technology risk management, and the design, implementation, monitoring, and maintenance of IS control. This 200-question, four-hour examination, is available only in English, and covers the following domain or knowledge requirement areas:

Domain 1: Risk Identification, Assessment, and Evaluation (31%)
Domain 2: Risk Response (17%)
Domain 3: Risk Monitoring (17%)
Domain 4: Information Systems Control Design and Implementation (17%)
Domain 5: IS Control Monitoring and Maintenance (18%)

Candidates must have three or more years of cumulative work experience performing the tasks of a CRISC professional across at least three CRISC domains. There are no substitutions or experience waivers.

CRISC-certified professionals should have the skills to manage risk, design, and oversee response measures, monitor systems for risk, and ensure that the organization's risk management strategies are met. CRISC is a newer certification, and since its inception in 2010 over 17,000 professionals have acquired it. This qualification is designed to help qualify professionals for jobs such as an IT security analyst, security engineer architect, information assurance program manager, and senior IT auditor.

29.8 CERTIFIED FRAUD EXAMINER

Concerns regarding fraud and fraud investigations are becoming increasingly important to all auditors. Chapter 27 discusses fraud detection and prevention and highlights how both external and internal auditors in the past had once stated that it was not their responsibility to investigate and detect fraud. However, in today's post–Sarbanes-Oxley

Act (SOx) era, both internal and external auditors now have a strong responsibility to investigate for fraud and to take appropriate actions when it is identified. This issue has been highlighted in the revised COSO internal control framework discussed in Chapter 3.

There is a professional organization that is very involved with fraud-related issues for the internal auditor, the Association of Certified Fraud Examiners (ACFE). The organization has its own professional examination and certification, the Certified Fraud Examiner (CFE). Obtaining a CFE designation is regarded as an indicator of excellence in the antifraud profession. CFE members experience growth both professionally and personally, and can position themselves as leaders in the antifraud community.

The CFE examination is based on four broad areas:

1. Criminology and Ethics
2. Financial Transactions
3. Legal Elements of Fraud
4. Fraud Examination and Investigation

To many internal auditors, these topic areas are beyond their experience and training. The ACFE, of course, has its own publications, conferences, and local chapters to provide an internal auditor with a greater level of information about fraud and fraud investigations.

With our increasing concerns with fraud issues, the ACFE has quickly gained prominence in this post-SOx era. While the ACFE has its own web site (www.acfe.com), much of the fraud materials published on AICPA Web pages on fraud and discussed in Chapter 27 are strongly based on ACFE materials. In addition, the ACFE web site contains a sample examination to allow an internal auditor to determine if he or she is ready to take the CFE test. The CFE test is an entirely online exercise where the candidate registers and takes the examination over a machine-timed interval.

29.9 CERTIFIED INFORMATION SYSTEMS SECURITY PROFESSIONAL

A professional organization known as the International Information Systems Security Certification Consortium, or (ISC)^2, is responsible for one of the more challenging and better-recognized internal audit–related professional certifications and examinations, the Certified Information Systems Security Professional (CISSP). This professional examination and its CISSP designation are well recognized but can be difficult to achieve. This certification is for information systems security professionals, not for the ordinary internal auditor.

With the possible exception of the CISM examination, the CISSP examination is on a much higher and much more technical level than the other internal auditor certification examinations discussed in this chapter. The examinations are tightly proctored, training materials are reviewed and approved by (ISC)^2, and the overall quality of the examination is high. If an internal auditor encounters someone in an auditee organization with CISSP certification, that person should almost certainly be someone with a high knowledge of information systems security.

29.10 ASQ INTERNAL AUDIT CERTIFICATIONS

Chapter 31 discusses the American Society for Quality (ASQ) and its quality auditor certifications. The ASQ sponsors a wide range of examinations and certifications for all aspects of its operations, including their Certified Quality Auditor (CQA) examination and certification. A Certified Quality Auditor (CQA) identifies a professional who understands the standards and principles of quality management auditing and the techniques of examining, questioning, evaluating, and reporting to determine a quality system's adequacy and deficiencies. The CQA analyzes all elements of a quality system and judges its degree of adherence to the criteria of industrial management and quality evaluation and control systems. The difference here between a regular, IIA-heritage internal auditor and a CQA is that the latter often works in a quality assurance group and spends more time on process-oriented reviews as opposed to the IIA internal auditor's financial and operational reviews. CQA auditors often work in enterprise production areas and perform more hands-on reviews as compared to the CIA level of internal auditor.

Chapter 31 discusses the differences and similarities between the IIA-heritage internal auditors who are the subject of many of these chapters and ASQ quality auditors. While many ASQ auditors also are IIA members, they often seek their own professional CQA certification. To achieve a CQA designation, the candidate is required to pass a five-hour multiple-choice written examination that measures comprehension of the quality audit profession. As the minimum professional expectations, a CQA quality auditor:

- Must possess the knowledge to effectively conduct different types of objectives, ethically based audits using and interpreting applicable standards/requirements.
- Must be able to develop and communicate an audit plan within a defined scope that identifies applicable standards, necessary personnel, required documents and tools, and an audit agenda.
- Must be able to effectively execute an audit plan, including the opening meeting, performing the audit, and the closing meeting using generally accepted auditing techniques and verifying, documenting, and communicating findings as appropriate for the audit.
- Must be able to objectively present verified nonconformance to the audited standard and evaluate the effectiveness of the resultant follow-up/corrective action activities in an ethical and timely manner.
- Must know and be able to apply basic auditing tools and techniques, such as flowcharting, the concept of variation, observation techniques, and physical examination techniques. A CQA must also demonstrate a general knowledge of quality control tools, descriptive statistics, and applicable sampling theories.

Many of the requirements listed here are similar to those of the IIA-oriented CIA internal auditor, but the CQA uses many different approaches and terminologies. For example, the previous list references such things as "verified nonconformance to the audited standard" or "the concept of variation." These are specialized ASQ terms, although many other concepts go back to standard IIA internal audit processes. The CQA examination is based on the ASQ's body of knowledge, a comprehensive set of key knowledge areas and practices for the CQA. This is a document that is reviewed by the ASQ professional organization and then updated after republication.

A CSQ-certified auditor has similar professional and continuing education requirements as a CIA. If nothing else, the ASQ is perhaps more stringent than the IIA, requiring recertification of all CSQs every three years. Professionals who have not completed required continuing educational requirements must retake the CSQ examination to regain their certification.

The ASQ has two other specialized Quality Auditor certifications, one for biomedical quality audits and the other for Hazard Analysis and Critical Control Points (HACCP) food safety standards. The ASQ is very responsive to member requests to build a separate certification when there appears to be a special demand. This is just a different area of quality auditing.

27.11 OTHER INTERNAL AUDITOR CERTIFICATIONS

As discussed at the beginning of this chapter, some professions have a large number of professional certifications available to them, depending upon an internal auditor's job requirements and skills. There is no one list here, but the certification depends on the auditor's needs and interests. The requirements for all are similar, usually consisting of specified requirements to take the examination, passing it, and receiving the "Certified" designation, followed by continuing education requirements to keep the certification current.

A professional certification is a good way for an internal auditor to demonstrate to peers and others that the audit professional has some unique and important professional skills. Professional certifications are important, and even more important, the knowledge gained through obtaining a certificate allows an internal auditor to work more efficiently and effectively in service to management. Certification and in particular the CIA is important for all internal auditors. All internal auditors should take the effort to become certified as CIAs and/or as CISAs. Individual internal auditors should use these certification examinations as a measure of their own professionalism. They are important indicators of one's knowledge, interests, and abilities. Whether with an organization's internal audit function or moving beyond it, certifications are measures of one's knowledge and interest in the profession.

We have concluded most of these chapters by talking about the chapter's subject as a strong or general knowledge internal auditor CBOK requirement. Every internal auditor should understand why a professional certification such as a CIA is important and should have a general knowledge of what it takes to achieve that certification. A general knowledge of the chapter topics throughout this book should help an internal auditor to achieve some of the general understanding necessary, but a strong professional auditor should study and take the steps to become a CIA and/or a CISA.

CHAPTER THIRTY

The Modern Internal Auditor as an Enterprise Consultant

AN INTERNAL AUDITOR'S ROLE AS a business consultant has been a bit ambiguous over time. Earlier versions of the *International Standards for the Professional Practice of Internal Auditing*, from the Institute of Internal Auditors (IIA), as discussed in Chapter 9, had until recent years prohibited internal auditors from acting as business consultants. The idea had been that an internal auditor was there to review and assess internal controls and then to make recommendations for controls improvements and corrective actions through their internal audit reports. However, this no-consulting standard was not followed very closely in those earlier years as many internal auditors often acted like consultants as part of their management-oriented reviews. This author recalls his earlier days as an information technology internal auditor. With five-plus years developing and designing IT applications, managing IT projects, and a strong understanding of systems development processes, it was difficult to not act as a consultant in those earlier internal audits. Many other internal auditors all but ignored the IIA's consulting prohibitions when making their internal audit recommendations.

The internal audit consulting prohibition became stronger in the early days of the Sarbanes-Oxley Act (SOx). While the early SOx legislation hardly mentioned internal audit, many felt that internal audit would be in violation of these no-consulting rules if it helped management to install effective SOx Section 404 internal control processes. The rules have since changed, however, and newer IIA standards, discussed in Chapter 9, now expressly permit internal auditors to act as management consultants in certain designated and specified audit reviews. Many of the IIA standards are now separated into distinct attest (i.e., auditing) or consulting guidance reviews.

Following revised IIA standards, this chapter discusses internal audit's alterrnative role as an internal consultant to the auditor's overall enterprise. We will discuss the IIA's consulting standards and how internal audit consulting services can fit in and interface with otherwise normal internal audit review activities. In addition, we will look at how internal audit can deliver internal consulting to the enterprise in a manner that is not in conflict with internal audit's normal audit attest functions.

Serving as an enterprise internal consultant is an expanded and important role for many internal auditors. We use the word *many* here because internal consulting activities may not fit into all internal audit functions. In some cases, the industry, audit committee concerns, or even the size of the internal audit function may restrict plans to offer internal consulting services. Where these arrangement seem to work, however, internal audit typically has the inside knowledge and experience to be an important and powerful internal consultant. All internal auditors should have a common body of knowledge (CBOK) level of knowledge of the distinctions between internal audit attest responsibilities and serving as internal consultants. In addition, when internal auditors elect to act as enterprise consultants, they need to have a good CBOK level of understanding of *consulting best practices*.

30.1 STANDARDS FOR INTERNAL AUDIT AS AN ENTERPRISE CONSULTANT

As has been mentioned throughout other chapters, the purpose of an internal audit is to assist management by providing analysis, information, and recommendations for the improvement of internal controls and operations. The adequacy and effectiveness of these associated internal controls to be evaluated may include:

- Compliance with policies and procedures, rules, and regulations
- Reliability and integrity of financial and operational information
- Adequacy and integrity of governance processes
- Effectiveness and efficiency of operations
- Safeguarding of assets

IIA international standards now specifically describe internal auditing as both an attest and a consulting activity. The standards allow internal auditors to provide consulting services relating to operations for which they had previous responsibilities, provided that they disclose any potential impairment to their independence or objectivity relating to proposed consulting services prior to accepting the audit engagement. The IIA standards define internal audit consulting as advisory and related audit client service activities, the nature and scope of which are agreed with the client and which are intended to add value and improve an organization's governance, risk management, and control processes without the internal auditor assuming management responsibility. Examples include counsel, advice, facilitation, and training.

There is often a large gap between effective attest-level internal auditing and what it takes to be an effective consultant. Internal auditors recommend changes in their internal audit reports, but often are not able to influence those audit report–recommended changes in other ways. Internal auditors often just perform an attest audit, and they collaborate with their clients to make an outcome better.

Serving as internal consultants, internal auditors can be held to higher standards of performance and accountability. In these situations, internal auditors need to act as objective and critical "outsiders" within their own enterprises, delivering the hard facts and bad news beyond audit report findings, including issues that management sometimes does not want to hear. Additionally, they need to be prepared to deliver the truth to management beyond what is presented by the facts. They also need to be good at off-the-record consulting-related conversations, which are sometimes more important than the written internal audit report. Internal auditors who master the principles of effective internal consulting can use the related methods and techniques to dig deeper and deliver the truth.

Serving as an enterprise consultant often places internal auditors in a rather different role than normal internal audit attest assignments. In that audit attest role, internal audit will use its audit planning and risk objective measurements to plan and schedule the audit review. Although management usually has some flexibility in delaying or slightly rescheduling a planned review, internal audit has the authority and responsibility to schedule a review. In addition, it can define its own scope, time schedules, and audit team assignments. While internal audit scheduling normally operates on a collaborative basis and local management can negotiate an audit visit or even appeal to senior management and ultimately the audit committee if they object to a planned internal audit visit, internal audit generally has the responsibility for launching an internal audit review.

Responsibilities for initiating and scheduling a consulting assignment are very different. Management will engage internal auditors to come and help as consultants in some area and the assignment objectives, timing, assigned team, scope of work to be performed, and almost everything else is subject to negotiation. In some respects, when internal audit acts as an enterprise consultant, management will seek it out and engage with it similar to contracting with an outside firm that is providing and offering consulting services. A consulting project will be launched through a formal engagement letter, as discussed in Section 30.2 of this chapter and also shown in Exhibit 8.3, and the project will proceed in an informal, almost collaborative basis. Going beyond that old joke by some management skeptics—"Hello, I'm from internal audit, and I'm here to help you"—an internal auditor acting as an enterprise consultant has really been brought in because management has requested that consulting help and recognizes that their internal auditors have a very good understanding of enterprise operations.

There are some other significant differences between internal audit operating as an internal consultant and management's use of an outside, independent consulting firm. Perhaps the strongest is that management can always decide that they do not approve of their external consultants and can fire them or send them home. Things are not so easy when using internal audit consulting resources. Although management can end an internal audit consulting engagement, the same audit team will still be part of the overall enterprise. On the positive side, however, internal auditors acting as internal consultants will better understand organization systems, culture, issues, and a wide range of other matters, including even the location of the facility's employee cafeteria. An external consultant often does not have such in-depth knowledge.

Internal audit consulting standards now clearly define internal audit's potential role as an internal consultant. However, some members of senior management and the audit committee, who are perhaps accustomed to external auditors doing this specialized internal consulting work, may not realize that internal audit standards now also allow such formal internal *consulting activities*. An internal audit function needs to plan and formally launch its internal consulting activities. Discussing such arrangements, of course, first with the audit committee, the chief audit executive should consider offering appropriate internal audit consulting services and should effectively manage this newer, expanded component of internal audit's service to management. Internal audit should never lose sight that its prime responsibility is to review the adequacy and effectiveness of internal controls in the enterprise. The internal audit attest role is very significant.

30.2 LAUNCHING AN INTERNAL AUDIT INTERNAL CONSULTING FACILITY

Before engaging in ongoing in-house consulting activities, internal audit needs to receive acknowledgment from its audit committee and to fully demonstrate to management that it has the capabilities and objectives to act as an internal enterprise consultant. Just because internal audit standards now allow internal audit consulting engagements does not mean that every internal audit function must engage to do so. The number of other internal audit opportunities may limit internal audit's ability to perform any consulting activities beyond normal audit attest reviews. In addition, as discussed, some members of management may not fully understand internal audit's potential role as an internal consultant, thinking of it only in an attest role.

If an enterprise's internal audit function wants to begin to regularly offer internal consulting, it should develop a consulting strategy and then strongly document that role and its capability through its audit charter. Chapter 14 discussed the importance of audit committee–approved internal audit charters and provided examples of such documents. However, with past IIA standards prohibiting internal auditors from acting as consultants, this expanded internal audit potential role may not be well understood by some internal audit functions, senior management, or by audit committees. Internal audit itself needs to develop a strategy for any planned internal consulting activity that is not in conflict with its main mission of internal controls review and that brings value to the overall enterprise. Some of the areas to consider when developing an internal consulting practice include:

- **What types of internal audit consulting should be considered?** Internal audit may have the skills to perform internal controls reviews in many specialized areas but not the necessary consulting expertise for those areas. For example, while internal audit can perform IT controls reviews in many specialized areas, it may not have the ability to provide detailed technical consulting help in those same areas.
- **How will resources be divided between attest-related internal auditing and internal consulting?** Internal audit needs to take extreme care that it is not viewed as auditors one day and consultants the next. With a larger audit organization, this

can be accomplished by creating a separate internal consulting section with the overall internal audit function. Otherwise, care must be given to separating these two different functions.

- **Budgeting and accounting for costs of internal audit consulting services.** Although external or independent consulting firms typically bill their services at fairly substantial rates, internal audit attest services are often delivered "free" to their enterprises, with the costs being covered out of centralized financial budgets. Internal consulting should perhaps be viewed as a value-added function, similar to how an enterprise imposes internal budget charges on graphics or computer time services. A charging and billing mechanism should be established for any such internal consulting activities.
- **Planning and scheduling internal audit consulting activities.** Separate but different planning and scheduling tools should be established for all internal consulting activities. Many of the same procedures for planning and performing internal audits that are discussed in Chapters 8 through 13 are applicable here. However, internal audit consulting activities should be kept separate from regular internal audit materials.
- **Reporting results and communication with management and the audit committee.** Consulting activities should go through a regular reporting process similar to the basic format of the internal audit reports discussed in Chapter 18. However, consulting reports do not carry the same type of audit report findings, recommendations, and expected responses as normal internal audit reports. In addition, it often is not necessary to provide management and the audit committee with any level of detailed consulting project reporting beyond high-level summaries.
- **"Selling" the internal audit consulting program.** If internal audit is going to provide consulting services to the overall enterprise, there is always a need to sell and promote these activities. While we are not at all suggesting power lunches to sell a program, internal audit should develop an informal services catalog to describe its consulting capabilities.

There are many options to consider when launching an internal audit consulting offering. The considerations listed here and others should be outlined and then discussed with both the audit committee and senior management. Once tentative approvals have been obtained, internal audit should request an approved audit charter that clearly specifies internal audit's role as an internal consultant to the enterprise. Exhibit 30.1 is an example of an internal audit charter that specifically authorizes internal audit's role as an internal enterprise consultant.

An internal audit internal consulting activity should not be an ad hoc exercise that only occurs for limited, special-purpose occasions. As an available offering in some areas of internal audit's skill set, internal consulting resources should be offered and then managed. When auditee management needs consulting help beyond internal audit's skill set, care should be exercised in not getting involved with activities that might better belong with other enterprise resources or with outside consultants.

EXHIBIT 30.1 The Modern Internal Auditor as an Enterprise Consultant

This charter is very similar to the sample internal audit charter for the Global Computer Products sample company as described in Exhibit 14.1. This version specifically authorizes internal audit to engage in internal consulting activities in addition to normal internal audit attest reviews. Consulting-related authorizations are displayed in bold.

Internal Audit's Mission

The mission of Global Computer Products Internal Audit is to ensure that company operations follow high standards both by providing an independent, objective assurance function and by advising **and consulting** on best practices. By using a systematic and disciplined approach, Internal Audit helps Global Computer Products accomplish its objectives by evaluating and improving the effectiveness of risk management, internal control, and governance processes.

Independence and Objectivity

To ensure independence, Internal Audit reports directly to the Board of Directors Audit Committee, and to maintain objectivity, Internal Audit is not involved in day-to-day company operations or internal control procedures. **However, Internal Audit may provide independent consulting help in certain specified areas that is independent from regular Internal Audit review procedures.**

Scope and Responsibilities

The scope of Internal Audit's work includes the review of risk management procedures, internal control, information systems and governance processes. This work also involves periodic testing of transactions, best practice reviews, special investigations, appraisals of legal and regulatory requirements, and measures to help prevent and detect fraud.

To fulfill its responsibilities, Internal Audit shall:

— Identify and assess potential risks to all areas of the enterprise's operations.
— Review the adequacy of controls established to ensure compliance with policies, plans, procedures, and business objectives.
— Assess the reliability and security of financial and management information and supporting systems and operations that produce this information.
— Assess the means of safeguarding assets.
— Review established processes and propose improvements.
— Appraise the use of resources with regard to economy, efficiency, and effectiveness.
— Follow up recommendations to make sure that effective remedial action is taken.
— Carry out ad hoc appraisals, investigations, or reviews requested by the Audit Committee and Management.
— Perform independent consulting projects at the specific request of management.

Internal Audit's Authority

In order to promote effective controls at reasonable cost, Internal Audit is authorized, in the course of its activities, to:

— Enter all areas of Global Computer Products operations and have access to any documents and records considered necessary for the performance of its functions.
— Require all members of staff and Management to supply requested information and
— explanations within a reasonable period of time.
— Engage in independent consulting reviews at the specific request and authorization of Management.

Accountability

Internal Audit shall prepare, in liaison with Management and the Audit Committee, an annual audit plan that is based on business risks, the results of other internal audits, and input from Management. The plan shall be presented to Senior Management, including the General Counsel, for approval by the Audit Committee. Any needed adjustments to the plan should be communicated to and approved by the Audit Committee.

Internal Audit is responsible for planning, conducting, reporting, and following up on audit projects included in the audit plan, and deciding on the scope and timing of these audits. The results of each internal audit will be reported through a detailed audit report that summarizes the objectives and scope of the audit as well as observations and recommendations. In all cases, follow-up work will be undertaken to ensure adequate response to Internal Audit recommendations. Internal Audit also will submit an annual report to Senior Management and to the Audit Committee on the results of the audit work including significant risk exposures and control issues. Internal audit also may complete independent consulting projects, at the specific authorization of management, that are not part of specific audit report recommendations.

Standards

Internal Audit adheres to the standards and professional practices published by the Institute of Internal Auditors as well as those of the Information Technology Governance Institute.

30.3 ENSURING AN AUDIT AND CONSULTING SEPARATION OF DUTIES

As an example of the potential problems regarding the need for an adequate separation of responsibilities between internal auditors acting as internal consultants and those doing audit attest work, we can look back at the public accounting industry. Before the 1970s, the American Institute of Certified Public Accountants (AICPA) separated public accounting firms between certified public accountant (CPA) auditors and professionals providing consulting services. A CPA firm would have a sort of line in its office separating the auditors who certified financial reports from the specialists, such as IT consultants. Over the years, however, this line grew fuzzier as specialist consultants, particularly those with IT skills, got directly involved in helping complete audits of heavy IT-bound enterprises. Similarly, strong CPA financial auditors became very involved in helping with specialized financial consulting projects.

This separation-of-duties barrier really slipped and sometimes became almost transparent before the fall of Enron and the passage of SOx in the early years of this century, and has been highlighted in Chapter 5 regarding SOx. One of the internal control breakdowns highlighted in the SOx legislative hearings was that public accounting firms often strongly suggested that one of their IT consultants visit a financial audit client to install a new financial application; the public accounting firm would send its CPA auditors back to review the internal controls over that same application. Not surprisingly, the financial auditors typically did not find many internal control problems in the applications their own consultants had just installed. SOx has forbidden this potential conflict of interest, and public accounting consulting practices have now moved off as independent consulting firms.

The point of this pre-SOx public accounting firm example is that separation-of-duties restrictions between auditing and consulting can very much break down over time. Care must always be given to separating the roles of internal auditors acting as consultants from those performing audit attest functions. Paraphrasing words directly from internal audit consulting standards that are summarized in Chapter 9, it is particularly important that internal auditors establish an understanding with consulting engagement clients about objectives, scope, respective responsibilities, and other client expectations. For significant engagements, this understanding should be documented.

30.4 CONSULTING BEST PRACTICES

Many people do not have a clear understanding of what it means to be a consultant. The person selling shoes at a retail store may have a job title of "sales consultant," and the Web contains many other definitions of the term. According to those definitions, a consultant is an individual who provides counsel and assistance to a client on specific assignments. Another more academic-sounding definition of consulting (from the Latin *consultare*) means "to discuss" and refers to a professional who provides advice in a particular area of expertise such as accountancy, the environment, technology, law, human resources, marketing, medicine, or finance.

The role of a consultant is a little different from that of an internal auditor. An internal auditor starts with a prepared audit program outlining areas to review or a set of standards. Much of the review is based on an assessment of compliance against those standards. As discussed previously, an internal auditor generally schedules a review, while a consultant comes at the invitation of management. Consultants may structure a review on the basis of compliance with some standards, but generally they approach assignments more like open books, discussing matters with management and developing solutions in a more collaborative manner.

In order to operate as effective internal consultants, internal auditors need to do more than change their title on a business card; they also need to develop some new approaches. While the scope of this book does not call for a treatise on how to be a consultant, the following sections define some key action steps for internal auditors operating as internal consultants. However, as discussed previously, internal audit should have fully defined its capabilities for consulting work and outlined them through an approved charter statement.

First Steps: Launching a Consulting Assignment

Internal consulting opportunities will typically come to internal audit because (1) it has completed an internal review with recommendations for corrective action that management needs help to implement; (2) other needs develop within the enterprise, such as significant deficiencies requiring correction that were highlighted during the external auditor's internal controls reviews; or (3) management often has specific needs where internal audit, based on its past review activities, may provide some important help. We would generally recommend that internal audit should not actively promote its consulting services beyond these basic areas and should operate primarily to fulfill specific management needs.

Consulting Help to Implement Internal Audit Report Recommendations

A major component of the internal audit process is audit's recommendations for corrective action, published and described in an audit report. Internal audit enterprise-specific standards and audit committee directions usually require that auditee management must respond to audit report findings with a plan for corrective action over a very short period of time. In some cases, an internal audit finding outlining the need for some form of corrective action puts a burden on management, which may be lacking the skilled resources to implement the suggested improvement.

In some situations, internal auditors acting as in-house consultants may be an appropriate resource to implement these audit report recommendations. This is particularly the case when an internal audit recommendation covers such areas as improving documentation, improving certain internal control procedures, or training staff in internal control–related areas. If their own departmental resources are limited, an internal audit internal consultant may be the best choice to implement the recommended corrective action. This is particularly true because bringing in a new, outside consultant might very well be much more expensive and time-consuming. If auditee management indicates that it does not have the resources available on a short-term basis to implement the internal audit recommendations, internal audit's consulting services might be proffered.

There are some major danger areas with this type of consulting work. First, internal audit recommendations should not be self-serving in a manner that appears to build consulting opportunities. Second, there must be a level of independence between the internal auditors who made the recommendation and the internal consultants helping to implement corrective actions. That level of independence should be strong enough such that an internal consultant helping to implement a suggested recommendation should be able to freely take exception to some area of a recommendation and to point out any shortcomings.

Other Consulting Needs within the Enterprise

There are often many areas within an enterprise where internal audit can meet needs and offer some specific skills and expertise. A good example might be when management formally requests help with its SOx Section 404 internal controls compliance review and where internal audit comes in not to perform and internal controls audit but to assist management in that Section 404 compliance work. (This process is discussed in Chapter 5.) Similarly, the external auditors might have found some significant control weaknesses in their assessments and have passed these on to the audit committee and management. These are both areas where internal audit often has the broad skills to help install internal control improvements not as internal auditors but as management consultants.

Specific Management Needs for Internal Audit Consulting Help

Internal auditors should have a wide set of skills and expertise in critical knowledge areas. Beyond specific internal audit risk-based audit assignments, internal audit can often provide consulting help over a wide variety of areas. Examples might include helping to build effective internal controls in a new IT application, discussed in Chapter 19, or helping to launch an ethics hotline function, as discussed in Chapter 26. Internal audit can be a major help to the overall enterprise in many of its particular expertise areas here through providing internal consulting support.

Any internal audit consulting project depends on management needs, the availability of internal audit resources, and the overall approval of the audit committee. When there is a perceived need or interest, internal audit representatives should meet with the requesting management group to understand its requirements and needs. The internal audit consultants should gain a high-level understanding of the consulting project's needs and requirements.

This preliminary process will usually require internal auditors as potential internal consultants to gather more information about the possible assignment in order to somewhat size the issue. For example, enterprise management may recognize a need to better organize the documentation processes that cover its product repair and return operation. With internal audit's background in preparing workpaper documentation, it could be an obvious choice to provide some help and direction here. However, after some very preliminary discussions, a member of the internal audit team—probably one of the potentially assigned consultants—should visit this customer service area to gain a greater appreciation of the specific nature of the request, the size of the problem, and whether an internal audit consultant can be of help. If things appear to be a good match, internal audit should formalize this internal consulting arrangement.

The Consulting Engagement Letter

Using a term that dates back to public accounting consulting practices, an authority or lead from the internal audit internal consulting team should draft a formal letter of understanding describing the upcoming internal consulting project. Because this is an internal understanding within the enterprise, such an engagement letter does not have the same legal basis that would be found when an outside firm outlines its work plans. However, a formal internal audit prepared engagement letter is an appropriate way to launch an internal consulting project between internal audit and an enterprise operation.

Exhibit 30.2 is an example of an internal audit consulting engagement letter. This is a document that describes what the internal audit consultant proposes to accomplish, who will be doing the work, its timing and duration, and the expected outcomes from the consulting project. If internal audit charges for its consulting services through some form of a budget cross-charge, expected cost factors should also be estimated. An engagement letter launches an internal consulting project and should require appropriate management approval.

The approved engagement letter should then become the basis for launching an internal audit consulting project. Chapter 8 talked about planning and performing a typical internal audit, and Chapter 16 talked about internal audit project management. An internal audit consulting project should be organized and tracked in the same manner as a normal internal audit. A major difference, however, is that the consulting project is subject to local management's request and priorities. If local management tells the internal auditors serving as consultants to ignore some area of operations or to give

EXHIBIT 30.2 Internal Audit Consulting Engagement Letter Example

Internal Audit Consulting
Consulting Engagement Authorization

The finished goods shipping department at the Metroville, PA, plant has identified a need to improve its customer service operations at that facility and has requested that specialists from the corporate internal audit department perform a detailed analysis of plant operations and then lead an effort to improve operations at that facility. Based on this request and on recommendations from a recent internal audit review of this same facility, a team of independent internal audit consultants propose to review these customer service facilities and to help improve controls and procedures as necessary.

A team of consultants, led by Tom Bell, plan to visit the Metroville, PA, plant during February, 20xx, to perform a detailed independent analysis of your operations and to suggest areas for improvement, including the identification and implementation of a new customer service computer system. We expect to complete this analysis and provide recommendations for approval approximately six weeks after the initiation of this project. The final selection and installation of a new computer system will take additional time and resources to be discussed at the time of our preliminary analysis.

We expect this work to require approximately xx hours, and our charges will be internally billed to your department through the corporate expense accounting system, based on our normal billing rate of $xx per hour as well as any out-of-pocket charges associated with this review. The charges associated with any new custom service computer system will be based on a separate estimate to be presented later.

I recognize that the internal audit consulting group will be operating independent from normal internal audit review activities, and I authorize them to begin this consulting project as described.

Name: ______________ Date: ______________

some discovered problem a pass, the internal auditor consultant does not have the same flexibility in bringing the matter to the attention of the audit committee.

The Consulting Process: Defining "As Is" and "To Be" Objectives

Consulting projects are almost always very different from internal audits, where the auditor starts with an audit program or set of standards. In a consulting project, senior or even local management will typically have some idea that an area of operations is wrong or could be performed more effectively or efficiently. With these broad concepts in place, the internal auditor as consultant needs to analyze the matter and develop a potential problem statement to begin the consulting exercise.

Although many different approaches can be used, a cause-and-effect analysis is often a useful approach to analyzing the current status of some problem area. The consultant internal auditor will be presented with a general problem statement and then reviews information, asks questions, and observes the problem environment to break a problem down into smaller pieces. For example, if there was a potential problem concerning enterprise staff training, the consultant might consider the training responsibilities that were formally established, whether general needs have been identified, and whether appropriate personnel are being brought into the training process.

Assume that an internal auditor consultant has been asked to identify customer service problems in a business unit operation. The consultant may decide that the major problems are due to a lack of training, design problems with the supporting IT system, document control problems, and customer input difficulties. These identified issues can be then organized into a fishtail cause-and-effect diagram, as shown in Exhibit 30.3. The idea is to identify the potential contributing problems in a graphic manner that suggests basic root causes. An internal auditor can then use such a diagram to discuss the problem and its root causes with members of management to obtain some general agreement on the current problem.

Often this type of high-level potential problem analysis will result in a series of "Have you thought about . . . ?" types of questions that will send the consultant back for further analysis. However, such a *root cause analysis* will often point the consultant in the direction of a recommendation.

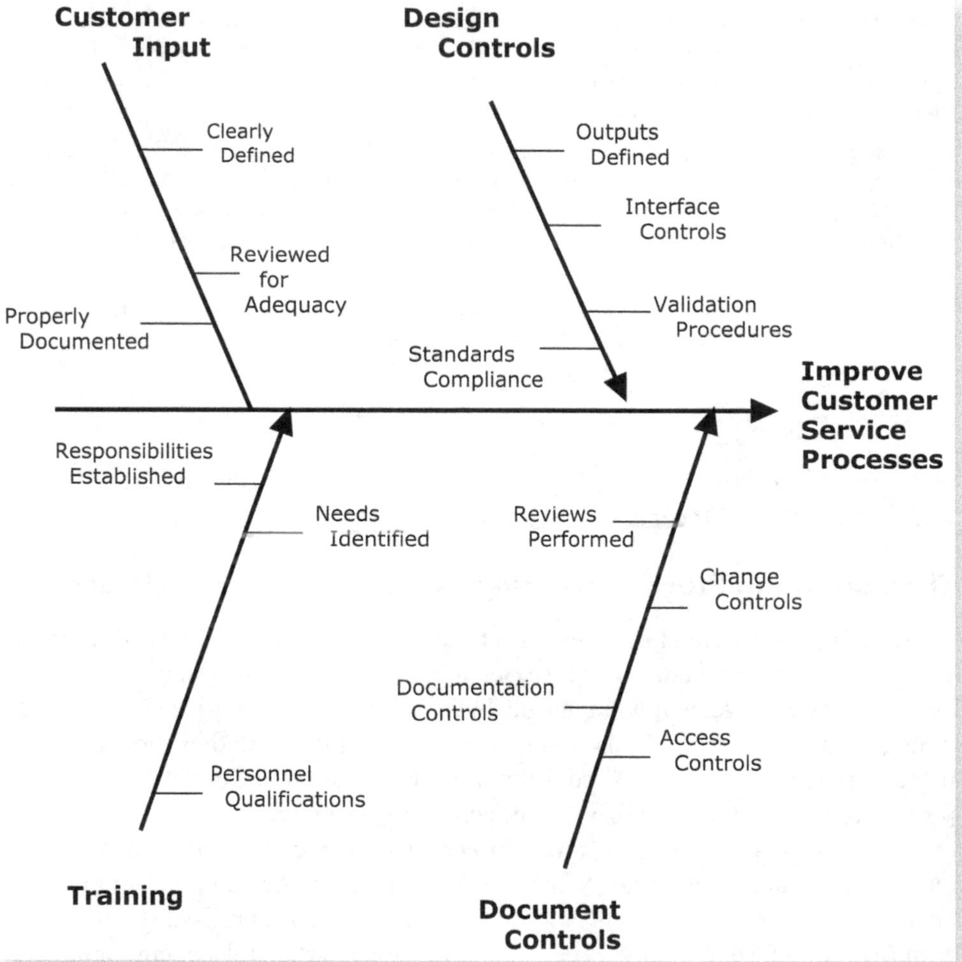

EXHIBIT 30.3 Cause-and-Effect Diagram

Implementing Consulting Recommendations

Recommendations from consulting projects should always be fairly well thought out, with consideration given to a wide variety of cost and feasibility considerations. They are often made after much more consultative discussions than sometimes occur on internal audits. Perhaps a difference is that an internal auditor will often review a draft audit report with management to discuss issues surrounding a recommendation. The internal auditor will finally issue the audit report and will expect management's responses regarding the corrective action plan.

A consultant making a recommendation often faces a difficult situation. If management agrees to those consulting suggested actions, it will often ask the same consultant to take an active role to lead the implementation of the suggested solution. Most internal auditors have encountered situations where management does nothing in regard to external auditor recommendations; as consultants, internal auditors often must help to take the lead role in implementing any recommended actions. This is a significant difference from many internal audit attest activities.

Documenting and Completing the Consulting Engagement

Chapters 17 and 18 talked about documenting internal audit results through formal workpapers as well describing them in a formal audit report. Consulting projects have similar but somewhat different requirements. In many instances, the consultant internal auditor may have implemented a new set of desk or other operating procedures. A major portion of the consulting project should be procedures that operating personnel can take and use going forward. In other cases, the consulting project should be documented in such a manner that management can go forward with the documented results and that the internal audit attest function will be able to fully accept the work if they elect to audit its internal controls.

Perhaps even more than for a traditional internal audit project, strong attention should be given to the hours and costs associated with the consulting engagement. There will often be direct cross-charges, and management may expect to see detailed accounting records supporting those charges. For a normal internal audit project, the auditee may receive communications that an audit will be completed after perhaps three weeks. When the internal auditors take four or five weeks, auditee management may grumble about why it is taking so long, but will often see no direct charges for that extended time and will move on.

In an internal audit consulting project, management will often be asked to absorb the costs of that work. The expansion of a project from the estimated three weeks to an actual five will result in crossover charges to the auditee's ledger, and there must be detailed documentation to support these activities. In addition, to support an adequate separation of duties between internal audit consulting and attest activities, consulting-related projects should be completed in such a manner that they always appear to be separate from the internal audit attest review.

30.5 EXPANDED INTERNAL AUDIT SERVICES TO MANAGEMENT

Consulting represents an expanded and important potential internal audit service to management. Internal audit should organize itself in some of the areas discussed, from a revised charter to detailed statements describing its consulting capabilities and offerings, which will allow it to provide consulting services to management beyond regular attest audits. Care must be given to supporting the independence of these two functions within internal audit. Although an internal audit professional may be working on attest projects at one point in time and consulting projects separately, extreme care must be given to assuring that these activities are separate and independent both in fact and in the perception of others.

Properly organized, an internal audit consulting project will provide resources to management in a way quite different from internal audit reviews with their often critical internal audit reports focused on findings and recommended actions. However, if an internal audit function wants to provide internal consulting as an additional offering, it must ensure that this work is at least as professional as its internal audit attest work. In addition, great care must be given to organizing this activity so that it is not perceived by others as self-serving. That is, internal audit attest findings should not be construed as promotional work to increase consulting projects.

Internal auditors should also have a CBOK understanding of consulting-related standards and of the consulting process. Even if the internal audit function has elected not to engage in internal consulting beyond normal attest work, all internal audits should understand the role and place of consulting as part of the overall internal audit process.

VIII

PART EIGHT

The Other Sides of Auditing: Professional Convergence

CHAPTER THIRTY-ONE

Quality Assurance Auditing and ASQ Standards

WHILE A MAJOR FOCUS OF this book has been on IIA international internal audit standards and Certified Internal Auditor (CIA) requirements, as well as the roles of Certified Public Accountant (CPA)–type external auditors in internal audit engagements, these are not the only professionals today who consider themselves auditors. There are many other audit professionals, including U.S. federal government contract auditors and the professionals who audit health care and hospital standards. These other auditors typically do not work in or with the corporate headquarters offices that are the domains of IIA-associated internal auditors or even the CPA-type external auditors. While the IIA-member or IIA-heritage internal audit professional discussed throughout this book often does not have a strong working relationship with them, quality auditors play an important role in many enterprises. Administered through the *American Society for Quality (ASQ)* professional organization, they are a unique internal audit practice–like professional group that has its own standards, codes of ethics, and professional certification designations. Once called quality auditors rather than just internal auditors, these professionals have responsibilities to review a wide range of International Organization for Standardization (ISO) standards-compliance, work-simplification, and quality-related processes in the enterprise. Quality auditors have historically primarily operated on the shop floor in manufacturing enterprises and often have had little contact with the IIA-type internal auditors who are part of the same enterprise but more often are based in enterprise headquarters operations.

Today quality auditors are becoming closer to IIA internal auditors. More accurately, both of these internal audit professional groups are changing in their objectives and approaches in ways that bring them closer together. The classic IIA internal audit professional should have an understanding of the activities of quality auditors and how their work fits in the overall environment of corporate governance.

This chapter reviews the role of quality auditors in an enterprise, their practices and standards. There are many similarities between the activities of these auditors and the IIA internal auditors that are the main focus of this book. As the convergence of enterprise activities to improve governance and internal controls grows, we may expect these two internal audit groups to become more closely aligned in the future. IIA-type of internal auditors should have a general common body of knowledge (CBOK) understanding of the roles, responsibilities, and activities of ASQ quality auditors.

In addition, this chapter will consider another key component of internal auditing—quality assurance (or QA) reviews of an internal audit function performed by members of the internal audit team itself or by contracted outside reviewers. These reviews answer the question "But who is going to audit the auditors?" Quality assurance reviews are internal audit reviews of internal audit functions. The terminology can be confusing here. A quality auditor, as described in this chapter, is a separate professional who is a member of the ASQ. Quality assurance refers to a process that should be practiced by many internal audit departments. Large internal audit functions in particular often bring real value to their overall enterprise by having an independent quality review of their internal audit practices and operations.

31.1 DUTIES AND RESPONSIBILITIES OF ASQ QUALITY AUDITORS

For many traditional IIA-heritage internal auditors, quality assurance terminology can be a bit confusing. While some ASQ quality auditors may belong to the IIA as well, they have their own separate professional organization, the ASQ's Quality Audit Division (QAD). The ASQ professional organization, with responsibilities for many activities in quality management, previously referred to their QAD professional affiliates as "quality auditors." The ASQ now refers to its audit members as just internal auditors. Confusing? Yes. In this chapter, we refer to the ASQ audit professionals as quality auditors to distinguish them from internal auditors.

The ASQ is the leading proponent of the quality movement in the United States. It has a wide range of publications, professional certifications, and separate divisions covering industries such as aerospace and pharmaceuticals as well as professional practices, such as the QAD. ASQ is very involved with the ISO quality standards, discussed in Chapter 33, and its QAD is responsible for compliance audits against those ISO standards.

The QAD's stated mission is "To support auditors and other stakeholders by defining and promoting auditing as a management tool to achieve continuous improvement, effective communication, and increased customer satisfaction." Again, the use of just "auditor" causes some confusion regarding the roles of these quality auditors. In addition, the ASQ and its QAD recognizes and defines several activity levels of auditing:

- **Self-audits.** This is a quality audit preformed within the enterprise to review compliance with ISO quality standards and the like.
- **Second-party audits.** Quality auditors often perform reviews to assess whether their suppliers or outside contractors are operating in compliance with some specified standards. A second-party audit occurs when an enterprise's own quality auditors visit a supplier to test their compliance with some standards.

- **Third-party audits.** These are audits performed at the enterprise by an independent organization, such as one of the ISO registrars, discussed in Chapter 33, or an auditor from a government agency such as the Department of Labor's Occupational Safety and Health Administration (OSHA) or the Federal Drug Administration (FDA).

As has been discussed, although the ASQ historically used the term *quality auditors*, the ASQ just calls them *auditors* today. This is due to the ASQ broadening its own professional designations. Exhibit 31.1 describes the classifications of these ASQ *quality audits* showing both outside customers, who need quality audit assurances, and suppliers. These areas of activity put quality auditors in a very different framework when compared to IIA internal auditors.

Quality audit terminology can be even more confusing because the ASQ designates its audit professionals as either internal or external auditors. An ASQ internal auditor reviews controls and standards within that auditor's enterprise or employer, while an ASQ external auditor, in this context, performs third-party reviews at other enterprises to establish such matters as ISO certifications as discussed in Chapter 33. While a quality auditor may be a member of the IIA in addition to the ASQ, their designation of being an *external* quality auditor has no regular relationship with the financial statement attest auditors, the American Institute of Certified Public Accountants (AICPA) and its CPA designation. When we refer to just an internal auditor in this chapter, we mean the IIA-heritage internal auditor that is the main focus throughout this book.

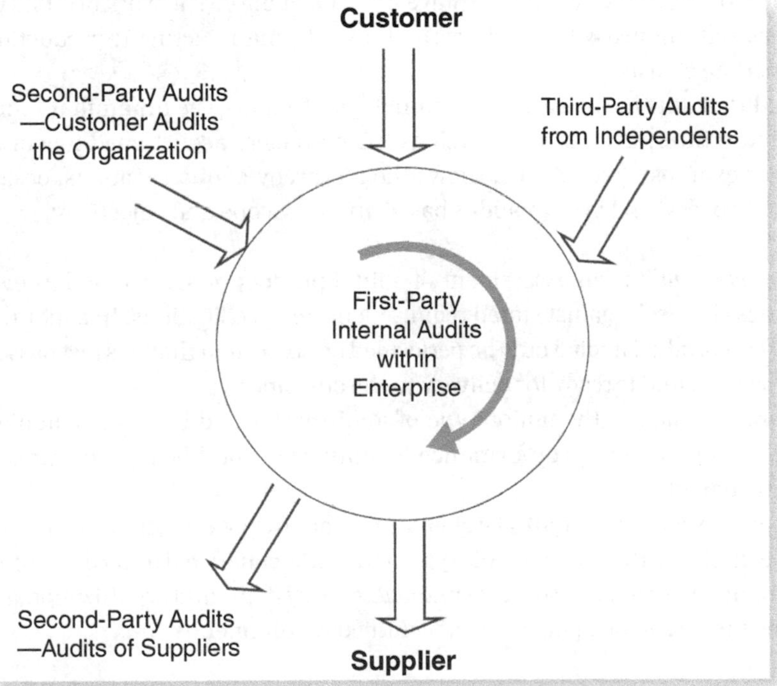

EXHIBIT 31.1 Classifications of Quality Audits

While the IIA has its Certified Internal Auditor (CIA) professional designation and the Information Systems Audit and Control Association (ISACA) has its Certified Information Systems Auditor (CISA), the ASQ also has the Certified Quality Auditor (CQA) professional certification. Chapter 29 outlines these more common internal audit professional certifications. In addition to holding a CQA, a quality auditor may earn several quality audit specialty subdesignations, such as for hazard analysis or biomedical auditing, among others. These certifications require designated levels of work experience and successfully passing an examination. ASQ quality auditors are involved in similar professional activities and have standards similar to IIA internal auditors. In addition, the ASQ has a series of specialized national meetings and conferences for ASQ quality auditors.

31.2 ROLE OF THE QUALITY AUDITOR

ASQ procedures, standards, and quality auditing guidance materials are similar to the standards used by IIA internal auditors. Quality auditors follow many of the same general internal audit steps as IIA-sponsored internal auditors in their procedures for developing programs, reporting findings, and the like. ASQ quality auditors usually are not involved with common internal audit issues such as reviews of financial internal controls, nor are they directly involved with audits covering many IT internal control areas. Quality auditors often follow published international industry standards such as ISO 9000, and their audits often tend to be much more quantitative and mathematical than the work of the typical IIA-heritage internal auditor. The work of quality auditors is often closely aligned with the classic tools used by manufacturing production quality assurance specialists.

Quality audits include a set of terminologies that may be unfamiliar to many IIA-background internal auditors as well as the managers accustomed to working with them. For example, Exhibit 31.2 shows the hierarchy of quality audits, designated as Product, Process, and System audits based on their scope and objectives:

- A *product audit* is an assessment of a final product or service and a review of its "fitness for use" against stated requirements or specifications. In a manufacturing sense, a product audit would be performed on some item that has just passed its final inspection and is ready for delivery to the customer.
- A *process audit* is the major type of audit performed by quality auditors. This is a review to verify conformance to standards, methods, procedures, or other requirements.
- A *systems audit* is not an IT-related systems review but an audit that covers all aspects of a control system. This type of review is conducted to verify, through objective evidence, that all aspects of management systems and organizational plans are implemented to adequately meet identified requirements.

ASQ defined quality audits are typically more analytical in their approaches than the usual IIA type of internal audit. Because many quality auditors have the mindset of

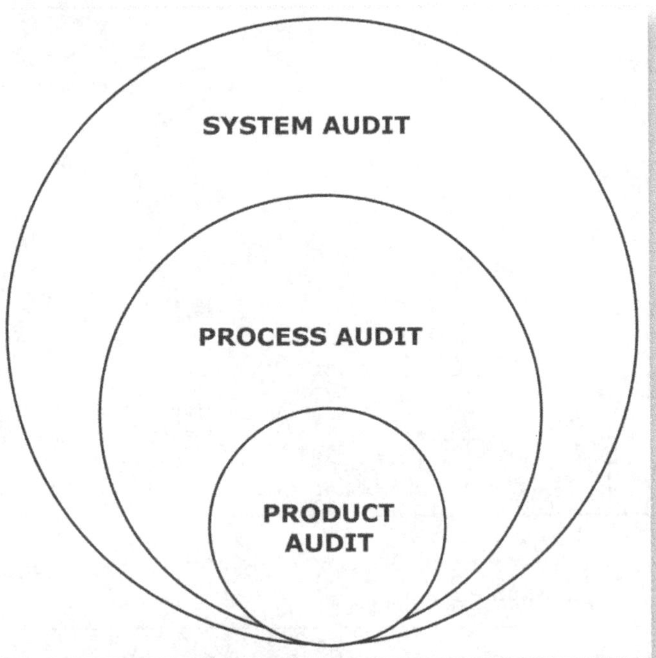

EXHIBIT 31.2 Types of Quality Audits

an engineering technician rather than an accountant, they tend to make greater use of analytical tools and techniques in their workpaper analyses and audit reports. Perhaps because many quality audits are performed in process and manufacturing environments, quality auditors are often much more production shop floor–oriented than the typical IIA-heritage internal auditors. An explanation for this is that today a quality audit function often does not report to the CAE or the audit committee but typically has strong ties to production operations.

Quality audit tools and techniques are also often different from those used in IIA-heritage internal audits. An example might help explain such a typical quality auditor tool, technique, and quality audit approach. Exhibit 31.3 shows a Pareto chart, a common diagram used in quality-related audit analyses. The idea of this common quality audit chart is to rank the types of errors or problems found by the auditor on the vertical axis, with the most severe problems listed first. In this example, there were 62 cases of defect 1 during the period reviewed. Similarly, there were 58 cases of defect 2, with increasingly fewer cases for the other defects. The numbers of cumulative defects are plotted on the vertical axis. The line goes from 62 to 120) for the second point and continues. The idea behind a Pareto chart is to see which defects require the most attention. The fewer than 10 instances of defect 6 shown here should require less management attention.

While quality auditors have traditionally used tools such as Pareto charts to review quality defects and make recommendations, in recent years the worldwide movement to ISO 9000 quality standards, as discussed in Chapter 33, has very much

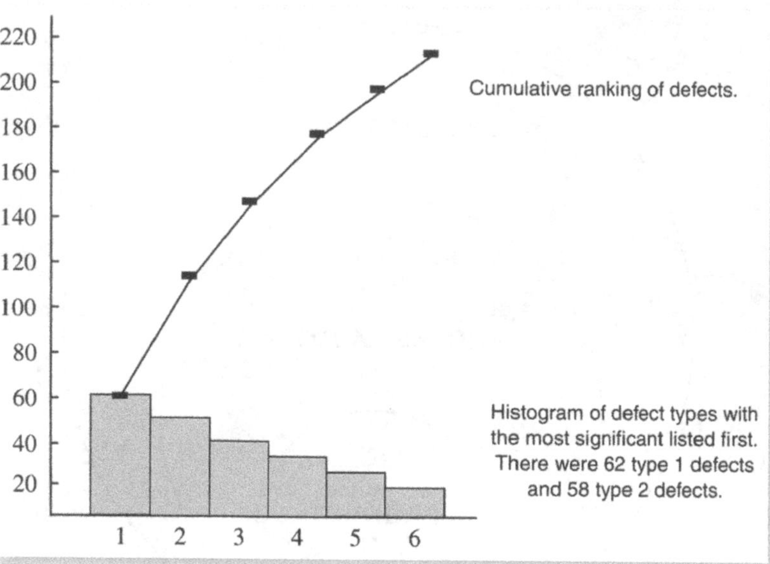

EXHIBIT 31.3 Pareto Chart Example

Source: Robert Moeller, *Brink's Modern Internal Auditing,* 6th ed. (Hoboken, NJ: John Wiley & Sons, 2005). Used with permission.

changed the role of quality auditors. For example, section 8.2.2 of ISO 9001:2000, shown in Exhibit 31.4, describes the requirements for internal audits of ISO standards. It also calls for management to conduct internal audits at planned intervals to determine whether the quality management system conforms to requirements of the standard and is effectively implemented and maintained. These standards also contain requirements for audit programs, management's responsibility, and other matters. Similar audit requirements exist for other quality management system ISO standards. For example, section 6 of the ISO 27001:2000 standards is titled Internal Security Management Systems (ISMS) audits, and the ISO standard states, among other matters:

> The organization shall conduct internal audits at planned intervals to determine whether the control objectives, controls, processes, and procedures of its ISMS:
>
> a) conform to the requirements of this International Standard and relevant legislation or regulations;
> b) conform to the identified information security requirements;
> c) are effectively implemented and maintained; and
> d) perform as expected.

Again, this section of the standard has more substance, and the extracts shown in Exhibit 31.4 illustrate the requirements of audits for ISO standards. Any enterprise that is launching and seeking standards certification must establish such a quality audit function.

EXHIBIT 31.4 ISO 9000 Standards Example: 8.2.2 on Internal Auditing

The organization must conduct periodic internal audits to determine if the QMS conforms to ISO 9001, and has been effectively implemented and maintained. Audit program planning must take into consideration the status and importance of activities and areas to be audited, and the results of previous audits. The audit procedure, scope, frequency and methodologies must be defined. These audits must be performed by personnel other than those who performed the activity being audited. Timely corrective action must be taken on deficiencies found during these audits, with follow-up actions including verification of corrective action implementation and reporting verification results.

ASQ-type quality audit functions are often organized more informally than IIA-trained internal audits with their board of directors' audit committee reporting relationships. The following sections will discuss this quality audit process. There is almost a disconnect today between quality auditors following ASQ standards and the IIA internal auditors following internal audit professional standards discussed in Chapter 9. Over time, however, we would hope to see a greater level of convergence between these auditing processes.

Quality auditors are often involved with tests for process improvement based on their findings from an earlier review. To accomplish this continuous improvement, the data in a new review must be analyzed for trends and identification of weaknesses. The quality auditor then compares results to goals and objectives, and analyzes process data to identify risks, inefficiencies, opportunities for improvement, and negative trends. The results may be recommendations for changes in procedures, or in other elements of the process, such as improvements in acceptance criteria or methods of monitoring. Recommended changes in equipment or technology issues may also be among the quality auditor's recommendations for continual improvement. In many respects, quality auditors recommend more significant changes to the improvement cycle than has been the case with internal auditors.

31.3 PERFORMING ASQ QUALITY AUDITS

Traditional internal auditing standards are well recognized among many professionals. The IIA's *International Standards for the Professional Practice of Internal Auditing*, discussed in Chapter 9, provide a good overview of those standards and the overall professional of internal auditing. The ASQ-sponsored practice of quality auditing brings a somewhat different perspective to auditing. Although it has its roots in earlier quality assurance and industrial engineering processes, quality auditing is particularly important for measuring compliance to the ISO standards, and there are both internal and external components to this auditing practice.

ASQ-driven audits—quality audits—are somewhat different. They are reviews performed to assess regulatory compliance rules or to meet requirements for ISO standards registration and certification. They are also important because they are a key feedback loop in an enterprise's quality system to keep management informed about compliance with their documented systems procedures. As discussed, quality audits composed of a number of different audits, including internal or self-audits and then second- or third-party audits. Under these rules, a quality audit may be performed, as a self-audit, by persons very close to the actual process operations. Quality audits are typically not performed by a separate internal audit department but by persons in the enterprise who can demonstrate a level of objectivity.

Quality audits often take place in the ISO standards environment where an enterprise must check that its suppliers and others are in compliance with certain standards. Second-party audits occur when an enterprise performs a quality audit on one of its suppliers. A third-party audit happens when an outside registrar or a regulatory agency, such as OSHA or the FDA, performs an independent review. The concept here is that an enterprise must determine that its suppliers are in compliance with some standard through a second-party review. However, in order to show to others that it is in compliance with a standard such as ISO 90001, an enterprise must contract with a certified independent registrar to certify that compliance.

Many quality auditing processes are based on the principles first established by *Frederick Deming* in Japan a long time ago in the years following World War II. We have discussed how the originator of these editions, Victor Brink, launched internal auditing in the years following the war; meanwhile, Deming worked as a consultant in the massively damaged postwar Japan with an objective to help repair and rebuild the country's shattered manufacturing resources. Deming introduced many quality management techniques that were initially ignored by traditional U.S. manufacturers such as General Motors, but those same Deming-led techniques led to very high-quality and innovative Japanese products at that time, such as the offerings of Toyota and Sony.

Although it appears very simple in its thought process, a basic concept in Deming's work and a component of quality auditing activities is his Plan-Do-Check-Act (PDCA) cycle. Illustrated in Exhibit 31.5, this is a continuous improvement cycle where a team of quality auditors, among others, would work to improve processes. They would use the *PDCA cycle* to review a process by following the steps:

1. **Plan.** What are the objectives of a quality audit team? What changes are desirable and what data are needed? What types of tests are needed? How will operations be observed? Plan tests as appropriate.
2. **Do.** Execute the planned tests.
3. **Check.** Observe the results of the tests to develop preliminary conclusions.
4. **Act.** Study all test results to assess what was learned and what can be predicted from the exercise. Based on these results, determine areas for process improvements.
5. **Repeat steps while gaining more knowledge.**

This is a simple procedure for process improvement but is quite different from the traditional internal audit steps discussed in Chapter 8. The quality audit process is one of process improvement. Quality auditors do not just review an area and then report results through a formal audit report. Rather, they look at some area, evaluate their findings, and seek to return and improve the process.

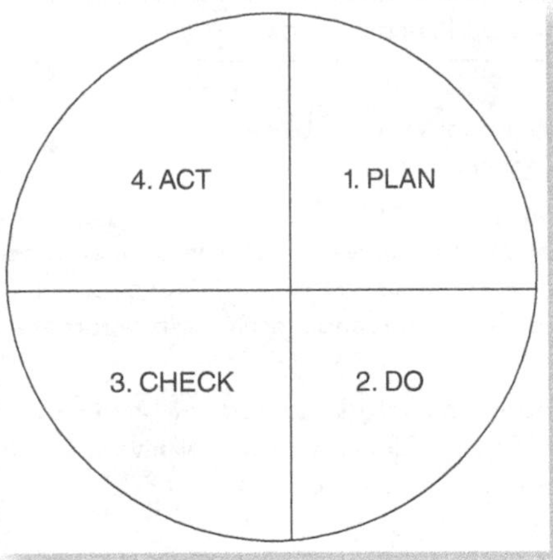

EXHIBIT 31.5 Deming PDCA Cycle

ASQ quality audits are often much more extensive than traditional IIA-heritage internal audits. Quality auditors are often interested in compliance with applicable standards with objectives to:

- Verify that the implemented system is working
- Verify that supporting training programs are cost-effective
- Identify people or groups not following procedures
- Provide evidence to management and others that processes are working as documented

While the quality audit process follows steps that are similar to IIA-heritage internal audits, they are not supported by the same level of detailed internal audit standards found with the IIA-heritage standards as discussed in Chapter 9. Quality audits are not required to follow that same level of standards for performing their reviews. In contrast, the quality auditing process is often much more analytical than IIA-heritage internal audits. The Pareto chart in Exhibit 31.3 is an example of a typical procedure that quality auditors might use to develop their audit findings. A typical quality audit often emphasizes statistical analysis and analytical techniques. The difference, perhaps, is that these audits often cover manufacturing and production operations where there is a great emphasis on technical procedures.

The process of launching and performing a quality internal audit, however, is very similar to IIA-heritage internal audits. Quality auditors start with developing an audit plan, then the development of audit procedures, and finally the concluding audit report and steps to achieve corrective actions. Exhibit 31.6 outlines these quality audit process steps. They are very similar to many familiar with a typical IIA internal audit or even some financial audit standards. Perhaps a major difference is that quality auditors are much more involved with correcting audit findings and launching corrective actions initiatives than many IIA-heritage internal auditors. In contrast to the IIA IPPF standards

EXHIBIT 31.6 Quality Audit Process Steps

- **Preaudit Activities**
  1. Preparation for audit—establish audit objectives
  2. Planning for all audit activities
- **The On-Site Audit**
  1. Opening meeting—meet with auditee and outline planned procedures
  2. The Audit—activation will depend on the nature of the review
  3. Closing Meeting—discuss findings and present draft report at end of fieldwork review
- **Post-Audit Activities**
  1. The Audit Report—report on findings and recommendations
  2. Management Review—discuss audit results with all levels of management
  3. Corrective Actions—negotiate plan to correct audit findings
  4. Follow-up/corrective action audits.

discussed in Chapter 9, quality auditors often have roles as the assessor of control weaknesses and as a consultant to help with implementing corrective actions.

As enterprise compliance with a growing number of ISO standards becomes more important, we will almost certainly see the role of the quality auditor moving more to an enterprise's front office. Audit committees and their management will increasingly understand that there are many common needs for both ASQ-trained quality auditors and IIA-trained internal auditors. We will almost certainly see these two professional groups move closer together in future years.

Although the IIA and the ASQ often had few professional contacts and little in common in the past, there should be an evolving level of integration today with IIA internal auditing and ASQ quality auditing. The term *quality auditing* is going away and the ASQ replaced it with just *auditing* in more recent ASQ publications and in some ISO standards. The terminology used in both IIA and ISO standards is becoming increasingly consistent with revisions to each in recent years. ISO has defined an audit as a "systematic, independent and documented process for obtaining audit evidence and evaluating it objectively to determine the extent to which audit criteria are fulfilled." The IIA's definition of internal auditing, discussed in Chapter 8, contains some quality-related words such as *assurance, adding value, risk management, systematic, disciplined, control,* and *process orientation.* There appears to be some integration of quality auditing and internal auditing terminology into a generic assessment and business process improvement model.

There will probably be a growing convergence of internal auditing and quality auditing over the next few years. An increasing number of enterprises worldwide are seeking ISO registrations, and ISO 9000 standards are becoming more process-oriented, customer-focused, and business-driven. An ISO 9000–registered company must be able to demonstrate its quality system effectiveness.

In some enterprises today, the chief audit executive (CAE) may also have been involved with an enterprise's quality audit function on at least at a courtesy level. In the future, internal audit functions will almost certainly become more acquainted with their quality audit functions and should give consideration to sharing resources.

Although their historical roots are different, both audit functions should become involved with value-added audit functions for the enterprise. If there are separate quality and internal audit functions in an enterprise, IIA-heritage internal auditors should develop a greater understanding of quality audit procedures, and the two audit groups should build some regular and ongoing communication links. While each type of auditor has different approaches and objectives, there may be some value to sharing ideas and even doing some joint review work.

31.4 QUALITY ASSURANCE REVIEWS OF THE INTERNAL AUDIT FUNCTION

Internal auditors have a special role in their service to the management of the modern enterprise. As has been described in many chapters of this book, internal auditors will visit a unit or component of an enterprise, review its controls, and make recommendations for improvements. The IIA-oriented modern internal auditor uses the *International Standards for the Professional Practice of Internal Auditing*, described in Chapter 9, as well as the supporting practices and procedures discussed throughout this book. Other members of the enterprise, and potential auditees, should have a basic understanding that internal audit will be following good practices when it performs its reviews. However, beyond a high-level review of internal audit activities by their external auditors, no one regularly audits the internal auditors to see if they are following both good practices and their own professional standards.

The effective modern internal audit function should look at itself from time to time to determine if all of its own components are following good internal audit practices and procedures. This is best accomplished if internal audit goes through an audit-the-auditors type of quality review over its own functions. The *International Standards for the Professional Practice of Internal Auditing* refer to what are called *quality assurance reviews*. IIA Standard 560 calls for the CAE "to establish and maintain a quality assurance program" to appraise the quality of the audit work performed through ongoing supervisory reviews, reviews by internal audit of its own work, and reviews by external parties. Chapter 12 discussed the concept of internal auditor control self-assessments where internal audit will review its activities on a more informal basis.

In addition, and perhaps even more important, the IIA's Standard 1312 requires that "External assessments must be conducted at least once every five years by a qualified, independent reviewer or review team from outside the organization." Further, the CAE must discuss with the board whether there is a need for more frequent external assessments as well as the qualifications and independence of the external reviewer or review team, including any potential conflict of interest.

IIA Standard 312 says that in addition to its own internal quality assurance review function, internal audit must arrange for another independent internal audit entity or contract with an outside provider to assess the overall quality of their internal audit function. This is a key requirement for all internal audit departments.

Going beyond those control self-assessments, *internal audit quality assurance reviews* are a special type of audit review—more than a normal management assessment of operations or an external auditor service organization's review. While the ASQ quality audit process calls for three levels of review, this section primarily focuses on internal audit *quality assurance reviews* performed by normal internal audit operations, including members of other enterprises or even a specialized department within internal audit. These reviews allow an internal audit function to assess the quality of its own procedures and its compliance with internal audit International Professional Practices Framework standards. This section describes the elements that should be included in an internal audit quality assurance program and describes how internal audit can establish a program to perform these reviews.

Benefits of an Internal Audit Quality Assurance Review

Internal audit departments are sometimes viewed as operating outside of other mainstream enterprise functions. Internal audit reports to the audit committee with close ties with very senior levels of management, and has contact with all other functions in the enterprise through its operational and financial reviews. However, as a very specialized function, internal audit is not always considered when other enterprise performance measurement policies and procedures are established. This is not to suggest that internal audit is ignored. However, a new enterprise program of employee incentive pay, a major quality assurance initiative, or some other employee benefit does not always consider the unique aspects of the internal audit function when designing the program. These programs are often focused on the enterprise's main functions, whether they are manufacturing, distribution, or financial.

As a key function in the enterprise, however, internal audit needs a way to measure itself and to establish incentives to do a better job. This is one of the real benefits of an internal audit quality assurance review. While internal audit itself is the prime beneficiary of these reviews, other stakeholders in an enterprise also benefit from a strong program of internal audit quality assurance reviews. These reviews allow internal audit to demonstrate to management that it is doing a good job or taking corrective action to improve if necessary. Other parties, such as regulatory agencies, also may benefit from these reviews, which provide a basis to better utilize the work of the internal audit department.

The main beneficiary of any internal audit quality assurance review program should be internal audit itself. As highlighted in Chapter 1, internal audit operates somewhat differently from many other functions in a typical enterprise and cannot measure itself by such common measures of success as sales, production, or administrative efficiencies. An external reviewer who understands the internal audit process and who has had exposure to other enterprises can review internal audit operations with the perspective both of internal audit's compliance with professional standards and of how its operations compare with other similar internal audit enterprises. A review of compliance with internal audit standards also is valuable. While an internal audit function should have a program in place to follow these standards in all of its own auditing activities, compliance with one or another specific standard may slip through inattention or just the pressure of completing audit projects. A quality assurance review will allow an outside assessment of day-to-day internal audit activities to evaluate how good a given internal audit function is doing in complying with internal audit standards. This can be a valuable benefit to the modern internal audit function.

The other area where internal audit can benefit from an internal quality assurance review is from the reviewer's comparison with other internal audit enterprises. Internal audit management does not always know how well it compares to other internal audit functions in terms of such things as its use of audit automation, efficiency in performing audit tests, or travel policies. CAEs can gather some of this information through their professional contacts at IIA meetings or other personal or professional contacts. However, these contacts do not always provide the same level of objectivity that would be found through the work of an independent reviewer who looked at several internal audit enterprises. Even though one-on-one contacts are valuable, there can be a tendency for professional peers in different enterprises to gloss over some faults or weaknesses when comparing their relative activities.

Internal audit quality assurance reviews, performed by either outside parties or by an independent reviewer in a larger internal audit department, can add significant value to the internal audit enterprise. The review should point to areas in the organization where some internal audits had been performed in a manner not fully in compliance with standards or where efficiencies could have been achieved by using different audit procedures. For example, the sample size selection approach used in a given audit may have been way too large. Although the audit's results were correct, a smaller sample might have produced the same audit conclusions but with greater efficiency and less cost. As a result of such quality assurance reviews, internal audit management may be able to take the recommendations and improve its own overall operations.

Several levels of management, ranging from the managers directly responsible for internal audit areas reviewed to the audit committee, can all be beneficiaries of internal audit quality assurance reviews. Although an internal audit team should certainly not show its latest quality assurance review report to the auditee management of the next audit project, the findings of a good program of quality assurance reviews should result in better and more efficient audits. All members of enterprise management—and managers directly responsible for units audited, in particular—will benefit from an efficient and effective internal audit function. A program of quality assurance reviews should help to ensure ongoing audit efficiency and affectivity.

The audit committee and senior management should realize even greater benefits from a strong program of internal audit quality assurance reviews. As has been discussed throughout this book, internal audit is a strong component in the system of internal controls. Senior management and the audit committee should understand the overall principles of internal control, but may not always fully understand the workings of the internal audit function. By sharing the summarized results of an internal audit quality assurance review with various levels of senior management, management will have a greater confidence in the quality of the reviews performed. This is a major benefit to the overall enterprise.

Elements of an Internal Audit Quality Assurance Review

An internal audit quality assurance review is a formal process similar to many of the internal audit procedures outlined in other chapters. The review should be properly planned, follow a formal plan or audit program, and be performed by qualified reviewers who can exhibit an appropriate level of independence. Whether performed by a special unit of internal audit charged with performing such reviews or by an outside consultant, the review should follow the same standards of independence and objectivity found in any internal audit. The only significant difference here is that the quality assurance review will focus its efforts on internal audit procedures. The establishment of these requirements is an important first step necessary to launch an internal audit quality-review function. Although management may want to vary the content of any review to reflect local concerns within an enterprise and its internal audit function, the review should concentrate on the internal audit's compliance with IIA international standards, and any quality assurance review should assess compliance with the principles outlined in those standards.

The specific details of how the quality of internal audit operations will be measured depend on many factors, including the size of the internal audit department, directions by the audit committee and senior management specifying more emphasis on one area over another, and other factors. Nevertheless, all internal audit activities should be measured against compliance with these IIA standards.

A quality assurance review is usually initiated through a detailed review of compliance with internal audit procedures. This would include such matters as an evaluation of the risk assessment planning process, reviews of other planning documents, staff assignment procedures, a review of selected workpapers and reports used in actual audits, and all other planning and administrative materials used by internal audit in the course of performing its audit assignments. The purpose of this review approach is to measure the overall quality of internal audit's own procedures. While the specific procedures to be performed will vary with the size and activities of the internal audit department, Exhibit 31.7 outlines the general procedures to be performed in an internal audit quality assurance review. In addition to reviewing workpapers and administrative procedures, the quality assurance review should focus on the auditees who either request reviews or have had reviews performed in their areas. An internal audit function contributes little to the quality of procedures in the overall enterprise if auditee management has serious concerns about the nature of the work performed, including the appropriateness of the audit conclusions reached and how those conclusions were communicated to management. The idea is not to determine that a representative group of auditees necessarily *like* the internal auditors who performed one or another review in their area but to assess whether the reviews were performed in an appropriately professional manner.

As a result of these review procedures and auditee surveys, the quality assurance reviewer should summarize the results and prepare a report for the CAE. Based on these report recommendations, a plan for improvement or corrective action should be established. In some cases, if the reviewers found that certain completed audits did not follow good internal audit procedures, a program of ongoing review or corrective

EXHIBIT 31.7 Internal Audit Quality Assurance Review Procedures

1. Define the areas to be included in the internal audit Quality Assurance (QA) review—whether the entire function or just a separate component of internal audit, such as a separate division or geographic area.
2. Define the time period for the audits to be included in the QA review—whether from the conclusion of the last QA review or for the 12-month period prior to the announcement of the audit.
3. Determine who will be performing the QA internal audit review and ascertain that the reviewer understands both IIA standards and supporting internal audit department procedures.
4. If internal audit has not had such a quality-assurance review within the last 24 months, take steps to assure that both members of the internal audit staff and management understand the purpose and nature of the QA review.
5. If the QA review team plans to survey or interview auditees outside the internal audit department, make some preliminary plans to inform all affected persons.
6. Based on internal audits completed and in-process, develop a general strategy for the number and types of audits to be selected for review. If special knowledge areas are to be included, such as IT security or wireless networks, determine that appropriate resources have been allocated.
7. Decide if the QA review will be on a top-level basis, checking for compliance to general standards or planned to include detailed reviews of selected audits, including workpaper reference checks or reperformance of tests.
8. If problems are encountered in the course of the planned QA review, such as audits requiring a more detailed review, procedures should be prepared to evaluate the QA review's scope or schedule.
9. Develop a general procedure for the format and nature of the QA final audit report.
10. Develop a strategy for reporting the results of the QA review to other members of the internal audit department and to selected members of senior management.

action should be established. If the quality assurance review points out the need for such improvements as increased continuing education, a plan for corrective action should be established.

Although a CAE should see the value of a quality assurance review, an independent party is often needed to perform the review. This is often fairly easy in a large, multiunit internal audit department where a team of centralized corporate internal auditors as well as others from differing divisional units can perform quality assurance reviews of other divisional units. Although there is always the possibility of jealousies and nonobjective appraisals, an in-house quality review, if properly managed, can be performed inexpensively as well as effectively and efficiently. For larger internal audit departments, in-house resources can even be devoted to performing periodic quality assurance reviews.

Many internal audit departments, however, are either not large enough to perform a separate quality assurance review or may face other challenges that prevent them from having members of their enterprise perform quality assurance reviews. A five-person internal audit group, for example, cannot realistically conduct an independent quality assurance review with one member of the staff reviewing the other four. Internal audit management has two options here. It can develop a self-assessment type of review and have all members of the smaller staff evaluate themselves, or it can contract with an outside party to perform the review.

The options available for outside parties to perform a quality assurance review include public accounting firms, consultants who specialize in such reviews, or internal auditors from other enterprises. As another option, the IIA has a review program where it will schedule a team of professionals to perform the review. In addition to very small internal audit groups, some large internal audit functions may find these outside source review approaches to be attractive. An internal audit self-assessment of its quality procedures can take the form of the control self-assessment reviews discussed in Chapter 12.

A large internal audit enterprise can perform quality assurance reviews using designated members of the department. In many respects, an internal auditor who is familiar with the enterprise, its procedures, and the industry—but also understands general internal audit procedures—is often the best, most qualified person to review internal audit operations. Just as internal audit performs a review of another function, such as the purchasing department, the purchasing department could review itself by assigning certain people from its organization to perform this task. However, unless the purchasing department has experience performing such self-assessments, the results of its review could be viewed as self-serving. Internal audit has an advantage over a function such as purchasing, because internal audit regularly exhibits its independence through its standards and other review activities. A large internal audit function can perform its own effective quality assurance reviews if it can demonstrate to others, both inside and outside of internal audit, that it is acting as an independent party.

Large internal audit functions can also establish effective quality-review programs internally by designating certain members of the enterprise the responsibility to perform quality assurance reviews throughout the department. The internal audit function must be large enough to allow one auditor, or a small specialized group of auditors, to perform the quality assurance reviews separate from normal audit activities. In a large internal audit department, there may be enough activity to justify a full-time quality assurance function. In addition to the reviews, it could perform other activities such as developing audit procedures. This internal-review arrangement will not work if members of the regular audit staff are often pulled from the normal schedule and asked to review their peers.

Although internal auditors have standards that require them to act independently, quality reviews of themselves can be viewed by some as either self-serving exercises or as programs to "get" one or another person in the audit department. As mentioned, the reviews are best performed by an independent function within the internal audit function and should otherwise follow normal internal audit procedures. That is, the internal audit quality assurance function would schedule each of its reviews in the same manner as internal audit plans and schedules a normal audit. Once the review is completed, the manager responsible for the unit reviewed would respond to the audit report as would any other auditee. Copies of the final report would go to the director of internal audit, who could take further action as necessary.

This is a particularly effective way to organize internal audit quality assurance reviews when the audit functions are distributed throughout the enterprise. An outside quality assurance reviewer would probably not get to all of the geographically remote units in the course of a single review, but an in-house set of quality assurance reviewers could.

Self-assessment reviews, as discussed in Chapter 10, are often the most realistic way for a very small internal audit function, perhaps with fewer than 10 members, to review its own operations. The staff might postpone normal scheduled audits and block out time to perform the self-assessment review. Time could be allocated for this type of review when the staff was not otherwise busy with scheduled audits.

A self-assessment review by the same internal audit staff responsible for normal audit procedures too often appears as if the auditees are auditing themselves. However, this is often the only way to review the quality of internal audit procedures in a small enterprise. Budget limitations usually prevent hiring outsiders to perform the review, and a small audit department could not justify the extra people resources. Members of the staff would be asked to step back and review all of the procedures performed in the course of a series of audits, including planning, workpaper documentation, audit report content, and a variety of other matters.

Rather than writing a report about itself, as is often done when people outside of normal internal audit operations perform this type of quality assurance review, findings from the self-assessment review are often shared through a series of introspective review meetings. Here, internal audit management and all parties involved would take steps to improve operations based on the self-assessment review findings. For a small internal audit enterprise, self-assessment is usually a cost-effective way to measure quality assurance. People are often their own best critics.

31.5 LAUNCHING THE INTERNAL AUDIT QUALITY ASSURANCE REVIEW

The CAE should take the lead in launching an internal audit quality review program if a formal quality assurance function is not already in place. While it does not matter who starts the review, the internal audit staff will recognize the importance of the CAE initiating the process. If the outside auditors, for example, suggest such a review to members of the audit committee, all parties will ask the underlying question "What's wrong with internal audit?" But if internal audit itself initiates the process, it will have much greater flexibility to suggest the most appropriate parties to perform the review. When an enterprise's external auditors propose an internal audit quality assurance review, the implication is that they will probably be contracted to do the work.

Internal audit may initiate a quality review of its own processes and procedures by proposing the review as part of the annual budgeting and planning process. A basic program can be outlined and resources allocated for either creating a separate quality assurance review function in the enterprise or contracting the review process to an outside provider. If such a process is not already in place, the CAE should think of this not as a one-time process but as a continuing mechanism to assess the quality of overall internal audit performance.

While any outside contractors should clearly be made to understand that they do not have annuity rights for these reviews once they receive the first assignment, internal audit should think of this quality assurance review process as an ongoing program rather than a one-time review. When a CAE proposes a program of internal audit quality assurance reviews to the audit committee and senior management, there may be mixed messages received in return.

If the work is planned to be performed by a specialized in-house group, the question may be asked why existing internal audit staff cannot be pulled off other audit work to perform the reviews. The CAE needs to emphasize the importance of performing these reviews independently and in a manner that will not limit other planned audit activities. If the review is planned to be performed by an outside consulting firm specializing in such reviews, internal audit may have to explain why they would be preferable to the outside auditors. In either case, the CAE may find that convincing management of the need for the reviews and the approach to be used will require some "selling."

An internal audit quality assurance review process will be readily accepted by management if internal audit presents a good plan to perform these reviews on an ongoing basis, if the reviews will allow auditees to provide some inputs regarding their impressions of the overall internal audit process, and if the quality assurance review process points to an improved internal audit function in the enterprise. In addition to selling management on the need for such a quality assurance function, internal audit management should inform all of the internal audit staff of the plans to form the function. Care should always be taken to emphasize that the reviews are not intended to be a witch hunt but are designed to improve the overall quality of all audits performed. Properly explained, the process should be enthusiastically accepted by members of thc internal audit staff.

Although an overall plan of performing quality assurance reviews over a period of time is needed, established procedures are necessary to perform a single, comprehensive review of an internal audit function. The necessary steps are to establish the objectives of a given review, to understand internal audit staff procedures, to survey or interview a selected group of auditees, and to report the results of the review to management and other interested parties. The quality assurance review process will often be performed by a specialized, independent group within internal audit. A section following discusses self-assessment reviews directly performed by members of internal audit on their own audit activities. These self-assessment reviews are particularly appropriate for a small enterprise.

Quality Assurance Review Approaches

An internal audit function launching a quality assurance review program needs to make some basic planning and organization-level decisions. In addition to deciding who will be performing the reviews, internal audit management also must decide on the scope, depth, and breadth of the reviews to be performed. *Scope* here implies the amount of detail to be included in any review. Should the review include primarily internal audit administrative procedures or should it extend to detailed reviews of such areas as IT audit practices or audit sampling approaches? *Depth* here refers to the amount of detail to be included in the quality assurance review of any area. With an extended scope, the quality assurance reviews might go down into the detailed audit procedures performed in each audit reviewed. It is one matter to determine that a selected audit project to be reviewed has a planning memo, a set of workpapers, and an audit report on file. In an extended scope review, the quality assurance reviewers might examine the audit procedures performed for each audit selected for the review. This might include a detailed review of workpapers and even the reperformance of some tests. *Breadth*, as used here, refers to the number of units to be included in any quality assurance review. Should the quality assurance review be just restricted to the large centralized internal audit function at headquarters or should it extend to remote units? In other large enterprises, the geographically remote units may be subject to quality assurance reviews but headquarters will not. In yet other instances, internal audit management will review only domestic units and not go overseas or will review one operating division but not others. Auditees may or may not be surveyed depending on the review approach selected.

Decisions should be made as to the frequency of planned quality assurance reviews. In a large, geographically dispersed enterprise, a quality assurance function will probably not be able to review every internal audit unit every year. The selection of who to review, and how often, should depend on the criticality of the internal audit function reviewed. The same risk assessment techniques introduced in Chapter 7 can be useful in helping internal audit management decide which areas are to be included as part of annual quality assurance review plans. If a given area was subjected to an earlier quality assurance review and areas in need of corrective action were identified, the quality assurance review function may want to schedule an additional follow-up review in that area. Even if an outside consultant is used to perform its quality assurance reviews, internal audit management should take a major role in deciding on the scope, depth, and breadth of the quality assurance reviews to be performed by the quality assurance reviewers over a specified, often a one-year time period. Internal audit management should take the lead in specifying the types of reviews to be performed as well as the expected outputs from those reviews. Sometimes outside reviewers will have a tendency to do the work according to their own agenda. Management should make it known that the CAE is responsible for getting the quality assurance review approach subject to risk-analysis studies and various other inputs from enterprise management.

While these comments have assumed that the CAE will have a strong input into the quality assurance review process, the role of that same CAE in administering and reviewing internal audits should also be considered within the scope of any reviews of overall quality assurance procedures. For example, if internal audit standards call for the CAE to sign the engagement memo and if the CAE ignores this duty, the quality assurance review should highlight this discrepancy. This scope allows the review to assess the overall quality of performance by the entire internal audit function.

The CAE should assure the quality team performing the work that it has an obligation to effectively assess the overall quality of the internal audit function. Once the reviews have been selected, an approach established, and a plan developed, senior internal audit management should inform all members of the internal audit function of these

EXHIBIT 31.8 Quality Review Engagement Memo

Corporate Internal Audit

To: XYZ Division Internal Audit Staff
From: Tom Goodguy, Quality Assurance Manager
Subject: Quality Assurance Review

As part of our established internal audit procedures, the internal audit quality assurance group periodically selects areas for review to assess compliance with audit department and general internal audit standards. Since we have not performed a review in your area for over two years, the XYZ Division internal audit function has been selected for a quality assurance review starting May xx, 20xx. I will be directly managing this review and will be assisted by two staff members.

Please send me a current schedule for internal audits completed over the past year as well as a copy of your current annual audit plan. We will select two audits completed in this period and will request to see the workpapers in advance.

We plan to arrive at the XYZ Division internal audit office on the morning of May xx and would like to meet with your team at that time. We expect that our fieldwork will require no more than two weeks, at which time we will arrange to meet with the XYZ Division Internal Audit team to discuss our initial findings and recommendations.

Thank you for your cooperation and please contact me if you have any questions.

Tom Goodguy

quality assurance review plans. For a large internal audit function with multiple units, that communication could be a formal memo announcing the review plans and the need for cooperation. A sample memo is shown as Exhibit 31.8. A similar note should be directed to auditee groups that may be asked to participate in interviews or surveys. All parties need to be informed of the objectives of the quality assurance review program. Even if internal audit has an ongoing review program, a similar notice will remind internal audit team members that this review program is starting another new, often annual cycle.

Quality Assurance Internal Audit Review Functions: An Example

This section describes how an example internal audit quality assurance review might be performed by internal auditors scheduled to review an internal audit department at a separate, semi-independent division of the enterprise. The unit to be reviewed is called Axylotl Specialties, an independent unit that is 75% owned by the headquarters company, with the remaining 25% held by outside investors. Assume Axylotl Specialties' internal audit function ultimately reports to the headquarters' CAE but does not have day-to-day audit project-related contact with the headquarters audit staff. As with many decentralized enterprises, the Axylotl Specialties internal audit function has been asked to follow general guidance from headquarters but has the freedom to establish some of its own local procedures based on the unique audit risks found in their business unit. In addition, Axylotl Specialties has its own audit committee.

This quality assurance example review will follow the general procedures outlined in Exhibit 31.7 and assumes that the headquarters review team has had little direct contact with Axylotl Specialties. While this example assumes that the group to be reviewed is an independent unit of the parent corporation, these same basic procedures can be used by a variety of different reviewers and for varying internal audit units.

As part of its quality assurance review preliminary planning, the internal audit quality assurance review team should follow some of the same procedures here that it would use when performing a normal internal audit, as has been described in previous chapters of this book. These might include:

- **Announce the planned quality assurance review.** The review should be announced to all impacted members of the internal audit staff. Audit staff members might be offended if they do not know about the planned review and its objectives. The review announcement should contain a strong message that the purpose of the review is not to "get" anyone on the internal audit staff but to help the overall internal audit organization to become more efficient and effective.
- **Assign resources to perform the review.** Concurrent with or even prior to announcing the review, decisions need to be made regarding who is to perform the work. If it is performed by an outside provider, objectives and review schedules should be defined. An internal audit quality assurance review should have designated persons who will be performing the work and who will not be distracted by other projects.
- **Meet with internal audit management.** In a larger internal audit group, the CAE is often responsible for initiating the review by scheduling it with the specialized function within internal audit that will perform the work or by contracting with an outside provider. Other members of the internal audit management team may not have much knowledge about the planned review. Before starting the actual work, the review team should meet with appropriate members of audit management to advise them of its review approach and to discuss any special considerations that might impact them. For example, the quality assurance team may schedule a review at a separate, divisional internal audit function. Local internal audit management may explain some special considerations that might suggest that the reviewers avoid looking at one or another area. If the request is reasonable, the quality assurance team should honor it, documenting that decision.
- **Meet with other members of management.** Enterprise management should normally be quite aware of their internal auditors' work products through their presence in various operational areas or through audit reports, but they may not be aware of the objectives of an internal quality assurance review. This is the time for the review team leaders to meet with appropriate members of local management to explain their review objectives. The review team should also request some input from management regarding any of their concerns about the performance of internal audit. For example, management may feel that certain audit reports took far too long to issue or that some members of the audit enterprise have not been acting in a professional manner. This type of input may point the review team to an examination of completion times for those audits mentioned or a review of training records for the audit staff.

After completing these first steps, the internal audit quality assurance team should be ready to perform the actual review. Assuming that it has established a starting audit program, it may want to modify the scope and extent of its planned review based on these inputs. If a branch unit audit manager has indicated a very critical audit is in process during the time of the review, the review team may want to avoid that review area so as to not disrupt other internal audit operations.

Effective internal audit review procedures are very important. An internal audit quality assurance review is an independent assessment of the audit department's performance in compliance with internal audit professional and departmental standards. There is no single approach that applies to all internal audit departments and reviews. Generally, a review will investigate internal audit procedures and enterprise standards and then will focus on individual completed audits to determine if the standards have been followed. Exhibit 31.9 describes some of the major review steps for a quality

EXHIBIT 31.9 Review Steps for a Quality Assurance Review of Internal Audit

1. Review internal audit department approved procedures to determine if adequate emphasis is devoted to accuracy and quality issues; summarize any areas for potential improvements.
2. Review the current and most recent past year of the completed audit plan:
   a. Assess reasons for any audits never launched or still in progress.
   b. Review the hours recorded for completed audits and compare to original plans; determine and document reasons for any major plan variances.
   c. Review the extent of special, unplanned audit performed and assess both their supporting documentation and reasonableness.
3. For the current period and the past two years, review the risk analysis and audit planning process. Assess whether appropriate attention was given to relative risks in all scheduled audits.
4. Select a sample of internal audits completed over past two years and review their complete workpapers to ascertain:
   a. Workpapers are in good order and follow internal audit department standards for both hard- and soft-copy formats.
   b. Audit programs were developed for each review that support audit scope, identified risks, and work performed.
   c. All potential findings have either been carried to the audit report or have otherwise been resolved through appropriate disposition.
   d. Appropriate audit reports or other communications were prepared following good internal audit standards.
   e. All audit documentation reviewed is controlled in secure repositories.
5. Based on the workpapers and other supporting materials reviewed, assess internal audit's use of special IT retrieval tools, audit sampling, and other audit techniques.
6. Interview key auditees from several of the selected audits completed to assess their impressions of both the professionalism of the assigned internal audit team and the results of the audit work.
7. Review overall internal auditing budgeting, travel expenses, and time-reporting procedures to determine the reasonableness and thoroughness of procedures.
8. Review the time budgets prepared for the selected review audits and compare them with the actual hours required for the selected reviews; review any documentation covering major differences.
9. Review the internal audit continuing education activities to determine appropriate attention is given to professional training.
10. Review internal audit staff turnover and assess potential causes for any high turnover.

assurance review of internal audit operations. The reviewers here need to understand specific internal audit departmental procedures. This requires an initial study of documentation and other materials, just as internal auditors would review available documentation as a first step in their operational audits. Even if members of the same overall audit enterprise are performing the quality assurance review, the review team should still review this internal audit documentation. It will reacquaint them with operations and will allow them to better define their audit tests. This documentation standards review may also point to additional areas to emphasize in their detailed testing procedures. For example, the reviews may find that internal audit's standards for auditor project timekeeping are too complex, and because of this complexity, they may see a red flag that might suggest that internal auditors may have trouble completing the time reporting and therefore may not be keeping accurate time records. This might point to an area for more detailed review.

Items reviewed within the internal audit department should be selected on a test basis. While this might not be an appropriate area to perform detailed statistical sampling test selection approaches, the review team should use judgmental sampling in the various areas reviewed. That is, internal audit might not care to reach an attributes sampling–type of conclusion, as was discussed in Chapter 10; however, the review teams should take care to make representative selections of all areas sampled. For example, if the quality assurance reviewers are interested in whether internal audit has been performing an adequate risk analysis in various areas of the enterprise, the review team might judgmentally select several areas of overall enterprise operations and determine if an adequate risk analysis had been performed in those areas selected as part of the annual planning process.

Internal audit quality assurance review procedures are essentially the same as for all other internal audit procedures described throughout this book. The reviewers should identify an area from their established review program, select a representative sample of actual items in that area, review or test the items selected, evaluate the tests, and document thc results. The quality assurance review team should take the same care in selecting and documenting its work as it would expect internal audit to follow in its regular audits. As with normal internal audits, when the review team finds what appear to be significant exceptions, it should discuss these potential findings with the internal auditors being reviewed to determine that there are no extenuating circumstances behind the potential findings. This is the same process normally followed in any internal audit, except that here the reviewers are auditing the auditors.

Reviews of Individual Completed Audits

In addition to reviewing overall internal audit group procedures, a quality assurance review should always include a detailed review of a sample of completed audits. This review should not be made to second-guess the findings of the auditors who performed the work but to determine that the review followed good internal audit standards, including planning, test procedures performed, workpaper documentation, and the completed audit report. While the steps described previously reviewed internal audit department standards, this phase of a quality assurance review will assess compliance with these standards in the completion of actual audits.

Normally, a quality assurance review team should select a representative sample of materials from completed audits over perhaps the past one-year period. This sample should include all types of audits, including operational, financial, IT, and other types of special reviews. A good starting point here is to look at an audit project report listing completed audits. From this, the quality assurance review team should select the sample and pull the workpaper files and any other related data to describe the audit procedures performed, the conclusions reached, and the method for communicating those audit conclusions. The reviewers should read enough of the workpapers to understand the audit objectives, the approaches used, and the conclusions reached. If the section reviewed has what appears to be a good process where audit supervisors or others reviewed all workpapers and appear to ask appropriate questions prior to the completion of normal audits, the quality assurance review team can look at this sample review and satisfy itself that it is working for all of the audits selected.

Once a review selection has been made, the quality assurance reviewers should examine a sample of completed audit workpapers. This exercise should very much depend on the reviewers' understanding of departmental procedures. Here, in a review of individual workpapers, quality assurance should determine if those standards are being followed and if good auditing practices are used. The number and extent of areas that might be included in such a review will vary with the overall type and scope of the audit. They might include:

- **Audit sampling procedures used.** Chapter 10 discussed audit testing procedures, including the use of statistical sampling procedures. The internal auditors who did the actual work may have made a decision to only pull a limited judgmental sample when a better audit result might have come from the use of some type of statistical sampling approach. An appropriate quality assurance comment is that the auditor in charge of the review did not appear to have considered the better results that might have been gained from statistical sampling techniques.
- **Compliance with generally accepted accounting principles (GAAP) or other accounting standards.** While internal auditors will generally not be performing financial audits, many internal audits have some financial accounting ramifications. In many cases, these reviews may have been performed for the external auditors who would be responsible for reviewing the work and signing off on the conclusions developed. However, if the financial accounting procedures performed were strictly part of internal audit's review, the quality assurance reviewer might want to consider the appropriateness of the financial accounting procedures as documented in the workpapers.
- **Appropriate consideration of IT risks.** Operational audits sometimes do not consider the IT risks associated with the area reviewed. For example, an operational or financial review might rely on the outputs of an IT system, with no attention given to the controls surrounding that system. An appropriate quality assurance review point is to comment on the assessment of IT risks.

- **Use of other audit automation techniques.** Chapter 17 discussed the preparation of process modeling and workpapers to understand and document audit activities. While many of the areas discussed there are appropriate for a quality assurance review, the chapter emphasized some of the automated techniques that could be used to make the audit and workpaper preparation process more efficient. Again, this is an area for potential quality assurance review and comment.

These examples are just a few of the many specific areas that might be included in a quality assurance review of completed workpapers. The quality assurance reviewers need to go through the selected workpapers in some detail and determine if internal audit best practices were followed during the review. In some instances, the quality assurance reviewers may want to discuss the work with the internal auditors who completed the review and prepared the workpapers. While the audit workpapers should speak for themselves, the internal auditors who did the work can often provide additional background information on their reviews. A need to ask specific questions about the audit procedures not documented in the workpapers may point to lack of documentation; however, these questions are sometimes necessary for clarification purposes. Also, the quality assurance reviewers will often want to interview or survey the actual auditees.

The actual audit report and its findings are also part of the quality assurance review of the completed audit workpapers. The reviewers should determine that all points covered in the workpapers and identified as potential report findings have been included in the final audit report or otherwise given proper disposition. The quality assurance review should not focus on style and small grammatical errors and the like; it should assess whether the report has been clearly written and is in accordance with internal audit department standards. The reviewers may want to consider the elapsed time between fieldwork completion and report release. Too long of a delay in this report production may indicate some overall internal audit quality problems. The review of workpapers should include all of the steps documented in the internal audit process, from risk assessment and initial audit planning to the release of the final report, including auditee responses.

A quality assurance review should include interviews or surveys with a sample of users of internal audit services. The internal audit quality assurance reviewers may want to select a sample of recent internal audits and interview both the auditees and the recipients of the issued reports from those selected internal audits. The quality assurance survey should contact members of enterprise management to better understand their impression of internal audit's services. These surveys with persons outside of the internal audit department can have different dimensions and may point to alternative potential conclusions regarding internal audit services.

After reviewing workpapers and other materials from a completed audit, the quality assurance reviewers will usually find it valuable to interview some of the auditees. These are the persons whose functions were reviewed as part of the completed audit selected for the review. The idea here is to assess the level of internal audit professionalism as seen through the eyes of the auditees. Even though the quality assurance team may have found the selected workpapers to be well organized and the audit report well written, internal audit has a potential quality problem if the auditees—the subjects of the audit—did not regard the internal auditors who performed the review as high-quality professionals.

Many factors can cause this type of feeling. For example, the field audit team may have worked late into the evening one day and arrived at the audit site late in the morning the following day. Because auditees do not know the team was working late, they might resent the auditors' late arrival work habits. Quality assurance interviews with selected auditees might reveal this type of information.

Auditee interviews are usually initiated following a quality assurance workpaper review. While not every auditee identified in the workpapers should be contacted, the review team might consider asking a small sample of these persons to participate in an interview. Even though quality assurance may want to talk to several auditees identified in a single set of workpapers, all quality assurance interviews should involve only a single auditee at a time. This one-on-one approach allows an auditee to be more open in expressing concerns regarding an audit.

Quality assurance auditee interviews can provide much information about the quality of the internal auditors performing a review, but they can present difficulties. First, an auditee may not give totally honest responses to the interviewer's questions. The auditee being interviewed may not want to hurt the members of the audit team and will be reluctant to express honest opinions. Even worse, if a group of auditees are interviewed together as a focus group, there is a danger that the session will transform itself into a "feeding frenzy" where a large amount of negative but unsupported bad news is communicated.

31.6 REPORTING THE RESULTS OF AN INTERNAL AUDIT QUALITY ASSURANCE REVIEW

An internal audit quality assurance review, as we have discussed, is a review of internal audit's own processes. Thus, such a quality assurance review should follow many of internal audit's normal procedures including planning, fieldwork, documentation of results, and issuing the audit report. A quality assurance review is of little value unless its results are reported to the audit committee and others in a formal audit report. Depending on the size of the internal audit department and the scope of the quality assurance review, the completed review might follow a normal internal audit report, as discussed in Chapter 18. That is, the quality assurance reviewers should prepare a draft report with their quality assurance review findings; the audit group reviewed would have an opportunity to respond to those findings, outlining the corrective action steps they plan to take; and the final product would be a quality assurance report similar to regular internal audit reports.

A key difference between an internal audit quality assurance report and a normal internal audit report, however, is the report distribution. This report will normally be addressed to the CAE, with copies given to the audit committee, but few if any other persons outside of internal audit would be on its distribution list. Since the report may cover some very specific and technical details of problem areas identified by the quality assurance team, it may go into far greater detail than should be included in a well-drafted internal audit report. The quality assurance review team is responsible for discussing areas where the internal audit area reviewed can improve its procedures; internal audit itself is responsible for making certain that appropriate corrective actions are taken. The CAE is normally responsible for deciding if persons outside of internal audit should receive a copy of the internal audit quality assurance report. The CAE is responsible for determining that all aspects of the internal audit department follow good practices and that any appropriate corrective actions are taken.

A smaller internal audit department or an enterprise that has not devoted formal resources to performing formal quality assurance reviews should still take steps to monitor the quality of its internal audit activities. The quality of the internal audits performed can be measured through self-assessment surveys, which can take many forms, ranging from an open discussion in response to a "How are we doing?" type of question raised at a departmental session, through the completion of a formal self-assessment review or questionnaire. While the open discussion will give the CAE some information on how well the small audit department is doing, a self-assessment survey is most useful.

The idea is to ask each member of the internal audit department to complete a survey where they will respond to questions regarding their audit practices and how well they think that they, the individual auditors, are doing, as well as how the department in total thinks they are doing. Despite the size of the department, all members of the team can evaluate how they feel they are performing as individuals and as a team on their audit assignments, and how the overall audit department is performing in the eyes of each individual auditor. Each member of the audit department would be asked to complete a survey, tailored to the individual internal audit department, which emphasizes compliance with internal audit standards and the overall perceived quality of the work performed. A limited number of users of internal audit services might also be polled through this type of survey.

A small internal audit enterprise may be faced with the question of who should complete the survey. If the internal audit department consists of the CAE and perhaps only a staff of six, that director would know which of the internal audit staff completed the surveys based on the nature of some criticisms or even the handwriting. These types of surveys are best run independently. The CAE might ask the human resources department to mail out the surveys and to compile the mailed-in results. This way, the survey responses would not be easily connected with the persons completing them and staff members would feel freer to express their opinions regarding the quality of internal audit department operations.

Once the survey results have been tabulated by the responsible nonaudit party, the CAE should share them with the audit staff. Although this type of assessment will not result in a formal findings and response type of audit report, members of the audit staff can collectively decide on various areas for internal audit improvement and should take steps to change internal audit operations as appropriate. Although not as comprehensive as a formal internal audit quality assurance review, an independent self-assessment review is a good exercise for the small internal audit department to evaluate the quality of its performance.

31.7 FUTURE DIRECTIONS FOR QUALITY ASSURANCE AUDITING

This chapter has looked at quality assurance from two different dimensions—the separate quality audits that had been the domain of the ASQ and the IIA-related quality assurance reviews—as a means of assessing the standards and performance of existing internal audit departments. While quality assurance standards and practices are important for all internal auditors, we can sometimes lose track of our objectives in this area because too many use the term *quality assurance* without fully understanding it.

This chapter started with a discussion of the role of ASQ members who once called themselves quality auditors and are now just auditors. They should be important members of the overall internal audit community, but because of their manufacturing and process industry heritage, they often operate separate from conventional IIA-heritage internal audit functions, and sometimes have only minimal contact with the CAE and audit committee. We have called this group *quality auditors* to distinguish them from the IIA-heritage *internal auditors*. Even though their IIA and ASQ professional organizations do not have any formal connections currently, we can only expect these two audit professions to grow close in the future. IIA-trained internal auditors need to learn and use some of the analytical and statistical tools that are common to ASQ quality auditors, and the latter needs some of the rigor and discipline demonstrated by the IIA's internal auditing standards.

An internal audit departments needs to measure how well it is performing. Internal auditors perform reviews of many other areas and freely make constructive suggestions, but they often do not take the opportunity to review themselves. A formal program of internal audit quality assurance reviews will allow internal audit to better assess its own performance; reviews are performed by a specialized function within internal audit, by various qualified outsider reviewers, or by means of a self-assessment survey. Who performs the review will depend on the size and enterprise of the internal audit department, as well as on management's commitment to this type of review program.

In addition to reviewing how an individual internal audit department is doing and how well it is operating in compliance with internal audit standards, an internal audit department often needs to assess how it is performing when compared to internal audit functions in other enterprises. This is where the concept of benchmarking is useful. An internal audit quality assurance function can meet with other internal audit groups and determine how those groups are performing. Similarly, the well-run internal audit function should hold itself open to share its ideas and practices with other internal audit functions that are doing their own benchmarking. This becomes even more important with the IIA international standards requirement that every internal audit function must arrange to have an external quality assurance review at least once every five years. Understanding these internal audit quality assurance requirements and the steps necessary to perform an effective quality assurance review is an important internal audit CBOK requirement.

CHAPTER THIRTY-TWO

Six Sigma and Lean Techniques for Internal Audit

ENTERPRISE OPERATIONS MANAGERS AT ALL levels are regularly looking for ways to improve their operations, whether in shop-floor production processes or office administrative procedures. Internal auditors have a major role here through their internal controls reviews and audit report–recommended corrective actions. As discussed in Chapter 30, they can also have a strong role in launching process improvements by serving as internal consultants to their enterprise. However, internal auditors must keep in mind that there is no single solution or methodology for implementing best practices to improve operations, and should recognize that many different approaches have been tried over the years. Some of the older approaches or methodologies, although launched years ago, are still active, while others are now little more than footnotes in business history.

An overall quality improvement approach called *Six Sigma* was first based on Japanese quality assurance techniques developed in the 1970s and now has been successfully been used in the United States and worldwide to reduce errors and improve efficiencies in all aspects of enterprise operations. Six Sigma has its roots in statistical quality control procedures but now is viewed as much more of a process improvement approach. However, because of its roots in Japanese quality manufacturing processes, knowledgeable Six Sigma practitioners are designated as Green Belt certified, using Japanese karate belt-achievement levels, and its experts are certified as *Black Belts*. When an enterprise adopts a Six Sigma approach, it can become an almost all-consuming exercise for many in operations. Six Sigma's designated black belts, after considerable training and expertise, are often recognized and respected as authorities within an enterprise's operations, and the overall Six Sigma process can become an important and valuable exercise for enterprise operations.

Chapter 31 discussed quality assurance processes and the role of American Society for Quality quality auditors—professionals who have some of the same professional standards and activities as those of the Institute of Internal Auditors (IIA) that have been the subject of most chapters of this book. While those quality auditors will normally have some understanding of the Six Sigma concepts that are the topic of this chapter, all internal auditors—IIA as well as quality auditors—should have a basic common body of knowledge (CBOK) understanding of Six Sigma concepts and how they are applied in many areas of an enterprise.

This chapter will provide a high-level introduction to Six Sigma concepts and how they should be applied in many aspects of enterprise operations. We will provide an overview of Six Sigma as well as some of what are called the Lean approaches to implementing it. *Lean* is a term that is increasingly used in business procedures today. It is an approach that takes a comprehensive but very document-oriented process and breaks things down to essential bare minimums. A concept that is useful in many areas of operations, Lean techniques are particularly valuable for understanding the important aspects of Six Sigma operations.

Even though an internal audit function may not be using Six Sigma concepts as part of its overall operations, internal auditors should have a basic CBOK understanding or familiarity of these important quality improvement concepts. An internal auditor will encounter auditees in all levels of operations in many enterprises who may talk about their Six Sigma achievements and activities. The professional internal auditor should have sufficient background information to understand Six Sigma concepts at a high level and to ask important review questions.

32.1 SIX SIGMA BACKGROUND AND CONCEPTS

Whether from knowledge gained from a college mathematics course or even college fraternity or sorority awareness, most internal auditors will recognize sigma as one of the letters in the Greek-language alphabet. As an uppercase Greek letter, sigma appears as Σ, and in mathematics this symbol normally refers to the sum of a series of numbers following it. In its lowercase form, sigma appears as σ. Here it is used to express the variability from some process. For example, Chapter 10 on statistical sampling described the manner in which variable data is often organized in a bell-shaped curve, a standard distribution illustrated in Exhibit 10.5. The σ, or sigma symbol, is used to describe the variability around the central points or averages in a standard distribution.

These σ-based variability measures have been used by enterprises to measure product or process quality. For example, enterprises traditionally accepted quality measures of 3 or 4 sigma level as a norm. That is, they would accept error or problem levels of between 6,200 and 67,000 problems per million opportunities. We can think of these measures in terms of some part rolling off a highly automated production. Whether in the United States or Europe, enterprises would accept that level of problems with these high-volume production parts, assuming they could fix or repair things later.

This concept of an acceptable level of quality changed in the 1970s when a Japanese company took over the production processing for what had been a Motorola production plant producing Quasar-brand television sets. The Japanese company installed its own production and quality procedures, and was soon producing products with only 1/20th of the number of defects that had been tolerated by Motorola production management. They were operating at Six Sigma.

Motorola enthusiastically implemented these Six Sigma quality standards throughout its production and other operations. It became a recognized leader in quality operations, and the company received the U.S. government's Malcolm Baldrige National Quality Award[1] in 1988. Many other major companies, such as GE and Allied Signal, then embraced Six Sigma concepts as an approach to improve customer service and productivity. Six Sigma received considerable press and other attention during the days when Motorola was in the press as a quality leader. It still remains an important improvement process today.

Although Six Sigma had its origins as a statistical quality assurance concept, its real importance is its use as a program to improve overall process quality, whether in manufactured products or service-related processes. It is not the kind of concept that the CEO announces at a major meeting with little action taken beyond some broad statements. Rather, an effective Six Sigma initiative is implemented through the efforts of small teams using what is known as a Define-Measure-Analyze-Improve-Control, or *DMAIC*, model where:

- **Define** the goals for the improvement activity.
- **Measure** the activity covering the existing system.
- **Analyze** the need to identify ways to eliminate gaps between the current performance of the system and the desired goal.
- **Improve** the system initiatives.
- **Control** the new or revised system.

These DMAIC steps define the overall philosophy behind Six Sigma. Although it got started as a precise—many decimal points—quality and process improvement process, Six Sigma today is much more about the steps necessary to improve existing enterprise processes by observing businesses processes of all types and levels, then developing a hypothesis to potentially improve the observed operation, followed by making predictions to improve the area of concern. The team responsible will then install the suggested changes, test the results of those changes, and repeat these steps as necessary to make effective improvements.

Internal auditors should recognize some very strong differences between a Six Sigma–led environment and their typical auditee review areas. Internal auditors typically review operations in an area and make recommendations for improvement through published audit reports. Internal auditors' recommendations are based on their experiences as well as suggested approaches that may be developed through discussions before the release of the published audit report. These are not flexible or best-guess recommendations, and it may be a long time before internal audit returns to see if its recommendations have been implemented.

Six Sigma process improvements do not come from outsiders—such as internal auditors or consultants—visiting an operation and then making tentative suggestions to improve processes. Rather, a team of trained specialists in an area of operations reviews operations and implements process improvements throughout that area. There are opportunities here for internal auditors on three levels. First, when internal audit discovers a Six Sigma process in place when reviewing some area of enterprise operations, internal audit, in its service to management objectives, might consider a review of the effectiveness of the existing Six Sigma program as part of its internal audit in the area. As a second area of opportunity, internal auditors may want to consider recommending Six Sigma processes as part of their reviews of internal controls in some area. Our third suggested area is that internal auditors should consider the use of Six Sigma processes to improve their own internal audit operations.

All of these opportunities, of course, require that an internal audit team have some understanding of Six Sigma processes. While quality auditors, discussed in Chapter 31, are typically very well aware of Six Sigma processes, IIA-heritage internal auditors have had limited exposure to these important concepts. This chapter will provide a high-level overview of Six Sigma concepts for internal auditors. A general understanding of Six Sigma processes should be part of every internal auditor's CBOK.

32.2 IMPLEMENTING SIX SIGMA

The concept of Six Sigma calls for an enterprise to implement processes that will deliver no more than 3.4 defects per million opportunities for a defective production product or process step. Although we are using the spelled-out term *Six Sigma* through this chapter, today the program's name is written as 6σ . At first glance, Six Sigma sounds like a very tough standard to meet. However, a Web search will provide information on thousands of companies that have successfully implemented Six Sigma programs. In most cases, the effort has been launched by a fairly senior manager who has heard about the success of other enterprises and will act as a catalyst for improving service quality. The whole idea is less about statistical-led quality management than the process of establishing a new initiative throughout the enterprise. For many enterprises, changing to the Six Sigma processes is akin to a family's adopting a new religion. One family member may have been exposed to the new religious philosophy, took some additional training, and then brought in missionaries from the new religion to teach and convert other family members. They will subscribe to the new philosophy, will establish goals, and will continue to actively follow and work under that new religion.

Our family religion conversion analogy for adopting Six Sigma is admittedly weak because the newly converted family will view their new religion as an approach to better spiritual values and other intangible future benefits. Six Sigma is an approach to make the overall enterprise more profitable and efficient and calls for an enterprise to establish some very definite goals that will begin to provide benefits once deployed. Exhibit 32.1 outlines the types of deployment and process goals an enterprise might attempt to achieve by adopting a Six Sigma program. These deployment and process goals are very high-level but point to the types of activities that virtually any enterprise, whether a production operation or not, can do to initiate improvements.

EXHIBIT 32.1 Six Sigma Deployment and Process Goals

- Six Sigma Enterprise Deployment Goals
  - Goals to enhance business needs
    - Increase shareholder value
    - Increase revenues, returns on investment, and profitability
    - Improve market share
  - Operations level goals
    - Reduce material and labor costs
    - Eliminate production rework at all levels
    - Improve production and process throughput
  - Process level goals
    - Improve cycle times
    - Reduce process resource requirements
    - Improve process yield through reduction in defects
    - Reduce all levels of variability and improve process capability
- Identify Operations Value Streams Deployment Goals
  - Define the processes that are critical to enterprise performance
  - Analyze how key processes bring value to customers
- Determine Metrics and Current Performance Levels
  - Develop techniques to measure key value streams
  - Identify processes that are stable and subject to statistical control
  - Establish process measures, such as cycle times, costs, and quality opportunities
  - Define process "should be" objectives where appropriate
  - Define benchmark or best-in-class performance measures
- Establish Breakthrough Strategies for New Performance Levels
  - Identify the variables that make the most differences to process performance and establish settings or goals for them
  - Identify areas where processes can be designed to become more robust
  - Define areas where process redesign will yield production of quality improvements
- Standardize New Production or Process Approaches
  - Develop and release operational procedures covering new approaches
  - Train people, as necessary, to use new approaches
  - When necessary, implement statistical measures to control process variation
  - Modify inventory, accounting, and other business systems to assure the improved process performance is reflected in overall operations

32.3 SIX SIGMA LEADERSHIP ROLES AND RESPONSIBILITIES

An effective implementation of Six Sigma in an enterprise requires designated leadership and a strong, trained team of employees who are launching Six Sigma projects in addition to their own normal job responsibilities. Just as Chapter 29 on internal auditor professional certifications introduced the CIA, CISA, and others, Six Sigma introduces its own series of new professional certifications based on its Japanese heritage. While there are special training responsibilities for each, an enterprise leadership team to launch and manage Six Sigma should include:

- **Six Sigma executive council.** A top-level group of senior managers across the enterprise should be formed to manage the Six Sigma initiative. This group suggests and approves high-impact Six Sigma projects, tracks progress, reviews the effectiveness of the program, and generally provides a communication message throughout the enterprise. Although the analogy is not at all complete, the Six Sigma executive council takes sort of an audit committee role to a Six Sigma initiative.
- **Six Sigma director.** This person directs and manages all Six Sigma efforts. The director is the Six Sigma program manager for multiple Six Sigma projects and leads overall deployment efforts, such as shown in Exhibit 32.1. The director leads and evaluates the overall initiative and communicates progress to customers, suppliers, and the enterprise.
- **Master Black Belt.** This is often the one full-time agent in an enterprise to lead a Six Sigma initiative. Certified Six Sigma Black Belts (CSSBBs) are persons who have displayed proven knowledge and expertise in implementing Six Sigma. This involves both "textbook" knowledge of the subject matter (methodologies, tools, principles, and related topics such as leadership and change management), as well as real-world, successful application of the methodology and tools in more than one Six Sigma project.

  An individual can be become a CSSBB in a variety of ways: from a professional organization, such as the American Society for Quality, from some consulting companies, or from their Six Sigma active company (e.g., GE, Motorola, etc.). No one way is necessarily better than another, but it is widely accepted that private companies with mature Six Sigma programs serve as the best vehicles for certification.
- **Six Sigma Black Belts.** These are the designated Six Sigma experts in an enterprise. Black Belts lead overall process improvement efforts and take direct responsibility for specific key Six Sigma projects. A Black Belt should have a demonstrated understanding of this body of knowledge, as shown in Exhibit 32.2,[2] and a proficiency in achieving the results of Six Sigma approaches. One should think of this body of knowledge description as similar to the internal auditor CBOK topics discussed throughout this book. Some topics here are essential, while others are areas where the Black Belt should have a good general understanding. Black Belts frequently serve their organizations for assignments lasting one or two years, then return to their regular job duties.
- **Green Belts.** These professionals have a basic understanding of Six Sigma processes and serve as part-time assistants to their enterprises while maintaining normal job responsibilities. They work on Six Sigma projects but on a more junior level than Black Belts.
- **Six Sigma improvement teams.** Following the leadership of Black and Green Belts, many other persons may be assigned to a Six Sigma project on a part-time basis. Depending on the nature of a Six Sigma project, there may be a need for detailed data gathering, process testing, or preparation of documentation to achieve Six Sigma results.

EXHIBIT 32.2 Black Belt Body of Knowledge

High-Level Six Sigma Understandings

- Overview of Six Sigma and Its Language
- DMAIC Methodology Overview
- Financial Benefits of Six Sigma
- Understanding the Impact of Six Sigma to the Enterprise

Define Six Sigma Elements

- Project Management
- Project Definition
- Project Charter
- Developing a Business Case
- Chartering a Six Sigma Team
- Defining Roles and Responsibilities
- Gathering Voice of the Customer and Support for a Project
- Translating Customer Needs into Specific Requirements
- Define Phase Review Elements

Measure

- Process Mapping (As-Is Process)
- Understanding Data Attributes (Continuous Versus Discrete)
- Defining Metrics
- Measurement System Analysis
- Gage Repeatability and Reproducibility
- Data Collection Techniques
- Calculating Sample Size
- Data Collection Plan
- Understanding Variation
- Measuring Process Capability
- Calculating Process Sigma Level
- Rolled Throughput Yield
- Visually Displaying Baseline Performance
- Statistical Software Training
- Measurement Phase Review

Analyze

- Visually Displaying Data (Histogram, Run Chart, Pareto Chart, Scatter Diagram)
- Detailed (Lower Level) Process Mapping of Critical Areas
- Value-Added Analysis
- Cause and Effect Analysis (a.k.a. Fishbone, Ishikawa)
- Affinity Diagram
- Data Segmentation and Stratification
- Correlation and Regression (Linear, Multiple)
- Process Performance (Cp, CpK, Pp, PpK, CpM)
- Short-Term Versus Long-Term Capability
- Non-Normal Data Distribution Transformations
- Central Limit Theorem
- Goodness of Fit Testing
- Hypothesis Testing
- Analysis of Variance (ANOVA), Two Sample T-Tests, Chi Squared Test
- Design of Experiments (DOE)—Full, Fractional Factorials
- Verification of Root Causes
- Determining Opportunity (Defects and Financial) for Improvement
- Project Charter Review and Revision
- Statistical Software Training
- Analyze Phase Review

(continued)

EXHIBIT 32.2 (*continued*)

Improve

- Brainstorming
- Multivoting
- Process Simulation
- Quality Function Deployment (House of Quality)
- Selecting a Solution
- Failure Modes and Effects Analysis (FMEA)
- Poka Yoke (Mistake Proofing Your New Process)
- Piloting Your Solution
- Implementation Planning
- Statistical Software Training
- Culture Modification Planning for Your Organization
- Improve Phase Review

Control

- Assessing the Results of Process Improvement
- Statistical Process Control (SPC)
- Rational Subgroupings
- Establishing Process Standards for Inputs, Process, and Outputs
- Developing a Process Control Plan
- Documenting the Process
- Statistical Software Training
- Control Phase Review

Beyond these designated Six Sigma leaders, many others in an enterprise are usually assigned to the project to analyze and achieve results. The whole concept here is that a team of designated Six Sigma belts should study areas of operations to identify a process or service areas with objectives to eliminate errors or waste to bring operations down to the Six Sigma standard of less than 3.4 defects per million opportunities. This is a very tight standard. Internal auditors who are accustomed to reviewing documents for internal control violations but who sometimes give small violations a pass may find Six Sigma rules quite tight. There is almost no tolerance for errors or exceptions of any types under Six Sigma rules. Even when an enterprise has not formally adopted an overall Six Sigma program, internal auditors should consider using some Six Sigma rules and concepts as part of their internal audit activities.

32.4 LAUNCHING AN ENTERPRISE SIX SIGMA PROJECT

A successful Six Sigma initiative in an enterprise cannot be successfully launched through one large senior management–mandated project. Six Sigma success is initiated through the implementation of many smaller efforts to make improvements. Similar to internal auditors performing reviews to improve internal controls, a Six Sigma team will look at virtually all processes and select a small number of critical ones as candidates to find opportunities for improvements. A critical difference is that internal audit generally starts with a high-level approach—such as a plan to review internal controls in some operating unit. The Six Sigma team will typically develop detailed flowcharts covering both large and small operations and then will ask the following questions to better understand a candidate Six Sigma process:

- For which stakeholder does a process primarily exist?
- What value does the process create or what outputs are produced?
- Who is the owner of the process?
- Who or what supporting area provides the inputs to the process?
- What are the inputs to the process?
- What resources—people, IT, or other—does this process use?
- Are there any subprocesses with their own discrete start and end points?
- What steps in the process create value?

Based on this preliminary information, the Six Sigma team should then attempt to establish some process improvement objectives. These can cover a wide variety of areas, and each process should be given a high-level objective, such as to "help customers better find the replacement parts needed for a product," to "improve product delivery times," or to "reduce office staff voice message telephone tag communications." The Six Sigma process then can look at all operations in the enterprise, ranging from major to almost mundane.

The Six Sigma team would next create high-level process maps for each area reviewed, developed similar to the process maps described in Chapter 17. However, because Six Sigma improvements often emphasize activities outside of the enterprise, such as customers and suppliers, the analysis should cover their needs and requirements.

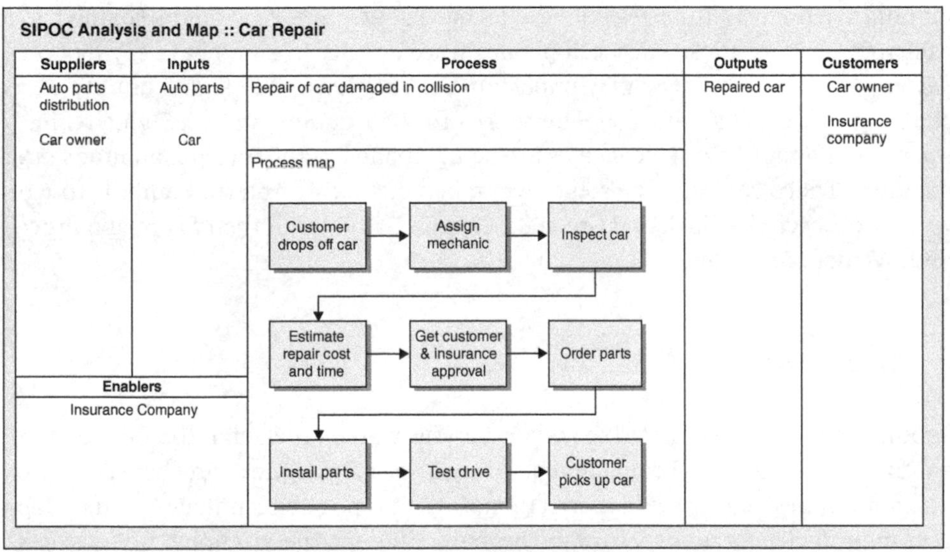

EXHIBIT 32.3 Six Sigma Example SIPOC Chart

Source: U.S. Army Business Transformations, www.army.mil/ArmyBTKC/focus/cpi/tools3_i1.htm#img.

Using Six Sigma terminology, a series of supplier-inputs-process-outputs-customer (SIPOC) charts should be created to describe the overall process. Exhibit 32.3 is an example SIPOC chart taken from a U.S. Army training document used to describe an automobile repair process.

Based on this *SIPOC analysis*, the Black Belts who performed the analysis should design and propose a Six Sigma process improvement project. Based on this proposal, an enterprise Six Sigma team should document opportunities to improvement, estimate the potential cost savings, and then identify a sponsor from the business area reviewed. Usually a senior manager from some area of operations will recognize potential savings and will take responsibility for the expected process improvements. The proposed project will then be reviewed and approved as an active Six Sigma project. The overall management of any Six Sigma project is similar to the project management processes discussed in Chapter 16.

Six Sigma projects follow the DMAIC steps of Define-Measure-Analyze-Improve-Control as illustrated in Exhibit 32.4. Six Sigma DMAIC project procedures represent a repetitive process based on an objective of constant improvement. The first steps of defining the project are particularly important. Project goals, potential rates of investment returns, and such expectations as customer or employee satisfaction levels should be defined. The steps of measuring, analyzing, and taking steps to improve the process follow. The final control steps call for the project team to implement and institutionalize the process improvements recommended and installed.

We have described Six Sigma here only at a very high level. To actually analyze and reengineer processes often requires very detailed mathematical and quantitative analysis procedures. Six Sigma procedures, as discussed, really got started many years ago in the United States through what was then Motorola's improved processes for the manufacturing of cellular telephones. We have now moved to far more sophisticated smartphones, but those early cell phones were even then small but very technical devices where quality was very important and achieving Six Sigma quality was a challenge. Internal auditors should work with their quality and Six Sigma teams to learn more about how the concepts are being applied in the internal auditor's organization. There can often be some strong benefits for an internal auditor to work with or observe the Black and Green Belt team's activities in their Six Sigma process improvement activities.

32.5 LEAN SIX SIGMA

Around the same time that Six Sigma processes were launched in the United States, another initiative called Lean manufacturing also started. The efforts here came from U.S. auto manufacturers who were attempting to replicate techniques used by Japanese manufacturers such as Toyota. The main difference between the two concepts is that Six Sigma emphasizes quality, while Lean manufacturing emphasizes the speed of production. Over time, these programs have somewhat merged together in the concept called *Lean Six Sigma*. This combined concept is based on the recognition by many industry leaders that you cannot do "just quality" or "just speed"; a balanced process is needed that can help an enterprise to focus on improving service quality, as defined by the customer within a set time limit. To cite one small but now older example, the July 2008 edition of *Fortune* magazine[3] contains an interview with Gary Reiner, then chief information officer of General Electric. One of the published questions was "What does Jeff Immelt [the CEO] want from you?" Reiner responded, "Three things. My responsibility for IT, Lean Six Sigma, and sourcing." The interview contains some other references to GE's use of the Lean Six Sigma technique.

The origins of what we call Lean manufacturing date back well into the twentieth century even though it wasn't called Lean then. The word *Lean* came from studies on the differences between some very successful Japanese carmakers and the traditional North American carmakers. The key thought processes within Lean are identifying "waste" or "non-value-added activities" from the customer perspective and then determining how to eliminate them effectively. Waste is defined as the activity or activities that a customer would not want to pay for and/or that add no value to the product or service from the customer's perspective.

The determination of *value* is a key concept behind Lean production or manufacturing. Value is defined as an item or feature for which a customer is willing to pay. All other aspects of the process are deemed waste. The Lean framework has been used as a tool to focus resources and energies on producing value-added features while identifying and eliminating non-value-added activities. Among other concepts, Lean production brought in an emphasis on improved quality assurance, manpower reductions, a focus on customer value, and the concept of just-in-time manufacturing. This latter concept holds that production materials should not be placed in stockrooms but introduced to the production process only when and as soon as needed.

For some time in the 1990s, Lean and Six Sigma had their own separate adherents, each arguing that one was better than the other. Eventually, specialists began to realize that Lean techniques alone cannot bring a process under the statistical controls that are so important in reducing exceptions. However, Six Sigma alone cannot dramatically improve process speeds or reduce the need for invested capital. Thus Lean Six Sigma was launched.

Lean Six Sigma uses many of the same tools and procedures we have discussed for Six Sigma. For example, a key component of any analysis here is the same basic DMAIC cycle approach shown in Exhibit 32.4. There is now much more emphasis on analyzing non-value-added components in a process and measuring process cycle efficiencies. The same Black and Green Belts still identify and develop process improvement projects. The overall difference is not just on reducing statistical error rates to six sigma levels but establishing dramatic improvements in process efficiency and eliminating waste in all levels of operations.

While efficiency improvements are sometimes hard to define with a strong set of statistical measures that form the backbone of Six Sigma, Lean Six Sigma also emphasizes improvements in the overall process value stream and the elimination of waste. Exhibit 32.5 contains some examples of process waste, some of the areas that Lean Six Sigma techniques attempt to reduce and that many internal auditors will see as potential areas for improvement.

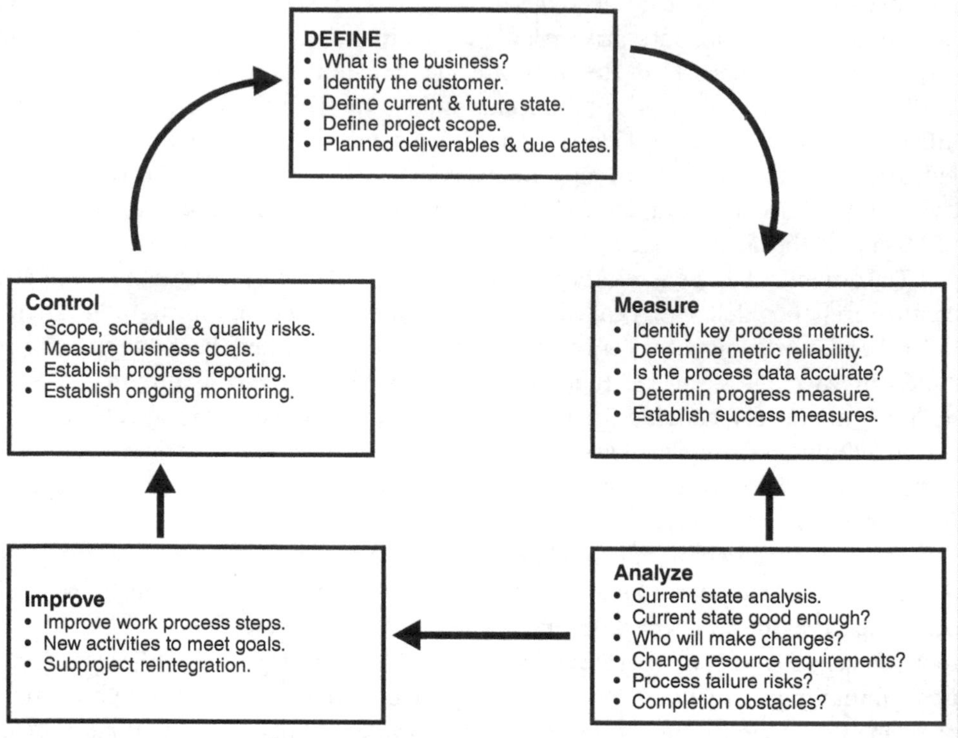

EXHIBIT 32.4 DMAIC Procedure for a Six Sigma Project

EXHIBIT 32.5 Examples of Lean Six Sigma Process Waste

Type of Waste	Process Improvement Waste Examples
Complexity	Unnecessary process or production steps, excessive or difficult to understand documentation, too many approval checkpoints.
Labor	Excessive headcount, ineffective operations, poorly trained personnel.
Overproduction	Producing more than customer demands or production in advance of customer needs.
Facility Space	Storage for inventory excess, parts awaiting disposition, production material waiting rework or scrap storage. Also, excessively wide aisles or other wasted, unused space.
Energy Resources	Wasted power requirements or demands for excessive human energy.
Process Defects	Repair, rework, multiple steps to resolve problems.
Materials	Scrap, ordering more than is needed.
Idle Materials	Excess inventory, material that does not match requirements.
Time	All human, machine, and IT processes that waste time.
Transportation	Movements of any sort that adds no value.
Safety Hazards	Unsafe or accident-prone environments.

Internal auditors learning about basic Six Sigma techniques may wonder what the differences are between it and Lean Six Sigma and why they should care. In many respects, some people in industry do not really understand the fine differences between the two and refer to everything described here as Six Sigma, whether Lean or not. Pure Six Sigma is much more statistically process-oriented, while the Lean approach emphasizes process improvements and the elimination of waste. When an internal auditor visits an auditee who claims they are implementing Six Sigma, it is often sufficient to know of these differences in approach. The next sections talk about auditing Six Sigma processes, but our references essentially cover both regular as well as Lean Six Sigma.

32.6 AUDITING SIX SIGMA PROCESSES

Internal auditors frequently encounter major Six Sigma initiatives at auditee locations. This has been particularly true for manufacturing-related operations, but it is becoming increasingly common in other areas of operations, such as financial service processing. Six Sigma has been beyond the sphere of interest for most IIA-heritage internal auditors. For example, we mentioned earlier that the IIA web site at the time of our publication contained only minimal internal auditor references to Six Sigma. Also, because Six Sigma operations are often structured as a special project outside of normal organization charts, many times they do not appear or are not a consideration when building an audit universe and developing internal audit plans. This is a deficiency that needs to be corrected for many internal auditors.

While a properly organized and structured Six Sigma project can bring some significant benefit to an enterprise, it can also quickly become an expensive and even risky undertaking if not well managed and controlled. While the benefits from a Six Sigma program should be strong, problems can develop due some of the following issues:

- **Limited project management.** Six Sigma requires well-thought-out projects with good objectives and detailed planning. These can sometimes be missed when Six Sigma teams work on these projects along with their regular work duties.
- **Poor budget controls.** The excitement of launching a Six Sigma effort can create an almost open-checkbook environment where no attention is given to costs because it is "Six Sigma." Projects sometimes will lack strong project management controls.
- **Limited supporting documentation.** Concepts such as Lean encourage professionals to trim down on the paperwork supporting Six Sigma results, and requirements here are very different from internal auditor supporting materials. Nevertheless, there always should be some level of documentation to corroborate Six Sigma results.
- **Failures to coordinate Six Sigma efforts.** There always will be a risk that multiple Six Sigma teams operate at almost cross-purposes among themselves and within normal enterprise operations. There is often a need for some multiproject program management.

Our comments here are not to criticize Six Sigma efforts but to highlight that in the frequent enthusiasm to launch such an initiative, matters can get almost out of control themselves. Internal audit can sometimes provide a strong service to overall management by scheduling an internal controls review of either the overall enterprise Six Sigma effort or of individual larger projects.

When planning to schedule a review of Six Sigma efforts, internal audit will often find that it is in danger of entering a minefield. Six Sigma proponents will argue that the overall effort is designed to promote efficiency within the enterprise and any internal audit efforts may only hamper things. Internal audit needs to point out its overall objective to review internal controls and its ability to assess the overall quality of such a program. Six Sigma efforts often take place primarily on the factory floor, while internal audit may be more corporate headquarters–oriented. Internal audit needs to bridge that gap.

A strong internal auditor understanding of the Six Sigma process should be an internal auditor CBOK general knowledge requirement. An internal auditor launching a review in this area, however, may very well encounter a comment along the lines of "I'm a Black Belt. What do you know about Six Sigma that qualifies you to audit me?" This, of course, is the same situation that an internal auditor will encounter in many areas, whether launching a review of an IT function or a specialized financial area. Through reading, general studies, and discussions with quality auditors, internal audit should exhibit enough knowledge of Six Sigma processes to have a general understanding of this area. However, any internal audit should be based on a good general assessment of the internal controls environment in that area, whether Six Sigma or any other.

Exhibit 32.6 contains some internal audit procedures for a review of an enterprise Six Sigma program. While many operational reviews, particularly in manufacturing or process areas, may cover specific Six Sigma projects, the review in Exhibit 32.6 might best be focused on the overall program, with an emphasis on project management processes, as discussed in Chapter 16, as well as general budget and financial controls covering the project. Depending on the nature and scope of the overall Six Sigma program, internal audit may want to either observe or participate in one or more selected Six Sigma projects. Properly executed, an internal audit review of an enterprise Six Sigma project should help to strengthen and add increased importance to the overall Six Sigma project.

32.7 SIX SIGMA IN INTERNAL AUDIT OPERATIONS

Six Sigma is a process to increase customer satisfaction by dramatically reducing the number of process exceptions. It has its origins in high-production-level manufacturing operations, such as smartphones. Lean Six Sigma is more process-oriented and has found use in high-volume financial services operations. However, there is no reason why some of these Six Sigma concepts cannot be directly implemented in internal audit operations. As was discussed in Chapter 9 on internal audit standards, there is a strong requirement for internal audit to establish effective quality assurance standards. Effective quality assurance can be enhanced by establishing Six Sigma–like programs to

EXHIBIT 32.6 Internal Audit Procedures for a Review of a Six Sigma Program

1. Plan and schedule the audit.
   a. Establish high-level objectives for the review
   b. Confirm planned review with audit committee, senior management, and persons responsible for Six Sigma activities.
   c. Arrange for Six Sigma training for audit staff members performing the review.
   d. Schedule audit per normal internal audit planning cycle.
2. Review and understand Six Sigma organization.
   a. Understand Six Sigma organization and meet with director to understand recent achievements and current projects.
   b. Understand the number and responsibilities of Master, Black, and Green Belts assigned to Six Sigma projects.
      i. Determine that adequate procedures are in place for belt certifications.
      ii. Review adequacy of Six Sigma team operating procedures for such areas as documentation of reviews, testing procedures, and documentation requirements.
   c. Review and assesses adequacy of Six Sigma budgeting processes in place and asses reasons for any significant variances.
   d. Review overall effectiveness of the Six Sigma deployment, including supporting systems, communications processes, and recognition systems.
3. Review and assess Six Sigma project management processes
   a. Review procedures for developing, planning, and managing Six Sigma projects to determine they are consistent with good project management procedures (see Chapter 14).
   b. Determine that appropriate objectives, such as cost per unit measures, have been established and are monitored in Six Sigma projects.
   c. On a sample basis, review project documentation for completed Six Sigma projects to determine adequacy and completeness of processes.
   d. Determine that adequate procedures are in place for reporting the progress and results of Six Sigma projects to the overall enterprise.
4. Select one or more completed Six Sigma projects and assess whether adequate attention was given to DMAIC steps for each selected project.
   a. Define steps. The objectives of each project should be clearly defined along with an analysis of the current state, planned future state, due dates, and deliverables.
   b. Measure steps. Key metrics should be established along with processes to use those metrics to achieve project success.
   c. Analyze steps. Evidence should be in place to determine that current state benchmarks were established as well as measurement results that will point to measurable process improvements.
   d. Improvement steps. Processes should be in place, including measurement tools, to implement suggested improvements or approaches.
   e. Control steps for new processes. Measurement steps should be in place to demonstrate new process is working as predicted, or if not, to revise for the next round of improvements.
5. Assess adequacy and completeness of Six Sigma deployment.
   a. Where appropriate, review the adequacy of selected completed Six Sigma projects for their emphasis on:
      i. Asset utilization improvements
      ii. Profit and revenue improvements
      iii. Service and customer relationship improvements
      iv. Product introduction and process improvements
   5.2. Determine that adequate processes are in place to analyze results and initiate corrective actions.
   5.3. One a sample basis, select several Six Sigma projects that have been recently implemented and assess if objectives have been adequately met.
6. Determine that adequate communication tools are in place to report results of Six Sigma work to all constituents.

better monitor performance, reduce exceptions, and improve the overall quality of internal audit operations.

Because almost every scheduled internal audit will be different, many of the Six Sigma principles discussed in this chapter will not apply to regular internal audit operations. However, the basic Six Sigma concepts of closely monitoring activities and eliminating errors and exceptions are very important. For example, both on an internal audit department and individual level, a strong emphasis should be placed on accurately planning internal audit start and completion dates, including the issuance of audit reports, and a major emphasis should be given to meeting or bettering those dates. Similarly, a strong no-errors emphasis should be placed on the accuracy of all audit findings and reported results. These actions will improve the overall quality of internal audit activities and will help to let others in the enterprise realize that internal audit is following Six Sigma principles.

Six Sigma, and in particular Lean Six Sigma, has been a major initiative at many enterprises worldwide for some years. With many demonstrated success stories surrounding it, we can only expect to see more of the initiative to improve customer service and massively reduce errors and exceptions. While they probably will not have Black or Green Belt levels of knowledge, internal auditors should develop a broad general CBOK understanding of Six Sigma principles. In this way, they can demonstrate a knowledge and understanding of this important concept in much of their internal audit activities.

NOTES

1. The Malcolm Baldrige National Quality Award is a national quality award that recognizes U.S. organizations in the business, health care, education, and nonprofit sectors for performance excellence. Find more information at www.nist.gov.
2. This exhibit contains references to some quality assurance terminology, such as fishbone and Ishikawa techniques, that is not included in this book. A Web search will provide more background information on any of them.
3. "Information Worth Billions," *Fortune* 158, no. 2 (July 21, 2008), 73.

CHAPTER THIRTY-THREE

ISO and Worldwide Internal Audit Standards

As we have summarized in earlier chapters, the Sarbanes-Oxley Act (SOx) is a U.S. law that was enacted in response to a spate of financial frauds in U.S. corporations at the turn of this century. Although U.S corporations such as Enron and WorldCom captured much of the attention, a non-U.S. corporation was involved too: Tyco, with its headquarters in Bermuda. Tyco, whose CEO was involved in flagrant financial excesses, was really a U.S. corporation that had recently transferred its corporate registration to Bermuda for tax purposes. At the time, journalists and politicians elsewhere in the world and particularly in European Union countries tut-tutted that this financial fraud was a U.S. problem. They particularly resented the SEC's plans to impose SOx rules on international corporations whose securities were registered in U.S. exchanges.

It did not take long to realize that the United States was not alone in regard to financial fraud. In February 2003, the major Dutch food distributor Royal Ahold admitted an "accounting irregularity" of some $500 million. Ahold had operations throughout the world and was found to have misstated its accounting and financial records to show better results. Also, a Sri Lankan–born billionaire businessman, Sanjay Kumar, former chief of a California-based company called Computer Associates International, was sentenced to 12 years in prison and fined $8 million for securities fraud and obstruction of justice.[1]

In addition and at about the same time, a corruption trial was initiated in France against some 37 people from the major oil company Elf Aquitaine, who were accused of siphoning off over $400 million of corporate funds through the 1990s.[2] The CEO was the main miscreant there. When asked at the trial to justify his use of Elf corporate funds for the purchase of a $9.3 million Paris mansion, a country chateau, and $4.5 million for a personal divorce settlement after 18 months of marriage, the ex-CEO stated, "I allowed myself to get carried away." As this book goes to press, similar financial fraud scandals are being investigated at the national petroleum exploration companies in both

Brazil and Mexico. The United States is very much not alone in experiencing corporate accounting scandals.

This chapter, however, will primarily look at financial internal control standards from an international perspective and will provide an overview of what the English-speaking world calls *International Auditing Standards*, a set of guidance applicable worldwide. Many professionals have seen the words "ISO Registered" in brochures and other advertising materials. While the United States often pushes its standards on the rest of the world, the International Organization for Standardization (known as ISO; www.iso.org) is responsible for issuing standards and guidelines in many businesses and technology areas. This chapter will discuss several ISO standards that are important to internal auditors.

A basic common body of knowledge (CBOK) understanding of ISO standards is important for internal auditors worldwide. ISO compliance is important for today's global economy, and internal audit can help to assure effective ISO compliance. This chapter introduces some ISO standards that are significant for internal auditors, the ISO registration process, and ISO quality audits.

33.1 ISO STANDARDS BACKGROUND

In the years following World War II, the United States emerged as the worldwide economic and political leader. Due to this dominance, many in the United States all but ignored the commercial best practice standards developed and used elsewhere in our globally connected economy. These international best practice standards are collaborative efforts that take into account a wide range of national needs and requirements. The source of many of these standards is the ISO, an international body based in Geneva, Switzerland, that has issued well-recognized standards covering a wide range of areas, ranging from specifications for fastener machine screw threads in an automobile engine, to the thickness of a personal credit card, to information technology (IT) quality standards. These standards have been expanded over the years to cover many areas that are important for enterprise governance and quality.

Senior enterprise executives should have an understanding of the role of any ISO standards that are appropriate in their business. This chapter will review three of these standards that are important for effective IT governance practices. After a background discussion of how ISO standards are developed and why they are important, we will look first at the international standard called ISO 9000. While not focused on IT governance issues specially, the principles outlined in this standard have encouraged many enterprises on a worldwide basis to build and continually implement quality practices in their manufacturing and other business processes.

ISO standards are developed through the collaborative efforts of many national standards-setting organizations such as the American National Standards Institute or other similar groups throughout the world. The standards-setting process gets itself started with a generally recognized need for a standard in some area. An example would be ISO 27001, which outlines the high-level requirements for an effective information security management system. The ISO 27001 standard was developed through the efforts of several international technical committees sponsored by ISO in cooperation with the International Electrotechnical Commission international standards-setting group. The standard is not specific in its detailed requirements but contains many high-level statements along the lines of "the organization shall . . ."

Because of the numerous international governmental authorities, professional groups, and individual experts involved in the ISO standards-setting process, the building and approval of any ISO document is typically a long and slow process. An expert committee develops an initial draft standard covering some area, it is sent out for review and comment with a review response due date, and the ISO committee then goes back to review draft comments before either issuing the new standard or sending a revised draft out for yet another round of reviews and suggested changes. Typically, after many drafts and comment periods, the ISO standard will be published. Enterprises can then take the necessary steps to comply with the standard, but to certify their compliance they must contract with a certified outside auditor, with skills in that standard, to attest to their compliance. This standards-setting process is similar to what happened for the release of the *COSO internal control framework*, discussed in Chapter 3, from its initial draft, released in December 2011, to the lengthy exposure draft and comment period following the final, revised internal control framework released 2013.

Many U.S. enterprises first got involved with these international standards through the launch of ISO 9000 quality management system standards in the 1980s. Companies at that time were faced with the high-quality design standards found in many non-U.S. products, such as Japanese automobiles. Japanese manufacturers then had designed many high-quality products following what became the ISO 9000 standards, and U.S. manufacturers finally began to step up to the plate by modifying their own processes to comply with these higher product quality standards. Compliance with the ISO 9000 standards allowed worldwide enterprises to design their operations in accordance with a single, consistent standard and then to assert that they have a quality management system in place in accordance with the international standard. ISO standards are published and controlled by the ISO organization in Geneva following strict copyright rules. These are not the kinds of materials that can be downloaded through a casual Web search; they must be purchased. Many of the actual ISO standards are just very detailed outlines of practices to be followed.

ISO standards contain much more content and details than the COSO internal control framework in Chapter 4 or the ITIL® recommended best practices in Chapter 19 of this book. They represent performance measures for an enterprise and its peers. These are worldwide standards that will allow an enterprise to hold itself out and qualify that it is operating in accordance with a consistent international standard. Although there are many different standards to select, ISO 13485 on quality management regulatory requirements for medical devices provides an example. This ISO standard defines the quality requirements covering human health care devices. For example, the standard calls for an enterprise manufacturing such devices to establish appropriate calibration controls. Because of the diversity of different calibration approaches, the standard cannot specify just one approach but only that enterprises should have appropriate mechanisms in place.

It is one thing for an enterprise to read an ISO standard and change its processes to follow it; they must demonstrate to others, such as customers and trading partners, that they are following the standard. In order to attest to their compliance to an ISO standard, an enterprise must contract with an authorized outside reviewer to assess the enterprise's adherence to that standard. This ISO certification is a process somewhat similar to an external audit of financial records performed by certified public accountants (CPAs). Financial statement audits in the United States require a licensed CPA external auditor to assess whether an enterprise's financial reports are "fairly stated," following good internal controls and recognized accounting standards. Those good internal controls, of course, are outlined in the COSO internal control framework. When either an investor or the Securities and Exchange Commission (SEC) finds such a signed external audit report along with the final reported results, there is a level of assurance that these financial reports are fairly stated and are based on good internal control procedures.

The ISO certification process also is similar to a CPA-led U.S. financial audit that is based on compliance with generally accepted auditing standards (GAAS) performed by a major public accounting firm. While we do not have a "Big 4" set of major ISO auditing firms in the United States, national standards-setting organizations qualify outside reviewers to perform external audits of various ISO standards. There is no ISO GAAS, however, but a wide degree of diversity in audit objectives since a reviewer for ISO 27001 on IT security management systems will be looking for different control procedures than would an ISO auditor for ISO 13485 on medical device quality management systems. In all cases, however, the qualified ISO outside auditor may identify areas for corrective actions and publish a report to management similar to the internal audit processes discussed in other chapters. Once the ISO auditor's recommendations are corrected, the outside reviewer will certify that the enterprise is in compliance with that standard.

Once certified, the enterprise can advertise to the outside world that they have an effective process in place that meets a specific ISO standard. For example, a customer for a medical diagnostic device would want to know if a potential supplier of such a medical device product is in compliance with ISO 13485. That same medical device manufacturer would also want to gain assurance that its prime component suppliers are similarly ISO qualified.

33.2 ISO STANDARDS OVERVIEW

Compliance with appropriate ISO standards is not the same level of requirement for an enterprise as is the need for an audited financial statement. Because of SEC financial reporting rules, the lack of an audited financial report or a report with an unfavorable auditor's opinion can be devastating for a publicly traded enterprise. While virtually all publicly traded enterprises are expected to have audited financial statements, the rules are not the same regarding compliance with ISO standards. In most instances, compliance with an ISO standard is voluntary but still often essential. We have cited the ISO standard covering the thickness and size of a personal credit card as an example. An enterprise that manufactured either cards or card readers that were not in compliance with such a standard would soon fail in the marketplace.

ISO standards covering quality management systems are a bit different. An enterprise can all but ignore a standard such as ISO 9000 calling for a quality management process and still succeed within a national marketplace. For example, in the United States some senior managers had historically looked at this ISO 9000 standard as requiring "too much paperwork" and only made minimal efforts to achieve compliance for some of these standards. However, as we move to a more worldwide business trading environment, many enterprises request such certification today. What was once just nice to have and yet carried the perception of needing too much documentation to obtain, has become almost mandatory in the United States for manufacturing and other enterprises.

Internal auditors should learn more about the status of any applicable ISO standards compliance within their enterprises or areas of internal audit activity. Some ISO standards, such as defining the thread pattern on a bolt or the thickness of a credit card, have become essentially mandatory and an enterprise would not be in business if it did not follow them. All too often, responsibility for ISO compliance standards is several levels down into the organization chain in engineering or quality assurance and may be viewed as too technically detailed by some members of management.

There is not a single ISO standard that is comparable to the COSO internal control framework, but several important standards that cover areas that support the COSO framework. The sections following outline several ISO areas where compliance with that standard will very much support adherence to the COSO framework.

ISO 9001 Quality Management Systems

ISO standards have a heritage dating back to World War II when both sides in the conflict required strong product uniformity while operating at extremely high levels of production volume. Even if the products produced were bullets and bombs, they still had to work correctly and there was a need for strict product quality control. The results on the Western Allies' side were some strong quality assurance standard procedures and the emergence of industrial engineers and production quality control specialists. After the war, the ISO was established as part of the General Agreement on Trade and Tariffs, one of the international agreements to bring the world into a peacetime environment. ISO 9000 on quality management systems was one of the earlier ISO standards. This international standard first received most of its attention in the newly recovering European countries.

Japan was another rebuilding and recovering postwar country that had strongly embraced quality management systems. In the 1950s and 1960s, the Japanese invited a series of U.S.-based quality systems experts such as Frederick Deming and others to help at many of their plants in Japan. In many instances, these quality systems experts were often all but ignored in the United States. However, their philosophies and techniques were heavily embraced by Japanese industry, and by the mid-1970s Japanese electronic and automobile manufacturers began to make deep inroads into U.S. markets due to the quality and value of their products. Despite its then dominant product offerings and market advantages, the United States began to recognize that these Japanese-manufactured products were superior in many respects to its own. ISO 9000 quality standards became an increasingly important factor measuring and assessing the quality of products worldwide.

ISO 9000 is not just one standards document but a family of standards for quality management systems. Maintained by ISO, these standards include requirements for such matters as:

- Monitoring processes to ensure they are effective
- Keeping adequate records
- Checking output for defects, with appropriate corrective action where necessary
- Regularly reviewing individual processes and the quality system for effectiveness
- Facilitating continual improvement

Each list item refers to processes, not specific actions. However, for enterprises to assert that they are in compliance with ISO 9000 (actually 9001), for example, that they are monitoring their key processes to be effective, they often must make significant changes to their management procedures and supporting documentation. It also creates a required level of expectation. Any enterprise, on a worldwide scope, that holds to such standards is stating that it has effective quality systems in place. A company or organization that has been independently audited and certified to be in conformance with ISO 9001, for example, may publicly state that it is "ISO 9001 certified" or "ISO 9001 registered." Certification to an ISO 9000 standard does not guarantee the compliance (and therefore the quality) of end products and services; rather, it certifies that consistent business and production processes are being applied.

The actual certification is achieved through a review by a registered ISO auditor certified for the particular ISO standard. As discussed, this process is similar to the CPA's review and certified audit of an enterprise's financial statements or a special internal audit specifically requested by the audit committee. Regulated by their national standards organizations, ISO auditors are authorized to register an enterprise's compliance with unique ISO standards.

ISO 9000, as well as other ISO standards, imposes heavy documentation requirements on an enterprise and certainly more than would be expected under the COSO internal control framework. It is not sufficient for an enterprise to just claim some process has been once documented. There must be an ongoing process to keep that documentation current over time. In past years, many enterprises went through one-time efforts to create documentation and then never kept it current. This is the kind of situation that many internal auditors have faced. Auditors frequently ask if some system or process they are reviewing is documented, and are met with an admission that the documentation is out of date or nonexistent. This lack of documentation would often become a minor audit report finding that would result in little definitive corrective action. ISO 9000 compliance raises documentation requirements for quality processes to a whole new level. An outside reviewer must certify that the enterprise and its supporting documentation are in compliance in order to show the outside world that the enterprise is following the ISO standard.

To clarify, ISO 9000 is not just one standard but really a series of "certifiable" standards and guidelines:

- ISO 9001: Certifiable standard dealing with design
- ISO 9002: Certifiable standard dealing with manufacturing

- ISO 9003: Certifiable standard dealing with manufacturing and assembly
- ISO 9004: Guideline defining a quality system

These standards are periodically updated, and updates are reflected in the name of the standard; for example, the current version of ISO 9001 is known as ISO 9001:2008, which means it was last updated in 2008. A few years into the future the current version may be ISO 9001:20XX, but we do not anticipate any significant changes to a strong standard. To add to the complexity of things, an enterprise can claim that it is only in compliance with an earlier version, ISO 9000:1994, and there is also the Quality Standard, or QS 9000 series of standards that are similar but pertain to just the automobile industry. A certifiable standard means it is subject to review by an outside ISO auditor, as discussed previously.

ISO 9000 is a set of standards for a continual improvement–driven quality system, no matter whether it is a manufactured component or a service process. Exhibit 33.1 shows such a quality management system process that is driven by internal procedures for ongoing improvements as well as customer requests. This is a continual process where existing processes should be monitored, actions planned for improvements, and the action items implemented for subsequent monitoring and further improvements. These are really the type of processes that should be in place when establishing and monitoring COSO internal controls and establishing an effective COSO control environment. IT systems development professionals have used essentially the same continual improvement quality processes ever since the early days of IT, in what was called the systems development life cycle (SDLC), as highlighted in Chapter 22, to develop new IT systems. However, many SDLC-developed application processes in older days called for a major amount documentation

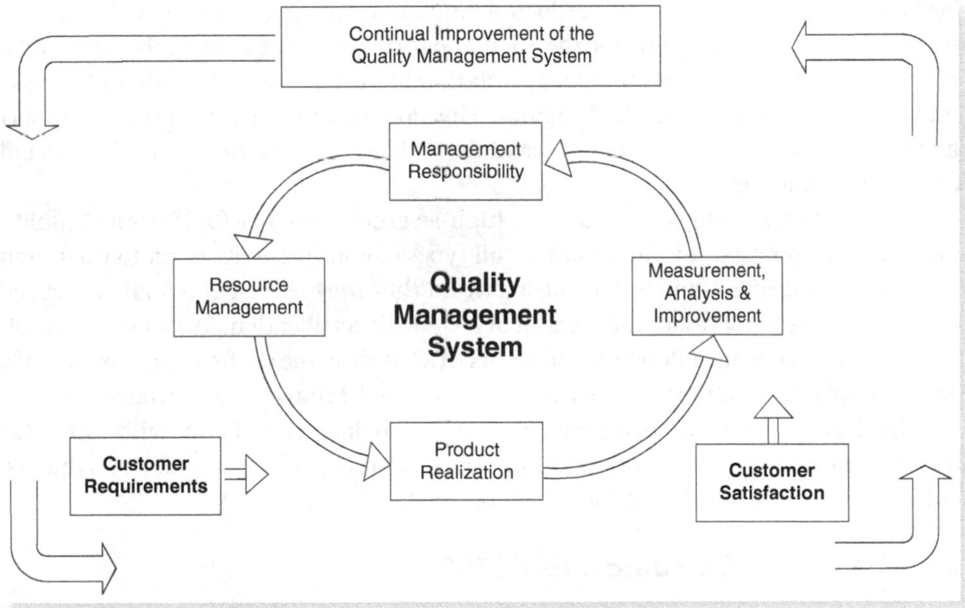

EXHIBIT 33.1 Quality Management System Processes

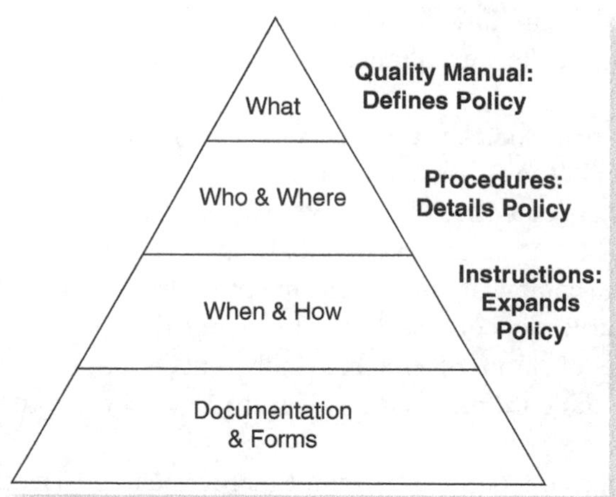

EXHIBIT 33.2 ISO Documentation Hierarchy

that was often ignored. Today, many IT applications are developed through more informal and iterative rapid application development processes. In either case, the documentation is an important part of the COSO internal control framework.

Solid and accurate documentation is extremely important for an enterprise seeking to claim ISO registration. ISO registration is a global requirement, and, for example, when ISO 9001:2000 section 4.2.3 states, among other provisions, that "A documented procedure should be established to define the controls needed," along with such subsections as "a) to approve documents for adequacy of issue," an enterprise or process documentation control system is needed to demonstrate compliance with that standard. ISO best practices call for a hierarchy of documentation in any area, starting with top-level manuals to explain the *whys*, and then down to instructions describing the *hows* of the practice. Exhibit 33.2 shows this documentation hierarchy with "Records and Forms" providing proof at the base of this matter. This documentation is essential to support a quality management system and certainly will be a requirement to ISO's external certification auditors.

This section has only provided a very high-level description of the ISO 9000 quality management process. It is important for all types of enterprises to assert to their own internal management and to the outside world that they represent a quality-focused enterprise. Just to represent the breadth of ISO 9000 certification, in 1995 the American Institute of Certified Public Accountants (AICPA) became the first major worldwide professional organization to become ISO 9001 certified. From an internal audit perspective, the IIA has made no such compliance efforts to date. Compliance with ISO 9000 does not mean compliance with COSO internal controls, and vice versa. Nevertheless, enterprises at all levels should consider adopting ISO 9000 processes.

ISO IT Security Standards: ISO 27002

ISO 27002 is an IT-related security standard designed to help any enterprise that needs to establish a comprehensive information security management program or improve its current information security practices. The ISO 27002 is a standard about both information and information security in a general and all-inclusive sense and similar to the Information and Communication component of COSO internal controls. Since such information can exist in many forms, the standard takes a very broad approach and includes a wide range of security standards covering security regarding:

- Data and software electronic files
- All formats of paper documents, including printed materials, handwritten notes, and even photographs
- Video and audio recordings
- Telephone conversations as well as e-mail, fax, video, and other forms of messages

The concept here is that all forms of information have a value and need to be protected just like any other corporate asset. Many enterprises today do not even consider security standards in many of these other broad areas, but the ISO standard suggests they should be covered when appropriate. In addition, the infrastructure that supports this information, including networks, systems, and functions, must also be protected from a wide range of threats including everything from human error and equipment failure to theft, fraud, vandalism, sabotage, fire, flood, and even terrorism. Similar to all other ISO standards, this published standard does not really prescribe what is specifically required but outlines areas where there are requirements for security-related standards.

As a first step to implementing ISO 27002, an enterprise should identify its own information security needs and requirements. This requires performing an information security risk assessment along the lines of the COSO Enterprise Risk Management processes discussed in Chapter 7. Such an assessment should focus on the identification of major security threats and vulnerabilities as well as an assessment of how likely it is that each will cause a security incident. This process should help to pinpoint an enterprise's unique information security needs and requirements.

Too often missed in getting ready for the ISO 27002 information security standards-setting process is that an enterprise should identify and understand all of the legal, statutory, regulatory, and contractual requirements that the organization, its trading partners, contractors, and service providers must meet. This requires an understanding and identification of an enterprise's unique legal information security needs and requirements.

ISO 27002 is an international standard meant for any enterprise that uses internal or external IT systems, possesses confidential data, depends on IT to carry out its business activities, or simply wishes to adopt a higher level of security by complying with a standard. Although a relatively new standard and not in common application, at least in the United States, ISO 27002 constitutes a mark of confidence in an enterprise's overall security, in a like manner that ISO 9000 has become a guarantee of quality. Compliance should promote an increased level of mutual confidence between partners, where each can attest that they have established security standards according to a recognized set of standards. ISO 27002 is a structured and internationally recognized methodology that should help an enterprise to develop better management of information security on a continuing basis. It is a code of practice that supports the information security management systems requirements of the related security standard, ISO 27001. Internal auditors should be aware of this standard and its relative level of implementation in an audit's enterprise.

IT Security Technique Requirements: ISO 27001

While ISO 27002 covers security controls, ISO 27001 is what ISO defines as a "specification" for what ISO calls an Information Security Management System (ISMS). That is, this standard is designed to measure, monitor, and control security management from a top-down perspective. The standard essentially explains how to apply ISO 27002 and defines its implementation as a six-part process as follows:

1. **Define a security policy.** A fundamental component of any standard is the need for a formal, senior management–approved policy statement. All other compliance aspects of the standard will be measured against this policy statement.
2. **Define the scope of the ISMS.** ISO 27002 defines security in rather broad terms that may not be appropriate or needed for all enterprises. Having defined a high-level security policy, an enterprise needs to define the scope of ISMS that it will implement. For example, ISO 27002 defines an element of its security requirements as video and audio recordings. This may not be necessary for an enterprise, and thus would be even specifically excluded from its ISMS scope.
3. **Undertake a risk assessment.** The enterprise should identify a risk assessment methodology that is suited to its ISMS environment and then develop criteria both for accepting risks and for defining what constitutes acceptable levels of risk.
4. **Manage the risk.** This is a major process that includes formal risk identification, risk analysis, and options for the treatment of those risks. The latter can include applying appropriate risk avoidance controls, accepting risks, taking other steps to avoid them, or transferring the risks to other parties such as insurers or suppliers.
5. **Select control objectives and controls to be implemented.** This is the same internal control process discussed in Chapters 3 and 4 on the COSO internal control environment. For each defined control objective, the enterprise should define an appropriate internal controls procedure.
6. **Prepare a statement of applicability.** This is the formal documentation that is necessary to wrap up the ISMS documentation process. Such documentation matches up control objectives with procedures to manage and implement the ISMS. From an internal audit perspective, this step is close to a final audit report.

As can be seen from these six outlined steps, risk analysis and security policies are fundamental to this ISO standard. While setting up these practices are not normal internal audit attest matters, internal management can provide strong help to enterprise management by offering to serve as an internal consultant and help in performing adequate risk assessment procedures.

Because of strict ISO copyright rules, we have not supplied any extracts of the ISO 27001 text or any other ISO standards in this chapter. The actual ISO standard documents are available for purchase through the Web and are presented in tight and unambiguous text. There is little specific detail, but enough to allow an enterprise to implement its ISMS. Each formal standard concludes with an Appendix section listing control procedures for each of the objective details in the standard. However, ISO 27001 should not be considered as a comprehensive set of control procedures that will change as technology changes but rather as an outline for the framework of ISMS that should be continually implemented, monitored, and maintained.

ISO 27002 and ISO 27001 are global standards, with established compliance and certification schemes in place, particularly in the United Kingdom and the European Union as a whole. Both of these standards will continue to evolve, to track technology, and will expand with even wider changes. The COBIT framework, discussed in Chapter 6, is tied closely with ISO 27002, and these ISO standards will continue to grow and their influence and adoption will continue to expand.

Service Quality Management: ISO 2000

While internal auditors are often looking for standards to support their recommendations, many other business professionals will agree that we live in a world with too many standards, many of which are similar to others with like objectives but are not connected to each other. ISO 2000 on service quality management introduces some of this much-needed standards convergence. This is an international standard for IT service management, and it introduces many of the ITIL® service management best practices that were discussed in Chapter 19. ISO 2000 consists of a Part I on implementing service management, and a Part II describing best practices for service management. Part I of this standard specifies the need for a series of service management documented processes, such as defining requirements for implementing such a management system, new or changed service requirements, and documented relationship, control, resolution, and release processes. Quite correctly, the standard takes the best practices approach of ITIL® and calls for formal documented processes to support them.

ISO 2000 calls for an enterprise to adopt and be certified that it has adopted the ITIL® best practices discussed in Chapter 19. Formally, this standard "promotes the adoption of an integrated process approach to effectively deliver managed services to meet the business and customer requirements." ISO 2000 is a global standard for IT service management, and is fully compatible with and supportive of the ITIL® framework. Although a newer standard, it will undoubtedly have a significant impact on the use and acceptance of ITIL® best practices and the whole IT service management landscape.

In future years, both enterprise management and internal audit in particular should see a growing level of recognition on the importance of ISO service-related standards. In our increasingly global economy, no matter what national restrictions may be imposed across borders from time to time, internal standards are needed to define common practices and to better facilitate communication. When an enterprise or service organization, anywhere in the world, has achieved ISO 9000 quality management certification, customers and users can expect a certain minimum level of documentation and process standards. The ISO 27001 IT security standards should soon reach a similar level of importance and recognition. With our comments on ISO 2000 on ITIL® and ISO 9000's similarities with SOx, we should see increasing convergence trends between ISO and standards in other areas. Internal auditors at all levels should understand and embrace these important ISO standards.

33.3 ISO 38500 IT GOVERNANCE STANDARD

ISO standards are developed and then issued in areas where there is a perceived need for best practices guidance on an international level. Sometimes these standards are released when there is a strong commercial need for product standardization. Our previously discussed ISO standard covering the size of consumer credit and debit payment cards is an example here. In the early days of consumer credit cards, they were issued in slightly different sizes, numbering schemes, and other factors. Standards of worldwide interchangeability were needed to promote e-commerce, and an ISO standard was released. In some other cases, ISO standards represent best practices where compliance is necessary for commercial purposes. Our previous discussion on ISO 9000 quality standards is an example of this. Virtually every product manufacturing enterprise today that wants to compete on an international basis must be certified to be in compliance with ISO 9000 quality management system standards.

While some ISO standards have been in place for many years, ISO 38500 on IT governance is relatively new, having been released after a long development period in 2008. It also has not received a great of a level of international attention at present, although the current versions of COBIT, discussed in Chapter 6, will incorporate ISO 38500 principles. In addition to the COSO internal control framework and principles discussed in Chapters 3 and 4, COBIT in Chapter 6, and ITIL® best practices in Chapter 19, ISO 38500 is another framework to help support effective IT governance practices for an enterprise. The standard to date has been released at a very high level, and more detailed sections and guidance are sure to follow. This section will provide a description of ISO 38500 and how it can help an internal auditor better understand the importance of effective IT governance practices.

ISO 38500 Objectives

This standard provides a framework of principles for both internal auditors and senior managers to use when evaluating, directing, and monitoring the use of IT in their enterprise. This should assist reviewers to understand and fulfill their legal, regulatory, and ethical obligations in respect of their enterprise's use of IT. The framework comprises definitions, principles, and a governance model with the objectives of:

- Providing assurances to all enterprise stakeholders that they can have confidence in their organization's corporate governance of IT
- Informing and guiding senior managers in governing the use of IT in their organization
- Providing a basis for the objective evaluation of the corporate governance of IT

ISO 38500 is also intended to guide those involved in designing and implementing senior management systems on effective policies and processes that support IT governance. That is, while its guidance refers to more senior-level management, all professionals involved with designing, implementing, managing, or reviewing an IT process should give some consideration to these broad standards.

This standard applies to the governance of IT management and decision processes that are controlled by IT specialists within the organization, by external service providers, or by other enterprise business units. The standard's objective is to provide guidance to IT professionals advising, informing, or assisting senior executives, including:

- Senior managers
- Members of groups monitoring the resources within the organization
- External business or technical specialists, such as internal auditors or legal staff
- Specialists, retail associations, or professional bodies
- Vendors of hardware, software, communications, and other IT products
- Internal and external service providers (including IT consultants)
- IT auditors

The objectives and scope outlined here are fairly broad and extensive for a relatively small and new standard. However, there are some major general principles buried in its current text, and we can expect to see much more detailed supporting definitions and guidance on ISO 38500 in future years.

The ISO 38500 Framework and IT Governance

The standard sets out six principles for good IT governance that are applicable to most enterprises. These principles express a preferred behavior to guide IT governance–related decision making. That is, a statement of each principle refers to what should happen, but does not prescribe how, when, or by whom the principles would be implemented, as these aspects are dependent on the nature of the organization implementing the principles. The standard is not drafted in the form of a set of internal audit control objectives but outlines principles important for a well-managed IT function.

- **Principle 1: Responsibility.** Individuals and groups within the enterprise should understand and accept their responsibilities in respect to both supply of and demand for IT services and resources. Those with responsibility for actions also have the authority to perform those actions.
- **Principle 2: Strategy.** An enterprise's business strategy should take into account the current and future capabilities of IT; these strategic plans for IT should satisfy the current and ongoing needs of the enterprise's business strategy.
- **Principle 3: Acquisition.** IT component or resource acquisitions should be made for valid reasons, on the basis of an appropriate and ongoing analysis, with clear and transparent decision making. There should be an appropriate balance between benefits, opportunities, costs, and risks, in both the short term and the long term.

- **Principle 4: Performance.** The enterprise IT function should be organized for the purpose of supporting the enterprise, providing the services, levels of service, and service quality required to meet current and future enterprise business requirements.
- **Principle 5: Conformance.** IT should comply with all mandatory legislation and regulations, with policies and practices clearly defined, implemented, and enforced.
- **Principle 6: Human behavior.** IT policies, practices, and decisions should demonstrate respect for human behavior, including the current and evolving needs of all the people in the process.

In addition to these basic principles, the standard provides a model for IT governance, as shown in Exhibit 33.3. The overall IT governance process is described in the exhibit's center triangle. The model shows business pressures and business needs

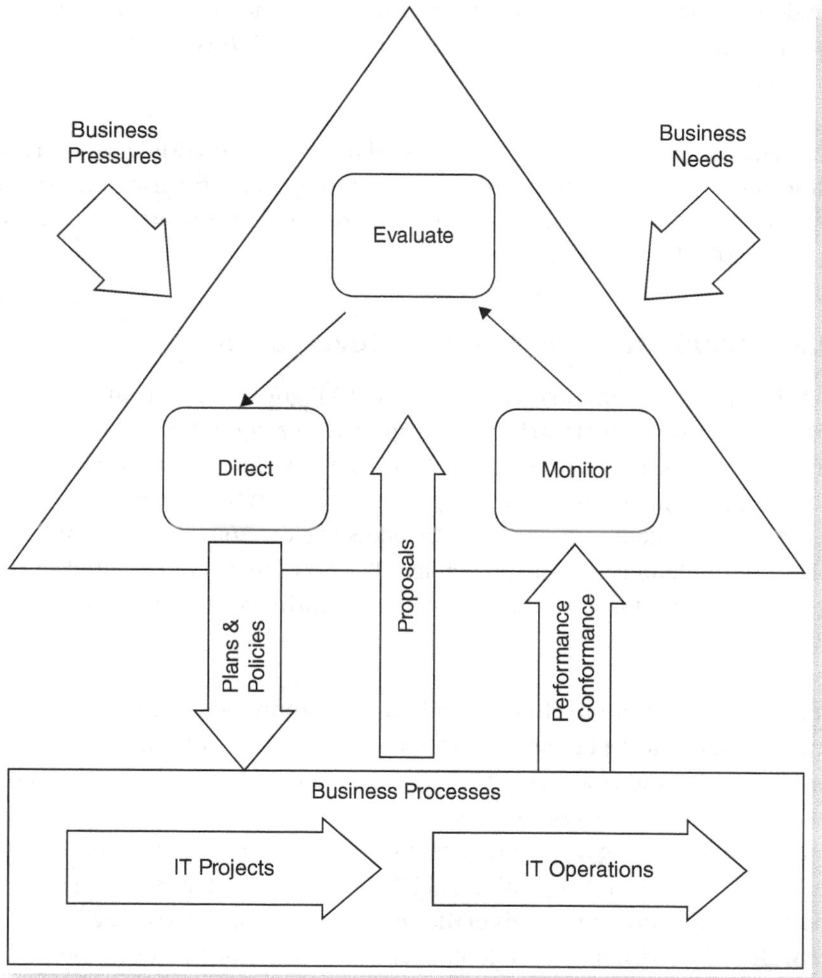

EXHIBIT 33.3 ISO 38500 Model

influencing the IT governance process. Governance processes then sit above overall IT processes where various proposals from within IT influence IT governance processes. In addition, the IT governance process provides plans and policies to IT, and the overall IT function provides performance and conformance information to IT governance. The basic overall process has been described in other chapters, but ISO 38500 does a good job in encapsulating this issue. Inside the IT governance triangle in Exhibit 33.3, there are three process functions named Evaluate, Monitor, and Direct. The ISO standard provides a definition for each of these.

IT senior managers should examine and make judgments on their current and future use of all IT resources, including strategies, proposals, and supply arrangements (whether internal, external, or both). In evaluating the use of IT, management should consider the external or internal pressures acting upon the business, such as technological change, economic or social trends, and political influences.

If an enterprise has taken steps to comply with ISO 38500, internal audit should determine that these evaluations take place continually, as pressures change. They should also take account of both current and future business needs—the current and future organizational objectives that they must achieve, such as maintaining competitive advantage, as well as the specific objectives of the strategies and proposals they are evaluating.

Following ISO 38500 guidance, senior management should assign responsibility for and direct preparation and implementation of IT governance plans and policies. Plans should set the direction for investments both in IT projects and operations. These policies should establish sound behavior in the enterprise's use of IT. IT management should ensure that the transition of all types of development and implementation projects in their transfers to operational status is properly planned and managed, taking into account impacts on business and operational practices as well as existing IT systems and infrastructure.

The ISO 38500 guidance calls for senior IT management to encourage a culture of good IT governance by requiring managers to provide timely information, to comply with direction, and to conform with the previously referenced six principles of good governance. Internal auditors, in their reviews of IT internal controls, should monitor, through appropriate measurement systems, the overall performance of IT. They should reassure themselves that this performance is in accordance with plans, particularly with regard to business objectives. Internal audit should also make sure that IT conforms with regulatory, legislative, and contractual external obligations as well as with internal work practices.

The ISO 38500 published standard defines six ISO principles and folds them into the IT governance model to provide more specific IT governance guidance. This guidance as well as all details of the standard can be purchased in hard copy or downloaded from the ISO web site.[3] ISO copyright rules do not allow us to reproduce this published guidance, but we have extracted a very small portion of it in this chapter to provide some insights into the actual materials.

The standard has a general style of language, with no specific rules or detailed procedures but rather just some general good guidance. But when a standard calls for senior management to "monitor the progress of approved IT proposals to ensure that they are achieving objectives in required timeframes," this language points to the need for IT project and program approval processes, project planning with established time frames, and regular senior management reviews. The enterprise's internal audit function can act as an internal consultant and provide help in implementing this standards guidance, as discussed in Chapter 30 and Chapter 16, which talks about the importance of project management procedures.

The many applicable ISO standards, and ISO 38500, can help and strengthen overall enterprise IT governance. Many managers have rejected some of these standards because they seem to call for too much documentation or are too paperwork intensive. That is, if a standard says that "management should monitor" some process or activity, the enterprise group support in this area should be in a position to demonstrate this monitoring activity through some level of documentation. Of course we are not talking about cabinets of paperwork, but forms of retrievable electronic evidence. Many enterprises today that provide products or services in international markets have gone through the process of an ISO external audit to attest to their compliance with ISO 9000. In future years we may see a similar compliance requirement for ISO *IT governance standards* as they are expanded and become more recognized.

The IIA did not say much about ISO standards for many years. In our past edition, we referenced that we could find little or no guidance about the appropriate ISO standards in the IIA's web site. Things have changed, however, and many IIA publications now reference the importance of appropriate ISO standards for certain internal control reviews. For example, an IIA practice guide on *Auditing IT Projects*[4] contains multiple references to appropriate ISO standards.

33.4 ISO STANDARDS AND THE COSO INTERNAL CONTROL FRAMEWORK

As we become a more globalized world of commerce with many interconnections and relationships, the ISO standards become more important for all enterprises. While standards describing component dimensions—such as the tread pattern and size of a bolt—are essential for commerce, the "softer" quality system standards such as ISO 9000 are equally important. Enterprises in one location will refuse to do business with enterprises elsewhere unless they can certify their compliance to some ISO standard.

Although many senior executives and even their internal auditors have not been very close to ISO standards in the past, we expect this to change. COBIT, introduced in Chapter 6, is becoming more closely aligned with ISO 27002, and we can see internal auditors becoming increasingly involved with ISO quality standards. When appropriate, internal auditors should try to incorporate appropriate ISO standards in their IT internal controls audits.

The concepts behind ISO quality and security standards are similar to the COSO internal control framework. A big difference is that ISO standards outline significant expectations. That is, under ISO the enterprise should have certain internal control processes in place, such as tested documentation for some process, and external ISO auditors reviewing that area will test and assure that those ISO standards are in place and are effective. COSO only outlines some general requirements, such as the need for risk assessment processes, but there are no requirements beyond COSO's better defining any requirements necessary to achieve COSO internal controls compliance.

One might argue that we are better off with a more general framework than with the more specific ISO standards. Of course, things could be even worse if governmental authorities wrote specific rules here, resulting in the drafting of many hundreds of pages of rules covering every detailed nuance.

An objective of this chapter has been to introduce some of the ISO standards that are similar to the COSO internal controls requirements and to introduce some of the difference between COSO and ISO. Internal auditors should be aware of ISO standards and should work to recommend compliance in areas when appropriate, but should focus an enterprise's internal controls on the COSO framework.

33.5 INTERNAL AUDIT AND INTERNATIONAL AUDITING STANDARDS

External auditors based in the United States had once thought of the AICPA and its then important Auditing Standards Board as the longtime body establishing auditing standards for U.S. organizations through its Statements on Auditing Standards, or SAS, numbered documents. At least that was prior to SOx and the Public Company Accounting Oversight Board (PCAOB) that now has the authority to establish auditing standards in the United States. Of course, the whole purpose of any audit is to review compliance against some recognized standard or principle. One of the major tenets of internal control, under COSO and any other internal audit for that matter, is compliance with laws and regulations. That legal compliance becomes a standard for audits of internal accounting controls. Financial audits also assess the fairness of accounting procedures per established accounting standards. Although we are transitioning to a worldwide set of international standards, standards in the United States have been based for many years on generally accepted accounting principles (GAAP), as well as very specific accounting rules proscribed by the Financial Accounting Standards Board (FASB). The current U.S. auditing and accounting standards do not match others around the world.

Standards such as double-entry bookkeeping are accepted and recognized throughout the world. Others may have the same intent but are different in various national entities. The practice of driving on the right- or left-hand side of the road is an example of a national practice. No matter which standard is followed, drivers can still easily get from point A to B as long as all drivers follow the same rule. The same is true for auditing and accounting standards and practices. It only becomes a bit more complex because today we are an increasingly global economy where accounting and auditing practices in Belgium, for example, need to be comparable to nearby neighbor France. In addition, there is a need for some consistency between Germany and the United States. As our individual organizations become increasingly global, internal auditors should at least have a general understanding of the differences and consistencies across international borders.

Accounting and auditing standards had been established over the years on a country-by-country basis by professional or governmental boards as well as by international standards-setting bodies. Individual countries may fully or only generally accept these international standards. The United States is an example of the latter. With strong established practices in many areas, the United States takes the lead for some, or goes its own way for others. All internal auditors, whether in the United States or elsewhere, should gain a general understanding of the current rules and how they might apply to an auditor's organization and the body that establishes the standards. The latter can be confusing.

As we move into a world of international organizations, we run into a gaggle of initials to describe them. One can just think of the United Nations (UN) with its UNESCO, FAO, UNICEF, UNCTAD, and many more. International auditing accounting and standards use the same often confusing sets of initials. There are International Standards on Auditing (ISA), as well as *International Accounting Standards (IAS)*. The ISA auditing standards are established by the International Federation of Accountants (IFAC) through its International Auditing and Assurance Standards Board (IAASB), which issues these ISAs as well as International Auditing Practice Statements (IAPSs). To complicate the picture, there is also the International Organization of Supreme Audit Institutions (INTOSAI), whose Auditing Standards Committee contributes to the work of IAASB.

The ISA has a lengthy list of auditing standards, fairly consistent with the old pre-PCAOB U.S. SAS documents. A Web search will provide copies of each of these standards. For example, ISA No. 610 is a standard on considering the work of internal auditors that is published in over 20 languages, including French, German, Russian, and Spanish. More than 70 countries have indicated that they have either have adopted IASs or feel there are no significant differences between their standards and the ISA international standards. The United States is one of the "no significant differences" countries. In many cases, the ISAs follow U.S. practices. The typical internal auditor does not at present need to have a detailed understanding of these international standards of auditing. However, as we work in a more global environment, they will become increasingly important.

To cite more acronyms, the International Accounting Standards Board (IASB) publishes accounting standards in a series of pronouncements called *International Financial Reporting Standards (IFRS)* Those pronouncements continue to be designated "International Accounting Standards" (IAS). To a certain degree they provide a basis or foundation for all countries worldwide, and in particular for developing countries that lack established accounting standards. Most developed countries have established accounting standards that generally follow U.S., British, German, Swiss, or French standards. The IAS standards historically were not inconsistent with those country-by-country standards. An auditor doing work in a developing country that does not have any strong accounting standards should look to the IAS materials to form a basis for appropriate accounting standards. Going forward, all countries that are members of the European Union are now required to adopt the IASB international accounting standards.

In a step toward eliminating the existing differences between U.S. GAAP and international standards, FASB and IASB have been working for some years to identify differences and bring their standards together. In the United States, the AICPA is going through a massive effort to educate all interested parties on the implications of transitioning to IFRS. Although the compliance date has been postponed multiple times, we should soon see the two sets of standards—international standards and U.S. GAAP—converge.

For internal auditors, the IIA's standards, as discussed in Chapter 9, are international standards and apply to internal audits no matter the country. Internal auditors may encounter different accounting standards or even different local financial statement auditing standards, but the overall IIA professional standards should always be followed. Regarding these accounting and auditing standards, we can almost certainly expect that they will take the place of country-by-country standards, with the exception of the United States in its international leadership role.

The objective of this chapter has been to introduce internal auditors to both some of the more significant ISO standards impacting their internal audit work as well to briefly introduce international auditing and accounting standards. An understanding of both of these areas is important for all internal auditors, no matter their country of residence, as we increasingly encounter a worldwide network of business and commerce and as we become more connected through the Web and other resources. While it is perhaps not a knowledge requirement today, a good CBOK general understanding of appropriate ISO standards as well as the evolving status of international accounting and auditing standards should be a priority for all internal auditors.

NOTES

1. On the Computer Associates financial scandal, see William M. Bulkeley, "Former CA Chief Is Sentenced to 12-Year Prison Term, Fined," *Wall Street Journal*, November 3, 2006, http://www.wsj.com/articles/SB116248304060911444.
2. On the Elf Aquitaine financial scandal, see David Ignatius, "True Crime: The Scent of French Scandal," *Legal Affairs*, May–June 2002, http://www.legalaffairs.org/issues/May-June-2002/story_ignatius_mayjun2002.html.
3. ISO Standards can be purchased through http://www.iso.org/iso/home/store/catalogue_ics.htm.
4. This reference is only available to IIA members at *Auditing IT Projects*, an IIA Practice Guide, https://na.theiia.org/standards-guidance/Member%20Documents/GTAG-12_PDF_TEXT_and_COVERS-CX.pdf.

CHAPTER THIRTY-FOUR

A CBOK for the Modern Internal Auditor

APRIOR CHAPTERS OF THIS BOOK have described the internal audit process as it exists for today's modern internal auditor. We have described areas where internal audit skills and understanding are essential, and other areas where internal auditors should have a strong general understanding. All of these become an internal audit common body of knowledge (CBOK).

Our internal auditor CBOK approach has been based on current and evolving governance, risk, and compliance areas important for internal auditors, this author's past experience in performing and leading internal audits, and his research on important and developing trends. Thus we have highlighted internal audit knowledge areas that should be important, if not essential, for internal auditors. An example here would be our Chapter 6 discussion on COBIT, an important alternative framework for documenting and understanding internal controls. While extracts from the IIA web site tend to view COBIT as just a specialized IT audit tool and not much else, we discuss the importance of COBIT as an alternative and important internal audit tool for evaluating and understanding internal controls. We suggest that all internal auditors should have a high-level CBOK understanding and familiarity with the COBIT framework.

This comment on COBIT references our approach to defining an internal audit CBOK. Rather than publishing the results from a fairly wide-open but not necessarily controlled survey, based on IIA members who responded to a "Tell us what you think is important" Web request, we have tried to outline knowledge areas that should be important to all internal auditors.

The IIARF CBOK publication was developed by hiring a consulting team to send surveys to selected IIA members worldwide and then published their IIA members-only CBOK[1] survey results about the same time that the seventh edition of this book was released. That 2006 *IIARF CBOK* seemingly collected survey response data on what internal auditors said they were doing, but with some sometimes troubling reported results. For example, although there are always ways to manipulate statistics and while we did not have complete access to all of the data, the now purged and obsolete 2006 IIARF CBOK survey found that some internal auditors were not even following their own professional standards. For example, the IIARF's 2006 CBOK study reported that only some 90% of the chief audit executives surveyed felt that their internal audit function "adds value" and "proactively examines important financial matters, risks, and internal controls" in the CAEs' enterprises. These are areas where we would have expected that nearly 100% of CAEs should be in agreement. These and other similar troubling reported statistics led to our objective to better define an internal audit CBOK as reported in this edition. As this book goes to press, the IIARF has again circulated some CBOK survey forms to its membership to publish an updated IIARF CBOK. Their original 2006 CBOK study has been purged from the IIARF's records and our criticism of this poorly structured is only available in this author's files in a hard-copy format.

Our internal auditor CBOK, as discussed throughout this book, is *not* based on the responses from multiple and fairly uncontrolled survey questionnaires but rather on published standards and information that are necessary internal audit knowledge areas. In addition, our CBOK recommendations are based on this author's 40-plus years of experience in many aspects of internal auditing. We have tried to define our internal auditor CBOK in terms of some key areas where all internal auditors must have a strong level of knowledge and understanding—such as adherence to internal audit standards—as well as other areas where we have recommended that internal auditors should have at least a good general knowledge.

Our description of an internal auditor CBOK is much greater than just a series of bullet points to be summarized on a single table or chart. The framework for this internal auditor CBOK has been discussed in previous chapters, and here we will summarize the CBOK by revisiting each of the eight parts of this book with a summary of CBOK needs described in those supporting chapters.

Some experienced internal auditors may disagree with our choice of some of our CBOK requirements, saying we have given certain areas too much emphasis or that we missed others. However, we feel these chapters provide a good overview of a CBOK for all internal auditors.

34.1 PART ONE: FOUNDATIONS OF INTERNAL AUDITING CBOK REQUIREMENTS

Chapters 1 and 2 in Part One discussed the background and origins of the internal auditing profession, as well as providing an introduction and discussion on the need for an internal audit CBOK. We gave some of the well-recognized definitions of the internal auditing profession. Professionals at all levels of their careers frequently receive questions along the lines of "What does an internal auditor do?" While this question was answered in much more detail in other chapters, these foundation chapters provide some basic internal auditor definitions—an essential CBOK requirement.

Chapter 2 provided background on the origins of and need for an internal audit CBOK. Due to the assorted industries and geographical areas where internal auditors operate in evaluating internal controls and assisting management, there can be many variations in their modes and styles of operations. However, all internal auditors should have some basic skills and competencies—the need for a CBOK. In addition, internal auditors should understand why a CBOK is important for their profession and why they should always try to follow CBOK best practices in every aspect of their internal audit work.

34.2 PART TWO: IMPORTANCE OF INTERNAL CONTROLS CBOK REQUIREMENTS

The five chapters here introduced some common practices that are essential knowledge requirements for every internal auditor. Chapter 3 discussed how many enterprises and their internal auditors went for years without a clear and consistent understanding of the meaning and concept of internal controls. Definitions were resolved and clarified, however, through the Committee of Sponsoring Organizations (COSO) internal control framework, a three-dimensional model of how an enterprise should organize and think of its internal controls.

Originally launched as sort of a best practice description of good internal controls, the COSO internal control frameworks became first a U.S. and now a worldwide standard for defining and establishing good internal controls. The COSO framework was revised in 2014 to better reflect changes in business operations, the pervasive growth of IT systems, and common organizational structural changes today. Chapter 3 described the revised COSO framework, a key internal auditor CBOK requirement.

Whether operating in an industry environment, as an IT specialist internal auditor, or in not-for-profit or governmental sectors, every internal auditor should have a CBOK understanding of the newly revised COSO internal control framework. As part of that internal control framework, COSO has introduced 17 internal control principles, key measures for understanding and evaluating internal controls. These COSO principles were discussed in Chapter 4. Understanding them is an internal auditor CBOK requirement as they will help to plan and build internal audits in many areas of operations.

In the early part of this century, a series of major accounting frauds and business failures in the United States and elsewhere became a clarion call for external auditing and corporate governance reforms. The result was the Sarbanes-Oxley Act (SOx) in the United States, as discussed in Chapter 5. While SOx's initial focus initially was on large U.S. corporations, it has defined rules and reporting standards that are requirements for many enterprises, large and small, in the United States and worldwide. Although the overall SOx legislation is very broad and has regulations and rules in some areas that may be of little interest to most internal auditors, a strong knowledge and understanding of the SOx internal control review procedures should be a CBOK requirement for all internal auditors who are working with public corporations. In addition, all internal auditors should have general CBOK understanding of the SOx internal control requirements and its corporate governance rules, as described in Chapter 5.

Chapter 6 introduced another very important internal control framework, control objectives for IT (COBIT). An understanding of COBIT, an internal control framework with origins tied to IT audit specialists, is important for all internal auditors because IT systems and processes are so pervasive in all aspects of virtually every enterprise today. Whether operational, financial, or IT specialists, all internal auditors should have at least a high-level CBOK understanding of the COBIT framework and how it might apply to their internal audit activities.

Part Two ends with Chapter 7, on the COSO enterprise risk management (COSO ERM) framework, a model to help understand risks not in just a single internal audit, but the overall enterprise. A basic understanding of these concepts and principles of risk management is important for all internal auditors today, as support to assess various areas to review and in making other internal audit decisions. Every internal auditor also should have a high-level CBOK understanding of COSO ERM.

34.3 PART THREE: PLANNING AND PERFORMING INTERNAL AUDIT CBOK REQUIREMENTS

Having a good knowledge and understanding of the COSO internal control framework will help an internal auditor to understand some basic internal audit principles, but internal auditors also need the knowledge of how to plan and perform actual internal audits. The six chapters in Part Three included some CBOK internal audit performance background information, starting with Chapter 8 on guidance on performing effective internal audits. The chapter emphasized that the ability to plan and perform an individual internal audit is a key CBOK requirement, whether one is an internal audit manager or an audit staff member.

Chapter 8 also discussed the importance of building and using audit programs, the step-by-step procedures that an internal auditor should use to perform current as well as potential future reviews in the same topic area. Internal auditors should perform their reviews using audit programs, the documented steps covering the audit procedures to follow. Internal auditors at all levels should have a CBOK understanding of how to build and use audit programs to serve as a guide for constructing consistent internal audit reviews.

A very strong understanding of the Institute of Internal Auditors' *International Standards for the Professional Practice of Internal Auditing* is *an essential* internal audit CBOK requirement. These standards, summarized in Chapter 9, are the rules outlining how an internal auditor should launch, conduct, and manage any review, whether in an audit attest engagement or while serving as an internal consultant. These are internal audit's marching orders, and a good knowledge and understanding of them is a strong CBOK requirement.

While their technical details can be a challenge for some, all internal auditors should have a CBOK high-level understanding of audit evidence sampling and testing techniques. Internal auditors should know how to appropriately look at a body of audit evidence, pull and review an appropriate sample of items from that evidence, and then make an audit decision and recommendations from that sample. Testing, assessing, and evaluating audit evidence were discussed in Chapter 10.

With the growth of highly automated systems, it is now a fairly common practice to build controls in those systems that flag audit exceptions and other warnings. Internal auditors encounter this situation when their corporate IT function tells them that they have too many open e-mails or when a credit card provider tells them they have exceeded credit charge limits. These kinds of controls and monitors can be built into IT systems to provide continuous auditing processes. Though this is area is not a CBOK knowledge requirement, these continuous auditing techniques, as described in Chapter 11, are an area where an internal auditor should obtain a good general knowledge.

Chapter 12 covered another important area in which internal auditors should have the knowledge and ability to perform self-audits and to assess how other peer groups are performing in similar internal audit functions. Called control self-assessments and benchmarking, these are internal audit CBOK knowledge areas. While not knowledge requirements in the sense of Chapter 9's standards, these self-assessment processes should be familiar to internal auditors. This is another area where we make a distinction between what we feel is a CBOK requirement and what we feel an effective internal auditor should understand more generally.

Internal auditors are confronted with a wide range of audit candidates, potential areas to review for their organization. Internal control needs, timing, audit committee management requests, and time and resource limitations prevent internal audit from launching such reviews for every such area in an enterprise, and internal auditors should establish what is called an audit universe listing or catalog for their enterprise. Chapter 13 describes audit universe concepts, an area where all internal auditors should have a good general CBOK understanding.

34.4 PART FOUR: ORGANIZING AND MANAGING INTERNAL AUDIT ACTIVITIES CBOK REQUIREMENTS

The five chapters in Part Four covered important CBOK areas on how an internal audit function should both manage and perform internal audits, as well as some individual internal audit skills. Starting the section, Chapter 14 discussed audit charters, the official enterprise audit committee authorization of an internal audit function. An internal audit charter is generally drafted and approved by the audit committee of the board of directors. It is the kind of document that an internal auditor can use when his activities are questioned in an internal audit engagement. As described in the chapter, internal auditors should have a CBOK understanding of the purposes and importance of internal audit charters.

Chapter 15 went on to discuss some key internal audit competencies, the kinds of attributes that internal auditors should have in order to be effective. In particular, the chapter described the importance of understanding and making risk management a factor to consider in any internal audit engagement.

Similar to the Chapter 14 and 15 descriptions of key internal audit competencies, Chapters 16 and 17 covered individual audit function activities. Project management, a very important CBOK activity, was presented and discussed in Chapter 16. Every internal audit should be thought of as a project that should be planned and organized in a well-structured, consistent manner. The chapter provides an overview of understanding project management—a CBOK requirement. Focusing on the individual internal auditor, Chapter 16 discussed the CBOK general steps necessary to plan and perform an individual internal audit, using a hypothetical example.

Chapter 17 covered another essential internal auditor CBOK area: documenting audit results through workpapers. Although detailed processes and techniques may vary from one internal audit function to another, all internal auditors should have the knowledge and understanding of how to develop effective workpapers to describe and document their individual audit activities.

Although formats can vary from one internal audit function to another, the ability to report internal audit results through effective audit reports is a key CBOK requirement. While much of the effort of developing and delivering formal internal audit reports is often delegated to more senior members of the internal audit team, all internal auditors should have a strong CBOK understanding of the purpose and role of their enterprise's internal audit reports.

This section concluded with Chapter 18 on developing and publishing effective internal audit reports. Whether its recipients are auditees of a review or the audit committee, a formal audit report describes the results of the review and includes recommendations for corrective actions. Although a final audit report may be the product of internal audit management, every internal auditor should have a CBOK understanding of how to develop and prepare effective internal audit reports.

34.5 PART FIVE: IMPACT OF IT ON INTERNAL AUDITING CBOK REQUIREMENTS

Because IT processes are so critical to all areas of business and other operations today, the six chapters of Part Five describes some very important CBOK areas. Chapter 19 discussed performing IT general controls as well as the Information Technology Infrastructure Library (ITIL®) best practices for understanding and installing IT infrastructure controls procedures. These are CBOK areas where every internal auditor should have a general understanding.

While the general controls that cover the overall IT function are important, internal controls covering specific IT applications are at least as crucial. For virtually all internal auditors, a CBOK understanding of these IT control concepts is particularly important because many IT applications and their internal control responsibilities have moved from traditional centralized IT functions to individual user-managed controls. Internal auditors should have a good CBOK understanding of IT application controls in today's environment of handheld wireless terminals and cloud-based storage resources.

With our heavy reliance on IT applications and processes as well as the use of the Internet and heavily networked applications and IT resources, these same IT resources face a multitude of security and privacy threats. Chapter 20 discussed cybersecurity and IT privacy controls. While IT security issues are often a very special and complex area, internal auditors should try to gain an overall high-level CBOK understanding of cybersecurity internal control issues.

IT technology is always changing and some areas considered important in the past are almost ho-hum today, while others are gaining in internal importance. Chapter 21 introduces one of these new areas, what we call big data. Many enterprise IT systems are growing at massive rates, and enterprises, their customers, and often regulators increasingly require that large, historical IT records be maintained. Big data raises internal control issues, and internal auditors should have a good CBOK understanding of these concepts.

Just as internal auditors need to understand key internal control principles, they also should be able to use that understanding to let IT processes aid them in their internal audit procedures. Chapter 22 discusses internal audit procedures for reviewing IT application management controls as well as software management internal controls. While there are many potential approaches and techniques here, internal auditors should have a CBOK general understanding of basic IT application controls as well as the use of report generators and other query tools that can potentially make internal audit application reviews more efficient and productive.

The vast numbers of application systems and IT resources connected to the Internet through wireless links, access controls, and security vulnerabilities are an increasing concern. Chapter 23 discusses cybersecurity internal controls as well as compliance requirements for some important privacy legislation. IT cybersecurity controls are an ever-growing and more complex area. Specialized knowledge and tools are needed, and while the typical internal auditor will not be an IT expert in these security and privacy areas, all internal auditors should have a good CBOK understanding of IT security and privacy controls.

The last chapter in Part Five, Chapter 24, discussed business continuity planning and disaster recovery. This is an area where technology has made it much easier than in past years for an enterprise to save its IT-stored data to recover operations after an unexpected event. While this was once very much the realm of IT specialist auditors, today every internal auditor should have a good CBOK understanding of IT continuity planning and recovery operations.

34.6 PART SIX: INTERNAL AUDIT AND ENTERPRISE GOVERNANCE CBOK REQUIREMENTS

There has been a growing recognition of the importance of enterprise-level fraud, and ethics issues have made many aspects of the business world increasingly complex and have added to an internal auditor's CBOK needs. The four chapters in Part Six look at the importance of GRC—governance, risk, and compliance—issues and associated areas where internal auditors should develop a CBOK general understanding.

Chapter 25 discussed internal audit communications and relationships with the board of directors' audit committee. While this is a critical requirement, particularly for the CAE, all members of an internal audit function should have a general CBOK understanding of the role of their enterprise audit committee in internal audit operations, and in particular that role in their own specific enterprise. Again, these are areas where all internal auditors need to develop a good CBOK understanding of effective programs and why they are important to internal audit.

In a similar sense, Chapter 26 discussed enterprise ethics and whistleblower programs, important initiatives in many enterprises. Starting with a strong code of conduct covering all parties, enterprise senior executives should be broadcasting a tone-at-the-top message about the importance of these policies. Internal auditors should have CBOK skills to look for effective polices in their reviews and should also make them part of their normal internal audit activities. These are really CBOK requirements, not general knowledge areas.

Understanding basic fraud detection and prevention controls, as discussed in Chapter 27, should be a CBOK requirement for all internal auditors. For many years, professional standards did not call for internal auditors to have the skills to look for fraud. Things have changed. While the typical internal auditor today need not be a sleuth, all internal auditors should gain a good CBOK level of skills in reviewing and detecting the red flags that indicate the possibility of fraud, as part of general internal audit fraud investigation review procedures.

Chapter 27 introduced the importance of effective GRC programs in an enterprise. While the concepts of governance, risk assessment, and compliance with enterprise rules and regulations are essential elements of all internal audit activities, internal auditors worldwide should develop a CBOK understanding of the processes and rules that govern compliance in their own enterprise as well as in relevant countries and locations.

34.7 PART SEVEN: INTERNAL AUDITOR PROFESSIONAL CBOK REQUIREMENTS

While the other parts in this book focused more on managing and performing internal audits, Part Seven looked at several other important CBOK areas. Chapter 29 discussed internal audit professional certifications, with an emphasis on the Certified Internal Auditor (CIA) and the Certified Information Systems Auditor (CISA) designations. While attainment of these is not necessarily a CBOK requirement, all internal auditors should at least have an understanding of these professional certifications and the requirements to achieve them. All internal auditors should strive to attain one or both of these credentials.

Chapter 30 discussed the role of the internal auditor as a business consultant. A practice that was banned by internal audit standards until recent years, serving as an internal consultant can be a very important role for internal audit and its enterprise organization in many situations. Internal auditors should have a good general CBOK knowledge of the internal audit standards rules for serving as an enterprise consultant.

34.8 PART EIGHT: THE OTHER SIDES OF INTERNAL AUDITING: PROFESSIONAL CONVERGENCE CBOK REQUIREMENTS

The last part of our CBOK requirements discussion introduced the need for internal auditors to have a greater understanding of some internal audit issues that go beyond just IIA-related internal auditing and its standards. Chapter 31 introduced the area of ASQ internal quality auditing. These internal audit procedures are controlled in the United

States by the American Society for Quality (ASQ), and have many common threads with the IIA processes discussed throughout most of the book. There will almost certainly be a convergence of some IIA and ASQ procedures in the future, and all internal auditors should develop at least a CBOK understanding of the ASQ quality internal audit standards and procedures.

Many internal auditors work in manufacturing and process control–related areas where concepts such as Six Sigma and what are called Lean techniques are very important to the enterprise. These processes, discussed in Chapter 32, are more familiar on the production shop floor than in the administrative office. Where appropriate, internal auditors should have a high-level CBOK understanding of these concepts and should incorporate compliance of them in their review activities.

Chapter 33 introduced International Organization for Standardization (ISO) international standards, with an emphasis on the organization's quality and IT management standards. These standards and compliance efforts to meet them have been in place worldwide for some years. They are increasingly appearing in U.S. environments, and internal auditors who have worked in an IIA-standards environment over the years should gain a greater CBOK understanding of these ISO standards and their supporting concepts. Chapter 33 also very briefly introduced some worldwide accounting and auditing standards. In particular, what are called International Accounting Standards have been the preferred standards almost everywhere in the world, with the exception of the United States, which uses what have been called generally accepted accounting principles (GAAP). The United States is now taking steps to move from GAAP to the international standards. While this does not have a major impact on internal audit procedures, all internal auditors should have a CBOK understanding of a few of the implications of this change.

34.9 A CBOK FOR THE MODERN INTERNAL AUDITOR

The topics summarized in this chapter and presented in more detail throughout this book outline a CBOK for internal auditors today. Some of these, such as Chapter 3 on the COSO internal control framework or Chapter 9 on the IIA's internal audit standards, are essential CBOK knowledge areas. Many others cover areas where an internal auditor should at least have a good general understanding.

Many knowledge areas are beyond the immediate needs and requirements of many internal auditors. However, all internal auditors, from the CAE responsible for a large enterprise internal audit function to the student considering internal auditing as a career choice, can see the large body of knowledge that is part of the world of internal auditing.

Exhibit 34.1 summarizes the overall CBOK topics discussed throughout this book, with references to the chapter where discussed and whether the issue should be a requirement or an area of understanding.

This edition has painted a big picture of the world of internal auditing in our ever-changing world today. While many of the internal audit CBOK requirements described throughout these chapters will continue to be important and significant, some areas of emphasis or topics may wax or wane in the years going forward. A future edition of this

EXHIBIT 34.1 Internal Audit CBOK Summary

Internal Auditor CBOK Knowledge Needs	CBOK Concentration Areas	CBOK Importance	Chap Ref
Analytical reviews	Organizing and Managing Internal Audit Activities	Internal Audit Knowledge Requirement	Chap 15
Assessing internal audit risks	Planning and Performing Internal Audits	Internal Audit Knowledge Requirement	Chap 7
Audit committee charters	Internal Audit Enterprise Governance Issues	General Understanding	Chap 14
Audit committee responsibilities	Organizing and Managing Internal Audit Activities	General Understanding	Chap 14
Audit committee responsibility for internal audit	Internal Audit Enterprise Governance Issues	General Understanding	Chap 25
Audit sampling techniques	Planning and Performing Internal Audits	General Understanding	Chap 10
Audit universe concepts	Planning and Performing Internal Audits	General Understanding	Chap 13
Auditing business continuity plans	Impact of IT Systems on Internal Audit	Internal Audit Knowledge Requirement	Chap 24
Auditing for fraud	Internal Audit Enterprise Governance Issues	Internal Audit Knowledge Requirement	Chap 27
Auditing GRC processes	Internal Audit Enterprise Governance Issues	Internal Audit Knowledge Requirement	Chap 28
Auditing in a wireless computing environment	Impact of IT Systems on Internal Audit	Internal Audit Knowledge Requirement	Chap 20
Auditing IT configuration management processes	Impact of IT Systems on Internal Audit	General Understanding	Chap 19
Auditing IT network access controls	Impact of IT Systems on Internal Audit	Internal Audit Knowledge Requirement	Chap 23
Auditing IT privacy controls	Impact of IT Systems on Internal Audit	Internal Audit Knowledge Requirement	Chap 23
Auditing the IT infrastructure	Impact of IT Systems on Internal Audit	Internal Audit Knowledge Requirement	Chap 19
Building an effective internal audit function	Organizing and Managing Internal Audit Activities	General Understanding	Chap 15
BYOD concepts	Impact of IT Systems on Internal Audit	Internal Audit Knowledge Requirement	Chap 20
COBIT internal controls guidance	Importance of Internal Controls	Internal Audit Knowledge Requirement	Chap 6
Common Body of Knowledge Concepts	Internal Auditing Foundations	General Understanding	Chap 2
Continuous auditing techniques	Planning and Performing Internal Audits	General Understanding	Chap 11
Control self-assessments	Planning and Performing Internal Audits	General Understanding	Chap 12

Internal Auditor CBOK Knowledge Needs	CBOK Concentration Areas	CBOK Importance	Chap Ref
COSO ERM risk management	Importance of Internal Controls	Internal Audit Knowledge Requirement	Chap 7
COSO internal control principles	Importance of Internal Controls	Internal Audit Knowledge Requirement	Chap 4
COSO internal control framework	Importance of Internal Controls	Internal Audit Knowledge Requirement	Chap 3
Definition of internal auditing	Internal Auditing Foundations	Internal Audit Knowledge Requirement	Chap 1
Developing audit programs	Planning and Performing Internal Audits	Internal Audit Knowledge Requirement	Chap 8
Disaster recovery plan testing	Impact of IT Systems on Internal Audit	Internal Audit Knowledge Requirement	Chap 24
Documenting internal audit results	Organizing and Managing Internal Audit Activities	Internal Audit Knowledge Requirement	Chap 15
Documenting internal audit results	Organizing and Managing Internal Audit Activities	Internal Audit Knowledge Requirement	Chap 17
Enterprise content management internal controls	Impact of IT Systems on Internal Audit	Internal Audit Knowledge Requirement	Chap 21
Familiarity with ASQ quality assurance audit standards	Internal Audit Professional Convergences	General Understanding	Chap 31
Familiarity with malware and IT hacking issues	Impact of IT Systems on Internal Audit	General Understanding	Chap 23
Familiarity with NIST cybersecurity framework	Impact of IT Systems on Internal Audit	General Understanding	Chap 23
Importance of corporate codes of conduct	Internal Audit Enterprise Governance Issues	Internal Audit Knowledge Requirement	Chap 26
Importance of enterprise compliance programs	Internal Audit Enterprise Governance Issues	General Understanding	Chap 28
Internal audit background and history	Internal Auditing Foundations	General Understanding	Chap 1
Internal audit charters	Organizing and Managing Internal Audit Activities	Internal Audit Knowledge Requirement	Chap 14
Internal audit code of ethics	Planning and Performing Internal Audits	Internal Audit Knowledge Requirement	Chap 9
Internal audit professional standards	Planning and Performing Internal Audits	Internal Audit Knowledge Requirement	Chap 9
Internal audit quality assurance reviews	Internal Audit Professional Convergences	Internal Audit Knowledge Requirement	Chap 33
Internal audit quality assurance techniques	Planning and Performing Internal Audits	General Understanding	Chap 12
Internal audit workpapers	Organizing and Managing Internal Audit Activities	Internal Audit Knowledge Requirement	Chap 17
Internal control documentation tools	Planning and Performing Internal Audits	Internal Audit Knowledge Requirement	Chap 8

(continued)

EXHIBIT 34.1 *(continued)*

Internal Auditor CBOK Knowledge Needs	CBOK Concentration Areas	CBOK Importance	Chap Ref
International auditing standards	Internal Audit Professional Convergences	Internal Audit Knowledge Requirement	Chap 33
International Professional Practices Framework (IPPF)	Planning and Performing Internal Audits	Internal Audit Knowledge Requirement	Chap 9
ISO 9000 quality audit standards	Internal Audit Professional Convergences	General Understanding	Chap 33
ISO standards for quality	Internal Audit Professional Convergences	General Understanding	Chap 31
IT governance standards	Internal Audit Professional Convergences	Internal Audit Knowledge Requirement	Chap 34
Modern internal audit CBOK requirements	Internal Audit Professional Convergences	Internal Audit Knowledge Requirement	Chap 34
Performing fraud investigations	Internal Audit Enterprise Governance Issues	Internal Audit Knowledge Requirement	Chap 27
Planning and establishing areas to audit	Planning and Performing Internal Audits	Internal Audit Knowledge Requirement	Chap 13
Planning and launching an internal audit	Planning and Performing Internal Audits	Internal Audit Knowledge Requirement	Chap 8
Preparing audit reports	Organizing and Managing Internal Audit Activities	Internal Audit Knowledge Requirement	Chap 18
Preparing internal audit flowcharts	Organizing and Managing Internal Audit Activities	Internal Audit Knowledge Requirement	Chap 17
Process modeling	Organizing and Managing Internal Audit Activities	Internal Audit Knowledge Requirement	Chap 17
Project management body of knowledge (PMBOK)	Organizing and Managing Internal Audit Activities	General Understanding	Chap 16
Reporting internal audit results	Organizing and Managing Internal Audit Activities	Internal Audit Knowledge Requirement	Chap 18
Reporting to the corporate audit committee	Internal Audit Enterprise Governance Issues	Internal Audit Knowledge Requirement	Chap 25
Reviewing application software management controls	Impact of IT Systems on Internal Audit	Internal Audit Knowledge Requirement	Chap 22
Reviewing big data validity and volume internal controls	Impact of IT Systems on Internal Audit	General Understanding	Chap 21
Reviewing ethics and whistleblower programs	Internal Audit Enterprise Governance Issues	Internal Audit Knowledge Requirement	Chap 26
Sarbanes-Oxley Act Internal control requirements	Importance of Internal Controls	Internal Audit Knowledge Requirement	Chap 5
Six Sigma Black Belt concepts	Internal Audit Professional Convergences	General Understanding	Chap 32
Statistical and attributes sampling	Planning and Performing Internal Audits	General Understanding	Chap 10

Internal Auditor CBOK Knowledge Needs	CBOK Concentration Areas	CBOK Importance	Chap Ref
Testing business continuity plans	Impact of IT Systems on Internal Audit	Internal Audit Knowledge Requirement	Chap 24
Understanding attest versus consulting roles	Internal Audit Enterprise Governance Issues	Internal Audit Knowledge Requirement	Chap 30
Understanding audit committee whistleblower rules	Internal Audit Enterprise Governance Issues	Internal Audit Knowledge Requirement	Chap 25
Understanding big data governance	Impact of IT Systems on Internal Audit	Internal Audit Knowledge Requirement	Chap 21
Understanding CIA, CISA, and other certifications	Internal Audit Enterprise Governance Issues	General Understanding	Chap 29
Understanding data leakage risks	Impact of IT Systems on Internal Audit	General Understanding	Chap 21
Understanding disaster recovery plans	Impact of IT Systems on Internal Audit	Internal Audit Knowledge Requirement	Chap 24
Understanding enterprise governance issues	Internal Audit Enterprise Governance Issues	General Understanding	Chap 28
Understanding IIA, AICPA, and ACFE fraud audit standards	Internal Audit Enterprise Governance Issues	Internal Audit Knowledge Requirement	Chap 27
Understanding importance of mission statements	Internal Audit Enterprise Governance Issues	General Understanding	Chap 26
Understanding internal audit's role as enterprise consultant	Internal Audit Enterprise Governance Issues	Internal Audit Knowledge Requirement	Chap 30
Understanding IT emergency response plans	Impact of IT Systems on Internal Audit	Internal Audit Knowledge Requirement	Chap 24
Understanding IT general controls	Impact of IT Systems on Internal Audit	Internal Audit Knowledge Requirement	Chap 19
Understanding IT service level agreements	Impact of IT Systems on Internal Audit	Internal Audit Knowledge Requirement	Chap 19
Understanding ITIL® best practices	Impact of IT Systems on Internal Audit	General Understanding	Chap 19
Understanding ASQ quality audit processes	Internal Audit Professional Convergences	General Understanding	Chap 31
Understanding PCI DSS cybersecurity and privacy controls	Impact of IT Systems on Internal Audit	General Understanding	Chap 23
Understanding project management	Organizing and Managing Internal Audit Activities	Internal Audit Knowledge Requirement	Chap 16
Understanding social media computing risks	Impact of IT Systems on Internal Audit	Internal Audit Knowledge Requirement	Chap 20
Understanding software as a service functions	Impact of IT Systems on Internal Audit	General Understanding	Chap 22
Understanding system development life cycle IT processes	Impact of IT Systems on Internal Audit	Internal Audit Knowledge Requirement	Chap 22

book may paint a slightly different picture, but we have tried to present in this edition a CBOK for internal auditors today to use in their internal audit service to management activities.

NOTES

1. The Institute of Internal Auditors Research Foundation, *A Global Summary of the Common Body of Knowledge* (Altamonte Springs, FL: 2006 published again by the IIARF as a CBOK study in 2007). However, the IIRF has purged this study and deleted all versions from its public records.

About the Author

Robert R. Moeller, CPA, CISA, CISSP, PMP, first was introduced to internal auditing when he had a new engineering degree, had completed his U.S. Army service, and was working at the then major computer manufacturer Sperry UNIVAC and was also attempting to learn more about managerial accounting. That was in 1975. Out of curiosity Moeller enrolled in an evening class on internal auditing at the University of Minnesota taught by Leon Radde, one of the pioneers of the internal audit profession. Moeller was fascinated by this introduction to internal audit processes and soon joined a team to help create an IT internal audit function at Sperry.

After several years as a lead on the Sperry internal audit team, Moeller then relocated to the Chicago area where he launched IT internal audit functions for several major corporations and also got involved with the Chicago IIA chapter. He gained CPA credentials, earned an MBA at the University of Chicago, and became national director of IT auditing for Grant Thornton. He subsequently joined Sears Roebuck, back in the days when Sears was a major retailer that owned Allstate Insurance, Discover Card, and major financial and real estate operations. Moeller launched Sears' first corporate IT internal audit function and went on to become Sears' internal audit director; he also reengineered the corporation's internal control processes and launched its corporate ethics function.

Since leaving Sears, Moeller has been involved with a wide range of audit, internal control, IT governance, and project management processes. A frequently published author and speaker, he provides insights into many of the issues and concerns impacting internal audit, enterprise governance, and risk and compliance processes.

Index

CPSIA information can be obtained
at www.ICGtesting.com
Printed in the USA
LVHW021315270122
709373LV00005B/25